THE OXFORD ENCYCLOPEDIA OF

ECONOMIC HISTORY

THE OXFORD ENCYCLOPEDIA

OF

ECONOMIC

HISTORY

Joel Mokyr

Editor in Chief

VOLUME 1

Accounting and Bookkeeping

—

Contract Labor and the Indenture System

OXFORD

UNIVERSITY PRESS

2003

OXFORD
UNIVERSITY PRESS

Oxford New York
Auckland   Bangkok   Buenos Aires   Cape Town   Chennai
Dar es Salaam   Delhi   Hong Kong   Istanbul   Karachi   Kolkata
Kuala Lumpur   Madrid   Melbourne   Mexico City   Mumbai   Nairobi
São Paulo   Shanghai   Taipei   Tokyo   Toronto

Copyright © 2003 by Oxford University Press, Inc.

Published by Oxford University Press, Inc.
198 Madison Avenue, New York, New York 10016
www. oup.com

Oxford is a registered trademark of Oxford University Press

Library of Congress Cataloging-in-Publication Data
The Oxford encyclopedia of economic history / Joel Mokyr, editor in chief.
p. cm.
Includes bibliographical references and index.
ISBN 978-0-19-510507-0 (set)
1. Economic history–Encyclopedias. I. Title: Encyclopedia of
economic history. II. Mokyr, Joel. III. Oxford University Press.
HC15 .O94 2003
330'.03–dc21
2003008992

3 5 7 9 8 6 4
Printed in the United States of America
on acid-free paper

EDITORIAL AND PRODUCTION STAFF

ACQUIRING EDITOR
Christopher Collins

DEVELOPMENT EDITORS
Mark Mones   Marion Osmun   Stephen Wagley

PROJECT EDITORS
Meera Vaidyanathan   Peter Rocheleau

ILLUSTRATION EDITOR
Ann Deborah Levy

COPYEDITORS
Laura Daly   Norma Frankel   Juanita Galuska
Martha Goldstein   Joan Hyman   Jean Kaplan   Constance McDonald

PROOFREADERS
Dorothy Bauhoff   Katharyn Dunham
Sue Gilad   Gareth Ridout   Rhoda Seidenberg   Ryan Sullivan

INDEXER
Katharyn Dunham, *ParaGraphs Indexing and Editorial Services*

COMPOSITOR
Macmillan India Limited

MANUFACTURING CONTROLLER
Chris Critelli

DESIGNER
Joan Greenfield

EDITORIAL, DESIGN, AND PRODUCTION DIRECTOR
John Sollami

DIRECTOR OF EDITORIAL DEVELOPMENT
Timothy J. DeWerff

PUBLISHER
Karen Day

Contents

THE OXFORD ENCYCLOPEDIA OF

ECONOMIC HISTORY

List of Maps

List of Articles

Preface

Economic history is much like a sparsely populated country: its inhabitants are small in number compared to its much larger neighbors in adjoining and related fields. The cultivators of its rocky soil are few and the area is vast: economic history encompasses all the material aspects of human existence through and before written history, describing a myriad of diverse forms of economic activity and organization. The "mainstream" fields of economics such as theory and applied microeconomics and the many fields and subfields of the history profession attract far more scholars than economic history. But as is true for many a small country, there are some of us who have elected to dwell there and love it dearly, and they would never live anywhere else. They feel its intellectual excitement, its many challenges, its sense of community, and its ability to attract young scholars despite the often hard and frustrating research involved.

To pursue the metaphor a bit further, this country could be likened to what economists like to call a "small open economy." Economic history has never been and should never be anything like a closed field in which practitioners converse mostly with one another. Instead, it stands at a busy intersection of history and the social sciences, where economists, political scientists, sociologists, anthropologists, demographers, and historians come and go. While the field has had its strongest intellectual and institutional roots in history and economics, it has always blithely ignored the artificial boundaries between academic disciplines. Economic historians, by the very nature of their field, ask questions that require a bewildering array of diverse specialists. The power and the glory of the discipline has always been its willingness to venture out far afield, to bring to the worlds of the economist and the historian insights and information originating in the netherworlds of engineers, physicians, agronomists, biologists, and geographers, as well as from the more lofty spheres of political philosophy, social thought, and game theory. If ever there was a bunch of eclectic intellectuals who will go almost anywhere to find their models, their evidence, and their inspiration, economic historians are it.

The need for such an interdisciplinary approach is related to the large size of the territory covered by this small field. Economic history has at least three dimensions it needs to span. First, it covers *all* of history, from the very first days of written records and before, using archaeological and even paleontological evidence, to recent statistical data and modern time series. Second, its ambitions have always been explicitly global and international. While the evidence that economic historians use is not spread evenly and uniformly over the planet, there has always been a tacit assumption that every economy and every society has an interesting story to tell. If this story can be illustrated in detail with statistical data and firsthand illustrations, all the better. If not, however, economic historians will work with whatever evidence can be found, reconstructing the past from the shards and debris that time has forgotten to sweep away. The more sparse the evidence, the more tantalizing the questions, the more challenging the answers. Third, economic history covers nothing less than the entire material existence of the human past: how have people made their living, eking out an existence in a constant struggle with nature, organizing into groups, markets, firms, and economic nation-states. The topical contours that economic historians have had to cover must therefore look much like economics itself: financial and labor markets, the organization of production in farms, workshops, and plants, the trade and transport of commodities and services, the variations of prices and wages, the occupation and deployment of workers over different sectors, the intricacies of money, taxes, social insurance, and technological progress, the measurement of prosperity and poverty, the terrors of famines and epidemics, the subtleties of political economy.

This breadth of topical coverage makes any attempt to sum up what is known a daunting task indeed. To start with, economic history must deal with the basic issues of technology: how have people over time succeeded in teasing out food and materials from an often recalcitrant soil and overcome the endless hardships of climate, pests, and natural disasters? How have they learned of the basic phenomena and regularities of their natural environment, from the most obvious ones such as tides and seasons, to the laws of thermodynamics and combinatorial chemistry, and then harnessed this knowledge to production in its widest sense? And yet, that story is only a first move. Economics is a *social* science, and economic history is a story of human interaction in the economic sphere. It needs to tell the story of markets, of organizations, of institutions, of small and large communities, from the tiny medieval village to the huge command economies of the totalitarian regimes of the twentieth century. Economic society depends on specialization and exchange, a division of labor and a concomitant need to coordinate and delegate the use of coins, credit, and capital.

In recent decades, the training of many young economic historians in formal neoclassical economics has greatly increased the fascination of economic historians with markets, in which rational actors do as well as they can and in the process enrich society. Yet economic history is far more than a story of markets and prices; it is a story of economic interaction within families, within hierarchical structures and institutions large and small. It is often a story of asymmetrical power and information in which people may behave opportunistically and strategically. It involves bargaining, learning from one another, signaling intentions, generating trust, sharing risk, threatening, monitoring, coordinating, and persuading. Economic behavior involves power, violence, graft, ignorance, and prejudice as often as it involves rational and predictable behavior. Moreover, in recent years the economic profession, including economic historians, has increasingly discovered that in many interactive situations, rational agents, each working in his or her own best interest, may bring about outcomes that are undesirable.

Such, then, is the richness and vastness of the field. So many topics, so few scholars, so little time. Many areas in the field still lie largely uncovered, vast patches of terra incognita surrounding little islets of knowledge. Any synthetic and synoptic work, such as an encyclopedia, must confront this reality. All the same, the editors of this work have made a concentrated effort to cover as much of the territory as possible. No serious subfield of human knowledge with relevance to economic history has been knowingly omitted, and the links between the field and other areas of learning have been explored as much as possible. Within economic history we have tried to cover an area that is as wide and as encompassing as possible. Beside the well-trodden fields of the history of agriculture, the cotton industry, banking, ocean shipping, and coal mines, we have included articles on service industries that provided a living for many thousands throughout history, from music and the arts to medicine and the law, to food processing, coinage, teaching, zoo keeping, prostitution, and newspapers. Throughout, our approach has been eclectic, panoptic, and catholic.

Economic history, by its very nature, is an area in which alternative interpretations and competing ideologies have often clashed. The Marxist approach to social sciences is in effect a debate about economic history, as is the anti-Marxist approach that views concepts such as class struggles and historical materialism as redundant but regards history as the ultimate vindication of the free market. Whether the competitive market or the class struggle is the correct approach to social science is a debate about which no synthetic work should take a position. Many other topics such as the economic history of slavery, economic imperialism, the standard of living, and the economic performance of collectivist economies are riven with controversy. But whereas we have no illusions of being able to write an "ideology-free" work, we have made a deliberate effort at a careful and balanced approach to the material, that will reproduce the facts as they are known to scholarship, without taking an obviously ideological position. Given human nature, such an attempt is doomed; but without making that effort, a synthetic work cannot claim to be "encyclopedic." Beyond that, it must strive for factual accuracy, completeness in coverage, and a balanced and fair approach to interpretation. Insofar as readers will judge us to have fallen short in fairness and balance, then, it has not been for lack of trying.

The other principle that has been followed as steadfastly as humanly possible was to eschew the "Western-centric" biases to which works like this tend to be prone. To some extent it is inevitable that the economic history of the "West" is over-represented. The bulk of modern research in the past decades has been on North America and Europe. Scholarship and research are what economists call "normal goods": as the rich countries in the Western world have become even richer, they have been able to afford to engage in the scholarship that looked in the material past of humanity, and naturally, this was biased toward their own past. And while a number of these scholars have actually turned their interest to non-Western areas, these have been a minority. The constraints of language, sources, and the self-perpetuating nature of a growing secondary literature are responsible for this bias. To partially compensate for this, the editorial board included two specialists on non-European economies, and the contributors were asked without exception to cover—wherever appropriate—non-Western economies as much as they could, and a large number of scholars have done so with remarkable success. While it would be overly ambitious to claim that the reach of this work is truly global, few corners of the planet are without coverage: the reader will find summaries of the economic history of virtually every "nation" and society, as well as many other geographical concepts, such as cities and rivers.

Some scholars have accused the economic history profession of a certain attitude of smugness, even triumphalism toward the achievements of modern post-industrialist society. The centrality of the notions of technological progress and economic growth is often cited as evidence of a certain "presentism" in this literature, and there is a literature that seems to imply that the wealth and prosperity of the modern age are the ultimate goals of thousands of years of development. In a work of synthesis, there is no room for such teleological approaches, and we have made an effort to avoid such pitfalls. All the same, this is not to deny the economic achievements that the industrialized West has made in the past two centuries in terms of affecting the standard of living in a considerable (and expanding) part of humankind. Without confusing material well-being and comforts with "happiness," "social harmony," "economic freedom," or any other encompassing measure of well-being, no serious work in economics can deny that the achievements of the past two centuries are as real and as momentous as they are incomplete and costly. In emphasizing the real accomplishments in material economic welfare, from reduced infant mortality and increased stature to an ever-expanding access to leisure, arts, and high-quality food and clothing, any work in economic history must acknowledge the irreversible impact that modern economic growth has had on the nature of the human condition—even if we confine it largely to the material side. Perhaps it is too simple and too confining to speak of economic Progress with a capital *P*, as if we could really assess the trend in economic change as a favorable development, the many horrors of the twentieth century notwithstanding. Yet surely we can, to cite the historian Robert Darnton in a famous essay, speak of "progress" with a small *p*, material and commercial. It consisted of small, incremental, local but real victories in the eternal struggle of humanity against disease, starvation, discomfort, infant mortality, malnutrition, bad housing, premature aging, and mind-numbing, backbreaking, and dangerous work that machines eventually took over in large part. The processes we may call—in the absence of a better term—"economic modernization" can be measured in part as rising productivity. Better economic organization and improved technology led to growing economic capabilities, teasing out more product per unit of input. It led to the gradual disappearance of the boredom and stupefying monotonousness of work and production in earlier times. It is the function of economic history to reveal the truth about the so-called good old times before the Industrial Revolution, just as it is its duty to fully display the costs of urbanization, the frustrations of commercialization and mass consumption, the horrors that modern technology and mass production can inflict during times of war, and the ambivalent impact that technological change has had on the majority of humanity who happened to live outside the industrialized world. Economic historians need to show the full effect of the many fluctuations and cycles in economic activity, the setbacks during wars and depressions, and the disruptions caused by inflation, unemployment, ill-conceived or evil economic policies, and the often ghastly social and economic experiments that all mark the modern era.

Economic history, in any event, deals with much more than just "how rich" a society was and how its riches were distributed. A great deal of research has been carried out on how the economic matrix of production and exchange functioned in the human past. What kind of contracts existed and how were property rights defined and enforced, how did society provide for public goods, how did it take care of its poor and unfortunate? Economic history needs to show how people allocated their time between work and leisure, their resources between consumption and investment, how they transferred assets between generations through inheritance practices. Every economy, moreover, rested its production system on certain bodies of skills and knowledge, yet because these skills resided primarily in the perishable human mind, mechanisms needed to be found to educate the young and, if possible, to expand the knowledge base. Similarly, in each society that ever was, there is an ever-present tension between those who tried to make their living by producing goods and services, either by the patient toil of farmers or the more entrepreneurial activities of merchants and bankers, and those who sought their riches through redistribution from one group to another, whether through violence, taxes, forced exclusions, or fraud. The prevalence of such opportunistic or "rent-seeking" behavior depended on the cultural beliefs and norms of each society, but also on the kind of incentive structures and distribution of political power prevailing in the institutions of each economy. Much of the material in this Encyclopedia surveys, in one form or another, these essential details from a historical perspective.

One institution to which economic historians have paid much attention in recent years is the family. It is now well understood that research in the economic history of the family is a legitimate field, and that the economics of population change cannot be understood without describing the details of the dynamics of the family: at what age did people get married, what kind of resources were exchanged and pledged before and during the marriage, how did the family allocate resources between man, woman, children, and other members, and how were demographic decisions made? In view of the enormous amount of evidence accumulated by demographic historians, we are much better informed about these pivotal developments in human history. A set of very different institutions, but equally central to the understanding of our past, are those that made accumulation and exchange possible: money, credit, contracts, insurance, law enforcement, and institutions that engendered trust and reciprocity and made local and long-distance trade possible. These institutions include those that lubricated the process of exchange: the emergence of coins and other means of exchange, the use of letters of credit, bills of exchange, and the emergence of financial institutions. We cover the full range of these institutions, from medieval contracts to modern exchange rates, from bimetalism to the working of the gold standard and post-1945 international monetary system. These topics have been given considerable space because they are of interest to students and scholars, and because they have been the subjects of a great deal of research. In the end economic history is largely what economic historians do.

Outside the social interactions in markets and other institutions, there are the interactions between people and their environment—though a precise boundary is, of course, hard to draw. Yet we have included a great deal of information on the physical environment and human biology, since economic activity and well-being by definition depends on the number of people around, as well as on their health and longevity. To understand that, economic historians have looked in the past at the causes and severity of diseases, the tendency of women to nurse their babies, the connection between nutrition and health, changes in climate and rainfall, pest and flood control, and many similar variables. Finally, we have a substantial number of entries about individuals, men and women, who for one reason or another are of importance as economic historians, entrepreneurs, inventors, financiers, and scholars. The entries are followed by brief bibliographies and listings of Internet sites that will allow interested readers to explore the topics further. The Encyclopedia in its entirety will be made available electronically online in 2004 through institutional subscriptions to its online site.

There are nearly nine hundred entries and subentries in *The Oxford Encyclopedia of Economic History*, arranged in alphabetical order letter by letter. Composite entries gather together discussions of similar or related topics under one headword. For example, under the entry "Radio and Television Industry" the reader will find three subentries: "Historical Overview," "Technological Change," and "Industrial Organization and Regulation." A headnote listing the various subentries introduces each composite entry.

The contributors have sought to write in clear language with a minimum of technical vocabulary. The articles give important terms and titles in their original languages, with English translations when needed. A selective bibliography at the end of each article directs the reader who wishes to pursue a topic in greater detail to primary sources, the most useful works in English, and the most important scholarly works in any language.

To guide readers from one article to related discussions elsewhere in the Encyclopedia, end-references appear at the end of many articles. Blind entries direct the user from an alternate form of an entry term to the entry itself. For example, the blind entry for "Coinage" tells the reader to look under "Money and Coinage." The Encyclopedia includes approximately 425 photographs and seventeen maps.

Volume 5 contains the topical outline of articles, a listing of Internet sites related to economic history, the directory of contributors, and the index. Readers interested in finding all the articles on a particular subject (e.g., natural resources and the environment or labor) may consult the topical outline, which shows how articles relate to one another and to the overall design of the Encyclopedia; the outline also appears at the beginning of volume 1. The list of Internet sites directs the reader to sites where more information on selected articles in the Encyclopedia can be found. The comprehensive index lists all the topics covered in the Encyclopedia, including those that are not headwords themselves.

Editors in chief of big collaborative projects such as this are little more than symphony orchestra conductors: the waving baton makes no music itself, and serves only as a coordinating device. I have had, however, the privilege of relying on an impressive row of first-chair string, brass, and woodwind players. Above all is my devoted board of area editors, seven brilliant and learned scholars, expert economic historians every one of them; they worked tirelessly for close to a decade, reading and re-reading essays, advising me and the staff on endless matters, from topics of serious substance to deciphering and translating the often impenetrable prose of some contributors. The fact that I can still count every one of them as a personal friend attests to their saintly patience and forbearance. The Associate Editor, my former graduate student and now close personal friend and colleague Maristella Botticini, moved mountains in the early stages of this project and was a tower of strength and support throughout the long years of its completion. Members of the board of advisers loyally counseled me on hundreds of thorny issues. Of the many names to whom I remain indebted for life I must mention above all two: Stanley L. Engerman and Eric L. Jones, two scholars who between them seem to know everything and everyone worth knowing in economic history. Among the research assistants who have spent not just their time but also their sweat and (less often) tears, I must mention Amit Goyal, who helped compile the Internet sites, and Elizabeth Brown-Inz, whose dedication and ingenuity helped complete this project during its final—and most difficult—stage.

At Oxford University Press, the list of hard-working and talented individuals who contributed to this project is long: Christopher Collins conceived of the Encyclopedia and was the one who persuaded me to take it on. It would probably be disingenuous to say that I have been grateful to him for this act of salesmanship for every single day of the past ten years; but looking back at it now, I recognize his foresight and common sense. Marion Osmun, a wise and skillful editor, taught me many things in the early days of this project. In its middle stages, Merilee Johnson and Peter Rocheleau worked night and day to help the project along and both saw it through during some tough times when the editor in chief was absorbed in college administration. In the final stages, Meera Vaidyanathan and Stephen Wagley were simply indispensable; it is only thanks to their dedication and perseverance that we have been able to refute the pessimistic predictions about the Encyclopedia made even by some of its close collaborators. In addition, their good cheer in putting up with the often difficult moods of an overcommitted and too-thinly-stretched editor reserves them a place in the hall of fame of human patience. The wisdom and leadership of Karen Day was essential in guiding us through the final stages of the project.

To end on a personal note, I need only to look over my shoulder and see the one friend and adviser who has stood beside me during the many years of this project and kept her faith in it and me: my wife Margalit B. Mokyr, who deserves as much credit as anyone for the successful completion of this Encyclopedia.

Joel Mokyr
April 2003

Topical Outline of Articles

The entries and subentries in *The Oxford Encyclopedia of Economic History* are conceived according to the general conceptual categories listed in this topical outline. Entries in the Encyclopedia proper are organized alphabetically. The outline is divided into eleven parts:

1. Geography: Countries and Regions
2. Geography: Cities
3. Agriculture
4. Production Systems, Business History, and Technology
5. Demography
6. Institutions, Governments, and Markets
7. Macroeconomic History and International Economics
8. Money, Banking, and Finance
9. Labor
10. Natural Resources and the Environment
11. Biographies

1. GEOGRAPHY: COUNTRIES AND REGIONS

EUROPE

Alsace
Austria
  Austria before 1867
  Austro-Hungarian Empire
  Modern Austria
Balkans
Baltic States
Bavaria
Belgium
Black Country
Catalonia
Czechoslovakia and the Czech and Slovak Republics
Danube
England
  Early and Medieval Periods up to 1500
  Early Modern Period
France
  Early and Medieval Periods
  Early Modern Period
  Modern Period
  The French Empire between 1789 and 1950
  The French Empire to 1789

Germany
  Early and Medieval Periods
  Early Modern Period
  Modern Germany
Great Britain
  British Empire
  Modern Period
Greece
  Byzantine and Ottoman Periods
  Classical Period and Earlier
  Modern Period
Hungary
Ireland
  Ireland before 1800
  Ireland from 1800 to 1922
  Ireland after 1922
Italy
  Classical Period
  Early Modern and Modern Periods (to 1861)
  Medieval Period
  United Italy
Lancashire
Lombardy

9. LABOR

BASIC CONCEPTS

Apprenticeship
Human Capital
Journeymen
Labor
Labor Productivity
Literacy

FORMS OF LABOR CONTRACTS

Contract Labor and the Indenture System
Serfdom
Slavery

LABOR MARKETS

Child Labor
Labor Markets
  Historical Overview
  Segmentation and Discrimination
  Integration and Wage Convergence
Labor Mobility
Unemployment
Women in the Labor Force

LABOR ORGANIZATIONS, UNIONS, AND INDUSTRIAL RELATIONS

Bargaining, Collective
Craft Guilds
Employers' Associations
Industrial Relations
Luddism and Social Protest
Unions

PAYMENT SCHEMES AND WAGES

Wage Legislation
Wage Systems
Wages

LABOR CONDITIONS

Labor Conditions and Job Safety
Labor Time
Retirement

10. NATURAL RESOURCES AND THE ENVIRONMENT

NATURAL RESOURCES

Fisheries and Fish Processing
Forests and Deforestation
Fossil Fuels
Natural Resources
  Historical Overview
  Property Rights
  Regulation
Nuclear Power
Quarries
Soil and Soil Conservation
Solar Power
Water Resources
Whaling
Wood as Fuel

ENVIRONMENT

Climate and Climate History
Environment
  Historical Overview
  Environmental Policies and Regulation
Fire Control
Pest Control
Pollution
Volcanic Activities and Earthquakes

11. BIOGRAPHIES

INVENTORS AND WRITERS ON TECHNOLOGY

Agricola, Georgius
Arkwright, Richard
Babbage, Charles
Bell, Alexander Graham
Bessemer, Henry
Boulton, Matthew
Brunel Family
Cort, Henry
Daimler, Gottlieb
Diesel, Rudolf
Eastman, George
Edison, Thomas A.
Gutenberg, Johannes
Haber, Fritz
Jacquard, Joseph-Marie
Kettering, Charles
McCormick, Cyrus
Newcomen, Thomas
Nobel, Alfred
Otto, Nikolaus August
Roberts, Richard
Singer, Isaac Merritt
Smeaton, John
Stephenson Family
Taylor, Frederick Winslow
Watt, James
Westinghouse, George
Whitney, Eli
Wright Brothers

ENTREPRENEURS, BANKERS, AND LABOR LEADERS

Agnelli Family
Armour Family
Astor, John Jacob
Bakunin, Mikhail
Brown Family
Brunner Family
Cadbury Family
Campbell, Joseph
Carnegie, Andrew
Chavez, Cesar
Chrysler, Walter
Coats Family
Cockerill, John
Courtauld Family
Debs, Eugene Victor
Deere, John
DuPont Family
Duisberg, Carl
Duke, James Buchanan
Dunlop, James
Ericsson, L. M.
Ford, Henry
Franklin, Benjamin
Gompers, Samuel
Gould, Jay
Gramsci, Antonio
Guggenheim Family
Guinness Family
Harriman, Edward
Hill, James J.
Kautsky, Karl
Krupp Family
Lenin, Vladimir Ilich
Lever, William Hesketh
Lewis, John L.
Liebknechts, The
List, Georg Friedrich
Luxemburg, Rosa
Mellon Family
Morgan, J. P.
Morris, William (Lord Nuffield)
Owen, Robert
Philips Family
Pilkington Family
Rhodes, Cecil John
Rockefeller, John Davison
Rong Family
Sassoon Family
Schlumberger Family
Schneider, Joseph-Eugène
Siemens Family
Slater, Samuel
Sloan, Alfred
Stinnes, Hugo
Swope, Gerard
Thyssen, August
Trotsky, Leon
Vanderbilt Family
Vickers Family
Wallenberg Family
Wendel Family
Zaibatsu

ECONOMISTS AND ECONOMIC HISTORIANS

Ashton, T. S.
Bloch, Marc
Braudel, Fernand
Chandler, Alfred D.
Clapham, John
Cliometrics
Fogel, Robert
Friedman, Milton
Gerschenkron, Alexander
Heckscher, Eli
Hughes, Jonathan
Keynes, John Maynard
Kindleberger, Charles P.
Lane, Frederic Chapin
Le Roy Ladurie, Emmanuel
Lewis, W. Arthur
Malthus, Thomas
Marshall, Alfred
Marx, Karl
Mill, John Stuart
Mumford, Lewis
North, Douglass Cecil
Pirenne, Henri
Polanyi, Karl
Postan, Michael
Power, Eileen
Ricardo, David
Schumpeter, Joseph
Smith, Adam
Sombart, Werner
Tawney, R. H.
Usher, A. P.
Veblen, Thorstein
Weber, Max
White, Lynn
Young, Arthur

Common Abbreviations Used in This Work

AD	*anno Domini*, in the year of the Lord		n.	note
ASEAN	Association of Southeast Asian Nations		NAFTA	North American Free Trade Association
b.	born		NBER	National Bureau of Economic Research
BCE	before the common era (= BC)		n.d.	no date
c.	*circa*, about, approximately		NGO	nongovernmental organization
CE	common era (= AD)		no.	number
CEO	chief executive officer		n.p.	no place
cf.	*confer*, compare		n.s.	new series
d.	died; penny (pl., pence)		OECD	Organization for Economic Cooperation and Development
diss.	dissertation			
EC	European Community		OEEC	Organization for European Economic Cooperation
ed.	editor (pl., eds), edition			
EEC	European Economic Community		OPEC	Organization of Petroleum Exporting Countries
EU	European Union			
f.	and following (pl., ff.)		p.	page (pl., pp.)
FAO	Food and Agriculture Organization		pt.	part
FDI	foreign direct investment		r.	reigned
fl.	*floruit*, flourished		R&D	research and development
FTA	free trade area		rev.	revised
GATT	General Agreement on Tariffs and Trade		s.	shilling
GDP	gross domestic product		SEC	Securities and Exchange Commission (United States)
GNP	gross national product			
G-10	Group of Ten industrialized countries		ser.	series
IMF	International Monetary Fund		supp.	supplement
ISI	import-substitution industrialization		UNESCO	United Nations Educational, Scientific, and Cultural Organization
l.	line (pl., ll.)			
LDC	less developed country (pl., LDCs)		UNRRA	United Nations Relief and Rehabilitation Administration
MDC	more developed country (pl., MDCs)		USD	U.S. dollar(s)
MFN	most-favored nation		USSR	Union of Soviet Socialist Republics
MITI	Ministry of International Trade and Industry (Japan)		vol.	volume (pl., vols.)
			WHO	World Health Organization
MNC	multinational company (pl., MNCs)		WIPO	World Intellectual Property Organization

THE OXFORD ENCYCLOPEDIA OF
ECONOMIC HISTORY

A

ACCOUNTING AND BOOKKEEPING. Over the course of established human history, accounting information and business have had an interdependent relationship, in which each has influenced the progress of the other. The development of business enterprises, from proprietary to corporate forms, has been a factor in the development of accounting; and as accounting has responded to such needs, it has supported the adaptation of business to increasingly complex market conditions. This complementary relationship causes continuing debate among historians about which has influenced the other more. One view claims that changes in the environment and in society have necessitated accounting development. The other argues that the evolution of commerce has been enabled as better accounting methods have been developed. Using improved methods, accounting has helped businesses to understand their operations, to improve, if not to flourish, and to respond to the needs of business owners, managers, and society. In either view, there is considerable agreement that accounting has played an important role in the history of business and the economy of the world.

Throughout history, accounting has had many multifaceted roles in the organization and business community, from the simple need to record transactions, to protect and control assets and activities, to the complex role of establishing decision and behavior parameters to direct the allocation of societal resources. Baladouni (1996) asserts that accounting serves four informational needs in the community: (1) fulfilling a wide variety of control objectives, (2) profit calculation and planning, (3) cost-benefit analysis, and (4) the formulation of major financial and economic policy decisions in various organizations and on many occasions.

Ancient Civilizations' Record Keeping. Accounting can be traced to the cradle of history, in its role in information generation. A prosperous and advanced society existed in ancient civilizations such as Mesopotamia, Egypt, and Greece, which employed an elaborate record-keeping system to manage complex interrelated governmental and commercial activities, as contemporary society does but with quite different technology. In fact, the record-keeping, verification, and internal control problems encountered by ancient societies were in many ways similar to those of the present day.

Information generation, an important function, defines the development of accounting. The invention of accounting as a record-keeping system preceded the development of writing. From her study of ancient Mesopotamian society, Schmandt-Besserat (1992) argues that writing emerged from counting. The need to account for something resulted in the invention of counting devices, which ultimately led to the development of writing, following interrelated economic and social changes.

In the crescent-shaped fertile area of the Middle East, Mesopotamian society flourished as a prosperous society for a long period. In that business environment, trade was encouraged as farmers regularly had surplus harvests. In addition, other types of business and services developed, such as brickmaking, barbering, weaving, carpentry, and banking. Religious institutions and governments collected various taxes, sacrificial offerings, and services from cities throughout the region. Such cities as Babylon and Ninevah became centers for regional commerce, and a Babylonian empire became the center of business and politics in the known world. Mesopotamian society was the first one known to develop its own bookkeeping system as the need for record keeping emerged to facilitate the extensive scale of business, religious, and governmental activities. This society had its own accounting profession, people called scribes, whose main duties were preparing and reading records as well as facilitating business transactions.

In addition to political stability and extensive business growth, several other factors helped the development of accounting in this period. There were legal codes that penalized the failure to memorialize transactions. Ancient Mesopotamian society also employed standard measures of gold and silver. Credit was used extensively in many business transactions, suggesting the need for information and records.

Other ancient societies developed their own record-keeping systems for assisting the governmental sector and managing the financial sector. Ancient Egyptian society developed its own governmental accounting in a fashion similar to that of the Mesopotamians. The Egyptians kept extensive records, particularly for the network of royal storehouses within which "in kind" tax payments of goods were kept. However, literacy, coin, and currency limitations affected ancient Egypt's accounting development.

Ancient Chinese society developed a record-keeping system to evaluate the efficiency of governmental programs and the civil servants who administered them. In the business community, the Chinese developed a simple commercial accounting method for calculating gain or loss in commerce and simple methods of calculating costs of handcrafted goods.

Similar needs led ancient Greek society in the fifth century BCE to employ record keeping. They had a designated profession, similar to that of "public accountants," to help citizens to maintain authority and control over governmental finances. For oversight of legislation for financial matters and control of receipt and expenditure of public monies, this society employed ten state accountants, who followed codified accounting procedures to fulfill their duties.

The Roman Empire improved upon the record-keeping methods developed by Greece and incorporated them as part of their system of financial administration and accounting. This system helped the empire to control a wide area of Europe and Asia. As the Roman Empire expanded, its system of financial administration and accounting also spread throughout the empire, laying the groundwork for the development of medieval accounting.

Medieval Accounting. Medieval accounting is considered a direct development of Roman accounting traditions. Teichmann (1978) claims that this tradition continued for a time in Italy and later in ecclesiastical organizations. The accounting profession, similar to that in the Greco-Roman era, was present and later expanded as business and trade advanced through venture partnerships and overseas trading. During this period, dating from as early as the twelfth century, advanced bookkeeping techniques were developed to support the development of these new types of venture business. Record keeping tended to be localized and centered around a number of specialized institutions serving entrepreneurs and moneylenders. The introduction of Hindu-Arabic numerals simplified calculations made cumbersome under the Roman numbering systems. The facilitation of mathematical calculation afforded by this new system of numbers represented a significant contribution to accounting method. Accounts were kept because merchants needed to monitor subordinates, acting as their agents, and to settle concluded joint-partner ventures.

The use of systematic accounting procedures also helped Charlemagne to manage his estate, in the ninth century in pre-Norman England. He issued an ordinance containing elaborate instructions for the management of royal states. In this ordinance, the Capitulare di Villis, there is a requirement for keeping and rendering accounts for income and expenditure and for the auditing of accounts.

Luca Pacioli and the Birth of Double-Entry Accounting (1400s). Double-entry accounting is dated and identified with medieval Venice, which inherited and gradually developed accounting as practiced in the Roman Empire. This region also had direct relationships with various commercial centers in many locations, from Africa to China. To support such long-distance business relationships, Italian merchants in the Middle Ages developed the partnership venture as a type of business organization. A partnership was used to form and manage each voyage and was dissolved when the venture/voyage was completed. This arrangement evolved to the development of a separate entity for control and reporting, in order to provide an accounting for each voyage. Later, changing conditions made more enduring partnerships necessary, because of established trade between Italy and trade locations. Voyage-based capital partnerships became the established entities for asset control and reporting purposes, and represented an important mercantile institution.

As trade became commonplace, capitalism emerged as the rationale for viewing a business enterprise. Italian capitalists formed agencies to channel their capital. Banks replaced moneylenders and began to play an important role in allocating capital among various new ventures, employing techniques to establish instruments of credit. As these developments occurred, the need to control partners and agents arose, and the practice of reporting to capital sources became institutionalized. Indeed, some scholars consider this the origin of the profit mentality that prevails in contemporary times. As banks required adequate records for their accounts, accounting and the accounting profession were about to undergo a modern transformation. Businesses used their services regularly, and customarily employed accounting system and information; and accounting methods transformed into double-entry bookkeeping. Littleton (1966) points out that double-entry bookkeeping was not an individual's invention but the result of a long evolution. The introduction of Hindu-Arabic numerals facilitated this development. This new numeric technology enabled accounting to handle far more transactions than before, and business records became extensive. Record keeping enabled merchants to handle transactions with more facility, and business could develop faster than before.

Luca Pacioli, a medieval mathematician, building upon the work of Cotrugli and others, developed a refined version of double-entry bookkeeping using the business mathematics of that era. After working on the treatise for thirty years, Luca Pacioli published his *Summa de*

ACCOUNTING. Luca Pacioli (c. 1445–c. 1514), portrait by Jacopo de' Barbari (c. 1440–c. 1516). (Gallerie Nazionali di Capodimonte, Naples/Alinari/Art Resource, NY)

Arithmetica, Geometria, Proportioni, et Proportionalita in Venice in 1494. Pacioli stated that the bookkeeping section was written as a collection of material and ideas from many sources and by many authors, including Leonardo da Pisa. Most of the techniques explained in the book for double-entry bookkeeping are related to practices used in modern record keeping that underlie accounting reports. The *Summa* quickly became popular throughout Italy, as the business community could easily use its techniques in their bookkeeping. The new technology of typeset printing helped to disperse the "Venetian method" widely. Its suggestion that Italian merchants held a competitive advantage may have made copying this technique an important competitive necessity. McMickle and Vangermeersch (1987) identify further adaptions, abetted by commercial typeset printing, in the text writings of Jan Ympyn Christofells in Antwerp, 1543, Simon Stevin in Leyden, 1607, and John Carpenter in London, 1632, who disseminated the Italian double entry system as trade developed to the East Indies. Spanish applications of voyage accounting have been attributed by Alistair Cooke to Columbus's journeys to the New World of the West Indies.

The *Summa* spread throughout Europe as intercountry trading increased. The double-entry bookkeeping that once contributed to the excellence of Italian business became commonplace outside that region. The spread of double-entry bookkeeping coincided with commercial voyages in Europe in the sixteenth and seventeenth centuries. Many European countries, such as England and the Netherlands, that had extensive fleets used and developed accounting methods around double-entry bookkeeping, once they embraced this type of bookkeeping for managing their venture and trading businesses. Double-entry accounting also assisted them in managing their trading colonies as well as local businesses developed in these colonies.

As the use of the corporate form of business emerged in England and other northern European countries, the notion of mutual association, as represented in the Italian partnership form of limited liability, was emulated and extended to corporate entities. Large companies, such as the Russian Company (chartered in 1555), the East India Company (1600), and the Hudson's Bay Company (1670), emerged through viable forms of incorporation that conferred a privilege of exclusivity as a royal prerogative and thereby granted monopoly status. Together, double-entry accounting and the corporate form of business led to ways to develop modern enterprises and support even more complex information needs.

The Development of Modern Accounting and the Influence of Information Technology. The corporate business form and the development of double-entry accounting were preconditions for the Industrial Revolution in the eighteenth century, particularly in England and the United States. Using the corporate form, a company was able to accumulate the needed capital to expand in a period of new technological developments, which led to "revolutionary" new methods of manufacturing, transportation, and communication. This was a period of unparalleled and rapid accumulation of wealth. Capital markets began to supply the needs of larger and larger entities. London became the center of the world's capital markets, just as Venice had been during the period of merchant venture kingdoms. By the early twentieth century, New York replaced London as the largest capital center; but most developed economies, including France, Germany, Japan, the Netherlands, and Spain, also had growing capital-market centers. Rapid geographic and demographic expansion and competitive political environments aided this development, all of which contributed to open global conflicts.

Accounting served the business community by providing information needed for decisions about capital allocation, as increasingly there was a separation of ownership from active management control. At this time, just as today, the need for periodic reports was established, and financial statements were an expected communication, especially in the United States. Many individuals who contributed capital, in public markets, needed information about their venture or investment. Accounting became a means of measuring and communicating useful information. As the corporate form of business organization combined with emerging large-scale technology, as in railroad, refining, and steel operations, the stage was set for substantial distribution of information. For example, information about railroad companies provided by John Moody and Henry Varnum Poor supplied investment banking and financial institutions with information about company conditions, which was further disseminated into the growing public-investment community.

Changes in public investing led the British government to enact the 1844 Companies Act. This law, designed to protect the providers of capital to corporations, required companies to keep books and to present a "full and fair" balance sheet at each ordinary meeting of shareholders. This law also required companies to appoint auditors to make a report on the balance sheet to be read at the meeting and to be filed, together with the balance sheet, with the legal "Registrar" of the company.

By the end of the century, a series of such acts codified the practices of the Industrial Revolution, namely, the requirements for financial statements, an audit of those statements, and the filing of the statements with an independent agency or a branch of the government. However, early in this period, an auditor was a layman, usually a shareholder acting on behalf of all shareholders. These laws initially were satisfied by the emphasis on financial reporting provided by the balance sheet.

By the beginning of the twentieth century, the business and investment community had discovered that an emphasis on earning power shifted the orientation of financial reporting to an income statement, especially in the United States, where large public stock holding by small investors meant that the most effective way of showing stockholder displeasure was to sell one's holdings. Prospective investors, speculators, bankers, and creditors are eager to evaluate the quality of management and its earning capacity. A clear statement of the details of operations thus was the next emphasis in U.S. accounting. This development was amplified by the enactment of federal income-tax laws in the early twentieth century. In the United Kingdom, the government enacted legislation in 1929 that called for an income statement for the purpose of selling and trading securities.

As the business community began to understand the importance of income statements, professional management teams developed and refined accounting methods for use in managing day-to-day operations and to communicate standard performance ratios, such as ROI (return on investment) and EPS (earnings per share). Accordingly, management accounting (cost accounting) was developed, and it was integrated into the general-ledger system of the Industrial Revolution as it increased in importance. New tax laws, as noted above, made it necessary that companies maintain adequate records to support their cost computations in tax returns.

In the years 1890 to 1910, publications describing cost-accounting methods often were initiated by engineers, and were distributed both within the traditional business community and in the newly formed academic business community. Procedures for integrating cost with financial accounting, as well as the basic methods for job orders and process cost, were laid down. Later (1909–1919), a standard cost system, using predetermined costs, was developed. Industry also started to develop and adopt a uniform system of cost determination and accounting. J. Hugh Jackson (1952) argues that this development represented a very definite awakening, or cost-consciousness, on the part of industry generally, and industry leaders' attempted to educate all units within their respective industries about the value and the use of modern, scientific methods of cost determination. This helped eliminate unfounded "cutthroat" competition, yet supported more efficient organization, better purchasing methods, and improved controls for many organizations. Methods were continually refined and improved, especially in computation and determination of standard costs, computation and distribution of overhead or burden expense, handling and pricing materials (FIFO, LIFO), recording cost variations, and preparing cost reports and summaries.

Following the stock market crash of 1929, the accounting profession was given a mandate by the U.S. government, under supervision of the Securities and Exchange Commission (SEC), to develop accounting practices and standards for the purpose of financial reporting and to conduct audits of financial statements, according to securities laws passed in the 1930s. This marked the beginning of an era of development and promulgation of accounting standards by independent accounting standard committees and boards. As the need for providing reliable information in capital markets became greater, the need for comparable accounting reports became clear. Accounting evolved into two branches: (1) financial accounting was developed around the need to communicate to capital markets; (2) management accounting was developed around the need to support the functioning of management in individual companies.

Conclusion. Throughout history, accounting has helped to satisfy society's information needs, aiding it in managing its allocation of investment capital and productive economic resources. From the cradle of civilization to the era of the Internet, accounting has evolved in its role, providing information to society for control, performance measurement, and key management decisions. The role of accounting professionals continues to develop, as the value of such information is considered essential to fair and full use of the world's limited physical and knowledge assets.

BIBLIOGRAPHY

Association of Chartered Accountants in the United States. "Luca Pacioli and 'The Method of Venice'." In *Accounting: A Virtual History*, 1999. <http://www.acaus.org/history/index.html>

Baladouni, Vahe. "Accounting and the Accountant Portrayals." In *The History of Accounting: An International Encyclopedia*, edited by Michael Chatfield and Richard Vangermeersch, pp. 4–6. New York and London, 1996.

Baxter, William T., ed. *Studies in Accounting*. London, 1950.

Cooke, Alistair. *America*. New York, 1973.

Cooper, W. W., and Yuji Ijiri, eds. *Kohler's Dictionary for Accountants*. 6th ed. Englewood Cliffs, N.J., 1983.

Edey, Harold C. "Company Accounting in the Nineteenth and Twentieth Centuries." In *Contemporary Studies in the Evolution of Accounting Thought*, edited by Michael Chatfield, pp. 135–143. Belmont, Calif., 1968.

Irish, R. A. "The Evolution of Corporate Accounting." In *Contemporary Studies in the Evolution of Accounting Thought*, edited by Michael Chatfield, pp. 57–85. Belmont, Calif., 1968.

Jackson, J. Hugh. "A Half-Century of Cost Accounting Progress." In *Contemporary Studies in the Evolution of Accounting Thought*, edited by Michael Chatfield, pp. 222–236. Belmont, Calif., 1968.

Littleton, Ananias C. *Accounting Evolution to 1900*. New York, 1966.

McMickle, Peter, and Richard Vangermeersch. *The Origins of a Great Profession*. Tuscaloosa, Ala., 1987.

Schmandt-Besserat, Denise. *Before Writing.*, vol. 1, *From Counting to Cuneiform*. Austin, 1992.

Taylor, R. Emmet. "Luca Pacioli." In *Studies in the History of Accounting*, edited by A. C. Littleton and B. S. Yamey, pp. 175–184. Homewood, Ill., 1956.

Teichmann, Max. "A Sketch of Accountancy." In *Readings on Accounting Development*, edited by S. Paul Garner and Marilynn Hughes, pt. 2, pp. 421–430. New York, 1978.

GARY JOHN PREVITS AND RAHMADI MURWANTO

ADOPTION. Adoption involves the complete absorption of a child or an adult from the family of birth into a new family. The full rights and responsibilities of parenthood and the social and kinship position of the person are transferred, and the adopted parents become full substitutes for the biological parents. Adopted children, therefore, need to be distinguished from children who have been fostered. The latter, although raised by adults who are not their biological parents, acquire no right to a share of the property of their foster parents.

Adopted children are found in many societies, from classical times to the twenty-first century, where they are present in both developed and Third World societies. Adoption is largely absent from Africa, both historically and contemporarily. In Africa, adoption was rendered unnecessary by the prevalence of fostering, in combination with polygamy, and the ready availability of heirs other than those in the direct line of descent. These heirs included both members of the wider lineage and widows in a situation where land was relatively abundant. The fostering of children occurs more widely than full adoption, and in the past it often involved children learning the trade of their foster parent or fulfilling the role of a servant while receiving a modicum of care. The biological family was thereby relieved of the expense of their maintenance. When the foster parent was reimbursed by the biological parent for the care they provided, the fostering arrangement had more elements of a child minding service.

Three reasons have been adduced for adoption: first, to provide homes for orphans, bastards, and abandoned children (foundlings); second, to allow childless couples the opportunity to raise children; and third, to provide heirs for property. The need to care for deprived children has constituted the principal motive for adoption in western societies since the latter part of the nineteenth century, whereas earlier the dominant motive had been the need to provide an heir. Heirship as a motive for adoption was particularly important in cultures where there was a duty to perpetuate the worship of the ancestors of a particular family line. Such substitute heirs were usually adopted when they were already adult because their capability was evident, they had survived the high mortality years of infancy and childhood, and they had little chance of succeeding to the property of their own father because another son was already the designated successor. Differences in the motives for adoption between twenty-first-century and historical societies should not be overstressed. The primacy of economic motives for adoption in past societies did not preclude the development of ties of affection, just as the child-centered approach to modern adoption does not mean there is no emotional satisfaction to be gained by adults who adopt a child.

Adoption, which had functioned effectively in pre-Christian Rome, is supposed to have been absent from medieval western Christendom. In a provocative thesis, Jack Goody attributed its absence to a drive by the church to divert the wealth of childless families into its own coffers and remove one mechanism that could promote the worship of ancestors as a rival to Christian worship by focusing attention on the continuity of the line of direct descent (Goody, 1983, pp. 34–47, 214–216). This argument has now been countered from a number of directions. First, it has been claimed that the medieval church was insufficiently well organized to pursue a coherent campaign against adoption. Second, there is evidence that families without children of their own were not left without heirs, even in the absence of adoption, because customs sanctioned inheritance by more distant relatives. In the case of Germanic tribes, for example, inheritance was sanctioned even if the relationship extended to the seventh degree. Throughout western Europe, peasants also enjoyed the freedom to dispose of property to nonrelatives in return for economic support in old age.

To solve the problem of orphaned or unwanted children, preindustrial societies developed solutions that circumvented the need for formal adoption. One solution involved care by siblings, grandparents, or other kin; others included various types of fostering, funded by the state or by charity. Placement in a foundling hospital or workhouse, which exposed the child to high risk of early death, was a less-satisfactory option. Infanticide was another possibility. Some instances are documented, but its actual prevalence is unknown. Evidence for England in the late nineteenth and early twentieth centuries (reminiscences, social surveys, and comments by middle-class observers) indicates that the care provided by relatives and neighbors to other peoples' children was sometimes viewed by the parties concerned as informal adoption, even though formal adoption was only first authorized in England by the Adoption Act of 1926. Such informal adoptions by relatives and neighbors are likely to have occurred in earlier centuries and in other societies.

The many different motives for adoption are revealed in a number of studies of the adoption process in specific time periods and countries. An examination of adoption contracts in sixteenth- and seventeenth-century Paris, for example, has shown that 30 percent of the small number of adoption contracts uncovered in notarial archives were made by widows, unmarried women over the age of twenty-five, and women separated from their husbands. The majority of these women chose to adopt girls and promised to provide basic care, a religious education, apprenticeship, a dowry, and in many cases an inheritance. Contracts could involve foundlings but also were made privately with the biological family.

Studies of adoption procedures in East Asia reveal that the major function of adoption was the provision of an heir. In China and Korea, where emphasis on the direct line of descent constituted an important element in the culture, custom prohibited the adoption of a male child who was not related to the family head. In Japan, by contrast, adopted sons were accepted from among the kinsmen of the wife of the family head or even from a nonrelative. The custom of adopting a son as a husband for a daughter was also common in Japan, although prohibited in Korea and rare in China. A detailed study of adoption in a region west of Tokyo has established that both forms of adoption not only enabled households without a son to recruit an heir, but also provided surplus sons from households whose succession was already secured to acquire the headship of other, though often poorer, households. Yet despite the prevalence of adoption and the existence of other males as potential candidates for adoption, a considerable number of low-status household lines became extinct.

In the United States, stress before 1850 on the importance of inheritance by blood relatives and the availability of a range of schemes for placing children in other households, such as apprenticeship and informal adoption, ensured the continued unpopularity of the idea of formal adoption. After 1850, however, adoption came to be viewed more favorably. The reasons for this were an increased emphasis on the welfare rights of children in custody cases, the desire to remove ambiguities in inheritance law, the ever-present problem of neglected and delinquent children, and the decline in apprenticeship. Nevertheless, adopted children did not secure all the rights of biological children in that they were debarred from inheriting from the blood relatives of their adopted parents and in a few states even from their adopted parents.

In the Soviet Union, adoption was outlawed in 1918 on the grounds that it would be used, as before the Revolution, to recruit cheap labor and preserve inheritances. Only eight years later, however, adoption was reinstated as a consequence of the problems of child homelessness, the need to reduce the cost to the state of child maintenance, a weakened belief in the merit of raising children in institutions, and a greater acceptance of inheritance. The adoption law was not designed to assist childless families, nor was it used to ensure equality for illegitimate children, as the distinction between illegitimate and legitimate children had been abolished by the Family Code of 1918. Important distinctions continued to be drawn, however, between biological and adopted children. For example, under the law of 1926, adopters did not secure similar rights to those held by biological parents to dispose of the child's property, while adopted children could inherit both from their adopted and from their biological parents.

The social disruption occasioned by World War II and profamily policies after the war introduced a more favorable attitude toward adoption in the Soviet Union. Ties between the adopted child and the biological parents were severed by a ruling in 1950, and adoptions by single people began to be discouraged. By 1968 adoptive and biological families had been granted legal equality. Ideological considerations did not provide the prime motivation for these changes, apart from a general desire to tailor the laws to reflect what was conceived at the time as likely to have been in the best interests of the child.

BIBLIOGRAPHY

Bernstein, Laurie. "The Evolution of Soviet Adoption Law." *Journal of Family History* 22.2 (1997), 204–226.

Bonfield, Lloyd. "Church Law and Family Law in Medieval Western Christendom." *Continuity and Change* 6.3 (1991), 361–374.

Gager, Kristin E. "Women, Adoption, and Family Life in Early Modern Paris." *Journal of Family History* 22.1 (1997), 5–25.

Goody, Jack. "Adoption in Cross-Cultural Perspective." *Comparative Studies in Society and History* 11 (1969), 55–78.

Goody, Jack. *The Development of the Family and Marriage in Europe*. Cambridge, 1983.

Grossberg, Michael. *Governing the Hearth. Law and the Family in Nineteenth-Century America*. Chapel Hill, N.C., and London, 1985.

Hanawalt, Barbara A. *The Ties That Bound: Peasant Families in Medieval England*. New York and Oxford, 1986.

Kurosu, Satomi, and Emiko Ochiai. "Adoption as an Heirship Strategy under Demographic Constraints: A Case from Nineteenth-Century Japan." *Journal of Family History* 20.3 (1995), 261–288.

Ross, Ellen. *Love and Toil: Motherhood in Outcast London, 1870–1918*. New York and Oxford, 1993.

Townsend, Nicholas. "Reproduction in Anthropological Demography." In *Anthropological Demography: Toward a New Synthesis*, edited by David I. Kertzer and Tom Fricke, pp. 96–114. Chicago and London, 1997.

RICHARD WALL

ADVERTISING. An old business adage declares that "It pays to advertise." It also *costs* to advertise. Advertisers must invest something, whether labor, goods, or money, to send a message through a selected medium into the marketplace. Thus advertising's history weaves together two mutually reinforcing and dependent themes: (1) market conditions that encourage investments in promoting goods or services; and (2) the evolving means used to project promotional messages. As long as marketers have sought audiences, message carriers have competed through innovation and quality for their patronage, each thereby fueling the other's ambitions. Thus advertising can advance both marketing and communication technologies if it rewards innovation and investment with competitive advantages.

Although marketing entails many decisions and efforts, from conceptualizing, producing, and pricing to promoting and distributing, advertising generally reigns as marketing's most high-profile component. As paid communications conducted through some channel or medium to a multiplicity of people, advertisements differ from publicity (unpaid and uncontrolled communications), sales promotions (special sales events and inducements), and personal selling (one-on-one communications). Advertisers can invest their own time and materials in creating and distributing a message, whether a fence-post sign or a direct-mail brochure. They also can barter labor or goods, or give money for the services of media providers, such as street criers, newspapers, radio networks, and Internet search engines. Since the 1890s, advertisers increasingly have paid, directly or indirectly, for professional assistance in designing and composing their messages, more and more often from advertising agencies. Advertisers thereby have exchanged complete control over their messages for greater effectiveness, but they always retain final authority and, therefore, responsibility. They who pay the piper call the tune, even if under advisement.

Street Media. In the short term, the mutual reinforcement of marketing and communications appears to have yielded ever more dynamic and persuasive impacts. Yet, in the longer view, not even four centuries of print—including more than a century of mass media—have given advertisers the potential for invasiveness, persuasiveness, and feedback of the ancient art of the street seller. Documented evidence of both street crying and peripatetic peddling extends as far back in Mediterranean and European history as recorded town life; and there is no reason to suspect that is has any shorter history elsewhere, despite the lack of surviving evidence. Because it typically announced official as well as commercial news prior to widespread literacy, street crying was often a well-respected trade into the 1800s. Criers' music, antics, ubiquity, and immediacy have yet to find their equal in mass media for creating advertising messages that aim both to inform and to persuade. So powerful were public criers in medieval Paris that tavern keepers had to pay criers who decided to sing their wines' praises. Throughout Europe shopkeepers hired criers both to wander the neighborhood and to stand at their doors enticing passersby with bells and horns, as well as voices.

Visual street media also have flourished for millennia. The world's most famous graffiti beckoned customers with images and text into commercial establishments and entertainments in the Roman resorts Herculaneum and Pompeii. Such hand-painted wall signs adorned other ancient towns, but only these survive in large numbers, preserved by volcanic disaster in 79 CE. Signs over shop doors everywhere date back to market stalls on ancient fair days, often attracting trade only with identifying icons. These images could be literal, such as a clockmaker's wood carving of a clock, or figurative, such as a cloud for bedding. Shop banners and signboards have served like functions in China at least since the eleventh century BCE. Shop signs and signboards (now billboards) still serve everywhere, if now enhanced by words and electricity.

Industrialization and Print. The rise of more ephemeral visual advertisements preceded movable type in such forms as painted, drawn, and written posters, as well as woodcuts and engravings. The small handwritten or printed *siquis* asked "if anybody" wished what was offered, and it could be found handed out or posted in European towns from late medieval times well into the eighteenth century. William Caxton, believed to have published the first book printed in English, generally receives credit for the first English poster printed with movable type, which in 1477 offered a set of ecclesiastical rules. In the mid-1600s, a densely printed handbill introduced the coffeehouse to London, promising "to prevent and cure the dropsy, gout, and scurvy" with this "simple, innocent thing" that "much quickens the spirits, and maketh the heart lightsome." By the 1700s, advances in printing and paper production allowed the broadside to flourish, selling goods, proclaiming entertainments, and fomenting rebellions throughout the world. Large typefaces eventually allowed broadsides' words to be espied from a distance, giving advertisers a new advantage from a relatively inexpensive medium, even though images remained rare, and color almost never appeared. Broadsides, like newspapers, sported only those illustrations for which their printer owned woodcuts; so all incoming ships looked alike in a given paper, as did horses, the two most common icons before the 1820s. Newspapers had begun as small single sheets in the 1600s. Then as paper supplies and printing presses grew in the next century, they became multiples of four pages, folded from large sheets. To maximize revenues, printers often gave the front page over to ads, as some still do. In Philadelphia in the 1700s, Benjamin Franklin admonished his readers more than once to pay up their subscriptions before they complained about advertisers' owning the front page.

Beginning around 1800, powerful demographic and business forces diminished the usefulness of street media and heightened advertisers' willingness to pay to expand their reach. Population centers throughout the world grew in size and density, and both rural and urban inhabitants depended increasingly on goods produced or processed at a distance. Railroads and steamships soon linked producers, retailers, and consumers; but, as an American authori-

ty (Harris, 1890) explained in 1890, "the producer and consumer should know each other. . . . Only the printer's ink can bridge the distance, and bring the producer and consumer into relations of intimacy. The locomotive and printing press must go hand in hand." The street crier could no longer canvas an entire market, and the range and the variety of goods and services becoming available exceeded the capacity of the unaugmented voice. Print's glory days were at hand.

Many advertisers perceived a growing need for greater reach through up-to-date media, if only because their competitors did, and newspapers grew in numbers and size. In the 1820s, advertising subsidized technical innovations that made penny presses possible in the United States. In contrast, stamp taxes on English newspapers between 1713 and 1855, and duties on notices therein until 1853, made that medium too costly for most merchants into midcentury, after which time rapid expansion occurred. Britons in India founded newspapers and solicited advertisements starting in 1780, but there poorly developed markets, not taxation, restrained advertising's growth.

Visual media other than periodicals burgeoned during this same era of market expansion. Ingenious printers competed for merchants' and manufacturers' promotional budgets with posters and countless premiums for inducing consumers' trade. Lithography, invented in Germany in 1796 to replace embossing and engraving, made it possible to print thousands of copies and ultimately hundreds of thousands. By the 1870s chromolithography gave advertisers the first relatively inexpensive multicolor medium, and they commissioned it with abandon for wide distribution and displays in stores and every other public place. Every imaginable item that could be made from paper, and, by the 1880s, from thin sheets of metal, became a potential message carrier. Colorful postcard-size trade cards exploded into the marketplace in the 1870s, and millions of them carried sales arguments with pictures and advertising copy into homes in Europe and America. Manufacturers generally commissioned lithographs to carry unique messages, whereas retailers typically purchased stock (generic) items by the thousand and had their own identities imprinted locally in spaces left blank by lithographers. Calendars, rulers, almanacs, posters, tin plates and cups, and lunch boxes were only some of the beautifully lithographed forms through which entrepreneurs reached the public.

Advertising Specialists and Trademarks. During market expansion prior to 1900, specialists arose as intermediaries between advertisers and periodical media. Developing the functions that later came to define advertising agents, most initially solicited merchants or manufacturers on behalf of newspapers and magazines in the expectation of receiving commissions from the publishers, who

AN ADVERTISEMENT. *Guinness for Strength*, advertisement designed by John Gilroy and produced by S. H. Benson. (Victoria and Albert Museum, London/Art Resource, NY)

were anxious to gain the trade. By the 1890s in both America and Europe, competitive agents increasingly assumed writing and design functions. Because agents are the specialists with whom advertising became most closely associated in the twentieth century, and because periodical media have always been their arena, retrospectives that rely solely on advertising agents see a trend to more color and persuasion since the mid-nineteenth century. However, just as nothing rivaled the dynamism of the street crier before color television, periodical ads did not challenge the visual intensity and narrative content of chromolithographic media until the 1910s. In addition to the often outrageous sales pitches of medicinal purveyors and entertainers, manufacturers, such as McCormick Harvesting Machine Company in the United States, sought to persuade their audiences with lithographed scenes showing their devices to advantage and often displaying their factories as evidence of their successes as industrialists. In 1865, for example, Thomas Barratt became a partner in a venerable English firm producing Pears' Soap; he not only expanded advertising expenditures beyond those of any other nonmedicinal firm, but he applied remarkable creativity. He purchased "fine" art for ads and wrote clever copy that became clichés on both sides of the Atlantic; for years, teasers gleefully asked "Good Morning! Have you used Pears' Soap?"

Advertisements generally contain identifying words and/or pictures—trademarks—that link their messages to what consumers see when they shop. Early on, only goods with high profit margins per unit and low practical demand, such as alcohol, tobacco, and nostrums, afforded the use of consumer-sized packaging on which sellers could affix trademarks. Nineteenth-century industrial capacities made such packaging possible for countless processed and manufactured goods and thus encouraged the growth of brand-name advertising. McCormick and Pears were family names, like most other early trademarks. Other sellers, however, applied descriptive or strongly connotative terms or icons as trademarks, from angels to demons, from flowers to hammers. By the end of the century, especially once mergers began absorbing owner-managed firms, such brand names and trademarks became commonplace. In 1898 the Michelin brothers, French inventors of the pneumatic tire, were inspired by stacks of tires to commission a cartoonist to create the Michelin Man. Since then, this chubby charmer has graced countless advertisements in more than 170 countries to become one of the ten most recognized symbols in the world.

Investments in building a trademark's "goodwill," or positive reputation with consumers, can pay off in enhanced market control. Thus, goodwill became a key marketing goal for nineteenth-century industrialists of consumer goods with low differentials from similar goods. By advertising so intensively that consumers became familiar with and trusted their brands, high-volume manufacturers tried to prevent retailers from substituting goods with lower wholesale prices. Moreover, if consumers insisted on a particular brand, their demand required retailers and wholesalers to carry it, thus effectively pulling the product through the distribution channels. Successful advertising thus could allow manufacturers to rely less on salesmen's pushing a product onto middlemen, who then pushed it onto consumers. In the United States of the 1880s and 1890s, businesspeople considered Royal Baking Powder a wonder of advertising prowess. Although the product was physically indistinguishable from its competitors, the goodwill associated with its trademark forced retailers to carry it while complaining that "there was not a living profit in handling the goods." Once self-service retailing became the norm in the 1920s, the value of such goodwill rose even higher.

Advertising professionalism developed in a variety of ways in the late-nineteenth and early-twentieth centuries. In the West, those manufacturers that grew from small owner-managed firms into large corporations increasingly relied on specialist practitioners to create their messages. For example, the National Biscuit Company (now Nabisco) formed from mergers in 1898, and soon thereafter it initiated an innovative campaign together with N. W. Ayer & Son, an early and prominent agency. Out of this partnership, unusual for the times, came the first major brand name so devised—Uneeda Cracker. A teaser campaign introduced the cracker, based on a traditional cracker, and its uniquely protective package, which effectively kept out both moisture and pests. Extensive follow-up advertising resulted in a level of consumer demand, or pull, that actually required building new factories. This campaign and other successes by agencies adding creative functions to their space brokering began to build a sense of professionalism among practitioners. Although American and British practitioners were notoriously competitive, French advertising agents operated through a series of quasi monopolies until after World War II. Agencies appeared in Canadian cities throughout the 1870s and 1880s, but for lack of sufficient trade, few enjoyed any longevity unless they possessed strong ties to prospering newspapers for which they also could solicit ads. In the 1890s, as truly independent agencies began to thrive, the first francophone agents succeeded, working with clients and media in both French and English. Modern-style Japanese agencies flourished in the 1880s and 1890s, propelled by a burgeoning press. In the mid-1920s, China's many agencies began two shifts: from space brokerage to full service, and from serving primarily Western advertisers to mixes of Chinese and foreign patrons. In 1936, C. P. Ling's China Commercial Advertising Agency celebrated its tenth anniversary, proclaiming "China has taken to advertising with a vengeance." Its "unbounded prospects," however, looked dimmer a few years later, as Chinese advertising would not recover from war and Maoism for forty years. Moscow's first advertising office opened in 1878 with the slogan "Advertising is the Engine of Trade." Interestingly, the Russian Revolution did not abruptly end commercial advertising in 1917; in 1923, ads provided two-thirds of *Izvestiya*'s revenues. But by the end of 1920s, Soviet industrial policies had largely reduced nonstate announcements to promoting entertainments.

Regulations, Persuasion, and New Media. State policies affected practices in the Western world as well as the East. For decades after 1890, reformers in the United States and Britain attacked misleading advertising, often through the very presses dependent on it. The U.S. Pure Food and Drug Act of 1906 evinced great popular support for protections regarding both claims and product content. Some magazines, most famously *Collier's*, *McClure's*, and the *Ladies' Home Journal*, took up the cause, banishing patent medicine and alcohol ads and asserting that any goods found in their pages were trustworthy. To improve public standing, ad professionals banded together in trade associations and in the 1910s advocated a nongovernmental Truth-in-Advertising campaign, in the hopes of fending off regulations and gaining tax credits. In 1917, the American Association of Advertising Agencies consolidated many groups' efforts.

State policies also determined the varied courses of the twentieth-century's signature medium, broadcasting. Early in the twentieth century, countries everywhere debated control of the airwaves; many countries, including both Britain and Canada, initially prohibited radio advertising, instead selling both transmitters' and listeners' licenses to found broadcasting. Britain elected to retain state control, providing content through the British Broadcasting Company but not providing a conduit for advertisers. Beginning in 1930, enterprising broadcasters set up in France and elsewhere, including ships at sea, to attract British advertising revenues; policy changed in 1971, allowing independent stations. Commercial broadcasting began in the United States in 1922, shortly after it was technically possible, although amid great controversy. Many citizens objected to using the airwaves to send advertisements into homes, commodifying what some considered a public cultural resource. Even so, strong economic pressures enabled advertisers to "buy" blocks of time from national networks and local stations and to produce the content, with each show having a single sponsor. Canada evolved a hybrid system of licenses with restricted advertising on all stations at first. In the 1930s and 1940s, private stations and the national network cooperated to build national public-service broadcasting alongside commercial shows imported from or modeled on U.S. programming. Japan banned commercial radio until 1951, yet by the end of the following year its advertising expenditures for radio already exceeded those for magazines.

Televising blossomed as an advertising medium after World War II. In the United States, television began with sponsor-produced programming, following radio's patterns. By the 1960s, however, "spot" commercials became the norm, breaking the link between individual advertisers and programming while increasing advertisers' reach. Britain's Television Act of 1954 allowed commercials but clearly disallowed any influence on programming whatsoever. British agencies' lack of experience in active presentations resulted in years of commercials that played like dramatized press advertisements. Commercial television in Japan expanded rapidly after its introduction in 1953, taking a 34 percent share of total expenditures in 1975, even topping newspapers. Its advertising profession likewise grew apace, so that by the mid-1990s ten Japanese agencies ranked among the world's top thirty in terms of billings (money value of ads placed). Dentsu, founded in 1901, has ranked at the top worldwide since the 1970s, in part because of its many initiatives since World War II to further profession's maturation and public stature.

Consumer purchase decisions result from evaluating many types of utility. When goods and services are in limited supply, advertisements tend merely to announce availability, assuming that demand exceeds supply. In fact, "to advertise" originally meant to announce or warn. Thus, prior to industrialization, advertisers functioned primarily to inform, with the exceptions of medicine sellers and entertainers. During industrialization, marketers—retail, wholesale, and manufacturing—often found it advantageous to ascribe meaning to products and services in order to generate demand that could absorb increasing supplies. (In some cases, however, entrepreneurs' promotional successes drove production.) In industrial and media systems uncongenial to commercial marketing, such as the Soviet bloc nations, however, a product often was offered simply as a product, with limited and objective instrumental value. Even an excess of a product could result in nothing more evocative than billboard copy such as "Drink Milk." Any persuasion derived from implications of what people *should* do, rather than what they might wish to do. In contrast, U.S. advertisers, first nostrum purveyors and then others, have long honed techniques for attaching meanings. For example, a 1923 magazine ad for Lifebuoy soap told parents to "Guard Your Children from City Contagions." It pictured a father riding on the trolley in close contact with various "nameless foes of health." Once home, he reached to embrace his lovely and vulnerable family without having taken precautions to "purify" himself from the "menace of dirt." Lifebuoy told mothers that, as "the *health doctors*" of their families, they must be wary of contagion and provide the "pure and wholesome" solution. Lifebuoy soap took similar strategies around the world, telling native Zimbabweans, for instance, that "Successful Men Use Lifebuoy," and "Keep Healthy . . . Keep Clean . . . Use Lifebuoy, the *Health* Soap."

Building the power of trademarks through countless promotions may well prove as potent a force in globalization as any other. The worldwide headway of Sony Walkman and the eternal battling of Coca-Cola and Pepsi certainly mark cultural convergence as propelled by advertising. Moreover, as varied as are the histories of the world's cultures, the strong dependence of advertising processes upon communications systems lends common patterns to local transformations. Having a communications medium available, both technically and legally, for advertising encourages entrepreneurs to reach potential buyers. Advertisers seek the most alluring medium available to add its meaning, as "up-to-date," to the meaning of their message. Henry Sampson wrote in his 1874 history of advertising: "In advertising there seems to be always something new springing up, and no sooner do we think we have discovered the last ingenious expedient of the man anxious to display his wares, or tempt others to display theirs, than another and more novel plan for publicity arrests the attention, and makes its predecessor seem old-fashioned, if not obsolete" (p. 597).

Some call this progress. It certainly explains the drive, beginning in the mid-1990s, to exploit Internet narrowcasting as an advertising medium. The Internet's potential for extending reach beyond many demographic borders—if not entirely across classes—to invade online activities with animated banners, and to embed feedback beacons, technically known as cookies, within consumers' computers, adds to its appeal as the latest state-of-the-art medium. Although turn-of-the-millennium Internet options remain primitive, by the time this essay is in print, some ingenious entrepreneur may have found a way, online, to match the street criers' advertising impact.

BIBLIOGRAPHY

Countless narratives about historical advertisements are easily located within the histories of specific brands or firms, both in print and on the Internet. In addition to sources focused on particular products or companies, the most reliable general sources include the *International Directory of Company Histories* and *Gale Business Resources* (see below).

Borden, Neil H. *The Economic Effects of Advertising*. Chicago, 1944. Classic study with a historical perspective that assesses advertising's importance to firms, entrepreneurship, and markets.

Burke, Timothy. *Lifebuoy Men, Lux Women: Commodification, Consumption, and Cleanliness in Modern Zimbabwe*. Durham, N.C., 1996. Rare and theoretically sophisticated analysis of advertising's interactions with social, cultural, and political variables in a non-Western nation.

Fox, Stephen. *The Mirror Makers: A History of American Advertising and Its Creators*. New York, 1984. Valuable resource for details on agency histories, but limited by lack of information or perspective other than that of the agents.

Frith, Katherine Toland, ed. *Advertising in Asia: Communication, Culture, and Consumption*. Ames, Iowa, 1996. The essays in this well-edited collection focus on present conditions in specific Asian regions, but each includes a historical perspective supplemented by a bibliography. Together the essays provide a uniquely useful access to historical information on the topic.

Garvey, Ellen Gruber. *The Adman in the Parlor: Magazines and the Gendering of Consumer Culture, 1880s to 1910s*. New York, 1996. Analysis of the successes of lithographed trade cards and then magazines in bringing advertisements into the American home.

Hanson, Philip. *Advertising and Socialism: The Nature and Extent of Consumer Advertising in the Soviet Union, Poland, Hungary, and Yugoslavia*. White Plains, N.Y., 1974. Detailed analysis of advertising outside its most congenial environments; important for showing the comparative role of the state.

Harris, E. P. "Random Thoughts on Trade and Advertising." *Inland Printer* 8 (December 1890), 202–203.

Hower, Ralph M. *The History of an Advertising Agency: N. W. Ayer and Son at Work, 1869–1939*. Cambridge, Mass., 1939. In-depth study of an important U.S. agency during the field's formative decades.

International Directory of Company Histories. Chicago. Published annually since 1988, these collections of business histories, based largely on secondary sources and trade journals, include discussions of important advertising campaigns. The series is available through public and academic libraries.

Laird, Pamela Walker. *Advertising Progress: American Business and the Rise of Consumer Marketing*. Baltimore, 1998. Detailed examination of the cultural, business, and technological contexts for advertising's evolution in the United States between 1860 and 1920.

Marchand, Roland. *Advertising the American Dream: Making Way for Modernity, 1920–1940*. Berkeley, 1985. A model interpretation of the field and its output, this classic elegantly shows how American advertising agents in the 1920s and 1930s played out their social ambitions and prejudices through the advertisements they created.

Nevett, T. R. *Advertising in Britain: A History*. London, 1982. Well-illustrated narrative that covers ancient to recent Britain.

Ohmann, Richard. *Selling Culture: Magazines, Markets, and Class at the Turn of the Century*. London and New York, 1996. Interpretation of the dynamics between American publishing and advertising within their ambient culture.

Pollay, Richard W. *Information Sources in Advertising History*. Westport, Conn., 1979. Detailed and lengthy annotated bibliography of published advertising resources in English before 1979.

Pope, Daniel. *The Making of Modern Advertising*. New York, 1983. Very useful analytical narrative of the business history of American advertising through the 1920s.

Sampson, Henry. *A History of Advertising from the Earliest Times*. London, 1874; reprinted, Detroit, 1974. History of the European, especially the English, roots of advertising in great detail up to the point of the modern takeoff.

Strasser, Susan. *Satisfaction Guaranteed: The Making of the American Mass Market*. New York, 1989. Study linking the business decisions of many advertisers with their marketing concerns, processes, and innovations.

Tedlow, Richard. *New and Improved: The Story of Mass Marketing in America*. New York, 1990. Detailed analyses of four major case studies of marketing innovation, including their advertising campaigns.

Yi, Xu Bai. *Marketing to China: One Billion New Customers*. Lincolnwood, Ill., 1990. For those involved with current marketing to China, this book provides useful general and case histories.

PAMELA WALKER LAIRD

AFGHANISTAN. *See* Central Asia.

AGE COMPOSITION. An important aspect of population structure is its composition according to the size of each age group. Any grouping by age can be employed, depending on the purpose of an inquiry, but one of the most commonly used is a five-year span calculated for both sexes. A population pyramid is a graphic expression of such an age-sex structure. A broad-based pyramid represents a young, faster-growing population as contrasted with a narrow-based pyramid, which represents a slower rate of population growth.

Dependency Ratio. For research and reporting purposes, a three-part broad-category classification is commonly employed: 0 to 14, 15 to 64, and 65-plus are the age groups widely adopted; for populations of the past, 0 to 14, 15 to 59, and 60-plus are also used. From the three-part grouping it is possible to define a dependency ratio, which relates the sum of the old and young age groups to the size of the central working-age category. Since most people under the age of fifteen and over the age of sixty-five are not in the workforce (hence called "an economically dependent population"), the statistic expresses how many dependents one working-age person has to support. This is a useful measure for historical studies of the relationship between population and economy.

According to United Nations estimates (*World Population Prospects*, New York, 1999), the mean dependency ratio for less developed countries from 1950 to 1955, calculated with the 0 to 14, 15 to 64, and 65-plus age groupings, was 71.3 per 100 as against 54.4 for more developed countries. The gap widened by 1965 to 1970, with 83.8 for the former and 57.5 for the latter. This meant that working men and women in the third world had to feed about 40 percent more dependents than their counterparts did in wealthier nations. The key factor explaining this contrast is differential population growth. In the 1950s and 1960s, the population of less developed regions grew at the average rate of well over 2 percent per year, while the average rate for the developed countries was 1 percent. Although a natural increase is determined by both birth rates and death rates, it is demonstrated that age structure is determined largely by fertility (because changing mortality affects, more or less, all the age categories—whereas only the young age groups are affected by a change in fertility). In other words, higher birth rates in the developing world resulted in higher dependency ratios, despite their death rates remaining comparatively high.

It is interesting to see that the proposition also holds for the so-called preindustrial period. According to Tony Wrigley and Roger Schofield in *The Population History of England, 1541–1871* (London, 1981), who chose age sixty rather than sixty-five as the lower end of the old-age category, England experienced a high dependency regime in the mid-sixteenth century. The ratio fell to a low in the late seventeenth and rose again to a peak in the 1820s. In both the mid-sixteenth century and the early nineteenth, England's population was growing with high fertility, while late-seventeenth-century England had a reduced fertility rate and population hardly increased. To put this differently, in both the early modern and the modern periods of population growth, English adults had to support up to 40 percent more dependents than they did in the middle, sluggish period.

This age-composition approach is only one way of measuring how population growth affects living standards. It should be remembered, however, that the dependency ratio is a crude measure, since it does not take into account the changing consumption needs and productive capacity of people—which vary with age and sex. In fact, by adopting appropriate age-sex schedules of consumption and production, Wrigley and Schofield demonstrated that changes in the age structure of preindustrial England affected the consumer-producer balance "far less than is suggested by the dependency ratio," although it still holds that an increase in fertility did have a negative effect on the balance between consumption and productive capacity of the population.

Aging of the Population. The Wrigley and Schofield study (1981) shows that while the dependency ratio fluctuated greatly with changing fertility rates, the proportion of the elderly to the total population did not change significantly from 1541 to 1871. A decline in fertility, for example, was largely absorbed by an increase in the size of the working-age population. Yet when fertility was further reduced, as was the case for England after the late nineteenth century, the relative proportion of old people did start to expand. This increase in the relative importance of the elderly is called an "aging of the population." The proportion of those aged 65 and over in England and Wales, for example, was 4.7 percent in 1871, and it did not change until 1901. In 1931, it rose to 7.4 percent, and it exceeded 10 percent during the 1950s. Appearing through this process was what Peter Laslett in *A Fresh Map of Life* (London, 1989) called the "Third Age," a new life-course stage that emerged between the period of working life and that of complete dependence. The process was based on an increase in the probability of a young adult's reaching an old age. Judging from available life tables, the probability of reaching age seventy from age twenty-five (a Third Age indicator) was modest before the twentieth century. In

England, it did not exceed 30 percent until 1891, but today a majority of twenty-five-year-olds will live on to their seventieth birthday and even into an age long after retirement (with a probability of 0.581 for men and 0.749 for women in England and Wales, as of 1961).

Aging of the population is rapid in countries where the decline of fertility started late. Post–World War II Japan, for example, has an accelerated aging of the population. In 1935, the country's proportion aged 65 and over was 4.7 percent, with the Third Age indicator being 0.365 for men and 0.483 for women; by 1990, the proportion over 65 was 12.1 percent with the probability of 25-year-olds reaching 70 years of age rising to 0.759 for men and to 0.879 for women (calculated from life tables published by Japan's Ministry of Welfare). Compared with the English experience, the length of Japan's aging process was halved. It is estimated that the process in China, where a dramatic fall in fertility took place as late as the 1970s, will be even more rapid. For a country having not yet reached the "more developed" stage in economic development, this will pose an unprecedented problem in relation to the balance between the productive-age population and the dependent.

[*See also* Baby Boom.]

BIBLIOGRAPHY

Laslett, Peter. *A Fresh Map of Life: The Emergence of the Third Age.* London, 1989. Chapter 6 is a good overview of the demographic history of aging based chiefly on the English experience.

United Nations. *World Population Prospects: The 1998 Revision.* New York, 1999. Demographic databank for all the countries of the world in the recent past, 1950–1995. Also contains projected numbers for 1995–2050.

Wrigley, E. Anthony, and Roger S. Schofield. *The Population History of England, 1541–1871. A Reconstruction.* London, 1981. Probably the only work so far available that enables us to trace centuries of changing age structures in the preindustrial period.

OSAMU SAITO

AGNELLI FAMILY. The origins of the Agnelli family can be traced to Villar Perosa, in Piedmont, where they were rich landowners from the beginning of the nineteenth century. There, on 13 August 1866, Giovanni Agnelli, the man who would make Fiat into the most important of the Italian automobile manufacturers and one of the biggest in Europe, was born. After service as an Army officer, Agnelli, together with other landowners and bankers who were strongly attracted by technical progress, founded Fabbrica Italiana Automobili Torino (Fiat) in 1899 in Turin. Initially just one of the shareholders, he soon emerged as the firm's leader.

Unlike others of his time, Agnelli was quick to understand that the automobile was not just a toy for wealthy people. He grasped the industrial features of production as well as the enormous possibilities of market expansion. He took note of the American model and strongly wanted to "do it like Ford," aiming for mass production and vertical integration. This strategy, in spite of the serious financial crisis of 1907, permitted Fiat to gain control of more than 50 percent of Italian automobile production by the eve of World War I.

The war brought in military orders—for trucks, airplanes, and machine guns—and allowed Fiat to move from thirtieth to third position in Italian industry, as employees, who had numbered 4,000 at the beginning of the war, increased to 40,000 by its end. Thanks to Agnelli, Fiat did not scatter its war profits into diversification in unrelated sectors. Rather, they were utilized to build up a highly integrated automobile complex (from steel production to dealerships) and a new installation in Turin, the Lingotto plant, the most modern in Europe when it started operations in 1923. In 1926 Agnelli created IFI (Italian Financial Institute), the holding company in which he concentrated all his investments, including 70 percent of Fiat.

In the postwar period, Agnelli had to deal with the problem of workers eager to imitate the Soviet experience. In September 1920, the factory—as happened in many Italian firms—was occupied by workers for a month. Agnelli was a liberal thinker who accepted social conflicts as normal in industrial life; but, when the workers' movement challenged his property rights, he became a supporter of Mussolini's dictatorship. Mussolini appointed him senator in 1923, granted him extensive control of the labor force, and did him several favors, including a 1930 decree that de facto prohibited foreign competitors from entering Italy and made Fiat a protected monopoly. Nevertheless, Agnelli maintained his independence from Fascism. Key positions in Fiat were never assigned for political reasons; and, going against Mussolini's fear of concentrations of workers, in 1936 Agnelli started construction of the Mirafiori plant in Turin, still the company's industrial heart.

Agnelli's designated heir was his son, Edoardo, who had married Virginia Bourbon del Monte, a noblewoman, and had seven children with her. Edoardo's untimely death in a 1935 plane crash forced his father to become directly involved in the education of the eldest grandson, Giovanni (Gianni), who was groomed as his successor. But when the elder Giovanni died in 1945, Gianni was only twenty-four years old. The reins of Fiat were taken over by Giovanni Agnelli's closest collaborator, Vittorio Valletta.

Under Valletta's leadership, the "Fordist" strategy of Giovanni Agnelli fully materialized. With the aid of the European Recovery Program (the Marshall plan), Valletta extensively renovated the plants. In this way, Fiat moved from production of 55,000 automobiles in 1939 to more than a million in 1963.

Finally, in 1966, Gianni Agnelli became Fiat's president, assisted by his brother Umberto and an experienced manager, Gaudenzio Bono. In the following years, Fiat coped with serious difficulties caused by a rigid and hierarchical company structure, an economy upset by oil crises, and strong conflicts inside the factories, which occasionally led to terrorism. This turbulence was brought on by Fiat itself, which had concentrated too much of its expansion in Turin, leading to social problems in the city. In this plight, Gianni Agnelli revealed himself to be a capable leader. He started a wide organizational decentralization, separated the role of ownership from that of management with the nomination of Cesare Romiti as chief executive officer, and found an important new investor in 1976 in Lafico, a financial holding company owned by the Libyan government.

Following a long strike in 1980, Fiat was able to convince the labor unions to accept thousand of layoffs. At the same time, an extensive process of automation inside the factories was begun, yielding excellent economic results for the entire decade.

The globalization of the 1990s compelled Fiat to search for a partner, an objective that may have been met with its recent alliance with General Motors. At the same time, through its IFI holding, the Agnelli family has built a conglomerate with interests in sectors as varied as banking, insurance, mass retailing, food processing, and tourism. At the beginning of the twenty-first century, the family still occupies a central role in Italian life, even identifying itself as owner and sponsor of the nation's most popular soccer team, Juventus. Giovanni Agnelli continues to be a recognized leader of the Italian business community. In 1992 he was appointed senator for life by the president of the republic, as his grandfather before him had been. Other Agnelli relatives have also served in public office. Fiat remains Italy's most important industrial group, second only to the Italian government in its number of employees.

BIBLIOGRAPHY

Bairati, Piero. *Vittorio Valletta*. Turin, 1983.
Castronovo, Valerio. *Giovanni Agnelli*, Turin, 1977.
Castronovo, Valerio. *Fiat, 1899–1999*. Milan, 1999.
Galli, Giancarlo. *Gli Agnelli: Una dinastia, un impero, 1899–1998*. Milan, 1997.
Ori, Angiolo Silvio. *Storia di una dinastia: Gli Agnelli e la Fiat*. Rome, 1996.
Romiti, Cesare. *Questi anni alla Fiat*. Milan, 1988.
Turani, Giuseppe. *L'avvocato*. Milan, 1985.
Pietra, Italo. *I tre Agnelli*. Milan, 1985.

FRANCO AMATORI

AGRIBUSINESS. In the late nineteenth and early twentieth centuries, it became clear that more and more activities once essential to agriculture were carried on outside the farm. The change appeared all the more dramatic because agriculture was usually considered as a pre-Smithian world, ignoring the division of labor. The notion

AGRIBUSINESS. Harvesting grain on the Hungarian plateau, 1985. (© Bill Weems/Woodfin Camp and Associates, New York)

of agribusiness emerged in this context. The term was coined to refer in a single word to encompass not only farming but also such diverse activities as food processing to the enterprises that produce farms' inputs or provide supporting services. More recently, the term became even more comprehensive and now also refers to farms, to agribusiness companies (formal or informal, large or small), to education/research institutions, to various profit or nonprofit organizations, and to public-sector agencies.

Agribusiness thus describes a major multifaceted transition. "Modern times" begins by replacing wooden plows with steel-gang plows, sickles with mechanical reapers, and manure with chemicals spread by planes (as in Alfred Hitchcock's 1959 movie *North by Northwest*). It ends when agribusiness replaces agriculture. While in traditional societies the food was mostly made of agricultural products prepared within the family, modern societies received more and more of their caloric intakes from agricultural products transformed by agribusiness firms. If, in the 1960s, the food consumed in western Europe was divided into two roughly equal parts—agricultural products processed by various industries on the one hand and raw agricultural products on the other—since then, the first one grew quickly at the expense of the second. In relative terms, agriculture thus shrank while agribusiness grew, and the part of agricultural value added in the food consumed declined.

It is noteworthy that the notion was used continuously for damnations and defense of capitalism. Indeed, it dates back to the late nineteenth century, when Karl Kautsky (1854–1938) and others underscored that fact that agricul-

ture's fate had come to depend on agribusiness for better but also for worse. After Kautsky's *Agrarfrage*, the notion of agribusiness put to the fore the question of monopoly power of large, often globalized firms producing farm inputs (such as seeds, chemicals, machinery, etc.) or transforming farm products (in the dairy industry, for instance).

If the notion of agribusiness helps to gauge how deeply agriculture is linked today to a number of activities, it also has interesting consequences for analyzing its past. First, it has contributed to a reassessment of the history of European long-term growth. Ironically, while it insists on the revolutionary characteristics of the recent modernization, it "de-revolutionizes" the past. Indeed, as it ties farming and the various enterprises that produce, process, and distribute farm products, the notion of agribusiness is particularly relevant for analyzing the very long period during which agriculture was the main source not only of food but also of the great bulk of the raw material used in manufacture. During the medieval and early modern period, industry was to some extent "agribusiness." Food-processing firms alone then played such a significant part in European growth that they can be seen as "industrialization before industrialization." For this reason, when historians started analyzing this sector, they were led to a quite different vision of the Industrial Revolution. The British brewing industry is a classical example. In the late seventeenth or early eighteenth century, it was both an important component of British agribusiness and of the British economy because the market for such goods as grains or beverages relied predominantly on domestic products and because the quantities involved were huge. Consumers' spending on drink alone (wine, beer, spirits, and cider) exceeded the value of the whole of English overseas trade. But if the rate of growth in this sector had little in common with the rate of growth in the cotton industry, it had long attracted a large amount of capital. The first industrial censuses made it clear. In mid-nineteenth century France, for instance, half of industrial capital was concentrated in agribusiness (a figure that is admittedly an upper bond since sources neglect both mining and railways).

When this sector was taken into account, agribusiness contributed to the downward revision of the rate of growth during the Industrial Revolution: first because it was already well developed in the pre-industrial period, and, second, because it also developed elsewhere besides the sectors usually seen as the birthplace of industrial revolution (textiles), where the pace of growth in the late eighteenth and early nineteenth century was much quicker. Moreover, regions where agribusiness firms were well developed early were threatened by knowing the bleak fate of early comers locked in outdated technologies and turned into "angry orphans" (to use Paul David's phrase) due to their early start.

If agribusiness was already so important in European economies in the early modern period, it gives more weight to Fernand Braudel's insight that says the choice of either wheat or rice as staple food had long-lasting consequences. Indeed, China has developed food habits that give place both to rice and wheat and share with Europe the same technology of milling wheat (which developed roughly in the same time in Europe and China, twenty-five hundred years ago). But it remains true that the investments required by wheat mills resulted in a more capital-intensive food-processing industry in Europe than in China. In this respect, the European historical experience is at odds with the classical model of growth put forth by Sir Arthur Lewis (1915–1991).

To the contrary, where rice is the staple food, one can be satisfied with Lewis's model of a two-sector economy: peasant agriculture (relying on labor and land but no capital) on the one hand, and industry (relying on labor and capital) on the other hand. In such a world, growth occurs as capital is accumulated in the modern sector, which absorbs the surplus labor removed from the traditional sector. Instead, where wheat is the staple food, one cannot imagine an agriculture without agribusiness. There is no such thing as peasant agriculture or a sector of the economy without capital. This has clear implications for the presumed dichotomy between peasant and capitalists that has been imposed on rural history by generations of sociological historians.

BIBLIOGRAPHY

Chanut, Jean-Marie, et al. *L'industrie française au milieu du 19e siècle: Les enquêtes de la statistique générale de la France*. Paris, 2000.

Gernet, Jacques. *Les aspects économiques du bouddhisme dans la société chinoise du Ve au Xe siècle*. Paris, 1956. Also available in Chinese and in English.

Kautsky, Karl. *Die Agrarfrage: Eine Uebersicht über die Tendenzen der modernen Landwirtschaft und die Agrarpolitik der Sozialdemokratie*. Stuttgart, 1899. Also available in English, French, and Italian.

Mathias, Peter. *The Brewing Industry in England, 1700–1830*. Cambridge, 1959.

Sabban, Françoise, and Silvano Serventi. *La pasta: Storia e cultura di un cibo universale*, Rome, 2000. Also available in English and French.

Wrigley, Edward Anthony. *Continuity, Chance and Change: The Character of the Industrial Revolution in England*, Cambridge, 1988.

GILLES POSTEL-VINAY

AGRICOLA, GEORGIUS (1494–1555), German physician and writer on mining and metallurgy.

Known as the "father of metallurgy," Agricola (Georg Bauer) was born in Glauchau, Saxony, and at the age of twenty entered the University of Leipzig. After a period of teaching and further study, he was appointed town physician at Joachimsthal in Bohemia, which was then in the midst of the most prolific metal-mining district of central Europe. He thereafter devoted most of his spare time to an extended study of written sources on mining and visits to local mines and smelters, combined with extensive conversations with the industry's leading practitioners. This early

GEORGIUS AGRICOLA. (Art Resource, NY)

phase of Agricola's lifelong study resulted in the publication of his dialogue *Bermannus* in 1530, which dealt with mineralogy and mining terms. After leaving his position at Joachimsthal in the same year, Agricola traveled extensively and carried out further research of mines and mining methods. In 1533, he became city physician in the town of Chemnitz, Saxony, where as a resident until his sudden death in 1555, he played a prominent part in local affairs. It is this latter part of his life that produced the studies on which his historical reputation is based.

In 1546, Agricola published a series of works that dealt with the fundamentals of physical geology, mining, and metals. The most important of these was *De natura fossilium*, which is the first systematic attempt at mineralogy. This classified minerals into five categories: "earths" (such as clays), "stones properly so-called" (such as gems), "solidified juices" (such as salts), "metals," and "compounds" (such as galena). Also noteworthy was *De ortu et causis subterraneorum*, a pioneering work on physical geography, which identified the erosive force of wind and water linked to landform development. *De natura eorum quae effluunt ex terra* dealt with subterranean waters and gases, *De veteribus et novis metallis* explained the history of metals and mineralogy, and *Rerum metallicarum interpretatio* listed a glossary of Latin and German mineralogical and metallurgical terms.

Agricola's most important and enduring publication is *De re metallica*, which was planned as early as the late 1520s but not completed until 1550. It was published posthumously in 1556, the delay caused by the time needed to prepare the numerous woodcuts that are a feature of the work. It consists of twelve "books" and is an extremely detailed account of mining and smelting techniques. The significance of the study was not in the advancement of new methods but in providing a comprehensive compendium of the mining and smelting technology then extant, which had previously been shrouded by considerable secrecy. The study's importance may be judged by the fact that it circulated widely in Europe during the sixteenth and seventeenth centuries, issued in at least ten editions in three languages, and was not superseded until the publication of Christoph Andreas Schlüter's metallurgical handbook in 1738. (Agricola's *De re metallica* was translated anew and edited in the twentieth century by Herbert Clark Hoover and Lou Henry Hoover.) Agricola, with his liberal religious views and his additional interests in classical scholarship, education, and music, is considered a scientific humanist of world significance.

BIBLIOGRAPHY

Halleux, Robert, and Albert Yans, trans. *Bermannus (Le mineur): Un dialogue sur les mines*, by Georgius Agricola. Paris, 1990. French translation with introduction, notes, and commentary.

Hoover, Herbert Clark, and Lou Henry Hoover, eds. and trans. *De re metallica* (1556), by Georgius Agricola. London, 1912. The English translation with introduction, commentary, and bibliographical and biographical notes.

Naumann, Friedrich, ed. *Georgius Agricola: 500 Jahre*. Basel, 1994. Proceedings of a conference held in Chemnitz. A comprehensive evaluation of Agricola's life and historical significance.

Singer, Charles, et al., eds. *A History of Technology*, vol. 3, *From the Renaissance to the Industrial Revolution, c. 1500–c. 1750*. Oxford, 1957. Contains a number of references to Agricola, which places his work in the broader context of technological development.

NICHOLAS GODDARD

AGRICULTURAL CREDIT. Agricultural credit institutions and issues evolve in a manner complementary to evolution of agricultural production systems. The range of contemporary developed and developing countries include each stage of these evolutionary processes. Thus, one can understand agricultural credit history by understanding current geographic differences and vice versa. However, the evolution of both agricultural production and credit systems is far faster for contemporary developing countries than was the case for the currently developed countries. That pace creates special problems of management and discipline of credit systems.

Stages of Agricultural Credit Development. Agricultural development and the related evolution of agricultural credit divides into four stages. These stages cover a continuum of increasing commercialization and intensification of agriculture, rapid technological change, steady decline in the relative size of the agricultural sector, and rapid increase in credit requirements.

As the economy develops, the size of a farm increases with respect to land and capital per farm unit. The size of the labor force per farm tends not to increase, on the average, beyond the order of two full-time persons. Agriculture remains widely dispersed geographically because of the importance of land in production. That dispersion is a primary reason for small labor forces per farm. It is difficult to manage a widely dispersed labor force. That is in sharp contrast to manufacturing, which experiences rapid increase in the labor force per enterprise. It is also in contrast to the many support services provided to a modern farm enterprise. Thus, complex relationships must be worked out to relate the farm enterprise to the support services. Systems of credit become increasingly intertwined with those interenterprise relations.

Thus, the big change in agriculture is in technology, including biological and mechanical technology. With technological improvement, a small labor force can manage large quantities of capital and labor and be highly productive. As these changes occur, the need for agricultural credit increases, the form of that credit changes, and the required institutional structures change.

Pure subsistence agriculture. Hunting and gathering societies, as well as early stages of settled agriculture, are largely subsistence. Each family unit produces essentially all of what it consumes, with little surplus for sale. However, in the family life cycle the relative size of consumption and production change. Good fortune or a calamity of health, hunting, or crop also brings a disjuncture between production and consumption. Those disjunctions provide opportunity for one family to provide consumption goods or even production goods to others on a temporary basis.

Such transfers were the first forms of credit. They were on a reciprocal basis with an expected symmetry in life cycle stage or good and bad fortune. Such credit systems evolved into multilateral arrangements, in which *A* might lend to *B* and *C* while at some later date *C* might lend to *D*. To facilitate such multilateral exchange, interest as a formal payment for loans was instituted.

Once interest entered the credit system, efficient transfer of resources could occur over life cycles, good fortune, and calamity. In such a multilateral world, lenders protected themselves from loss by requiring security in the form of the borrowers' assets, such as land, or consumption goods, including jewelry, that could be taken if the loan and interest were not repaid.

The recipient of a loan would prosper if he or she could invest it in productive processes at a rate of return higher than the interest rate. However, that was not likely in a subsistence economy with limited improvements in technology. On the other hand, some might suffer sequences of misfortune from health or crop damage and thereby accumulate debt and interest so that more and more production is needed for repayment. In such a downward spiral, borrowers would relinquish their meager assets in payment of the debt or possibly provide labor in payment, moving into bondage. That circumstance generated the literature of protest in earlier stages of commercialization that revolved around the rapacious moneylender. We see such a literature in nineteenth-century Europe, Japan, and North America. It is a recurrent literature in contemporary low-income countries of Asia and Africa. Of course, concurrently come nostrums about becoming debt free.

Early stages of commercialization. As agriculture evolves, it gradually becomes more specialized, buying inputs and selling output. The need for production credit grows. That stage proceeded rapidly in North America, Europe, and Japan in the early decades of the twentieth century. In Asia, it began forcefully in the early decades after World War II and the end of colonialism. It is barely underway now in much of Africa.

Production credit allows an increase in income that can soon diminish debt. Credit increasingly becomes an instrument for increased prosperity rather than an instrument of exploitation in the context of bad luck and improvidence.

Contemporary with the increasing commercialization of agriculture, the total demand for credit began to outpace the capacity of local moneylenders to provide credit. Moneylenders worked adequately as long as there was a need for modest levels of consumption credit and perhaps some small production loans. They lacked the capacity to expand rapidly with increased commercialization. Moneylenders were also poorly placed to productively absorb increased savings that normally follow periods of rapid farm-income growth.

There was increasing need to tap larger capital markets within a region, across urban and rural communities, and finally internationally. Institutions developed to integrate capital markets. Moneylenders saw a decline in the interest they could charge. Commercial banks already serving urban commerce began to lend to farmers. Specialized institutions, some established by governments, started to meet farmers' needs. Such institutional innovation came on rapidly in the 1920s and 1930s in the developed countries. A similar evolution is now underway in the developing countries of Asia and Africa. However, the sheer rapidity of development has brought poor supervision, mounting problems of late payments, bad debts, and failing financial institutions.

Even as credit institutions evolve, agriculture continues to suffer from the vicissitudes of weather and other sources of calamity as well as continued problems with individual improvidence. In addition, farmers are especially vulnerable to major price fluctuations. Prices of products farmers produce fluctuate more than the products they buy, with consequent large changes in net incomes. All of these forces leave farmers in a position of losing their assets to lenders, with lenders continuing to risk an unsavory reputation if they claim those assets on a universal basis.

Late stages of commercialization. In the late stages of commercialization of agriculture, it becomes possible for farmers to take up mechanical innovation, including tractors and highly complex harvesting machinery, that allows the amount of land farmed per family to increase dramatically. At the same time, rapid growth of urban industry provides attractive jobs for farmers' children. The result is a period of rapid consolidation of farms.

In that stage, credit needs become immense. Production inputs for crops and livestock—as well as land acquisition on a large scale—must be financed. And as children leave agriculture, they demand compensation for their share of the land inheritance. Thus, the whole farm asset, including the immensely valuable land resource, must undergo refinancing every generation. That is a major function of agricultural credit systems in late stages of commercialization. New institutional forms of credit develop and old ones expand. Government again plays an important role in expanding the agricultural credit system.

Industrialization of Agriculture. As economies develop further, technology becomes increasingly complex and fast moving, the farm business expands, capital requirements grow, and the need to control quality and the flow of produce on the part of processors increases. New ways of providing capital come to the fore. The old system of borrowing from intermediaries who provided links to the national and international capital markets gives way to an integration of farm production with input supplies and marketing. That ultimately leads to contract farming.

Contract farming is often described as the industrialization of agriculture. It is not that the individual farm production unit starts to employ large labor forces. Rather, the family farm, with several full-time employees and massive capital requirements, undertakes a contract, usually with a marketing agency, that supplies inputs, provides the market and quality control (including the training of farmers), and finances the whole effort.

The farmer puts up only a modest proportion of the total capital required. The processor, as the orchestrator of the operation, provides the financing on a contract basis that specifies the delivery schedule. In this case, the financier is the processor, who in turn relies on the global financial markets for capital through equity, bonds, and bank credit. Thus, the credit system is vertically integrated to efficiently provide credit as well as operate the total input and marketing chain.

The industrialization stage moves from financing of agriculture into the realm of industrial finance. Agricultural credit, then, has few distinguishing features. Prior to that stage, a multitude of special problems arise. Those problems are especially relevant to evolving low-income countries and still have relevance for significant portions of the agriculture of Europe, North America, and Japan.

Institutions. Formal rural lenders and integrated rural financial markets emerge through deliberate public policy rather than unguided market forces. That is partly because financial market transactions deal with future events that are innately imperfect in their operation and the difficulty of small farm units in developing their own credit systems. It is also because of the large political role of agriculture arising from its geographically dispersed nature and large number of small farms, and perhaps because of a harking back to days when consumers were worried about their food supplies.

In the early stages of commercialization, farmers rate access to credit as their most important concern. That requires many branches. The cost of credit tends to be high if it is not competitive, requiring multiple providers. Successful agricultural credit systems, in such divergent countries' institutions as the United States, Japan, South Korea,

and Taiwan, have a variety of forms, including private banks, cooperatives, government institutions, and private nongovernmental organizations. As a result, volume per branch may be low, with consequently high overhead costs per unit of lending.

Overhead per loan can be reduced by ensuring both a high intensity of agriculture with consequent need for large amounts of credit per unit of area and widespread participation of farmers in credit programs. Offering a range of services also spreads overhead. Lending institutions in developing countries tend to provide only lending services. Volume could be built and concurrently render a desirable service by mobilizing deposits as well. Intensity of lending can also be increased by combining credit with other services, such as input supply.

Interest rates. Interest rates serve three functions: to cover the costs of lending and provide a return on money; to attract deposits for further lending; and to attract borrowers.

In low-income countries, borrowing tends to be more elastic with respect to the interest rate than in high-income countries. Conversely, savings or deposits tend to be more inelastic with respect to interest in low-income countries than in high-income countries. Thus, in low-income countries growth is fostered by keeping interest rates low. This is achieved by reducing the costs of borrowing through scale economies, as stated above, and efficient management. Similarly, the upward manipulation of interest rates by central banks is unfavorable to rapid agricultural development in low-income countries. Of course, if farmers are to obtain adequate credit, the credit institutions must be financially healthy. Therefore, their costs must be covered.

Traditional moneylenders tend to have relatively high interest rates primarily because they are not integrated into national markets and lend seasonally, with their funds idle in off-seasons.

Risk. Risks are high in agriculture because of weather, health, and related risks to the family and the rapid change in technology and markets. Lenders also face a moral hazard—borrowers who intend not to repay. The latter is a serious problem in low-income countries with poorly adapted legal systems and substantial political interference in farm lending. Crop insurance is generally not successful, partly because of moral hazards. Credit is itself often the farmer's best source of risk reduction. Loans may be renegotiated with payments spread further in the future.

Theories of Credit and Interest. There is a large and complex body of theories on credit and finance and interest rates. This literature is widely applied to agricultural credit.

A major issue is whether development of financial systems and credit should precede, and hence lead, enterprise and technology, or the reverse. A substantial literature and logic supports each. In the case of agricultural development, in which improved technology plays the critical role, it seems clear that finance and credit should accompany improved technology. Improved technology requires credit to proceed rapidly, and loan payments tend to be slow and overdue if profit-increasing technologies are not available.

Another important issue is the role of interest rates. In recent years, emphasis has been on high interest rates to favor increased saving, providing the finance for expanded application of technology and hence production increases. A few decades ago, the emphasis was on lowering interest rates to encourage borrowing for improved technology.

In developing countries, in contrast to developed countries, the empirical evidence is that borrowing to apply improved technology is interest-rate sensitive. That is, a given percentage reduction in the interest rate will bring a more than proportionate increase in borrowing. Conversely, saving is inelastic with respect to the interest rate. That is because farmers save for specific purposes irrespective of the interest rate. Also, increased saving by farmers is at the expense of productive investment in physical assets of the farm.

Of course, interest rates must cover the costs of obtaining money and the costs of lending if financial institutions are to be viable over the long run. Therefore, there is limited scope to change interest rates. However, the evidence is that central banks need to keep basic interest rates low to encourage investment in agriculture, and lending institutions need to constantly search for means of reducing their costs through the devices stated earlier.

Institutional Development. Low-income countries are evolving toward agricultural credit systems similar to those of high-income countries. However, considerable variation exists among countries. Institutional development is in part driven by the economics of the situation and in part by historical accident. The United States provides a rough idea of the institutional structure for agricultural credit in a developed country, and India offers an example as a developing country.

United States. Commercialization of agriculture increased rapidly in the 1920s and later in response to improving technology that derived from the federal government's actions in technology generation and dissemination as evidenced in the Morrill Act of 1863. In 1913, the United States Congress authorized a careful look at agricultural credit systems abroad, particularly the Landeschaft System of Germany, which served as the prototype for systems in France, Denmark, and other European countries. The commissions' findings ultimately led to the Federal Farm Loan Act of 1916, which established the Federal Land Banks and Joint-Stock Land Banks. The Farm Credit Administration (FCA), created by executive order in March 1933, brought nearly all federally sponsored farm credit agencies under the one agency. FCA included the Federal Land Banks for long-term loans and the Production Credit Associations for short-term loans. Provisions were also made for lending to farmers' cooperatives in the June 1933 Farm Credit Act.

The governing body of the FCA is composed of one member, nominated by the president, from each of the twelve Farm Credit Districts and an appointee by the secretary of agriculture.

The powers of the FCA are mainly supervisory and regulatory, and it does not directly distribute loans. The history of the FCA shows a gradual enhancement of its powers. While farmers took over ownership, financing, and management, the government, through a succession of acts continuing to the present, provided important oversight and assistance in times of general economic stress. The government in effect guaranteed borrowings on the major money markets and constantly acted to protect farmer access to credit.

In response to concern for less creditworthy farmers, including those just beginning to farm, the Farm Security Administration was created in 1935. Its successor, the Farmers Home Administration (FHA), established by the Farmers Home Administration Act of 1946, remained a government program of some size even as the FCA became farmer owned and farmer run. While the FHA is a centralized, federal government agency, it operates through a highly decentralized system, devolved first to the states and then further to the county level.

Funds for the FHA come in small part from congressional appropriations and in large part by refinancing in the national capital markets. For that purpose, the underlying loans are guaranteed by the FHA. Loans are made at somewhat below market rates, with the subsidy coming from the federal government. Some funds also come from commercial banks with FHA guarantees. In recent years, the FHA has broadened its mandate to cover providing funds for a wide range of rural community services.

With the development of these institutions, the agricultural credit system of the United States provides multiple institutional forms to farmers: direct lending from the government, farmer-owned and -financed credit systems with government guaranteed access to the major money markets, commercial banks (particularly small rural banks), credit unions, and others. Such multiplicity of institutions and combinations of private, public, and quasi-public institutions characterize all the successful developed countries and an increasing proportion of developing countries.

India. The rural finance system in India has had a profound effect on the agricultural sector. The Indian rural institutional finance system is made up of vertically organized cooperatives, cooperative land development banks, private banks, nationalized commercial banks, and government-sponsored regional rural banks. From 1961/1962 to 1981/1982, rural financial institutions (RFIs), which tap national money markets, have increased their share of lending from approximately 5 percent in 1951 to over two-thirds by 1981. Japan was up 90 percent by 1981 from one-third in 1912. Moneylenders have declined commensurately. Institutional credit has enhanced and increased productivity and the use of fertilizer, irrigation, and other agricultural investment. RFIs and farm-level credit have greatly increased in rural areas.

However, these positive trends have been undermined by high loan delinquency rates, while scale economies with low transaction costs are still in transition. High delinquency rates derive from complex and varied reasons: natural factors (i.e., disasters), inadequate increases in production and marketable surplus, mismatches between time schedule for loan recovery and loan repayment deadlines, inadequate credit due to an outdated formula for scale economies, unavailability of complementary credit, lack of available inputs and extension services, and inadequate supervision and attention to the selection, and perhaps low interest rates.

[See also Informal Credit.]

BIBLIOGRAPHY

Adams, D. C., D. J., Graham, and J. D. Von Pischke, eds. *Undermining Rural Development and Cheap Credit*. Boulder, 1984.

Battles, Ralph, and Robert C. Thompson. *Fundamentals of Agribusiness Finance*. Ames, Iowa, 2000.

Brake, John R, and Emanuel Melichar. "Agricultural Finance and Capital Markets." In *Agricultural Economics Literature*, edited by Lee R. Martin, vol. 1, pp. 416–494. Saint Paul, 1977.

Desai, B. M., and John W. Mellor. *Institutional Finance for Agricultural Development: An Analytical Survey of Critical Issues*. Washington, D.C., 1993.

Hoag, W. Gifford. *The Farm Credit System*. Danville, Ill., 1976.

Lee, Warren F., et al. *Agricultural Finance*. 8th ed. Ames, Iowa, 1988.

Nelson, Aaron G., and William G. Murray. *Agricultural Finance*. 5th ed. Ames, Iowa, 1967.

JOHN W. MELLOR

AGRICULTURAL LABOR. Agricultural labor takes place in a bewildering variety of ways. The list includes family farms, community cooperation, slave estates, feudal dependents, full-time wageworkers, casual wageworkers, pieceworkers, contract workers, and sharecroppers. Moreover within one country and one epoch different forms of labor frequently coexist: slave and free, family and hired, pieceworkers and day workers, sharecroppers and wageworkers, males and females.

Historians, some influenced by Karl Marx's interpretation of history, have identified a broad historical evolution from nonmarket systems of labor—family, community, slaves, and feudal dependents—toward labor motivated and rewarded purely by financial incentives. The social bonds of family, community, and obligation fell away, replaced by the impersonal forces of the market. But it is not clear that the movement has been as unidirectional and unequivocal as this. In the United States, for example, it is true that family labor was 75 percent of the farm labor force in 1910 but dropped to 61 percent by 1970. But in England family labor was at a maximum of only 33 percent of the labor input in 1851, while for the United Kingdom in the year 2000, 63 percent of farming labor was family labor. Thus in recent years in England, family has been replacing market.

The Gender of Agricultural Labor. In England from the Middle Ages to the twentieth century, farm labor was mainly conducted by males, and women played a modest role. Thus the 1851 census shows 77 percent of the labor was male (assuming woman worked as many hours as men), but given men's higher wages, this implies that more than 85 percent of labor measured by wage costs was male. Not all agricultural systems have such a male-dominated labor supply. In many African societies agricultural work was mainly done by women. As late as the 1970s at least half the labor input in crop production in Uganda and the Upper Volta was from women. In Asian peasant societies women were also seemingly a more important share of the labor supply than in northern Europe. Thus in India in 1950–1951, 30 percent of man-days supplied by agricultural workers were from women. But there was great variation across different districts. In the Punjab women were only 4 percent of man-days and in Uttar Pradesh 7 percent, while in Hyderabad they were 34 percent and in Mysore 50 percent.

There are two potential sources of this variation in female participation in agriculture across time and place. First, there is variation in the supply of female labor. This can be created by social barriers to women outside the home or in "male" occupations and by women's alternative employment opportunities in industry or services. Second, there is variation in the demand from agriculture for female labor. Some agricultural operations require mainly strength, others mainly dexterity. In jobs involving dexterity, female labor is as productive as male. Thus agricultural systems that involve a lot of brute strength have fewer demands for female labor at any given wage. Figure 1 shows how higher participation by females can be created by shifts in labor supply, by shifts in labor demand, or by both. If the variation in female participation across societies is mainly a product of differences in labor supply, then agricultural systems that employ many women will have if anything a relatively low female wage. If the variation is mainly because of technologically based differences in labor demand, then agricultural systems that employ

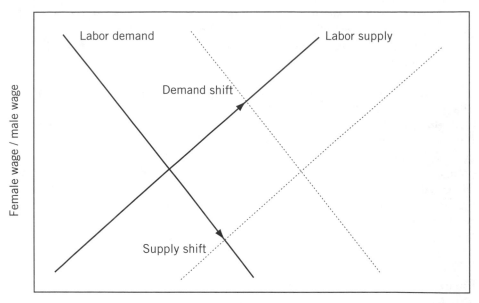

FIGURE 1. Demand and supply of female labor in agriculture.

many women will have a relatively high female wage. The evidence for Britain around 1851 on this question is summarized in Figure 2. This shows the relative wages of women compared to men in fieldwork outside harvest by country versus the fraction of the hired labor that was female. There is a large variation in the fraction of the hired labor force female, from 0 to 33 percent. For counties with higher female labor force participation, the relative wage is slightly lower, but the effect is not statistically significant. The most plausible interpretation of this picture, informed by knowledge that the climate and topography was similar in areas with different levels of female labor force participation in agriculture, is that labor supply varied greatly across countries in Britain. Female labor supply was higher in the north of England and in Scotland, but that extra supply in these areas led to only modest declines in women's relative earnings because men and women were easily substitutable in many agricultural operations.

Figure 3 shows a similar picture drawn for Indian regions in 1950–1951. Here again there is a modestly lower relative wage where women were more prevalent in agriculture. This again suggests labor supply was the main factor varying across Indian regions. The conclusion is reinforced by the fact that it was in the north (in India the social status of women is much lower in the south) that female agricultural labor participation was low even though relative wages were high. Thus both these examples suggest that variations in labor supply, as opposed to labor demand, explain the great variations in female labor participation in agricultural history.

Bound and Free Labor. Dependent labor was common in some agricultural systems and took several forms. First, there was outright slavery, where the workers had the same legal and practical status as the farm animals. This was the system of slavery in the classical world of Greece and Rome and black servitude in the New World. Second, there were systems where, while the labor might legally have no greater status than an animal, custom and usage gave the owners only limited rights in labor. This was serfdom in western Europe until the late Middle Ages and in eastern Europe from the late Middle Ages until the nineteenth century. Why, however, does bound labor dominate in some societies—the Caribbean Islands of the eighteenth century or Russia of the early nineteenth century—while free labor prevails in others—preindustrial India and China and Roman Egypt?

One condition required for bound labor, it has been argued, is some kind of central authority in a society. Otherwise slaves can simply run away from their current masters and make a better deal with another. On these grounds Douglass North and Robert Thomas (1973) argue that medieval serfdom in western Europe was less a form of oppression than a contractual relationship. They contend that serfdom represented a voluntary exchange of labor services from the peasants for protection from the lords. Given the decentralized nature of medieval society in western Europe, the peasants could flee from one lord to another. Lords could thus not extract any surplus from the peasants, however nominally unfree peasants might be. Instead lords provided the local public good of protection, and the labor tax they collected from the peasant was the precise analog of the property taxes modern towns extract from homeowners for the public goods of police and fire protection. Thus the serfs could find no landowner who did not exact labor services.

North and Thomas's argument depends on the assumption that protection was a public good. Interesting in the years 1311 to 1322, when the Scots frequently raided northern England, private castle owners would charge "access money" for sheltering people and goods when the Scots were on the loose. So protection in the medieval period seems to have been much more of a private good than North and Thomas assume.

Evsey Domar (1970) argues that a second necessary condition for slavery is that the wage of free labor in the society be well above the physical subsistence level. Slavery is found in the poorest societies. That is why preindustrial India and China, even though they often had a strong central authority, were still largely free labor societies. An analytical presentation of the Domar argument, that simplifies a little from his original article, is the following. Suppose that for a given technology, area of land, and capital the average output of free labor per day is higher than the average output of serf or slave labor. This implies that the marginal product of free labor is higher than the marginal product of slave labor. Thus

$$mp_f > mp_s$$

where mp_f and mp_s are respectively the marginal products of free workers and of slaves or serfs This implies that slavery is a socially inefficient system, in the sense that the total output of the society would be larger if the slaves or serfs were freed. But the owners will only free their slaves or serfs if the marginal product of serfs falls below their subsistence costs. Let s be the amount that must be spent on slave or serf workers to just allow them to reproduce themselves (the subsistence allowance). Also assume w_f is the wage of free workers. Then, since in a competitive labor market $mp_f = w_f$, for slavery to continue requires

$$w_f > mp_s > s$$

In the poorest societies the wage of free workers will approach the wage that has to be paid to maintain slaves. Thus if a society becomes poor enough that free workers receive simply the subsistence allowance a slave would receive, there is no economic value in owning people, and the slaves will be freed. A very low wage for free labor will come about with a stagnant technology (as in the Malthusian economy) and a high birthrate of free labor. This, argues Domar, explains why, even though there were no legal barriers against slavery in preindustrial India and China, slaves were a small share of the population. Domar also argues that this explains why serfdom was reimposed in

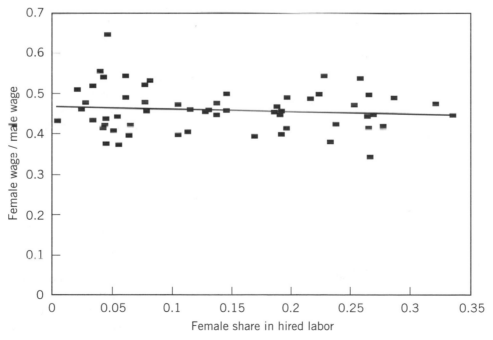

FIGURE 2. Relative female wage versus percent female workers, Britain, 1851. The line indicates the trend of the observation. SOURCE: *Census of Great Britain, 1851: Ages, Civil Conditions, Occupations, etc.* Sessional papers, vol. 88, 1852–1853. "The Value of Agricultural Labour." *Gardeners' Chronicle and Agricultural Gazette* (27 April 1850), 266–267.

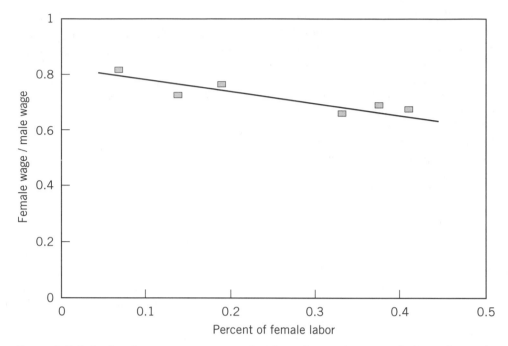

FIGURE 3. Relative female wage versus percent female workers, India, 1950. The line indicates the trend of the observation. SOURCE: Government of India, 1954.

eastern Europe after the Black Death struck in 1348–1349. The enhanced value of labor, resulting from higher death rates after 1349, gave the eastern lords an incentive to once again claim property in people.

The crucial assumption of Domar's theory that slaves are less productive than free labor is problematic, however. This assumption is derived from the experience of eastern Europe serfdom, where serf labor does seem to have been unproductive. Owners sold off a day of forced serf labor at much less than the going rate for a day of free labor. Yet basic economic reasoning would suggest that bound labor should always produce more per day than free workers. Free workers will not want to maximize just their daily earnings, since they also value leisure. But slave owners give no value to slave leisure. They should thus force the slaves to produce more than free workers. In the U.S. South after the Civil War, labor productivity in agriculture fell in those areas where there were large numbers of freed slaves, exactly as would be predicated from this consideration.

An alternative theory for why slavery was limited to a few societies, which does not rely on the idea that slaves are inherently less productive than free workers, is implicit in the work of Robert W. Fogel and Stanley L. Engerman (1974) on slavery in the pre–Civil War United States. The most rigorous form of slavery only persists if it is profitable for the owners to encourage the reproduction of the slave population. This is only the case if the value of a slave at birth is greater than zero. Otherwise the incentive for

owners is to discourage reproduction by having labor forces of predominantly one or the other gender and by neglecting (or even killing) slave children.

The price of a slave at birth, P_0, will be the net present value of the slave at birth, which is the discounted sum of the slave's marginal product in each year minus the slave's maintenance cost. Let:

λ_t = fraction of slaves who are still alive at year t
mp_t = output of slave in year t (= marginal product of the slave in year t)
s_t = subsistence allowances to slave in each year
r = rate of return on capital (interest rate)

Then the value of a slave at birth will be

$$P_0 = \sum_{t=0}^{n} \frac{\lambda_t(mp_t - s_t)}{(1 + r)^t}$$

= net present value of output – net present value of subsistence payments

At younger ages the net income from the slave ($mp_t - s_t$) is negative and only becomes positive sometimes after age ten. Thus the profitability of slave reproduction is sensitive to the interest rate. Maintenance costs of $1 at age 0 need to be repaid with $5.7 of earnings above maintenance costs at age 30 at a rate of return on capital of 6 percent. People are a long-lived investment compared to most other types of capital, which makes the value of their output compared to their maintenance costs very sensitive to the rate of return on capital. The profitability of slavery is also dependent on life expectancy. The more slaves die in their childhoods or early working years, the higher will have to be the profits generated by the surviving slaves in their work years to pay off the maintenance costs of these slaves. In the U.S. South 40 percent of slaves died before age nineteen.

The slave economy of the U.S. South was the most efficient ever observed. The marginal product of slaves in the South was much higher than for most free farmworkers in Europe in 1860. In the United States a thirty-year-old field hand produced twice as much as the maintenance costs incurred by the owner. At the prevailing interest rate of 6 percent and with a life expectancy for slaves of thirty-six years, the value of a slave at birth was positive. But it was positive by a surprisingly small amount. Indeed had the interest rate been 7.5 percent, then at birth even a slave in the U.S. South would have had no economic value. Alternatively had maintenance costs in the work years been as high as 56 percent of output, then the value of the slave at birth again would have been negative.

The implication of the work of Fogel and Engerman is thus that, while slavery was profitable in the U.S. South and encouraged the reproduction and growth of the slave labor force, it was very nearly unprofitable even there to reproduce slaves. Indeed Fogel and Engerman argue that, in such Caribbean colonies as Jamaica (under British rule), the much lower life expectancies for slaves of only twenty-one years at birth (partly from nature conditions, partly from the lower efficiency of the plantation agriculture there) created a disincentive for owners to encourage reproduction. Owners found it cheaper to import adult slaves from Africa than to encourage higher fertility among the existing slave population. They thus maintained a sex imbalance, preferring male slaves to female.

Considering most other preindustrial societies, locked in the Malthusian equilibrium, shows that slave owners would have no incentive to reproduce the slave population. The wage of free labor, and hence the marginal product of slaves, would be far below that of the U.S. South. Also interest rates tended to be high in preindustrial economies. Thus, for example, the interest rates for money lent on land security by temples in southern India in the tenth century CE were typically 15 percent (Sharma, 1983, pp. 199–200).

The above argument does not depend on the idea that slaves are less productive than free labor and can indeed hold even if slaves are more productive. But it raises a puzzle. If there is no economic incentive in most societies for slave labor to reproduce itself, how are free workers able to reproduce themselves? The answer is that in the

FARM LABOR. *Two Peasant Women Digging Potatoes*, painting by Vincent van Gogh, 1885. (© Stichting Kröller-Müller Museum, Otterlo, The Netherlands/Tom Haartsen)

free population children are supported out of the current surplus of income over maintenance costs for adults, but without requiring the children to pay back these costs with interest or to cover the expenses (with interest) of their siblings who died in their youth. Instead, each generation finances the next as a gift. As long as

$$\sum_t \lambda_t(mp_t - s_t) \geq 0$$

this is possible. This is a far less-restrictive condition than for the slave owner. Thus in a labor market where there are both free and slave workers, the free population can generally keep on growing even when the point has been reached where there is no incentive to slave owners to reproduce the slave population.

A problem with all such accounts of bound labor, pointed out by Stefano Fenoaltea (1984), is that they do not explain why slave owners insist on directly extracting labor from their workers, especially if such labor is less efficient than free labor. An alternative to direct extraction would be to allow slaves to buy their freedom in return for a fixed annual payment or a lump-sum fee. If serfs or slaves are less productive than free labor, as Domar assumes, there is a potential surplus of

$$mp_f - mp_s$$

that can be divided between the lord and the serf, making them both better off. In the new arrangement the serfs will work as free workers for the lords, simply remitting their fixed labor dues each year. Even if slaves are more productive than free workers because they can be forced to put in more hours, as long as slaves value controlling their own activities, a similar deal could be done.

One explanation for the persistence of slavery or serfdom in societies such as Russia in the light of the seeming profitability of manumission in return for a fixed labor rent is that the owners perceive that, without direct control of the serfs or slaves as a class, they will eventually lose their property rights. There is no way to make a binding agreement that frees the serfs that can be upheld in the long run. The freed serfs or slaves will combine politically to frustrate the payment of the contracted labor rents and perhaps indeed seize all the property of their former masters.

[*See also* Agricultural Wages.]

BIBLIOGRAPHY

Agricultural Labor Enquiry: Report on Intensive Survey of Agricultural Labor, vol. 1. Government of India. New Delhi, India, 1954.
Boserup, Ester. *Women's Role in Economic Development.* London, 1970.
Clark, Colin, and Margaret Haswell. *The Economics of Subsistence Agriculture.* 3d ed. London, 1967.
Domar, Evsey. "The Causes of Slavery or Serfdom: A Hypothesis." *Journal of Economic History* 30 (1970), 18–32.
Ellis, Frank. *Peasant Economics: Farm Households and Agrarian Development.* Cambridge, 1988.
Fenoaltea, Stefano. "Slavery and Supervision in Comparative Perspective." *Journal of Economic History* 44.3 (1984), 635–668.
Fogel, Robert W., and Stanley L. Engerman. *Times on the Cross: The Economics of American Negro Slavery.* Boston, 1974
North, Douglass, and Robert P. Thomas. *The Rise of the Western World.* Cambridge, 1973.
Ransom, Roger, and Richard Sutch. *One Kind of Freedom: The Economic Consequences of Emancipation.* Cambridge 1977.
Sharma, Ram Sharan. *Perspectives in Social and Economic History of Early India.* New Delhi, India, 1983.

GREGORY CLARK

AGRICULTURAL MARKETING *[This entry contains three subentries, overviews of regional and international trade, and a discussion of agricultural marketing boards.]*

Regional Trade

The marketing of agricultural produce probably goes back to the earliest days of agriculture, when Neolithic settlements were established near foraging tribes. Such patterns of interdependence are still found, as for example in the relationship between the Mbuti pygmies of the Congo region and their horticultural Bantu neighbors or between the Agta of the Philippines, who specialize in hunting and fishing, and the grain-growing Palanan. Trade of this kind is usually conducted between small numbers of individuals, with a minimum of formal apparatus.

Among settled rural populations in preindustrial economies, much trade has been independent of formal markets, since inequalities of land endowment create opportunities for exchange between neighbors. These could take the form of poor households buying from wealthy peasants or from landlords, but it could also occur, conversely, when large households acquired produce from tenants. Most past currency systems, being dependent upon scarce media of exchange, such as precious metals, were poorly adapted for small sales of low-value foodstuffs like vegetables and eggs, so that trade in such goods was difficult except by barter, a form of exchange that crosses the boundaries between trade and other categories of transaction. Labor has often been paid in kind, whether in full board given to resident farm servants, in meals during working hours, or in agreed allowances of grain. Rents too have often been paid in produce, either by custom or by agreement. In these ways, much of the food exchanged in the countryside in past societies has bypassed the marketplace. Informal exchange of these kinds has, however, often been augmented by the development of informal trading at public ceremonies. In Christendom, the celebration of Sunday mass encouraged sellers of produce to assemble around well-attended churches, and such commercial enterprise sometimes anticipated the establishment of a more formal marketing organization.

Periodic marketing institutions for foodstuffs are a universal feature of developing civilization, associated with the growth of urban settlements where the division of labor is more marked than in the countryside. The institution of a market fixes the place and time at which buyers and sellers meet, and it often places restrictions on trade in other places and at other times. The balance between public systems of redistribution and institutions of private exchange is debatable for the early theocratic civilizations—those with powerful palace or temple administrations at the core of their urban development—and the existence of public markets in their early cities is only sporadically attested. For example, the ancient Egyptian archive from Deir el-Medina records trading at "the riverside" in the late second millennium BCE; there, fabric might be exchanged for a predictable quantity of grain. The best-known marketing structures in an empire lacking coinage is that of the Aztec, whose numerous urban markets were commonly held every five days, though sometimes daily. They were described, in 1519, with some amazement, by Fernando Cortés in his *Second Letter* from Mexico.

In the Old World, during the centuries following the adoption of metallic currencies, the regional marketing of food in Europe attained a peak of sophistication. Roman food markets are well known from both the archaeological and the literary record, and they were of primary importance for feeding the numerous towns of the empire. Their status as part of the public administration is apparent from the status of the official *aediles*, who were appointed to administer them in the public interest. They were held every eight days, that being the length of the Roman week. When the imperial system collapsed during the early Middle Ages, local markets had to be reinvented—and the modern marketing economy of western Europe can trace its institutional evolution back only as far as the eighth century CE. The new structure depended upon markets every seven days (according to the new Christian calendar, once a week), with annual fairs held for a few days around some regular festival. Of these two institutions, the weekly market was the most important for the sale of agrarian produce, although some annual fairs were developed for a specialist role in livestock trades. Much of the impetus behind the reconstruction of a European system of local trade came from rulers and landlords who could increase their income by drawing people together in towns, instituting markets and fairs, and charging tolls on trade and additional rents. Such inducements to commercial development continued to be operative in much later periods in regions of low monetary circulation, such as Highland Scotland during the eighteenth century.

The multiplication of periodic markets was widespread throughout the more urbanized regions of the world between the tenth century and the fourteenth. Considerable scope exists here for the comparative analysis of such developments in Europe, northern Africa, the Near East, India, China and southeastern Asia—all of which had monetized rural economies, highly developed urban civilizations, and state-controlled taxation on trade. Urbanization in parts of China was particularly advanced and by the twelfth century there, a high level of market dependence and market integration is in evidence. In China's southern province of Kiangnan, there was a variety of market types whose periodicity was characteristically every third, sixth, or tenth day. In medieval Europe, the establishment of weekly markets was extended spatially—for example, from France, western Germany, and southern England westward to Wales and Ireland, northward to northern England, Scotland, and Scandinavia, and eastward to the lands beyond the Elbe River, sometimes in the wake of conquest and colonization. The establishment and developing sophistication of marketing institutions was a major engine of world economic development; it encouraged the expansion of agricultural production and manufactured goods and permitted the growth of both urban and rural populations. The combination of requirements for harmonious trading—providing space, maintaining the peace, policing the rules of trade, standardizing weights and measures, protecting the environment against pollution by traders, and adjudicating in disputes between buyers and sellers—have all been subject to centuries of innovation, imitation, modification, and regional variation, though the course of evolution is very imperfectly known. Both the practice of institutional marketing and particular forms of market are necessarily culturally specific, and the spread of marketing institutions has often been imposed from outside (as on the fringes of medieval Europe and, more extensively, in the course of modern European colonialism).

Although usually established and developed to enhance the wealth of the already wealthy, some benefits of marketing institutions were widely diffused beyond landowning circles. Formal marketing, by reducing the costs of searching for buyers and sellers, eases exchanges between agricultural producers, but its most significant effect has been to stimulate trade between agricultural producers and the suppliers of manufactures and services. The stimulus to both rural enterprise and productivity growth that is implicit in such exchanges was of major significance for the early commercialization of agrarian societies. Once local markets became important for the livelihoods of their users, they attracted high public concern, for political reasons, and their development was spurred on by public pressure as well as by the lure of financial gain to their owners. The safeguarding of market institutions in ancient and medieval societies was one of the few recognized duties of a good ruler; much of their early development occurred without the benefits of administrative records, although written trading regulations have since then proliferated in literate cultures.

Despite the importance of formal markets for supplies to large concentrations of population, the development of towns also encouraged the operations of middlemen, who became intermediaries between rural producers and urban buyers. Such enterprises have taken many forms, from that of the urban baker who secures his supplies by contracting with a local farmer to the corn monger who buys up the crops of whole estates. Middlemen dealing in agricultural produce were active from the beginnings of recorded history—they occur as early as the Mesopotamian archives of the late third millennium BCE. By about 160 BCE, Marcus Cato's *De agricultura* relates how middlemen contracted in olives, grapes, and wine under the Roman republic. Wholesale trade was always more likely than retail trade to bypass the formal institutions of trade, by purchasing at the source. In western Europe, the emergence of auctioning as a means of selling in bulk could only have occurred outside the operating rules of weekly markets, which were expressly designed to prevent the bidding up of prices; the auction seems to date there only from the sixteenth century. Although governments and urban authorities have commonly been suspicious of mercantile suppliers and have done what they could to discourage the emergence of monopolies, however temporary—as in the widespread medieval hostility to forestalling—large cities were bound to depend on merchants for some of their supplies. Mercantile enterprise became of dominant importance for provisioning towns only when urban requirements outgrew purely regional trade and came to depend on the shipment of produce over long distances. This was conspicuously the case with the greatest cities of antiquity, notably imperial Rome, and it was true of the large medieval cities, especially in years of poor local harvests. Western European trade in fine wools and wine acquired a regular interregional structure beginning in the twelfth century, appreciably earlier than that in basic cereals, meat, and dairy produce. Dependence on merchant enterprise and trade over long distances for most agricultural produce has grown steadily since the sixteenth century. After the discovery of the New World by Europeans and the opening up of intercontinental trade, supply conditions were transformed. From the mid-nineteenth century onward, local trade in agricultural produce has become peripheral to the supply of industrial populations.

The distance over which peasants are prepared to market their own goods sets a limit to their direct trade with urban consumers. With similar transport technologies, the distribution of market trade is also likely to be similar; for example, close analogies have been found between traditional Chinese marketing structures and those of preindustrial Europe. Geographers analyzing the spatial relationships among local markets, and between the lesser markets and the larger urban centers, characteristically use the central-place model of Walter Christaller (1966), which has proved helpful in a wide variety of contexts. Transport constraints relevant to the emergent patterns of agrarian specialization around major centers of consumption were modeled by Johan Heinrich von Thünen (1826), whose work is the foundation for most modern analysis of spatial relationships of this kind. Despite the apparent cell-like structure of local marketing regions, the multiplication of markets, the growth of formal local trade, and the growth of larger towns are closely associated with interregional price convergence; this is due to the increased amount of reliable information available to urban middlemen who are able to move among alternative sources of supply. Where communications were easy, especially where there was unobstructed contact by sea or river, large areas of Europe and adjacent lands, with a common price regime, had emerged by 1300—replicating, to some extent, earlier features of Roman trade. The coastal regions of the Mediterranean Sea constituted one such region through the activities of merchants who supplied the cities of Italy, southern France, Catalonia, and Aragon (Spain). To the extent that local markets became part of more integrated regional economies, they lost any capacity to determine prices autonomously, which could be a source of confusion among local leaders who were inclined to blame outsiders and merchants for unaccountable price changes.

By the 1770s, Adam Smith, the Scottish economist, establishing his liberal principles of economic theory, regarded the laws against forestalling (interfering with free trade by buying up produce on the market) as equivalent to laws against "witchcraft"—the analogy deriving from the propensity of public authorities to personalize and, so, misspecify the causes of high prices. Little comparative work has been done to establish how markets actually operated throughout Europe to establish their prices, or to respond to price changes elsewhere, although it has long been recognized that this was one of their important functions. In fact, there has been considerable diversity of practice in formal markets; in some cultures, buyer and seller have negotiated individually, but in others, buyers and sellers have been obliged to respect a current price approved by the officers of the market, and haggling has been illegal. For all its loss of autonomy, the local marketplace long remained, for most sellers and consumers, the point at which authoritative prices became available.

[*See also* Urbanization.]

BIBLIOGRAPHY

Belshaw, Cyril E. *Traditional Exchange and Modern Markets*. Englewood Cliffs, N.J., 1965.

Bromley, Ray J. *Periodic Markets, Daily Markets, and Fairs: A Bibliography*. Melbourne, 1974; reprint, Swansea, 1977; also *Periodic Markets, Daily Markets, and Fairs: A Bibliography Supplement to 1979*. Swansea, 1979.

Christaller, Walter. *Central Places in Southern Germany*. Translated by Carlisle W. Baskin. Englewood Cliffs, N.J., 1966.

Clark, Hugh R. *Community, Trade, and Networks: Southern Fujian Province from the Third to the Thirteenth Century*. Cambridge, 1991.

Frayn, Joan M. *Markets and Fairs in Roman Italy: Their Social and Economic Importance from the Second Century BC to the Third Century AD*. Oxford, 1993.

Gregg, Susan Alling. *Foragers and Farmers: Population Interaction and Agricultural Expansion in Prehistoric Europe*. Chicago, 1988.

Kaplan, Steven L. *Provisioning Paris: Merchants and Millers in the Grain and Flour Trade during the Eighteenth Century*. Ithaca, N.Y., 1984.

Kowaleski, Maryanne. *Local Markets and Regional Trade in Medieval Exeter*. Cambridge, 1995.

Morley, Neville. *Metropolis and Hinterland: The City of Rome and the Italian Economy, 200 BC–AD 200*. Cambridge, 1996.

Plattner, Stuart, ed. *Economic Anthropology*. Stanford, Calif., 1989.

Postgate, J. N. *Early Mesopotamia: Society and Economy at the Dawn of History*. London, 1994.

Rathbone, Dominic. *Economic Rationalism and Rural Society in Third-Century AD Egypt*. Cambridge, 1991.

Shiba, Yoshinobu. *Commerce and Society in Sung China*. Translated by Mark Elvin. Ann Arbor, 1970.

Thirsk, Joan, ed. *The Agrarian History of England and Wales*. 8 vols. Cambridge, 1967–1991.

Thünen, Johann Heinrich von. *Isolated State: An English Edition of Der Isolierte Staat*. Translated by Carla M. Wartenberg. Edited by Peter Hall. Oxford and New York, 1966.

RICHARD H. BRITNELL

International Trade

Marketing is the business of selling a product. It can take the simplest of forms, such as a brief conversation with a friend, or be as complicated as investing in the most sophisticated of consumer information-gathering and promotional campaigns aimed at boosting profits through differentiating one's product from that of others. Marketing farm products, particularly before processing, is typically at the less sophisticated end of the spectrum. As economies develop, however, the proportion of sales value allocated to marketing costs at each point in the supply chain tends to increase for agricultural as for most other products.

For millennia people have exploited the opportunity that trade provides for expanding real incomes via specialization in production and subsequent exchange in the marketplace. Long-distance trade between nation-states is not quite as old as intranational trade, because it involves larger transactions costs (of overcoming language, culture, geographic distance, and trade tax barriers). Nonetheless, marketing the most fundamental of products—namely, food and the technology to produce it internationally—has a long history.

The motivation for engaging in international trade in goods, services, and productive factors (including technologies) is there whenever the domestic price differs from that of a similar foreign product by more than the costs of making a sale. Price differentials for agricultural products arise from time to time for a range of reasons. The most common is seasonality. Crops ripen at different times in places with different climates, so it is common for fresh fruit and vegetables to be imported in the off-season. Also, weather variations cause cereal harvests to vary from year to year. Even countries that are normally food self-sufficient may import after an especially poor season. Less common are natural disasters. The eruption of Mount Vesuvius in CE 79, when Pompeii was the Bordeaux of the world wine market, is a famous example. Its vineyards and cellars were buried, causing an immediate hike in the price of wine and the importing of wine from abroad (Johnson, 1989, pp. 66–67).

In addition to natural causes, price differences that affect international trade in farm products can be the result of technological changes, particularly in the provision of international transport and communication services, and of changes in governmental taxes and subsidies at a country's border.

The Impact of Transport Costs. Falls in transport/travel costs have had increasingly dramatic effects on agricultural trade over the centuries. Examples of products so affected are wines, fibers, spices, and grains.

Travel west from the region between the Caspian and Black seas brought vine cuttings and the technology of wine grape cultivation and winemaking to the Mediterranean by 2500 BCE. Over the next three millennia, the technology gradually moved as far north as Germany. Then another millennium passed before wine production spread with Europe's mariners to other continents with suitable climates: South America in the 1500s, South Africa in the 1650s, Australia in 1788, and California and New Zealand in the 1820s.

Even so, wine exports from the New World were slow in developing. Production was undertaken mainly to obviate the need for colonials to import European wines, which were expensive and suffered badly from their long sea voyage. Prior to the 1980s, wine exports grew only during periods when Europe offered preferential tariffs (e.g., as Britain did for South African wine in the three decades to 1841 and for Australian fortified wines from the mid-1920s to the mid-1940s). Such exports typically were shipped in bulk, were of low quality, and, in the absense of brand marketing, generated low returns for their producers.

By contrast, European wine producers developed relatively sophisticated marketing techniques. Indeed, promoting wine by its characteristics, including where it was produced, has been going on there for at least five millennia (Unwin, 1991, p. 68). As early as the second millennium BCE, the Greek island of Thasos only allowed wine to be exported in standard-sized amphorae and sealed with the name of the magistrate. This was done ostensibly as a guarantee of authenticity, although it also made taxing those exports easier (Robinson, 1994, p. 465). Even by the first century BCE wine was not cheap: the price of a (roughly 22 liter) jar of standard wine exported from Italy to France was one Gaul slave (Johnson, 1989, p. 83).

The second example is fiber trade. The technology of silk production was well developed in the Far East when the caravan routes controlled by the Persians, Arabs, and Syrians linked China and Europe. Light and highly valued, silk began to be exported from China to the Italian republics of Genoa and Venice during the Mongol period, along the so-called Silk Road. This early example of intercontinental agricultural trade launched a process of international specialization in the production of textiles and clothing that is still evolving. Countries with a strong comparative advantage in natural fibers export them to countries with a strong comparative advantage in textile products. Initially the latter were in Europe, starting with Britain. But since those manufacturing activities have become standardized they tend to be intensive in the use of low-skilled labor. That means the optimal location of production keeps shifting to labor-abundant countries at the first stage of industrial development. The densely populated economies of the Far East have dominated that transition over the past century: first Japan, then Hong Kong, Taiwan, and Korea, and most recently China. Ironically, these formerly silk-exporting economies became instead the world's major importers of natural fibers (Anderson, 1992).

A third example of transport costs falling, leading to growth in international agricultural marketing, is in the spice trade. Cinnamon and cassia found their way from South and Southeast Asia to the Middle East at least 2,000 years before Christ (as mentioned in the Bible's Old Testament). Arabs managed to control that spice trade for many centuries. With the Venetians they were instrumental in getting spices to Europe from the thirteenth century, albeit at exorbitant prices. Those prices by the late fifteenth century contributed to the stimulus to build ships and search for the spice-producing countries. The Portuguese were in the race first, bringing spices from India by way of the Cape of Good Hope. Meanwhile, Columbus failed in his search because he chose to sail west. Then the Dutch and English vied for power over spice sales in Europe, aided by support from their respective monarchies to establish monopolistic East India companies. The recent popular history of the spice trade by Milton (1999) is a reminder of the brutal lawlessness with which international agricultural

trade was conducted in centuries past. Even when the United States entered the spice market at the end of the eighteenth century, huge profits were still to be made by returning ships. The trade did not stabilize until the twentieth century, first around London and later New York.

The final transport cost example is with grain. After the American Civil War, in the 1870s and 1880s, the American rail network spread rapidly, making it possible to transport wheat to tidewater at less cost than by canal. Railroad construction from the Ukranian wheat fields to Crimean ports had a similar effect. Coupled with the shift from wooden to iron ships, these developments substantially lowered the cost of getting wheat to western Europe. So in the 1880s, when weather patterns generated low yields in western Europe, wheat farmers there did not receive the usual partial compensation in the form of increased wheat prices. On the contrary, with less natural (transport cost) protection from import competition, and coincidentally high yields in America, they faced real wheat price declines of around 15 percent between 1873 and 1896. Thus began the period when some European governments (e.g., France and Germany) responded by protecting their farmers with higher import tariffs. Others, most notably Britain, allowed grain farming to shrink and consumers to enjoy lower food prices (Kindleberger, 1951).

The Impact of Government Intervention. That episode introduces the other major influence on the growth in international marketing of agricultural products—government policies. The history of industrial development has been overlaid with a history of the growth of protection for agricultural products. Much government intervention in agricultural trade over the centuries has been aimed at stabilizing domestic food prices and supplies, but generally, poor agrarian economies have typically taxed agriculture more than other sectors of the economy. As nations industrialize, however, their policy regimes have tended to change gradually from negatively to positively assisting farmers relative to other producers.

From the late 1100s to the 1660s, prior to the first industrial revolution, Great Britain used export taxes and licenses to prevent domestic food prices from rising excessively. Between 1660 and 1690, a series of acts gradually raised food import duties (making imports prohibitive under most circumstances) and reduced the export restrictions on grain. The Corn Law of 1815 further strengthened the protective aspects of these acts. The famous repeal of the Corn Laws in the mid-1840s heralded a period of relatively unrestricted food trade for Great Britain, but agricultural protectionism returned in the 1930s and has continued to increase in recent decades.

Similar tendencies have been observed in many other west European countries. In France and Germany the period of free trade was considerably shorter, and agricultural protection levels during the twentieth century have remained somewhat higher on the Continent than in Great Britain. Meanwhile, tariffs on west European imports of manufactures have been reduced progressively since the GATT came into force in the late 1940s—further encouraging agricultural manufacturing production (Lindert, 1991).

Japan provides an even more striking example of the tendency to switch from taxing to increasingly assisting agriculture relative to other industries. Its industrialization began later than in Europe, as the economy opened up following the Meiji Restoration in 1868. By 1900 Japan had switched from being a small net exporter of food to becoming gradually more dependent on rice imports. Farmers and their supporters soon called for rice import controls. Their calls were matched by equally vigorous calls from manufacturing and commercial groups for unrestricted food trade, since the price of rice at that time was a major determinant of real wages in the nonfarm sector. The heated debates were not unlike those that led to the repeal of the Corn Laws in Britain six decades earlier. In Japan, however, the forces of protection triumphed, and a tariff was imposed on rice imports from 1904. That tariff gradually rose over time, lifting the domestic price of rice to more than 30 percent above the import price during World War I.

Even when there were food riots because of shortages and high rice prices just after World War I, the Japanese government's response was not to reduce protection but instead to extend it to its colonies and to shift from a national to an imperial rice self-sufficiency policy. That led to accelerated investments in agricultural development in the colonies of Korea and Taiwan behind an ever-higher external tariff wall that, by the latter 1930s, had driven imperial rice prices to more than 60 percent above those in international markets.

After postwar reconstruction Japan continued to raise its agricultural protection, Western Europe did the same, but Japan raised it to even higher levels. Domestic prices exceeded international market prices for grains and meats by about 50 percent in the late 1950s, by about 100 percent in the early 1970s, and by more than 200 percent in the 1990s. In liberated South Korea and Taiwan, by contrast, an import-substituting industrialization strategy was adopted in the 1950s that harmed agriculture. But it was short-lived, replaced in the early 1960s with a more neutral trade policy that resulted in rapid export-oriented industrialization. That development strategy imposed competitive pressure on the farm sector, which, as in Japan earlier, prompted farmers to lobby (successfully, as it happened) for ever-higher levels of protection from import competition in those newly industrialized economies as well (Anderson and Hayami, 1986, chapter 2).

Agricultural protection growth in the advanced and newly industrialized economies contrasts markedly with what is happening in still-poor agrarian economies. For example, once the sub-Saharan African colonies of European powers were given independence after World War II, many of them were inclined to reduce their economy's dependence on trade with rich industrial countries, to provide cheap food to urban consumers, and to create an industrial sector. They could raise funds for the latter by trade taxes. For countries with a strong comparative advantage in agriculture, these taxes also contributed to the government's goal of being less agrarian and less dependent on trade. The export taxes did not need to be explicit; often they took the form of government monopoly marketing boards simply paying farmers less than the price received minus the cost of getting produce to the point of export (Bates, 1981). It took more than a generation for the costliness of that development strategy to become obvious to its supporters, and only since the 1980s have the majority of developing countries adopted more open policies.

The long history of government intervention in agricultural markets and the way it distorted international trade in farm products entered a new phase in 1995, when the World Trade Organization came into being. Its members began implementing the Uruguay Round Agreement on Agriculture. With the slump in international food prices in the mid-1980s, caused partly by North America matching the agricultural export subsidies provided by the European Union, agricultural protection levels soared to dizzying heights (Tyers and Anderson, 1992). Food-exporting countries were galvanized into a coalition that ensured agriculture remained high on the agenda of the multilateral trade negotiations known as the Uruguay Round. Whether the Uruguay Round Agreement brings to an end the long-run growth of agricultural protectionism and its tendency to limit the contribution of international agricultural markets to human well-being remains to be seen.

BIBLIOGRAPHY

Anderson, Kym, ed. *New Silk Roads: East Asia and World Textile Markets.* Cambridge and New York, 1992.

Anderson, Kym, and Yujiro Hayami. *The Political Economy of Agricultural Protection.* Boston, London, and Sydney, 1986.

Bates, Robert H. *Market and States in Tropical Africa: The Political Basis of Agricultural Policies.* Berkeley, Calif., 1981.

Johnson, Hugh. *The Story of Wine.* London, 1989.

Kindleberger, Charles P. "Group Behaviour and International Trade." *Journal of Political Economy* 59. 1 (February 1951), 30–47.

Lindert, Peter H. "Historical Patterns of Agricultural Policy." In *Agriculture and the State: Growth, Employment, and Poverty,* edited by C. P. Timmer. Ithaca, N.Y., 1991.

Milton, Giles. *Nathaniel's Nutmeg.* London, 1999.

Robinson, Jancis. *The Oxford Companion to Wine.* London, 1994.

Tyers, Rod, and Kym Anderson. *Disarray in World Food Markets: A Quantitative Assessment.* Cambridge and New York, 1992.

Unwin, Tim. *Wine and the Vine: An Historical Geography of Viticulture and the Wine Trade.* London and New York, 1991.

KYM ANDERSON

Agricultural Marketing Boards

There are three types of agricultural marketing boards: (1) those run entirely by producers who join on an entirely voluntary basis; (2) statutory boards having the sole right to buy and sell a particular product, generally for export; and (3) those established with government support and managed by producers with some form of penalty for producers who do not join. The primary justification of these boards is they sustain farm incomes by maintaining stable prices for farm products.

The first type of marketing board was a self-help measure adopted by farmers in the depressions of the late nineteenth and early twentieth centuries. Both regional and national producers' cooperative associations were established in Sweden, the Netherlands, Denmark, and the British Commonwealth, mainly for selling their produce in the U.K. market. In return for a guaranteed price, farmers agreed to deliver given quantities of output to central depots for processing, grading, and packaging standardized ranges of products. The requirements of war in 1914 provided the first example of the state undertaking direct marketing of an agricultural product and established the second type of board. In 1915 the Australian Wheat Board transferred to the Commonwealth government the responsibility for marketing the country's crop of that year, and for the duration of the war. All Australian wheat producers were compelled to sell to the board for a guaranteed price and the board delivered its wheat to Great Britain for a price guaranteed by the British government. The board was disbanded in 1921 when the fall in wheat prices made guarantees too expensive, and Australia returned to a free market.

In the interwar years, marketing boards and schemes of the third type appeared in the Australian Commonwealth, Europe, North America, and Great Britain, particularly in the severe depression of the 1930s. In Denmark, British bacon import quotas in the 1930s made it necessary to limit production. "Pig cards" or licences were issued to farmers, and only those animals delivered to bacon factories accompanied by a card received a preferential price that corresponded to the price that could be obtained on the British market. The rest received a lower price that was available on other markets. Under this scheme, the number of pigs fell from 5.4 million in 1932 to 3 million in 1934 and the bacon price rose from seventeen cents to thirty-five cents per kilogram. This was probably the first agricultural marketing quota scheme for any product in any country and it led to inevitable difficulties and disputes between producers over numbers of licences.

Throughout the 1920s, British farmers had shown themselves incapable of any joint enterprise and governments held almost without exception to the policy of laissez faire.

The Agricultural Produce (Grading and Marking) Act of 1928 failed to convince British farmers of the advantage of "National Mark" grades and standards, leaving the British market for standardized and advertised bulk lines of agricultural produce to overseas producers. Marketing boards in Britain were first established under the Agriculture Acts of 1931 and 1933. These bodies were controlled by producer representatives, and by 1938 applied to potatoes, hops, pigs, and milk. Their primary purpose was to control production and regulate prices, although at a later stage they were given some quality-control powers. In all countries in the interwar years agricultural marketing boards need to be seen as a part of a general program of market organization alongside subsidies, import quotas, and tariffs. In Germany under National Socialism and in Italy under fascism, state control was taken further and agricultural markets were regulated in accordance with general political aims and an overall economic plan in which all farmers had to participate.

During World War II, the British government set up marketing boards of the second type in its West African colonies. These boards had sole rights to buy for export a number of commodities needed for the British war effort, such as cocoa, palm oil, palm kernels, groundnuts, and cotton. In the postwar years, this state export monopoly was extended to a number of other countries in Africa and also to Burma. After independence, the boards were retained and used as a convenient source of revenue by the new governments, which purchased products from farmers at (low) fixed prices, exported and sold the produce at (higher) world prices, and pocketed the balance. Governments justified their actions on the grounds that the producer received a stable price from the board, but critics saw it as a way of taxing farmers. In Nigeria and Ghana, low prices caused farmers to cease investment and the planting of new acreages of cocoa and oil palms, which brought about an eventual decline in the export of these products.

In many Western countries after the war, governments wishing to promote food production and maintain agricultural incomes continued a range of semiofficial marketing boards of the third type. For this reason, and as producers were largely responsible for their management, they never had the harmful effects associated with their African counterparts and were highly popular with the great majority of farmers, who regarded them as essential for the maintenance of rural prosperity. By the 1990s, the Canadian province of Ontario had twenty-two marketing boards administered under state acts covering virtually all agricultural products; Alberta under its 1965 Marketing of Agricultural Products Act had fifteen producer commodity groups that operated boards and commissions. Some regulated both production and marketing, while others simply collected levies to fund commodity research and promotion activities. They, like similar boards in the United States, Australia, New Zealand, and the United Kingdom, were associated with political regimes that bestowed positive assistance and benefits on farmers. However, they were disliked by consumer interests, who said that where boards used production quotas to regulate output, they raised consumer prices and shielded inefficient producers. Despite these objections, the popularity of this form of producers' agricultural organization, with state support, has remained strong. But they have also been unpopular with international bodies when their activities seem to conflict with postwar aims of freer international trade, which makes their future uncertain.

When the United Kingdom joined the Common Market in 1973, its remaining marketing boards for milk and potatoes were ruled to be inconsistent with the Common Agricultural Policy of free domestic markets and were dismantled in the 1980s and 1990s. In the mid-1990s Canadian provincial boards were challenged by the World Trade Organization, which ruled the higher price paid for milk sold in Canada acted as an unfair subsidy for the much lower price they received for milk sold on the world market.

BIBLIOGRAPHY

Alberta Agricultural Products Marketing Council (AAFRD) <http://www.agric.gov.ab.ca/ministry/apmc/>

Astor, Viscount, and B. Seebohm Rowntree. *British Agriculture: The Principles of Future Policy.* London, 1938.

Bauer, Péter T. *West African Trade: A Study of Competition, Oligopoly, and Monopoly in a Changing Economy.* Cambridge, 1954.

Bauer, Péter T., and Basil S. Yamey. *Markets, Market Control, and Marketing Reform: Selected Papers.* London, 1968.

Giddings, Philip J. *Marketing Boards and Ministers: A Study of Agricultural Marketing Boards as Political and Administrative Instruments.* Westmead, U.K., 1974.

Martin, John. *The Development of Modern Agriculture: British Farming Since 1931.* Basingstoke, U.K., 2000.

Ontario Ministry of Agriculture Food and Rural Affairs, Farm Products Marketing Commission. *Agricultural Marketing Boards in Ontario.*, Factsheet 97–011. ISSN 1198-712X. June, 1997. <http://www.gov.on.ca./OMAFRA/english/busdev/facts/97-011.htm>

Tracy, Michael. *Government and Agriculture in Western Europe, 1880–1988.* 3d ed. New York, 1989.

Tsokas, Kosmas. "Wheat in Wartime: The Anglo-Australian Experience." *Agricultural History* 66.1 (1992), 1–18.

World Trade Organization <http://www.wto.org>

RICHARD PERREN

AGRICULTURAL POLICY. From remotest antiquity, governments have nearly always intervened everywhere in the organization of agricultural systems and in the distribution of agricultural products. Whether the focus is irrigation, land distribution, or market regulation, evidence from Mesopotamia, as well as republican and imperial Rome, proves that governing authorities have always been concerned with agrarian issues. The stated objectives were not, however, fundamentally economic, but political (to avoid food shortages that would provoke civic unrest) and social (to protect certain categories of citizens through land redistribution and price controls). In imperial China also, the government regulated market supply, and in the Incan empire, all agricultural production was controlled by the state.

The Policy of Control. A similar situation prevailed in the modern era. Nearly everywhere the wheat trade was closely overseen to protect the interest of urban consumers. In most Italian cities, an annonary policy obliged farmers to convey their grain to the city to be stockpiled and resold by the authorities, who speculated on prices and deliveries to bakers. In France, strict control was exercised over the cereal markets, with a prohibition from selling outside the market and taxation of bread. In the case of a shortage, forceful intervention by the government was justified: requiring private individuals to report their inventory; encouraging them to supply the markets; requisitions, and so forth. The wine market was similarly controlled.

In England, internal commerce was totally free. Since the middle of the seventeenth century, and especially since the Glorious Revolution, the state had ceased to exercise control over economic life. Enlightenment circles of the eighteenth century strove to liberalize their wheat trade as England had done so successfully. In France, the physiocrats advocated a policy of elevated prices to encourage producers, calling for the end of state control of markets and prices. But measures favoring the free movement of wheat, decreed in 1763, 1774, and 1787, were in large part revoked in 1768, 1776, and 1788, because of food shortages. Under the French Revolution, the wheat shortages necessitated total government control that encompassed requisitions, taxation, and imposition of a ceiling price called the maximum. Even if the markets enjoyed a certain amount of freedom in the nineteenth century, they remained under government control, to regulate the wheat supply. In general, foreign trade was also government controlled. All trade policy in the European countries, yielding to strong demographic pressure, fought against runaway inflation and the famine it would cause. Grain exports were generally government regulated; in times of scarcity, grain was retained to feed the populace. In France, the freedom to export was won for a short time in 1764, and then sought again in 1775. In periods of famine, such as during 1661, 1694, 1709, and 1740, the government bought grain from Barbary (through the Mediterranean) or from Northern Europe (through the Baltic) to lower prices. In England, the inverse more often prevailed. The government tried to guarantee a minimum price to producers, thus keeping the market profitable in a country with a relatively small population, which normally maintained a surplus. Beginning in 1663, export premiums were instituted, and in the following century, customs tariffs were imposed, on a sliding scale, on imported wheat when price reductions fell short of projections.

Until the middle of the nineteenth century, the Corn Laws protected English agricultural production. These laws were repeatedly reinforced and adjusted, particularly in 1790, 1815, 1822, and 1828, thus preventing price collapses. But in 1846 the government decided to open the borders to foreign import and repealed the laws. It opted for cheap bread, favoring domestic industry by lowering its production costs, thus sacrificing the interests of large landholders and farmers. At the same time, France gravitated in the opposite direction, toward closing its borders. The goal was to protect farmers, even though it would drive up agricultural prices for consumers, requiring them to work harder to feed themselves. In 1819, customs tariffs were established. Despite several attempts at liberalization (such as the free trade treaty of 1860), the tariffs were reinforced by successive governments, especially during the depression of 1882, which resulted in the Méline laws of 1892. In nearly all of Europe, a similar situation prevailed, including Germany beginning in 1879, where assorted import taxes accompanied support measures for grain exports, and, a little later, Italy and Austria-Hungary. Tariff wars pitted nations against each other at the end of the nineteenth century, particularly France against Italy and Spain. A few countries resisted the protectionist wave that submerged Europe—England, the Netherlands, Denmark, and Switzerland. The Great Depression of 1929 definitively condemned free trade in democratic countries as well as in totalitarian states in search of autarky (economic self-sufficiency and independence).

Some blame this protectionism for the discernible moratorium on agricultural development, if not archaic structures of production, particulary in France. Inversely, free trade doubtless helped increase English productivity and satisfied consumers on a long-term basis. It also burdened British farmers with unforeseen difficulties and harmed a sector that by the 1930s could supply only about 40 percent of the total food consumption in a country that had become dependent on imports.

The Policy of Incentives. During the second half of the eighteenth century, government policies in Europe encouraged agriculture. The ambient mercantilism had long pushed the states to increase development of uncultivated lands to reduce imports and to cultivate new crops to increase exports. From the beginning of the seventeenth century in France, the monarchy pushed for the drainage of swamps, bringing in technicians from the Netherlands, and encouraged the rapid development of the mulberry tree and the silkworm. But after 1750, government support for agriculture intensified and became more extensive with the French Revolution. From 1761, tax exemptions were granted for clearing land or draining marshy areas. The intendants who administered the provinces played an active role in the circulation of agronomic knowledge. They gave financial assistance and distributed seed.

Governments encouraged the creation of agricultural societies, which multiplied throughout Europe at the end of the eighteenth century. They encouraged the development of new crops (potatoes, cultivated forage, and sugar beets) and also concerned themselves with improving animal breeds (the creation of the sheepfold of Rambouillet, near Paris, in 1786, and the introduction of Spanish merino rams) and with the fight against livestock diseases. In 1761, the first veterinary school was established in Lyon, followed by another in Alfort near Paris (1765).

The example was followed in other countries. From the beginning of the nineteenth century, agricultural training programs appeared in Piedmont, following the example of the previous French programs. These spread throughout Europe during the period of the First Empire (1804–1815), supported by both private initiatives and public incentives, before the governments took over the major part of that effort. In France, agricultural schools were created to improve and modernize the methods of cultivation, but doubly important to the country was the campaign to encourage the profession of farming and train farmers. The state supported farm schools, which private individuals had established, by purchasing the required lands or by paying the instructors; an example is the famous Royal Agronomic School of Grignon, established in 1827 on estate land purchased by Charles X. Other specialized schools were created (the stud farm of Le Pin in 1715, the royal forestry school of Nancy in 1824, the horticultural school of Versailles in 1874, and so on), a network of agricultural establishments was put in place in 1848 (model farms, regional schools), as was the agronomic research institute beginning in 1876. In Italy, the minister of agriculture was charged in 1861 with organizing agricultural training, and the first secondary school of agriculture (dedicated to viticulture) was founded in 1876. In Germany, agricultural chemistry stations distributed information about fertilizers, and in Austria-Hungary, agricultural schools proliferated: by 1910 there were fifty-three in Moravia alone.

The Policy of Intervention. Governments also concentrated on developing uncultivated lands, from the nineteenth century at least. In (Mussolini's) Italy, the focus was hydraulic planning in the north and, particularly in the south, improving marshy lands, either directly or by requiring the cooperation of large landholders. After World War II, in southern Italy, the Cassa per il Mezzogiorno (Italy Development Fund) encouraged or financed reforestation, the creation of villages and infrastructures, and the distribution of material, seeds, fertilizer, and other agricultural commodities. After the German empire was proclaimed in 1871, that state played a major role in the agricultural development of Brandenburg and Pomerania, and in the efforts to drain the marshy lands of eastern Prussia. In France, the government focused on the reforestation of Sologne and of Landes under the Second Empire, and on the development of the plains of the Lower Rhone in the twentieth century. In the Netherlands, polders were created; and in Spain, beginning in 1932, the government undertook the irrigation of orange plantations.

In England, the state intervened far less, despite the action of the voluntary Board of Agriculture, instituted in 1793, and the repeal of the Corn Laws in 1846. But beginning in 1880, faced with the fall of prices and the distress of farmers, the English government was obliged to intervene. It created a ministry of agriculture in 1889 that took the following measures to help producers: requirement of landowners, and no longer farmers, to pay the tithe beginning in 1891; protection against seizures beginning in 1893; acquisitions of lands and concessions to farmers through county councils beginning in 1908; loan facilities for modernizing operations; help against agricultural diseases; and the development of an agricultural training program tied to the universities. At the same time, the tax system became an instrument for restructuring farming operations in favor of medium-sized farms. World War I, then the collapse of prices again obliged the British state to intervene, beginning in 1921, with a policy of support for agricultural prices, before the crisis of 1929 forced them to tax imports and return to protectionism in the 1930s.

In the twentieth century, the state's role as director was obvious in countries under dictatorship, but also evident in democratic countries. In France, in 1936, the state instituted the ONIB (Office National Interprofessionel du Blé [National Interprofessional Office of Wheat]), which brought together the state and representatives of the producers to fix the prices of cereals and regulate them. Supplies were built up and vine stocks uprooted to support the price of wine. Even in the United States, where state intervention traditionally aroused scorn, indeed hostility, the Great Depression that began in 1929 obliged the government to resort to customs tariffs and to take innovative measures. The Agriculture Adjustment Act of 1933 permitted action on prices. Government agencies bought surpluses and built up supplies to support prices. They granted compensation so that producers would reduce their cultivated areas, and granted long-term loans to reduce indebtedness.

The Policy of Support for Farmers. After World War II, agriculture underwent considerable transformations that reopened the question of its economic place and function. In most European countries, as well as in the United States, agriculture survived only through the aid and protection of the state. It benefited from subsidies, price guarantees, and surplus management, all intended to reserve a decent income for farmers. But during the same period there was a drastic, rapid, and apparently irreversible reduction in the number of effective farmers. Efforts were made to render farm operations competitive and dynamic, to increase their size, and to reduce the distribution of lots (in France, called the policy of *remembrement*, or regrouping of lands), and to further agronomic research and improve and increase the amount of training of farmers.

Even in England, government measures sustained agriculture: control of production and of product quality, the policy of planning, furnishing fertilizers and equipment, tax exemption, prices guaranteed by marketing boards, and granting deficiency payments when prices fell too low. Agricultural training was encouraged in agricultural technical colleges and county agricultural institutes, as was research by the Agricultural Research Council.

Outside industrial countries, demographic growth exacerbated the food problem. To avoid famines and coordinate production with rapidly growing need, governments in developing nations had to choose between developing either subsistence agriculture or commercial crops from the plantations owned by colonizers. Desired effects were not always achieved, however. These policies frequently forced countries to increase dependence on the market and on multinational corporations, or even on other countries that supplied foodstuffs or the means of production. Aside from the use of food as a weapon against recalcitrant countries, the policy of development has led to other harmful consequences. If the "green revolution" made it possible to notably improve yields, it also made farmers dependent on imports such as more productive seeds and fertilizers and ruined those who were incapable of meeting the required expenses.

In Europe, the creation of the Common Market (European Economic Community [EEC]) in 1957 and the definition of a common agricultural policy a few years later profoundly influenced the agricultural system. A panoply of measures aimed to organize the markets of certain products, such as grains and dairy products. Grants were allocated to compensate for differences with general prices that were usually lower, and thus to sustain exports, while customs duties on imports from places outside the common area protected the member countries. A policy of price intervention and of stockpiling surpluses was put into affect, which avoided at great expense overproduction and the collapse of prices.

In spite of its undeniable success, the system thus implemented within the EEC aroused both criticism and fierce opposition. It not only drained the financial resources of the most effective farmers, it was unable to solve the problems of overproduction (it even accentuated them) other than by destroying surpluses, fixing quotas, or compensating farmers for letting lands lie fallow. It required a considerable expenditure to finance members' intervention in the market and the management of stocks. It struggled from the beginning with hostility from Great Britain, which joined the EEC in 1973. EEC preferences had harmful effects for Great Britain: it was obliged to buy its foodstuffs at higher prices, which penalized its consumers, used to cheap food purchased from the international market; it was forced to reduce its outside imports and to contribute heavily to the common budget. Great Britain therefore opposed the costly policies, risking the future of European agriculture anew through reviving its policy of free trade initiated in 1846.

Alternative Policies. United States demands for free trade lent support to those critics of the EEC agricultural policy. The United States pressured Europe to eliminate all customs restrictions to allow their agricultural products to enter freely. The system of free trade was assumed, as in the nineteenth century, to create fair competition, thus favoring the largest producers and stimulating economic progress. The United States therefore retaliated against European opponents of free trade, forgetting that its own agribusiness depended heavily on government subsidies. The recourse to "globalization" by countries outside the various agricultural trade conferences reopened the debate over the merits of the productivist policy supported by free trade proponents, again experiencing the dimension of associated risks, such as the crisis of mad cow disease and other health problems, the introduction of genetically modified organisms, and the use of animal feed laced with agrochemicals. Globalization was also an attempt among countries anxious to free themselves from the tyranny of the agribusiness multinationals, and to rescue farmers they victimized. Governments found themselves at a crossroads: either redefine agriculture in terms of new priorities, similar to new policies in health care and ecology, by regulating trade and exercising precautions, though this risks slowing supply side growth; or persevere with free trade and the bold industrial innovations that increase productivity at any cost, including the ecological equilibrium of the planet.

BIBLIOGRAPHY

Braudel, Fernand, and Ernest Labrousse, eds. *Histoire économique et sociale de la France*. Paris, 1970–1982.

Duby, Georges, and Armand Wallon, eds. *Histoire de la France rurale*. Paris, 1975–1976.

Engerman, Stanley L., and Robert E. Gallman, eds. *The Cambridge Economic History of the United States*. 3 vols. Cambridge, 2000.

Léon, Pierre, ed. *Histoire économique et sociale du monde*. Paris, 1978.

Mathias, Peter, and Michael M. Postan, eds. *The Cambridge Economic History of Europe*. Cambridge, 1978.

Thirsk, Joan, ed. *The Agrarian History of England and Wales*. Cambridge, 1967–1999.

GÉRARD BEAUR
TRANSLATED FROM FRENCH BY SYLVIA J. CANNIZZARO

AGRICULTURAL PRICES. Agriculture was the largest sector of the preindustrial economy, typically supporting three-quarters of the population. With incomes low, food accounted for a large share of consumption. Textiles, constituting the major manufacturing industries, largely consisted of processed agricultural products, such as wool, flax, silk, and cotton, although many European producers had to import their raw materials (cotton in particular from Asia and then the Americas). Economic development generally involves a transfer of resources from agriculture to industry, and the speed of that development depends in part on relations between the sectors. Agricultural prices are indicators of the success that agriculture had in supporting the population and also of its relations with the rest of the economy.

Agricultural price data are relatively abundant, which explains why they have been studied so extensively by economic historians. Since the nineteenth century, governments and the business press have continuously published the prices of the major crops. For earlier years, price circulars recorded agricultural prices in some major markets, but other sources provide the bulk of the data. Because most large institutions usually purchased grain, fibers, and other food products, their records are the bases of price histories going back to the Middle Ages. In addition, grain was an important traded good, so that its prices were entered in the records of wholesale and retail markets. Finally, governments often regulated the grain trade because of its centrality to the food supply, and their activities generated further information on prices. Much ingenuity has been devoted to using this information to explore many issues regarding agriculture.

Agricultural output is influenced by climate and weather; grain output, in particular, is subject to wide variations from one year to the next. The impact of these fluctuations on prices depends on the extent of the market compared to the spatial pattern of weather variation. When markets are broad but weather is local, weather fluctuations have no influence on price: A hailstorm that destroys the harvest in one village has no effect on the price there if grain can be brought in from neighboring villages to meet local demand. On the other hand, if bad weather cuts output throughout the whole marketing region, prices will rise to equate supply and demand.

Over the past millennia, the human population has expanded enormously, and the standard of living of most people in the world today is higher than that of their ancestors before the Industrial Revolution. Food consumption per head has increased over time, to provide an important component of the growth in living standards. The counterpart is that the prices of agricultural products have fallen relative to wages.

The Growth of Agricultural Output. Direct calculation of agricultural output is usually impossible before the nineteenth century, because the production of the various crops is unknown. Early work on the growth of output inferred it from the growth of population on the assumption that consumption per head was a constant, with some allowance made for imports and exports. That calculation, however, ignores the impact of income and prices on the demand for food. Between 1746 and 1821, for example, the population of England and Wales virtually doubled, from 6.2 to 12.3 million. It would be a mistake to regard that as the result of a rise in agricultural output, however, since food prices rose substantially over the period, thus reducing the demand for food. Making allowance for the dampening effect of rising agricultural prices implies that there was no growth in agricultural production. Indirect estimates of agricultural output must take agricultural prices into account to be accurate.

Standard of Living, Nutrition, and Famines. Famines represent acute failures of food provisioning. The common view emphasizes natural causes: bad weather or some other catastrophe that results in a poor harvest and insufficient food for the population. On the other hand, recent research has emphasized the role of markets in producing famines. Most famine victims are laborers who die because their wages are too low to allow them to buy enough food. Famines, in other words, are the result of agricultural prices that are high relative to wages.

Any factor that can produce high food prices or low wages can cause a famine. The Bengal famine of 1943 was at first blamed on a failure of the rice crop, but there was no harvest shortfall. Instead, the famine was caused by a large increase in British expenditures to fight World War II. The high incomes of employees in the military effort bid up the price of rice, so that rural farm laborers could no longer afford it and therefore starved. Speculation in food grains during suspected harvest failures can also raise prices and cause famines. Harvest failures can cause famines by eliminating the food crop of the poor (as in the potato famine of 1846) or by eliminating jobs in harvesting or threshing a crop that has failed. The failure of a crop can cause a famine by increasing its price only if the crop failure occurs over a sufficiently broad geographical range. Local failures—even national failures in a global economy—are not extensive enough to cause a famine if imports are drawn from other regions and prevent a rise in price. Peel's repeal of the Corn Laws in 1846 was intended to fight the Irish potato famine by allowing grain imports that would prevent food prices from rising. Famines cannot be understood without considering the impact of harvest failures and other developments on the price of agricultural products.

Market Integration. One of the earliest uses of agricultural prices was to study market integration. If markets are integrated, the "law of one price" should prevail; that is, the prices should be the same everywhere except for the cost of shipping between the markets. The rationale is simple: Larger divergences in price are unsustainable because they would induce shipments from the low-price market to the high-price market, and the shipments would drive the differential down to the cost of conveying the grain. Grain prices are available for many European cities back to the Middle Ages, and this material has been scrutinized to determine when European markets became integrated. The simplest procedure is to graph prices and see whether the differences decline over time. Indeed, that is what happened: Price differences were pronounced in the mid-fifteenth century, but they had largely disappeared by the mid-nineteenth century.

Price convergence has been used to study the impact of transportation improvements on markets. Railroad building and improved shipping in the nineteenth century cut regional differences within countries, such as India and Russia, and reduced differences between the exporting countries like Australia and importing countries like Great Britain. By the late nineteenth century, not only were wheat markets and rice markets integrated around the globe, but markets for the two basic food grains were also closely connected, so that a shortfall in the world rice crop would raise the price of wheat as well as the price of rice.

Agricultural Productivity. The growth of agricultural productivity is a central issue that has been studied directly with data like crop yields, calculations of output per worker, and so forth. These approaches are often precluded by the absence of the required information. Agricultural prices have been pressed into service to fill the gap.

One approach is to estimate agricultural production from income and prices, as discussed earlier, and relate the estimated output to inputs. Dividing agricultural output by demographically based estimates of the agricultural population, for instance, implies estimates of labor productivity in agriculture.

Another approach relies entirely on prices. When an economic activity becomes more efficient, firms—or farms—can sell their products at lower prices or pay higher prices to the owners of factors of production—land, labor, and capital. Indeed, the growth of farm input prices minus the growth of agricultural product prices equals the growth in agricultural productivity—specifically, total factor productivity.

Calculations of this sort have been used to measure productivity growth in several European countries. France, for instance, shows an erratic pattern of advance and retreat from the sixteenth to the nineteenth century. England, on the other hand, experienced steady productivity growth from 1500 to about 1750, then a pause until 1800, followed by further advance to 1850.

Terms of Trade between Agriculture and Manufacturing. Rapid urban-industrial growth may cause a sharp rise in the demand for food and a rise in its price relative to the price of manufactured goods; that is, an improvement in agriculture's terms of trade. The classical economist David Ricardo thought that economic development normally had that effect, since he believed that agricultural supply was relatively inelastic, so that an urban boom would raise food prices and would ultimately benefit landlords through higher rents.

Agriculture's terms of trade have shown considerable fluctuation. They improved during the Price Revolution (c. 1520–c. 1650), but deteriorated in the following century. Agricultural prices inflated more rapidly than manufactured goods prices during the British Industrial Revolution era but then declined in the mid-nineteenth century. Between 1896 and 1913, world trade expanded as improvements in transportation cut shipping costs. Agriculture's terms of trade improved in grain-exporting regions but declined in importing countries like Great Britain that were committed to free trade. Tariffs in many continental countries preserved high agricultural prices by excluding cheap American grain. Falling farm prices during the interwar period reduced agriculture's terms of trade everywhere.

Agriculture's terms of trade were of great concern in developing countries in the twentieth century; for instance, in the Soviet Union in the 1930s. The collectivization of agriculture was justified on the grounds that peasants would withhold crops, thus turning the terms of trade in their favor and choking off industrialization. The same concerns were common in the developing world until the Green Revolution produced such large increases in farm output that agricultural prices fell even as urbanization proceeded.

Distribution of Income. The logic underlying the use of prices to measure total factor productivity can be reversed to throw light on the distribution of the gains of agricultural revolutions. From this perspective, a rise in productivity can produce either a fall in agricultural product prices—in which case consumers gain from the agricultural revolution—or a rise in the wages of agricultural workers, the profits of farm capitalists, or the rents of landlords. In the latter cases, it is the workers, capitalists, or landlords who gain from the productivity growth. The division in any historical case depends on the character of the technological change, the demand curve for farm products, and the supply of inputs to agriculture.

This scheme has been applied to income distribution in England from the Middle Ages to the nineteenth century. While there were fluctuations around the trend, the real price of agricultural products remained steady since output barely kept pace with population; indeed, from 1750 to 1800, output stood still while population and income expanded, so that agricultural prices rose to choke off demand. Although agriculture's terms of trade improved, consumers did not gain; neither did farm laborers or farmers. From the 1520s to the 1840s, landlords were generally the main beneficiaries of agricultural productivity growth as rents rose briskly. Ricardo would not have been surprised.

[*See also* Agricultural Risk Management; Crop Failures; Crop Yields; Engel's Law; Famines; *and* Total Factor Productivity.]

BIBLIOGRAPHY

Abel, Wilhelm. *Agricultural Fluctuations in Europe from the Thirteenth to the Twentieth Centuries*, translated by Olive Ordish. London, 1980. An important early effort to compare price movements across European markets.

Allen, Robert C. *Enclosure and the Yeoman*. Oxford, 1992. Uses prices to measure agricultural productivity and then uses prices to show that landlords rather than consumers gained.

Allen, Robert C. "Tracking the Agricultural Revolution in England." *Economic History Review*, 2d series, 52.2 (1999), 209–235. Uses agricultural prices to estimate the growth in English agricultural output from 1520 to 1850 by specifying the demand curve.

Allen, Robert C. "Economic Structure and Agricultural Productivity in Europe, 1300–1800." *European Review of Economic History* 3.1 (2000), 1–25. Extends the demand curve method across Europe.

Braudel, Fernand P., and Frank C. Spooner. "Prices in Europe from 1450 to 1750." In *Cambridge Economic History of Europe*, vol. 4, edited by E. E. Rich and C. H. Wilson, pp. 378–486. Cambridge, 1967.

Clark, Gregory. "Agriculture and the Industrial Revolution, 1700–1850." In *The British Industrial Revolution: An Economic Perspective*, edited by Joel Mokyr, pp. 227–266. Boulder, 1993. Uses prices to measure total factor productivity growth in English agriculture and to estimate growth in demand.

Hoffman, Philip T. *Growth in a Traditional Society: The French Countryside, 1450–1815*. Princeton, 1996. Uses prices to measure the growth in total factor productivity in French agriculture.

Hurd, John. "Railways and the Expansion of Markets in India, 1861–1921." *Explorations in Economic History* 12.3 (1975), 263–286.

Latham, A. J. H., and Larry Neal. "The International Market in Rice and Wheat, 1868–1914." *Economic History Review* 2d series, 36.2 (1983), 260–280.

Li, Lillian M. "Integration and Disintegration in North China's Grain Markets, 1738–1911." *Journal of Economic History* 60.3 (2000), 665–699.

Metzer, Jacob. "Railroad Development and Market Integration: The Case of Tsarist Russia." *Journal of Economic History* 34.3 (1974), 529–550.

Persson, Karl G. *Grain Markets in Europe, 1500–1900: Integration and Deregulation*. Cambridge, 1999.

Ravaillion, Martin. *Markets and Famines*. Oxford, 1987. Analyzes food price movements and mortality during famines.

Sen, Amartya K. *Poverty and Famines: An Essay on Entitlement and Deprivation*. Oxford, 1981.

Wang, Yeh-chien. "The Secular Trend of Prices during the Ch'ing Period (1644–1911)." *Journal of the Institute of Chinese Studies of the Chinese University of Hong Kong* 5.2 (1972), 347–371.

ROBERT C. ALLEN

AGRICULTURAL RENTS. When all the technicalities involving the economists' definitions are removed, agricultural rent seemingly becomes an easy and practical concept to understand. It is the contract that one person had with another for the hire of land. But that simplicity is confounded when we realize that the two main contracts involved were quite different. They were fixed rent contracts, and what are known as share contracts, of which sharecropping was the most common. And even within these contracts there were quite important variations and historical developments. We illustrate the first from the English experience and the second by casting a wider net, predominantly over Europe.

Rack Rents and Archaic Tenures. Typically in English villages over the last several centuries, rent day was viewed as a social and economic ritual. It usually took place twice a year, and if the farmer had the cash to pay, he could relax and enjoy the rent dinner. But if he could not pay, or could not pay now, or could only pay a proportion of the rent, then rent day must have been filled with apprehension. Before the Industrial Revolution there is unlikely to have been a more substantial transfer of resources from one social group—the tenant farmers—to another—the landlords—as millions of pounds changed hands every year. While this concept of exchange is easy to state, the mechanics involved in the contract are quite another thing. It was a private agreement between landlord and tenant. No returns were required by the tax man, and so we know little about how rents were assessed, or how the contractual agreement between tenant and the landlord or his agent came about. We also know little about the precise methods of payment or the techniques used for agreeing abatements, remissions, and, occasionally, evictions.

On closer inspection, even the concept is not so straightforward. The rack rent is the most familiar rent contract. It is supposed to represent a return on land based on its market value. But in turn market value was often assessed according to the rent it commanded. Thus in eighteenth- and nineteenth-century England, land was sold for anything between twenty-five and forty years' purchase, that is between twenty-five and forty annual rent equivalents. But landlords might not exact the maximum rent indicated by value, especially when rent contracts were renewed, because they might reward their tenants for their loyalty and good service. Or they may have wished to attract good tenants by bestowing inducements or favors. Conversely, sometimes the maximum rent was sought. Sometimes land was rented by auction. This was prevalent with chari-

PAYING RENT. Frontispiece to Sir Anthony Fitzherbert's *The Boke of Surveying*, 1523. (North Wind Picture Archives)

ty lands where a system of trusteeship obliged those trustees to seek the maximum income possible for the beneficiaries of the charity.

But not all land was tenanted at rack rents. Archaic tenures and rental arrangements were common, and they were replaced only gradually from the sixteenth century onward by rack rents. In many places, these archaic tenures continued to operate well into the nineteenth and even into the twentieth centuries, particularly on the property of the major institutional landowners of the day: the major charities, the principal educational establishments, and the church. These old tenures embraced what were known as leaseholds and copyholds. Leasehold tenures, often called beneficial leases, were held by lessees of their landlords either for terms of years or for lives. The latter could run for the duration of the lives of the named persons, none of whose names need necessarily be the name of the lessee. Three-life leases were the most common. When the lease was for a term of years, it was not unusual for them to extend for long periods, such as ninety nine years.

Upon entering into the lease, the lessees paid a premium fee, known as an entry fine, and thereafter paid an annual, but relatively modest rent known by various terms: ground rent, quit rent, annual rent, or reserved rent. Upon the death of one of the named lives, or at the expiration of the term of years, it was usual to pay a "top-up" or reentry fine to maintain the tenancy. The annual rent was modest by comparison. And as long as the terms of the lease allowed it, the lessee could sublet the land to a third party for the same rent or even on a rack-rent basis. It may seem strange that the lessor allowed this, and thereby passed up the opportunity to maximize income. The advantage was that he would not bear any of the transaction costs for repair and maintenance of the property, for rent collection, or for the costs of distraint if tenants defaulted on their rents. Such a situation was especially attractive to charitable, educational, and church estates whose properties were often geographically disbursed and ordinarily would be costly to administer.

Copyhold was the other main archaic tenure. There were various kinds of copyholders, but they were all tenants of manors. The lords of the manors retained the fee simple of the various properties, and their tenants enjoyed a customary ownership of that part to which they were admitted as copyholders. For this they paid a fee upon entry, known as a fine—akin to the premium fee that leaseholders paid—and a small annual rent. Sometimes they were also obliged to make other small payments, and in medieval times in England (and much longer in central Europe where similar manorial customs existed) they would have been required to give labor services to the lords. Copyhold tenants enjoyed considerable independence as long as they fulfilled certain customary obligations.

Copyholds were predominantly of three kinds, copyholds for years, copyholds for lives, and copyholds of inheritance. The first two can be equated with leases for years or for lives. There could come a moment when the lords allowed such copyholds to expire, not to admit further tenants under such arrangements and instead convert the tenure to rack rents. Copyholds of inheritance were different. These conferred a status to the copyholder not far short of freeholder, but without the attendant fee-simple rights. Unless otherwise controlled by special custom of the manor, copyholds of inheritance obeyed the common laws of inheritance but were subject to money payments, rents, and services to the lord of the manor. As long as the tenants of the land (or put another way, the owners of the copy) paid their annual charges and carried out their other obligations, this land could remain in perpetuity outside the grasp of the lord of the manor. And if the custom of the manor allowed, the copyholders could sublet at rack rent. The charges that were paid to the manor were often fixed in the distant past and were not subject to revision according to price changes.

The annual rents and other services did not necessarily reflect current land values in the same way that rack rents did. Because the annual rent more or less descended by custom and therefore had often been fixed at a remote time without subsequent review, it might bear little relationship to the reputed economic value of the land. This understandably was a bone of some contention should a

lessor or lord wish to reevaluate the property and adjust the contract. It was the entry fine that was the principal element of the payment, the principal cost to the lessee or copyholder, and the principal income to the landowner or lord. It was a lump-sum payment made at regulated intervals. Those intervals were determinate—based on the length of term of the lease or the copyhold in years—or indeterminate, according to the expiration of a life or lives.

Fines. A fine was levied when a new lease was granted or a new copyholder was admitted, or when a new life was added to the existing lease or copy, such as at the death of one of the named "lives" already entered on the lease or copy. When contracts for years ran their course, new ones could be arranged and new entry fines paid. This was, in theory, the opportunity to equate the fine element of the contract to the current market level, but in practice these agreements were rarely founded on sound economic information since absentee landlords of this kind did not carry out regular surveys.

A disadvantage of this fine system was that the lessee had to find a large sum of money in a lump at the beginning of the process. The advantage to the lessor or the lord was that he would receive a one-off, but large payment. His disadvantage was that successive large payments, on lives at least, came at indeterminate intervals, and in the meanwhile the lord had to be content with a small annual rent. It was normal to add new lives to existing leases at the death of an already named life, but also at other times with or without a death. The latter situation allowed lessors or lords to acquire interim income between entry fines, by offering their tenants added security of tenure. Thus this was a mutually beneficial arrangement.

Inflationary price changes at the end of the eighteenth century made the modest annual rents on archaic tenures more or less a liability to fee-simple owners in terms of their asset strength. But for tenants it was a boon, giving them almost the ownership of a free good for the duration of the lease. Under this pressure, English rental practices changed significantly. Long leases and leases for lives were allowed to run out. In the 1840s, legislation was introduced to enfranchise copyholds whereby either tenants bought out the fee simple and became freeholders, or the lords bought out the remaining terms of the lease. The former arrangement became by far the more common, but it was a slow process. Copyholds lingered on well into the twentieth century until legislation in the 1920s declared that on 1 January 1926 all remaining copyhold land would become freehold.

Rents in the Age of Industrialization. This confusion of tenures makes it very difficult to construct an index of land rents in the period of greatest interest to economic historians, the century or so of industrialization. Rack rents emerged gradually as the common contract, but were far from universal even in eighteenth-century England.

Nonetheless, economic historians have used the course of rack rents as a barometer for economic change. In the eighteenth century, tenancies, even rack-rent tenancies, may have been contracted for a number of years. The famous Norfolk tenancy was a twenty one-year lease, often split into seven-year periods. In the nineteenth century the annual tenancy became dominant. Why?

As long as the general price level remained fairly flat, there was not a great risk for either party in taking on a long contract. The rent was the principal cost to the tenant, and in times of flat prices it was a fixed real cost. But in times of general price inflation the tenant had an advantage because in real terms that fixed cost would have fallen. Conversely, the rent was the principal income to the landlord, and during the same period of general price inflation that fixed income would have fallen in real terms. There appears to have been a fifteen-year lag or period of adjustment in rent levels relative to agricultural prices in the eighteenth century. The crisis came toward the end of the eighteenth century when price inflation took off and was exacerbated by the wars with France. Landlords who had to wait a number of years before tenancies expired saw their real income diminish severely. Conversely, tenants with a number of years yet to run saw their real costs plummet. Contracts that came up for renewal during the war were bid up, and the length of leases was reduced. The conversion to annual rack-rent tenancies meant that rents more closely shadowed agricultural prices. That is, they rose when prices rose, though they were sticky on the downturn and did not immediately follow price falls. This stickiness came to a head when agriculture experienced a depression in the 1820s and especially in the 1830s. Tenants were generally permitted rent abatements, rent holidays, or remissions, before the landlord turned, as a last resort, to actual rent reductions. In time landlords and tenants alike became more uncompromising. The otherwise paternal attitude of landlords toward their tenants and the deference shown by the tenants to their landlords gave way to a more commercial contract between the two parties.

Rent Rates from 1700. The one continuous annual rent series available for England in the period of industrialization suggests that rents rose gently from 8 to 10 shillings per acre from about 1750 to 1790. They then doubled in the next twenty years or so, more or less in line with inflation. Thereafter, unit acre rents remained at 20 to 21 shillings per acre from 1815 to 1850, but the general agricultural price level declined. Rents rose again from 1850 to 1878, reaching a high point of just over 28 shillings per acre, but agricultural prices remained more or less flat. Thus there was effectively a transfer of land-derived income from the tenants to the landlords from 1815 to the 1870s. A crisis hit agriculture in the 1870s and 1880s. Unseasonal conditions were accompanied by massive foreign imports of cheap grain. Prices tumbled, rents followed quickly and bottomed out at below 20 shillings per acre by the turn of the new century, and remained at or near this level until 1914, even though prices recovered from about 1896. Therefore, effectively the reverse transfer of income took place. However, the damage to landlords and tenants alike was severe and agriculture ceased to be a major component of British national income.

Slave Tenancy. The development of the English model of rent contracts here defined was perhaps the earliest to discard archaic forms of rent contracts. In much of the rest of Europe there was also a general transition away from manorial-controlled agriculture to landlord/tenant and owner-farming agriculture, but the rate of change was slower or responded to different economic and social stimuli. In the process other rental contracts can be identified, the most important of which was payment of rent in kind, of which the most widespread form was sharecropping. Payment in kind was common in manorial situations as a supplement to money rent, and it also included labor services. The payment of tithes was perhaps the most common form of payment in kind. But sharecropping became a very common form of rent contract outside of Britain. There are so many different theories in land and labor economics to explain the incidence of sharecropping that it is invidious to attempt an overall generalization. Sharecropping in vine agriculture in fifteenth-century Italy can hardly be directly equated with the dramatic rise of the system in France before 1700, or indeed with its development in post-bellum southern United States agriculture, in all three regions of which different socioeconomic conditions prevailed. This wide spatial and chronological incidence of the system did not end there since at times it was also found in India and throughout the New World. But there are general principles that can be applied throughout its use. The most important is that the landlord took a share of the harvest in lieu of rent.

Under fixed-rent systems the landlord expected a certain payment regardless of the state of the harvest, but under sharecropping the landlords' expectations depended on both the state of the harvest and the quality of the farming. The two are related, but are compromised by environmental influences. Since the landlords' return was dependent on the tenants' involvement there was an encouragement for the landlord to take a partial and direct control over the management of the land. Under fixed-rent contracts the main form of landlord control was through lease covenants and therefore exercised control at a distance.

If we must generalize then we can say that fixed-rent contracts developed in northern Europe, and share contracts in southern Europe. One distinguishing feature of sharecropping seems to be the management of the fixed capital. That is, the capital that is sunk into grain production is quite different from the capital sunk into vine or olive production. In the former, the crops were rotated from field to field, and annual sowing prevailed, but in the latter the basic crop was in place for many years. The greater involvement of landlords through share leasing in such agricultural pursuits was more likely to prevail where they provided, and therefore needed to ensure the safety of, significant fixed capital other than the land itself. Such conditions applied to vine, olive, cotton, and livestock production, but less to grain production.

While the archaic tenures of England are a thing of the past, sharecropping is still quite widespread. In 1970 it was calculated that 79 percent of the world's farms were owner cultivated, especially in Asia, but practically not at all in Africa, where squatting or communal tenures dominated. Conversely, 7 percent of farms were pure tenancy, but 36 percent of those involved a form of share tenancy, especially in Europe and North America.

[*See also* Tenant Farming.]

BIBLIOGRAPHY

Allen, Robert C. *Enclosure and the Yeoman: The Agricultural Development of the South Midlands 1450–1850.* Oxford, 1992.

Cheung, Steven N. S. *The Theory of Share Tenancy.* Chicago, 1969.

Clay, Christopher. "'The Greed of Whig Bishops'?: Church Landlords and their Lessees 1660–1760." *Past and Present* 87 (1980), 128–157.

Clay, Christopher. "Lifeleasehold in the Western Counties of England, 1650–1750." *Agricultural History Review* 29.2 (1981), 83–96.

Galassi, Francesco, Kyle Kauffman, and Jonathan Liebowitz. *Land, Labour, and Tenure: The Institutional Arrangements of Conflict and Cooperation in Comparative Perspective.* Seville, 1998.

Hoffman, Philip T. "The Economic Theory of Sharecropping in Early Modern France." *Journal of Economic History* 44.2 (1984), 309–319.

Otsuka, K., H. Chuma, and Y. Hayami. "Land and Labor Contracts in Agrarian Economies: Theories and Facts." *Journal of Economic Literature* 30 (1992), 1965–2018.

Reid, Joseph D. "Sharecropping in History and Theory." *Agricultural History* 49 (1975), 426–440.

Turner, Michael E. "Corporate Strategy or Individual Priority? Land Management, Income and Tenure on Oxbridge Agricultural Land in the Mid-Nineteenth Century." *Business History* 42.4 (2000), 1–26.

Turner, Michael E., John V. Beckett, and Bethanie Afton. *Agricultural Rent in England, 1690–1914.* Cambridge, 1997.

Wordie, J. R. "Rent Movements and the English Tenant Farmer, 1700–1839." *Research in Economic History* 6 (1986), 193–243.

MICHAEL TURNER

AGRICULTURAL REVOLUTION *[This entry contains two subentries, dealing with the agricultural revolution in Europe, and in Asia, Africa, and the Americas.]*

Europe

Agricultural revolutions are technological and organizational. Feeding a growing population and shifting a large portion of the workforce from agriculture to industry re-

quires more output per unit of land and higher labor productivity. The technical improvements in farming that raise productivity are closely associated with transformations in rural society. The relationship between productivity growth and social change is a fiercely debated question.

The technological revolution in European farming began between 1500 and 1800. Figure 1 shows output per worker in agriculture for important countries based on early twenty-first-century boundaries. Italy, Germany, and Spain had declining productivity during this period as agricultural output failed to keep pace with the farm population; in France, Austria, and Poland, output per worker fluctuated without a falling or a rising trend. Present-day Belgium, in contrast, had very high productivity at the end of the Middle Ages. Productivity slumped in the next three centuries under the impact of rising population, but the level of Belgian productivity remained above that of most of Europe. England and the Netherlands stand out as successes. Each had an agricultural revolution before 1800 and achieved the highest labor productivity in 1800. In the nineteenth century, the agricultural revolution spread from northwestern Europe to the rest of continental Europe. Output per farmworker increased throughout Europe and contributed to the growth of urban-industrial society.

Often agricultural modernization has been accompanied by far-reaching changes to the rural society, agricultural tenure, and farm size. Many commentators and theorists have argued that these institutional changes were preconditions of the technological revolution. Manorialism, communal tenure, open fields, owner-occupation, and sharecropping have all been identified as inhibitors to innovation, and their replacement by large-scale enclosed farms is the recipe for modernization. These claims, however, have been controversial, and recent research has contradicted them by showing that agricultural productivity has increased in various institutional settings—even those that appear the most backward.

England. England occupies a central position in the study of the agricultural revolution due to the conjunction of three developments: the enclosure of the open fields and the creation of a unique rural social structure, the high productivity of its farming, and the early industrialization of the country. Consequently, England has been regarded as the "classic case" in which the overthrow of traditional rural society precipitates a rise in farm productivity and unleashes an industrial revolution.

The enclosure of the open fields was the most idyosyncratic feature of English rural history. At the end of the Middle Ages, about half of England's farmland was open fields and commons. By 1850, virtually all of the arable land and much of the grass had been enclosed. Enclosures in the late fifteenth century were often effected by manorial

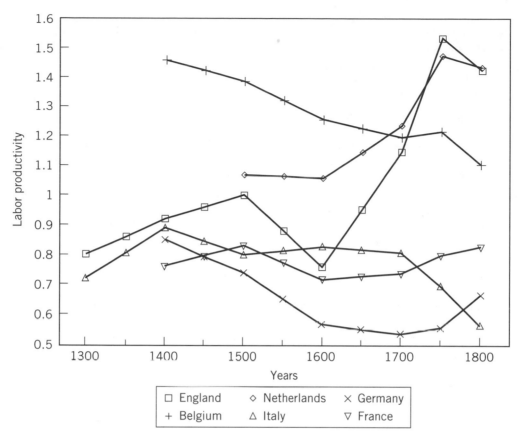

FIGURE 1. Output per worker in agriculture. England in 1500 set to 1.00. SOURCE: Allen, 2000.

lords who evicted their customary tenants, or, less dramatically, as marginal land was abandoned. By the seventeenth century, enclosure required agreement among all property owners and customary tenants. To overcome the required unanimity, landowners turned to private acts of parliament. Such acts could be secured with the agreement of the owners of about three-quarters of the land; and on this basis, most of the remaining open fields and commons were enclosed in the century after 1750.

Proponents of agricultural improvement, such as the eighteenth-century writer Arthur Young argued that enclosure led to higher productivity by eliminating communal control over cropping and the problems of drainage, weed control, and animal breeding that arose from intermixed cultivation and village herds. The new crops of the eighteenth century, such as clover and turnips, were adopted more rapidly by enclosed farms than by open, and they were critical to the success of the more intensive crop rotation systems, alternate husbandry, and convertible husbandry that raised output per unit of land. The overall efficiency advantage of enclosure per se was small, however, and most of the gains in efficiency between the Middle Ages and the nineteenth century could be introduced by small-scale farmers in the open fields.

English landownership was also transformed between 1500 and 1800. Much land in the Middle Ages was divided into small family farms of ten to twenty acres. While many of these farmers owed various dues to manorial lords, the properties passed from generation to generation on customary terms. By the nineteenth century, manorial lords had acquired much of this customary land and leased it to tenants who cultivated farms of hundreds of acres. These farms were worked by hired landless laborers who were the descendants of the medieval customary tenants. The tripartite structure of great estate, large-scale tenant farmer, and landless laborer was unique to England and has been regarded as a uniquely modern set of institutions that facilitated agricultural progress. Comparisons of large and small farms show that employment per acre declined as farms got larger, while output per acre was the same for all sizes.

Much debate has centered on the timing of the agricultural output and productivity increases. A long-standing view identifies the years from 1750 to 1850 as the decisive period. This century coincided with the parliamentary enclosures, with the ascendancy of the great estate, and with the Industrial Revolution, and so supports the interpretation that enclosure led to productivity growth, which in turn spurred industrialization. An alternative view locates the technological revolution in the preceding century, 1650–1750. Proponents of this view tend to question the progressive role of the great estate and emphasize instead the capacity of small-scale, open-field farmers to generate rising productivity. On this reading of the evidence, the technological revolution of agriculture may have been a precondition for the Industrial Revolution, but it was not a concurrent development.

The Low Countries. The province of Flanders in modern-day Belgium was renowned for the productivity of its agriculture in the Middle Ages, and that superior efficiency may have contributed to the dense urbanization and manufacturing prowess of the region. Adjacent parts of northeastern France, as well as eastern England, also stood out for their high productivity, but these successes are often lost in the general averages of the countries.

Medieval Flanders was largely enclosed, but otherwise the rural society was traditional with the land being divided into small peasant farms. The farmers were essentially owner-occupiers, unburdened with significant feudal dues. The gains from efficiency accrued to the peasants themselves, rather than to the nobility or treasury, so the incentive to raise productivity was high.

The Netherlands was very sparsely populated before 1500, and manorialism was of little importance. Most of the farmland was enclosed, although there were extensive commons in the western region. As in Flanders, tenure systems protected the cultivators. They had a high incentive to innovate, and they did so after 1500.

France, Italy, and Spain. Manorialism in France was comparatively light at the end of the Middle Ages, and peasants were essentially owner-occupiers. This viable tenurial situation collapsed, however, as the nobility and bourgeoisie bought up peasant property and converted the cultivators to tenants. In northern France, large farms were assembled by leasing small properties. Warfare and taxation reduced the rate of agricultural productivity growth, but satisfying the Paris market produced strong incentives to improve; and by the middle of the eighteenth century, efficiency was probably just as high in the Paris Basin as in the English midlands. This favorable achievement is obscured in Figure 1 by the less satisfactory performance of southern and western France. There, the predominant tenure was sharecropping in which the tenant paid the landlord a predetermined fraction of the crop—usually a third or a half. Sharecropping may have reduced the incentive to innovate since the farmer gave up much of the output gain to the landlord, but this view is controversial. It is clear that warfare and high taxation contributed to low productivity, as did poor transportation, which inhibited the formation of a national market. As a result, grain was grown everywhere, even when it was manifestly unsuited to local conditions. Also, agricultural progress

along the Mediterranean required irrigation, and the legal system of seventeenth- and eighteenth-century France frustrated efforts to construct the necessary canals.

The agricultures of Spain and Italy suffered from many of the same problems as southern France, which they resembled. Spanish agriculture also may have been adversely affected by state policy. Price ceilings on grain reduced its cultivation, and grazing rights granted to the Mesta, the guild of shepherds, also may have hurt agriculture by allowing sheep to run across land that would otherwise have grown crops.

Germany. Religious warfare in the sixteenth century, and the Thirty Years' War (1618–1648) devastated Germany and accounted for its low productivity in the early modern period. In the eighteenth and nineteenth centuries, rural society developed in very different ways in eastern and western Germany.

In western Germany, state policy favored the peasants at the expense of the nobility, with the result that feudal tenants were transformed into peasant proprietors, although they were then burdened with high taxes. In eastern Germany, the peasantry remained ensurfed until the nineteenth century. The defeat of Prussia by Napoleon in 1806 precipitated the Stein-Hardenburg reforms, which freed the serfs but deprived them of much of the land. The Junker nobility emerged from these "reforms" with greatly enlarged estates and a near landless workforce of former peasants. While very different, the agrarian regimes of both western and eastern Germany supported rising productivity in the nineteenth century.

Russia. Before 1860, the productivity of Russian agriculture was low and stagnant. The countryside was divided into large estates, and most of the population were serfs. In the last half of the nineteenth century and in the twentieth century, Russian agriculture passed through several institutional revolutions as successive governments refashioned the system in the hope of stimulating economic development.

The first revolution began in 1863 with the emancipation of the serfs. The result, however, was an incomplete modernization of rural life, for the ownership and management of most farmland was transferred to the village community, which, in many cases, periodically redivided the land among its members and limited their movements. The "peasant question" was concerned with whether the system of equal family farms was stable or would inevitably polarize rural society into rural capitalists and landless laborers. Dramatic changes did not occur, but the issue is still debated.

Commentators in the late nineteenth century believed that the village communes were obstacles to improvement and that output and productivity were stagnant in the Russian countryside. This view has been undermined by aggregate statistics, which show a significant increase in farm output, and by studies of individual communes, which indicate important improvements in practice. The history of the tsarist peasantry supports the view that technological progress is possible in traditional peasant society, but successive generations of scholars have found ideological reasons to deny this possibility.

The second institutional transformation was initiated during the revolution of 1905–1907, when the imperial government stopped supporting the commune and actively sought its demise. The prime minister, Pyotr Arkadyevich Stolypin, introduced laws in 1906 and 1910 that encouraged peasants to commute their communal land into purely private property and to remove their strips from the open fields and consolidate them into enclosures. About 10 percent of the peasants left communes with their land between 1906 and the 1917 Revolution. These reforms were too short lived to affect productivity.

The Stolypin reforms were not popular with most peasants. After the 1917 Revolution, the third agrarian reorganization occurred as village communes throughout Soviet Russia reintegrated enclosed and separated lands, as well as property that had been owned by the nobility, into the village fields. Holdings were radically equalized. Livestock output expanded significantly during the 1920s, and the mechanization of grain production began as Russian farmers purchased about one million horse-drawn reapers.

The fourth institutional revolution occurred in the 1930s with the collectivization of agriculture. Peasant sales of grain did not meet the state's expectations in the 1920s. Stalin and many other communists blamed this on the hoarding of grain by a reemerging class of capitalist farmers called *kulaks*. In the early 1930s, the peasants were dragooned into "voluntarily" joining collective farms. These farmers acquired ownership of most land, horses, and much other livestock, while the peasants retained their houses, small plots, and a portion of the cattle, pigs, and small animals. The collective farms received substantial delivery quotas for grain and other produce and received low prices for these sales from state procurement agencies, and the peasants could sell the surplus production from their private plots at high, free-market prices. The peasants resisted collectivization by slaughtering about 40 percent of the livestock and reducing sowing. State procurements were maintained and the result was famine in 1933–1934.

Farm production dropped as agriculture was collectivized, but recovered by the late 1930s. Tractors and combines were widely used by 1940 and greatly abridged farm labor. There has been much debate about the long-run impact of collectivization on productivity. There was little growth in grain yields in Russia from the 1880s to 1940s after which they rose sharply. The history of yields was similar on the American Great Plains and the Canadian prairies where the climate was similar.

[*See also* Open-Field System *and* Young, Arthur.]

BIBLIOGRAPHY
Allen, Robert C. *Enclosure and the Yeoman*. Oxford, 1992. Nominates the small-scale, open-field farmers as the real heroes of the agricultural revolution.

Allen, Robert C. "Economic Structure and Agricultural Production in Europe, 1300–1800." *European Review of Economic History* 3 (2000), 1–25. Overview of productivity, growth, and economic change.

Aston, Trevor H., and C. H. E. Philpin, eds. *The Brenner Debate*. Cambridge, 1976. Vigorous debate on the causes and significance of alternative development patterns of rural society.

Bloch, Marc. *French Rural History: An Essay on Its Basic Characteristics*. Translated by Janet Sondheimer. Berkeley, 1966. Pioneering study of changing agrarian structures since the Roman Empire.

Finberg, H. P. R., gen. ed. *The Agrarian History of England and Wales*, Cambridge, 1967–2000. Indispensable and voluminous compendium on the subject, but rarely a source of pathbreaking interpretation.

Gerschenkron, Alexander. *Bread and Democracy in Germany*. Berkeley, 1943. Agrarian structure, tariff policy, and political reaction.

Gerschenkron, Alexander. "Agrarian Policies and Industrialization: Russia, 1861–1917." In *Cambridge Economic History of Europe*, vol. 6, pt. 2, edited by H. J. Habakkuk and M. Postan, pp. 706–800. Cambridge, 1965. Affirms the backwardness of Russian peasants.

Grantham, George W. "Agricultural Supply during the Industrial Revolution: French Evidence and European Implications." *Journal of Economic History* 49.1 (1989), 43–72.

Gregory, Paul R. *Russian National Income, 1885–1913*. Cambridge, 1982. Establishes the rapid growth in agricultural output in Imperial Russia.

Hoffman, Philip T. *Growth in a Traditional Society: The French Countryside, 1450–1815*. Princeton, 1996. Views French peasants as innovative but held back by war and taxation.

Jasny, Naum. *The Socialized Agriculture of the USSR. Plans and Performance*. Stanford, Calif., 1949. Helpful overall account.

Le Roy Ladurie, Emmanuel *The Peasants of Languedoc*. Translated by J. Day. Urbana, Ill., 1974. Demography, farming, and culture united in a total history.

Nove, Alec. *Was Stalin Really Necessary? Some Problems of Soviet Political Economy*. London, c. 1964. Explains why the answer is yes.

O'Brien, Patrick K., and Leandro Prados de la Escosura. "Agricultural Productivity and European Industrialization, 1890–1980." *Economic History Review* 45.3 (1992), 514–536. The twentieth-century story.

Rosenthal, Jean-Laurent. "The Development of Irrigation in Provence, 1700–1860: The French Revolution and Economic Growth." *Journal of Economic History* 50.3 (1990), 615–638. The French Revolution consolidated decision-making power in Paris and accelerated the construction of irrigation systems.

Simpson, James. *Spanish Agriculture: The Long Siesta, 1765–1965*. Cambridge, 1995. Modern analysis of the lateness of the agricultural revolution.

Veblen, Thorstein. *Imperial Germany and the Industrial Revolution*. Ann Arbor, 1966. Traces reactionary politics to the agricultural revolution.

Vries, Jan de. *The Dutch Rural Economy in the Golden Age, 1500–1700*. New Haven, 1974. The major work on the subject.

Vries, Jan de. *The Economy of Europe in an Age of Crisis, 1600–1750*. Cambridge, 1976. Overview of alternative patterns of institutional change.

ROBERT C. ALLEN

Asia, Africa, and the Americas

Agricultural revolution, the transition from traditional agricultures to modern farming, has been, much like its well-known demographic analog, a universal phenomenon. Although its beginning and speed, as well as some of its important features, are country specific, its general attributes are readily recognizable around the world. From a fundamental physical point of view, this grand global transition can be best defined as a change of energy foundation (Smil, 1991, 1994). All traditional agricultures, regardless of their outward features or productivity, were powered solely by photosynthetic conversion of solar radiation, which produced food for people, feed for animals, recyclable organic wastes for the replenishment of soil fertility, and fuel for households. Fuel needed for small manufactures and for the smelting of metals to make simple farm tools also was derived from the photosynthetic conversion, by cutting fuelwood and producing charcoal.

Consequently, if properly practiced, traditional agricultures were energetically fully renewable, as they did not require any depletion of accumulated energy stocks and did not use any nonsolar subsidies. However, this renewability, and inherent resilience, did not guarantee either sustainability of the traditional practices or a reliable supply of food. Poor agronomic practices and overgrazing reduced soil fertility and also commonly resulted in excessive erosion (and desertification) and the abandonment of arable or pasture lands. Low yields, often hardly changed over centuries, typically provided only marginal food surpluses in good years; and they led to recurrent food shortages, widespread malnutrition, and, during times of natural catastrophes or wars, periodic famines. Intensification of traditional farming through fertilization and irrigation, multicropping and plant rotations, and mechanization of some basic tasks, accompanied by more efficient use of draft animals, could sustain higher population densities but demanded higher inputs of human and animal labor than traditional practices.

Four universal measures that revolutionized traditional agriculture and turned it into a modern economic activity include: the use of inorganic fertilizers, particularly synthetic nitrogen compounds; mechanization of field and crop-processing tasks energized by engines and motors; development of new high-yielding cultivars; and application of agrochemicals to combat pests and weeds. None of these advances could have occurred without still-increasing inputs of fossil fuels and electricity and without the introduction of new prime movers. Consequently, modern farming is not just a skillful manipulation of solar energy flows; it is now an activity unthinkable without massive fossil fuel energy subsidies channeled directly from fuels and electricity used to power farm machinery and, more important, indirectly from energy embedded in numerous industrial products and used to support extensive agricultural research.

A discussion of the key ingredients of this agricultural revolution follows, and then some of its specific trends are illustrated by post-1750 developments in the United States and China. These important countries are emblematic of agricultural revolutions that took place on their respective continents, but with a uniqueness that suggests the highly individual paths that many countries have followed during their transition from traditional to modern farming.

Inorganic Fertilizers. Only the introduction of inorganic fertilizers made it possible to remove the limits imposed on crop yields by the recycling of organic wastes and the planting of nitrogen-fixing legumes. Treatment of phosphate rock by diluted sulfuric acid to produce ordinary superphosphate became common after 1870, and this new demand led to discoveries of huge phosphate deposits in Florida in 1888 and in Morocco in 1913, still the largest sources of the rock. Concurrently, potash mining began to expand in both Europe and North America. The most important advance, breaking the nitrogen barrier, came only with the synthesis of ammonia from its elements (Smil, 2001). The impact of this process, first demonstrated by Fritz Haber in 1909 and rapidly commercialized by a BASF team led by Carl Bosch, was delayed by the two world wars and the intervening economic crisis. Global consumption rose rapidly, from five million to eighty-five million tons of nitrogen between 1950 and 1990, as solid urea became the world's leading nitrogen fertilizer.

About half of all energy used directly and indirectly in farming now goes into the synthesis of fertilizers. By the year 2000 about half of all nitrogen used annually by the world's crops and about 40 percent of the element available in the world's food proteins originated in the Haber-Bosch synthesis of ammonia. The United States and other affluent countries could easily reduce their dependence on synthetic nitrogen by lowering their high meat consumption, but in all populous low-income countries the dependence will only grow. In addition to nitrogen, the world's crops now receive also close to fifteen million metric tons of phosphorus and about eighteen million metric tons of potassium a year (IFA, 2001). Rising fertilizer applications have been accompanied by the expanding use of chemicals synthesized to reduce weeds and to combat insect and fungal infestations of crops. The first—and still widely used—commercial herbicide, 2,4-D (introduced in 1945), kills many broad-leaved plants without serious injury to crops. The first insecticide was DDT, released in 1944. By the year 2000, more than fifty thousand different pesticides were on the market.

Mechanization. Mechanization removed one of the greatest bottlenecks of traditional farming, its extraordinarily high seasonal demand for labor needed to harvest

AGRICULTURAL REVOLUTION. Moerbecke Sugar Company plantation, Zaire (present-day Democratic Republic of the Congo), 1967. (Eliot Elisofon/Eliot Elisofon Photographic Archives/National Museum of African Art, Smithsonian Institution, Washington, D.C.)

and plant crops. Before its introduction, for example, between March and September, 94 to 98 percent of all the available labor supply was needed in China's double-cropping area; and in parts of India, the two peak summer months required 110 to 120 percent of actually available labor (Buck, 1937; Clark and Haswell, 1970). This need could be met only if entire families worked almost around the clock or by relying on migratory labor, as even a week's delay beyond the optimum harvesting and planting period could substantially reduce yields. Draft animals could work only a limited number of hours a day, often lacked sufficient power for the needed tasks, and required high-quality feed for optimum performance.

Mechanization based on animate power began in earnest only after 1850, relying mostly on steel plows, seed drills, reapers, and harvesters. Horse-drawn combines and steam-powered plows and threshing machines came later. Substitution of tractors for draft animals began in the United States just after 1900; but in the populous countries of Asia and Latin America, it started only during the 1960s, and in most countries of sub-Saharan Africa, it still remains beyond the reach of individual subsistence farmers. Today's global agriculture operates with more than twenty-six million tractors, some seven million of which are in low-income countries. Shares of the agricultural labor force mirror different stages of the mechanization process: by the late 1990s, they had fallen to just 2 percent in North America and 20 percent in Latin America, but they were still nearly 60 percent in both Africa and Asia (FAO, 2001).

Mechanization also transformed crop irrigation, whose global extent grew more than sixtyfold between 1750 and 2000, from about 4 million to more than 270 million hectares, or from just over 1 percent to about 18 percent of the world's harvested cropland (FAO, 2001). Half of this area (and 70 percent in Asia) is now irrigated with mechanical pumps. In all places where water is drawn from deeper aquifers, fuel or electricity for these pumps is the largest energy input in cropping. Most pumps still deliver water to traditional ridges and furrows, but sprinklers are much more efficient (both water- and energy-saving) means of modern irrigation than pumps.

High-Yielding Cultivars. Mechanization alone could not have released so much rural labor. Higher crop yields, brought by new crop varieties responding to higher fertilization and to more widespread irrigation, were also necessary. Hybrid corn, introduced in the United States during the 1930s, was the first improved crop variety that made a large yield difference. Prehybrid yields averaged less than 2 tons per hectare; the recent U.S. mean is around 8 tons per hectare, and Iowa harvests 10 tons per hectare. A systematic development of short-stalked, high-yielding varieties (HYVs) of wheat and rice began in Japan during the 1920s, with the first early maturing varieties responsive to high rates of fertilization released during the 1930s. After World War II this effort was carried on primarily by

CIMMYT (The International Maize and Wheat Improvement Center) in Mexico (for wheat) and IRRI (International Rice Research Institute) in the Philippines (for rice), and both centers released their now globally dominant HYVs during the 1960s. All HYVs share a higher harvest index, commonly containing 50 percent, or even 60 percent, of all above-ground biomass in harvested parts, compared to 25 to 35 percent in traditional plants (Smil, 1999a).

With adequate fertilization, irrigation, and protection against pests, HYVs respond with much increased yields and have lifted the food output of scores of developing countries above subsistence minima. This combination of new agronomic practices, introduced during the 1960s, became widely known as the Green Revolution, as it radically improved agricultural prospects in populous low-income countries (Borlaug, 1970). The global mean harvest of all cereals more than doubled between 1950 and 2000, while China's rice yields roughly tripled; only sub-Saharan Africa's harvests remain in the pre-HYV era. Higher reliance on intensively cultivated grain monocultures, narrowing of the genetic base in cropping, and environmental impacts of agricultural chemicals have been the most worrisome consequence of this innovation; but all of these concerns can be addressed by better agronomic practices (Smil, 2000).

Transformation of U.S. Agriculture. During the last decades of the eighteenth century, agricultural practices in the new United States lagged behind the European performance. A century later, rapid and accelerating innovation gave the United States the world's most labor-efficient crop cultivation (Rogin, 1931; Schlebecker, 1975); and the no less revolutionary advances of the twentieth century further strengthened this primacy (USDA, 1950–2001). Mechanical innovations arrived first: interchangeable cast-iron moldboard plows before 1820 and mass-produced grain reapers, steel-blade plows, and seed drills after 1840. The first mechanical harvester was patented in 1858, and the twine knotter, which eliminated hand binding of cut grain, was introduced in 1878. Large steel moldboard plows could cut the heavy sod of North America's vast plains, and mechanical harvesters could gather the grain from vast fields. Horse-drawn combines, first sold during the 1880s, further accelerated the harvesting.

Productivity contrasts between 1800 and 1900 are impressive. In 1800, New England farmers needed 150 to 170 hours of labor per hectare to produce a good harvest of wheat; by 1900, this took less than nine hours in California. These rates translated, respectively, to more than seven minutes and less than half a minute of labor to produce a kilogram of wheat, roughly a twentyfold improvement of labor productivity in a century. However, these achievements required large numbers of draft animals, averaging about twenty-five million, during the first two decades of

the twentieth century; and their feeding required about one-quarter of America's cultivated land. This burden declined rapidly as tractor power surpassed horse power during the late 1920s. Finally, by 1963 the U.S. Department of Agriculture had stopped its count of draft animals.

Key transformations of post-1950 U.S. cropping have included the following changes: increasing size of individual holdings; greater size and installed power of agricultural machinery; large increases in fertilizer applications and in reliance on herbicides and pesticides; introduction of center-pivot irrigation, whose distinct circles cluster throughout the country's arid regions; and dramatic changes in cropping patterns, with larger areas devoted to corn and wheat monocultures, and with soybeans—cultivated on only a few thousand hectares in the early 1930s—becoming the second largest crop, now planted on one-fifth of all arable land. Animal farming saw the rise of mass poultry production, concentration of all feeding operations in huge enterprises, and general use of specifically formulated high-protein feeds.

Continuing modernization cut the rural labor force from more than 60 percent of the total in 1850 to less than 40 percent in 1900, 15 percent in 1950, and a mere 2 percent since 1975 (U.S. Bureau of the Census, 1975). At the same time, higher productivities have kept the planted area well below its historic peaks, lowered food prices, and delivered a surfeit of food to the population, whose every third adult is now overweight (Flegal, 1996). The U.S. agricultural revolution has been perhaps too successful.

China's Agricultural Intensification. Not every traditional society could intensify its farming by relying on higher inputs of animal labor. Cropping intensification based on more elaborate cultivation of a limited amount of arable land became the norm in rice-growing Asia. This approach, called agricultural involution by Geertz (1963), rested on highly labor-intensive cultivation of paddy rice and on constructing and maintaining the requisite irrigation systems, wet fields, and terraces. The process supports progressively higher population densities, but it brings extreme impoverishment. Labor productivity first stagnates and then declines as larger populations rely on increasingly marginal diets.

China's intensively cultivated southern provinces showed clear signs of agricultural involution long before the fall of the Qing dynasty in 1911. After stability returned to China following the conflicts of the first half of the twentieth century, new Maoist policies based on mass rural labor in communal farming perpetuated the involution. They also caused the death of at least 30 million people during the world's largest famine between 1959 and 1961 (Smil, 1999b). After Mao's death (1976), nearly 800 million peasants still represented more than 80 percent of China's total population, and they continued to subsist on barely adequate, although more equitably distributed, rations. Although China developed independently its own HYVs of rice, shortage of fertilizers and institutional weaknesses made it impossible to take advantage of this achievement. Only Deng Xiaoping's abolishment of communes and privatization of farming during the early 1980s radically reversed the trend.

By the mid-1980s, China's average per capita food availability rose to within 10 percent of the Japanese mean. By 1989, China became the world's largest producer of nitrogen fertilizers; and, with some 75 percent of the country's protein supplied by crops, more than half of all nitrogen in China's food now comes from synthetic fertilizers. China also irrigates 40 percent of its arable land and is diverting increasing amounts of its crops to animal feeding. Between 1980 and 2000, China's average per capita purchases of meat more than doubled, and the supply of aquacultured fish and fruits grew more than fivefold. Although serious challenges lie ahead, post-Mao China is an excellent illustration of the efficacy and the benefits of fossil-fueled agricultural revolution (Smil, 2000).

What the Revolution Accomplished. Between 1750 and 2000, the world's population increased 8.4 times (from 725 million to 6.1 billion), but the global crop harvest rose nearly eighteenfold. This increase became possible because the total cultivated area as well as the average crop yields expanded more than fourfold. Most of the productivity gains took place after 1900, thanks to a roughly hundredfold increase of fossil energy inputs to field farming. This achievement profoundly changed the global availability of food. In 1750, the average global crop output (before storage and distribution losses) did not cover even bare subsistence food needs. Today's global harvest produces more than enough food for the world's population, but a substantial productivity gap still divides the average agricultural performances of rich and poor countries.

Although North America and Japan have a surfeit of food energy and dietary protein, persistent socioeconomic inequalities in Asia and Latin America and failing states and chronic civil wars in Africa result in unequal access to food, with widespread and continuing malnutrition and even recurrent famines. The latest FAO (Food and Agriculture Organization of the United Nations) estimate of undernourished people totals 826 million, or about 14 percent of the world's population in 1998 (FAO, 2000). The highest shares of undernourished population (about 70 percent of the total) are in Afghanistan and Somalia, whereas the rates for India and China are, respectively, about 20 percent and just above 10 percent. With just over 200 million undernourished people, or roughly a quarter of the world's total, India ranks first. As India will add more people by the year 2050 than any other nation (about half a billion), its continuing agricultural revolution must be accompanied by more equitable income distribution, a challenge shared by most of the countries in Asia, Africa, and Latin America.

[*See also* Open-Field System.]

BIBLIOGRAPHY

Borlaug, N. E. "The Green Revolution: Peace and Humanity." A speech on the occasion of the awarding of the 1970 Nobel Peace Prize in Oslo, Norway, on 11 December 1970. <http://www.theatlantic.com/issues/97jan/borlaug/speech.htm>

Buck, J. L. *Land Utilization in China*. Nanking, 1937.

Clark, C., and M. Haswell. *The Economics of Subsistence Agriculture*. London, 1970.

Food and Agriculture Organization of the United Nations. *The State of Food Insecurity in the World, 2000*. Rome, 2000.

FAO. *FAOSTAT Database*. Rome, 2001.

Flegal, K. M. "Trends in Body Weight and Overweight in the U.S. Population." *Nutrition Reviews* 54 (1996), S97–S100.

Geertz, C. *Agricultural Involution*. Berkeley, 1963.

International Fertilizer Industry Association (IFA). *World Fertilizer Consumption*. Paris, 2001.

Rogin, L. *The Introduction of Farm Machinery*. Berkeley, 1931.

Schlebecker, J. T. *Whereby We Thrive*. Ames, Iowa, 1975.

Smil, Vaclav. *General Energetics*. New York, 1991.

Smil, Vaclav. *Energy in World History*. Boulder, 1994.

Smil, Vaclav. "Crop Residues: Agriculture's Largest Harvest." *BioScience* 49 (1999a), 299–308.

Smil, Vaclav. "China's Great Famine: 40 Years Later." *British Medical Journal* 319 (1999b), 1619–1621.

Smil, Vaclav. *Feeding the World. Challenge for the Twenty-first Century*. Cambridge, Mass., 2000.

Smil, Vaclav. *Enriching the Earth: Fritz Haber, Carl Bosch, and the Transformation of World Agriculture*. Cambridge, Mass., 2001.

U.S. Bureau of the Census. *Historical Statistics of the United States: Colonial Times to 1970*. Washington, D.C., 1975.

U.S. Department of Agriculture. *Agricultural Yearbook*. Washington, D.C., 1950–2001.

VACLAV SMIL

AGRICULTURAL RISK MANAGEMENT *[This entry contains three subentries, a historical overview and discussions of agricultural price stabilization and storage.]*

Historical Overview

Agricultural production is highly susceptible to natural "accidents" such as climatic shocks and noxious insects and fungi that make the relationship between work effort and yield, output and income uncertain. Prices of agricultural goods typically varied more than output. These conditions cause both incentive problems and welfare losses for producers as well as consumers and inspire risk control, risk sharing, and price and consumption stabilizing strategies. Modern agricultural techniques have reduced crop yield variance but single crop output normally displayed a standard deviation of 15 to 20 percent in preindustrial agrarian regions with uniform conditions in terms of soil or climate.

Harvest shocks are largely uncorrelated across such regions and sometimes even at different locations in a single village. Therefore the harvest variation of a single farm is usually greater than in a village. Unplanned aggregate crop output variance in a large geographical unit—say, the Mediterranean area—is usually quite small, as Aristotle already noted. Output shocks for a single crop are almost uncorrelated over time, and there is little covariation between the output shocks of different crops in a given agricultural region—for example, between wheat and rye, or between winter and spring crops.

These conditions set the stage for the basic strategies to manage risk: interregional trade, storage and crop diversification. However, historically the scope for these strategies was limited by the high cost of transport and storage. Before the railroads, land transport would add about 10 percent to grain price per 100 km, restricting long-distance trade to waterways.

Risk Pooling and Insurance. Unlike in animal husbandry, viable private insurance for harvest failures has been rare throughout history. In continental Europe formal insurance emerged as a local and spontaneous cooperative enterprise from the middle of the eighteenth century covering both cattle and draught animals. This institution spread to Scandinavia in the nineteenth century, but remained a local concern throughout the century. Its absence in arable farming was because of the familiar problems with private insurance. Adverse selection and moral hazard are particularly pronounced when it is difficult to detect to what extent damage is self-inflicted. Moreover, and perhaps more important, the incidence of risk among the insured tends to be highly correlated in an entire agricultural region. Modern attempts to introduce insurance against crop failures stem from the 1930s and insurance has since been widely used in developed and developing nations, but they rely crucially on public subsidies with indemnities outweighing premiums in the long run.

Rural communities developed less formal ways of mutual assistance. Given the informal nature of such self-help institutions the historical documentation is scarce. Studies of contemporary developing nations reveal a wide variety of support, in kind or in money, to households with transitory income shortfalls. However, these studies also indicate that informal self-help is unstable if the institution does not adhere to a principle of balanced reciprocity over time. Some farmers do tend to remain deficient in their net contributions over time (J-P. Platteau, 1997).

Risk can be pooled within a community of farmers by minimizing the exposure to risk of single households. European agriculture, at least from the early medieval period until the enclosure movements consolidated land holdings for each household at the dawn of the Industrial Revolution, had a partial answer. Characteristically, it scattered individual plots over the entire arable area of a village, a method also called the open field system. Households held a large number of narrow strips of land on open fields alongside other households' possessions. Eighteenth-century reformers suggested that it was detrimental to the efficient use of land, a view that is shared by many scholars although it has been challenged.

The persistence of the open field system has invited a search for some efficiency property compensating for an alleged productive disadvantage. In one interpretation, originally suggested by D. McCloskey (1976), the scattering of holdings is a risk-pooling device that works when natural "accidents" are local. By holding land in varying locations and of different soil characteristics a household minimized exposure to large shocks that hit a particular part of the village or a single type of soil or location. S. Fenoaltea (1976) opposed that interpretation on the grounds that other ways of coping with risk, such as informal mutual assistance, might be less costly. However, as noted above, informal agreements of mutual assistance are unstable. K. G. Persson (*Pre-Industrial Economic Growth*, Oxford, 1988) advanced the interpretation that mutual assistance faces the problems of free riding and shirking from obligations if effort and output of members are not observable. Scattered fields made for concerted labor—for example, in ploughing and harvesting—and therefore permitted costless monitoring.

Labor Contracts and Risk. The long-term and worldwide coexistence of different contractual arrangements invites interpretation in terms of risk sharing. Basically, labor has been contracted in agriculture under three forms: a wage contract, sharecropping, and a fixed rental arrangement. Of these forms, sharecropping, or output sharing, is unique to agriculture and fishery. Again, the apparent inefficiency of the share contract has been in the forefront of inquiry since the days of Adam Smith and Arthur Young. Under sharecropping, tenant and owner of land share the output—for example, by dividing output in two halves. This system violates the marginal conditions for efficient use of resources in that labor is used until its cost equals half the marginal output. Modern theoretical and empirical research has looked for compensating advantages with the sharecropping system, forced to do so by its widespread and continued use across time and civilizations.

The three contractual forms differ in the distribution of risk from output and revenue variations. In the wage contract the landowner bears the entire risk, being the claimant on the residual income, if any. Furthermore, the landowner bears the cost, sometimes high, of monitoring labor effort. The sharecropping contract divides the risk between landowners and labor. In the fixed rental system labor effort and output are greater because labor is expended on land until its marginal cost equals the marginal output, but the laborer bears the entire risk from revenue and output variation. However, if fixed rental contracts are short, the landowner faces the risk that labor may exhaust land and fixed investments, such as vine or olive trees.

Attempts to explain the coexistence of the three contractual forms proceed along two lines. J. D. Reid (1976) and others have argued that although the three forms coexist, labor typically passes through the three contracts over its lifetime. A sequence of contracts represents a learning by doing process that increasingly enables labor to cope with risk. Inexperienced labor does not take on a risk-sharing arrangement; it starts with a wage contract, benefiting from the monitoring of the landowner. With growing experience labor is able to take on more risk as a sharecropper, eventually ending up as a fixed rent tenant.

The other line of explanation looks at monitoring costs and the varying risks of opportunistic behavior in different crops and deduces contractual form from crop distribution. Although the evidence is not conclusive, Galassi et al. (1998) suggest that the high incidence of sharecropping in wine growing revealed in the 1427 Florentine *Catasto*—a population and property registry—can be interpreted by the implicit tax on labor effort that this type of contract imposes, since labor cost at the margin is lower than marginal output (see above). Because short-term output maximization might hurt the long-term return of long-life investments such as vine, a contract that discourages short-term overexploitation of resources is preferable to rental contracts.

Managing Price Variations from Output Shocks. Given the variations in output, price responses of a single good will depend on the quantities traded and stored and the availability of substitutes. Since most agrarian goods are necessities demand is price inelastic; that is, small quantity shocks have large effects on prices. The price fluctuations will affect revenue for producers and consumption for nonfood producers with rigid nominal wages. The French late-eighteenth-century physiocrats were the first to advocate free trade to stabilize prices, relying on the observation that output shocks in a large area like Europe canceled out, opening up the possibility of trade between surplus and deficit regions.

K. G. Persson (1999) documented a substantial decline in price volatility of grain from the early modern period in Europe and particularly in the nineteenth century as a response to increased trade and fall in transport cost despite continued harvest variation. However, with high transport costs, carryover storage from abundant harvest years to crises was the obvious alternative. This alternative, by smoothing out the supply over time, would be expected to diminish price volatility.

The length and cost of storage vary between different agrarian goods. Potatoes, at one extreme, are impossible to carry over from one harvest year to the next. Grain, under good storage conditions, can be carried over several years. There is little consensus as to the extent and nature of grain storage because most of the evidence is indirect. Tony Wrigley (1981) argued that given the fact that output shocks are uncorrelated, the high autocorrelation in price movements reveals carryover stocks. However, autocorrelation of price seems to be a fairly general property in prices observed in nonstorable goods and services such as day wages and potatoes as well as in storables such as grain. On the other hand, scattered documental evidence indicates that private and public storage has been used over long stretches in history and in most civilizations. The extent of that storage is not known, but most scholars side with a rather conservative estimate of perhaps 5–10 percent of the average harvest.

Elaborate forms of publicly subsidized granaries are found in antiquity and from early modern times in Europe and China, but they were gradually scaled down in Europe from the end of the eighteenth century. Many contemporary developing nations, for example India, use buffer stocks operations to stabilize prices and help with subsidized procurements to the poorest sections of the population, a policy many city councils practiced in seventeenth- and eighteenth-century Europe. Although the scale of these operations differed over time, their operating principles have been fairly similar, buying during abundant harvest years in order to stop a free fall of prices and selling in periods of scarcity.

Modern buffer stock and commodity price stabilization schemes have attracted a great deal of theoretical critique but the empirical assessment of their price-stabilizing effect is mixed and the schemes tend to be rather short-lived. According to one line of argument public granaries crowd out private storage, with little net effect on the level of inventories. Evidence suggests that eighteenth-century European grain markets, which practiced public granary intervention, experienced lower price volatility than markets that did not. R. A. Fogel (1992) assigns a positive role in reducing price and consumption volatility to public regulation of grain markets in the early modern period and Ejrnaes and Persson partly corroborate that claim (1999), showing considerably higher price volatility in sixteenth-century England before the introduction of grain price stabilization according to the so-called Book of Order policies than after.

Following up on that result one interpretation is that publicly subsidized storage emerged because private storage failed. The reason for this failure might be the prohibitive risks associated with carryover. Grain price series do not normally reveal a deterministic seasonal pattern, which is what one would expect for a good that has positive storage costs, is produced once a year, but is consumed over an entire harvest year (Samuelson, 1957). Neither do

AGRICULTURAL RISK. Chicago Board of Trade in session, circa 1900. (Geo. R. Lawrence/Prints and Photographs Division, Library of Congress)

grain prices *ex post* reward carryover, since the only deterministic pattern of grain prices is that they drop below trend at harvest, making it profitable for speculators to buy after harvest rather than carry over. One clue to the puzzle of carryover storage not showing signs of overall profitability is that stocks generate a so-called "convenience yield"; that is, the positive utility of having inventories available in a risky environment in excess of the economic return, which can be negative.

The welfare impact of price volatility differs, depending on whether price shocks are local or global and on whether we are concerned with producers or consumers. In poorly integrated markets price volatility is endogenous, having its origin in local supply shocks: a poor local harvest will send prices up, compensating the farmers for the drop in output, while a bumper harvest can actually reduce revenue for peasants. A decrease in price volatility would stabilize consumption for wage earners with rigid nominal wages and restore a positive relationship between output and revenue for farmers. A reduction in income volatility improves the welfare of the people who are averse to risk, providing the traditional rationale for achieving price stability. In modern development economics (Ravallion, 1988) the focus is on the relationship between price stability and consumption smoothing, which is believed to be increasing the chances for survival of individuals.

Typically in poorly integrated economies the ruling elite was mainly concerned with the reaction to price volatility of the net consumers of food—that is, the urban crowds—who could unsettle local and central governments. The food riot, endemic in European societies, practically disappears by the middle of the nineteenth century (Tilly, 1971). With the nineteenth-century integration of grain and food markets, price shocks are increasingly global in origin, an example is the long-term fall in European grain prices as a response to the North American grain invasion in the last third of the nineteenth century. Global price shocks tend to change the concern of public policy away from consumer support to producer subsidies to stabilize farmers' revenues. Tariffs were the preferred means to that end in the closing decades of the nineteenth century. Direct subsidies and price support have been the main policies in the twentieth and twenty-first centuries. They have been practiced widely in the United States and Europe since the 1930s, although political opposition to them is increasing.

Crop Diversification. Price movements of close substitutes are highly correlated but that does not hold for nonsubstitutes. Therefore, a risk-reducing strategy typically involves a combination of food products and agricultural raw materials for industrial use or export. Observed diversification in history often follows that pattern, and can be interpreted in terms of rational portfolio adjustment. R. A. McGuire (1980) suggested as much in a study of nineteenth-century farmers' output mix of corn and cotton in the southern United States. However, diversification to industrial raw material or export crops relies on the extension of trading networks and urban growth. In medieval Europe farmers who clustered around the big urban centers benefited from increased demand for poultry, dairy products, and raw materials for the textile industry. They could intensify land use, improve crop rotation and productivity, and reduce risk at the same time.

Futures and Forward Contracts. A futures contract allows for selling (or buying) a good at a fixed price for delivery at some future date, typically after harvest. It protects the seller (buyer) from an unexpected fall (rise) in market price in the future. Having entered a futures transaction, one has to fulfill the contractual obligation—normally not by actual delivery, but by a matching or offsetting transaction at the closure date. As the seller you cannot reap the benefit from an eventual increase in spot price above the futures price. Modern agrarian option and hedging instruments do not have that limiting property. Although futures trading was in use at the busy European marketplaces, such as Amsterdam, from early modern times ordinary farmers did not rely on it as a risk-reducing institution until the twentieth century. In its modern form futures trading in grain and other agricultural products originated in the United States in the mid-nineteenth century; the Chicago Board of Trade was the leading institution. From the end of the nineteenth century agrarian futures were traded on the major European markets. Agrarian producers criticized the early phase of nineteenth-century futures trading because of the alleged tendency to increase spot price volatility. Before futures trading was regulated, market manipulation was endemic and caused large price volatility. However, on theoretical grounds and in the absence of such behavior, futures can be expected to depress spot price volatility because they make storage less risky.

Since medieval times grain merchants have offered farmers advance cash payment for future deliveries. This procedure differs from a futures contract because payment precedes delivery. Political authorities normally did not approve of this institution. The reason is obscure, but contemporaries suggested that the advance payment for the future harvest, while reducing the risk of a future fall in prices, usually meant that the farmer paid a high premium by taking far less money than the expected price of the good. In that respect it might be considered just a concealed loan at usurious rates of interest, with the harvest as collateral.

[*See also* Agricultural Prices; Crop Failures; Crop Yields; *and* Famines.]

BIBLIOGRAPHY

Ejrneas, Mette, and Karl Gunnar Persson. "Grain Storage in Early Modern Europe." *Journal of Economic History* 59.3 (1999), 762–772.

Fenoaltea, Stefano. "Risk, Transaction Costs, and the Organization of Medieval Agriculture." *Explorations in Economic History* 13 (1976), 129–151.

Fogel, Robert A. "Second Thoughts on the European Escape from Hunger: Famines, Chronic Malnutrition, and Mortality Rates." In *Nutrition and Poverty*, edited by S. R. Osmani, pp. 243–286. Oxford, 1992.

Galassi, Francesco L., et al. "An Econometric Model of Farm Tenures in Fifteenth-Century Florence." *Economica* 65 (1998), 535–556.

Garnsey, Peter. *Famine and Food Supply in the Graeco-Roman World: Response to Risk and Crisis*. Cambridge, 1988.

McCloskey, Donald N. "English Open Fields as Behaviour towards Risk." *Research in Economic History* 1 (1976), 124–170.

McGuire, Robert A. "A Portfolio Analysis of Crop Diversification and Risk in the Cotton South." *Explorations in Economic History* 17 (1980), 324–371.

Netz, Janet S. "The Effect of Futures Markets and Corners on Storage and Spot Price Variability." *American Journal of Agricultural Economics* 77 (1995), 182–193.

O'Rourke, Kevin. "The European Grain Invasion, 1870–1913." *Journal of Economic History* 57 (1977), 775–801.

Persson, Karl Gunnar. *Grain Markets in Europe, 1500–1900: Integration and Deregulation*. Cambridge, 1999.

Platteau, Jean-Philippe. "Mutual Insurance as an Elusive Concept in Traditional Rural Communities." *Journal of Development Studies* 33.6 (1997), 764–796.

Ravallion, Martin. *Markets and Famines*. Oxford, 1988.

Reid, Joseph D. "Antebellum Southern Rental Contracts." *Explorations in Economic History* 13 (1976), 69–83.

Samuelson, Paul M. "Inter-temporal Price Equilibrium: A Prologue to the Theory of Speculation." *Weltwirtschaftliches Archiv* 79 (1957), 181–219.

Tilly, Louise. "The Food Riot as a Form of Political Conflict in France." *The Journal of Interdisciplinary History* 2 (1971), 184–200.

Will, P.-E., and R. B. Wong. *Nourish the People: The State Civilian Granary System in China, 1650–1850*. Ann Arbor, 1991.

Wrigley, Sir Tony. *People, Cities and Wealth*. Oxford, 1987.

KARL GUNNAR PERSSON

Agricultural Price Stabilization

In almost every advanced economy, whatever the era, the state has intervened, usually through buffer stocks or restrictions on trade, in the name of "price stabilization." *Price* presupposes exchange between individuals who have specialized, such as the urban artisan or the tenant farmer growing cotton. Were all independent subsistence farmers, they might suffer from fluctuating harvests, but not to the extent of artisans whose income might not cover the cost of their staple or of tenant farmers whose large crops might contribute less revenue than their expenses for inputs.

Stabilization presupposes inflexibilities. Price movements would be much less pronounced if consumers would happily substitute abundant barley for scarce wheat, if farmers' access to credit allowed them to store at nominal expense, if merchants could easily transport wheat from regions with an abundance, or if farmers could sow and harvest wheat within a few weeks. The various public interventions in the name of price stabilization do not address the inflexibilities directly. Indeed they often exaggerate some of them.

State Systems. Interventions in the name of price stabilization are exemplified by those of eighteenth-century Qing China. In the context of considerable regulation of the private grain trade, the emperor established in each county seat a granary under magistrates appointed centrally and acting locally. Ideally the magistrates would procure grain locally at harvest time, especially in years of abundance, thereby supporting prices for farmers. Ideally the magistrates would release some grain—recommended was an administrative rule of 30 percent of stocks—each spring and summer to dampen seasonal price variability, but they could release much more grain during years following poor harvests. Magistrates were instructed to release grain at set percentages below high prevailing prices, influencing the local market price thereby, yet were expected to lose little money on average. Magistrates could authorize releases in the form of loans to producers, to be returned to the granary from the next harvest, at implied interest rates less than market rates for money loans. To achieve more than token intervention, the magistrates needed to have substantial quantities in hand, indeed to achieve an "ever-normal" granary. In practice many provinces achieved close to the ideal quantities, which collectively represented a substantial investment by the state. State-run reserves had been an objective in China for over two thousands years, but only in the eighteenth century were the reserves so substantial and the magistrates so focused.

Although it may seem odd that anyone would question the usefulness of the state granary system in Qing China, many did over concerns common in other times and places and in the theoretical as well as practical literature. Magistrates worried that their own irregular buying contributed to the price instability they hoped to dampen. Magistrates wondered whether or not grain itself was the best buffer; many began to hold what they called silver-grain. Magistrates feared that the ever-normal granaries discouraged the very community-supported granaries the emperor desired as part of his efforts at political decentralization. And did everyone in fact benefit from price stabilization? It sounds good for all, to support the producer during times of low prices and supplement the consumer during times of high prices. But the consumer bought at a price higher than otherwise when the producer was helped, and the producer sold at a price lower than otherwise when the consumer was helped. Much as the social gains from free trade are dwarfed by the negative and positive effects on particular groups, the main point of price stabilization interventions is in their disproportionate impacts on particular groups.

Fiscal Incidence. On closer inspection, state interventions in the name of price stabilization are usually better classified as "poor relief." Those who received releases from Qing granaries at their peak effectiveness are estimated to represent 5 percent of the population for 15 percent of their food needs in a year. (Given how little grain entered marketing channels in eighteenth-century China, the state thus distributed as much as 10 percent of marketed grain.) These Chinese recipients were predominantly the poor, whether temporarily or chronically. Similarly the price stabilization schemes of sixteenth-century Venice were explicitly tied to the network of charities. In the Hellenistic age *euergetism*, namely the public munificence of the rich, was often expressed through grants of grain or gifts of money to city grain funds. In 123 BCE Gaius Gracchus, as tribune of the plebs, began the construction of state granaries and the monthly sale of grain to citizens in Rome at a fixed low price, the beginnings of the "dole."

On closer inspection, state interventions in the name of price stabilization have disproportionate spatial effects. Qing granaries were in urban areas, not the countryside, where the poorest lived. Meanwhile grain in the form of tribute ensured supplies to Beijing, just as the Roman and eighteenth-century French systems aimed to quiet the politically important crowds in Rome and Paris, no matter the consequences to landless rural laborers in Sicily and northern France. In regions more distant from Paris, which might export grain only when closer crops failed, the magistrates tolerated the *entave*, a nearly ritualistic form of riot by rural consumers to prevent shipments to Paris. Similarly the many twentieth-century marketing boards—such as the Canadian Wheat Board—"pooled" their sales across farmers with minimal regard for transport expenses, thereby favoring those farther away from export ports.

Releases from Qing granaries could be made only to residents of the particular county. The private grain shippers meanwhile were often harassed as the cause of local price rises; coastwise shipment of grain was prohibited. Similarly mid-twentieth-century regulations in India prohibited shipments across state boundaries. In eighteenth-century France grain on the road required a passport. Sixteenth-century Venice, in times of high prices, prohibited exports, despite the city's principal activity as an entrepôt. In ancient Greece the diversion and forced unloading of a grain vessel from another city-state was not viewed as an act of war but a necessity in the face of local shortage. Needless to say all such interventions add to inflexibilities and undercut trade itself as a buffering mechanism. Moreover such interventions mainly serve to transfer the price instability elsewhere. Developed countries in the twentieth century, say for sugar, have devised import restrictions in bad years and export subsidies in good years that keep their local sugar prices remarkably stable (not to mention extremely high on average) but with the result of extremely unstable prices elsewhere.

Notwithstanding the use of phrases such as *price stabilization* and *orderly marketing*, many state interventions have monopoly profits for select groups as their aim, pure and simple. The Agricultural Adjustment Act of 1933 was the first in the United States to allow growers of a particular crop to form a "marketing board," which could coordinate and time shipments in ways that in the industrial sector would be prima facie evidence of an antitrust violation. Similarly the various International Coffee Agreements, negotiated from the 1960s to a collapse in 1989, stabilized, which is to say restricted, exports through a quota system, in line with Brazil's long-standing efforts to gain from its dominance in coffee production. The International Coffee Agreements were an unusual example of consumers, notably in the United States, acquiescing to the extraction of those monopoly profits. More often a state export monopoly has provoked a state import monopsonist, as happened in Britain after World War II with the formation of the Raw Cotton Commission in response to statutory export boards Britain itself had established in its colonies.

Often missed, by economists at least, is the dynamic incidence of price stabilization. The Qing granaries could not release grain they did not yet have; the accumulation of significant quantities took several decades. In the 1930s, proponents of similar ever-normal granaries in the US wanted the immediate boost in price from immediate substantial State purchases, whatever their pronouncements about the symmetry of purchases and releases in later years.

Sometimes the fiscal incidence is less obvious, but is present nonetheless. Qing granaries were often filled with grain presented in lieu of cash land taxes and sold below the market price. The magistrates had every reason to extract more implicit tax, say by grading the grain lower, because it allowed them to cover the granaries' storage and operating costs. In ancient Athens and eighteenth-century France an implicit tax fell on bakers, because of regulations determining the maximum price of bread as a function of the price of wheat. Another group in eighteenth century France, namely religious foundations and hospitals, were required to keep three years of their own estimated food needs, reserves that the magistrates could call upon at any time for sale at below market prices. This

"community" granary system transferred the storage and interest expenses of a buffer stock from the state to those private organizations. Elsewhere, private organizations that began as attempts at cartelization of a commodity business, such as the Federación Nacional de Cafeteros de Colombia, became captured by the state. Coffee prices within Colombia were stabilized, to be sure, but at a low average, while concern shifted to the instability in the state's fiscal flows.

Rationales. Why, it might be asked, do private traders not stabilize prices sufficiently? "It is an outstanding fault of the competitive system that there is no sufficient incentive to the individual enterprise to store surplus stocks of materials, so as to maintain continuity of output and to average, as far as possible, periods of high and low demand" (Keynes, 1938, p. 459). John Maynard Keynes, however, offered no evidence for this proposition in favor of state storage. If anything the evidence is that state policy itself discourages private stockholding. In Qing China magistrates often made the argument that they themselves should buy in times of abundant harvest, for otherwise private traders would take advantage of low prices to speculate. In ancient Athens regulations prohibited the amount any single grain merchant could hold. A regulation common throughout Europe in the Middle Ages prevented "regrating," namely the buying of a commodity for later resale. (Similar crimes included "engrossing" and "forestalling," not to mention the catchall "profiteering.") In eighteenth-century France, in the face of high prices, mobs imposed a "just" price on those with grain to sell, a form of civil disobedience known as *taxation populaire*. As there was no symmetric *subvention populaire*, such attacks on "hoarders" surely reduced the quantities available during the next crisis. Throughout the ages, that those in the commodity business were often minority outsiders was both cause and effect of the popular disrespect of such commercial activity.

"The need for stabilizing prices arises from the inherent incapacity of the open competitive market alone to keep the production of agricultural products constant when the demand is constant, and changing in the right direction and the right amounts when the demand changes" (Shepherd, 1942, p. 589). But this common criticism sets an impossible standard for private traders, namely that they make beforehand the allocations obvious after the fact, when the weather is known. Price stabilization is easy for anyone with foreknowledge, as for Joseph interpreting Pharaoh's dreams (Gen. 41). Had seven even better years followed the accumulation of stocks over the seven good years, as ordered by Pharaoh under Joseph's direction, and those stocks had had to be dumped at a loss, Joseph would have ended back in prison or worse. (That Pharaoh bought those stocks from his subjects without telling all Egypt of his dreams, only to sell the grain back at higher prices, looks close to "profiteering" or even "insider trading.") And by no means is the state's forecasting skill clearly superior. Even though the creators of the Raw Cotton Commission in Britain expected it would "adjust the forward buying programme with knowledge of the requirements of the whole [spinning] industry," the commission discovered "size works no such magic in foreknowledge" (documents quoted in Wiseman and Yamey, 1956, p. 15).

Effects of War. In yet another dimension, state intervention in the name of price stabilization receives little scrutiny. The major source of price instability is not weather but war. The Qing dynasty promoted ever-normal granaries as a way to restore institutional and social stability after the Manchu conquest. In Babylon from 464 to 72 BCE (monthly agricultural prices have been preserved on clay tablets for those years), the principal spike coincides with the political turmoil following the death of Alexander in 323 BCE. In ancient Greece prices reached record highs as a result of sieges and in ancient Rome as a result of civil war. The price instability in the following twenty-five years made that of 1789 in France seem minor. In the twentieth century the major price spikes came during World Wars I and II, even without allowance for rationing's suppressive effects.

In addition to the mindset of centralized decision making, the legacy of World War II included the exchange controls in the United Kingdom and production controls in the United States that encouraged the formation of such organizations as the Raw Cotton Commission. The legacy of World War I included the massive shifts in production worldwide and the resulting surpluses and low prices in the 1930s. For that matter, among the many origins of World War I can be discerned the German government's decision for high tariffs on agricultural commodities, ostensibly to stabilize its own agricultural sector and to protect its population from supply disruptions. Besides antagonizing Russia, this stabilization intervention left Germany too little transportation infrastructure in the east; left its agricultural sector, already achieving maximum yields through imported fertilizer, too inflexible to increase production; and left its population near starvation. Meanwhile England's free trade in agriculture, which during the nineteenth century caused pasture to replace much wheat production and which seemingly exposed it to the U-boats' sinking of food imports, had unintentionally left it with a buffer stock in those animals, a capacity for a one-time surge in wheat production, and a port and rail infrastructure flexible at redirecting imports. Many such ironies can be found in the history of state intervention in the name of price stabilization.

[*See also* Agricultural Prices; Crop Failures; Crop Yields; *and* Famines.]

BIBLIOGRAPHY

Bardsley, Peter. "The Collapse of the Australian Wool Reserve Price Scheme." *Economic Journal* 104.3 (1994), 1087–1105.

Garnsey, Peter. *Famine and Food Supply in the Graeco-Roman World.* Cambridge, 1988.

Graham, Benjamin. *Storage and Stability: A Modern Ever-Normal Granary.* New York, 1937.

Gras, Norman Scott Brien. *The Evolution of the English Corn Market, from the Twelfth to the Eighteenth Century.* Cambridge, Mass., 1915.

Kaplan, Steven Laurence. "Lean Years, Fat Years: The 'Community' Granary System and the Search for Abundance in Eighteenth-Century Paris." *French Historical Studies* 10.2 (1977), 197–230.

Keynes, J. M. "The Policy of Government Storage of Food-Stuffs and Raw Materials." *Economic Journal* 48.3 (1938), 449–460.

Khusro, A. M. *Buffer Stocks and Storage of Foodgrains in India.* Bombay, 1973.

Miller, Judith A. *Mastering the Market: The State and the Grain Trade in Northern France, 1700–1860.* Cambridge, 1999.

Newbery, David M. G., and Joseph E. Stiglitz. *The Theory of Commodity Price Stabilization.* Oxford, 1981.

Persson, Karl Gunnar. *Grain Markets in Europe, 1500–1900.* Cambridge, 1999.

Samuelson, Paul A. "The Consumer Does Benefit from Feasible Price Stability." *Quarterly Journal of Economics* 86.3 (1972), 476–503.

Shepard, Lawrence. "Cartelization of the California-Arizona Orange Industry, 1934–1981." *Journal of Law and Economics* 29.1 (1986), 83–123.

Shepherd, Geoffrey. "Stabilization Operations of the Commodity Credit Corporation." *Journal of Farm Economics* 24.3 (1942), 589–610.

Taylor, Alonzo E. *Corn and Hog Surplus of the Corn Belt.* Stanford, Calif., 1932.

Tilly, Louise A. "The Food Riot as a Form of Political Conflict in France." *Journal of Interdisciplinary History* 2.1 (1971), 23–57.

Waugh, Frederick V. "Does the Consumer Benefit from Price Instability?" *Quarterly Journal of Economics* 58.4 (1944), 602–614.

Will, Pierre-Étienne, and R. Bin Wong. *Nourish the People: The State Civilian Granary System in China, 1650–1850.* Ann Arbor, 1991.

Wiseman, J., and B. S. Yamey. "The Raw Cotton Commission, 1948–52." *Oxford Economic Papers* 8.1 (1956), 1–34.

Wright, Brian D., and Jeffrey C. Williams. "The Incidence of Market–Stabilising Price Support Schemes." *Economic Journal* 98.4 (1988), 1183–1198.

JEFFREY C. WILLIAMS

Storage

The richness of the world's cuisine can be traced in large part to the need to convert perishable foods into more stable, storable forms. Means of storage—granaries, oil and wine jars—are prominent in the archaeological evidence of ancient societies. Ancient governments saw the provision of adequate food stocks as a crucial part of public policy; an early and atypically successful example of economic analysis and forecasting is Joseph's biblical interpretation of the pharaoh's dream.

The cultivation of annual cereal crops, which directly or indirectly furnish the major part of human food needs, depends upon the ability to save seed, suitable for planting, from one harvest at least until the start of the next season.

To cope with harvest failure, a longer span of storage is necessary.

Economists have been slow in achieving an adequate understanding of the economics of storage, even the simplest types of food storage such as the competitive storage of grains. A fundamental analytical difficulty is due to the impossibility of holding negative stocks. In a market with random supply or demand, this nonnegativity constraint is occasionally binding, when there is a "stock-out." At such times, the equality generated by competitive arbitrage between current price and expected price, net of storage cost and interest, breaks down.

It was not until 1958 that a way was found to model this type of behavior successfully. In a remarkable paper, Gustafson (1958) presented a method of numerical approximation that ensured that expectations of future prices were consistent with the storage behavior that influenced those future prices. That is, Gustafson constructed a model with rational expectations, anticipating Muth (1961), using an approach soon to be known as dynamic programming. More recently, the numerical approach has been modified to take account of producer supply response, coexistence of public and private storage activities, and spatial dispersion of storers and producers. In the past two decades, advances in this area have run ahead of the numerical approaches used in macroeconomics to solve stochastic models with occasionally binding constraints (such as limits on aggregate borrowing). Along the way, economists have learned how difficult it can be to deduce whether market behavior is competitive. For example, price correlations are highly unreliable indicators of spatial or temporal market integration. And when transport costs are demand-sensitive, rankings of "economic distance" between points in space can fluctuate wildly over time, often changing storage incentives in different directions at different locations (Brennan et al., 1997).

Given the often counter-intuitive nature of market signals, it is not surprising that governments have very often viewed the activity of private hoarders as suspect. Regulation of private hoarders still receives significant support from economists usually perceived as protagonists of the "free market." For example, the World Bank (1991) credited the policy of forced delivery of grain to local markets, mandated by the first *Book of Orders* of the English Privy Council when necessary for the relief of dearth, with the avoidance of hunger in England between 1600 and 1640.

The rationale for such interventions is often unclear. Adam Smith saw them as directed against storage monopolization, a concern he viewed as misguided. Corn merchants were too numerous to collude. Furthermore, the monopolistic hoarder who hoarded excessively would depress the market for his stocks (Smith, 1784). As usual, Smith's intuition was correct; a monopolist of storage would supply too little of it, not too much.

Besides monopolization, another rationale for intervention in storage decisions is perceived irrationality of private expectations regarding future market conditions. This is difficult to test. Expectations are never exactly fulfilled. A test based on a small time-series sample will show substantial *ex post* deviation from expectations with high probability, even if expectations are perfectly rational. Moreover, there is no convincing evidence that the agents of intervention (usually governments or international organizations) have more accurate expectations than the private sector.

A third rationale for mandatory sales from stocks is short-run redistribution of wealth, a credible motive when some are starving. However, the level of private stocks, given any history of harvests, may be reduced or even eliminated by anticipation of confiscation or forced sales in times of high demand. Hence, a policy of public intervention may improve the distribution of existing stocks yet reduce the consumption of the whole population via its previously anticipated effects on storage incentives.

A fourth rationale for public intervention, the perceived inadequacy of private stocks, may be attributed to other "market failures" in the economy. Private storers, if competitive, equate the cost of storage, including interest on the value of their stocks, to the expected price increase. If potential private storers have a high cost of capital, due, for example, to taxes on capital income, lack of access to financial markets, or fear of expropriation, their private stocks may well be below what would, in a perfect market, be their socially optimal level. McCloskey and Nash argued that in medieval England, a "shockingly high" interest rate meant that peasants' food stocks, at no more than two years' supply, were inadequate for smoothing consumption (McCloskey and Nash, 1984, p. 174). Risk-averse peasants had to resort to inefficient scattering of farm plots in an open-field system to try to reduce weather-related disturbance of their consumption. In a study of eighteenth-century China, where interest rates were apparently reasonable, Shiue (2000) inferred that high-cost transport and difficulties in other aspects of market access increased storage among subsistence farmers in regions not accessible to waterways. A recent survey of farm families in Shaanxi province in China reveled that they held on average about two years' production (nearly one-third of their assets) to buffer consumption (Park, 1996).

Commercial farmers and other speculators might, in an imperfect capital market, plausibly find that investment in commodity stocks is reduced by risk aversion, in contrast to the case for subsistence-oriented peasants. John Maynard Keynes viewed risk aversion as one reason for socially inadequate private storage. However, storage interventions in developed countries in the past century have usually been motivated, at least in part, by a desire to redistribute income to farm operators, or wealth to current owners of land and other fixed assets used in agricultural production.

Finally, even if a credible commitment not to intervene in storage were socially optimal, governments unable to make such a commitment might be forced to continue a policy of public storage. Anticipation of such intervention reduces private storage below optimal levels; this compensatory private response might offset half or more of public additions to stocks at moderate supply levels, as indicated by dynamic-programming models of petroleum storage and experience of U.S. grain-market responses to fluctuations in Commodity Credit Corporation policies (Williams and Wright, 1991, Table 13.2, p. 368).

As the understanding of storage economics advances, a more critical assessment of past storage interventions is becoming possible. In an innovative study, Nielsen (1997) found that although harvests appear to be independent in English data from the thirteenth century to the nineteenth century, prices had substantial positive serial dependence, consistent with the operation of a private storage market in a consumption-smoothing role. Furthermore, he found the market effects of the *Book of Orders* from 1600 to 1640 to be negligible; this was a time of stable food supply in the wider European market, which could not have been greatly affected by the English law but was demonstrably influenced by private storage.

Apart from constraining private storage, government policy has included subsidized loans to storers, as seen in the rural reform introduced in China in 1069 by Wang An-Shih, and in contemporary U.S. commodity policy. More often, the government directly controls its own storage activity. For a long-lasting example, the Chinese Han dynasty in 54 BCE institutionalized an "ever-normal granary" system that became a permanent feature of Chinese administration, and similar policies have been pursued by other states and cities throughout recorded history (Liu and Fei, 1978).

John Maynard Keynes advocated an international commodity-market-stabilization policy that would stabilize the price of a commodity by an open offer to buy at one price and sell at another (higher) price—a "price band" scheme. International schemes of this type were adopted after World War II, and their operational history reflects confusion about the operation of commodity markets evident in the minds of their designers, including Keynes. Virtually all schemes of this type by now have failed. Recent advances in analytical studies of the role of storage (in particular, Scheinkman and Schechtman, 1983) have helped show that purely private storage is optimal in a competitive market economy with no missing markets, contrary to the intuition of Keynes and countless other economists and regulators before and since.

A yet unsolved puzzle, was identified by Holbrook Working (1934), is that for many commodities, significant stocks appear to be held, even if the futures–spot price spread is negative. Nicholas Kaldor (1939) hypothesized that, besides the measured monetary returns, storers receive a nonmonetary "convenience yield" from stocks on hand (as distinct from contingent claims on stocks held elsewhere).

A more recent competing hypothesis is that the typical "supply of storage" graph is an artifact of aggregation of stocks with different shadow prices, due to differences in costs of transportation or transformation (Wright and Williams, 1989); testing of this hypothesis, using data from Australia and the United States, began in the mid-1990s. Econometric tests of simple versions of the general storage model also began in the 1990s, notably in the work of Deaton and Laroque (1992, 1996), with results suggesting that economists have still more to learn about how markets for storable commodities behave.

[*See also* Agricultural Prices; Crop Failures; Crop Yields; *and* Famines.]

BIBLIOGRAPHY

Brennan, Donna, Jeffrey C. Williams, and Brian D. Wright. "Convenience Yield without the Convenience: A Spatial–Temporal Interpretation of Storage under Backwardation." *Economic Journal* 107.443 (1997), 1009–1022.

Deaton, Angus, and Guy Laroque. "On the Behavior of Commodity Prices." *Review of Economic Studies* 59.1 (1992), 1–23.

Deaton, Angus, and Guy Laroque. "Competitive Storage and Commodity Price Dynamics." *Journal of Political Economy* 104 (1996), 896–923.

Gras, Norman Scott Brien. *The Evolution of the English Corn Market from the Twelfth to the Eighteenth Century*. Cambridge, 1915.

Gustafson, Robert L. "Carryover Levels for Grains: A Method for Determining Amounts That Are Optimal under Specified Conditions." U.S. Department of Agriculture. Technical Bulletin No. 1178. Washington, D.C., 1958.

Kaldor, Nicholas. "Speculation and Economic Stability." *Review of Economic Studies* 7.1 (1939), 1–27.

Keynes, John M. 1974. "The International Control of Raw Materials." *Journal of International Economics* 4 (1974), 299–315.

Liu, Ts'ui-jung, and John C. H. Fei. "The Public Granary Institution of the Ch'ing Dynasty, 1644–1911." Economic Growth Center, Yale University. Discussion Paper No. 299. New Haven, 1978.

McCloskey, Donald N., and John Nash. "Corn at Interest: The Extent and Cost of Grain Storage in Medieval England." *American Economic Review* 74 (1984), 174–187.

Muth, John F. "Rational Expectations and the Theory of Price Movements." *Econometrica* 29.3 (1961), 315–335.

Nielsen, Randall. "Storage and English Government Intervention in Early Modern Grain Markets." *Journal of Economic History* 57.1 (1997), 1–33.

Park, Albert. "Household Grain Management under Uncertainty in China's Poor Areas." Ph.D. diss. Food Research Institute, Stanford University, Palo Alto, Calif., 1996.

Scheinkman, Jose A., and Jack Schechtman. "A Simple Competitive Model with Production and Storage." *Review of Economic Studies* 50.3 (1983), 427–441.

Shiue, Carol H. "Transport Costs and the Geography of Arbitrage: Trade and Storage in 18th Century China." University of Texas, Austin, 2000.

Smith, Adam. *Wealth of Nations.* London, 1776.

Williams, Jeffrey C., and Brian D. Wright. *Storage and Commodity Markets.* Cambridge, 1991.

Working, Holbrook. "Price Relations between May and New-Crop Wheat Futures at Chicago since 1885." Food Research Institute. *Wheat Studies* 10 (1934), 183–228.

World Bank. *World Development Report.* New York, 1991.

Wright, Brian D., and Jeffrey C. Williams. "A Theory of Negative Prices for Storage." *Journal of Futures Markets* 9.1 (1989), 1–13. Reprinted in millenium issue of *Journal of Futures Markets* 20.1 (2000), 59–71.

BRIAN D. WRIGHT

AGRICULTURAL WAGES. Agricultural wages constitute the payments needed to secure labor when that labor is obtained in some kind of market. Wages can be paid in many forms: food, beer, shelter, money, access to land, a share of the output, or use of animals or other inputs. Thus in nineteenth-century Great Britain, farm laborers in the southeast were paid in money; those in the southwest received part of their wage in beer or cider; those in the northeast received cottages, potatoes, oats, and milk; and those in Scotland received food and lodging in a bothy (hut). In Ireland, the wage often included access to tilled and manured potato ground. Wages can be paid by the unit of time worked or by the unit of work accomplished. In eighteenth-century England, grain threshers in the northeast were often paid a twentieth of the grain threshed. Wages can be paid at different periods: annually, monthly, weekly, or daily.

Wage payments in kind have coexisted with payments in cash across millennia. Estates in Roman Egypt in the third century CE, for example, paid workers both goods and cash. But economic historians regard these variations in the form and frequency of payment—while often colorful—as incidental to the major question, which is the total value of the wage payment per day or per hour.

A distinction must be made between nominal wages, which are wages measured in the local monetary unit (10 sous, 9 shillings, 5 dollars), and real wages, which are wages measured in the goods the wage can buy. To know real wages, we must know the prices of the farm workers' consumption goods and the share of each in expenditure. In northern Europe, the standard consumption goods from the time of the earliest records were bread, beer, cheese, meat, clothing, shoes, housing, and fuel. The real wage of a worker is an index of how much of such a standard basket of consumption goods the nominal wage will buy. If I tell you only that agricultural laborers in Jiangnan, China, in 1750 earned 3 taels per year, then you know little about workers' wages. Only when I also tell you the price of rice,

tofu, cloth, fuel, and housing do I tell you anything significant. One rough method of comparison is to convert wages into their equivalent in one standard commodity, such as wheat or rice, or to convert wages for poorer workers into a calorie equivalent.

Marginal Productivity Theory. The dominant theory on the determination of agricultural wages is the marginal productivity theory. It holds that wage payments to farm labor will equal the net extra output that the last worker hired adds to the value of farm output. If hiring another worker adds ten bushels of wheat to net output, then the workers should all receive a wage equivalent to ten bushels of grain. The reasoning to establish this is simple. If the wage is below the net added value from the last worker, then the farmer profits by hiring more labor. If the wage is above the net added value from the last worker, then the farmer profits by firing some workers. Only when the wage equals the net value added by the last worker will the farmer have maximized the surplus realized from hiring labor. But at an arbitrarily chosen wage, the total demand from farmers following this rule may exceed the supply of labor. In that case, the wage offered will be bid up until demand equals supply.

An implication of the marginal productivity theory is that there is no necessary connection in agrarian history between the sophistication of agricultural technology and the wages received by workers. Wages can be high when the technology is primitive, and they can be low when the technology is sophisticated. Table 1 shows some measures

TABLE 1. *Wages Measured in Wheat Equivalents*

LOCATION	PERIOD	DAY WAGE (IN LBS. OF WHEAT FLOUR)
Roman Egypt	c. 250 CE	8.0
Egypt	1900–1914	8.3
Egypt	1930s	7.8
Egypt	1960s	9.0
England	1300–1309	7.7
England	1400–1409	19.6
England	1500–1509	16.2
England	1600–1609	8.7
England	1700–1709	12.7
England	1800–1809	9.2
England	1900–1909	40.8
France–Languedoc	1480–1500	17.9
France–Languedoc	1630–1650	9.0
India–Behar	1900–1909	5.0
India–Decan	1900–1909	4.9
India–Punjab	1900–1909	12.3

SOURCES: Clark, 2001; Le Roy Ladurie, 1977; Rathbone, 1991; Richards, 1982.

THE HARVESTERS' WAGES. Painting (1882) by Léon Lhermitte. (Hôtel de Ville, Château-Thierry, France/Lauros-Giraudon/Art Resource, NY)

of wages for a day of labor given in terms of the number of pounds of wheat flour that the wage would buy for different times and places. Wages in Roman Egypt, for example, were nearly as high as those in Egypt of the 1960s, even though in the interim there had been the large-scale introduction of artificial fertilizers, pesticides, and some mechanization. Wages in England in 1400–1409 greatly exceeded those of 1800–1809, even though crop yields perhaps doubled in that interval.

The marginal productivity theory also implies that with a static agrarian technology, as most of Europe had between 1200 and 1600, the main determinant of wages is the level of population. For this reason, proponents of this view of wage determination for the medieval and early modern periods in Europe, such as M. M. Postan and John Hatcher in the case of England, have been labeled *demographic determinists* or *neo-Malthusians*.

There have been attempts to develop alternative theories of wage determination based on moral economy or class power. The moral economy theory argues that wages are set with reference to social norms about the "value" of different types of labor. Even with an excess supply of labor, workers will refuse to work for wages less than the norm. Thus, it is reported in modern Indian villages that the same wage is paid to all workers, regardless of their work abilities, and that even in slack periods workers get a standard wage, resulting in involuntary unemployment. The class power theory argues that wages are set in a contest between a class of land owners and a class of workers. The resulting wage depends on a variety of elements: the degree of solidarity within the respective classes, the state exercise of power on one side or the other, and social institutions that favor one class or the other. This theory has been applied to modern Indian villages by Gaurav Datt (1996).

It is empirically possible to derive some insight into which theory of wage determination best describes wage determination. The marginal productivity theory has more concrete predictions than the others, however, so it is possible to test it much more severely than any of the specific alternatives. The following are all predictions of the marginal productivity theory.

1. For a given agricultural technology, an increase in the supply of workers will reduce the wage received.
2. There will be no involuntary unemployment of labor. If workers do not work in any season, it is because the wage offered is less than the value of leisure to them. No workers would work at the prevailing wage but cannot find employers. The class power and moral economy theories both imply that involuntary unemployment will sometimes be observed.

3. If workers are hired on a daily or weekly basis, then the wage will vary across the year, being higher at periods of peak labor demand.

4. Individual workers get paid for their individual marginal productivity when this is easily observable by employers. Thus, for example, wages will follow an inverse U shape over workers' careers. When they are young, they lack in strength and art and should be paid little. When they get older, they may retain acquired skills, but they lose strength.

5. The ratio of men's to women's wages for various tasks will depend on their relative productivities rather than set social norms. Thus, women's wages relative to men's may vary across the year or by the dominant type of agricultural activity in a region.

6. There will be no money illusion in the determination of wages. Long-term declines in prices will be accompanied by proportionate declines in nominal wages, unless the supply of workers has also changed. Conversely, long-term increases in prices will see a proportionate rise in wages. In time of general price movements, agricultural wages will thus be flexible both upward and downward.

Predictions Discussed. The first prediction—that with a given agricultural technology, wages will depend on the supply of workers relative to the land area—is well attested in the case of England from 1200 to 1600. Figure 1 shows the real wages per day of male farm workers versus the English population between 1200 and 1600. When the onset of the Black Death in 1349 kept population low for the next two hundred years, real wages of farm workers more than doubled.

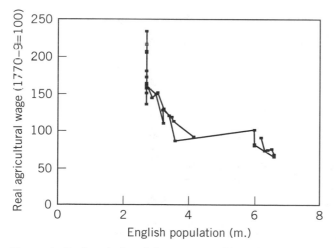

FIGURE 1. Real agricultural day wages and population, 1260–1599. SOURCE: Clark, Gregory. "The Long March of History: Farm Laborers Wages in England, 1208–1850." Working Paper, University of California, Davis, 1999.

The second prediction, that workers will be fully employed across the agricultural year, seems at variance with a widespread belief that peasant societies mostly operated with a labor surplus. Indeed, even in England in the nineteenth century, it is generally believed that there was much rural unemployment in winter. As per the marginal productivity theory, this should have forced winter wages down and stimulated demand for employment.

Measuring when workers are truly involuntarily unemployed is not easy, however. If wage workers also occupy land on their own, then they may be employed on their own holdings on days when they do not work for wages. Further, there is little evidence regarding the seasonal pattern of labor inputs of farm workers in any country before the twentieth century. And the presence of market-distorting factors, such as relief payments to the unemployed in England before 1834, can reduce the downward flexibility of wages in the slack seasons that would be required if there was to be full employment. Rather than accept lower wages in the winter to compensate for the lower marginal productivity of labor, workers may prefer to seek relief from the local parish.

One test of the full employment theory is the ratio of the wages of workers employed by the year to those of workers employed by the day. If day workers face involuntary unemployment in the slack seasons of the year, then they will seek annual employment unless the day wage is high enough to compensate them for this employment risk. Thus, the ratio of the yearly wage to the weekly wage should indicate the number of days farm workers typically can find employment each year. In British agriculture in the eighteenth and nineteenth centuries, this ratio was typically about 290, indicating that day or weekly workers were typically employed for most of the year. For England in the sixteenth and seventeenth centuries, the ratio found in the magistrates' wage assessments is a little lower at about 260–270. However, this may reflect fewer days worked per year by annual workers. There is some sign that, in these years, Saturday was worked only as a half day.

The presumption that, before the reform of the poor law in 1834, there was widespread unemployment in nineteenth-century England during the slack seasons of the year may also be less evident than historians assume. Figure 2 shows the percentage of adult male manual workers who received poor relief in each week of the year in Ardleigh, a rural village with high poor rate payments relative to most, in 1821. There is significant unemployment in the months between December and July, when 5 to 8 percent of male workers were unemployed. But this still means that, even with the distortions of the English poor law, if a fully employed worker worked 300 days per year, Ardleigh laborers worked on average 283 to 288 days per year.

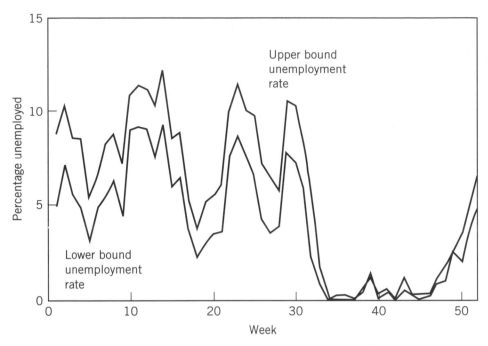

FIGURE 2. Male unemployment in Ardleigh, Essex, 1821. SOURCE: Ardleigh Overseers Accounts, 1820–1821.

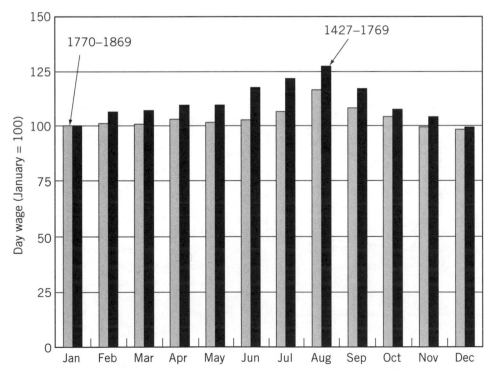

FIGURE 3. Wages as a function of season in England,1427–1869. SOURCE: Clark, Gregory. "The Long March of History: Farm Laborers Wages in England, 1208–1850." Working Paper, University of California, Davis, 1999.

For the third prediction wages certainly varied over the course of the year in English agriculture in the preindustrial period. Figure 3 shows the average recorded wage paid per month for 101 farms in England in the years 1427 to 1769, for which the January wage has been normalized to 100. The seasonal movement of wages clearly shows August average wages about 28 percent higher than those in December. Only some of these workers were hired on a casual basis, so the season movement of wage rates in the free labor market would be greater than this. When the same comparison is made for a set of farms in the years 1770 to 1869, a similar seasonal movement of rates occurs, but the swing is less pronounced, August being only about 18 percent higher than December. The English labor market appears to have evolved from one in which spot-labor hires dominated to one in which more workers were hired on implicit annual contracts.

The fourth prediction of the theory, that wages for workers will correspond to their individual marginal productivity, finds support in wage records in England and the United States. Wages, for example, do follow an inverse U shape with age of the worker. In 1894, farm workers in their twenties in Michigan (United States) were paid the most. Those in their sixties earned one-third less than this. A smaller study of two farm wage books in England in the nineteenth century shows a wage profile with a more moderate peak. But workers in their sixties clearly earned less than those age twenty to fifty-nine.

English farm wage books also reveal that many employers paid an individual wage rate to each of their workers. It is claimed that this individual setting of farm wages may not be a timeless feature of rural societies. It is reported, for example, that in modern rural India employers do not differentiate wages by person. Rather, they pay a fixed wage per day for a given type of labor. However, these workers were typically hired in a spot labor market, in which individual workers work for many employers, so that the costs of negotiating individual wages may have been too high. And the wages reported by Gaurav Datt (1996) for North Indian villages in the 1970s suggest male workers there in their sixties did receive wages that were 11 percent less than those workers in their twenties.

The ratio of women's to men's wages on the marginal productivity theory of wages should depend on the relative productivity of men and women on a given task. It should not be dictated by social norms about their relative standing or about the needs of men for more income to support their families. In preindustrial European agriculture, women's wages were less than half of those of men. Table 2 shows some observations on the ratio of men's to women's earnings by season and country. European women's wages are generally so low that it would seem they must be lower than women's marginal productivities. Note also that Eu-

TABLE 2. *Women's Earnings Relative to Men's*

PLACE	YEAR	FIELD WORK, OUTSIDE HARVEST	GRAIN HARVEST
England	1561–1599	—	[a]0.71
England	1600–1699	—	[a]0.68
England	1770	0.46	0.58
England	1800	0.43	0.45
England	1832	0.38	0.42
England	1850	0.44	0.36
England	1860	0.42	0.39
Ireland	1860	0.56	0.56
Scotland	1850	0.45	0.66
Scotland	1860	0.43	0.65
Southern Italy	1900	0.36	—
Northern India	1970s	0.73	—

[a]Relative wages in grain reaping only.
SOURCES: Wage Assessments; Arthur Young; Board of Agriculture; Poor Law Commission; Agricultural Gazette; Petrusewicz, 1996; Datt, 1996.

ropean women farm workers received significantly less relative to men than women workers in India in recent times. But several sources suggest that these wages could be consistent with the relative productivities of men and women in the heavy manual labor involved in European agriculture. Thus, modern studies show the average man can lift about twice as much as women. And studies of the actual productivity of female compared to male workers in agriculture find a ratio of 0.60 for the United States in the nineteenth century and 0.46 for modern Peruvian peasant agriculture.

If the marginal productivity theory of wages is correct, the relative pay of men and women over the course of a year varied, since farm tasks varied in the amounts of dexterity as opposed to strength that they required. In reaping grain, for example, a task that involved cutting grain with a sickle using a sawing motion, the nineteenth-century farming expert Henry Stephens even claimed that women could do just as much work as men. Reaping was displaced by mowing, a task only performed by men, as the nineteenth century progressed. But before then, women's earnings in the harvest season should have been higher relative to men's. Arthur Young does report a higher ratio for 1770. And the wage assessments set by local magistrates in England show a prescribed ratio of women's to men's wages for reaping of 71 percent in the sixteenth century and 68 percent in the seventeenth century. Thus in the minds of magistrates setting these wage assessments, the appropriate wage for women in reaping was much higher relative to men than average women's wages, at least as observed later. The issue of whether women's wages were set by their

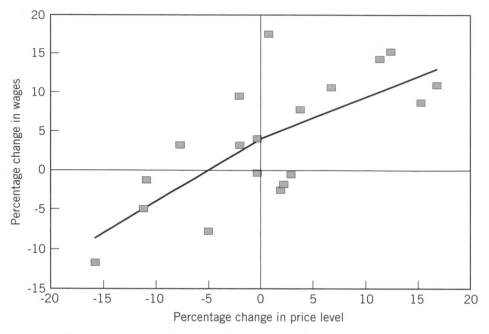

FIGURE 4. Changes in wages with price levels, 1770–1869. The graph shows by quinquernia the percentage change in nominal farm wages compared to the percentage change in the general price level. SOURCE: Clark, 2001.

marginal productivity is still open, but the variation in relative earnings over the year suggest that productivity rather than custom was at work.

To test for the absence of money illusion (the sixth prediction) in determining wages, one must look at what happens to wages when the general price level changes as a result of an expansion or contraction of the money supply alone. Such pure money-supply changes absent other economic effects are rare. The money supply in Great Britain, for example, expanded in the Revolutionary and Napoleonic Wars when the pound was forced off the gold standard, but the strains of the wars might also have influenced wages. But graph by five-year intervals the percentage change in farm day wages from 1770 to 1869 against the percentage change in the general price level in England (leaving out volatile grain prices that are heavily influenced by the weather), a clear association appears between the two. Wages move up and down with prices, as Figure 4 shows. There are indeed three quinquennia with significant declines in nominal wages. The solid line in the figure shows the best fit for periods of price increases and decreases. In neither case are wages fully responsive. A full response would mean that the slope of the line linking price increases and wages was 45°. That means that on average workers tended to get higher real wages in periods of price declines and lower real wages in periods of inflation. But since the movement of the price level cannot be measured perfectly, the lack of full response may reflect just this measurement problem. Wages were certainly closer to being fully responsive than to being unresponsive.

Theory Holds. Overall, the marginal productivity theory seems to hold up reasonably well as a description of how agricultural wages were determined in countries like pre industrial England. Indeed, these labor markets seem to fit the classic model of competitive labor markets better than modern industrial labor markets. Whether it holds for all preindustrial agricultural labor markets is yet to be determined.

An interesting implication of the finding that women's wages seem plausibly to have been determined by their marginal productivity in agriculture is that the emancipation of women in modern industrial society may in part owe to the increased importance of industrial employment in which women's marginal productivity was relatively much higher. In the classic factory industry of the Industrial Revolution, for example, women's marginal productivity was close to or equal to that of men in many tasks, such as weaving or ring spinning, by the late nineteenth century. As women's wages rose relative to men's, the incentive for them to specialize in child care and domestic chores, with their husband specializing in market work, would correspondingly decline. Thus in the Lancashire textile towns in the late nineteenth century, the proportion of married women who worked was much greater than in areas where women's wages were lower relative to those of men.

[*See also* Agricultural Labor.]

BIBLIOGRAPHY

Aston, T. H., and C. H. E. Philpin. *The Brenner Debate: Agrarian Class Structure and Economic Development in Pre-Industrial Europe*. Cambridge, 1985.

Burnette, Joyce. "An Investigation of the Female-Male Wage Gap during the Industrial Revolution in Britain." *Economic History Review* 50.2 (1997), 257–281. Considers whether women's wages relative to men's depended on women's relative marginal products.

Clark, Colin, and Margaret Haswell. *The Economics of Subsistence Agriculture*. 3d ed. London, 1967. Includes some discussion of wages across countries in various periods and of the ways of comparing real wages.

Clark, Gregory. "Farm Wages and Living Standards in the Industrial Revolution: England, 1670–1869." *Economic History Review* 3 (2001), 477–505. Includes discussion of wage variation by season, seasonal unemployment, and the conversion of money wages into real wages.

Datt, Gaurav. *Bargaining Power, Wages, and Employment: An Analysis of Agricultural Labor Markets in India*. Thousand Oaks, Calif., 1996. Proposes an alternative to the marginal product theory of wages for rural India.

Le Roy Ladurie, Emmanuel. *The French Peasantry, 1450–1660*. Berkeley, 1977.

Petrusewicz, Marta. *Latifundium: Moral Economy and Material Life in a European Periphery*. Translated by Judith C. Green. Ann Arbor, 1996.

Rathbone, Dominic. *Economic Rationalism and Rural Society in Third-Century AD Egypt*. Cambridge, 1991. This book includes a discussion of laborers on a rural estate.

Richards, Alan. *Egypt's Agricultural Development, 1800–1980*. Boulder, 1982.

Shirras, George Findlay. *Report on an Enquiry into Agricultural Wages in the Bombay Presidency*. Bombay, India, 1924.

Stephens, Henry. *The Book of the Farm*. Edinburgh, 1860.

GREGORY CLARK

AGRICULTURE *[This entry contains six subentries: a historical overview and discussions of technological change; main tools and implements; agricultural production systems; property rights and tenure systems; and agricultural inputs, productivity, and wages.]*

Historical Overview

Until the late nineteenth century, farming was the predominant economic activity of almost every economy. Among the economically advanced nations, only Great Britain employed less than 30 percent of the labor force in the sector in 1850, and in most countries the proportion exceeded 50 percent. And although the share of agricultural output in gross domestic product (GDP) did not quite equal its share of the labor force, it was large enough that agricultural performance crucially affected overall economic performance. The amount of land in cultivation and the yield of that land set a maximum to the population an economy could sustain at a given nutritional standard without having recourse to imports. Similarly, the level of agricultural labor productivity set an upper bound to the share of the workforce that could be employed in nonagricultural occupations. Because sustained economic expansion depended on supporting improvements in agricultural productivity, the pre-twentieth-century economic history of developed economies has been largely dominated by the economies' agricultural history.

The most important economic consequence of agricultural predominance in pre-modern economies was the location of economic activity. The land- and labor-intensive agricultural production function has always caused farming to be a highly dispersed mode of production. And since most farm produce consists of water-laden organic foodstuffs that lose almost all weight and volume when consumed by people and livestock, consumption sites were inevitably drawn toward the point of production in an age when transport costs were still prohibitively high for commodities produced away from navigable waterways. As a result, the overwhelming majority of the population in the agrarian age thus resided in the countryside. A dispersed pattern of settlement, however, increased the costs of distributing goods and services from a small number of locations, where suppliers could exploit potential economies of scale, so that the production of non-agricultural as well as agricultural goods was also highly dispersed. Early agricultural economies were thus a congeries of disjointed local economies connected by traffic in a few high-value commodities. The sputtering trade in luxuries provided little encouragement for a more extended regional division of labor and the growth of urban districts, where economies of scale were most likely to emerge. The dispersion of the population also protected agricultural economies from each other by sheltering local institutions that restricted the mobility of farm labor and the untrammeled exercise of property rights in land. It thus reinforced an economic stasis, the original cause for which was the glacial pace of improvement of agricultural technology. These constraints started to lift around 1830, when seemingly unrelated improvements in transportation, agricultural machinery, and concentrated commercial fertilizers first appeared. With these developments, the premodern history of agriculture began to come to an end. I begin my analysis, therefore, by considering the salient features of premodern agricultural technology.

Farming distinguishes itself from other activities by its exceptional space requirements, by the nonreproducibility of that space, and by an exacting seasonal sequencing of tasks. Moreover, the life processes that farming exploits are highly complex and not readily revealed by casual observation, and they resisted scientific methods of investigation almost to the end of the nineteenth century. These intrinsic characteristics of the agricultural production function had important economic consequences. For one, they inhibited large-scale farming operations owing to the high cost of adequately supervising field operations at a distance. For another, the inelastic supply of land caused the fruits of general economic improvement to be transferred to landowners in the form of rent rather than as profits and wages to the suppliers of reproducible and presumably improvable inputs. The marked seasonality of agricultural operations made it impossible to specialize workers by task and impeded regional specialization in crops whose seasonal peak demand for labor exceeded the local supply. Finally, the refractoriness of the life processes to scientific methods of investigation made it almost impossible to develop new farming techniques from general biological principles. Moreover, it was difficult, though not impossible, to introduce radical improvements into new environments. These features tended to reduce the rate of productivity growth by limiting the degree of specialization and the rate of technical change. Another feature limited the desire to specialize and innovate. Unlike other producers, subsistence farmers could retreat from the world of market exchange if the terms of trade became too unfavorable to them. Such regression to a less specialized form of farming was invariably accompanied by lower productivity. The physical constraints constitute the matrix within which the decisions determining the crop mix, methods of cultivation, and agricultural investments were taken.

Forms of Agricultural Organization. The units of agricultural production fell into three broad types: the family farm, the great estate, and the slave plantation. The predominant type was the family farm. Because co-residence of family members working on family farms gave rise to economies of scale in the provision of room, board, and social insurance, the family farm could supply seasonally variable amounts of agricultural labor at an annual cost significantly below what could be achieved by any other form of agricultural organization. It also enjoyed a considerable advantage in managing workers, since unsupervised family members were less likely to shirk on the job than unsupervised hired hands. These advantages were only partly offset by the economies in cultivation, storage, and marketing possessed by large farms staffed by hired labor. The latter were generally profitable when there was an abundant supply of labor willing to work for wages. When this condition was absent, as in the United States for most of its history, the family farm dominated the "capitalistic" farm.

The capitalist or large tenant farm originated in the Middle Ages. While specialized capitalistic farms are known to have flourished in certain sectors of farming during classical antiquity, large cereal-producing operations after 1000 CE were a by-product of the accumulation of landed wealth during the early Middle Ages. The consumption requirements of the large households maintained by the higher aristocracy and monastic communities, into whose hands much land had fallen, led to the assessment of quotas on farms in their possession. Historians disagree as to the origin of these quotas: Some argue that they descend from the Roman fiscal system; others say that they resulted from the expropriation of peasant farmers. In either case, it was easier to draw regular provisions from a few large farms than from many small ones. As the medieval economy became more commercialized in the centuries following 1000 CE, such demesnes grew in size and attracted investments, making them more productive. According to conventional historiography, they were cultivated by serfs. Recent studies, however, have thrown doubt on the importance of serfdom as a means of holding and managing farm labor. By the mid-fourteenth century, the largest farms were leased out to tenants employing hired labor. Their economic viability rested on the strength of commercial outlets for their produce and the availability of wage labor. They thus flourished in regions where the development of an urban population presented large and stable markets for cereals, the cultivation of which was subject to significant economies of scale. Declining transport costs after 1550 and the growth of specialized farms serving cities permitted large-scale farming to be extended to more regions. An outstanding example of this was in England, where comparatively low-cost transport, precocious urbanization, and industrialization caused farms in districts specialized in raising cereals to be consolidated into large holdings during the seventeenth and eighteenth century.

Slave plantations were the most specialized farming enterprises of the premodern era. Owners decided how much labor slaves had to supply and where and when they had to supply it. The economic significance of the power to compel work from an unwilling workforce lay in the ability of slave owners to direct labor to the financially most profitable employments, without regard to the nonpecuniary returns that restricted the mobility and hours worked by free labor. As a result, slave-based agriculture was exceptionally responsive to commercial opportunities, as manifested in its high degree of specialization—which in the case of sugar plantations was almost total—and in the large size of slave-based farms. Similar to the specialization of labor in early factories, one can argue that the economic advantage of slave plantations resided in economies of scale associated with "gang" labor, considered distasteful to free workers. Analysis of cotton plantations in the United States, however, indicates that the advantages of plantations were mainly due to their higher degree of specialization on risky but highly remunerative cash crops. From this perspective, the scale economy in slavery was essentially a pecuniary advantage accessible to any large-scale farming enterprise, though the extra work extracted from slaves probably accounts for some of the differential. These elements were later reproduced on farms employing contract or indentured workers, whose legal condition in certain temporary respects was similar to that of slaves. As a mode of agricultural organization, slavery disappeared in the second half of the nineteenth century.

The Scale of Agricultural Organization. The scale of individual farms ran the gamut from tiny truck gardens to vast sheep runs and cattle ranches. In normal mixed farming, the maximum area that could be tolerably well managed before the advent of the tractor was about 400 hectares (1,000 acres). The lower bound was about 1 hectare, which when cultivated by hand produced enough food to supply a family's annual subsistence. For arable farms, the size of the holding depended on whether it was worked with animals or tilled by hoe or spade. Each method had its advantages and disadvantages. The advantage of manual cultivation was an extremely high yield; its disadvantage was that only a small area (about 2.5 hectares) could be worked up with family labor, and that crops raised by hand were much more costly, in terms of person-hours, than those grown on land prepared with plow and harrow. Plowing, on the other hand, yielded less produce per hectare—often half to two-thirds less—but allowed farmers to make up the deficit by keeping more land in crops. Thus, a family farm employing plows could plant four to ten times more land than a family farm worked by hand. And although the yield was lower, the additional land produced double to eight times the produce of a hand-tilled farm. Even when one subtracts the fodder for draft animals, the substitution of plowing for manual cultivation represented a huge gain in labor productivity. Yet, from the perspective of self-sufficient farms, the substitution secured little advantage beyond additional leisure. It was only by enabling more workers to specialize in non-agricultural work that higher labor productivity mattered greatly for the economy as a whole. The plow was the source of the agricultural surpluses that supported towns, lords, officials, and industrial populations from the Neolithic period to the late nineteenth century. The plow team and its complement of implements and driver constituted a technical indivisibility that defined a natural unit of farming. Indeed, in some countries the term "plow" designated a fiscal unit of land assessment, the actual area varying according to the amount of land locally cultivated by a single team. By this measure, labor productivity grew with increasing farm size to about five or six "plows." The advantages of scale seem mainly attributable to faster cultivation and more expeditious handling of farm materials, though there were also economies to be had from larger and better situated barns and buildings. And large farms typically enjoyed superior marketing facilities. Economies of this type increased the productivity of agricultural labor even when there was no fundamental technical improvement.

Data from a large farm near Paris, atypical only in its meticulous records, reveal that consolidation of plots and growing size of the arable fields raised the productivity of farm hands by one-third over the course of the eighteenth century. Analysis of English farms described by Arthur Young in the 1770s indicates that labor productivity rose with farm size up to about 300 acres. These improvements were mainly situated in operations of tillage and transporting farm materials, where the tractive power of animals could be most efficiently applied. In reaping, mowing, and threshing, by contrast, the gains from increased farm size were small and, in specialized dairying, wine making, and gardening, virtually nonexistent. By lowering the demand for permanent hands relative to seasonal workers, the growth in farms that specialized in cereals intensified the seasonal imbalance in labor requirements. This imbalance was perhaps the chief constraint on the growth of large farms.

Questions of scale also appear at suprafarm levels of organization. Before the establishment of state-sponsored agricultural cartels in the twentieth century, the only suprafarm institutions with significant allocative functions were the medieval lordship and the agricultural village. The impact of lordship was largely confined to the labor market and to restrictions on the methods and place of processing agricultural produce. A lord's subjects might be required to perform work for the lord at specified times of the year as an incident of their status and be required to mill their grain, press their grapes, and bake their bread in his mill, winepress, and oven. These regulations are best viewed as legal monopolies and monopsonies enjoyed by the lord as the local ruler over the farming population.

More long-lasting than these seigniorial nuisances were village rules regulating the right of villagers to gather fuel and fodder from undeveloped land and to pasture their stock on temporarily uncropped fields or on meadows that had already been mown. Where individual holdings consisted of numerous intermingled small plots, village regulations reduced the damage caused by the passage of men and plow teams by requiring individual farmers having plots in the same field to conduct similar farming operations at the same time. This usually necessitated placing certain restrictions on the choice of crops sown. Such regulations were usually subsumed under the rubric of communal farming, though there was little communal in their application and on the whole tended to correspond to the interests of the largest farmers. The impetus to regulation seems to have come not from any ingrained communal "spirit" but from the practical difficulties of farming. Individual plots were small, scattered, and intermingled. This pattern of landholding was common in districts where the

AGRICULTURAL SOCIETY. Country meeting of the Royal Agricultural Society of England at Bristol, 1842. Painting by Richard Ansdell. In the foreground lie several agricultural tools and implements. (Royal Agricultural Society of England/Salford Museum and Art Gallery, Manchester, U.K.)

rural settlement took the form of agglomerated or "nucleated" villages. Why this pattern emerged in some regions and not in others is a matter of dispute. Considerations of defense, access to water, and the lords' need to more efficiently control their subjects have all been suggested.

Perhaps the most common pattern is the correspondence between nucleated settlement and "champion" or open country dedicated to growing cereals for the market. In any event, nucleated settlement was a comparatively late development, which archeologists situate between the eighth and twelfth century CE. Before that time, villages tended to be impermanent and peripatetic. Although archaeological data are inadequate to support strong generalization, it is likely that nucleation was due to the growing commercialization of cereal production associated with the medieval boom. Open-field regulations were gradually dismantled between 1400 and 1900 as farms became larger and more compact as a result of consolidation by purchase and exchange. At the same time, governments enacted private and public legislation to consolidate individual farms by extinguishing collective rights and those rights of private property that impeded efficient reorganization of the land.

Market Structure. Prior to the nineteenth-century revolution in transport and long-distance communications, the costs of establishing new farms and shipping produce over any considerable distance conferred a degree of monopoly power on farmers who marketed their produce locally. The degree of market power varied with the cost of obtaining alternative supplies and was therefore lowest along waterways and near great cities drawing provisions from many farms, and in markets for readily transported produce such as wool, dyestuffs, or wine. Market power was further sustained by significant product differentiation, since commercialized produce varied greatly in quality, and the differences were prized by consumers. As a rule, produce sold on local markets was of lower quality than produce sold to distant consumers because only higher

qualities could support the cost of transport. Thus, while in a broad sense, the small size of farms relative to total agricultural demand made agriculture a competitive industry, locally individual farms faced less than perfectly competitive markets. This meant that they could expect to be paid lower prices for significantly higher output. This circumstance provoked two typical responses. On the one hand, farmers tended to defer costly investments until the demand schedule moved out far enough to warrant them; on the other, they lobbied for "internal improvements" that, by lowering the cost of transportation, opened up new markets for their surplus produce. The latter response was especially strong in the United States.

With the improvement of transport and communication after 1840, agricultural markets became more competitive. By the first decade of the twentieth century, the markets for nonperishable produce like wheat, cotton, and vegetable fibers, were global. When global prices were lower than the customary local prices or when long-established markets were captured by foreign suppliers, however, the global market could be a mixed blessing. Worse,

global output might rise so much faster than global demand, or general trade depression originating in another part of the world might inhibit global demand, that farmers could be forced out of farming by falling prices. Not surprisingly, in the late nineteenth century agricultural tariffs began to go up, and in the 1930s governments instituted production controls intended to curtail farm output under the euphemistic term "supply management." By this date, however, the rate of technological progress was so rapid that no system of supply management could sustain the existing number of farms and farmers at acceptable standards of income. Agricultural markets in most industrial countries today combine competition in some commodities with strict production quotas and legal barriers to entry for other types of produce. Despite the growing importance of extremely large farms in nearly all sectors, the structure of the industry is still basically competitive, despite oligopolistic tendencies in food processing.

Technology. Until the decisive nineteenth-century breakthroughs in chemical and mechanical technologies that ushered in the modern era of agricultural development, the pace of technological change was slow. The major advances in farming technique occurred in three prehistoric waves during the eighth, fourth, and first millennium BCE. The initial wave introduced the short list of domesticated plants and animals that still account for the greatest part of agricultural product. A "secondary products revolution" after 4000 BCE added the domesticated olive and the grapevine to the list of cultivated plants and extended the purposes of livestock husbandry to include production of wool, dairy products, and traction.

The invention of plowing and the introduction of crops valuable enough to support the costs of long-distance carriage encouraged greater specialization in agriculture and a more pronounced social division of labor, which left its marks in the copper and bronze age civilizations of Europe and the Near East. The final wave of innovation occurred in the first millennium BCE, and was a by-product of the perfection of ferrous metallurgy after 1300 BCE. Improvements in smelting technique lowered the cost of iron enough for it to be employed in agriculture, and by 500 BCE, local fabrication of iron-tipped spades, hoe blades, plow shares, sickles, and scythes had spread to nearly every corner of Europe. The scythe was especially critical to the emergence of mixed husbandry. By speeding up the cutting of forage grasses, it permitted farmers to make enough hay in late spring to keep large stocks of animals through winter, thereby increasing the supply of meat, milk, manure, and animal power. Iron also strengthened the parts of implements subject to stress, strain, and abrasion, thereby permitting a greater application of animal power in field operations. By the end of the first millennium CE, rural wrights and smiths had devised wheeled plows with iron shares and coulters capable of slicing and turning stiff soils.

Iron tools greatly raised the productivity of traditional farming methods. At the cost of a large expenditure of labor, the iron-tipped spade produced a deep, well-drained, and aerated seedbed that was virtually weedless. The iron plow accomplished much the same work with less labor, though not to the same degree of perfection. The resulting improvement in the seedbed extended the range of crop rotations by permitting weed-sensitive plants to be sown as field crops and by permitting farmers to sow two cereal crops in succession in three- and four-course rotations. The extra produce was largely directed to feeding animals, which encouraged the development of intensive mixed husbandry based on the recycling of animal manure as fertilizer. This development was significantly enhanced around 500 BCE by the introduction of clover, alfalfa, and sainfoin into Europe from west Asia. These forage legumes, which had earlier been domesticated as fodder for horses, laid the foundation for sustained increases in crops by virtue of their ability to fix atmospheric nitrogen. The full realization of this fertility-restoring attribute came only in the first half of the nineteenth century; but its introduction dates to the early Iron Age. The only significant additions to the classical list of crops were maize and potatoes, introduced from the Americas in the sixteenth and early seventeenth centuries along with tomatoes and squashes. Buckwheat arrived from west Asia in the fifteenth or sixteenth century and contributed to the food supply in regions of marginal fertility.

Until recently, historians believed that a fourth wave of agricultural innovation occurred between 700 CE and 1000. The innovations were thought to include the heavy plow, the horse collar, and the three-course crop rotation. It is now known that these improvements were products of classical antiquity, although there is nevertheless some evidence that agricultural technique regressed toward the end of the Roman era. Similarly, the developments in intensive mixed husbandry during the early modern era seem to be the result of the introduction or reintroduction of forage legumes that had been extensively planted and traded in antiquity but were abandoned in most parts of Europe after 500 CE. How the plants were diffused from the Mediterranean basin to northern Europe is not known, though there is evidence of trade in legume seeds in the late sixteenth century. Farmers sometimes reseeded their meadows with the seeds that fell from hay stored in barns. But because the forage legumes were cultivated for their leaf and stem, they were usually harvested before the seeds formed, so most seeds would have had to be secured by deliberately cultivating the plants for their seeds.

By the beginning of the Christian era, then, the fundamental elements of European mixed husbandry were in place. Subsequent improvements consisted mainly in adapting them to new economic conditions by changing the intensity of cultivation, changing the proportion of land cultivated by hand and by plow, and by increasing or decreasing the size of farms. Such adjustments were a flexible response to changing patterns of demand and population density. Changes in farm size mainly affected the productivity of labor; changes in the crop mix and in the intensity of cultivation, weeding, and seeding rates mainly affected yields. This fine-tuning of agricultural routine and farm organization tended to raise the average level of productivity. The evidence suggests a secular upward drift in labor productivity of up to 25 percent per year. This largely was due to learning by doing in districts undergoing specialization. But endogenous improvements in productivity also implied the possibility of reversals. Techniques profitable under one set of circumstances might cease to be so under others, causing them to be abandoned, and if abandoned long enough, forgotten. This seems to have been the case with the forage legumes cultivated in antiquity and is also evident in the changing size of domestic animals as

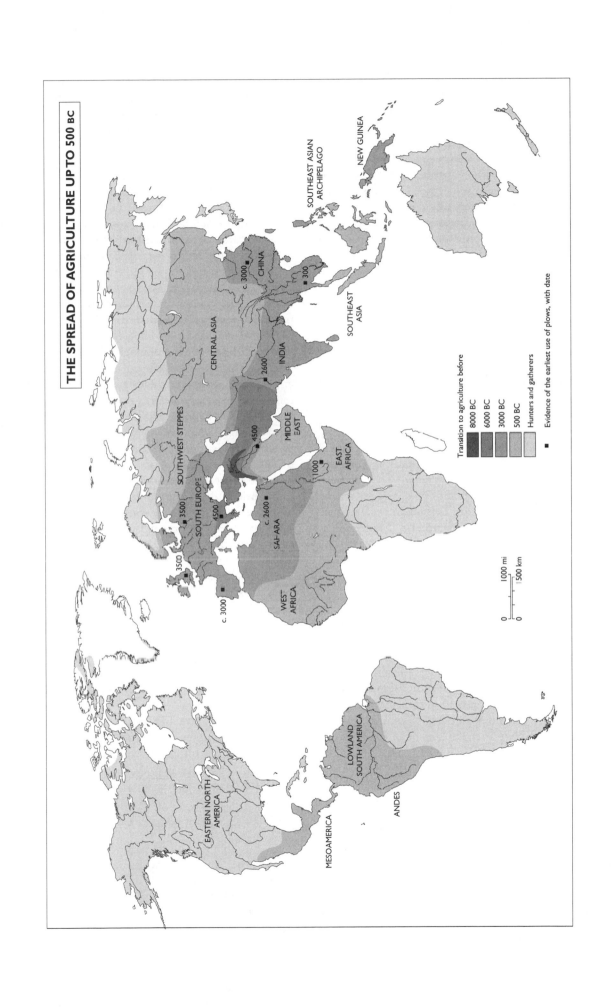

THE SPREAD OF AGRICULTURE UP TO 500 BC

Transition to agriculture before

- 8000 BC
- 6000 BC
- 3000 BC
- 500 BC
- Hunters and gatherers

■ Evidence of the earliest use of plows, with date

NEW GUINEA

SOUTHEAST ASIAN ARCHIPELAGO

SOUTHEAST ASIA

CHINA
c. 3000
300

CENTRAL ASIA

INDIA
2600

MIDDLE EAST
4500
1000

EAST AFRICA

SOUTHWEST STEPPES

SOUTH EUROPE
3500
4500
3500

SAHARA
c. 2600

WEST AFRICA
c. 3000

1000 mi
500 km

EASTERN NORTH AMERICA

MESOAMERICA

LOWLAND SOUTH AMERICA

ANDES

reconstructed from dated bone samples. Oxen, which in later Roman times were as large as the heavy draft animals of the nineteenth century, lost half their weight between CE 500 and 750 and did not regain the late Roman weights until after 1800. In the fourteenth and early fifteenth century, English fleece weights, which had increased in the twelfth and thirteenth century, declined significantly. These reversals, which were subsequently themselves reversed, suggest that productivity movements were endogenous to other features of the agricultural economy, of which the most important were changes in population and the extent of the market.

Although the fundamental elements of European agricultural technology remained basically unchanged from the early Roman era to 1800, there were improvements in implements and methods of farm management from about 1600. Efforts to devise seed drills can be dated to the seventeenth century, and improved plows that reduced the amount of traction needed to turn the soil began to appear in the course of the eighteenth. Commercial plant breeding became a profession in the seventeenth century, as did breeding of animals in the eighteenth, though owing to the ignorance of the laws of particulate inheritance and the inability to distinguish genetic from environmental causes of plant and animal performance, progress was slow. The major breakthroughs in agricultural technology occurred between 1780 and 1840, when a variety of new fertilizers, some organic, others mined or manufactured, became available, along with a series of innovations in mechanical threshing, reaping, mowing, and tillage implements. The latter were a product of the Industrial Revolution. Even in this period, however, the major source of productivity growth continued to be based on gradual improvements in the management of systems of mixed husbandry and greater specialization of production in response to growing urbanization and declining transport costs.

Population and Colonization. It is natural to suppose that in an era when technological change was minimal, the chief dynamic factors affecting agricultural evolution were population growth and agricultural colonization of empty land. The latter was for the most part a one-time event, as regions brought under the regime of plow and pasture rarely reverted permanently to waste and forest before the present era of rapid productivity growth. Population growth, on the other hand, has been a recurring historical phenomenon that, in the context of a comparatively stable amount of land dedicated to agricultural production, has produced significant changes in the man/land ratio. It is commonly believed that when technological change is negligible, changes in this ratio cause opposite changes in the productivity of agricultural labor. This Malthusian doctrine is encapsulated in the hypothesis of diminishing returns, according to which additional inputs of labor per unit of land under cultivation render diminishing amounts of extra produce. Because it asserts a continuous propensity of population to grow to the limit (or beyond it) set by the means of subsistence, this hypothesis is usually deployed to explain the apparent long swings in agricultural production, yields, prices, rents, and real wages. In periods of population growth, production, prices, and rents rise, while wages and, under certain conditions, yields decline; in periods of demographic contraction, the pattern is reversed. This regime is thought by some to have dominated European agricultural dynamics until the late eighteenth century. At that time, additional land supplies became available as a consequence of the substitution of coal for land-intensive organics fuels and the opening of new food-growing territories in southern Russia and the New World, which provided a temporary respite from the Malthusian trap until the age of rapid technological change.

The evidence for the demographic hypothesis consists mainly in secular fluctuation of food prices and wages that appear to be roughly consistent with what is known of contemporaneous movements in population and land settlement. But the hypothesis that population in the agrarian age was regulated by positive rather than preventive checks is not supported by ethnological investigations of primitive societies in modern times, and there is little evidence to suggest that this was true of agricultural societies in historical times. Agricultural regions characterized by high rates of population growth prior to the twentieth-century introduction of mortality-reducing public health programs into tropical underdeveloped countries almost always had an abundance of land available to be settled. In Europe, deep rural poverty was usually associated with the collapse of rural industry.

A variant of the population-push model of agricultural development holds that declining living standards provoked by rising man/land ratios may in some circumstances have induced agricultural innovation. This hypothesis is associated with the Danish economist Ester Boserup, who argued that the development of increasingly intensive crop rotations in European mixed husbandry was provoked by growing population pressure.

Demographic pressure is thought to have had other effects through the impact of living standards on the relative price of livestock and cereals. The income elasticity of demand for meat and dairy products greatly exceeds that of cereals. Thus, a period of declining per capita income associated with increasing population density should cause land to be reallocated from pasture to arable. It has been argued that population pressure was one factor responsible for the late medieval agricultural collapse, on the grounds that farmers planted so much land in grain pasture was lacking to feed the livestock whose manure was required to maintain soil fertility. Using the same logic, historians have argued that the diffusion of forage legumes after 1650 at a time when population growth was stagnant was due to the decline in the price of cereals relative to the price of meat and dairy produce. Both hypotheses have proved difficult to demonstrate. The medieval manure deficit seems to be definitely disproved by the fact that after 1350, when population contracted and the supply of land was no longer a binding constraint on agricultural output, yields did not rise but continued to decline. The effects of overall changes in the relative price of grain and pastoral products in the seventeenth and early eighteenth century are difficult to distinguish from effects resulting from the differential transport costs of the two classes of agricultural produce, which caused the farm gate price of bulky or perishable pastoral produce like hay and milk to be higher than that of cereals in the vicinity of large towns, the growth of which was perhaps the chief dynamic factor affecting agriculture at that time.

Overall, population growth in the preindustrial era seems to have been an effect rather than a cause of agricultural evolution. The overpopulated rural districts that characterized many countries in the nineteenth century seem on the whole to have resulted from the collapse of rural by-employments that had permitted families to divide their time between work on small holdings and other occupations, rather than from excessive pressure on agricultural resources.

Markets. The association between traditional agricultural societies and high levels of local self-sufficiency in modern times has encouraged the view that with the exception of "colonial" regions, agricultural markets were marginal to agricultural development until recently. This view has been fortified by the persistence of nineteenth-century sociological theories holding that markets encourage individualistic values that are incompatible with the maintenance of traditional social relations, causing them to be resisted by the community. These hypotheses have not withstood empirical scrutiny. Economic studies demonstrate that both contemporary and traditional farmers allocate resources along the lines predicted by the conventional hypothesis of wealth-maximizing behavior, while archaeological and historical investigations reveal much greater involvement by traditional farmers in market exchange and higher levels of specialization than was previously believed possible. It is impossible to identify periods when agrarian economies were so self-sufficient as to be considered a "natural economy" in the older sense of the term. Markets evolve faster than traditional technology or population, so they are perhaps the most important dynamic factor in the evolution of premodern agriculture.

The existence of markets for specialized farm produce can be traced back at least as far as the third millennium BCE, by which time farmers on some islands in the Aegean Sea were producing olive oil and wine in amounts greatly exceeding domestic consumption requirements. The evidence for trade in agricultural produce from the second millennium is even more abundant. The greatest signs, are from the Hellenic and Roman eras, when grain was traded by sea over long distances in huge transports, and large specialized olive and grapevine plantations emerged in North Africa, Spain, and around the northern rim of the Mediterranean. The trade in wine and olive oil is especially well documented, as it was transported by sea in specially designed freighters, some of which have been excavated from the ocean floor. Iconographic evidence, inscriptions, and archaeology all support the view that the era was one of market expansion for agricultural producers, and that the expansion was met by increased specialization and rising productivity.

The same evidence indicates a sharp decline in trade and specialization in the later Roman era and through the early medieval period. While a full retreat to economic autarchy is implausible given the present state of evidence, the collapse of urban demand and the contraction of specialized nonagricultural production clearly reduced the scope of commercial opportunity for farmers. This opportunity seems to have revived toward the end of the tenth century. Growing signs of trade in grain and other produce accompany evidence of urbanization in northern Italy, Flanders, northern France, and southern England. The effect of medieval urbanization on agricultural markets was far-reaching. Thirteenth-century Tuscany drew a significant proportion of its cereals from Sicily; the Flemish towns imported grain from northern France and southeast England; London's influence on the patterns of agricultural production extended 200 kilometers into the nation's interior, while the growth of Paris stimulated the creation of the largest farms in Europe.

These developments had a marked impact on agricultural productivity. The growth in market demand was contemporaneous with the replacement of oxen by horses on large specialized farms in northern Europe. It is also no doubt responsible for the proliferation of plows, harrows, and other implements of cultivation that showed up in significant numbers after 1200 as agriculture became more specialized. It has been inferred from likely movements in the relative urban and rural populations of northern Italy and Flanders that agricultural labor productivity probably rose at a rate of 0.25 percent per year between 1050 and 1300. Yields also rose, as farmers cultivated the land more intensively and planted pulses that restored nitrogen to the soil. In livestock husbandry, growth in the size of sheep can be measured by the changing dimension of parchments used as supports for record keeping and by increased fleece weights. The effects of demand can also be seen in the intensive land-clearing and drainage projects of the late twelfth and early thirteenth centuries. Although these phenomena were once viewed as responses to population pressure, the evidence suggests that they represent growth in agricultural specialization in response to the expansion of urban markets for produce.

These developments were arrested in the early fourteenth century by the outbreak of major dynastic conflicts in the central Mediterranean between the kingdom of Naples and the kingdom of Aragon and in northern Europe between France and England. The resulting disruptions to trade exposed the vulnerability of towns and districts whose prosperity depended on long-distance commerce. Their economic implosion had profound effects on the agricultural regions that served them. The contraction was intensified by the demographic collapse following the introduction of the bubonic plague in Europe in 1348. The economic disorganization caused by this calamity and the continuing European wars lasted nearly a century, during which time agricultural productivity stagnated or contracted. Crop yields fell in the specialized grain-growing regions, as did fleece weights. Many large farms were broken down into smaller, less specialized holdings and farming on the whole became more self-sufficient. This pattern began to reverse itself with the revival of trade and urban activity in the second half of the fifteenth century, which was especially marked in the Low Countries. In this region, the availability of cheap grain imports shipped from the eastern Baltic region permitted many farmers to dedicate more land to pastoral products and cash crops. Cheap transport in this land of many waterways relieved them of the need to be totally self-sufficient in grain, while providing a means of importing urban waste to fertilize their soils. It was also about this time that forage legumes were introduced (or reintroduced) to the region.

The positive effect of commerce on agricultural productivity was due to the high marginal productivity of capital and labor released into agriculture by contracting household production of nonagricultural goods that could now be acquired through the market. This effect is especially well documented for the Low Countries, but it was present wherever the size of the urban market and the ease of transport facilitated farm specialization. The growth of urban markets provided premia that rewarded the breeding of specialized livestock yielding a greater quantity and better quality of dairy products than traditional breeds. It also encouraged breeding animals exclusively for draft services and meat production. The same specialization can be seen in crops. From the seventeenth century, farmers sowed forage legumes for seed, and by the early eighteenth century, seed merchants were supporting attempts to select and propagate better varieties of cereal.

Because of the importance of animal power and manure in premodern agriculture, the crucial factor affecting the intensity of production was the ratio of the price of animal products to cereals. The relative price of meat and dairy products was higher near great towns, where the demand for butchered meat and fine dairy produce was higher than in the countryside. Since the prosperity of towns was linked to general economic prosperity, it is not surprising that, as the European economy began to expand vigorously after 1740, agricultural productivity also rose. Whether the growth in output kept pace with demand between 1770 and 1815 is in dispute. But on the whole, it seems as though it did. In England, the output of high-quality fodders such as barley and oats rose faster than wheat, which suggests it was stimulated by growing demand from the transport sector. The most difficult years occurred when international trade in foodstuffs was interrupted by the war and embargo during the Revolutionary and Napoleonic era. After Waterloo, food prices everywhere declined. By this time, however, urbanization and industrialization were far enough along to support continued investment in agriculture. Over the next half century, most of the investment went into the perfection of the traditional methods of mixed husbandry. After 1870, falling grain and meat prices, better agricultural machinery, and the growing supply of manufactured fertilizer eroded traditional husbandry, which survived in isolated patches of Europe into the 1950s and 1960s. By this time, the role of the market as the major source of change had been supplanted by technological advances.

[*See also* Agriculture, *subentries on* Agricultural Inputs, Productivity, and Wages *and* Technological Change; Enclosures; Malthusian and Neo-Malthusian Theories; *and* Markets.]

BIBLIOGRAPHY

Allen, Robert. "Tracking the Agricultural Revolution in England." *Economic History Review* 52 (1999), 209–235.

Ambrosoli, Mauro. *The Wild and the Sown: Botany and Agriculture in Western Europe, 1350–1850*. Cambridge, 1997.

Astill, Grenville, and John Langdon, eds. *Medieval Farming and Technology: The Impact of Agricultural Change in Northwest Europe*. Leiden and New York, 1997.

Amouretti, Marie-Claire. *Le pain et l'huile dans la Grèce antique: De l'araire au Moulin*. Paris, 1986.

Barker, Graeme. *Prehistoric Farming in Europe*. Cambridge, 1985.

Campbell, Bruce M. S. *English Seigniorial Agriculture, 1250–1450*. Cambridge, 2000.

Campbell, Bruce M. S., and Mark Overton. *Land, Labour, and Livestock: Historical Studies in European Agricultural Productivity*. Manchester, 1991.

Chorley, Patrick. "The Agricultural Revolution in Northern Europe, 1750–1880: Nitrogen, Legumes, and Crop Productivity." *Economic History Review* 34 (1981), 71–93.

Duby, Georges. *Rural Economy and Country Life in the Medieval West*. Translated from the French by Cynthia Postan. London, 1968.

Grantham, George. "Contra Ricardo: On the Macro-Economics of Europe's Agrarian Age." *European Review of Economic History* 3.2 (1999), 199–232.

Grantham, George. "Divisions of Labour: Agricultural Productivity and Occupational Specialization in Pre-Industrial Europe." *Economic History Review* 46.3 (1993), 478–502.

Grantham, George. "Long-Run Agricultural Supply in the Industrial Revolution: French Evidence and European Implications." *Journal of Economic History* 49 (1989), 1–30.

Grantham, George, and Carol Leonard, eds. *Agrarian Organization in the Century of Industrialization, Research in Economic History*. 2 vols. Greenwich, Conn., 1989.

Henry, Donald O. *From Foraging to Agriculture: The Levant at the End of the Ice Age*. Philadelphia, 1989.

Hoffman, Philip T. *Growth in a Traditional Society: The French Countryside, 1450–1815*. Princeton, 1996.

Magnou-Nortier, Elizabeth. "Le grand domaine: Des maîtres, des doctrines, des questions." *Francia* 15 (1987), 659–700.

Moriceau, Jean-Marc. *Les fermiers de l'Île de France, XVe—XVIIIe siècle*. Paris, 1994.

Overton, Mark. *Agricultural Revolution in England: The Transformation of the Agrarian Economy, 1500–1850*. Cambridge and New York, 1996.

Parker, William. N. "Agriculture." In *American Economic Growth: An Economist's History of the United States*, edited by Lance E. Davis, Richard A. Easterlin, and William N. Parker, pp. 369–417. New York, San Francisco, and London, 1972.

Postel-Vinay, Gilles. *La terre et l'argent: L'agriculture et le crédit en France du XVIIIe au début du XXe siècle*. Paris, 1998.

Raftis, J. Ambrose. *Peasant Economic Development within the English Manorial System*. Montreal, Kingston, and Buffalo, N.Y., 1996.

Sherratt, Andrew. "Plough and Pastoralism: Aspects of the Secondary Products Revolution." In *Pattern of the Past: Studies in Honour of David Clarke*, edited by Ian Hodder, Glynn Isaac, and Norman Hammond, pp. 261–308. Cambridge, 1997. Reprinted in *Economy and Society in Prehistoric Europe: Changing Perspectives*, by Andrew Sherratt. Princeton, 1997.

Simpson, James. *Spanish Agriculture: The Long Siesta, 1765–1965*. Cambridge, 1995.

Slicher van Bath, B. H. *The Agrarian History of Western Europe, 500–1850*. London, 1963.

Spur, M. S. "Arable Cultivation in Roman Italy, c. 200 BCE–c. AD 100." *Journal of Roman Studies Monographs* 3 (1986).

Vries, Jan de. *The Dutch Rural Economy in the Golden Age, 1500–1700*. New Haven, 1974.

Wright, Gavin. *The Political Economy of the Cotton South: Households, Markets, and Wealth in the Nineteenth Century*. New York, 1978.

Zanden, J. L. van. "The First Green Revolution: The Growth of Production and Productivity in European Agriculture, 1870–1914." *Economic History Review* 44.2 (1991), 215–239.

GEORGE GRANTHAM

Technological Change

From the earliest beginnings as hunters and gatherers, human beings have slowly developed a series of different farming systems, each one adapted to the soil and climate of its specific region. As the human population grew, peoples who occupied the drier regions of North Africa, the Middle East, Central Asia, and the Arctic zone moved to a system of nomadic pastoralism that still may be practiced today by Mongol tribesmen, the Masai in East Africa, the bedouin in Arab lands, and the Saami of Finland, whose system differs only in that they follow herds of wild caribou rather than driving their own domesticated stock of sheep, cattle, or goats. Like hunting and gathering, pastoral nomadism can scarcely be described as a form of "agriculture" at all, and in the drier areas of the world it was superseded by the work of the world's first true farmers. These people began to deliberately cultivate cereal crops such as barley and wheat, which were native to the region, in what has become known as the "fertile crescent"—that is, the curving arch of land that carries the rivers Nile, Tigris, and Euphrates, taking in territory that today is occupied by Egypt, Israel, Lebanon, Syria, Jordan, and Iraq. Because of the early development of true agriculture in this region, at some date between 10,000 and 8000 BCE, it is also sometimes referred to as the "cradle of civilization."

It was here, for the first time, that a substantial food surplus was created by the settled farmers, enabling the release of some of the population from the land, a diversification of economic activity, the building of cities, and the earliest development of the arts of "civilization", which included writing, calculation, astronomy, and manufacturing. The cities of Giza, Jericho, and Ur, for example, are certainly among the oldest in the world, and by 3000 BCE, great civilizations had been established in Egypt and Mesopotamia. This transition is represented metaphorically in the biblical story of Cain and Abel, in which Cain, the settled farmer, disposes of Abel, the herdsman. In truth, however, nomadic pastoralism was never totally eliminated in the Middle East, where traces of it still survive to the present day.

Dependence on Rivers. The first truly agricultural societies were riparian; that is, they depended heavily on their close proximity to rivers, whose valleys provided a rich alluvial soil for cultivation and were subject to natural seasonal flooding for irrigation. Ironically, the desert soils of the Middle East are potentially very fertile. The low rainfall of this region means that soil nutrients are not leached away in the kind of tropical downpours experienced by the equatorial zone. Instead, they remain locked in the soil, requiring only one key ingredient to release them: water. Beyond the river valleys, fertility may be brought to these soils by the building of irrigation channels. For this reason, farming in the low-rainfall lands between the Temperate Zone and the Tropics is often referred to as "dry belt" or "irrigated" farming. It is most typical of the Middle East, but it was also developed independently in several other parts of the world.

The idea of extending the cultivable area beyond the natural flood plain in river valleys by the digging of irrigation ditches is a simple one that suggested itself to all of the early riparian farmers. The technique certainly arose spontaneously and simultaneously in several parts of the Middle East and shortly afterward in the Indus Valley of present-day Pakistan, in India, and in China. No elaborate technology was employed here; only simple hand tools were used, and the channels were dug by human manual labor. However, the system did evolve with the passing years. At first, only simple ditches were dug, but later these were lined first with clay and later with kiln-baked bricks. Later still, the first piece of simple technology was introduced, the *shaduf*, essentially just a bucket dangling from a rope at one end of a pole. The pole pivoted on a tall support and was counterweighted at its other end to assist in the lifting of the heavy bucket, which was filled with water from a lower channel. By this means, water could be raised from reservoir to reservoir up the sides of a hill and stored in a large reservoir on high ground. Finally, naturally occurring water sources at higher levels were tapped, and the water was transported many miles via brick-built canals and aqueducts to reach the arable land where it was needed.

The control of water supply became, in fact, a fundamental element in several of the world's major agricultural systems. In monsoon Asia, for example, heavy rainfall is concentrated into just a few months of the year, with the remaining months very dry. An obvious solution to this problem is the building of reservoirs to store the monsoon rains, with associated waterways to distribute the water in dry months. Such systems were built in western India and Sri Lanka from the fourth century BCE. An alternative system is the building of terraces to trap and hold such rainfall and also to make possible the controlled distribution of water. Terracing is also instrumental in preventing soil erosion, a consideration of the utmost importance in areas of higher rainfall. Terracing as a means of water control is found in southeastern India, South China, Southeast Asia, and Indonesia, as well as in the dry-belt lands. This technique was even developed independently in the New World, where in the fourteenth century the Inca of the high Andes irrigated their terraces on the mountainsides by means of canals of hewn stone, which brought water from distant glacial lakes. Farther north on the American continent, another variant of irrigated agriculture was practiced. From the sixth century CE, first the Toltec and then the Aztecs of Mexico brought their gardens to the water rather than bringing water to the gardens. On the marshy borders of the lakes of central Mexico, they gathered mud to make an island, held together with walls of reed and secured by lines of trees, whose roots bound the gardens into discreet units, interspersed by irrigating water channels. The resulting garden was known as a *chinampas*, and these were steadily built out onto the Mexican lakes such as Lake Texcoco and Lake Xochimilco, which still provides Mexico City with vegetables from its chinampas today.

Farming in Tropical Regions. All of these water-controlling or "hydraulic" societies (as Karl Wittfogel has dubbed them) gave rise to great civilizations, but in the tropical regions of the world, an entirely different form of early agriculture was practiced. This is sometimes known as "swidden farming," but its more descriptive name is "slash and burn." Under this technique, a small area of dense tropical forest is cut down and left to dry during the short dry season. The cut foliage is then burned, and the resulting ash is raked into the soil to provide a fertile seedbed. A wide variety of crops are then grown together, sown, and harvested in turn throughout the long wet season. These crops might include yams, taro, manioc, and sorghum, but their variety was almost infinite and included a range of root crops and fruit trees. These would grow well for a year or two, but the heavy tropical rains would soon leach the nutrients out of the soil, and it would be necessary to move on to the next swidden.

The cleared area would then be reclaimed by the forest. The only form of natural vegetation that could survive in the Tropics was in fact the tall trees of the rain forests. These had long and powerful roots, which could reach down to the nutrients that had been leached far below the surface, while their spreading canopies protected the ground below from the lashing tropical rains that would otherwise have caused soil erosion. Thanks to the protection of these trees and their supply of a constant layer of leaf litter, an infinite host of minor plants could flourish in their shade. Swidden farming proved to be a successful form of agriculture for the tropical forest dwellers of Africa, Indonesia, Southeast Asia, and the Amazon basin, but the food surplus that it produced was small, never more than 10 percent above the needs of the farmers who produced it, and over the long term it could not sustain an advanced, city-based culture. In some tropical areas, where it was possible to supplement swidden farming with some hydraulic agriculture, great civilizations flourished for a time, such as those of the Maya in the Yucatán Peninsula, the Khmer of Cambodia, and the people of Anuradhapura in Sri Lanka. A large temple complex has even been found in tropical Zimbabwe. These civilizations flourished between about 500 CE and 1600, but all of them collapsed, succumbing to overpopulation, harvest failure, starvation, disease, or war. The jungle reclaimed their proud temples, and their civilizations were forgotten until recent times, when their buildings have been rediscovered and restored, and their histories reconstructed by archaeological research.

Societies based upon swidden farming therefore offered mankind no hope of long-term cultural or technological progress. Most of the land occupied by a swidden-farming community remained under unproductive forest, and the system supported a population density of only 15 persons per square mile on average. By comparison, the hydraulic farming systems appeared to be much more successful.

The irrigated province of Shaanxi in North China, which grew wheat, millet, and dry rice, supported 183 people per square mile in the thirteenth century, while the wet rice growing province of Zhejiang in eastern China supported 554 people per square mile. It has been calculated, however, that in the first century BCE the irrigated wheat and barley fields of the Nile Delta probably maintained a population density of 725 people per square mile. Although Egyptian agriculture could be practiced only in the valley of the Nile, farming here was probably the most productive in the ancient world. It seemed that the dry-belt civilizations would be certain to lead the way in bringing cultural and technological progress to the world, but surprisingly this did not prove to be the case. The principle of settled farming, and the key cereal crops on which it was based, spread northward across Europe from its native origins in the dry belts. But the hydraulic societies themselves tended to ossify into regimented hierarchies, in which freedom of thought among the closely organized toiling masses was discouraged: the classic "oriental despotism" according to Karl Wittfogel. A certain level of development was reached, but these societies then became locked in to an excessively rigid social and political structure, victims in a sense of their own success.

Farming in the Temperate Zone. This meant that the leadership role in technological progress was taken over by societies based on one-third of the world's major farming systems, what might be described as the "rainfall farming" of the Temperate Zone, where agriculture could be practiced with a less intensive input of labor. Large parts of western Europe and North America fall within this zone, where rainfall levels offer certain natural advantages to farmers. In the Southern Hemisphere, Argentina, South Africa, eastern Australia, and New Zealand also lie in temperate zones, but their development was delayed due to underpopulation. In terms of the world's wind belts, the temperate regions lie in a low-pressure zone, where air has a tendency to ascend, cool, and condense the water vapor held within it, which then falls as rain. It shares this property with the tropical zone, while high pressure is found over the poles and the dry belts of the world. Here, the circulating air from the Tropics and Temperate Zones begins to descend once more, warming as it falls and absorbing water vapor, leaving little to fall as rain or, over the poles, as snow, although in polar regions the snow permanently accumulates as glaciers because of the low temperatures. The tropical zones, therefore, suffer from too much rainfall and the dry belts from too little. But in the Temperate Zones, rainfall is moderate—not enough to cause severe leaching of nutrients out of the soil but enough to water cultivated crops without the assistance of irrigation channels. This would appear to give a great natural advantage to farmers in the Temperate Zone, but European agricul-

ture in the Middle Ages was not, in fact productive. A seed-yield ratio of four to one was regarded as high, and the yield was often lower than this.

Use of Stone Tools in Europe. The story of technological evolution in Europe began with the mounting of Neolithic stone hand axes onto wooden shafts to produce the long-handled, swingable axe, which is still familiar today. It was the invention of this implement that enabled Stone Age man to begin a program of forest clearance and to transform the environment for the first time. Swidden farmers, of course, used the same Stone Age technology, and in Europe, too, the felled timber was often burned to remove the debris and provide an ash seedbed. In Europe, however, forest clearance was followed by the introduction of domesticated livestock, sheep, cattle, pigs, and, most damaging of all, goats, which nibbled down the young tree shoots of cleared areas, keeping them as permanent grassland. The first European farmers relied heavily on their livestock and were more akin to nomadic pastoralists than to the true farmers of the dry belts. Swidden farmers, on the other hand, were unable to keep domesticated livestock at all because of the endemic animal diseases of the Tropics, spread by insect vectors such as the tsetse fly.

In Great Britain, through a combination of clearance and livestock grazing, by the time the Romans first arrived in force in 55 BCE, most of the country's natural forest cover had already been removed, particularly over the thin soils of the chalk and limestone hills. These light soils could be cultivated with the aid of the primitive plow in use at that time, named by the Romans as the *ard* or *aratrum*. This was a light wooden implement, easily pulled by a pair of small oxen, and sometimes known disparagingly as a "scratch plow." From about 500 BCE, it was sometimes tipped with a bronze or, later, iron share, but it was never able to cope with the heavy clay soils of areas such as the English midlands or the north European plain.

The evolution of the plow was, therefore, a key factor in the progress of European farming systems. By the time of the Norman Conquest of England in 1066, a heavier wheeled plow had been developed in Europe, fitted with a coulter in front of the share, which made a deep vertical cut into the soil. The sheared earth was then undercut by the share, and turned over onto its side by the addition of a moldboard behind the share, designed for this purpose. Three operations were thus combined into one, and the deep plowing of heavy clay soils became possible for the first time. The new plows required a much heavier draught, but this could be supplied by a larger team of oxen, usually eight, or by horses. The pulling power of the latter was improved some three-fold by the widespread adoption of the horse collar from the thirteenth century. The development of the heavy plow enabled the Europeans to cultivate the whole of their land surface if they wished, apart from mountainous areas, since all of it was naturally watered by moderate rainfall. Dry-belt farmers remained confined to regions close to a water supply, but the mainly alluvial soils that they worked were light, and it was never necessary to develop a heavy plow here. Swidden farmers never used plows at all, but only simple dibblers and digging sticks. Both farming systems reached their maximum output levels without the assistance of any sophisticated technology. Only the European system demanded the application of advanced technology as an essential prerequisite to the raising of productivity levels. The soils of Europe were less fertile than those of dry-belt lands or of newly made swiddens. Additional productivity had to be coaxed out of them.

Strip Farming in Europe.   The origins of strip farming in Europe, with three great open arable fields divided into individually owned strips, has been associated with the spread of the heavy plow from the Rhineland area during the Dark Ages, but this link remains speculative. Certainly, the heavy plow was so efficient that one strip-plowing of the soil was sufficient, while farmers of Roman times had been obliged to cross-plow even the light soils of small square fields with the ard in order to get a good tilth. The main point of the three-field system however, was, to facilitate the rotation of arable crops between the three fields as a means of preserving soil fertility. A common early rotation was wheat, barley, fallow, with animals grazed on the fallow field as soon as it threw up a few weeds and grasses, so that their dung would restore some fertility to it. By the seventeenth century, however, the three fields had often been divided into four, five, or even six, and much more sophisticated crop rotations had been introduced into them. These would include breaks with leguminous crops such as peas, beans, lentils, and chickpeas, which captured atmospheric nitrogen and transformed it into soluble nitrates through their root nodules, leaving the soil actually richer than before. Animal fodder crops, such as clover, vetches, lucerne, and lupines were also introduced into these new rotations. These, too, were leguminous and beneficial to the soil. At the same time, the devotion of some arable land to fodder crops, which were stored for the winter, enabled farmers to keep more livestock. The animals provided more dung, and so a beneficial cycle was set in train.

Not all of the land of Europe was farmed under the open-field system, however, with its arable portion confined permanently to the strips in the open fields, while adjacent areas of common grazing and meadowland were used for permanent grass or hay. Small irregular fields dating from Celtic or Roman times, which had never been replaced by the medieval system, could still be found over much of Europe in 1600, and new enclosed fields were continually being created from former forest, waste, or common land. These enclosed fields, which could be farmed

under quite different systems from those employed on the open fields, accounted for about half of the cultivated land of Europe in 1600. In enclosed regions, a new technique known as "convertible husbandry" was developed during the seventeenth century. Under this system, the land spent most of its time under a mixture of grasses and clovers, being grazed and dunged by livestock, and building up its fertility for the following cereal crops of wheat, barley, oats, or rye. Cereal yields were, on average, twice as great under this system as those produced by the strips of the open fields, which were never rested long enough to fully regain their fertility.

Enclosed fields also offered other advantages, among them the possibility of introducing further crop rotations in addition to convertible husbandry, which worked best on heavy soils. On lighter soils, other rotations, such as the famous "Norfolk four course" of turnips, barley, clover, and wheat, could be introduced, although this was only one of a wide variety of rotations that were being used across Europe in the eighteenth century. Many of these rotational crops, such as turnips, clover, lucerne, and sainfoin, were new to field culture. New World crops, such as potatoes, maize, and tomatoes, were added to the European repertoire in the eighteenth century. As the advantages of enclosed fields became clearer, the open fields and commons themselves were enclosed across Europe in the seventeenth and eighteenth centuries, sometimes with the aid of national legislation, as in Great Britain, so that enclosure itself became a technique of agricultural advance. The Europeans were also studying the possible advantages of adding fertilizing agents, such as clay marl on light soils; sand, rags, or ashes on heavy soils; and lime on both, to change the structure of their often difficult soils. Night soil from the growing towns, malt dust, seaweed, and leather shreds were added to the traditional animal dungs to improve both the texture and the fertility of European soils.

Although the Europeans were by no means hydraulic farmers, water control did have a marginal importance even here. Rainfall levels in parts of Europe could be surprisingly low: Over much of eastern England and central Spain, for example, rain levels averaged only 25 inches per year, while geographers' official definition of a desert is an area with 10 inches of rain a year or less. Irrigation was, therefore, sometimes a helpful technique to employ, especially in the "floating" or flooding of water meadows near to streams, which were deliberately damned to flood the land with a thin layer of water in the spring, bringing on early grass and doubling the hay yield. From 750 CE, with the Arab conquest of Spain, Middle Eastern irrigation practices were introduced there, but this technology was lost with the Christian reconquest of the country, completed in 1492. In general, however, drainage techniques were far more important than irrigation to European farmers.

AGRICULTURAL TOOL. At work in the fields, Taiwan, 1983. (© Chuck Fishman/Woodfin Camp and Associates, New York)

An excess of rainfall onto heavy, ill-drained soils was much more of a problem for them than aridity. In fact, extensive areas, such as the Pontine marshes of the Romagna, the polders of the Netherlands, and the Fens of England, were subjected to large-scale drainage engineering projects over the course of European history. At the local level, individual wet fields were drained first by open ditches and later by covered ditches, rendered "hollow" at the base by the addition of brushwood or rubble below ground level. Later, they were lined with drainage tiles, and in the nineteenth century pipe drainage was used.

Increase in Productivity Levels. Through the intensive application of techniques such as those outlined above, the productivity levels of the unpromising soils of Europe were gradually forced upward. On extensively cultivated large fields, the late medieval seed-yield ratios of three or four to one had been increased to ten to one on average in western Europe by 1800, and a great deal of additional land had been brought into agricultural use through enclosure, drainage, and fertilizing techniques. In the most fertile parts of Europe, such as the Po Valley in northern Italy, yields were higher than this. And on intensively cultivated land, such as the market gardens of the Netherlands and England or the small peasant holdings of France, seed yields of twenty to one or more were obtained. These were achieved through heavy inputs of labor and capital. French peasants did not plow their few-acre holdings but rather cultivated them garden-style with a mattock and lavished fertilizers upon them.

So great had been the progress of European agriculture that some have spoken of an agricultural revolution taking place in these centuries. Certainly, the population of Europe west of the Urals increased from about 80 million in 1500 to some 200 million by 1800, but the use of the term "agricultural revolution" is unhelpful. Rather, there was slow but steady progress over a long period of time. In the nineteenth century, the chemical and engineering industries came to the aid of agriculture, providing a number of artificial fertilizers, such as the superphosphates and nitrate compounds, and a wide range of labor-saving agricultural implements. The wooden plows and harrows of the eighteenth century were replaced by lighter and stronger versions made of iron, and entirely new inventions, such as the steam-powered threshing machine and the multi-furrow iron seed drill, came into use. The scythe and the sickle, which for centuries had been used for mowing hay and reaping cereals, were slowly replaced by horse-powered mowing and reaping machines, later versions of which also bound the crops into sheaves, saving still more labor. In 1900, however, despite some experiments with a steam plow, steam power was still little used in European farming, and labour was still done by human power or horsepower, although aided now by a variety of mechanical contrivances.

These new machines, coupled with the use of many more horses to power them, greatly increased the productivity of labor in European farming. In Great Britain, for example, although one-third of the labor force had been engaged in agriculture in 1800, this proportion had fallen to only 8 percent by 1900. It is a tribute to the achievement of former centuries, however, to note that despite all the technological advances of the nineteenth century and the rise in labor productivity, seed-yield ratios in England increased from ten to one to only eleven to one over this one-hundred-year period. The population of Europe roughly doubled in the nineteenth century, from about 200 million to about 400 million, but by 1900, Europe could barely feed itself and was relying on imports of cereals from North America, Argentina, Australia, and even India. Great Britain was particularly reliant on imports, realizing from as early as 1846 that the country could no longer feed itself entirely from its own resources, as the urbanization rate neared 50 percent. This situation continued until World War II, with European agriculture remaining in a generally depressed condition owing to an increasing reliance on imports, despite the introduction of petrol-powered tractors and other vehicles. It has been only since 1945 that agriculture in Europe and across the world has experienced a triumphant revival with the advent of the so-called "green revolution." This has been associated with the introduction of new crop strains, new measures of pest control, advanced irrigation schemes, and new fertilizing agents, making it possible to increase dramatically, by several orders of magnitude, the yield of all crops in all areas of the world on a scale entirely unknown in historical terms. If the concept of an agricultural revolution has any validity at all, it should surely be applied only to developments in the second half of the twentieth century and to no earlier period. In recent years, genetic engineering has also come to the aid of the plant scientists, a technique that promises enormous potential for the future, if it can win public acceptance.

The wide range of new plant species that has been developed, particularly the new strains of drought- and pest-resistant rice, offers new hope to farmers in all of the world's climate zones. The last century has seen a world population of 1.6 billion in 1900 rise to 6 billion by 2000, unchecked by the onset of severe famines—although many have gone hungry. This rate of increase looks likely to continue. That it has been sustained at all is a great tribute to the new technologies of the world's agricultural communities.

[See also Agriculture, subentries on Main Tools and Implements and Agricultural Production Systems.]

BIBLIOGRAPHY

Astill, Grenville, and John Langdon, eds. Medieval Farming and Technology: The Impact of Agricultural Change in Northwest Europe. Leiden, 1997.

Bruce, M., S. Campbell, and Mark Overton. eds. Land, Labour, and Livestock: Studies in European Agricultural Productivity. Manchester, 1991.

Burford, Allison. Land and Labor in the Greek World. Baltimore, 1993.

Collins, Edward John T. Power Availability and Agricultural Productivity in England, 1840–1939. Reading, U.K., 1996.

Fussell, George E. Farming Techniques from Prehistoric to Modern Times. Oxford, 1966.

Grigg, David. The Agricultural Systems of the World. Cambridge, 1974.

Grigg, David. The Transformation of Agriculture in the West. Oxford, 1992.

Hoffman, Philip T. Growth in a Traditional Society: The French Countryside, 1450–1815. Princeton, 1996.

Langdon, John. Horses, Oxen, and Technological Innovation: The Use of Draught Animals in English Farming from 1066 to 1500. Cambridge, 1986.

Manshard, Walther. Tropical Agriculture. London, 1974.

Morgan, Raine, ed. Farm Tools, Implements, and Machines in Britain: Pre-History to 1945, A Bibliography. Reading, U.K., 1984.

Overton, Mark. Agricultural Revolution in England: The Transformation of the Agrarian Economy, 1500–1850. Cambridge, 1996.

Rowley, Trevor, ed. The Origins of Open-Field Agriculture. London, 1981.

Russell, William M. S. Man, Nature, and History. London, 1967. This is an excellent short survey of the subject, lavishly illustrated, which deals with the social outcomes of different farming systems.

Thomas, William L. Man's Role in Changing the Face of the Earth. Chicago, 1956. Although an old work now, this is still the most detailed single history of world agriculture available, running to 1,152 pages.

Watson, Andrew M. Agricultural Innovation in the Early Islamic World: The Diffusion of Crops and Farming Techniques, 700–1100. Cambridge, 1983.

Webster, C. C., and P. N. Wilson, eds. Agriculture in the Tropics. Oxford, 1998.

Wittfogel, K. A. Oriental Despotism: A Comparative Study of Total Power. New Haven, 1957. This is a classic work, which deals extensively with dry belt or "hydraulic" agricultural systems in China and the Middle East and the social and political consequences that have flowed from this farming system. His conclusions remain, however, somewhat controversial.

J. R. Wordie

Main Tools and Implements

From prehistoric times to the present, production of the world's food grains has necessitated the use of tools and implements to perform a range of discrete operations. Some agricultural implements predate settled farming: sickles were used to harvest the wild ancestors of the major western cereals, and shifting agriculture could operate with a minimum of specifically agricultural implements beyond pre-existing tools to clear natural vegetation. The basic means of achieving the seasonal tasks necessary to arable farming remained essentially unchanged over long periods of time, and virtually all the tools and implements of medieval and modern western agriculture were already in existence at the end of the Roman era. Later development was more concerned with efficiency and economy of operation than with basic principles. The numerous and highly detailed variations in agricultural tools and implement represent adaptation to environmental conditions and cultural traditions.

The Ard and the Plow. The preparation of the soil prior to sowing was first achieved with digging sticks of varying degrees of sophistication including weighting and the strengthening of points by means of stone, metal, or fire hardening. Spades and forks press into the earth and lift it with a combination of hand and foot action with the operator moving backward; picks and mattocks dislodge the ground with a striking action and the operator working forward. These early implements are thought to have gradually developed into the ard and plow, the emergence of which is difficult to date with precision. However, animal-drawn ards—which break the ground by means of a pointed share—appear to have been in use in Iraq and Egypt c. 3000 BCE and there is evidence for ard tillage in China during the Yangshao period five hundred to six hundrd years ago. It is notable that the ard or plow was unknown in the New World prior to European colonization; neither were draught animals used. In Central- and South America, aboriginal cultivators used a wide variety of handtools, including planting and digging sticks, the *coa*, a one-piece bladed implement halfway between a planting stick and a shovel, and the *chaquitaclla* (or *taclla*), a relatively late (Inca) invention that featured a metal point, curved handle, and footrest. The use of the foot in turning the sod has given rise to the term *footplow*, remarkably effective in framing the difficult Andean highlands.

The distinction between the ard (sometimes termed the "scratch-plow") and the plow proper is fundamental. The ard (Fr. *araire*, Lat. *aratrum*) is symmetrical in design and pushes soil to either side of the dividing plow-share. The western plow (Fr. *charrue*, Lat. *carruca*), in contrast, turns the soil by means of a curved *moldboard* and also incorporates a *colter*, a sort of vertical knife that helps to achieve deeper tillage. In that the action was asymmetrical, ground was thrown up into ridges, which was useful where good drainage was important; reversible moldboards allowed a flatter finish. Plows could be wheeled or wheel-less, wheeled plows allowing for a larger team of draft animals. The additional powerforce provided was particularly valuable on the heavy lowland soils of northern Europe, while the ard was better suited to light soils, where deep cultivation is not required, or in dry regions where soil moisture conservation is all-important. The action of these implements also influences fieldshape; to achieve uniform division of the surface, use of the ard often necessitates cross-plowing, which is most efficient in square fields. The plow, on the other hand, particularly when large teams of draft animals were utilized, was more effective on rectangular blocks of land, particularly the "strips" of lowland northern Europe in medieval times. Although it has been argued that the Chinese plow was diffused from the Middle East, more recent evidence points persuasively toward independent origins. Neolithic stone ard shares have been found in China, and Francesca Bray has itemized a range of detailed points of variation between Chinese and European plows—for example, the absence of the colter from the Chinese implement.

Plows did not necessarily displace spades or other hand implements—as in the distinctive "Flemish husbandry"—particularly where deep cultivation was required or where there was emphasis on the individual plant, as in potato growing in western Ireland. On many soils repeated plowing was necessary to produce fine ground, tilth, for planting small seeds; the separate implement of the harrow was developed to achieve this and also extirpate weeds. In its simplest form the harrow consisted of brushwood mounted on a frame. Roman agriculture employed wooden frames with numerous teeth drawn by oxen for this purpose, although harrows were not common throughout northern Europe until the tenth century. Not until the eighteenth century was more attention given to better preparation of the soil for the reception of seed, particularly with the development of Jethro Tull's "horse-hoeing husbandry," which anticipated later mechanization. Harrowing could also bury and redistribute broadcast seed; Tull's development of the seed-drill brought more precision to sowing, although the concept of putting the seed in regular lines was not in itself new. In the second part of the twentieth century, when herbicides became widely used to control weeds in growing crops, seed-drilling equipment with spacer bars was developed to allow the admission of spraying machinery through the growing crop, which gave rise to the appearance of now-familiar "tramlines" in fields of wheat and barley.

Reaping Tools. Of reaping tools, the sickle is the oldest implement; those with smooth edges were more generally employed in humid areas where they would bite into the stalk; serrated sickles were better adapted to arid areas. It remained the most used harvesting implement in medieval times, but in fourteenth-century Europe the Flemish hook or scythe was employed when straw became utilized as an ingredient of manure rather than being left in the fields. Although mechanical harvesting was essentially a nineteenth-century innovation, the Romans had an animal-driven reaping machine, the *vallum*, which consisted of a large frame fitted with teeth and mounted on a pair of wheels, with the animals pushing from behind. Use of the *vallum* was restricted to large estates in Gaul.

Threshing and Winnowing Tools. After harvesting, the finishing of the crop prior to consumption or processing has throughout history been difficult. There are two distinct operations: threshing, the separation of grain from its surrounding inedible husk, and winnowing, the production of a clean sample of the final product by the removal of chaff and dust. The simplest threshing consists of using animals to trample the harvested crop; the Roman *tribulum*, or threshing sledge, consisted of a heavy wooden board equipped with flints or iron teeth on its underside to

FIELD WORK. The Jethro Tull plow (fig. 1), invented in the early 1700s by the English agrarian reformer, profoundly altered agricultural practice in England. Horses had replaced oxen, and seeds were planted using a device (fig. 4) that dropped seeds evenly and at a controlled rate. In the background, a worker sows grain (fig. 5), a light spike-harrow (fig. 6) distributes and covers the seed, and a roller (fig. 7) firms the ground. Plate from Diderot and d'Alembert's *Encyclopédie*, 1762–1772. (Prints and Photographs Division, Library of Congress)

release grain from the straw, an implement that remained essentially unchanged in parts of the Mediterranean and Middle East until the recent past. The flail became the most ubiquitous threshing implement, essentially two sticks joined together by a chain or rope with which the corn was beaten, which was generally adopted in Europe and Scandinavia between c. 1000 and 1200 CE. Threshing, which was particularly laborious work, was the first agricultural operation to utilize nonbiological sources of

motive-power (although water and wind power were used for milling in medieval times). In the eighteenth century, Andrew Meikle developed a system by which flails fixed to a beam were turned by water wheel. Threshing machines most often used horsepower, however, until portable steam engines became viable in the mid-nineteenth century. Compared with mechanized threshing, the hand flail was slow and ineffectual, but the adoption of the threshing machine sparked considerable protest in rural Britain.

The simplest form of winnowing was to toss the grain in the air across the wind using a winnowing shovel (Lat. *ventilabrum*). A draft could be obtained by opening the barn door under suitable conditions, or by using canvas sails. Evidence suggests that winnowing fans were used in China much earlier than in Europe, and Chinese winnowing machines appear to have been introduced to Scandinavia and other parts of Europe in the eighteenth century. After 1850 steam-driven combined threshing, winnowing, and dressing machines became commonplace on British and North American farms.

Mechanization. Agricultural tools and implements in the pre-industrial age underwent adaptation and improvement and were sometimes rediscovered, but with little that was essentially new; where labor was abundant and cheap, there was not much incentive to mechanize established operations. Traditional implements were adapted to local conditions and agricultural practices; the European plow held little attraction for the aboriginal inhabitants of Central- and South America, where individual plants were cultivated in small intermontane basins or on narrow terraces. The publication of L. White's study, *Medieval Technology and Social Change*, in 1962 aroused a great deal of interest in the extent of the "agricultural revolution" in medieval Europe. Research over the last forty years has revealed a complicated pattern of uneven regional development of innovative agricultural practice and a number of cumulatively significant developments, including the substitution of the plow for the ard (exclusively so in England) and the increased use of the horse in place of oxen, which depended upon innovation in harnessing equipment and the adoption of horseshoes.

Developed during the "classical" agricultural revolution of the eighteenth century, the "Rotherham" plow has been viewed as one of the greatest single advances in fundamental design. This utilized a new frame, triangular rather than rectangular, and merged the share into the line of the moldboard to reduce friction. The lighter, faster plow that resulted produced significant savings of both human and animal effort. The Industrial Revolution of the late eighteenth and nineteenth centuries brought the expectation that science and technology, which had so transformed the manufacturing industry, could do the same for farming; ultimately, the nature of farm tools and implements in the Western world was indeed transformed, but the process was more protracted than is generally appreciated. Agricultural mechanics made significant progress in Great Britain in the 1840s and 1850s, decades that witnessed the emergence of a full-fledged agricultural engineering industry producing tools and implements for export as well as home consumption.

The most obvious area for development was the application of steam power to agricultural operations, and after 1850 steam engines were used for a wide range of "belt work": to drive bone mills, guano breakers, and various cutters, crushers, and grinders, but it was in threshing and finishing where steam power had the greatest impact on traditional farm tasks. The technical difficulties associated with steam plowing proved more difficult to solve. Their adverse power: weight ratio made early steam engines impossible to use for hauling farm equipment across fields except in areas of light soil and low rainfall, as on the western plains of the United States and Canada. Steam cultivation was achieved by confining the engines to the headlands and using them to haul plows across the fields by means of steel cable and windlass systems; the one developed by the firm of John Fowler was most successful in Britain. Because steam cultivating equipment required substantial capital investment, the work was most usually carried out by contracting companies. Large fields and smooth terrain were also prerequisites for successful steam plowing, conditions that were more widely encountered in North America than in Europe, where animal-hauled plows were not displaced by steam power.

A reaping machine was patented by Patrick Bell in Scotland in 1826 but attracted little interest. Obed Hussey and Cyrus McCormick demonstrated successful reaping machines in North America during the early 1830s, but they did not gain popular acceptance there until the 1850s. This hiatus has been explained by the need for the price threshold to fall enough to make them economical on smaller farms; improved reliability was also important. Reaping and mowing machines for the hay harvest also attracted interest in Britain in the 1850s and 1860s following their demonstration at the Great Exhibition of 1851 and as additional harvest labor became less accessible. Adoption of non-human-powered harvest technology was relatively slow at first—about 25 percent of the British harvest was mechanically harvested in 1870, a figure that rose, however, to 80 percent by the turn of the century, by which time self-binding reapers, which tied the cut corn into sheaves, were generally employed. As in steam-plowing, uneven terrain and small irregular fields were initially barriers to adoption and additionally, up to the 1870s, there were also important social considerations—employers were wary of labor-saving machinery following the earlier countryside protests against the threshing machine, and some felt an obligation to augment harvest earnings to tide the laborer over the lean period of winter. Harvest efficiencies were, however, achieved by the "intermediate technology" solution of improvement or by substitution of traditional handtools.

Twentieth-Century Advances. The concept of combining the harvesting operation with threshing and finishing is attributed to Hiram Moore and John Hascall of Kalamazoo County, Michigan, in 1836. There were also important

Australian influences on the early "combine harvester" that employed huge teams—up to thirty-two horses to one machine—to drive the cumbersome mechanism. The first self-propelled combine was seen in 1886, using a straw-fired steam engine. By the 1890s combine harvesters were most widely employed in California, where large fields and dry conditions provided an optimum environment. By 1930 about one-third of all the combines in use in the United States were in Kansas; they slowly advanced across the northern plains as prejudice against the quality of combined grain was overcome. Acceptance was encouraged by the development of windrow or swath harvesting, whereby the crop was first cut and allowed to ripen on the ground to produce a higher quality sample and prevent grain loss. The first combine was not used in Great Britain until 1928, and only about one hundred were in operation at the outbreak of World War II—the threshold size of field and farm was generally too small to allow their economic operation; the 1950s, however, saw their rapid adoption.

The application of the internal combustion engine to farming operations brought the greatest change to agricultural technology and the tractor, along with the combine, became the joint symbol of agricultural progress in the twentieth century. Initially stationary gas engines were applied to the range of operations that had been successfully accomplished by steam power, to be followed by gasoline and oil engines in the 1890s. The first tractor was produced by the Charter Engine Company of Chicago in 1889, with a number of North American tractor manufacturers established by 1914. Many of these early machines were not, however, "tractors" in the modern sense and it was the "Ivel Agricultural Motor" perfected by Dan Albone in Great Britain in 1902 that set a new standard of lightness and versatility. This design eventually superseded the unwieldy "American Primitives," as C. L. Caward termed them, although they remained popular on the huge open fields of the western plains. In 1970 the same author cited a 1908 South Dakota wheat ranch as the world's first fully mechanized farm.

Early tractor design, particularly in the United States, demonstrated a huge diversity, with many creations incorporating eccentric and impractical design elements. The latter part of World War I encouraged the employment of the tractor in Great Britain as grassland was converted to arable because of the reduced labor supply. In 1917 the British government commissioned six thousand Fordsons from the firm of Henry Ford and Son, which had been established in Dearborn, Michigan, in 1915 specifically to produce farm tractors. This model became the most influential of conventional tractor designs in the interwar period, produced for Europe at first in Cork, Ireland, and later at Dagenham, England. Important developments in overall tractor design included the adoption of the low-pres-

sure pneumatic tire, which was adapted to yielding soils and permitted higher speeds, and the hydraulic lift and linkage developed by Harry Ferguson. The tractor did not, however, supersede the horse in Great Britain until after World War I. There were also the "crawler," as opposed to wheeled, tractors developed at the start of the twentieth century, most notably by Holt and Best of California. After 1925 the "Caterpillar" became well known and the basic design has not been superseded; it proved particularly useful in opening up previously uncultivated areas.

"Mechanized" farming, however unsatisfactory the term, became synonymous with conventional agricultural progress during the twentieth century. At the British Association at York in 1932, H. J. Denham observed that the farming industry was within "measurable distance" of the day where the labor requirement for cereal production would be 0.002 men per acre, but this level of operation—one man per 500 acres—was not generally reached in Great Britain until the 1980s, and in Western Europe and the Mediterranean the post-1950s spread of mechanization was uneven regionally. In many parts of the world, handtools remain in use, with human and animal power providing the greatest part of the motive force. At the start of the twenty-first century, the view from the air-conditioned tractor cab on the U.S. plains or the English eastern counties presents a far from typical picture of the use of tools and implements in world agricultural production.

BIBLIOGRAPHY

Astill, Greville, and John Langdon. *Medieval Farming and Technology: The Impact of Agricultural Change in Northwest Europe.* Leiden, 1997.

Bray, Francesca. "The Evolution of the Mould Board Plough in China." *Tools and Tillage* 3.4 (1979), 227–239.

Brown, Jonathan. *Farm Machinery, 1750–1945.* London, 1989. A useful pictorial guide with commentary.

Cawood, Charles L. "The History and Development of Farm Tractors." *Industrial Archaeology* 7 (1970), 264–291 and 397–423.

Collins, Edward John T. *Sickle to Combine.* Reading, 1969.

Collins, Edward John T. "Diffusion of the Threshing Machine in Britain, 1790–1880." *Tools and Tillage* 3 (1972), 16–33. Analyzes chronological phases of the spread of this important innovation.

Collins, Edward John T. "The Age of Machinery." In *The Victorian Countryside*, edited by G. E. Mingay, vol. 1, pp. 200–213. London, 1981.

David, Paul A. "The Mechanization of Reaping in the Ante-Bellum Midwest." In *Industrialization in Two Systems: Essays in Honor of Alexander Gerschenkron*, edited by Henry Rosovsky, pp. 3–39. New York, 1966.

David, Paul A. "The Landscape and the Machine: Technical Interrelatedness, Land Tenure and the Mechanisation of the Corn Harvest in Victorian Britain." In *Essays on a Mature Economy: Britain after 1840*, edited by D. M. McCloskey, pp. 145–205. Princeton, 1971. Two extremely influential essays.

Donkin, Robin A. "Pre-Columbian Field Implements and Their Distribution in the Highlands of Middle and South America." *Anthropos* 65 (1970), 505–529. A comprehensive guide to, and interpretation of, pre-Columbian handtools.

Fussell, George E. *The Farmer's Tools: The History of British Farm Implements: Tools and Machinery Before the Tractor Came*. London, 1952. Despite later research, this work has never been fully superseded.

Fussell, George E. *Jethro Tull: His Influence on Mechanised Agriculture*. Reading, 1973. A comprehensive and readable assessment.

Langdon, John. *Horses, Oxen and Technological Innovation*. Cambridge, 1986. An important contribution to research on the "medieval technical revolution" debate inaugurated by Lynn White.

Marshal, Geoffrey. "The Rotherham Plough. A Study of a Novel 18th Century Implement of Agriculture." *Tools and Tillage* 3.3 (1978), 150–167. A definitive article on an important development.

Moorhouse, Robert. *The Illustrated History of Tractors*. Edison, N.J., 1996.

Morgan, Raine. *Farm Tools, Implements, and Machines in Britain. Prehistory to 1945: A Bibliography*. Reading, 1984. An invaluable guide to further research. The University of Reading supports the Rural History Centre, which has a large collection of otherwise inaccessible pamphlets and articles on agricultural implements and machinery together with an extensive range of manufacturers' records. The Museum of English Rural Life attached to the center has a permanent exhibition of tools and machinery. The British Agricultural History Society publishes the *Agricultural History Review* (1953–), which contains article on farm practice. The North American equivalent is *Agricultural History* (1927–), the Quarterly Journal of the Agricultural History Society, edited at the Center for Agricultural History, Iowa State University.

Payne, F. G. "The British Plough: Some Stages in its Development." *Agricultural History Review* 5.2 (1957), 74–84.

Partridge, Michael. *Early Agricultural Machinery*. London, 1969.

Steensburg, Axel. *Ancient Harvesting Implements: A Study in Archaeology and Human Geography*. Copenhagen, 1943. Over his long career, Axel Steenburg (1906–1999) contributed more than any other individual scholar to the study of early agricultural tools and implements. Especially notable was his pioneering of experimental approaches to the subject. The journal that he founded, *Tools and Tillage* (1968–) is particularly useful for its worldwide coverage. See Alexander Fenton, "Professor Axel Steensburg, 1 June 1906 March 1999," *Review of Scottish Culture* 13 (2000 2001), p. 129.

Tyler, Colin, and Haining, J. *Ploughing by Steam: A History of Steam Cultivation over the Years*. Hemel Hempstead, 1970.

Xing-guang, Wang. "On the Chinese Plough." *Tools and Tillage* 4.2 (1989), 63–93.

White, K. D. *Agricultural Implements of the Roman World*. Cambridge, 1967. An indispensable guide.

NICHOLAS GODDARD

Agricultural Production Systems

This article provides a historical overview of worldwide production systems; the types defined by the American geographer Derwent Whittley follow. The earliest production system, the Mediterranean type, appeared in the Middle East; wheat and barley, sheep, goats, and cattle were the earliest domesticates, and the olive, grape, and fig were added in the fourth millennium BCE. The ox-drawn *ard*, or simple plow, followed. By the end of the Roman Empire, these crops and livestock had spread around the shores of the Mediterranean. Most villages grew cereals and legumes on the better land surrounding the houses.

Grapes for wine and olives were grown on surrounding hilly slopes, while livestock, mainly sheep and goats, were kept on the higher lands in the summer drought and in the lowlands during the winter rainfall. In the sixth and seventh centuries CE, the Arabs introduced citrus fruit, sugar cane, and rice and established elaborate irrigation systems in parts of Spain, although irrigation was not characteristic of most Mediterranean agriculture. Sedentary agriculture declined in North Africa after the Arab invasion, and nomads predominated. There was little change in the Mediterranean farming system until the nineteenth century, when the growth of demand from northern Europe led to the specialization in fruit, vegetables, flowers, and viticulture. The areas of Mediterranean agriculture abroad, in California, Chile, South Africa, and Australia, never had the self-sufficient villages rearing livestock, growing cereals, and fruit and vegetables. In California, sheep rearing in the early nineteenth century gave way to large-scale grain production, but in the twentieth century, the region specialized in the production, with irrigation, of fruit and vegetables and viticulture.

Nomadic Herding. It was once thought that sedentary agriculture in the Middle East evolved from nomadic herding, but the geographer Edward Hahn showed in 1892 that the practice of nomadic herding occurred later than the domestication of crops. The earliest nomads first appeared in Central Asia; sheep, cattle, and goats in varying combinations were tended by herdsmen mounted on horses in Turkestan and eastward, and on camels in the Middle East and North Africa. Livestock were milked but meat rarely eaten, and natural vegetation held in common provided the grazing; herds followed the seasonal movement of rain in well-established patterns. Nomads obtained grain either by force, by trade, or by leaving part of the group to grow crops at a base camp, while the herds migrated. The arrival of European powers in the Middle East and North Africa led to the enforced settlement of tribes and their increasing impoverishment as they lost income from transportation, slavery, and protection. Now found in small numbers, they represent an insignificant type of agriculture with an illustrious—politically—past.

Shifting Cultivation. Also known as "swidden" or "slash and burn," shifting cultivation has shown a similar decline. The earliest farmers cleared woodland or shrub with axes and fire, planted with a minimum of cultivation with hoe or digging stick, sowed a number of crops by hand, and abandoned the land after two or three years, as weeds and falling soil fertility led to falling crop yields. In regions with low population density, it was possible to clear new land, allow the forest to regenerate, and return some twenty years later when the forest cover had restored soil fertility. Livestock were not kept, no manure was used, no weeding was done. Shifting cultivation gave way before rising population densities and the spread of the ox-drawn plow and survives in the upland areas of Southeast Asia and the remaining lowland forest of the Americas. In Africa, a far more complicated version, rotational bush fallow, has much shorter fallows, sometimes planted with leguminous shrubs, permanent fields, and has incorporated cash crops. But livestock and cropping are still separated, and the plow advances slowly.

Wet-Rice Cultivation. In southern China, lowland Southeast Asia, and the eastern and southern parts of the Indian subcontinent, shifting cultivation was replaced in river valleys and deltas by wet-rice cultivation. Rice can be grown in the same way as other cereals, but it gives higher yields if the stalk is partially submerged for much of the growing period. As water has to be withdrawn for weeding and, later, harvesting, this requires an elaborate system of water control—small, flat fields surrounded by bunds and a system of channels to supply and withdraw the water. The water supply is derived either from heavy rainfall in the growing season, provided by the monsoon, or by controlling the natural flooding of rivers or less commonly by reservoirs. Flat land is necessary, but can be created on valley slopes by terracing. However, this is not common. Soil fertility is maintained by silt brought in with water and by blue-green algae in the paddy fields. Wet-rice systems appeared in south China, Japan, and Korea early in the first millennium CE, rather later in India, and later still in some deltas of Southeast Asia, which expanded rice cultivation only in the nineteenth century. The distinctive feature of wet-rice cultivation has been its ability to continuously increase yields by additional labor inputs, thus just maintaining output per head over long periods, a process described by Clifford Geertz as involution. Thus, extra yields have been obtained by using extra manure from humans and pigs, by terracing, by double cropping, by adopting varieties with shorter growing seasons, by transplanting, and by irrigation. This system, with scavenging pigs and poultry, provided a low standard of living for very dense and increasing populations in east and south Asia for more than a millennium; there was little or no attempt to save labor until the 1960s, when much-improved rice varieties, the use of nitrogen fertilizers, and more effective irrigation not only increased crop yields but also was accompanied by some mechanization.

The Plantation System. Europeans had long imported products from the tropics; the spice trade was particularly important, and when the American tropics and subtropics were settled in the seventeenth century, high-value crops that would survive the long journey home, after some processing, were sought. Sugar in the West Indies and tobacco and cotton in the British North American colonies were the solution. The failure of white and indigenous labor led to the import of slaves from Africa. The plantation system became established throughout the tropical Americas and the subtropics, characterized by a large residential labor force, some processing before export, comparatively large farms, and concentration on one crop, although food crops were raised by the slaves for their own subsistence. After the abolition of slavery, at various times in the nineteenth century, the production on farms was undertaken by tenants or independent small holders for central processors. In the nineteenth century, plantations became established in Asia. Often joint-stock companies, they mobilized large labor forces in thinly populated areas and exported to the eastern United States or western Europe. Tea from Assam (after the end of the British East India Company's monopoly of Asian trade), rubber in Malaysia, and coffee in Ceylon are examples. Plantations were less successful in Africa, where colonial governments encouraged small holders to produce such export crops as cacao and opposed the introduction of plantations, except in the Belgian Congo. In the late nineteenth century, small holders began to compete effectively with plantations in Asia. When colonial empires disappeared after 1945, many plantations were nationalized.

Mixed Farming. Farming spread slowly from the Middle East northward to Europe; after the fall of Rome, there slowly emerged a system of mixed farming north of the Alps, based on the manor and villein labor; villages were surrounded by arable fields divided into three unfenced fields, each subdivided into strips, with every farmer having strips in each field. Spring and winter cereals were grown and pulses broadcast on land broken by ox-drawn wheeled plows with colter and moldboard. Every third year, land was left fallow but cultivated to remove weeds. Livestock grazed on the common land that surrounded the open fields, as well as on the fallow and the arable after harvest. Crop yields were low. After the fourteenth century, rent began to replace villein services, and serfdom declined, lasting longest in Russia. The slow adoption in northern Europe of alfalfa and clover provided hay for cattle feed and nitrogen for the soil. The fodder roots, and later potatoes and sugar beet, and the use of the drill in the eighteenth century allowed cultivation of the land during crop growth and eliminated the need for fallow. Animal and crop husbandry were integrated, with roots and legumes feeding more animals, which provided more manure that raised cereal yields. Horses replaced oxen, iron plows were adopted in the eighteenth century, and drills and harrows became commonplace. These advances were made easier where the enclosure of land took place, eliminating collective regulations and allowing the consolidation of fragmented farms, a process not completed in much of Europe outside Great Britain and Scandinavia until after 1945. This long process of change was begun mainly on small farms in the Netherlands in the seventeenth century, was adopted in eighteenth-century England, and spread in the nineteenth and twentieth centuries to the rest of Europe. In North America, the abundance of land meant there was less intensive farming, but from the 1860s there evolved a system used in the growing of maize to feed pigs and cattle; the Corn Belt was a form of mixed farming.

Specialized Methods. In the mid-nineteenth century, the impact of industrialization began to have a profound impact on agricultural production systems; farms sold an increasing proportion of output off the farms; manufacturing industry provided machinery and chemical fertilizers; the fall in oceanic freight rates and the expansion of the railway network encouraged international trade; and after the 1850s, higher wages in the manufacturing industry attracted agricultural labor into the towns. Eventually, the agricultural labor force declined in developed countries, prompting the introduction of labor-saving machines. These processes also led to specialization on the farm and by region, and the emergence of new types of farming from mixed farming. There had been milking since the fourth millennium BCE, although rarely in tropical Africa or East Asia, where a high proportion of the population suffers from lactose malabsorption. In Europe, cattle were valued as draft animals, milk yields were very low, and there was no controlled breeding. Dairying as a specialization occurred only in areas unsuited to cereal production. Milk consumption remained low; but in the nineteenth century, the rise of incomes prompted an expansion of demand for fresh milk, aided by the railway, and for butter and cheese, which could be produced in less-accessible areas with good grass growth. A series of inventions on the farms, such as milking machinery, the breeding of specialist dairy cattle, including the Friesian and Brown Swiss, and the introduction of cheese and butter factories in the 1850s led to the increasing importance of dairying, especially in the Netherlands, Denmark, New Zealand, and the eastern United States.

Ranching. In the newly settled areas overseas, two quite new production systems emerged in the nineteenth century. Ranching began with the Spanish, who took long-horned cattle to the Americas in the sixteenth century, which rapidly multiplied. They were herded on open ranges by mounted herdsmen, rounded up annually, and calves were branded. These techniques and the herdsmen's distinctive dress were derived from Andalusia. Kept initially for their hides, cattle were numerous in the llanos, *sertao,* and pampas grasslands of South America and were also taken north into Texas. Ranchers in the United States raised cattle on the prairies after the American Civil War, and ranching later became intensified. Herefords replaced longhorns, cattle were fattened on feedlots, and the open range was replaced by enclosed private properties. But industrial growth meant ranching flourished, with markets for meat in the eastern United States and western Europe; in Australia and New Zealand, sheep were raised in a similar manner, though mainly for wool. But ranching was pushed ever outward into less-humid areas by advancing farmers.

Large-Scale Grain Production. Large-scale grain production emerged as a form of agriculture on the prairies of North America, the steppes of Russia, the pampas of Argentina, and in southeastern Australia, all thinly populated. Much of this grain was exported to Europe, initially for flour and later also as animal feed. From the 1860s, a series of inventions, including the combine harvester, led to the establishment of large mechanized farms with few workers, producing mainly cereals, especially wheat, and with no livestock. In the twentieth century, these systems became more diversified and intensified; in Australia, for example, wheat and sheep production were combined on the same farm.

Farmers have not added to the crops and livestock available from two or three thousand years ago, although they have dispersed from their source regions around the world. The way in which these crops and animals are raised—the production systems—has changed substantially, prompted by growing commercialization, slow advances in technology, and changes in institutions, such as the decline of serfdom or the abolition of slavery. But perhaps the major changes came in the nineteenth century as industrialization increased demand and made available the inputs to increase output, allowing the emergence of regional specialization in production systems.

[*See also* Open Field System.]

BIBLIOGRAPHY

Courtenay, Percy Phillip. *Plantation Agriculture.* 2d ed. London, 1980. Modern account but with useful chapters on historical development.

Dale, Edward E. *The Range Cattle Industry: Ranching on the Great Plains from 1865 to 1925.* Norman, Okla., 1960. One of many books on American ranching.

Dovring, Folke. "The Transformation of European Agriculture." In *Cambridge Economic History of Europe,* vol. 6 (2), *The Industrial Revolutions and After,* edited by H. J. Habakkuk and M. M. Postan, pp. 603–672. Cambridge, 1965. Good account of the emergence of modern farming in Europe.

Dunsdorf, Edgars. *The Australian Wheat Growing Industry, 1788–1948.* Melbourne, 1956.

Geertz, Clifford. *Agricultural Involution: The Process of Ecological Change in Indonesia.* Berkeley, 1963.

Grigg, David. *The Agricultural Systems of the World: An Evolutionary Approach.* Cambridge, 1974. Discussion of modern (1960s) characteristics of major types of farming with much on their historical evolution.

Jensen, Einar. *Danish Agriculture: Its Economic Development.* Copenhagen, 1937. Excellent account of emergence of dairying in Denmark.

Needham, Joseph. *Science and Civilisation in China,* vol. 6, *Biology and Biological Technology,* part 2, *Agriculture,* by Francesca Bray, pp. 1–724. Cambridge, 1984.

Slicher van Bath, Bernard H. "Agriculture in the Vital Revolution." In *Cambridge Economic History of Europe*, vol. 5, *The Economic Organisation of Early Modern Agriculture*, edited by E. E. Rich and C. H. Wilson, pp. 42–132. Cambridge, 1981.

Spencer, Joseph E. *Shifting Cultivation in Southeastern Asia*. University of California Publications in Geography, no. 19. Berkeley, 1966. More modern than historical but useful.

Stamp, Laurence D. *A History of Land Use on Arid Regions*. Arid Zone Research, no. 17, UNESCO. Paris, 1961. Several essays covering major types of farming. Especially good on North Africa.

Whittley, Derwent. "Major Agricultural Regions of the World." *Annals of the Association of American Geographers* 26 (1936), 199–240.

DAVID GRIGG

Property Rights and Tenure Systems

Both today and in the past, agricultural land has been farmed under a wide variety of property rights and tenure systems. In some places, farmland is owned individually; in others, it belong to groups, such as tribes and lineages in parts of modern Africa. At times, the ownership of agricultural property is widespread; in others, only a minority possess land. This variation in property rights and the distribution of land ownership in turn leads to enormous differences in the way agriculture is organized. In many cases, fields have been cultivated by the sort of owner-operators who have predominated in the American Midwest and in much of western Europe since the nineteenth century. But in others, they have been tilled by serfs or slaves, or worked by tenants, sharecroppers, day laborers, or hired hands.

To make sense of this enormous variation in agricultural property rights and tenure systems across the world and throughout the past, the place to begin is at the idealized world of perfect markets. A look at the actual distribution of land ownership and its effects on farm operation and tenure systems is next. After surveying the economics of farm tenancy and the variation in tenancy over time and space, we turn to the question of individual ownership versus group property. Throughout, the emphasis is on the economic impact that property rights and tenure systems have.

Labor, Land Sales, and Rental Markets. Given the breadth of the subject, some sort of guide is necessary. Although there are many places to which one could turn (the subject has intrigued anthropologists, historians, sociologists, and political scientists), it is economics that draws the clearest map of property rights and tenure systems in agriculture. To read the map, imagine an idealized world of perfect markets and clearly defined and costlessly enforced property rights in agriculture. This is, of course, a world that has never existed, but it will nonetheless lead the way through the thicket of actual property rights in real-world agriculture. Assume that land and labor are unevenly distributed, with some individuals having little or no property and others possessing too many fields to cultivate themselves. In this idealized world, one could imagine three sorts of transactions that would resolve the uneven distribution of property. First, property owners with too much land could sell it to the land poor on a land-sales market. Second, they could rent it out in a land-tenancy market. Third, they could turn to the labor market and hire the landless to work their land as hired hands or day laborers. Any of the three types of transactions would suffice; it would not be necessary to use more than one of the three markets for land sales, land tenancy, and labor.

Reality, of course, is quite different, for in the real world all three markets are often in operation simultaneously, even though in theory only one of them would suffice. Why then do labor, land-sales, and land-rental markets exist when one alone would do? One plausible answer is that in the real world, it is more difficult to monitor workers in agriculture than in other occupations. Because they are dispersed across fields, it is costly to supervise them and to keep them from loafing on the job. Worse yet, if they mistreat animals or do a poor job of sowing seeds, the resulting damage may not appear until months later, when it is impossible to tell who was at fault. Problems of this sort have vexed land owners for centuries, and because they do raise the cost of farming with hired labor, they give an advantage to the owner-operator, who can employ family labor and dispense with the monitoring.

We might therefore expect that owner-operators would predominate in farming as land owners sold off the property that they could not farm with their own family labor. But that has not been the case in the past, and even today a significant fraction of farmland is farmed by tenants or by hired labor. According to the 1970 World Census of Agriculture, only 61 percent of the world's agricultural property was farmed by owners who did not rent any land, and even some of them may in fact have been disguised tenants or mere employers of hired labor.

One reason ownership does not triumph everywhere is that land-sales markets are often inactive. Although they have long existed, land-sales markets are often dormant for a variety of reasons: failure of credit markets that are needed to fund sales; legal or institutional limits on who can possess farmland; and social, cultural, and political obstacles to establishing widespread individual ownership of land. Particularly in the past, rulers and states have often given agricultural land to elites and then intervened to keep it from falling into the hands of peasants, who would otherwise have become owner-operators. Elites received land grants or exclusive rights to choice farmland in Asia and Europe during the Middle Ages, and in Latin America and Africa after colonization. Peasants were then typically forced to pay tribute in the form of higher taxes or required labor duties on elite estates. To keep the peasants from

SERFS AND LORDS. Peasants receive orders from their lord before going to work in the fields. Miniature from *Propriétaire des choses*, fifteenth-century manuscript. (Bibliothèque de l'Arsenal, Paris/North Wind Picture Archives)

moving away or from devoting all their effort to their own farmland, their mobility or their right to own or rent land was often restricted. Alternatively, their access to crop markets might be limited, as in colonial Africa, or they might be denied access to public goods and services. The precise details of their treatment varied greatly from place to place, but the effect was to keep large farms in the hands of elites and to diminish the amount of land cultivated by owner-operators. The situation would be likely to change only with land reform, as in South Korea after World War II, or during political upheavals, such as the French Revolution.

Where peasants ended up tied to the soil and owing labor duties, they provided the work force on large elite farms, as in parts of eastern Europe from the end of the Middle Ages up until the nineteenth century. Many historians also believe that a similar kind of serfdom existed in much of western Europe in the Middle Ages, but Douglass C. North and Robert P. Thomas argue that serfdom in the medieval West was actually quite different. In their view, western serfdom was not the sort of involuntary servitude found in eastern Europe; rather, it was a voluntary contract brought on by the collapse of product markets and of centralized political authority. They contend that without product markets, bargaining costs were too high for lords of medieval manors to use tenants or wage labor. Instead, the lords offered peasants hereditary serfdom in return for

the protection that higher political authorities could not provide. Peasants entered into serfdom voluntarily, committing themselves and their heirs to give the lord fixed labor duties in return for protection. Serfdom in the West disappeared, according to North and Thomas, only when population growth and the revival of product markets cut the relative cost of alternative contractual arrangements. Here other historians stress somewhat different reasons for serfdom's ultimate disappearance in western Europe, such as the return of centralized political authorities who intervened on the serfs' behalf, or the ease with which serfs could flee manors and seek refuge in western Europe's growing towns.

Obviously, serfdom is not the only way that elites have worked their estates. Where slavery was permitted and the agricultural technology made it feasible, elite farms used slaves, as in the American South, the Caribbean, and parts of Latin America before emancipation in the nineteenth century. Such elite estates could survive the emancipation of the slaves or the end of labor duties, if they were large enough to take advantage of economies of scale in monitoring labor. The elite could then hire free workers to work their farms, as in parts of Latin America today. (In Latin America, hired labor might have the added advantage of protecting landlords against pressure to redistribute land to tenants during land reform.)

Tenancy. What happens if an elite farm is too small to realize economies of scale in monitoring and the land market was too thin to break the farm up and sell it to owner-operators? What does a landlord do in that case? Renting the property out to tenants is the obvious alternative, and it turns out to be widespread in those parts of the world where the distribution of farmland is not so unequal that hiring labor becomes economical, for example, in much of South and Southeast Asia and parts of Latin America today, and from the end of the Middle Ages on in much of western Europe. Tenancy is also common even in areas of owner occupancy because it evens out variations in the distribution of family labor over the life cycle and corrects for difficulties with the land-sales market and changes in the efficient scale of farming.

Tenancy, however, has its own problem. It might at first glance seem an easy matter to rent out agricultural property: the landlord would simply charge a fixed rent, and the tenant would then have all the incentives to farm properly. At the margin, the tenant would pay all the costs and reap all the benefits from his decisions, for he would not have to share the increased output from working an additional hour or applying another wagonload of fertilizer. Economic theory then suggests that he would farm in the same way that an owner-operator would.

But tenancy is not that simple. To begin with, there are problems with long-lived capital that belonged to the landlord, particularly toward the end of a lease. The tenant might be tempted to misuse this capital because he could do so without bearing the costs. To consider a particular example, consider western Europe in the early modern period (roughly 1500 to 1800), when tenancy had grown common. Fixed-rent tenants were often accused of neglecting buildings and of ignoring problems with ditches that caused flooding and erosion long after their leases had expired. They were also charged with cutting grape vines too short, which boosted the yield during their tenure but reduced productivity thereafter. Worst of all—at least according to manuals for landlords and records of property administration—was the risk that tenants would go broke and not pay the fixed rent to which they had agreed.

Nor are these the only problems with tenancy. It may simply prove to be very difficult to find a tenant who will agree to a fixed-rent lease. Paying a fixed rent means assuming all the risks of farming, and in the absence of perfect insurance markets, a prospective tenant may well hesitate before engaging in such a gamble. Alternatively, he may have difficulty raising the working capital needed for a farm, either because credit markets have failed or because there is no rental market for certain kinds of agricultural capital, such as livestock. The landlord may then have to supply him credit, capital, or other inputs—even untraded ones, such as managerial skill. All of these problems may make a fixed-rent lease much less attractive for the landlord, and both he and the tenant may prefer a lease in which they share the output—a sharecropping contract. Such a contract reduces the risks the tenant faces, while still giving him an incentive (albeit a reduced one) to work the farm. After all, if he does absolutely nothing, there will be no crops to share.

We might therefore expect to find more share tenancy where tenants were poor. Indigent tenants would presumably be more risk averse, in part because they would not possess assets that could be sold during crises. They would also lack capital and the collateral needed to borrow. Other things being equal, they would therefore be more likely to sharecrop than to pay a fixed rent. The frequency of sharecropping would also depend on the landlord's characteristics. A landlord who could monitor tenants at lower cost might prefer sharecropping (or even wage labor) to a fixed-rent lease. His monitoring costs might be lower, for example, if he lived on or near his farm property, or if he had to check on long-lived capital, such as vines, no matter what sort of contract he had to use. They were presumably low, too, for small-scale landowners and for those engaged in an ongoing relationship with their tenants, for example, landlords who were relatives or close friends of their tenants.

Predictions of this sort have been subjected to a number of empirical tests. Sometimes the evidence has been gathered in developing countries. In other instances, it has been historical, coming from Renaissance Italy, from early modern France, and from the American South after slavery was outlawed and tenancy took its place. Whatever the source, the studies usually confirm the predicted relationships between the characteristics of landlords and tenants and the choice of agricultural tenancy (or wage) contracts.

Obviously, the choice of a tenancy contract or the decision to hire wage labor depends on more than just landlords' and tenants' characteristics. We have already mentioned how these decisions are influenced by the distribution of property. They can be affected by wages and relative prices and by social and legal constraints, too. In sixteenth- and seventeenth-century Japan, agrarian laws limited tenancy, and much agricultural land was therefore cultivated by hired laborers. De facto tenancy gradually developed, however, and many laborers became de facto tenants, particularly when the Meiji government (1868–1912) modernized property rights and legitimized tenancy. Similarly, in parts of India, social sanctions prevented members of lower castes from owning or renting land, and they ended up working for higher caste landowners as farm laborers. Land reform in India created further incentives to hire labor because land cultivated by labor was usually exempt from laws that transferred agricultural property to tenants and did not fully compensate landlords.

What effect did these agricultural contracts and land tenure systems have on the efficiency of farms? Unfortunately, tests for efficiency are difficult, even with current-day evidence, and most of the tests have at best simply compared sharecropping, fixed-rent leases, and owner cultivation. One of the best studies (Shaban, 1987) finds little difference between ownership and fixed-rent leases, but sharecropping turns out to be less efficient than either of them. The evidence, however, is Indian, and Indian land reform laws discourage landlords from entering into certain kinds of contracts, such as fixed-rent leases. The peculiarity of the Indian situation may well explain why studies elsewhere have found no differences in efficiency between sharecropping and fixed-rent leases.

Group Ownership. So far, we have implicitly assumed that each piece of agricultural property belongs to a particular individual who has exclusive rights to sell it, profit from it, and cultivate it as he sees fit, without interference from other people. We have supposed, in other words, that property rights are absolute, private, and individual and that any one individual's rights do not overlap another's. Such an assumption is not unreasonable, for individual rights to own and sell farmland are widespread, and contrary to what such scholars as Karl Polanyi have maintained, they have a long history. Still, for much of history—and for much of the world today—individual ownership is not the only type of property right one encounters.

Often groups of individuals—a village, an extended family, a serf and a lord—may share rights to use a piece of property, as with common grazing land. Such group rights tend to prevail in a variety of situations: where agriculture makes extensive use of land, as with herding; where the cost of fencing or of registering title to land is high; where low land values reduce the benefits from establishing individual rights; and where groups maintain rights to property. They are particularly common in current-day Africa. There, property in pastoral regions may be managed by large ethnic groups, and arable land can often be reallocated by chiefs or heads of lineages, even though households may have rights to use it or even pass it down to their descendants.

In addition to group rights, one person's farming may interfere with his neighbors, creating what economists call an externality. In parts of medieval and early modern Europe, for example, each peasant farmed a collection of scattered strips of land, in a land tenure system known as open-field agriculture, since the tiny strips were too expensive to fence. Peasants farmed this way (so Deirdre McCloskey has argued) because the scattering provided a form of insurance: a strip near a hilltop survived a flood, for example, while one in a damp valley bottom bore crops in a drought. With such a land-tenure system, reaping grain on one strip would have obviously meant trampling the crops on adjacent strips—an externality—had it not been for regulations that coordinated harvest on every piece of land. Similar problems arise with drainage and irrigation. To take the example of the open fields again, it was often impossible to drain one marshy strip of farmland without doing the same for all the neighboring ones. The drainage is what economists call a public good: if one person gets it, so must all of his neighbors.

These group rights, externalities, and public goods can create serious political and economic problems. Although public goods, such as irrigation and drainage, may be highly profitable investments, it may prove impossible to get landowners to agree on a drainage or irrigation project. Each owner may prefer to let others bear the costs of getting the project going (in the jargon of economics, this is called free riding). Worse yet, he may be able to use the legal system to hold the project up for ransom by demanding a disproportionate share of the benefits from draining or irrigating. The clearest examples of such strategic behavior come from eighteenth-century France, where it was encouraged by the legal system until the judicial reforms of the French Revolution.

Can these economic problems be solved by creating individual private property rights to land? In some cases, the answer is certainly yes, for there are examples of individual private property rights boosting agricultural productivity and agricultural investment—at Jamestown Colony

in colonial Virginia, for example, and in developing countries in current-day Southeast Asia. But in other instances, individual property rights have not had such an effect. In early modern England, for example, enclosures brought an end to the open fields and their regulations by consolidating the scattered strips and fencing them in. But contrary to the hope of agricultural reformers, farm productivity usually did not rise greatly. The creation of individual property rights has apparently failed to stimulate investment and agricultural productivity in a number of African countries, also.

The moral here may well be that the group agricultural property rights one sees in small societies may be nearly optimal much of the time. The same may hold for the sort of regulations adopted in small societies to deal with externalities in agriculture (in open-field villages, for example). Repeated interaction among the members of the society is what keeps the group rights and regulations close to optimal, and in some cases it can even bring about adjustment of property rights as relative prices change. Simply imposing individual property rights may not always increase agricultural productivity. In some cases, it will, as in Southeast Asia. But in others it will not, and it can cause enormous political problems by redistributing wealth.

BIBLIOGRAPHY

GENERAL STUDIES

Binswanger, Hans, Klaus Deininger, and Gershon Feder. "Power, Distortions, Revolt, and Reform in Agricultural Land Relations." In *Handbook of Development Economics*, vol. 3B edited by Jehre Behrman and T. N. Srinivasan, pp. 2659–2772. Amsterdam, 1995. Overview of the history and current state of agricultural land relations throughout the world.

Ellickson, Robert C. "Property in Land." *Yale Law Journal* 102.6 (April 1993), 1315–1400. Clear analysis of the law of property rights and its evolution.

Otsuka, Keijiro, Hiroyuki Chuma, and Yujiro Hayami. "Land and Labor Contracts in Agrarian Economies: Theories and Facts." *Journal of Economic Literature* 30 (December 1992), 1965–2018. Theory and facts about land tenancy today.

Ray, Debraj. *Development Economics*. Princeton, 1998. The economics of contract choice in agriculture and how it is influenced by the distribution of property.

STUDIES OF DEVELOPING COUNTRIES

Alston, Lee J., Gary D. Libecap, and Bernardo Mueller. "Violence and the Development of Property Rights to Land in the Brazilian Amazon." In *The Frontiers of the New Institutional Economics*, edited by John N. Drobak and John V. C. Nye, pp. 145–163. San Diego, 1997.

Bates, Robert. *Beyond the Miracle of the Market: The Political Economy of Agrarian Development in Kenya*. Cambridge, 1989.

Ensminger, Jean. "Changing Property Rights: Reconciling Formal and Informal Rights to Land in Africa." In *Frontiers of the New Institutional Economics*, edited by John N. Drobak and John V. C. Nye, pp. 165–196. San Diego, 1997. Overview of changing agricultural property rights in Africa.

Shaban, Radwan Ali. "Testing between Competing Models of Sharecropping." *Journal of Political Economy* 95.5 (1987), 893–920. Test of the efficiency of tenancy contracts in India.

HISTORICAL STUDIES IN EUROPE AND NORTH AMERICA

Allen, Robert C. *Enclosure and the Yeoman*. Oxford, 1992.

Aston, T. H., and C. H. E. Philpin, eds. *The Brenner Debate: Agrarian Class Structure and Economic Development in Pre-industrial Europe*. Cambridge, 1985.

Clark, Gregory. "Commons Sense: Common Property Rights, Efficiency, and Institutional Change." *Journal of Economic History* 58.1 (March 1998), 73–102.

Domar, Evsey D. "The Causes of Slavery or Serfdom: A Hypothesis." *Journal of Economic History* 30.1 (March 1970), 18–32. Model of serfdom in eastern Europe.

Fenoaltea, Stefano. "The Rise and Fall of a Theoretical Model: The Manorial System." *Journal of Economic History* 35.2 (June 1975), 386–409. Criticism of North and Thomas.

Hoffman, Philip T. *Growth in a Traditional Society: The French Countryside, 1450–1815*. Princeton, 1996.

Kantor, Shawn Everett. *Politics and Property Rights: The Closing of the Open Range in the Postbellum South*. Chicago, 1998. Best example of the politics of agricultural property rights reform.

McCloskey, Donald (Dierdre). "The Economics of Enclosure: A Market Analysis." In *European Peasants and Their Markets*, edited by William N. Parker and Eric L. Jones, pp. 132–133. Princeton, 1975.

McCloskey, Donald (Dierdre). "The Persistence of English Common Fields." In *European Peasants and Their Markets*, edited by William N. Parker and Eric L. Jones, pp. 73–119. Princeton, 1975.

North, Douglass C., and Robert Paul Thomas. "The Rise and Fall of the Manorial System: A Theoretical Model." *Journal of Economic History* 31.4 (December 1971), 777–803.

Rosenthal, Jean-Laurent. *The Fruits of Revolution: Property Rights, Litigation, and French Agriculture, 1700–1860*. Cambridge, 1992. Drainage, irrigation, and agricultural property rights in France.

PHILIP T. HOFFMAN

Agricultural Inputs, Productivity, and Wages

Agricultural output is obtained in all societies by combining three fundamental inputs: land, labor, and capital. The first two of these inputs are obvious and tangible: acres of land and man-days of labor. The third, capital, is a little mysterious to those not versed in economics. But its presence is real to actual cultivators. Capital is required as an input because production takes time. Seed must be planted in the ground and labor applied in tilling and fertilizing the soil, long before the resulting crops are sold. Thus, the wages of farm laborers must be paid months before the output they produce is sold. Similarly, fixed capital such as buildings, fences, roads, land drainage, animals, and tools must be provided. The money tied up in fixed capital and crops in progress could be invested to produce income elsewhere. Thus, the provider of capital is just as much a contributor to the production enterprise as the owners of land and labor. Since the late nineteenth century, agriculture also has used large amounts of purchased inputs such as manufactured fertilizers, and this complicates the measurement of productivity. But for most agricultural systems in the world before 1900, purchased inputs were negligible. So the focus here is on land, labor, and capital.

Measuring Productivity. The productivity of an agricultural system is a measure of how much output is obtained per unit of each of these three inputs. Measuring output would be easy if there were only one output, such as wheat. But all agricultural systems produce multiple outputs, and a measure of output has to combine them in some way. The normal way of aggregating the various outputs into one measure is to weight them by their relative prices. Thus, if one wanted to compare output across different economies, one might calculate output as bushels of wheat-equivalent, weighting other outputs on the basis of their prices relative to wheat. Unfortunately, relative prices of products will vary across different countries and epochs depending on the climate, demand conditions, and the agricultural technology. So converting everything into wheat equivalents is still an imperfect way of comparing outputs.

There are, however, other possible weightings of outputs. A researcher interested in the capacity of an agricultural system to feed a population might want to weight outputs by the calorific content of each food. Output in this case would be expressed in kilocalories. Such a measure has been used by some historians, such as Paul Bairoch. In this case, spices such as garlic or pepper would get zero weight, as would fibers and wood, while foods rich in calories such as grains would get a high weighting. (Thus the claim made by some ethical vegetarians that the agricultural systems of rich economies are inefficient because of their wasteful production of meat and dairy products, which require much more input of land per calorie produced than do grain and root crops.) A researcher interested in human stature might even weight by the protein content of different outputs.

Economists generally use the price weighting for two reasons. First, in a competitive market for agricultural output, the relative price of products will reveal, on the margin, how much consumers value each type of output. Filet mignon may be a wasteful agricultural output in terms of the calories produced per acre, but a product that yields much satisfaction to its consumers is revealed by how much they are prepared to sacrifice to get their bloody treat. Poor people eat foods that incur the lowest costs to produce per unit of calories: grains and potatoes. So if output is measured in kilocalories, early agricultural systems will seem much more productive compared with modern systems if price weighting is used. Second, if one assumes that cultivators manage their holdings with the objective of maximizing their profits, then they will try to maximize the productivity of land measuring output by price weighting. Farmers will not care about the calorie content of their output. Their concern is how much money their output fetches in the market. Price-weighted output weighting is thus the best measure of how well cultivators are doing, measured in terms of what they are trying to maximize.

Measuring inputs of land, labor, and capital similarly encounters these same issues of how to aggregate different types of land, different types of labor done at different times of the year, and different types of capital. In the case of labor, for example, the wage often varies greatly across the year. Should a day of harvest labor, paid in England in 1720 at 20d. per day, count the same as a day of winter labor when the pay was only 10d. in measuring the total labor input? And should the labor of a woman, paid for at perhaps only 30 to 40 percent of the wage of a man's labor, count for as much labor input as a man's? Again, the principle that should be applied in the case of profit-maximizing farms is to measure the total quantity of all inputs by weighting them using their relative prices. Thus, women and children would count as a minor labor input in most preindustrial agricultural systems because of the wage disparity between men and women. The reason for weighting labor inputs according to the relative wages is again that profit-maximizing cultivators will try to minimize total labor costs in making their hiring decisions. If the value in producing output of a day of woman's labor was really the same as a day of man's labor, then cultivators would prefer to hire women only and would bid up the wage ratio until it equaled the relative productivities of women and men.

Output per acre is land productivity, output per man-day of labor input is labor productivity, and output per unit of capital is capital productivity. Treatments of agricultural history by historians have tended to focus on land productivity alone as a measure of the development and sophistication of agricultural systems. Thus, the early studies of medieval European agricultural productivity, for example, focused almost exclusively on the productivity of grain cultivation per acre (van Bath, 1963). Because of difficulties in knowing the area corresponding to local land measures and the quantities corresponding to local grain measures, these studies of early arable yields often express them in terms of yields per seed.

Medieval Europe seemed to have a miserably unproductive agriculture on this basis since across most of medieval Europe, grain yields were low. On the estates of the bishop of Winchester and of Westminster Abbey in southern England, for example, the gross yield averaged only 3 to 4 grains per seed sown. The yield per sown acre was only about 11 bushels on the Winchester manors in the years from 1208 to 1452. In contrast, estates in Roman Egypt typically yielded about tenfold for wheat, equivalent to 17 bushels per acre. The work on medieval and early modern English grain yields has been improved by later researchers such as Bruce Campbell and Mark Overton, who widen the measure of land productivity to include the effects of crop mix and of the amount of land kept fallow. But

pastoral agriculture was important also, and here the yield evidence tends to be poorer. Van Bath and others quote evidence on the size of animals, but this says little directly about the production of pastoral products per acre. Good indications exist regarding the numbers of animals per acre for medieval estate agriculture, for example, but little evidence on the sizes or productivity of the animals. (There are signs that farm animals in medieval England may have been much smaller than even their eighteenth-century counterparts.) But even a wider measure of land productivity incorporating pastoral products and timber would still measure only one aspect of agricultural productivity.

Where data are unavailable on these wider measures of output, a reasonable measure of land productivity in preindustrial agriculture will simply be the population supported per acre of land. This measure is imperfect since even in preindustrial societies, food consumption per capita varied considerably. But when one learns that circa 1800 there were 166 people per square mile in England, compared with 226 in Japan, one knows that land productivity in Japan was likely higher than in England (given the large share of unproductive mountainous land in Japan). That there were 875 people per square mile in Jiangsu in China in 1787 shows that the coastal regions of China (such as Jiangsu) likely had an even higher land productivity compared with England. One may argue that these densities were based on paddy rice cultivation, an option not open to most of Europe. But even in the wheat regions of Shantung and Hopei, Chinese population densities in 1787 were more than double those of England and France. Similarly, a population of 14 per square mile in Tahiti, when the Europeans first made contact, implies a much lower land productivity than in Europe, despite the favorable climate in Tahiti.

The high population densities of coastal Japan and China compared with Europe circa 1800 does not, however, necessarily imply that Japanese and Chinese agriculture systems were more productive overall. Any overall assessment of the achievement and development of preindustrial agricultural systems has to look also at labor and capital productivity, for it is possible in a given agricultural system to increase output per acre by reducing output per worker or per unit of capital. Thus, land farmed as market gardens by spade cultivation will produce many times the value of output per acre than regular cropland. But it does so by the application of huge amounts of labor per acre and often large quantities of organic manures. If farmers are seeking to maximize profits, they will use intensively any input that is relatively cheap, thus driving down the productivity of that factor, but driving up the productivity of the other factors of production. For this reason, the correct way to examine the performance of agricultural systems over time is to take a weighted average of the productivities of land, labor, and capital, weighting by the share of each factor in production costs. Thus, if we denote by Q, output; L, labor; K, capital; and T, land, the productivities of labor, capital, and land will be given by (Q/L), (Q/K), and (Q/T). The overall or "total factor productivity," $\mathbf{A}$, can thus be measured either through an arithmetic weighting as

$$\mathbf{A} = \alpha_K \left(\frac{Q}{K} \right) + \alpha_L \left(\frac{Q}{L} \right) + \alpha_T \left(\frac{Q}{T} \right),$$

or more conventionally by a geometric weighting as

$$\mathbf{A} = \left(\frac{Q}{K} \right)^{\alpha_K} \left(\frac{Q}{L} \right)^{\alpha_L} \left(\frac{Q}{T} \right)^{\alpha_T}.$$

The two indexes will show different measured productivity gains only if the productivity gains differ across the inputs. In this case, the geometric index always shows a smaller gain in overall productivity. But in most practical cases, particularly for preindustrial agriculture where productivity gains were limited, the two methods will give similar measures. Thus, suppose output per unit of capital increases by 100 percent, while output per acre and per worker does not change, and capital, labor, and land each get paid one-third of the output. Then on the arithmetic index, total factor productivity has increased by 33 percent. On the geometric index, it has increased by only 26 percent. The geometric weighting is generally preferred because productivity gains tend to differ across the inputs, and this index assumes that an input whose productivity increases more than the others is used proportionately less in production.

Difficulties in Measuring Productivity. Measures of output per worker in preindustrial agriculture have been much more difficult than measures of output per acre. The labor input on family farms in the farming enterprise is hard to measure from the surviving documents, since many accounts of labor use were constructed as checks on the honesty of managers or as records that workers had indeed been paid for their labor. It is thus generally impossible to determine who was working on family farms and how long they worked per year before the arrival either of population censuses, which detailed those residing on farms and their occupations, or of modern survey research methods as practiced by Chayanov in Russia in the 1900s or John Lossing Buck in China in the 1920s. On large estates, the accounting system makes these calculations possible in an earlier epoch. Thus, medieval English manors kept accounting records of the amount of labor purchased. But even here the difficulties are legion, so that no direct measure of labor productivity even in a country as well documented as medieval England is available. On English manors, some workers such as threshers or reapers were paid by the piece, so that the days of their labor input must be inferred from an estimate of their productivity on these

tasks. Some workers were hired year round: shepherds, carters, and plowmen. But the number of days per year these workers were expected to work is unknown. In nineteenth-century England, a year-round worker worked nearly three hundred days per year. But these medieval estate workers likely had their own holdings that they worked on part time. (The reason for suspecting that their labor was not a full three hundred days is, first, that this would make their day wage much lower than for workers hired for shorter periods, a phenomenon that we do not see in the nineteenth century. Second, some of these workers were possessors of their own farms, which they would need to work on sometimes.) Finally, on many estates the dependent peasantry were required to contribute labor rents each week. Even when the number of days the peasants worked is known, there is dispute over whether peasants so engaged put in a full day's work. Many medieval scholars believe the day of corvée labor was only half a regular day.

These difficulties in measuring labor productivity in preindustrial agriculture by direct measurement of the labor input have led to indirect methods that use the share of the population employed in agriculture, or the share living in urban areas, as the basis for an estimate of labor productivity. In recent years, it has been learned that in societies in which agriculture is a small share of employment, people reside in cities. When agriculture takes up a large share of employment, people reside in the countryside. If one is willing to assume that this relationship between urbanization and employment in agriculture holds for earlier societies, then one can estimate the agricultural labor force from the fraction of the population living in cities. Going further, one of the first proponents of this method, Anthony Wrigley, assumed that food consumption per capita would be constant in preindustrial economies. In this case, labor productivity in agriculture is given only by the degree of urbanization, with some allowance for imports or exports of food.

The assumption of constant food consumption per capita is not realistic, however, since urbanization is also an index of the level of income per capita in a society, and richer societies consume more food than poorer ones. Gunnar Persson adjusted Wrigley's method to account for this. More recently, Robert Allen also allowed food consumption per capita to vary with the price of food relative to other products. Looking at the agricultural systems of Austria, Belgium, England, France, Germany, Italy, the Netherlands, Poland, and Spain, he concludes that most of these countries saw little increase in labor productivity in agriculture from 1300 to 1800. Indeed, Austria, Italy, Germany, and Spain all saw declines in labor productivity. Surprisingly, despite the poor reputation of agriculture in eastern Europe, Poland generally ranks in the top half of these countries in terms of labor productivity.

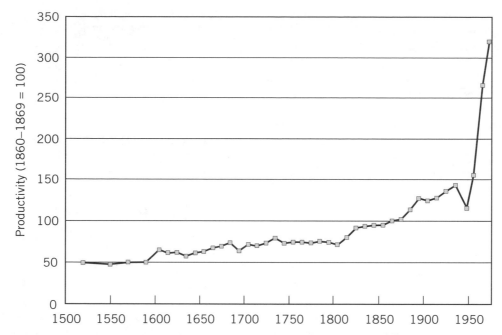

FIGURE 1. The overall productivity of English agriculture, 1500–1974. The productivity index is set at 100 from 1860–1869. The decline in measured productivity from the 1930s to the late 1940s is presumably a result of the disruptions caused by World War II. SOURCE: Clark, n.d.

In practice, it is hard to measure the capital inputs used in agriculture. Thus, it is hard to estimate the overall productivity of an agricultural system from the formulas given above. But there is a result from economic theory that can be utilized here. That is, if the outputs and the inputs are purchased in competitive markets, then the overall productivity of the system can be measured equivalently by the formula

$$\mathbf{A} = \prod_{i,j} \frac{\omega_j^{\theta_j}}{p_i^{\alpha_i}}$$

where $\mathbf{A}$ is an index of productivity, p_i is the price of output i, and α is the share of output i in the value of output, ω_j is the renumeration paid to input j, and θ_j is the share of input j in the total payments to inputs. In particular, if there is only one output, price p, and the traditional three inputs of capital, labor, and land, whose respective costs are r, w, and s, then productivity will be given by

$$\mathbf{A} = \left(\frac{r}{p}\right)^{\alpha_K} \left(\frac{w}{p}\right)^{\alpha_L} \left(\frac{s}{p}\right)^{\alpha_T}.$$

To apply this price measure exactly requires knowledge of the cost shares of each input in production. This share, as seen above, is not available for capital. But assuming that the cost shares did not vary too much over time, or to use ancillary evidence on cost shares, then this formula will approximate productivity movements even if only the cost of various inputs is known, not the amounts actually used. In England, for example, it is possible to get output prices and cost data all the way back to the thirteenth century.

Once the productivity of agricultural systems is measured, one can ask what determines the overall productivity level. Three basic facts stand out here.

1. From 1300 to the present, there have been enormous gains in the overall productivity of agriculture in the advanced economies. The overall productivity of English agriculture now, for example, is at least six times what it was before 1500.

2. Despite the proclamation of various earlier agricultural revolutions by historians, most of these productivity gains, in the English case at least, took place since the late nineteenth century. The overall productivity of English agriculture, for example, more than tripled between the 1860s and the early 1970s. Productivity growth occurred in earlier years but at a much slower pace. Thus in 350 years between the early sixteenth century and the 1860s, overall productivity roughly doubled. Figure 1 shows the overall productivity of English agriculture from 1500 to 1974 calculated by the price and cost method. The gains since the 1860s were the result first of the application of a new scientific understanding of the factors that control growth to the design of plants, crop rotations, and chemical fertilizers. This

knowledge stems from the 1840s and, in particular, to the pioneering work of the German Justus von Liebig (1803–1873), who is regarded as the father of agricultural science. The Rothamsted experimental station in England, founded in 1843, explicitly sought to test his theories, which were first published in English in 1840. Second, productivity advances since the 1860s have owed much to the mechanization of agriculture that, for example, doubled labor productivity in England between 1911 and 1971.

3. At any given time, agricultural productivity varies markedly across societies. This is true in Europe as early as the 1850s. Even before the large-scale application of science and mechanization, there were marked differences in the productivity of agriculture across different countries. Advanced economies such as Great Britain, the United States, and the Netherlands had productivity levels two or three times those of much of eastern and southern Europe by the mid-nineteenth century. This continues to be true in the present day, with the productivity differences now being even larger. The sources of these differences in productivity at any given time have been the subject of much debate. Institutions, culture, and education have all found champions as the primary causes. But no satisfactory explanation of these differences has yet been developed.

[See also Agricultural Labor; Agricultural Wages; Farm Capital; Farm Management; and Wages.]

BIBLIOGRAPHY

Allen, Robert. "Economic Structure and Agricultural Productivity in Europe, 1300–1800." *European Review of Economic History* 4.1 (2000), 1–27.

Bairoch, Paul. "Les trois revolutions agricoles du monde développé: Rendements et productivité de 1800 à 1985." *Annales: Économies, sociétiés, civilisations* 44 (1989), 317–353.

Bath, Slicher van. *The Agrarian History of Western Europe, A.D. 500–1850.* Translated by Olive Ordish. London, 1963.

Buck, John Lossing. *The Chinese Farm Economy: A Study of 2,866 Farms in Seventeen Localities and Seven Provinces in China.* Chicago, 1930.

Campbell, Bruce M. S. *English Seigniorial Agriculture, 1250–1450.* Cambridge, 2000.

Campbell, Bruce M. S., and Mark Overton, eds. *Land, Labour, and Livestock: Historical Studies in European Agricultural Productivity.* Manchester, 1991.

Chaianov, A. V. *A. V. Chayanov on the Theory of Peasant Economy.* Edited by Daniel Thorner, Basile Kerblay, and R. E. F. Smith. Madison, Wis., 1986.

Clark, Gregory. "The Agricultural Revolution and the Industrial Revolution: England, 1500–1912." Manuscript, University of California, Davis, n.d.

Persson, Karl Gunnar. *Pre-Industrial Economic Growth, Social Organization, and Technological Progress in Europe.* Oxford, 1988.

Rathbone, Dominic. *Economic Rationalism and Rural Society in Third-Century A.D. Egypt.* Cambridge, 1991.

Titow, Jan. *Winchester Yields.* Cambridge, 1972.

Wee, H. van der, and E. van Cauwenberghe, eds. *Productivity of Land and Agricultural Innovation in the Low Countries, 1250–1800.* Louvain, 1978.

Wrigley, E. A. "Urban Growth and Agricultural Change: England and the Continent in the Early Modern Period." *Journal of Interdisciplinary History* 15 (1985), 683–728.

GREGORY CLARK

AIR TRANSPORTATION *[This entry contains three subentries, a historical overview and discussions of technological change and industrial organization and regulation.]*

Historical Overview

Since the 1960s, commercial air transportation has entirely replaced shipping as the principal long-distance passenger transport mode, and it has made substantial inroads into the railroad passenger market over medium-length routes. As an industry, it has a remarkable growth record and boasts an unparalleled rate of technological innovation. However, decent profits are notoriously difficult to make in this industry, and demand for its services is subject to sharp, especially seasonal, fluctuations; airlines have always operated close to the break-even point so that any downturn in the economy can leave them with excess capacity and sudden losses.

Commercial air transportation is two highly interdependent but separate industries: aircraft manufacturing and the airline business. The history of both has been marked by persistent involvement with government, and in both cases governmental support often has been vital to industry survival. Although international airlines have been subject to the rules of supply and demand, they also have been instruments of national prestige, and "showing the flag" remains a basic *raison d'être*. The hand of government also has weighed heavily on airframe and aero engine manufacturing, primarily because they represent a very prominent high-tech industry. No other manufacturing sector can match aircraft manufacturing in the amount of capital spent or the number of highly skilled workers employed. No other products combine such refinement in the techniques of aerodynamics, metallurgy, and electronics, and no other industry equals aircraft production in the enormous risks taken—for in deciding to build a new airliner, a manufacturer often is betting the entire future of the company.

1919–1938. Powered flight began in America with the Wright brothers' short flights in December 1903. Following the Wright brothers, the commercial market was limited to sport and exhibitions until after World War I. Although there were passenger flights in the years before the war—such as the short-lived flying-boat service between the Florida towns of St. Petersburg and Tampa in 1914—it was not until 1919, in Europe, that commercial air transport really took off. Shortly after the war ended, embryonic airlines offering passenger services sprang up, and they immediately faced a struggle for survival. Passenger demand was low, and the costs of operating the primitive aircraft were high. If the European airlines were to remain in business, the only solution was subsidies; and almost immediately national governments felt obliged to help. Starting with the Deutsche Luft Reederei in 1919, the airlines began to receive government assistance, and over the course of the next fifteen years the pioneer operators in Holland, Belgium, Britain, Germany, Switzerland, and France evolved, usually through a process of government-induced amalgamation, into the state-sponsored flag-carriers KLM (1920), SABENA (1923), Imperial Airways (1924), Deutsche Lufthansa (1926), Swissair (1931), and Air France (1933). By the late 1920s, Britain, France, Holland, and Belgium had begun long-distance air services for mail and passengers to their colonies in Africa and Asia, and the Germans had laid the foundations of a national intercity network as well as international services in central Europe and to South America.

Meanwhile, the U.S. Post Office Department was the first customer for American air transport. In the early 1920s, airmail services were developed across the nation with pilots who followed railroad tracks in rickety biplanes. Then came the Kelly Contract Air Mail Act of 1925, which transferred American airmail services from U.S. Army aviators to the first commercial airlines. In 1930, Postmaster General Walter Folger Brown pushed through a rationalization of the airmail payment system, which encouraged the formation of a few well-financed domestic passenger airlines. Three transcontinental carriers emerged from this process: United Air Lines, Transcontinental & Western (TWA), and American Airways. These three were granted rights to develop parallel, coast-to-coast routes, to the exclusion of other, less favored airlines. In addition, a fourth company, Eastern Air Lines, received the rights to develop services along the Atlantic seaboard. The formation of the "big four" trunk operators was dependent on finance from banking interests, railroads, and a combination of aircraft builders and air transport undertakings. However, in 1934 the Black-McKellar Act broke up these "aviation companies" and separated airlines from aircraft manufacturers. It also cut airmail rates substantially, providing a further incentive for the development of passenger services. The legislative structure for American air transportation was completed in 1938 when the Civil Aeronautics Act confirmed the "big four" in being and set the oligopolistic shape of the domestic airline industry. The act established the Civil Aeronautics Board (known until 1940 as the Civil Aeronautics Authority), which was responsible for tight regulation of fares and market entry in

the U.S. airline industry for the next forty years. By 1939, U.S. air fares were cheap enough to appeal to businesspeople who needed to get somewhere in a hurry, and U.S. airlines were carrying many more passengers than those of any other country. In contrast, European aviation, with less stimulation from geography and more competition from the railways, was carrying the flag (and a lot of mail) to far-flung colonies.

American international passenger services were launched in 1927 when Pan American Airways began flying from southern Florida to Cuba. In 1930, Pan American was able to buy its chief competitor, NYRBA (the New York, Rio and Buenos Aires Line), and gain for itself a practical monopoly on American international services in the Caribbean, South America, and later the Pacific. Thanks to generous airmail contracts and the firm leadership of its founder, Juan Trippe, Pan American quickly became the "chosen instrument" of U.S. overseas aviation policy.

The first aircraft capable of carrying fare-paying passengers were biplanes made of wood, wire, and doped fabric, with cabin space for four passengers, a range of 500 miles and a cruising speed of 100 mph; their technical limitations eliminated any possibility of profitable passenger operations. In the 1920s, aeronautical engineering was dominated by European firms such as Junkers, Fokker, de Havilland, Handley Page, and Farman. The monoplanes of Junkers and Fokker set the standard for aircraft design and were copied in early American planes such as the Ford Trimotor (1925). Initially aircraft had water-cooled in-line engines, which were heavy and temperamental. It was the development of reliable air-cooled radial engines by Wright and Pratt & Whitney in the United States, and by Bristol in Britain, that gave commercial air transport its first technological step forward. Then, in the early 1930s, further innovations in airframe manufacturing, such as stressed skin construction and the use of lightweight alloys and retractable undercarriages, brought forth a new generation of American airliners. Starting with the Lockheed Vega in 1927, a series of streamlined monoplanes took to the skies from America's West Coast. In 1933, the Boeing 247 brought together all the latest developments in a twin-engined, all-metal monoplane with seating for ten passengers. It seemed to be the state-of-the-art in aircraft design until the Douglas company was prompted to go one better with the DC-2 (1934) and then the legendary DC-3 (1936). The latter cruised at 190 mph and had seating for twenty-one passengers. It was first, economical to operate, and the first airliner that could be operated profitably by carrying passengers only.

1939–1958. Until World War II, American and European aviation developed separately. The Atlantic Ocean that separated them had been crossed many times, and

AIRPLANE TRAVEL. Passengers boarding a TWA Constellation, 1946. (Prints and Photographs Division, Library of Congress)

Charles Lindbergh's famous flight in 1927 had proved that the feat even could be done single-handedly; but there was no aircraft with sufficient range to permit regular transatlantic passenger service until the summer of 1939, when the huge Boeing 314 flying boat was introduced into service by Pan American Airways. In the war years this "bridge" across the ocean was quickly reinforced, and transatlantic flights became routine as thousands of U.S. aircraft were ferried to Europe. American transport aircraft were produced in great numbers during the war, and technical advances were accelerated as experience with military craft spilled over into the civil sector. Thanks to higher wing loadings, nose-wheel undercarriages, new navigational aids, and cabin pressurization, more passengers now could be carried farther. The four-engine Douglas DC-4 (flying in 1942 as the C-54 Skymaster military transport) and its rival the Lockheed Constellation (1943) signaled the advent of the true long-distance airliner. The Constellation was the first fully pressurized passenger aircraft and represented an important advance for the industry as airliners now could cruise at twenty thousand feet, greatly reducing the incidence of airsickness among their customers.

As World War II appeared to be consolidating America's lead in commercial air transportation, Britain responded after 1943 with its own program of civil aircraft development, named after its initiator Lord Brabazon. The Brabazon program was not a great success in reversing the American advantage, but it did lead to the production of two noteworthy airliners in the postwar years: the de Havilland Comet and the Vickers Viscount. The Comet 1 is a classic example of a bold innovation coming tragically ahead of its time. It was the first civil aircraft to be powered by jet engines, and although it was comparatively small (carrying thirty-six passengers) and lacked sufficient range to cross the Atlantic, it captured the world's imagination with its speed in 1952–1953. Unfortunately a series of crashes in 1954, whose cause eventually was attributed to metal fatigue, banished the Comet from the sky until a revised version was ready in 1958. A commercially more successful British airliner, also utilizing the new gas turbine technology, was the Vickers-Armstrong Viscount, powered by four Rolls Royce Dart turboprop engines. This short- to medium-range airliner sold well in Europe in the 1950s and even secured orders from American airlines. A third European airliner developed in the 1950s, combining the Viscount's range with the Comet's Rolls Royce Avon engines, was the French Sud-Aviation Caravelle. However, despite the appearance of these advanced European aircraft, the international airline industry remained loyal to American piston-engined craft, now at their peak of development; and the Boeing Stratocruiser, the Douglas DC-6 and DC-7C, and the Lockheed L-1049 Super Constellation served most of the world's long-distance carriers in the 1950s.

The postwar airline industry in which these aircraft operated was highly regulated. In the 1944 Chicago Conference and later in 1946 at the Anglo-American meeting in Bermuda, the foundations were laid for an international civil aviation structure in which entry to routes would be limited to designated national carriers, traffic rights and capacity would be determined in bilateral negotiations, and international air fares would be held at a uniform level by a cartel of airlines known as the International Air Transport Association (IATA). IATA has existed before the war, but when it was revived in 1945 it was a more powerful organization because it now had the sanction of the American carriers. Although its jurisdiction was limited to scheduled international air services, the force of IATA's authority in the regulation of postwar civil aviation hardly can be exaggerated. Thanks to its fare regime, price competition in scheduled air services was minimal; however mutually agreed-upon price cuts were introduced by IATA in 1952 with tourist-class and in 1958 with economy-class fares.

1959–1978. As air fares grew cheaper, air travel became available to lower-income groups, and air transportation was democratized. This revolution received vital assistance from technology, in the shape of the jet engine. The jet age began in October 1958 with the opening of Pan American Airways' New York to London and Paris services with the Boeing 707. The 707, and the identical Douglas DC-8, were not only fast but also big (the original 707 carried 130 passengers at 600 mph); so they were much cheaper to operate, on a unit-cost basis, than the piston-engined aircraft they replaced. In the 1960s the 707 and DC-8 were complemented with a broad range of jet aircraft. Boeing followed with the tri-jet 727 (1964) and the short-range 737 (1968), Douglas with the DC-9 (1965), and the British Aircraft Corporation (BAC) with its long-range VC-10 (1964) and its One Eleven short-range twin jet (1965). Of the major U.S. manufacturers, only Lockheed seemed to get it wrong at this stage by pursuing the turboprop alternative to the pure jet with the L-188 Electra (1959).

A comprehensive international air network was in place by 1960, but the supply of scheduled airline seats did not reflect the true size of the market. Demand was expanding and changing in composition. In Europe, where air transport had remained the preserve of an exclusive minority, there was demand for cheaper tourist flights. Further capacity was provided by independent nonscheduled charter airlines catering to the new leisure air travelers. By the mid-1970s, charter airlines, flying package tourists to the Mediterranean beaches, were well established in Britain, Germany, Holland, and Scandanavia; and charter air traffic comprised over 50 percent of the total passenger market in Europe. Slowly the old distinction between scheduled and nonscheduled services became blurred and new entrants such as Freddie Laker's Skytrain (1978) showed that there was a pressing demand for cheap "no-frills" passenger services.

Accompanying the low-fare movement in the 1970s was a shift toward increased aircraft size. The tremendous increase in speed represented by the Boeing 707 was not pursued by the airlines, except in the single case of the supersonic Concorde, an Anglo-French prestige project, which eventually entered service with Air France and British Airways in 1976. Instead manufacturers concentrated on wide-bodied aircraft that could carry more economy-class passengers. Heading the list was Boeing's 747, the original jumbo jet, which could carry up to five hundred passengers and entered service with its sponsoring airline, Pan American, in 1970. Two smaller wide-bodied jets that followed were the McDonnell Douglas DC-10 and the Lockheed L-1011 TriStar. Critical to the launch of all three was growth in the size and the power of jet engines, culminating, in the early 1970s, in the production by all the major manufacturers of high-ratio bypass turbofan engines. However, the Americans were no longer alone in the field. In 1975, the European Airbus consortium, led by France and Germany, brought the twin-engined, wide-bodied A300B into service with Air France; and, in the following years, a whole range of Airbus aircraft appeared, signifying Europe's return to a position of meaningful contention in the civil aerospace market.

1979–2001. In 1978, the corset of regulation that had bound the airline industry since 1945 finally burst with passage, by the U.S. Congress, of legislation deregulating America's domestic airline industry. In the next decade, the spirit of deregulation spread to Europe and had a worldwide effect on international air transportation. Slowly, in the 1980s, the European market for scheduled air services was transformed into a more liberal and competitive environment; and, in 1993, the European Union (EU) launched a phased introduction of a fully deregulated market. This process of market liberalization coincided with a shift toward greater reliance on market forces and a trend toward the privatization of state-owned airlines, the first major European flag-carrier to revert completely to private ownership being British Airways in 1987. Accompanying the movement toward deregulation in the last two decades of the twentieth century was a trend to make airliners cleaner, quieter, and more economical in operation. For newly privatized airlines, concerned about profit levels, there is constant pressure to reduce running costs, and aircraft that are economical to fly are at a premium. Jets originally conceived in the 1960s, such as the Boeing 737 and the Douglas DC-9, were "stretched" and re-engined to meet the lean commercial requirements of the 1990s, and radically new types such as the enormous twin-jet Boeing 777 were launched to bring greater economy to the all-important transatlantic route.

Deregulation caused a tremendous upheaval in air transportation and the demise of some famous names among the airline community, including Pan American Airways in 1990. In America, formerly domestic airlines such as United and American became international giants, whereas in Europe deregulation encouraged new entrants to the market, including no-frills, low-price operators such as EasyJet in Britain. Deregulation also has led, in an age of globalization, to an unprecedented level of concentration among airlines and the appearance of so-called megacarriers, produced by the merger or alliance of previously independent operators. In the United States and to a lesser extent in Europe, it has hastened the growth of hub-and-spoke route networks and the domination of some major airports by single airlines.

The deregulation that took place in the 1980s in the United States occurred in a market with at least six well-founded domestic carriers capable of withstanding open competition with one another. In Europe, by contrast, no country had that depth of corporate strength in air transportation, and most had only a single flag-carrier and perhaps one or two smaller independent airlines, often deliberately nurtured by the state to compete with the national airline. Since 1990 in Europe, there has been an inevitable eclipse of the airlines' prestige role and their transformation from state-owned flag-carriers into privately-owned "brand carriers." The challenge for the air transportation industry, in both Europe and the United States, is to complete the ongoing process of realignment and consolidation—strikingly reminiscent of the formation of the American "big four" in the early 1930s—and to do so in such a way that the industry's pattern of low profitability is finally changed. Airlines long ago lost their aura of glamour and romance and became a mass-transportation system. What remains is for the industry to become a stable, predictable, and profitable sector of the service economy.

BIBLIOGRAPHY
Bender, Marilyn, and Selig Altschul. *The Chosen Instrument*. New York, 1982.
Bilstein, Roger E. *Flight in America: From the Wrights to the Astronauts*. Rev. ed. Baltimore, 1994.
Davies, R.E.G. *A History of the World's Airlines*. London, 1967.
Dienel, Hans-Liudger, and Peter Lyth, eds. *Flying the Flag: European Commercial Air Transport since 1945*. Basingstoke, U.K., 1998.
Doganis, Rigas. *Flying Off Course: The Economics of International Airlines*. 2d ed. London, 1991.
Gibbs-Smith, Charles H. *Aviation: An Historical Survey from Its Origins to the End of World War II*. London, 1970.
Hanlon, Pat. *Global Airlines: Competition in a Transnational Industry*. Oxford, 1996.
Hayward, Keith. *The British Aircraft Industry*. Manchester and New York, 1989.
Heppenheimer, T.A. *Turbulent Skies: The History of Commercial Aviation*. Sloan Technology Series. New York, 1995.
Lyth, Peter, ed. *Air Transport*. Aldershot, U.K., 1996.
Morrison, Steven A. and Clifford Winston. *The Evolution of the Airline Industry*. Washington, D.C., 1995.
Rae, John B. *Climb to Greatness: The American Aircraft Industry, 1920–1960*. Cambridge, Mass., 1968.
William F. Trimble, ed. *From Airships to Airbus: The History of Civil and Commercial Aviation*, vol. 2. Washington, D.C., 1995.

PETER LYTH

Technological Change

One of history's great ironies is that the first consistent reports on the Wright brothers' achievement of powered flight came not in scientific journals but in a local beekeeping paper published near their home in Dayton, Ohio; most authoritative observers remained firmly convinced that the brothers were perpetrating a hoax. When the Wrights made a triumphant public appearance in Le Mans, France, in 1906, many spectators gaped in stunned silence.

Early History. The three-year standstill following the Wrights' first successful flight at Kitty Hawk, North Carolina, in 1903 was symbolic of the long road that flight technology would take as it evolved from an object of scientific curiosity and wishful imagination to a viable form of transportation, a journey that would last roughly thirty years. The slow pace of early development depended partly on the nature of aviation technology: crude flying machines were not only unsatisfactory but also usually lethal. The social and economic context of aviation's prehistory also played a key role. Although compelling to nearly everyone who watched a bird soar through the air, air travel offered little as a means of alternative transportation. Its signature advantage, the ability to transfer people and high-value goods rapidly, meant less in an age before the telephone and the telegraph had created distended commercial and political empires. Consequently, aviation remained largely the scientific pursuit of wealthy hobbyists, and most attempts to fly revolved around trying to imitate birds.

Indeed, scientific curiosity played the largest role in the first controlled ascents into the air. Two children of the scientific revolution, the Montgolfier brothers of France, seized upon the idea that hot air would rise—and, if kept in a bag, would carry a balloon along with it. Ascending over Versailles in September 1783, a sheep, a duck, and a rooster bore the honor of becoming the world's first true aeronauts, and, by surviving, banished worries that the upper atmosphere was poisonous. Two months later, a physician and an infantry major took a twenty-five-minute hot-air-balloon flight. Experiments with hydrogen balloons followed, and by the middle of the following century balloon ascents had become relatively commonplace. The first widespread and practical use of balloons occurred during the U.S. Civil War, when the Union Army used tethered balloons to map troop movements.

Going up and down or merely floating with the winds proved of little use to commercial fliers, however. Controlling shaped balloons through the use of a propeller held more promise, but the absence of sufficiently lightweight engines held back development. Even small steam engines were very heavy; and, although the advent of workable internal combustion engines in the 1880s offered some promise, their low efficiency and heavy construction meant that development was slow. Indeed, the leader in powered ballooning at the end of the nineteenth century was the picaresque Brazilian Alberto Santos-Dumont, who used a small engine to power a semirigid balloon on spectacular laps around the Eiffel Tower. More serious work was carried out by Count Ferdinand von Zeppelin, who began experimenting in 1900 with the rigid airships that later would bear his name. Within ten years, German zeppelins were regularly carrying passengers and freight; but their slow speed and military vulnerability eventually limited their use.

A second major avenue for human flight came through the application of airfoils, or wing shapes, to the air's mass. Experimenters dating back to Leonardo da Vinci had worked with propellers, which showed the possibility of gripping the air if correctly shaped. Centuries of kiting, and later gliding, led to the development of serviceable airfoils by the end of the nineteenth century. The British baronet Sir George Cayley and later the German engineer Otto Lillenthal proved the most important innovators in gliding in the nineteenth century, applying consistent means to measure the efficiency of various airfoils. Before his death in a crash in 1896, Lillenthal was making controlled glides of several hundred feet.

Propellers, wings, rudimentary engines—most of the pieces of the puzzle were in place by the end of the nineteenth century. Yet the genius of Orville and, particularly, Wilbur Wright in placing them together cannot be underestimated. The Wrights made several important contributions to the incipient science of flight, but their greatest insight came in the area of control. Unlike other competitors such as Samuel Langley, president of the Smithsonian Institute, the Wrights eschewed the possibility of designing an inherently stable aircraft. Instead, drawing on their background as bicycle-shop owners, the Wrights designed means of controlling pitch, roll, and yaw—the three axes on which a craft in flight can rotate. The Wrights incorporated their control mechanisms into a gliderlike craft,

mounted it with a lightweight engine they had designed and manufactured, and began the era of powered flight on a windswept beach in North Carolina in December 1903.

The Wrights would continue to improve their craft, and several other Americans, most notably the New York motorcycle mechanic Glenn Curtiss, would follow their lead and make important innovations of their own. Nonetheless, the locus of innovation shifted largely to Europe in the following decade. In part, this change was due to a well-developed culture of competition among European elites, who competed strenuously in a series of flights across the English Channel. European aircraft makers such as Louis Bleriot and Gabriel Voisin made important improvements, including the development of the monoplane, in an attempt to seal a number of aerial firsts.

World War I and Its Legacy. To make a complete transition from scientific curiosity to accepted means of transport, a major source of support for aerial innovation was needed—which airplane makers found with the outbreak of war in the summer of 1914. Visions of aerial war had preoccupied science-fiction writers and other thinkers for the two decades leading up to the outbreak of hostilities. Most such ideas were highly fanciful, relying on prophesies of what future flying machines might look like rather than extrapolations of current technologies. When fragile aircraft began flying reconnaissance missions in the early months of World War I, European governments and public opinion were primed to translate fiction into reality. The British, French, and German aircraft ministries quickly grew as their nations developed aircraft production programs, and other combatants followed suit as best they could. Bombers, fighters, and observation aircraft all incorporated dramatic innovations in speed, size, and range as designers figured out how to attach more powerful engines to stronger airframes. Aerial warfare, heroic and decisive in comparison to the mechanized attrition in the trenches below, quickly captured the public's attention. Lighter-than-air technologies also advanced in the form of the German zeppelins.

By the time the United States entered the war in the spring of 1917, America's technological standing had fallen precipitously. The insuffiencies of American technology were painfully demonstrated as an enormous aircraft production program failed to deliver as promised. Until the end of the war, the Americans relied on British and French firms for their most advanced fighting aircraft. An important legacy of this failure, however, was a renewed commitment on the part of the American government to foster aeronautical supremacy.

With Congress reluctant to fund a large peacetime military, this commitment bore fruit in the form of the U.S. Air Mail Service, which by the end of the 1920s was flying some of the world's most advanced aircraft over some of its longest and most demanding routes. Subsidies to the mail service and, later, to the commercial airlines that carried the mail, filtered large sums to the engineering departments of American aircraft makers. From these firms flowed numerous innovations, including the highly reliable air-cooled engine that allowed a young airmail pilot, Charles Lindbergh, to cross the Atlantic in 1927. Given further incentives to carry passengers, many of the subsidized mail lines began flying larger craft, best typified by the famous trimotors of the period.

With the need to deliver mail in all weather conditions and around the clock, a complex ground and navigation infrastructure developed. The first radio-controlled guidance systems were crude, relying on the pilot to navigate between a left and a right signal to find the route to the airport; but the stage was set for further safety improvements that would allow pilots to navigate through cloudy or nighttime skies.

The greatest legacy of the airmail program was the Douglas DC-series aircraft, generally recognized as the first modern and commercially feasible airliner when introduced in 1933. The aircraft incorporated several innovations that had been in development since World War I: adjustable-pitch propellers allowed for more efficient operations at higher speeds; high-octane fuels permitted greater horsepower engines that weighed less; duralumin skin and flush riveting improved airflow; monocoque construction obviated the need for weight- and space-consuming bracing; cantilevered wings allowed designers to do away with drag-producing external struts; engine cowlings improved airflow around air-cooled radial engines while reducing drag; retractable landing gear improved streamlining; and wing flaps allowed higher wing loadings, or wing area relative to aircraft weight, and slower landings. Taken together, the innovations allowed the DC-3 to carry large loads at high speed over substantial distances. More important, they made the journey reasonably comfortable, making air travel appealing not just to adventurers but to a wide range of prosperous travelers able to afford the high fares.

On a largely distinct track of development, the 1930s also saw the advent of the giant Clipper ships, large seaplanes designed to fly in hops across the Pacific in the service of Pan American World Airways. Using multiple engines and unencumbered with landing-strip limits, the craft, which came to resemble luxury cruise ships, became the largest built to date. However, the Clippers soon lost their appeal, when pressurized versions of the DC-based airliners became available. Beginning in the mid-1930s, the U.S. Army Air Corps sponsored work on pressurized cabins. These cabins made their way into two commercial aircraft, the Boeing 307 Stratoliner and the Douglas DC-4E, before World War II stopped further development. Pressurized craft offered the key advantage of being able to fly above most rough weather, sparing passengers the worst jolts caused by turbulent air.

The innovations that made for fast and reliable passenger-carrying airmail planes also took aerial warfare to a new level. Based largely on technologies designed for American civilian airliners, the first effective, high-speed, long-range bombers came under development in the United States and Europe. The ability to deliver large amounts of explosives through such aircraft was first made clear in Spain and Manchuria, where German and Japanese aircraft subjected civilian populations to the world's first large-scale terror bombings. The development of smaller, speedier aircraft using the same technologies continued apace. By the time the Battle of Britain began in 1940, British fighter aircraft were able to engage German bombers at altitudes of up to forty thousand feet and speeds of 440 miles per hour. The American B-29 bomber, designed for high-altitude bombing, incorporated a pressurized crew cabin.

With the growing use of strategic bombing and tactical combat came competition for aircraft that could outmaneuver the enemy, through either higher range, faster speed, or sheer numbers. With the majority of the world's industrial might on their side, the United States, Britain, and their Allies relied increasingly on numbers, sending huge waves of fighters and bombers on raids over German cities and military targets. Mass-produced B-17 bombers proved a particularly notable example of the Allies productive prowess; but so did the DC-3 in its incarnation as the Dakota transport, which ferried troops and supplies across battle theaters. The Germans, on the other hand, sought to make great leaps in aviation technology in the hopes that miracle weapons would compensate for smaller numbers.

The idea of the turbine gas engine dated from the early 1930s, when aeronautical engineers began to foresee problems for propellers at speeds above 400 to 450 miles per hour. By providing the thrust produced by igniting compressed gas, jets promised to do away with the propeller altogether. Frank Whittle, a Royal Air Force officer, proved an important innovator in the field, conducting research with minimal government support until just before the outbreak of war. In Germany, researcher Hans von Ohain began work at roughly the same time but with significant funding from the German Air Ministry. The Germans conducted the first gas turbine flight in 1939, and unveiled a highly effective although short-range jet fighter in 1944.

Post–World War II Development. In the same way that the legacy of World War I would have unforeseen effects on postwar technological development, so would World War II shape the coming decades in unforeseen ways. Predictably, the successful wartime operation of jet fighters by Germany and, to a lesser extent, Britain encouraged military planners in the United States, Europe, and Russia to fund jet-aircraft development. Wartime experience suggested that the appeal of jets would come first in fighter development, but European and American aircraft soon were able to bring jet technology to larger bombers such as the American Boeing B-47 and the British Vickers Valiant. Mounting jets on aircraft subjected them to new challenges because of stresses and high speeds, but solutions soon appeared in innovations such as swept-back wings and new techniques for producing stronger and smoother surfaces.

Treading a well-worn path, military innovations soon ventured again into commercial airline development. Many observers thought advances in jet development would first appear in the commercial realm in the hybrid turboprop, which used compressed gas to turn traditional propellers; but problems in gearing the jets down to efficient prop speeds meant that development was slow. Instead, engineers began to develop cowled fan engines, which proved quieter and more fuel-efficient than the jets used on military craft.

Jets could not be simply strapped onto aircraft designed for traditional piston engines; but military-influenced advances in aircraft structures, such as swept wings and stronger skins, proved highly useful. Reflecting their lead in jet engines, the British first introduced a commercial jet airliner, the Comet, in 1949, but a series of spectacular crashes due to structural failure doomed it. Basing its design on plans for a military tanker aircraft, Boeing introduced the first stable and successful jet airliner, the 707, in 1954, a craft that would not look out of place on a tarmac at a major airport almost fifty years later. Boeing's domestic competitor Douglas followed with a successful rival craft, the DC-8, in 1958.

With jet aircraft soon displacing turbine craft on long-haul routes around the world, engineering development turned to making aircraft larger and faster. Although these were twin goals for many aircraft makers, they soon veered into disparate visions of the future of air transportation. Faced with competitive incentives to fly larger, more comfortable craft, the procurement divisions of American airlines argued mainly for larger airplanes. Boeing met this demand most spectacularly in its design of the 747, which entered service for Pan Am in 1970. Size could offer more seats as well as luxury, however; so the craft soon gained appeal with airlines concerned with reducing seat-mile costs. Douglas and Lockheed countered Boeing in the mid-1970s with virtually identical tri-jets, the DC-10 and L-1011, a competition so costly that it helped drive Lockheed from the commercial airline business.

Greater speed proved a larger challenge for the airlines, for it meant bridging the sound barrier. Smaller military craft had succeeded in doing so since Chuck Yeager's celebrated flight in 1947, but only at the cost of significant control problems, airframe stresses, and fuel consumption. Larger supersonic military planes, such as the ill-fated XB-70, proved notoriously unstable. With research support from the U.S. government, Boeing began work on a supersonic transport, the SST, in the 1960s, but soon abandoned the effort because of cost and environmental concerns—the first time that the latter had been allowed to intervene in the progress of air transport. A cooperative state-led effort joining Britain and France did proceed, however; and the resulting aircraft, the Concorde (1969), proved a technical triumph, able to fly at two and one-half times the speed of sound. Yet its extremely high operating costs and environmentally driven route limitations kept production of the plane limited.

As air transport deregulation around the world proceeded in the 1970s and 1980s, attention turned toward cost efficiency in design. Another Anglo-French venture, this one including other European nations as well, seized the lead in this area with the Airbus series, efficient planes that proved highly popular on short- and medium-range routes. Limiting engines for maintenance purposes and using computerized controls to reduce crew size became the hallmarks of engineering development, not simply going farther and faster. Boeing took Airbus's cue by designing the first twin-engined, long-range jets, the 767 and 777, while introducing further refinements to the company's popular short-range craft, the 737.

As technical developments in commercial air transportation focused increasingly on cost reductions, the field further distanced itself from the symbiotic relationship it had long experienced with military aviation. Additionally, smart bombs, cruise and ballistic missiles, stealth technologies, and other focuses of military development proved less useful to commercial designers than the older pursuits of speed and size. At the same time, the enormous resources necessary for developing new commercial aviation technologies meant that only two major manufacturers—Boeing and Airbus—remained as the century ended, both of which focused on stretching current designs or otherwise basing their work on existing platforms. These factors combined to suggest that future improvements would be more incremental in nature when compared to the field's remarkable achievements over past decades.

BIBLIOGRAPHY

Bilstein, Roger E. *Flight in America, 1900–1983: From the Wrights to the Astronauts*. Baltimore, 1984.

Brooks, Peter. *The Modern Airliner: Its Origins and Development*. London, 1961.

Caves, Richard. *Air Transport and Its Regulators*. Cambridge, Mass., 1962.

Crouch, Tom D. *The Bishop's Boys: A Life of Wilbur and Orville Wright*. New York, 1989.

Miller, Ronald, and David Sawers. *The Technical Development of Modern Aviation.* New York, 1970.

Newhouse, J. *The Sporty Game.* New York, 1982.

Rae, John B. *Climb to Greatness: The American Aircraft Industry.* Cambridge, Mass, 1968.

Vincenti, Walter G. *What Engineers Know and How They Know It: Analytical Studies from Aeronautical History.* Baltimore, 1990.

C. DEREK JOHNSON

Industrial Organization and Regulation

Sporadic ventures in air transport appeared before World War I, but its continuous development began in 1918 when the U.S. government introduced regularly scheduled airmail service. In 1919, passenger routes opened in Europe between major cities. The difference between the two approaches was significant. Because of American commitment to limited government and free enterprise, federal policy aimed at turning the airmail system over to private contractors as soon as possible. This was done in 1925 when the Kelly Act opened bidding on routes. In Europe, by contrast, only Great Britain tried to maintain privately operated airlines, and even it soon embraced government control. Motives for developing European airlines varied. Germany created Lufthansa partly to evade provisions in the Treaty of Versailles inhibiting its aerial rearmament. Britain, Belgium, France, and the Netherlands used Imperial Airways, Sabena, Aeropostale, and KLM to build air connections with far-flung overseas empires. The Soviet Union pursued interior development by creating air routes across its enormous landmass, flown by Aeroflot, the world's largest airline. Expanding foreign trade was also a European goal. After Aeropostale linked French possessions in Africa, Gallic aviators pioneered routes to South America. Germany penetrated Brazil and Colombia by using dirigibles and airplanes. Strong central government made these efforts possible.

The United States used airmail routes to pursue its interests in Latin America by fostering the growth of Pan American Airways, its international flag carrier. Mainly, however, the government aided private enterprise with airmail contracts to domestic carriers. Not until 1930 did it throw its weight behind passenger transport with the Watres Act, which paid contractors according to the space provided for mail, thus forcing them to acquire large aircraft. Under this act, Postmaster General Walter F. Brown, favoring "big business," created three major transcontinental systems and a north-south route from New York to Miami. Giant holding companies compounded their earnings by simultaneously making planes and running airlines. Government officials saw no conflict of interest.

International and national regulation helped make complex air transport systems possible. In 1919, at Paris, twelve countries negotiated a Convention Relating to the Regulation of Aerial Navigation, based on control by each signatory of its own airspace. Forty-three articles governed safe and efficient operation of aircraft across national boundaries. An International Commission for Air Navigation (ICAN) supervised observance of the rules. Neither the United States nor the Soviet Union ratified the convention. In 1928, the United States and twenty countries in the Western Hemisphere adopted a Pan American Convention on Commercial Aviation. It recognized national control of airspace and adopted vague rules administered separately by the signatories. No provision was made for a permanent secretariat. This convention was so flexible that it created more confusion than order.

Private Interests and Domestic Regulation. Domestic regulation of aviation was difficult in the United States because of conflicts over federal and state powers and demands of private interests. The Air Commerce Act of 1926 settled such disputes by asserting federal authority over airways, certifying airworthiness of planes, licensing pilots (who had to pass medical examinations), and providing navigational and meteorological services. The Bureau of Aeronautics in the Commerce Department oversaw enforcement. William P. MacCracken, the bureau's first administrator, was sympathetic toward aerial enterprise and promoted private interests. Economic regulation was limited to the power of the Post Office Department over airmail contracts.

A major change occurred after 1933. Franklin D. Roosevelt, who became president amid the Great Depression, brought a new attitude toward free enterprise. Accusations about Brown's interpretation of the Watres Act led to cancellation of airmail contracts, a congressional witch hunt, a failed attempt to have the U.S. Army fly airmail routes, and eventual restoration of contracts to private contractors under punitive conditions, with lower subsidy rates. Holding companies could no longer make commercial aircraft and run airlines at the same time. These measures were a blessing in disguise because they forced airlines to increase efficiency. Concurrently, a revolution in aircraft design enhanced productivity. The first airliner to provide such benefits was the Boeing 247, a streamlined, all-metal, twin-engine airplane capable of carrying more passengers and mail at less unit cost than earlier planes. Competition between airlines yielded aircraft with even better features, culminating in the legendary Douglas DC-3, which was so economical that it could earn profits without carrying mail. Because mail contracts constituted the only government regulatory mechanism, airline owners feared an invasion of hard-won markets by new companies that needed only to buy DC-3s to create havoc in an industry that had fought hard to survive. Seeking federal protection, airlines got it in the Civil Aeronautics Act of 1938, requiring any air carrier to secure a Certificate of

AIR TRANSPORTATION. Although the Boeing 707 (top) cost twice as much as the DC-7 (bottom), the 707 provided more than three times as many seat miles. Idlewild Airport (renamed John F. Kennedy Airport in 1963), New York, 1958. (John Ross/Look Magazine Photograph Collection/Library of Congress)

Public Convenience and Necessity (CPCN). The law confirmed existing companies in possession of current routes by grandfathering them. The benefits of the law came at a heavy price because airlines now had to submit to unprecedented regulation. All tariffs and charges for transport of passengers and goods required approval by the Civil Aeronautics Board (CAB), a federal agency established in 1940. The CAB carefully scrutinized business records and practices. Because grandfathering did not give carriers exclusive rights to their routes, the CAB could discipline them by admitting other firms.

Commercial Aviation Frameworks. The new order, however, facilitated a cozy relationship with the government for executives who knew how to play the game. The Air Transport Association (ATA) lobbied effectively for management with federal officials. As World War II approached, airlines became part of a tight-knit family of government agencies and defense-related industries. Carriers avoided nationalization during the war by helping create the Air Transport Command (ATC), a commercial-military hybrid that enlisted personnel and aircraft from privately owned carriers to conduct airlift operations that kept huge numbers of people and materiel moving to and from far-off theaters of war. As victory neared, the aircraft industry had funds and facilities to produce commercial planes of a quantity and a quality that foreign nations could not match. Roosevelt wanted American airlines to carry American-made goods to all corners of the earth. His representatives at an international conference at Chicago in 1944 sought a new order in international aviation permitting American carriers to invade foreign markets as freely as possible. Britain, seeing the end of an era in which it had dominated world markets, resisted. Canada, which had ties with both sides in the debate, played a moderating role.

A compromise confirmed national sovereignty over airspace, and the right of a country to refuse to let scheduled international airlines operate in or out of its territory; but it also provided for bilateral treaties and important "freedoms" (which were really privileges). One freedom gave international airlines the privilege of overflying a treaty partner's territory without landing; the other, that of refueling in its territory without enplaning or discharging revenue traffic. Two other freedoms gave international airlines reciprocal privileges to carry revenue traffic to or from a country of origin and a treaty partner's territory. A fifth freedom permitted international airlines to add other nations to routes operating into or out of a treaty partner's domain. Other freedoms emerged but were seldom permitted. An International Civil Aviation Authority (ICAO), headquartered in Canada, oversaw rules governing safety, flight plans, uniform tickets, tariffs, and other details. A convention containing most of these agreements became effective in April 1947. Meanwhile, the United States and Great Britain agreed in Bermuda in 1946 to liberalize carrier designation, route allocation, capacity and frequency levels, and tariff regulation. This protocol became a model for other nations.

Competition over International Routes. Just as the Civil Aeronautics Act had established a framework for American commercial aviation that would last four decades, the Chicago and Bermuda conventions yielded an era of relative stability that endured for thirty years. Disagreements continued between nations, particularly because many parts of the world permitted pooling arrangements for apportioning revenues among carriers, a practice forbidden on international air routes entering or leaving the United States; but harmony generally prevailed. The United States, committed to international as well as domestic competition, ended Pan American's monopoly over foreign routes. Believing that air transport was a public service as well as a way of making money, the CAB promoted service competition by allowing more than one airline to fly a commercial route, the premise being that carriers offering better amenities, more convenient schedules, and faster and more comfortable planes would attract more traffic than airlines that did not.

During the 1970s, increasing debate arose in the United States about whether market forces should prevail in the airline industry. Critics claimed that, in encouraging service competition, the CAB permitted airlines to raise prices to provide amenities and preserved stability by protecting inefficient airlines that obeyed antiquated rules. Mounting controversy produced the Airline Deregulation Act of 1978, phasing out the CAB and its regulatory authority. By 1980, American airlines were free to choose their own routes and set their own fares.

After abolishing airline regulation at home, the United States pushed to liberalize bilateral treaties with foreign countries. More American airports became international gateways, and more American airlines entered foreign markets. Other countries followed the trend amid the decline of command economies and a resurgent belief in free markets. By the end of the century, the American faith in competition and capitalism was at least temporarily ascendant.

BIBLIOGRAPHY

Doganis, Rigass. *Flying off Course: The Economics of International Airlines*, 2d ed. London and New York, 1991.

Groenewege, Adrianus D. *Compendium of International Civil Aviation*, 2d ed. Montreal, 1999.

Leary, William M., ed. *The Airline Industry*. New York and Oxford, 1992.

Lewis, W. David, ed. *Airline Executives and Federal Regulation: Case Studies in American Enterprise from the Airmail Era to the Dawn of the Jet Age*. Columbus, Ohio, 2000.

W. David Lewis

ALGERIA. *See* France, *subentries on* The French Empire to 1789 *and* The French Empire between 1789 and 1950; *and* North Africa.

ALKALOIDS. Plant use for medicinal purposes is an age-old human endeavor. Artefacts denoting poppy use in the eastern Mediterranean date to the Bronze Age—in Crete (c. 1400–1350), in Egypt in the first half of the Eighteenth Dynasty (c. 1567–1320 BCE), and in Anatolia during the Hittite Empire (c. 1400–1200 BCE). A first-century Greek army physician, Dioscorides, recommended a "poultice of the leaves of a Mediterranean plant" for some eye diseases. This plant, identified in the seventeenth and eighteenth centuries as *Argemone mexicana* ("prickly poppy"), came to Europe from the Caribbean in the sixteenth century and reportedly caused epidemic dropsy or glaucoma outbreaks in India in 1866 and 1935 because cooking oil was contaminated with oil from *A. mexicana* seeds.

In the early nineteenth century, efforts by J. F. Derosne (1803 and 1806) and Friedrich Wilhelm Sertürner (1817) showed that the aqueous opium extract, "morphium," was a plant alkali that turned red litmus paper blue. This paved the way for scientists to isolate alkaloids from medicinal plants. The term *alkaloid* was subsequently coined in 1819 by a pharmacist, W. Meissner, and means "alkali-like."

Over 40 percent of all plant families include at least one alkaloid-bearing species. Many of these are found in Southeast Asia, South America, and Africa. Some alkaloids occur in plants combined with sugars (e.g., *Solanum tuberosum L.* in potato) or as amides (e.g., piperine from *Piper nigrum L.*), or esters (e.g., cocaine from coca leaves, *Erythroxylon coca Lam.*). Over five thousand alkaloids of all structural types are known today.

Alkaloids constitute only a small percentage of plant materials. In terms of dry weight, there is only 10% of morphine in opium, 5 to 8 percent of quinine in cinchona bark, and about 0.2 percent of hyoscyamine in *Atropa belladonna* leaf. Despite the increasing reliance on chemical synthesis as the main source of the alkaloid supply for medicinal use, plant sources continue to be an important raw material base for alkaloids.

Alkaloids occur in different parts of plants. The alkaloids of the tobacco plant, *Nicotiana tabacum*, are found in the roots and are translocated to the leaves. Opium poppy (*papaver somniferum*) alkaloids form in the latex of the fruit, and in the cinchona tree, they accumulate in the bark. Those of the autumn crocus (*Colchicum autumnale*) accumulate in both the seeds and corm. Other alkaloids manifest in different parts of the plants during the daily alterations between day and night.

Many alkaloids have a pharmacological effect on organs and tissues of both animals and humans and hence serve as important agents in medical practice. The alkaloid cocaine, from the *Erythroxylon coca* leaves, blocks nerve conduction upon application and stimulates the central nervous system, but is not used for clinical purposes because the alkaloid is too toxic in its side effects, including addiction.

The pharmacological action of opium derives from its morphine content. Morphine exerts a depressant action on the central nervous system, especially on the cerebral cortex, hypothalamus, and medullary centers. This depression is effective against pain and for this reason it is often used in hospitals. Morphine also stimulates the spinal cord and the vomiting center. A related alkaloid, codeine, resembles morphine in its action, but it is much weaker. It is prescribed as a pain killer. A synthetic derivative of morphine, heroin (diamorphine), is more toxic and has a greater risk of addiction, and as such it is outlawed in the United States and Canada but used in some European countries as a therapeutic agent.

Quinine, one of over twenty cinchona alkaloids of the cinchona bark, acts on almost all forms of protoplasm with a transitory stimulation followed by depression and cessation of activity. Its pharmacological effects on various tissues and organs of the animal and human bodies include a weak increase in uterine contraction, and a local anesthetic effect. Quinine sulphate is used principally for its antimalarial action.

Nicotine's pharmacological action consists of a primary transient stimulation and a more persistent paralytic action on the skeletal muscles. It is very toxic, and very large doses may prove fatal in a few seconds. The principal use of nicotine is as an insecticide. It is commonly used in the form of a 40 percent solution of nicotine sulphate.

The alkaloid of the kola nut helps to treat stomach disorders, including dysentery. Kola powder is brewed as a tea in Jamaica for stomach disorders and food poisoning. Similarly, arecoline of the areca or betel nut is used as an anthelmintic for the treatment of tapeworm and roundworm infestation in animals but not in humans. Its pharmacological interest derives from the fact that its parasympathomimetic action stimulates the smooth intestinal muscles and exocrine gland cells innervated by postganglionic cholinergic nerve fibers.

The use of coca leaves, poppy, areca or betel nut, kola, and other psychoactive substances by ancient communities in the Americas, Asia, and Africa sparked interest in pharmacological and therapeutic properties of such plants.

BIBLIOGRAPHY

Green, Maurice B., and Paul A. Hedin, eds. *Natural Resistance of Plants to Pests. Roles of Allelochemicals*. Washington, D.C., 1986.

Henry, Thomas Anderson. *The Plant Alkaloids*. Philadelphia, 1949.

Ginsburg, David. *The Opium Alkaloids*. New York, 1962.

Phillipson, John D., Margaret F. Roberts, and M. H. Zenk, eds. *The Chemistry and Biology of Isoquinoline Alkaloids*. Berlin, 1985.

Sim, Stephen K. *Medicinal Plant Alkaloids*. Toronto, 1965.

Taylor, William I., and Norman R. Farnsworth. *The Catharanthus Alkaloids*. New York, 1975.

EDMUND ABAKA

ALSACE. Alsace is one of the earliest industrialized regions on the European continent. The first Alsatian manufacture of calico printing appeared in 1746 at Mulhouse. The Alsatian textile industry's breakthrough on the French markets occurred in the first two decades after the end of Napoleonic wars (1815), when its share of the total cotton spindles in France increased from less than 7 percent to more than 20 percent. The performance of the Alsatian metal-working industry, particularly machine building and the production of railroad equipment, was as spectacular as that of the cotton sector. During the second quarter of the nineteenth century, Alsace ranked among the foremost producers in France of a large number of products related to the machinery industry, including locomotives, locomotive wheels, and wagon wheels, as well as textile machinery. The Strasbourg-Mulhouse railway, inaugurated in 1841, was equipped with locomotives built by André Koechlin in Mulhouse. After its annexation by Germany in 1871, the departure of numerous entrepreneurs to other parts of France caused a prolonged decline in industrial output. But in the 1890s, the Alsatian economy revived, and its growth continued until World War I (1914–1918). Thereafter, Alsace was returned to France, but its frontier setting made it risky to produce there. Alsace's location became an advantage only with the end of World War II (1945). Located in the heart of Europe, Alsace is again a dynamic industrial region and has replaced textiles with electronic devices, cars, and pharmaceutical products.

If we explore Alsace's comparative advantage, which might have contributed to its successful industrialization drive, it is noteworthy that the region completely lacked both the energy supplies and the raw materials its factories needed. It had no coal, and local hydraulic power was insufficient for factories after the middle of the nineteenth century. But the quality of the rural labor force seems to have been an important factor of Alsatian industrialization.

Population growth accelerated in most rural districts of Alsace during the last quarter of the eighteenth century, leading to a proliferation of small holdings. The cultivation of cash crops by increasing work input and the manufacture of handicrafts within the household economy using underemployed labor in off-season was the typical solution Alsatian farmers chose in response to the increasing land shortage. The Alsatian labor force developed important skills that served them well once industrialization proceeded in earnest. The mentality of the regional bourgeoisie was another factor conducive to rapid industrialization. The Alsatian bourgeoisie was mostly Calvinist and, as Max Weber already asserted in 1904–1905, the Protestant ethic appears to have fostered industrial capitalism. Imbued with a tradition of study and intellectual curiosity, the Alsatian entrepreneurs became very active in implementing the new technologies of the Industrial Revolution. The strict endogamy practiced within the old Mulhouse patriarchy and parental authority over grown children facilitated the recruitment of motivated managers and the training of successors. The prolonged existence of Alsatian industrial dynasties (Dollfus, Koechlin, Schlumberger, de Dietrich) reveal the strength of this family-based capitalism.

BIBLIOGRAPHY

Hau, Michel. *L'industrialisation de l'Alsace, 1803–1939*. Strasbourg, 1987.
Ott, Florence. *La société industrielle de Mulhouse, 1826–1876*. Strasbourg, 1999.
Stoskopf, Nicolas. *La petite industrie dans le Bas-Rhin (1810–1870)*. Strasbourg, 1987.
Stoskopf, Nicolas. *Les patrons du Second Empire, Alsace*. Le Mans, France, 1994.
Selig, Jean-Michel. *Malnutrition et développement économique dans l'Alsace du XIXe siècle*. Strasbourg, 1996.

MICHEL HAU

AMERICAN INDIAN ECONOMIES *[This entry contains five subentries, an overview and discussions of Inca, Aztec, Maya, and indigenous North American economies.]*

General Overview

The pre-European cultures of the New World exhibited considerable variation in their economic institutions and processes. This variation is strongly correlated with the level of sociopolitical evolution of individual societies. Indigenous groups ranged from small bands of hunter-gatherers to large territorial empires. The case studies in the accompanying entries provide a cross section of this diversity, emphasizing the state-level societies most comparable to the Bronze Age civilizations of the Old World. The Aztec and Inca, for example, both ruled extensive empires, but their political economies were radically different. The Aztec Empire, financed through tribute in goods and long-distance trade by merchants, was part of an extensive commercial economy. The economy of the Inca Empire, by contrast, was organized by the state. Tribute was paid in labor, and institutions of commerce were largely absent.

The Classic Maya were organized into city-states ruled by charismatic kings whose level of control over the economy was probably intermediate between the Inca and Aztec examples. The Cahokia polity of North America illustrates another major form of economic organization, the complex chiefdom. Although social classes and bureaucratic organization were absent, craft specialization and trade were extensive, organized by a powerful chief who resided in an urbanized center.

Technology and Agriculture. Metallurgy had a long history in South America, and by the sixteenth century the Incas and other peoples were highly adept at smelting and working gold, silver, bronze, and other alloys through a variety of techniques. Metals were employed primarily for ritual objects and jewelry. Around 900 CE metallurgy spread from South America to Mesoamerica (Mexico and northern Central America), where again its utilitarian uses were minimal. One reason bronze was not put to use in weapons and cutting tools was the effectiveness of obsidian tools. A volcanic glass, obsidian occurs geologically in mountainous areas throughout the New World. All obsidian tools have sharp edges, and one particular form—the difficult-to-manufacture prismatic blade—has the sharpest edge known to science (sharper than a surgical scalpel). Obsidian was one of the technological highlights of ancient New World cultures.

The evolution of societies from Paleo-Indian hunters through states was accompanied by innovations in agricultural technology and agricultural intensification. Irrigation technology in the Andes and central Mexico was quite advanced, involving canals that ran for tens of kilometers, aqueducts, and a variety of dams, dikes, and other control features. These areas also saw the extensive use of terracing, both hill slope terraces and cross-channel terraces (check dams). The most important technique of intensive agriculture in the ancient New World was raised fields. This labor-intensive swamp-reclamation method produces dramatically high yields. Raised fields were used widely in South America wherever topography and hydrology permitted, and in Mesoamerica raised fields supported the cities of the Classic Maya and the Aztec capital Tenochtitlan. Although the overall level of technological development was equivalent to the Bronze Age civilizations of the Old World, New World economies lagged in two areas—the small number of utilitarian uses of metal and the rudimentary technology of transport. The concept of the wheel was known (wheeled toys existed in

Mesoamerica), but it was not put to use for transport, probably because of the mountainous terrain and a lack of suitable draft animals. Only the Inca and other Andean societies had an effective pack animal, the llama.

Production, Distribution, and Consumption. The household was the basic unit of production and consumption in most New World societies. Artisans in many areas were proficient in the technology of ceramics, chipped stone, lapidary art, textiles (using cotton and, in the Andes, the wool of camelids), and other materials. The production of utilitarian goods was widespread in both rural and urban areas, and artisans for the most part were independent producers working out of their homes. Many were farmers who worked on their crafts part-time. Luxury goods—whose production required costly raw materials and more difficult methods—were typically manufactured in urban settings under the patronage of the elite or the state. In societies with strong governmental control over the economy (for example, the Inca) luxury goods were produced by commoner specialists under the direct supervision of the state. Among the Mixtec and Maya city-states of Mesoamerica, on the other hand, junior members of royal families were the skilled artisans who produced luxury goods. In the commercial economy of the Aztecs, artisans producing jewelry, sculptures, and feather work worked both for elite patrons and independently. There is little evidence for the involvement of temples in the organization of craft production, a common pattern in the Bronze Age economies of the Old World.

All ancient New World societies engaged in long-distance trade. High transport costs, however, limited the volume of exchange and affected the types of trade goods in most cases. The organization of exchange varied with sociopolitical complexity. Egalitarian (family-level) groups used trade partnerships and other forms of face-to-face exchange to obtain needed goods. In chiefdoms and many states trade, controlled by rulers and elites, was largely limited to luxury goods. Elite gift giving was a major form of exchange. The Aztec and Inca Empires illustrate contrasting state-level distribution systems. The Aztec commercial economy fostered extensive exchange by professional merchants, leading to perhaps the highest volume of exchange (in both luxuries and necessities) in the ancient New World. The Inca redistributive economy, on the other hand, kept exchange within the polity. Imperial bureaucrats assembled goods in state storehouses and supervised their movement within the empire using a state-built infrastructure of roads, bridges, and administrative cities.

Patterns of consumption, like production and exchange, varied with sociopolitical context. Most states for which written evidence exists had some forms of sumptuary rules limiting consumption of certain goods to certain social categories, typically elites. Even where commoners and elites had access to the same goods (for example, the Aztec economy), their patterns of consumption differed. Feasting played a major role in the political and social dynamics of many societies, and this was an important factor in the organization of consumption.

Processes of Change. The most widespread and fundamental processes of economic change in the ancient world were population growth and agricultural intensification. Increases in sociopolitical complexity were almost invariably accompanied by larger populations and intensified agriculture, just as the collapse of cities and states was associated with the reverse processes. The causal relationships among these processes are much debated. In Mesoamerica several other long-term economic trends have been identified. One concerns the status of obsidian goods in the Maya region. In the Classic period (200–900 CE) obsidian was a scarce luxury, often used in ritual activities. In Postclassic times (900–1520 CE) commercial exchange intensified, the supply of obsidian increased, and the cost of obsidian declined as it became more of a necessity than a luxury to Maya households.

Another case of long-term change was an agrarian cycle in Aztec central Mexico. At the start of the Aztec period (ca. 1100 CE) populations were low. Increased rainfall coupled with an abundance of land and a scarcity of labor led to population growth, the clearing of new land, urbanization, and rising prosperity in a commercial economy. By the Aztec imperial period (1430–1520 CE), however, an abundance of labor was coupled with a shortage of land. Agriculture was heavily intensified, famines occurred, standards of living declined, and most regions fell victim to the expanding Aztec Empire. These are but a few of the cases of economic change documented by continuing archaeological and historical research on the ancient economies of the New World.

BIBLIOGRAPHY

Baugh, Timothy, and Jonathan E. Ericson, eds. *Prehistoric Exchange Systems in North America*. New York, 1994. Collection of useful chapters on the archaeological study of exchange in ancient North America and Mesoamerica.

Denevan, William M. *Cultivated Landscapes of Native Amazonia and the Andes*. New York, 2001. Masterful synthesis of indigenous agriculture in South America by the leading scholar in the field; particularly important for the analysis of raised field agriculture.

Doolittle, William E. *Cultivated Landscapes of Native North America*. New York, 2000. Major summary of indigenous agriculture based on archaeological and historical sources.

Earle, Timothy. *Bronze Age Economics: The Beginnings of Political Economies*. Boulder, 2002. Important new theoretical and empirical synthesis of ancient economies and social evolution focusing on chiefdoms; includes chapters on the Wanka and Inca of Peru.

Hirth, Kenneth G., ed. *Trade and Exchange in Early Mesoamerica*. Albuquerque, 1984. Collection of influential chapters on Formative period Mesoamerican exchange systems; includes important works on obsidian and transport.

Masson, Marilyn A., and David A. Freidel, eds. *Ancient Maya Political Economies*. Walnut Creek, Calif., 2002. Chapters describe new data and document current understandings of ancient Maya economic organization.

Peregrine, Peter N., and Gary M. Feinman, eds. *Pre-Columbian World Systems*. Madison, Wis., 1996. Analyses of ancient New World economies from a modified world-systems perspective that emphasizes the importance of trade across political borders.

Smith, Michael E. "Trade and Exchange." In *The Oxford Encyclopedia of Mesoamerican Cultures: The Civilizations of Mexico and Central America*, edited by Davíd Carrasco, vol. 3, pp. 254–257. New York, 2001. Summary of patterns of ancient exchange among the societies of ancient Mesoamerica.

Smith, Michael E., and Frances F. Berdan, eds. *The Postclassic Mesoamerican World*. Salt Lake City, 2003. Collection of chapters on the explosion of commercial exchange and stylistic interaction throughout Mesoamerica in Late Postclassic (1200–1520 CE) times; uses a modified world-systems perspective.

Stanish, Charles. "The Origin of State Societies in South America." *Annual Review of Anthropology* 30 (2001), 41–64. Useful review article summarizes current archaeological understandings of the earliest South American states and their economic organization.

Whitmore, Thomas M., and B. L. Turner II. *Cultivated Landscapes of Middle America on the Eve of Conquest*. New York, 2001. Comprehensive new survey of the ancient agricultural systems of Mesoamerica by two of the leading researchers.

MICHAEL E. SMITH

Inca Economy

The Inca empire, called Tawantinsuyu (The Four Parts Together), was a latecomer to Andean history, emerging in the early fifteenth century CE and ending with the Spanish invasion of 1532. According to most narratives told to the Spaniards, the empire lasted primarily through the reigns of three emperors: Pachakuti, Topa Inca Yupanqui, and Wayna Qhapaq. Although the Incas were innovative, the brevity of their reign meant that the imperial economy relied on millennia of cultural developments and adaptations to the complex Andean environment. Broadly speaking, the imperial Inca economy was preindustrial and precapitalist. The key features organizing economic relations were control of labor, productive resources, and distribution of products to support state projects, personnel, and political ceremony. Money, markets, and industrial-scale production of commodities were largely outside the scope of Andean economic practice (Murra, 1980; D'Altroy, 2002).

The Andean environment set challenging conditions for its inhabitants. Within a narrow band along the continent's western margin are found, from west to east, a sere desert, the highest mountain ranges in the Americas, a high plateau (altiplano), tropical forests, and low eastern plains. All of the staple foods and industrial crops used in Tawantinsuyu had been domesticated by 3000 BCE. The natural conditions favored an agricultural and maritime strategy on the coast, a mixed agropastoral economy in the highlands, and an agricultural and foraging regime along the eastern slopes of the Andes. Coastal agriculture was possible only with irrigation, and farming in the mountains was intensified through terracing and irrigation. Up to 3,600 meters (3,960 yards), a maize crop complex was preferred, while potatoes, other tubers, and chenopods were farmed at higher altitudes; maize and manioc were favored staples in the eastern lowlands. Llama and alpaca herding was widely practiced in the highlands and became a source of wealth and status for mountain peoples.

The Inca economy was rural, even though the capital city of Cuzco (Peru) housed about 100,000 people, since most of Tawantinsuyu's approximately 10 million people lived in small towns and villages. When the imperial expansion began, the Incas intensified the highland economies they knew best and left the more integrated systems of coastal societies largely alone. Each highland community owned its own resources and allocated access to them through kin relations or marriage. Specialized production was organized at a community or cottage industry level; these societies did not typically have markets, taxation in goods, a temple economy, or any other institution that would allow the Incas to easily divert their products to Cuzco's ends. In contrast, the Chimú people of Peru's north coast had economies that were more integrated; individual settlements may have specialized in the production of certain commodities, such as farm or marine products, or cloth. In Ecuador, some small-scale societies had market systems and special-purpose moneys, such as gold and shell beads, but those were not adopted in the Inca imperial economy. Even at the height of the imperial era, peasants still produced and consumed most of the products of the Inca era in their self-sufficient communities.

At least as early as the reign of Topa Inca Yupanqui (estimated conventionally as 1471–1493), the Incas made efforts to broadly apply certain policies throughout the empire. When the Incas annexed new peoples, they claimed all farmlands, pastures and flocks, and wild and mineral resources of the region (Polo, 1965; Cobo, 1979). Inca ideology maintained that all resources were divided among the state, the state religion, and the local societies, but practices varied among regions. Large tracts of farmlands and pastures were dedicated to the state and its solar religion and to royal and aristocratic manors, but most resources stayed within peasant communities. In some valleys, such as Cochabamba (Bolivia), Abancay, and Vilcashuaman (Peru), the populace was vacated and the lands were turned over to state production. The entire province of Chiquicache (Peru) may have been dedicated to the Sun, but state resources were generally greater than those of the religion.

The llama and alpaca lay at the heart of the Inca economy, and people devoted considerable energy to breeding large herds that could be used for the armies, sacrifices, and transport. Since the greatest flocks grazed in the altiplano, the Incas turned their eyes to that region to enhance the herds already husbanded near Cuzco. Although the vast state and Sun herds were tabulated each November, it is hard to come by reliable numbers, but figures in excess of one million are reasonable. The prime uses of the herds were military. Armies on the move regularly used trains of thousands of llamas to pack supplies and to serve as food when they were no longer needed for portage. Herding for the state was at least partially a specialized duty conducted by adults, a practice that contrasted with the typical community practice, in which children and adolescents tended the flocks.

The economy was administered through provincial governors, usually ethnic Incas, aided by a coterie of assistants. Prominent among the aides were the *khipu kamayuq*, or keepers of the mnemonic knot records (*khipu*). These individuals used a base-ten system to keep track of the populace, labor obligations, resources, and stored goods, among other things. Officials below the governor were typically local elites confirmed in their positions by state representatives.

The basic taxpaying unit was a married couple. Most of the services and products that the Inca state required were obtained through a corvée system that tabbed the heads of households for rotating service, called *mit'a*. The products of the peasantry's own fields and flocks were generally untouched, but subjects lost considerable resources through alienation. In return for their subjects' labors, the state owed largess, security, leadership, and support during the discharge of duties. The rationale was that the Incas were extending traditional relationships of mutual obligation between local lords and their subjects to a grander system (Murra, 1980). A householder's duties required two to three months of his time annually, and his family could help discharge his obligations. Some chroniclers wrote that there were more than forty standard categories of duties. The most important were farming on state lands, portage, military duty, and construction. Tax obligations were tailored to the resources of individual provinces and the perceived skills of their inhabitants, so that taxes were not applied uniformly throughout the empire.

To determine the available resources and manpower, the Incas undertook periodic censuses. There were apparently ten categories each for males and females, with classifications based on an individual's productive capabilities. Because married men about twenty-five to fifty years of age made up about 15 to 20 percent of the empire's population, the Incas could call on the labor of about two million workers. Many households were organized into a pyramid of units that encompassed from ten to ten thousand households; each unit was headed by an official appointed by the state. Despite its renown, the decimal hierarchy has been identified principally in the central part of the empire, not in the far north or south.

Over time, the Incas appeared to move away from an economy based on the productive capacities of the general populace toward a more independent economy (Murra, 1980). To that end, they created several special labor categories. Most important were resettled colonists (*mitmaqkuna*), lifelong servants (*yanakuna*), and sequestered young women (*aqllakuna*) dedicated to weaving and brewing before being awarded in marriage. State-sponsored mass production arose from the Incas' interest in controlling the quality, nature, and circulation of products in the state style, not from efforts to reduce costs in a market economy, even though local exchange was widespread below the mantle of state oversight. The state retained thousands of weavers, metalsmiths, wood and lapidary workers, sandal makers, potters, feather and pigment workers, dyers, and makers of weapons, hunting gear, and personal adornments. The system worked because many tributaries were already masters of a particular craft, and weaving was the essence of feminine skill.

The Incas resettled entire communities of farmers and artisans who were set to work for particular needs. The largest enclaves, such as the weaving community at Milliraya (Peru), contained as many as one thousand workers dedicated to a single craft. About one-quarter to one-third of the empire's populace was ultimately resettled. Crafts made for the Incas combined high quality with labor intensity and mass production. The simplicity and repetition of the basic elements lent themselves to duplication by artisans throughout the empire. The products were then used to supply state activities or aristocrats or were distributed through ceremonial largess to favored elites or individuals who had distinguished themselves in service to the state. The ruler and other lords also retained personal artisans who produced goods for household consumption or gifts. Even so, most artisans worked part-time at their crafts, alternating farming and herding with seasonal or intermittent craft work. Full-time artisans working for themselves, the state, or elite patrons were rare, perhaps even in Cuzco.

The imperial expansion also put vast resources in the hands of the Inca elites, some of which were converted into private reserves for living and deceased emperors and other aristocrats. Every province set aside lands for each ruler, but the most elegant estates lay in a hundred-kilometer (62-mile) stretch of the Vilcanota/Urubamba drainage basin between Pisac and Machu Picchu. The estates were used to support the monarchs in a manner suited to their deified stature, while providing sustenance and wealth for their descendants and the underwriting of their political and ceremonial activities (Cobo, 1990).

A vast storage system provided the bridge between state-sponsored production and use throughout the empire. As with farms and herds, the state and church storehouses were administratively and physically separated. Most of the storehouses were built at Cuzco, at state installations along the roads, and next to state farms. The largest known facilities contained two to three thousand buildings (e.g., Hatun Xauxa, Cotapachi), within which the Incas stored all manner of provisions, including foodstuffs, armaments, raw materials for artisans, and finished luxury goods.

[*See also* Andean Region; Argentina; Central South American States; *and* Chile.]

BIBLIOGRAPHY

Cobo, Bernabé. *History of the Inca Empire: An Account of the Indians' Customs and Their Origin, Together with a Treatise on Inca Legends, History, and Social Institutions*. Translated by Roland Hamilton. Austin, 1979.

Cobo, Bernabé. *Inca Religion and Customs*. 1st ed. Edited by Roland Hamilton. Austin, 1990.

D'Altroy, Terence N. *The Incas*. Oxford, 2002.

Murra, John V. *The Economic Organization of the Inka State*. Greenwich, Conn., 1980.

Polo de Ondegardo, Juan. "A Report on the Basic Principles Explaining the Serious Harm Which Follows When the Traditional Rights of the Indians Are Not Respected." In *Information concerning the Religion and Government of the Incas*, translated by A. Brunel, John Murra, and Sidney Muirden, pp. 53–196. New Haven, 1965.

TERENCE N. D'ALTROY

Aztec Economy

The Aztec economy was divided into two distinct sectors: the capital, and cities more generally, and the countryside and tributary empire. The great challenge to understanding this economy has been to integrate the evidence from Tenochtitlán, the imperial capital, and from the countryside into a comprehensive interpretation. Tenochtitlán lived on the tribute or surplus of its subject towns, but in a very distinctive way. Most of the people in small towns were farmers and part-time specialists, whereas in the cities, the economy was dominated by the activities of artisans, masons, merchants, and practitioners of different trades, as well as providers of every kind of urban service.

The attention of scholars has focused on three issues: food production and supply, trade, and tribute.

Food Production and Supply. In regard to food production and supply, there are two general themes: agriculture, with an emphasis on cultivation techniques and types of plants and yields, with little attention paid to storage and transport, and the nature and quality of the diet. The Aztec agriculture was Mesoamerican, based on maize, squashes, chili, and beans, often seeded together, and a variety of vegetables and fruits, mainly maguey (a sort of cac-

tus) and cacao. The main techniques were fallowing and irrigation. The most intensive cultivation, practiced in the lakes around Tenochtitlán, was the *chinampas*, or plots of land claimed from the shallow waters of the lakes, frequently misnamed "floating gardens," and still in use in Mexico today. Using seedbeds and transplanting only germinated plants, it was possible to have several crops in a single year.

The adequacy of the diet was hotly debated in the 1970s and 1980s. The focus of research was on the lack of cattle and a consequent shortage of protein in the diet. The Aztecs raised only turkeys and dogs for human consumption. Several scholars postulated that cannibalism was a response to the lack of meat (Michael Harner, Marvin Harris), whereas others claimed that the diet was actually very rich, based on maize and beans, complemented by insects, reptilians, and waterfowl. One important nutritional source documented by Fray Bernardino de Sahagún, a sixteenth-century Spanish friar, was the alga spirulina (Santley and Rose). These researchers concluded that the Aztec diet was proper and could support high population levels.

Trade in the Aztec Economy. A great deal of agricultural and craft production entered into trade. Short-distance dealers moved food, local crafts, and raw materials, often as part-time specialists, whereas long-distance merchants (Nahuatl: *pochteca*) supplied luxury items and enjoyed a high status, even reaching the nobility.

The marketplace was the distribution center, varying in size from Tenochtitlán to the smaller towns. The Spanish conquerors Hernán Cortés and Bernal Díaz del Castillo described their astonishment when they saw the Tlatelolco market. There were every kind of food, clothes, raw materials, jewels, animals, firewood, luxury and utilitary wares, and services like barbers, artisans, masons, porters, and vendors of cooked food, all arranged by items. Several judges and lesser officials supervised the markets. Barter was present, but the Mesoamericans used cacao beans and certain cloaks as money. Some researchers have added copper axes and quills filled with gold dust as currency equivalents in the Aztec economy. Cacao and cotton cloaks continued being used as money after the Spanish Conquest, besides Spanish coins.

The main function of the market in Tenochtitlán was to provide food, tools, and raw materials to the urban population, composed of nonagricultural specialists. At Tenochtitlán were many artisans, porters, merchants, and practitioners of almost every kind of urban service, from cleaning the streets, to supplying water, to constructing and maintaining buildings.

It seems clear now that the short-distance dealers were most active at markets held daily in the great cities and every five, ten, or twenty days in smaller towns. Some of the dealers were also producers, and others were fulltime

AZTEC AGRICULTURE. The lake marshes on the outskirts of the Aztec capital of Tenochtitlán at Xochimilco, Mexico, were reclaimed and converted into raised agricultural fields (*chinampas*) in the early 1400s. (Nick Saunders/Barbara Heller Photo Library, London/Art Resource, NY)

merchants. Not so clear is the relationship between long-distance merchants and markets. Sources indicate that the *pochtecas* worked at the marketplaces in these major cities and also at their destination towns. These merchants also traded at neutral points with peoples outside the empire. This foreign trade sometimes merged into spying in enemy territories and even into open warfare. We do not know if such trade was carried on regularly, with expeditions meeting at trading sites at an appointed time, or if the long-distance traders maintained permanent trading posts. The character of the traders' convoys is also debated. One view holds that the merchants set out to trade at a specific destination, another that they engaged in a sort of peddling at many points along their routes. At any rate, we know that these trading expeditions often lasted for several years.

More research has been done on transportation. In the Aztec Empire, all transportation was done by water, in canoes or on rafts, where it was possible, or with human porters (Nahuatl: *tlameme*). Ross Hassig (1985) studied the weight of the burden the porters carried (around 50 pounds), the wages, the distances (variable, depending on the terrain, load, and weather), and the organization. Other scholars have studied transportation apart from the activities of the merchants. It is believed that the great *pochtecas*, mainly dealers in luxury items, must have had some control of their porters. Thus, there must have been merchant enterprises, embracing several levels of trade: local and long distance, markets, porters, and producers, in Tenochtitlán and abroad.

Tribute. Tribute was the major source of income of the Aztec elite. Conquered provinces owed the empire large quantities of goods and services. Two pictorial manuscripts (the Codex Mendoza and the *Matrícula de tributos*) and one prose document (*Información de los tributos que pagaban a Moctezuma*), all of them written in the sixteenth century, show the kinds of tributed goods and their amounts: maguey fiber cloaks, cotton cloaks, ceramics, grains (maize, chia, and beans), warrior costumes and shields, quetzal feathers, eagles, jaguar skins, gold dust and gold jewels, raw cotton, cacao beans, clothes, paper, mats, firewood, strings of jade beads, and so on. The amounts listed in these documents remain the object of speculation. The texts in Nahuatl and Spanish accompanying the pictures in the *Matrícula de tributos* appear to suggest that each picture is a unit of the represented product, while the Spanish text in the Codex Mendoza suggests that each is a *carga*, that is, a load of twenty units each. In addition, these documents appear to be schedules of taxes due rather than accounts of taxes received. The Codex Mendoza indicates that it lists the tributes paid to Moctezuma, the Aztec emperor when Hernán Cortés arrived, but some authors argue that many of the goods remained in the provinces and never were carried to Tenochtitlán.

Until recently, most scholars believed that the tribute mentioned in the cited manuscripts was all the imperial tribute the subjects paid, but now we know that there were many types of tribute, with different sorts of obligations, such as maintaining garrisons and defending commercial routes. Local rulers also received goods and labor from their subject states and people. Thus, the study of the Aztec tribute system is linked to the analysis of the political units and their evolution. If there were multiple types of political relationships in the Aztec Empire, there must have been different degrees of autonomy or subjection of local rulers.

One of the items we must elucidate is the transformation of the tribute paid. Prose documents from the sixteenth century indicate that the vassals (Nahuatl: *macehualli*) paid in mainly agricultural labor, including the provision of wood and water, to their masters. Local rulers paid in goods to their superiors, mainly cotton cloaks, clothes, turkeys, and cacao beans. The Codex Mendoza shows the goods arranged by provinces; some of the goods, such as beans and maize, may be the result of an accumulation process, whereas others, such as live eagles and pieces of amber, must have another provenance. The document describes the tribute the whole province paid, not the addition of the tribute of the towns painted in each page. Scholars have surmised that every page in the Codex Mendoza offers two types of information: the places with officials representing the empire and the total tribute of the province.

We cannot discuss the Aztec economy without mentioning the Aztec political system. The most recent model, proposed by Frances Berdan and colleagues (1996), supports the importance of the ruling elites over the towns. Conquests and alliances were between people, and so were the duties: the *macehualli* paid to their masters, who paid to the local ruler, who in turn paid to the regional governor, who paid to the emperor.

In summary, the Aztec economy was based on agriculture and craft production. The movement of goods was done in three ways, which formed a single system: trade, tribute, and marketplaces. Barter and some forms of money (mainly cacao beans) were used, and there had to have been a system of storage, which we know very little about.

[*See also* Central American Countries *and* Mexico.]

BIBLIOGRAPHY

Berdan, Frances F. *The Aztecs of Central Mexico: An Imperial Society.* New York, 1982.

Berdan, Frances F., and Patricia R. Anawalt. *The Essential Codex Mendoza.* Berkeley, 1997.

Berdan, Frances, Richard Blanton, Elizabeth Boone, et al. *Aztec Imperial Strategies.* Washington, D.C., 1996.

Carrasco, Pedro. "La economía del México prehispánico." In *Economía, política e ideología en el México prehispánico,* edited by Pedro Carrasco and Johanna Broda, pp. 15–76. Mexico, 1978.

Davies, Nigel. *The Aztecs: A History.* Norman, Okla., 1973.

Harvey, Herbert H. *Land and Politics in the Valley of Mexico.* Albuquerque, 1991.

Hassig, Ross. *Trade, Tribute and Transportation: Sixteenth-Century Political Economy of the Valley of Mexico.* Norman, Okla., 1985.

Hassig, Ross. *Aztec Warfare: Imperial Expansion and Political Control.* Norman, Okla., 1988.

Hodge, Mary G., and Michael E. Smith. *Economies and Polities in the Aztec Realm.* Albany, N.Y., 1994.

Sanders, William T., Jeffrey R. Parsons, and Robert S. Santley. *The Basin of Mexico: Ecological Processes in the Evolution of a Civilization.* New York, 1979.

Smith, Michael F. *The Aztecs.* Oxford, 1996.

JOSÉ LUIS DE ROJAS

Maya Economy

The Maya inhabit the area of Mesoamerica that includes Guatemala and Belize, the Mexican states of Yucatán, Campeche, Quintana Roo, Tabasco, and Chiapas, and parts of El Salvador and Honduras. They built a great ancient civilization but in modern times have been mostly reduced to a peasantry, a servant class, and a rural proletariat employed on plantations.

Mayan-speaking people of various dialect groups have inhabited this region for three millennia and developed a productive economy based on food crops, especially maize, beans, and squash. The technology used for maize was simple but effective: After clearing the land, the farmer made a hole with a digging stick, dropped a few seeds into the hole, and then with a foot covered the hole with dirt. The plant was productive, usually yielding harvests of forty to one or more. However, the land in the Maya area was usually easily exhausted, thus requiring the farmers to move on and clear new lands only a few years after the first clearing and planting. Beans, squash, tomatoes, onions, and chile peppers were also regularly produced to yield a largely well-balanced vegetarian diet. Production was carried out through a rigid sexual division of labor: Males cared for the fields of maize and beans, while females raised vegetables and fruits in the area around the family house. The extended family, therefore, was the essential unit of production. In addition, Maya grew, raised, or hunted various animals — turkeys, peccaries, deer, and fish — which provided the vitamins not found in vegetables. Fish farming and fishing at sea and in rivers, streams, and lakes were also important activities. Food production was productive enough to generate a substantial surplus, which allowed for the emergence of social classes and a complex civilization.

In addition to food, the Maya economy also included production of cotton textiles of high quality. The Maya cultivated cotton for thousands of years, and cotton cloth was virtually the only article of clothing for basic, rather than ceremonial, use. It was also one of the most important exports from the region until modern times. Production once

MAYAN CITY. Remains of the step pyramids of the ancient Mayan center, Tikal, Guatemala. (SEF/Art Resource, NY)

again was in accordance with a sexual division of labor: Males carried out the harvesting of cotton, while women and girls removed the seeds, spun the thread, and wove the cloth in their houses using a back-strap loom.

The ancient Maya belonged to a trading network that linked local production to regional and broader Mesoamerican markets. In addition to cotton textiles, the Maya traded or exported salt, jade, slaves, fish, quetzal feathers (highly prized in central Mexico), and cacao. The latter, produced in Tabasco and northern Honduras, was used throughout Mesoamerica not only to make a beverage but also as coins in the marketplace, for the ancient Maya economy was largely monetized. These trade routes diminished in importance in the ninth century and afterward because of the collapse of the Classic Maya city-states, but then recovered somewhat in the post-Classic period. The Maya population also declined in numbers as a result of the Classic Maya collapse, but it, too, recovered

somewhat in the two centuries before the arrival of Europeans.

After the conquest, the Spaniards found the Maya economy to be useful and thus worth preserving. Although the Maya could not be made to produce great riches for the colonists, their production provided income for the provincial Spanish upper classes that emerged throughout the area. Therefore, the colonial regime kept the already existing tributary system in place and recognized the Maya as the owners of their village lands (so that they would be able to pay their taxes). Tribute consisted of payments in kind (maize, turkeys, salt, fish, cacao, and textiles) in the first century after the conquest and increasingly in money after that.

Cotton textiles proved to be the most commercial and therefore most useful and lucrative of the tributary goods. In the late sixteenth century, cotton production became even more important in the lowland Maya area because demographic decline in the lowland Gulf Coast area reduced production there. At the same time, the opening of the silver mines of Honduras and northern Mexico created considerable demand. In order to increase production, the Spaniards employed a system known as the *repartimiento* (a frequently coercive putting-out system requiring Indians to pay tribute debts in cloth). This meant that the Yucatan Peninsula, far from being isolated from the world economy, was in fact an export platform, sending large quantities of cotton textiles to central and northern Mexico, one of the most important places in the world economy at that time. Lesser quantities were sent to Honduras from Guatemala. The Maya of Chiapas sent cloth to both Mexico and Honduras.

The viability and profitability of the lowland cotton industry declined significantly in the late colonial period. Political and economic reforms designed to encourage competition, stimulate Spanish textile production, and diminish governmental corruption resulted in the elimination, in the 1780s, of the *repartimiento* system, which had boosted output beyond what was required as part of the tributary system. As a result, the Maya, now given a choice, continued to pay their tribute in cloth but chose not to produce beyond what was necessary. Total output, therefore, declined significantly. Then, in the early nineteenth century, English textiles began arriving in large numbers and effectively eliminated the traditional Maya textile industry, although production for domestic consumption continued for a long time afterward.

Throughout most of history, forced labor was a significant feature of the Maya economy. In the precolonial era, people were required to perform community service and sometimes work on the lands of the local and regional elites. This practice continued after the Spanish conquest and into the twentieth century. During the colonial period, the Spaniards increased forced labor by requiring the Maya to work in the few gold and silver mines of the highlands and on indigo plantations in the lowlands. Many people also had to work to build the Spaniards' houses and churches and then to build churches in their own villages. However, in the late sixteenth century forced labor tended to abate somewhat in the lowlands and in Chiapas because of the decline or virtual disappearance of Spanish enterprises. In the Guatemalan highlands, on the other hand, virtually all Spanish-owned landed estates received annual allotments of laborers from surrounding villages. This practice continued into the twentieth century.

The Maya, whose population totaled 1 million or more before the Spanish invasion, declined to around 300,000 after the conquest because of disease and destruction. Since fewer people required less land, Spaniards in most cases could establish landed estates without dispossessing the indigenous people. In the eighteenth century, however, the Maya population increased rapidly, which resulted in a land shortage. Increasingly, the Maya had to rent or work on the properties of Spaniards. At the same time, new markets for Spanish-owned rural enterprises opened up. Thus, non-Indians increasingly desired the land held by the Maya. In the nineteenth century, the demand for forced labor increased dramatically, and the Maya had to work even more for the non-Indians.

This began first in Yucatán, which, because of its location, has always been more integrated into the world economy than the rest of the Maya area. Sugar planters in the late colonial period expanded production, a process that the government aided by organizing labor drafts from the surrounding villages. After independence (1821), the non-Indian planters expanded production and acquired land in new areas. Once again, the government helped by changing the law, making it easier to claim supposedly unused lands. This expansion, however, helped contribute to a massive Maya rebellion called the Caste War (1847–1901), which resulted in the destruction of the sugar economy.

In the latter half of the century, Yucatán's estate owners began production of henequen (made into binder twine, which was exported to the United States) on a massive scale. Legal changes allowed them to acquire land from the Maya. As a result, the Maya usually had to work half-time or full-time (as resident laborers) on the estates. The resident workers were usually peons, who were sometimes subjected to considerable abuse by their bosses until the Mexican Revolution (1910–1940). Subsequent agrarian changes and foreign competition destroyed the profitability of the henequen industry, leaving the Maya with neither jobs nor a viable economic base. In the last decades of the twentieth century, many emigrated to work in the service or construction industry in Cancún, Mérida, Mexico City, and southern California.

The intensification of estate agriculture occurred later in Guatemala and Chiapas, where it involved production of coffee for export to Europe and later to the United States. As in Yucatán, the government aided the process by authorizing forced labor and making it easier for non-Indians to acquire land at the expense of the Maya. Once again, much abuse of the labor force took place, and forced labor did not end until after 1944. Political instability, resulting from social and economic inequalities, caused the deaths of thousands of Maya since the 1960s and the disruption of the economy. As a result, many people migrated to the United States.

The Maya peasant economy still survives, and the Maya peasants make up the majority of the population throughout much of Guatemala and Chiapas and, to a lesser extent, Yucatán. However, they are among the poorest people in their respective countries.

[*See also* Central American Countries *and* Mexico.]

BIBLIOGRAPHY

Benjamin, Thomas. *A Rich Land, A Poor People: Politics and Society in Modern Chiapas*. 2d ed. Albuquerque, 1996.

Lovell, W. George. *Conquest and Survival in Colonial Guatemala: A Historical Geography of the Cuchumatán Highlands, 1500–1821*. 2d ed. Montreal, 1992.

McCreery, David. *Rural Guatemala, 1760–1940*. Stanford, Calif., 1994.

MacLeod, Murdo J. *Spanish Central America: A Socioeconomic History, 1520–1720*. Berkeley, 1973.

Patch, Robert W. *Maya and Spaniard in Yucatan, 1648–1812*. Stanford, Calif., 1993.

Patch, Robert W. "Imperial Politics and Local Economy in Colonial Central America, 1670–1770." *Past and Present* 143 (1994), 77–107.

Sherman, William L. *Forced Native Labor in Sixteenth-Century Central America*. Lincoln, Nebr., 1979.

Wells, Allen. *Yucatan's Gilded Age: Haciendas, Henequen, and International Harvester, 1860–1915*. Albuquerque, 1985.

Wortman, Miles L. *Government and Society in Central America, 1680–1840*. New York, 1982.

ROBERT PATCH

Indigenous North American Economy

Alfred Marshall's observation that economics "is a branch of biology broadly interpreted" (1948, p. 772) applies with special force to Native American economic history. The first Americans lived closely connected to their environment, continuously adapting to changes in climate, geography, and the arrival of Europeans by developing new modes of production supported by evolving cultural, legal, and political institutions. A variety of Amerindian modes of production and institutions emerged in response to changing incentives facing the tribes of present-day Canada and the continental United States from prehistoric times to the present.

Early History. Advanced paleolithic people first migrated to America by crossing the Bering land bridge that connected Siberia to northern Alaska around 10,000 BCE (before present). These people expanded their range to the rest of Canada and the continental United States by approximately 9000 BCE. Native Americans who stayed in the Arctic (the Inuit or Eskimo) spread eastward across the Arctic region, hunting marine mammals such as whales and seals. Others, who migrated southward, used stone weapons with fluted points attached to spears to hunt a variety of large mammals. Prey animals included the mammoth, mastodon, caribou, two species of larger-than-modern bison, stag moose, deer, and pronghorn antelope. Paleo-Indians hunted in small, interdependent groups of fifteen to fifty members that covered ranges up to 30,000 square miles (77,700 square kilometers) over an annual cycle. The size of hunting groups increased where economies of scale in killing large prey such as bison existed. For example, pedestrian hunters stampeded herds of bison over cliffs in the present-day western United States as long ago as 6500 BCE. This technique required cooperation among several bands to locate herds, drive them toward trapping sites, initiate stampedes, and process meat. Surplus meat was preserved to ensure against shortfalls due to erratic herd migration patterns. The spiritual life of these communities was focused on rituals to ensure hunting success.

A warmer global climate caused glaciers covering much of North America to recede through 6000 BP, resulting in changes in the mode of production in different regions. Hunting large game continued to be the primary subsistence activity for Amerindians in western North America, but groups in other locations responded differently to changing opportunity costs resulting from climate change. For example, agriculture first appeared in Mexico from 5000 BCE and gradually spread north to other Amerindian communities, enabling them to adopt a more sedentary existence. Town-centered life with higher population densities took hold among the Pueblo Indians in the Southwest with irrigated cultivation of corn, beans, squash, cotton, and tobacco. The Indians of the Southeast and Midwest grew corn, beans, squash, and tobacco. Plains Indians, typically associated with bison hunting, were also accomplished riverine farmers in the period leading up to contact with Europeans. Agriculture played a less important role the farther north Amerindians lived and in areas close to other food sources that could be procured by gathering (e.g., acorns for tribes in California and shellfish for coastal Indians) or by fishing. Fishing was especially important to the tribes of the Northwest. Clearly, Indians specialized according to the absolute and comparative advantages that nature conferred.

Prior to contact with Europeans, farming not only generated surpluses to support larger communities in the Southwest, Southeast, and Midwest, but also allowed interregional trade to flourish. For example, the Pueblo Indians exchanged locally produced cotton cloth and maize for imported bison hides and meat from the Great Plains, shells from California, and exotic feathers from Mexico. Extensive trade networks supported successive cultures in the Southeast and Midwest based around cosmology characterized by ritual burial practices, human sacrifice, and extensive mound building over many centuries. Work on mounds located at present-day Poverty Point, Louisiana, began about 1200 BCE. Mound building in the Ohio River Valley dates from approximately 500 BCE. Mississippian civilization, the last of the mound-building cultures, climaxed between 900 and 1400 CE. centered around Cahokia in present-day southern Illinois. Cahokia supported a population between 15,000 and 38,000. Other Mississippian population centers existed in Moundville (in northern Alabama) and Etowah (in northern Georgia). The Mississippians traded over long distances in raw materials like shells and a variety of stone types, finished blades, sculptures, furs, dried meats, and other foodstuffs. Specialization and

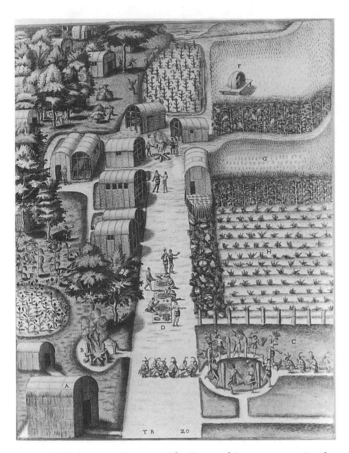

AMERICAN INDIANS IN VIRGINIA. *The Town of Secota*, engraving by Theodore de Bry (1528–1598) based on eyewitness drawings of John White, who traveled to Virginia in 1585. From Bry's *America*, pt. 1, 1590. Fields of tobacco, corn, and pumpkins lie adjacent to special areas set aside for ceremonies, prayer, and feasting. (Service Historique de la Marine, Vincennes, France/Giraudon/Art Resource, NY)

division of labor were widespread in Mississippian culture, alongside a hierarchical political structure that enforced surplus production and investment in public works.

Cahokia's power declined over the thirteenth and fourteenth centuries as other Mississippian communities in the Southeast gained relative political and military strength. Cahokia may have overexploited local resources or may have encountered growing disaffection from neighboring communities with Cahokia's requirements for sacrificial victims to serve dead elites in the next life. Chiefdoms emerged in the Southeast in the wake of Cahokia's decline that were precursors to the town-centered agricultural tribes, including the Chickasaws, Choctaws, Creeks, and Cherokees.

Prior to the entry of European explorers and colonists to North America in the sixteenth and seventeenth centuries, Native Americans had adapted to local climate and resource bases in ways that facilitated enough surplus pro-

duction to support significant trade activities, although accumulations of wealth were notable only in the Southwest, Midwest, and Southeast, where agriculture predominated. Surplus production by the Amerindians also supported persons devoted to art, religion, and the continuation of culturally significant rituals. Estimates of population size for the North American native population prior to European contact vary widely from 1.25 million to 10 million. Life expectancies at birth were in the mid-twenties, similar to other subsistence populations in the late fifteenth century. Dramatic changes in modes of production, institutions, and living standards for Amerindians followed the arrival of Europeans.

Effects of European Contact. Native Americans along the Atlantic and Gulf coasts had sporadic contact with Europeans during the sixteenth century. Inland contacts were limited to Hernando de Soto's expedition in the Southeast from 1539 to 1543 and Francisco Vasquez de Coronado's wanderings in search of gold in the Southwest from 1540 to 1542. Both of these expeditions led to the spread of deadly pathogens, especially smallpox, among the Indians they encountered. Thus, the tribes in the Southeast and Southwest were weakened considerably by population losses immediately after first contact with Europeans.

European settlement greatly expanded along the Atlantic coast during the seventeenth century and drastically changed the economic life of Amerindians. For example, by the 1620s, the French were trading manufactured goods for tens of thousands of pelts each year with Montagnais, Algonquins, and Hurons along the St. Lawrence and in the upper Great Lakes region. The Dutch used wampum, sacred shell beads used in rituals and exchanges, to facilitate trade of European goods for pelts with the Iroquois and other tribes in the Hudson Valley and along the Mohawk River. Somewhat later, English colonists in Massachusetts moved easily into the Connecticut River Valley after a smallpox epidemic had decimated local Indian populations in the 1630s. Farther south along the Atlantic coast, English colonists negotiated transfers of land rights with various tribes. As encroachments on Indian land increased, Native Americans responded violently, with disastrous results for tribes like the Powhatan in Virginia, who were virtually wiped out by 1646. Trading dominated in South Carolina, where the coastal Yamasee tribe, equipped with firearms by the British, captured members from the inland Cherokees for sale into slavery on Caribbean sugar plantations. Over time, the Cherokees also established trade relations with the English to gain access to firearms that allowed them to defeat the Yamasees and begin trading valuable deerskins for export from Charlestown (Charleston).

Supplies of Western goods and the strong European demand for furs dramatically altered the incentives facing

Native Americans. Instead of subsistence hunting for food, Indians shifted to trapping and hunting activities to support the fur trade with Europeans. Competition for access to furs among various tribes in Canada and the Great Lakes region ensued, with the French, British, Dutch, and later, the Americans vying for supremacy on the buyers' side of this lucrative market. The British Hudson's Bay Company emerged as a dominant force by the early eighteenth century, trading mainly with the Cree Indians in Canada. Town-centered agriculture diminished as Native American communities scattered to engage more effectively in the fur trade. Extensive trapping led to the gradual depletion of the common-property populations of fur-bearing animals.

Imperial conflicts between European powers, especially the British and the French, created a new employment opportunity for Native Americans as mercenaries. The Iroquois were among the most active as mercenaries, having established a confederacy among their tribes (the Senecas, Cayugas, Onondagas, Oneidas, and Mohawks) in the seventeenth century. The Iroquois were able to unite militarily against other tribes and to ally with the English against the French and, later, against the revolutionary American colonists. During the American Revolution, tribes along and to the west of the Proclamation Line of 1763 correctly perceived their self-interest as British allies. However, decades of warfare and the British defeat in 1783 left the Indians in the eastern United States weakened as a result of disease, war losses, and disruptions in traditional modes of production.

Early United States policy toward Native Americans in the administrations up to Andrew Jackson's first term in 1828 focused on assimilation. The intention was to instruct Amerindians in agriculture so that they would abandon subsistence hunting and gathering, thus decreasing their land requirements. Then, Indian title to surplus land could be extinguished through negotiation, thereby opening large expanses of land west of the Appalachian range to white settlement. Some tribes, including the Cherokee, Creeks, Choctaw, and Chickasaw, successfully adopted agriculture practiced by nuclear families rather than the traditional community-based agriculture that existed prior to white contact. Cherokee farmers produced large surpluses of food by the mid-1830s. These Southeastern tribes had significant numbers of households that owned African slaves and practiced limited plantation agriculture. Northern tribes, including the Iroquois, Shawnee, Miami, and Potawatomi, had more difficulty adopting agriculture and faced intense pressure from white settlers moving into the Northwest Territory. An agricultural lifestyle was harder for men from these tribes to accept, given a historical sexual division of labor where women were charged with farming and men focused on hunting and warfare. By 1828, most northern tribes had been pushed west or had been decimated by warfare, disease, and alcoholism. Jackson adopted a controversial policy of negotiated removal to Oklahoma for the remaining Indians in the Southeast. Removal treaties were negotiated with the Creeks, Chickasaws, Choctaws, Cherokees, and finally, after a bitter war that lasted into the 1840s, the Seminoles in Florida. Farming communities were reestablished in Oklahoma alongside the remnants of the northern tribes.

Contact with Spanish explorers, missionaries, and colonizers in the arid Southwest and California affected Amerindians primarily through the introduction of the horse (which extended to the Plains Indians) and by the influence of the Catholic Church. The horse eliminated the scale advantages from large-group buffalo hunts, making possible more productive hunting by smaller bands of Indians. The nature of warfare also changed as warriors from the Southwest and Plains tribes, especially the Apaches and Comanches, advanced to be among the world's most-skilled cavalry troops. The Plains Indians thrived as a result of the new horse culture. Anthropometric evidence shows that they were the tallest people in the world as late as the second half of the nineteenth century, stature being an indication of healthful living conditions. Indians in California were less fortunate as a result of early contact with the Spanish in the eighteenth century. Catholic missions were established along the California coast, and the extraordinarily diverse California tribes were encouraged to abandon their traditional hunting, gathering, and fishing modes of production in order to settle and farm close to the missions. Between 1769 and 1832, California's Indian population fell from some 300,000 to 98,000 due largely to epidemic diseases and the disruption of traditional modes of subsistence production.

Native Americans in the Pacific Northwest, including coastal Alaska, had regular contact with Europeans after the Russian Vitus Bering's explorations in 1741. An active fur trade developed between the numerous tribes (especially the Chinooks) in the Northwest and Russian, Spanish, and British traders. Except for the spread of disease among the Indian populations of the Northwest, the fur trade was mutually beneficial to Europeans and Indians, who proved to be highly skilled traders. However, as settlement in Oregon, Washington, and British Columbia increased through the middle of the nineteenth century, trade relations were strained by conflicts over land tenure between whites and Indians. The warfare that ensued resulted in the restriction of Northwest Indians to reserves in Canada and reservations in the United States. Indians in the Northwest continued to practice traditional forms of primary production (fishing, hunting, and trapping) in connection with the growing European economy.

From Devastation to Rebirth: The Nineteenth Century to Today. The Indian wars in the western United States after the American Civil War had a devastating impact on tribes ranging from the Sioux in the northern Plains to the Apaches in the Southwest. American policy shifted from negotiated removal to one that verged on outright extermination. Surviving Amerindians were confined to reservations. Conflict on a lesser scale between Indians and whites occurred on the Canadian Plains in the late nineteenth century.

The Dawes Act of 1887 attempted to convert Plains Indians in the United States to farmers through an allotment policy that gave nuclear households title to 160 acres. Indian title to remaining reservation land was then extinguished to the extent possible. Native Americans lost some 90 million acres of their land in this manner from 1887 to 1934. The Dawes Act caused breakdowns in tribal governments, extended family relations, and as title to land. Similar attempts in Canada to establish agriculture among Native Americans during the late nineteenth century met with general failure. Although many Canadian Plains Indians were willing to become farmers, given declining buffalo populations, too few resources were provided by the Canadian government for agriculture to succeed.

The Amerindian population probably hit a historic low in 1890 with only 228,000 Indians in the United States. The economic circumstances for Amerindians from 1890 to 1950 can be characterized as grinding poverty. Amerindians in the United States and Canada existed as wards of the state, whereby the relationship between tribes and the federal governments largely determined their economic possibilities. Some improvement in economic circumstances for Indians in the United States came after the Indian Reorganization Act (IRA) of 1934. The United States adopted a new approach in this legislation with the abandonment of the goal of assimilation. The IRA reorganized tribal governments and ended sales of Indian land to non-Indians under the Dawes Act. The act allowed traditional Amerindian institutions to reemerge and guide economic progress with support from the federal government. Although this policy was reversed during the Eisenhower administration with a push to terminate the federal relationship with Native Americans, termination proved disastrous for the few tribes involved and was abandoned. Today, policy has shifted to treat Indian tribes more like sovereign powers with greater political and economic self-determination in both the United States and Canada.

In 1990, the Indian population in the United States stood at just over two million, and the Canadian Indian population was just under one million. The dramatic recovery in population is due largely to more people identifying themselves as Indian, although birth rates are high within the largely rural Amerindian communities. Statistical measures of living standards show that Native Americans have reached economic parity with African Americans. The re-

silience of Native American culture is displayed in an ongoing economic, political, legal, and artistic renaissance that is testimony to the adaptiveness of the Amerindians and their institutions to radically altered environments.

[*See also* Canada *and* United States.]

BIBLIOGRAPHY

Anderson, Terry L., ed. *Property Rights and Indian Economies*. Lanham, U.K.,1992.

Anderson, Terry L., ed. *Sovereign Nations or Reservations? An Economic History of Native Americans*. San Francisco, 1995. Anderson's work is representative of the property rights and new institutional economics approaches to understanding Amerindian economies.

Barrington, Linda, ed. *The Other Side of the Frontier: Economic Explorations into Native American History*. Boulder, 1999. This collection of articles combines new economic history, traditional economic history, and the new institutional economics in a wide-ranging presentation of topics related to Amerindian economies.

Barrington, Linda, ed. "The Mississippians and Economic Development before European Colonization." In *The Other Side of the Frontier: Economic Explorations into Native American History*, edited by Linda Barrington, pp. 86–102. Boulder, 1999.

Carlson, Leonard A. *Indians, Bureaucrats, and Land: The Dawes Act and the Decline of Indian Farming*. Westport, Conn., 1981. Carlson presents a new economic history of the impact of the Dawes Act on Indian agriculture.

Carlos, Ann M., and Frank D. Lewis. "Indians, the Beaver, and the Bay: The Economics of Depletion in the Lands of the Hudson's Bay Company." *Journal of Economic History* 53.3 (1993), 465–494. The authors argue that Indians were unable to establish private rights to beaver populations; hence the tendency for the common property resource to be overexploited.

Carter, Sarah. *Lost Harvests: Prairie Indian Reserve Farmers and Government Policy*. Montreal, 1990. Carter's book is a highly detailed account of the Canadian government's attempts to effect a transition to agriculture for Indians on the Canadian Plains in the late nineteenth and early twentieth centuries.

Fenton, William N. *The Great Law and the Longhouse: A Political History of the Iroquois Confederacy*. Norman, Okla., 1998. The definitive work on the Iroquois Confederacy.

Hurt, R. Douglas. *Indian Agriculture in America: Prehistory to Present*. Lawrence, Okla., 1987. This extensive agricultural history of Amerindians includes an excellent bibliography.

Johansen, Bruce E. *The Encyclopedia of Native American Economic History*. Westport, Conn., 1999. This compact volume contains numerous short entries with an extensive list of sources.

Milner, George R. *The Cahokia Chiefdom*. Washington, DC, 1998.

Muller, Jon. *Mississippian Political Economy*. New York, 1997.

Pauketat, Timothy R. "Refiguring the Archaeology of Greater Cahokia." *Journal of Archaeological Research* 6 (1998), 45–89.

Pauketat, Timothy R., and Thomas E. Emerson, eds. *Cahokia: Domination and Idelogy in the Mississippian World*. Lincoln, Nebr., 1997.

Smith, Vernon L. "Economy, Ecology, and Institutions in the Emergence of Humankind." In *The Other Side of the Frontier: Economic Explorations into Native American Economic History*, edited by Linda Barrington, pp. 57–85. Boulder, 1999. Combines anthropological economics and the new institutional economics to examine the behavior of hunter-gatherer communities in prehistoric North America.

Steckel, Richard, H., and Joseph M. Prince. "Tallest in the World: Native Americans of the Great Plains in the Nineteenth Century." *American Economic Review* 91.1 (2001), 287–294. The authors use anthropometric history to show that Plains Indians adopted the horse culture effectively to achieve high levels of nutrition despite extreme demographic stress from warfare and disease.

Trigger, Bruce G., and Wilcomb E. Washburn, eds. *The Cambridge History of the Native Peoples of the Americas*, vol. 1, *North America*, parts 1 and 2. Cambridge, 1996. The editors have compiled an excellent collection of articles that covers Amerindian history from prehistoric times to the present. Each entry includes a bibliographic essay.

Wishart, David J. *The Fur Trade and the American West, 1807–1840.* Lincoln, Nebr., 1979. An examination of the fur trade in the western United States from an economic geography perspective.

Wishart, David M. "Evidence of Surplus Production in the Cherokee Nation Prior to Removal." *Journal of Economic History* 55.1 (1995), 120–138. Examines a detailed census of the Cherokees from 1835 to find evidence of surplus food production in order to challenge arguments that Jackson's removal policy was humanitarian.

DAVID M. WISHART

AMSTERDAM, constitutional capital and largest city (pop. 1 million) of the Netherlands, a major port that is joined to the North Sea and Rhine River by canals. One of Europe's great intellectual, commercial, and artistic centers, it has a major stock exchange and important financial institutions. Amsterdam was located on a reclaimed peat-bog area of Holland, at the spot where the river Amstel flows into the IJ, a branch of the Zuiderzee (now IJselmeer). Archaeological research suggests that by 1225 CE, people had settled there. The foundation of the settlement's commercial expansion was established about 1270, when a dam was built to separate the mouth of the Amstel from the sea, to protect the reclaimed hinterland from floods and create an inner and outer harbor. Compared to similar dam-towns in Holland, Amsterdam had a locational advantage; it served as a gateway for Holland and as a center of transshipment to and from northern Germany via the Zuiderzee, IJ, and inland waterways to the populous Low Country cities of Flanders and Brabant (both now in Belgium). Amsterdam also had ready access to the Rhineland, where Cologne was a major staple market.

Amsterdam developed into an important center for shipping and trade, notably with northern Germany and the Baltic ports. Its commercial expansion was fueled by the late medieval increase of Holland's population and because the subsidence of the peat made Holland less suitable for arable farming, generating an ever-growing demand for imported (Baltic) grain. That need promoted the development of a competitive shipping and shipbuilding industry and established a tradition in the Baltic Sea trade. During the early 1500s, when the demand for Baltic grain was rising both in the Low Countries and elsewhere in Europe, Amsterdam reaped the fruits of this development and became a major market for Baltic commodities in Western Europe.

In the second half of the sixteenth century the Dutch Revolt, a rebellion against the Habsburg government, forced a profound transformation of the spatial economy of the Low Countries. The northern part of the Low Countries emerged as an independent state, the Dutch Republic, while the southern part, including Antwerp (now in Belgium), was restored to Habsburg rule. While the economy in the Southern Netherlands declined, and Antwerp lost its eminent position in international trade, the economy of the Dutch Republic flourished and Amsterdam's trade rapidly expanded to include almost every port of the known world, including the Americas and the East Indies. From a medium-size town with 25,000 to 30,000 inhabitants in 1585, it grew into a metropolis of 175,000 inhabitants by the mid-1600s. By then, it was one of the largest cities in Europe, the port of call for some five thousand ships annually.

The large volume of trade was partly the result of Amsterdam being a staple market, where merchandise from many parts of the world was brought, stored, and ultimately redistributed. From the late 1500s until the mid-1600s, the Dutch met with little serious competition from the other European countries, where trade was hampered seriously by political turmoil and religious strife. In this relatively short period, Dutch merchants, shipowners, and sailors, backed up by a responsive regional economy and by the inflow of commercial assets and skills from elsewhere (many Antwerp and Jewish merchants expelled from Spain), were able to create an extensive and well-developed trading network that linked regional economies throughout Europe and maintained contacts with the extra-European world as well. This multilateral trading system made Amsterdam-based merchants excellent intermediaries in the settlement of international payments, while it gave them easy access to vital information about markets throughout the system. As a consequence Amsterdam developed into an international clearing house and a center of information exchange. At bottom, this expansion was built on Amsterdam as the gateway for a hinterland that not only comprised the Dutch Republic but also included a major part of Germany and the Southern Netherlands. The Dutch Republic may have been small in size, but by 1650 its urban population was larger than the urban populations of Great Britain and Scandinavia together. Moreover, during the first half of the 1600s, Dutch agricultural and industrial outputs rose to new heights. Since Dutch farmland and natural resources were scarce, many industries both imported and produced for the international markets—thus the large total turnover in Dutch ports.

From the mid-seventeenth century onward, the economy of the Dutch Republic was faced with high labor costs, falling prices, and restricted access to foreign markets. The British seized the New Netherland colony, including New

AMSTERDAM. *View of the Dam, the Old Weighhouse, and the Damrak,* painting by Jacob van Ruisdael (c. 1628–1682). (Staatliche Museen zu Berlin-Preussischer Kulturbesitz Gemäldegalerie/Jörg P. Anders)

Amsterdam in 1664 (which soon became New York). A long period of economic stagnation then lasted well into the nineteenth century. Dutch intermediation in international trade had been challenged by the mercantilist policies adopted by many countries, especially France and Britain. The merchant community of Amsterdam responded by making the most of their financial, informational, and locational assets. During the eighteenth century, many merchants moved from commodity trade into finance; others used their financial and informational resources to draw commission trade to Amsterdam. They were most successful in those branches of trade for which Amsterdam was an entrepôt based on location (German hinterland) or political force (East India trade). During the Napoleontic Wars and the Continental System (1806), when Amsterdam was blockaded from the sea, its commercial life reached its nadir. After the French left Amsterdam in 1813, not much was left of the city's foreign trade and shipping. Economic recovery was slow and in the 1800s largely restricted to Dutch colonial trade and related industries (with the Dutch East and West Indies).

Only in the late nineteenth century did the economy of Amsterdam regain its vitality, with an expanding East In-

dia trade, the industrialization of the German hinterland, modern deepwater routes to the sea and the Rhine River, growing demand on the home market, and the booming diamond industry. During the twentieth century, Amsterdam could not continue to compete with Rotterdam in shipping and transit trade, but Schiphol Airport became Amsterdam's gateway to the world. At the turn of the twenty-first century, air transport and distribution, banking and finance, tourism, and the new media are the strong sectors in the city's economy.

BIBLIOGRAPHY

Barbour, Violet. *Capitalism in Amsterdam in the 17th Century* (1950). Reprint, Ann Arbor, 1963.

Christensen, Aksel E. *Dutch Trade to the Baltic about 1600: Studies in the Sound Toll Register and Dutch Shipping Records.* The Hague, 1941.

De Vries, Jan, and Ad van der Woude. *The First Modern Economy: Success, Failure, and Perseverance of the Dutch Economy, 1500–1815.* Cambridge, 1997.

Israel, Jonathan I. *Dutch Primacy in World Trade, 1585–1740.* Oxford, 1989.

Price, Joseph M. "Multilateralism and/or Bilateralism: The Settlement of British Trade Balances with 'The North,' c. 1700." *Economic History Review* 14 (1961), 254–274.

Smith, Woodruff D. "The Function of Commercial Centers in the Modernization of European Capitalism: Amsterdam as an Information Exchange in the Seventeenth Century." *Journal of Economic History* 44 (1984), 985–1005.

Sperling, J. "The International Payments Mechanism in the Seventeenth and Eighteenth Centuries." *Economic History Review* 14 (1961), 446–468.

Wilson, Charles. *Anglo-Dutch Commerce and Finance in the Eighteenth Century*. Cambridge, 1941, 1966.

CLÉ LESGER

ANDEAN REGION. The Andean region, if a true economic unit, is composed of the present-day republics of Ecuador, Peru, and Bolivia, an area larger than France. Andean social or cultural zones also exist in parts of Colombia, Venezuela, northwest Argentina, and Chile as vestiges of former Incan outposts. Within the core Andean nations, three main climatic or economic geographies dominate: the *sierra* (the fragmented high mountainous Andes themselves at twenty-five hundred to four thousand meters); a dry coastal strip (tropical in Ecuador); and *selva* or *montaña* (the western edge of Amazonian rain forest). Yet even within the *sierran* highlands, Andean territory is often described—in the terms of archaeologist John Murra—as a "vertical archipelago," composed of scores of usable microregions or niches, connected across heights and distances by elaborate social webs and customs.

Despite, or because of, these geographic challenges, the Andes emerged some five thousand years ago as a cradle of human civilization, based on intensive agriculture, exchange, complex cosmologies, and aggressive state building. Irrigated coastal cotton, beans, squashes, fruits, highland tubers, grains, and camelids (llamas and alpacas) provided a prosperous basis for the rise of trade, towns, and religious and military expansionism. Behind these large-scale transformations, Andean social organization was characterized by the *ayllu*, the local kinship labor sharing unit among peasants and herders, led by ethnic *kurakas*. In the 1420s, the Inca lineage from highland Cuzco managed to establish a remarkable century-long hegemony over the Andes. At its peak, the Incan realm Tawantinsuyu controlled as many as 8 million subjects in a polity stretching from Chile to Colombia. The Incas were the classic Polanyi redistributive state, using an efficient road system and conquest pacts to forge a vast exchange area and "Pax Incaica" across the settled Andes. Some local markets carried on, but the Incas took credit for having integrated and systematized Andean "vertical" exchange between ecological zones and kinship groups.

The Spanish conquest of Peru in the 1530s, which took four decades to perfect in strong colonial institutions, brought the isolated Andes into contact with an expanding world system. Spain constructed a Habsburg-style mercantilism here, based on extraction of silver and indigenous tribute, from communities reorganized into a million-strong Indian labor caste by 1600. The massive Viceroyalty of Peru, covering most of western South America, was regulated from the new coastal capital, Lima. Despite disasters (such as the loss of Incan populations to newly introduced diseases), by 1600 the Viceroyalty was supplying more than half the world's silver bullion, in a century long bonanza that was felt throughout the early modern European economy. In the Andes, historians now stress the surprisingly integrative impact of the Spanish silver imperium, even if colonial and exploitative. Silver mining at high-altitude Potosí (in today's Bolivia) spurred the world's largest camp city, which demanded inputs, labor, and linkages from all corners of the Andean world: Huancavelica mercury, Argentine mules, foodstuffs of sierran haciendas (Spanish landed estates), *montaña* coca leaf, Pacific plantation wines and oils, and textiles from *obraje* workshops of Quito. However, historians rarely regard this complex as "capitalist," driven as it was by political edict and labor coercion, notably the *mita* Indian mine draft. Moreover, by 1800 the Andes had over time become a backward bulwark of the Spanish Empire, in decline with the rise of more competitive Atlantic economics.

By 1825, the Spanish Empire collapsed in South America, superseded in the Andes by the region's three main national states—Peru, Ecuador, and Bolivia—with about 5 million predominantly Indian inhabitants overall, and whose borders roughly corresponded to late vice-regal administrative divisions. These new states did not prosper, wracked by endemic political instability, internal wars regionalism (known as *caudillismo*), and a severe fiscal and institutional debility. For much of the nineteenth century, the fragmentation of the Andes continued, despite varied attempts to build conservative "nationalist" economic regimes (harking to colonial forms of social integration) or liberal regimes (borrowing on North Atlantic market ideals). After 1860, firmer elite central states arose, usually around the sudden availability of import-export revenues. Novel exports underwrote free-trade relationships with the world economy: Peruvian guano (a lucrative bird-excrement fertilizer) and sugar, cacao plantations in coastal Ecuador, and the foreign-owned tin mines of Bolivia. Business and governing classes revived and enacted modern commercial and legal codes; capital cities became Europeanized in architecture and consumer styles, and moribund haciendas rebounded at the expense of traditional Indian or mixed mestizo communities in the countryside. Reforming governments strove to bring majority indigenous peoples into the market by privatizing their *ayllu* lands and abolishing discriminatory colonial caste distinctions, though the impact of these acts is still obscure. Slowly, markets and capitalist relations (if still often coercive labor regimes) spread deeper into the Andes. The dramatic and costly construction of railways sought to physically reintegrate the Andean region, with mixed results, especially in Peru, which mortgaged its entire export base on this idea before going broke (with the world's second-largest debt) in the mid-1870s. Peru's mid-century, Lima oriented, guano-age state, and most of its modern economy, collapsed in the Pacific War (1879–1883) with Chile, fought over nitrate lands, which also cost Bolivia its former desert outlet to the sea.

As the first post-Colonial century closed, Peru's losses symbolized its ephemeral "enclave" development, though new and socially deeper export enterprises began to thrive again from 1895 to 1920; in turn-of-the-century Bolivia, power groups launched stronger "civilizing" campaigns against its Aymara peoples; Ecuador finally moved beyond its colonial regional factionalism with the forceful Liberal Revolution of 1895. The apogee of these liberal-aristocratic Andean republics, from 1890 to 1920, came with the peak of European ties. These experiences are often seen, particularly by Andean historians, as thinly based oligarchic and distorted varieties of Western capitalism, or as a vehicle for continuing neocolonial control from abroad and against their own indigenous majorities. Though national governments and economies likely consolidated in these years, the results were not well-integrated Andean societies, and average living standards (except for the few) likely remained at or about colonial norms.

To generalize about the Andean region since the 1930s is not a happy story. The Andean region shared less than successfully in the prototypical movements, ideologies, and transformations of modern Latin America: the rise of labor, limited industrialism, and middle classes; on-off military regimes, political parties, populism, peasant movements, revolution (though only Bolivia's of 1952 merits capitalization); urbanization, migration, "development," and agrarian reform. By the 1940s, modern health, educational and communications systems were taking root. Populations grew swiftly—by the late 1990s, there were more than 22 million Peruvians, a third of whom lived in Lima—and in all three countries Amazonian frontiers receded after 1960 to land colonists and foreign oil companies. Yet no Andean state has managed to find durable political stability or economic formulas that bring their poor majorities into the mainstream; nor have they forged stable growth-enhancing ties to the post-1929 global economy, despite passing export booms in such products as bananas, fish meal, and petroleum. Bolivia is the extreme case, with no export sector to speak of after the decay of tin in the 1960s. Older oligarchies have faded (for example, in post-1952 Bolivia or Peru after its 1968 reformist military experiment), but major land reforms in all three countries failed to revive or transform agriculture, or to reduce inequality. Short-term attempts ensued after 1960 to expand

state services and bring development projects to wider sectors of growing populations. But former peasants flocked to the cities, where large numbers hang on in motley urban "informal sectors" by contraband activities, or in the case of poor Ecuadorians, exported en masse as workers to New York City and Spain. Inequality is rampant throughout the Andes, aggravated by historic ethnic and regional disparities and by the new wave of "neoliberal" market reform and state downsizing that hit the region during the 1980s. Unlike other parts of Latin America, little recovery followed in the 1990s, and graft, pauperization, and despair are ubiquitous. Institutional democratization is fragile in the Andes. It is not surprising that illicit drug trades—the Andes as coca patch and cocaine mart—had come to symbolize the chaos, corruption, and unworkability of Andean economies and societies by the close of the twentieth century. The present-day Andean countries (now including Colombia) are defined less by common heritage or shared geography than by their seemingly intractable national crises in the modern world.

[*See also* American Indian Economies, *subentry on* Inca Economy *and* Spain, *subentry on* Spanish Empire.]

BIBLIOGRAPHY
Assadourian, Sempat. *El sistema de la economía colonial*. Lima, 1982.
Contreras, Carlos, and Manual Glave, eds. *Estado y mercado en la historia del Peru*. Lima, 2002.
Gootenberg, Paul. *Between Silver and Guano: Commercial Policy and the State in Post-Independence Peru*. Princeton, 1989.
Larson, Brooke, Olivia Harris, Enrique Tandeter, eds. *Ethnicity, Markets, and Migration in the Andes*. Durham, 1997.
Mörner, Magnus. *The Andean Past: Land, Societies, and Conflicts*. New York, 1985.
Murra, John V. *The Economic Organization of the Inca State*. Chicago, 1955.
Painter, James. *Bolivia and Coca: A Study in Dependency*. Boulder, 1994.
Sheahan, John. *Searching for a Better Society: The Peruvian Economy from 1950*. University Park, Penn., 1999.
Thorp, Rosemary, and Geoffrey Bertram. *Peru, 1890–1977: Growth and Development in an Open Economy*. London, 1978.

PAUL GOOTENBERG

ANIMAL AND LIVESTOCK DISEASES. The economic importance of animal disease cannot be underestimated, for the losses to farmers down the centuries have been immense. The costs of controlling disease are also great, and in turn these have raised the political importance of serious animal disease, as governments have had to assume much of the responsibility for the management of epidemics. Scientific understanding of most animal diseases, and from that, the development of successful treatments and control measures have been established only during the last 250 years. Systematic implementation of control and eradication programs came about from the second half of the nineteenth century.

Infectious Diseases. The diseases that have been most prominent, and which have inflicted the greatest damage, have been the serious infectious diseases. Among the most prominent of these have been anthrax, rinderpest (cattle plague), pleuro-pneumonia, foot-and-mouth disease in cattle, foot rot and liver fluke in sheep, and swine fever (hog cholera) affecting pigs. There have been cycles of virulence of the different diseases, and new diseases have from time to time arisen, such as swine fever, which appeared in the 1830s and was a scourge for more than a century before being brought under control.

In the medieval and early modern centuries, it can be difficult to identify the diseases suffered. There was a tendency to lump diseases together under a general term, such as "murrain" in sheep, which seems to have embraced liver fluke, foot rot, and scab at the very least (Lloyd, 1977–1978, pp. 10–13). Some diseases have sufficient characteristics in common to make them difficult to distinguish from one another. Rinderpest and foot-and-mouth disease were two that could be confused. The first positive identification of foot-and-mouth as a separate disease by Hieronymus Fracastorius in 1514 may not have been its first appearance. Rinderpest had been counted, along with invasions of locusts and floods, among the great natural catastrophes that could cause famine and general distress. Major outbreaks recurred in Europe through the medieval centuries.

Losses to disease were high in medieval and early-modern times. Rinderpest took a heavy toll on cattle, which for medieval farmers was doubly disastrous, as they lost not only the meat but their draft animals. Large estates could in bad years lose as many as 40 percent of their lambs and 20 percent of adult sheep. Losses, however, had to be accepted, as veterinary knowledge was limited. The spread of that knowledge to the general farming population was slower. The belief that disease in animals was caused by witchcraft rather than contagion prevailed into the seventeenth and eighteenth centuries, and lingered even in the nineteenth. Magic and ritual, the use of amulets, ceremonial willow wands, and other effects remained common in the treatment of diseases, along with herbal remedies. Elecampane (*Inula helenium*) has been an ingredient in treatments for several diseases of horses, cattle, and sheep, including scab (Drury, 1985, pp. 243–247). Herbal remedies could be effective in treating some conditions, but they had little use against the major infections.

This was still the situation at the beginning of the eighteenth century when Europe was subject to particularly severe outbreaks of rinderpest, or cattle plague. The epidemic that began in 1709 was particularly vigorous and had devastating results. Starting in Italy, it spread across continental Europe, killing three hundred thousand cattle in the Netherlands and seventy thousand in England between 1711 and 1714. It was not the last outbreak. There was another in the 1740s, again spreading across continental Europe until it reached England and Wales in 1745. Here the worst period seems to have been from 1747 to 1748, but the plague was not finally eradicated until 1758, thirteen years after the first occurrence. In parts of central Europe, meanwhile, rinderpest had become endemic by the mid-eighteenth century.

Control and Treatment. However, the epidemic of 1709–1714 stimulated new interest in methods of control and treatment. Veterinary science hitherto had been very limited, dominated by astrological and alchemical thinking. At the beginning of the eighteenth century, Bernardino Ramazzini in Italy studied the pathology of rinderpest and demonstrated that it spread from animal to animal and was not caused by astrological influences. At the same time, Giovanni Lancisi recommended the adoption of quarantine measures to contain the spread of the disease and was thus one of the progenitors of veterinary sanitary policy. It took some time, and the work of many veterinarians, before the principle of infection became widely accepted.

Rinderpest remained one of the major diseases throughout the nineteenth and early twentieth centuries. It was, however, supplanted by foot-and-mouth disease as a dominant scourge. Foot-and-mouth is one of the most contagious of diseases. It was first recorded in Germany in 1751 and appeared in Great Britain in 1839 in an epidemic that broke out in the dairies around London. The disease became more prominent during the nineteenth century, an effect in part of the growth of world trade, which brought increased contact with countries where the disease is endemic. Foot-and-mouth spreads very quickly. The outbreak in England in 1839 started in August and affected most of the country by the end of that year, remaining prevalent until 1841. In the United States, twenty-one states were affected within three months in the epidemic of 1915–1916. Foot-and-mouth remained virulent throughout much of the twentieth century, endemic in a number of countries, such as Argentina, Brazil, France, and Italy, and appearing as severe epidemics in others, including Great Britain, the United States, and Canada.

Swine fever, or hog cholera, made its first appearance in the United States in 1833, although its precise origins remain unclear. It spread like wildfire and was found throughout the United States within ten years. It reached England in the 1860s, then spread to Scandinavia and across Europe. The devastatingly high mortality rates prompted international research into the causes and nature of the disease, which ultimately produced antidotes.

The severe outbreaks of animal disease in the nineteenth and twentieth centuries brought about major changes in their treatment and control. The expansion of agricultural

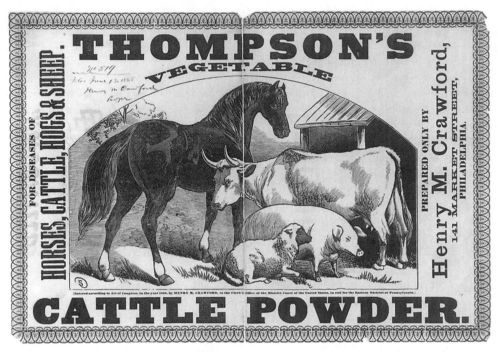

FIGHTING ANIMAL DISEASE. Advertisement for Thompson's Vegetable Cattle Powder, circa 1868. (Prints and Photographs Division, Library of Congress)

production and trade, both nationally and internationally, caused governments to assume responsibility for the control of contagious diseases. Concern for public health was another factor encouraging governments to take action, and was behind, for example, campaigns to eradicate bovine tuberculosis in the twentieth century. State veterinary departments and laboratories were established in most countries.

Veterinary science made significant advances during the nineteenth and early twentieth centuries, and was finally able to achieve acceptance among governments and farmers as providing a basis for measures to control disease. Although such diseases as rinderpest had long ago been shown to be infectious, debate still raged in the veterinary profession in the 1850s and 1860s. Many adhered to theories of spontaneous generation and "atmospheric corruption," and thus looked for causes and cures for infectious diseases in accordance with those theories. Louis Pasteur had to fight against the theories of spontaneous generation when he published the results of his research into the microbiology of fermentation. The ultimate acceptance of Pasteur's theories opened the way to the development of bacteriology and immunology in both human and veterinary medicine. Robert Koch in Germany, investigating anthrax, and Theobald Smith in the United States, who worked on Texas fever and swine fever and discovered salmonella, were among the most prominent in establishing bacteriological practices in veterinary science. Two of

Koch's assistants, Friedrich Loeffler and P. Frosch, in 1898 discovered the virus at the heart of foot-and-mouth disease, and from that the science of virology developed.

The measures to control and eradicate the major infectious diseases were quarantine and slaughter, to which was added vaccination during the twentieth century. Policies of quarantine and slaughter were advocated by some of the early discoverers of the infectious nature of the diseases. They were sometimes applied with some success in the eighteenth and early nineteenth centuries. In England they had been applied first during the outbreak of cattle plague in 1714–1715, under the direction of Dr. Thomas Bates, one of the royal surgeons. Bates proposed that diseased cattle be slaughtered, that the farmers be paid compensation, and that potential contacts be put in quarantine. This policy proved so successful that the cattle plague of 1714 was stamped out in six months. Similar steps were taken in 1745, but with less consistency and consequently less success. However, because theories of contagion were far from universally held, the political will to apply such policies rigorously and consistently was not always present. Farmers, likewise, could not always see the point of controls and resented them. Foot-and-mouth disease, for example, although highly contagious, also has a good recovery rate, and farmers preferred to wait for their cattle to get better rather than have them slaughtered. Without some of these basic quarantine precautions being applied, epidemics continued to spread very rapidly. It was the shock of some of the more virulent of them and the increasing scale of economic loss that forced governments to take a more determined approach during the later nineteenth century.

By the end of the nineteenth century, most governments of the Western world had introduced measures to control infectious animal diseases. Restrictions on the import and export of live animals were common, and internal quarantine controls and the slaughter of infected animals were also usual. The worldwide nature of many of the serious diseases, and the effect of increasing international trade in helping epidemics to spread, also required international cooperation in programs to control them. International veterinary congresses during the late nineteenth century raised this issue, but no concrete international agreements were made before World War I. Disease-control policies were still a source of tension between countries long after that.

Vaccines. Vaccines, the third main weapon against major animal diseases, were first investigated by some of the veterinary scientists of the late eighteenth century. Paul Adami in Hungary was one of the first who experimented, unsuccessfully, with inoculation against rinderpest in the 1780s. Successful research into serums did not result until a century later. A vaccine for bovine tuberculosis was made available in 1902. The first vaccines for foot-and-mouth disease were developed in the 1920s. New generations of live attenuated vaccines introduced in the 1950s became widely used, and in 1981 the first vaccine against foot-and-mouth using genetic modification was produced. By this time, vaccines were a serious part of the armory against animal disease, especially for countries where infections were endemic, or nearly so.

The effect of these measures has been to bring the major infectious diseases under control. Many of the countries where they have been epidemic became effectively free of foot-and-mouth disease, rinderpest, and swine fever from the 1960s onward. The attention of veterinary science began to turn more to lesser infections and the diseases of hygiene management, such as mastitis. Then a new epidemic broke out—bovine spongiform encephalopy (BSE), or "mad cow disease." This is a progressive degenerative disease, not infectious, but caused apparently by a virus. It is closely related to scrapie in sheep and to Creuzfeldt-Jakob Disease (CJD) in humans. But whereas scrapie had been known for decades, the first confirmed appearance of BSE was not until 1985 in Great Britain. It was here that the full force of the epidemic was felt over the following decade, but there were many cases also in France, Switzerland, and other western European countries. The likely cause of this epidemic, lying in contaminated feeding stuffs, and concern that the disease might be transmissible to humans in the form of CJD meant that the political and economic repercussions have been immense. The advance of science has certainly not lessened the importance of animal disease and its management.

[*See also* Crop and Plant Diseases.]

BIBLIOGRAPHY

Andrews, A. H. "A Century of Cattle Practice." *Veterinary Record* 110 (1982), 603–605.

Drury, Susan. "Herbal Remedies for Livestock in Seventeenth and Eighteenth Century England: Some Examples." *Folklore* 2 (1985), 243–247.

Karasszon, D. *A Concise History of Veterinary Medicine*. Budapest, 1988.

Lloyd, T. H. "Husbandry Practice and Disease in Medieval Sheep Flocks." *Veterinary History* 10 (1977–1978), 3–13.

Mowat, G. N., and A. J. Garland. "The Development of Foot-and-Mouth Disease Vaccines." *Veterinary Record* 102 (1978), 190–193.

JONATHAN BROWN

ANIMAL HUSBANDRY. Domesticated animals today outnumber the ancestral creatures from which they were first tamed, and their existence is a major expression, perhaps the major expression, of humankind's dominion over the planet. The wild have retreated before the tame—both those species truly domesticated, whose breeding is entirely under human control (cattle, pigs, and horses), as well as the "exploited captives," (elephants, caribou, or dolphins). Abandoned by humans, feral dogs, cats, cattle, goats, and horses have all flourished in the wild, often placing fragile indigenous ecologies, especially of the world's arid margins, under additional stress. If zoos, nature preserves, and other sanctuaries represent the best prospect for the long-term survival of the wild species most under threat (including all 160 kinds of non-human primate), this route to survival ensures that what remains of the wild will become ever more tame. In fact, the selection pressures associated with captivity shape the character of both exploited and unexploited captives.

The dog is the oldest domestic animal; the number and diversity of its breeds (at least 400) testify to time (at least 15,000 years) since humans first began to shape the wolf to their own purposes (the wolf being the ancestor of all dogs, including the seemingly unlikely Pekingese and Chihuahua). Animals drawn into closer association with humans experience reduced environmental stress, meaning that some of their traits become accessible to selection that were suppressed by the exigencies of life in the wild. As Charles Darwin observed in the mid-1800s, much impressed by the diverse and often outlandish creations of pigeon fanciers, "under domestication the whole organism becomes in some degree plastic." In the case of dogs, much effort has been dedicated in recent centuries to shaping their plasticity to human aspirations as companionable status symbols. It is now difficult to imagine that the poodle was originally bred for hunting, one of a number of breeds fashioned to various and contrasting demands. Canine breeds designed to assist farmers have fared well, since the demand remains for their originally intended functions. Even so, many farm dog breeds are now selected for appearance, not utility, since such functions as flock guarding and droving are no longer required in most parts of the world.

While other farm animals have not been immune to selection by fanciers for nonproductive traits, these tendencies have been balanced by the need for growth and performance. Changes in their appearance and character do, however, reflect shifting economic and functional demands. Before twentieth-century developments in breeding science, trial and error was the sole means of achieving these. The extended trial-and-error period fell into three phases, each phase laying the foundations for its successor. The first was domestication, which occurred independently in the ancient Near East, sub-Saharan Africa, the Americas, India, and China at various times, from 12,000 to 6,000 years ago. The small number of species that have been domesticated relative to the large number in existence has often been noted. As Francis Galton noticed in the mid-1800s, few species with useful qualities breed readily and thrive when living as adjuncts of human society; the remainder were "doomed to be gradually destroyed off the face of the earth."

The second phase, which Andrew Sherratt (1981) called the "secondary products revolution," was associated particularly with the ancient Near East (West Asia). The five key species—sheep, goat, pig, cattle, and horse—were all domesticated there, as were wheat and barley, the basic Western farm crops. Partly in consequence of their juxtaposition, by about 3000 BCE a society where animals had been kept mainly for meat and where transport and cultivation were supplied by human muscle became a society that depended on the secondary features of the animal economy—wool, milk, transport, and traction, including plowing. The two types of societies and subsistence systems that emerged—plow-based agriculture (as across the northern European plain) and pastoralism (as on the inner Eurasian steppelands)—were not part of precontact America, where the camelid keepers of the Andes were part of high civilizations where plowing was not practiced. Pictorial representations of animals from both Babylon and Egypt suggest that by 2000 BCE, the intensification of animal husbandry in both early civilizations had resulted in the development of distinctive breeds of dogs, cattle, and sheep. The selective breeding of bulls for religious and ceremonial purposes is documented in both ancient Egypt and ancient Greece. Breeds are the result of deliberate selection for desired characteristics—they differ from geographically confined subspecies, which arise as a response to natural environmental variation. Breeds are least numerous in the horse, the most recently domesticated of the main domestic species.

While the second phase in the development of animal husbandry resulted in the appearance of breeds, the third witnessed their proliferation and the improvement of those already established. The main factor was increased demand for animal products within the context of commercializing, urbanizing, and less exclusively agricultural economies. Such Classical-era writers as Aristotle, Varro, and Columella discussed the mechanisms of animal breeding; but enduring, improved, or high-performance breeds only appeared in northwestern Europe about 1800. Several centuries of prior theoretical debate and praxis had laid the foundations, and two developments were crucial. First, the number of functions any one type of animal was expected to perform were reduced, as breeds proliferated. One or a few high-performance traits proved easier to imprint on a breed than a great many. There would, for example, have been little prospect of developing cattle with either good milking or early-maturing beefing properties had they also been expected to serve as efficient draft animals. For horses, the invention of the padded collar harness and the iron horseshoe enabled heavy horses, initially bred for war service, to displace oxen as the main suppliers of draft and traction from 1000 to 1900 CE. One result was that in the 1500s and 1600s, young cattle once bred in the north and west of England and in Wales to provide the main arable areas of south and east England with replacement plow animals became increasingly destined for graziers and stall fatteners, who raised beef animals for the London market.

Second, agriculture was transformed by the increased cultivation of fodder crops—the cereal grains, vetches, sainfoin, clover, and turnips. The integration of animal culture and arable culture sustained increased animal numbers and the quantity of manure available as fertilizer; it also reduced winter feed shortages and boosted the number of breeding stock that might be carried through the year, so a higher proportion of adult animals were able to transmit their genetic traits to the next generation. Breeds vary in their responses to different feeding regimes, thus a highly segmented animal agriculture became possible. For example, in Britain, summer and autumn beef was increasingly supplied by animals of the Hereford type, fattened to slaughter weight on grass, while winter and spring consumers were more likely to be eating Shorthorns, the more efficient converters of arable crops and oilcake. Beyond Britain, the Hereford did well in areas like the American West, where feed was meager, while the Shorthorn was the dominant breed in Argentina, where the export-oriented meat trade was grafted onto a pre-existing landscape of cereal production. In the early nineteenth

ANIMAL HUSBANDRY. Shropshire pig produced by using selective breeding techniques. Colored aquatint (c. 1795) by W. Wright after W. Gwynn. (Institute of Agricultural History, University of Reading, U.K.)

century, the fine-wooled Merino sheep was taken to European colonies and settlement frontiers, where its voracious feeding habits earned the breed John Muir's tag of "hooved locusts." Wider diffusion of the English middle-wool and short-wool breeds, which were sources of sustaining the soil's fertility in the mixed-farming systems of the eighteenth century European agricultural revolution, had to await expanding markets for wool clothing and reliable long-distance refrigerated transport for meat.

In many parts of the world, animal husbandry remained substantially untouched by improved breeds or by the process of improvement. In areas where production for the market was limited and farms were small, as in India and much of Africa, the versatility of the unimproved breed was sufficient. Russia's substantial nineteenth-century export trade in bones, tallow, and hides was founded on cost, not quality. British livestock improvers had great influence beyond Britain's shores, which owed less to the activities of Robert Bakewell (1725–1795) of Dishley, Leicestershire (whose reputation says as much of his skills as salesman and self-publicist as of his achievements as a breed improver), than to those who recognized that the success of an improved breed implied geographical spread and that this was not compatible with improvers' restrictive attitudes toward their intellectual property. Though sometimes spurious and likely to attract the attention of hobbyists and fanciers, published pedigrees (beginning

with George Coates's *Shorthorn Herd Book* in 1822) were an essential precondition for the worldwide spread of breed elites that were improved by close and careful selection. The common or scrub stock could then be upgraded by crosses with the elites. These improvements to livestock allowed countries to participate in markets for the highest levels of livestock products.

Sheep. In Britain, breeds and breed elites became sharply defined as a result of the overseas demand for pedigree breeding stock. Only as breeders in the United States began to shift their attention away from fine-wooled sheep during the decades after the American Civil War (1861–1865) did British breeders of middle- and short-wool types seek to formalize their breeds, by identifying breed elites and then publishing flock books (the Oxford Down flock book was first published in 1883, although the improved breed dated to the 1830s). By 1920, the fine-wooled breeds (Merino and Rambouillet) comprised no more than 36 percent of the pure-bred U.S. flock, the residue being English breeds, almost exclusively downland types, like the Oxford and the Shropshire.

Pigs. The effects of international trading relationships on the breeding of pigs are equally striking. The pig's status as household scavenger to the prudent British poor meant that pig breeds in Britain long remained loosely defined and breed characteristics poorly fixed. As late as the middle of the nineteenth century, "breed" names of the exhibitor's own choosing often appeared in British show schedules. Between 1846 and 1854, the breed identities of pigs exhibited by Queen Victoria's husband Prince Albert changed almost yearly, although there is no evidence of any marked change in the identity or appearance of the pigs themselves. The first British breed of pigs to gain permanent recognition as a breed was the Berkshire; the breed type was fixed and then improved by a cluster of breeders living in and around the upper Thames Valley, among whom Russell Swanwick of the Royal Agricultural College, Cirencester, was the most influential. The Berkshire was granted its own class at the shows of the Royal Agricultural Society in 1862, but a breed society and a published pedigree register did not begin until 1884. This belated development was prompted by the possibilities of major exports of breeding stock to North America.

In Canada, the Berkshire and the Yorkshire, another British breed, met with considerable success because of Canada's dedication to the production of quality bacon and ham for export. The two breeds accounted for three-quarters of Canadian pedigree pigs in 1911. In the United States, where the Berkshire made some inroads during the 1880s, a continuing presence proved more elusive. The Poland China, Duroc Jersey, and Chester White were breeds developed in the United States during the first half of the nineteenth century, largely on the basis of earlier importations of unimproved British strains. Those fast-maturing breeds of corn-fattened "lard" pigs were the bedrock of an industry that supplied mass markets, both domestic and foreign, with products notable principally for their high fat content—whether lard, packed pork, or low-quality bacon and ham.

When the United States began to supply high-quality pork products, it was at first on the basis of within-breed selection, designed to "lengthen" indigenous lard pigs. Then, during the 1930s, imported Danish landrace hogs were crossed with American breeds to produce, in due course, the American landrace. Interestingly, the original terms of the Danish exportation did not allow the release of pure landrace swine for general use in the United States. Britain, however, showed no qualms about possible damage to its domestic farming interests from the export of British breeding stock; British policymakers were more concerned for the security of their own export markets in pedigree livestock than for the possibility of reducing import demand by the more productive use of pedigree at home. Free-trade ideology remained a feature of British agricultural policy until World War II.

[*See also* Cattle; Horses; *and* Sheep and Goats.]

BIBLIOGRAPHY

Clutton-Brock, Juliet, ed. *The Walking Larder: Patterns of Domestication, Pastoralism and Predation*. London, 1989.

Clutton-Brock, Juliet. *A Natural History of Domesticated Mammals*. 2d ed. Cambridge, 1999. A comprehensive but highly readable and attractively illustrated account of the origins of domestication and its global spread, treated species by species.

Hall, Stephen J. G. "Why Are There So Many Breeds of Livestock?" In *Skeletons in Her Cupboard: Festschrift for Juliet Clutton-Brock*, edited by Anneke Clason, Sebastian Payne, and Hans-Peter Uerpmann, pp. 99–107. Oxford, 1993.

Harris, David R., ed. *The Origins and Spread of Agriculture and Pastoralism in Eurasia*. London, 1996.

Jones, Steve. *Almost Like a Whale. The Origin of Species Updated*. London, 1999. A lively representation of Darwin's *Origin* (1859) in the light of current knowledge; as in the original, the breeding of domesticates receives much attention.

Langdon, John. *Horses, Oxen, and Technological Innovation: The Use of Draught Animals in English Farming from 1066 to 1500*. Cambridge, 1986. Scholarly exploration of the early centuries of the slow takeover of heavy horses for draft and traction tasks in England.

Ritvo, Harriet. "Possessing Mother Nature: Genetic Capital in Eighteenth-Century Britain." In *Early Modern Conceptions of Property*, edited by John Brewer and Susan Staves, pp. 413–426. London, 1996. An exploration of Robert Bakewell's activities, written from the viewpoint of a cultural historian.

Russell, Nicholas. *Like Engend'ring Like: Heredity and Animal Breeding in Early Modern England*. Cambridge, 1986. Explores breed improvement before Robert Bakewell, showing that he was less of an innovator than he claimed.

Sherratt, Andrew. "Plough and Pastoralism: Aspects of the Secondary Products Revolution." In *Pattern of the Past: Essays in Honour of David Clarke*, edited by Ian Hodder, Glyn Isaac, and Norman Hammond, pp. 261–305. Cambridge, 1981.

Smih, Vaclav. "Millennium Essay: Horse Power." *Nature* 405 (11 May 2000), 125. Short but thought-provoking article on the millennium of gradually expanding use of horses.

Smith, Bruce D. *The Emergence of Agriculture*. New York, 1995. Attractively packaged synthesis of recent research on agricultural origins, globally.

Walton, John R. "Pedigree and Productivity in the British and North American Cattle Kingdoms before 1930." *Journal of Historical Geography* 25.4 (1999), 441–462. Argues that fanciers' involvement in pedigree had more damaging consequences for British than for North American agriculture, though influential in both.

Whetham, Edith H. "The Trade in Pedigree Livestock, 1850–1910." *Agricultural History Review* 27.1 (1979), 47–50.

JOHN R. WALTON

ANTHROPOMETRIC HISTORY. Attempts to define and estimate the standard of living originated more than three centuries ago, and eventually led to the system of national accounts in the twentieth century. Although economists recognize the great achievements of the accounts, research momentum has shifted to alternatives or supplements that address shortcomings in gross domestic product (GDP) as a welfare measure or that indicate living standards in time periods or among groups for which conventional measures cannot be calculated. Stature is an example now used extensively in the fields of economic history and economic development.

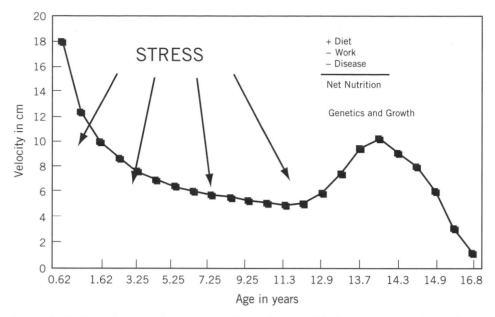

FIGURE 1. Height velocity under good conditions. SOURCE: Tabulated from data for males in National Center for Health Statistics (1977, p. 37).

Readers unfamiliar with the methodology of anthropometric history should not be sidetracked by genetic issues. Genes are important determinants of individual heights, but genetic differences approximately cancel in comparisons of averages across most populations, and in these situations heights accurately reflect health status.

Many studies show that measures of health are positively correlated with income or wealth. Less well known are the relationship between stature and such conventional measures as per capita income, and the ways that stature addresses certain conceptual inadequacies in gross national product (GNP) as a welfare measure. Stature adeptly measures inequality in the form of nutritional deprivation; average height in the past century is sensitive not only to the level of income but also to the distribution of income and the consumption of basic necessities by the poor.

Unlike conventional measures of living standards based on output, stature is a measure of consumption that incorporates or adjusts for individual nutritional needs; it is a net measure that captures not only the supply of inputs to health but also demands on those inputs. Moreover, heights are available in settings, such as eighteenth-century America, where income data are lacking (or of low quality) and for groups, such as slaves, for which conventional income or wage concepts do not apply. Because growth occurs largely during childhood, stature also provides valuable insights into resource allocation within the family, an interesting phenomenon obscured from household-level data on income or earnings, much less aggregate statistics on output or inequality.

Development of the Discipline. A distinguished intellectual tradition of height studies existed prior to the mid-1970s, but the research was conducted mainly by human biologists or physical anthropologists, and its contributors largely ignored questions of interests to economics, history, and other social sciences. The 1970s witnessed a revival of interest in social accounting. Moderation of business cycles and high rates of economic growth with accompanying disamenities in the form of urban sprawl, pollution, congestion, and crime stimulated interest in broad welfare measures. In a similar vein, the United Nations created the human development index, which weighs life expectancy, literacy, and income, and subsequent refinements incorporated a broader definition of education, and made adjustments for gender discrimination and income distribution. Thus, interest in stature was boosted by disaffection with national income accounting and a return to the debate over measures of human welfare.

The fortunes of anthropometric research in the formative period depended heavily on engaging debates of interest to historians and economists, and its success hinged on novel and credible results. The four areas of important applications were slavery, the standard of living during industrialization, inequality, and mortality. Slavery was the most contentious, at least in the United States. Heights recorded on slave manifests added much to the debates over demography and quality of life. Scholars have long debated the quality of life during industrialization, and despite considerable effort using such traditional sources as per capita income and real wages, they have failed to reach anything approaching a consensus. Despite great interest, measures of inequality are often difficult to acquire, and when available they often pose problems of interpretation. Height data did not resolve the problems of measuring inequality in historical settings; they merely added new, useful information. Anthropometrics also clarified explanations for the substantial long-term improvement in life expectancy that began in Europe after the middle of the nineteenth century.

Sources and Methods of Analysis. Modern studies establish that two periods of intense activity characterize the growth process following birth. Figure 1 shows that the increase in height, or velocity, is greatest during infancy, falls sharply, and then declines irregularly into the preadolescent years. During adolescence, velocity rises sharply to a peak that equals approximately one-half of the velocity during infancy, then declines rapidly and reaches zero at maturity. The adolescent growth spurt begins about two years earlier in girls than in boys, and during their spurt girls temporarily overtake boys in average height. As adults, males are taller than females, primarily because they have approximately two additional years of growth prior to the adolescent growth spurt.

Although genes are important determinants of individual height, studies of genetically similar and dissimilar populations under various environmental conditions suggest that differences in average height across most populations are largely attributable to environmental factors. Important for interpreting stature in the United States is the fact that Europeans and people of European descent, as well as Africans and people of African descent who grew under good nutritional circumstances have nearly identical stature.

Height at a particular age reflects an individual's history of *net* nutrition, or diet minus claims on the diet made by work (or physical activity) and disease. Metabolic requirements for basic functions, such as breathing and blood circulation while at rest, also make claims on the diet. The synergy between malnutrition and illness may further reduce the nutrition left over for growth. Poorly nourished children are more susceptible to infection, which reduces the body's absorption of nutrients. The interaction implies that analyses of stature must recognize not only inputs to health, such as diet and medical care, but also work effort and related phenomena, such as methods of labor organization. In addition, exposure to infectious disease may place claims on the diet.

The sensitivity of growth to deprivation or biological stress depends upon the age at which it occurs. For a given degree of deprivation, the adverse effects may be proportional to the velocity of growth under optimal conditions. Thus, young children and adolescents are particularly susceptible to environmental insults. The return of adequate nutrition following a relatively short period of deprivation may restore normal height through catch-up growth. But ingestion of toxic substances, such as alcohol or tobacco, in utero or in early childhood often creates permanent stunting regardless of subsequent nutritional conditions. If conditions are inadequate for catch-up, individuals may still approach normal adult height by an extension of the growing period by as long as several years. Prolonged and severe deprivation results in stunting, or a reduction in adult size.

Because GDP per capita is the most widely used indicator of living standards, it is particularly useful to compare and contrast this measure with stature. Income is a potent determinant of stature that operates through diet, disease, and work intensity, but one must recognize that other factors, such as personal hygiene, public health measures, and the disease environment, affect illness, while work intensity is a function of technology, culture, and methods of labor organization. Extremely poor families may spend two-thirds or more of their income on food, but even a large share of their very low incomes purchases inadequate calories. Malnutrition associated with extreme poverty has a major impact on height; but at the other end of the income spectrum, expenditures beyond those needed to satisfy calorie requirements purchase largely variety, palatability, and convenience.

At the individual level, extreme poverty results in malnutrition, retarded growth, and stunting. Higher incomes enable the parents of growing children to purchase a better diet, and height increases correspondingly; but once income is sufficient to satisfy caloric requirements, individuals often consume foods that also satisfy many vitamin and mineral requirements. Height may continue to rise with income because a more complete diet or better housing and medical care are available. As income increases, consumption patterns change to realize a larger share of genetic potential, but environmental variables are powerless after individuals attain the maximum capacity for growth. The limits to this process are clear from the fact that people who grew up in very wealthy families are not physical giants.

While the relationship between height and income is nonlinear at the individual level, the relationship at the aggregate level depends upon the distribution of income. Average height may differ for a given per capita income, depending upon the fraction of people with insufficient income to purchase an adequate diet or to afford medical care. Because the gain in height at the individual level increases at a decreasing rate as income rises, one would expect average height at the aggregate level to increase with the degree of equality of the income distribution (assuming there are people who have not reached their genetic potential).

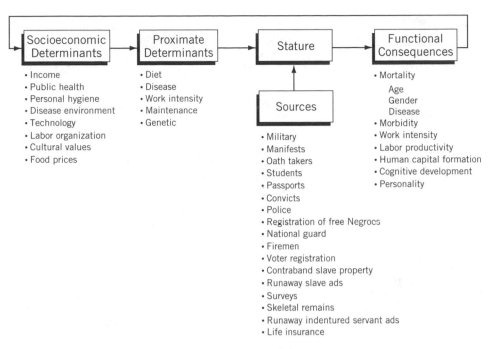

FIGURE 2. Relationships involving stature. SOURCE: Steckel, 1995.

Real per capita GDP and life expectancy at birth are two widely used measures of the standard of living or quality of life. Both are highly correlated with average height in data from developing and developed countries of the mid- and late twentieth century. Simple correlations between a country's average height and the log of its per capita GDP are in the range of 0.82 to 0.88. Similarly, simple regressions of average height at age twelve on life expectancy at birth have an R^2 of about 0.82 and show that an increase in life expectancy of one year was associated with an increase in average stature of about 0.56 centimeters.

Figure 2 is a useful organizing device for understanding the relationship of height to living standards. Stature is a function of such proximate determinants as diet, disease, and work intensity during the growing years, and as such it is a measure of the consumption of basic necessities that incorporates demands placed on one's biological system. Because family income heavily influences purchases of basic necessities, such as food and medical care, stature is ultimately a function of access to resources. It is noteworthy that stature recognizes or adjusts for consumption of products, such as alcohol or drugs, that are harmful to health, but excessive consumption of food, while leading to rapid growth, may impair health in later life. Public health measures, personal hygiene, and the disease environment affect the incidence of disease that claims nutrition. In addition, human growth may have functional consequences for health, labor productivity, mental development, and personality, which in turn may influence socioeconomic conditions.

Applications. Scholarly debate over slavery came to a head with the publication of *Time on the Cross* (Robert William Fogel and Stanley L. Engerman, New York, 1974), and its aftermath featured debates over the fertility behavior of young-adult slaves, living conditions, work effort, and mortality. Heights recorded on slave manifests added much to the debates over demography and quality of life. The age of the maximum increment in the adolescent growth spurt in girls precedes menarche by approximately one year. Analysis of heights by age shows that the peak increment was 13.3 years, and that menarche occurred on average prior to age fifteen (2 to 3 years earlier than estimates for European populations of the era) and that young slave women could have borne children by age sixteen or seventeen on average (Trussell and Steckel, 1978). Second, they showed that age at first birth was nineteenth to twenty-one years, depending on plantation size. Thus, slave fertility was not maximized, and many women abstained for a period of time prior to cohabitation or marriage.

Adult slave men were approximately 67.2 inches (170.7 centimeters), which was about half an inch to an inch (depending on social class) smaller than northern whites of the antebellum period (Steckel, 1979). Thus, slaves did experience some nutritional deprivation relative to whites, but on balance their diet was reasonably adequate for the work effort and disease load they faced. Subsequent research showed that children were remarkably malnourished—comparable in stature to the most disadvantaged groups of poor developing countries—a phenomenon he linked to seasonal growth retardation in utero, early interruption of

HUMAN MEASURE. Goethe's drawing of the measurement of recruits for the duke of Sachsen-Weimar's army in 1779. (Goethe-Nationalmuseum, Weimar, Germany/Stiftung Weimarer Klassik)

breastfeeding, and a low protein diet (Steckel, 1986). As teenagers, the slaves overcame much of their early childhood height deficit, which suggests that the diet of working slaves was nutritionally adequate, if not exceptional for their physical effort.

Anthropometrics clarified explanations for the substantial long-term improvement in life expectancy that began in Europe after the middle of the nineteenth century. The trends have inspired numerous hypotheses about the contributions of man and nature. Some scholars advocate advances in medical technology, while others favor greater immunity through natural selection or less virulent pathogens. It seems clear that personal hygiene, public health, and improved diet were relevant. Robert Fogel used height data to measure the independent contribution of nutrition to the mortality decline. Applying knowledge that heights are a proxy for net nutrition, he regressed mortality rates on heights and other factors to estimate the strength of the relationship. By applying changes in height observed over the period of declining mortality, he calculated that improved nutrition accounted for approximately 40 percent of the English mortality decline between 1800 and 1980.

Debate over the standard of living during industrialization has been intense in part because the raw data series are meager in quality, especially for the crucial early and middle phases of change. Traditional measures also fail to capture several important aspects of the quality of life, such as inequality, hours of work, effort, health, and safety while at work, and psychological adjustments to an urban-industrial way of life. In addition, the type and quality of goods available changed radically during industrialization, and accurate measurement of the cost of living is difficult over long periods of time. One of the great virtues of stature is that it provides a reasonably consistent measure of health, making it comparable over time and across vastly different societies. Stature is far from comprehensive, but everyone agrees that nutritional status is an important aspect of the standard of living.

The report on nutritional status and nineteenth-century industrialization for Sweden was rather optimistic (Sandberg and Steckel, 1980). Adult heights in that country increased with only minor interruptions after the 1840s, providing a good nutritional foundation for worker productivity that was to follow. Moreover, heights continued to increase during the strong industrial growth of the late nineteenth century, contradicting claims of immiserization through industrialization made by Marx and Engels.

Results for England and the United States were more pessimistic. Addressing one of the most controversial topics in English history, Roderick Floud and Kenneth Wachter found that the stature of poor London boys declined during the early and middle nineteenth century, suggesting that the poor became worse off during the heart of the Industrial Revolution. Figure 3 shows the trend in heights for the United States, which shows a half-century height decline that began for those born in the early industrial period (c. 1830) and affected many occupational categories. Verified in other studies and various data sources, the American pattern has given rise to what John Komlos has called the "early industrial growth puzzle." On the other hand, stature increased continuously or with no more than modest interruptions in many industrializing countries, including the Netherlands, France, Germany, Australia, and Japan.

Despite great interest, measures of inequality are often difficult to acquire, and when available they often pose problems of interpretation. Unlike aggregate data on income, which might be estimated from census data on production, measures of inequality must be estimated from data on individuals (or families). Tax records, probate records, and census manuscript schedules have proven useful, but it is difficult or impossible to assemble consistent time series from these sources. Of course, height data do not resolve the problems of measuring inequality in historical settings, they merely add new, useful information.

Regressions demonstrated that a country's average height in the mid-twentieth century was a nonlinear function of average income and a linear function of inequality, measured by the Gini coefficient of household income (Steckel, 1983). Average height is a sensitive barometer of the share of the population that lacks the basic necessities of life, and for this reason it can be used as a measure of human welfare. In very poor countries, the health of a large share of the population is significantly constrained by inadequate diet, housing, and medical care. As income increases, a growing share of the population acquires the basic necessities of life, and average height increases.

In rich countries, most people attain their genetic potential for growth unless there is considerable inequality, which limits opportunities for growth among the poor. Differences in average heights by occupation, region, ethnicity, and so on are a measure of inequality in biological aspects of the standard of living. Class differences in stature exceeded 10 centimeters in eighteenth century England, more than twice the difference ever observed for the United States. In America, heights were virtually identical across occupations during the late Colonial period, whereas they were less than 4 centimeters in the mid-nineteenth century. Free blacks faced considerable obstacles to social and economic mobility but achieved reasonably good nutritional status, with heights falling between those of slaves and whites of the same era.

The average heights of American men have stagnated, increasing by only a small fraction of an inch over the past half century. Figure 3 refers to the native born, so recent increases in immigration cannot account for the stagnation. In the absence of other information, one might be

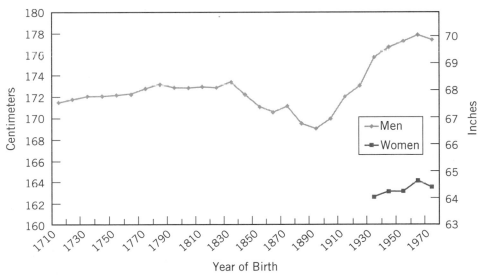

Figure 3. Heights of native-born American men and women, by year of birth. SOURCE: Steckel, 2003.

tempted to suppose that environmental conditions for growth are so good that most Americans have simply reached their genetic potential for growth. But data on heights of military conscripts in Europe show that this is not the case. Heights have continued to grow in Europe, which has the same genetic stock from which most Americans descend. By the 1970s, Americans had fallen behind Norway, Sweden, and Denmark, and were on par with Germany. While American heights were essentially flat after the 1970s, heights continued to grow significantly in Europe. The Dutch are now the tallest, averaging 6 feet, about 2 inches more than American men.

Note that significant differences in health and the quality of life follow from these height patterns. The comparisons are not part of an odd contest that emphasizes height, nor is big *per se* assumed to be beautiful. Instead, we know that on average, stunted growth has functional implications for longevity, cognitive development, and work capacity. Children who fail to grow adequately are often sick, suffer learning impairments, and have a lower quality of life. Growth failure in childhood has a long reach into adulthood because individuals whose growth has been stunted are at greater risk of death from heart disease, diabetes, and some types of cancer. Therefore, it is important to know why Americans are falling behind.

Research and Policy Needs. The new anthropometric history has reached the quarter-century mark, with publication of several books and more than fifty articles. Yet ample research opportunities exist. Abundant data are available from military records and other sources to document historical patterns of heights. Often, some socioeconomic variables are also available for analysis of historical height patterns. While very few measurements were taken before the eighteenth century, when height was widely used for identification purposes, the time frame can be extended backward for several millennia by using skeletal remains. In the area of methodology, much more work is needed on the functional implications of stature. This measure will be understood by social scientists only after its relationship has been thoroughly mapped to more familiar measures. Some work has been done on height and income, and height and longevity, but research opportunities exist on height as a predictor or explanatory factor in health quality of life while living, educational attainment, and social and economic mobility. Progress in this area will require longitudinal data, which are often difficult to obtain.

Given the huge literature on poverty and inequality, it is encouraging to see interest expand in using height to monitor living standards, to investigate inequality, and to evaluate social policy. A UNICEF project recently used anthropometric data to express detailed baseline measurements of child malnutrition against which progress can be measured. An ongoing children's growth surveillance program (National Study of Health and Growth) for this purpose has existed in England since 1972, but few systematic efforts are in place in industrialized countries. Even in wealthy societies, disadvantaged groups are exposed to fluctuations in socioeconomic circumstances, which creates a need for assessing nutritional status. Such a program has a sound methodological base, and I expect would be sensible given the ease of collecting anthropometric data. This article therefore concludes with a call for study of the costs and benefits of incorporating measures of the biological quality of life into our social accounting apparatus.

BIBLIOGRAPHY

Bodenhorn, Howard. "A Troublesome Caste: Height and Nutrition of Antebellum Virginia's Rural Free Blacks," *Journal of Economic History* 59 (1999), 972–996.

Floud, Roderick, Kenneth W. Wachter, and Anabel S. Gregory. *Height, Health, and History: Nutritional Status in the United Kingdom, 1750–1980*. Cambridge, 1990.

Fogel, Robert William. "Nutrition and the Decline in Mortality since 1700: Some Preliminary Findings." In *Long-Term Factors in American Economic Growth*, edited by Stanley L. Engerman and Robert E. Gallman, pp. 439–527. Chicago, 1986.

Komlos, John. *Nutrition and Economic Development in the Eighteenth-Century Habsburg Monarchy*. Princeton, 1989.

Komlos, John, and Peter Coclanis. "On the Puzzling Cycle in the Biological Standard of Living: The Case of Antebellum Georgia." *Explorations in Economic History* 34 (1997), 433–459.

Margo, Robert A., and Richard H. Steckel. "Heights of Native-born Whites during the Antebellum Period." *Journal of Economic History* 43 (1983), 167–174.

National Center for Health Statistics. "NCHS Growth Curves for Children, Birth–18 Years, United States." DHEW "Publication No. (PHS) 78–1650, 37. Hyattsville, Md., 1977.

Sandberg, Lars G., and Richard H. Steckel. "Soldier, Soldier, What Made You Grow So Tall? A Study of Height, Health, and Nutrition in Sweden, 1720–1881." *Economy and History* 23 (1980), 91–105.

Steckel, Richard H. "Slave Height Profiles from Coastwise Manifests." *Explorations in Economic History* 16 (1979), 363–380.

Steckel, Richard H. "Height and Per Capita Income." *Historical Methods* 16 (1983), 1–7.

Steckel, Richard H. "A Peculiar Population: The Nutrition, Health, and Mortality of American Slaves from Childhood to Maturity." *Journal of Economic History* 46 (1986), 721–741.

Steckel, Richard H. "A Dreadful Childhood: The Excess Mortality of American Slaves." *Social Science History* 10 (1986), 427–465.

Steckel, Richard H. "Stature and the Standard of Living." *Journal of Economic Literature* 33 (1995), 1903–1940.

Steckel, Richard H., and Roderick Floud, eds. *Health and Welfare during Industrialization*. Chicago, 1997.

Steckel, Richard H., and Jerome C. Rose, eds. *The Backbone of History: Health and Nutrition in the Western Hemisphere*. New York, 2001.

Steckel, Richard H. "Health, Nutrition, and Physical Wellbeing." In *Historical Statistics of the United States: Millennial Edition*, edited by Susan Carter et al. New York, 2003.

Trussell, James, and Richard H. Steckel. "The Age of Slaves at Menarche and Their First Birth." *Journal of Interdisciplinary History* 8 (1978), 477–505.

RICHARD H. STECKEL

ANTIQUES TRADE. With the fall of the Greek Empire in the second century BCE, the Romans became enthusiastic collectors, as captured works of art were brought to Rome. Bronze and marble statues were highly prized, as the appropriated symbols of foreign cults, as well as pictures, curiosities, rare plants, and weapons, were collected for public display. Imperial Rome, however, possessed no museum. The captured spoils of war were divided between various temples and frequently found their way onto a vigorous art market, which comprised auction sales, retail shops, and specialized dealers. Copies, particularly of statues, were accepted with enthusiasm and frequently realized high prices, and archaic Greek works were much favored, as Horace tells us. Interest in contemporary art, however, was limited.

During the early Christian centuries, objects associated with the pagan classical world were regarded as corrupting. To the medieval mind, as Bazin (1967, p. 29) put it, history began with the Christian era, "preceded by a prehistory that was the world of the Bible." The Italian Renaissance began with an effort to reconcile Greek and Roman history with biblical narratives, but antiquarian and archaeological work on the monuments of Rome were of central importance. Leon Battista Alberti and Flavio Biondo's surveys from the 1430s to the 1450s marked the beginnings of systematic recording, prior to Raphael's memorandum to Pope Leo X recommending a comprehensive survey of the city's monuments, in 1519. The dividing line between scholarship and souvenir hunting was narrow, however, and a vigorous trade in art and antiquities between Italy and other parts of Europe developed during the sixteenth century, which the pope unsuccessfully attempted to ban in 1534. Interest in books and manuscripts was especially strong in Florence, with enthusiasts such as Niccoló Niccoli and Poggio Braccolini leading the "codex hunt," in a trail that stretched from the eastern Mediterranean to England.

By the second half of the sixteenth century, the humanist impulse had spread from Italy to the rest of Europe, from the princely courts of the Medici and d'Este, to the Austrian Habsburgs and the Landgraves of Hesse, and to bourgeois collectors from Basel and the Netherlands. Agents such as the Flemish engraver Hubert Goltzius and the Augsburg merchant Philip Hainhofer increasingly supplied a socially diverse clientele with antiquities and curiosities. Goltzius listed all the collectors whom he visited between 1556 and 1560, in an account that included 968 names in the Netherlands, Germany, Austria, Switzerland, Italy, and France. Collecting was slow to develop in England and inclined toward the fine arts rather than curiosities, under the influence of Thomas Howard, Earl of Arundel. But the Society of Antiquaries was formed in 1586, the year that also saw publication of William Camden's

ANTIQUES TRADE. Display in auction window, New York City. (Prints and Photographs Division, Library of Congress)

Britannia, which associated a sense of national pride with the Roman-British past.

The European encounter with the New World stimulated new patterns of collecting through the "cosmological uncertainty" created by new knowledge of indigenous peoples and their artifacts. Aztec treasure, pre-Hispanic featherwork, mosaic masks, clothing, and jewelery were imported in large quantities, but much was reworked, melted down, and subsumed into an adjustable category of "pagan" artifacts. A minority of antiquarians, however, including Michele Mercati, Isaac de la Peyrere, Sir William Dugdale, and Robert Plot, suspected that stone implements suggested the existence of a race of "pre-Adamite men," and therefore a more realistic view of human origins than the biblical account. The importance of natural history specimens from the New World also led to the development of new classification systems.

By the early eighteenth century, market growth was producing a more specialized international trade in works of art and antiquities, distinct from the assembly of embryonic scientific collections. Italy continued to supply antiquities and modern art through a network of dealers' shops, but in northern Europe, the auction room became the principal means of distribution. The first printed auction catalog appeared in Holland in 1616, and Amsterdam remained the preeminent auction center until the 1740s, before London and Paris rose to prominence. In Paris, the success of public sales inhibited the rise of the art dealer, although Jean-Michel Picart, Charles Hérault, and Edmé-François Gersaint emerged as important dealers in the late seventeenth and early eighteenth centuries. By the 1720s and 1730s, an infrastructure of dealers and regular auction sales had emerged in London, and the disposal of several important collections, such as those of the Dukes of Portland (1722), Chandos (1747), and Rutland (1759), attracted international attention. The London picture sales often included bronzes, busts, antiquities, books, and engravings, as well as old masters.

For much of the eighteenth century, the upper classes of northern Europe found the lure of Italy irresistible, particularly the English and the French. The grand tour formed a "wandering academy" for generations of young Englishmen, and numerous collections of ancient marbles found their way to English country houses such as Duncombe, Ince, Blundell, and Petworth. The years 1764–1798 saw an unprecedented number of excavations in and around Rome, and restorers like Giovanni Battista Piranesi and Bartolomeo Cavaceppi maintained enormous workshops for the repair and copying of antique sculpture. Resident British dealers and antiquarians such as Thomas Jenkins and James Byres were less discriminating in supplying fakes and forgeries, in what one commentator described as a "wonderful system of imposition and villainy."

The number of important old masters leaving Italy before the French Revolution was small, but the upheavals of the 1790s and the Napoleonic Wars resulted in a flood of works of art from France, Italy, and Egypt. Unrequisitioned crown and church property, together with that of emigré aristocrats, was auctioned and exported abroad, and Napoleon's Egyptian campaign produced a staggering quantity of plundered material, including the Rosetta Stone, acquired by the British Museum in 1801. By the 1870s, art dealing was divided principally between London and Paris, before New York completed the "golden triangle" in the years immediately following World War I. During the next forty years, Britain's slow economic decline was accompanied by a loss of imperial power, yet it was in the 1960s that London emerged as the epicenter of the world art market. In the long run, the British market has benefited from conditions of internal political stability and the saprophagous character of collectibles, which thrive on the decomposition and dismantling of cultural capital.

BIBLIOGRAPHY
Bazin, Germain. *The Museum Age*. Brussels, 1967.
Impey, Oliver, and Arthur MacGregor. *The Origins of Museums: The Cabinet of Curiosities in Sixteenth- and Seventeenth-Century Europe.* London, 1985.
North, Michael, and David Ormrod, eds. *Art Markets in Europe, 1400–1800.* Aldershot, U.K., 1998.
Pomian, Krzystof. *Collectors and Curiosities: Paris and Venice, 1500–1800.* London, 1990.
Schnapp, Alain. *The Discovery of the Past: The Origins of Archaeology.* London, 1996.
Wilton, Andrew, and Ilavia Bignamini, eds. *Grand Tour: The Lure of Italy in the Eighteenth Century.* London, 1996.

DAVID ORMROD

ANTITRUST. Antitrust theory and policy occupies a distinctive place in economic history. Since the first Industrial Revolution originated in Great Britain during the eighteenth century, the owners of firms had managed the processes of production, distribution, transportation, and communications personally; but during the closing decades of the nineteenth century, a separation occurred between owners and operators. In the new form of corporate capitalism, managers were the primary decision makers, laying the foundation for what historian Alfred Chandler has called the managerial revolution in American business. In the United States, antitrust legislation first emerged out of popular concerns about the rise of corporate big business. Throughout the second half of the twentieth century other nations enacted antitrust laws, and by the turn of the twenty-first century the internationalization of antitrust had become central to the process of globalization associated with the World Trade Organization (WTO). Whenever governments have established an antitrust regime, its primary concern has been the control of private market power, holding a firm accountable to an authority outside of itself. Antitrust policy employs economic theory to create and enforce formal standards of business behavior; such economic theories, nonetheless, have changed over time and differed from place to place; and antitrust, increasingly defined broadly as competition policy, gradually emerged as a global policy issue by the end of the twentieth century.

Antitrust and Managerial Capitalism before 1914. American antitrust policy first developed in response to two principal modes of business combination. In late-nineteenth-century America, a rapid rise in urban population, the spread of technological innovation, and a tremendous expansion of transportation facilities transformed the factory system and mass production, enabling a single firm greatly to increase its potential rate of production and thereby supply the rapidly expanding urban market. Simultaneously, however, the decades following the Civil War witnessed a precipitous decline in the wholesale price index for all commodities, from 185 in 1865 to about 80 during the early 1890s. Increasingly, firms addressed the demands of economic uncertainty through forms of combination. By building their own marketing organizations, for example, manufacturers were able to handle their buying and selling more effectively than could specialized middlemen. Many big firms were little more than loose confederations or cartels formed to eliminate competition and to fix prices. Even so, the fundamental problem was that cartel members might seek to gain advantage by undercutting agreed prices, thereby unleashing the very competition the cartel had sought to prevent.

The second path of combination involved forms of corporate consolidation through merger. In 1882 Standard Oil used trust agreements to transfer ownership and managerial control from independent firms to a centralized board of directors, creating the first formal trust. As state prosecutions destroyed the original trust device, Standard Oil and other leading industrial firms then pursued ways to adapt the corporate merger to greater managerial centralization. In 1889 New Jersey became the first state to seize this opportunity, by enacting a statute permitting corporations to form holding companies. By establishing a holding company, a firm incorporated in one state could purchase stock in companies incorporated in other states. Such mergers created a centralized enterprise officially based in one state but in fact operating throughout the nation or even around the world. Since mergers eliminated the independence of the firms absorbed, internal interference with enforcement of contractual agreements was not a problem. Moreover, mergers gave the managing directors of the parent firm direct control over assets and earnings of subsidiaries, which usually were located in different states. Managerial control facilitated a wide range of intercompany contractual transactions, including the sale of assets of one subsidiary to another, the routing of profitable business to one subsidiary in preference to another, the concealment of losses, or giving the appearance of nonexistent deficits (to alter tax liability).

The convergence of successful state prosecutions of the formal trust, private suits against cartels, and New Jersey's holding-company law spurred demands for federal antitrust legislation. Small business, farmers, and labor groups nonetheless fragmented in their search for effective antitrust measures. Thus, by 1890, interstate legal conflict and party politics and ideology had diffused the antitrust issue among both Democrats and Republicans. Accordingly, in that year Congress passed by overwhelming bipartisan majorities, and Republican President Benjamin Harrison signed, the Sherman Antitrust Act. It declared that every "contract, combination in the form of trust or otherwise, or conspiracy, in restraint of trade or commerce among the several states, or with foreign nations," was illegal. Although these phrases seemed straightforward, their meaning was subject to diverse interpretations primarily because the language was taken from the common law, which in America and England had always been ambiguous.

In England, Parliament overturned portions of the common law in the Joint Stock Companies Act of 1844, establishing the principle of limited liability; ironically, during the nineteenth and twentieth centuries, most British businesses did not seek the benefits of the law, favoring instead the personal accountability inherent in partnerships. The U.S. Supreme Court confronted this uncertainty in the Knight Sugar Trust case of 1895. The firm was a holding company whose sugar production monopoly was confined principally to the state of Pennsylvania. Because such monopolies were traditionally subject to state regulation under the commerce clause, the Court decided eight to one that the Sherman Act did not apply. Soon thereafter, however, the Court upheld unanimously an injunction against Eugene V. Debs's support of the Pullman strike, leaving open the question of whether the Sherman Act might be used against striking workers. The very next year, in the Trans-Missouri Freight Association case, the Court by a five-to-four majority construed the Sherman Act to strike down the railroads' interstate rate fixing.

The Court's ambivalent merger and cartel decisions transformed American business. Corporate lawyers read the Court's Knight Sugar Trust decision to mean that the Sherman Act did not prohibit a holding company of the sort sugar producers had established to achieve economies of scale, even if the result was a production monopoly based principally in a single state. The consistent state and federal decisions, especially the Trans-Missouri Freight opinion, against looser cartel practices led such lawyers to conclude also that the law sanctioned organizational consolidation of small firms to establish large-scale corporations. Thus, between 1895 and 1904 antitrust law ironically encouraged a great turn-of-the-century merger wave; at its peak, in 1899, some 1,208 firms valued at over $2.064 million were absorbed.

Antitrust and Comparative Economic Policy before 1914. Compared to other nations, moreover, the American antitrust response to big corporate business was distinctive. In Britain the turn-of-the-century merger wave was much smaller, involving fewer industries, principally textiles and brewing. Indeed, in 1899 the number of British firms consolidated was roughly one quarter of that in the United States; the comparative value of the British mergers was about 5 percent of the American. British business also increasingly relied on cartel practices. The German and, to a lesser extent, Japanese governments expressly encouraged cartel combinations, with the result that in those nations the number of large, managerially centralized corporations was even smaller. Meanwhile, Canada and Australia experimented with American-style antitrust legislation in an effort to curb the reach of U.S.-based corporations in their domestic markets; but both nations soon abandoned meaningful enforcement of these laws, relying instead on protectionism within the British Empire.

This divergent international response carried over into economic theory. Outside the United States, most professional economists and publicist journals reflecting their opinion, such as the *Economist*, agreed with Britain's Alfred Marshall that although combinations to form large firms were "natural," they eventually would succumb to competitive pressures and break up. Economists and publicists espousing socialism agreed although they contended that combination paved the way to public ownership of industry. Both sides concurred nonetheless that government intervention on the scale of American-type antitrust legislation was unnecessary, even ill-advised. In contrast, not only were most American economists—including John Bates Clark and Richard Ely—less sanguine about whether such new corporate giants as Standard Oil were subject to competitive pressures, but they broadly concurred that some form of government intervention was essential. Moreover, once the consequences of the merger wave became apparent, American professional economists and economic publicists increasingly shared the conviction that the emergence of corporate big business broadly challenged the moral foundations of both the nations's business order and republican self-government itself.

The basic contours of American antitrust policy were established by the end of World War I. Over the years before the war, public anxiety concerning the transformation of the business order wrought by the merger wave made antitrust policy a dominant issue in American life. Republican President Theodore Roosevelt initiated a record number of antitrust cases. The government won a major victory in the Northern Securities case of 1904, where the Supreme Court decided against a railroad holding company. This first-ever dissolution of a holding company through federal prosecution ended the great merger wave, but Roosevelt and many of his fellow Progressives nonetheless argued that large-scale corporate consolidation itself was not wrong. The purpose of antitrust policy, then, was to eradicate immoral business conduct these Progressives identified with unfair and predatory business practices. The leading Progressive and "people's lawyer" Louis D. Brandeis, however, condemned the "curse of bigness" as a profound threat to small business and the virtues of free government that it represented. Accordingly, the chief goal of antitrust enforcement should be the breakup of big corporations. Brandeis even went so far as to advocate that lawmakers should permit, as did their counterparts in Britain, anticompetitive price agreements among members of trade associations composed of small dealers. Finally, the most influential argument employing economic theory was that of the nation's foremost neoclassical economist, John Bates Clark, who distinguished between good (efficient) combination and bad monopoly.

Out of this controversy emerged a new consensus on antitrust policy. Although more conservative than Roosevelt's, the Republican administration of William H. Taft prosecuted and won in 1911 the major Standard Oil and American Tobacco cases. The two firms, both holding companies engaged in national and worldwide business, each within their respective industries had entered into anticompetitive agreements involving distribution and production, which they defended on grounds of efficiency. The Court declared, however, that the anticompetitive conduct represented an *undue* restraint that was unreasonable and, therefore, a violation of the Sherman Act. The decisions established a standard of legality that depended on a blend of moral and economic factors. The two firms were, accordingly, broken up because the Court found evidence of undesirable consequences due to intentional pernicious conduct. Even so, interpreting the law according to a "rule of reason" left the Court considerable flexibility. Moral considerations such as those showing criminal intent in the Standard Oil and American Tobacco cases thus were distinguishable from efficiency concerns in separating reasonable from unreasonable conduct. Also in 1911 the Court reaffirmed, contrary to the policy Brandeis had urged, that cartel practices were *per se* illegal. Meanwhile, despite vigorous criticism from many Progressives, the Court sanctioned a loose construction of the Sherman Act to grant businesses injunctions against the secondary boycotts of unionized workers supporting the strikes of other unions. By contrast, state prosecutions against cartels and big corporations—such as Texas's success in preventing Standard Oil's takeover of the state's oil industry—continued, but their significance declined as compared with federal action.

The Interwar Period's Antitrust Policy Balance. The balance between merger and cartel decisions that the Court established in 1911 prevailed until the Great Depression. In the much-contested election of 1912, Democrat Woodrow Wilson won on an antitrust platform supporting J. B. Clark's distinction between "good combinations" and "bad monopolies." In order to more effectively enforce the difference, the Wilson administration amended the Sherman Act with the Clayton Antitrust Act of 1914. The new law prohibited the effects of such practices as price discrimination, interlocking directorates, exclusive dealing contracts, and mergers that could be proved to "lessen" competition or create monopoly. In the same year, the Wilson administration achieved passage of legislation to establish the Federal Trade Commission, to protect consumers and business itself from unfair trade practices. However, World War I required suspension of the antitrust laws; and with the return of peace, the Court's narrow construction virtually emasculated the two new laws, including the Clayton Act's admittedly ambiguous attempt to protect unions from the labor injunction. Otherwise, in the U.S. Steel decision of 1920, the Court held that, despite being one of the largest corporations in the world, the company evidenced no intentional pernicious conduct toward competitors, against whom, indeed, it competed "fairly." Thus, the Court decided that bigness truly achieved and maintained through efficiency was reasonable. Even so, from 1890 to 1919 the government won about 80 percent of its antitrust cases; moreover, six out of seven of these suits were against cartel agreements among small firms in the furniture, lumber, and apparel—wholesale and retail—trades. After the war, Congress enacted antitrust exemptions for agriculture cooperatives and trade exporters. Meanwhile, the Court decided that antitrust law did not apply extraterritorially to conduct occurring beyond the borders of the United States; it also found that many trade associations' practices did not violate antitrust policy, while generally benefited small business. The government continued to grant patent monopolies, but the Court's decisions limited patent protection under the antitrust laws.

The impact of antitrust policy on American business was apparent by the end of the 1920s. More so than either patent laws or the tariff, it shaped the distinctive development of large-scale industrial enterprise in the United States. The federal and state success in closing off cartel combinations to smaller firms while the Court initially sanctioned holding-company mergers encouraged large-scale corporate consolidation in the turn-of-the-century merger wave, establishing the basic structure of managerially centralized, vertically integrated corporations, which came to dominate the nation's economy throughout the twentieth century. The Court's application of the "rule of reason" from 1911 on, moreover, encouraged large industrial firms generally to abandon the holding company, which, in conjunction with World War I, facilitated a second major merger wave. As a result, most leading industrial firms adopted even more centralized managerial organization, thereby creating an oligopolistic market structure throughout the American economy. Significantly, antitrust policy prevented monopoly and increased competition within oligopolistic industries, but it never returned oligopolistic markets to traditional ones predominately controlled by smaller firms. Brandeisians, to be sure, lamented that the curse of bigness had befallen America, but ongoing federal and state effectiveness in cartel prosecutions ensured that the nation's economy would continue to benefit from thriving small enterprise. Meanwhile, it was small business that gained most from the antitrust sanction of the federal court's labor injunction against organized labor.

During the twentieth century's middle decades, American managerial capitalism and antitrust policy gradually gained international influence. The Great Depression of the 1930s brought about the most significant drop in America's gross national product in the entire twentieth century; but it did not prevent American corporate management from maintaining an efficient divisional organization adaptable to both national and international operations, particularly in the leading science-based industries—electrical equipment and chemicals. Early in the Depression, Franklin Roosevelt's Democratic administration promoted federal cartelization of the nation's economy. Coincidentally, certain U.S. chemical and oil firms secretly joined their British and German counterparts to form international cartel agreements. The Supreme Court's invalidation of most of Roosevelt's initial New Deal legislation, followed by his dramatic 1936 reelection victory and the Supreme Court's constitutional revolution—reversing its opposition to those earlier laws—beginning in 1937, however, resulted in a more competition-centered New Deal. In a bid to gain the support of small business, Congress enacted the Robinson-Patman Act of 1936 and the Miller-Tydings Act of 1937. Generally, these laws loosened the restrictions against resale price maintenance and other restrictive practices along lines Brandeis had urged.

Also, in 1938 Roosevelt appointed as head of the Justice Department's Antitrust Division Yale law professor Thurman Arnold, who transformed antitrust policy-making, setting it on a course of active enforcement lasting throughout the next thirty years. He used new economic theory to emphasize more directly market results rather than the moralism inherent in the original "rule of reason" the Court had established in 1911. Arnold and his successors ensured that American managerial capitalism would attain international post–World War II dominance through competition rather than cartelization.

The Internationalization of Antitrust since 1945. As World War II ended the Depression, Arnold's antitrust enforcement policies thus drew upon two schools of economic theory. The main sources were institutionalist theories identified with Thorstein Veblen, Wesley Clair Mitchell, and others, for whom the legal rules governing the marketplace rather than the market itself were most important. However, the newer, Depression-driven theories of Joan Robinson and E. H. Chamberlin also were influential; these theories recognized that imperfect competition characterized by oligopoly or monopoly shaped a firm's pricing practices in ways that displaced the classical competition described as rivalry between small units. During World War II and the following decades, American antitrust enforcement amalgamated these theories to develop a policy that increasingly excised moralism from standards of proof in favor of concerns about efficiency. Nevertheless, because the interests of the institutionalists predominated, the goal of antitrust was to balance market efficiency and social-welfare interests, including support for smaller enterprise. In addition, during the Depression, Congress had abolished the labor injunction and broadly exempted labor relations from antitrust jurisdiction. In wartime, antitrust enforcement remained active, partly in defense of small contractors but especially because it energetically pursued members of international cartels.

This international action converged, moreover, with the wider postwar goal of creating international organizations to further democracy and liberal free trade throughout the world. The United States attempted to incorporate antitrust provisions into the charter of the International Trade Organization (ITO); but when the ITO itself failed to be enacted, interest in an international antitrust regime dissolved. Nevertheless, the United States succeeded in establishing antitrust regimes in Germany and Japan, as part of Allied Occupation efforts to create democratic institutions strong enough to resist a recurrence of militarist-racist dictatorships in those nations. The United States also encouraged passage of Great Britain's first rather limited antitrust law in 1948, which nonetheless imposed accountability throughout an economy that, since the Joint Stock Companies Act of 1844, had become increasingly cartelized. Americans also facilitated the adoption of antitrust provisions in measures that culminated in creation of the European Economic Community, established in the 1957 Treaty of Rome.

Throughout the postwar era antitrust policy went through two broad phases. During the 1950s and 1960s, American antitrust enforcement—empowered in the Celler-Kefauver Act of 1950 with new authority to combat mergers involving corporate asset acquisitions—employed social-welfare and efficiency theories to address a third major merger wave. This period, the most active era of American antitrust enforcement to that time, witnessed successful private actions on an unprecedented scale, and saw the federal antitrust authorities winning significant cases in the Supreme Court, which focused on the structure of market power. As a result, finance-oriented managers such as Harold Geneen of International Telephone and Telegraph Corporation (ITT) developed new strategies leading to widespread diversification and conglomerate mergers. In addition, by the end of the 1960s European and Japanese business gradually closed the international competitive gap with the United States. The European Community's Commission employed antitrust theory to integrate a common market, as Australia and eventually Canada began reviving their antitrust laws. All these developments broadened the law's application into a more general competition policy. Meanwhile, Japanese antitrust policy survived primarily because it protected the interests of small business, leaving most economic policy-making authority to the Ministry of International Trade and Industry (MITI). Even so, antitrust authorities everywhere used prevailing economic theories to balance social-welfare and market efficiency in order to achieve "workable competition."

The second phase of postwar antitrust policy began during the 1970s and was still underway by the turn of the twenty-first century. In America, the oil shocks of 1973 and 1979, in conjunction with the Hart-Scott-Rodino Antitrust Improvement Act of 1976 instituting a merger notification system, converged with the growing market impact of knowledge-based industries, which World War II had promoted, and which within two decades amounted to a third Industrial Revolution grounded on information technology (IT). The chaotic business cycle of recession and boom persisted between the seventies and the early nineties, when the longest period of prosperity in American history began. Even so, corporate governance was transformed: more than ever managerial effectiveness was tied to the short-term performance of the stock market. As a result, advocates of theories identified with R. H. Coase, spread by the teaching of Aaron Director, popularized by Robert Bork, and broadly associated with the Chicago School of economics succeeded in making efficiency the dominant policy goal of antitrust from the 1970s on. During the 1980s the antitrust authorities of Ronald Reagan's Republican administration institutionalized this theory in virtually every field of antitrust enforcement. Although the administration did break up AT&T, in cases involving the relationship between monopoly and oligopolistic competition its antitrust officials allowed mergers to the greatest extent since the turn of the twentieth century. Meanwhile, globalization accompanying the IT revolution and the emergence of the so-called New Economy facilitated a reworking of the antitrust rules pertaining to patented intellectual property, which in turn profoundly promoted the computer industry. including IBM and Microsoft.

Globalization also furthered the internationalization of antitrust policy. In the member states of the European Union (EU), antitrust was more significant than ever—in part because the end of the Cold War opened Eastern European nations to future EU membership, but only if the former Communist states met strict accession standards that included adopting effective antitrust regimes. Similarly, in Japan a long recession began during the 1990s that ended the postwar economic miracle, but which in turn resulted in the most effective antitrust enforcement since the Allied Occupation forces departed in 1952. By the early 1990s, in the United States a reevaluation of Chicago-inspired economic theories also was gaining ground. Under Bill Clinton's Democratic administration, this facilitated—as demonstrated by the famous case against Microsoft—reinvigorated antitrust enforcement in which consumer welfare defined more broadly than market efficiency alone was the policy goal. The administration pursued its policy, moreover, to counter a historic global merger wave and the proliferation of international cartels. Accordingly, international cooperation among antitrust regimes increased as never before, prompting demands for some sort of global antitrust authority that would address the full scope of competition policy on the level of the WTO. Although the future of such an organization remained problematic as a new millennium dawned, antitrust policy's traditional concern with curbing economic power—and not solely with the maintenance of narrowly defined market efficiency—had achieved global importance.

BIBLIOGRAPHY

Arceda, Philip, and Louis Kaplow. *Antitrust Analysis*. 5th ed. New York, 1997.

Bork, Robert H. *The Antitrust Paradox: A Policy at War with Itself*. New York, 1978.

Chandler, Alfred D., Jr. *The Visible Hand: The Managerial Revolution in American Business*. Cambridge, 1977.

Chandler, Alfred D., Jr., Francis Amatori, and Takashi Hikino, eds. *Big Business and the Wealth of Nations*. Cambridge, 1999.

Eisner, Marc Allen. *Antitrust and the Triumph of Economics: Institutions, Expertise, and Policy Change*. Chapel Hill, N.C., 1991.

Ernst, Daniel R. *Lawyers against Labor: From Individual Rights to Corporate Liberalism*. Champaign, Ill., 1995.

First, Harry, Eleanor M. Fox, and Robert Pitofsky, eds. *Revitalizing Antitrust in its Second Century: Essays on Legal, Economic, and Political Policy*. New York, 1991.

Fligstein, Neil. *The Transformation of Corporate Control*. Cambridge, 1990.

Freyer, Tony. *Regulating Big Business: Antitrust in Great Britain and America, 1880–1990*. Cambridge, 1992.

Hannah, Leslie, *The Rise of the Corporate Economy*. London, 1983.

Hovenkamp, Herbert. *Enterprize and American Law, 1836–1937*. Cambridge, 1991.

Jones, Clifford A., and Mitsuo Matsushita, eds. *Competition Policy in the Global Trading System: Perspectives from Japan, the United States, and the European Union*. The Hague, 2002.

Lamoreaux, Naomi R. *The Great Merger Wave in American Business, 1895–1904*. Cambridge, 1985.

Letwin, William. *Law and Economic Policy in America: The Evolution of the Sherman Antitrust Act*. New York, 1965.

May, James. "Antitrust Practice and Procedure in the Formative Era: The Constitutional and Conceptual Reach of State Antitrust Law." *University of Pennsylvania Law Review* 135 (1987), 495–593.

McCraw, Thomas K. *Prophets of Regulation: Charles Francis Adams, Louis D. Brandeis, James M. Landis, and Alfred E. Kahn*. Cambridge, 1984.

Peritz, Rudolph J. R. *Competition Policy in America, 1888–1992, History, Rhetoric, Law*. New York, 1996.

Sklar, Martin J. *The Reconstruction of American Capitalism, 1890–1916: The Market, the Law, and Politics*. Cambridge, 1988.

Thorelli, Hans. *The Federal Antitrust Policy: The Organization of an American Tradition*. Baltimore, 1954.

TONY A. FREYER

ANTWERP. Although the great Belgian scholar Henri Pirenne had always linked the origins of towns with the revival of international trade during the tenth and eleventh centuries, historians now agree that Antwerp also had Roman precedents. *Terra sigillata* found on a sandhill, in the actual center of the town, provides the oldest traces of human occupation, which can be dated to between 150 and 250 CE. For reasons that are still uncertain, the place was soon abandoned. A new settlement was founded in the middle of the seventh century on a place probably situated more than a thousand meters to the south. By the time this *civitas* was destroyed by Viking raids (836) a *vicus* had developed in the neighborhood of the present *steen* (castle), very near in fact to the first Roman settlement. This Carolingian *vicus*, also called *emporium*, evidently had a commercial character since both archaeological data and written sources refer to the presence of merchants. Population growth stimulated territorial expansion. When, at the beginning of the twelfth century, a church (the present cathedral of Our Lady) was built, it was still situated outside the town proper; but one century later it was completely incorporated by new houses, streets, canals, and walls.

The further development of the town would be determined by its favorable location near the river Scheldt, one that linked the town downstream with the North Sea and the mouths of the Rhine and the Meuse, and upstream with the rich hinterland of Brabant and Flanders. Hydrographic elements also favored the town. Storm floods altered the shallow Honte at the end of the fourteenth century to

ANTWERP. Port and market at Antwerp. Anonymous painting, Flemish School, seventeenth century. (Mayer van den Bergh, Antwerp, Belgium/Erich Lessing/Art Resource, NY)

become the easily navigable Western Scheldt, which became an ideal connection with the North Sea.

The real breakthrough took place with the establishment of the famous fairs around 1317. At that moment regional trade was still dominating. Traces of a growing international importance soon became apparent when Italian and Hanseatic merchants came to the town. Flanders's annexation of Antwerp, as a result of the Flemish-Brabantine war in 1356, was a temporary setback; but the growth of the fairs could not be stopped. Before the end of the century, numerous Dutch, Spanish, and English merchants had found their way to Antwerp. Moreover, the fairs of Antwerp also fitted well into the cycle of the important central German fairs, as a result of which commercial contacts between Antwerp, the Rhineland, and the Frankfurt region expanded strongly. The irresistible growth of south-German industry and commerce proved especially promising for the future of the town. Subsequently, Antwerp could not avoid some involvement in the Flemish and Brabantine civil wars (1482–1492). Since the town remained loyal to the regent Maximilian, it succeeded in taking advantage of the defeat of Bruges and the ruin of its money market. At the end of the fifteenth century, Antwerp was ready to supersede Bruges as leading economic center in the Low Countries.

Antwerp's brilliant economic expansion in the sixteenth century initially (1485–1520) was dominated by the transit function of its harbor in servicing European trade. This function derived its importance from the presence of various merchants belonging to the so-called new generations in European commercial history. Although English cloth exports to Flanders and Bruges frequently had been hindered by several cloth bans, Antwerp had welcomed the Merchant Adventurers, who, after some political maneuvers, selected this port as their main distribution center in marketing English woolens on the Continent. Furthermore, most of these cloths were dyed and finished there, in the best textile traditions of the Low Countries. The Portuguese, having discovered new direct sea routes to India at the end of the fifteenth century, first showed a clear preference for Bruges; but they decided to stay in Antwerp once the civil war was over. In 1501, the first Portuguese ship arrived in Antwerp, with pepper and cinnamon; seven years later, the Portuguese king established the *Feitoria de Flandres* in Antwerp, thereby giving the town official monopoly of the Portuguese spice trade in Europe. The reason for this shift is that the Portuguese were interested in the massive amounts of silver and copper now being brought to Antwerp by south-German merchants, who had been the chief investors in the new technology that had produced central-European mining (c. 1460–c. 1530).

The transit function, however, remained very vulnerable, as was clearly proved by subsequent crises (from c. 1520 to 1540). A new period of intensive warfare between the French and the Hapsburgs in Germany brought an end to two of Antwerp's initial commercial foundations: the Portuguese spice monopoly and the overland trade with southern Germany. After 1540, however, Antwerp benefited once again from the ongoing English export boom in cloth (favored by the Great Debasements of Henry VIII). The town even managed to broaden the narrow base of its first growth cycle by integrating the revival of the urban export industries of the southern Netherlands into its own development. Antwerp thus became an international market for the export of light draperies (says, serges, fustians, linen), as well as tapestries, furniture, printed books, and the fine products of the Low Countries' renowned painters and sculptors. Import substitution was important as well. Most noticeable was the silk industry, followed by glass, mirror, and crystal manufactures.

By the middle of the sixteenth century, Antwerp had become the commercial metropolis of western Europe, with more than eleven hundred foreign and some four hundred domestic merchants. Commerce brought prosperity within its walls, rising real wages, and full employment. Wages in Antwerp were clearly higher than in other towns. Despite the onset of the highly inflationary Price Revolution era, wages were in fact increasing more rapidly than prices. The famous new Bourse of 1531 would later inspire the Exchange of Thomas Gresham in London. Demographic growth followed commercial success. Antwerp probably had no more than seven thousand inhabitants in 1374, some twenty thousand in 1437, and about thirty thousand at the end of the fifteenth century. By 1526, however, its population had risen to fifty-five thousand; and between 1565 and 1570, approximately one hundred thousand people lived there. The expansion of the town was so remarkable that the rhythm of its economic development corresponded to a large extent with the pattern of the general economic history of the Low Countries. Nevertheless, many small towns in traditionally backward regions such as the Hageland and the Campine area fell into a deep shadow in the glare of Antwerp's splendor. They were sharply hit by Antwerp's competition and saw their most qualified workers emigrate.

The golden age of Antwerp came rapidly to an end with the outbreak of the Eighty Years' War (1568–1648). Military operations and a large exodus of merchants and craftsmen ruined the export industries. Antwerp was itself plundered, during the so-called Spanish Fury of November 1576, and then conquered by the Spanish (1585), after which the Dutch closed the river Scheldt, to blockade this port, still a rival of the now expanding Amsterdam to the north. In spite of this last handicap, the town did more than just survive. In fact, it remained the greatest harbor and the most important financial center of the southern Netherlands. Antwerp even managed to enjoy a real "Indian summer" in the first half of the seventeenth century, thanks to its industrial tradition (with the export of silk, lace, linen, tapestries, cut diamonds) and artistic potential (with the Officina Plantiniana, but also the school of Rubens, Van Dyck, and Jordaens); and it benefited from using family commercial-financial networks and from trade with the Spanish Empire and its colonies. In the second half of the seventeenth century, with the spread of mercantilism in Europe and Spain's worsening economic and political problems, Antwerp's decline became inevitable. The downward trend would continue into the first half of the eighteenth century, when Antwerp turned into an important regional center without ever regaining its international status. Its population declined from some sixty to seventy thousand in the seventeenth century to just forty-six thousand in 1755 although it increased somewhat afterward (to fifty-four thousand in 1784) with the appearance of some new large-scale, mechanized industries. A new and impressive growth process, however, would commence only after the reopening of the Scheldt (1792) and with the industrialization of the Walloon part of Belgium, the Ruhr area, and northern France in the nineteenth century.

BIBLIOGRAPHY

Isaker, Karel van, and Raymond van Uytven, eds. *Antwerp: Twelve Centuries of History and Culture.* Antwerp, 1986.

Suykens, F., G. Asaert, et al. *Antwerp, A Port for All Seasons (Ortelius Series).* Antwerp, 1986.

Wee, Herman van der. *The Growth of the Antwerp Market and the European Economy (Fourteenth–Sixteenth Centuries).* 3 vols. Louvain, Paris, and The Hague, 1963.

Wee, Herman van der. (in collaboration with J. Materné). "Antwerp as a World Market in the Sixteenth and Seventeenth Centuries." In *Antwerp, Story of a Metropolis: Sixteenth-Seventeenth Centuries*, edited by J. Van Der Stock, pp. 19–31. Ghent, 1993.

ERIK AERTS

APICULTURE is the keeping of bees. Beekeepers may be hobbyists, maintaining a few colonies for pleasure; sideliners, keeping modest numbers for income enhancement; or commercial beekeepers, earning their livelihood from hive products and pollination rentals. Hive products include honey, pollen, royal jelly, venom, propolis, queen cells, mated queens, and bulk bees. However, honey bees' greatest value is their role in commercial crop pollination. Nearly one-third of the U.S. daily diet relies on honey bee pollination, with an annual U.S. value of $14 billion.

Whether honey bees originated in Africa or in Europe, as is suggested by a recent discovery of a 40-million-year-old honey bee in Baltic amber, they colonized Europe, Africa, and Asia long before human existence. Humans documented their relationship with honey bees only within the last 5,000 years. Honey bee historian Dr. Eva Crane describes a rock painting of a honey gatherer from Barranc Fondo, Castellón, eastern Spain (Crane, 1983, 1999a) that is estimated to be 4,000 to 4,500 years old. Investigators also have found a stone bas-relief from Egypt dating from about 2400 BCE and a clearer tomb painting of Egyptians visiting hives from about 1450 BCE (Crane, 1999b).

Honey is the only known ancient source of abundant sugar. It was consumed as a sweetener and fermented into an alcoholic beverage called mead. Its medicinal properties led to its use internally and externally to heal many infirmities. Honey is especially good for treating wounds and burns because it accelerates healing and reduces scarring. Propolis, bee-collected plant resins, also has a history of medicinal uses, as its antiviral, antibacterial, and antifungal properties made it an inexpensive active ingredient for tinctures and salves.

It was not until 1851 that the American Lorenzo Lorraine Langstroth determined that an appropriate "bee space" would prevent the bees from connecting adjacent combs or fastening combs to hive walls. Now bees could be kept in movable frame hives, instead of hollow tree trunks, pottery vessels, straw skeps, and solid boxes. Removable frames allowed combs to be taken from the hives, uncapped, extracted by centrifugation, and returned to the bees.

Immediately following the bee space discovery, inventors rapidly developed beeswax comb foundation, the honey extractor, slotted queen excluders, and the bee escape. Since 1900 about the only advances in beekeeping have been refinements of preexisting equipment, transition from animal-powered to petroleum-powered vehicles, and substitution of plastics for wood and metal equipment and for comb foundation. Beekeepers also take advantage of modern antibiotics and pesticides to help subdue honey bee diseases, pests, and parasites.

Up to the 1900s, hive products were processed and consumed locally. The current global economy has brought those products to the world market. The cost of production of hive products in countries with high standards of living exceeds the world market price. International trade of hive products has become an active political issue. Subsidies, import quotas, import tariffs, locally advantageous quality standards, and phytosanitary considerations affect distribution to a greater extent than simple supply and demand.

BIBLIOGRAPHY

Crane, Eva. *The Archaeology of Beekeeping.* London, 1983.
Crane, Eva. *The World History of Beekeeping and Honey Hunting.* London, 1999a.
Crane, Eva. "Recent Research on the World History of Beekeeping." *Bee World* 80.4 (1999b), 174–186.

ERIC C. MUSSEN

APPRENTICESHIP. A form of initiatory training under legal agreement in a trade, apprenticeship as a means for transmitting tacit skills is most closely associated with the craft guilds of medieval and early modern Europe. Children in premodern Europe normally were employed outside their homes, either by apprenticeship or by a work contract negotiated by a parent or a guardian, the latter arrangement distinguished from apprenticeship by its lack of an element of professional training. Large numbers of children were never apprenticed because they were trained within their parents' homes, or because some crafts (particularly those involving trade) did not require formal training. This fact accounts for the low number of apprentices with practicing masters relative to the number of trained masters and journeymen needed to reproduce trades over time, and for the low number of working girls recorded. Conversely, apprenticeship could exist outside guild structures although it faced the problem of enforcement outside a formal institutional framework. For these reasons and because of the nature of the skills involved, apprenticeship was mainly an urban, craft-based phenomenon, although in seventeenth- and eighteenth-century England it also was undertaken by the children of the rural poor under the remit of the national Poor Laws. Finally, apprenticeship was the prime means by which boys were trained to enter into the better-paying professions.

Parents or guardians, including people acting for religious foundling institutions, would present a child for apprenticeship between the ages of thirteen and fifteen; girls were apprenticed somewhat younger than boys. However, not all apprentices were adolescents, and guild statutes never specified the maximum age at which the indenture could begin. Most statutes specified the term of service, usually proportional to the craft's skill requirements and to its expected returns. The average length, which appears to have increased slowly over time, was variable; the English Statute of Artificers (1563, repealed 1814), which prescribed a national norm of seven years, terminating at age twenty-four or older, was unique. Even in England the actual length of service was negotiated individually on the basis of the apprentice's age and prior experience, the premium (if any) the parents could advance, and the master's reputation. Most statutes required longer terms for outsiders than for sons of members, who would have experienced some basic induction to the craft in their fathers' shops. Apprenticeship years could be bought out at a later date, or condoned if the trainee could demonstrate sufficient skills. The duration was further influenced by the fact that, before the dissolution of craft guilds, apprenticeship was not just a traineeship for a skilled occupation but also a means for socializing children and adolescents into adulthood and the world of work, so that the younger the age at entry, the longer the term.

The duration of training does not capture the intensity of resources expended on it. Apprentices could learn only when their masters were working; so the ups and downs of the trade cycle affected the learning process. Nor should one underestimate the complexity of specific, transferable skills in preindustrial crafts and the difficulties of transmitting tacit, unformulated knowledge. Such factors help explain the three stages or components of premodern apprenticeship. Initially, apprentices were assigned menial tasks in the house, such as cleaning, serving, and running errands; after several months or years, they would be given small, marginal craft tasks; finally, they would be promoted to more skilled jobs, but often were not taught how to do them and had to learn in ad hoc ways (described in the sources as "stealing with one's eyes") or by getting journeymen to help them. Apprentices were nonetheless enjoined not to divulge the masters' secrets, and some masters went as far as forbidding their apprentices from working for another craftsman within a given geographic radius for some years after the term had ended. The practice of secrecy suggests that by the end of their term many apprentices would not achieve the skills needed to become full masters, and that apprentices trained in their fathers' shops with privileged access to the master craftsman would have had a strong technical advantage over outsiders.

The fact that the length of the apprenticeship generally exceeded the duration of actual learning became a source of controversy and misunderstanding among eighteenth-century political economists, who contended that the contract was long, expensive, and superfluous. Adam Smith, who understood that apprenticeship was the institutional base of the guild system, argued that since it was out of proportion to the requisite training, it must serve primarily to restrict job entry and thus to provide craftsmen with monopoly rents. However, although Smith implied that apprenticeship would wither away without legislative backing, its longevity in premodern Europe and its persistence and ubiquity in modern European industrial societies indicate that he may have underestimated apprenticeship's efficiency advantages in providing skills.

Recent analysis suggests that apprenticeship offered a solution to market failures arising from capital-market imperfections and skewed distributions of wealth. Since future human capital could not act as collateral, resource-poor but potentially able workers might be incapable of bearing the costs of their investment in training, leading to a socially suboptimal supply of skilled workers. Apprenticeship allowed trainees to indenture their labor in

APPRENTICES. Industrial workers learning the trade, Soviet Union, circa 1930. (David King Collection)

exchange for subsistence, that is, to exchange initially subsidized training for below-market wages for a period after training was concluded. However, if trainees were able to quit before repaying the training costs, firms still would supply suboptimal amounts of training because they could not capture the full return on their investment. Trainees with transferable skills (neither entirely general nor wholly specific to one firm) would be poached by firms that did not have to recover the training costs and could pay the trainees less than their marginal product but more than the wage paid by the original training firm. For apprenticeship to be viable, poaching must be constrained through legally enforceable indentures, allowing the firms that provided the training to appropriate the benefits in the immediate posttraining period. The decline of apprenticeship in postcolonial North America has been explained along these lines, in the absence of legislation enforcing contracts across state boundaries and with the presence of a large pool of immigrant skilled labor, which was in effect being "poached" from its countries of origin.

Premodern European guilds appear from this perspective to have been essential in overcoming training externalities in transferable skills. Crafts registered apprenticeships and carried out periodic inspections of job performance, work conditions, and quality of instruction. They enforced binding contracts through a combination of statutory penalties, compulsory membership, and blackballing and boycott of poachers. They acted as guarantors and established a set of rights and duties for both parties, albeit strongly unbalanced in the master's favor. Live-in apprentices had the right to be lodged, fed, housed, clothed, and heated on a par with members of their master's family, but they were equally subjected to his disciplinary rule as a surrogate father. Even those apprentices who lived at their parents' home (which they did in increasing numbers from the late seventeenth century on) were expected to be unquestioningly obedient to the master's orders and to respect the craft's rules. The apprentices' minority status explains the universal ban on marriage, and why breaches of the rule were treated severely; and the contract's educational features explain why younger trainees were given longer terms. The master controlled the apprentices' work time, and could offer their labor to another guildsman; apprentices had to work to the master's benefit and profit, and the guild enforced the master's right to keep apprentices on after their training had been completed so as to repay the master's training costs.

Guilds were more effective in banning poaching by their members than in stopping apprentices from quitting before their terms ended. Masters attempted to raise trainees' cost of default by demanding entry fees (de facto bonds posted to ensure the apprentices' commitment for the full term), by setting apprentices' wages on a rising scale for the contract's duration, and by promising a payoff upon completion; but there was little they could do to stem the hemorrhage permanently. The rate of attrition in early modern England (the only country for which data currently exist) has been estimated at 30 to 50 percent in sixteenth- and seventeenth-century London, Bristol, and Norwich. Although a significant proportion of apprentices who quit early were simply unable to cope, were mistreated, or moved to another occupation, many left in search of work in rural and small-town provinces where skills requirements were lower than in larger towns; crafts in premodern towns acted as training centers for their regional or even, in the case of London and other capital cities, national hinterlands, which they provided with a constant flow of skilled and semiskilled labor. The practice of secrecy (described above) responded to a situation of moral hazard that underpinned the outflow of trainees from the workshops, namely, that the better the training provided, the more likely it was that the apprentice would leave before the contract's expiry.

Many departing apprentices had originally immigrated to the training site from the urban hinterland. Immigration gave rise to problems of adverse selection and asymmetric information, which guilds and governments addressed by stipulating entrance requirements that signaled the laborer's quality or provided surety against misbehavior, such as place of residence, family income, or father's occupation; the Statute of Artificers specified all three. In some highly specialized and cyclical industries, such as mining and iron making, shipbuilding, and high-quality masonry, skills training often was kept within closely knit kin networks, probably because the higher risks of those industries restricted the supply of apprentices.

Craft guilds also protected apprentices against the opportunism of masters. Like masters, apprentices had to be vested with appropriate rights (including a guarantee of proficiency and security of employment over at least one economic cycle) for them to invest their capabilities willingly. Masters could use protection of trade secrets as an excuse for providing poor training, possibly because undertrained workers were more productive to their current masters than elsewhere, whereas well-trained apprentices were more likely to quit early. Undertraining was also a way to exploit apprentices by paying them less than the current rate for generic labor, and discharging them before they had gained the agreed-upon skills; since they learned craft-specific skills within oligopsonistic labor markets, they suffered serious loss if they were discharged early or were poorly trained. The guilds passed rules to enforce adequate training and in extreme cases had the apprentice transfer to a new master; if the first master died, the guilds placed the apprentice with a new one. From the seventeenth century on, English, French, and German craft guilds began to enforce supralocal and supraregional systems of compulsory skill certification, sometimes including an examination to become a journeyman. On the other hand, the doubling or tripling of wages sometimes seen after the end of apprenticeship terms indicates that apprentices might have been exploited, and guild rules forbade masters from keeping apprentices beyond their statutory term.

Although formally indentured women generally comprised less than 5 percent of the labor force, and no women with the exception of masters' widows were allowed to keep apprentices, women had many ways to learn skills informally, either in male-controlled workplaces (as daughters and wives in family workshops where they learned by example, observation, and possibly direct employment) or more commonly in traditionally female work (housewifery). The lack of written records of indentures seriously underestimates the extent of skilled female labor employed by premodern crafts.

Despite the efficiency benefits of craft-based apprenticeship, regulation of entry was undeniably among its lesser objectives. It was achieved by limiting the number of apprentices (usually one to three) a master could train at one time, by introducing employment moratoria, and, in seventeenth- and eighteenth-century France, by using the *alloué*, a youth who was similar to an apprentice in terms of training and skills but was forbidden to take up a mastership and thus fell outside guild restrictions. However, given the limits on the number of apprentices a normal craftsman could usefully employ and teach on his premises, the fact that the restrictions excluded the master's children and step-children, and evidence of widespread infringement by wealthy artisans that produced a constant buzz of hostility among skilled journeymen, the practical impact of these regulations must be questioned.

[*See also* Craft Guilds *and* Journeymen.]

BIBLIOGRAPHY

Booth, Alison Lee, and Dennis J. Snower, eds. *Acquiring Skills: Market Failures, Their Symptoms, and Policy Responses.* Cambridge and New York, 1996. Theory and case studies in the economics of modern apprenticeship.

Brooks, Christopher. "Apprenticeship, Social Mobility, and the Middling Sort, 1550–1800." In *The Middling Sort of People: Culture, Society, and Politics in England, 1550–1800,* edited by Jonathan Barry and Christopher Brooks, pp. 52–83. London, 1994. A detailed survey of apprenticeship in early modern England.

Dunlop, O. J., and R. D. Denman. *English Apprenticeship and Child Labor: A History.* London and Leipzig, 1912. A classic study, from a legal-institutional angle.

Elbaum, Bernard, and Nirvar Singh. "The Economic Rationale of Apprenticeship Training: Some Lessons from British and U.S. Experience." *Industrial Relations* 34.4 (1995), 593–622. A model of industrial apprenticeship based on nineteenth- and early-twentieth-century experience.

Epstein, Stephan R. "Craft Guilds, Apprenticeship, and Technological Change in Preindustrial Europe." *Journal of Economic History* 53.4 (1998), 684–718. An interpretation of craft guilds in light of their contribution to skills training and technological progress.

Hamilton, Gillian. "The Decline of Apprenticeship in North America: Evidence from Montreal." *Journal of Economic History* 60.3 (September 2000), 627–664.

Kaplan, Steven. "L'apprentissage au XVIIIe siècle: Le cas de Paris." *Revue d'histoire moderne et contemporaine* 40.3 (1993), 436–479. A model study.

Krausman Ben-Amos, Ilana. "Failure to Become Freemen: Urban Apprentices in Early Modern England." *Social History* 16 (1991), 155–172.

Nicholas, David. "Child and Adolescent Labour in the Late Medieval City: A Flemish Model in Regional Perspective." *English Historical Review* 110 (November 1995), 1103–1131. A general view of late-medieval northwestern Europe.

Rappaport, Steve. *Worlds within Worlds: Structures of Life in Sixteenth-Century London.* Cambridge, 1989. Apprenticeship training in London, which supplied up to two-thirds of the skilled labor force in sixteenth-century England.

Schulz, Knut. *Handwerksgesellen und Lohnarbeiter: Untersuchungen zur Oberrheinischen und Oberdeutschen Stadtgeschichte des 14. bis 17. Jahrhunderts.* Sigmaringen, 1985. Apprenticeship in the context of skilled-labor markets in central Europe.

Steinfeld, Robert J. *The Invention of Free Labor: The Employment Relation in English and American Law and Culture, 1350–1870.* Chapel Hill and London, 1991. A fascinating analysis of the "feudal" and coercive aspects of medieval and early-modern labor contracts, including apprenticeship.

Westermann, W. L. "Apprentice Contracts and the Apprentice System in Roman Egypt." *Classical Philology* 9.3 (1914), 295–315. An example from the classical world.

S. R. EPSTEIN

ARABIA. The first known civilization to arise on the Arabian Peninsula was that of the Sabeans, around 750 BCE, in the fertile region in Southwest Arabia (modern Yemen). Agriculture was highly developed, with complex irrigation systems and livestock breeding. The main crops were cereals, such as wheat, barley, and sorghum; corn, dates, and other fruits and vegetables; and frankincense and myrrh for export. In addition to its agricultural production, the Sabean civilization took advantage of its location along an overseas trade route connecting the East to the West. The peninsula, with the Persian Gulf on the east and the Red Sea on the west, provided access to the neighboring civilizations of the Nile and the Tigris and Euphrates. The Sabeans monopolized trade on the Red Sea, as pearls from the Persian Gulf; condiments, fabrics and swords from India; silk from China; and slaves, monkeys, ivory, gold, and ostrich feathers from Ethiopia passed through on the way to markets in the Mediterranean area. After the fall of the Sabeans in 115 BCE, the Himyarite kingdom ruled most of Arabia until 525 CE but lost the monopoly on Red Sea trading in the first century CE.

In the first century CE improved understanding of the patterns of the monsoon winds enabled an expansion of maritime commerce, overland trade declined, and port cities, such as Aden and Mocha, began to thrive. The Roman Empire exported textiles, metals, wine, oil, grains, and luxury items, such as gold and silver goods, in exchange for myrrh from Yemen as well as exotic animals, precious stones, wood, ivory, silk, spices, sugar, cotton, and fruit, which passed through Arabia on the way from China to Rome. Ships from Muza brought glassware, iron tools, and weapons to Africa in exchange for ivory and shells. After the fall of Rome, trade among Arab merchants declined until the Quraysh tribe unified the region.

Agriculture was centered on the southern part of the peninsula, present-day Yemen, Oman, and southern Saudi Arabia, while central Arabia prospered from trade routes. Other than in the coastal areas, harsh climate and desert terrain limited agriculture. Up until the growth of Islam in the seventh century, the population was primarily pastoral and nomadic. The people lived in small, isolated communities, raised camels, and migrated seasonally in search of pasturage. In the summer they camped near villages or oases, where they exchanged animal products for grains, dates, utensils, weapons, and cloth. Pastoral nomads had used the one-humped camel for milk and meat since 3000 BCE, but the development of camel saddles around 1000 BCE enabled its use for riding and transport. The camel can travel without water for up to a month in winter and can subsist on parched grass only, which allowed Arab pastoralists to penetrate more deeply into the interior of Arabia. Camels could reliably cross the barren land, and Arabs could therefore benefit from some of the overland trade that had previously circumvented the Arabian Peninsula. Trans-Arabian trade led to the rise of cities, the most important of which was Mecca, which evolved to service the trains of camels moving across the desert.

In the sixth century the Hejaz region was controlled by the Quraysh tribe, the ruling tribe of Mecca, who made agreements with northern and southern tribes that enabled Arabia to be open to trade. Under Quraysh protection, caravans could move freely from the southern coast of Yemen to Mecca, carrying coffee, medicinal herbs, and perfumes, and then move north to Byzantium or east to Iraq. Quraysh agreements also allowed for trade with Axum, in modern Ethiopia, and along the African coast, promoting commerce outside of Arabia. Spices, leather, drugs, cloth, and slaves from Africa or the Far East were brought through Mecca into Syria in exchange for money, weapons, cereals, and wine. Mecca became one of the most important caravan cities of the Middle East, with a sphere of political as well as commercial influence over the tribes participating in the trade.

Islamic Arabia. In 571 CE Muhammad was born to the Quraysh tribe and began to gather supporters of his new religion after hearing messages from God in 610. By the time of his death in 632 most of Arabia had been conquered, a process that was completed under the caliphate of Muhammad's successor, Abu-Bakr. Under Abu-Bakr's leadership Arab tribes began a career of conquest to convert others to their new faith. Organizing their strength against the Byzantine and Persian Empires, Islamic armies quickly pushed through these empires and established Arab control. Many Arabs from the peninsula settled in the newly conquered areas, a migration that led to a decline in agricultural productivity, as neglect to irrigation systems resulted in erosion of fertile lands. However, the holy cities of Mecca and Medina thrived as loot from the conquests poured in. The cities became wealthy centers of Arabian culture and learning. Under the Umayyad dynasty, which lasted from 661 to 750, Islamic power expanded still further. To the east they extended their influence into Transoxania and in modern Russia, and went on to reach the borders of China. To the west they took North Africa and continued to the shores of the Atlantic Ocean, including Spain. However, the Umayyads were centered in Syria, so the capital of the empire was moved to Damascus, decreasing the importance of Arabia in the Islamic world.

In 750 CE the area controlled by the Umayyads was conquered by the Abbasid dynasty, centered in Baghdad, which ruled until 1258. Because much of the Middle East and Southwest Asia were united under Islam, trade was freer and more extensive than it had been since the time of Alexander the Great. Muslim traders established trading posts as far away as India, the Philippines, Malaya, the East Indies, and China. Maritime trade was improved as the compass was borrowed from the Chinese and the lateen sail was borrowed from Southeast Asian and Indian sailors. Pearls from the Persian Gulf, livestock (particularly Arabian horses and camels), and cloth were exported from Arabia. The Arabs also traded medicines, based on Abbasid progress in medical science, as well as paper, sugar, spices, and silk. This expansion of commercial activity led to other developments, such as a system of banking and exchange that allowed letters of credit issued in Baghdad to be honored from Central Asia to North Africa and inspectors to make sure that weights and measurements were given correctly. The flourishing of trade also stimulated the development of crafts and industry. In areas with large urban populations, such as Baghdad, there were metalworkers, leather workers, bookbinders, papermakers, jewelers, weavers, druggists, bakers, and many more. As they grew in importance to the economy, these craftspeople eventually organized themselves into societies similar to Western guilds.

After the first millennium trade with the West expanded to a level unknown since Roman times. During the period of the Crusades (1095–1270), many new plants were brought to the West, such as sesame, carob, millet, rice, lemons, melons, apricots, and shallots. A new European market was created for goods, such as perfumes, spices, ginger, sugar, fabrics, rugs, tapestries, and dyes. Europeans had little to offer in return, except for slaves; precious metals, especially silver; wood; and furs, the last two both extremely scarce in the Arabian deserts. At the beginning of the sixteenth century the Portuguese penetrated the Indian Ocean and the Red Sea. Although their attempted capture of Aden failed, they blockaded the Indian trade routes to Europe via the Persian Gulf and the Red Sea, which caused severe and lasting damage to the economies of Muslim Middle Eastern countries. Arabia began to come into contact with other European nations as the Dutch, English, and French followed the Portuguese into commercial penetration of the Indian Ocean. They began to trade with Yemen through the port of Mocha, which traded coffee beginning in the seventeenth century. During the eighteenth century British rule in India and the growth of the East India Company brought coastal Arabia increasingly into contact with the world economy through commerce in coffee, slaves, pearls, and dates.

During the sixteenth century the Ottomans expanded their empire southward from Anatolia as far as the eastern and western edges of Arabia, along the Persian Gulf and Red Sea, including the Hejaz region containing Mecca and Medina. Ottoman rule was challenged in the late eighteenth century by the Wahhabis, a fundamentalist sect formed by Muhammad ibn 'Abd al-Wahhab in alliance with the prince Muhammad ibn Sa'ud. When ibn Sa'ud died in 1765, only a few areas in central and eastern Arabia had been brought under Wahhabi control, but the process of expansion was sustained by ibn Sa'ud's son, 'Abd al-'Aziz I (reigned 1765–1803) and further continued by his son Sa'ud I (reigned 1803–1814). In 1802 the Wahhabis captured Mecca from the Ottomans, and although they were expelled from the city in 1812, they were not defeated. The Wahhabis and Saudis retreated to Riyadh, where they founded their capital in 1824. From there the Saudis reconquered most of the land they had lost. However, this success was short-lived, and the remainder of the century was a chaotic period of struggle for control of Arabia between the Wahhabi and Ottoman Empires.

Kingdom of Saudi Arabia. 'Abd al-'Aziz (also known as ibn Sa'ud) regained rule of Arabia under the Sa'ud dynasty, conquering Najd in 1905, Hail in 1921, and the Hijaz in 1924. On 18 September 1932 the kingdoms of the Hejaz and Jajd were officially unified as the Kingdom of Saudi Arabia. In the years before oil was found, Saudi Arabia was a poor land. The main sources of government revenue were the charges paid by pilgrims to Mecca and taxes on goods they brought to pay for their journeys, the tithe of one sheep per forty or one goat per five, and a monthly subsidy of five thousand pounds from the British beginning in 1917. This payment was suspended in 1924 until World War II, when Saudi Arabia received irregular subsidies and shipments of rifles from Britain. In 1920 worldwide conditions improved, and more and more Muslims made pilgrimages to Mecca, raising government revenues. An average of 100,000 pilgrims per year came during the 1920s, but with the onset of the Great Depression, this number fell to 40,000 in 1931 and continued to decline.

Discovery of oil completely altered the economic situation of Saudi Arabia. After the 1908 discovery of oil in Iran, sporadic exploration for oil began in Saudi Arabia, but none was found. In 1932 oil was found on the island of Bahrain near the eastern shore of Arabia and was exploited by the Standard Oil Company of California (SOCAL). Despite pressure from Wahhabi leaders not to allow Western interests into Saudi Arabia, the finance minister 'Abd Allah Sulayman and business interests persuaded the king in favor of development. SOCAL beat out the Iraq Petroleum Company in negotiations with a concrete proposal of a loan and specified future payments in gold in return for a sixty-year concession covering a large part of eastern Saudi Arabia with preferential rights in other areas. To conduct operations SOCAL formed a subsidiary company, the Arabian American Oil Company (Aramco), which started drilling in 1935. Oil was first found in commercial quantities in 1938, and SOCAL was granted rights to additional areas that had the best prospects for oil in 1939.

The underdeveloped infrastructure of Saudi Arabia meant that Aramco had to construct all the facilities needed to produce and sell oil itself. A port was built to bring in equipment, water was found and delivered to work areas, and housing, hospitals, and offices were constructed. There were almost no local construction firms, and few Saudis were familiar with the equipment used in oil wells. Aramco began to train Saudis to take over as many tasks as possible through training programs, scholarships to foreign universities, and social service programs. Saudis were trained as doctors, supply experts, machinists, ship pilots, truck drivers, oil drillers, and cooks. Many of these Saudis later established businesses of their own, while others remained with Aramco and advanced in the ranks. By 1984 the president of Aramco was a Saudi citizen.

Government revenues in 1938 were around $7 million, of which 50 percent came from pilgrims and 37 percent from customs duties. Only $340,000 of revenue came from oil royalties, but this increased rapidly to $3.2 million in the next year and $4.79 million in 1940. During World War II markets and production could not be greatly increased since the war interfered with the flow of supplies and shipments, but geological exploration and mapping continued. However, overseas pilgrimages were reduced during the war, and customs revenue dropped from the decrease of the duty paid by pilgrims. Non-oil revenues fell from $7 million in 1938 to $2 million in 1941. Once again 'Abd al-'Aziz turned to foreign aid, receiving $37 million from Britain between 1943 and 1944, $5 million from the United States in silver, gold, and cereals, and $12 million in advances on royalties from SOCAL.

After the war oil production increased dramatically, especially due to the 1941 construction of the Tapline, which crossed Jordan, Syria, and Lebanon to the Mediterranean Sea, saving about 3,200 kilometers of sea travel and the transit fees of the Suez Canal and ending Saudi Arabia's need for foreign aid. 'Abd al-'Aziz pressured the finance minister for more money, and he pressed Aramco for larger payments, receiving $3 to $5 million during the war, $10.4 million in 1946, and $56.7 million in 1950. On 1 January 1951 a new agreement was reached with Aramco after they paid more in taxes to the U.S. government in 1949 than Saudi Arabia received in royalties. Under the new agreement Aramco was required to pay an income tax of 50 percent of net operating income to the Saudis, which greatly increased government revenues. Between 1950 and 1951 oil production rose 39 percent, but government revenues from oil rose from $56.7 million to $110 million. In 1952 the Saudi Arabian Monetary Agency (SAMA) was established as the kingdom's central money and banking authority. Islamic law forbids the payment of interest on money lent or invested, so the bank is a nonprofit service institution. Its functions are to issue and regulate the money supply, stabilize and maintain currency value, and regulate commercial banks and other financial institutions.

In 1960 the Organization of Petroleum Exporting Countries (OPEC) was formed to coordinate the petroleum policies of its members and to provide them with technical and economic aid. In the next decade oil revenues rose from $377.6 million to $1.2 billion. Despite the vast oil wealth, extravagant government spending on development through a series of five-year development plans led to deficits and foreign borrowing. The first development plan was begun in 1970 to modernize the economy through industrial diversification. This plan cost $20 billion to implement, slightly over the budget of $16 billion. It improved agriculture and water resources, including plants to desalinate seawater; built new ports; established industries based on petrochemicals and minerals; built health centers; and improved the defense of the nation. Most of the country's basic transport, power, and communications facilities were established at this time. A substantial educational program was also initiated, with more than 125 elementary and secondary schools built annually, including some for girls along with vocational training centers and institutes of higher education.

During the early 1970s, as U.S. demand for oil increased, OPEC had enough monopoly power to raise prices drastically, and oil revenues reached $22.6 billion by 1974. The second development plan (1975–1980) was budgeted at $141.5 billion, though it eventually cost over $200 billion to implement. This plan attempted to develop and diversify the economy in an effort to reduce dependence on oil, including the development of agriculture-based industry, such as flour milling. The plan also attempted to strengthen human resources through education to reduce dependence on skilled foreign labor. Other social goals included free medical service, interest-free loans and subsidies for the purchase of homes, interest-free credit for people with limited incomes, extended social security benefits, and support for the needy. Imports increased so rapidly that the bottleneck of the ports caused ships to wait four to five months to unload, and additional facilities had to be constructed.

High oil prices stimulated the rapid growth of non-OPEC oil suppliers, such as Siberia and Alaska, and demand for Middle Eastern oil decreased. In 1982 OPEC began to lower production quotas in an attempt to stabilize prices, but various members produced beyond their quotas. Because of this, Saudi Arabia was forced to act as a swing producer, cutting production to stem falling prices, and oil production fell from ten million barrels per day in 1980 to three million in 1985. The third development plan (1981–1985)

coincided with the downturn in Saudi oil production, which caused real GDP to decline 1.5 percent annually during the period of the plan, instead of the planned annual increase of 1.3 percent. Despite the decrease in revenues, the plan continued the work of the previous two at a cost of at least $285 billion. It gave aid to light and labor-intensive industrial businesses to develop the private sector and continued the development of large projects, both oil-related and otherwise, in conjunction with major foreign firms. The plan also provided for the maintenance of buildings, roads, airports, ports, schools, and hospitals and set up water, sewage, and drainage facilities. One-sixth of the project's total expenditures went to the education of children and adults, and social service and community development centers were established. During the period of the fourth plan (1985–1990) oil revenues plummeted following the oil price crash of 1986. Government spending was cut with reduced expenditures on infrastructure. This hit commercial banks especially hard, as construction firms experienced delays in government payments for state projects. This once risk-free, profitable activity became a major liability for commercial banks, and they began to shift their investment overseas to more profitable ventures in Europe.

The fifth plan (1990–1995) was shaped by Saudi Arabia's reduced resources. The Gulf War of 1991 had a considerable impact on the Saudi economy, as Saudi Arabia housed foreign troops as well as Kuwaiti civilians, purchased new weapons, increased the size of the armed forces, and gave subsidies to a number of foreign governments. Additional expenditures on social programs pushed the total close to $64 billion in 1990–1991. A rise in oil prices and production compensated for some of the higher spending, but the deficit rose from $6.75 billion in 1991 to $10.6 billion in 1994. Large cuts were made in government investment in economic enterprises, transportation, and communications, while spending on human resources development, health and social services, and housing was maintained.

Until the 1970s there were few changes in agriculture, which declined due to foreign imports, urbanization, and lack of investment. However, during the late 1970s and early 1980s the government undertook a modernization and commercialization program for agriculture. Infrastructure expenditures indirectly supported agriculture through electricity supply, irrigation, drainage, and transportation facilities that aided in distributing and marketing produce. Land was distributed to individuals, special projects, and farming companies through the 1968 Public Lands Distribution Ordinance, with the requirement that the land be developed. This ordinance also had the effect of imposing political control over various nomadic tribes through sedenterization caused by the loss of pastureland. Modern technology and new transportation networks rendered useless the primitive transport services of the bedouin to aid in trade and pilgrimages. The government also mobilized sizable financial resources to support the raising of crops and livestock, providing interest-free loans to farmers and purchasing locally produced wheat and barley at guaranteed prices for domestic sales and exports. Additionally desalinated water was provided at a low cost, and electric companies were required to supply power at a reduced price. This program provoked a substantial response from the private sector. Between 1983 and 1989 wheat production rose from 1.4 million to 3.5 million tons per year, and growth rates for sorghum and barley accelerated even more quickly, although the overall amounts produced were much smaller.

Saudi Arabia has the largest reserves of petroleum in the world (26 percent of the proved reserves) and plays a leading role in OPEC. In 2002 it ranked as the largest exporter of petroleum, exporting to Japan, the United States, Italy, France, and the Netherlands. The petroleum sector accounts for roughly 75 percent of budget revenues, 45 percent of GDP, and 90 percent of export earnings. About 25 percent of GDP comes from the private sector. Seventy percent of food needs are still imported, but the country is self-sufficient in wheat, eggs, and milk. Wheat is the primary cultivated crop, followed by sorghum, barley, and millet, and watermelons, tomatoes, dates, grapes, onions, pumpkins, and squash are also important crops.

BIBLIOGRAPHY

Abu-Lughod, Janet L. *Before European Hegemony: The World System AD 1250–1350*. New York, 1989.

Chaudhry, Kiren Aziz. *The Price of Wealth*. Ithaca, N.Y., 1997.

Hitti, Philip K. *History of the Arabs: From the Earliest Times to the Present*. London, 1970.

Hoyland, Robert G. *Arabia and the Arabs: From the Bronze Age to the Coming of Islam*. London, 2001.

Young, Arthur. *Saudi Arabia: The Making of a Financial Giant*. New York, 1983.

ARCHITECTURE. *See* Construction Industry.

ARGENTINA. Its early growth and its later stagnation make Argentina one of the most interesting case studies in economic history. The country features an abundance of land, and its development came about largely through gradual intensification of initially scarce labor and capital. Argentina is one of the few Latin American nations where per capita income once approached that of the more developed countries.

Early Economic Growth: 1810–1874. In the early nineteenth century, Argentina's population was small, reaching about 500,000 people in 1820. It was divided into two distinct regions, the seacoast and the interior. The coastal zone benefited from rich soil and a temperate climate with abundant rainfall. In addition, its access to the Atlantic Ocean and to navigable rivers kept transportation costs low. Conditions in the interior were less favorable, with limited arable land, a harsher climate, and a largely mountainous terrain. About half the population lived in the interior in 1820, having settled there in colonial times because of its proximity to the mining operations in Bolivia, such as at Potosí. With independence, the economy was given a major boost. In the 1810–1825 period, terms of trade increased dramatically owing to the abandonment of the Spanish mercantile system and the decline in shipping costs following the Napoleonic wars. This led to the convergence of local prices of exportable goods with their international prices, a change that altered the use of the factors of production. Labor, capital, and land now concentrated on the production of exports, while the production of import substitutions, such as wheat and textiles, was limited. These years witnessed the first westward shift of the frontier, as settlers gradually occupied the lands west of the Salado River, a trend that continued throughout the nineteenth century. A military campaign in 1879–1880 expelled the last native peoples from their lands on the Pampas. Until 1875, growth was based chiefly on exports of animal products, initially hides and, to a lesser extent, salted meat. The importance of wool and lard exports also gradually increased. Exports in this period are estimated to have grown by some 5 to 6 percent annually or some 3 percent per year in per capita terms. Growth stemmed not only from the accumulation of land and especially labor and capital but also from greater rural productivity from the crossbreeding of sheep, which sharply raised the output of wool. This growth of exports and of the economy in general was sporadically interrupted by civil wars and blockades of the Buenos Aires port by foreign powers.

Economic development was especially noteworthy in the coastal region, where annual population growth reached 3.1 percent. Virtually all European immigrants settled in this region, which also absorbed many immigrants from the interior. In coastal areas, people living in towns of one thousand inhabitants or more accounted for 36.8 percent of the population in 1819, and this reached 45.7 percent in 1869. In the country as a whole, the proportion of town dwellers grew from 25.3 percent in 1819 to 30.4 percent in 1869. This trend caused Buenos Aires to lose some of the absolute predominance it had enjoyed at the start of the century as other cities sprang up throughout the territory. Meanwhile, the interior region was severely affected by the exhaustion of the Bolivian mines. Many inhabitants emigrated to the coastal region, and those who remained engaged in subsistence agriculture. There was little growth of population centers in the interior.

The Rapid Economic Growth of 1875–1913. Between 1875 and 1913, Argentina's gross national product (GNP)

BUENOS AIRES, ARGENTINA. Sunflower pellets being loaded on ships for export, 1985. (Enrique Shore/Woodfin Camp and Associates, New York)

grew at an annual rate of 7 percent. The primary sector expanded at a similar pace, and agriculture alone grew at the spectacular annual rate of 11 percent. Hitherto an importer of cereals, the country became the world's largest exporter of maize and flax and a major shipper of wheat. With the advent of refrigeration, Argentina soon became the world's largest supplier of beef. The increase in exports brought a steady opening of the economy. While exports had accounted for 15 percent of the country's GNP in 1884, by 1913 the proportion had reached 21 percent. The crisis of 1890 momentarily halted this growth, however, causing a collapse of production, a decline in immigration, and a rise in unemployment. The crisis had its origins in a new banking law that led to a speculative bubble. When it burst, the resulting wave of bank failures shook international financial markets, especially the City of London. Only when the crisis was overcome did Argentina achieve monetary stability, adhering to the gold standard between 1900 and 1914. Many factors explain Argentina's development in this period, including the final drawing of its borders, the reduction in the cost of shipping and overland transportation, the influx of capital and modern agricultural machinery, and the increase in the supply of labor. While the area of occupied rural land increased significantly, more important was the intensification of the use of both labor and capital. Argentinean agriculture was far more labor intensive than that of other developed countries. Capital investment often took the form of fencing, mills, silos, refrigeration facilities, harbors, and the improvement of livestock through breeding programs. The railroad constituted another major improvement to the country's infrastructure. In 1875, there were only about two thousand kilometers of track in service, but by 1913, this number exceeded thirty thousand kilometers, making Argentina's railroad system one of the world's largest transportation networks. Most of the railroads were built and exploited by British and French companies, whose investments were guaranteed by the Argentinean state. Foreign investments, particularly British, accounted for much of the growth of Argentina's capital stock. Economic development led to a sharp rise in consumer demand, which was chiefly met with imported goods. There was some industrial development in this period, centering mainly on products that could not easily be transported by sea and others that were needed by exporters. Factories were built to produce or process food and beverages, such as beer, wine, and sugar. The new industries also included printing plants, refrigeration plants, and, to a lesser extent, textile plants and metalworking facilities. In the services sector, there was considerable expansion of transportation and trade.

Between 1869 and 1914, Argentina's population grew at an annual rate of 3.4 percent, from 1.7 million to 7.8 million people. This was chiefly owed to the large numbers of immigrants arriving from Europe, especially Italy and Spain. In the same period, the proportion of immigrants grew from 12 percent to 29 percent of the population. Immigrants were attracted by high wages, so the influx reacted sensitively to the country's economic fortunes and diminished sharply during the crisis of 1890.

Stagnation: 1914–1989. The spectacular growth of the Argentinean economy brought income levels close to those of the most developed nations, a trend that peaked in 1913, when Argentina's per capita income reached 70 percent of that of the United States. But the economy subsequently entered a period of stagnation, and its growth lagged behind that of most other countries. By 1945, per capital income had fallen to 32 percent of that of the United States, and in 1990, it had slipped to 30 percent. The initial stage in this process encompassed World War I and the worldwide depression of the 1930s. During these years, the country suffered a series of external setbacks, and the sharp reduction in international trade had a particularly severe impact on Argentina's open economy. During the war, Argentina was unable to import many essential goods, and the 1930s brought a steep decline in world demand for its agricultural and meat exports. The terms of trade turned against the country, which was also badly affected by the collapse of the world capital market on which it depended so heavily. However, in comparative terms the Argentinean economy did not perform badly. This has been ascribed to successful monetary and fiscal measures, such as support prices for agriculture, a flexible exchange rate, and a trade agreement with Britain that helped curb the decline in beef exports.

A second stage, known as "the decline," should be attributed more to internal causes since it began in the 1940s, when new economic measures effectively prevented the country from taking full advantage of production factors. On the one hand, a multiple exchange rate system sharply diminished exports of agricultural and livestock products by pushing producer prices below international levels. On the other hand, strongly protectionist policies intended to encourage import substitution spawned new industries that were ill equipped to compete internationally. The closing of the economy is reflected in the ratio of exports to GNP, which fell from 17 percent in 1929 to 9 percent in 1950 and to 5 percent in 1992. Meanwhile, state intervention in the economy engendered increasingly important public sector enterprises for the production of goods in such key industries as transportation, petroleum, telephone services, and electric power. In addition, macroeconomic instability mounted, causing a steady rise in the inflation that began at midcentury and ran out of control in the 1970s. Between 1975 and 1990, the inflation rate never fell below 90 percent, and in 1989, it exceeded 3,000 percent. Successive rises in prices, caused by lack of fiscal discipline, had a severe impact on capital markets and microeconomic decisions. However, the period of stagnation was not a homogeneous one, since between 1963 and 1973 the Argentinean economy took part in the growth of the post–World War II world economy, while the 1980s witnessed a steep decline in income levels. In 1991, the country's population reached thirty-two million people, largely concentrated in Buenos Aires and its environs, a result both of internal migration and of immigration from neighboring countries.

An Aborted Return to Prosperity: 1990–2001. In 1990, Argentina's economic policies were changed dramatically in an effort to overcome past shortcomings. An initial step was to set a fixed exchange rate between the Argentinean peso and the U.S. dollar, accompanied by statutory limits on the issue of unbacked currency. These measures effectively curtailed hyperinflation, reducing the inflation rate to 10 percent in 1993 and to nearly zero in 1995. Under a far-reaching privatization program, nearly all state-run companies were sold to the private sector and were stripped of their subsidies. The relaxation of customs duties and import quotas helped to revive international trade, and exports increased by more than 300 percent between 1987 and 1997, coming to account for more than 9 percent of the GNP in 1998. In the first half of the 1990s, the economy responded well to these structural changes, as was reflected by the sharp rises in worker productivity and capital goods output along with the expansion of the financial markets. But from 1995 onward, a series of external shocks damaged local markets, plunging the economy into a new period of stagnation and leading to a sharp rise in unemployment. The nation's external debt rose rapidly, forcing the abandonment of the dollar-backed peso in early 2002, which resulted in a devaluation of more than 200 percent. During that year, the country suffered a very severe macroeconomic crisis, with the GNP falling by about 10 percent.

[*See also* Spain, *subentry on* Spanish Empire.]

BIBLIOGRAPHY

Brown, Jonathan. *A Socioeconomic History of Argentina, 1776–1860*. New York, 1979. The early economic history of Argentina.

Cortés Conde, Roberto. *La economía argentina en el largo plazo: Siglos XIX y XX*. Buenos Aires, 1997. A recent source for the statistical data cited.

Cortés Conde, Roberto. *Progreso y declinación de la economía argentina*. Buenos Aires, 1998. A recent source for the statistical data cited.

Díaz Alejandro, Carlos. *Essays on the Economic History of the Argentine Republic*. New Haven, 1970. A classic on the country's economic development.

Gerchunoff, Pablo, and Lucas Llach. *El ciclo de la illusión y el desencanto: Un siglo de políticas económicas argentinas*. Buenos Aires, 1998. A recent source for the statistical data cited.

Randall, Laura. *An Economic History of Argentina in the Twentieth Century*. New York, 1978.

Tella, Guido Di, and Manuel Zymelman. *Las etapas del desarrollo económico argentino*. Buenos Aires, 1967. Another classic on the country's economic development.

CARLOS NEWLAND
Translated from Spanish by Dwight Porter

ARKWRIGHT, RICHARD (1732–1792), barber, wigmaker, and publican of Preston, England.

Arkwright has enjoyed a controversial reputation as an inventor and mill operator. Karl Marx (*Capital*, vol. 1, New York, Vintage Books edition, 1977) called him the "greatest thief of other people's inventions and the meanest character" in Britain; Andrew Ure (*The Philosophy of Manufactures*, London, 1835), in contrast, described the introduction of a "successful code of factory discipline . . . a Herculean enterprise, a noble achievement."

During the first half of the eighteenth century, there was a great demand for yarn owing to improvements in weaving capacity. Arkwright took up the challenge and mechanized spinning operations. His exact role in developing the "Arkwright water-frame" in 1776 and carding machines later in the decade has been contested both by contemporaries and by subsequent generations of historians. To shield his investments, Arkwright sought patent protection, which ensured the holder sole entitlement to the use of the invention for fourteen years. A series of famous patent trials ensued. The first trial challenged Arkwright's role as inventor and confirmed the validity of the patent. But he lost the second trial, which was about the improvements he had made to the frame in the 1770s. After a series of court battles, in 1785 the patents became freely available to all.

The chief use of cotton in the mid-1770s was in the weft of materials of which the warp was linen, worsted, or silk. The water-frame, or throstle spinning, transformed the manufacture of yarn because it helped to create an industry based solely on cotton. Unlike Hargreave's jenny and Crompton's mule, the water-frame spun yarn continuously, drawing the rovings out, then imparting the twist. The jenny and the mule drew and twisted simultaneously. The weakness of the untwisted thread limited the length of the draw. Consequently, the water-frame could not produce fine counts and was used primarily for the production of warps. The mule gave more play to the twist, producing a more regular thread that was better suited to spinning fine weft yarn. Very early on, Arkwright's machine was exploited outside Britain; it was a key technology in U.S. and continental European industrialization. Within Britain, it became less popular over the course of the nineteenth century. The British developed a strong preference for the mule, but ring spinning, a direct descendant of Arkwright's water-frame, was widely used elsewhere.

The Arkwright system centered on a prototype mill built for a ten-horsepower water-wheel. His first watermills were built in Derbyshire. At Cromford, his mill employed more than one thousand workers, many of whom were women and children, although he claimed to avoid employing children under ten years of age and parish apprentices. His mills were in operation long hours and at night. Based on his initial success, Arkwright built other mills in Yorkshire, Worcestershire, Lancashire, and Scotland and, by 1782, his empire totaled more than five thousand workers. Many others copied his model mill and, according to one account, two hundred mills were built on the Arkwright system in England in 1787.

BIBLIOGRAPHY

Fisk, Karen. "Arkwright: Cotton King or Spin Doctor?" *History Today* 48.3 (1998), 25–36.
Fitton, R. S. *The Arkwrights: Spinners of Fortune.* Manchester, 1989.
Fitton, R. S., and A. P. Wadsworth. *The Srutts and the Arkwrights.* Manchester, 1973.

MICHAEL HUBERMAN

ARMENIA. The Republic of Armenia (capital: Yerevan), along with the economically integrated Nagorno-Karabakh Republic (capital: Stepanakert), is situated in the northeastern part of the Armenian Highland, constituting one-tenth of historical Armenia. According to the most recent statistics (1991), the Republic of Armenia has an area of 29,800 square kilometers and a population of about 3.3 million; Nagorno-Karabakh has an area of 12,520 square kilometers, and a population of about 150,000.

Armenia is a cradle of civilization. According to Genesis (8:4, 9:20), Noah's Ark came to rest upon the mountains of Ararat and Noah planted a vineyard in the valley there. Mount Ararat (5,165 meters [17,044 feet]) is the highest peak of the Armenian Highland, which is the homeland of the Armenian people. The highland is situated between Asia Minor, the Black Sea, the Caucasus, the Iranian plateau, and Mesopotamia. Climate favored agriculture. Rivers and lakes provided fish. Mineral deposits (copper, iron) promoted metallurgy (Metsamor).

Armenian obsidian was exported to the Levant and Mesopotamia. The ancient state of Aratta (Ararat) exported precious metals (gold, silver) and lapis lazuli to Sumer. The archaeological monuments and Hittite inscriptions testify to Armenia's (kingdom of Hayasa) active political and economic life during the third and second millennia BCE.

The excavations of the cities (capital Van, Erebuni-Yerevan, Argishtekhinele-Armavir), citadels and temples (Ardine-Musasir, Teyshebaine), artifacts, and canals attest as well to the highly developed political and economic system of Armenia (Ararat, or Urartu Kingdom, from the ninth to seventh centuries BCE). In the sixth century BCE, the Armenian Kingdom's wealth amounted to about 3,000 talents.

From 519 to 331 BCE, the administrative system of Achaemenid Persia also included western Armenia. The independent eastern Armenian kings and the governors of western Armenia struck their own coins. Armenia was rich in food and horses. The Royal Road (from Susa in Elam to Sardeis in Lydia) traversed Armenia, which permitted trade with Mesopotamian cities. The Euphrates River was also an important waterway, along which international trade was conducted.

During the third and second centuries, the Armenian Kingdom (capital Ervandashat, later Artashat) continued to prosper. The international importance of the kingdom of Great Armenia reached its peak during the reign of Tigran the Great (95–55 BCE). He built cities, took a part of the Silk Road under his control, struck coins in capitals Artashat, Tigranakert, and other cities (Antioch, Damascus). The Greek writer Plutarch mentions Armenia as a prosperous country.

The economy of medieval Armenia (capital Dvin) was based on royal, feudal, monastic, and communal landowning systems. The Persian-Byzantine policies resulted in the abolition of the Armenian Kingdom in 428 CE. The struggle against Persian, Byzantine, and Arab political and economic domination, however, led to the restoration of the Armenian Kingdom (885–1045). Crafts and agriculture prospered. Its capital, Ani, famous for Armenian classical architecture, became one of the biggest cities in the world.

Because of the devastating invasions by the Seljuk-Turks during the second half of the eleventh century, many Armenians left for Cilicia, where the Armenian Princedom (1180–1198) and the Armenian Kingdom (1198–1375) developed a prosperous economy based on agriculture, crafts, and sea trade with European countries. Caravan routes passed from Cilicia to the East. Armenian kings struck their own coins.

During the Turkic-Persian wars and conquests in the sixteenth through eighteenth centuries, Armenia suffered both severe human and economic losses. During the periods from 1804 to 1813 and from 1813 to 1828, the Russian-Persian wars led to eastern Armenia's incorporation into the Russian Empire. The Ottoman Empire's persecutions forced many Armenians to resettle in eastern Armenia. By 1913, Armenians accounted for 23 percent of Transcaucasia's population and 40 percent of its urban population. Armenian invested capital dominated the industries and commerce of Transcaucasia, while the Yerevan province remained chiefly agricultural.

During World War I and its aftermath (1915–1920), more than 1.5 million western Armenians under Turkish rule perished in what many observers deemed as genocide. More than 1.5 million western Armenians were exterminated in western Armenia and other parts of the Ottoman Empire (1915–1920) under the cover of World War I. Their property was plundered. The survivors became dispersed all over the world (the Armenian diaspora-*spyurk*).

The first Republic of Armenia (1918–1920) suffered a difficult time, sheltering thousands of refugees while enduring epidemics and Turkish invasions. Under Soviet rule (from December 1920), Armenia's economy was modernized, though with considerable human suffering. In 1921, the Soviet government assigned the Armenian regions of Nakhijevan (since 1924, Nakhichevan Autonomous Soviet Socialist Republic) and Karabakh-Artsakh (since 1923, Nagorno-Karabakh Oblast, or NKO) to the neighboring Soviet Republic of Azerbaijan. With the Stalinist repressions during the 1930s and the casualties (about 300,000 Armenian soldiers who served in the Soviet Army were killed in battles) of World War II, Armenia experienced a tangible decrease in its population in the 1940s. Tens of thousands of Armenian repatriates were also persecuted.

By the 1960s, Armenia began to thrive economically and culturally. In 1979, the population of Armenia was estimated to be approximately 3 million (Armenians 89.7 percent, Azerbaijanis 5.3 percent, Russians 2.3 percent, Kurds 1.7 percent, and others 1 percent). The economy was based on modern industries, a highly educated intelligentsia, and collectivized agriculture. The Yerevan subway, Armenian Atomic Power Station (AAPS), hydroelectric and terminal electric power stations, reservoirs, canals, and tunnels were constructed. Yerevan prospered as the center of Armenia's political, industrial, scientific, and cultural life. Industrial facilities were built in Leninakan (Gumri), Kirovakan (Vanadzor), Spitak, and Kapan. The NKO's constitutional right to reunite with Soviet Armenia was opposed by massacres (Sumgait, 26–28 February 1988) and deportation of Armenians from Soviet Azerbaijan. Azerbaijanis emigrated from Armenia with much of their property. On 7 December 1988, a major earthquake killed 25,000 to 30,000 people, and Leninakan, Spitak, and Kirovakan were destroyed. The AAPS was closed. (It reopened in 1995.) Many countries sent humanitarian aid. In 1989, Armenia's population was estimated to be 3.4 million (Armenians 95.8 percent, Kurds 1.7 percent, Russians 1.6 percent, Azerbaijanis 0.5 percent, and others 0.4 percent). In January 1990, thousands of Armenians fled to Armenia after Armenian massacres in Baku.

After the breakup of the former Soviet Union, the independent Republic of Armenia suffered an economic decline. NKO's legal secession from Azerbaijan was opposed by a war, which resulted in many victims and a new wave of refugees. In 1994, a cease-fire was agreed, but the blockade by Azerbaijan and Turkey inflicted more damages on the Armenian economy and led to another wave of emigration.

Privatization in Armenia started with agriculture. Problems still exist with irrigation, insufficient credit financing, and equipment. Industrial privatization has been even slower but more advanced in trade, small- and medium-sized enterprises, transport, and communication. Armenia trades with several countries including Russia, Belgium, the United States, Iran, Great Britain, Germany, Georgia, and Turkmenistan. Imports exceed exports three-fold. According to the experts of the World Bank and the International Monetary Fund, Armenia will double its export if the economic blockade is lifted.

Machine tools, electric motors, chemicals, diamond cutting, microelectronics, metal mining (molybdenum), agribusiness, food processing, energy and construction, cognac, software development, information technology, and tourism are the main areas of industrial and commercial interests and foreign investments.

BIBLIOGRAPHY

Dickson, J. E., J. R. Cann, and Colin Renfrew. "Obsidian and the Origins of Trade." *Scientific American* 218. 3 (1968) 44–48.

Hewsen, Robert H. *Armenia: A Historical Atlas*. Chicago and London, 2001.

Kavoukjian, Martiros. *Armenia, Subartu, and Sumer: The Indo-European Homeland and Ancient Mesopotamia*. Montreal, 1987.

Khojabekyan, Vladimir E. *The Reproduction and Movements of the Population of Armenia in the Nineteenth and Twentieth Centuries and at the Threshold of the Twenty-first Century* (in Armenian with an English summary). Yerevan, 2002.

Kramer, Samuel N. *The Sumerians: Their History, Culture, and Character*. Chicago and London, 1970.

Lang, David M. *Armenia: Cradle of Civilization*. London, 1970.

Manandyan, Hakob. *About the Trade and Cities of Armenia in Relation with the World Trade of the Ancient Times* (in Russian). Yerevan, 1954.

Masih, Joseph R., and Robert O. Krikorian. *Armenia at the Crossroads*. 1999.

Perrin, B., trans. *Plutarch's Lives*. 11 vols. Cambridge, Mass., and London, 1950. Book 19.4, "Demetrius and Antony."

Walker, Christopher J. *Armenia: The Survival of a Nation*. 2d ed., rev. New York, 1990.

EDUARD DANIELYAN

ARMOUR FAMILY. Philip Danforth Armour (1832–1881) was born on a farm in Stockbridge, New York, and was educated at the Cazenovia Academy. At age twenty Armour journeyed to California, where he made several thousand dollars in gold mining. He returned home in 1856 but left shortly thereafter for Milwaukee. After investing in a soap factory that burned, Armour sold hides in Saint Paul before returning to Milwaukee in 1859, where he went into the provision business with Frederick Miles.

In 1863 Armour ended his partnership with Miles and formed with John Plankinton the provisioning firm of Plankinton, Armour & Company. In the spring of 1865 pork was selling for approximately $40 per barrel, and many easterners, frustrated by the slow progress of the Civil War, foresaw that the price could reach $60 per barrel. Armour, believing the war would end soon, sold short at $40. After the war he purchased pork at $18 per barrel to meet his obligations, which generated a profit of approximately $1.8 million.

When Plankinton retired in 1877, the firm had grown beyond Milwaukee and opened satellite operations in Kansas City overseen by Armour's brothers Simeon B. Armour and Andrew Watson Armour. Beginning in 1867 a factory in Chicago operated under the direction of Armour's brother Joseph F. Armour. Another brother, Herman O. Armour, who had been in Milwaukee, started working in Chicago as a livestock commission merchant in 1862 and moved to New York in 1865 to oversee the company's interests there. Rolla Armour died while serving in the Union army. One sister, Julia Armour, died as a child, but the other, Marieta Armour, married S. B. Chapin, another Chicago packer.

Philip Armour moved to Chicago in 1875, when he was convinced the city would be the nation's preeminent meat-packing center. He also became involved in the Chicago Board of Trade and in the Chicago, Milwaukee, & St. Paul Railroad. Armour & Company was among the first to use a conveyor system in the slaughterhouse and refrigeration for storage and shipping. Most importantly it was the pioneer in vertical integration in meatpacking. In 1884 the firm purchased the Wahl Brothers glue works in Chicago and began funneling a large quantity of bones and low-quality hides into this plant. The same year Armour hired a chemist to investigate the various alternative uses of animal wastes. Eventually all the large packers were involved in such activities as soap production and selling hides to the leather industry and tails to the paintbrush industry. Within a short period of time the price packers paid for live animals exceeded the value of the dressed beef. Armour and the other packers also became involved with such goods as butter, eggs, and cheese to fill the bottoms of their refrigerator cars.

In his later years Philip Armour supported the Armour Mission established by his brother Joseph Armour, who had died in 1881. The mission included a medical dispensary, a day nursery, a kindergarten, and a library. Around it were the Armour Flats, housing for the workers. The Armour Institute of Technology (later the Illinois Institute of Technology) opened in 1893 and provided relatively inexpensive education and career training in engineering and architecture.

Philip Armour had two sons, Philip D. Armour, Jr., and Jonathan Ogden Armour. Philip Armour, Jr., a partner in the company, died suddenly in January 1900 while visiting his parents in California. After his death the company was reorganized as a corporation. Following the death of Philip Armour, Sr., in 1901, the firm continued to prosper under the leadership of J. Ogden Armour, who brought his two nephews, Philip D. Armour III and Lester Armour, into the business. At J. Ogden Armour's retirement in 1923, the company was the largest meatpacking firm in the world, but much of his personal fortune was lost in the 1921 recession. He had borrowed heavily to finance a fifty-four-thousand-acre reclamation project in the Sutter Basin in California, but the return of peace brought a depression in farmland. Banking interests acquired large blocks of the company's stock in payment of his personal debts. By 1925 Armour & Company had ceased being a family firm.

BIBLIOGRAPHY

Armour, J. Ogden. *The Packers, the Private Car Lines, and the People*. Philadelphia, c. 1906.

Leech, Harper, and John Charles Carroll. *Armour and His Times*. New York, 1938.

Hubbard, Elbert. *Philip Armour*. East Aurora, N.Y., 1909.

LOUIS P. CAIN

ARMS INDUSTRY *[This entry contains two subentries, an overview of the history and a discussion of the organization of the arms industry.]*

Historical Overview

Insofar as the purpose of economic history is to explain the growth of human welfare, the development of the arms industry is a subject loaded with ambiguity. On the one hand, the possession of arms provides a society with a measure of security, thus enhancing the welfare of its members. On the other hand, the manufacture of arms diverts resources from the production of other goods and services, while the use of arms destroys lives and property. By the 1950s, the arms industry, particularly in the United States and the Soviet Union, was producing weapons capable of setting the world economy back by many centuries and, in the worst case, of extinguishing life on Earth.

Arms in Antiquity. Sticks and stones, the first human weapons, were employed both defensively and offensively against animals and other humans. More effective weapons were fashioned by sharpening the ends of sticks, by shaping the stones, and eventually by combining them to form spears. A Spanish cave painting, believed to be twenty thousand years old, shows fighting among a group of archers, which indicates further technological development.

Conflict between humans was on a small scale until hunter-gatherer society, in which it was easy for rival groups to avoid contact, gave way to a settled form of agriculture. Property now had to be defended against intruders. Armies were raised, and elaborate fortifications, such as those of the biblical city of Jericho, constructed. (The building and arms industries have often worked for the same master.) Territory occupied by neighboring groups was a temptation to ambitious rulers. Organized warfare, as opposed to skirmishing, may have started between seven and nine thousand years ago. Copper also began to be used in the manufacture of blades. A breakthrough occurred in Mesopotamia around fifty-five hundred years ago, when copper was alloyed with tin to produce a stronger metal, bronze, which proved ideal for making weapons and armor. Access to supplies of copper and tin became crucial, encouraging the growth of long-distance trade. Iron blades, originating in Anatolia, were introduced around forty-five hundred years ago; however, iron only gradually replaced bronze for military purposes. The Romans went one step further, equipping their legionnaires with even stronger steel swords, manufactured in Spain. Other technological developments in the ancient world included chariots, catapults, battering rams and other types of siege engine, Greek fire (a sort of flamethrower), and warships sporting bronze-tipped rams.

Technology transfer appears to have been relatively rapid within the Eurasian world, aided by the passage of armies back and forth across the Middle East.

Weapons, armor, and warships were expensive, often customized items, made by craftsmen. Most arms production was conducted on a small scale, though some governments (for example, in Greece) supplemented private enterprise by building and operating state armories and naval shipyards, with a view to overcoming capital shortages, boosting output, experimenting with new designs, and ensuring uniform quality standards. Naturally, the best armor and the most glamorous weapons, such as the chariot, were reserved for warriors of high birth, while the other ranks had to make do with inferior equipment. A few armies, including the Roman, were more particular about the quality of weapons issued to the rank and file. Overall, however, expenditure on arms did not pose a great economic burden on ancient society. Warfare was labor intensive. Most ancient arms could be reused, unlike shells and bombs in the twentieth century. Ancient warfare imposed other, probably more onerous, economic burdens. Armies contributed nothing to the cultivation of the land, yet they demanded food for themselves and fodder for their horses. Millions of labor hours were spent building fortifications. Most important, war killed large numbers of young men, permanently removed them from the agricultural workforce and thus, temporarily at least, raised the dependency ratio.

From the Lance to the Musket and the "Man of War." Until the conversion of European and, to a lesser extent, Asian armies to firearms, the weapons technology of the ancient world continued to reign supreme. Massive armies and navies were sent into action by the world's great empires, including the Chinese and the Ottoman, but these forces relied on traditional weapons.

One of the cheapest, but most far-reaching, technological developments with a military application was the invention in Central Asia (500–600 CE) of the stirrup. Though the stirrup cannot be classified as a product of the arms industry, its adoption enhanced the stability and fighting power of mounted warriors. The Mongols made spectacularly good use of the stirrup, without which they could not have fielded armies of mounted archers in battles with European and Asian opponents. In Europe, however, the stirrup facilitated a rather different development—the emergence of the cumbersome, heavily armored knight who rode into battle, lance in hand. Knights were equipped as much for social display as for combat. The armor and weapons required by a single knight cost the equivalent of twenty oxen or the plowing teams of ten peasant households. (Even the knight's steed wore armor.) Italian craftsmen were considered the best armorers in Europe. Foot soldiers were generally of a lower social status and, for reasons of economy, wore less-elaborate armor.

Gunpowder, a product of the chemical industry, was first used to fire projectiles by experimenters in China and in Europe in about 1300 CE. This was one of the turning points in the history of warfare. Once a reasonable standard of reliability was attained, heavy guns proved more capable than other siege weapons at reducing castles and fortified towns. Although the fire from handheld guns, like the harquebus, was not as accurate as from longbows drawn by expert archers, it was easier to train the average soldier to load and fire a gun than to master the art of archery.

Firearms were adopted sooner and in greater quantities in both Europe and the Ottoman Empire than in the more technologically conservative environment of China. Both cannon and small arms were loaded at the muzzle until well into the nineteenth century. The best artillery pieces were cast in bronze by artisans employing similar skills to those used in the casting of church bells. Cannon manufacture required significant sums of capital, and the constructors were for many years expected to accompany their temperamental weapons to war and to operate them in combat. Iron artillery pieces were much cheaper, but generally of a lower quality, and did not completely supersede bronze artillery until the nineteenth century. Cannon designers vied with one another to build ever more specialized weapons, including light guns for use in the field and howitzers for accurate bombardment. The harquebus started to give way to the more powerful musket after 1530. Pistols were issued to cavalry units. Iron was the material used in the manufacture of small arms.

The production of firearms, like the manufacture of swords and armor, was the province of skilled artisans, scattered across Europe, the Middle East, and Asia. Gun manufacturers built on and extended earlier traditions of metalworking. The process by which certain districts came to specialize in a particular industry is complex. Agglomeration economies in arms manufacturing emerged in some localities, including Liège, now in Belgium, but once an independent bishopric. Liège was in the Low Countries, the military cockpit of western Europe, which was fought over at various times by French, German, Dutch, Austrian, and British armies. In 1492, Liège disarmed and declared itself neutral. This did not prevent occasional periods of occupation but, over the next 250 years, the Liège arms industry thrived, as orders were taken from all sides in the wars that swirled across the Low Countries. Liège clearly benefited from its proximity to large and discerning markets, and from external economies generated by the concentration of complementary skills and craft traditions.

Government arsenals were opened for research and development and for the construction of the most expensive and complex weapons systems. Venice Arsenal, opened in 1104, was an exemplar of state enterprise in the arms industry. The arsenal at Venice was responsible for designing and building several new types of vessel, including an improved naval galley and, in the early sixteenth century, the galleon. Naval guns were also produced at the arsenal. Other powers followed the example of the Venetians. Until the nuclear age, major warships and their weapons systems were the most costly instruments of war, with the exception of large fortifications. Their construction involved the labor of hundreds, if not thousands, of workers. Before the emergence of large business corporations in the nineteenth century, the risks of constructing and equipping large warships, or men-of-war, tended to be borne by state-owned yards and factories.

The Arms Industry in the Era of Industrialization. The quickening pace of technological change and industrial activity during the late eighteenth and nineteenth centuries led to the transformation of the arms industry. Crucial to this process was the growth of the European iron industry. A series of innovations, mostly originated in Great Britain, enabled the production of large quantities of cheap, good-quality iron and, later, of steel. In the case of the Bessemer converter (1856), there was a direct link between inventive activity in the metallurgical and arms industries. The English inventor Sir Henry Bessemer (1813–1898) developed the converter to reduce the price of steel. He wanted cheaper steel for the special guns required to fire another of his inventions, an improved shell. Advances in the engineering industry, including the development of accurate machine tools (e.g., Wilkinson's borer), the industrial application of steam power, and the invention of steamships, also had a momentous effect on the arms industry. The technological lead of Europe (especially northern Europe) and the United States over the rest of the world in arms technology widened during the early nineteenth century, resulting in the military humiliation of China and Japan in the 1840s and 1850s. Organizational changes, including a more disciplined approach to management and greater division of labor, enabled private and state-owned arms producers to exploit the new technological environment.

Combat during the Napoleonic Wars was dominated, both on land and at sea, by two long-established weapons systems—the musket and the wooden sailing ship. After 1815, however, a technological revolution took place in warfare, most visibly in the naval sphere. Sail was gradually superseded by steam power; warships were clad in armor and equipped with breech-loading guns of rising caliber; then the heavy guns were put in revolving armored turrets. The torpedo was introduced, initially for deployment on fast boats, and then as the main weapon of the submarine, which had ceased to be a curiosity by 1900. The early twentieth century saw the introduction of steam turbine and oil engines, the advent of even more powerful vessels, such as the *Dreadnought* battleship, and the use of wireless technology for communication at sea. The quality of armor was continually improved.

Change was less dramatic on land, although the firepower available to a general in 1914 was immensely superior to that available to Napoleon in 1815. The rifle, which was more powerful and accurate than the musket, eventually became the main infantry weapon. Rifles were not new, but until the invention of the Minié ball by a French officer, they could not be loaded and fired quickly enough to justify their general adoption. The introduction of breech-loading rifles further enhanced the infantry's potential rate of fire, giving the Prussians a decisive advantage over the Austrians in the 1866 campaign. During the late nineteenth century, the machine gun was transformed from a novelty into an efficient and deadly weapon. Artillery also became much more potent. Explosives became more destructive, while muzzleloaders gave way to quick firing breechloaders. Technology transfer among the major powers was fairly rapid, since it would have been fatal to be left behind.

Innovation extended to the organization of arms production. In many countries, the established approach to small arms manufacture involved an elaborate network of subcontractors. Small producers, based in workshops or their own homes, made individual components, using hand tools. These components passed through several hands before the final product was assembled and then inspected by government representatives. Many subcontractors were highly skilled; however, each individual weapon was unique. In the late eighteenth century, the French showed interest in the production of guns with interchangeable parts, which would have facilitated the repair of damaged weapons. The U.S. government was intrigued by this concept. During the early decades of the nineteenth century, American arms factories, including the Federal Armory at Springfield and the Harpers Ferry Rifle Works, experimented with new production methods. The division of labor was extended, and skilled workers were replaced by machine tools operated by unskilled workers. Mechanization did not guarantee interchangeability, which also depended on the use of accurate gauges and meticulous inspection procedures. Nor did the "American system of manufactures," as it was known, necessarily reduce production costs, for which large runs were necessary. After 1850, the principles of the "American system" were copied in European arms works, like the government arsenal at Enfield, London. The lessons learned in the manufacture of small arms at Harpers Ferry and Springfield were also applied to other industries, including bicycle production, and constituted a stage on the road to mass production.

At the apex of the arms industry, namely the production of warships and heavy guns, large private firms with origins in the iron and steel, shipbuilding, and engineering industries posed a growing technological challenge to state-owned factories after 1850. In Great Britain, for instance, Armstrong-Whitworth and Vickers were far more innovative and efficient than the Royal Dockyards and the royal gun foundry (Woolwich Arsenal). These corporations won a rising share of British government contracts, though in slack years the state allocated as much work as possible to its own facilities. In Germany, which lacked a strong naval tradition, the main private contractor, Krupp of Essen, enjoyed an even more dominant position. The growth of large arms firms was partly a reflection of the increased efficiency and scope of capital markets in industrial economies. Since it was much harder to routinize the manufacture of warships and large guns than the production of small arms, the leading firms hired thousands of skilled crafts workers. Relations between the arms industry, the defense ministries, and the services became increasingly complicated. Senior officers were offered lucrative jobs in the arms industry in the hope that they would influence the distribution of orders. Firms both colluded and competed with one another. Mutual dependence between the state and the arms industry was the norm. By 1914, the "military industrial complex" was an established fact.

Countries that were industrially backward, such as Brazil, Chile, Greece, and Turkey, relied on Europe's core industrial countries, Great Britain, Germany, and France, for supplies of the most sophisticated weapons. The obvious interest of western European firms in selling weapons to deadly rivals, such as China and Japan or Greece and Turkey, attracted much criticism, and these so-called "merchants of death" were accused of fomenting the outbreak of wars in order to enhance profits. However, the arms producers' influence over political events was not that strong. Intermediate states, including Japan, Russia, and Italy, all of which were rapidly industrializing, soon graduated from importing weapons systems to manufacturing their own, usually with the aid of such major arms producers as Armstrong-Whitworth and Vickers. Joint ventures were established in those countries between the multinationals and local arms producers, with a view to obtaining and assimilating the foreigners' superior technology. In the long run, this strategy was successful. Italy, for example, had moved ahead of Great Britain in submarine technology by 1914.

Changes in technology and organizational methods ensured that the armies and navies of 1914 were many times more powerful than those of 1815. Each soldier had the capacity to fire more shots in a given period, with greater accuracy, than his predecessors. The battleship represented the apogee of Victorian technology—it was the most sophisticated machine in the world.

Two World Wars. World War I was the first genuinely industrial war. To many contemporaries, the battlefield (or the trenches) seemed an extension of the factory, which was not the case in earlier wars. During the first few months of the war, ammunition was expended at a rate unheard of in previous conflicts. The size of armies had also increased. Modern warfare consumed weapons and ammunition, not to mention lives, much more rapidly than most authorities had expected in August 1914. The arms industries of the belligerents were too small to meet the demands of the generals and admirals. Hence it was necessary (as it would be in World War II) to invest in new capacity, often with financial assistance from the state, and to employ firms from other branches of the engineering and chemical industries as auxiliary producers.

At the highest level, total war raised questions of resource allocation that were inadequately resolved in societies that were as yet unaccustomed to economic planning. A balance needed to be struck between, for example, the amounts of labor devoted to fighting, producing munitions, digging coal, growing food, and so on. Munitions production was disrupted when armies were particularly desperate for cannon fodder and insisted on calling up key engineering workers. Front-line units were depleted when governments gave priority to arms production and sent troops back to the factories. Though governments took powers to direct munitions-related industries, they generally proceeded by persuasion. Groups of firms, consisting of experienced arms producers, supplemented by some newcomers, were encouraged to cooperate in the supply of certain weapons. The production of simple components was subcontracted to inexperienced firms. Labor was diluted by means of an increase in the division of labor, which facilitated the employment of unskilled workers, including women. Quality often suffered, but there was no alternative. Bottlenecks occurred when firms in the supply chain failed to meet deadlines, and when shortages emerged in the supply of such basic inputs as steel and coal. Though the impression was created on the public mind that arms firms and their workers did very well out of the war, it should be stressed that excess profits were heavily taxed and workers were compelled to put in grueling hours of overtime.

The output of munitions expanded rapidly, even in the United States, which remained neutral until April 1917, but nonetheless won large orders from the Allies. The production of new weapons presented special difficulties. Demand for poison gas had to be met by the chemical industry. Aircraft production imposed demands on a range of industries, including the manufacturers of internal combustion engines, textiles, and chemicals. The first tank

constructors included Fosters (agricultural machinery), Metropolitan Carriage and Wagon (railway equipment), Renault, and Ford. Among the suppliers of components for tanks was a producer of baking machinery.

Overexpansion of the arms industry between 1914 and 1918 was followed by a period of chronic excess capacity until rearmament began in the 1930s. Under the Treaty of Versailles (1919), tight restrictions were placed on the German army and navy, and the air force was disbanded. The technical capacity of the German arms industry was maintained during the 1920s through cooperation with the Soviet Union. In the Allied countries, defense contractors also led a hand-to-mouth existence during the 1920s. Some firms attempted to diversify into related engineering activities, such as the manufacture of motor vehicles, but without much success. The main wartime innovations had few commercial applications. Rapid strides were made in aircraft technology between 1914 and 1918, but it would be some time before commercial services would be profitable in the absence of subsidy. An improved type of caterpillar track for farm and construction machinery was the only spinoff from the tank program. Efforts to develop insecticide from poison gas ended in failure, though disabling gases were successfully produced for riot control. The aircraft carrier was a complete white elephant.

Rearmament and World War II provided an even bigger test for the arms industry than World War I. Government direction of munitions output was in general much more systematically organized during World War II. Many of the economic lessons of the previous conflict had been absorbed. Except in the Soviet Union, however, war production in the belligerent countries was planned on a cooperative basis by the state in conjunction with the private sector. Capacity was requisitioned from nonessential industries, labor was diluted, and supplies of labor, coal, and steel were rationed. The electrical industries played a significant part in the war effort, not least because of the development of radar. Despite exhibiting many similarities, the arms programs of the belligerents were by no means identical. The Soviet performance was remarkable. Soviet arms output recovered strongly in 1942–1945, after the loss of several key industrial centers to the invading Nazis during the early stages of the war. Central planning, mass production techniques, and an iron discipline were responsible for the Soviets' achievement. Taylorism and Stalinism were successfully combined in the Russian context. The Americans also relied on mass-production techniques. Once harnessed to the war effort, America's huge industrial capacity churned out standardized weapons of all types in unrivaled quantities. The German arms program was hampered by bureaucratic rivalries between the various Nazi barons, at least until the latter stages of the war. German industry was less reliant on mass production

INDIA'S ARMS INDUSTRY. A worker in one of India's fast expanding munitions plants, early 1940s. During World War II, India produced more than fifty kinds of arms and ammunition and supplied 75 percent of its own wartime requirements. (Prints and Photographs Division, Library of Congress)

techniques than either the Americans or the Soviets. German plants produced several weapons of the highest quality, for instance, the Tiger tank, which was far superior to its American and British opponents (though not superior to the Russian T34). Significantly, however, weapons like the Tiger were made by craft methods in small batches. British production techniques occupied a position midway between the American and German models. Though Great Britain's munitions performance was creditable, especially in aircraft production, the British needed to supplement the output of their own factories with arms supplied under aid programs by the United States and Canada. Japan began the war with well-equipped armed forces but could not hope to compete with the United States in volume production. The Japanese industrial base was simply too small to sustain a lengthy war against the strongest economy in the world. Since World War II was even more arms-intensive than World War I, the ratio of arms workers to combatants, which had been rising since the nineteenth century, continued to rise. Industrial capacity, as well as sheer weight of numbers on the battlefield, was a major influence on the outcome of both world wars.

The Nuclear Age. The development of nuclear weapons by American and Western European scientists in the mid-

1940s, and the copying of this technology by Soviet scientists, led to a further increase in the capital intensity of defense preparations. Defense budgets did not return to traditional peacetime levels after 1945. They remained high because of the arms race between the North Atlantic Treaty Organization (NATO) and the Soviet Bloc, and the rising sophistication and cost of both nuclear and conventional weapons. Each side in the Cold War amassed nuclear arsenals capable of destroying the world many times over. Arms producers in the United States and the USSR were the beneficiaries of their governments' proclivity for overkill.

Between the 1930s and the 1950s, there was a decisive shift in the center of gravity of the world arms industry. After 1945, severe restrictions were placed on the military capabilities of Germany and Japan. Though these controls were subsequently relaxed, especially over Germany, arms production in Germany and Japan remained subdued. Moreover, during the Cold War the arms industries of Great Britain, France, and Italy failed to keep up with those of the nuclear superpowers. Nuclear warhead and missile production required technical expertise of the highest order. In the Soviet Union, research and development (R&D) and production were conducted within state-owned facilities. Nuclear weapons programs in the United States and in the minor Western nuclear powers (Great Britain and France) were based on collaboration between the state and private sectors. Thompson Ramo Wooldridge (TRW), for instance, provided systems engineering and technical assistance for the U.S. intercontinental ballistic missile (ICBM) program. Missile construction was contracted out to private corporations. Boeing manufactured, installed, and maintained the Minuteman ICBM, which was introduced in the early 1960s.

Complex weapons systems, including nuclear missiles, combat aircraft, and military communications networks, relied on advanced electronics. Some of the earliest computers were designed for military applications, including the University of Pennsylvania's ENIAC (1946), developed with financial assistance from the government, which was used for calculating ballistic trajectories. Indeed, the stimulus of frequent large military orders materially contributed to the expansion of the U.S. computer industry in the 1950s and 1960s. Computer manufacturers elsewhere struggled in the absence of an equivalent military demand. Department of Defense orders played a significant role in the development of the electronics and computing cluster in Silicon Valley, California. Silicon Valley was the birthplace of microwave electronics and the semiconductor. These technologies had critical military and civilian applications. Fairchild, one of the early Silicon Valley semiconductor producers, soon became a major defense contractor. Among the other military-industrial firms in the district were Watkins-Johnson, which supplied electronic warfare products, and Electronic Systems Laboratories, which produced electronic reconnaissance software. The district also attracted firms producing missile, satellite, and armored fighting vehicles. Silicon Valley was a modern version of Liège—though clearly neither agglomeration relied solely on military orders.

Research and development costs escalated, not least in the military aircraft industry. American and Soviet producers could spread fixed costs over long production runs, but British, French, and Swedish manufacturers, who received much smaller orders from their respective governments, could do little to contain unit fixed costs. Faced with high prices, European governments responded by placing even smaller orders at longer intervals. Western European governments began, in the 1960s, to cooperate in the design and production of new aircraft types, like the Jaguar and the Tornado, in an attempt to spread fixed costs.

European arms industries devoted a great deal of energy to the search for export orders, in competition with American and Eastern Bloc suppliers. It was common for exports to be subsidized, either for strategic reasons, or in order to preserve jobs in the arms industry. The dismantling of the European empires led to political fragmentation and to the emergence of new regional rivalries in Asia, Africa, and the Middle East between, for instance, Israel and the Arab states, and India and Pakistan. A substantial new market for arms was created. India, China, Israel, and South Africa also established their own arms industries. China obtained Soviet arms technology in the 1950s. Despite breaking with the Soviets in the early 1960s, the Chinese forged ahead in arms technology, developing a full range of products, including nuclear weapons.

The relationship between defense spending, technological change and economic performance attracted increasing attention from economists after World War II. It seems unlikely that the arms industry provided a major technological stimulus, or exerted a powerful economic impact, whether for good or ill, until the twentieth century. During the two world wars, the rapid expansion of arms production occurred at the expense of other goods and services, and therefore brought about a fall in economic welfare, which more than offset the benefits of accelerated technical change, such as the development of jet propulsion. After World War II, several important civilian spinoffs, especially in information technology, were derived from research into defense electronics and satellite technology. However, the positive externalities of defense R&D must be compared with the costs. The Western countries that spent the most on military R&D and weapons systems after World War II, namely the United States and Great Britain, experienced much slower economic growth than those that spent the least in this area, namely West Germany and Japan. Insofar as the American arms complex had first call on the services of the best U.S. scientists and technologists, the pace of innovation in firms making consumer products may have been held back—an effect known as "crowding out." By contrast, Japanese firms could focus on developing consumer electronics unhindered by competition for key inputs from arms contractors. Japan and other countries were able to "free ride" on scientific and technological research carried out under the U.S. defense program, while U.S. corporations often failed to fully exploit the civilian applications of such research. Crowding out was far more severe in the Soviet Union, a relatively backward economy that insisted on competing with the United States across the entire range of defense systems, including nuclear weapons. Soviet weapons were of a high quality, but the ultimately one-sided arms race with Americans imposed a heavy economic burden. Living standards in the USSR were suppressed in order to release human and physical capital for use by the arms complex. High levels of expenditure on imported weapons were equally detrimental to economic welfare in the third world.

The collapse of the Soviet Union was followed by a stringent economy drive in the Russian armed forces. Moreover, the end of the Cold War also allowed NATO countries to make economies in weapons procurement. New threats soon emerged, however, as the proliferation of nuclear, chemical, and biological weapons proceeded. These "weapons of mass production" were becoming relatively cheap and simple to manufacture. Arms producers quickly adapted to the new market environment.

Aggression and Security. The arms industry came into existence to satisfy demands arising from two apparent constants of human behavior—aggression and the need for security. Relations between the arms industry and the state have always been very close. Arms production has since ancient times been conducted in both state-owned and private establishments, the balance depending on the circumstances and the prevailing ideology. Until the twentieth century, the arms industry was responsible for relatively few important technological spinoffs and was not a major user of factors of production. During the two world wars, however, rising arms production crowded out the supply of other goods and services and—setting aside political considerations—exerted a clearly detrimental impact on welfare. More recently, the demands of the "military industrial complex" have contributed to the growth of the electronics and information technology industries. At the same time, however, the high levels of defense R&D and arms production in the leading military powers have continued to crowd out other economic activities, possibly to the detriment of economic growth, though the evidence on this point is not conclusive.

BIBLIOGRAPHY

Black, Jeremy. *War and the World: Military Power and the Fate of Continents, 1450–2000*. New Haven, 2000.

Hardach, Gerd. *The First World War, 1914–1918*. London, 1977.

Harrison, Mark, ed. *The Economics of World War II: Six Great Powers in International Comparison*. Cambridge, 1998.

Hartley, Keith, and Nick Hooper, eds. *The Economics of Defense, Disarmament, and Peace: An Annotated Bibliography*. Aldershot, U.K., 1990.

Hartley, Keith, and Todd Sandler, eds. *Handbook of Defense Economics*. Amsterdam, 1995.

Heinrich, Thomas. "Cold War Armory: Military Contracting in Silicon Valley." *Enterprise and Society* 3.2 (2002), 285–317.

Holmes, Richard, Hew Strachan, Chris Bellamy, and Hugh Bicheno, eds. *The Oxford Companion to Military History*. Oxford, 2001.

Hounshell, David A. *From the American System to Mass Production, 1800–1932: The Development of Manufacturing Technology in the United States*. Baltimore, 1984.

Kaldor, Mary. *The Baroque Arsenal*. London, 1983.

Koistinen, Paul A. C. *The Military-Industrial Complex: A Historical Perspective*. New York, 1980.

Mayer, Kenneth R. *The Political Economy of Defense Contracting*. New Haven, 1991.

McNeill, William H. *The Pursuit of Power: Technology, Armed Force, and Society since A.D. 1000*. Oxford, 1983.

Mokyr, Joel. *The Lever of Riches: Technological Creativity and Economic Progress*. Oxford, 1990.

O'Connell, Robert L. *Of Arms and Men: A History of War, Weapons, and Aggression*. Oxford, 1989.

Parker, Geoffrey. *The Military Revolution: Military Innovation and the Rise of the West, 1500–1800*. Cambridge, 1996.

Singleton, John. "The Tank Producers: British Mechanical Engineering in the Great War." *Journal of Industrial History* 1.1 (1998), 88–106.

Stevenson, David. *Armaments and the Coming of War: Europe 1904–1914*. Oxford, 1996.

Stockholm International Peace Research Institute, <http://www.sipri.org> An essential source of information on the contemporary arms industry.

Unger, Richard W. *The Ship in the Medieval Economy, 600–1600*. London, 1980.

Van Creveld, Martin. *Technology and War: From 2000 B.C. to the Present*. New York, 1991.

JOHN SINGLETON

Industrial Organization

In his farewell speech to the American nation in 1961, President Dwight D. Eisenhower coined the phrase "military industrial complex" to describe the close, and in his view politically dangerous, relationship between large U.S. arms producers and the state. Thirty years earlier, critics of the international arms industry were arguing that Europe's leading arms firms has colluded to foment World War I and other conflicts in order to boost profits. They described these corporations as "merchants of death." The collaboration between munitions producers, Nazis, and Japanese militarists received considerable attention at the end of World War II. Only the British aircraft industry, which could take some credit for saving Britain from invasion in 1940, was insulated from criticism.

Origins of the Military Industrial Complex. The crucial phase in the development of the modern arms industry occurred between 1850 and 1900. Land warfare became more capital-intensive during this period, because of the rising ratio of artillery to other arms. But the pace of mechanization was slower on land than at sea, and in 1914 most soldiers still fought on foot with rifle and bayonet. Indeed, the modern arms industry originated in the naval sphere.

France launched *La Gloire*, the world's first armored warship, in 1859. The British and those on both sides of the American Civil War scurried to emulate this breakthrough. In the years that followed, there was a gradual convergence between warship building, which was traditionally a function of large state-owned shipyards, and capital-intensive private industries such as iron and steel and engineering. The state did not produce armor and steam engines, so government dockyards had to purchase these items from private contractors. Anglo-French, and later Anglo-German, naval rivalry fueled such rapid technological change, that most large warships were obsolete within a decade of construction. Instead of expanding the state dockyards in line with rising demand, governments awarded some warship contracts to private yards owned by, or associated with, the suppliers of armor. These large firms also gained a technical lead over the state arsenals in the design and production of heavy naval guns and their mountings. The demand for naval armaments was subject to large swings, reflecting the vagaries of the political process, so governments found it advantageous to shift the burden of excess capacity during periods of low demand from the state dockyards to private contractors.

Major Arms Firms before 1914. Only the most technologically and industrially advanced nations succeeded in establishing self-sufficient armaments sectors before World War I. Krupp of Essen, Germany, was the world's largest arms maker, boasting a full range of naval and military products of the highest quality. The largest British firms, Vickers and Armstrong-Whitworth, were on a par with Krupp in terms of technology and product range. Schneider was the largest French firm; William Cramp & Sons, Bethlehem Steel, and New York Ship were the principal American warship builders; and Skoda was the dominant arms producer in Austria-Hungary. In their day, these complex organizations were among the largest manufacturing firms in the world. Their success was based on skilled labor, technological excellence, close ties with government, and vigorous marketing overseas. Although rivals in many respects, they cooperated in others, for instance, through the Harvey syndicate, an agreement on prices and market sharing between British, U.S., French, and German armor plate producers. Smaller firms supplied components, or attempted, with mixed success, to compete with the major producers, especially in niche markets. However, the arms industry was highly concentrated, with one or two firms exerting a stranglehold in each advanced country.

Less economically advanced countries like Italy, Russia, Japan, and Spain imported capital, technology, and know-how from foreign firms, particularly Vickers and Armstrong-Whitworth, in order to develop their own armaments industries. After World War I Italy, Russia, and Japan achieved technological independence in arms production.

Arms Firms in Two World Wars. War was not an unmitigated blessing for the major arms firms. Orders increased dramatically, but so did uncertainty about taxation and supplies of materials, fuel, and skilled labor. Moreover, any new capacity attained during wartime would probably become redundant when peace came. Arms producers in defeated nations could expect harsh punishment.

Total war required an increase in munitions output that was simply beyond the capability of existing arms manufacturers. Firms in other branches of the shipbuilding and engineering industries had to be incorporated into the munitions effort. Metropolitan Carriage and Wagon Co.

(Britain), a rolling stock producer, was the largest tank assembler during World War I. Automobile manufacturers, including Ford and General Motors, were among the main producers of armored fighting vehicles during World War II. Consumer goods factories were converted into shell filling works, while the state opened new munitions factories. The definition of the arms industry became blurred during World War I as governments ordered poisoned gas from chemical companies. In both world wars, the major belligerents devoted a substantial share of industrial output, either directly or indirectly, to the support of the armed forces. The services could not fight without ample supplies of coal, uniforms, and pharmaceuticals.

The development of the aircraft industry was accelerated by the competitive challenge of two world wars. By the 1940s, aircraft producers were taking over from firms with their origins in the naval industrial complex as the dominant arms suppliers. Some established arms companies, including Vickers, succeeded in diversifying into aircraft production, but most of the leading aircraft producers, including Messerschmitt and Boeing, were relatively new entrants to the arms industry.

Peace, which returned in 1918 and in 1945, brought dramatic changes to the arms industry. Future arms production in the defeated countries was restricted by treaty. After 1945, the American occupation authorities dismembered the Japanese conglomerates or zaibatsu, including Mitsubishi, which had been heavily involved in wartime arms production. Arms suppliers in the victorious countries also suffered—from canceled orders—particularly in the aftermath of World War I. After World War II, however, they did not have long to wait before the Cold War stimulated the resumption of business.

Postwar Developments. U.S. corporations dominated the global arms industry after 1945. British and French companies, which were next in importance in the capitalist world, struggled to keep abreast with their American rivals. The American firms' advantage stemmed from the vast size of their domestic arms market. As aircraft and other weapons systems became increasingly sophisticated, research and development costs soared. U.S. firms were able to spread these fixed costs thinly over large domestic orders. But British and French companies, which had smaller home markets, could not avoid high unit fixed costs. During the 1960s, West European military aircraft producers began to cooperate in the design and production of new models, including the Jaguar, and later the Tornado, in an attempt to counter American industrial leadership. The Soviet Union and China also developed massive arms industries, which were to some extent sustained by the poaching of Western technology.

Convergence between the arms and the electronics industries was a significant feature of the military industrial complex after World War II. Computer technology was incorporated into a wide range of weapons systems, including guided missiles, and was an integral part of radar and communications installations. The success of the U.S. computer industry owes much to the initial stimulus provided by defense-related orders. In European countries with a more limited R&D capacity, including Great Britain, research into defense electronics may have been at the expense of the development of consumer electronics products.

In the 1990s, after the Cold War ended, the pressure of international demand for arms weakened, prompting the acceleration of moves to merge and rationalize the industry. Four of the five largest arms producers in the world in 1997, measured by sales, were American (Lockheed Martin, Boeing, General Motors, and Northrop Grumman); the fifth was British Aerospace.

Arms Procurement. Private arms producers had no option but to work in close collaboration with the state, which was in the position of a domestic monopsonist. Retired generals and admirals were often appointed to senior positions in the arms industry. Whether this incestuous relationship resulted in the exploitation of the taxpayer by the "merchants of death" remains uncertain. But it seems likely that the state had as much influence over the arms producers as they had over the state. In some circumstances, as in Germany during rearmament in the 1930s, there was a natural coincidence between the aims of political leaders and of arms salesmen.

A Natural Oligopoly. The sophisticated, and often secret, nature of the technology involved, the high levels of fixed capital investment required, and the close nature of business-government relations made the modern arms industry an oligopoly. Although it is debatable whether the arms industry contributed much to global economic welfare, its historical significance is undeniable.

[See also Zaibatsu.]

BIBLIOGRAPHY

Ball, Nicole, and Milton Leitenberg, eds. *The Structure of the Defense Industry: An International Survey.* London, 1983.

Gatrell, Peter. *Government, Industry, and Rearmament in Russia, 1900–1914: The Last Argument of Tsarism.* Cambridge, 1994.

Harrison, Mark, ed. *The Economics of World War II: Six Great Powers in International Comparison.* Cambridge, 1998.

Hartley, Keith, and Nick Hooper, eds. *The Economics of Defence, Disarmament, and Peace: An Annotated Bibliography.* Aldershot, U.K., 1990.

Hartley, Keith, and Todd Sandler, eds. *Handbook of Defense Economics.* Amsterdam, 1995.

Koistinen, Paul A. C. *The Military-Industrial Complex: A Historical Perspective.* New York, 1980.

Manchester, William. *The Arms of Krupp, 1587–1968.* London, 1968.

Overy, Richard J. *Goering: The "Iron Man."* London, 1984. Goering was head of the Luftwaffe and a major figure in the Nazi war economy.

Ritchie, Sebastian. *Industry and Air Power: The Expansion of British Aircraft Production, 1935–41.* London, 1996.

Scott, J. D. *Vickers: A History.* London, 1962.

Singleton, John. "Full Steam Ahead? The British Arms Industry and the Market for Warships, 1850–1914." In *Entrepreneurship, Networks and Modern Business,* edited by Jonathan Brown and Mary B. Rose, pp. 229–258. Manchester, 1993.

Stevenson, David. *Armaments and the Coming of War: Europe, 1904–1914.* Oxford, 1996.

Stockholm International Peace Research Institute (SIPRI). <http://www.sipri.org> For information on the contemporary arms industry.

Weir, Gary E. *Building the Kaiser's Navy: The Imperial Naval Office and German Industry in the Von Tirpitz Era.* Annapolis, Md., 1992.

Zeitlin, Jonathan. "Flexibility and Mass Production at War: Aircraft Manufacture in Britain, the United States, and Germany, 1939–1945." *Technology and Culture: The International Quarterly of the Society for the History of Technology* 36.1 (1995), 46–79.

JOHN SINGLETON

ART MARKETS. Before offering an account of its historical development, it is first necessary to define what is meant by *art market*. An art market differs from the situation in which art is chiefly produced on commission in that the prices charged for works of art in an art market are wholly determined by the forces of supply and demand. Artists working for such a market produce their work on behalf of an anonymous clientele rather than for a specific patron, with whom they would have reached a prior contractual agreement regarding the theme of the piece, the materials to be used, the size, the price, and so forth. The customers in this market purchase works at the artist's workshop or through dealers as finished products, without having to order them in advance.

Market Emergence. Taking this definition as a basis, the first signs of an art market emerged in thirteenth- and fourteenth-century Italy, where the desire for paintings of the Virgin Mary, the Crucifixion, and Saint John the Baptist encouraged Florentine artists to standardize their production of paintings on these and other devotional themes. In the 1370s and 1380s, Francesco Datini regularly exported these paintings to Avignon. Moreover, in fifteenth-century Northern Italy, works of art were often bought as finished products. Paintings, especially those of a low quality, and copies were exhibited and sold at fairs. Merchants specializing in the art trade found customers chiefly among the courts of the Renaissance princes. This trade expanded during the sixteenth century, but there is no evidence from Florence, Venice, or Mantua that an anonymous public market displaced the commissions ordered by public and ecclesiastical patrons as the dominant impetus for art production.

Signs of market production are also visible in fifteenth-century Bruges, the most diversified artistic production center and the most international art market north of the Alps. This region witnessed a tremendous demand for art stemming from the Burgundian court, a rich commercial bourgeoisie, an exceptionally large community of foreign merchants, and an extraordinarily well-to-do and broad middle class. Along with the Burgundian court, whose role should not be overestimated, local elites and institutions, such as the religious fraternities, where various segments of the Bruges society intersected, patronized art. Accordingly, the patrons of Hans Memling consisted above all of foreign merchants, of Bruges burghers, and of Bruges religious institutions. At the same time, art developed into an export commodity in fifteenth-century Bruges. An expanding and hence guild-regulated art market can be identified around 1450. The paintings it offered were relatively cheap canvases on popular themes aimed at customers of more modest means. Canvas paintings, or *panni*, of this kind turn up as often in Italian estate inventories as they do in Flemish wills. It is clear that they were systematically exported to the south—to Spain and Italy—where their mixture of worldly and religious subjects adorned many citizens' walls. In 1482, the city of Bruges opened a special space, or *pandt*, physically modeled on a cloister, dedicated to the display and sale of artistic goods. There artists were allowed to participate without any guild restrictions.

By the sixteenth century, the commercialization of artistic production was well under way in the southern Netherlands. In Antwerp, from 1485, artists sold paintings along with other luxury items, such as carved altarpieces, at Our Lady's *pandt*, a rectangular courtyard building next to the church of that name and the first art market housed in a building constructed expressly for the purpose. The proportion of commissioned pictures declined, and standardized production, involving the repetition of parts and patterns, especially in altarpieces, increased. Some famous artists overcame guild restrictions to become full-time art dealers. The Antwerp Exchange became the first permanent exhibition of works of art in 1540, yet prior to that, artists and dealers exhibited works for display and sale at fairs held in churchyards. Despite the expansion of the Antwerp art market, however, patronage remained the dominant form of art production in the Antwerp guild up to the seventeenth century.

Remarkably, the artistic crafts recovered quickly following the fall of Antwerp in 1585 and the sudden exodus of many of its most industrious and talented inhabitants to the north. Up to the 1640s, gold- and silversmiths, engravers, and especially painters worked for an international market focused on the Iberian Peninsula, the Americas, and Paris. The workshops of Jacob Jordaens, Anthony Van Dyck, and most significantly, Peter Paul Rubens all made famous contributions to the recovery.

Most German city guilds in the fifteenth century forbade the sale of works of art at church fairs and weekly markets and also forbade works commissioned by out-of-town dealers. Nearly all of the paintings produced by the flourishing artistic community at Nuremberg were commissioned. When Albrecht Dürer exhibited a triptych at the Frankfurt fair, he hoped to attract new commissions, not potential buyers. However, there was a lively trade of art objects and especially of antiquities (including everything from coins, medals, and cameos to major pieces of sculpture), which were channeled by Italian and upper German merchants from Italy into the collections of Augsburg and Nuremberg humanists and patricians and further into the *Kunst-* and *Wunderkammern* of the German princes. Nuremberg and Augsburg supplied German markets with local artistic (graphic) productions and, in the case of Augsburg, with silver and golden objects, cabinets, harnesses, and armors, a trade that declined during the Thirty Years' War.

Dutch Market. The Dutch Republic witnessed the emergence of an unprecedented anonymous art market in the seventeenth century that nourished a large proportion of its artists. This resulted from a tremendous growth in the demand for paintings. Seventy thousand pictures were painted every year, many of which were cheap works acceptable to a broad segment of Dutch society.

One of the most striking features of the emergent art market is the fact that the majority of painters did not paint for private patrons. Instead, they painted for an anonymous public market. The necessary preconditions for this were low production costs, a broad and stable market demand, and prices high enough to cover material expenses and the artists' costs of living. All these conditions appear to have been present in the seventeenth century.

Product innovations—characteristic of the Dutch economy—generated new demand, while specialization lowered the costs of producing paintings. For example, the introduction of the so-called tonal style cut down the time necessary to produce a painting, thus raising the painters' productivity. The new techniques became widespread in the northern Netherlands in the 1640s with the landscape paintings by Jan van Goyen and Pieter Molijn. The consumer gained by paying lower prices for landscapes, and this reduction contributed to the rising importance of landscapes in Dutch collections.

The average price of paintings sold in auctions and assessed in inventories was less than ten guilders. At this price, many seventeenth-century Dutch would have been able to afford a painting or at least a copy—perhaps several—during a lifetime. Moreover, the expanding art market generated the new profession of art dealer. Although most painters bought and sold the pictures of their colleagues from time to time, professional art dealers became much more common in the 1630s and 1640s, when printers, engravers, frame makers, and unsuccessful painters, like Gerrit Uylenburgh, Crijn Volmarijn, and Abraham de Cooge, specialized in the art trade. This new trade in art also developed its own areas of specialization. Whereas secondhand dealers bought cheap paintings at estate sales and sold them on the street, other art dealers bought works of art directly from the artists' studios and exported them to other cities, selling paintings to collectors all over the country and even abroad. Another group increased the supply of works available in the market by creating putting-out systems for art production. At the highest level of the art market were the international art dealers, who had masterpieces of the Renaissance and works by the most famous contemporary artists, at least as copies, in their stock and who offered them to the kings and princes of Europe.

While most painters painted for the public market, others worked at least temporarily for patrons. There were different kinds of patronage in the Dutch Republic. Whereas the Calvinist church offered only a few organs to decorate, the stadtholders of the House of Orange engaged Flemish painters and painters of the Utrecht school to embellish their palaces. The cities commissioned the decoration of the city halls with allegoric paintings symbolizing the omnipotent and just city government. Moreover, different social groups, such as the town militia, the aldermen of the guilds, and the directors of charitable foundations, commissioned group portraits. Individual and family portraits formed another substantial part of commissioned art.

It was not only the portrait painters who worked for individual commissioners but also the "fine painters" Gerard Dou, Frans van Mieris, and Johannes Vermeer. They sold most of their works to single patrons, who often paid in advance. This limited the risk for the painters, whose highly finished paintings were time consuming and expensive and therefore did not meet the conditions required in the anonymous art market. Despite the considerable proportion of patronage in seventeenth-century Dutch art, the majority of master painters seem to have produced paintings for commercial speculation, assisted by art dealers who channeled their works on the market.

Although the Dutch art market was characterized for the first time in history by a variety of institutions, such as auctions, lotteries, and exhibitions, it is unwise to underestimate the Antwerp art market. Here, art production and collecting were regarded as a part of the noble lifestyle of the Antwerp elites. However, a mass market for paintings in seventeenth-century Antwerp also emerged. A characteristic feature of Antwerp art production was the so-called workshop, in which cooperation or collaboration featured in the production of a painting. In this respect, artistic production in Antwerp differed from the rest of Europe, where studios rivaled for important commissions (Italy) or individual masters successfully exploited personal market niches (Holland). Instead, in Antwerp "collaborative

circuits" (Honig, 1998) existed, whereby two or more colleagues worked together on paintings (Rubens–Frans Snyders, Rubens–Jan Brueghel, Jan Brueghel–Hendrick Van Balen). If a patron wanted to have certain masters represented in his or her collection, collaborative paintings offered two names instead of one. And if a patron was not able to get the desired painter this way, he or she had to solve the problem with a copy after a canonical painting, produced at large scale in painters' workshops, thus meeting the high demand for their works and those of their predecessors.

English Market. When the Dutch art market contracted in the last decades of the seventeenth century, the rising English market formed one outlet for Dutch painters and paintings. An indigenous painting tradition hardly existed in seventeenth-century England. However, a number of Dutch and Flemish portrait painters and engravers immigrated into England, and Dutch paintings were also imported in growing quantities. The market grew rapidly at the end of the century, when the auction, a sales mechanism hitherto primarily used to sell off the household effects of the recently deceased or the bulk import commodities of the English East India Company, became recognized as a regular fixture of the fashionable London social life. During speculation booms, tens of thousands of paintings might change hands. In 129 extant auction catalogs from 1689 to 1692, 35,797 pictures were mentioned, including Dutch genre. After this explosion of interest in selling and buying paintings, the number of art sales per annum dropped substantially. By the early years of the eighteenth century, an entire generation of immigrant artists had substantially enlarged the stock of home-produced paintings, while Joseph van Aken and Pieter Angellis refined the low-genre Dutch drolls into the English conversation piece. The number of picture auctions rose steadily from the 1720s, and by the 1730s the auction had become the dominant method for selling and buying pictures in London. In this period, a number of virtuosi and artist-dealers, such as Andrew Hay, Arthur Pond, Samuel Paris, and Robert Bragge, established themselves, purchasing works of art on commission for clients or for resale by public auction. Dealing in antiquities, medals, manuscripts, prints, drawings, and paintings, or combining portraiture, decorative painting, and picture restoration with dealing, collecting, and print selling, these dealers profited from a growing market for decorative arts. In the 1740s, the emphasis shifted from imports to the recirculation of existing stocks, as prominent collections of high-quality paintings entered the market (for example, the collections of Lord Halifax, the painter Charles Jervas, the earl of Oxford, and the duke of Chandos). At the same time, a circle of connoisseurs of Dutch art formed in London, comprising city merchants, gentry, and artist-dealers.

The second half of the eighteenth century saw the emergence of auction houses, such as Cock's, Christie's, and Sotheby's, and the struggle of British painters for appreciation. As only the more successful painters, like Joshua Reynolds, had private showrooms, the majority was looking for exhibition places to reach the public. In the 1750s, painters, sculptors, and architects recommended the establishment of a public academy. When the project failed, artists engaged themselves for public exhibitions and founded societies, such as the Society of Artists and the Free Society of Artists in Great Britain. Both societies used the auction rooms of Cock's and Christie's as exhibition places, but they still lacked adequate exhibition spaces, even after the Royal Academy of Painting was established in 1769. Finally, in the 1780s, the new academy quarters in Somerset House enabled the Academy Exhibition to attract between forty thousand and fifty thousand visitors per season. The commercialization of art in Britain, however, was not confined to paintings and prints. The commercial application of arts opened the luxury trades, such as ceramics, glass, enameling, and japanning, for painters and sculptors and provided new tasks for intermediaries in this trade, like the upholder, as the eighteenth-century interior designer was called.

France. While in England the foundation and success of the Royal Academy created a far more elevated artist and increased his independence from patrons, in France the academy traditions and the Salon for a long time tended to petrify art taste and the art market. Like the other European countries, except the Netherlands, France, especially Paris, was characterized by the absence of a specialized group of professional art dealers. The large number of public sales, which art dealers were not permitted to conduct, inhibited the rise of professional dealers. Although dealers in the seventeenth century had occasionally held sales of important paintings, only in the early eighteenth century did dealers overcome sales restrictions by joining the *merchands-merciers*, who were permitted to sell a variety of goods. One of the pioneers of the Paris art market was Edmé-François Gersaint, who joined the mercers' guild in 1720 and contributed to the gradual erosion of the academic taste standards set by Jean-Baptiste Colbert and Charles LeBrun on behalf of the Académie Royale de Peinture et de Sculpture. In the beginning, Gersaint dealt in a wide range of luxury goods, like Oriental porcelain, lacquered cabinets, marquetry, bronzes, mirrors, clocks, paintings, gems, shells, and other naturalia. By the 1740s, he began to specialize in the trade of paintings and prints. He frequently traveled to Holland and bought paintings, which he resold in auctions that differed significantly from earlier sales of paintings. Gersaint's auctions were characterized by preceding viewing days and informative and advisory catalogs. Other dealers, like Pierre Remy, Jean-Baptiste-Pierre Lebrun, and Alexander Paillet, imitated Gersaint in this respect. Although Gersaint was more interested in the quality of paintings than in attributions, he shaped taste by promoting Netherlandish paintings and the immigrant Fleming Watteau. Gersaint's marketing efforts coincided with a growing interest in the Salon, which became not only the dominant entertainment in Paris but also "the first regularly repeated, open, and free display of contemporary art in Europe" (Crow, 1985, p. 3).

The commercialization of arts continued in the second half of the eighteenth century. For the period from 1740 to 1780, more than 70 art dealers are known by name, while 581 auctions are documented by surviving catalogues for the years from 1750 to 1770. The auction boom reached its climax in the years 1776 and 1777 with the sales of the famous collections of Blondel de Gagny, Randon de Boisset, and Prince Conti. Thereby, paintings by Gerrit Dou, Philips Wouwerman, Gabriel Metsu, Adriaen van de Velde, and Paulus Potter reached the highest prices and reflected the success of the *écoles de nord* on the Paris art market, which had become the major market for Dutch paintings apart from Amsterdam.

Germany. In the eighteenth century, an art market emerged in Germany. While it began regionally in territorially scattered Germany, it can be traced above all in the two major artistic and commercial centers of the Holy Roman Empire: Frankfurt (Main) and Hamburg. Behind them, Leipzig and Cologne played minor roles. The development of a German art market was hampered by both the small supply of paintings and the modest demand, especially in German cities. Therefore the import of paintings and an increasing local art production were the preconditions for a growing art market. These conditions seem to have been present in the eighteenth century.

As in the seventeenth-century Netherlands, in eighteenth-century Germany the expanding art market generated the new profession of art dealers, mainly in the middle of the century, when painters and merchants specialized in the art trade. This new art trade developed its own areas of specialization. While "international" art dealers supplied the courts and private collectors, the local art trade in cities like Frankfurt or Hamburg expanded, supplying not only local collections but also the courts in their neighborhoods, and art auctions became most important for this kind of local supply, in addition to patronage of local painters. Although auctions of paintings had taken place in Germany in the seventeenth century, in the eighteenth century, especially in its later half, the number of art auctions grew significantly. The eighteenth-century German auction catalogs, collected by the Getty Provenance Index, clearly document this development. From a total of 298 recorded auctions, 234 took place between 1770 and 1800. Hamburg, with a total of 140 auctions, was the leading art market in the Holy Roman Empire, followed by Frankfurt with 40 auctions, Leipzig with 27 auctions, and Cologne with 9 auctions.

Which factors influenced the importance of the auction places and thus the professionalization of the art trade? Hamburg, for example, was favored by its convenient location for transit trade and attracted, among foreign merchants, art dealers such as Gerhard Morell. Morell settled in Hamburg to sell paintings of the highest quality from Dutch auctions to the German princely collections, such as Hesse-Cassel and Mecklenburg-Schwerin, but also to private collectors. Moreover, the art market in Hamburg profited from its liberal auction laws, owed to the great tradition of auctioning import commodities. By 1785, more than thirty brokers were registered in the Hamburg art trade, most prominent among them Peter Heinrich Packischefsky, Michael Bostelmann, and Peter Texier, who are mentioned on the title pages of several auction catalogs. Most of the collections were probably brought to Hamburg from outside, but Hamburg private collections were recycled in auctions. Thus auctions helped satisfy the growing demand for paintings in urban households. After 1789, an increasing number of French collections were brought to Hamburg, often by Hamburg merchants taking advantage of the favorable exchange rate and low prices in France.

The Frankfurt art market mainly profited from the annual fair and the continuous flow of import commodities. That is why painters and art dealers, such as Justus Juncker and Johann Christian Kaller, held a series of auctions of imported paintings in Frankfurt between 1763 and 1765. The most striking feature of the Frankfurt art market is the huge turnover of paintings from notable collections. Even prominent collections were quickly dissolved by auction after the deaths of their owners. At these auctions, art dealers and collectors were the most active purchasers.

Leipzig, however, was hampered as an art market by its rigid auction laws. The guilds of the booksellers and shopkeepers watched carefully that only the estates left by local people were auctioned. Accordingly, only in the 1780s were art auctions started by the art dealer Christian Heinrich Rost, who publicly called for works of art for his first auction on, according to the catalog, 1 August 1783, where he sold engravings, drawings, paintings, and books. This auction likewise represents the beginning of Rost's art trading enterprise, the *Kunsthandlung*. The *Kunsthandlung* represented a new business type in the German art trade. It combined production, publication, and sale of graphical productions with the auction of paintings and sometimes antiquarian books. The prototype of the *Kunsthandlung* was probably the Prestel publishing business in Frankfurt. In the 1780s, the painter and engraver Johann Gottlieb Prestel specialized in the facsimile reproduction first of drawings and later of paintings in files. In this publishing enterprise, reproductions of Dutch landscapes took a prominent position and satisfied as well as stimulated the *Holländermode* among the German public. In the nineteenth century, Prestel became one of the leading German auction houses. Even broader was the supply the Kunsthandlung Dominik Artaria, founded 1793 in Mannheim, offered to potential collectors visiting its exhibition: paintings, engravings, etchings, sculptures, plaster copies of classical sculptures, portraits of princes, and more.

The importance of prices differed with respect to market segments. In the upper market segment, in the range of masterpieces, prices counted and added up to several hundred gulden. However, there were always alternatives available at reasonable prices in the middle segment of the market, including imitations by a local master or anonymous copies. The majority of paintings sold at Frankfurt auctions was worth less than ten gulden, and the *Kunsthandlungen* offered reproductions between one gulden twelve kreuzer and five gulden thirty kreuzer.

World Leaders. In the nineteenth century, Britain developed into the leading art market of the world, rivaled, as reflected in the auction sales, in the second half of the century by France and at the end by the United States. Other nations, such as Holland, Belgium, Germany, and Austria, remained far behind. With the growth of the British art market (the number of annual auctions rose from less than one hundred at the beginning to just over three hundred by the end of the eighteenth century), a professionalization of art dealers took place. They became more numerous and more specialized. By the end of the century, family-run firms were replaced by professional enterprises, and a new hierarchy developed. On the top ranked a small number of large dealers, like Joel Joseph Duveen, who operated in several national markets and had branches in Paris and New York. Below them worked quite a number (more than sixty) of professional dealers with a medium-range clientele and prices, selling mostly national schools. This dealer network was connected with the London scene, on the one hand, and the urban centers of Dublin, Edinburgh, Manchester, Liverpool, and Birmingham, on the other. At the bottom, a large number of smaller dealers successfully exploited specific market niches. The most important intermediaries of the art market were auctioneers. In the first decade of the nineteenth century, eighty-four auctioneers working in thirty-four cities can be traced only in the painting sector. From the 1830s, a concentration process to thirty or forty firms took place. However, they still auctioned a wide range of goods, including books, wines, drawings, etchings, porcelain, bronzes, enamels, ceramics, furniture, carpets, glass, paintings, and other objects of art, since property sales after death remained an important

AN AUCTION HOUSE. Auction sale in progress of a painting (at top right) at Sotheby's. (Photograph Courtesy of Sotheby's, Inc. © 2002)

source of the auction houses. Even at Christie's, the leading auction house, paintings constituted only 40 percent of the sales in 1910. Guido Guerzoni (1996, p. 107) estimates that on average fourteen thousand paintings were sold in British auctions annually during the nineteenth century, while the British living painters nourished the market with thirty to thirty-five thousand paintings a year. Additionally, Britain annually added by import six to seven thousand paintings (net) to its stock. Only from the 1890s, when exports to the United States increased, did the import and export of paintings begin to constitute equal flows.

As regards the demand side, private collectors remained the major group on the market. Besides patronizing artists, they bought at auctions, at exhibitions, and from dealers. In the 1830s, however, a new force appeared: museums. They began to remove masterpieces from the market to revaluate masters, schools, countries, and periods that made up the world of collecting. For example, between 1824 and 1888, the National Gallery, founded in 1824, purchased 508 paintings, including 108 from Italy. The competition among British, European, and American museums and the new, rich industrialist collectors (like John Pierpont Morgan, Andrew Mellon, Henry Frick, and Samuel Kress), who entered the market with huge fortunes, moved prices up from the 1880s. Masterpieces disappeared from the market and gradually from private collections into public museums.

This was, however, not confined to Britain. In France in 1793, the Revolution turned the Louvre into a national museum (for the nationalized former royal collections) that was subsequently filled with art from all parts of the world during Napoleon's victories. Even the repatriation of many objects of art in 1815 did not really affect its role as national museum. The second important institution for the French artistic art market remained the Salon. It still dictated official taste, influenced by academy members, but became, as a regular exhibition, the big marketing institution for France whereby the state purchased paintings by the prize winners. Thus exhibition and prizes (medals) in the Salon meant success on the market, which the numerous secessionist painters who withdrew from the Salon and exhibited outside imitated in later years.

In addition, the Paris market played an important role (second behind London) as the center for the trade in old masters and, in the early twentieth century, also for French impressionists. Between two thousand and three thousand paintings were exported annually to England, and all major museums of the world had agent-dealers at the Paris market. For example, the emerging Gemäldegalerie in Berlin bought paintings of the Flemish primitives and Dutch masters, among them several Rembrandts, with the help of its Paris dealer-agent Charles Sedelmeyer, although the majority of Berlin's purchases came from London. Germany had a deficit with respect to national institutions in the art sector. While states such as Bavaria and Saxonia could easily convert their princely collections into public museums by including the public, in Berlin the Royal Picture Gallery did not open its doors until 1830. There two private collections, bought in 1815 and 1821, formed the stock of a collection of old masters that was gradually enlarged but reached an international reputation only after the formation of the Deutsche Reich in 1871, when Wilhelm Bode acted as a global player on the European art market. In 1861, the Berlin collector Joachim Wagner bequeathed 262 modern pictures as the basis for a national gallery that received its own building at the Museumsinsel (1866–1876). In the following years, the bigger German states purchased contemporary paintings with the help of special art funds. Another factor of prestige was art exhibitions, such as in the Munich Crystal Palace or the centenary exhibition of the academy in Berlin (1886), respectively the emergence of secessions in the 1890s, when painters formed new communities in opposition to the academies in Munich, Berlin, and Vienna. Between 1879 and 1908, the exhibition sales in the Glaspalast totaled eleven million marks. Before this state engagement, the Kunstvereine organized regular exhibitions and sometimes formed their own collections. Additionally, they patronized painters and distributed their output via lotteries to the members. Quite important for the upper segments of the contemporary market were art dealers, such as Commeter in Hamburg, Arnold in Dresden, Flechtheim in Düsseldorf, and Heinemann in Munich. The last supplied not only German industry and commerce (Krupp, Thyssen, Ballin, and Rothschild) with German contemporary masters (Wilhelm Leibl, Hans Thoma, Arnold Böcklin, and Bismarck portraits by Franz von Lenbach) but also foreign buyers interested in South German landscapes. Flechtheim, who opened a gallery in 1913, supplied the French and German avant-garde artists but later added safer items.

Private generosity played a great role in the art market and in support of museums. Art lovers and friends associations were founded, and private benefactors bought important paintings. When the Berlin Gallery was losing the international competition in paintings to British and American museums, Bode convinced private collectors to buy masterpieces in the hope that the pictures would later be bequeathed to the museum. Before World War I, patrons of contemporary art, such as Karl Ernst Osthaus, August von der Heydt, Bernhard Koehler, and Markus Kruss, entered the scene. They built up collections and supported artists and museums. Even during the war, the German art market boomed because art was regarded as security. The neutrals also bought art in Germany.

After World War I, buying and patronage declined all over Europe, and the prices for conventional paintings slumped worldwide. The United States succeeded Britain as the leading art market. The withdrawal of American capital during the Great Depression worsened the situation for the European art trade, which gradually revived in the 1950s. With the spectacular impressionist sales of the late 1950s and the 1960s at Sotheby's, London regained some of its previous importance, which the regionally divided German art market never enjoyed. London, however, could not challenge New York. On the contrary, Sotheby's became in the 1970s an American enterprise with its headquarters in New York. Christie's, which after 1998 belonged to a French entrepreneur named François Pinault, held together with Sotheby's a market share of 35 percent of the European and 42 percent of the American sales in 1998. To widen its market position, Christie's collaborates with marketing firms, such as Saatchi, and buys progressive galleries in New York, where it holds special auctions for contemporary art.

The galleries of art dealers that organize (sales) exhibitions of contemporary art to promote new artists gained importance all over the world in the second half of the twentieth century. Following the example of Daniel-Henry Kahnweiler, who promoted the cubists, especially Pablo Picasso, from the 1910s, the New York galleries have made art from the 1960s. Leo Castelli, for example, represented artists like Robert Rauschenberg, Andy Warhol, Jasper Johns, Roy Lichtenstein, Frank Stella, and Claes Oldenburg even before they became famous and thus contributed heavily to the success of pop art. New intermediaries and marketing devices are emerging, whereby online purchases and international art fairs will gain in importance.

[*See also* Antiques Trade *and* Museums.]

BIBLIOGRAPHY

Bok, Marten Jan. *Vraag en aanbod op de Nederlandse kunstmarkt, 1580–1700.* Utrecht, 1994.

Blockmans, Wim. "The Burgundian Court and the Urban Milieu as Patrons in Fifteenth-Century Bruges." In *Economic History and the Arts*, edited by Michaël North, pp. 15–26. Cologne, 1996.

Burke, Peter. *The Italian Renaissance.* Cambridge, 1987.

Brewer, John. *The Pleasures of Imagination: English Culture in the Eighteenth Century.* London, 1997.

Craske, Matthew, and Maxine Berg. "Art and Industry—The Making of Modern Luxury in Eighteenth-Century Britain." In *Economia e arte*, edited by Simonetta Cavaciocchi, *Secc. XIII–XVIII*, pp. 823–835. Prato, Italy, 2002.

Crow, Thomas E. *Painters and Public Life in Eighteenth-Century Paris.* New Haven and London, 1985.

De Marchi, Neil, and Hans J. Van Miegroet. "Art, Value, and Market Practices in the Netherlands in the Seventeenth Century." *Art Bulletin* 76 (1994), 451–464.

De Marchi, Neil, and Hans J. Van Miegroet. "Rules versus Play in Early Modern Art Markets." *Louvain Economic Review* 66 (2000), 145–165.

Fairchilds, Cissie. "The Production and Marketing of Populuxe Goods in Eighteenth-Century Paris." In *Consumption and the World of Goods*, edited by John Brewer and Roy Porter, pp. 228–248. London and New York, 1993.

Fredericksen, Burton. *The Index of Paintings Sold in the British Isles during the Nineteenth Century.* 3 vols. Santa Barbara, Calif., 1989–1993.

Goldthwaite, Richard. *Wealth and the Demand for Art in Italy, 1300–1600.* Baltimore and London, 1993.

Guerzoni, Guido. "The British Painting Market, 1789–1914." In *Economic History and the Arts*, edited by Michaël North, pp. 97–132, Cologne, 1996.

Honig, Elizabeth Alice. *Paintings and the Market in Early Modern Antwerp.* New Haven and London, 1998.

Jacobs, Lynn F. *Early Netherlandish Carved Altarpieces, 1380–1550: Medieval Tastes and Mass Marketing.* Cambridge, 1998.

Ketelsen, Thomas, and Tilmann von Stockhausen. *Verzeichnis der verkauften Gemälde im deutschsprachigen Raum vor 1800: The Provenance Index of the Getty Research Institute.* Munich, 2002.

Lenman, Robin. "Painters, Patronage, and the Art Market in Germany, 1850–1914." *Past and Present* 123 (1989), 109–140.

McClellan, Andrew. "Watteau's Dealer: Gersaint and the Marketing of Art in Eighteenth-Century Paris." *Art Bulletin* 78 (1996), 439–453.

Montias, J. Michael. *Artists and Artisans in Delft: A Socio-Economic Study of the Seventeenth Century.* Princeton, 1982.

Montias, J. Michael. "Cost and Value in Seventeenth Century Dutch Art." *Art History* 10 (1987), 455–466.

Montias, J. Michaël. "Auctions of Works of Art in Seventeenth-Century Amsterdam, 1597–1638." *Nederlands Kunsthistorisch Jaarboek* 50 (1999), 145–193.

North, Michaël. *Art and Commerce in the Dutch Golden Age.* New Haven and London, 1997.

North, Michaël, ed. *Economic History and the Arts.* Cologne, 1996.

North, Michaël, ed. *Kunstsammeln und Geschmack im 18. Jahrhundert.* Berlin, 2002.

North, Michaël, ed. " The Long Way of Professionalisation in the Early Modern German Art Trade." In *Economia e arte*, edited by Simonetta Cavaciocchi, *Secc. XIII–VIII*, pp. 459–471. Prato, Italy, 2002.

North, Michaël, and David Ormrod, eds. *Markets for Art, 1400–1800.* Aldershot, U.K., 1998.

Ormrod, David. "The Rise of the London Art Market, 1660–1760." In *Economia e arte*, edited by Simonetta Cavaciocchi, *Secc. XVIII–XVIII*, pp. 303–321. Prato, Italy, 2002.

Pears, Iain. *The Discovery of Painting: The Growth of Interest in the Arts in England, 1680–1768.* New Haven and London, 1988.

Pomian, Krzysztof. *Collectors and Curiosities: Paris and Venice, 1500–1800.* Translated by Elizabeth Wiles-Portier. Cambridge, 1990.

Sfeir-Semler, Andrée. *Die Maler am Pariser Salon, 1791–1880.* Frankfurt and New York, 1992.

Schnapper, Antoine. *Curieux du grand siècle: Collections et collectionneurs dans la France du XVIIe siècle*, vol. 2, *Oeuvres d'art.* Paris, 1994.

Thurn, Hans Peter. *Der Kunsthändler: Wandlungen eines Berufes.* Munich, 1994.

Vermeylen, Filip. "Marketing Paintings in Sixteenth-Century Antwerp: Demand for Art and the Role of the Panden." In *International Trade in the Low Countries, Fourteenth–Sixteenth Centuries: Merchants, Organization and Infrastructure*, edited by P. Stabel, B. Blondé, and A. Greve, pp. 193–213. Louvain, Belgium, and Apeldoorn, Netherland, 1998.

MICHAËL NORTH

ASHTON, T. S. (1889–1968), leading expert on the economic history of the Industrial Revolution and of eighteenth-century Great Britain.

Trained at Manchester, Thomas Southcliffe Ashton was one of the most influential economic historians of his age. He taught at the University of Sheffield (1912–1919) and Birmingham (1919–1921) and then returned to Manchester, where he taught for twenty-three years. In 1944, he moved to the London School of Economics to occupy the chair in economic history until his retirement in 1954.

Ashton's work focused on the industrial history of Great Britain in the eighteenth and early nineteenth centuries, and much of it is still in print and a valuable source of information for students and scholars alike, even if new research has done much to fill in the details. Among his lasting works of scholarship are *Iron and Steel in the Industrial Revolution* (1924) and *The Coal Industry of the Eighteenth Century* (joint with Joseph Sykes, 1929). These two books for many years were the standard works on the subject. His later works include *An Economic History of England in the Eighteenth Century* (1955) and his *Economic Fluctuations in Britain, 1700–1800* (1959).

His best-known and most widely read work remains a small book, *The Industrial Revolution, 1760–1830*, published in 1948, which affected the profession's thinking about the Industrial Revolution more than any other publication since Paul Mantoux's pathbreaking work at the be-

ginning of the twentieth century. It defined the Industrial Revolution and its historical significance and appeared on hundreds of student reading lists. It was translated into many languages and epitomized Ashton's approach to the field. Always searching for quantitative evidence as well as telling representative anecdotes, he was rarely given to theorizing with pretentious or sweeping arguments. Yet he was unfailingly able to see the forest from the trees and possessed a powerful intuition on the economic significance of historical events.

Ashton also maintained a strong interest in financial and monetary history and edited with R. S. Sayers a volume on *English Monetary History* (1953). A complete bibliography can be found in the Festschrift presented to him in 1960, *Studies in the Industrial Revolution*, edited by L. S. Pressnell.

Ashton had little sympathy for ideas such as class struggle and the pessimist wailings about the "disasters of the Industrial Revolution." Left-wing denunciations of industrialization and technological progress left him cold, since he believed that they were informed by neither a knowledge of history nor an economic sense. While fully aware of the costs of economic change and the injustices and follies of the people he was describing, he did not believe that Marxist concepts added much to the analysis and felt a deep admiration of the industrial and commercial entrepreneurs of whom he wrote: Ambrose Crowley, Abraham Darby, Benjamin Huntsman, Henry Cort, and other pioneers of the iron industry of the time. For him, the Industrial Revolution was a defining moment in the transition from a subsistence economy to one marked by the comforts and security of a modern industrialized economy. The closing words of that little book are characteristic of Ashton's depth of insight and eloquence:

> There are today [1948] on the plains of India and China men and women, plague-ridden and hungry, living lives little better, to outward appearance, than those of the cattle that toil with them by day and share their paces of sleep by night. Such Asiatic standards, and such mechanized horrors, are the lot of those who increase their numbers without passing through an Industrial Revolution.

BIBLIOGRAPHY

Ashton, T. S. *Iron and Steel in the Industrial Revolution.* Manchester, 1924.

Ashton, T. S. *The Industrial Revolution, 1760–1830.* Oxford, 1948.

Ashton, T. S. *An Economic Study of England: The Eighteenth Century.* London, 1972.

Pressnell, L. S., ed. *Studies in the Industrial Revolution.* London, 1960.

ASIENTO. The first cargo of enslaved Africans who labored in the Americas disembarked in Hispaniola in 1502.

Those Africans were dispatched in response to a request for them from the governor Nicolás de Ovando. The indigenous population of the islands had begun to decline rapidly as a consequence of the new diseases introduced by the Spaniards as well as from mistreatment. This created a severe labor crisis for the colonists, who sought to exploit their newly acquired possessions but disdained manual labor. Since Spain had a long history of using enslaved African workers, the request by governor Ovando was neither new nor unusual. The arrival of these slaves, however, inaugurated almost four centuries of African slavery in the Americas.

These early arrivals did not come directly from Africa. Rather, they were transshipped from Spain after having been acculturated to that society's religion, language, and culture. Individuals received licenses from the crown to deliver a fixed number of slaves to the colonists in Hispaniola, and later to Jamaica, Peru, Mexico, and elsewhere. In some cases, the license indicated the port to which the slaves would be delivered, but in others it merely stipulated "the Indies."

The nationality of the successful applicants for these licenses varied, but the vast majority were either Spaniards, Portuguese, or Genoese. The crown received a fee for each license awarded. And a new license was required for each voyage to the Americas. Typically, individuals received licenses to deliver from ten to thirty slaves, but some traders received permission to supply as many as three thousand over a period of time varying from one to five years. Generally speaking, the contracts required the recipient to deliver slaves between the ages of fifteen and twenty-six, with two-thirds being male and the remaining third female. These licenses were not monopoly contracts; several were awarded simultaneously.

The individually based licensing system was not without its problems. The colonists complained about its inefficiency, stating that it was cumbersome and undependable. Some licensees failed to fulfill their contractual obligations, and unhappy colonists denounced the haphazard and unpredictable nature of the deliveries. Responding to these persuasive complaints, the crown introduced the Asiento system in 1595.

The Asiento was a monopoly contract awarded by the Spanish crown to individuals, joint stock companies, or to selected nations to supply the Spanish colonies with a stipulated number of slaves over a given period of time, usually several years. In accordance with Spanish practice, the Asiento contracts did not count slaves by individual heads but by *piezas*. Not every slave constituted a *pieza*. Much depended on their height, age, and physical condition. Thus, the number of heads of slaves delivered could actually be in excess of the number of *piezas* indicated in the contract since some slaves formed only a proportion of a *pieza*. The

Spanish crown collected a duty on each *pieza*, and not on each individual slave delivered.

Portuguese traders were the recipients of the six Asiento contracts awarded between 1595–1640, years when the Portuguese and Spanish crowns were united. The first *asentista* was Pedro Gómez Reynel, who signed a contract to deliver 4,250 *piezas* annually to the Indies until he reached a maximum of 38,250. In order to exercise this privilege, Reynel paid the crown 900,000 ducats. Reynel failed to execute his contract satisfactorily and it was terminated after a few years. In fact, most *asentistas* experienced difficulties in living up to their contractual obligations, some preferring to engage in contraband trade in other goods. At least two of the six *asentistas* filed for bankruptcy. The dissolution of the union of the Spanish and Portuguese crowns in 1640 ended this first phase of the Asiento system, which Portuguese traders had dominated.

The Spaniards did not sign another Asiento contract until 1662. Two Genoese merchants, Domingo Grillo and Ambrosio Lomelia, won the contract. They were expected to deliver 24,000 *piezas* to the colonies over a seven-year period—like several of their predecessors, they failed to execute the contract satisfactorily and it was not renewed when it ended in 1670. The Portuguese merchant Antonio Garcia inherited the contract, holding it until 1675. The Spaniards signed an Asiento contract with two Seville merchants, but it was really the Dutch who provided the capital for the venture. During the 1690s, the Portuguese regained control of the Asiento, only to lose it in 1701 to the French West India Company. In 1713, as a result of the Treaty of Utrecht, the English were awarded the Asiento contract. It gave the English the sole rights to supply the Spanish colonists with slaves for the ensuing thirty years. Under the terms of the contract, the colonists would receive 4,800 *piezas* annually, or an overall total of 144,000 *piezas*. Although the Asiento had been awarded to the English crown, Queen Anne gave the South Sea Company (chartered in 1711) the responsibility for the conduct of the trade.

The South Sea Company fared hardly better than its predecessors. It dispatched ships to the African coast to convey slaves to the Americas and purchased some of its cargo from individual or private traders. Still, the company appeared less interested in trading in slaves than in the contraband trade in other goods. Hostilities between Spain and England interrupted the Asiento trade between 1718 and 1721 and again between 1729 and 1739. The War of Jenkin's Ear, which began in 1739, resulted in the suspension of the trade for ten years, permanently crippling it. During the twenty-two years of actual trading, the South Sea Company never at any time met its annual contractual obligation to deliver 4,800 *piezas*.

The Asiento system never recovered from the blow it received during the war. Spain awarded Asientos in 1772 and again in 1773, but the era of the monopoly contract had passed. Spain had begun to question her dependence on foreigners for supplying slaves, a practice that had opened the empire to contraband trade with other nations. But there were other forces at work. The second half of the eighteenth century saw the ascendancy of free trade so that monopoly contracts had become increasingly anachronistic.

The Asiento system was designed to ensure that the Spanish colonists received a steady and dependable supply of African slaves to meet the needs of their expanding economies. The *asentistas*, however, never exercised monopoly control of the trade at any time since interlopers challenged them. Some *asentistas* went bankrupt and others confronted political difficulties not of their making. Still others preferred to engage in contraband more aggressively than they did in the human commerce. In the end, a largely inefficient commercial system could not surmount the vigorous challenges of a new age that was beginning to reject national exclusiveness in favor of free trade.

BIBLIOGRAPHY

Palmer, Colin. *Human Cargoes: The British Slave Trade to Spanish America, 1700–1739*. Urbana, 1981.

Rawley, James A. *The Transatlantic Slave Trade: A History*. New York, 1981.

Vila Vilar, Enriqueta. *Hispanoamerica y el comercio de esclavos*. Seville, 1977.

COLIN A. PALMER

JOHN JACOB ASTOR. Portrait (c. 1825) by John Wesley Jarvis (1780–1840). (National Portrait Gallery, Smithsonian Institution, Washington, D.C./Art Resource, NY)

ASTOR, JOHN JACOB (1763–1848), best known of America's early capitalists.

Astor is the prototypical American merchant who grew up with the early American republic and who died as America prepared for an urban-industrial society. He also created the first American family fortune, a German immigrant who came to the land, acquired his money in that quintessential frontier occupation—the fur trade—branched out into the China trade, and then speculation in New York City real estate.

John Astor first arrived in New York City in 1784 from Waldorf, near Heidelberg and immediately became involved in the fur trade, first with Canadian partners from Montreal. His interest was in the purchase of furs in Canada and on the New York frontier for sale in New York City and European markets, where they brought high prices. Astor expanded his markets, and by the 1790s he was shipping furs to China, where they could be exchanged for teas and spices for shipment to the United States and Europe. As the China trade expanded, Astor built his own ships, stocked goods in warehouses in New York City and in Europe, and grew a fortune of considerable size.

In 1808, Astor entered a world stage of geopolitical as well as corporate innovation. Astor was well aware of the Lewis and Clark expedition by late 1806. He eyed the vast lands to the West as potential sources of supply and, eventually, new markets on the path to China. Given the tenuous state of British-American relations and Canadian competitors, Astor moved quickly. He formed the American Fur Company to expand his fur business westward through the Great Lakes, up the Missouri River, and eventually to an outlet on the Pacific Ocean. He simultaneously formed the Pacific Fur Company, along with Canadian partners (many of whom were part of his initial venture), and authorized both an overland group and a sea voyage to the Pacific coast. Eventually Astoria was founded at the mouth of the Columbia River.

However, the War of 1812 intruded, and the British moved quickly to take Astoria. American policymakers, such as James Madison, did not have the political or economic vision after the war to reclaim Astor's Pacific venture. The American Fur Company pulled back from the Pacific strategy but became a force in the Great Lakes through the 1830s. But John Astor became less involved in business as his son, William, and his trusted lieutenants, Robert Stuart and Ramsay Crooks, continued to deal with the day-to-day operations.

Astor lived much of the 1820s and 1830s in Europe. He remained active in the fur trade, but more often he was involved in new enterprises, such as the buying and selling of New York City real estate, the construction of the Astor House Hotel, and the building of the New York Public Library. His later years were spent in recrimination about the lost opportunities on the Pacific coast. Nevertheless, Astor's life reflected the transition from a commercial economy to the urban and industrial economy of the later nineteenth century.

BIBLIOGRAPHY

Haeger, John. *John Jacob Astor*. Detroit, 1991.
Porter, Kenneth W. *John Jacob Astor: Businessman*. 2 vols. Cambridge, l931.
Ronda, James. *Astoria and Empire*. Lincoln, Nebr., l990.

JOHN HAEGER

AUSTRALIA. The central theme of Australian economic history during the past two centuries has been the expansion of European settlement subject to the maintenance of high and rising incomes. In 1800 the non-Aboriginal population numbered five thousand; in 1900 almost four million; by 2000 almost twenty million. As in other regions of recent European occupation, key early events included the occupation of territory and displacement of existing inhabitants, an early reliance on agricultural and mining activities, the transplanting of European language and institutions, and the early integration of the domestic economy into the international economy. Initial factor supply conditions were natural resource abundance and labor and capital scarcity. Australia's subsequent development also shared prominent features with other settler economies. Agricultural productivity was high almost from the outset, generating high incomes, high levels of urbanization, and a prominent service sector. Thus Australia did not follow the more common growth sequence whereby an initially dominant peasant-agriculture gradually gives way to urban-based industrial and commercial activities as resources are reallocated to higher productivity sectors, raising average incomes. It has therefore not experienced the agricultural, commercial, or industrial "revolutions" that conveniently bracket historical epochs of many developed and developing countries.

History. When European settlement began in New South Wales in 1788, the Australian continent was inhabited by approximately half a million Aborigines. They were hunter-gatherers with no villages or significant permanent structures. Hence population density was low even in well-watered temperate-zone areas. Their major economic achievement was survival and adaptation over millennia in a land much of which is subject to extremely harsh and variable environmental conditions. In the face of introduced disease, and the superior weaponry and organization of the Europeans, the brutal competition for control of the land was accompanied by a dramatic fall in the Aboriginal population in areas favored by the settlers.

Early colonization through nineteenth century. One distinguishing economic feature of the first decades of pioneer European settlement was the presence of convicts and ex-convicts in the labor market. Over 160,000 convicts were "transported" to Australia, beginning with the first fleet to Sydney in 1788 and winding down in the 1840s. They provided much of the initial workforce at a time when the colony's establishment and survival benefited from a high proportion of the population being economically active and possessing attributes such as good health and physical strength. Unlike slaves, convicts usually faced fixed terms of sentence, retained many legal rights, enjoyed considerable freedom of movement, and their children were born free. They faced a variety of pecuniary incentives in relation to work assignment and effort, while the range of their skills or experience was relevant to the various types of labor needed.

A second distinguishing feature of the early colonial economy was the emergence in the 1820s of an export-oriented wool industry. The natural grasslands of a swathe of southeastern Australia well accommodated low-cost sheep-raising, especially the fine-wool merino breed. The traditional Aboriginal occupiers were displaced from these abundant grazing lands, which were reoccupied by pastoral "squatters" who eventually gained leases to their properties. Production methods economized on scarce labor and capital, and wool output expanded simply by the method of allowing the flock size to grow: there were 100 million sheep by 1890. Distance from the nearest port or (later) railway, let alone the principal market in Great Britain, was not a serious economic impediment to profitability, given the high value-to-bulk ratio and nonperishability of wool. By 1850 Australia was the dominant source of wool imports to Great Britain. This one industry figured prominently in the economy's fortunes in most decades until the mid-twentieth century.

The European population had reached only four hundred thousand by 1851 when gold was discovered. However, the short-run demographic and economic effects were as dramatic as those following the discovery of gold in California three years earlier. The longer-range effects were no less dramatic. The labor that rushed in during the 1850s stayed on after the surface gold was removed, finding employment in the expanding agricultural and urban industries. The age and gender mix of the population following the rushes was heavily skewed toward young adult males, bequeathing a highly favorable workforce participation rate. Gold displaced wool as the principal export for the following two decades. And gold production declined only slowly from its peak in the 1850s until discoveries in Western Australia led to a second rush in the 1890s. A renewed expansion of the wool industry in the 1870s and 1880s makes clear that rapid exploitation of the natural resource base was driving Australian growth throughout the nineteenth century.

The population explosion at midcentury stimulated the growth of farming activities other than wool growing. Cereal, meat, and dairy production had begun in the first years of settlement, but remained primarily targeted to the domestic market. By the end of the nineteenth century, and with the advent of refrigerated shipping and the extension of the railway network into inland areas best suited for grain growing, Australia was a major exporter of wheat, frozen meat, and dairy products, primarily to the British market. This phase of rural development occurred on family-farm enterprises smaller than the vast sheep "stations" typical of the pastoral frontier, which had moved farther inland to semi-arid areas throughout eastern Australia.

Despite the importance of mining and farming, Australia was a relatively urbanized society by the end of the nineteenth century. Moreover, much of the country's industrial and service sector activities came to be concentrated in just a few large cities. By 1911, 38 percent of Australia's population was living in five urban areas. Today, this figure has risen to more than 60 percent, with populations ranging from one million to four million in the same five urban areas. The urban concentration was partly due to geography (an arid interior and few natural harbors along the coastline), and partly to the labor-saving production technology of Australian farming such that only a small proportion of the workforce were ever required to work the actual farmland. Though very different from Europe, the size distribution of Australian cities was similar to that observed in some other regions of recent European settlement, such as Argentina, Canada, and the western United States.

Early-nineteenth-century manufacturing activities were confined to the processing of agricultural commodities (e.g., flour milling, brewing), and the production of items expensive to import (e.g., timber milling, brick making). Although gold and wool remained the principal exports, there were few demand or supply linkages to domestic manufacturing. In the later nineteenth century, some diversification in manufacturing and the emergence of larger scale enterprises accompanied the growth of the export trade in meat, butter, and cheese (meat-freezing and dairy factories), the mechanization of farming (agricultural machinery production), and the expansion of the railways (engineering workshops). It was not until 1915 that the first iron and steel mill was constructed.

Australian cities in the nineteenth century thus did not flourish in conformity with the industrial expansion that dominated either the first or second industrial revolutions of northwestern Europe or the northeastern United States. Australians at this time primarily relied on imports for their supplies of iron and steel products, machinery, and other capital goods, textiles and clothing, and ship and railway equipment. Rather, the major cities were commercial and service centers, though containing some small-scale and light manufacturing activities. Prominent in the former group were specialist institutions that catered to the financial, shipping, and marketing needs of farming, especially the wool industry. Of course, the rapid pace of population growth created a large construction sector that encompassed residential and commercial building, road and railway construction, and the provision of urban water, gas, and sewerage systems. The high incomes attained in the colonies must also partly explain the early prominence of the services sector. In 1861, 60 percent of GDP originated in services (including transport and construction). Australia already had an economy with some twentieth-century characteristics.

In the early 1890s, the first major phase of Australian economic growth ended. A depression set in that lasted over a decade. The reasons for the end of the long economic boom include an array of domestic and foreign influences, but their interaction makes any neat separation of causes impossible. During the 1880s, economic expansion became increasingly based on speculation in assets (rural land and urban property), fueled by extremely high volumes of British capital inflow and rapid immigration. Returns to pastoral investment declined in the face of falling world prices and the expansion of wool-growing into climatically marginal areas. The bubble was pricked by the London banking crisis in 1890 (originating in Argentina), which occasioned a reappraisal of British investments in Australia and reduced capital inflow.

The institutions financing the boom were largely unregulated, and so many banks failed with the crash in asset values. The colonial governments did not have control over the exchange rate and did not renegotiate their debt with the London capital market, and thus Australians bore the full deflationary pressure of the necessary downward adjustment in economic activity, which was especially pronounced in Victoria. The gloom was lightened by the gold rush to the rich fields in Western Australia, and the upturn in world commodity prices from the mid-1890s. However, an especially severe drought delayed sustained recovery until several years into the new century.

Throughout the nineteenth century, the Australian economy had been very open to international influences, with few barriers to trade, few restrictions on immigration levels or composition, and few impediments to foreign capital. Likewise, the colonial economies were relatively unregulated. Government was important primarily for promoting economic expansion, that is, extensive rather than intensive growth. The goals were to settle and develop—increasing the population via immigration and exploiting the generous natural resource endowment. Some hoped that Australia would become a second United States. Despite the similarity in their sizes, however, the resource base of Australia was much smaller when assessed in terms of land suitable for farming, soil quality, water supplies, climate, and known mineral resources.

By the 1890s, much of the pastoral and agricultural land was occupied—further rural development would require the application of additional capital and technology to land already settled. The severe depression of the 1890s also witnessed an acceleration of the moves to federation by the six Australian colonies (completed in 1901). These events at the turn of the century ushered in a new era. The emergence of a Labor Party, the strengthening union movement, and the broadened electoral franchise created a new consensus on economic development. The objective remained to expand the (European) population and to maintain high wages, but it was recognized that the capacity to absorb immigrants on the agricultural frontier was now limited. Hence manufacturing was seen as the future source of employment. And supply shortages during World War I emphasized Australia's dependence on imports for much of its capital equipment and other industrial requirements.

Twentieth century. By the 1920s, Australia had, piecemeal, adopted an inward oriented growth strategy. This rested on import-substituting industrialization induced by tariff protection; the imposition of strict controls on immigration to ensure existing workers' protection against the competition of low-wage labor (the "White Australia" policy); and the centralization and regulation of the national labor market to ensure that workers' real wages were maintained (especially in the face of the higher prices that resulted from tariff increases). The manufacture of iron and steel, chemicals, textiles, clothing and footwear, electrical goods, and farm equipment, as well as the number of automobile assembly plants, all expanded. Some rural development continued, especially "closer settlement" schemes to give more people (especially veterans) access to farmland.

When the world depression arrived in 1929, the Australian economy already faced serious economic problems. These included falling world commodity prices, rising foreign debt levels, misdirected public investment in rural development, and a worsening of the balance of payments deficit. The slump of the early 1930s, transmitted to Australia by the cessation of capital inflow and decline in export prices, was severe by world standards, with unemployment reaching 25 to 30 percent. The recovery was not helped by contradictory domestic economic policies on wages, interest rates, the exchange rate, the tariff, and government spending. But the banking system did not collapse as in the 1890s. Given the balance of payments constraint, and the commitment to fully service debt obligations, it is likely that there was limited freedom of action for policy makers: Australians had to await a recovery in the world economy.

During World War I, Australia suffered a severe economic downturn due to the disruption of trade with its principal export market and source of imports, Great Britain. By contrast, World War II stimulated domestic growth, partly because the expansion of manufacturing during the interwar period had reduced the economy's vulnerability to trade disruption, and partly because the war came to Australia's doorstep. Australia was now in a position to feed, clothe, and equip both its own and U.S. forces fighting the Japanese in the South Pacific. A considerably expanded domestic industrial capacity resulted.

Postwar expansion was also assisted by the resumption of large-scale immigration, no longer solely British, but also including Italians, Greeks, and other Europeans. These immigrants provided labor for the manufacturing and construction sectors and boosted the demand for the cars, houses, and durables that those sectors generated. The rural industries also flourished, especially the wool trade during the Korean War. Rising living standards, low unemployment, and low inflation meant that Australia shared in the international prosperity of the 1950s. This trend continued through the 1960s, not just because international conditions remained favorable, but also because Australia exploited new mineral discoveries for which strong foreign demand existed, especially from the rapidly industrializing Japanese economy. Australian prosperity was thus underpinned by export diversification away from agriculture (to iron ore, coal, bauxite, copper, oil, gold, natural gas, and uranium) and away from Great Britain (to Japan and other East Asian markets). Mineral exports became more important than farm exports, just as gold had overtaken wool a century earlier. Australia experienced its second great natural resource–based and export-oriented economic boom.

From the early 1970s, Australia encountered the same deterioration in economic performance as did other advanced industrial countries. In addition to the energy price shocks and increased competition from manufactured imports from Asia, however, deindustrialization resulted from the domestic minerals boom, which raised domestic wages and other costs, in turn making import-competing manufacturers less competitive despite high tariffs. Of course, the rising energy prices were not all bad news for Australia, a net energy exporter. However, policies that prevented the adjustment of the exchange rate and boosted wages in the early 1970s contributed to inflation, unemployment, and the slowdown in income growth. Both international and domestic forces were increasing the pressure for major structural changes that favored the minerals and nontraded services sectors but caused serious difficulties for manufacturing.

After 1983, recognition of these forces led to a major change in economic policy direction. Australia abandoned many of the regulations and policies dating from early in the twentieth century (having already abolished the restrictions on Asian immigration) and reverted to a more outward oriented growth strategy. The exchange rate was floated, foreign banks allowed to compete in the retail end of the capital market, and tariff protection was steadily reduced, even on the most highly protected industries (autos, textiles, clothing, and footwear). The strategy was designed to increase the openness of the economy, thus making manufacturing and traded service industries as internationally competitive as farming and mining had always been. To this end, domestic labor market regulations were reformed, attendance at high schools and institutes of higher education increased markedly, and governments (both federal and state) shed functions and privatized public enterprises. As initial results of this policy shift, manufacturing and agricultural employment shrank, new regional economic disparities emerged, unemployment stayed stubbornly high, and average incomes grew only slowly.

During the 1990s, however, the economy reaped the benefits of economic reform, with strong growth in incomes, productivity, and employment, as well as low inflation and stabilized economic activity. Even the relative stagnation of Japan (Australia's principal trading partner) and the Asian economic crisis of 1997–1998 had little domestic effect as a more diversified and flexible export sector diverted output to other markets. And the restructured manufacturing sector had become increasingly export oriented, securing significant foreign sales even of such previously heavily protected products as cars and car parts.

By century's end, only a tiny proportion of Australians worked in the rural and mining industries; the decline in the share of the workforce in manufacturing that had begun in the late 1960s had halted; the share of public-sector employment declined; and the (nongovernment) services sector became even more dominant—as in other advanced economies. Other prominent features of the 1990s economic experience in Australia were also common among many OECD (Organization for Economic Cooperation and Development) economies. There was evidence of a rising inequality in income and wealth after decades when trends had been toward greater equality. There was also economic distress in some rural areas and in those urban areas reliant on manufacturing employment. And household employment patterns changed, with an increased women's labor force participation partly reflecting increased employment opportunities and partly a desire to maintain or raise household income by adding a second wage earner. Much of the increased female employment was part-time or temporary and in the service sector. As the shares of blue-collar manufacturing jobs and jobs in the public sector both declined, so too did the proportion of the workforce in unions. Australia thus acquired an economy that was substantially liberalized, though not to the degree manifest in the United States.

Issues and Perspectives. From this broad view of the evolution of the Australian economy since European settlement, several important themes and issues arise. The first is how, in most international comparisons of per capita income during the nineteenth century, Australia came to rank number one, ahead of Britain and the United States. There are probably several related causes. The known endowment of natural resources of current economic value was high relative to the small population. Further, these land and mineral resources could, for the most part, be exploited at low cost. In addition, there was high and sustained international demand for the products intensive in these natural resources, such that neither transport cost disadvantages because of distance from final markets, nor the scarcity and high cost of labor, nor the underdeveloped infrastructure constituted serious impediments to successfully exploiting the advantages of specialization of production for international markets. Moreover, the favorable sex and age characteristics of the convicts, later reinforced by those of the gold miners, generated a high labor force participation rate, which, at the prevailing level of labor productivity, raised measured GDP per person. It is not clear how much of Australia's high average incomes relative to those in Britain or the United States were attributable to the favorable age distribution and high masculinity ratio, to the level of labor productivity, or to the resource endowment per worker.

These favorable influences were not sustained into the twentieth century. As stated earlier, most of the better quality land suitable for agricultural or pastoral production had been occupied by the 1890s. The Western Australian gold rush of the 1890s did not usher in a sustained period of mineral discoveries. And with the exception of the decade before 1914, and the early 1920s, immigration rates were low from the early 1890s to the late 1940s, removing that source of growth. Thus it is not surprising that trend aggregate growth rates were lower, and that improvements in real GDP per capita slowed, though other measures of living standards continued to improve across the first half of the century.

VICTORIA, AUSTRALIA. Women spread grapes on a wire rack to prepare them for making wine, 1983. (© David Austen/Woodfin Camp and Associates, New York)

From this perspective, the return to rapid population and economic growth in the post-1945 period has a nineteenth-century feel about it, both in the high levels of immigration and foreign investment, and the new era of resource-based development. Some of this involved the further diversification of rural industries—important new products included beef, sugar, cotton, and wine. Most dramatic was the rapid expansion of the minerals sector, substantially for export, but much more diversified than in the nineteenth century when gold dominated. By the 1990s, minerals accounted for 40 percent of Australian exports, twice the value of farm exports. (Exports of manufactured goods and of services each accounted for a further 20 percent of the total.) Thus Australia remained, as in the nineteenth century, an export-oriented small open economy, specializing in the export of resource-intensive products. The efficiency of the export industries remained high by world standards. Hence Australian incomes, though no longer the highest in the world, remained comparable with those recorded by other members of the club of rich, advanced economies.

Although Australia's natural resources exerted a major influence on the course of the economy's development, their existence did not alone ensure its success. The discovery and utilization of resources are determined by many factors, including the institutional and legal environment within which exploration, investment, and production decisions are made. Nineteenth-century tensions over ownership of the pastoral lands initially occupied by "squatters" and the Goldfields Riots over miner's grievances both illustrate the importance of appropriate property rights to successful resource-based growth.

The distribution of the resource rents was also important to the Australian success story. Access to both agricultural land and alluvial gold was widely shared. The early extension of the electoral franchise was one further factor preventing the concentration of economic and political power, and the social tradition of a rough equality of opportunity for all was established early. State regulation of economic activity was limited in the nineteenth century, although the reactions to the depressions of the 1890s and 1930s led to increased intervention for both social and economic ends. In the 1980s and 1990s, the opposite tendency has resulted from a perception that continued prosperity was threatened by excessive or inappropriate government regulation of the economy.

From a comparative perspective, Australian economic history contains features both common and unusual. For the nineteenth century, Australia is appropriately regarded as a European settler economy. Similar national or regional economies emerged in New Zealand, Argentina, Canada, and the United States. These economies shared many initial conditions, and successfully achieved economic development by broadly similar means, and as vital components of the pre-1914 international economy. In the twentieth century, Australia experienced the major economic shocks of war, depression, postwar boom, stagflation, and pressure for structural adjustment, as did all advanced economies. Thus, in any general comparison with other OECD economies, Australia is no anomaly.

However, on closer inspection, the history of Australia's economy differs in countless ways from that of other settler economies in the nineteenth century and other industrialized economies in the twentieth century. Australia faced environmental and climatic challenges unlike the United States, in that most of the continent is desert or semi-arid, and water the one vital natural resource that is in short supply. Further, settlement has been scattered, fragmenting the small domestic market and, unlike Canada, there has been no large foreign market on Australia's doorstep—though this has begun to change with the economic modernization of Southeast Asia. And unlike many other similar societies, Australia has experienced two centuries without wars, revolution, or serious regional or sectional strife, but with a remarkable social and political stability accompanying a relatively equitable sharing of the benefits of an impressive economic achievement.

BIBLIOGRAPHY

Blainey, Geoffrey. *The Tyranny of Distance: How Distance Shaped Australia's History*. Rev. ed. Sydney, 1983.

Boehm, E. A. *Prosperity and Depression in Australia, 1887–1897*. Oxford, 1971.

Butlin, N. G. *Australian Domestic Product, Investment, and Foreign Borrowing, 1861–1938/39*. Cambridge, 1962.

Butlin, N. G. *Investment in Australian Economic Development, 1861–1900*. Cambridge, 1964.

Gregory, R. G., and N. G. Butlin, eds. *Recovery from the Depression: Australia and the World Economy in the 1930s*. Cambridge, 1988.

Maddock, Rodney, and Ian W. McLean, eds. *The Australian Economy in the Long Run*. New York, 1987.

Meredith, David, and Barrier Dyster. *Australia in the Global Economy: Continuity and Change*. Cambridge, 1999.

Nicholas, Stephen, ed. *Convict Workers: Reinterpreting Australia's Past*. Cambridge, 1988.

Schedvin, C. B. *Australia and the Great Depression: A Study of Economic Development and Policy in the 1920s and 1930s*. Sydney, 1970.

Schedvin, C. B. "Midas and the Merino: A Perspective on Australian Economic Historiography." *Economic History Review* 32.4 (1979), 542–556.

Vamplew, Wray, ed. *Australians: Historical Statistics*. Sydney, 1987.

IAN W. MCLEAN

AUSTRIA *[This entry contains three subentries, on the economic history of Austria before 1867, during the Austro-Hungarian Empire, and in modern times.]*

Austria before 1867

The Austrian monarchy ranked among the European Great Powers from the beginning of the early modern period up until the outbreak of World War I. Austrian *monarchy* and *empire* are used interchangeably in this article to refer to the whole of the central and east European lands ruled by the Habsburgs. *Austria* itself is taken to include the Alpine provinces, the Bohemian lands, the Karst provinces in the south, Lombardy and Venetia (lost 1859 and 1866), and Carpathian lands in the east (Galicia, Bukovina). *Hungary* refers to the lands of the Hungarian crown (i.e., Hungary proper, Croatia-Slavonia, Slovakia, and Transylvania). Characterized by profound regional differences in geography and resource endowments and inhabited by at least eleven different nationalities, the central and east European lands under Habsburg rule formed the second-largest country in Europe by area, after Russia. This sprawling empire comprised 23 million inhabitants in 1800, or about 14 percent of the European total, and by 1870 their numbers had increased to 36 million.

However, the Habsburg economy displayed wide divergencies in the level of development between its western and northwestern regions and those in the east and southeast. These gaps widened as industrialization in the Bohemian and Alpine lands gathered momentum in the eighteenth and nineteenth centuries. There, the timing of initial industrial advance, if not its intensity, coincided broadly with the experience elsewhere in western Europe. The eastern regions, however, remained overwhelmingly agrarian. The largely rural basis of the Habsburg economy as a whole is underlined by urbanization rates that were markedly lower than the west European average between 1600 and 1850.

After the end of the Thirty Years' War (1618–1648), mercantilist thinking began to influence state policy. Initially, this had little impact on the complex system of internal tariffs that stifled intraempire commercial exchange. However, prompted by the loss of Silesia (1742), the empire's economically most advanced region, and impending economic crisis, the scope of reform increased dramatically during the reign of Maria Theresa (1740–1780) and Joseph II (1765–1790). Domestic economic integration was fostered through the removal of most internal tariffs, a lowering of the customs barrier between Austria and Hungary, a common external tariff, and improvements in waterway and road communications. The government encouraged the immigration of skilled artisans, loosened guild restrictions on industrial activity, and offered incentives for the adoption of up-to-date techniques in manufacturing. The institution of serfdom was transformed, improving the peasants' legal position and, eventually, converting their obligations into money rents.

While the impact of government policy is hard to quantify, there is evidence pointing to increased division of labor between the empire's eastern agrarian regions and the western lands. In the latter, proto-industrialization was clearly under way in the second half of the eighteenth century. However, while the Napoleonic Wars and the continental blockade had a differential impact on the glass,

REVOLUTION OF 1848. A day-laborers' uprising is broken up by the National Guard in the Vienna Prater on 23 August 1848. Hand-colored lithograph, nineteenth century. (Historisches Museum der Stadt Wien, Vienna/Erich Lessing/Art Resource, NY)

linen, cotton, woolen, sugar, and iron industries, overall industrial expansion ground to a halt at around the turn of the century and was not to accelerate again until the 1820s. The pre-1800 "industrial momentum" is mostly viewed as the precursor to self-sustained growth in the nineteenth century. Komlos (1989) recently reinterpreted the significance of socio-economic change in the eighteenth century, arguing that the government reforms in industry and agriculture removed the food constraint on population growth and economic expansion in Austria. The issue rests largely on the extent to which the reversal in human height decline, as a reflection of improved nutritional status, can be interpreted as evidence of irreversible economic growth.

Earlier historical works tended to link the onset of modern economic growth in Austria to the institutional reforms following the Revolutions of 1848. More recent quantitative research suggests, however, that the rate of economic expansion was largely independent of state policy. The creation of the Austro-Hungarian customs union (1850) had little impact on the growth of either Austrian industry or Hungarian agriculture because the barriers to internal trade were already fairly low. Similarly, the full emancipation of the peasantry did not mark a watershed since feudal obligations had already been reduced in the later eighteenth century to the extent that they no longer posed a major obstacle to growth. Austrian industrial output accelerated from the late 1820s and grew at about 3 percent per annum up to 1870. Aided by foreign capital, expertise, and technology, the main growth impetus came from the textiles and metallurgical sectors. In the cotton textile industry, the modernization that had begun in the 1790s was resumed, and mechanization, the use of steam power, and the shift to the factory system intensified. The similarly rapid expansion of iron output (about 5 percent per annum to 1870) occurred against a background of limited technical change in the much larger charcoal-based industry in Alpine Austria and a faster adoption of coke smelting and the puddling refining process in the Bohemian lands, where bituminous coal was relatively abundant. The spread of mechanization and the increased use of steam power in industry and, after 1840, in rail transport was reflected in the growth of coal consumption by 10 percent annually as well as the emergence of an indigenous machine-building industry. However, by the 1870s, total steam capacity in the empire was about one-third of that in Germany, and most of it was employed in railway locomotion rather than industry.

The growth of an urban industrial labor force in Austria after 1820 provided the stimulus for the expansion of Hungarian agriculture, especially grain production. Austria offered a market to Hungarian producers that was largely uncontested by foreign competitors because of the common external tariff and geographical proximity. Later, the link to Austria also proved crucial for Hungary's transition to sustained industrial growth from the late 1870s. Austrian capital, seeking safe and profitable outlets after the 1873 Vienna stock market crash, underpinned a major surge in railway construction and the flour milling and iron industries.

Yet, despite the advances made over the previous century, by the time of the Dual Settlement (1867), the empire's economic position relative to western Europe had deteriorated. There were several proximate causes that may have accounted for this. First, industrial growth was largely confined to Austria's western regions. The wider diffusion of modern technology was slowed by less well-developed markets, less favorable resource endowments, and an institutionally less receptive environment in the eastern parts of the empire. Second, aggregate productivity gains from structural change were limited. A high proportion of labor remained in an agricultural sector that in the empire as a whole, stark regional differences notwithstanding, displayed both low levels and low growth of average output per worker. In 1870, more than 76 percent of the total labor force was still engaged in agriculture, contributing less than 35 percent of the empire's total gross domestic product.

BIBLIOGRAPHY

Good, David F. *The Economic Rise of the Habsburg Empire, 1750–1914.* Berkeley, 1984. A wide-ranging, well-documented synthesis of modern Habsburg economic history.

Gross, N. T. "The Habsburg Monarchy, 1750–1914." In *The Fontana Economic History of Europe,* edited by C. M. Cipolla, vol. 4, pt. 1, *The Emergence of Industrial Societies,* pp. 228–278. London, 1973.

Ingrao, Charles W. *The Habsburg Monarchy, 1618–1815.* 2d ed. Cambridge, 2000.

Komlos, John. *The Habsburg Monarchy as a Customs Union: Economic Development in Austria-Hungary in the Nineteenth Century.* Princeton, 1983. A rigorous quantitative examination of the dynamics of nineteenth-century growth.

Komlos, John. *Nutrition and Economic Development in the Eighteenth-Century Habsburg Monarchy.* Princeton, 1989. Adopts anthropometric approach in the analysis of economic and institutional change, and argues that industrial revolution in Austria began in the eighteenth century.

Sandgruber, R. *Ökonomie und Politik: Österreichische Wirtschaftsgeschichte vom Mittelalter bis zur Gegenwart.* Vienna, 1995. A comprehensive survey of the economic history of Alpine Austria since the medieval period.

Sked, Alan. *The Decline and Fall of the Habsburg Empire, 1815–1918.* 2d ed. Harlow, U.K., 2001.

MAX-STEPHAN SCHULZE

The Austro-Hungarian Empire

On the eve of the Compromise of 1867 (Dual Settlement) that created the Austro-Hungarian Empire out of the Habsburg Monarchy, the institutional foundations for economic integration—the customs union, the monetary union, and the final emancipation of the peasants—were in place. The actual degree of economic integration, however, remained rather modest because of high transportation costs; in 1866, the length of the empirewide railroad network was a little more than six thousand kilometers; two-thirds in Austria and one-third in Hungary.

Because of their close proximity to the more developed regions of western Europe, sustained economic growth had been underway in the Bohemian and Alpine lands since the 1820s, and perhaps even the late eighteenth century. By contrast, growth impulses in the eastern, Hungarian lands were weak. As a result, by 1867 the Habsburg Monarchy had fallen further behind more advanced economies, such as England, Belgium, France, and even Prussia, especially in the 1850s and 1860s, when it fought costly wars to preserve its influence among the German states, on the Italian peninsula, and in the Balkans.

Economic Growth after the Compromise of 1867. After the overwhelming defeat by Prussia in 1866, the monarchy's elites turned their attention to internal affairs, and a year later reached an accommodation with the restive Hungarians, whose revolution in 1848 had been crushed and autonomy severely restricted. The resulting Compromise of 1867 preserved the empire as a customs union and a monetary union, mandating a single foreign policy and military policy for the empire as a whole, but dividing it into two semisovereign political units: Austria (the "Kingdoms and Lands represented in the Parliament") and Hungary (the "Kingdom of Hungary"), each with its own parliament, executive, and judiciary branches of government.

A central bureaucracy in Vienna administered "common" affairs (the military and diplomacy) and "dualistic" affairs (setting tariffs, determining consumption taxes, and regulating the currency and the Austro-Hungarian National Bank) based on identical legislation passed by the two governments. Tariff revenue financed the common expenditures, with the shortfall covered by each government (70 percent by Austria and 30 percent by Hungary). All taxes and other public-sector spending, for example, on education, transportation, social affairs, agriculture, and industry, were under the control of the governments in Vienna and Budapest or governmental authorities at the regional or local levels in the two semisovereign states.

Once the Compromise was put in place, the two governments promoted vigorous programs of railroad expansion. During the boom years from 1867 to 1873, both networks doubled in size, so the basic outlines of an empirewide rail system were in place. By World War I, both rail systems had more than doubled again. Even in the eastern regions of the empire, rail density compared favorably with the more developed regions of western Austria, and greatly exceeded levels prevailing in the independent Balkan states.

The expansion of the railroads fostered interregional flows of goods, capital, labor, and high levels of economic and financial interdependence within Austria-Hungary. Reflecting its standing as a relatively low-income economy, the empire was a net exporter of primary products and a net importer of manufactured goods until World War I. Because of its large size, diverse resource base, and substantial regional income disparities, a relatively low percentage of its total output entered international trade compared with other European states. Within the customs union, Hungary was a net exporter of agricultural goods to Austria, and Austria was a net exporter of raw materials and manufactured goods to Hungary. The interdependence of the two trading partners was high. Austria accounted for almost 75 percent of Hungary's total exports, while Hungary accounted for almost 40 percent of Austria's total exports.

Financial integration moved apace, too, as capital markets facilitated the flow of surplus capital from high-income regions in Austria, especially around Vienna, into low-income areas where local savings could not fully accommodate the growing demand for capital. The big Viennese joint-stock banks spearheaded the interregional flows by investing directly in private firms and by establishing a branch bank network that channeled investment into the Austrian hinterland and eventually Hungary. The share of Austria in the total investment in Hungary increased dramatically from 1867, peaked in the early 1890s, and then declined as economic growth fueled domestic savings in Hungary. Although Austrians provided the lion's share of foreign capital for Hungary's industrialization prior to World War I, they did so indirectly by acquiring relatively safe Hungarian state bonds and bank shares rather than riskier shares of industrial firms.

The railroad also facilitated the migration of people inside Austria-Hungary and eventually emigration abroad, especially to the United States, beginning in the 1890s. Both Vienna and Budapest acted as magnets in attracting surplus population from the rural hinterland. More generally high-income areas in the empire tended to experience net in-migration or lower rates of net out-migration than low income areas.

These flows of goods, financial capital, and people within Austria-Hungary brought a narrowing of regional differences in commodity prices, interest rates, and wages after 1867. The empire was becoming economically and financially integrated in the decades before World War I.

Beginning in the 1960s, economic historians trained in economics and statistics used standard national income accounting methodology or proxy-based approaches to generate quantitative estimates of growth. Their estimates largely overturned the more pessimistic views of the Monarchy's economic development that typified the older historiography. However, the most recent estimates of gross domestic product (GDP) per capita for the period from 1870 to 1910 (see Schulze estimates of Table 1) suggest the need to temper these optimistically revisionist views. On balance, it seems fair to conclude that the Habsburg economy was neither a success nor a failure but a mix of both.

On the positive side, growth rates of GDP per capita in Austria, Hungary, and the empire during the four decades prior to World War I (Table 1) had never been so rapid. Of course, the growth paths were not smooth over time. Hungary grew faster than Austria in the 1870s and 1880s as capital flowed from Austria to Hungary after the crisis of 1873 in Vienna. When capital flows reversed in the 1890s, so did relative growth rates: Austria's accelerated and Hungary's slowed down.

The iron industry was increasingly important in both Austria and Hungary, but each economy also had its own special niches, for example, textiles in Austria and flour milling in Hungary. Overall, in the period from 1870 to 1914, regional income disparities narrowed within the empire. Hungary grew faster than Austria and, more generally, the empire's low-income regions tended to grow faster than its high-income regions. Finally, microlevel studies show evidence of success in certain key sectors. The food processing industry was the locus of innovation in both Austria (sugar beets) and Hungary (flour milling), while the bentwood furniture industry pioneered the introduction of the modern

TABLE 1. *Estimates of GDP per Capita Growth, 1870–1910 (percent per annum)*

	1870–1890	1890–1910	1870–1910
Austria			
Kausel	1.24	1.38	1.31
Good and Ma	1.10	1.31	1.20
Schulze	0.70	1.35	1.03
Hungary			
Katus	—	—	1.67
Good and Ma	1.49	1.51	1.50
Schulze	1.48	1.26	1.37
Austria-Hungary			
Good and Ma	1.20	1.36	1.28
Schulze	0.99	1.32	1.15

SOURCES: Schulze (2000) based on estimates of Good and Ma (1998); Katus (1979); Kausel (1979); and Schulze (2000).

TABLE 2. *GDP per Capita Levels (1990 Geary-Khamis $) and Growth Rates (percent per annum)*

	1870	1890	1913	GROWTH RATE 1870–1913
AUSTRIA	1,421	1,635	2,222	1.05
HUNGARY	978	1,313	1,722	1.32
AUSTRIA-HUNGARY	1,230	1,498	2,008	1.15
Belgium	2,640	3,355	4,130	1.05
Denmark	1,927	2,427	3,764	1.57
Finland	1,107	1,341	2,050	1.44
France	1,858	2,354	3,452	1.45
Germany	1,820	2,412	3,647	1.63
Italy	1,467	1,631	2,507	1.25
Netherlands	2,640	3,228	3,950	0.94
Norway	1,303	1,617	2,275	1.30
Spain	1,376	1,847	2,255	1.16
Sweden	1,644	2,086	3,096	1.48
Switzerland	2,172	—	4,207	1.55
United Kingdom	3,263	4,099	5,032	1.01
Russia	1,023	925	1,488	0.88

SOURCES: Austria, Hungary, and Austria-Hungary from Schulze (2000). Remaining countries from Angus Maddison, *Monitoring the World Economy, 1820–1992*, Paris, 1995. The values in Geary-Khamis $ reflect adjustments for differences in purchasing power across countries and for changes in price levels over time within countries.

industrial enterprise and mass production technology in a consumer goods industry where they were unknown even in the United States. In both Austria and Hungary, the machine-building industry was a dynamic sector that promoted industrial growth through substantial backward and forward linkages to the rest of the economy.

Although the central and eastern European lands under Habsburg rule grew at unprecedented rates in the late nineteenth century, they could have grown even faster given the potential inherent in their relatively low income levels. Between 1870 and 1910 (see Table 2), Austria's growth rate was greater than only three of the fourteen other European states: the Netherlands, the United Kingdom, and Russia. Hungary grew faster than Austria, so its performance looks somewhat better in a Europeanwide perspective—slow compared with Germany, France, Switzerland, and the Scandinavian countries except Norway, but fast compared with Belgium, the Netherlands, the United Kingdom, Russia, Italy, and Spain.

Economic Policy under Dualism. The Compromise of 1867 retained the empire as a customs union, which meant that the governments in Vienna and Budapest had to agree on common external tariffs rather than pursuing independent tariff policies. Following a period of liberalizing trade after the Revolutions of 1848, which reflected the dynasty's interest in shoring up its position in the German

states against Prussia, the Monarchy returned to its more traditional protectionist stance, especially after the crisis of 1873, when deflationary pressures set in. Powerful economic interests—the textile and iron manufacturers in Austria and the grain-producing large landowners and flour millers in Hungary—fueled protectionism. Debates on tariff policy after 1867 were contentious. Hungary's policy of import substitution cut into Austria's market for manufactured goods, and the great power aspirations of the Monarchy demanded tariff concessions for the independent Balkan states at Hungary's expense. Whatever the impact on the politics of dualism, economic interdependence between the two partners remained high. Hungary's industrialization did not reduce it, and the imperial tariff policy tended to reinforce it. The Compromise also maintained Austria-Hungary as a monetary union with a single currency and a central bank organized along dualistic lines. Until 1892, the florin was nominally on a silver standard, although after 1879 it lost its convertibility and floated freely against other currencies. The value of the florin was actually quite stable against the pound sterling in this period compared with the 1850s and 1860s. In 1892, Austria-Hungary formally severed its link with silver and adopted the gold standard with the crown as the new currency. Although the crown was never fully convertible into gold, the Austro-Hungarian Bank successfully managed a de facto gold standard and maintained the value of the crown within a half a percentage point above and below parity until the outbreak of World War I.

One source of this stability under both the de facto "paper standard" before 1892 and the subsequent de facto gold standard was that the Compromise severely restricted the ability of the Austro-Hungarian Bank to hold public-sector debt issues. Equally important was the fundamentally changed political context within which these legal strictures operated. The defeat of the Habsburg Monarchy by Prussia in 1866 ended two decades of domestic turmoil and/or shooting wars abroad, which enabled government finances to be put on a much sounder basis. In both Austria and Hungary, periods of modest surplus alternated with periods of modest deficit. This fiscal discipline fostered a sound currency and greatly smoothed the functioning of capital markets in the empire.

Having no ability to set tariffs or pursue an independent monetary policy, policymakers in Vienna and Budapest concentrated on other public-sector functions. Historians view economic policy in Hungary as being coherent and highly focused because Magyar policymakers in Budapest did not have to pay much attention to the relatively powerless non-Magyar nationalities and regional elites. By contrast, they view economic policy in Austria as being more ad hoc and unfocused because of the relatively strong bargaining power of its non-German national elites, for example, the Czechs and the Poles, and of elites in its historic crown lands. Do these differences in economic policy explain why Hungary grew faster than Austria from 1870 to World War I? The evidence, as least for railroad and industrial policy, suggests not.

Railroad construction was a major priority for both governments. The initial years of post-Compromise Austria-Hungary, as noted above, saw a spectacular boom in railroad building by private firms under the old system of state interest guarantees. The economic crisis of 1873 called into question the financial health of many rail lines and eventually led the state to return them to state ownership, Austria beginning in 1878 and Hungary in 1883. The railroads facilitated the ongoing economic integration of the empire, but except perhaps in the boom years of 1867 to 1873, they were not a "leading sector" with strong backward linkages to industry.

Because of disparities in levels of industrial development within the Austro-Hungarian customs union, the two governments followed quite different approaches to industrial policy. In industrially advanced Austria, the government promoted export markets for its already sizable industrial sector. In agrarian Hungary, the government pursued import substitution in the face of competition from Austrian industry.

In neither half of the empire, however, did the government provide much direct assistance to industry. In Hungary, industrial policy began later because of its initial focus on infrastructure. Even so, only a small percentage of new factories were founded with state subsidies, and the total amount was only a small percentage of the total investment in joint-stock companies. In addition, much of it was directed to such industries as textiles that were simply not competitive, even with help. Indirect aid—tax holidays for a period of years, low interest loans, "buy-at-home" provisions for public contracts—were more significant.

At first glance, the Austrian government seems to have been less supportive of industry. After 1873, it taxed joint-stock (corporate form) companies more highly than other companies, and from the 1880s, its policies favored small-scale enterprise. Yet the government indirectly supported large-scale industrial firms by encouraging cartels and by pushing for higher industrial tariffs. In addition, even adjusting for Austria's larger industrial sector, the Austrian government spent more than the Hungarian government on direct promotion and industrial education.

The evidence suggests that neither the political foundations of economic policy nor direct policy measures explain the ability of Hungary to begin catching up with Austria. Instead, the consensus among historians is that fiscal discipline in both states and the "hard" currency policy of the Austro-Hungarian National Bank greatly improved the investment climate throughout the empire, which benefited Hungary more because of its lower income and greater capital scarcity.

Economy and Politics in Austria-Hungary. For no other European state in the pre–World War I era has the study of politics so dominated subsequent historiography than in the case of the Habsburg Monarchy. The reason lies in its ultimate fate in World War I and the Paris Peace Treaties. Like the German and Russian Empires, dynastic rule ended in the Habsburg lands; but unlike these two states, which emerged from the war and the Paris Peace Treaties with new political arrangements on territories that were merely reduced in size but still intact, Austria-Hungary collapsed in the war and was completely carved up by the treaties. Narratives of the Monarchy's fate tend to focus on the politics of its great power status in Europe and the growing conflict among its nationalities. Its economic history has not been central to the debates on these big political issues. Does Austria-Hungary's status as a great power and its character as a multinational state explain its economic performance? Does Austria-Hungary's economic performance explain its ultimate collapse and dismemberment as a political entity? Answers to these questions are fundamental to understanding the last half century of the Habsburg Monarchy but they remain speculative given the current state of knowledge.

Great power politics may explain both the Monarchy's modern economic growth and its propensity to fall behind other, faster-growing economies in the late nineteenth century. From the middle of the eighteenth century, elites both inside the Habsburg lands and abroad were very conscious of the Monarchy's role in central Europe as a "European necessity" in stabilizing international relations. In the tradition of mercantilism, promoting economic development became a means for preserving the Monarchy's great power status up to World War I. This was most obvious in the case of major external threats and/or internal crises that seemed to challenge the Monarchy's great-power status—the institutional changes under Maria Theresa (1717–1780) and Joseph II (1741–1790) after the defeat by Prussia, the reforms following the revolutions of 1848, and the Compromise of 1867 after a second major defeat by Prussia.

That the Monarchy grew but fell further behind in its last half-century may have been the result of a mismatch between its great power aspirations and its economic capacity to attain them. Fighting wars on a relatively small economic base seems to have crowded out productive investment and slowed growth between 1848 and 1867. But after 1867, the argument is less compelling. In Austria-Hungary as elsewhere, crude data show that military spending most likely decreased as a percentage of GDP because of the absence of major shooting wars prior to World War I.

The Monarchy's multinational character, too, may explain both its modern economic growth and its propensity to fall behind. National competition in the economic sphere may actually have been productivity raising. The demands by various national groups for education, for example, led to relatively high levels of literacy and enrollments in higher education compared with other European states, which may have fueled high rates of technological change, the key source of modern economic growth.

Consistent with its prominence in the historiography of the empire, the growing conflict among its nationalities may explain why Austria-Hungary lagged behind in the European growth league. The terms of the Compromise of 1867, for example, were not fixed but had to be renegotiated every ten years by the two parliaments sitting in Vienna and Budapest. The high levels of uncertainty about the "rules of the game" implicit in this requirement and the acrimonious debate that surrounded each renewal led to high levels of uncertainty about the future, which may have disrupted the functioning of markets and raised the cost of doing business. Within both partners to the Compromise, but especially in Austria, national passions ran high, which meant that elites seemed to engage more readily in rent-seeking behavior aimed at redistributing income than in efforts to raise productivity.

The link between politics and economics may have run in the other direction. Austria-Hungary's political collapse and dismemberment, for example, may have had roots in its uneven economic development. Regional income inequalities were, to a large extent, national inequalities because the empire's nationalities tended to live in clearly defined regional pockets. Less-well-off national groups tried to narrow these economic gaps by confronting those in power. According to the standard view, national conflicts paralyzed parliamentary government in both Austria and Hungary and inevitably eroded the long-term viability of the imperial structure. Others argue that in addition the Monarchy's limited economic power was insufficient to support its great power aspirations and survive intact under conditions of modern warfare.

Yet, the link between economics and politics is much more complicated. Recent scholarship sees these nationality conflicts as part of a broad process of modernization and a slow but persistent democratization of policymaking and administration in much of the empire. There is little evidence that the nationality conflicts in Austria-Hungary were actually any more intense and violent than the conflicts along regional, sectoral, and class lines that were typical of other modernizing societies in Europe. In multinational Austria-Hungary, these socioeconomic conflicts increasingly became contested in the rhetoric of nation, not of class, sector, or region. Also, the national rhetoric was actually quite moderate. Only nationalists on the radical end of the spectrum called for independent national states; the vast majority sought more autonomy within the empire and a bigger slice of the economic pie.

Although Austria-Hungary may have been doomed to disappear at some point, recent scholarship argues that in 1914 it was not on the verge of collapsing or even remotely close to a revolutionary situation. Some suggestive economic evidence supports this conclusion. The Austro-Hungarian currency (the crown) enjoyed high credibility under the de facto gold standard up to 1914 as it fluctuated within a narrow band above and below parity. The striking stability of the crown on the eve of World War I indicates that foreign exchange markets were not forecasting a collapse of the empire. Also, considering how ill-prepared the empire was for war in 1914, and the brutal and protracted nature of the war itself, the Austro-Hungarian economy performed remarkably well in sustaining the military and the imperial structure until very late in the conflict.

[*See also* Czechoslovakia and the Czech and Slovak Republics *and* Hungary.]

BIBLIOGRAPHY

Cohen, Gary B. "Neither Absolutism nor Anarchy: New Narratives on Society and Government in Late Imperial Austria." *Austrian History Yearbook* 29 (1998), 37–61.

Eddie, Scott. "Economic Policy and Economic Development in Austria-Hungary, 1867–1913." In *The Cambridge Economic History of Europe*, vol. 8, edited by Peter Mathias and Sidney Pollard, pp. 814–886. Cambridge and New York, 1989.

Gerschenkron, Alexander. *An Economic Spurt That Failed*. Princeton, 1977.

Good, David F. *The Economic Rise of the Habsburg Empire, 1750–1914*. Berkeley, Los Angeles, and London, 1984.

Good, David F., and Tongshu Ma. "The Economic Growth of Central and Eastern Europe in Comparative Perspective, 1870–1989." *European Review of Economic History* 3.2 (1999), 103–137.

Good, David F., and Tongshu Ma. "New Estimates of Income Levels in Central and Eastern Europe, 1870–1910." In *Von der Theorie zur Wirtschaftspolitik—ein Österreichischer Weg. Festschrift zum 65. Geburtstag von Erich Streissler*, edited by Franz Baltzarek, Felix Butschek, and Gunter Tichy, pp. 147–168. Stuttgart, 1998.

Gross, Nachum. "Industrialization in the Nineteenth Century." Unpublished Ph.D. thesis. University of California, Berkeley, 1966.

Huertas, Thomas. *Economic Growth and Economic Policy in a Multinational Setting*. New York, 1977.

Katus, László. "Economic Growth in Hungary during the Age of Dualism, 1867–1913: A Quantitative Analysis." In *Social and Economic Researches on the History of East-Central Europe*, edited by E. Pamlényi, pp. 35–127. Budapest, 1970.

Kausel, Anton. "Österreichs Volkseinkommen 1830 bis 1913." In *Geschichte und Ergebnisse der zentralen amtlichen Statistik in Österreich 1829–1979*, pp. 689–720. Vienna, 1979.

Komlos, John. *The Habsburg Monarchy as a Customs Union: Economic Development in Austria-Hungary in the Nineteenth Century*. Princeton, 1983.

Komlos, John. *Stature, Nutrition, and Economic Development in the Eighteenth-Century Habsburg Monarchy: The "Austrian" Model of the Industrial Revolution*. Princeton, 1989.

Kyriazidou, Ekaterini, and Martin Pesendorfer. "Viennese Chairs: A Case Study for Modern Industrialization." *Journal of Economic History* 59.1 (1999), 143–166.

März, Eduard. *Österreichische Industrie und Bankpolitik in der Zeit Franz Josephs I*. Vienna, 1968.

Matis, Herbert. *Österreichs Wirtschaft: Konjunkturelle Dynamik und gesellschaftlicher Wandel im Zeitalter Franz Josephs I.* Berlin, 1972.

Pammer, Michael. "Austrian Private Investments in Hungary, 1850–1913." *European Review of Economic History* 2.2 (1998), 141–169.

Rudolph, Richard. *Banking and Industrialization in Austria-Hungary.* Cambridge, 1976.

Schulze, Max-Stephan. *Engineering and Economic Growth: The Development of Austria-Hungary's Machine-Building Industry in the Late Nineteenth Century.* Frankfurt am Main, 1996.

Schulze, Max-Stephan. "Patterns of Growth and Stagnation in the Late Nineteenth Century Habsburg Economy." *European Review of Economic History* 4.3 (2000), 311–340.

DAVID F. GOOD

Modern Austria

The new frontiers of the 1918 peace treaties interrupted a century's development of Central Europe's interregional division of labor. The problem with which most of the new national states were confronted was that they had to build up functioning institutions in a new economic environment. In the 1920s most of the successor states pursued protectionist policies with high tariff barriers and neomercantilist policies aiming at economic autarky. Of all of the former Habsburg Empire's successor states, the newly founded Austrian republic suffered most from political dissolution and economic disintegration. The former political, economic, and cultural core of a European great power found itself reduced to a small country depending on foreign aid. From that experience derived the conviction that Austria ("the state that nobody wanted") would not be able to survive on its own and could only be integrated into a Danubian federation or into greater Germany. The economic challenge was to adapt to the reality of what was now a small state with a heterogeneous structure, which involved on the one hand scaling down surplus capacities and on the other carrying out an export initiative. With a stagnant population of 6.8 million and an area of 83,850 square kilometers, modern Austria had a very small agricultural base but was rich in forests, iron ore, and hydraulic energy. Almost all industrial capacity was concentrated in a small zone in the east, in an area including the oversized capital Vienna (with 2.1 million inhabitants, also the biggest consumer market) with its highly developed handicrafts and service industries and extending to the Vienna basin in Lower Austria and the heavy-industry districts in Upper Styria. In the west, only Vorarlberg with its textile industries provided an export-oriented industrial cluster. Compared to former Cisleithania and most of the other successor states, modern Austria's gross domestic product (GDP) was higher and its industrial structure much more developed. This is underlined by official data: Austria with 12.9 percent of the total population inherited 23.7 percent of the Habsburg monarchy's GDP.

MODERN AUSTRIA. Karl-Marx-Hof, the largest and most important apartment block built by the socio-democratic city administration of Vienna as low-rent workers' housing between 1926 and 1930. The block contains 1,325 apartments. (Karl-Marx-Hof, Vienna/Erich Lessing/Art Resource, NY)

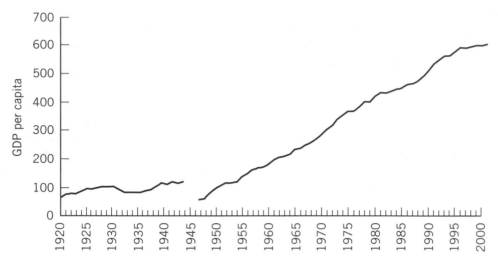

FIGURE 1. Austria's real GDP per capita (1918 = 100). SOURCE: Austrian Institute of Economic Research (WIFO).

In spite of favorable preconditions, Austria did not succeed in solving the problems of disintegration and adaptation. This failure was a consequence not only of political mismanagement but also of unfavorable global economic conditions. Although the Austrian government was able to stop postwar hyperinflation with the help of a League of Nations loan, it failed to initiate economic growth by its strict monetary regime, favorable only to the interests of foreign capital. Such policies, also forced by the League of Nations commissioner in Austria, contributed to growing social conflict and to political polarization. During the interwar period, Austrian real per capita GDP decreased by an annual average rate of 0.4 percent. For the years 1929–1937 alone, the rate of decrease was 1.8 percent. Industrial production in 1925 only reached 83 percent of the output of 1913. In 1929 it came very close to the prewar level (98 percent), but then fell again until the incorporation of Austria into the German Reich in 1938. Unemployment was already high during the twenties (around 9.5 percent of the labor force between 1925 and 1929), but reached a peak of 23.5 percent after the onset of the Great Depression. The fall of the Creditanstalt, the country's most important bank, marked the nadir of the economic crisis. Thus, the first Austrian Republic displayed a picture of economic decline and, consequently, political radicalism, demonstrated by such events as the forced dissolution of parliament in 1933, the establishment of the "Staendestaat" and the civil war in 1934, and finally the "Anschluss" to Germany in 1938. The German rearmament boom initiated a brief spurt in industrial production, and full employment was achieved. It had a lasting impact on Austria's industrial structure by encouraging the founding of power plants and new industries in the western part of the country. However, as a result of the war, Austria's real per capita GDP in 1946 only reached 58.4 percent of the 1913 level (see Figure 1).

Austria experienced better external conditions after World War II. The joint efforts of European countries in connection with the distribution of Marshall Plan aid not only helped Austria to participate in the ongoing Western integration process but also to develop a new national identity within this transnational context. Despite extensive war damage, the cost of ten years' presence of Allied troops and partition into zones of occupation until the state treaty of 1955, confiscation of industrial enterprises by the Soviets, and the country's exposed location next to the Iron Curtain, Austrian real GDP exceeded the prewar level by one-third as early as 1951. During the 1950s the economy grew faster than those of all other Organization for European Economic Cooperation (OEEC) countries, by an average of 7.7 percent per annum. No one now doubted the country's economic viability.

Although the pace of growth slowed after this first stage of economic reconstruction, expansion continued at a faster speed in Austria than in the rest of Europe. As a founding member of the European Free Trade Association (EFTA), Austria boasted a prosperous and stable market economy with a sizable but declining proportion of nationalized industry and with extensive welfare benefits. Thanks to its raw materials endowment, a technically skilled labor force, and export-oriented small- and medium-sized industries, it occupied niches in European industry and services (tourism). Austria had developed into one of the most dynamic modern economies before its accession to the European Union in 1995 and its participation in the Euro-zone. The ongoing integration of eastern European countries may provide further markets for Austrian exports and services.

Future problems include an aging population as well as an appreciable level of immigration from the Balkans, high labor costs, and the struggle to keep welfare benefits within the country's budgetary capabilities. It is questionable whether the recently adopted political system can master this challenge. The room for maneuver is tight: a "grand coalition" of Social Democrats and the conservative People's Party as well as a "social partnership" between trade unions and employers' associations guaranteed stable political conditions but did not provide the impetus for necessary reforms. Other coalitions that would include the far-right Freedom Party would not find international acceptance. Therefore, at the beginning of a new century Austria is confronted with unstable political conditions that could affect its economy.

BIBLIOGRAPHY

Butschek, Felix. *Die österreichische Wirtschaft im 20. Jahrhundert.* Stuttgart, 1985.

Komlos, John, ed. *Economic Development in the Habsburg Monarchy and in the Successor States: Essays.* East European Monographs 280. New York, 1990.

Teichova, Alice, and Philip C. Cotrell, eds. *International Business and Central Europe, 1918–1939.* New York, 1983.

Matis, Herbert, ed. "The Economic Development of Austria since 1870." In *The Economic Development of Modern Europe since 1870,* vol. 4, edited by Charles Feinstein. Aldershot, U.K., 1994.

Rothschild, Kurt W. *The Austrian Economy since 1945.* London and New York, 1950.

Steiner, Kurt, ed. *Modern Austria.* Palo Alto, Calif., 1981.

HERBERT MATIS

AUTOMOBILE AND TRUCK INDUSTRY *[This entry contains three subentries, a historical overview and discussions of technological change and industrial organization and regulation.]*

Historical Overview

This article offers a broad overview of the origins and development of the automobile and truck industry and of the importance of autos and trucks in economic history. The industry is interesting for a number of reasons. Among these are the emergence of large-scale (and indeed eventually global) firms from an industry initially characterized by something like free entry, the responses to the problems posed by manufacturing, organization, and sales on this scale, and the complications that came with commercial success. The article is divided into four principal sections, taking up first broad supply-side considerations, then organization *per se*, then demand, and finally the main consequences and complications of the industry's growth. Separate essays discuss technological change in the industry, its industrial organization and regulation, and certain of the figures mentioned below.

Supply Considered Broadly. An automobile is a transportation vehicle that carries its own source of motive power. Carriages and wagons were commonplace in nineteenth-century Europe and North America. The late nineteenth-century bicycle craze may have prepared the consuming public. It certainly whetted the imagination of some inventors, who experimented with steam engines and electric motors. But not until a series of inventive efforts culminated in the internal combustion engines of Carl Friedrich Benz and Gottlieb Wilhelm Daimler in the 1870s and 1880s did a truly suitable power source emerge.

Conditions of entry were relatively unconstrained. In Europe engines were easily procured, but the patents apparently did not extend to North America. An American named George Selden unsuccessfully attempted to obtain a patent in the United States on the very idea of an automobile powered by an internal combustion engine. On both continents early autos were manufactured by extant metalworking firms or were assembled from parts and components manufactured by extant firms. There was much to be improved upon in the earliest models, but the problems lay in fundamental elements of design rather than in manufacturability *per se*.

Manufacturing methods were a constraint upon intensive growth, however. Parts were not generally manufactured to high tolerances, and assembly therefore required the intervention of skilled mechanics. On the other hand, financial resources were not the constraint one might have imagined. Particularly in the United States, parts and even components were often purchased on trade credit. An enterprising manufacturer could sell the final product before the bills came due.

The development of demand was an urgent task. In the mid-1890s races with open entry were staged, and annual trade shows began not long thereafter. Also in the 1890s a trade press devoted entirely to the new category developed, complete with news of products and manufacturers, comparative statistical issues, and paid advertising.

Most of the production between 1890 and 1910 was marketed to professionals and well-to-do consumers. The vehicles were large and heavy, and the manufacturers were happy to customize to please. The real cost was high relative both to general income levels and to the prices that followed. At least one American firm, the Olds Motor Works, experimented with a light and inexpensive popular model as early as 1901, but when a fire destroyed the factory and the plans, the directors, thinking themselves conservative, dropped this initiative. It was a decision they must surely have come to regret.

An American mechanic and tinkerer named Henry Ford opened up the market. He built a prototype in 1896 and was chief engineer and an increasingly powerful shareholder in auto firms in the early 1900s. His early cars were in the old style, but he eventually conceived the idea of making a modest car (the Model T), suitable for the masses and the circumstances in which they lived. He wanted to make the car in immense numbers and at low unit cost. The design objectives required somewhat different materials (in particular vanadium steel alloy), dramatic standardization in product variety, and tremendous routinization in production methods and tasks. Skill requirements on the shop floor shrank, and fixed-cost dedicated capital increasingly replaced variable-cost labor. The most famous element of the latter was the moving assembly line, but equipment to produce parts to extremely high tolerances was at least equally important and far more expensive.

The more intensively Ford implemented his basic vision, the more unit costs went down. The decline was, in the event, sharp. The company dropped prices sharply too. At first the car sold for as much as $1,000; not long thereafter, it was "one day, one dollar; one year, one Ford." The demand curve indeed sloped downward, and orders and output levels exploded. Ford soon produced many more cars per year than his closest competitor and dominated the low end of the market. He owned 58.5 percent of the company by that point and was briefly thought, when the expansion was at flood tide, to be the wealthiest man on the planet.

What was originally the low-end market became most of the market overall. The Ford company's position was eventually displaced by the General Motors Corporation (GM), initially a conglomerate firm assembled by William C. Durant in the first two decades of the twentieth century and then rationalized and made successful by Alfred Sloan, a manager of genius. GM, unlike Ford, was a self-consciously multiproduct firm, and most of its innovations derived from this fact. It remains the largest American company in the industry. The third large firm in the American market was assembled in the 1920s by Walter Chrysler, a successful executive who specialized in fixing broken firms. Chrysler too was firmly established before the Great Depression and, unlike the small and medium-sized firms of that day, decisively survived it.

The automobile industry in Europe—primarily in France and to a lesser extent in Germany, Italy, and Great Britain—developed more slowly. In all cases there was sooner or later a shakeout. The earliest French companies, most notably Panhard et Levassor and Peugeot, entered the industry from closely related manufacturing businesses, as did Citroen after World War I. Renault, originally just an assembly firm, began with money from the family textile business. None of these was large by the scale of Ford. This was also true of the leading firms in Germany (Daimler, Benz, and Opel), Italy (FIAT), and the United Kingdom (Morris and Austin). Fragmentation of the European market probably played a large role in this outcome, as did the interruptions of World War I. In the 1920s, by which time some manufacturers had learned the lessons of wartime mass production, both Ford and GM had overseas plants and used them to further exploit economies of scale.

The origins of an indigenous industry in Japan were different. Both Ford and General Motors had branch assembly plants in place by the 1930s, when it became government policy to encourage a domestic industry. The Toyoda textile firm in Japan was interested but felt a need to develop a flexible manufacturing practice suited to short production runs. The full flowering of these efforts, led by the engineer Taiichi Ohno, was extremely good at high-quality production as well. Late in the twentieth century Toyota (as the company was known by then) cars made major inroads into the North American market, still the largest and richest in the world.

Design improvements, among them Rudolf Diesel's development of the diesel engine in 1896, made it feasible by about 1905 to produce motor vehicles strong and powerful enough principally to carry freight. Trucks were initially used in urban areas for pickup and delivery, mainly displacing horse-drawn carriages. As the quality of roadway infrastructure gradually improved, trucks began to be used over longer distances and began to compete with railroads. The engines and certain components were sufficiently different from those in passenger cars and the markets were sufficiently distinct that truck manufacturing was not necessarily parasitic on auto manufacturing. Many of the leading firms of the twentieth century were either specialist producers or functionally separate divisions of car firms.

There have been two major developments on the production side of the industry subsequent to World War II. The first is an ongoing shakeout in which the number of substantial firms has shrunk while the scope of their sales (and often manufacturing operations) has grown global. (Even the giant American firms have not been immune, as Chrysler is now effectively controlled from Stuttgart.) Economies of scale that would be familiar to earlier industry participants are an important component of this development, but another involves much greater costs of new product development (in part a consequence of the growing complexity of the product itself). The second change concerns the American marketplace, which was served for many years almost entirely by domestic firms. Starting in the 1950s Volkswagen, as part of its own globalization, made considerable inroads with a small and somewhat

AUTOMOBILES. Row of completed "Tin Lizzies" or Model T's come off the Ford assembly line in Detroit, circa 1917. (Prints and Photographs Division, Library of Congress)

odd-looking car that bore some resemblances, mutatis mutandis, to the Model T. The Americans responded with a new set of products, and the incursion was limited. The American firms did not do as well in the aftermath of the oil price increase of the early 1970s. The American offerings all had low miles per gallon because petroleum had theretofore been cheap by world standards. American consumers promptly discovered Japanese cars, designed for a clientele demanding light, fuel-efficient vehicles. The American consumers also discovered that Japanese manufacturing standards, especially those of Toyota, were much higher than the domestic ones and that the companies, again especially Toyota, were much better at delivering timely product variety. This was partly a matter of assembly practice, partly supply chain organization, and perhaps partly something more elusive in the company culture. It took decades for the American industry significantly to catch up, by which point Toyota was well established in the domestic marketplace. It seems unlikely the GM or Ford market share will ever again be what it was.

Organization. The changing skill requirements in production, as Ford-style mass production methods displaced the prior artisanal ones, posed problems for labor organization and motivation. The increasing coordination required in such high-volume manufacturing made assuring the cooperation of the workforce of great importance.

Ford was an early and prominent exponent of what came to be called welfare capitalism, teaching English and preparation for the citizenship exams to his immigrant workforce and more than doubling their maximal take-home pay to the then large sum of $5. Ford characterized the new compensation system to the public as a profit-sharing scheme, though it soon emerged as more scheme than profit sharing. Labor-management relations in the American industry became more adversarial, though formally unorganized, until the New Deal, when labor legislation and the legal environment facilitated industry-wide organization by the United Auto Workers. The principal developments subsequent to World War II involved patterned bargaining (that is, across manufacturers) of multi-year contracts with cost-of-living adjustments, annual improvement factors (as a counterpart to technical progress in manufacturing), and highly formalized grievance procedures. Employee representation in Europe was more fragmented across unions, Germany excepted, and more politicized, though relations have gradually become turbulent. Company unions are more common in Japan. The extent to which shop floor employees now make suggestions and contribute something other than their labor to the production process varies, with Toyota and Volvo standing in contrast to the Taylorist style of traditional mass production.

General Motors had a number of distinct product lines, and the lack of coordination among them posed major internal problems from the early 1920s. Sloan's product line policy—"a car for every purse and purpose"—brought order. The firm implemented what is now known as the multidivisional form of organization for internal governance and capital allocation and became in fact the most well-known exemplar. This organizational model eventually diffused worldwide, though recent scholarship suggests it was neither as effective nor even as stable at GM as had been generally understood.

Several different models of relations with upstream suppliers can be observed in cross section and in time series for the population (and even for some individual firms). The two basic models are one of arm's-length transactions, with the downstream firm focused on obtaining parts of given specifications at minimal cost, and one in which upstream firms undertake significant developmental work and profit from this at least in part through long-term relationships with their customers. The latter approach has at least officially been widely in favor since the rise of Toyota.

GM's problems with the multidivisional form can be understood as deriving from the entrenched interests within the firm. The industry is large enough that the firms, their employees, their suppliers, and their dealers can themselves represent an entrenched interest in matters of trade and environmental policy within nation-states. The peculiar form taken by America's commercial policy vis-à-vis Japan, apparently little understood by consumers, is an excellent example.

Demand. The automobile emerged after the heyday of the second Industrial Revolution, but the industry has a number of the classic features. From early on, two striking features downstream of manufacturing have been the extent of investment in advertising and the intricate relationships with dealers. In the earliest years of the industry almost all firms made some sales direct from the factory, but independent dealers were valued, first, for their marketing and sales efforts and, second—often at least as important—for their willingness to finance inventory. A common quid pro quo was exclusive dealing rights within a geographical territory. This created the difficulty known to economists as the problem of successive monopoly, in which the dealers maximized profits by selling less in their territory than the manufacturer would prefer. The mutual dependence and struggle in the American industry went through many forms and epochs, the latter punctuated by federal investigations (elicited by the dealers), legislation (the "Automobile Dealers' Day in Court Act"), and efforts to restructure dealer ownership patterns. The Internet has only complicated matters, and the situation continues to evolve.

It seems that initially firms manufactured products of particular specifications and lived or died passively by whether or not those products found market acceptance. From the 1920s, however, after GM encouraged the R. L. Polk Company's research into the local patterns of registration (as a window onto what was actually selling to consumers), systematic consumer research increased. More active research into consumer tastes and investment in design followed and continues actively.

This consumer research impulse was lent salience by the increasing saturation of the market for new cars and the development, often at the hands of the new car dealers, of a market in used cars. Manufacturers responded in part by investing more in (highly touted) annual model changes and thus in planned obsolescence. Particularly during the scores of years between the advent of the automatic transmission in the 1930s and the infusion of electronics into the control systems of vehicles, the innovations were in fact modest and the impulse was seen, at least by outside observers, as wasteful and exploitative from the social perspective.

Consequences and Complications. An industry that scarcely existed in 1895 was by forty years later producing output for a mass market in all the major industrialized countries of the world. The growth induced demand for high-quality roadways and related facilities. As highway systems improved, the location of manufacturing activity in the broader economy was little constrained by the location of railway lines and ports. Similarly, patterns of residence over the course of the century and the sprawl of suburbs into once pristine countryside have been vastly facilitated by private automobile ownership. Retail follows residence. The development and diffusion of the automobile has exercised a tremendous influence on the spatial development of twentieth-century life.

All this incremental driving has had its costs. Indirectly highway construction firms have systematically insinuated lobbyists into public spending decision making, most notoriously in Japan. But the most direct costs concern gasoline, the fuel that in retrospect seems to have made it all possible. Decades after the rise of environmentalism as a political movement, automotive exhaust is still a major and burdensome source of atmospheric pollution, and there seems to be no political will to tax the externality efficiently. And the apparently insatiable—indeed still growing—demand for fuel gives countries that control the supplies of the crude petroleum from which it is refined tremendous economic and political influence.

BIBLIOGRAPHY

Bardou, Jean-Pierre, Jean-Jacques Chanaron, Patrick Fridenson, and James M. Laux. *The Automobile Revolution: The Impact of an Industry*. Chapel Hill, N.C., 1982.

Chandler, Alfred D., Jr. *The Visible Hand: The Managerial Revolution.* Cambridge, 1977.

Clark, Kim B., and Takahiro Fujimoto. *Product Development Performance: Strategy, Organization, and Management in the World Auto Industry.* Boston, 1991.

Fine, Sidney. *Sit-Down: The General Motors Strike of 1936–1937*. Ann Arbor, 1973.

Freeland, Robert F. *The Struggle for Control of the Modern Corporation: Organizational Change at General Motors, 1924–1970.* New York, 2000.

Fridensohn, Patrick. "The Coming of the Assembly Line to Europe." in *The Dynamics of Science and Technology: Social Values, Technical Norms, and Scientific Criteria in the Development of Knowledge*, edited by Wolfgang Krohn, Edwin T. Layton, Jr., and Peter Weingart, pp. 159–173. Dordrecht, Netherlands, 1978.

Fujimoto, Takahiro. *The Evolution of a Manufacturing System at Toyota*. New York, 1999.

Laux, James M. *The European Automobile Industry*. New York, 1991.

Nevins, Allan. *Ford: The Times, the Man, the Company*. New York, 1954.

Raff, Daniel M. G., and Manuel Trajtenberg. "Quality-Adjusted Prices for the American Automobile Industry, 1906–1940." in *The Economics of New Goods*, edited by Timothy F. Bresnahan and Robert J. Gordon, pp. 71–101. Chicago, 1996.

Report on the Motor Vehicle Industry. U.S. Federal Trade Commission. Washington, D.C., 1939.

Womack, James T., Daniel T. Jones, and Daniel Roos. *The Machine That Changed the World*. New York, 1990.

DANIEL RAFF

Technological Change

According to David Landes (1969, p. 443), no other mid-twentieth-century product has yielded so rich a harvest of forward and backward linkages as the automobile. The car played a role analogous to that of the railroad in the mid-nineteenth century. It was a huge user of intermediate products, had an insatiable appetite for petroleum products, required an army of mechanics and servicemen, gave powerful impetus to investments in the social infrastructure, and posed new technical problems in metallurgy, organic chemicals, and electrical engineering.

Internal combustion, steam, and electric vehicles at the end of the nineteenth century all came from a merger of technologies and components developed and produced for other uses: carriage bodies, wheels, steering, motive power, and so on. The modern car continues to draw on technologies from outside the industry: global positioning system (GPS) terminals, radio and compact-disc players, computers, and air conditioning. Not only did the automobile borrow technologies, but it also fostered their development; for example, the first generations of mobile telephones had heavy electrical demands, conveniently supplied by the car battery, and were too big to carry comfortably, so for many decades the mobile telephone was a car phone.

Early Influences and Innovations. The driving forces behind the development of the motor car are numerous. Flink (1976) points out that the car offered mobility to the individual while demanding small initial investments from society. From the beginning of the industry, public interest was supported by exhibitions, races, and reliability tests. Speed was and continues to be an important feature, despite the fact that most cars can easily surpass maximum legislated speeds. Initially safety was not a major preoccupation, but it has grown in importance. However, safety is not the primary sales argument for the car manufacturers; in recent years the increased sales of vans and 4 × 4s have resulted in many deadly accidents.

In 1860–1890, many inventors tried to substitute a motor for the horse, and "no one could claim to have invented the automobile" (Flink, 1976, p. 10). The most important German inventors, Gottlieb Daimler and Karl Benz, developed their vehicles in the 1880s independently although they were living only sixty miles apart. The cars they developed in 1885 and 1886 both had single-cylinder internal combustion engines.

Daimler's car had an improved Otto four-stroke (induction-compression-ignition-exhaust) engine. The original 1876 Otto design used coal gas, but Daimler and his assistant Maybach adapted the motor to gasoline and significantly increased the number of revolutions per minute (rpm). The Otto gas engine had a maximum of 180 rpm; the Daimler operated up to 900 rpm and gave 1.1 horsepower (hp) at 650 rpm. The first Benz car used a two-stroke engine: induction and compression, ignition and exhaust. In 1888–1889, Daimler produced an engine with two cylinders in a V-shape, which proved to be an extremely malleable design. Cylinders could be added to form bigger and bigger engines: in 1898, Maybach designed a four-cylinder engine that gave 28 hp. In 1903, the British firm Napier produced the first six-cylinder car. Cylinders could be added, and important components such as the carburetor and the ignition could be developed with no change in the basic engine design. Many early improvements later became standard; for example, Bugatti's "Type 13" in 1910 had four overhead valves per cylinder driven by an overhead camshaft.

From the start, the ignition was of a battery type, though early batteries were very sensitive and often malfunctioned. Consequently, many inventors tried to develop new ignition systems. The most successful of them was Robert Bosch, who developed a low-tension magnetic ignition at the end of the nineteenth century. This device had the disadvantage that it was very difficult to produce a spark powerful enough to start a car with a big engine; so a double system, using both low-tension magnetic and battery ignition, was constructed. This system made it easier to start the car but was much more complicated than the earlier systems. In 1904, Bosch found a solution with a high-tension magnetic ignition; and this system was the standard for a decade until Charles Kettering invented the starting-lighting-ignition, the first system with an electric self-starter. The arrival of the SLI in gasoline cars in 1912 eliminated the need for a crank start, one of the most undesirable features of the gasoline-powered car. This innovation removed one of the perceived advantages of the electric vehicle, namely, that they were so easy to start that anyone could drive them.

An important step in the development of the motor car occurred when the French firm of Panhard et Levassor acquired a concession to manufacture and sell Daimler engines in France. Panhard et Levassor changed the design of the car radically in 1891, placing the engine vertically in front of the chassis, which put the crankshaft parallel with the axles. He built a friction clutch into the flywheel and followed it with a sliding-pinion gearbox, and a final drive to the rear wheels. This configuration not only allowed for larger engines and better weight distribution but also marked a radical aesthetic departure from the carriage silhouette. These changes were all adapted from other cars and practices in other industries, and, according to Rolt (1964, p. 23), the "famous *système Panhard*, as it was called, did not exhibit a single original feature."

Influences for the car design came from the bicycle industry, for example, Henry Ford's Quadricycle (1896), or the carriage-maker industry, for example, Daimler's first car (1886). These early automobiles had a disjointed look, owing to the assembly of components purchased from different companies—carriage makers, machine shops, wheel manufacturers, and so on.

Integrated Design. Integration of production and design has been crucial for the technical evolution of the car. Sloan (1964, p. 220) writes that the car in the 1920s usually "got somewhere and back; fortunately it was unable to go fast or far enough for many of its deficiencies to become serious drawbacks. It was roughly adapted to its environment—and its major parts were reasonably adapted to each other, at however low a level of integration and efficiency. The problem of the development of the automobile was to raise its level of efficiency, and this often meant raising the level of its integration."

The mass production of the Ford model T resulted in an integrated production process for cars, but the design continued to be fragmented. By 1912, most mass producers had transformed the car body from a hand-shaped wooden frame with aluminum body panels to a wooden frame with machine-pressed steel panels. In the following years, the composite steel-over-wood body was replaced by a lighter, stronger, and cheaper all-steel body.

Integrated designs appeared after World War I with the European "vintage" luxury cars that combined high performance with complete reliability. The Hispano-Suiza from 1919 included many technical improvements: a six-cylinder engine derived from an aero engine, a low chassis upswept over the rear axle, and four wheel brakes activated by a servomechanism.

A few years later, mass-produced American cars followed this movement toward integration. In 1927, Harvey Earl designed the La Salle car for General Motors, which is regarded as the first mass-produced integrated design. The next important step was production of the streamlined Chrysler Airflow. To attain a tapered aerodynamic tail, the engine was moved up over the front axle, allowing the rear seat to be moved forward from the top of the rear axle (Gartman, 1994, p. 121).

Fuel and Equipment Innovations. The oil industry was growing rapidly from the mid-nineteenth century on, in part because of demand for kerosene in paraffin lamps and for gasoline as fuel in steam engines. At this point, because of its negligible commercial value and the danger from its extreme volatility and low flash point, gasoline was simply a waste product of the huge (24 million barrels a day in the United States) kerosene industry. Its distribution for use in early motor cars was simple: the waste product was packaged in cans and sold in stores. In the 1920s, research at General Motors under Kettering showed that adding tetraethyl lead to gasoline solved the problem of engine knock and made it possible to increase the engine's compression. Leaded fuel was the norm until the 1980s, when it began to be phased out for environmental reasons.

The first pneumatic tires appeared and were patented in 1845. They consisted of an inner tube of vulcanized rubber and an outer cover of leather. In the patent application, they were designated to be used on steam carriages. At this time, however, there were no steam carriages on the British roads, and the tires were to be used on horse-drawn broughams although they did not go into production. At the same time solid rubber tires were developed, but these tires also had no commercial success. (Nicholson, 1982, p. 241f).

Thin solid rubber tires were put on the Benz car in 1885; Daimler used iron tires. Dunlop reinvented the pneumatic tire in 1888, expecting to use them on bicycles. He did not believe they would be practicable on heavier vehicles. The tire initiative passed to France and the Michelin Brothers firm, which tested pneumatic tires on three different cars. The brothers competed with a Peugeot in the 1895 Paris-Bordeaux-Paris race, but gave up after fitting twenty-two new tubes and mending innumerable punctures. The trial showed that pneumatic tires were better than solid ones, but only if they were holding air. During the next nine months the Michelin firm developed the tires, and in the competitions in 1896 more than 50 percent of the cars had pneumatic tires. With pneumatic tires the ride became smoother, and an important effect was that car construction could be less solid, and, in particular, the engine could be lighter than earlier ones.

In 1895 before the arrival of the pneumatic tires, the normal internal combustion engine weighted 250 kilograms per horsepower. This figure dropped to 166 in 1896, to 120 in 1897–1898, and to 40 in 1900. However, it would take many decades to solve problems with tire punctures. A first solution was to carry many spares. The next idea was to use either a system of detachable rims or fully detachable wheels. Pneumatic tires on trucks were developed during World War I because of a dramatic increase in freight transport demand. When the trucks were driven at high speeds (60–70 kilometres per hour) for long distances, the use of solid tires resulted in many breakdowns. The solution was to develop a giant balloon tire for the trucks. This innovation was later introduced on buses, radically increasing their comfort.

Steering, in the form of a tiller, was adapted from the horse and steam carriages. On the first models the whole front part of the car turned, as on a stage coach; but this design was changed early on to a system with front wheels that turned in parallel but independently of the body. The greatest disadvantage with the tiller was that a driver needed to hold on to it firmly at all times; otherwise, he could lose control of the car if there was a hole or a bump in the road. The tiller was gradually replaced by the steering wheel between 1895 and 1905.

A legal battle over patents led to information sharing. George B. Selden, a patent attorney and neophyte inventor, applied for a patent for a car using a two-stroke Brayton engine in 1879, later selling the patent to the Electric

AUTOMOBILE PLANT. Assembly line at the Ford automobile plant in Mexico City. (© Stephanie Hall/Woodfin Camp and Associates, New York)

Vehicle Company. In 1903, a trade association (ALAM) was formed under the Selden patent to control the automobile market, and it kept many important producers, including Henry Ford, outside the organization. In 1911, a court found that Ford had not infringed the Selden patent because he (and nearly all other gasoline car manufacturers) had used the Otto four-stroke engine whereas the Selden patent mentioned the two-cycle Brayton engine. Thereafter, a new trade organization (NACC) instituted a cross-licensing agreement between its members that made it possible for the automobile firms to use other firms' patents. For several decades this patent sharing provided an important collective source of technological information.

Safety aspects became more important in the 1960s. The first safety belts were lap belts, which had been promoted by different U.S. organizations for a number of years. Vol-

vo was the first firm to market cross-chest diagonal belts in 1956, and in 1959 Volvo introduced the first three-point belt as standard in Sweden. Airbags became an important safety device in the 1990s although the first airbag had appeared in a Mercedes Benz in 1981.

Throughout the twentieth century automobile technology continued to improve incrementally. The automatic gearbox was invented by József László Bíró in 1910; power steering appeared in 1926 on the Pierce-Arrow; individual front-wheel suspension was launched by General Motors in 1933; front wheel drive appeared on the American Cord in 1929 and was mass-produced by Citroën in 1933; catalytic cleaning of the exhaust introduced by General Motors in 1974; fuel injection appeared in 1954 on the Mercedes 300SL—to name a few examples.

Early Alternative Technologies: Electric and Diesel. The diesel engine was invented in the first half of the 1890s, but for 40 years was unsuitable for cars because of its much higher compression ratio (15–25 to 1 compared with the gasoline engine's 8–9 to 1). The higher compression required a much heavier and more expensive engine that proved difficult to fit into the body of a car. Diesel engines did not become viable for the car industry until Bosch invented the fuel-injection pumps in 1927. The first diesel engine car, the Mercedes-Benz 260 D, was produced in 1936 and sold roughly 2,000 units before World War II. By the 1990s, cleaner more efficient diesel engines had been developed and cars equipped with these engines began to have significant market penetration.

Electric cars appeared before the gasoline car in the 1830s and 1840s. These cars used nonrechargeable electric cells and had little impact on the development of the car. The invention of better storage batteries by the Frenchmen Gaston Planté in 1865 and Camille Faure in 1881 created an opportunity for commercial electric vehicles. Electric cars and steam cars dominated the U.S. market at the nineteenth century: for example, 1,575 electric cars were sold in 1899. Electric cars were popular among wealthy female drivers because they were easy to start.

Another important market was the 200 vehicles ordered by the Electric Vehicle Company to be used as taxis. The market for electric cars doubled in the first decade of the twentieth century, but the sales of cars with internal combustion increased more than 120 times in the same period. Despite intermittent attempts to develop the technology over the course of the century, (particularly in the 1980s and 1990s in response to emission regulations) the electric vehicle continues to have only a marginal place in the car market.

The automobile has shown continuous technological change, adopting technologies from outside the industry and developing its own. Through a long history of incremental improvements, it has changed from a dangerous, expensive, unreliable toy for the rich to a machine that became a key part of the world's transportation system.

BIBLIOGRAPHY

Automobile Manufacturers Association Inc. *Automobiles of America*. Detroit, 1962.

Flink, J. J. *The Car Culture*. Cambridge, Mass., 1976.

Gartman, David. *Auto Opium*. London, 1994.

Landes, David S. *The Unbound Prometheus*. Cambridge, 1969.

Nerén, John. *Automobilens historia*. Stockholm, 1937.

Nicholson, T. R. *Revival and Defeat of the Birth of the British Motor Car 1769–1897*, vol. 2. London, 1982.

Nitske, W. Robert. *The Complete Mercedes Story*. Rev. ed. New York, 1956.

Rolt, L. T. C. *Motoring History*. London, 1964.

Sloan, Alfred P., Jr. *My Years with General Motors*, edited by John McDonald and Catherine Stevens. New York, 1964.

ROBIN COWAN AND STAFFAN HULTÉN

Industrial Organization and Regulation

The automobile and truck industry has undergone three distinct phases in its evolution from a small-scale handicraft industry to mass production for a global market. The first was a period of experimentation and consolidation and lasted until about 1907. Entry into the industry was relatively easy, vehicles were produced by skilled labor in small numbers, and no firm dominated the market. The second phase was a period of American dominance that began in 1908, the year Ford began producing the Model T in Detroit, and lasted until the mid-1960s. Within five years of introducing the Model T, Ford was producing five times as many cars than the next-largest American company and more than forty times as many cars than the largest non-American producer. For much of the period, the industry operated unconstrained by government regulations regarding safety, environmental standards, or fuel efficiency. The third phase, beginning in the mid-1960s, saw the emergence of a global industry and the erosion of American dominance. In the 1970s, the Japanese became major players in the supply of vehicles. American dominance was further eroded in the 1990s with the emergence of new "global" firms operating in the major regional markets. Chrysler merged with the larger German firm Daimler, while Ford entered into alliances with Volvo, Jaguar, and Mazda. The growing popularity of automobiles since the mid-1960s has led to new concerns regarding their safety, their impact on the environment, and their use of oil.

Before 1907: Experimentation and Consolidation. European pioneers, such as Daimler in Germany and Peugeot in France, began making cars in the 1880s. Hundreds of firms tried their hand at vehicle production before 1907; few made more than a couple of vehicles. Some, such as Morris, entered the industry with a background in bicycles. Others, such as Studebaker, had a background in wagons. Still others, such as Ford, were self-taught and had no manufacturing background. After more than a decade of experimentation, Benz, the leading German producer, had an annual output of 135 vehicles in 1895; while Peugeot, the leading French producer, was assembling seventy-two vehicles per year. Beginning around 1890, the center of production gradually shifted from Europe to the United States; but in 1900, vehicle production was still evenly split between the United States and Europe.

Vehicle ownership was limited to a wealthy elite. In 1907, total vehicle ownership was probably less than three hundred thousand, equally split between the United States and Europe. In Great Britain and the United States, there was approximately one vehicle per 600 inhabitants. Most producers aimed to serve this elite market; and such firms as Rolls Royce and Daimler in Britain, and Cadillac in the United States made names for themselves in the process. They used skilled labor to produce stylish and handcrafted vehicles. Mass production and standardization were still in the future. The industry was largely unregulated, although in Great Britain, concern that these new machines would terrorize the population led to the temporary enforcement of the Red Flag Law, which limited the speed of vehicles to two miles per hour in urban areas and four in the countryside, a limit raised in 1896 to fourteen miles an hour.

1907–1965: A Period of American Dominance. Even before the outbreak of World War I, there were signs of the future structure of the industry. By 1914, total vehicle ownership had increased to nearly 2 million with twice as many vehicles registered in the United States compared with Europe. There was one vehicle for every 77 inhabitants in the United States. An important milestone was reached in 1912, when the price of a Ford Model T fell below the average annual U.S. wage. Twenty years later, vehicle ownership was widespread in the United States, with one vehicle for every 5.3 inhabitants, far surpassing European ownership levels. The spread of vehicle ownership was associated with important changes in market structures. Successful firms shifted to the mass production of standardized products. It was also associated with important cultural shifts as vehicle ownership became synonymous with American culture.

The rapidity with which U.S. firms came to dominate the automobile and truck industry is stunning. Ford, the most successful of the new American firms, controlled less than 10 percent of the U.S. market prior to 1910. By 1913, the company was producing almost half the vehicles in the world, and U.S. producers accounted for more than 90 percent of world production. In 1913, Peugeot, the largest non-American firm, produced just over 2 percent of Ford's annual output. As late as 1950, the United States still produced more than 90 percent of the world's vehicles. Its dominance began to erode after this as European production increased, capturing 25 percent of world output in the mid-1960s.

The success of American producers was based on their enthusiastic support of mass production based on long production runs, standardization, interchangeable production, and the employment of less-skilled workers. In 1913, the ten largest British firms together produced a total of 15,800 vehicles. In the United States, six firms each produced more vehicles than this in 1913. The new system of mass production created new barriers to entry into the industry. Minimum efficient scales of operation increased, and only firms able to sell enough vehicles to exploit these economies of scale survived. Firms began producing a smaller range of vehicles and targeted middle-class consumers. The automobile became the mark of success for young American males. The need for mass markets and mass production techniques led to a wave of mergers and rationalization. General Motors and Chrysler were created in this way. Of the 239 firms that tried to make cars in Detroit between 1890 and 1933, only seven survived in 1933.

By 1939, the U.S. market was dominated by three companies, General Motors, Ford, and Chrysler. For a few years, a number of independents, (Nash, Packard, Studebaker, Hudson) remained in business, each selling fewer than 100,000 vehicles in 1955. The ending of Studebaker production in South Bend, Indiana, in 1963 marks the end of any real challenge to the "Big Three" dominance. The last Studebaker rolled off the lines in South Bend in December of 1963. Production continued for a few more years from the company's Canadian plant in Hamilton, Ontario, but production there ended in 1966.

The growth in plant size and the spread of mass production methods brought with it new labor relations problems. Following the introduction of the moving assembly line in 1913, Ford faced both high levels of labor turnover and the threat of unionization. The famous Five Dollar Day, implemented in January of 1914, doubled real wages overnight and stabilized relations until the mid-1930s. However, competition between producers and the collapse of the vehicle market in the 1930s led to new cost-cutting measures. These contributed to growing labor unrest and a renewed interest in unionization as the industry emerged from the Great Depression. Concerned about the lack of purchasing power in the U.S. economy and growing labor militancy, the U.S. government passed the Wagner Act in 1935 and created the legal framework for collective bargaining in mass-production industries. By the early 1940s, the United Automobile Workers union (UAW) had successfully organized the "Big Three" plants in both Canada and the United States. When it became clear after World War II that unions were a permanent fixture, General Motors moved to strike a bargain with union president Walter Reuther and the UAW. The 1948 agreement, often referred to as the Treaty of Detroit, resulted in Reuther and the UAW backing off from their demand for a greater labor say in how vehicles were produced. In return, General Motors agreed to a formula that protected wages from inflation (the COLA clause) and gave workers a share of any increases in productivity through an Annual Improvement Factor. This compromise created stability in the industry and made possible massive investments in automation beginning in the early 1950s. It also gave workers the purchasing power to buy the vehicles they were making.

Until the mid-1950s, there was almost unquestioning support in Europe and the United States for the industry and for public investment in roads. However, by the mid-1950s, the growing concern regarding the social and environmental impact of automobiles led to new and more restrictive regulations. In 1956 there were more than thirty thousand traffic fatalities on American roads, leading to demands for safer cars and highways. Led by consumer advocate Ralph Nader, a campaign was launched to force vehicle producers to pay more attention to safety. The state responded with a series of regulations in the 1960s, intended to force reluctant manufacturers to improve safety standards. In 1963, the passage of the Clean Air Act marked the beginnings of state attempts to regulate the industry's environmental impact. In the 1970s, the focus turned to fuel efficiency, and again the U.S. government turned to regulations, forcing new fuel standards on the industry with the passage of the Energy Policy and Conservation Act in 1975. These regulations influenced industry structure. The cost of finding engineering solutions to the mandated regulations, particularly those dealing with pollution and fuel efficiency, have raised the minimum efficient scale of operation. Chrysler, the smallest of the Big Three in the United States, found these demands challenging, which may partially explain its weakness in the 1970s and eventual merger with Daimler. Similar forces were at work in Europe, resulting in the virtual disappearance of a British-owned manufacturing capability and the merger of a number of independent firms on continental Europe.

After 1965: A Global Industry. The continuing evolution of the industry's structure was shaped by the globalization of vehicle consumption and production. Total global ownership of vehicles remained below 50 million until after World War II, when it began a steep assent, reaching 420 million by 1980. By 1979, there was more than one vehicle for every two Americans, around one vehicle for every three people living in France and Germany, and one for every four people in Great Britain. Global vehicle production remained below 5 million per year for much of the pre-1945 period, after which it began rising dramatically, reaching nearly 45 million in 1980. This rise in vehicle ownership and production raised new environmental concerns. By 1980, the world's vehicle fleet was consuming more than 5 billion barrels of oil per year.

Beginning in the 1960s, the industry moved from national to regional markets. In Europe, rationalization was driven by the European Common Market. In North America, regionalization was based first on the passage of the Autopact in 1965, which created a single market for cars and trucks in Canada and the United States. Mexico joined the club in 1992 with the signing of the North American Free Trade Agreement. U.S.-based production peaked at just under 13 million units in the early 1970s. Thirty years later, U.S.-based production was virtually unchanged. Over that same period, vehicle production in Canada more than doubled to 3 million units, and Mexican production increased sixfold to nearly 2 million units. Combined, Canada and Mexico represented just 5.3 percent of total North American production in 1960, growing to 27.6 percent in 2000 as both regions moved from net importers of finished vehicles to net exporters. Over the same period, the United States became a net importer, producing three vehicles for every four consumed domestically.

The industry also shifted to a more global structure reflected in the growth of imports into both North America and Europe. As late as 1955, imports into the U.S. market accounted for less than 1 percent of domestic sales. There was a surge after 1965, largely the result of growing imports from Canada following the U.S.–Canada Autopact. However, a more important trend was the growing share of the market being captured by Japanese imports into the United States. From virtually nothing in the mid-1960s, Japanese imports grew to just over 10 percent of the U.S. market in 1976 and over 20 percent by 1980. Another major change in the industry was the shift toward truck production. In 1960, more than 80 percent of the vehicles produced in the United States and Canada were passenger cars. The popularity of minivans and light trucks changed the product mix, so that by the year 2000, less than 45 percent of production represented passenger cars.

The growing importance of non–Big Three firms as suppliers of vehicles was naturally accompanied by a shift in the geography of vehicle production, with Japan becoming a key source of product. Production in Japan was minuscule prior to World War I, and as late as 1955 total Japanese production was less than 70,000 vehicles. Within twenty-five years, Japanese production would top 10 million units and represent 25 percent of world output. Other nontraditional areas, such as Korea, Brazil, and Mexico, accounted for around 20 percent of global output in 1980. Following a path first exploited by American producers after 1919, Asian producers moved aggressively to produce vehicles in North America and Europe. By 2000, Asian firms with plants in North America assembled nearly 20 percent of the cars and trucks produced in the region.

BIBLIOGRAPHY

Alshuler, Alan, et al. *The Future of the Automobile: Report of MIT's International Automobile Program.* Cambridge, 1984.

Bardou, Jean-Pierre, et al. *The Automobile Revolution: The Impact of an Industry.* Chapel Hill, N.C., 1982.

Cusumano, Michael. *The Japanese Automobile Industry: Technology & Management at Nissan & Toyota.* Cambridge, 1985.

Davis, Donald Finlay. *Conspicuous Production: Automobiles and Elites in Detroit, 1899–1933.* Philadelphia, 1988.

Foreman-Peck, J., Sue Bowden, and Alan McKinlay. *The British Motor Industry.* Manchester, 1995.

Gartman, David. *Auto Opium: A Social History of American Automobile Design.* London, 1994.

Lewchuk, Wayne. *American Technology and the British Vehicle Industry.* Cambridge, 1987.

Ling, Peter J. *America and the Automobile: Technology, Reform and Social Change.* Manchester, 1990.

Meyer, Stephen, III. *The Five Dollar Day: Labor Management and Social Control in the Ford Motor Company, 1908–1921.* Albany, N.Y., 1981.

Nevins, Allan. *Ford: The Times, The Man, The Company.* New York, 1954.

Rae, John B. *The American Automobile: A Brief History.* Chicago, 1965.

Wayne Lewchuk

B

BABBAGE, CHARLES (1792–1871), English mathematician, inventor and economist.

Charles Babbage was born in Devonshire, the son of a banker. He showed an early aptitude for mathematics and produced important work in algebra and the theory of functions.

In the early 1820s, Babbage embarked on the project that was to provide his claim to fame as an inventor: the design and construction of a mechanical "calculating engine" that could routinize simple mathematical operations. One of Babbage's motivations for the project lies in his insight that progress in both science and industry would soon be constrained by the speed and cost of performing calculations, and he believed his engine would have wide applicability. His first effort, the "difference engine," calculated mathematical tables and set them directly into type. In 1832, Babbage turned his attention to an even more ambitious project, the "analytical engine." This was a programmable mechanical calculator that pioneered principles on which the modern electronic computer is based: punched-card programming (a concept borrowed from the Jacquard loom), a memory device in which numerical variables could be recorded on banks of counters, and a separate processor in which mathematical operations could be performed on numbers taken from the memory. Despite years of effort, neither of these machines was constructed successfully during Babbage's lifetime.

The problems he faced in constructing these machines led directly to Babbage's interest in the general state of manufacturing in Great Britain. He set up his own machine shop and visited workshops throughout Great Britain and continental Europe. These experiences formed the basis for Babbage's principal contribution to economics, his book On the Economy of Machinery and Manufactures (1832). In addition to including useful descriptions of manufacturing technologies used in Industrial Revolution–era Great Britain, Babbage outlined a more general analysis of the division of labor. This theory, which explicitly inspired his work on calculating engines, was also offered as an organizing principle for factories. When the division of labor is limited, he argues, each worker has to perform a number of tasks that involve a variety of physical and mental skills. Since the worker must have enough skill to perform the most complex task (and be compensated accordingly), unbundling the tasks by increasing the division of labor allows the employer to reduce costs by paying, for each separate task, only the wage associated with the lower-skill levels.

Babbage's *Economy* also contributed what is probably the first theory of increasing returns to scale in economics, based on the production indivisibilities inherent in his notion of the division of labor. Babbage explored additional sources of economic advantage for large firms as well, including the greater ability to bear fixed costs and the risks of innovation. Both John Stuart Mill and Karl Marx relied openly on Babbage's analysis of the economies of large-scale production.

Babbage also includes a groundbreaking analysis of the economics of technological change, again based on the division of labor, this time applied to the fields of science and engineering. Babbage also outlined how basic economic variables, such as expected demand growth, relative factor prices, and the potential for production cost reductions should shape the direction of innovation. Unlike many of his contemporaries, Babbage was quite optimistic about the potential for scientific and technological progress to increase industrial productivity and living standards, rejecting the notion of economics as a "dismal science."

BIBLIOGRAPHY

Babbage, Charles. *On the Economy of Machinery and Manufactures*. 4th ed. New York, 1963.

Hyman, Anthony. *Charles Babbage: Pioneer of the Computer*. Princeton, 1982.

Rosenberg, Nathan. *Exploring the Black Box: Technology, Economics, and History*. Cambridge, 1994.

THOMAS GERAGHTY

BABY BOOM. From the late 1940s and into the 1960s, following the Great Depression (1929–1941) and World War II (1939–1945), a marked upsurge in fertility rates occurred in the leading industrialized countries, from levels of about two or less children per woman, on average, to about three of more. Commonly termed "the baby boom," the increase was partly due to a rise in marriage rates, but even more to a higher rate of childbearing within marriage. The post–World War II peak in childbearing occurred from 1955 to 1965—earlier in that decade for the United States, Canada, Australia, and New Zealand, and later for most of the countries of western, northern, and central Europe. By 1930, all these countries were already far along in the demographic transition—a shift from initially high to eventually low levels of both mortality and fertility; with the Great Depression of the 1930s, fertility rates plunged to unprecedented lows. Projections of total population size at that time foresaw a leveling off and decline in many of those countries by as early as 1960. The unexpected baby boom undercut those projections.

Several new circumstances common to the economic and demographic history of those countries appear to have been responsible for the baby boom. After World War II, young adults enjoyed an unusually favorable labor market, which resulted from two circumstances: (1) the rapid growth of aggregate product and labor demand that accompanied a protracted postwar economic boom, and (2) an exceptional scarcity of young workers, caused by the depressed fertility rates of the 1920s and 1930s and the war losses in the 1940s. In addition, their goods aspirations were abnormally low, because their economic socialization had occurred during the extended consumer goods deprivation of the depression and war years. Their favorable labor-market experience plus their limited material aspirations resulted in record marriages and immediate families—hence, the baby boom.

In turn, the baby boom had major consequences in the countries in which it occurred (sometimes likened to a pig-in-the-python phenomenon, as the baby-boom bulge worked its way through the population's age distribution). As baby boomers entered the working ages, this turned around the labor-market experience of young adults, by causing a marked increase in the supply of young workers. The increased supply occurred from the late 1960s to the mid-1980s, when the growth of aggregate demand was being constrained by monetary and fiscal authorities fearful of inflationary pressures. The consequent weakening of employment and promotion opportunities among the baby boomers—whose material aspirations had grown by virtue of their upbringing during the post–World War II economic boom—led to new pressures on those of family-forming age. For example, to supplement household income, young women turned increasingly to participation in the labor force at the expense of childbearing, so fertility rates plunged—a "baby bust." The growth of aggregate demand, which had benefited from the sharp rise in household formation associated with the baby boom, now suffered from much lower rates of demand for new household goods, housing, schools, and associated infrastructure.

In the first decades of the twenty-first century, the impact on society on the large baby-boom generation would still be felt, as the baby boomers began to move into retirement.

The ratio of aged dependents to the working-age population would rise noticeably, placing an unprecedented burden of old-age support on workers and increasing the need for health-care, age-related, and retirement services. In these and other ways, the baby boom has left its imprint on the history of the leading industrialized countries.

[*See also* Age Composition.]

BIBLIOGRAPHY

Easterlin, Richard A. *Birth and Fortune: The Impact of Numbers on Personal Welfare*. 2d ed. Chicago, 1987.

Elder, Glenn H. "Scarcity and Prosperity in Postwar Childbearing: Explorations from a Life Course Perspective." *Journal of Family History* 6 (1981), 410–433.

Lee, Ronald, and Jonathan Skinner. "Will Aging Baby Boomers Bust the Federal Budget." *Journal of Economic Perspectives* 13.1 (Winter 1999), 117–140.

Macunovich, Diane J. "The Fortunes of One's Birth: Relative Cohort Size and the Young Labor Market in the U.S." *Journal of Population Economics* 12.2 (1999).

Pampel, Fred C. "Relative Cohort Size and Fertility: The Socio-Political Context of the Easterlin Effect." *American Sociological Review* 58 (1993), 496–514.

RICHARD A. EASTERLIN

BAGHDAD was founded in 762 CE, by Caliph Mansur, the first of the Abbasid dynasty, on the west bank of the Tigris River. The site was chosen for its good water supply and freedom from malaria. The capital of the Islamic caliphate was moved from Damascus to Baghdad at the very time of Baghdad's founding. The city was circular in design with a surrounding stone wall that measured 3.5 kilometers in diameter. The city soon spread onto both banks of the river, and its location made it a center of trade for items coming from China and India by sea and overland. Several bridges crossed the Tigris, and a canal was constructed between it and the Euphrates near Baghdad. Early in the city's life the canal system in the surrounding countryside was expanded, enabling orchards and gardens in the city and surrounds to flourish. Within thirty years of its founding Baghdad was the second largest city in the Mediterranean and Near East with a population estimated by some as high as 1 million. Early Baghdad was a world center for scientific study with a focus on mathematics, astronomy, and medicine. Paper production began in 795 CE, and bookshops and libraries soon followed. Baghdad became a major banking center, with ownership mainly in the hands of Christians and Jews. By the tenth century CE Baghdad was a world leader in weaving, ceramics, and brick and wood sculpture.

Sporadic floods caused major problems, and succession disputes and religious warfare between Shiite and Sunni Muslims occurred in the city almost from its founding. By the twelfth century the economic prosperity and population

BAGHDAD. View of the city's auto repair shops, 2001. (© Mike Yamashita/Woodfin Camp and Associates, New York)

was much diminished. In 1258 the city was captured by the Mongols, with massive loss of life and destruction of infrastructure. The surrounding canal system was seriously damaged by this invasion and was never fully rebuilt. The Black Death struck in 1348, and the city was again sacked by Mongols in the early fifteenth century.

In 1534 Baghdad was conquered by Suleiman the Magnificent, introducing the Ottoman administration that lasted almost four centuries. As a provincial town in the Ottoman Empire, Baghdad stagnated, and by some estimates the population fell to around twenty thousand in the early seventeenth century. In 1831 the city was struck by the bubonic plague again and by a flood, which limited but did not stop a gradual population increase driven by migration from the countryside.

In the late nineteenth century Baghdad began to industrialize, linked by telegraph and steamships from the Persian Gulf. The last census before World War I indicated a city of 202,000, of whom 80,000 were Jewish. Following that war a constant stream of people, attempting to escape rural poverty and attracted by economic opportunities, flowed from the countryside into the city. In the twentieth century Baghdad became the center of higher education in Iraq as well as an industrial hub. Almost all the Jews left Baghdad for Israel upon the latter's founding after World War II. Baghdad was extensively bombed during the 1991 Gulf War and 2003 Iraqi War.

BIBLIOGRAPHY

Longrigg, Stephen, and Frank Stoakes. *Iraq*. London, 1958.

Simons, Geoff. *Iraq: From Sumer to Saddam*. New York, 1994.

Wiet, Gaston. *Baghdad: Metropolis of the Abbasid Caliphate*. Translated by Seymour Feiler. Norman, Okla., 1971.

LYNDON MOORE

BAKUNIN, MIKHAIL (1814–1876), Russian anarchist theorist and activist.

From a conventional gentry upbringing, Bakunin became one of the most extreme proponents of libertarian ideas. He emphasised that individual freedom could only be achieved through the freedom of all. He developed a materialist-determinist philosophical framework that was an uneasy accompaniment to his voluntaristic activities.

Concepts of class and of the internationalism of the oppressed were important to Bakunin. Unlike his near contemporary, the German economist Karl Marx, the founder of the nineteenth-century communist movement, Bakunin considered the *lumpenproletariat* (lower ranks of workers) as potentially revolutionary; he was also open to the revolutionary potential of the peasantry. He envisaged associations of agricultural and industrial producers as postrevolutionary owners of the means of production—the state being replaced by a free federation of producers' collectives. Bakunin's most characteristic point was his emphasis on the direct struggle against state and church, which also brought him into theoretical conflict with Marx, for whom politics, class struggle, and state ownership of the means of production were the priorities. Bakunin stressed strikes and direct economic struggle outside conventional politics, since politics would lead to the contamination of the proletarian movement through contact with the bourgeoisie. Terrorism was not excluded. Bakunin considered it a law of nature that the birth of the new often came about at the expense of the old, hence his best known dictum, "the urge to destroy is a creative urge."

Bakunin was an active revolutionary. He became involved in the support of the 1848–1849 rebellions in many parts of Europe during those turbulent years, until he was captured. He then spent eight years in the tsar's most debilitating prisons, which broke his health. His revolutionary spirit, however, was not broken and, after his release, he was involved in further adventures in Lyon (France) in 1870; however, his health gave out, and he died prematurely in 1876. During this last part of his career, the contradictions of his thought and activities became most obvious. Though an extreme libertarian, Bakunin had a lingering infatuation with conspiracies. He believed that they were a necessary instrument to promote revolution. Although never amounting to anything in practice, it appeared to put Bakunin in the camp of those who thought it necessary to introduce freedom by force.

Bakunin was, in many ways, the prototype of the Russian radical of the nineteenth and early twentieth century. The near-theocratic nature of the Russian autocracy and its deeply repressive activities meant that, in Russia, direct confrontation with the state and its increasingly subservient (and established) church were high priorities. That was in contrast to the more industrially advanced areas of Europe, where church influence had declined and the indirect mechanisms of capitalist oppression—notably owners of capital and their associates—were seen as a greater threat than the state itself. It was no accident that Bakunist ideas were also taken up in some relatively underdeveloped areas of Europe that were still subject to church domination, most notably in parts of Italy and Spain; Bakuninist inspiration remained important there until the triumph of fascism in the 1920s and 1930s, respectively.

BIBLIOGRAPHY
Bakunin, Mikhail A. *God and the State*. New York, 1970. An English translation.
Bakunin, Mikhail A. *Statism and Anarchy*. Cambridge, 1990. An English translation.
Kelly, Aileen. *Mikhail Bakunin: A Study in the Psychology and Politics of Utopianism*. Oxford and New York, 1982.
Marshall, Peter. *Demanding the Impossible: A History of Anarchism*. London, 1992.
Mendel, Arthur P. *Michael Bakunin: Roots of Apocalypse*. New York, 1981.

CHRISTOPHER READ

BALANCE OF PAYMENTS. A country's balance of payments is the record of market transactions (imports and exports of goods, services, and capital) between that nation and the rest of the world. It is composed of three accounting categories: the current account, the capital account, and the official reserves balance.

The current account records the sum of net exports in three categories: merchandise trade, services, and unilateral transfers. Unilateral transfers consist of the net amount of gift transactions between the home country and foreign counties. Examples of this include foreign aid donated from one country to another and remittances sent by immigrants in one country to their relatives in another country.

The capital account measures net exports of capital in two basic areas: portfolio investment and direct investment. Portfolio investment includes purchases and sales of securities changes in bank deposits. Direct investment involves control and ownership of productive facilities outside the home country. This category thus would include purchases and sales of factories, mines, and plantations, for example.

The official reserves balances measures the net changes in a country's foreign reserve holdings. These assets currently include gold, foreign exchange holdings, and since 1970 Special Drawing Rights issued by the International Monetary Fund. Historically gold was the most important reserve holding, with foreign exchange holdings (especially of pounds sterling and dollars) becoming dominant from 1900 onward.

The term *balance* comes from the fact that each international transaction creates both a debit and a credit in the country's international account and thus the sum of all debit transactions should equal the sum of all credit transactions over the course of a given time period. For example, if Britain exports £100,000 of goods to another country, this creates a credit of £100,000 in the current account (from the sale of the goods) and a £100,000 debit in the capital account (with the creation of a claim on foreign assets.)

How then can a nation experience a balance of payments "crisis"? The answer is that while the overall balance of payments must balance, the individual accounts (that is, the current account and the capital account) do not have to balance. For example, during the 1960s the United States experienced a balance of payments crisis when it began running current account deficits in order to finance the Vietnam War. The deficit in the current account was financed first by flows of reserves from the United States and eventually through capital imports.

The sizes and directions of international capital flows have varied over time and place. Before 1800 capital account flows were relatively small relative to GDP. This changed with European industrialization. According to Angus Maddison (2001, Table 3-3, p. 128), foreign-owned capital as a percentage of GDP in developing countries was

8.6 percent by 1870 and reached 32.4 percent by 1914. These figures fell to 4.4 percent in 1950 and then rose again during the past fifty years, to 10.9 percent in 1973 and 21.7 percent in 1998. Different regions of the world were at various times net importers or net exporters of capital. Europe generally has exported capital to the rest of the world. North America imported capital until 1914 and then exported capital until the 1980s, when it again began importing capital on a net basis. Asia historically has imported large amounts of capital; however, since the 1970s Japanese capital exports pushed the region toward balance and in many years to net export status. South America suffered through regular periods of large inflows, debt default, and capital outflows and then a resumption of capital inflows from the 1840s through the present. Finally, Africa imported capital until the 1980s. Beginning in the early 1980s, exports and imports balanced out until, in the 1990s, repayments of debt actually outstripped new capital flows and made the continent a (small) net capital exporter.

Economists have developed two basic theories of balance of payments adjustment: the expenditure method and the monetary approach. Both of these theories are based on David Hume's price-specie-flow mechanism. It is easiest to understand this mechanism through an example. Suppose the world is composed of two countries: one has a current account surplus, the other has a current account deficit. The deficit country sends gold to the surplus country to pay for its imports, and the surplus country absorbs gold in return for its exports. The increase in the surplus country's gold stock then causes an increase in its money supply. Assuming that the country is at full employment, the increase in the money supply causes inflation and thus a rise in the surplus country's export prices relative to prices of similar goods in the deficit country. At the same time the gold outflow from the deficit country causes deflation in that county and thus also works to make domestic goods relatively cheaper. Taken together the export surplus in the surplus country shrinks, the deficit in the deficit country shrinks, and the two countries move toward current account balance.

Notice that, in this version of the story, causation runs from spending to gold flows to changes in money stocks to changes in prices to changes in spending patterns. This is the expenditure approach to the balance of payments.

This story misses a crucial element: instead of gold flows, the deficit country could pay for its deficit by borrowing funds from abroad. This is exactly how current account imbalances were settled beginning in the nineteenth century. This meant that, if imports were used for productive purposes, they would yield a stream of revenue adequate to service the debt payments. If, however, the imports were for consumption purposes, no productive

assets were purchased, and a debt crisis was almost inevitable.

There is another way to view the price-specie flow mechanism. Again suppose that there are two countries, each with a zero balance in the current account. Then if there is a change in money demand or money supply in one of the countries, interest rates will adjust, causing either an outflow or inflow of gold or foreign exchange. The country that begins absorbing gold will experience a rise in its relative prices, making imports cheaper and exports more expensive and thus producing current account deficit, while the country that exports gold will see its relative prices fall and find itself with a current account surplus.

This is the foundation for the monetary approach to the balance of payments. In this theory current account and capital account movements are driven by changes in the worldwide demands for and supplies of money. Changes in spending patterns are then caused by the changes in relative prices that result from capital and reserve flows.

This article has only touched on the most important aspects of a large subject. More details are available in the sources in the bibliography.

BIBLIOGRAPHY

Eichengreen, Barry, and Marc Flandreau, eds. *The Gold Standard in Theory and History*. 2d ed. London, 1997. This is an excellent source for understanding how the balance of payments operated under the gold standard. See especially the editors' introduction and chap. 2 (Hume's original essay on the price-specie flow mechanism).

International Financial Statistics. International Monetary Fund. Washington, D.C., 2001. This is the best source for balance of payments data on individual countries after 1960.

Lindert, Peter H. *Key Currencies and Gold, 1900–1913*. Princeton, 1969. Describes and analyzes the change from gold to foreign exchange as the predominant reserve holding.

Maddison, Angus. *The World Economy: A Millennial Perspective*. Paris, 2001. This is an excellent source of aggregate data on exports, imports, and capital flows from 1870 to 1998 for all regions of the world.

Mitchell, B. R. *International Historical Statistics*. 2d rev. ed. New York, 1995. This is the best source for balance of payments data on individual countries before 1960.

Newman, Peter, Murray Milgate, and John Eatwell. *The New Palgrave Dictionary of Money and Finance*. London, 1992. See the entries "Balance of Payments," "Monetary Approach to the Balance of Payments," and "Current Account of the Balance of Payments: Normative Theory."

LOUIS D. JOHNSTON

BALKANS. The region now best identified as southeastern Europe has historically been called the Balkans. That Turkish word for "wooded mountains" alerts us to geographic and political distinctions that have marked the region's premodern and modern economic history. Its rugged uplands are more extensive and its arable lowlands relatively smaller (with less annual rainfall) than those of northwestern and central Europe. Prolonged imperial domination (Ottoman but also Habsburg and extending to World War I) distinguished these Balkan lands from the Italian and Iberian Peninsulas. For this entry, the region is further defined to exclude Greece, and hence its peninsular links to the Mediterranean. Its largely landlocked territory extends from the former Yugoslavia to Albania, Bulgaria, and Romania, all economies proceeding under Communist regimes from 1945 to 1989.

We turn first to two earlier periods: a long premodern era dating from native feudal regimes as early as the tenth century and then a modernizing century (1839–1939) of centralized states and growing economies, both native and late imperial, that still left a largely rural population of peasants to rely primarily on traditional agriculture.

Command and Market in the Premodern Borderlands. During the first half of this premodern millennium, five native elites protected and controlled enough peasants beyond the extended family to create feudal kingdoms. Only the Romanian boyar regime survived the advance of the Ottoman and also the Habsburg empires. True, the Croatian nobility kept its local authority and a majority of their holdings from the Hungarians and eventually Austrian-Germans, who took some of their best land following their monarchy's acceptance of a Hungarian King in 1102. Feudal and Orthodox church estates from the second of two Bulgarian kingdoms and the longer Serbian and briefer Bosnian regimes, however, were swept aside by the Ottoman conquest that followed decisive battles in 1371, 1389, and 1463, respectively.

Ottoman and Habsburg agrarian regimes. By the sixteenth century, the Ottoman regime had imposed a command economy dedicated to support the Sultan's military forces in the field and to supply food to the huge capital of Constantinople. Unless specially designated, all arable land became *miri*, the sultan's (or state) property. The *timar* system divided it into smallholdings whose delivery to the state of one-tenth of annual crops was the responsibility of a resident *sipahi*, or cavalry officer. His holding was not heritable, nor was he allowed to take more than subsistence for himself and his small detachment from the large share thereby left to the native, mainly south Slav peasantry. That population, however, was sparse and scattered (still less than ten per square mile by the early sixteenth century apogee of the Ottoman advance), the officers' tenure limited, and bulk transportation difficult. We therefore find no incentives for intensive cultivation or improved methods within this initially less exploitative system of land tenure.

The imposition of the *timar* system varied across this region from the start and then gave way to a heritable, less widespread, regime of seriously exploitative sharecropping by the end of the seventeenth century. Its classic application under Turkish *sipahi* extended across the Bulgarian

lands into Slav and Greek Macedonia. Grain from these lands and independent Romanian estates supplied Constantinople. Farther away, the Serbian lowlands and the few lowlands in Montenegro would remain largely forested. There, with the exception of more cleared valleys in Kosovo, the extended family, or *zadruga*, focused on raising livestock outside the Ottoman regime more than cultivating grain within it. But from Bosnia-Herzegovina down into the Albanian lands, all equally uncleared, the Ottoman regime made relatively numerous native converts to Islam its agents for *timar* holdings—holdings that quickly became heritable and exploitative. During the seventeenth century, these heritable *chiftlik* holdings replaced the *timar* system, most prominently in the original Bulgarian and Macedonian lowlands, and demanded half of peasant crops. But Marxist scholars of the region abandoned their original assumption that these holdings were larger or more commercially organized holdings comparable to Poland's "second serfdom." *Chiftliks* did, however, divert their collections from state deliveries to Mediterranean trade, thus prompting the Ottoman regime to make *ayan*, typically native village leaders, its tax collectors by the eighteenth century.

The agrarian regimes of the rival Habsburg empire exhibited even greater variety in the lands across which they had advanced by the end of the seventeenth century. The core areas of Slovene and western Croat lowlands had never been lost to the Ottomans. They remained under a feudal system of sharecropping and demesne labor that would continue until the end of serfdom per se in 1848. Croatian estates comparable to those in the Romanian Principalities of Walachia and Moldavia faced the loss of some of their peasantry to the broad Habsburg Military Border to the south, where free smallholdings and other privileges were granted in return for lifetime military service in a border regiment. From a small sixteenth-century base, the border spread across Slavonia and the Vojvodina with Habsburg reconquest from 1697 and around the Transylvanian demarcation from the Romanian Principalities after 1762. Most peasants attracted to this land and service came from Ottoman territories, Serbs from Bosnia and Serbia in particular.

The one migration along these imperial borderlands that served to advance agricultural modernization was the movement of Germans, Slovaks, and others from the Habsburg lands attracted to the Vojvodina and the Romanian Banat. Starting slowly in the early eighteenth century, the Habsburg policy of initially tax-free land and other inducements brought largely Swabian immigrants to populate this fertile but largely deserted plain with whoever would oppose Ottoman (or Hungarian) recapture. Serbs from Serbia were welcome as well, and soon were the largest single group in the Vojvodina. But it was the German immigrants, some seventy-five thousand by the 1780s, who brought with them the first devices for intensive cultivation of crops seen in most of our wider region, from iron plows to seed varieties, crop rotation, and deep wells. Wells allowed some irrigation of land that, like the wider region, receives less annual rainfall than the Great Northern Plain of Western Europe.

Premodern growth: Trade, mining and population. Although the data are scarce, it seems doubtful that any sustained increase in real per capita income, that is, modern economic growth, occurred during this premodern period. Markets nonetheless grew and modern commercial practice spread inland from the Dalmatian coast and later from both sides of the Ottoman-Habsburg border to the north. Typical of the minerals and animal products that were the region's principal exports, Bosnian silver, salt, and wool supported the rise of Split and other Venetian-controlled ports on the Adriatic. They were responding to the commercial challenge of the independent city-state of Ragusa (later Dubrovnik) during the fourteenth century. The Ragusan reaction in turn was to cut back its craft-guild production of cloth and concentrate instead on creating a network of inland traders across most of the Ottoman Balkans. The carrying trade for its merchant fleet, Europe's third largest by 1580, grew with this network. Neither survived the seventeenth century's Venetian ascendancy and disorder across the Ottoman interior.

By the eighteenth century, however, a new nexus for trade, minus Ragusa's Italian-style credit and accounting practices, had appeared along the new Ottoman-Habsburg border dividing Serbia from the Vojvodina and Walachia from Transylvania. Largely Greek, Serbian, or Bulgarian traders from the Ottoman side provided the large export surplus of wool and other animal products exchanged across a border whose minimal tariffs aided the populations that Habsburg policy wished to collect in the Vojvodina and Banat. The larger Bulgarian connection, however, was with Constantinople. By the early nineteenth century, its upland traders had begun organizing the household, or proto-industrial production of wool cloth. A similar development, focused on Trieste, spread through some Slovene towns.

This trade, let alone the scattered craft manufacture of textiles, hardly touched the bulk of the region's population. Its Ottoman numbers, roughly estimated at four million by the start of the sixteenth and again at the start of the eighteenth centuries, had indeed risen by some 20 to 25 percent during the course of both centuries. The later increase made up for demographic decline during the seventeenth century. Yet this last increase was more the result of improved political order and easier taxation than access to trade routes and commercial opportunity. Population in the Habsburg's far smaller Slovene, Croat, and Vojvodina/

Banat area exceeded six million by 1790, with a density about double the still meager ten per square kilometer reckoned for the Ottoman Balkans, excluding Greece. Yet the very small urban proportion on the Ottoman side was even smaller on the Habsburg side, just half of the former's 10 percent. There, aside from Bucharest in autonomous Walachia, only Sarajevo approached fifty thousand and Ottoman regulation restricted urban commercial development more than the Habsburg policy.

Modernizing States and Traditional Agriculture, 1839–1939. A century of consolidating state power, expanding trade, repeated land reforms, and industrial stirrings began with the Ottomans' Tanzimat reforms (1839–1856). Imperial reform within the large Habsburg and Ottoman territories joined with the emergence of small national economies in Serbia, Bulgaria, Romania, and even Montenegro to define the region until World War I. The war's disruptions and the new borders that followed left a set of new or enlarged nation-states to deal with reduced foreign trade and investment during the 1920s and then the Depression of the 1930s.

Imperial versus national growth to 1914. The growth of international and interregional trade (the former far better recorded), enabled the economies of still Ottoman or Habsburg lands and the newly independent Balkan states to grow from the 1850s to 1914 at rates that may have allowed aggregate income to keep pace with an unprecedented, still largely rural, increase in population. A certain population growth of 1 percent a year roughly doubled density to exceed fifty per square kilometer as a regional average by 1914, but still holding the urban share to less than 20 percent. The economic growth that did occur was unarguably labor extensive, drawing very little on investment in mechanized industrial production or intensive agricultural methods. But its extent and its distribution within the region and between time periods are open to dispute in the absence of a satisfactory statistical record.

At issue are the respective fortunes of the Ottoman and Habsburg lands, the latter occupying the former's Bosnia-Herzegovina in 1878, and the Balkan states carved from Ottoman territory (Serbia and Greece from 1830 and enlarged in 1878, Bulgaria in 1878 and enlarged in 1885) or freed from domination (the Romanian Principalities in 1828, united in 1859). In works cited in the bibliography, Michael Palairet argues for the relative advantages of the Ottoman lands to 1878, John Lampe and Marvin Jackson for the independent Balkan states after 1878, and David Good for the Habsburg lands throughout the period.

One Ottoman advantage was the growing urban market of Constantinople coupled with the demand created by the standing army, which the Porte established by the 1820s to replace unruly local warlords. Proto-industrial production of woolen and other household or military goods did indeed spread to a number of upland villages near the Bulgarian Balkan mountains. Its trade moved some Bulgarian merchants to Constantinople and also to Salonika and Bucharest. From the late 1850s, these urban centers began to import a significant part of their grain supply from Macedonian as well as Bulgarian lands. Overland routes were now more secure. More controversially, Palairet finds agricultural production expanding from newly consolidated sharecropping estates of now Bulgarian or Greek owners taking over under the Ottoman land reform of 1858 from Turkish *chiftlik* holders who had extracted more exploitative shares (Palairet, 1997).

The Bulgarian loss of Ottoman markets after 1878 was clearly a blow to proto-industrial production for which the stirrings of a small sector for factory-based, mechanized industry from the 1890s on clearly failed to compensate. Across the region, modern industry accounted for just 3 to 7 percent of rough estimates of gross domestic product (GDP) during the last pre-1914 decade. Until then, a one-third or higher increase in arable land cultivated per capita had sustained a comparable rise in real exports per capita in the independent Balkan economies after the European depression of 1873 to 1879. After 1900, as Lampe and Jackson admit, agricultural indicators leveled off or began to decline slightly, even in Romania where large estates still predominated. Livestock numbers declined across the region, dragging down farm household income and suffering further in Romania and Serbia from tariff wars with Austria-Hungary in 1886 to 1891 and 1906 to 1911.

All independent states had attracted sizeable loans from European capital markets but turned their use from railway construction in the 1880s to expanding their budgets, military expenditure in particular, and servicing a growing debt. The creation of modern central and commercial banks reflected a level of financial practice that allowed their governments to stave off the bankruptcy and prolonged international debt supervision that confronted the Ottoman Empire from 1881 on.

Inclusion in the large Austro-Hungarian customs union of fifty-one million by 1910 offered one obvious advantage to the Habsburg Slovene and Croat lands, plus the Vojvodina and since 1878 Bosnia-Herzegovina. Bosnia's access to this market allowed external trade per capita to be double that of independent Serbia. At the same time, the lack of data on Croatian grain exports to the rest of the monarchy makes it unclear whether Croatia-Slavonia's largely rural economy took full advantage of the latter's growing integration, as Good assumes, or whether the Hungarian Agricultural Revolution just to the north barred the way to Austrian markets. More certain was the large emigrant outflow, more than 5 percent of the population by 1910 for Croatia and also Slovene lands, despite the latter's substantial urban and industrial shares of population (27 and 15 percent, respectively).

Interwar trade problems, land reforms and state sectors. Four states struggled to create national economies during the brief interwar period that followed the disruption and deaths (two million from a prewar twenty-five million) of the Balkan Wars and World War I. The newly created Kingdom of Serbs, Croats, and Slovenes (Kingdom of Yugoslavia from 1929) and a Romania greatly enlarged by Transylvania faced initial problems of accommodating the currencies, commercial frameworks, and transportation systems of former Habsburg lands to centralized governments in Belgrade and Bucharest. A defeated and reduced Bulgaria faced the influx of 220,000 refugees from Greek Thrace and now Yugoslav Macedonia, plus the specter of reparations. The small Albanian state created on Habsburg initiative in 1912 struggled with the region's least-modern economy and the prospect of Italian financial penetration. That penetration, symbolized by the location of the Albanian central bank in Rome, would provide the largest proportional European investment in an interwar Balkan economy, but at the cost of economic sovereignty after 1925 and political sovereignty by 1939.

The region as a whole, however, would suffer from the sharp reduction in lending from a shrunken European capital market. Limited lending from the new League of Nations came too late to aid postwar recovery. In hopes of attracting private investment, all four governments stabilized their new currencies by the mid-1920s at overvalued rates of exchange. These rates placed a further restriction on agricultural exports already confronting reduced West European demand and lower prices after the war itself had disconnected rail and shipping links. Overvalued currencies also encouraged the protective tariffs that all save Albania placed on most manufactures by 1926–1927.

Sharing responsibility for the reduction of gross crop output in Romania by 5 percent and in Yugoslavia by 10 percent from the 1909–1913 level by 1926–1930 were land reforms that affected nearly 20 percent of their agricultural land. The subdivision of presumably consolidated and efficient estates into peasant smallholdings was long considered the primary cause of the region's poor performance—overpopulated holdings with an underemployed labor force. But in addition to the international constraints noted above, more recent research counters that many prewar estates were unconsolidated and finds smallholdings close to urban markets potentially more efficient. It remains true, however, that most redistributed smallholdings did not give clear title to their new owners until the late 1920s, who thereby suffered from lack of mortgage or affordable commercial credit.

One exception were the already predominant smallholdings of Bulgaria. Linked by a cooperative network that set up the regime of Aleksandar Stamboliiski's Agrarian party (1919–1923), they yielded gross crop outputs during the 1920s that were one-third above prewar levels. Then came the Depression's halving of international commodity prices, for which only a new state-controlled agency (Hranoiznos) for marketing first grain and then other agricultural exports could partly compensate. Similar agencies in Yugoslavia and Romania did even less well.

Small industrial sectors drew primarily on credit and some capital from domestic and European commercial banks to achieve growth rates that by 1929 had doubled their real output for Yugoslavia and Bulgaria and increased it by one third for Romania. Only the latter's accounted for more than 10 percent of national product estimates before 1914. Yugoslavia and Bulgaria probably reached that proportion by the onset of the Depression. But with the departure of most West European credit and the collapse of the Austrian Creditanstalt in 1931, the leading commercial banks of Zagreb and Bucharest also retreated or went under. Bulgaria's state-supported Agricultural Bank survived, while newly created ones in Romania and Yugoslavia served regions in political favor.

For industry, too, state support now became essential. It was already established in mining, and for Romania in petroleum production since 1924. Rising international demand for oil allowed Romania's government to resist Nazi overtures longer than its neighbors. Those overtures primarily took the form of bilateral clearing agreements for trade with Germany that also strengthened the state's role. The agreements required all the Balkan governments to expand such mechanisms as Hranoiznos for the direct control of agricultural exports to include industrial imports. In fact, Bulgarian trade made the most pronounced turn under a clearing agreement. Germany accounted for two-thirds of its trade turnover by 1939, while achieving more than 40 percent for Yugoslavia and belatedly Romania. Meanwhile, all three governments enforced cartel agreements for major industries and funded rearmament through state enterprise. As a result, the share of commercially accountable private enterprise declined in industrial sectors whose combined total output grew by one-third in real terms from 1935 to 1938.

The Rise and Fall of the Communist Economies. In 1945, these four states emerged with state sectors that had grown even more during World War II but with their interwar political institutions destroyed and their leaders discredited. Repairing the war's immense physical damage strengthened the logic of state initiative that new Communist governments wished to pursue in any case. Yugoslavia suffered the greatest damage, losing half of its industrial capacity, transportation network, and agricultural infrastructure, as well as a million of its people dead. By 1947, its population of 15.8 million was still 600,000 short of the 1939 total on postwar territory. Romania with 15.9 million, Bulgaria with 6.7 million, and Albania with 1.1 million had all regained their prewar population levels. But none of them had urban populations or modern industrial sectors that surpassed 25 percent of the national totals.

Extensive growth and rapid urbanization. After rebuilding infrastructure and nationalizing the remaining private industry, all four Communist regimes launched wildly ambitious Five-Year Plans based on the Soviet model between 1947 and 1949. This centralized hierarchy channeled 40 to 55 percent of the state budget, virtually the only source of investment, into large enterprises in heavy industry. Consumer goods and an agricultural sector still largely uncollectivized received much less, the latter only 6 percent in Romania. Yugoslavia's break with the Soviet Bloc in 1948 subsequently led the Tito regime to abandon collectivization beyond a minority of state farms and to dismantle its apparatus for centralized planning. But once the three remaining Bloc members had reallocated some investment to consumer goods and agriculture after 1953, Yugoslavia continued to match their still large shares of 30 to 40 percent devoted to heavy industry. Through the 1960s, these large investments, joined after 1956 for Yugoslavia and Bulgaria by a growth of foreign trade even faster than in western Europe, allowed all four economies to record annual rates of growth in net material product (NMP, or goods without services) of 6 to 9 percent.

From the late 1960s on, however, all four economies and societies bumped into barriers that weakened their Communist regimes and helped to bring them down by 1989. Their common fault was a failure to turn the corner from extensive to intensive industrial growth. Led by Bulgaria, whose urban population exceeded 50 percent by 1970, a flood of new workers from the countryside had supported increasingly oversized enterprises. This migration declined, along with birthrates, to a trickle by the 1970s. Then a new source of investment capital beckoned. But loans from China to Albania were misperceived as grants; loans from Western commercial banks to the other three were misperceived as renewable under any circumstances. By the 1980s, only the increased productivity of both capital and labor could have serviced the accumulated debts and sustained growth according to detailed Western analysis and statistical calculation.

Varieties of decline and crisis. Each of the four economies failed to increase the productivity of labor and capital, but in its own way. Albania, which was sustained in questionable measure from 1948 to 1975 first by Soviet and then by Chinese aid, possessed an industrial sector that remained the least modern and the least connected to international trade. With the Chinese departure and a continuing refusal to turn to Western lenders, the economy's isolation deepened. Heavy industry continued to receive the largest single share of state investment, leaving the majority of the population on inefficient collective farms, which at least promised them a food supply, but often lacked towns.

The Bulgarian and Romanian economies followed surprisingly divergent paths downward given their common commitment to central planning and heavy industry. The smaller Bulgarian economy relied far more on foreign trade than did Romania's. Its per capita value doubled the Romanian figure by 1980, making its smaller Western share (roughly 20 percent versus 40 percent) equal in absolute value. This larger international commitment may explain the far greater Bulgarian efforts at economic reform. After experimenting with incentives tied to export earnings alone from 1963 to 1968, the Bulgarian regime introduced a New Economic System in 1979 that was to reward and penalize enterprise management on this basis. Yet these incentives and a successful arrangement to lease land for private production from Agro-Industrial Complexes could not overcome a heavy-industrial sector that wastefully absorbed too much imported energy and too much state investment. Even the official Bulgarian growth rate for net material product (goods without services) fell below 3 percent per year from 1971 to 1980.

The Ceausescu regime persisted even more with an emphasis on heavy industry. Romania's collectivized agricultural sector received little incentive or investment, despite the fact that its productivity was higher than industry's. By the mid-1980s, moreover, too much of the farm output and energy supply needed to sustain the urban majority was diverted to insure the huge export surplus that the regime used not just to service but also to pay off its entire Western debt. Deadly domestic hardship ensued. Overall, the economy recorded literally zero growth according to Western estimates for the period from 1981 to 1988.

Estimates of gross national or domestic product (GNP or GDP) for all the pre-1989 Soviet Bloc economies have now undergone a major downward revision. Western estimates before 1989 concentrated on rates of growth rather than per capita levels, and typically trimmed official percentages in part to factor services into the Council for Mutual Economic Assistance (CMEA) accounts for NMP based on goods alone. All estimates of NMP or GDP per capita now appear to have been much too high. Official aggregates, even after recalculation by Western sources, resulted in estimates for Bulgarian and Romanian GDP per capita in 1988 that were respectively double and triple the revised levels ($2,200 and $1,600) reduced to account for overvalued exchange rates and a wider range of artificial prices than had been assumed.

Controversy still surrounds the systemic problems of a Yugoslav economy whose GDP per capita for 1989 realistically exceeded $3,000 after declining by one-third in real terms since 1980. More reliable official data also revealed growing regional disparity since 1960, from 4:1 to 9:1 in Slovenia's per capita income versus Kosovo's, and accelerating inflation, from 12 percent a year for 1965 to 1970 to 63 percent by 1984 to 1985. One critique concentrates on the political manipulation of self-managed enterprises and the misuse of domestic and international borrowing (Lydall, 1989). An opposite view stresses the rise of regional unemployment as the principal socialist failing (Woodward, 1995). Woodward also indicts the Western response to Yugoslavia's international debt crisis of the 1980s, specifically the IMF's insistence on some repayment of Yugoslavia's principal and on its keeping the domestic interest rate above the rate of inflation.

The bloody breakup of Yugoslavia that followed the collapse of Communist regimes across the Soviet Bloc in 1989 made the transition to a market economy a far greater challenge for the entire region during the 1990s than for its nearest northern neighbor, Hungary. Western assistance was at least sufficient to prevent the accumulation of unserviceable new foreign debt, and the new governments, even in Yugoslavia's successor states, were able to establish stable and convertible currencies, albeit with Western-backed Currency Boards in Bulgaria and Bosnia-Herzegovina. But the gains in factor productivity needed for the turn from extensive to intensive growth, overdue since the 1970s, failed to materialize. With the exception of Slovenia, GDP per capita lagged well behind the levels needed to qualify for the much-desired membership in the European Union. High unemployment levels of 20 percent or more made the privatization of large, often loss-making industrial enterprises more difficult politically. Decollectivized agriculture also struggled to keep its labor force and to secure credit. Warfare and criminalized commerce in the former Yugoslavia made domestic credit more expensive and legal frameworks more uncertain across the region, discouraging the private Western investment that flowed readily into Hungary. Despite these difficulties, the region's leaders seemed determined to persist in moving their economies away from rather than back to the legacy of state ownership and political control.

BIBLIOGRAPHY

Carter, Francis W., ed. *An Historical Geography of the Balkans*. New York, 1977.

Good, David. *The Economic Rise of the Habsburg Empire, 1750–1914*. Berkeley, 1984.

Inalchik, Halil. *An Economic and Social History of the Ottoman Empire*, vol. 1, *1300–1600*. Cambridge, 1994.

Joint Economic Committee of the House and Senate. *East European Economic Assessments*, parts 1 and 2. Washington, D.C., 1981.

Kaser, M. C., and E. A. Radice, eds. *The Economic History of Eastern Europe, 1919–1975*. 3 vols. Oxford, 1985–1986.

Lampe, John R. *The Bulgarian Economy in the Twentieth Century*. London, 1986.

Lampe, John R., and Marvin R. Jackson. *Balkan Economic History, 1550–1950: From Imperial Borderlands to Developing Nations.* Bloomington, Ind. 1982.

Lydall, Harold. *Yugoslavia in Crisis.* Oxford, 1989.

McGowan, Bruce. *Economic Life in the Ottoman Empire: Taxation, Trade, and the Struggle for Land, 1600–1800.* Cambridge, 1981.

Palairet, Michael. *The Balkan Economies, c. 1800–1914: Evolution without Development.* Cambridge, 1997.

Pearton, Maurice. *Oil and the Romanian State, 1895–1948.* Oxford, 1971.

Plestina, Diana. *Regional Development in Communist Yugoslavia: Success, Failure and Consequences.* Boulder, 1992.

Roszkowski, Wojciech. *Land Reforms in East Central Europe After World War I.* Warsaw, 1995.

Sjoberg, Orjan, and Michael L. Wyzan, eds. *Economic Change in the Balkan States: Albania, Bulgaria, Romania, and Yugoslavia.* New York, 1991.

Stoyanovich, Traian. *Balkan Worlds: The First and Last Europe.* Armonk, N.Y., 1994.

Todorov, Nikolai. *The Balkan City, 1400–1900.* Seattle, 1983.

Tomasevich, Jozo. *Peasants, Politics, and Economic Development in Yugoslavia.* Stanford, Calif., 1954.

Turnock, David. *The Making of Eastern Europe: From Earliest Times to 1815.* London, 1988.

Turnock, David. *Eastern Europe: An Historical Geography, 1815–1945.* London, 1989.

Woodward, Susan L. *Socialist Unemployment: The Political Economy of Yugoslavia, 1945–1990.* Princeton, 1995.

JOHN R. LAMPE

BALTIC STATES. The Baltic States—Estonia, Latvia, and Lithuania—are situated in the southeast corner of the Baltic Sea. In the westernmost end of the east European plain, the landscape is flat with mixed forests. Once, it was almost entirely covered by forest and marshes. Today, the forest covers one-third of the land; almost half is agricultural land, meadows, and pastures. The soil is not particularly rich in natural resources; there is some oil shale in the northwestern part and some phosphorite used for fertilizers.

The Baltic countries are maritime nations, with Riga and Tallinn as main ports. The seaports are not the only important transportation hubs. The largest rivers are still used as traffic routes. Most important is the Western Dvina (Daugava), followed by Neman (Nemunas), Emajõgi, and others. In the eighth century, this river system constituted the eastward routes of the Vikings to the Russian inland and further south to the coasts of the Black Sea and the Mediterranean.

Political History. The political history of the Baltic States is complicated. The indigenous peoples consisted of Finno-Ugric and Baltic tribes, consolidating into three larger language groups and several smaller ones, which are almost extinct. In the north, the Estonians with a Finno-Ugric language, in the middle Latvians, and in the south Lithuanians with Baltic languages have different ethnic and linguistic roots. Their small strip of land has been a contest area for larger powers. Russian and German invaders dominated, but Nordic and Polish armies also crossed and subjugated the area. With this history, the area is highly diversified, with many cultures, religions, languages, and minorities. They existed as independent nations only for thirty years—from 1919 to 1940 and from 1991 on—in the twentieth century. Most of the time, they have been parts of larger empires, while preserving their indigenous languages and cultures through the centuries.

At the turn of the thirteenth century, the Baltic realm was heathen, autarchic, and independent but had no statehood. At this point, it became the target for German crusaders and colonization. The Lithuanians in the south founded their own state and withstood the attacks for almost another two centuries, whereas the Estonians, Latvians, and Livs in the north were conquered and baptized by force by the Teutonic order in cooperation and competition with Scandinavian rulers. With the invasion, a feudal order with German knights as landlords and Catholic bishops as rulers was introduced in the German-dominated area, which was named Livonia. Due to Lithuanian resistance, Livonia was cut off from other German-speaking areas, which meant that peasant colonization and assimilation did not take place.

The Grand Duchy of Lithuania, meanwhile, expanded eastward to include most of Byelorussia and large parts of Ukraine, developing a similar kind of feudal rule with an indigenous and Polish aristocracy. It merged with Poland in 1385. At this point, the Lithuanians, as the last heathen people of Europe, were finally Christianized.

The feudal rules introduced in the dominated area gave vassals of German origin jurisdictional rights and the right to extract duties in money, kind, and labor from the peasantry. Peasants retained their hereditary rights to land use, so as a rule a farm was kept in the family. The village communities did not have intermediary rights of land use, and the duties were not of a collective nature. On donated land, feudal lords built manors and constructed mills and barns. The land was taken from peasant villages; peasants were relocated and had to reclaim new land.

In the large Lithuanian Empire, feudalism in the thirteenth and fourteenth centuries was relatively mild in character. A large number of lower-level noblemen, free armed peasants, and the somewhat fluid borderline between these two groups added to the military strength of the rulers, needed in the upkeep and expansion of one of the largest countries in Europe of its time. Whereas social divisions between the indigenous peasantry and the foreign lords were sharp in Livonia, the social system of the Lithuanians was less oppressive but tended to change after its alliance with Poland.

The emergence of towns between the thirteenth and sixteenth centuries meant an intensification of economic activity. The German towns in Livonia joined the Hanseatic

League, which drew the area into world trade. The first important exports, like tar timber and furs, were related to the forests. When the building of fleets in Europe increased in the fifteenth century other continents were discovered and colonialism began. The Baltic area was important because of its ability to produce naval supplies: timber to build ships, tar to make them waterproof, hemp for ropes, and flax to make sails. These were strategic raw materials of the time. Although they were not exclusively produced by the Baltic area, the Baltic trade was important enough for a rivalry to arise between the Hanseatic League and the Netherlands. When the importance of the league decreased, the Baltic area became a large-scale provider of grain to the Dutch. Part of it came from Livonia; the major share was cultivated in the Russian inland. The grain exports were based on heavy duties on the peasant households, not on manorial cultivation.

When the Reformation swept through the Baltic area in the sixteenth century, the Teutonic Order dissolved, and Livonia fell prey to another large-scale attack from neighboring powers, ending in a century of Swedish rule. The Swedish military state took advantage of Livonia as a granary. In Sweden, peasants were free, and Swedish rulers made promises to increase the freedom of Livonian and Estonian peasants as well. However, the rulers succumbed to the local aristocracy and to the influence of increasing oppression of the peasantry in surrounding areas such as Poland and Muscovy, for instance. What is commonly known as the second serfdom was not officially introduced during the seventeenth century in Livonia, but in practice, it became the rule.

Estonia and Livonia became Protestant, and one important corollary of this change was the elementary education provided by the church, eventually leading to impressive rates of literacy. Lithuania and Poland, meanwhile, remained Catholic. In the Swedish period, a certain amount of *Gutsherrschaft*, manorial cultivation of grain and other crops with the help of peasant labor, was introduced in the area.

In the Great Northern War in 1720, Sweden lost its Baltic possessions to Russia. Population losses in the Northern War have been estimated at almost 50 percent, the whole social system collapsed, lands lay waste. With peace, new organizational patterns were introduced. Baltic German rule survived in the Baltic provinces of Russia, but the freedom of movement of the peasantry was completely lost. In the towns, the guilds continued to reign. But trade changed, and the Baltic towns became transit ports for Russian trade.

In the seventeenth century, Lithuania lost most of its sovereignty as it merged with Poland in the so-called *Rzeczypospolita*. It followed the Polish path of a powerful aristocracy and a slower development of towns as a result of the aristocratic monopoly on trade. The wars around 1700 caused a scarcity of labor on the land and momentarily reduced feudal duties. But these were increased again during the next fifty years, due to the rising demand for grain on the world market and the high prices paid.

With the successive partitions of Poland in the late eighteenth century, Russia eventually gained the whole territory of Lithuania. The easternmost part of it included a substantial Jewish population, which was now compelled to stay inside the Russian Empire. A lively Jewish culture, the Litvak culture, developed with Vilnius as one of its main centers.

The manorial economies of the Baltic provinces of Russia were in crisis in the mid-nineteenth century as increases of peasant duties could no longer yield higher production and productivity was at a standstill. In Estonia, Livonia, and Curonia, serfdom was abolished in the early nineteenth century. The situation of the peasantry, which lacked the means to buy land, did not change. By mid-century, flax was bought by merchants in the countryside and became a peasant cash crop. Agrarian reforms by the Baltic German *Ritterschaft* in charge in Estonia, Livonia, and Curonia, inspired by Prussian reforms, made it possible, between 1860 and 1870, for peasants to buy land in Livonia first, then other parts of the Baltic provinces later. This group became the mainstay of the nationalist movement, achieving statehood in the twentieth century. Still, the German Baltic nobility owned most—and the best—of the land. In Lithuania, reforms of Crown lands in midcentury provided similar reforms, while serfdom was abolished later.

Movement to Industrialization. At the end of the nineteenth century, the Baltic provinces took part in the rapid, state-led industrialization effort in Russia, specializing in shipyards for the Baltic fleet, textiles (including the largest textile mill of its time, Kreenholms in Narva), and railway equipment for the whole empire. Riga became one of the largest industrial centers of the empire. The whole Baltic rim was part of the most industrialized areas of tsarist Russia, with Lithuania lagging a little bit behind. Urbanization followed industrialization. For the first time, Estonians, Latvians, and Lithuanians started to move into the towns, previously populated mostly by Baltic Germans and other minorities.

The revolution of 1905 in Russia had enthusiastic followers in the Baltic provinces. Above all, the landless peasant population, constituting a majority of the peasantry, directed its wrath toward landlords. Manors were burned down and peasant brutality occurred. In the large industries, social democratic movements started to spread. A special case was the Jewish socialist movement in southeastern Lithuania. In 1917, a Bolshevik revolution occurred in the Baltic provinces, but between the receding Red Army and attacking Germans, Estonian, Latvian, and

BALTIC STATES. Kreenholms textile mill, Narva, Estonia. Built in the1860s, the mill was the largest factory in northern Europe; part of it is still in operation. (Kersti Morger/Stockholm University)

Lithuanian nationalist governments and armies succeeded in gaining independence in 1919.

With independence, the large-scale industries lost their imperial market in Russia and had difficulties in surviving. The agrarian program of the independent states was more successful, carrying through major scale land reforms in which manors were broken up into middle-sized family farms. With the aid of a rapidly developing cooperative movement, providing capital equipment and loans, and a transformation from grain production to dairy farming—both using an intensive agriculture system from Denmark as a model—Baltic farmers achieved a certain success selling butter and meat on the difficult world market in the interwar period. Great Britain and Germany were their main trade partners.

The Great Depression was severe in the Baltic republics. As agrarian countries, they suffered from price cuts that hurt agrarian exports, as well as from the difficulties on the export market. Even Great Britain introduced restrictions on agrarian imports. The clearing system of Germany, whereby trade between two countries was conducted on an account basis, made the Baltic republics fear political dependence. Estonia reacted to these problems by leaving the gold standard in 1934. Latvia and Lithuania devaluated their currencies later, which had no impact on the Depression.

High rates of urban unemployment led to social unrest and eventually to authoritarian regimes, mild in character compared with their neighbors in Germany or the Soviet Union, but nevertheless restrictive of democracy. These authoritarian regimes, now in all three countries, launched state-led industrialization programs to reduce unemployment and promote exports. Industries based on local raw materials such as oil shale and wood, and import substitution were priorities. As Germany started its rearmament programs, its demand in the Baltic area for raw materials and agrarian products increased, and a period of economic growth followed. This progress was led by domestic, regulated, protected—and ethnically national—industries. When World War II broke out, it looked as if the Baltic countries had succeeded in overcoming their most pressing economic problems.

Soviet Occupation. In the summer of 1940, Soviet troops entered the Baltic countries and seized power.

Industries were nationalized, and a new land reform—taking land from *kulaks*, peasants owning more than 30 hectares (12 acres)—was carried through in a short time. Bourgeois elements were deported to Siberia in a large-scale operation. German occupation followed in 1941 but did not reverse the Soviet measures in a permanent way. Their plan was to settle the area with German peasants, and the indigenous peoples were to be moved farther eastward. The Jewish population of Lithuania in particular was practically wiped out. Local Communists and Gypsies also were targets of the German occupation. The Red Army came back in 1944, and a large number of Baltic citizens fled to Sweden, Germany, the United States, and other nations worldwide. This meant a loss of educated and enterprising people in addition to the young men conscripted in both armies, lost in battle, or held in prisoner-of-war camps. The area was of strategic importance to the Soviet Union, crucial for providing Leningrad with energy and food, so a large number of Soviet workers and cadres were moved into the Baltic countries. Major industries were restored and new ones were built in a typical Stalinist shock-industrialization campaign after the war. The Baltic countries had a higher standard of living, a different culture, and became the *Sovetskij zapad*, the Soviet West.

In 1949, tens of thousands of Baltic people, most of them from the countryside, were deported in a massive collectivization campaign. Agriculture was collectivized but remained more productive than in most parts of the Soviet Union. A relatively high level of education and good infrastructure were reasons to direct investment to the area. As a result, investment rates were higher in the Baltics than elsewhere. Simultaneously, labor power was brought into towns like Tallinn, Riga, or Narva. Heavy industry and metallurgy predominated, and there were advanced branches such as electronics and radio. These were all-union industries, under the submission of the central ministries in Moscow, with a high proportion of Russian employees. They had separate housing, schools, day-care centers, and shops and were not integrated in the surrounding society.

From the early 1980s, agricultural production fell, shortages became more acute, and the industries experienced crises. In the era of *glasnost*, protest movements surfaced and took a nationalist direction, with demands for independence.

With independence in 1991, large-scale industries catering to the whole Soviet Union went bankrupt. Restitution of land owned in 1940 was decided in all three countries. Privatization programs were launched, foreign investment invited, and separate currencies introduced. Estonia went through a liberal, shock-therapy transition and combined comparatively high rates of growth with high rates of economic differentiation along with an agricultural crisis. Lithuania had a more gradual transition, with protection

of agriculture and somewhat lower growth. Latvia, with an in-between policy, experienced the slowest growth in the 1990s. Still, these differences were small, and together these countries were the most successful post-Soviet economies. The large exile populations from World War II have to some extent contributed to investment, technical, and administrative aid. Estonia, Latvia, and Lithuania have applied to become members of the European Union and the North Atlantic Treaty Organization, and belong to the cooperative organizations of the Baltic Sea area. Main trade partners are the Nordic countries, Germany, the United States, and Russia.

BIBLIOGRAPHY

Baltic Facts, 1998. Tallinn, Estonia, 1999.

Dreifelds, Juris. *Latvia in Transition.* Cambridge, 1996.

Hiden, John, and Patrick Salmon. *The Baltic States and Europe: Estonia, Latvia, and Lithuania in the Twentieth Century.* London, 1994.

Johansson, Anders, Karlis Kangeris, Aleksander Loit, and Sven Nordlund, eds. *Emancipation and Interdependence: The Baltic States as New Entities in the International Economy, 1918–1940.* Uppsala, 1994.

Kahk, Juhan, and Enn Tarvel. *An Economic History of the Baltic Countries.* Stockholm, 1997.

Karlsson, Mats, and Brian van Arkadie. *Economic Survey of the Baltic States.* London, 1992.

Kirby, David. *Northern Europe in the Early Modern Period.* London, 1990.

Kirby, David. *The Baltic World, 1772–1990.* London, 1995.

Kõll, Anu Mai. *Peasants on the World Market: Agricultural Experience of Independent Estonia, 1919–1939.* Stockholm, 1994.

Kõll, Anu Mai, and Jaak Valge. *Economic Nationalism and Industrial Growth: State and Industry in Estonia, 1934–1993.* Stockholm, 1997.

Loit, Aleksander, and Helmut Piirimäe, eds. *Die Schwedischen Ostseeprovinzen Estland und Livland im 16.–18. Jahrhundert.* Uppsala, 1993.

Misiunas, Romuald, and Rein Taagepera. *The Baltic States: Years of Dependence 1940–1980.* London, 1983.

Schwabe, Arveds. *Grundriss der agrargeschichte Lettlands.* Riga, Latvia, 1928.

Soom, Arnold. *Der Herrenhof in Estland im 17. Jahrhundert.* Lund, 1954.

ANU MAI KÕLL

BANGLADESH emerged as an independent nation on 16 December 1971 after a nine-month civil war against Pakistan. The country inherited a legacy of foreign rule by the Mughals and the British.

The British rule ended in August 1947 with the creation of India and Pakistan. Pakistan, consisting of East Pakistan (the erstwhile East Bengal; now Bangladesh) and West Pakistan (now Pakistan), was created in northeastern and northwestern parts of India with Muslims as the majority. Peoples in two parts of Pakistan were socially and culturally different. Pakistan's government, dominated by West Pakistan, continued a dualistic policy to oppress the Bengalis in East Pakistan. The civil war was caused by the denial of the right to govern the country after parliamentary election in 1970 was won under political leadership from East Pakistan.

Bangladesh borders India on its north, east, and west. Myanmar is on the southeast. A mangrove forest and a long sea beach lie along coast of the Bay of Bengal on the south. The country is a deltaic land with a high drainage density, providing fertile lands and fresh water. The major part of the country is flood plain with hills in the eastern part and highlands in the central and northern areas. The climate of the country is influenced by the monsoons, which cause heavy rains from June to September. Bangladesh is prone to floods, cyclones, tidal inundations, and droughts. The country has a good reserve of natural gas, hard rock, and coal.

Politics and Administration. Bangladesh inherited administrative and political systems from British India and Pakistan. Its self-governed rural communities lived in religious and social harmony. They contained in miniature all the materials of state and were sufficient to protect their members, if all other governments were withdrawn (Tinker, 1968). The indigenous village institutions continued their activities until the end of Mughal rule (Huque, 1984).

Political instability has held back social and economic progress in Bangladesh for many years. The country initiated parliamentary democracy after independence, changed to a presidential system in January 1975, and returned to a parliamentary system in April 1991. The first constitution, adopted in 1972, declared democracy, socialism, secularism, equal rights, freedom of expression, and independence of judiciary as national goals. No genuine efforts were made in the early years of independence to prepare the country for a transition to socialism (Alamgir, 1978). The country moved away from socialistic policy after the assassination of the leader of the liberation war, Sheikh Mujibur Rahman, in August 1975. It is believed that the killing was masterminded by political conspiracy and army rebellion. Rahman attempted to establish a one-party authoritarian government.

Amidst civil-military unrest, General Zia ur-Rahman, a liberation war hero, came to power in November 1975. He restored democracy and freedom of the press, which were affected earlier by one-party political authority. Zia formed a political party, was elected president, changed nationality from Bengali to Bangladeshi, and was assassinated in May 1981. It is believed that the assassination of Zia was a result of dissatisfaction among army officers.

General Hossain Mohammad Ershad grabbed power from an elected government in March 1982, formed a political party, was elected president, made Islam the state religion, and ruled the country in an autocratic manner until he was removed in December 1990 by mass movement.

Since Bangladesh has returned to parliamentary democracy, two elections held under neutral government in 1991 and 1996 resulted in two women as prime ministers. It worth noting that in a Muslim country female leadership is well respected. Both leaders are considered symbols of unity in two major political camps. Begum Khaleda Zia, widow of the late president, leads the Bangladesh Nationalist Party and served as the first woman premier from April 1991 to March 1996. Her government adopted an open-economy policy and implemented food for education at the primary level and girls' scholarships at the secondary level. Khaleda's successor, Sheikh Hasina, daughter of Sheikh Mujibur Rahman, is chairperson of Awami League and acted as prime minister from June 1996 to July 2001. She settled a water dispute with India and enacted a law for direct election of women representatives in local governments. Begum Zia was reelected prime minister after her political coalition won an absolute majority in the election of October 2001. Her government committed to, among other things, a crackdown on corruption and terrorism, economic recovery, and more transparency in politics and administration.

A constitutional change in 1991 shifted executive power of the republic to the prime minister. The president has no executive authority during parliamentary period but is constitutionally authorized to appoint a caretaker government for ninety days to hold national elections after the expiration of each parliament. The major challenge for Bangladesh today is to strengthen political institutions to achieve faster economic growth.

Economic Development. Bangladesh used to produce high-quality jute and textiles, which were in demand worldwide before synthetic fibers swamped the international market. Its agrarian economy was neglected under both British and Pakistan regimes. During the British regime, West Bengal received priority in industrial development, while the Pakistan regime deprived erstwhile East Pakistan in all aspects of development.

Bangladesh has experienced difficulties in socioeconomic development because of political instability. It failed to adopt rational policies in economic development from the beginning. Overemphasis on the public sector, following the socialistic model of development, ruined its economy in the initial years. The country started encouraging the private sector economy in the second half of the 1970s. The country's strong network of non-governmental organizations (NGOs) has been contributing increasingly to contain poverty, operating microcredit programs.

Bangladesh, with a low industrial base, depends on imported technology and raw materials. The public sector industries incur a heavy loss and consume about one-fourth of the revenue budget as subsidies. Privatization encounters intense pressure from unions and political parties.

Agriculture still remains the backbone of the Bangladeshi economy. In the early 1950s, about 60 percent of national income, 95 percent of foreign exchange earnings, and 90 percent of national employment were contributed by agriculture (Ahmed, 1980). The sector was a major contributor to gross domestic product (GDP) even in the 1970s. In recent years, the contribution of agriculture to GDP has decreased to one-third but has continued to absorb more than 50 percent of employment (Government of Bangladesh, Dhaka, 1998). Significant progress made in crop production is leading the country toward self-sufficiency in food.

Bangladesh adopted an open-economy policy in the early 1990s and has been making steady progress. Once called a "bottomless basket" in the early 1970s, Bangladesh is now considered a potential developing economy. It maintained an average GDP growth of more than 5 percent during the last ten years. Contribution of the informal sector and women's unpaid domestic labor has recently been included in GDP. In 2000, per capita income was estimated at U.S. $386, up from $286 in 1999 (*The Daily Star*, Dhaka, 31 March 2000). Though the unemployment and underemployment rates have continuously declined from 38.78 in 1972–1973 to 27.95 in 1996–1997, the figure is still high to contain impoverishment. More than 40 percent of the country's population is below the poverty line.

The private sector is currently a major contributor to the national economy. Some export-processing zones (EPZ) are providing opportunities for foreign investments. In recent years, the energy sector has attracted investment by multinational corporations. The country may realize economic fortune if it can utilize the potential of this sector. Bangladesh enjoys the status of a most-favored nation in the markets of the developed world. This has helped the growth of exports, particularly ready-made garments. The country needs to develop forward and backward linkages for this sector. Other important export items include jute, tea, leather, and fish.

Bangladesh at times faces poor economic and financial management. The government in recent years has had to borrow huge amounts of money from commercial banks. Revenue collection suffers from inefficiency, malpractice, and corruption. Bureaucratic delay and corruption, deteriorating law and order, and political conflicts, strikes, and armed clashes are major constraints to foreign investment. Export growth, recorded at around 20 percent annually during the first four years in the 1990s, declined to around 10 percent in 2000 (*The Daily Star*, Dhaka, 5 July 2000). The country faces an acute problem of debt servicing.

Demographic Changes. Bangladesh has a population of about 130 million in an area of about 145,000 square kilometers (58,000 square miles). Over the past few years, there has been significant improvement in demographic characteristics. The population growth rate has reduced to 1.48 in 2001 from 2.60 in 1970. Crude birth and death rates and child death rates have been reduced due to improved health facilities. Progress has been made in maternal health and the use of contraceptives. Life expectancy increased to sixty-one years in 1998 from forty-five years in 1974, and literacy rates have risen to 60 percent in 2000 from 25.8 percent in 1974. Concerted efforts by the government and the NGOs in recent years have contributed to this dynamic change in literacy. New education programs have supported economic development, family welfare, and socio-politics. Poor families have been encouraged by the free supply of books and food for education at the primary level and scholarships for female students at the secondary level.

The higher literacy rate is helping the family planning program become successful, contributing to the reduction of family size, and discouraging early marriage. Family size decreased to 4.8 in 2001 from 5.5 in 1991, and the average age at first marriage for males and females increased to 27.6 and 20.0, respectively, in 1996.

Urbanization. Urbanization in Bangladesh is a recent phenomenon. Only a few urban centers existed before the British introduced a modern administration. Modern administration helped the distribution of urban centers all over India. The independence of India and Pakistan resulted in the redistribution of Hindus and Muslims between the two countries. Some cities in East Pakistan experienced negative growth because of the migration of Hindus to India and others gained in Muslim migrants from India.

Unprecedented urban growth took place in independent Bangladesh. Famines in the early years of independence were a major cause of rural to urban migration. The trend continued owing to widespread rural poverty and natural calamities, such as floods, cyclones, erosion, and droughts. Decentralization of administration in the face of rural poverty helped urban migration by improving transport and communication. The country's urban population increased from 9.3 percent in 1975 to 23.39 percent in 2001. About 10 million people live in the Dhaka Statistical Metropolitan Area.

Today, cities in Bangladesh suffer from inadequate infrastructures, overcrowding, chaotic traffic, pollution, and health hazards. About one-third of the population in the capital, Dhaka, lives in slums. Urban local governments suffer from inefficiency, corruption, and a lack of planning controls. Currently, NGOs are undertaking slum improvement programs in major cities.

Human Rights, Gender Issues, and Child Protection. Governmental control in public and private affairs is a major impediment to establishing human rights in Bangladesh. During the past few years, some laws have been enacted to prevent the discrimination of men and women and to protect children from abuses. Women's unpaid contribution in the economy is currently recognized in the GDP. Progress has been made to educate and empower women, and provision is made for direct elections of women representatives in local governments. Civil society believes that poor and landless people are capable of taking leadership and working with the upper echelon in rural society (Rahman, 1994). There are difficulties, however, to implement natural and legal rights because of deep-rooted traditional and religious values espoused by the patriarchy (Huda, 1998). The country must move faster to eliminate criminal offenses related to women's physical oppression, child abuses, and the trafficking of women and children. Although Bangladesh has ratified the convention on the rights of children, it has not done enough to establish child rights in society (Khair, 1998). There must be effective enforcement to implement the rights of women and children. An independent judiciary, free media, and fair politics may help improve the situation.

Within the backdrop of political and administrative weaknesses, the recent move to an open economy has created new hope of national progress for Bangladesh. Future success depends much on the political leadership's respect for democratic culture and the utilization of new opportunities in the global market.

[*See also* India *and* Pakistan.]

BIBLIOGRAPHY

Ahmed, Emajuddin. *Bureaucratic Elites in Segmented Economic Growth: Bangladesh and Pakistan.* Dhaka, Bangladesh, 1980.

Alamgir, Mohiuddin. *Bangladesh: A Case of Below-Poverty-Level Equilibrium Trap.* Bangladesh, Dhaka, 1978.

Huda, Sigma. "Legal Rights and Gender Equity." In *Towards Gender Equity: Poverty, Rights and Participation,* pp. 87–101. Dhaka, Bangladesh, 1998.

Huque, Ahmed S. "The Problems of Local Government Reforms in Bangladesh: The Failure of Gram Sarker." Ph.D. diss., University of British Columbia, Vancouver, 1984.

Jansen, Erik, G. *Rural Bangladesh: Competition for Scarce Resources.* Dhaka, Bangladesh, 1990.

Kalam, A. K. M. Abul. *Decentralisation and Development: With Special Reference to the Experience of Bangladesh since 1982.* Ph.D. diss., University of Salford, 1990.

Khair, Sumaiya. "Taking Children's Rights Seriously: Areas of Concern." In *Towards Gender Equity: Poverty, Rights and Participation,* pp. 102–109. Dhaka, Bangladesh, 1998.

Rahman, Muhammad, A. *People's Self-Development: Perspectives on Participatory Action Research.* Dhaka, Bangladesh, 1994.

Siddiqui, Kamal. *Local Government in Bangladesh.* Dhaka, Bangladesh, 1994.

Tinker, H. *The Foundations of Local Self-Government in India, Pakistan, and Burma.* London, 1968.

A. K. M. Abul Kalam

BANK FAILURES. These events are an occupational hazard of the system of modern, fractional reserve banking. Under fractional reserve banking, banks receive funds from depositors, whom they promise to repay upon demand. The majority of these funds are used in profitable activities: the banker either makes loans at interest or purchases interest-yielding securities. The remaining funds are held as reserves, as either cash or other liquid (i.e., easily convertible into cash) assets, in order to meet the demands of depositors. Reserves earn little or no return.

The banker is torn by two competing urges with regard to the allocation of funds between earning assets and reserves. On the one hand, the bank would like to minimize its reserve holdings in order to maximize profits. On the other hand, the bank needs to hold enough reserves to meet the withdrawal demands of depositors. Typically, banks that cannot meet deposit withdrawal demands are forced to close their doors. If the bank cannot very quickly arrange to meet withdrawals, then it has failed.

Thus, banks fail when they have insufficient reserves on hand to meet the demands of their depositors; and they can have insufficient reserves because their earning assets fail to perform, thus lowering the value of their assets and impairing their earnings. This failure can result from default of one or more borrowers, collapse in value of securities in the bank's portfolio, mismanagement, or fraud. Alternatively, banks can fail when depositors attempt to withdraw funds in excess of the reserves on hand. Such a "run on the bank" can occur when depositors suspect fundamental problems with a bank's assets (e.g., the failure of a prominent borrower). Whether the suspected problems are genuine or imagined, large-scale withdrawals can force the bank to close and, ultimately, to fail.

The consequences of an isolated bank failure are typically limited to individuals and institutions associated with the failing bank. Depositors that did not withdraw their funds prior to closure may not be paid until the bank's assets have been liquidated, and even then may not receive the full value of their deposits. Bank shareholders also will suffer losses; and bank borrowers may suffer, as outstanding loans are called or not renewed and credit lines withdrawn. The more extensive a bank's operations, the greater the economic impact of the failure.

Although isolated bank failures typically arise from problems with a specific bank, clusters of bank failures (i.e., a banking crisis) can result from economic downturns in particular regions, industries, or an entire economy. For example, a severe decline in a particular industry could lead to the demise of several banks that had made extensive loans to companies in that industry. Similarly, a localized shock could lead banks that are not geographically diversified to substantial declines in asset values

BANK FAILURE. *The Stoppage of the Bank*, painting by Rolinda Sharples, 1822. (City Museum and Art Gallery, Bristol, U.K.)

and/or simultaneous deposit withdrawals (i.e., bank runs). Finally, since depositors typically do not know about the internal workings of their banks, the failure of one bank may lead others to suspect their banks' solvency. This asymmetry of information between banks and their customers can lead to large-scale deposit withdrawals from, and thus failures of, banks that are otherwise perfectly healthy (Mishkin, 1991).

Banking crises can affect the overall economy through a variety of mechanisms. A monetarist school stresses the fact that bank failures lead to a decline in the money supply, which has a negative effect upon the macroeconomy (Friedman and Schwartz, 1963). Others emphasize the importance of the intermediation function undertaken by banks, and view bank failures as raising the cost of banks' intermediation between borrowers and lenders (Bernanke, 1983). Whatever the mechanism, the consequences of banking crises can be severe. One study of nineteenth-century U.S. banking crises places the cost of a small banking crisis at about 2 percent of real gross domestic product (GDP), and the consequences of a large crisis at approximately 20 percent of real GDP (Grossman, 1993).

The economic history of the developed world is filled with examples of bank failures and banking crises. Banking crises occurred frequently in the United States during the nineteenth and early twentieth centuries. During the national banking era (from 1863 to 1914), for example, the United States endured crises at regular intervals, in 1873, 1884, 1890, 1893, and 1907 (Sprague, 1910). Individual failures and crises were a common feature of the industrialized and industrializing world during the nineteenth and early twentieth centuries. Some of the well-known failures include the City of Glasgow Bank (1878), France's Union Générale (1882), and the Home Bank of Canada (1923). Kindleberger (1984, 1996) provides detailed chronologies of banking crises.

The most famous, and widespread, episode of banking crisis occurred during the Great Depression, when the banking systems of many countries endured record numbers of failures. Banking crises during this period included those in Austria, Belgium, Estonia, France, Germany, Hungary, Italy, Norway, Poland, Romania, Switzerland, and the United States. Many countries that did not suffer full-scale banking crises during this period—including

Canada, Britain, Denmark, the Netherlands, and Sweden—nonetheless suffered severe banking problems (Grossman, 1994).

Banking crises have led policy makers to adopt a variety of supervisory and regulatory mechanisms both for preventing crises and for responding to them once they have occurred. Countries frequently establish numerous balance-sheet regulations, including reserve and capital requirements as well as limits on the types of assets banks can hold in their portfolios, in efforts to ensure that the banks have adequate resources to meet depositor demands. Central banks can act, and have acted, to avert crises by serving as lenders of last resort. The Bank of England was the first central bank to take on this role, lending funds to the market when individual bank reserves were low and the probability of a crisis was high, beginning in the second half of the nineteenth century (Bagehot, 1873). Finally, countries have adopted various systems of deposit insurance, both to protect depositors in the event of bank failures and to prevent bank runs by assuring depositors that their deposits are safe.

[*See also* Barings *and* Great Depression.]

BIBLIOGRAPHY

Bagehot, Walter. *Lombard Street*. London, 1873. First, and still classic, work on the lender of last resort.

Bernanke, Ben S. "Nonmonetary Effects of the Financial Crisis in the Propagation of the Great Depression." *American Economic Review* 73.3 (1983), 257–276. Describes the consequences of banking crises, focusing on increased cost of credit intermediation.

Friedman, Milton, and Anna Schwartz. *A Monetary History of the United States, 1867–1960*. Princeton, 1963. Describes the consequences of banking crises, focusing on the monetary channel.

Grossman, Richard S. "The Macroeconomic Consequences of Bank Failures under the National Banking System." *Explorations in Economic History* 40.3 (1993), 294–320. Provides an estimate of the macroeconomic costs of banking crises in the nineteenth-century United States.

Grossman, Richard S. "The Shoe That Didn't Drop: Explaining Banking Stability during the Great Depression." *Journal of Economic History* 54.3 (1994), 654–682. Explains the pattern of banking stability and instability during the turbulent years of the Great Depression.

Kindleberger, Charles P. *A Financial History of Western Europe*. London, 1984. General reference on European banking and monetary history, including chronologies of banking crises.

Kindleberger, Charles P. *Manias, Panics, and Crashes*. 3d ed. London, 1996. General overview of theory and history of financial crises.

Mishkin, Frederic. "Asymmetric Information and Financial Crises: A Historical Perspective." In *Financial Markets and Financial Crises*, edited by R. Glenn Hubbard, pp. 69–108. Chicago, 1991.

Sprague, O. M. W. *History of Crises under the National Banking System*. Washington, D.C., 1910.

RICHARD S. GROSSMAN

BANK FOR INTERNATIONAL SETTLEMENTS.

The Bank for International Settlements (BIS), in Basel, Switzerland, is the world's oldest international financial institution and the principal center for international central bank cooperation. The BIS was established in the context of the Young Plan (1930), which dealt with the issue of reparation payments imposed on Germany by the Treaty of Versailles. The new bank was to take over the functions previously performed by the Agent General for Reparations in Berlin and to act as a trustee for the Dawes and Young Loans. In addition, the BIS was to promote central bank cooperation in general. The reparations issue quickly faded into the background, focusing the bank's activities entirely on central bank cooperation.

The bank's main tasks, as they have developed over seven decades, can be summarized as follows:

1. The BIS provides a forum for central bank cooperation. Through regular meetings, bringing together governors and officials of its member central banks, the BIS acts as the prime forum for information exchange and cooperation among central banks worldwide. Central bank cooperation at the BIS aimed at defending the Bretton Woods system in the 1960s and early 1970s, and managing capital flows following the two oil crises and the international debt crisis in the 1980s. More recently, the thrust has been to stabilize financial markets in the wake of economic integration and globalization. To achieve this, the BIS, in recent years, has extended its membership to include systemically important economies in Latin America, the Middle East, and Asia, and has increasingly involved financial supervisory authorities in its work.

2. Within the context of central bank cooperation, the BIS conducts research on monetary policy, collects and publishes statistical material on international finance, and, through its expert committees, formulates recommendations to the financial community aimed at strengthening international finance. For example, the Basel Committee on Banking Supervision has recommended a risk-weighted capital ratio for internationally active banks that has become an international standard (1988 Basel Capital Accord; a new Basel Capital Accord will be finalized in 2002 and is expected to be implemented in 2005).

3. The BIS performs traditional banking functions, such as reserve management and gold transactions, for the account of its central bank customers. The total of currency deposits placed with the BIS amounted to U.S. $131 billion as of 31 March 2001, representing about 7 percent of world foreign-exchange reserves. In addition, the BIS has performed trustee and agency functions. Thus, the BIS was the agent for the European Payments Union (EPU, 1950–1958), helping the European currencies restore convertibility. Likewise, the BIS acted as an agent for various European exchange-rate arrangements, including the European Monetary System (EMS, 1979–1998), which preceded the move to a single currency.

4. The BIS has provided or organized emergency support to shore up the international monetary system when needed. During the 1931–1933 financial crisis, the BIS organized support credits for both the Austrian and the German central banks. In the 1960s, the BIS arranged special support credits for the Italian lira (1964) and for the French franc (1968) and two so-called Group Arrangements (1968 and 1969) to support sterling. More recently, the BIS has provided finance in the context of IMF-led stabilization programs (for example, for Mexico in 1982 and Brazil in 1998).

The Bank for International Settlements has the legal structure of a limited company with issued-share capital. At the same time it is an international organization governed by international law. The entirety of the bank's issued-share capital was registered in the names of fifty central banks and monetary authorities as of 31 March 2001. The BIS's head office is in Basel, Switzerland, and its Representative Office for Asia and the Pacific is in the Hong Kong Special Administrative Region of the People's Republic of China. The BIS has announced its intention to establish in 2002 a Representative Office for the Americas in Mexico City.

BIBLIOGRAPHY

Baer, Gunter D. "Sixty-five Years of Central Bank Cooperation at the Bank for International Settlements." In *The Emergence of Modern Central Banking from 1918 to the Present*, edited by Carl-Ludwig Holtfrerich, Jaime Reis, and Gianni Toniolo. Aldershot, U.K., 1999.
Bank for International Settlements. <http://www.bis.org>.

PIET CLEMENT

BANKING *[This entry contains three subentries dealing with banking in classical antiquity, during the Middle Ages and early modern period, and in the modern period.]*

Classical Antiquity

The origins of ancient banking were intimately linked with the need to verify the fineness and weight of out-of-town coins and to exchange them for domestic coinage. Banking cannot therefore be found in ancient Mesopotamia and other ancient Near Eastern civilizations, which did not use die-struck coins before the Hellenistic era (see Egypt below). The businesses of two entrepreneurial families in Babylonia in the sixth and fifth centuries BCE were sometimes erroneously described as banks, but their activities do not fulfill the criteria for banking. They did not accept deposits in order to grant credit and to facilitate financial transactions. Credit was granted instead by various individuals and institutions for commercial and nonproductive purposes, usually on a short-term basis throughout the history of the ancient Near East from the third until the first millennium BCE.

Banking in Athens. True banking was born in ancient Greece, toward the end of the fifth and beginning of the fourth century BCE; and its origins were prompted by the widespread use of out-of-town coinage in trade, other economic transactions, and political relations between the more than 265 Greek *poleis*, each having its own coinage. The most decisive change was the issue of coins by the rulers of the Hellenistic empires from the fourth century BCE, that were accepted as valid throughout the empire. The sources for Greek banking are more or less restricted to Athens (Greek orators) and Greco-Roman Egypt (papyri and *ostraca*). The table (*trapeza*) on which bankers undertook their business gave them their name, *trapezites*.

The emergence of banking in fourth-century BCE Athens also coincides with a fundamental change in the structure of the Athenian economy and society, a change from agricultural subsistence patterns to a more money-based agricultural economy. The foundations for such a change were the outbreak of the Second Peloponnesian War (431 BCE) and the great Athenian plague (430 BCE), which together prompted large parts of the rural population of Attica to move into Athens. The money payments that the state necessarily made to its relocated citizens thus helped to monetize the economy much more effectively. From the beginning of the fourth century BCE, Greek moneychangers acting as bankers accepted deposits destined for future payments, such as repaying a debt or other obligations. Payment was made in the presence of these bankers, who authenticated both the quality of the coins and the payment transactions. Along with these transactions, the bankers established deposit accounts for their customers.

There is no convincing evidence that bankers were attracting funds by paying interest. Traders (*emporoi* and *naukleroi*) deposited amounts of coined money at such banks for safekeeping (without interest). Willingness to grant credit was a social virtue in classical Athens; and wealthy men often sought out their own borrowers, calculating their risk in doing so. Thus the demands of the Athenian economy for credit were met not by banks but by private individuals. Most of the coins in circulation never found their way into a bank; instead, they were kept at hand for immediate use or were hoarded. In general, moneylending was noninstitutional and was discontinuous Security was substitutive, not collateral. Short-term lending was the rule in order to minimize the risk of debtors defaulting.

The very limited number of documents has led to disagreements about the purpose of bank credits and about the relative importance of productive and nonproductive loans, that is, loans for personal consumption and/or ostentatious display. Some economic historians, such as Raymond Bogaert and Moses Finley, contend that the vast majority (99 percent) of credits granted—by banks and by individuals—were for nonproductive purposes, but Wesley Thompson has contested such interpretations. A completely separate type of credit was "bottomry" or nautical loans, which bore great risks—indeed, too great a risk for banks and their depositors ever to undertake.

Social Position of Athenian Bankers. Athenian society consisted of three distinct social strata: citizens, who were farmers; slaves in domestic service; and merchants, who were either foreigners or metics (resident aliens in a Greek polis), but not Athenian citizens. Athenian social philosophy developed a clear correspondence between social status and economic roles. Since bankers were often former slaves, they stood outside the social system. Their business was not embedded in civic social relations; it was purely economic. They were thus able to offer opportunities not otherwise available within Athenian society. Banking was usually a one-man enterprise, although some slaves served as employees. The banker's business depended on a trust and reputation that had to be established over a considerable length of time.

Banking in Hellenistic-Roman Egypt. There is a marked difference between banking practices in Athens and those found in Hellenistic and Roman Egypt, as revealed by thousands of *ostraca* and papyri. Banks accepted written orders from depositors to pay specified amounts of money to a third party out of their account (first attested in 254 BCE); banks would transfer money from account to account (attested in the second century BCE); and, from the first century BCE, they accepted checks drawn on the account of the emittent, which could be exchanged between business partners in lieu of cash. Checks could not, however, be endorsed; and there was no giro. Legal contracts from Hellenistic Egypt stipulate repayment of a loan to be paid in cash or through a bank. Checks became necessary because of the difficulty of handling large amounts of circulating copper coins. In contrast to Athens, where bank customers were generally merchants and members of the social elite, all social levels in Egypt, from the late third or second century BCE, used these banking facilities.

Public or State Banks. There were two reasons to explain why public funds were entrusted to private banks in return for certain "dues,"—to gain interest or a share of bank profits and to obviate the arduous efforts and high costs of establishing a public treasury. The state also established public banks, modeled on the private banks, to manage the budgets of urban magistrates, who handled their accounts like private individuals. In Ptolemaic Egypt, the royal banks (*basilikai trapezai*) were hierarchically organized, with a network of branch offices. Their function was to collect fees, dues, and taxes owed to the king (taxes could be paid directly to the tax collector's account at the state bank); to pay wages and salaries to state officials; and to pay the bills for goods and services rendered to the king.

Banking in Rome. In ancient Rome, banking regulations and procedures are reflected in the provisions of Roman law. The first moneychanging bankers can be documented by the end of the fourth century BCE, an era that coincides with the initial commercialization of Roman society. In many cases, the bankers were freed slaves. In general, Roman banking followed the same principles found in Athens: holding deposits without interest; granting interest-bearing credits using the deposits; maintaining accounts whose registers were accepted as proof in court; and managing customers' assets. As is the case for ancient Greece, there is still much scholarly dispute about the quantitative and qualitative roles of banking in the Roman economy. Evidently, as in Athens, members of the Roman elite, rather than banks, supplied most of the credits for commercial and nonproductive purposes.

BIBLIOGRAPHY

Andreau, Jean. *La vie financière dans le monde romain: Les métiers de maniers d'argent.* Rome, 1987. The authoritative work on Roman financial affairs and banking.

Andreau, Jean. "Mobilité sociale et activités commerciales et financières." In *La mobilité sociale dans le monde romain,* edited by Edmond Frézouls, pp. 21–32. Strasbourg, 1992. The essay stresses the social position of bankers in the Roman world.

Bogaert, Raymond. *Banques et banquiers dans la cités grecques.* Leiden, 1968.

Bogaert, Raymond. *Grundzuege des Bankwesens im alten Griechenland.* Konstanz, Germany, 1986.

Bogaert, Raymond. *Trapezitica Aegyptiaca—Recueil de recherches sur la banque en Égypte gréco-romaine.* Florence, 1994. A collection of the more recent essays of Bogaert, the most prominent scholar in the field of banking in classical Greece and in Greco-Roman Egypt, from the years 1965 to 1989.

Bogaert, Raymond. "Banking in the Ancient World." In *A History of European Banking,* edited by Herman Van der Wee and G. Kurgan-Van Hentenrijk, pp. 13–70. 2d ed. Antwerp, 2000.

Finley, Moses I. *Economy and Society in Ancient Greece,* edited by Brent D. Shaw and Richard P. Saller. New York, 1981.

Humphreys, Sally C. "Economy and Society in Classical Athens." In *Anthropology and the Greeks,* edited by Sally C. Humphreys. London, 1983.

Thompson, Wesley E. "A View of Athenian Banking." *Museum Helveticum* 36 (1979), 224–241. Critical assessment of the writings of Bogaert, especially those focusing on the quantitative relationship between productive and nonproductive credits and interest paid on short-term deposits. Thompson regards credits for commercial purposes more important to the banks (in Athens) than consumptive loans.

JOHANNES M. RENGER

Middle Ages and Early Modern Period

Even in the Middle Ages, the terms *bank* and *bankers* were being used. They were related to *bancus* (Lat.), *banco* (It.), *tavola* (It.), and *taula* (Catalan), the exchange tables on which money changers (Lat. *bancherii*) conducted their exchange transactions. The services of a bank were never narrowly defined or completely specialized. In the early Middle Ages, for example, a mint master (*monetarius*) often acted as money (coin) changer, bullion dealer, goldsmith, and moneylender to kings and princes. However, in the course of the Middle Ages one can distinguish three main categories of bankers: international merchant-bankers, local money changers and/or deposit bankers, and pawnbrokers. Out of these developed further categories such as public (deposit) banks and nonprofit pawn banks, the *monti di pietà*.

International merchant-bankers combined long-distance trade with foreign exchange transactions. By 1200, Italian (Asti, Genoa, Siena, Lucca) merchants advanced money to merchants traveling to the Champagne fairs by accepting obligations (*instrumenta ex causa cambium*, precursors of the bill of exchange), payable at the fairs. The fair became a market for goods, currencies, and information (about prices and exchange rates) and a clearing center for claims and debits; at the end of the fair due balances could either be settled in cash or be deferred as a credit to the following fair by a *lettre de foire*.

The decline of the Champagne fairs, because of shifts to maritime trade routes and to the Italian-German alpine route, and because of growing fiscal pressure from the French crown, led to the rise of large Florentine family companies, from the early fourteenth century on. In this "commercial revolution" (Raymond de Roover), the sedentary merchant-banker replaced the traveling merchant because he could utilize superior business techniques such as the bill of exchange and subsequently double-entry bookkeeping, maritime insurance, and new forms of company partnerships. By the 1330s, the predominant firms were the Bardi, Peruzzi, and Acciaiuoli—veritable "super-companies" (E. Hunt) in terms of their geographical range, stretching as far as England, Spain, and the Aegean, as well as the wide range of their economic activities.

These activities included commodity trading, tax farming, revenue collections for the papacys and banking services for princes, and commerce in bills of exchange. Partnership capital, the *corpo*, was drawn from family members, relatives, and third parties. Profits and losses were divided in proportion to investments. Cash flow and trade were indissolubly linked, and only careful accounting made operations on a Europe-wide scale possible. Cash, however, was often immobilized for longer periods—for example, when the finishing process of imported cloth tied up capital before the cloth could be reexported to consumers. Moreover, in the case of Bardi and Peruzzi, the loans to the Florentine commune and to various monarchs, especially Edward III, who refused to pay principal and interest on his debt, as bankers had sought, drew

JAKOB II FUGGER. Often called the Rich, Jakob Fugger (1459–1525) made loans that assured the election of the Holy Roman Emperor Charles V in 1519. Portrait (1538) by Dosso Dossi (Govanni di Luteri; 1480–1542). (Museum of Fine Arts [Szepmueveszeti Muzeum], Budapest, Hungary/Erich Lessing/Art Resource, NY)

them into a financial morass that contributed to bankruptcies in the 1340s.

Their places were taken by new companies, generally smaller, which organized their branches on the basis of separate partnership contracts. Examples are the Alberti, Francesco di Marco Datini, merchant of Prato, and the Medici Bank. The last began by the end of the fourteenth century with investments in wool manufacture and silk production and a local bank in Florence, which gained huge profits from papal finance. The Rome branch provided up to 50 percent of the Medici's total profits by 1420. The Medici also opened branches in Milan, Naples, Geneva, Bruges, and London with the primary objective of advancing funds by bills of exchange. The fortunes of the bank declined after the death of Cosimo de' Medici in 1464, one reason being inefficient management and a lack of central control and another being an unfavorable set of developments in the branches. Unauthorized loans to the English king and to Duke Charles the Bold of Burgundy compromised both the London and the Bruges branches. Furthermore, the establishment of the Lyon fairs by Louis

XI of France diverted business away from the Geneva fairs and Geneva's Medici branch. When the Medici opened another branch in Lyon in the 1460s, specializing in the exchange market in the new international clearing center Lyon, it failed miserably. However, a broad portfolio of investments and a broad spread of independent branches generally did reduce the risk that a crisis in one branch would mean a disaster for the entire enterprise, as in the age of the Bardi and Peruzzi. In 1494, however, when the Medici were expelled from Florence, and the bank was closed during the French invasion, the Medici Bank was already in bankruptcy. The Medici themselves, who later became dukes of Tuscany, were replaced by other merchant-bankers, among them the South German Fuggers. The Fuggers represented the most developed form of late-medieval family mercantile companies, differing from their predecessors only with respect to their investments in silver, copper, and mercury mining and their concentration on Habsburg rulers.

Below the international merchants ranked local money changers or deposit bankers. Once money changers began accepting deposits, as they did in Genoa in the mid-twelfth century and in Venice during the thirteenth century, the move to the transferability of deposits on current account was almost inevitable. Operating on a fractional reserve system, granting overdrafts, a successful banker liberated his clients more and more from dependency upon cash. Clients opened accounts not only to safeguard moneys and valuables but especially to utilize such deposits in making payments to creditors in bank money by giro or assignment. In most places, clients gave their orders to the bankers orally, but in Tuscany they drew sums on a bank by a written check. The banker transferred the money by the mere stroke of a pen (for which the banks in Venice were called *banchi di scritta*). Clients periodically compared their accounts with those of their bankers, and bankers cleared their debits and credits informally among themselves. Because of their crucial role in the local payments system, deposit banks were more or less subject to strict control by the government, which licensed the bankers. Their location was usually in the central business square (Rialto at Venice, Mercato Nuovo at Florence, Piazza Banchi at Genoa).

The most important centers for deposit banking were Venice, Genoa, Barcelona, and Bruges, and, in the Holy Roman Empire, Cologne and Nuremberg. Unlike those of the Italian and western European deposit bankers, the services of Cologne and Nuremberg money changers were not confined locally since they also dealt internationally in bills of exchange at the Frankfurt fairs. Deposit bankers who were also money changers were often subject to panics and crises. Especially as result of the "great bullion famine" and thus chronic coin scarcities, western Euro-

pean deposit banking waned in importance during the early- to mid-fifteenth century, and survivors faced increasing state restrictions (as in the Burgundian Low Countries, with the monetary reforms of 1433–1435). In Italy, deposit banking encountered its major crises in the sixteenth century, and did not survive there in many cities. Civic governments responded by establishing public deposit and exchange banks, modeled on those previously founded in the fifteenth century, in Aragon (in Barcelona, Taula de Cambi, 1401; in Valencia, 1408) and in Italy. The Aragonese Banks did not survive the bullion famine, and even the Casa di San Giorgio of Genoa, dating from 1407 and functioning as a public bank, had to give up the experiment in 1444. The establishments of the late sixteenth century were more successful: Banco di San Giorgio in Genoa (1586), Banco della Piazza di Rialto in Venice (1587), Banco di Messina (1587), Banco di Sant'Ambrogio in Milan (1593), and so on, thus shaping the model for public exchange banks of the seventeenth century (Wisselbank in Amsterdam, 1609; Hamburg Bank, 1619; Banco Giro in Venice, 1619; Nuremberg Banco Publico, 1621).

On the lowest level of credit institutions there was the pawnbroker, who granted loans on the security of movable property for a fixed rate of interest. Consumer credits were crucial for the survival of the poorer strata of society, especially during the seasonal fluctuations of agrarian production. Although there was a sophisticated scholastic debate on the role of usury in the commerce of merchant-bankers, the role of the pawnbroker was evident. He belonged to an "infamous profession." Pawnbroking was officially forbidden everywhere, yet it received special licenses because people depended upon the services of pawnbrokers. Moreover, cities offered special contracts or *condotte* to Jewish pawnbrokers, who guaranteed regular payments to the city and a stable of interest rate (20 percent), thus bettering the rates of 25 percent that in 1366 Christian usurers had demanded in Mestre. All over western Europe, princes and urban governments granted privileges to "Lombards," Italian pawnbrokers who were usually citizens of Asti and Chieri in Piemonte. Thus there was a rigorous competition between Christian and Jewish pawnbrokers, one in which the Jewish merchants usually emerged victorious because of strong family networks.

In Italy, however, Jewish moneylenders faced severe pressures from the Franciscan Order, which tried to replace them with the new charitable institution of the *monte di pietà*. The first effort was the *monte da' poveri*, founded in Perugia in 1462. The attempt was not really successful since the institutions operated harmoniously together, each satisfying demands for different forms of credit. Also the *monti di pietà* offered different services: small consumer credits (money) in the cities, demanding 3 percent interest and later repayment, and wheat for seed corn in the country, to be given back after the harvest. In the sixteenth century many *monti di pietà* branches started to accept deposits (at interest), thus enlarging their working capital. Moreover, the idea spread to the southern Netherlands, where Ypes (Ieper) (1534) and Bruges (1573) opened public pawnshops after the withdrawal of the Lombards.

In the early modern period, these banking institutions and instruments developed further, and new types emerged. There were two models, the Italian deposit and clearing bank system and the discount and issuing banking system, which originated in Antwerp and was brought to perfection in London. The Italian traditions were spread through Europe by immigration, mercantile contacts, and communication at the great fairs, which were dominated by Italian merchant banking houses. The principle of the fairs of Geneva and Lyon as Besançon and Piacenza in the late sixteenth and early seventeenth centuries was a stable money of account, which the international setting-off for credits and debits was based upon. Thus the Lyon fairs developed into *foires de change*, while the Besançon and Piacenza fairs were dominated by trade in bills instead of goods. A further step was development of a permanent system of multilateral clearing, concentrating all accounts at a single bank, which was introduced by such public exchange banks as the Banco della Piazza di Rialto and the Amsterdam Wisselbank. The civic ordinances that established the Wisselbank in 1609 abrogated the unregulated exchange activities of the private *kassiers* (moneylenders) and transferred them to the new public bank. Out of the monetary chaos of the early seventeenth century the bank created stable silver coins, which the Dutch needed for their commerce in the Baltic, the Levant, and the East Indies. The bank also established an international clearing system since all transactions over 600 guilders (florins) had to be cleared by the bank, thus forcing all the important companies to open accounts. Moneylending was not so important since it was contrary to the bank's founding statutes. However, institutions such as the city of Amsterdam or the East India Company were able to borrow money through overdrafts, paying penalty fees as interest. A final important function of the Wisselbank concerned the precious metals trade. From 1683 onward, bank clients were allowed to deposit precious metals, and their value was credited to the clients' accounts. The bank traded with the precious metals deposited, and the clients used their receipts to settle debts.

Besides the Wisselbank, private bankers, offering cash deposits, discounting and acceptance credits, contributed to the banking success at Amsterdam, which became the major European center for international government finance in the eighteenth century. The success of Amsterdam spread from the Low Countries to Germany, where the Italian banking tradition was received either directly or by Dutch middlemen. During the sixteenth century, Frankfurt, the leading banking center in central Europe, was integrated with its fairs with the clearing system of Lyon, Besançon, and Piacenza. From 1585 on, Frankfurt merchants created a setting-off system *sui generis*, which was centralized at the Frankfurt exchange in the periods between the fairs at weekly paydays. Even more innovative was the foundation of exchange banks in Hamburg and Nuremberg. In Hamburg, where Dutch immigrants had contributed to the diffusion of the bill of exchange in northern commerce, a public exchange bank was founded—on their initiative—in 1619. The bank created two moneys of account: a stable bank money (mark banco) and a current money (mark courant). Because of the obligation to settle bills over four hundred *Marks lübisch* through the bank, it served as a successful clearing institution for northern and eastern Germany up to 1875.

In the long run, even more important than the Italian/ Amsterdam tradition in banking were the financial innovations of the Habsburg Low Countries, which led— from the early sixteenth to the mid-sixteenth century—to the legal and full negotiability of credit instruments. At the Brabant fairs of Antwerp and Bergen-en-Zoom, the use of bills obligatory (promissory notes) had long been in common practice, usually with three-month maturities set for the dates of the cycle of fairs. The hand-to-hand circulation of these bills was, however, very limited, because of various legal problems that left third parties with an insecure claim to payment. In 1507, the law merchant court of Antwerp removed these obstacles with a *turba*, evidently based on the precedent set by the London mayor's law-merchant courts in 1437, that provided "the bearer of writings obligatory [with] the same rights as the original creditor with regard to the prosecution of an insolvent debtor" (H. van der Wee). In 1537 and 1541, the Estates General of the Habsburg Netherlands went a step further with ordinances that granted the status of legal tender to payment made by the transfer of commercial bills with a bearer clause, while also requiring that all prior transferring creditors were to be and remain jointly liable for payment. Before the end of the sixteenth century, discounting became an increasingly common practice for the longer-term bills obligatory—an early example dates from the 1530s. The key feature of negotiability of commercial bills, with discounting, was the acceptance of written endorsement (making each endorsee liable) in the Antwerp money market, around 1600.

Following Antwerp's decline, clearly evident by that date, London rather than its rival Amsterdam proved to be more successful in profiting from Antwerp's financial innovations. In the first half of the seventeenth century, London goldsmiths began to assume various functions of modern banking; but only during the Restoration era, after

1660, did they acquire their major role as financial intermediaries in the English economy—in offering monetary remittances and clearing services, by discounting promissory notes and "inland bills," and then by issuing interest-bearing deposit certificates, which finally became non-interest-bearing bearer bank notes. From 1694, however, the new Bank of England, as England's first and only joint-stock bank (before 1826), quickly surpassed, though did not fully supplant, the goldsmiths in many financial roles, especially in discounting both private and government bills but above all in discounting the newly issued exchequer bills (from 1695), trading in bullion, and issuing legal-tender bank notes, thereby forcing most goldsmith banks to cease issuing notes by the 1720s. By the mid-eighteenth century, the resources (with much increased capitalization), the credit, and the stability of the bank had allowed it to become the institutional heart of the financial city. From the 1760s on, it was able to perform as an effective "lender of last resort" in ways that the Amsterdam Wisselbank, as a strictly giro bank, could not. During the financial crises of 1763, 1773, and 1783, its success in that role—in replenishing the cash reserves of its own clients, including some Dutch banks, through rediscounting their inventory of bills—drew much of the financial commerce away from now-threatened Amsterdam. Protected by the state, the bank serviced the credit needs of the merchant community, as British merchants overseas were at the same time diversifying into different private banking activities. Thus by the later eighteenth century, the English banking system consisted of an embryonic central bank and a well-developed set of private banking institutions, one having matured over a century, that furnished both internal and international trade with substantial forms of liquid credit and mechanisms of exchange, in both discounted bills and legal tender currency.

In continental Europe, this model was introduced only gradually. Even in the nineteenth century, merchant or private bankers long remained dominant, with regional specialization. In Germany, for example, Frankfurt became the center for public finance (Bethmanns, Rothschilds), and Cologne concentrated upon industrial finance (Oppenheims, Schaafhausens), leaving the finance of trade and other services to Hamburg (Joh. Berenberg, Gossler & Co).

BIBLIOGRAPHY

Abulafia, David. "Italian Banking in the Late Middle Ages." In *Banking, Trade, and Industry: Europe, America, and Asia from the Thirteenth to the Twentieth Century*, edited by A. Teichova, G. Kurgan-Van Hentenryk, and D. Ziegler, pp. 17–34. Cambridge, 1997.

Bowen, H. V., and Cottrell, P. L. "Banking and the Evolution of the British Economy, 1494–1878." In *Banking, Trade, and Industry: Europe, America, and Asia from the Thirteenth to the Twentieth Century*, edited by A. Teichova, G. Kurgan-Van Hentenryk, and D. Ziegler, pp. 89–112. Cambridge, 1997.

De Roover, Raymond. *Money, Banking, and Credit in Mediaeval Bruges*. Cambridge, Mass., 1948.

De Roover, Raymond. *Rise and Decline of the Medici Bank, 1397–1494*. Cambridge, Mass., 1963.

Hunt, Edwin S. *The Medieval Super-Companies: A Study of the Peruzzi Company of Florence*. Cambridge, 1994.

Lane, Frederic C., and Mueller, Reinhold C. *Money and Banking in Medieval and Renaissance Venice*, vol. 1, *Coins and Moneys of Account*. Baltimore and London, 1985.

Mueller, Reinhold C. "Bank." In *Von Aktie bis Zoll: Ein historisches Lexikon des Geldes*, edited by M. North, pp. 32–35. Munich, 1995.

Mueller, Reinhold C. "Larghezza." In *Von Aktie bis Zoll: Ein historisches Lexikon des Geldes*, edited by M. North, p. 213. Munich, 1995.

Mueller, Reinhold C. "Ricorsa." In *Von Aktie bis Zoll: Ein historisches Lexikon des Geldes*, edited by M. North, pp. 343–344. Munich, 1995.

Mueller, Reinhold C. "Strettezza." In *Von Aktie bis Zoll: Ein historisches Lexikon des Geldes*, edited by M. North, pp. 385–386. Munich, 1995.

Mueller, Reinhold C. "Usance." In *Von Aktie bis Zoll: Ein historisches Lexikon des Geldes*, edited by M. North, p. 403. Munich, 1995.

Mueller, Reinhold C. *The Venetian Money Market: Banks, Panics, and the Public Debt, 1200–1500*. Baltimore and London, 1997.

Munro, John H. "The International Law Merchant and the Evolution of Negotiable Credit in Late-Medieval England and the Low Countries." In *Textiles, Towns and Trade: Essays in the Economic History of Late-Medieval England and the Low Countries*, edited by J. H. Munro, pp. 49–80. Aldershot, U.K., 1994.

Munro, John H. "Inhaber-Klausel." In *Von Aktie bis Zoll: Ein historisches Lexikon des Geldes*, edited by M. North, pp. 171–172. Munich, 1995.

Munro, John H. "Inhaber-Schuldschein." In *Von Aktie bis Zoll: Ein historisches Lexikon des Geldes*, edited by M. North, pp. 172–174. Munich, 1995.

Munro, John H. "Wechsel." In *Von Aktie bis Zoll: Ein historisches Lexikon des Geldes*, edited by M. North, pp. 413–416. Munich, 1995.

North, Michaël, ed. *Das Geld und seine Geschichte: Vom Mittelalter bis zur Gegenwart*. Munich, 1994.

North, Michaël, ed. *Von Aktie bis Zoll: Ein historisches Lexikon des Geldes*. Munich, 1995.

North, Michaël. "The Great German Banking Houses and International Merchants, Sixteenth to Nineteenth Century." In *Banking, Trade, and Industry: Europe, America and Asia from the Thirteenth to the Twentieth Century*, edited by A. Teichova, G. Kurgan-Van Hentenryk, and D. Ziegler, pp. 35–49. Cambridge, 1997.

North, Michaël, ed. *Kommunikation, Handel, Geld und Banken in der frühen Neuzeit*. Oldenburg, Germany, 2000.

Teichova, Alice, Ginette Kurgan-Van Hentenryk, and Dieter Ziegler, eds. *Banking, Trade, and Industry: Europe, America, and Asia from the Thirteenth to the Twentieth Century*. Cambridge, 1997.

Wee, Herman Van der. *The Growth of the Antwerp Market and the European Economy (Fourteenth–Sixteenth Centuries)*. 3 vols. The Hague, 1963.

Wee, Herman Van der. "Monetary, Credit and Banking Systems." In *The Cambridge Economic History of Europe*, vol. 5, *The Economic Organization of Early Modern Europe*, edited by E. E. Rich und C. Wilson, pp. 315–322. Cambridge, 1977.

Wee, Herman Van der. "The Influence of Banking on the Rise of Capitalism in North-west Europe, Fourteenth to Nineteenth Century." In *Banking, Trade and Industry: Europe, America, and Asia from the Thirteenth to the Twentieth Century*, edited by A. Teichova, G. Kurgan-Van Hentenryk, and D. Ziegler, pp. 173–188. Cambridge, 1997.

MICHAËL NORTH

Modern Period

Contemporary financial intermediaries, including commercial banks, that operate in developed countries are large-scale, multidivisional, international corporations. The form of today's banks reflects the breadth of customers they serve, and the services they provide reflect the changing needs of those customers. Whereas technological change within banking has been an important force in shaping the size, scope, and structure of financial intermediaries, other historical trends and particular historical events have contributed to the development of modern banking. One especially important factor shaping the development of commercial banks has been their relationship to government. Banks often have been chartered as instruments of government policy. More fundamentally, government regulatory restrictions, grants of special privileges, and financial dealings between government and banks have played a crucial role in financial innovation, and in the rise or demise of important financial institutions.

The demonstrated usefulness of the first public clearing banks of Venice, Genoa, Seville, Barcelona, Basel, and Strasbourg combined with legal innovations in the creation of negotiable instruments and joint-stock companies to set the stage for an international revolution in banking in the seventeenth and eighteenth centuries. That revolution took place throughout northern Europe and especially in London, Amsterdam, Hamburg, Stockholm, and Paris, which saw the development of important new institutional forms. The burdens of financing war, along with mercantilist links between sovereign and growing commercial interests, provided impetus for these changes. Marketable sovereign debts, such as those of the Habsburg Charles V in the mid-sixteenth century, created a large new market for transferable and heritable annuities. Banks, in turn, relied on these securities markets to float their stock and debt offerings. The growth in public finance exerted an important developmental influence on European securities markets up to the end of the Napoleonic Wars.

The most ambitious early advocate of a strong financial partnership between private and public interests was John Law, a Scotsman who rose to control the finances of France during the early eighteenth century. Law's "system" was a set of economic doctrines embodied in novel debt-management practices and financial institutions. Law was among the first to consider how bank chartering, debt-management policies, and the chartering of other joint-stock companies could be used together to effect domestic macroeconomic objectives and spur internal economic development. His system depended on the use of monetary powers and banking to reduce sovereign debt service costs and to promote greater liquidity and economic activity. Thus, Law's system can be viewed as the origin of two important applications of the power of banks: countercyclical monetary policy and development banking.

John Law's *Money and Trade Considered* (1705) pointed to the potential use of bank charters to finance land development as well as commerce. Although chartered land banks did not take hold in either England or France in the eighteenth century, the idea was embraced in the American colonies, where the developmental advantages of land banks received the eloquent support of a young Benjamin Franklin (see *A Modest Inquiry into the Nature and Necessity of a Paper Currency* [1729]). Law's doctrines also reemerged in French development banking schemes of the mid-nineteenth century (e.g., Crédit Mobilier, Crédit Foncier, and Crédit Agricole).

Public land banks (with mortgages as assets and bank notes as liabilities) offered two advantages in the American colonies, where wealth was largely land-based. First, the use of paper money freed resources that were being devoted to importing specie money, thereby increasing the wealth of colonial inhabitants. Second, mortgages provided a means to finance expansion on the frontier by relaxing capital-market constraints faced by land speculators and farmers. This logic was also extended to colonial government bills of credit (paper money not backed by land). These bills were used in lieu of taxes to finance government expenditures, especially war expenses. They also economized on resources by displacing specie and permitted the colonies to avoid current taxation and borrow against future taxes, which relaxed liquidity constraints on development. Land banks and bills of credit were opposed, and eventually prohibited, by Britain.

Banking in Scotland and America, 1700–1840. Other important innovations in banking can be traced to Scotland and America, which were exceptional in several respects. Like America, and unlike England, Scotland was an important primary commodities producer. The Scottish banking system, like the American, developed as part of a "peripheral" economy, based initially on agriculture and increasingly on commerce and industry. The English banking system, particularly in the London banks, was involved in public finance and imperial commerce, but the banking systems of America and Scotland were active participants in the process of industrial finance from the first Industrial Revolution. In Scotland, the textiles, iron, coal, whiskey, and brewing industries were all heavily bank-dependent. In New England, the cotton textiles industry was the main user of industrial finance (Lamoreaux, 1994). Recent research on New England's banks emphasizes that bankers and industrialists often were the same people, and many bankers lent almost exclusively to the companies in which they were involved.

The banking system of Scotland was unusual in other respects. Its first chartered bank, the Bank of Scotland, chartered in 1695, had no link to the Scottish government and was prohibited by its charter from lending money to the state, under heavy penalty. This restriction was largely an artifact of the absence of independent sovereignty. This relative independence from imperial concerns put the Scottish banking system on a different path from England's from an early date and left it free.

Perhaps the most important and unique feature of Scottish banking was the intensity of competition among banks. Soon after the founding of the Bank of Scotland, a competing bank, the Royal Bank (1727), was chartered. Another bank, the British Linen Company, was chartered in 1746. Alongside the three specially chartered banks, private banks, provincial banks, and joint-stock banks arose. Despite some differences in their roles within the banking system, these various types of banks engaged in similar activities. Joint-stock, private, and provincial banks typically were organized as permanently capitalized partnerships or companies, but joint-stock banks alone among the three had publicly traded shares. By 1826, there were thirty-five banks operating in Scotland; but that figure understates the extent of Scottish banking.

A distinctive feature of Scottish banking was the ability of banks to branch freely, 134 bank branches having been established by 1826. The advantages of branching—first illustrated in Scotland—included increased competition, greater diversification of bank portfolio risk, and ease of coordinating payment transfers within a small number of institutions.

Scotland's banks appear to have been uniquely stable, whether measured by the probability that a bank would fail over a given time interval or by the propensity for runs on individual banks or systemwide panics (runs on all banks at once). The relative stability of the Scottish system likely reflects the greater diversification within banks and coordination among banks that large-scale, branch banking allows.

Scotland's banks also financed themselves differently from England's. They were the first banks to rely upon small-denomination bank notes and interest-bearing deposits to fund their activities, which reflected the intense competition among banks for funds. The use of bank notes as bank liabilities led to additional experimentation. Scottish banks organized a note exchange to facilitate the circulation of each other's notes. These banks also were the first to experiment with explicit option clauses in bank notes. These controversial clauses were outlawed in Scotland in 1765, but they had set the important precedent that during times of systemic crisis, the legal requirement of convertibility of bank debts on demand could be suspended. This became a common practice throughout the world by the nineteenth century, although the legal authority charged with determining whether to permit suspension of convertibility varied.

Another important innovation associated with Scotland's three chartered banks was the limited liability of bank stockholders for losses incurred by depositors or noteholders. In general, limited liability protects bank stockholders from unlimited claims against the stockholders' personal assets. In Scotland, limited liability took the form of no personal liability of the stockholders for corporate debt, but in the United States, limited liability laws varied and included double liability and other rules by which stockholders could be liable personally for bank losses in proportion to their capital contributions to the bank. This innovative feature of Scottish chartered banking was not permitted for other banks in Scotland; and it was not imitated in Britain until the statute of 1858, which admitted banks to the privilege of limited liability with respect to their general obligations, which did not include banks' promissory notes.

Although Scotland invented it, the United States made the greatest use of limited-liability banking in the early nineteenth century. American independence from England permitted the establishment of private corporations (including banks), which had hitherto been prohibited by Parliament. The extent of the liability of stockholders in American chartered banking corporations was unclear until the 1820s, by which time the precedent was established and the practice widespread. Initially, bank incorporation under limited liability was viewed as an important special privilege to be granted by government in pursuit of activities that served the commonweal—a source of public revenue and lending and a means to finance favored public works projects. Because early America was a capital scarce economy with few large concentrations of wealth, banking corporations were useful for concentrating wealth for certain purposes.

Congress established the first incorporated bank, the Bank of North America, in 1781 as a financing vehicle for the government on Robert Morris's recommendation. At that time, there was no general agreement over whether the federal government had the power to charter banks. Without resolving the matter legally, after the Revolution, the Bank of North America became a state-chartered institution. At the same time, other states were chartering banks under their individual laws (most notably, Alexander Hamilton's Bank of New York in 1784). Under the new Constitution, federal authority to charter banks was left murky, but the prodding of Hamilton, the first secretary of the Treasury, led to the formation of the Bank of the United States in 1791. Not only did the Bank of the United States assist in the collection of government revenue, the placement of national debt, and the supply of credit to the government, but the federal government also owned shares in the bank, which it later liquidated at a handsome profit.

From the beginning, Americans objected to the federal chartering of banks because of the potentially antidemocratic consequences of creating a powerful financial monopoly within the United States. These objections led to the failure to renew the Bank of the United States' charter in 1811. Its value as a fiscal coordinator and source of funds was revealed by its absence during the War of 1812, and a new Second Bank of the United States was chartered in 1816, again for twenty years. At the time the Second Bank was chartered, there was a general suspension of convertibility of bank notes, a consequence of the war. The Second Bank was expected to restore convertibility of bank notes within the country by maintaining redemption facilities for notes; but it was merely a large private bank, and did not possess a "widow's cruse" of specie with which to redeem notes of insufficient underlying value. In 1819, the Second Bank retreated from this activity, and thereby helped to precipitate a general suspension of convertibility. Blame for the crisis set in motion opposition to the continuation of the bank. This, combined with Jackson's opposition to some features of the Second Bank's charter, culminated in the "bank war" between President Jackson and Nicholas Biddle, and resulted in Jackson's vetoing the bank's rechartering in 1832.

State-chartered banks also received their share of criticism; accusations of political influence peddling and abuse of authority were leveled against state legislators. As Sylla (1975) observed: "The new republic's rapid growth made the local bank monopolies highly profitable, to the pleasure of legislators who collectively and quite often individually shared in the good fortune that derived from controlling the issuance of bank charters . . . . But Americans demanded more banks . . . ." The demands for free access to banking underlay the free banking movement in the northern United States in the 1830s and 1840s.

The operation of a dual banking system in America (the parallel chartering and regulation of banks by state and federal authorities) is one of the great institutional peculiarities of bank-chartering history, and it was extremely important in creating an economically as well as a politically fragmented banking system. Dual banking was made possible by an early Supreme Court ruling, which held that state-chartered authorities could control banking activities within their borders, with the important exception of the activities of federally chartered banks.

Bank Fragmentation in America. The vesting of banking authority largely at the state level contributed to the uniquely fragmented quality of American banking in two ways. First, to protect their own chartered institutions, states effectively prevented interstate banking. Second, decentralization made it easier for certain special interests (unit bankers and landowning farmers) to succeed in restricting bank branching within states—a political movement that would not become important until the 1880s. Thus, dual banking was an important precondition for producing a fragmented banking system in the United States, which persisted despite its inefficiency for two centuries. Although there were eras of bank consolidation (especially the 1920s), unit bankers and their allies succeeded in preventing significant changes in branching laws until the 1980s and 1990s.

The fragmentation of American banking, especially in the Northern states, brought several related problems, some of them apparent in the early national era. These complications included the higher probability of bank failure, the more frequent incidence of banking panics and suspensions of convertibility, and the problems of transacting in a multitude (first hundreds, and eventually thousands) of different banks' notes. The high failure rate of U.S. banks relative to banks operating in other countries and the higher incidence of banking panics reflected the lack of asset diversification under unit banking, as well as the difficulty of coordinating large numbers of banks to deal with collective problems attendant to banking panics.

Complications in transacting bank notes arose not only from the number of different issuers, but from their geographical isolation from one another. Because bank notes were demandable debt obligations redeemable at par at the bank's headquarters, they traded at par in the cities where they were issued. However, bank notes that drifted to other locations could only be redeemed with a lag; and this lag meant that bank notes would be discounted from par when used at points distant from their point of origin, and that those discounts would reflect the perceived risk of the underlying value of the bank's credit. Empirical evidence has shown that the discount on a bank's notes was positively related to the distance the note had traveled, the riskiness of the bank's assets, and the ratio of assets to capital of the bank. Special note brokers emerged to transact in notes, and many of them published newspapers, called bank note reporters, that quoted weekly or monthly transaction prices in a particular location for notes of all banks of issue. Note reporters also provided information on bank failures and securities prices and gave detailed accounts and illustrations of note forgeries.

The Suffolk System was a note-clearing network developed for New England by Boston banks. Beginning in 1819 and reaching its fully integrated form by the mid-1820s, the system enabled Boston banks to coordinate New England's note clearing among themselves. Each peripheral New England bank was required upon joining the system to deposit funds at one of the Boston clearing banks and to submit to additional rules regarding note issuance. In return for its agreeing to become a member of the system, a New England bank's notes were redeemed by all member banks at a uniform discount throughout New England (with the discount set at zero in 1825). This system operated successfully in two senses. First, it made transacting in bank notes within New England easier by making New England a uniform currency area where all banks' notes traded at par. Second, the discipline of interbank self-regulation within the system made New England's notes less risky and thereby increased the demand for the notes, within and outside New England.

Some observers, especially the Jacksonians, found objectionable both the private concentration of banking power, as in the Suffolk System, and the discounting of bank notes. With respect to the latter, they viewed note discounting as an opportunity to cheat the "common man." For the Jacksonians, the answer to the dilemma was to purge the financial system of all small-denomination bank notes and rely more on federally produced coins or currency. Indeed, some of Jackson's followers advocated the creation of a new government-chartered monopoly bank of issue, with government bonds for assets and small-denomination notes for liabilities. Although this specific proposal was never realized, it was effectively achieved during the Civil War in the form of the national banking system.

With respect to both the convertibility of notes and the instability of the banking system, state governments developed other schemes to mitigate the effects of fragmentation. Beginning with the creation of New York's Safety Fund system in 1829, six Northern states (New York, Michigan, Vermont, Indiana, Ohio, and Iowa) established insurance systems for some of the banks chartered in their states. Three of these systems (New York, Michigan, and Vermont) adopted a flawed approach to providing mutual protection among member banks, and these schemes resulted in free riding on collective insurance and the rapid collapse of the systems. Indiana enacted a different kind of liability insurance plan in 1834, one based on the principles of credible self-regulation by member banks and unlimited mutual liability for each other's losses; this plan was imitated by Ohio (in 1845) and Iowa (in 1858). Banks within these systems fared well. They enjoyed low and uniform discounts on their currencies in other locations, virtually never experienced bank failures, and even avoided suspension of convertibility during panics when other banks were suspending or failing en masse.

Free-banking laws were another government intervention. The first free-banking statute was passed in New York in 1838, partly as a response to the large numbers of specially chartered and Safety Fund banks that failed during the Panic of 1837. The new system not only permitted banks to enter freely under general incorporation laws, but it set restrictions on note issue that were designed to simultaneously aid the state government and provide more

security to noteholders. Banks were required under the new law to maintain on deposit with the state a 100 percent reserve in the form of bonds, including state bonds, against their note issues. Although there is some evidence that noteholders received greater protection under this arrangement, banks organized under this new law (which spread through much of the North in the 1840s and 1850s) experienced similar failure risks and susceptibility to panics as their predecessors.

In the antebellum South, these problems were less serious than in the North because the South relied on branch banking, which was permitted in some Southern states from the beginning of their chartering history and was adopted by virtually all of the South by the 1840s. This adoption of branching was attributable to two factors: first, contact with Scottish merchants exposed Southerners to the concept of branching; second, Southerners saw special advantages of branch banking in enhancing interregional flows of loans for cotton production and export. Branching provided an alternative means for accomplishing the same ends that motivated free banking, deposit insurance, and clearinghouses in the North.

The Transformation of Banking in the Nineteenth Century. The relationship between government and the banking system underwent an important transformation in much of the world during the nineteenth century. Prior to the early nineteenth century, modern banks were the primary tool of government finance. Over time, however, the privileged chartered banks, both public and private, lost their monopoly over banking privileges. New banks became chartered under general laws of incorporation under which anyone qualifying under the law had access to a bank charter. This new movement generally is termed free banking, although the U.S. incarnation of free banking discussed above had many additional aspects. Free banking in general refers to freedom of entry in banking and does not mean that banks were free of government regulation or taxation. Indeed, the free-banking movement often was characterized by increased taxation of banks and by more restrictive government regulation and supervision of bank activities than the earlier banks experienced.

The essential changes in government–bank relationships were twofold. First, government relied less on specially chartered banks as unique partners in financial affairs. Although central banks such as the Bank of England retained their special relationship with the government vis-à-vis monetary powers, the banking system became more competitive with respect to public and commercial finance. Banks, like other corporations, were taxed or forced to hold government debt. Second, chartered banks and government became less directly dependent upon one another; and in some cases, in the United States, their relationship could be described as adversarial. Existing banks with special privileges, such as the Bank of England, were increasingly called upon to exercise new macroeconomic responsibilities in the public interest as "central banks."

In England, these changes were a natural outgrowth of the transition from a developing imperial economic system to a developed one. The granting of monopoly rights to banks or other joint-stock companies may be regarded as a necessary but temporary evil that helped to ensure an alignment of interest between the bank and the government during the high-risk era of constant war, exploration, and settlement. Once development had occurred, the inefficient restricting of competition became more costly, and the need to provide special incentives for investment lessened. By the mid-nineteenth century, the political constraints of empire building had eased enough to allow England to imitate Scotland's system, based on free entry and branching.

The Bank Acts of 1844 and 1845 were the brainchild of Lord Overstone and the British "currency school," which sought to link the quantity of notes in circulation to the quantity of available specie. These acts restricted the note expansion of English joint-stock banks and required the Bank of England and Scottish banks to maintain 100 percent reserves in gold against note issues. This eliminated any profits the Bank could earn on notes, and helped to further spur the development of deposit banking. In 1858 British joint-stock banks were permitted to obtain limited-liability charters, but on the condition that they would publish periodic statements of their balance sheets and submit to government inspections. Entry into banking and competition among banks in England increased dramatically in the mid-nineteenth century. By 1836, some 61 registered joint-stock banks operated 472 banking facilities (headquarters and branches); by 1870, there were 111 joint-stock banks operating 1,127 facilities. For Britain as a whole in 1870, there were 378 banks operating 2,738 facilities.

Industrial Banking in France and Germany. In the latter half of the nineteenth century, France, Germany, and Austria became a source of important bank innovation, particularly with respect to industrial finance. After a long hiatus from actively promoting the expansion of chartered banking in France, the French government moved aggressively in that direction in the 1850s, with the establishment of the Crédit Mobilier (1852), Crédit Foncier (1852), and its subsidiary, the Crédit Agricole (1861). Of these, the most significant for the historical development of banking was the Crédit Mobilier, which served as a model for limited-liability, large-scale industrial banking throughout Europe in the late nineteenth century. That model was perfected in Germany and elsewhere in the late 1800s in the form of the German Kreditbanken and similar Austrian banks, such as the Creditanstalt.

The German banking system was divided into several separate types of institutions that specialized in different activities, including commercial banks with note-issuing power, credit cooperatives, and industrial credit banks (Kreditbanken). The Kreditbanken were depository institutions that made commercial and industrial loans, underwrote corporate and government securities issues, and managed trust accounts for individual investors. They lacked the power to issue banks notes but faced few other categorical restrictions on their activities. They were organized under limited liability and became the premier financiers of German industrialization in the late nineteenth and early twentieth centuries.

Limited liability was important because it constrained the size of loss that shareholders could experience. This was crucial for German industrial banks because it provided a means to attract capital contributions from "outsiders" (small shareholders without a direct managerial role in the bank), thus allowing the banks to become large quickly. Large size was crucial to successful industrial banking as practiced by late-nineteenth-century banks, as it allowed them to finance firms in important new industries with high minimum scales of efficient production without sacrificing bank portfolio diversification.

The second half of the nineteenth century saw the rise of securities markets for government and corporate finance on a new scale in Europe and America, propelled by war-financing needs and by the need to finance large railroad networks. The creation of these new networks of brokers and dealers changed the way corporate finance was organized, but the form of these changes differed across countries. The banks of Germany and Austria played a central role as financial innovators of universal banking, which combined traditional bank lending with underwriting and trust activities in a novel way. Banks lent to firms in the early stage of the firm-bank relationship, often in the form of very short-term credit, which facilitated bank control over the firm's use of funds. As firms developed, the involvement of banks deepened, as banks underwrote their clients' stock issues and placed the issues within their own trust networks. This allowed a bank to continue to exercise influence over the industrial firm via stock voting proxies that it held in trust. The large size of these nationwide limited-liability universal banks made it possible for the banks to finance industrial lending to large-scale firms. The ability to concentrate funds in the hands of new industries, particularly in the case of electrical equipment and power plants, propelled some German industries to overtake their American and British competitors, despite the head start those competitors enjoyed.

Investment Banking and Commercial Banking in America. In America, the use of securities markets in corporate finance was different from the German model, owing to the fragmentation of the U.S. banking system "Finance capitalism" of the American variety was epitomized by the operations of large investment banking houses such as J. P. Morgan. Like German universal bankers, the investment bankers often played important roles on boards of directors of the firms they helped finance. Unlike their German counterparts, American investment banks' early involvement in firm finances was constrained by branching restrictions that prevented them from becoming nationwide depository institutions and, therefore, limited the scale on which they could lend. Moreover, because investment banks did not operate nationwide branching networks in America, securities were sold through decentralized networks involving several layers of buyers and sellers that transferred securities from the underwriter to the ultimate holder.

This multitiered network for placing securities made it more costly to sell risky securities in America for three reasons: higher physical transaction costs, higher costs of communicating credible information, and greater difficulty of controlling corporate behavior after the issue. Germany avoided such high costs because its banks sold securities within their own networks of customers and retained control over the proxies sold to those customers. These differences were reflected not just in the cost for floating stocks (5 percent in Germany and 25 percent in the United States) but also in the fact that German firms—especially relatively new, small industrial firms—were much more likely to place stock in the market than American firms.

One of the peculiar adaptations of the American banking system was the use of double liability as a standard feature of limited-liability banking, an attribute that national banks and state banks shared. Under double liability, bank stockholders could be assessed to repay bank debt holders up to an amount equal to the stockholders' capital contributions to the bank in the event of bank failure. Double liability allowed bank stockholders to provide protection to depositors without tying up all their wealth in the form of capital contributions to the bank, and thus made it possible for bank lending to expand more than it otherwise could. Double liability disappeared in the 1930s in the United States, in the wake of large bank losses and increasing reliance—beginning in the late 1920s—on small shareholders as a source of bank capital. During the Depression it became clear that extended liability was not always effective because small shareholders had insufficient wealth to support extended liability. Furthermore, the losses borne by small shareholders through extended liability were regarded by some as an unfair burden.

National Bank Chartering and the U.S. Civil War. From 1863 to 1865, the federal government radically transformed the banking system by chartering "national banks" with special note-issuing privileges. Like state banks, national banks only operated within individual state boundaries. Entry into the new system was free, and state banks were encouraged to enter the national banking system by the prohibitive tax on the note issues of state banks imposed by the federal government.

Some of the provisions of the new system traced their roots to the Jacksonian movement to create a uniform currency with credible backing. National banks were required to maintain 111 percent backing for notes in the form of government bonds held on deposit by the Treasury Department, and had to maintain additional reserves in legal tender currency. Note holders had a first claim not only on bond reserves but on all assets of the bank, in the event of bank failure. The government, redundantly, insured the notes issued by the national banks. The chartering of national banks created a captive demand for government debt (bonds and legal tender notes) by the newly chartered banks, which helped to finance rising Civil War expenditures. Political opposition to the chartering of national banks and federal monopolization of currency production was overcome by arguments that this was the best way to fund the war effort.

The financing of the Civil War had other important effects. The U.S. government's Civil War bond campaign permanently transformed the business of banking through its effect on the development of securities markets. The network of securities sellers and buyers established during the Civil War laid the foundation for private securities flotations, especially railroad financing and industry consolidations, that characterized American finance capitalism in the late nineteenth and early twentieth centuries.

The National Banking System did not alter the fragmented structure of the American banking system. The Comptrollers of the Currency, who oversaw national banks, interpreted Congress's intent as not to allow branching, and so branching by national banks was effectively prohibited until the McFadden Act of 1927, which allowed national banks to branch only where state-chartered bank branching was also permitted.

The costs of unit banking became increasingly apparent in the United States during the late nineteenth century. It made the United States unusual in several important respects. As U.S. territorial expansion proceeded, new regions in the West remained isolated financially, as evidenced by large persistent interest rate differentials between the Eastern financial centers and the new territories and states. The high costs of establishing banks rather than low-cost branch offices made access to banking facilities difficult and made credit more costly. Industrial firms in the United States experienced increasing difficulty in raising funds from banks; as the size of industrial firms grew, small unit banks were unable to meet large-scale industrial financing needs and became increasingly focused on commercial lending. American banks, relative to those in other countries, were uniquely vulnerable to panics and to waves of bank failures.

The Federal Reserve System, World War I, and the Bank Consolidation Wave. In the wake of the Panic of 1907, a National Monetary Commission was established to study the functioning of the U.S. banking system in international perspective and to propose changes. The Federal Reserve System (1913) grew out of the findings and recommendations of the National Monetary Commission. Taken as a whole, the reports of the National Monetary Commission emphasized the seasonal inelasticity of the supply of reserves available to U.S. banks and the consequent inelasticity of bank loan supply. The main weaknesses of the financial system were perceived to be the insufficient seasonal response of lending and the increased seasonal risk in the banking system during times of high loan-to-reserve ratios. The new policy instrument designed to solve these problems was the lending of reserves from the Federal Reserve (the Fed) to member banks at the discount rate. The founding of the Fed was associated with a permanent decline in the seasonality of interest rates and an increase in the seasonality of lending. In this sense, the Fed succeeded in meeting one of its key objectives.

At the end of World War I, as with virtually every previous war, there was a sharp decline in the prices of agricultural products and severe agricultural distress. Agricultural banks suffered great losses, and many banks failed. In the face of banking disasters, the politics and the economics of support for unit banking were undermined in many states. The economic argument in favor of branching was furthered by the low failure rates of branching banks, and by the collapse of the eight state-sponsored deposit insurance systems. The change wrought by the bank consolidation and branching movement was revolutionary. From 1921 to 1929, the number of banks in the United States declined from 29,788 to 24,504. At the same time, the number of banks operating branches rose from 547 to 764, and the total number of branches rose from 1,455 to 3,353. Changes in bank practice related to consolidation were just as revolutionary. Large-scale banking made new banking activities viable for many banks. Banks expanded their role in industrial lending, trust activities, and underwriting. Yet, despite the increased elasticity of loan supply, the Fed did not succeed in stabilizing the banking system. Waves of bank failures in the 1920s and 1930s and banking panics in the 1930s demonstrated the continuing weakness of the system.

The Great Depression and the Banking Acts of 1933 and 1935. The worldwide economic collapse of 1929 to 1933, and the U.S. regulatory response that followed it, brought an end to the consolidation of banks and the expansion of banking activities in the United States. The Banking Act of 1933 was the single most important piece of banking legislation in U.S. history. It established federal deposit insurance, required a complete separation between underwriting and traditional commercial bank activities, and imposed "Regulation Q" interest ceilings on deposits, including zero interest on all demand deposits. Federal deposit insurance subsidized small banks at the expense of large banks and slowed the bank consolidation movement, and the separation between commercial and investment banking and Regulation Q of the act limited both the scale and the scope of large reserve-center banks. The Banking Act of 1935 extended some of the previous changes and reorganized the Federal Reserve System to concentrate power over monetary policy in the Board of Governors.

The goals of the 1933 act were not new, but the failure of many banks from 1929 to 1933 offered advocates of particular banking reforms an opportunity to press their case. Senator Carter Glass had long opposed the links between securities markets and bank activities, and the use of interbank deposits to finance Wall Street transactions through the reserve pyramid. By blaming the banking collapse of the Great Depression on the connections between banks and securities markets, Glass furthered his objectives of disconnecting banks from securities activities. Prohibiting interest on demand deposits (including interbank deposits) undermined the chief advantage of correspondent banking compared to reserve deposits at the Fed. Recent research on the determinants of bank failures during the period 1929 to 1933 has not supported Glass's view. Several recent studies have found that involvement in underwriting helped banks to diversify and thereby avoid failure, and that the securities underwritten by banks fared at least as well as those underwritten by nonbank underwriters.

Congressman Henry Steagall and his populist colleagues in the House and the Senate had been advocating federal deposit insurance unsuccessfully for thirty years; there was virtually no support for federal deposit insurance among bank regulators. President Franklin Roosevelt and the Secretary of the Treasury opposed it, as did Senator Glass. Deposit insurance won the day because Congressman Steagall was able to engineer a compromise. Essential to Steagall's success was his manipulation of the public perception that large banks had caused the Great Depression through imprudent lending and securities speculation, and that small bankers, like depositors, were unwitting victims. That perception drew support for fixed-premium deposit insurance, which was an unapologetic attempt to prop up small banks with insurance protection paid disproportionately by large banks.

Banking Deregulation in the United States. The defining influences on American banking since the 1930s have been reactions to the regulatory environment created in the 1930s. Because bank regulations imposed costs on banks, they encouraged entry by other intermediaries to perform functions that banks had performed. In reaction to that competition, banks introduced innovations to try to reduce the costs of regulation. This competitive process ultimately resulted in significant deregulation and reform in the last quarter of the twentieth century.

The declining fortunes of banks led the Federal Reserve Board and other influential parties to advocate relaxation of branching restrictions and limitations on bank entry into new areas. Many restrictions on deposit interest rates were phased out in the early 1980s. Acting on its own, the Federal Reserve Board reinterpreted the meaning of the Banking Act of 1933 to allow limited underwriting activities by certain banks and advocated the wholesale elimination of remaining barriers to bank holding company entry into underwriting. As in the 1920s, banking difficulties helped to propel deregulation, this time at both the state and the federal levels. An added element in the 1980s and 1990s was foreign entry into U.S. markets and the declining international prominence of U.S. banks, which galvanized support for expanding the scale and scope of U.S. banks. Many states relaxed branching restrictions during the 1980s and early 1990s, allowing increased branching within states and across adjacent states. In 1994, Congress approved unlimited interstate branching legislation, to be phased in over a period of three years. Government regulators also became more favorably disposed to allowing mergers of large banks to occur unchallenged. The result was a wave of bank consolidation in the late 1980s and 1990s reminiscent of the 1920s. Further relaxation of restrictions on bank underwriting, the expansion of banks into insurance sales, and bank holdings of equity in nonfinancial enterprises were enacted in the 1999 Gramm-Leach-Bliley banking act.

The Japanese Main Bank System. Japan developed a unique banking system in the post–World War II period, based on close ownership links between banks and the firms they finance. Many large Japanese firms operate as parts of conglomerates known as *keiretsu*s. Each *keiretsu* is organized around a large commercial bank, which takes on the role of main bank for each firm within the *keiretsu*. The main bank is the primary lender to the firm, or the organizer of a lending syndicate for the firm, and typically holds a significant amount of equity in the firm. The firms within the *keiretsu* also hold each other's shares. Even firms that operate outside *keiretsu*s may have strong affiliations with banks that hold large amounts of debt and equity in the firms.

During the 1980s and early 1990s, the general perspective on the Japanese main bank system was favorable, emphasizing the advantages of information processing and corporate governance that come with direct ownership by banks of firms. With the collapse of the Japanese banking system in the 1990s, the flaws of the main bank system became apparent. The desire for a more arms-length process of screening and monitoring, and for greater reliance on market credit instruments, underlay the so-called big bang in Japan of the late 1990s, which brought universal banking and deregulation of the entire financial services industry.

Summary. Common current features of the mature banking systems of developed economies include: (1) funding of on-balance-sheet activities through the issuing of negotiable instruments other than paper currency (which has largely been monopolized by state-controlled central banks) and bank capital; (2) the dominance of large-scale, publicly held, limited-liability corporations; (3) the use of branching networks, nationally and internationally, and involvement in a great variety of activities; (4) the determination of bank entry, privileges, and burdens by general statutes and regulations rather than special chartering provisions; (5) the clearing of bank checks, giro accounts, debit card payments, or credit card payments through highly automated and centralized clearing networks.

Despite differences across countries, there has been an international "convergence" in the functions and organization of the banking systems of developed economies over the last two centuries (especially in the 1980s and 1990s). Recent acceleration in this trend reflects increased global competition in financial services that has forced domestic regulators to conform to the "best practice" techniques and strategies of international competitors.

An interesting difference between banking systems before and after Britain's Peel Act of 1844, which imposed a 100 percent specie reserve requirement on note issues, concerns the role of government in financial innovation. In the early period, government had an interest in fostering innovations and encouraging new banking practices, and often was itself the source of innovation. In the later period, government became less active in promoting banks and often encouraged innovation unwittingly through regulatory burdens. Another difference relates to the fiscal role of private banks. Although private banks still must meet many government regulations, in most countries— with some significant exceptions—the social objectives that governments used to achieve through privately chartered banks are now pursued mainly by government programs or government lending institutions.

[*See also* Central Banking.]

BIBLIOGRAPHY

General references that are useful for defining terms and concepts, outlining important theories and empirical findings, and providing brief histories of particular institutions include: G. G. Munn and F. L.

Garcia, *Encyclopedia of Banking and Finance* (1983); J. Eatwell, M. Milgate, and P. Newman, *The New Palgrave Dictionary of Economics* (1987) and *The New Palgrave Dictionary of Money and Finance* (1992); L. Neal, *International Library of Macroeconomic and Financial History: War Finance* (1994); L. Schweikart, *Encyclopedia of American Business History and Biography: Banking and Finance* (1990); R. G. Hubbard, *Money, the Financial System and the Economy* (1994); A. Saunders, *Financial Institutions Management: A Modern Perspective* (1994); G. G. Kaufman, *The U.S. Financial System: Money, Markets, and Institutions* (1992); and S. I. Greenbaum and A. V. Thakor, *Contemporary Financial Intermediation* (1995). An excellent early bibliography of banking and related topics is M. Masui, *A Bibliography of Finance* (1935).

With respect to the practice and history of investment banking, see: V. P. Carosso, *Investment Banking in America: A History* (1970); R. Chernow, *The House of Morgan: An American Banking Dynasty and the Rise of Modern Finance* (1990); I. Friend, ed., *Investment Banking and the New Issues Market* (1967); S. L. Hayes and P. M. Hubbard, *Investment Banking: A Tale of Three Cities* (1990); and M. D. Bordo and R. Sylla, eds., *Anglo-American Finance: Financial Markets and Institutions in twentieth Century North America and the U.K.* (1995).

Useful references on the early history of banking and money include: A. P. Usher, *The Early History of Deposit Banking in Mediterranean Europe* (1943); J. G. van Dillen, ed., *History of the Principal Public Banks* (1934); R. D. Richards, *The Early History of Banking in England* (1958); J. K. Horsefield, *British Monetary Experiments, 1650–1710* (1960); R. DeRoover, *Business, Banking, and Economic Thought in Late Medieval and Early Modern Europe* (1974) and *The Rise and Decline of the Medici Bank, 1397–1494* (1966); S. Dean, ed., *History of Banking and Banks, from the Bank of Venice to the Year 1883* (1884); C. A. Conant, *A History of the Modern Banks of Issue* (1896); R. W. Goldsmith, *Premodern Financial Systems* (1987); C. Nettles, *The Money Supply of the American Colonies before 1720* (1934); A. M. Davis, *Currency and Banking in the Province of the Massachusetts Bay* (1900); H. Phillips, *Historical Sketches of the Paper Currency of the American Colonies* (1865); L. Brock, *The Currency of the American Colonies, 1700–1764* (1975); and J. McCusker, *Money and Exchange in Europe and America, 1600–1775* (1978).

Studies of European banking in the eighteenth, nineteenth, and early twentieth centuries include: C. P. Kindleberger, *A Financial History of Western Europe* (1984); F. Capie and A. Webber, *A Monetary History of the United Kingdom, 1870–1982* (1985); Sir J. H. Clapham, *The Bank of England: A History* (1944); A. Andreades, *History of the Bank of England, 1640–1903* (1966); W. T. C. King, *History of the London Discount Market* (1936); W. F. Crick and J. E. Wadsworth, *A Hundred Years of Joint Stock Banking* (1936); L. Neal, *The Rise of Financial Capitalism: International Capital Markets in the Age of Reason* (1990); A. E. Murphy, *Richard Cantillon: Entrepreneur and Economist* (1986); L. S. Presnell, *Country Banking in the Industrial Revolution* (1956); A. W. Kerr, *History of Banking in Scotland* (1884); S. G. Checkland, *Scottish Banking: A History, 1695–1973* (1975); C. W. Munn, *The Scottish Provincial Banking Companies, 1747–1864* (1981); L. H. White, *Free Banking in Britain: Theory, Experience, and Debate, 1800–1845* (1984); R. E. Cameron, *France and the Economic Development of Europe, 1800–1914* (1961); R. E. Cameron, ed., *Banking in the Early Stages of Industrialization* (1967); Y. Cassis, ed., *Finance and Financiers in European History, 1880–1960* (1992); O. Jeidels, *Das Verhaltnis der deutschen Grossbanken zur Industrie, mit besonderer Berucksichtung der Eisenindustrie* (1905); J. Riesser, *The Great German Banks and Their Concentration, in Connection with the Economic Development of Germany* (1911); P. B. Whale, *Joint Stock Banking in Germany* (1930); R. H. Tilly, *Financial Institutions and Industrialization in the Rhineland, 1815–1870* (1966); and C. W. Calomiris, "The Costs of Rejecting Universal Banking: American Finance in the German Mirror,

1870–1914," in *Coordination and Information*, edited by N. R. Lamoreaux and D. M. G. Raff (1995).

A useful review of the documents surrounding American banking history is contained in H. Krooss, ed., *Documentary History of Banking and Currency in the United States* (1969). Classic contributions to the history of American banking include: D. R. Dewey, *State Banking before the Civil War* (1910); J. J. Knox, ed., *A History of Banking in the United States* (1900); F. Redlich, *The Molding of American Banking* (1947); B. Hammond, *Banks and Politics in America from the Revolution to the Civil War* (1957); M. Myers, *The New York Money Market: Origins and Development* (1931); E. W. Kemmerer, *Seasonal Variations in the Relative Demand for Money and Capital in the United States* (1910); and R. Goldsmith, *Financial Intermediaries in the American Economy since 1900* (1958). More recent works on American banking history include: J. James, *Money and Capital Markets in Postbellum America* (1978); R. Sylla, *The American Capital Market, 1846–1914* (1975); E. N. White, *The Regulation and Reform of the American Banking System, 1900–1929* (1983); N. R. Lamoreaux, *Insider Lending: Banks, Personal Connections, and Economic Development in Industrial New England* (1994); B. J. Klebaner, *American Commercial Banking: A History* (1990); L. Schweikart, *Banking in the American South from the Age of Jackson to Reconstruction* (1987); L. P. Doti and L. Schweikart, *Banking in the American West from the Gold Rush to Deregulation* (1991); G. J. Benston, *The Separation of Commercial and Investment Banking: The Glass-Steagall Act Revisited and Reconsidered* (1989); and C. W. Calomiris, *U.S. Bank Deregulation in Historical Perspective* (2000). Useful discussions of Jacksonian banking policy include: C. Duncombe, *Duncombe's Free Banking* (1841); P. Temin, *The Jacksonian Economy* (1969); and L. Schweikart, "Jacksonian Ideology, Currency Control and Central Banking: A Reappraisal," *The Historian* (1988). Works that analyze American banking in the context of monetary or fiscal history include: M. Friedman and A. J. Schwartz, *A Monetary History of the United States* (1963); E. Wicker, *Federal Reserve Monetary Policy* (1966); D. C. Wheelock, *The Strategy and Consistency of Federal Reserve Monetary Policy, 1924–1933* (1991); and P. Studenski and H. E. Krooss, *Financial History of the United States* (1963).

A comprehensive review of the key elements of the Japanese banking system in comparison to other systems is found in M. Aoki and H. Patrick, eds., *The Japanese Main Bank System: Its Relevance for Developing and Transforming Economies* (1994); H. Patrick and Y. C. Park, eds., *The Financial Development of Japan, Korea, and Taiwan: Growth, Repression, and Liberalization* (1994); and T. Hoshi and H. Patrick, *Crisis and Change in the Japanese Financial System* (2000).

Works that treat the origins and consequences of panics include: O. M. W. Sprague, *History of Crises under the National Banking System* (1910); J. G. Cannon, *Clearing Houses* (1910); H. P. Minsky, *John Maynard Keynes* (1975); C. P. Kindleberger, *Manias, Panics, and Crashes* (1978); M. D. Bordo, "The Impact and International Transmission of Financial Crises: Some Historical Evidence, 1870–1933," *Revista di storia economica* (1985); C. W. Calomiris and G. Gorton, "The Origins of Banking Panics: Models, Facts, and Bank Regulation," in *Financial Markets and Financial Crises*, edited by R. G. Hubbard (1991).

On the question of the general necessity, and proper role, of a central bank, see (in addition to previously cited works): J. Law, *Money and Trade Considered, with a Proposal for Supplying the Nation with Money* (1705); A. E. Monroe, *Monetary Theory before Adam Smith* (1923); L. W. Mints, *A History of Banking Theory in Great Britain and the United States* (1945); E. Wood, *English Theories of Central Banking Control, 1819–1858* (1939); F. W. Fetter, *Development of British Monetary Orthodoxy* (1978); L. A. Helms, *The Contributions of Lord Overstone to the Theory of Currency and Banking* (1939); Lord Overstone, *Tracts and Other Publications on Metallic and Paper Currency* (1857); W. Bagehot, *Lombard Street: A Description of the Money Market* (1873); C. Goodhart,

The Evolution of Central Banks: A Natural Development? (1985); F. Capie and G. Wood, eds., *Unregulated Banking: Chaos or Order?* (1991); and J. Miron, "Financial Panics, the Seasonality of the Nominal Interest Rate, and the Founding of the Fed," *American Economic Review* (1986).

On the functioning of the classical and interwar gold standards and the Bretton Woods System, important works include: A. I. Bloomfield, *Monetary Policy under the International Gold Standard: 1880–1914* (1959); L. B. Yeager, *International Monetary Relations: Theory, History, and Policy* (1976); M. D. Bordo and A. J. Schwartz, eds., *A Retrospective on the Classical Gold Standard, 1821–1931* (1984); B. Eichengreen, *Golden Fetters: The Gold Standard and the Great Depression, 1919–1939* (1992) and *A History of the International Monetary System* (1995); M. D. Bordo and B. Eichengreen, eds., *A Retrospective on the Bretton Woods System* (1993); and M. D. Bordo and F. Capie, eds., *Monetary Regimes in Transition* (1993).

On the role of contemporary banks in economic development, and the costs of "financial repression" in developing economies, see: R. I. McKinnon, *Money and Capital in Economic Development* (1973); G. Caprio, I. Atyas, and J. A. Hanson, eds., *Financial Reform: Theory and Evidence* (1994); and D. O. Beim and C. W. Calomiris, *Emerging Financial Markets* (2000).

The recent literature on the bank safety net, debates over its reform, and related debates regarding the deregulation of bank powers from a variety of perspectives are represented by: J. Barth and R. D. Brumbaugh, eds., *The Reform of Federal Deposit Insurance: Disciplining the Government and Protecting Taxpayers* (1992); P. L. Brock, ed., *If Texas Were Chile: A Primer on Banking Reform* (1992); G. G. Kaufman and R. E. Litan, eds., *Assessing Bank Reform: FDICIA One Year Later* (1993); J. Barth and P. Bartholomew, eds., *Emerging Challenges for the International Financial Services Industry* (1992); L. J. White, *The S&L Debacle: Public Policy Lessons for Bank and Thrift Regulation* (1991); J. Barth, *The Great Savings and Loan Debacle* (1991); M. Klausner and L. J. White, eds., *Structural Change in Banking* (1993); A. Saunders and I. Walter, *Universal Banking in the United States: What Could We Gain? What Could We Lose?* (1994); G. Benston, H. Benink, and G. Kaufman, eds., *Coping with Financial Fragility: A Global Perspective* (*Journal of Financial Services Research*, 1995); and G. Kaufman, ed., *Banking, Financial Markets, and Systemic Risk* (*Research in Financial Services*, 2001).

CHARLES W. CALOMIRIS

BANK NOTES. *See* Money and Coinage, *subentry on* Money and Coinage after 1750.

BARBADOS. Since gaining independence from Great Britain in 1966, Barbados has established a reputation within the Caribbean as a development success, using such indices as access to quality health care, housing, education, nutrition, and leisure. The modern lifestyle that is shared by the social majority reflects the country's achievement of the most equitable income distribution in the English-speaking subregion.

Substantial increase in economic output and per capita income led to the growth of a robust middle class against the background of widespread poverty that typified the colonial dispensation. Slow rates of population growth between 1966 and the beginning of the twenty-first century, largely the result of effective family-planning policies, enabled the effective training and education of the labor force for new forms of employment. A discernible outcome has been the growth of labor productivity and the political stability of civil society.

From the 1640s to the 1940s, the colonial economy revolved around the sugar industry, which relied on enslaved African labor until 1838 when emancipation legislation converted slaves into a landless proletariat that remained impoverished in very much the same way a century later. Independence as a political project was associated with considerable social and ideological hostility toward a sugar sector that for the same period showed no serious signs of technological innovation and entrepreneurial adaptation.

The collapse of the sugar industry followed the rise of the nation-state. Sugar, however, represented centuries of accumulated skill and knowledge, and its demise took with it the sustainability of an agricultural sector that was crafted around its subsidiary products. Tourism, newly bolstered by the arrival of jet aircraft technology, followed the nation-building enterprise and emerged by the 1970s as the most important industry in terms of foreign-exchange earnings. Despite disturbing fluctuations in the fortunes of this industry in the past thirty years, it remains the core of economic activity on the island.

From the outset, government was attracted to the Puerto Rican model of industrialization, which emphasized the central role of foreign investment, as outlined by the eminent Saint Lucian economist Sir Arthur Lewis (1915–1991). This development plan was based on the assumption that the island's economic expansion would rely on an industrialization model rather than a persistent plantation economy. This was a significant departure in the conception of a development strategy that now invited government to invest in the modernization of infrastructure, foreigners to invest in tourism and large-scale manufacturing, and local elites to invest in public utilities, housing, and small-scale manufacturing.

The first national government wasted no time in going about the task of revising and expanding previous legislative provisions for the encouragement of tourism and agriculture. Tourism was promoted as a major industrial sector during the first four years of the regime, and government revenues increased at a remarkable rate. A hotel construction boom helped to stimulate the local manufacturing sector and contributed to reduced unemployment levels. In general, this policy meant that an assault was launched upon the sugar industries' dominance of the economy.

Though the tourist industry was targeted as an employment generator for youth and a major foreign-exchange earner, industrialization by invitation was the policy instrument designed for economic takeoff. Light manufacturing industries were encouraged—especially those with labor-intensive bias and an import substitution potential. More liberal tax holidays and duty-free incentives on raw materials were offered to the foreign private sector in order to promote industrialization. This policy was implemented alongside direct government action through the Industrial Development Act and the Export Industries Act of 1963. Within three years of these legislations, some forty-four industrial plants were established, providing more than two thousand jobs.

Early successes in significantly increasing the annual rate of growth of the gross domestic product distinguished early national governments' economic performance from that of their colonial predecessor. There had also been marked expansion in nonsugar agriculture, especially livestock, poultry, and vegetables. Sugar, nonetheless, still dominated the economy, earning $37 million in 1963 compared with $26 million in 1960.

No serious efforts were made to restructure the distribution of economic resources, though occasional mention was made of the need to nationalize the sugar industry. In general, the traditional planter-merchant elite that grew up within the sugar sector remained firmly entrenched. At the beginning of the twentieth century, it had incorporated its ownership in the form of two major conglomerates: Plantations Company Limited and the Barbados Shipping and Trading Company Limited. These two groups dominated the local economy at the end of the century and provided the social arena for the reproduction of a white elite within a largely black populace.

Job creation was associated with the development of a manufacturing sector built around food processing, garment production, and low-technology screwdriver industries within the electronic industry. In these industries, women found employment for the first time outside of domestic service and, to a lesser extent, basic clerical activities. Thousands of working women experienced considerable income enhancement from factory work. The garment industry expanded during the 1970s to meet growing regional demand, especially from Trinidad and Tobago, and absorbed the majority of female workers.

The collapse of oil prices in the 1980s led to the contraction of the Trinidad and Tobago oil-based economy, and Barbados garment manufacturers lost much of their market share. Unable to compete in the extraregional markets, garment producers, and the manufacturing sector in general, experienced systematic decline. Unsuccessful attempts to attract large-scale foreign investment to the sector left behind low sector morale and a reputation associated with low wages and unreliable employment. Barbados, however, at the beginning of the twenty-first century had achieved the highest wages in the subregion, with the exception of the Bahamas, in terms of real purchasing power and U.S.-dollar value.

According to DeLisle Worrell, a leading expert on the Barbados economy, the information services sector has been "heralded by many as the best prospect for export diversification and the replacement of lost manufacturing jobs." The sector, he suggests, seems "just right for the high quality labor Barbados can provide." Government has done a great deal to promote the potential of the sector. Legislative approaches have been effective in promoting the country as a site for international commercial and financial services, and information industries in general.

The nonforeign exchange sectors of the economy, construction, distribution, public-sector services, utilities, education, personal services, banking, and insurance, have played an important role in developing the modern identity of the economy. The growth of the local corporate elite was a direct result of considerable expansion in these sectors. But it was the steady expansion in the number of foreign multinational companies in tourism, banking, finance, and manufacturing that stimulated economic development and transformed the social structure.

Recent emphasis upon the provision of international quality services in the economy have enhanced the idea that Barbadians are experiencing economic relations that are comparable with those obtained in North Atlantic countries. Banks and insurance companies have opened up the market for credit facilities, mortgages, and portfolio investments to a level that has placed unprecedented levels of disposal income in the hands of the average consumer.

The result has been that consumer durables expenditures continue to be a reliable source of activity that drives the expansion of the distributive sector. With the recent introduction of a value-added tax (VAT) regime, government indicated its intention to extract revenues from the consumer revolution. The general view among economic stakeholders is that the VAT has been very successful and has enabled government to expand the provision of quality social services at a time when cuts have become the norm.

A number of key institutions were developed to sustain the economic progress of the postindependence era. The Barbados Development Bank was established in 1969 with a mandate to promote the indigenous small business sector in order to grow the national corporate culture. The provision of long-term loan finance to this sector did not generate the outcomes expected. The failure of the local manufacturing sector to secure a competitive regional or global competence was attributed to circumstances within the bank's purview. By the mid-1990s, the bank was dissolved. Emerging from its ashes were new development institutions that operate within the paradigm of microenterprise financing. It is still understood that government has a special role to play in the development of the small business sector that in general is another way to describe the local nontraditional economic agents.

Three years later the Barbados Central Bank was established to provide a regulatory framework for macroeconomic policy, to encourage public sector fiscal discipline, and to protect the trading value of the national currency. This institution has grown in the number of roles it performs as well as in reputation and now supervises the entire financial system of the country that comprises dozens of foreign multinational banks, finance and mortgage agencies, and offshore investment houses.

This pattern of institutional formation in the financial sector serves as evidence of the continuing dependence of the Barbados economy upon foreign investment and entrepreneurship in order to sustain development. It points to the extent to which the country is as globally integrated in the postcolonial era as it was in the mid-seventeenth century when it emerged as the most profitable cane sugar producer in the fledgling world economy.

[*See also* Caribbean Region.]

BIBLIOGRAPHY

Beckles, Hilary. *A History of Barbados*. Cambridge, 1989.
Downes, Andrew. "Industrial Growth and Employment in a Small Developing Country: The Case of Barbados, 1955–1980." Ph.D. diss., University of Manchester, 1985.
Howard, Michael. "Industrialization and Trade Policy in Barbados." *Social and Economic Studies* 40.1 (1991), 63–92.
Watson, Hilbourne. *The Caribbean in the Global Political Economy*. Kingston, Jamaica, 1994.
Williams, Martin. "From Manufacturing to Producer of Services." In *Barbados: Thirty Years of Independence*, edited by Trevor A. Carmichael, pp. 30–52. Kingston, Jamaica, 1996.
Worrell, DeLisle. "Barbados at Thirty: The Economy." In *Barbados: Thirty Years of Independence*, edited by Trevor A. Carmichael, pp. 3–29. Kingston, Jamaica, 1996.
Worrell, DeLisle, ed. *The Economy of Barbados, 1946–1980*. Bridgetown, Barbados, 1982.

HILARY McD. BECKLES

BARGAINING, COLLECTIVE. Collective bargaining, the determination of wages and working conditions through direct negotiations between groups of workers and their employers, is a term originally coined by Beatrice Webb (1911) in her study of the origins of the British trade union movement. Collective bargaining takes many forms. It can be centralized nationally or decentralized to the shop floor; it may occur at the level of occupations, industries, or establishments; agreements may be formal or informal and they may be detailed or limited to a few topics such as wages and working hours. Governments may participate directly in the substance of bargaining, facilitate or mediate agreement, or be limited to establishing a legal framework for bargaining.

Collective bargaining typically emerges during or after industrial revolutions and is associated with unions that have the ability to strike. Because the structure of unions and the amount of economic power that labor and management are allowed to exercise depend heavily on the political and legal institutions of different countries, collective bargaining tends to have distinctive national characteristics (Dunlop, 1958; Slichter, 1961). Despite both these institutional differences and some ambiguity in the objective functions of unions, collective bargaining is intended to alter labor market outcomes, and this intervention can affect the dynamics of industrialization (Kerr, Dunlop, Harbison, and Myers, 1960).

There are competing theses about the relationship between collective bargaining and industrialization. For some, unions and collective bargaining are sources of market inefficiencies from wage distortions, strikes, inflexible work rules, and rent-seeking behavior (Hirsch and Addison, 1986). According to this monopoly view of unions, collective bargaining reduces social welfare and hinders growth. For others, collective bargaining provides a forum for developing creative solutions to the inevitable conflicts between employers and wage labor that arise during industrialization (Kerr, Dunlop, Harbison, and Myers, 1960; Polanyi, 1944). Still others see unions, strikes, and collective bargaining as catalysts for restructuring economies in which accumulated changes in technology, markets, and power relationships have eroded the efficiency and acceptability of established systems of economic regulation (Boyer, 1990; Braverman, 1974; Piore and Sabel, 1984).

Historically, unions and collective bargaining have served all three of these functions with some success. However, unions and collective bargaining are now in relative decline in many countries (Freeman, 1994; Katz and Darbishire, 2000). Whether this reflects the erosion of union bargaining power by global competition, a reduction of the underlying differences between labor and management, or a lull between economic crises remains a matter of considerable debate (Freeman, 1994; Strauss, 1995).

The Case of Nineteenth-Century Craft Unions. Although no single economy can fully represent the evolution of collective bargaining, the American traditions of strong property and contract laws, competitive labor markets with relatively little governmental market regulation, and the market or "business" orientation of trade unions offer a clear and well-documented illustration of the relationship between collective bargaining and industrialization. The origins of collective bargaining in the United States can be traced to the unionization of atomistic preindustrial markets for highly skilled labor. Early nineteenth-century unions were originally fraternal organizations established by local groups of skilled workers in occupations such as printing, carpentry, shoemaking, and brewing (Ulman, 1955). These fraternal craft "unions" lacked the economic power to compel collective bargaining in their small-scale and volatile industries and also faced legal barriers to bargaining in the common law doctrines limiting interference with employers' property rights and individual employment contracts.

Under these circumstances, U.S. craft unions sought to benefit their members by improving labor market efficiency, rather than following the older European traditions of market regulation by guilds (Bloch, 1961; Webb and Webb, 1911) or of political reform (Hobsbawm, 1984). They provided rudimentary life insurance programs, facilitated job matching by established hiring halls, and improved labor market information by certifying the skills of journeymen and publishing standard wage rates. Their most important contribution to efficiency, however, was the development of apprenticeship programs that produced more productive human capital at a lower cost than the alternatives of indentured apprenticeship and haphazard learning-by-doing (Elbaum, 1995).

Economic theory shows that these improvements in market efficiency can promote growth and improve social welfare, but it is also unlikely that union members can capture the full benefits of these efficiency gains. In practice, nineteenth-century employers took advantage of the efficiencies of union hiring halls and apprenticeship programs and paid union wages when forced to by competition. However, they paid below union rates whenever possible and substituted capital and nonunion labor for union labor when it was profitable to do so.

To secure a larger share of their efficiency contributions for their members, unions sought to control the supply of labor through "members only" hiring halls, limitations on the number of apprentices, and stricter standards for journeyman certification. However, supply control could not successfully address the substitution of other factors for skilled union labor.

Restricting factor substitution meant extending union monopoly power from the labor market to the workplace. Unions defined the amount of production that would constitute a standard day's work for a standard day's pay, and required employers to operate "closed shops" where only union members could be hired. Closed shop agreements marked the transition from supply control in otherwise introduced "job control" through collective bargaining (McCabe, 1912; Perlman, 1928; Ulman, 1955).

This combination of union efficiency practices, monopoly control of labor supply, and job control through collective bargaining became known as "business" unionism and is a distinctive feature of U.S. industrialization (Slichter, 1961). Under business unionism, unions organized and bargained in demand-inelastic sectors when substitutes for skilled labor were highly imperfect, skilled labor accounted for only a small fraction of production costs, and product-demand elasticities were low. Inelastic demand for union labor reduced the employment losses from raising wages through collective bargaining. And because rising wages increased the total wage bill, unions could compensate members for job losses.

Business unionism in the nineteenth century survived several rounds of competition from radical or reform unionism, which favored political action to benefit broad classes in society (Commons, et al., 1918; Taft, 1957). Collective bargaining, however, continued to be severely constrained by common law doctrines favoring employers and, after 1890, by the monopoly restrictions of the Sherman Antitrust Act (Gregory and Katz, 1979). By 1900, union membership accounted for only about 7 percent of the nonagricultural workforce (Wolman, 1924), and labor markets were largely unfettered by collective bargaining (Fishback, 1998).

Shift from General to Firm-Specific Skill. The idiosyncrasies in the division and specialization of labor that accompanied mass production resulted in the gradual replacement of general skills by firm-specific skills and shifted responsibility for training investments from workers to employers (Edwards, 1979; Williamson, 1975). The returns to employer training investments took the form of "efficiency rents" (in which the marginal productivity of labor exceeds the wage), and employers maximized these rents by designing efficient on-the-job training procedures and by limiting labor turnover through the sharing of efficiency rents with their trained employees.

The changing composition of skills also reduced craft union control over labor supply, and falling costs of replacing strikers eroded union job control (Edwards, 1979; Montgomery, 1987). Falling market power and the inhospitable legal climate for unions limited collective bargaining to the most critical skilled workers, and there was little collective bargaining in mass production industries through the first part of the twentieth century when unions represented only about 11 percent of the nonagricultural workforce.

Beginning in the 1930s and 1940s, New Deal labor policies and wartime mobilization replaced organizing based on power with organization based on elections and resulted in widespread collective bargaining in mass production industries. Industrial union membership began to climb (Kochan, Katz, and McKersie, 1986), and by 1970, about one-third of the workforce belonged to unions and an even larger fraction was covered by collective bargaining. Since then, however, unions and collective bargaining have declined steadily toward the level of the 1920s.

Efficiency of Collective Bargaining and Strikes in the Postwar Period. The primary objective of U.S. unions is to improve wages and other labor market outcomes of their members, and this is often thought to lead to deadweight losses in efficiency. Estimates are that postwar collective bargaining raised wages of union members by

COLLECTIVE BARGAINING. Negotiations at the Ford Motor Company, Detroit, 1967. (Walter P. Reuther Library, Wayne State University)

about 15 percent and that further market distortions result from increased fringe benefits, seniority practices, union work rules, and strikes (Freeman and Medoff, 1984).

However, an important offset to the market distortions of collective bargaining is the contributions to efficiency. Job matching and training by craft unions are examples of such efficiencies. Collective bargaining and the incentives of negative-sum strikes can help to secure efficient compromises among different labor and management constituencies, as well as between labor and management (Dunlop, 1967).

Newly unionized employers often reported union "shock effects" on efficiency as managers economized on labor that had suddenly become more expensive (Slichter, Healy, and Livernash, 1960), and productivity improvement can be included in the bargaining agenda (Walton and McKersie, 1965). New developments in management theory during the 1970s and 1980s extended productivity bargaining to include new forms of worker voice, such as quality circles, for solving production problems and improving employee satisfaction (Kochan, Katz, and McKersie, 1986). A large body of research has documented that such employee involvement practices result in substantial efficiency improvements (Black and Lynch, 1999; Ichniowski, et al., 1997; Ichniowski, et al., 2000; Osterman, 2000). Similarly, the grievance procedures, which were an early innovation under collective bargaining and which became nearly universal in collective bargaining agreements by the 1950s, and other forms of collective voice have long been a means of reducing inefficient practices that contribute to employee

dissatisfaction and spontaneous strikes (Slichter, 1941). In addition, grievance procedures have a powerful effect in reducing quit rates (Freeman and Medoff, 1984).

Will Collective Bargaining Survive Globalization? There are frequent debates over whether the monopoly or the efficiency effects of collective bargaining are dominant. As global economic integration increases, this debate is being extended to the question of which national systems of collective bargaining are most competitive (Aoki, 1990; Doeringer, Evans-Klock, and Terkla, forthcoming).

National systems of collective bargaining fall into three categories—craft, bureaucratic, and flexible. The craft model (found in Germany, Denmark, and parts of eastern Europe) illustrates a pattern of industrialization in which many of the elements of craft bargaining have been adapted to large-scale mass production industries. Apprenticeship training with strong union involvement is the basis for skill formation, skills are high, and a large component of general skill is retained (Winkelmann, 1996). In this modern version of the craft model, unions represent a cross section of industrial skills, and collective bargaining is highly centralized by industrial sector. Centralized bargaining is largely limited to compensation, while a second tier of bargaining occurs at the workplace through "workers councils," which discuss issues of working conditions and productivity.

The bureaucratic model of collective bargaining has arisen where industrialization is based on highly specialized labor with firm-specific skills. This model is characteristic of much postwar bargaining in the United States and is most dramatically illustrated in France, where labor markets are heavily regulated by government as well as through collective bargaining (Lorenz, 2000; Reynaud, 1981). France has industrial unions that bargain nationally with employer associations, and the terms of national agreements are extended by law to all employers in a sector. French law also mandates plant-level collective bargaining and committees for discussing shop-floor issues, and governmental machinery exists for resolving grievances. However, both national bargaining and extensive government regulation of wages, hours, and fringe benefits circumscribe plant-level bargaining.

Japan illustrates the model of flexible collective bargaining. Japan was a late-developing country in which industrialization was led by large industrial conglomerates with strong traditions of industrial feudalism and little interest in bargaining with workers. In the absence of union apprenticeship programs or public vocational training, large enterprises were pivotal to the development of modern industrial skills (Dore, 1973). Large employers did not focus on specializing labor to nearly the same degree as those companies in the United States or France, and they invested substantially in general, as well as firm-specific, training to ensure a highly productive and flexible workforce. In order to ensure that quits and labor market competition did not undermine their investment returns, employers instituted seniority-based wage structures and lifetime employment guarantees that penalized job changing.

Collective bargaining was introduced in Japan after the end of World War II, when a wave of strikes led to a new policy governing unions and collective bargaining patterned after that in the United States (Sumiya, 1981). Japanese unions often strike, but they have generally accommodated employers' preferences for a highly productive and flexible workforce (Koike, 1988, 1994). Wages and bonuses often contain strong performance incentives through their links to enterprise profits and employee merit. Employees are intensely involved in quality circles, in which the priority is to improve efficiency, and it has even been argued that lifetime employment practices reduce principal-agent inefficiencies by fostering employee commitment.

Although union membership, collective bargaining, and strikes have declined under each of these models during the postwar period, the broad outlines of national systems of collective bargaining have persisted in the face of increased global competition. It seems unlikely that future industrialization will replace these national systems in the foreseeable future with either union-free labor markets or a single globally efficient model of collective bargaining. Instead, what appears to be happening is that improved efficiency practices are being selectively transferred from one country to another, where they are modified to accommodate traditional collective bargaining practices (Doeringer, Evans-Klock, and Terkla, forthcoming). What is less certain is the direction and extent to which national systems of industrial relations will be modified by these changes.

[*See also* Employers' Associations; Industrial Relations; *and* Unions.]

BIBLIOGRAPHY

Aoki, Masahiko. "Toward an Economic Model of the Japanese Firm." *Journal of Economic Literature* 27 (March 1990), 1–27.

Atack, Jeremy, and Peter Passell. *A New Economic View of American History.* New York, 1994.

Black, Sandra E., and Lisa M. Lynch. "What's Driving the New Economy: The Benefits of Workplace Innovation." November 1999. Authors' mimeo.

Bloch, Marc. *Feudal Society.* Translated by L. A. Manyon. Chicago, 1961.

Boyer, Robert. *The Regulation School: A Critical Introduction.* Translated by Craig Charney. New York, 1990.

Braverman, Harry. *Labor and Monopoly Capital.* New York, 1974.

Commons, John R., David J. Saposs, Helen L. Sumner, et al. *History of Labor in the United States.* New York, 1918.

Doeringer, Peter B., Christine Evans-Klock, and Terkla. *Startup Factories: High Performance Management, Job Quality, and Regional Advantage.* Forthcoming.

Dore, Ronald P. *British Factory, Japanese Factory.* London, 1973.

Dunlop, John T. *Wage Determination under Trade Unions.* New York, 1950.

Dunlop, John T. *Industrial Relations Systems.* New York, 1958.

Dunlop, John T. "The Function of the Strike." In *Frontiers of Collective Bargaining,* edited by John T. Dunlop and Neil W. Chamberlain, pp. 103–112. New York, 1967.

Edwards, Richard. *Contested Terrain.* New York, 1979.

Elbaum, Bernard. "The Economic Rationale of Apprenticeship Training: Some Lessons from the British and U.S. Experience." *Industrial Relations* 34.4 (October 1995), 593–622.

Fishback, Price V. "Operation of 'Unfettered' Labor Markets." *Journal of Economic Literature* (1998), 722–764.

Freeman, Richard B. "How Labor Fares in Advanced Economies." In *Working under Different Rules,* edited by Richard B. Freeman, pp. 1–28. New York, 1994.

Freeman, Richard B., and James L. Medoff. *What Do Unions Do?* New York, 1984.

Gregory, Charles O., and Harold A. Katz. *Labor and the Law.* New York, 1979.

Habakkuk, H. J. *American and British Technology in the Nineteenth Century: The Search for Labour-Saving Inventions.* Cambridge, 1962.

Hirsch, Barry T., and John T. Addison. *The Economic Analysis of Unions: New Approaches and Evidence.* Boston, 1986.

Hobsbawm, Eric J. *Workers: Worlds of Labor.* New York, 1984.

Ichniowski, Casey, Katherine Shaw, and Giovanna Prennushi. "The Effects of Human Resource Management Practices on Productivity: A Study of Steel Finishing Lines." *American Economic Review* 87.3 (June 1997), 291–313.

Ichniowski, Casey, David I. Levine, Craig Olson, et al. *The American Workplace: Skills, Compensation, and Employee Involvement.* New York, 2000.

Katz, Harry C., and Owen Darbishire. *Converging Divergences: Worldwide Changes in Employment Systems.* Ithaca, N.Y., 2000.

Kerr, Clark, John T. Dunlop, Frederick Harbison, et al. *Industrialism and Industrial Man.* Cambridge, Mass., 1960.

Kenney, Martin, and Richard Florida. *Beyond Mass Production*. New York, 1993.

Kochan, Thomas, Harry Katz, and Richard B. McKersie. *The Transformation of American Industrial Relations*. New York, 1986.

Koike, Kazuo. *Understanding Industrial Relations in Modern Japan*. New York, 1988.

Koike, Kazuo. "Learning and Incentive Systems in Japanese Industry." In *The Japanese Firm: Sources of Competitive Strength*, edited by Masahiko Aoki and Ronald Dore. Oxford, 1994.

Lorenz, Edward. "Societal Effects and the Transfer of Business Practices to Britain and France." In *Embedding Organizations: Societal Effects of Actors, Organisations, and Socio-Economic Context*, edited by Marc Maurico and Arndt Sorge, pp. 241–256. Amsterdam, 2000.

McCabe, David A. *The Standard Rates in American Trade Unions*. Baltimore, 1912.

Montgomery, David. *The Fall of the House of Labor*. New York, 1987.

Perlman, Selig. *A Theory of the Labor Movement*. New York, 1928.

Piore, Michael J., and Charles F. Sabel. *The Second Industrial Divide*. New York, 1984.

Polanyi, Karl. *The Great Transformation*. New York, 1944.

Reynaud, Jean-Daniel. "Industrial Relations Research in France, 1960–1975: A Review." In *Industrial Relations in International Perspective*, edited by Peter B. Doeringer, pp. 246–286. London, 1981.

Slichter, Sumner H. *Union Policies and Industrial Management*. Washington, D.C., 1941.

Slichter, Sumner H., "The American System of Industrial Relations: Some Contrasts with Foreign Systems." In *Potentials of the American Economy: Essays in Honor of Sumner H. Slichter*, edited by John T. Dunlop, pp. 271–286. Cambridge, Mass., 1961.

Slichter, Sumner H., James, J. Healy, and E. Robert Livernash. *The Impact of Collective Bargaining on Management*. Washington, D.C., 1960.

Strauss, George. "Is the New Deal System Collapsing and with What Might It Be Replaced?" *Industrial Relations* (1995), 329–349.

Sumiya, Mikio. "The Japanese System of Industrial Relations." In *Industrial Relations in International Perspective*, edited by Peter B. Doeringer, pp. 287 323. London, 1981.

Taft, Philip. *The A. F. of L. in the Time of Gompers*. New York, 1957.

Ulman, Lloyd. *The Rise of the National Trade Union*. Cambridge, Mass., 1955.

Walton, Richard, and Robert B. McKersie. *A Behavioral Theory of Labor Negotiations: An Analysis of a Social Interaction System*. New York, 1965.

Webb, Beatrice Potter. *The Co-operative Movement in Great Britain*. London, 1911.

Webb, Sidney, and Beatrice Webb. *The History of Trade Unions*. London, 1911.

Williamson, Oliver E. *Markets and Hierarchies*. New York, 1975.

Winkelmann, Rainier. "Employment Prospects and Skill Acquisition of Apprenticeship-Trained Workers in Germany." *Industrial and Labor Relations Review* (July 1996), 658–672.

Wolman, Leo. *The Growth of American Trade Unions, 1880–1923*. New York, 1924.

PETER B. DOERINGER

BARINGS. Baring Brothers, was one of a small group of London-based merchant banks that dominated the London capital markets from the late eighteenth century until the early twentieth. In particular, it assisted sovereign, quasi-sovereign, and business entities in countries experiencing capital shortage to raise funds that would finance vital infrastructure development and general expenditure.

In 1717, John Baring emigrated from Bremen, Germany, to Exeter in the West of England, where he emerged as a leading textile merchant and manufacturer. In 1762, his sons, led by Francis, established a sister house in London that initially acted as agents for the family business in Exeter; that emerged as a leading merchant house in its own right, trading in commodities internationally and acting as London agents for other merchants. As such, Barings arranged warehousing and shipping services and made and collected payments. This led to providing merchants with trade finance through either advances or, much more often, through the acceptance of bills of exchange. The size and prestige of Barings grew quickly and, during the War of American Independence, the firm marketed securities issued by the British government to fund war expenditures. Contracts were also won to supply the British army in North America. Francis Baring became well known in political circles and was close to Prime Minister Lord Shelburne, whom he advised on commercial matters, especially those regarding North America. He also became well acquainted with leading merchants and politicians in the United States after the Revolution.

During the Napoleonic Wars (1793–1815), Barings was the most important merchant house in Europe, yet it worked closely with its chief rival, Hope & Company of Amsterdam. The firm had become the principal marketer of British government securities, and it issued bonds for Britain's allies (e.g., the Kingdom of Portugal in 1802.) In those years it also emerged as the most important "American" house in London, in 1803 issuing bonds to enable the young U.S. government under President Thomas Jefferson to purchase the one million square mile territory of Louisiana from France. As the nineteenth century progressed the firm's merchanting business declined, but its trade finance business remained highly important. The firm was a major financier of European and U.S. trade with Asia, as well as of the North Atlantic cotton trade, which it facilitated by establishing a sister house in Liverpool in 1832. The most visible part of the firm's business continued to be the issuance of bonds. Barings, with the Rothschilds Bank, emerged as the most important issuing house in London, which was by far the leading international capital market. It became capable of exercising great influence. In 1818, the French first minister referred to the six great powers in Europe as Britain, France, Russia, Austria, Prussia, and Baring Brothers.

Although the firm specialized in raising finance for governments and businesses in the United States, Canada, Russia, and Argentina, there were also other connections, including the governments of China, Chile, Italy, and Japan. Funds were raised to enable governments to balance budgets, to wage war, or to construct infrastructure. From the mid-nineteenth century, the firm also issued bonds for companies building the railways, tunnels, bridges, and other infrastructure which opened the interior of continents and enabled the growth of cities. Some of the first railways of Canada, Russia, the United States, and France were financed through bond issues handled by Barings. From the mid-1880s onward, bond issuing for overseas businesses led to similar activity for large British-based businesses. Transactions included straightforward debt issues for such businesses as Manchester Ship Canal Company and Mersey Docks & Harbour Board, in order to finance canal and port construction. More complex operations were the conversion of large private partnerships, such as the Guinness and the Whitbread brewing businesses, into public companies, through their flotation on the London Stock Exchange. Additional services provided by Barings were security management and private banking facilities for private clients. Such clients were often associated with sovereign and business clients; they included Napoleon III of France, several U.S. presidents starting with James Monroe, Talleyrand, and the king of the Belgians. The firm also acted as the financial agent for governments—administering their financial affairs generally in London and Europe, providing them with advances, paying interest to their bondholders, and managing sinking funds for debt redemption.

In 1890, Barings suffered a liquidity crisis and was rescued by a Bank of England loan, which had been guaranteed by the British banking community. The business was reconstructed as a limited liability company, known as Baring Brothers & Company Limited. Within a decade, it was again a leading London merchant bank, still owned and managed by the Baring family. For most of the twentieth century, acceptance finance and security issuance remained core activities for Barings. During World War I, the firm was preoccupied with assisting the imperial Russian government in raising finance from the British government, to fund munitions purchases and to make the associated supply arrangements. From the late-1920s, the firm's activities became increasingly focused on the United Kingdom, since the British authorities restricted international lending in order to support their own currency in pounds sterling.

Barings soon emerged as a leader in London in providing corporate-finance services to U.K. companies. Its most complex transactions included the 1920s reorganization of the giant engineering company Armstrong Whitworth & Company Limited and the 1930s rationalization of the Lancashire cotton-textile industry through the establishment of the Lancashire Cotton Corporation. There was a similar shift in the firm's banking business from finance of international trade to finance of U.K. manufacturing. In the 1950s and 1960s, Barings participated fully in advising companies during the wave of mergers and acquisitions that then swept British business. A new core activity, asset management for U.K. pension funds, institutions, and individuals, was developed at that time, alongside corporate finance and banking. In the 1970s, the firm's activities again became internationally spread when subsidiaries were established in the Pacific Basin, the United States, and Europe.

In 1969, the majority of the equity of Barings was transferred by the Baring family to a charitable entity called The Baring Foundation. In 1984, following a major reorganization and the formation of a new holding company, Barings PLC (public limited company), the foundation received the remaining 26 percent of the firm's equity. In the early 1980s, further major diversification occurred, into security broking, with the formation of a security brokerage known as Baring Securities Limited. Initially, it specialized in East Asian securities but subsequently expanded, with considerable success, into the so-called emerging markets of Latin America and eastern Europe. In 1995, Barings PLC collapsed, following the accumulation of massive debts incurred as a result of unauthorized and concealed dealing by a staff member in Singapore. Barings PLC was placed in administration, its business was acquired by ING, the Dutch financial-services group, and it was subsequently renamed ING Barings.

[*See also* Bank Failures *and* Banking, *subentry on* Modern Period.]

BIBLIOGRAPHY

Chapman, Stanley. *The Rise of Merchant Banking*. London, 1984.

Gapper, John, and Nicholas Denton. *All That Glitters: The Fall of Barings*. London, 1996.

Hidy, Ralph. *The House of Baring in American Trade and Finance: English Merchant Bankers at Work, 1763–1861*. Cambridge, Mass., 1949.

Kynaston, David. *The City of London, 1815–2000*. 4 vols. London, 1994–2000.

Orbell, John. *Baring Brothers & Co. Limited: A History to 1939*. London, 1985. Privately printed.

Orbell, John. *A Guide to The Baring Archive at ING Barings*. London, 1997. Privately printed.

Platt, D. C. M. *Foreign Finance in Continental Europe and the USA, 1815–1870*. London, 1984.

Pressnell, L. S. "Gold Reserves, Banking Reserves, and the Baring Crisis of 1890." In *Essays in Money and Banking*, edited by C. R. Whittlesey and J. S. G. Wilson. Oxford, 1968.

Ziegler, Philip. *The Sixth Great Power: Barings, 1762–1929*. London, 1988.

JOHN ORBELL

BARTER AND BARTER ECONOMIES. Barter is defined as the direct exchange of goods or services for other goods and services. Unlike monetary economies, it has no widely accepted medium of exchange for settling payment.

There is a general presumption in economies that a medium of exchange improves economic efficiency. Alchian (1977) presents perhaps the most cogent argument for the existence of net social benefits from the emergence of monetary economies (see also Mélitz, 1974). The need to explain the net benefits from a monetary economy may be obvious, but it stems partly from old classical notions in economics. In these theories, for example, general equilibrium models of the economy, such as the Walrasian model, resorted to some existing commodity as the "numeraire," that is, something in relation to which all prices were set. Money was then simply a "veil" that served no special purpose. Economists would later demonstrate how the existence of money might improve social welfare or, conversely, how barter economies might hamper economic activity.

The chief disadvantage of barter, and of barter economies more generally, lies in the relatively high transactions costs of exchange. Such costs manifest themselves in a variety of forms.

The value of what is sold by an individual may vary according to what is exchanged, or the particular individual or institution with which the exchange is negotiated. In addition, individuals who have the right mix of goods or services that will result in a transaction need to locate each other. This is the familiar "double coincidence of wants" requirement in a barter economy that may be overcome through a medium of exchange. The two parties to a transaction have to negotiate the "price," a time-consuming process involving judgment about the intrinsic value of what is exchanged. Perhaps just as important is the potential for a far greater number of transactions under a barter system than in an economy with a widely accepted medium of exchange. A simple example, familiar to most students in economics, illustrates the point. Consider a simplified economy with only three goals, called A, B, and C. A sale of a good under a barter system would potentially consist of the following transactions:

$$
\begin{array}{ccc}
- & B \to A & C \to A \\
A \to B & - & C \to B \\
A \to C & B \to C & -
\end{array}
$$

The arrows indicate the direction of the transaction, and the dashes reflect the reasonable assumption that no good is exchanged for itself. A total of six transactions is possible. Now, suppose society decides that A is money in the sense that it is a medium of exchange that, perhaps with the aid of the device of legal tender, is acceptable by all in society as the means of payment. Any good can be purchased or sold with money to obtain a different good. As a consequence, there is no longer a need for goods B and C to be traded for each other. Therefore, buyers and sellers now face the following transactions:

$$
\begin{array}{ccc}
- & B \to A & C \to A \\
A \to B & - & - \\
A \to C & - & -
\end{array}
$$

Having a monetary system has reduced the number of potential transactions considerably. Clearly, in a complex society with millions of goods and services, the resulting "savings" in transactions costs would be considerable.

Although the foregoing illustration is useful, it cannot deal with the forces that lead societies to adopt some monetary standard. Indeed, a literature exists suggesting that money, as now known, emerged as a "civilizing" device—though the view continues to be somewhat controversial (e.g., see Goodhart, 2002). Nevertheless, it is clear that several sophisticated societies, such as the Incas and the Egyptians, operated barter economies. For example, Egyptians used grain, and granaries functioned as banks. The Ptolemies essentially developed a type of central bank in Alexandria where payments could be made from one account to another without money, thereby perpetuating the barter approach. For the Incas, a rigid and planned economic system facilitated reliance on barter much as it did for trade between centrally planned economies in the second half of the twentieth century.

Barter-type transactions potentially limit the geographic size of the marketplace since barter trading is facilitated by proximity to the goods and services demanded and supplied (but see below). Barter also requires additional search costs in locating a match that will ensure exchange of the desired set of goods and services. It is possible to retain the main features of a barter system, even in an economy where spatial considerations become important, via the emergence of specialists who are presumably trustworthy and can ensure that goods or services are redistributed elsewhere. Einzig (1966), Hicks (1969), and Clower (1995) have stressed the role of the division of labor and the role of specialists (i.e., merchants) in overcoming some of the constraints that emerge in barter economies. Finally, barter imposes additional information costs to ensure that the necessary characteristics of a product, such as quality and reliability, are known to buyers and sellers prior to completion of the transaction. Perhaps nowhere is the warning "buyer beware" more pertinent than in barter transactions.

Yet, the continued presence of barter is testimony to the resilience of alternative means of exchange, besides indicating that a simple exercise that focuses only on the reduction in the number of transactions under a monetary system does not tell the whole story.

The success of a monetary economy depends not only on its universal acceptance but also on its performance as a store of value. Hence, if what is "money" loses its value rapidly, as in a hyperinflation, a society either will seek out a more stable store of value or revert to barter. Although alternative stores of value, such as gold or a major currency, are normally available, they may not exist in sufficient quantity to permit the maintenance of continued economic activity or its growth over time. Barter then becomes a feasible alternative. Indeed, when Argentina ceased to operate under a currency board system at the end of 2001, and access to any form of monetary liquidity proved difficult to impossible, barter began at once to emerge as a means of exchanging goods and services.

Barter arrangements have also proved important as a trading technique either because the buyer did not have any credit standing, or because the alternative of exchanging currencies was not feasible as the currencies in question did not trade on foreign exchange markets. In that case, it would have been difficult, if not impossible, to place a currency value on the goods and services being traded. For example, prior to the collapse of the Soviet Union, barter trade was the rule among the COMECON (Council for Mutual Economic Cooperation) countries. Such a trading system also had the effect of forcing a form of specialization in the production structure of the economies in question. For example, Czechoslovakia would specialize in streetcar production, Hungary in the production of buses, Poland in trucks, and Cuba in sugar cane production. In return the Soviet Union usually would export oil to these countries, all of which were oil-poor. Nevertheless, owing to the relative size and power of the Soviet Union, there was little effort to ensure that the relative values of what was being traded were equal. To the extent that there was a "price" for the products being traded, oil tended to be overvalued and the finished goods obtained from other countries undervalued. It is widely acknowledged that COMECON was designed to benefit the Soviet Union at the expense of the satellite countries.

To a certain extent, barter arrangements also reflect a desire to avoid the "official" economy and, hence, are a reflection of the desire in some societies for tax avoidance. One difficulty in this connection is that transactions in the so-called underground economies can be completed via money in the form of an exchange of currency, as well as through the method of barter. Currency coexists as a medium of exchange in the underground world, along with barter transactions. Nevertheless, it is quite likely that a considerable fraction of underground economic activity involves the direct exchange of goods and services. Moreover, since estimates of the size of the shadow economy (see, e.g., Schneider and Enste, 2002) are a function of the degree of monetary sophistication and, hence, the stage of economic development, it is likely that barter-type transactions represent a greater fraction of "official" gross domestic product (GDP) in developing countries than in industrial countries.

Technology has both facilitated barter and reduced the transactions and search costs incurred in barter transactions. A simple click of a mouse can put individuals and firms in touch with organizations that enable the direct exchange of goods and services. Nevertheless, it is not always obvious that no medium of exchange exists even under such barter-type arrangements. Instead, an alternative medium of exchange often may be involved, but perhaps not one that is widely or universally acceptable. Moreover, even if such transactions are referred to as barter, the problem of confidence—which is essential for the survival of a monetary economy—also exists under such quasi-barter systems.

BIBLIOGRAPHY

Alchian, Armen A. "Why Money?" *Journal of Money, Credit, and Banking* 9 (February 1977), 133–140.

Clower, Robert W. "On the Origins of Monetary Exchange." *Economic Inquiry* 33 (October 1995), 525–536.

Einzig, Paul. *Primitive Money in Its Ethnological, Historical, and Economic Aspects.* New York, 1996.

Goodhart, Charles A. E. "The Constitutional Position of an Independent Central Bank." Working paper, London School of Economics, London, 2002.

Hicks, John. *A Theory of Economic History.* Oxford, 1969.

Mélitz, Jacques. *Primitive and Modern Money: An Interdisciplinary Approach.* Reading, Mass., 1974.

Schneider, Friedrich, and Dominik Enste. "Hiding in the Shadows: The Growth of the Underground Economy." *Economic Issues* 30 (2002).

PIERRE L. SIKLOS

BAVARIA. Today's Bavarians are proud. Their real income per capita ranks high among the large German lands. Only Hesse, with its banking concentration around Frankfurt, is richer. Bavaria's unemployment rate was only 7.3 percent in 1998, the lowest in Germany (11.7 percent). Bavaria was not always so prosperous. From the seventeenth to early twentieth century, this region in southeastern Germany was more famous for its negative characteristics: Bavaria suffered from one of the highest infant mortality rates in the world. During the nineteenth century, it was clearly a low-income region within Germany. And Bavaria was the last German region to stop the practice of burning witches. In short, during these three centuries, Bavaria was backward and poor. Going still further back—to the fifteenth and sixteenth centuries—the region now known as Bavaria as well as the surrounding countries (Switzerland, Bohemia) were in many respects leading European regions.

These developments suggest that Bavarian economic history has a U-shape. This article will review possible explanations for this. Note that "Bavaria" is defined here as the people living in the modern territory, including Franconians and Swabians. This territory was undoubtedly important for the European economic history of the fifteenth and sixteenth centuries. The Augsburg merchant families organized international trade networks that reached from the Americas to eastern Europe. The Fugger family monopolized the copper trade and operated mines in Hungary, Austria, and many other countries, yielding such an enormous wealth that the emperor Charles V and several popes needed the Fuggers to achieve their positions. Jakob Fugger (1459–1525) and Anton Fugger (1493–1560) amassed six million goldkronen and vast land possessions in 1560. But their famous names were also symbols for the prosperity of the region in which they lived. Augsburg became the largest city in Germany by 1600 with forty-five thousand inhabitants, and Nuremberg ranked in the top five. Others were Hamburg, Cologne, and Magdeburg. Among the next seven German cities of twenty to forty thousand inhabitants, three of them were Bavarian: Munich, Regensburg, and Ulm. These large urban agglomerations were sustained by a booming regional economy.

The seventeenth century brought a crisis to the region that lasted for three centuries. Urban population declined more than in other parts of Germany: Between 1600 and 1700, Bavaria's urban population was reduced by 11 percent, whereas Saxony's urban population increased by 37 percent, northern Germany's by 22 percent, and the central and eastern area lost 4 percent. Only in the southwest and the Rhineland was the decrease in population similar to Bavaria's: 10 percent. There was clearly a shift in urbanization from the south to the north and to Saxony.

Several reasons could have caused this decline in Bavaria's population. The Thirty Years' War (1618–1648) and the bubonic plague inflicted severe population decline. However, this was also the case in other regions of Germany, especially in the central German area, but their urban population declined much less between 1600 and 1700. The Thirty Years' War cannot explain why Bavaria did not recover as fast as the other affected territories.

Another reason for Bavaria's relative decline in the seventeenth century could be the strong recatholicization and counterreformation that cut trade routes and expelled Protestant entrepreneurs. The Upper Palatinate, a heavily industrialized region in the previous period, was converted to Catholicism by force, and at the same time this region lost much of its industrial activity. A related policy issue is the antitrade policy of the Bavarian government that historian Schremmer described. Especially in the eighteenth century, Bavarian officials believed that distributors of goods were not necessary, and farmers and craftsmen should sell their goods directly. This policy did not create efficient markets and a transparent price system.

However, the decline was a phenomenon of the larger region. Switzerland, Bavaria's southwestern neighbor who did not participate in the Thirty Years' War or Counterreformation, also found its population stagnant during this time, after sharing the previous dynamic urbanization of the fourteenth and fifteenth centuries. A third set of circumstances is more related to the whole region: with the discovery of America, the most important European trade centers shifted to the northwestern coastal zone of Europe. The import of cheap metals from the New World also caused central European mining to decline strongly, removing one of the previous bases of Bavaria's urban prosperity. The metal-processing industries of Nuremberg and other Bavarian towns were later challenged by new imports from northwestern Europe, and the rural textile industries in Swabia and northeastern Franconia suffered from low producivity and lack of entrepreneurial investments. Agriculture, the most important source of income, did not keep pace with the increase in northwest European productivity. Economists do not know much about agricultural productivity in the fourteenth and fifteenth centuries, but recent estimates suggest that it was—relative to England—significantly higher than in the seventeenth and eighteenth centuries. Otherwise, it would not have been possible to nourish the large urban population. Robert Allen estimated German agricultural output per capita to be 83 percent in 1400 and 72 percent in 1500, but only 48 percent in both 1700 and 1750, relative to England in 1500 (Allen, 2000, pp. 18–19).

Climate was very influential in Bavaria and other cold continental countries: when the weather was relatively warm during the fifteenth and sixteenth centuries, grain yields and cattle farming achieved higher productivity levels, but during the "Little Ice Age" (seventeenth to mid-nineteenth centuries) malnutrition was more widespread than in the maritime climates of the northwest. This could explain why Switzerland experienced a similar development—a flourshing, urbanizing economy with rapid growth rates during the fifteenth and sixteenth centuries, a long period of stagnation thereafter—in spite of not suffering from the Thirty Years' War or other political events.

One reaction to the economic decline could have been the strange demographic system of very high infant mortality rates. As late as 1864 to 1870, 33 percent of infants died during their first year of life (in Prussia 23 percent). Haines and Kintner confirmed the contemporary view that lack of breastfeeding was the primary cause. But why did Bavarians not breastfeed? Lee attributed the similarly high East Prussian infant mortality rates to increasing female physical exertion from intensified agricultural work, and Boehm's findings suggest a similar explanation for Bavaria. Relative to the German average, Bavarian infant mortality remained high until the 1930s, and thereafter declined to the national average.

Nutrition was poor in Bavaria during the 1600–1900 crisis period. The lowest point was reached around 1800 and in the early part of the nineteenth century, when in some regions of Bavaria adult male height was as low as 165 centimeters (about 5'4"). We are well informed about Bavarian male anthropometric history because the country had adopted a general draft system since Napoleonic times, and a large proportion of conscription lists survived both World Wars I and II. In addition, there is valuable evidence on female prison inmates that can be compared with male convicts. The famine crisis of the 1840s had particularly negative effects on women (especially in the potato-dependent regions), while the recovery of the 1860s was more beneficial to women than to men. During this period, women achieved a higher life expectancy than men for the first time in history.

In the twentieth century Bavaria developed from a low-income region to a rich one. It has been argued that the absence of "old industries" (coal, iron, textiles) and a convergence effect helped Bavaria to surpass more traditional industrial regions, such as Rhineland and Westphalia. Nevertheless, the question remains why most other German regions that also lacked "old industries" (among others Schleswig-Holstein and Lower Saxony) did not share Bavaria's success.

An additional factor that made a contribution to Bavaria's growth was the attractiveness of Munich and its surroundings to entrepreneurs and wealthy people in general. A first wave of millionaire migration toward Munich began during the late nineteenth century. After German unification in 1871, the wealthy migrated more to the south and to Berlin. While other southern German towns (Freiburg, Baden-Baden) also benefitted, Munich was the largest attractor in southern Germany. Apart from Bavaria's natural beauty and the romanticism connected to the "fairy king" Ludwig (Louis II), there was a certain uneasiness of new millionaires who lived close to the northeastern Junkers and the west German industrial laborers. The overall economic effects initially were not large, but this migration helped to attract similar social groups from Berlin, Bohemia, and other places who were threatened by the Soviet expansion after Word War II. Many electronic and aircraft companies moved to Bavaria. The upper class of Bavarian and immigrant origin dominated the government and generated a climate that was friendlier to entrepreneurial activity than in other German regions. (The dark side of it— the appearance of some corrupt figures—appears not to have had too strong an impact on economic development.) The immigration from Bohemia after 1945 contributed a large number of new citizens. Those seeking dependent employment often had difficulties finding jobs, so a higher proportion than normal switched to entrepreneurial activity. Those new entrepreneurs competed with Bavarian firms and helped to make the whole economy more innovative and competitive.

The Bavarian government pursued a strong industrial policy. The universities played a large role, as did the schooling system. But one should note that other German *Länder* also attempted this kind of policy. In the Bavarian case, the development was more successful because a critical mass of entrepreneurs was already living in Munich when the cards were newly distributed after Word War II.

BIBLIOGRAPHY

Allen, Robert C. "Economic Structure and Agricultural Productivity in Europe, 1300–1800." *European Review of Economic History* 3 (2000), 2–26.

Baten, Joerg. *Ernährung und wirtschaftliche Entwicklung in Bayern, 1730–1880*. Stuttgart, 1999. An economic and anthropometric history of living standards. Most recent bibliography.

Baten, Joerg, and John Murray. "Bastardy in South Germany Revisited: An Anthropometric Synthesis." *Journal of Interdisciplinary History* 28-1 (1997), 47–56. Explores the relationship between illegitimacy and nutrition.

Boehm, Max. *Bayerns Agrarproduktion, 1800–1870*. St. Katharinen, Germany, 1995. Agricultural history of Bavaria.

Haines, Michael R., and Hallie K. Kintner. "The Mortality Transition in Germany, 1860–1935: Evidence by Region." *Historical Methods* 33.2 (2000), 83–104. Explores determinants of the high infant mortality rates in Bavaria.

Imhof, Arthur E. *Die verlorenen Welten*. Munich, 1985. Discusses reasons of high infant mortality in Bavaria.

Lee, W. Robert. *Population Growth, Economic Development, and Social Change in Bavaria, 1750–1850*. New York, 1977. A detailed study on the demographic development of a number of villages.

Ruppert, Karl, et al. *Bayern: Eine Landeskunde aus sozialgeographischer Sicht*. Darmstadt, 1987. An economic geography of Bavaria that also discusses historical issues.

Schremmer, Eckart. *Die Wirtschaft Bayerns: Vom hohen Mittelalter bis zum Beginn der Industrialisierung*. Munich, 1970. An economic history that reviews much of the older literature.

Spindler, Max, ed. *Handbuch der Bayerischen Geschichte*, vol. 2. Munich, 1966. An overview of Bavarian history, mainly political history.

Zorn, Wolfgang. *Kleine Wirtschafts- und Sozialgeschichte Bayerns*. Munich, 1962. An overview of Bavarian economic history.

JOERG BATEN

BAZAARS. *See* Fairs.

BEER AND BREWERIES. Beer is any undistilled, fermented malt beverage of relatively low alcohol content. It can be made with almost any vegetable matter, though most commonly it is made with malt, grain allowed to germinate partially. Water is the most abundant constituent, but there are more than four hundred different compounds that can occur in beer. Mesopotamians made beer by 3500 BCE and probably earlier, while by 3000 BCE Egyptians were producing beer as well. Beer making was known in Israel, in classical Greece, and in Rome. Hops was known in the Roman

Empire but do not seem to have been a common ingredient. Typically, brewing was done at home on a small scale, commercial brewing and trade being almost unknown.

Brewing as a domestic chore continued in the countryside throughout the Middle Ages in Europe and perhaps through much of the Middle East and Africa. Methods of production were simple. In European villages by the thirteenth century, some producers, typically women, sold or traded surplus beer. Monasteries, where larger quantities were made, could sell extra beer to neighbors. Urbanization of the twelfth and thirteenth centuries led to commercial production by specialist brewers who took advantage of potential gains from greater investment in bigger and now often copper kettles.

Brewing with Hops. Brewing was transformed in the thirteenth century by the success of brewers in such north German towns as Bremen, Hamburg, and Wismar in making beer with hops. They found the right combination of ingredients and timing of processes to make a beverage that would not go bad for three months or more. Using hops as a flavoring and preservative also made it possible to decrease the alcohol content of the beer and so decrease the amount of grain used. By the fourteenth century, beer was a product of international commerce, with Hamburg a major exporter. Hopped beer made inroads in markets traditionally dominated by wine, first in the Low Countries and then Germany, reaching Bavaria by the late sixteenth century. As early as the mid-1400s in Munich and in 1516 for all of Bavaria, beer had to be made of only barley, water, yeast, and hops. The *reinheitsgebot* did assure purity, but it also assured the duke of Bavaria the proper tax income. Since levies were often made on hops, the substitution of other additives would affect government receipts.

By the early sixteenth century for the majority of towns in the beer zone, taxes on beer typically provided more than half of income. Governments therefore had a strong interest in the production of beer and in tax avoidance. Controls of brewing for tax purposes could at times restrict exchange as well as technical change. Despite increases in output, breweries at the end of the Middle Ages remained small with rarely more than ten workers. In the sixteenth century, the scale of production and investment increased. The growth in the size of units led to the gradual exclusion of women from commercial brewing.

Effects of Spirits and Other Drinks. In the seventeenth and eighteenth centuries, first spirits and then tropical drinks, such as tea, coffee, and cocoa led to declining beer consumption. Per capita levels of three hundred liters per year were common in the fifteenth century, but by the late eighteenth in many parts of northern Europe the figure was below one hundred liters per year. Many breweries collapsed. Some brewers shifted to the production of spirits. Many called for tax decreases. The exception to the pattern of decline was England and especially London with a large and growing population close to breweries. Transportation always added significantly to the selling price of beer. London brewers, by mixing beers of different types and strengths, produced porter, which was stronger and more durable. Success in porter brewing depended on large-scale production and on the large scale of vats. The largest London brewer, Whitbread's, produced more than 320,000 hectoliters of beer in 1796. The five largest London brewers in 1800 averaged an output of 163,000 hectoliters. Burton-on-Trent was also quickly a center of beer production, thanks to the presence of water with the correct chemicals to produce a clearer beer. Brewers there as throughout the British Isles enjoyed the advantage of having a rapidly growing population, as well as exceptionally high tariffs on imported wine.

Brewers elsewhere in northern Europe copied the technology of English porter brewing. English practice could not be easily transferred to Bavaria since there brewers used a type of yeast that stayed at the bottom of the trough during fermentation. The heavier variety required cooler temperatures and a longer period to act than did yeast that rose to the top, the typical kind used throughout Europe outside of Bohemia and Bavaria.

Technology and Biochemistry. From the 1850s, brewing was marked by ever more rapid technical change. First brewers brought the Industrial Revolution into the brewery through the use of steam power to shift raw materials and finished products, and to stir ingredients. Breweries still used large numbers of horses, especially for delivery to public houses, the principal outlets for sale, as they had been since the Middle Ages. The biochemistry of brewing became a topic worthy of study by scholars. It was the French chemist Louis Pasteur who made the greatest contribution by identifying and isolating yeast. The next step was to bring the laboratory into the brewery. That was accomplished by the chemist Emil Hansen in 1871 at Carlsberg in Copenhagen. Hansen found a way to propagate yeast and was thus able to control the exact strain. That reduced contamination and the resulting loss due to spoilage, significant since in the mid-nineteenth century even the most modern of English breweries had some 20 percent of output go bad. A pure yeast became a valuable commodity and a market developed in yeasts by the end of the century. Effective and efficient commercial refrigeration based on the machines of the German engineer Carl Linde solved the problem of erratic and often expensive supplies of ice. Linde's success from the 1870s on was partially the result of financing for prototypes and then purchase of machines by a group of brewers interested in promoting technical advances in the industry. The group included Gabriel Sedlmayr in Munich, Anton Dreher

ADVERTISING BEER. Poster, early-twentieth-century France. (Musée de l'Île de France, Sceaux, France/Giraudon/Art Resource, NY)

bottled beer contributed even further to concentration in production and spawned giant brewers like those in the United States, started by German immigrants in the mid-nineteenth century. Small brewers went out of business. High profits and potential for growth created an investment boom in brewing. In 1886 the Guinness brewery of Dublin put shares on the market and the offering was oversubscribed almost twenty-two fold. Brewers in Britain, Germany, and the United States moved quickly to take advantage of the availability of investment funds. With the new capital, brewers bought up smaller competitors, bought new equipment, and above all in Great Britain bought retail outlets that became exclusive channels for sale of their beers. The United Kingdom was the one place where bottled beer and pilsner did not sweep the market, so pubs remained important to success. Technical change and improved distribution contributed to an increase in beer consumption from the historically low levels of the early nineteenth century. So, too, did changes in the tax regimen in many jurisdictions and by the temperance movement, which saw beer as a healthy alternative to spirits.

Brewing's Effect on National Economies. Brewing made a major contribution to national incomes—in Germany in the late nineteenth century—as much as iron and steel. Brewing has always made a major contribution to tax income for governments. Success in Europe led to the spread of the new brewing technology to the rest of the world. Brewing was most successful in North America, especially after the influx of German immigrants in the mid-nineteenth century. High temperatures meant that exports to tropical and very distant regions were simply not practical. By the late nineteenth century, the new technology made it possible to set up pilsner breweries and sell beer in regions as distant as Shandong province, China, to Mexico to the Philippines and Brazil.

In the twentieth century, rising costs of marketing and further technical changes, which promoted larger scale production, such as using larger vessels, and continuous brewing increased the pressure for consolidation. In some parts of Europe with high levels of per capita consumption, such as southern Germany and Belgium, the number of breweries stayed high. A merger mania in Great Britain in the 1950s coincided with the disappearance of many smaller brewers in the United States. There a handful of big firms, especially Anheuser-Busch and Miller, dominated the market. Big breweries in Great Britain, such as Scottish and Newcastle, Allied, and Bass, were in a position to exploit a shift to pilsner from top-yeasted bitters. In Belgium Interbrew, in the Netherlands Heineken, and in Denmark Carlsburg expanded, often buying competitors. In Germany, Becks and Löwenbrau, like their counterparts elsewhere in Europe created international brands by setting

in Vienna, J. C. Jacobsen in Copenhagen, and Wilhelm Feltmann, Jr., who worked for Heineken in Rotterdam. Their background in science, education, access to sizeable capital, and interest in exchanging information generated highly successful breweries.

The combination of better knowledge of biochemistry and effective refrigeration made it possible to produce beer with yeast that fell to the bottom of the fermenting trough, pilsner or lager beer, all year round. The ability to maintain quality was enhanced even more with pasteurization. Pilsner was different from the drink commonly consumed before, so it was not always popular in all markets. Growing railroad networks made distribution easier in the era of free trade. In the late nineteenth century, breweries began to mass produce bottled beer, which made possible sales in small quantities to consumers at home. Production in the United States increased 600 percent from 1870 to 1900 and in Germany 300 percent. The capital and marketing requirements created by selling up breweries worldwide, by acquiring breweries in other countries, or by licensing production of their beer. Canadian Breweries' Carling brand was an early example of what became common practice by the 1970s. Internationalization and consolidation with breweries merged into large drinks and entertainment conglomerates became common at the end of the twentieth century, with small brewers surviving in parts of Germany and Belgium.

Limited consumer choice in many markets in the 1960s led to a reaction and calls for a return to variety and to older types of beer. It began with a revival of home brewing, which had never completely disappeared. Agitation in England for a return to "real ale" and to having it available in pubs made possible the revival or even the founding of new small brewers. A similar pattern in Canada and the United States generated local or regional brewers, with only a very small share of any market, while some expanded, creating national or international brands. The growth in small breweries was part of an increase in total output in the closing years of the twentieth century, up 163 percent in the United Kingdom and 237 percent in Germany from 1960 to 1990. Total world output reached 1.15 billion hectoliters in 1995, with output per person in exporting countries like the Netherlands and Denmark at 150 and 191 liters, respectively, while in the United States the level of production was 88 liters per person in 1996, a third of the figures for the zenith of European brewing in late medieval and Renaissance northern Europe.

BIBLIOGRAPHY

Aerts, Erik. *Het bier van Lier: De economische ontwikkeling van de bierindustrie in een middelgrote Drabantse stad (eind 14de-begin 19de eeuw)*. Verhandelingen van de Koninklijke Academie voor Wetenschappen, Letteren en Schone Kunsten van België, Klasse der Letteren, Jaargang 58, 1996, Nr. 161. Brussels, 1996.

Baron, Stanley. *Brewed in America: A History of Beer and Ale in the United States*. Boston, 1962.

Bennett, Judith M. *Ale, Beer, and Brewsters in England: Women's Work in a Changing World, 1300–1600*. New York, 1996.

Glamann, Kristof. *Jacobsen of Carlsberg: Brewer and Philanthropist*. Translated by Geoffrey French. Copenhagen, 1991.

Gourvish, Terence R., and Richard G. Wilson. *The British Brewing Industry, 1830–1980*. Cambridge, 1994.

Huntemann, Hans. *Das deutsche Braugewerbe vom Ausgang des Mittelalters bis zum Beginn der Industrialisierung: Biererzeugung—Bierhandel—Bierverbrauch*. Nuremberg, 1971.

King, Frank A. *Beer Has a History*. London, 1947.

Lynch, Patrick, and John Vaizey. *Guinness's Brewery in the Irish Economy, 1759–1876*. Cambridge, 1960.

Mathias, Peter. *The Brewing Industry in England, 1700–1830*. Cambridge, 1959.

Nordlund, Odd. *Brewing and Beer Traditions in Norway: The Social Anthropological Background of the Brewing Industry*. Oslo, 1969.

Richmond, Lesley, and Alison Turton, eds. *The Brewing Industry: A Guide to Historical Records*. Manchester, 1990.

Unger, Richard W. "Technical Change in the Brewing Industry in Germany, the Low Countries, and England in the Late Middle Ages." *Journal of European Economic History* 21:2 (Fall 1992), 281–313.

Unger, Richard W. *A History of Dutch Brewing, 900–1900: Economy, Technology, and the State*. Leiden, 2001.

RICHARD W. UNGER

BEGGAR-MY-NEIGHBOR POLICIES. The expression "beggar-my-neighbor" (or "beggar-thy-neighbor") was defined by Joan Robinson in 1937 to describe international economic policies "designed to benefit one nation at the expense of the rest." Robinson adopted the term from the popular children's card game (also known as "beat your neighbors out of doors") to characterize attempts by nation-states during the Great Depression to shore up employment through manipulation of currency rates and the prices of tradable goods; her pioneering essay extended and generalized Keynes's interpretation of international trade in his "Notes on Mercantilism" as "a desperate expedient to maintain employment at home by forcing sales on foreign markets and restricting purchases, which . . . shift[s] the problem of unemployment to the neighbor who is worsted in the struggle."

Beggar-my-neighbor conceptions were a major element in the doctrine of mercantilism in the preindustrial era, originating from the combination of two basic premises: that the accumulation of bullion was the measure of a state's economic strength and that the volume of commercial activity in the world was fixed. In a hard-money environment, in which the sole sources of bullion were found in international trade, the best means of accumulating additional wealth was through maintenance of a positive balance of trade. The best way to increase the size of one's trade balance was to reduce the amount of trade of commercial (and state) rivals: to beggar-my-neighbor.

The concept of mercantilism has often been criticized as a historian's fancy—a hodgepodge of ideas lacking intellectual coherence. Yet simple beggar-my-neighbor tenets were much in evidence. Jean Baptiste Colbert, controller general under Louis XIV and considered the leading exponent of continental mercantilism, argued in a 1669 memorandum that "Commerce . . . is carried on by 20,000 vessels and this number cannot be increased. . . . Each nation works incessantly to have its legitimate share of commerce or to gain an advantage over another nation." The English thinker John Locke famously declared in the *Lowering of Interest* (1696): "Riches do not consist in having more Gold and Silver, but in having more in proportion than the rest of the World, or than our Neighbours, . . . who sharing the Gold and Silver of the World in less proportion, want the means of Plenty and Power, and so are Poorer." Other examples abound.

The specific application of these policies is less well known. Colbert's famous dictum "Trading companies are the armies of the King" called out for state sponsorship and direction of joint-stock companies, colonial enterprises, and the merchant marine. French mercantilism also underwrote the introduction of new industries and the regulation of established ones. Continental mercantilism was in general motivated by state control of overall economic activities, rather than just trade.

Perhaps the most refined version of mercantilism in practice was the Old Colonial System of the first British Empire, with the Navigation Acts at its core. Here the state regulated access to intercolonial trade and shipping in order to exclude the Dutch (the target also of Colbert's policies), who dominated early modern commerce and shipping. The British also established prohibitive tariffs, such as the Molasses Act (1733), which banned non-British molasses from the North American colonies, thus depriving French, Spanish, and Dutch West Indies planters of a market for their products. By placing a cordon around the territories of the British Empire and excluding foreign rivals from participating in trade and commerce within it, the imperial government was practicing a version of beggar-my-neighbor policies, designed to exclude foreign competition from third markets and to stimulate transatlantic trade. Similar principles were later applied in Alexander Hamilton's repatriation of the Navigation Acts for the new American republic, although in this case the argument for protective tariffs and state-regulated shipping and fisheries was couched in infant-economy terms and directed principally at import substitution.

Beggar-my-neighbor policies need not be state-mandated, as demonstrated by the call of Philadelphia shoemakers, in response to the crisis of 1819, for tariffs to exclude "imports" from New England. Tax policies applied at the level of the individual state or province, designed to attract business to its locality rather than to another in the same federal system, can be perceived as a local manifestation of beggar-my-neighbor logic: the volume of investment is fixed, and steps must be taken to allocate it most favorably to local interests, at the expense of commercial rivals. In this case, as with the classic examples, individual states are measured relative to each other, using a common metric, and it is commonly perceived that each can improve its status only by reducing the position of others.

The underpinnings of mercantilist logic were gradually discredited, via Adam Smith's attack on the confusion of income flows and bullion stocks and by David Hume's declaration that "as a British subject, I pray for the flourishing commerce of Germany, Spain, Italy and even France," reflecting the crude awakening of the notion of mutual gains from trade, and by the visible expansion of international trade, undermining the idea of trade as a zero-sum game. Thus the appeal of systematic beggar-my-neighbor policies declined, although the impetus was not eradicated entirely. The call for general free trade in the nineteenth century was at times compromised by the dictates of practical politics, especially in times of cyclical downturns or in response to "invasions" of foreign goods in the home market.

Free trade became a casualty of the Great Depression, which signaled for some the resuscitation of mercantilism in a new and more troublesome form. The beggar-my-neighbor policies of the 1930s were no longer designed to increase stocks of bullion, but rather to reduce stocks of unemployment; no longer directed to exclude competitors from third markets, but rather to reduce foreign competition at home; no longer predicated on a belief in the constant size of world markets, but rather in response to a perceived decline in the size of the cake. Policies were motivated by expediency rather than doctrine, a short-term response to crisis under the particular constraints afforded by the existing system of international trade.

The balance of trade was the key to the process, as the means by which global dislocation was translated to national economies. Exports fell; unemployment in export sectors rose; a trade deficit was created. Governments attempted to restore balance by curtailing imports, via tariffs or quotas, or by stimulating exports, via subsidies, or by both at once, via exchange depreciation or wage cuts. Once adopted by one country, such policies were likely to be introduced in others, in retaliation or as a precaution. Their diffusion in turn generated a general deterioration in trade and a worsening of the global economic situation, thus intensifying the call for trade restrictions and causing the downward spiral in trade volumes and global economic activity characteristic of the 1930s. The same cumulative effect could also result from competitive devaluations, as noted by Kindleberger (1934) and Nurkse (1944), although, as Eichengreen and Sachs (1985) observe, these actions need not be beggar-my-neighbor in outcome if accompanied by monetary expansion at home. In Robinson's (1937) terms, depreciation accompanied by "an increase in home investment brings about a net increase in employment for the world as a whole." But policy makers were restricted by orthodox assumptions that largely precluded such behavior (the Roosevelt administration's monetary expansion after 1933 being a notable exception).

The destructive power of beggar-my-neighbor policies during the Depression, and a perception that untrammeled free trade was susceptible to a repetition of the same process, generated a movement for international organizations, such as the General Agreement on Tariffs and Trade (GATT) and the International Monetary Fund (IMF), as well as the entire Bretton Woods system of currency regulation, to frame rules to outlaw the practice. States still practice beggar-my-neighbor policies, however (e.g., by writing tax rules to attract foreign investment, or by subsidizing the production of export commodities), albeit in the comfortable belief that the world economy is immune to the form of cumulative breakdown suffered in the 1930s.

BIBLIOGRAPHY

Eichengeen, Barry, and Jeffrey Sachs. "Exchange Rates and Economic Recovery in the 1930s." *Journal of Economic History* 45 (1985), 925–946.

Kindleberger, Charles P. "Competitive Currency Depreciation between Denmark and New Zealand." *Harvard Business Review* 12 (1934), 416–426.

Nurkse, Ragnar. *International Currency Experience: Lessons of the Interwar Period.* Geneva, 1944.

Robinson, Joan. "Beggar-My-Neighbour Remedies for Unemployment." In her *Essays in the Theory of Employment*, pp. 156–170. London, 1937.

MARK THOMAS

BELGIUM. At the time of Belgian secession from the United Kingdom of the Netherlands (1830) the process of industrialization was well under way. In the second half of the eighteenth century, the introduction of steam engines in the coalfields of Liège and especially Hainaut marked the beginning of the so-called Belgian industrial revolution. In the first decade of the nineteenth century, industrialization gained momentum as the cotton (Ghent) and woolen (Verviers) sectors mechanized rapidly. In the 1820s John Cockerill modernized the iron, metal, and machine construction industries in a spectacular way.

The Early Years. The Belgian separation plunged the economy into a severe depression. Cut off from the Netherlands and its colonies, Belgian manufacturing lost important sales markets at a moment when the domestic economy was paralyzed by political uncertainties. Mechanized firms faced particularly bad losses as a plunge in revenues coincided with continuing high fixed costs. Moreover, several mechanized companies had financed long-term investments with short-term credits, and so fell into a severe liquidity crisis. To prevent large scale bankruptcies the Société Générale, Belgium's most important bank, decided in some instances to accept shares as debt settlement. In subsequent years this emergency strategy born out of the 1831–1832 crisis became common practice. Consequently, the Société Générale acquired large blocks of shares of coal mines and iron manufacturing firms and in doing so became Europe's first mixed bank.

Another factor explains the Société Générale's appetite for participation in heavy industry. As the Netherlands closed down its waterways for Belgian ships, the Belgian government decided in 1834 to build a railroad network to restore communication with Germany overland. The project presented the prospect of large orders for the depressed coal and iron industry. Backed by the Belgian mixed banks, iron manufacturing was completely restructured in the second half of the 1830s. A merger wave paved the way for quick replacement of the old charcoal furnaces by far more productive, but expensive, coke furnaces. Moreover, under the guidance of John Cockerill Belgium's machine-

building industry became an important producer of railroad equipment and locomotives. Consequently, Belgian manufacturing was in an excellent position to benefit fully from the European railroad boom in the next decades.

An important exception to this rosy picture was the collapse of the Flemish rural linen industry in the late 1840s. Since the 1820s growing competition from cotton cloth and from the mechanized British linen industry had been driving down linen prices on international markets. Flemish rural spinners, however, clung to traditional production methods to maintain their independence (the Verlag system). By the late 1840s the unequal battle between manual and mechanized production ceased, as wages of rural spinners fell below subsistence level. To make matters worse, the collapse coincided with a series of severe harvest failures. It would take decades for the Flemish economy to recover, as the area fell victim to widespread structural underemployment and poverty.

The depression of the late 1840s also shook up the financial sector. A banking panic swept the country, resulting in massive conversion of banknotes into metal coins. The mixed banks proved unable to meet their obligations because their funds were virtually frozen in shares and loans. In order to prevent future liquidity crises, a modern central bank was established in 1850 (National Bank of Belgium). Consequently, mixed banks lost the right to issue banknotes.

Economic Expansion. The long economic expansion of the 1850s and 1860s profoundly changed the economic structure of Belgium. Manufacturing surpassed agriculture in both value added and employment, with coal mines the most important employers. Technologically, the Walloon coalfields were very much at the forefront in continental Europe, with the development of new machinery and improved ventilation systems. Iron production also exploded, propelled by Europe's railroad boom and the rise of free trade. Participation in foreign markets, however, demanded a minimum firm size. Moreover, the continuing growth and the modernization of production capacity entailed enormous costs. All these factors provoked a new merger wave, consolidating all stages of production—from extraction of raw materials to machine construction—in large-scale integrated firms.

The end of massive railroad construction in western Europe around 1870 was a serious blow for Belgium's heavy manufacturing, but demand factors tell only part of the story. In the 1850s and 1860s, Belgian technicians and entrepreneurs had contributed to the industrialization of the Ruhr area, northern France, Lorraine, and the Grand Duchy of Luxembourg. Now these regions became serious competitors for Belgian manufacturing. The difficult shift from iron to steel production contributed to the ongoing structural crisis in Belgium's heavy industry. Bessemer converters only produced good results when high-quality iron ore was used, but it was found only in Sweden or North Africa. The Walloon industrial areas were difficult to reach for bulk sea transport; so they continued to depend heavily on Lorraine's low-quality "minette" ore. Therefore, iron production remained dominant in Belgium in the 1870s and 1880s, contrary to the international trend.

In the mid-1890s, large-scale adoption of the Thomas-Gilchrist process enabled Belgian heavy manufacturing to rebound. Converters turned phosphorus "minette" ore into high-quality steel, so that steel production rose exponentially. The Belgian economy also participated vigorously in the development of new sectors related to the so-called second industrial revolution. Ernest Solvay built an international empire in soda production, and Lieven Gevaert started a leading company for photographic products. Electrical engineering and the refining of nonferrous metals also took off. The revitalization allowed Belgian firms to conquer distant markets. In Russia, Belgian entrepreneurs established large coal and steel complexes, and played an important role in the construction of tramways. In Latin America and China, they participated substantially in railroad building and other construction.

Wartime Belgium. For Belgium, World War I was not only a human tragedy but also an economic one. As a result of systematic dismantling by the German occupying force, the country was stripped of most of its industrial equipment; and during the hostilities other suppliers took over markets traditionally served by Belgian firms. Moreover, many foreign assets were lost because of the Soviet revolution, unrest in China, and nationalization in Latin America. Despite all these difficulties postwar reconstruction was undertaken with enthusiasm. By 1923 the real gross domestic product (GDP) per capita had reached its prewar level.

This impressive growth performance, however, concealed major macroeconomic imbalances. The money supply soared during and immediately after the war, causing severe inflationary tensions. During the first half of the 1920s public finances suffered. As reconstruction and expensive new social programs consumed large quantities of money, fiscal revenues fell short because of precipitate tax reform and naive reliance on German reparations. The resulting explosion of public debt was primarily financed with short-term credits. In addition, massive imports of machinery and consumer goods caused substantial current account deficits.

Not surprisingly financial markets regarded the Belgian economy with suspicion. The value of the Belgian franc fell almost continuously on international exchange markets. Finally, in October 1926 the government adopted a severe austerity program and consolidated Belgium's large public debt. Both measures allowed for stabilization of the Belgian franc at one-seventh of its prewar parity. The whole operation was a success, with economic growth soon resuming.

In the late 1920s an investment boom modernized the country's industrial structure. The chemicals industry, together with the production and distribution of electricity, took the lead. The nonferrous metals sector also surged ahead, thanks to the exploitation of rich cobalt, copper, radium, and tin deposits in the Congo. Nevertheless, Belgian manufacturing failed to rid itself of its nineteenth-century outlook. It remained very much geared toward the production of capital goods and neglected the rapidly rising market for consumer goods.

The collapse of world trade in the early 1930s hit Belgium's export-dependent economy particularly hard. The Belgian government worsened the situation by maintaining the gold exchange standard as major trading partners such as the United Kingdom abandoned it. Belgian firms thus faced a serious decline in competitiveness. Falling exports and increasing import penetration forced many companies out of business, and unemployment soared. These events in turn undermined domestic demand, further deepening the depression. To restore Belgium's international competitiveness the government pursued a deflationary policy, which only exacerbated the problem.

With the stock market crash and the wave of business failures, many banking assets were either lost or frozen. Gradually, members of the public lost confidence in the financial sector and started to withdraw their deposits. In 1934–1935 a panic erupted that brought the banking sector to the brink of total collapse. Thorough reform of Belgium's financial and monetary system thus became inevitable. On the one hand, mixed banks were split into a deposit bank and a holding company; in addition, the deposit banks were put under government supervision. Belgium also left the Gold Bloc, and the franc was devalued by 28 percent. As a result of these measures the banking panic subsided, and Belgium experienced a short-lived economic recovery in 1935–1936.

In contrast to World War I, Belgium's industrial areas suffered relatively little damage during World War II. Moreover, during postwar reconstruction Belgium's specialization in the production of coal, steel, nonferrous metals, cement, and glass coincided perfectly with Europe's demand structure. Labor shortages and a considerable extension of social benefits soon pushed up wage costs.

In the late 1940s the so-called Belgian miracle came to an end. As the other European economies got back on their feet again, the era of "easy exports" disappeared. In addition, Belgium only partially followed the 1949 devaluation of most European currencies vis-à-vis the U.S. dollar. This de facto revaluation of the franc worsened Belgium's labor-cost handicap. Consequently, the country suffered from relatively high unemployment rates in the 1950s. Another blow, especially for Wallonia, was a rapid shift in energy use from coal to oil. For the mining sector this marked the start of a long and painful death.

Postwar Period. Despite these difficulties economic prospects brightened in the late 1950s. Belgium's competitive position gradually recovered as continuing high unemployment rates put downward pressure on wage demands. At the same time, many multinational enterprises were seeking a stronghold in the emerging Common Market. Belgium, with its trained labor reserve and flexible financial arrangements (easy repatriation of profits), was able to attract a substantial share of these investments. In the 1960s and early 1970s the activities of multinational firms especially modernized the Flemish manufacturing structure. The production of chemicals, petrochemicals, automobiles, and other consumer durables in the region soared; and Flanders surpassed Wallonia in per capita income.

In the early 1970s lax monetary and fiscal policies together with high wage demands gradually gave rise to inflation. The first worldwide oil crisis abruptly intensified the problem; in combination with automatic wage-indexing and continuing large real wage increases, it triggered a wage-price spiral. Once again Belgium's labor costs rose much faster than those of its main competitors. Loss of market share abroad and increased import penetration created not only massive job destruction in the private sector but also a growing current account deficit. Public spending soared as expenditures on unemployment benefits exploded, and numerous civil servants were hired in an attempt to put the brakes on unemployment growth. A second oil crisis, in 1979–1980, made these macroeconomic imbalances unsustainable, leaving the Belgian franc an easy victim of speculative attacks.

In February 1982, the franc was devalued by 8.5 percent. At the same time, the government imposed strict wage restraints in order to reduce real wages. The operation succeeded in restoring corporate competitiveness. Export growth resumed, and the massive current account deficit vanished. Brussels, as the (unofficial) capital of the European Community, succeeded in attracting many service companies. However, unemployment and the public deficit stayed high throughout the 1980s.

The Maastricht Treaty (1992) was an important turning point for public finances. As only countries with a budget deficit of a maximum 3 percent of GDP were allowed to join the European Monetary Union, the government finally imposed a painful austerity policy. At a cost of slow economic growth and continuing high employment, the target was reached: in 1999 the euro was introduced.

[*See also* Low Countries, *subentry on* The Low Countries before 1568.]

BIBLIOGRAPHY

Blomme, Jan. *The Economic Development of Belgian Agriculture, 1880–1980. A Quantitative and Qualitative Analysis*. Brussels, 1992.

Buyst, Erik. "Economic Aspects of the Nationality Problem in Nineteenth- and Twentieth-Century Belgium." In *Economic Change and the Nationality Question in Twentieth-Century Europe*, edited by A. Teichova, pp. 145–174. Cambridge, 2000.

Buyst, E., et al. *The Générale Bank, 1822–1997*. Tielt, Belgium, 1997.

Cassiers, I., Ph. Devillé, and P. Solar. "Economic Growth in Postwar Belgium." In *Economic Growth in Europe since 1945*, edited by N. Crafts and G. Toniolo, pp. 173–209. Cambridge, 1996.

Gadisseur, Jean-Florent. *Le produit physique de l'économie belge, 1830–1913: Présentation critique des données statistiques. Industrie. Premières conclusions*. Brussels, 2000.

Goossens, Martine. *The Economic Development of Belgian Agriculture: A Regional Perspective, 1812–1846*. Brussels, 1992.

Mokyr, Joel. *Industrialization in the Low Countries, 1795–1850*. New Haven and London, 1976.

Wee, H. van der, and J. Blomme, eds. *The Economic Development of Belgium since 1870*. Cheltenham, U.K., 1997.

ERIK BUYST

BELL, ALEXANDER GRAHAM (1847–1922), American inventor.

On 14 February 1876, Elisha Gray, an established inventor and a founder of Western Electric, and Alexander Graham Bell, a teacher of the deaf, filed competing patents for a device covering "the method of, and apparatus for, transmitting vocal or other sounds telegraphically . . . by causing electrical undulations, similar in form to the vibrations of the air accompanying the said vocal or other sounds" (U.S. Patent No. 174,465). Independently, both men had realized that electrical waves moving down a telegraph wire were analogous to sound waves moving through air. Since sound comprised a spectrum of frequencies, or tones, the electrical wave also could comprise a spectrum of frequencies—and each frequency might carry an independent message. Bell was awarded the patent. It was his second patent; the first, concerning telegraphic multiplexing, was issued in 1875.

The impetus for the invention was a combination of economics—the United States had entered a depression in 1873—and the technological limitations of telegraphy, then controlled by Western Union. In 1872, Western Union had effectively doubled its capacity by acquiring Joseph Stearns's duplex system, and the economic returns from multiplexing became obvious. One significant aspect of the invention was that its capacity was limited only by the number of distinguishable frequencies. Bell and Gray were known rivals from prior patent filings; and in Bell's case, the competitive edge was deepened in that one of his backers, Gardiner Hubbard, an entrepreneurial patent lawyer, was the prime mover behind the United States Postal Telegraph Company. In Bell's inventions, Hubbard saw a technological way to challenge Western Union's

ALEXANDER GRAHAM BELL. Bell at the opening of the long-distance line from New York to Chicago, 1892. (Prints and Photographs Division, Library of Congress)

Soon after the family settled in Ontario, Aleck accepted a teaching position in Boston, Massachusetts, where he was employed at the prestigious School for Deaf Mutes (later the Horace Mann School) and began to circulate within Boston and Cambridge's small but growing community of scientists. In 1872, he conducted experiments focused on the relationship between acoustics and electricity, based on arrays of tuning forks and vibrating reeds, which were modeled after Hermann Helmholz's electrical tuning fork apparatus. Fearful of Gray, Bell worked largely in secret, filing the patent application in February 1876 for a device that he had not yet tested; he did not make his famous call to Mr. Watson—saying that he had accidentally spilled acid on his trousers—until 10 March 1876.

Initially, Bell presented the telephone as a novelty, first demonstrating it at a meeting of the American Academy of Arts and Sciences in Boston on 10 May 1876. A month later, he presented it at the Centennial Exhibition in Philadelphia, where he won the exhibition's coveted gold medal. He then took the telephone on the road, showcasing it, for example, at the annual meeting of the American Association for the Advancement of Science in Nashville in September 1877. Bell continued to refine his invention, by designing a telephone box that was both a transmitter and a receiver. The first instrument had functioned rather like a broadcast medium. Indeed, for a period in the 1880s and 1890s, the telephone was used for subscriber broadcasts of news, information, and entertainment.

Bell had obtained backing from parents of two of his students, Thomas Saunders and future father-in-law Gardiner Hubbard. The three men had entered into an agreement in February 1875, which stipulated that they would share equally in any profits obtained from Bell's experiments. Following Bell's 1876 successes, they organized the Bell Company in 1877 to hold the potentially lucrative patents; manufacturing was undertaken entirely by one shop, operated by Charles Williams, Jr. The investors' strategy was to profit primarily from the royalties on the technology, which they controlled, while limiting their own investment and risk by allowing others to create the service-delivery systems.

Plagued by inadequate capital, the company was reorganized in 1878 and 1879 before it was restructured in 1880 as American Bell and finally placed on a secure financial footing. The company began to assume greater control over its licensees and to move away from profits based on patent royalties and toward a corporate model of delivering telephone service. Bell was not named to an executive position during the reorganizations of the company in 1879 and ended his salaried relationship with it in 1880. He retained substantial company stock, however, which enabled him to maintain his wife and two daughters comfortably and to support his professional interests.

monopoly. In May 1877, Bell married Hubbard's daughter Mabel, who had been one of Bell's students.

Alexander Graham (known as Aleck, born 3 March 1847) was the second of three sons of Alexander Melville Bell of Edinburgh, Scotland, and his English wife, Eliza Grace Symonds, a miniaturist. Both Aleck's father and his grandfather (also Alexander) were teachers of speech, and his grandfather had become known for his ability to help stammerers. Aleck's father, a teacher of the deaf, developed a system called Visible Speech, which he expected his son, who had begun teaching at the age of sixteen, to develop further and to publicize. Aleck's mother was deaf and had learned to play the piano by holding her ear horn close to the keys. Thus, early in life, the boy was exposed to music and acoustics and to the challenges of the deaf, of speech, and of speech impediments. After his older and younger brothers died, Aleck was prevailed upon to join his parents in migrating to Canada in July 1870, and thus gave up his ambition for a formal university education.

For the rest of his life, Bell maintained an active interest in education of the deaf and in inventions, which included precursors to modern optical fiber systems for the transmission of sound. He was granted eighteen patents in his own name as well as twelve in collaboration with others. Among them were patents for a "photophone," a phonograph, aerial vehicles, airplanes, and selenium cells. In 1888, he founded the National Geographic Society. Bell died on 2 August 1922 and, with his wife, is buried at their summer estate, Beinn Bhreagh, in Nova Scotia, Canada.

BIBLIOGRAPHY

Alexander Graham Bell's Path to the Telephone. University of Virginia, Charlottesville. <http://jefferson.village.virginia.edu/albell/homepage.html>. Excellent Web site, built with support from the National Science Foundation, on the invention itself, which includes an online version of Bell's notebooks.

Bruce, Robert V. *Bell: Alexander Graham Bell and the Conquest of Solitude*. Boston, 1973. Detailed biography of Bell, based on manuscript collections at the National Geographic Society, Library of Congress, and other major archives.

Fagen, M. D., ed. *A History of Science and Engineering in the Bell System: The Early Years (1875–1925)*. 1975. Standard Bell Telephone Laboratories work on technologies within the Bell System, including detailed discussion of the basic invention.

Frommer, Myra. "How Well Do Inventors Understand the Cultural Consequences of Their Innovations? A Study of Samuel Finley Breese Morse and the Telegraph, Thomas Alva Edison and the Phonograph, and Alexander Graham Bell and the Telephone." Ph.D. diss., New York University School of Education, Health, Nursing and Arts Professions, 1987.

Garnet, Robert W. *The Telephone Enterprise: The Evolution of the Bell System's Horizontal Structure, 1876–1909*. Baltimore, 1985. One of several historical studies investigating the origins of the Bell system.

Hoddeson, Lillian. "The Emergence of Basic Research in the Bell Telephone System, 1875–1915." *Technology and Culture* 21 (1981), 512–544. Includes discussion of the circumstances of the famous Mr. Watson anecdote.

Hounshell, David. "Bell and Gray: Contrasts in Style, Politics, and Etiquette." *Proceedings of the IEEE* 64 (September 1976), 1305–1314. Includes a detailed discussion of the rivalry between Bell and Gray.

Smith, George David. *The Anatomy of a Business Strategy: Bell, Western Electric, and the Origins of the American Telephone Industry*. Baltimore, 1985. Covers some of the early manufacturing history.

AMY FRIEDLANDER

BEQUESTS. *See* Inheritance Systems.

BESSEMER, HENRY (1813–1898), English inventor and manufacturer.

Bessemer's name is indelibly associated with his steelmaking process, but his experiments in this field came in the middle of his career. Bessemer was born on 19 January 1813, at Charlton, Hertfordshire. His childhood was spent largely in the manufacturing shops of his father, a talented mechanical inventor who made gold chains and cast type. After coming to London in 1830, Bessemer gained a reputation for artistic castings, electroplating, and embossing. For the next twenty four years, many of his inventions were aimed at cutting the manufacturing costs of premium-priced articles. His notable financial successes included making pencil leads, embossing velvet, and manufacturing bronze powder. Around 1833 he devised, on the suggestion of his fiancée, a way of date-stamping tax stamps that prevented their fraudulent reuse and, he claimed, saved the British government £100,000 per year. From 1838 to 1853 he gained thirty four patents for casting type, making glass, ornamenting textiles, making paints, and refining sugar.

In August 1854, at age 41, with no prior experience in iron or steelmaking, Bessemer began the experiments that would make him rich and famous. During the Crimean War he invented a novel way of imparting spin to a projectile

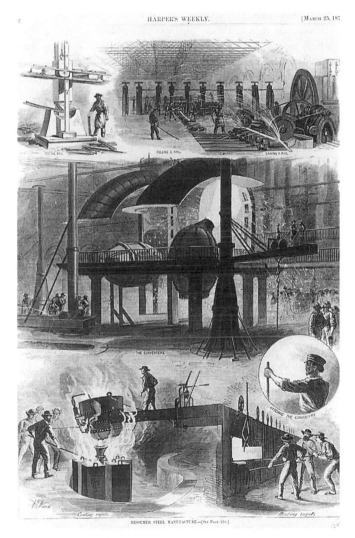

BESSEMER PROCESS. Six illustrations of operations in a steel mill, by Alfred R. Waud (1828–1891), appeared in *Harper's Weekly*, 25 March 1876. (Prints and Photographs Division, Library of Congress)

shot from a nonrifled cannon but then learned that the cannon metal itself was the real weakness. At his London laboratory, he applied himself to this problem. Bessemer's first two iron and steel patents (10 January and 18 June 1855) dealt with mixing wrought iron and steel together. A chance observation of an unmelted bar in his heating furnace led to his insight, embodied in a famous third patent (17 October 1855), that air *alone*, blown through the liquid metal, could remove excess carbon from pig iron and thus turn it into "malleable iron" or steel. His subsequent patents for a tilting converter, mechanical improvements, and adding a manganese-rich iron compound (15 March 1857) completed the key details of the Bessemer process. Bessemer was simultaneously inventing applications for his iron- and steelmaking process, with patents in 1855 alone for ordnance shells, screw propellers, railway wheels, anchors, railway bars, beams, and girders.

Bessemer launched a high-profile publicity campaign with a paper before the British Association for the Advancement of Science in August 1856, and soon received £27,000 in patent-licensing fees. But Bessemer had by chance used a high-grade foundry iron low in phosphorus and when other manufacturers tried his process with common high-phosphorus iron their results were disastrous. Hot or cold the brittle metal could not be rolled. Forced to return the patent fees, Bessemer embarked on a series of experiments, first to rid iron of phosphorus and then, more successfully, to identify British iron ores naturally low in phosphorus. (In 1879 the cousins Percy Gilchrist and Sidney G. Thomas developed chemically "basic" furnace linings that removed excess phosphorus and permitted a wider range of raw materials.)

Bessemer himself in 1858 set up a steelworks in Sheffield, its success persuaded steelmakers worldwide to adopt his process in the next decade, but many others also helped make the "Bessemer process" a real success. Robert Mushet is best credited with the manganese step that Bessemer patented in 1857, while the Swede Goran Göransson helped Bessemer's factory successfully make steel two years later. In the United States Alexander L. Holley virtually reinvented the Bessemer process for mass-producing railroad rails. (The notion that an American ironmaster named William Kelly, who gained the American patent on Bessemer steelmaking, was its "true" inventor is empirically unfounded.) By 1899 world wide production of Bessemer steel stood at 10 million tons, while the price for steel rails was one-fifth that of 1860.

Bessemer helped found the British Iron and Steel Institute in 1868 and was its president from 1871 to 1873. He received many honors from engineering societies in Great Britain and abroad, and was knighted in 1879 (for his dated tax stamp), and named Fellow of the Royal Society the same year. He died on 15 March 1898, at his residence, outside London. No modern biography of Bessemer exists, and his boastful *Autobiography* (published in 1905 and reprinted by the London-based Institute of Metals in 1989), which lists his 117 patents, must be consulted with extreme caution.

[*See also* Bessemer Process; Metallurgic Industry; *and* Steelmaking.]

BIBLIOGRAPHY

Barraclough, K. C. *Steelmaking: 1850–1900*. London, 1990.

Dredge, James. "Henry Bessemer, 1813–1898." *Transactions of the American Society of Mechanical Engineers* 18 (1898), 881–964. Unusually thorough, balanced, and detailed obituary notice.

Lange, Ernest F. "Bessemer, Göransson, and Mushet: A Contribution to Technical History." *Memoirs and Proceedings of the Manchester Literary and Philosophical Society* 57.17 (1913), 1–44. A much-needed evaluation of Bessemer's and his two principal rivals' work in perfecting the Bessemer process.

Misa, Thomas J. *A Nation of Steel: The Making of Modern America, 1865–1925*. Baltimore, 1995.

Wengenroth, Ulrich. *Enterprise and Technology: The German and British Steel Industries, 1865–1895*. Cambridge, 1994.

THOMAS J. MISA

BESSEMER PROCESS, a process of steelmaking, patented in 1855–1856 by the British inventor Sir Henry Bessemer (1813–1898); it made possible the mass production of steel and yielded "mild steel," a type more durable than wrought iron and less expensive than traditional steels. Because of this process, steel eventually replaced wrought iron as the basic material of engineering throughout the industrializing world. Before the Bessemer process, in early nineteenth-century Europe and North America, steelmaking involved the infusion of additional carbon into a low-carbon wrought iron, to achieve the requisite steely hardness. This "blister steel" was then melted in clay crucibles so that the added carbon was evenly distributed throughout the metal. The process was lengthy, expensive, and awkward; to make a large casting might require hundreds of crucibles and the close coordination of dozens of workers.

Henry Bessemer was not a specialist in ferrous metallurgy but a professional inventor whose attention was directed toward the properties of steel during the Crimean War (1853–1856), when he became interested in heavy gun manufacture. Bessemer reversed traditional steelmaking procedures by taking high-carbon cast iron as his raw material and lowering its carbon content to levels appropriate for steel by oxidizing most of the carbon with an air blast. His converter was made in the form of a large egg-shaped vessel, into which tons of molten cast iron could be poured. When air was forced at high pressure through perforations in the bottom of the converter, a violent chemical reaction ensued, causing a plume of flame to issue from the open mouth of the converter. When the flame subsided, after perhaps half an hour, the conversion was complete.

Bessemer's process offered huge fuel savings, since as a pneumatic process it used no fuel at all—the chemical fury generated its own heat. Moreover, Bessemer made bulk production possible; his earliest converters had a capacity of 2 to 3 tons, whereas the clay crucibles of old held no more than 70 pounds. Bessemer was not the only person to investigate pneumatic techniques. The rival claims of William Kelly, a Kentucky ironmaster, were to plague him in the United States, and Bessemer used the ideas of such rival steelmakers as R. F. Mushet for controlling the oxidization process. Bessemer was an able businessman who quickly persuaded the leading British iron companies to take out licenses under his patent, although the first trial of his process, at the Dowlais ironworks in South Wales in 1858, had been a failure. Bessemer's own experiments had, quite by chance, used iron made from nonphosphoric ores, but when the more common phosphoric ores were used, the steel proved brittle. So, the first successful industrial application of Bessemer's process was at Edsken in Sweden, where nonphosphoric ores abounded. Although the Bessemer process came to be adopted in most modern steel centers by the mid-1860s, licensees were restricted to using nonphosphoric irons. Not until 1879 did the Bessemer process became universally usable—when the British chemist Sidney Gilchrist Thomas (1850–1885) introduced the "basic" process, one that provided a chemically basic lining within the converter to absorb and neutralize the phosphoric acid that resulted from phosphorus-rich ores.

[*See also* Bessemer, Henry; Metallurgic Industry; *and* Steelmaking.]

BIBLIOGRAPHY

Birch, Alan. *The Economic History of the British Iron and Steel Industry, 1784–1879*. London, 1967. Places Bessemer's achievement within the broader context of iron- and steelmaking in Britain and Europe.

Gale, W. K. V. *Iron and Steel*. Harlow, U.K., 1969. A clear introduction to the technology.

Tweedale, Geoffrey. "Bessemer, Sir Henry." In *Dictionary of Business Biography*, vol. 1, edited by D. J. Jeremy, pp. 309–314. London, 1984. A concise biographical note.

CHRIS EVANS

BILLS OF EXCHANGE. The bill of exchange developed in medieval Europe, initially in Northern Italy, as an instrument of remittance and credit. Its use depended on a network of intermediaries—merchant banks—that would accept (or advance) funds in one city for payment (or repayment) in another at a later date, generally in a different currency. Its use also depended on a network of exchange markets that provided mechanisms for price discovery and for settlement—either "in bank" or through netting and as-

signment. For those wishing to defer settlement, the market offered credit—either bank overdraft or rolling the debt over for later settlement.

As a relatively inexpensive means of international remittance, the bill of exchange freed trade from the constraint of bilateral balance. This facilitated complex patterns of bilaterally unbalanced multilateral trade, and it enabled merchants to specialize as importers or exporters. Also, by lowering the cost of moving funds, it allowed merchant bankers to arbitrage exchange-rate and interest-rate differentials across markets, thereby integrating financial markets throughout Europe. By the fourteenth century, most of the traffic in bills of exchange was related to finance rather than trade.

As an instrument of credit, the bill of exchange, with its associated network of money markets, played a vital role in financing working capital—both that of merchants and, through them, that of producers. The network of intermediaries and markets integrated and augmented the informal trade credit that was the backbone of commercial finance. It provided merchants with backup liquidity, mobilized the resources of merchants with excess funds to finance those who needed funds, and tapped nonmercantile sources of finance to the benefit of commerce. By specializing in the assessment and extension of credit, merchant bankers facilitated trade among strangers when informal trade credit would not have been feasible.

The bill of exchange underwent a transformation in sixteenth-century Antwerp. Because banks had been banned there, settlement had to rely on the assignment of bills of exchange. To overcome the initial difficulties, a number of new practices evolved and came to be recognized by the courts—making bills "payable to bearer"; transferability (the assignee obtaining full legal rights to collect the debt); and negotiability (the assignee having recourse to the assigner if the debtor defaults). Such changes greatly enhanced the safety and the liquidity of the bill of exchange, expanding considerably its range of use. Each additional assignment increased a bill's security, giving the holder one more guarantee of payment. The safety and ease with which it could be assigned—both because of its legal status and because of the existence of a well-developed market—made it highly liquid. As a result, the bill of exchange became a means of payment, passing from hand to hand repeatedly in the settlement of debts, much like currency. It also became an attractive short-term asset: by holding bills of exchange, merchants could earn interest on their cash reserves with very little sacrifice of liquidity. In fact, some began to purchase bills specifically with this purpose in mind—a practice known as discounting. By the early seventeenth century, the endorsement of bills (to trace the chain of assignment) was common, as was the use of standardized printed forms. During the eighteenth century, use of the negotiable bill of exchange spread throughout Europe, although more rapidly in some countries than in others; England and the Netherlands, for example, were quick to embrace it, while France was a laggard.

The increased security afforded by endorsement made it easier for ordinary merchants, rather than merchant banks alone, to issue bills of exchange. Ordinary merchants used bills of exchange as an instrument of trade credit, to schedule payments on other types of debt, and to provide guarantees to others. Merchant banks, rather than being intermediaries issuing their own paper, increasingly provided credit enhancement by endorsing the bills of others—a practice known as acceptance. In this fashion, the great acceptance houses of Amsterdam, and later of London, were able to facilitate the financing of a huge volume of international trade on the basis of quite limited capital.

Private deposit banking had earlier largely died out in Europe: the lack of safe, liquid assets had made small banks too vulnerable to failure. However, the negotiable bill of exchange proved to be just such an asset. Consequently, from the early seventeenth century onward, commercial banking was reinvented in England, on the basis of the discounting of bills of exchange—which allowed English country banks to contribute significantly to the financing of the Industrial Revolution. The banks were supported by an interbank market for such bills that served to integrate the banking system: country banks in the rapidly growing industrial regions would rediscount most of their bills of exchange in London; there, country banks from prosperous agricultural regions would purchase the bills to hold as an investment. The Bank of England had long discounted bills on a large scale, and when it began to play the role of Britain's central bank in the late 1800s, its main instrument was the discounting and rediscounting of bills of exchange.

By the late nineteenth century, however, the bill of exchange passed the zenith of its importance—at least in domestic finance. As the need to finance fixed capital became increasingly important, the capital market played a growing role. Moreover, in many countries, large national branch banks emerged, which were stable enough to finance working capital directly through advances. The United States, where regulation kept banks small and localized, was an exception in this respect; an interbank market in bills of exchange developed, centered on New York, to integrate an otherwise fragmented banking system. During the twentieth century, this evolved into today's market in commercial paper and bankers' acceptances.

Some non-Western economies developed instruments similar to the bill of exchange. In the eighth century, the government of T'ang China introduced a paper instrument of remittance for use between the capital and the provinces (called "flying cash"). In Islam in the same period, the *suftaja* emerged as an instrument of remittance and credit: merchant banks provided intermediation, and endorsement and discounting were common. Mughal India had a version known as the *hundi*.

BIBLIOGRAPHY

Ashtor, Eliyahu. "Banking Instruments between the Muslim East and the Christian West." *Journal of European Economic History* 1 (1972), 553–573.

Chapman, Stanley. *The Rise of Merchant Banking*. London, 1984.

De Roover, Raymond. *Gresham on Foreign Exchange: An Essay on Early English Mercantilism*. Cambridge, Mass., 1949.

De Roover, Raymond. *L'évolution de la lettre de change, XIVe–XVIIIe siècles*. Paris, 1953.

Einzig, Paul. *The History of Foreign Exchange*. 2d ed. London, 1970.

James, John A. *Money and Capital Markets in Postbellum America*. Princeton, 1978.

Kindleberger, Charles. *A Financial History of Western Europe*. London, 1984.

Neal, Larry. *The Rise of Financial Capitalism: International Capital Markets in the Age of Reason*. Cambridge and New York, 1990.

Pressnell, L. S. *Country Banking in the Industrial Revolution*. Oxford, 1956.

Price, Jacob M. "Transaction Costs: A Note on Merchant Credit and the Organization of Private Trade." In *The Political Economy of Merchant Empires*, edited by J. D. Tracy, pp. 276–297. Cambridge, 1991.

MEIR KOHN

BIRTH CONTROL AND CONTRACEPTIVES. Humans have not universally believed that they could control reproduction, but individuals and groups in innumerable societies have reduced fertility by deliberate measures as well as by unconscious mechanisms such as rules governing who could marry and when, proscriptions on sexual activity within marriage, ritualized sexual abstinence, and prolonged breastfeeding and late weaning practices. In addition to cultural practices indirectly affecting fertility, men and women over the centuries have drawn from a large and diverse repertoire of behaviors to prevent conception and induce abortion.

Individuals and groups in societies everywhere in the world have tried to control fertility through magic and incantations, botanical remedies used externally and internally, and exercise and bodily manipulations. Methods have been lost and reinvented, whereas others have remained in variant forms across cultures for centuries. Some methods worked, although standards of effectiveness and safety are culturally and historically relative. The dangers posed by historic methods of contraception and abortion must be weighed against the equally grave health dangers posed by repeated pregnancies, childbirths, and postpartum infections.

Perceptions of the dangers of pregnancy and childbirth relative to abortion and contraception have changed over time, too, complicating all historical assessments of birth control techniques. Likewise, assessment of the effectiveness of methods is complicated by recognition that although simple contraceptive methods require careful and consistent use, birth control effectiveness is not necessarily dependent on accurate physiological knowledge. Coitus interruptus (withdrawal of the penis before ejaculation) was practiced for centuries with apparent success before knowledge of sperm mobility became widespread. Simple methods reducing the probability of pregnancy by 50 percent or prolonging intervals between conceptions continue to be valued and used in much of the world today.

In the twenty-first century, birth control has come to be associated principally with contraception, but the most important methods of fertility interventions in world history have been infanticide, abortion, and the simple contraceptive method of coitus interruptus. Infanticide has long been a way societies and individuals controlled family and population growth. Infanticide is particularly difficult to reconstruct because child neglect, overlaying (smothering while the infant slept with parents), and use of deliberately neglectful wet nurses may have caused as many infant deaths in earlier eras as deliberate abandonment and child murder. In China, Japan, and throughout Asia, infanticide remained a widespread practice after it declined in the West. High rates of female infanticide remained especially common, just as in areas of India and China today abortion of female fetuses has been widespread.

Abortion and Methods of Contraception. For most of world history, the distinction between preventing conception and procuring abortion was blurred and ambiguous, both regarded as part of the same interventionist continuum. Well into the nineteenth century abortion remained one of the most important methods of fertility intervention in Asia, especially in China and Japan, as well as in Europe, North America, Australia, and New Zealand. Abortion methods and lore constituted a significant part of secret medical knowledge among indigenous peoples in many parts of the globe, from the Bengalis in precolonial and colonial India to native tribes in North America.

On many continents for centuries certain botanicals had illicit reputations in folklore and folk medicine as abortifacients. Drunk as teas or swallowed as medicinal oils or pills, savin, tansy, rue, cottonroot, ergot, pennyroyal, and blue and black cohosh, among others, maintained reputations as abortives from antiquity through the nineteenth century. Women hoping to cause miscarriage drank herbal teas, applied herbal plasters to their bodies, and exercised strenuously. Once they felt fetal movement (known in earlier eras as "quickening"), some women stopped trying to induce miscarriage, but others intensified the drug dosages and the vigor of exercises, or turned to more drastic remedies such as the insertion of objects into the cervix.

Mentioned in the Bible as the crime of Onan ("spilling the seed on the ground"), withdrawal may well have been the single most influential and best-known method of preventing conception. It remained a widespread practice even in the late twentieth century in parts of Europe, the United Kingdom, and less developed nations.

In the United States and parts of western Europe, commercial birth control products became more available after the mid-nineteenth century. Condoms made of rubber as well as the traditional animal intestines, known to European elites since the seventeenth century, but expensive and associated with prostitution, began to be available. Barrier methods of contraception (the vaginal sponge, early versions of the cervical cap, and the contraceptive diaphragm) were manufactured for reproductive control and became increasingly available at declining prices from diverse sources. Spermicides became commercially available in the form of simple homemade douching solutions and vaginal suppositories. Contraceptive douching became one of the best-known birth control methods in the United States in the nineteenth century and in Europe in the twentieth century. The rhythm method, by which a woman's fertility could be tracked according to her menstrual cycle, grew in use among Roman Catholic populations in many parts of the world in the decades after the 1930s.

In the last half of the twentieth century, birth control practices worldwide, but particularly in developed nations, were significantly affected by new inventions: the anovulatory oral contraceptive pill, intrauterine devices (IUDs), the "morning after" pill (a one-time only drug dose to prevent fertilization after an unprotected coitus), and the so-called abortion pill such as mifepristone or other antiprogesterone drugs that prevent implantation of the newly fertilized ovum or otherwise induce early trimester abortion.

Although dramatically popular around the globe in the first decades after its introduction in 1960, the birth control pill declined in use by the mid-1970s as fears escalated about its long-term impact on women's health. Severe medical complications similarly limited the popularity of IUDs. Voluntary female sterilization grew in popularity worldwide as a birth control method in the 1970s, becoming by 1980 more common for birth control than use of the contraceptive pill and the IUD combined. By the 1990s, the most significant birth control methods globally were abortion, condoms (used for contraception and for protection against HIV infection), and sterilization in the form of vasectomy for men and tubal ligation for women.

Methods for Measuring Birth Control in Historical Populations. Where sufficient historical vital records exist, researchers use family reconstitution techniques to compile individual and family histories, yielding indices of family limitation. One such measure is the changing number of women in given cohorts who had large families. Another indicator of family limitation is the age of married women at their last childbirth. Even in preindustrial England and France, researchers found evidence of family limitation practices in some areas where the women who married youngest stopped childbearing well before menopause, presumably because they no longer desired additional children.

Although demographers continue to debate the significance of stopping behavior (couples achieving smaller families by terminating reproduction before the end of the reproductive life span) compared to spacing (deliberately prolonging intervals between conceptions), preindustrial people reduced fertility using both.

Economics and Birth Control. Correlating birth control behavior with economic issues at both the macro and micro levels has a long history. Economists and political philosophers have long studied the relations between population growth and economic growth. In 1798, British political philosopher Thomas Malthus predicted mass starvation and national decline because population growth occurred exponentially, whereas food supplies increased arithmetically. Malthusians, as his followers came to be called, believed the only remedy to be reduced rates of marriage and enforced sexual abstinence. Neo-Malthusian reformers in the second half of the nineteenth century in Europe and the United States mitigated some of the harshness of earlier policy proposals by promoting marriage with contraception, but they too feared the economic consequences of excess population growth.

In opposition to Malthusian predictions, European governments in the nineteenth century began to view population growth as a sign of national strength and sought to promote fertility among those they regarded as the fittest and most able. From the 1860s through the 1930s, population decline appeared highly threatening to many Western governments, and they turned to legal, cultural, and financial incentives to encourage fertility. By the mid-twentieth century, however, officials in developed countries began to question pronatalist theories and policies, believing that unrestrained population growth threatened economic and social advancement in all countries, especially those in the developing world.

At the micro level, economic concerns have long been associated with individual and family desires for fertility control. At times, families in rural and agricultural communities with high childhood mortality rates wanted a large number of children to ensure sufficient child labor for the family economy and care for parents in their old age. Children, however, required dowries and perhaps the division of property and land. In industrializing economies,

the economic costs of children increased with the passage and enforcement of child labor laws, with compulsory education, and with cultural shifts sentimentalizing childhood.

When family financial stability required fewer children, couples drew upon the fluctuating but always available contraceptive and abortifacient repertoire. Historically, people restricted fertility for many reasons besides economic concerns, including new attitudes about the well-being of children already born in a family, new attitudes toward motherhood and maternal health, and changing views of women's sexual, marital, and reproductive rights.

Few topics have received more attention and generated fewer conclusions in the social sciences in the last thirty years than the meaning and causes of the fertility decline since the nineteenth century, especially the relationships between economics and changes in fertility. The theory of the demographic transition, for example, occasioned much study and debate among economists, demographers, sociologists, and historians for much of the second half of the twentieth century. The theory postulated that as nations go through relatively predictable stages of industrial development, there are predictable demographic shifts from high mortality/high fertility to low mortality/low fertility. Supporters of the demographic transition theory created empirical models to disentangle the main structural features of industrializing economies under differing demographic circumstances.

As historical demographers and historians analyzed fluctuations in fertility in world history, however, it became increasingly evident that economic factors alone, especially per capita wealth, or gross national product, or levels of industrialization, could not explain the variety of fertility responses in Europe and the United States since the late eighteenth century or in the developing nations of Asia, Africa, and Latin America since World War II. Historical evidence, therefore, has complicated economic theory, suggesting more complex relationships between the adoption of marital birth control and economic factors.

As Europe experienced declining fertility in the nineteenth century, individual nations varied dramatically in levels of child mortality, urbanization, education, per capita income, and other indicators of economic development. A Princeton University project studying the European fertility decline concluded that social and cultural variables, including "mentality," held significant sway in determining historical fertility behavior (Coale and Watkins, 1986).

Other historical studies underscored the inadequacy of simple economic models in explaining the wide diversity of fertility behavior in world history. In some areas, and among some populations, deliberate family limitation was practiced well before the onset of any factors identified with industrialization. In the words of historical demographer

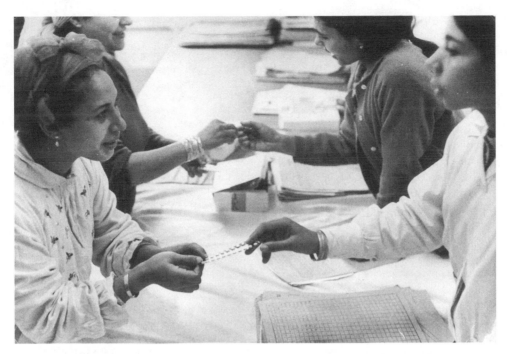

BIRTH CONTROL. Women receiving a supply of birth control pills at a family planning clinic in Egypt, late twentieth century. (M. Jacot/World Health Organization/Courtesy of the National Library of Medicine, Bethesda, Maryland)

E. A. Wrigley, the industrial revolution did not stimulate a sharp break with the past in European fertility behavior. Rather, it "created conditions conducive to the adoption of family limitation upon an unprecedented scale" (Wrigley, 1969, p. 181).

Economists' models have not identified specific and identifiable common economic thresholds to explain the complex and intertwined social, cultural, and economic factors that led to lower demand for children in past history. Demographer Donald Bogue, critical of economic causal explanations for fertility behavior, argued decades ago that "the only valid explanation we have for international differences in fertility is the extent to which contraceptive practices have been adopted," but otherwise "we do not know why some nations have high birthrates and others low birthrates" (Bogue, 1969, pp. 678–679).

Promotion of and Opposition to Birth Control. Throughout much of world history birth control was a secret and illicit activity rousing at times fierce opposition from religious, medical, and civic groups. To the religious, birth control interfered with God-given "natural" fertility, and the separation of sexuality from reproduction appeared to promote licentiousness. Birth control raised fears about female chastity, the sanctity of marriage, bloodlines, and property. Beginning in the seventeenth century, when birth control became part of marriage in some areas of Europe, it came increasingly under the critical scrutiny of the Catholic Church, although local parish priests differed greatly in

their attention to and punishment of such practices. In the twentieth century, the Catholic Church throughout the world became a consistent force against birth control.

Nation states participated actively in birth control, at times passing pronatalist measures to stimulate high fertility among specified groups, sometimes criminalizing both abortion and contraception. France in the nineteenth century became the first modern nation to use deliberate incentives and punishments to encourage higher fertility. European countries, the United States, Australia, and New Zealand passed laws restricting abortion and sometimes contraception when faced with declining fertility in the nineteenth century. Such laws were repealed gradually in the decades after World War II.

Official and quasi-official public agencies, secular reform groups, and private individuals also both promoted and opposed birth control. Eugenicists sought reproduction only from those deemed fit, feminists sought reproductive control as empowerment for women, economists began to associate fertility control with a nation's economic strength. The earliest nongovernmental promotion of birth control came from neo-Malthusian reformers in nineteenth century Europe and the United States who argued for simple contraceptive "preventive checks" as the way to balance population growth with natural resources and the food supply.

The first organized campaigns to promote birth control came from Margaret Sanger in the United States and

Marie Stopes in England, which led the way in the 1920s to the founding of Planned Parenthood. In the second half of the twentieth century, governments in developing countries, with incentives from international organizations and powerful U.S.-based organizations (the Ford Foundation, the Rockefeller Foundation, the Population Council, and the World Bank), subsidized family planning and birth control. In many countries national health insurance programs subsidized birth control, relying on advertising and peer pressure campaigns, financial incentives, and at times overt coercion to increase rates of sterilization along with use of the IUD and anovulatory pill. In 1952, India became the first nation to provide full governmental sponsorship of a widespread birth control campaign, emphasizing male sterilization and female use of the IUD. The Chinese government, after hesitation in the 1950s and 1960s, began an intensive campaign for one child per family, enforced by high rates of abortion and sterilization.

In the early twenty-first century, opposition to contraception is essentially quiescent. Even the Catholic Church, long opposed to contraception and abortion, has focused its effects on repealing the legality and cultural acceptability of abortion. The birth control debate has recently been refocused (and reconfused) by the introduction of mifepristone, which has once again blurred the distinction between contraception and abortion. This important new method, which promises to place reproductive decisions of contraception/abortion back in the hands of individual women, may once and for all effectively end the public birth control debate.

BIBLIOGRAPHY

Bergues, Helene. *La prévention des naissances dans la famille: Ses origins dans les temps modernes*. Paris, 1960.
Bogue, Donald J. *Principles of Demography*. New York, 1969.
Brodie, Janet Farrell. *Contraception and Abortion in Nineteenth-Century America*. Ithaca, N.Y., 1994.
Carlsson, Gosta. "The Decline of Fertility: Innovation or Adjustment Process?" *Population Studies* 20 (1966–1967), 149–174.
Coale, Ansley J., and T. James Trussell. "Model Fertility Schedules: Variations in the Age Structure of Childbearing in Human Populations." *Population Index* 40.2 (April 1974), 185–258.
Coale, Ansley J., and Susan C. Watkins, eds. *The Decline of Fertility in Europe*. Princeton, 1986.
Das Gupta, Monica. "Fertility Decline in Punjab, India: Parallels with Historical Europe." In *Reproductive Change in India and Brazil*, edited by George Martine, Monica Das Gupta, and Lincoln C. Chen, 65–95. Delhi, 1998.
Easterlin, Richard A. "The Economics and Sociology of Fertility: A Synthesis." In *Historical Studies of Changing Fertility*, edited by Charles Tilly, pp. 57–133. Princeton, 1978.
Engelen, Theo. "Family, Production and Reproduction: On the Relationship Between Economic and Demographic Processes." *Economic and Social History in the Netherlands* 6 (1994), 61–82.
Farooq, Ghazi M., and George B. Simmons. *Fertility in Developing Nations: An Economic Perspective on Research and Policy Issues*. New York, 1985.
Gautier, Etienne, and Louis Henry. *La population de Crulai, paroisse normande: Étude historique*. Paris, 1958.
Grossmann, Atina. *Reforming Sex: The German Movement for Birth Control and Abortion Reform, 1920–1950*. New York, 1995.
Guha, Supriya. "The Unwanted Pregnancy in Colonial Bengal." *Indian Economic and Social History Review* 33.4 (1996), 403–435.
Harsch, Donna. "Society, the State, and Abortion in East Germany, 1950–1972." *American Historical Review* 102.1 (1997), 53–84.
Hollingsworth, T. H. *Historical Demography*. Ithaca, N.Y., 1969.
Jones, Elsie F. "Fertility Decline in Australia and New Zealand, 1861–1936." *Population Index* 37 (October–December 1971), 301–338.
Lesthaeghe, Ron J. *The Decline of Belgian Fertility, 1800–1970*. Princeton, 1977.
McLaren, Angus. *Birth Control in Nineteenth-Century England*. New York, 1978.
Mosk, Carl. "The Decline of Marital Fertility in Japan." *Population Studies* 31 (March 1979), 24–28.
Nag, Moni. *Factors Affecting Human Fertility in Nonindustrial Societies: A Cross-Cultural Study*. New Haven, 1962.
Pommerenke, W. T. "Abortion in Japan." *Obstetrical and Gynecological Survey* 10 (April 1955), 145–175.
Santow, Gigi. "Coitus Interruptus in the Twentieth Century." *Population and Development Review* 19.4 (1993), 767–792.
Toth, Istvan Gyorgy. "Peasant Sexuality in Eighteenth-Century Hungary." *Continuity and Change* 6.1 (1991), 43–58.
Walle, Étienne van de, and Helmut V. Muhsam. "Fatal Secrets and the French Fertility Transition." *Population and Development Review* 21.2 (1995), 261–279.
Wrigley, E. A. "Family Limitation in Pre-Industrial England." *Economic History Review* 19.1 (April 1966), 82–109.
Wrigley, E. A. *Population and History*. New York, 1969.

JANET FARRELL BRODIE

BLACK COUNTRY, a region of central England situated on the South Staffordshire coalfield, bounded by the Bentley Fault to the north, by the eastern and western boundary faults, and by the River Stour to the south. The River Tame runs immediately to the northeast. The region was rich in minerals, and an outcrop, exposing a 2-meter (6-foot) seam of coal was easy to exploit. The earliest settlements were scattered, small hamlets. There were five small market towns: Dudley in the center of the region, and Wolverhampton, Walsall, Halesowen, and (after 1500) Stourbridge at its periphery. Coal was dug there from at least the thirteenth century, and the other minerals worked included iron ore, limestone, refractory clay, and sandstone. Local waterpower was intensively exploited. The manufacture of small metalware was well established by 1550, and glassmaking was successfully introduced in the early 1600s. By 1650, the products of the region were being sold throughout England and abroad in Europe and in new English colonies. Manufacture was carried on in small family workshops and was combined with subsistence agriculture to sustain a household. The distribution of goods was organized by commercial capitalists.

Local coal was mined for fuel for both workshops and homes. The first Newcomen steam-pumping engine was built near Dudley in 1712 and, from 1776, Watt engines were applied to power the blast furnaces. Some 120 coal-fired furnaces and their associated puddling furnaces, rolling mills, and foundries were smelting ores and converting pig iron to wrought iron by 1830. Coal was then exploited in both large and small-scale mines. The small metalware manufactures were stimulated to greater growth and specialization. New chemical industries were introduced, the glass industry was expanded, and the region was linked with the major seaports by both canals between 1766 and 1840 and railways from 1838. Waste products and smoke blackened the air and the landscape, which gave the Black Country its name. Commercial farming ceased, although kitchen gardens and allotments (plots) continued to play a part in feeding the industrial workers; pigs and hens were usually kept.

The Black Country had an almost insatiable market with the growth of the British Empire and trade with South America. By 1860, however, the local minerals (especially the iron ore) were overexploited. From 1875 to 1885, primary iron production in the area collapsed against the competition of other districts, and all but one of the blast furnaces closed. Coal production on the plateau ceased in 1918, though deep-coal mining was continued beyond the fault lines. After a severe slump, the region recovered its prosperity when traditional skills and premises were adapted to new products, notably bicycles and motor cycles. By 1918, factories with machinery driven by gas or electricity were the normal units of production. Large corporate partnerships absorbed the family firms, and the domestic workshops slowly declined to extinction by 1960.

From 1970 to 1990, the economy of the region was again transformed by the decline of both vehicle production and the steel industry. The last blast furnace was closed, and coal mining was ended. New industries were opened, including chemicals and electronics, but the numbers of workers engaged in manufacture were overtaken by those in the service sector.

The long history of this industrial region demonstrates the persistence of an industrial culture. It has been characterized by repeated adaptations of established skills and contacts, as well as the organization of production to meet successfully new economic circumstances.

BIBLIOGRAPHY

Allen, George C. *Industrial Development of Birmingham and the Black Country, 1860–1927*. Birmingham, 1927. Reprinted, 1966.

Johnson, B. L. C., and M. J. Wise. "The Black Country." In *Birmingham and Its Regional Setting: A Scientific Survey*. Wakefield, U.K., 1950.

Rowlands, M. B. "Continuity and Change in an Industrialising Society: The Case of the West Midlands." In *Regions and Industries*, edited by P. Hudson, pp. 103–132. Cambridge, 1989.

Timmins, Samuel. *Birmingham and the Midland Hardware District*. Birmingham, 1866. Reprinted, 1967.

Trainor, Richard. *Black Country Elites, 1830–1900*. Oxford, 1993.

MARIE ROWLANDS

BLACK MARKETS, UNDERGROUND ECONOMIES, AND THE INFORMAL SECTOR.

In every market economy, there are rules that regulate and constrain economic transactions, such as taxation, labor legislation, and quality and price controls, as well as certain goods and services for which markets are formally prohibited. The underground economy consists of transactions that do not observe these rules and are therefore untaxed, unregulated, and un-measured by official government statistics. It contains many types of economic activity, such as employing workers off the books while they are collecting welfare or unemployment benefits; tax evasion; informal trade between friends; and smuggling, bootlegging, and black-market trading, which have little in common beside being outside the realm of the formal economy. The transactions that should be included in the underground economy vary with changes in institutional boundaries that realign the division between the formal and informal. The growth of underground economies, also known as shadow, hidden, parallel, black, and informal economies, is a universal trend in the twentieth century. It is found in many different countries at different levels of economic development, with participants from every level of the social structure. Any transaction outside the view and formal control of the government is considered part of the underground economy.

Reasons for the Emergence of Informal Economies. Government regulation grew enormously in the twentieth century as governments assumed more and more responsibility for general welfare when politicians increasingly came to believe that free markets did not invariably produce an outcome they considered socially or politically desirable. New forms of labor legislation such as health codes, laws against racial and sexual discrimination, minimum wage laws, and laws banning child labor, sent employers to illegal labor markets. Informal employment benefited from hiring underground workers by avoiding payroll taxes and mandated fringe benefits, paying piece rates, avoiding constraints from unions and labor laws, and enjoying maximum flexibility in hiring and layoffs. Underground labor is most common in labor-intensive industries without much benefit from economies of scale. It is also more common in industries with volatile demand conditions in which much of the work is seasonal. Immigration restrictions and various legal limits imposed on foreigners are two important reasons for the recent growth of the informal sector in wealthy countries. As the income gap between rich and poor countries has increased, there have been growing incentives for workers from poor countries to take the risks involved in flouting these regulations.

The other cause for the emergence of informal sectors is the rise in the tax rate and the desire to avoid taxes. After World War II, for example, the U.S. government added payroll taxes to the personal income tax, which prompted some workers to work off the books. However, until the 1970s, the underground labor market was mainly composed of minorities, unskilled workers whose jobs had been replaced by technology. During the 1970s, the supply of underground workers grew because of rapid tax increases. The demand by firms for informal labor began to rise as big businesses began subcontracting from small firms, which relied on cheap labor and sweatshop conditions to compete with third world countries.

The underground labor market in developed nations consists of two disjoint sectors. The first includes workers employed in sweatshops and outwork, often for wages far below those of the formal sector or even the legal minimum wage, laboring in harsh, unsafe working conditions without union or legal protection. This group includes primarily illegal immigrants and minors who are not allowed to enter the labor market any other way. The jobs in this sector include seasonal help in agriculture, work in hotels and restaurants, garment making, and construction. For this group, taxation is largely irrelevant with the possible exception of payroll taxes. The second sector includes skilled workers who are moonlighting to earn additional, untaxed, off-the-books income, usually white males. In addition to the onerousness of the taxes or regulations that the informal sector can avoid, this economy's size depends on several economic and social variables, the respect that individuals have for the law and their government, and the severity of the penalties meted out for participating.

The underground economy has created a decentralized model of economic organization. Successful production and distribution are possible in the informal sector through personal networks of economic activity and coordinated clusters of workers. The informal sector leads to lower labor costs, because it avoids fringe benefits and payroll taxes to the state and undermines the power of organized labor. It increases the amount of currency in circulation, especially big bills, since underground markets use mainly cash.

The effects of these markets on productivity and price levels are ambiguous. Productivity could be lowered because informal and illegal producers might not have access to advanced production techniques but could be raised by reducing the costs imposed by regulation and red tape. Its effects on government revenues are equally indeterminate. The government suffers, of course, from revenue loss owing to unpaid taxes, but this loss may be offset by the additional purchases made from "hidden" disposable income (which is subject to value-added or other direct taxes that are rarely evaded in industrialized countries). The underground economy causes a distortion of economic indicators that are used to create economic policy. It causes gross national product (GNP), national income, and productivity to be underestimated and unemployment and inflation to be overstated, which could cause the government to create a policy that attempts to stimulate the economy more than necessary. Therefore, it is important to measure the size of this sector of the economy.

After World War II, American, European, and Japanese businesses attempted to spread modern production facilities to developing nations in Asia, Africa and Latin America. In the 1950s and 1960s, these international companies put up modern facilities next to smaller, less sophisticated ones. These attempts did not, however, help to reduce the informal sector in third world countries, which remained mixed in poverty. Beginning in the 1970s, however, these companies began to subcontract various phases of production to factories around the world. This allowed greater flexibility of output and left subcontractors to hire labor from informal labor markets, limiting the risk of work slowdowns due to labor strikes. While some subcontracted factories remained in the formal sector, many moved into the informal sector, further subcontracting to tiny underground workshops and homework enterprises. In the garment industry of the Philippines, for example, the majority of workers perform their work in sweatshops or at home on a piecework basis. This kind of work in third world countries is often supported by the local government even though the conditions would be illegal in the corporation's country of origin.

Thus, underground economies have proliferated in many countries, both developed and developing. In Italy, efforts of large industries to control union power led to decentralization. Artisanal enterprises with fewer than fifteen workers were exempted from parts of the tax code, and small enterprises working for larger formal firms increased rapidly. There is a large, diversified informal economy in which low-skilled jobs are filled by housewives and children, producing hosiery, garments, and textiles as well as bicycle, motorcycle, and car parts, while better-trained, experienced workers become small-business entrepreneurs.

In Soviet-type command economies, central planners fixed wages and prices, regulated production and trade, and, for all intents and purposes, prohibited free markets. In these economies, the underground economy—despite the risks—was huge, circumventing these inefficient rules and allocating resources to bring supply and demand into equilibrium. Underground economies continued to flourish in these countries during the transition to market

UNDERGROUND ECONOMY. Black market money exchange in progress in Sulaymaniyah, Iraq, 1999. (© Mike Yamashita/Woodfin Camp and Associates, New York)

economies. In Croatia, throughout the recovery from a devastating war and the transformation from socialism to a market economy, researchers estimated that at least 25 percent of economic activity was unrecorded, with markets flooded with goods smuggled from neighboring countries, unregistered workers, and employers neglecting to pay taxes. Noncompliance with the new institutional framework made new rules ineffective, increasing uncertainty and weakening property rights. This created the opportunity for criminal elements to seize existing wealth, rather than use resources to create new wealth.

Effect of Price Controls. One form of government intervention in markets that has created a parallel underground economy is price controls. During periods of war and in a few cases of high inflation, governments have set market prices by decree, hoping to subvert the operation of the price mechanism. When the government sets a price ceiling that is lower than the market price, it creates excess demand, and black markets arise, in which there are buyers willing to pay more than the ceiling price and sellers who would profit from selling to them. The American government imposed price controls during World Wars I and II, as well as the Korean and Vietnam Wars, in order to stem inflation, to make sure that even low-income consumers had access to goods it deemed essential, and to ensure that there would be adequate supplies for the war. Black markets existed during every stage of price controls but were most severe during World War II, when the Emergency Price Control Act of 1942 fixed prices on more than eight million items of food, clothing, shelter, fuel, and consumer durables. The black market acted as a way of raising prices to bring supply and demand into equilibrium and allocate resources productively, although not as efficiently as the free market system. Similar outcomes can be observed everywhere else price controls were introduced during and after World War II.

Smuggling is another paradigmatic black market. When import tariffs or sales taxes become sufficiently high, smuggling ensues. For example, beginning in the 1960s, the tax rate differential on cigarettes between states grew large enough to make smuggling from one state to another profitable, with a fee paid to clerks for looking the other way. In 1975, the estimated loss in high-tax states was $391 million.

Another part of the informal economy is foreign exchange. After the collapse of the gold standard, many governments, in an attempt to control exchange rates, set the exchange rate by legislative fiat. Dealers were not allowed to trade in foreign exchange and individuals were not allowed to hold it, leading to excess demand for foreign currency. The black market often sets a price for foreign exchange several times the official one, especially in less developed countries. In the 1980s, for example, the black market premium in Sierra Leone was 545 percent and in Nicaragua, 2,100 percent. Black markets for American dollars are common in South American countries such as Brazil and Bolivia, where export smugglers use the black market to remit their earnings, and smugglers of manufacturer's imports use it to acquire foreign exchange.

Outlawed Markets. Certain markets, rather than being regulated by the government, are simply outlawed. In the ill-fated American experiment in prohibition, alcohol became illegal between 1921 and 1933, creating a huge demand for illicit supply. Initially, bootleggers smuggled foreign-made commercial liquor into the United States across the Canadian and Mexican borders, but as this became more risky owing to searches by the U.S. Coast Guard, bootleggers turned to other sources. Little reliable information on prohibition exists, but expenditures for alcohol have been estimated at $5 billion in 1929, approximately what spending would have been in the absence of prohibition. And evidence indicates that Prohibition may have even had a slightly positive effect on alcohol consumption. Bootlegging helped lead to the establishment of American organized crime syndicates, such as the Mafia, which persisted long after the repeal of prohibition.

One of the largest sectors of the world economy today is the trade in illegal drugs. Production of illicit drugs is ubiquitous but thrives especially in countries with weak central governments, such as Afghanistan, Colombia, and Lebanon. It is controlled by a relatively small number of people who reap most of the financial gains but depends on the labor of hundreds of thousands of peasants for growing and processing. Heroin is produced from opium, derived from poppies that are grown in only a few parts of the world, such as Southeast Asia, Iran, Pakistan, and Mexico, and is imported into the United States. Because of the great distances and the difficult production process, U.S. production and distribution are controlled by large, oligopolistic firms. This market operates entirely outside the law and is subject to violent forms of contract enforcement.

Marijuana, the most commonly used illegal drug in the United States, is grown in many parts of the world, including the United States and Canada, although the main sources are Mexico and Colombia. Widespread production and limited processing needed for use allow for a number of producers and distributors, but bulk and odor make marijuana more expensive to transport and easier to detect. In the United States, the illegal narcotics trade costs billions of dollars through expenses for prison, law enforcement, and the resources wasted through violence and the need to evade law enforcement agencies. In countries that produce illegal drugs, the sector has produced huge profits for only a few people, increasing the gap between rich and poor.

Other Prohibited Markets. There are other informal markets in goods that for one reason or another are prohibited or taboo. These often include markets in things that are not considered eligible for sale, such as prostitu-

tion, as well as markets in transplantable organs and adoptable children. Prostitution ranges from streetwalkers to call girls and well-organized brothels and are often marketed and controlled by pimps, who take a portion of the earnings. In 1976, the Internal Revenue Service estimated the unreported income from prostitution at $1.1 to $1.6 billion.

Other markets that are banned are focused on "human products." More than eighty thousand Americans needed organ transplants in 2002, but studies show that one-third of patients die while awaiting the transplant, since the demand for organs (at a legally mandated price of zero) far exceeds the supply. In countries such as China, India, and Brazil, organs are sold on the black market, taken from both the living and dead. The United Network for Organ Sharing in the United States estimates that two hundred to three hundred Americans a year buy organs from the poor in third world countries, where organs can be included in dowries. In China, the organs of executed prisoners are sold, while in Brazil, a new law renders every adult a donor after death, which people fear will decrease the attempts of doctors to save their lives.

Another such market is the one for adopted babies. After World War II, demand for adoptions began to exceed supply, and black-market adoption arose to aid couples who did not meet the standards of government adoption agencies, such as couples of mixed religious denominations. In the 1970s, due to better contraceptive measures along with the legalization of abortion and increasingly liberal attitudes toward single motherhood, the supply of infants available for adoption decreased. By the mid-1970s, New York adoption agencies were averaging five white infant adoptions per year, compared with an average of fifty before abortion was legalized. In black-market adoptions, couples pay large sums of money to an adoption attorney, who finds them a child and transfers a portion of his fee to the mother. Today, in countries such as Guatemala, unprincipled attorneys, adoption agencies, foster home networks, and even smuggling rings help produce twenty-three hundred children a year for adoptive parents, mostly in the United States. The adoptions generate at least $25 million a year in these nations.

The underground economy is difficult to measure, since by nature it is intended to defy measurement, but economists have developed both direct and indirect methods to estimate its size. Direct methods use microeconomic data such as individual surveys, tax returns, and unemployment records to look for discrepancies between income measured with audits and income declared for tax purposes. Limits to this approach include difficulty in tracking down income when it is unreported by both the payer and the recipient, such as barter trade, as well as low data quality because of unsophisticated methods of collection. Indirect methods rely on macroeconomic data such as monetary aggregates collected for unrelated purposes. One method to isolate unrecorded income is to check for discrepancies in official statistics between production and consumption figures, but this approach disregards purchases made in the underground market, which are not included in expenditures. Since the underground economy primarily involves cash transactions, another method is to examine the currency/deposit ratio and isolate excess demand for currency by choosing a base year in which there was assumed to be no underground economy. Using this method, the underground economy as a percentage of gross domestic product (GDP) for 2001–2002 was estimated at 8.7 percent for the United States, 12.5 percent in Great Britain, 27 percent in Italy, 11.1 percent in Japan, 16.3 percent in Germany, and 28.5 percent in Greece.

This is one of the most commonly used approaches to estimating the underground economy, but it has several problems. One is that this method has to rely on the rather strong assumption that the velocity of money is the same in both underground and formal economies. Moreover, there are transactions in the hidden economy that are not paid in cash, such as barter trade or informal credit lines. Finally, the assumption of no underground economy in a base year cannot be verified, which could raise the size of the underground economy.

Another approach, the physical input method, measures electricity consumption, isolating the electricity supply used in underground activities. This produced estimates for 1990 of 10.5 percent in the United States, 13.1 percent in Great Britain, 19.6 percent in Italy, 13.2 percent in Japan, 19.6 percent in Italy, and 21.8 percent in Greece. Among transition economies, former Soviet Union economies had an average underground economy size of 44.8 percent of GDP in 2000–2001, and central and eastern European countries averaged 29.2 percent. However, not all underground economies require a large amount of electricity, and other energy sources can be used. Also, there may be considerable differences in the ratio of electricity/GDP in different countries or changes over time. Most economists seem to agree that for the United States, 10 percent of GDP is a good working estimate for the underground economy but exact numbers await more precise measuring methods.

[*See also* Prostitution *and* Smuggling.]

BIBLIOGRAPHY
Alessandrini, Sergio, and Bruno Dallago, eds. *The Unofficial Economy*. Aldershot, U.K., 1987.
Bawley, Dan. *The Subterranean Economy*. New York, 1982.
Dallago, Bruno. *The Irregular Economy*. Aldershot, U.K., 1990.
Feige, Edgar L., ed. *The Underground Economies*. Cambridge, 1989.
Mattera, Philip. *Off the Books: The Rise of the Underground Economy*. New York, 1985.
Miron, Jeffrey. "Effect of Alcohol Prohibition on Alcohol Consumption." NBER Working paper 7130. Cambridge, Mass., 1999.
Portes, Alejandro, Manuel Castells, and Lauren A. Benton, eds. *The Informal Economy: Studies in Advanced and Less Developed Countries*. Baltimore and London, 1989.
Rockoff, Hugh. "Price and Wage Controls in Four Wartime Periods." *The Journal of Economic History* 41.2 (1981), 381–401.
Schneider, Friedrich. "Dimensions of the Shadow Economy." *Independent Review* 5.1 (2000), 81–91.
Schneider, Friedrich. "The Size and Development of the Shadow Economies of Twenty-two Transition and Twenty-one OECD Countries." *IZA Discussion Paper No. 514* (2002).
Simon, Carl P., and Ann D. Witte. *Beating the System: The Underground Economy*. Boston, 1982.
Tanzi, Vito, ed. *The Underground Economy in the United States and Abroad*. Lexington, Mass., 1983.

BLAST FURNACES are facilities for producing cast iron. A shaft holding substantial quantities of fuel, its combustion accelerated by an air blast, the early blast furnace was able to generate the high temperatures needed to smelt iron ore and reduce the metal to a liquid state. The outcome was a metal that was high in carbon and therefore brittle, quite unlike the malleable irons produced at the small, low hearths characteristic of humankind's first steps in metallurgy. Cast iron required further refining before it could be used by a smith, but the blast furnace, which lent itself to continuous, large-scale production, had countervailing cost advantages.

The blast furnace originated in China in the fifth or sixth century BCE as a spinoff from an already developed tradition of bronze casting. Chinese superiority over other civilizations in iron casting was maintained for many centuries, but during the Ming period (fourteenth to seventeenth centuries), as Chinese technology stagnated, blast furnaces appeared in northern Europe. Whether knowledge of the blast furnace diffused from Asia or whether European metalworkers spontaneously produced cast iron in the course of heightening the smelting hearths at which they worked and harnessing advances in waterwheel technology to power the air blast is still disputed. The remains of blast furnaces dating from the thirteenth century, perhaps the twelfth, have been identified in central Sweden and Westphalia. By the start of the sixteenth century the indirect technique (the production of malleable iron at a furnace and forge) was well established in northern Europe. Yet the blast furnace did not automatically supplant the bloomery hearths that yielded malleable iron via direct reduction. Market conditions did not always favor the bulk production associated with the blast furnace, enabling bloomery operators to survive in the shadow of blast furnaces for several centuries, even into the late nineteenth century in parts of the United States and southern Europe.

European blast furnaces of the early modern period were fueled with charcoal, requiring the careful husbandry of forest resources. The substitution of mineral coal held out the promise of a vastly increased output, provided a means could be found of counteracting coal's damagingly sulfurous quality. Abraham Darby, master of the Coalbrookdale works in Shropshire, England, found a solution in 1709. His coking of coal opened the way for an abandonment of vegetable fuel and heralded the industrialization of the iron industry, first in Britain, then in the coal basins of Belgium, Germany, and further afield. Charcoal was not immediately ousted, however, as a fuel. Several major innovations of the industrial age, such as the "hot blast" (1828), boosted the productivity of charcoal furnaces as much as coke furnaces, ensuring the viability of charcoal smelting in much of central Europe and North America until the eve of the twentieth century.

Since the 1870s blast furnaces have supplied the key input for mass steel production. Modern furnaces, producing one thousand tons per day where their predecessors two centuries earlier managed just two or three, remain a fundamental feature of ferrous metallurgy and industrial society.

BIBLIOGRAPHY

Björkenstam, Nils. "The Blast Furnace in Europe in Medieval Times. Part of a New System for Producing Wrought Iron." In *The Importance of Ironmaking: Technical Innovation and Social Change*, edited by Gert Magnusson, pp. 143–153. Stockholm, 1995.

Hyde, Charles K. *Technological Change and the British Iron Industry, 1700–1870*. Princeton, 1977. Contains an important discussion of the transition from charcoal to coke smelting in Britain.

Tylecote, R. F. *A History of Metallurgy*. 2d ed. London, 1992. A useful guide to the technical problems of iron smelting.

Wagner, Donald B. *Iron and Steel in Ancient China*. Leiden, 1993.

CHRIS EVANS

BLOCH, MARC (1886–1944), French historian and cofounder with Lucien Febvre of the journal the *Annales d'Histoire Économique et Sociale* (from 1929, with several name changes, to the present).

A soldier in both world wars and a martyred leader of the French Resistance, Marc Leopold Benjamin Bloch was a specialist in medieval and comparative history who taught at the University of Strasbourg (1919–1936) and the Sorbonne (1936–1939). Under the German occupation, he taught at the University of Strasbourg-in-exile in Clermont Ferrand (1940–1941) and Montpellier (1941–1942) before entering the underground movement in Lyon, where he was captured in March 1944 and shot by the Germans three months later.

Throughout his scholarly career, Bloch valued economic history for its concreteness and comparative potential. Absorbed by the crisis unleashed by the Depression, he read voraciously in the literature of economics and finance,

participated in debates among specialists, and solicited contributions to the *Annales* by academics and practitioners. In his posthumously published manual *The Historian's Craft* (1953), Bloch insisted on the links between the present and the past. Nevertheless, while urging the importance of history in tackling contemporary problems, Bloch warned against building facile analogies with the past. Conversely, although he encouraged his university colleagues to interest themselves in contemporary issues, he was quick to criticize anachronistic interpretations of historical phenomena. An opponent of all forms of historical determinism (economic, geographic, racial, or political), Bloch followed a rigorous method of critiquing all his sources for fraud and error as he pursued an unending search for human tracks in the material world.

Bloch's major contributions to European economic history lay in the subjects of money, technology, and agrarian history. A convinced, but not uncritical, monetarist, he added a social and political dimension to the causes and consequences of medieval Europe's acute shortage of gold. He was fascinated by the currency mutations of Europe's rulers from the Middle Ages to his own time. He placed these "inevitable and necessary" devaluations in political perspective but also in a larger context of prices, overall gold supply, and volume of trade, as well as the various, and increasingly sophisticated, exchange and credit devices that were developed to manage a limited stock of precious metals.

Bloch considered technical change a problem of "collective psychology." In studying Europe's advances and lags as well as the suppression of particular innovations in such realms as land cultivation, power production, architecture, arms, transportation, and manufacturing, he stressed the mental habits of a particular era over the traditional factors of intellectual, material, and labor resources. Bloch's signal contribution to European agrarian history was his characterization of different field systems by their social, political, and environmental roots and consequences. He examined the comparative history of European feudalism, slavery, and serfdom. He also added to the history of western Europe's agricultural revolution, detailing the transformation of communal farming and the three-field rotation system into the modern pattern of enclosed, intensively cultivated private holdings.

Bloch's explanations, many corrected and superseded by new generations of scholars, nevertheless remain model attempts at applying critical intelligence and an open mind to achieve tentative syntheses of large-scale human and structural historical problems.

BIBLIOGRAPHY

Bloch, Marc. "The Rise of Dependent Cultivation and Seignorial Institutions." In *The Cambridge Economic History of Europe*, edited by M. M. Postan, vol. 1, chap. 6, pp. 224–277. Cambridge, 1941.

Bloch, Marc. *Esquisse d'une histoire monétaire de l'Europe*. Paris, 1954.

Bloch, Marc. *Land and Work in Medieval Europe: Selected Papers by Marc Bloch*, translated by J. E. Anderson. London, 1967.

Bloch, Marc. *French Rural History: An Essay on Its Basic Characteristics*. Berkeley and Los Angeles, 1970.

Fink, Carole. *Marc Bloch: A Life in History*. Cambridge, 1989.

CAROLE K. FINK

BOLIVIA. *See* American Indian Economies; Central South American States; Spain, *subentry on* Spanish Empire.

BOMBAY (Mumbai), island city on India's western coast, on the Arabian Sea, the capital of the state of Maharashtra, India's economic hub, largest city, premier commercial and financial center. According to the census of 1991, the population of Greater Bombay was 9.92 million, making it one of the largest cities of the world. The name Bombay was changed to Mumbai in 1995, which was probably derived from Mumba Devi, a Hindu goddess. From the ninth century CE until 1348, Bombay's rulers were Hindu. It then became part of the sultanate of Gujarat. In 1534, Sultan Bahadur Shah of Gujarat ceded it to Portugal. In 1661, Portugal gave it to Charles II of England, as part of the dowry of Catherine of Braganza, sister of the king of Portugal. Only with some effort were the English able to take possession of the island in 1664.

On 27 March 1668, Bombay was leased to the British East India Company (a trading company) by the Crown for the nominal rental of 10 pounds sterling per year. In 1672, Gerald Aungier, the president of the company's trading station at Surat, then western India's leading port, transferred his establishment to Bombay and became the modern city's real founder. In 1686, hostilities broke out between the company and the Moguls (Mughal, the Muslim empire in India, 1521–1857). In an attempt to put pressure on the Mogul emperor to stop English interlopers, who were trying to trade at Surat, the governor of Bombay, John Child, ordered the capture of eighty Indian vessels sailing to Surat. In retaliation, the Mogul emperor, Aurangzeb, ordered the stoppage of all English trade. He then directed the Abyssinian sealord, the Siddi of Janjira, who was his tributary, to attack Bombay; those troops succeeded in occupying most of the island but did not capture the city and its citadel. Frantic negotiations and British offers to pay reparations ended the affair. A few years later, Bombay was again in trouble. The European pirate attacks on Surat shipping—as well as the unauthorized minting of rupees at Bombay, which adhered to the Mogul standards for fineness and weight but bore the insignia of the English monarch—persuaded Aurangzeb to order Siddi Yakut Khan to attack Bombay again. Yet the Bombay fortifications held and the attack was repulsed.

In the course of the eighteenth century, Bombay's defences were made formidable and its trade grew. Gradually, Bombay supplanted Surat as the leading port of trade for western India. From 1834 to 1856, India's recorded foreign trade tripled in value from 12.3 to 36.5 million

BOMBAY (MUMBAI). Women cleaning shrimp for sale at the fish market near the Sassoon Docks, 2000. (© Catherine Karnow/Woodfin Camp and Associates, New York)

pounds sterling. Bombay and Calcutta (in eastern India) were the two seaports through which the bulk of this traffic was moved. In the case of Bombay, the trade with Europe was controlled by British merchants. Yet the sea trade of eastern and western Asia was jointly shared by Indians and non-Indians, (Arabs, Europeans, Persians, etc.). With this trade came the multiplication of facilities and institutions necessary to sustain it, and Indians participated in their development. As early as 1836, a group comprising ten Indian and fifteen European merchants organized the Bombay Chamber of Commerce. By the early 1850s, some Indians were involved in modern banking, in steam-shipping along India's western coast, and in steam-ginning and hydraulic-pressing enterprises (for the textile industry).

A great deal of India's export trade (in raw cotton and opium, primarily by the British to China, and the re-export trade of British products throughout Asia) was handled by Indian merchants in Bombay, either on their own or in partnership with, or as agents for, British firms. Knowledgeable about the supply of India's cotton from the interior, which entered into international trade, and largely involved in England's marketing of Lancashire's yarn and cloth, it was not long before those merchants recognized the commercial possibilities of local Indian factory production of cotton yarn and cloth. The first successful textile entrepreneur was C. N. Davar, a Parsi merchant of Bombay, who was active in a large number of enterprises. He was broker to two English commercial firms, his own company traded to eastern Asia, and he participated in promoting four Bombay banks from 1846 to 1863. Active in the formation of the Bombay Steam Navigation Company, he also organized a company that imported machinery and, in early 1854, opened the first steam-powered cotton press in Bombay. Davar had tried to establish a cotton mill as early as 1851 but was unable to gain financial support. By July 1854, he floated a spinning company with a capital of 500,000 rupees, contributed by fifty of the city's leading traders; the company started production in February 1856. Of the ninety-five cotton-textile mills established in Bombay before 1914, at least thirty-four were promoted by Parsis (Zoroastrian refugees from Muslim persecution in Persia during the eighth century). A high degree of inter-communal cooperation was involved; for example, the Oriental Mill, the second established in Bombay, is listed as promoted by Parsis, but among those involved were two Englishmen, E. D. Sassoon, a successful Jewish merchant from Baghdad whose commercial activities extended from the Persian Gulf to eastern Asia, and Veerjeewandas Madhowdas, a wealthy Hindu merchant banker. Another modern industry promoted from Bombay but located in Jamshedpur in Bihar was the iron and steel industry. The promoter J. N. Tata was an extraordinarily creative Parsi entrepreneur with a vision. He floated the Tata Iron and Steel Company in the early years of the twentieth century exclusively on the basis of Indian capital.

Bombay continues to be India's leading commercial and financial center, apart from being a main center of industrial production. In addition to textiles, major industries there include general engineering, printing, automobiles, chemicals, and paints. It is also the center of the Indian film industry, called Bollywood. Bombay's natural deep-water harbor handles a large volume of shipping traffic. Bombay is the headquarters of both the Central Railway and the Western Railway. The city houses the headquarters of the Reserve Bank of India and the nation's leading banking institution, the State Bank of India. The offices of the Life Insurance Corporation of India, the Bombay Mint, Air India, and a number of private commercial houses are also located in the city. The Bombay Stock Exchange is India's leading stock and share market and is considered the financial barometer of the country.

BIBLIOGRAPHY

Census of India. New Delhi, 1991.

Morris, Morris D. "The Growth of Large-Scale Industry to 1947." In *The Cambridge Economic History of India*, vol. 2. Cambridge, 1983.

Prakash, Om. *European Commercial Enterprise in Precolonial India*. In *The New Cambridge History of India*, vol. 2.5. Cambridge, 1998.

OM PRAKASH

BONDS. Bonds are written legal instruments pledging certain payments over time by the issuer to the holder, typically giving the holder recourse to specific forms of redress in case of default. As such, their origin must be found very close to the origin of both writing and the development of legal codes, that is, to the rise of civilization. Indeed, the code of Hammurabi, from at least 1750 BCE, specified the rules for a wide variety of private bonds that could pledge assets of land, goods, slaves, concubines, children, or wives in case of default. The detail of the code shows that bonds then were already long-established financial instruments to help people meet the risks of their economic enterprises by borrowing funds or assets from others unwilling to take those risks. The changing characteristics of bonds over time reflect the development of economies and their legal systems, as well as their cultures' perception of risk. For example, Hammurabi set usury limits on the annual interest, making a distinction between whether repayment was to be in terms of wheat or of silver. The interest rate in wheat was allowed to be substantially higher than that for silver, presumably to allow for a fall in the price of wheat at harvest time, when a bond most likely would be redeemed by the issuer. The implied maturity of the bond was no more than a year, and the issuer was allowed to pledge all kinds of tangible, easily identifiable assets against default.

Later evidence of private bonds comes from Athenian Greece, which indicates longer durations, a lack of usury limits, and payment specified in terms of standard coins. Further, escape clauses from repayment were added in case of shipwreck. This evolution may be evidence of a rise in civilization but also may reflect the legal and financial norms appropriate for a society based more on maritime commerce than on irrigated agriculture. Roman bonds, arising from both maritime commerce and settled agriculture, followed the Athenian example, but with usury limits, albeit much lower than those in Hammurabi's time. In these ancient examples, there is little evidence of transferability of bonds from one holder to another; and death of the issuer typically extinguished the claim of the holder as well.

In medieval Europe, the combination of the Roman legal legacy and the rise of monasteries and guilds as communal organizations for the protection of their members led to the development of several variants of bonds, first as life annuities (*rentes viagères* or *lijfrenten*) and then as heritable or even perpetual annuities (*rentes perpetuelles* or *erfrenten*). The life annuities expired without repayment on the death of the named insuree; but since the perpetual annuities were heritable, they were transferable and thus potentially negotiable. The liquidity premium arising from the possibility of transfer of perpetual *rentes* helped sustain lower interest rates compared to the life-*rentes*, reinforced by the universal usury laws, which were applied to perpetual *rentes* but not to life-*rentes*. Because perpetual annuities were callable, however, the upper limit of the resale price was the par value. Purchasing a perpetual *rente* at a higher price exposed the buyer to the risk that the *rente* would be redeemed at par, in addition to the risk that the issuer might default on payments. Default risk was minimized as well if the issuer were a perpetual institution with obvious sources of revenue—a port city republic, for example, such as Genoa or Venice, or the Pope. Absolute monarchs in Spain and France had to devise close substitutes for issuing such *rentes*. Francis I assigned his royal revenues in Paris to the city government, which in turn issued *rentes sur l'Hôtel de Ville*; Charles V created *juros de resguardia*, securing interest with revenues assigned to his Italian and German bankers, which did not prevent his successor, Philip II, from periodically revaluing, taxing, or converting them into less attractive *juros*.

Debt to Equity Conversions. The various city-states and provincial governments of the Habsburg Netherlands responded to the pressures of war finance in the sixteenth century by raising their own excise taxes, which were pledged specifically to regular payment of perpetual annuities. These annuities were made financially attractive enough to be bought willingly not only by local citizens but also by citizens in adjacent and more distant provinces. The further pressures of the Thirty Years' War encouraged towns and cities throughout northern Europe to raise funds in this manner. When the stadholder of the United Provinces of the Netherlands became William III of England in 1688, Parliament provided him with specific revenues for the duration of his reign; but the additional funds needed to finance his continuing warfare had to come from financial innovations drawn from both British and Continental experience. The most successful of these efforts was conversion of large amounts of the accumulated short-term debt of the government into long-term debt bought by chartered joint-stock companies, which issued their own equity shares to the general public, domestic and foreign. In addition to the interest they received on the long-term government debt, the companies could pass on to shareholders whatever profits they gained from their monopoly. Shareholders could sell their shares at any time in a secondary securities market centered in London. In addition, the companies could issue certificates of short-term debt, the most popular of which were the East India Company bonds redeemable at par at the semiannual auctions of company cargoes.

When the South Sea Company, formed in 1710, tried to consolidate all the remaining government debt in exchange for tripling its capital stock in 1720, a market bubble in its stock occurred but quickly collapsed. This event embarrassed the government but rid it of most of its high-interest debt. In the reorganization of the South Sea Company that followed the famous "bubble" catastrophe, the government's payment on its debt to the South Sea Company was passed on to shareholders in the form of Three Per Cent Perpetual Annuities. So successful was this conversion of government debt to company equity and then back to government debt, but now in the form of readily transferable perpetual annuities, that it became the basis for all future issues of British government debt. The various Three Per Cent Perpetual Annuities issued to finance subsequent wars were consolidated into one fund in 1752, creating the famous Three Per Cent Consol Annuity. The huge stock of this homogeneous, widely held and readily negotiable annuity laid the basis for an active securities market in London, one that expanded with each succeeding war through the Napoleonic Wars, ending in 1815. Attempts to imitate the British example were frustrated elsewhere, either by lack of perpetually living taxing authorities such as the British Parliament or by political fragmentation and competition among city, state, and provincial governments, as in the Netherlands and the United States. When a federal government was created in the United States, it assumed all existing state debts. To make conversion attractive to holders of each outstanding state bond, Alexander Hamilton created a variety of new bonds, some with lottery incentives, others backed by land grants, and one a zero-coupon bond; but the standard was the 5-20, a twenty-year bond bearing 5 percent nominal interest.

Continental Debt and the World Wars. Following the Napoleonic Wars, British debt was drawn down rapidly, but Continental debt was increased by reorganized, larger national units, which imitated the British Consol in the case of France, the Netherlands, Belgium, Austria, and Naples. Political resistance to giving the necessary taxing authority to national legislatures, however, limited the rise of a bond market outside Britain, while its own bond market was dwindling rapidly. The railway age revived first the British and then the Continental bond markets, starting in the 1830s. All railways began as joint-stock companies, but continued issues of new bonds were always necessary to complete construction and then provide rolling stock. The variety of bonds led to many opportunities for investors but increased the range of risks they faced. Issuers responded with further innovations—bonds backed by claims on branch lines, terminals, switching yards, and different types of rolling stock. Governments at all levels assisted with guarantees as well. Information services arose that published summary information on each railroad company and the financial claims outstanding on it. Private councils of bondholders were formed to protect the interests of bondholders as a class. Bearer bonds that were transferable without brokerage or stamp fees and were therefore instantly negotiable became standard.

Legal issues then arose on each class of bond issued, as to whether it was or was not subordinate to previous issues. Issuers responded by creating bonds that were convertible on the initiative of the holder to new issues of either bonds or equity shares in the company, which became useful instruments when mergers or reorganizations were required.

By the eve of World War I, the bond market was global, mostly denominated in gold-standard currencies, and dominated by railroad issues, which had largely displaced government bonds in capital markets around the world. The demands of war finance for the Great War, combined with government controls over the operation of their respective railroads, converted bond markets back to government issues. The peace treaties, regime changes, and currency disturbances following the war essentially destroyed the international bond market, creating insulated national bond markets dominated by issues of domestic government debt. Increasingly, government regulations were devised to maintain orderly markets and close loopholes exploited by market dealers trying to reopen trading opportunities interrupted by the war. By concentrating information about bond issues and making it transparent to potential investors, government regulations laid the basis for the rapid revival of bond markets when the opportunity again arose, following World War II. These markets, however, remained mostly domestic because of effective capital controls maintained by most industrial countries until the collapse of fixed exchange rates in the early 1970s. Government debt and corporate bonds coexisted in the respective national markets.

Deregulation. With the exchange rate volatility that began in the 1970s, governments increasingly deregulated their financial markets to allow financial intermediaries greater latitude in devising ways to cope with interest-rate shocks, which became extreme by 1980. The first innovations came, however, from private initiatives to exploit loopholes in existing regulations. The euro-dollar market expanded explosively, with foreign corporations and state enterprises issuing dollar-denominated bonds that could be purchased and held offshore by American financial institutions. Money market funds arose in the United States to retail shares in purchases of high-yield, large-denomination government bonds. With deregulation of the U.S. savings and loan industry in 1980, many new forms of bonds were devised to enable its small, closely regulated firms locked into long-term mortgages with low yields to find new sources of revenue so they could compete for deposits against the money market funds. Junk bonds, whose exceptionally high yields reflected the thinness of their collateral base, were issued by aggressive firms seeking to acquire underperforming firms with steady cash flows. Existing mortgages were repackaged by bundling them and then securitizing and selling separately the interest payments and the amortization payments from the bundle of mortgages. Outside the United States new bonds, denominated either in a weighted basket of currencies or in a choice of currencies for potential investors, were created.

As the twentieth century ended, a global bond market had once again emerged, with an even more bewildering array of bond instruments available for investors the world over, with even greater amounts of information available and more rating services at work than ever before. Whether this variety signaled a new peak in the progress of human civilization and its moral and legal codes remained to be seen; but benchmark interest rates were once again at levels close to those found on the eve of World War I.

[*See also* Government Borrowing.]

BIBLIOGRAPHY

Banner, Stuart. *Anglo-American Securities Regulation: Cultural and Political Roots, 1690–1860*. Cambridge, 1998.

Baskin, Jonathan Barron, and Paul J. Miranti, Jr. *A History of Corporate Finance*. New York, 1997.

Dickson, P. G. M. *The Financial Revolution in England: A Study in the Development of Public Credit, 1688–1756*. London and New York, 1967.

Homer, Sidney, and Richard Sylla. *A History of Interest Rates*. 3d ed. New Brunswick, N.J., 1990.

Millet, Paul. *Lending and Borrowing in Ancient Athens*. Cambridge, 1991.

Neal, Larry. *The Rise of Financial Capitalism: International Capital Markets in the Age of Reasons*. New York, 1990.

Tracy, James D. *A Financial Revolution in the Habsburg Netherlands: Renten and Renteniers in the Country of Holland, 1515–1565*. Berkeley and Los Angeles, 1985.

Yago, Glenn. *Junk Bonds*: *How High Yield Securities Restructured Corporate America*. New York, 1991.

LARRY NEAL

BOOK INDUSTRY *[This entry contains three subentries, a historical overview and discussions of modern book publishing and on libraries and book stores.]*

Historical Overview

Histories of book publishing commonly start with Johannes Gutenberg and the invention of movable type in Europe during the 1440s. Yet the technology had long been known elsewhere. Conventional accounts exaggerate the abruptness of change in the book industry and neglect the special conditions that permitted books printed on paper to bring about a knowledge explosion in early modern Christendom rather than earlier, in some other civilization.

Libraries had appeared whenever a civilization had records to preserve. China's first national library, founded about 100 BCE, needed 2,000 carts to shift books and manuscripts when the capital moved about 50 CE. Printing began in China some five hundred years later, movable type came in the eleventh century, but neither was much exploited. Books flowed from China to Japan before printing, from the fifth century CE. Printing began in Japan during the eighth century, but only 800 titles were produced in five hundred years, mostly Buddhist scriptures not meant for the public. Carved blocks were used (seventeenth-century examples were still in use in the nineteenth century). Common features of the publishing industry, such as banding together to share risks, nevertheless developed early. Urban Japan was penetrated by print as intensively as in Europe and North America soon after 1700, although only in the early nineteenth century did a national network of booksellers and circulating libraries create a large readership. Printed instructional works for, and indeed by, farmers were published in eighteenth-century Japan.

Japan was far ahead of the rest of the non-Western world. For example, printing and papermaking had diffused from China into the Islamic world. Examples of block printed religious works in Arabic have been dated to 900–1350 CE, but insistence on hand copying the Qur'ān helped to check the uptake of printing, which was not sanctioned for that purpose until 1825. Printing was extremely limited in eighteenth-century Constantinople, and only 243 titles were printed in Cairo before 1842.

China, Korea, and Japan, however, had no religious objections to printing, and all made intermittent use of movable type over several centuries. Furthermore, no absolute barrier was erected by the complexities of Chinese script that necessitated casting thousands of individual letters. In eleventh-century China, the alphabetic Uighur script was used, and in fifteenth-century Korea, King Sejong ordered his literati to create an alphabet suitable for mass literacy. In three years they came up with a twenty-nine character syllabary, Han'gul, only for it to be abandoned on Sejong's early death by scholars with personal investments in Chinese writing. The reason why printed books seldom took hold was thus less technological than the lack of literate publics large enough to establish markets. Outside Europe, then, there was technological potential, but its application was sporadic, and book production typically depended on government subsidy. In Europe, it was the advent of the technology that was delayed relative to a manifest popular appetite for reading.

In classical times, groups of publishers in Augustan Rome gathered Greek manuscripts in order to distribute books as far afield as Britain. Beginning in the first century BCE, the Roman Empire possessed large scriptoria selling commercially. A reader dictated to slave copyists, the resultant unit producing some thirty copies per week. After the sixth century CE, monastic scriptoria were in operation, some of them also selling to the public. Lay entrepreneurs later joined them. Charlemagne's standardization of script provided the model for the first Italian and French type founders seven centuries later.

By the early fourteenth century, scribes in London had their own trade guild. Before 1400, a union catalog included 600 authors represented in 180 English libraries. Forty professional scribes were present in Milan by the mid fourteenth century, and the output of manuscript books was at its height in Italy during the quarter century before the start of printing in 1464. In Paris, there were twenty-eight booksellers as early as 1323, some offering up to 125 separate texts for students to rent. Individuals owned large collections: two private libraries with 800 manuscripts are known, and 200 copies survive of a single manuscript translated from the Greek. Purchasers of books included merchants.

The scale of this trade inspired one authority to urge that the Renaissance might not have been another passing revival of learning even if printing had not been invented. Extravagant claims of the standardizing effect of print are commonplace, but manuscripts were not necessarily unstandardized, and scholars were establishing classical chronologies by means of critical comparison. The needs

BOOKBINDING. At left, a worker pounds the pages on a marble block before they are sewn into signatures using a special frame (at center). At right, the pages are bound, cut, and compressed in the press to prevent warping. Plate from Diderot and d'Alembert's *Encyclopédie*, 1762–1772

of clerics or rich collectors who sought works of art could be met by the scribal workshops that persisted into the age of print. Carrels for copyists were included in a cloister built at Canterbury as late as 1485, but by then the print revolution was under way, and the real price of books was falling. It was demand among urban professionals for grammars, dictionaries, encyclopedias, and texts in mathematics, astronomy, medicine, law, and history that swelled the European book market. Printing was to supply this market abundantly, but, without detracting from the scale of the change, books were not new, and too little notice is taken of the way print substituted for existing manuscript production.

Spot estimates exist of the volume of output and falling prices that printing made possible, for example, six million books by 1500, undoubtedly more than had been produced since the fall of Rome. At one time in the sixteenth century 4,000 copies of a work by Martin Luther were sold in five days, and an exceptional 10,000 copies of *ABC* and *Little Catechism* within eight months in 1585. During the early eighteenth century, over 800,000 copies of a religious work were produced in Halle in a short space. By the late eighteenth century, 109 volumes of *The Poets of Great Britain*

were selling widely at six shillings each at a time when a single slim book typically cost twenty-one shillings.

Limitations of Early Publishing. Ease of entry and accompanying undercapitalization were persistent problems in publishing: most firms started and stayed small. Printers initially formed firms to reduce the risks of an industry where they always found it hard to forecast demand. Moreover, difficulties in distribution and marketing restricted long runs to intermittent gambles on potential best-sellers or popular works whose copyright had expired. An alternative throughout western Europe and North America was to publish very cheap works such as chapbooks, which were sold by peddlers. The eighteenth century saw a considerable extension of books meant for entertainment, fiction for adults and amusing books for children.

With few technological improvements before 1800, the important changes were in modes of business organization. Specialist publishing houses, as distinct from print shops, had already appeared in the fifteenth century. In Milan, a publishing company was formed not merely to hedge against the financial risks but also to select titles and fix prices. Likewise, specialist booksellers broke away from printers and publishers, although every possible combination was to be found somewhere. Before 1500, there was a hierarchy of publishers with different lengths of lists. By the mid-sixteenth century, book fairs and catalogs of titles had become routine. Yet for a long time many towns had printing works without separate publishing concerns. Out of the tangled arrangements of printers, publishers, and booksellers, it was the publishers who became dominant from the end of the seventeenth century.

Piracy was rife, although copyright to combat it had emerged in Italy in 1481. By the mid-eighteenth century, English publishers were paying royalties rather than a flat fee because they could rely on domestic copyright. However, the lack or inadequacy of international copyright inspired cross-border piracy: nineteenth-century American publishers notoriously pirated British books, and the favor was returned; for example, in 1852, one and a half million copies of *Uncle Tom's Cabin* were quickly pirated in Britain.

The replacement of Latin by vernacular languages had meant that in its organization the industry had become less international by the mid-seventeenth century. Only in the broadest sense is there a single history of publishing, because allowance has to be made for different levels of literacy, size of national market, and the political and legal environment. Big differences lay in experiences with censorship. The trade was commonly regulated to prevent what the authorities feared would be seditious publishing. Commercial risks apart, publishers almost everywhere had to struggle against varying degrees of ecclesiastical or civil censorship, or both. Censorship acted as an additional trade barrier, though it encouraged smuggling.

England was a special case where censorship was challenged and significantly beaten earlier than in most countries. In 1557, Stationers Hall had been incorporated to regulate all those involved in the making of books. Its role from 1586 until the Licensing Act was abolished in 1695 can clearly be seen. Between those dates, sets of licensers were usually in existence, empowered to raid premises and scrutinize products, backed by severe punishments for convicted suppliers. An act of 1649 even imposed fines on purchasers of unlicensed works. Ironically, during the Civil War era, Parliament had let censorship lapse, only to be affronted by the flood of Royalist propaganda, whereupon it reaffirmed the licensing monopoly: this inspired John Milton's blast against censorship in *Areopagitica*, although it was not for half a century that press freedom was secured, and only then because revenue could be raised by substituting taxation for suppression. Political ideas could thenceforth appear in book form, but many people were unable to afford them. Not until 1861 did customs and excise impositions on the purchase of paper cease.

The French experience with censorship was similar. The monarchy controlled presses tightly. Abolishing censorship after the revolution of 1789 provoked an "explosion of print" like that following the English Revolution of the 1640s. The Paris book guild tried to regain control but lost when in 1793 publishing was declared free of everything except taxes. The number of booksellers and publishers tripled, to the usual publishers' lament of "too much competition." It was Napoleon who reasserted control in 1810.

Expansion of the Book Industry. The spread of literacy meant, however, that the market did expand. But it also fragmented. Accordingly, a specialist directing agent, namely, a publisher, who would organize production and distribution and assume (or lay off) the financial risk, was appropriate. For a long time books typically had been available only from the printer, although as early as 1717 a Leipzig publisher announced volumes "available in every bookshop." In other respects, German publishing changed only slowly.

In England, the trend toward proliferating titles pushed the crucial task for publishers away from manufacturing books as artifacts to organizing distribution and sale: one response was the emergence of wholesaling as early as the 1690s. Seventeenth- and eighteenth-century publishing in England produced the "conger," an association of publishers founded to share stock and spread risk. As distribution outside London became more common, larger stocks and more capital were needed. An entire run was printed at once, and suppliers were eager to sell it as soon as possible; they did not fund extra copies out of revenues from those sold earlier. The conger bought the books from the publisher and was thus not simply a passive vehicle for distribution. By 1705, the conger was handling 20,000 books per year.

In the mid-eighteenth century, the "modern" pattern took over: a small number of independent, copyright publishers appeared, all in London. Printers were their agents and booksellers their customers. Another milestone was reached in the 1790s with the invention of remaindering to clear unsold stock. The perpetual problem of the uncertain demand for individual titles led in 1829 to a group of publishers and booksellers developing the "Bookselling Regulations." These aimed to establish greater certainty by fixing both trade and retail prices but broke down in the late 1830s.

For a long time the only significant means of cutting costs and bringing down prices had been the longer print runs that entrepreneurial publishers risked bringing out from time to time. Until the start of the nineteenth century, there was little change in physical production methods. Thereafter the Fourdrinier papermaking machine and the steam press were adopted. Paper production greatly increased as a secondary effect of the augmented supply of rags from cheap cotton textiles, and although the quality fell throughout the nineteenth century, so did the price. Cheapness meant that a best-seller of the 1850s might sell fifty times the copies of one in the 1810s. Paper had constituted 50 to 66 percent of the cost of a book in 1800 but was only 7 percent by 1910, and leather covers were replaced by cheaper cloth. Between 1875 and 1897 the cost of wood pulp went down dramatically by over 80 percent.

By the 1860s and again in the 1880s, proliferating titles and longer print runs had occasioned such competition among booksellers that many were squeezed out of business. Publishers complained that there was too much competition, too low prices, and too few outlets. Once again their response was price fixing. Frederick Macmillan introduced the "net," or fixed retail price. Between 1880 and 1900 the pattern of the British industry froze into its modern assembly of trade bodies with the establishment of the Society of Authors, the Booksellers Association, and the Publishers Association, plus literary agents working for commission, all operating within the new anticompetitive net book agreement. Macmillan's very first "net" book was Alfred Marshall's *Principles of Economics*.

Colonial book markets long remained the creatures of metropolitan publishing. Colonial America relied on England for imports, and books were therefore expensive. One calculation is that in mid-eighteenth century Virginia, over five months of common labor was needed to pay for Tobias Smollett's *Complete History of England*, which was one of the titles most often sought. Only the upper 25 percent of the white population could readily afford to buy even schoolbooks. In 1775, there were only fifty printing houses in the entire country, heavily concentrated in Massachusetts, although after 1783 the spread was rapid elsewhere. Reductions in the costs of printing, distribution, and paper gradually cut prices, until in the early nineteenth century there was an "explosion of print." The expanding market meant that long runs became possible if investment was marshaled to finance them: the period 1800 to 1820 saw the rise of specialized publishers coordinating authors, printers, and booksellers. By 1859 there were 4,000 presses and 400 publishers. Significant book publishing developed later in other European colonies—the first printing press in Australia was established in 1795, in South Africa in 1796—and although the priesthood established presses for its own purposes in Spanish and Portuguese colonies as early as the sixteenth century, such areas wrestled with acute problems of censorship and low levels of literacy.

The Consequences of Printing. The question remains, what difference did the book industry make in economic history? Rephrased as a question about its role in economic growth, the topic is still extraordinarily diffuse; no well-known studies attempt to isolate the impact of the book from other effects. Most studies concentrate on the impact of printing, which, although this was clearly enormous, is an artificial limitation. The impact of increased scribal output in mid-fifteenth century Europe would be a study in itself, highlighting the central importance of lay literacy and merging more gradually than is usually implied into the greater impact of books that happened to be printed. Economic historians have largely left these matters to other specialists, especially those interested in printing qua printing.

Most discussions of the subject thus concern broad cultural effects of printing and, as noted, fail to separate economic effects from those affecting religion or literature. Moreover, most studies focus on Europe, which, because other parts of the world long had books, including printed ones, means that the relevant point is Europe's exceptionally increased output. What did it matter that the real price of books fell by so much in early modern Europe? That it did fall can be deduced from the fact that quite ordinary people came to own, read, and annotate so many volumes: about 1500, a sample of 337 French libraries revealed that 66 were owned by shopkeepers and artisans. There are also many indications of a shift during and after the fifteenth century in the composition of book output away from religious subjects toward practical, secular works: of 335 editions produced in Paris about 1500, 75 were on subjects other than religion or the classics. Works about machinery, architecture, and agriculture, together with many atlases, had been appearing there since 1480. It cannot be doubted that the existence and expansion of a lay market and the growing secularization of books imply that publishing had important economic effects. Practical works helped commerce, for example, by affording merchants readily available, uniform tables from which to calculate wages, weights, and distances between towns.

This effect was real. We should be impressed by the new scale and cheapness of output and the quickly enlarged circle of readers. Two widely spaced examples: in Paris, by 1470, a printed Bible cost only 20 percent as much as one in manuscript; in 1546, a shepherd in England had just bought a brand-new translation of a treatise entitled *Invention of Things*. Much attention has been devoted to the collective scientific effort now made possible by the standardization of knowledge in printed form. Certainly, wherever they might be, scientists could work from what were effectively the same texts; but in principle they could do so from manuscripts. Cheap books did overcome the greater errors of oral transmission and diffuse knowledge far more widely, but old, wrong beliefs could be fixed in print too.

Historical changes involved far more than printing, much more than just books. Economically speaking, just how far book publishing affected these changes remains moot. Many of its effects were indirect, via such influences as the role of print in upheavals like the Reformation, political revolutions, colonial rebellions, and the market-splitting consequences of fixing vernacular languages. But we may reasonably accept that the enormous expansion of the book trade in early modern times increased the intellectual productivity of Europe and North America well before powered machinery increased industrial productivity.

[*See also* Information and Communication Technology; Magazines; Newspapers; *and* Printing Industry.]

BIBLIOGRAPHY

Darnton, Robert, and Daniel Roche, eds. *Revolution in Print: The Press in France, 1775–1800.* Berkeley, 1989. Particularly interesting on responses to censorship and freedom.

Eisenstein, Elizabeth L. *The Printing Press as an Agent of Change: Communication and Cultural Transformations in Early-Modern Europe.* 2 vols. Cambridge, 1979. Classic source that makes large claims for effects of printing in Europe but not comparative and (like almost all specialist works) gives scant consideration to economic consequences.

Erickson, Lee. *The Economy of Literary Form: English Literature and the Industrialization of Publishing, 1800–1850.* Baltimore, 1996. Relevant sections demonstrate effect of technological change in forcing down book prices dramatically.

Feather, John. *A History of British Publishing.* London, 1988.

Febvre, Lucien, and Henri-Jean Martin. *The Coming of the Book: The Impact of Printing, 1450–1800.* London, 1976. The most useful such study of the early modern period.

Johns, Adrian. *The Nature of the Book: Print and Knowledge in the Making.* Chicago, 1998. Comprehensive modern study.

Joyce, William L., et al., eds. *Printing and Society in Early America.* Worcester, Mass., 1983.

Kornicki, Peter. *The Book in Japan: A Cultural History from the Beginnings to the Nineteenth Century.* Leiden, 1998. The most thoughtful book on the subject, skeptical about the role of printing and excellent as an offset to purely Western treatments.

McMurtrie, Douglas C. *The Book: The Story of Printing and Bookmaking.* New York, 1943. Very useful on early periods.

Myers, Robin, and Michael Harris, eds. *Development of the Book Trade, 1700–1899.* Headington, U.K., 1981. Deals with the British case.

Putnam, George Haven. *Books and Their Makers during the Middle Ages.* Vol. 1. New York, 1896–1997.

Robinson, Francis. "Technology and Religious Change: Islam and the Impact of Print." *Modern Asian Studies* 27. 1 (1993), 229–251. Rare treatment of a crucial topic though, as usual, not economic in focus.

Schottenloher, Karl. *Books of the Western World: A Cultural History.* Translated by W. D. Boyd and T. H. Wolfe. Jefferson, N.C., 1989.

Steinberg, S. H. *Five Hundred Years of Printing.* Harmondsworth, 1955. Most accessible broad coverage of Western experience.

ERIC AND SYLVIA JONES

Modern Book Publishing

The volume of book production increased substantially during the twentieth century despite the fact that for some commentators, particularly from the 1960s on, the advent and rapid development of new electronic technologies suggested that the demise of the book was imminent. Starting in the 1980s, the pattern of book publishing changed through internal reorganizations and mergers, many of them involving other media besides books. These changes seemed more far-reaching in their consequences than any changes since the invention of printing, or at least since the differentiation of printing, publishing, and bookselling during the eighteenth century. And in the 1990s, although the volume of book production continued to increase, the Internet raised a variety of further questions about print and its future at the same time that it opened up new opportunities, particularly in bookselling.

It was always easier to raise questions concerning publishing and to give impressionistic answers than it was to produce convincing statistics concerning numbers of new titles, of books in print, and of turnover. The statistics that exist—and they were more plentiful in the 1990s than ever before—are inadequate, inconsistent, incomplete, and almost impossible to compare analytically year by year or country by country. According to the International Publishers' Association, located in Switzerland, the 1997 total of book titles in the United Kingdom amounted to 100,102, in Germany to 77,515, in Japan (new titles only) to 65,438, in the United States to 64,711, and in France to 47,214.

Comparative figures for a century earlier are far patchier. For 1895 the *Publishers' Circular* figure for Great Britain was 5,581 new books and 935 new editions, and five years later the total had risen to 7,926 as against a total in France of 13,362. In the mid 1980s, a critical decade in publishing and, more broadly, communications history, according to a different source, the United States headed the international table with 72,382, the Soviet Union came second with 58,372, Germany third with 48,900, Great Britain fourth with 44,482, and Japan fifth with 42,217.

Book production at that time was still a comparatively small industry, and most publishers operated on a limited scale with little up-front capital. In May 1981 the entire U.S. industry ranked forty-sixth in *Fortune* magazine's list of the 500 largest American business corporations, and in Great Britain, where 30 percent of output was exported—an unusually high proportion—government statistics calculated that the 41,000 people engaged in printing and publishing constituted only 1 percent of the people employed in the manufacturing industry. There was a clear distinction, however, as there had been throughout the whole century and earlier, between big and small firms, the biggest proudly describing themselves, as they had done since the eighteenth century, not as firms, but as "houses." There was pride too in the adjective "traditional" and in the sense of belonging not to an industry but to a gentlemanly "trade" that generated anecdotal gossip as well as publishing projects.

The success of any particular firm, whether it was concerned with fiction or nonfiction, with "trade" or with "academic" publishing, or with mainstream or with what came to be called niche publishing, deliberately restricted in range, depended on the strength of its book list, set out in a catalog, along with old titles still in stock. The editorial function, on which the quality of the list depended, received separate attention from that of marketing, which depended on the knowledge and enterprise of booksellers, the name once used for publishers themselves, and the drive of publishers' "reps" who visited them. On the editorial side, publishers' readers were employed, some of them so-called men of letters, but it was recognized, as the distinguished American publisher Cass Canfield put it, that a good publisher needed "an animal instinct" for spotting the writers who had not yet displayed their full talents.

Publishing, as it developed, was always fragmented, but there was a balance between competition and cooperation, informal as well as formal, expressed in the selection of titles and authors, pricing, and promotion. The first continuous institutional publishing association was German. In 1825 a *Bössenverein des Deutschen Buchhandels* was set up, which served as a model, particularly in Scandinavia. In Great Britain, the Society of Authors, founded in 1884, preceded the Associated Booksellers, founded in 1895, and the Publishers' Association, founded in 1896.

The first objective of the Publishers' Association was to introduce a Net Book Agreement, binding on its members. It came into force in January 1900 and, ratified by the courts in 1955 and 1962, was to hold for almost a century. It specified that net books, so identified by the publisher, could not be sold by booksellers, other than under exceptional circumstances, at a price below that set by the publisher. After intense pressures, the agreement finally collapsed in 1995.

In a court judgment of 1962 upholding the agreement, it had been accepted that "books are different" from other forms of merchandise. It did not need the law, however, to demonstrate that different kinds of books were—and are—different from each other. They never fit into one single category, and in the twentieth, as in the nineteenth, century, various groupings were used for different purposes. The simplest twofold grouping was that between so-called "trade publishing" in hardcover and in paperback, and "academic publishing," including textbooks and monographs. Books were also grouped by subject, including religion, the oldest heading. Bibles came first in the category order of the British Department of Industry.

Paperback publishing, the history of which has been studied most, never seemed likely to supplant hardcover, and there were improvements in printing technology, including accurate electronic prepress systems and multicolor printing presses that made possible the production of huge illustrated volumes, sold simultaneously in translation, in print runs that compared with those of paperback editions. It is necessary to span long periods of time in re-lating text to pictures, and although the word "revolution" has been applied to breakthroughs in technology, it is generally agreed that still bigger changes in technology associated with digitalization are already drawing book publishing into a multimedia operation through technology as well as through corporate mergers.

As early as 1946, before the spectacular rise of television, the first of the post–World War II technological and corporate breakthroughs, the American novelist James T. Farrell, with his eyes on Hollywood rather than on television, forecast that "the tendency toward combinations and concentration in the book industry" would "increase the difficulties of operation for small and independent producers," that "money would talk more than ever," that there would be "increased efforts to minimize risks," that small bookstores would be driven out of business, and that "more than ever [before] publishers would be forced to be receptive to bestseller books." Farrell did not foresee, however, the emergence of a multimedia culture, which would involve massive mergers, or consider the future of academic books as well as of fiction.

There had been many mergers in the nineteenth century—in academic as well as in general publishing—but the number of mergers during the 1960s was higher than ever before. In the United States between 1965 and 1969 at least twenty-three publishing mergers took place annually. The year 1968 marked a peak, with forty-seven. The mergers of the 1970s, a very different decade, were of a different kind. Amicable or hostile, they often involved massive media interests in television and cable as well as in film and in home computing and home video.

With the further increase during the 1970s and 1980s in the scale of what were now often global conglomerations, book publishing became increasingly a division, even a minor division, in multimedia conglomerates. Relations with authors, mediated increasingly through literary agents, paralleled in sport, were less direct than they had been before World War II, which gave a great impetus to American publishing but slowed it down in all other countries. As "blockbusters" were sought, the production and marketing strategy, increasingly integrated, for selling one particular book, one for which a large advance had been paid, through the media (including celebrity advertising) became of crucial economic importance.

What was seen as a landmark date was 1966, when Random House in New York was taken over by the Radio Corporation of America, founded in 1919. Yet this was only the first step in a continuing process, involving many publishing businesses, old and new. Increasingly, Wall Street and Europe's stock exchanges came into the picture. In 1980, RCA sold Random House to the Newhouse newspaper and magazine chain, which in turn sold it to the Bertelsmann Group, based in Germany. On another landmark date, 1987, Random House acquired four British firms, including Chatto, Cape, Bodley Head, and the publisher of feminist literature, Virago.

Some of the late-twentieth-century conglomerates had nineteenth-century origins. For example, Bertelsmann was founded in 1884. Yet neither longevity nor profits were by themselves enough to ensure survival. The oldest British publishing firm, Longman, which celebrated its two hundred and fiftieth anniversary in 1974, had already on its own initiative been incorporated in 1968 within a Pearson conglomerate that had its origins not in publishing but in civil engineering. During the 1980s, Pearson moved increasingly into multimedia, beginning with newspaper operations. At first, Pearson Longman had substantial autonomy. With the financial support of the Pearson conglomerate, it merged in 1988 with the American firm of Addison-Wesley, which had a totally different business culture. It disappeared, however, in 1994, when both firms were incorporated within a Pearson Education division.

At the end of the 1970s, the American critic Alfred Kazin described "the book world" in 1980 as "like so much else in American life . . . big, busy, and commercially driven, not likely to be too aware of its compulsiveness, special interests, many blunders." A similar comment had been made almost a century earlier. When the then most established American publishing firm, Harper and Brothers, founded in 1817, was driven by cutthroat competition and overexpansion to the verge of bankruptcy in 1899, the name of the firm, now reincorporated, was preserved by J. Pierpont Morgan. Morgan's action provoked the comment that publishing had now been placed, "like other business, under the control of finance capitalism, with the result that the banks and investment trusts, which supplied it with capital, insisted on greater efficiency in the interest of surer profits."

This seemed a portent, and although there were relatively few basic structural changes in publishing from the late 1890s to the early 1920s, much was made of change by authors and publishers alike. One British novelist, George Gissing, focused in *New Grub Street* (1891) on the perils of authorship in a society less concerned with a reading public than with a publishing market, dominated by journalism. The sense of opposition between commerce and culture was itself not new, and in an age when both newspaper and magazine journalism was changing significantly, old business partnerships in book publishing, often family partnerships, remained strong, albeit alongside new entrants to publishing, some of them radically different in style. The cost of entry was low, making possible the entry of independent firms in the late twentieth century, some of them pioneering in their range and style, although always vulnerable to takeover if they succeeded. Meanwhile, bookselling too became dominated by large chains,

like Borders and Barnes & Noble in the United States, although in Britain, in particular, independent booksellers survived.

The position of the author in the late twentieth century was very different from that in Gissing's time, when the royalty system had not established itself. In Britain, authors waged a successful campaign between 1951 and 1979 to establish a "public lending right," offering them a return on books of theirs that had been borrowed from public libraries. In 1979, an Act of Parliament granted this right, and a national fund was set up to finance it. No payments to authors were made until 1982. Thereafter, since the fund was not increased until 1993, payments per page fell. Australia and Canada set up their own schemes, different in character, in 1974 and 1976. By 1994, Austria, Denmark, Finland, Germany, the Netherlands, Iceland, Israel, Norway, and Sweden all had their own versions of this right.

An international conference brought these countries together in London in 1994, and similar conferences were held to deal with issues relating to copyright, made more complex by the rise of new technologies, including photocopying. Copyright encompassed issues far broader than piracy of texts, particularly in Asia, as more countries subscribed to the Berne Convention of 1885, including the United States and China. Yet with the distribution of subsidiary or ancillary rights obtained through other media than books, the handling of individual rights in intellectual property became a matter for lawyers as well as for agents. In discussing his own experience as an agent before the 1980s, Ed Victor, based in London and New York, remarked that when he had begun his career a contract was a contract, but now it was a hundred pages.

By the late 1970s, before the Internet had dramatized all communications issues, predictions were being made in Great Britain that the electronic book would replace the printed book. Yet, except in the United States, electronic awareness was limited, particularly on the part of authors. The editor of *The Electronic Author*, started in London as a supplement to *The Author* by the Society of Authors in 1993, anxious to stimulate discussion, noted that the Frankfurt Book Fair in 1992 had for the first time staged an Electronic Book Fair in 1992 alongside the main event. In the face of technological hyperbole, the most sensible forecast of the future was that electronic publishing, which had registered more losses than gains, would be a new and additional market that would not rule out paper. The "e-novel" would not supplant the printed novel.

The use of the term *electronic publishing* had itself changed within a short period of time. Originally, it suggested the demise of the typewriter and the advent of desktop publishing, but with the CD-ROM it came to cover content as well as arts or techniques, implying that authors would become members of teams, not individual producers.

With the Internet, it became possible in reverse for them to dispense with publishers, if not with agents, and move on-line. While these controversial changes were taking place, the study of the history of the book became more searching and more sophisticated. French scholars led the way. Books were now treated historically and analytically as cultural products, remarkable for their variety and their adaptability, while more attention was paid to changes in the economics of the book industry. It was now impossible to examine the book industry in isolation from the economics of the media as a whole.

[*See also* Information and Communication Technology; Magazines; Newspapers; *and* Printing Industry.]

BIBLIOGRAPHY

Altbach, Philip G., and Edith S. Hoshino, eds. *International Book Publishing: An Encyclopedia*. London and New York, 1995. An essential general survey.

Coser, Lewis A., Charles Kadushin, and Walter P. Powell. *Books: The Culture and Commerce of Publishing*. New York, 1982. A thorough and illuminating volume concentrating more on sociology than on economics, but relevant to both.

Curwen, Peter J. *The United Kingdom Publishing Industry*. London, 1981. The first attempt to deal quantitatively with British book production and distribution.

Dessauer, John P. *Book Publishing: What It Is, What It Does*. New York, 1974. An informative introduction.

Eliot, Simon. *Some Patterns and Trends in British Publishing, 1800–1919*. London, 1994. A pioneering examination of limited and contentious statistics, stopping unfortunately at the end of World War I.

Kobtak, Fred, and Beth Luey, eds. *The Structure of International Publishing in the 1990s*. New Brunswick, N.J., and London, 1992. Very useful but already dated in rapidly changing circumstances.

Madison, Charles A. *Book Publishing in America*. New York, 1966. One of several surveys, intermittently published, along with autobiographies, on the state of the publishing industry.

Norrie, Ian. *Mumby's Publishing and Bookselling in the Twentieth Century*. 6th ed. London, 1974. The last edition of a standard guide to the history of British publishing.

Schreyer, Alice D. *The History of Books: A Guide to Selected Resources in the Library of Congress*. Washington, D.C., 1987. A useful survey that is more comprehensive than its title.

Tebbel, John. *A History of Book Publishing in the United States*. 4 vols. New York, 1972, 1975, 1978, 1981. The standard guide to the history of American publishing; the last volume takes the story to 1981.

ASA BRIGGS

Libraries and Bookstores

For much of the twentieth century, pundits predicted the decline of reading because of the overwhelming popularity of new leisure activities. Beginning with radio and Hollywood movies, and continuing with television and the Internet, observers mourned the impending death of the printed book. Nothing has been further from the truth, and in many respects other forms of entertainment have supported and encouraged reading. In recent years, the popularity of J. K. Rowling's *Harry Potter* series and J. R. R. Tolkien's *Lord of the Rings* trilogy attests to this fact, as film adaptations have encouraged blockbuster book sales. Rowling's four *Harry Potter* books, for example, sold 4 million copies in 2001, a book trade record in the United Kingdom, and worldwide sales exceeded 130 million copies, including several million in China.

In 2000, book sales of every kind—paperback and hardcover, fiction and nonfiction—exceeded $25.3 billion in the United States alone, an increase of 3.4 percent over 1999. The number of books published in the United States in 2000 exceeded 96,000 titles; in Great Britain, 116,415 titles were published. In terms of language, English books took the lion's share, with 27 percent of all books published. Chinese was second (13 percent), and German, third (12 percent).

How do readers obtain their books? They buy (from a bookstore, actual or "virtual" on the Internet) or they borrow (from a library—public, school, or other kind). In either case, readers are guided in their selection by choice, advertising, recommendations, and convenience.

The United States, as world leader in the number of bookstores and libraries, possesses the best statistics. In 2001, according to the *Bowker Almanac*, there were 25,921 bookstores in the United States, including 6,433 general ones. In 2000, 34 percent of readers purchased their books at a bookstore, followed by book clubs/mail orders (24 percent). Internet sales amounted to 6 percent, compared to 4 percent in 1999. The largest book chains were Barnes & Noble (900 stores, $3.5 billion in sales, 2000) and Borders Group (350 stores, $3.2 billion).

According to the American Library Association, there are an estimated 122,265 libraries of all kinds in the United States today, including 98,169 school libraries. Between 1999 and 2000, public library acquisition expenditures exceeded $1 billion, divided among an estimated 16,000 public libraries. There are 750 million books in circulation, or 2.7 million volumes per capita.

Libraries. For as long as records and books have been maintained and protected, there have been libraries. From ancient Egypt, Babylonia, and China to classical Greece and Rome, official repositories of books and records, prepared on papyrus, parchment, or clay, preserved culture and the law. The most famous of these libraries included Alexandria in Egypt (c. 300 BCE) and Pergamum in Asia Minor (c. 150 BCE). Julius Caesar authorized the creation of a large public library in Rome, a practice followed by subsequent emperors. In 159 CE, the Imperial Library was established in China.

During the Middle Ages, monasteries, notably the Benedictine foundations, carried on the tradition of libraries and, as manuscripts were copied, culture was preserved. The rise of universities launched the tradition of great school libraries, including those in Oxford, Cambridge, and Heidelberg. National libraries gained prominence in France (Bibliothèque Nationale, 1735), Great Britain (British Library, 1753), and the United States (Library of Congress, 1800).

All of these library foundations had limited public access. Public libraries, a revolutionary concept, date to the nineteenth century. Several factors at the time promoted publishing and reading and, therefore, both retail and library sales. Literacy levels increased throughout the century, as the commitment to public education expanded. The growth of the railways and extension of the telegraph afforded better distribution and communication. Increased rail travel also created a market for light reading to while away the journey. Improved methods of lighting, in the home and in public areas, encouraged reading. In the 1850s, better papermaking machinery was developed, and paper was cheapened with the use of wood pulp. The invention of the rotary printing press, which printed on continuous rolls of paper, speeded production considerably and made possible larger editions.

With disposable income for the purchase of costly books limited, entrepreneurs in Britain saw the possibilities of a new market for borrowing books and moved to exploit it. In 1860, the W. H. Smith Circulating Library was founded, operating through company bookstalls, in competition with freestanding branches of Mudie's Circulating Library (1842). Both libraries were the principal purchasers of the first, three-volume editions of novels (or "three-deckers"). Given the cost of an annual subscription (at least £1 per year, per volume), patrons of these libraries were largely from the middle class. In 1899, the main competitor of Mudie's and W. H. Smith, Boots Booklovers Library, was founded.

In Britain, the Public Libraries Act of 1850 empowered councils of towns with populations of 10,000 or more to levy a halfpenny rate for the provision and maintenance of a museum or library. The intention was to provide workers with a wholesome and edifying alternative to the public house during their spare time. Library growth remained slow, however, until the end of the century. Opposition stemmed from the dislike of increased taxes and an innate fear of the consequences of edifying the masses. The public library movement was spurred by further growth in public education, the 1889 Technical Instruction Act (which increased demand for nonfiction holdings), and private benefactions from philanthropists such as the Scottish industrialist Andrew Carnegie, who funded 380 libraries throughout Britain. Borrowers were not predominantly from the working classes, and the majority of issues—in some cases, as high as four-fifths—were of works of fiction.

At the same time, public libraries experienced growth in other parts of the world, notably in the United States. In 1852, the Boston, Massachusetts, Public Library was founded as a department of the city government. The beautiful and ornate building was dubbed "the People's Palace." Similarly, the New York Public Library was founded in 1895 in a grand edifice on Fifth Avenue. Not until 1956 did the U.S. government become directly involved with the Library Services Act, which targeted areas of the country that were still without a public library.

As in Britain, Carnegie was active in the United States, where he funded the construction of 1,689 libraries in 1,419 communities between 1893 and 1919. Carnegie committed to construction only if communities donated the land, purchased the books, and provided funds for staff and operations. His philanthropic goal was clearly stated: "The main consideration should be to help those who will help themselves; to provide the means by which those who desire to improve do so; to give those who desire to rise the aids by which they may rise; to assist, but rarely or never to do all."

Policies in terms of book acquisition have always been prominent—and controversial. Libraries make quality judgments in selecting books for purchase. In many cases, librarians provided what they thought the public should have, rather than what the reading public wanted. Popular fiction, for one, has always been controversial, as many libraries have resisted the use of public funds for recreation rather than edification.

In 1939, the American Library Association addressed these concerns and stronger claims of outright censorship by public libraries when it proposed a "Library Bill of Rights." Censorship, it said, "must be challenged": "In no case should any book be excluded because of the race or nationality, or the political or religious views of the writer." The landmark document was used as a model for library systems in other countries.

The reluctance of public libraries to stock "light fiction" enhanced the popularity of commercial or subscription libraries, especially in Britain, an indication of the growth of reading activity among the lower-middle and working classes. These libraries were run as adjuncts to newspaper vendors, tobacconists, or department stores. During the Great Depression, borrowing books was preferred over buying, and many subscribers read two books each week. "[In] practically every town in England there is now a well run commercial library," the Commercial Libraries' Association observed in 1938. By 1935, Boots Booklovers Library was purchasing more than 1 million books a year, with its headquarters handling over 700,000 volumes per month for 400 branches. The libraries proved to be "loss leaders," encouraging business in other parts of the hosting shop.

World War II rationalized library usage. The shortage of books, propaganda against unwise spending, difficulties of supply, and an increase in nonfiction interests (such as current affairs) all worked in the public libraries' favor. Public libraries recorded peak levels of usage. It was estimated that by 1949 only 60,000 people in Great Britain were "not" provided with library service, and that nearly 25 percent of the population were registered borrowers. The largest number of issues from public libraries remained within the fiction category.

In the 1950s and 1960s, public libraries were forced to compete with publishing's "paperback revolution" and dropped their resistance to stocking cheap paperback novels and books. This was the ultimate acknowledgment of the public library's recreational role.

Today, public libraries are ubiquitous, a fixture in nearly every community and region around the world. Readers no longer visit a library just to borrow books or consult reference collections. They also take advantage of computer workstations with high-speed Internet access to surf the Web, send e-mail, or consult library catalogs in any country around the world.

Benefactions remain important to public libraries, as they were in Carnegie's day. In 1999, Bill Gates, founder of Microsoft, and his wife, Melinda, gave $1.1 billion to provide public-access computers to public libraries in all fifty U.S. states by 2003. The Gateses' intention is to support poorer libraries without computers. The average donation per library buys five computers and peripheral equipment such as printers. The results so far have been encouraging: at the public library in Bay Minette, Alabama, where one in four adults is functionally illiterate and 21 percent of the 8,000 residents live below the poverty line, attendance has dramatically increased.

Bookstores. So long as books remained expensive (and therefore rare), libraries thrived. This was the case for at least 400 years after Johannes Gutenberg issued the first printed Bible in 1455. Not until the nineteenth century, when publishing became more commercialized (and the mass market emerged) and readers more widespread (with disposable income to spend), would a new kind of merchant emerge: the commercial bookseller. At this stage, publishing and bookselling, united for centuries, began to diverge.

As the railroad expanded across countries, entrepreneurs saw the possibilities. In 1848, the first W. H. Smith railway bookstall was opened at Euston Station in London, the beginning of a network of stalls and bookshops throughout England and Wales. In early years, this firm prided itself in stocking a "better" selection of reading matter than the vulgar penny magazines and books in great demand; in later years, it carried the full range of popular fiction and magazines. W. H. Smith's Scottish counterpart, John Menzies, opened his first bookstalls at Perth and Stirling in 1857.

It was the fall of the "three-decker" novel in the 1890s, which had the greatest impact on the future of the publish-

ing industry and bookselling. The displacement of the costly, three-volume novel by a one-volume edition, which was followed by even cheaper editions if demand warranted, encouraged the distribution of literature among all classes. Although cheaper editions were now established, the Net Book Agreement, introduced in 1900, prevented pricing wars between booksellers and publishers by forbidding the sale of any new book at less than the fixed price. It would remain in effect in Britain for ninety years.

The commercialization of publishing following World War I encouraged book sales. To meet the costs of production, a title needed to sell at least 1,000 copies, which necessitated the adoption of aggressive advertising efforts. Publishers would pay large sums to booksellers for prominent displays of their titles in bookstore windows or on front shelves, or a mention on a list of new and recommended books and authors. Series publishing, such as Hodder and Stoughton's *Yellow Jackets* novels, encouraged repeat sales. Similarly, Mills & Boon, the principal publisher of romantic fiction, promoted its list as a group, achieving rare brand-name recognition for its imprint. Readers learned to ask for "Another Mills & Boon, please," rather than for a particular author.

In 1895, in the United States, *The Bookman* launched the first "best-seller" list, based on sales reports from a representative number of bookstores. Though largely criticized by publishers (when their titles did not make the list, of course) as inaccurate and difficult to verify, best-sellers were nonetheless a boon to booksellers. Tie-ins with Hollywood films also sparked sales of popular books, such as *Gone with the Wind* by Margaret Mitchell (1936) and *The Citadel* by A. J. Cronin (1937). In the 1920s, the Book of the Month Club and the Literary Guild provided new outlets for bookselling to a captive market—one that romantic fiction publishers such as Mills & Boon and Harlequin would exploit decades later in direct-marketing subscription programs to their loyal readers.

Sales were further boosted between the wars by the unprecedented success of the revolutionary new paperback series, Penguin Books. Allen Lane pioneered the introduction of inexpensive quality paperbacks with Penguin Books. His success captivated the book trade: in the first year, 3 million copies of fifty titles were sold, price sixpence each, a turnover for the trade of £75,000. The company's innovative marketing techniques changed the traditional nature of bookselling, for Penguins were also sold not only at bookstores but also through newspaper vendors and at department stores. A Penguin vending machine was installed on London's Charing Cross Road. Following World War II, technological developments spurred book production. Photocomposition and offset printing enabled higher print runs (100,000 copies and more) than ever imagined, prompting what observers called the "paperback revolution." The paperback format was now used for light fiction as well as for the second edition of hardbound books. Their cheap price and "disposable" quality encouraged book sales.

As common as public libraries, bookstores were once a fixture of every High Street and Main Street, as there were few alternatives to consumers for buying books (apart from book clubs). In the 1980s, the rise of book chains, and subsequently book superstores, changed the landscape dramatically. Booksellers learned the lesson of other retailers: higher volume and lower prices attract consumers, at the sacrifice of the small store owner. With comfortable armchairs, cafes, and late night opening hours, book superstores play a social role as much as a retail role.

Ironically, the bookstore giants of today started as small stores. A bookshop owner in rural Illinois, Charles Barnes, launched Barnes & Noble in 1917, when he bought a stake in Noble & Noble, a New York–based educational bookstore. Today, Barnes & Noble is the largest bookseller in the United States, employing more than 32,000 booksellers in 900 stores in forty-nine states under the Barnes & Noble and B. Dalton names. The chain also possesses the biggest single bookstore in the world: 67,500 square feet, in Union Square, New York City. Similarly, Tom and Louis Borders started their empire in 1972 with an 800-square-foot bookstore on the campus of the University of Michigan. Today, Borders, which also runs the Waldenbooks and Books, Etc., chains, has 350 stores and 17,000 employees.

A more recent phenomenon, which appears to threaten the once invincible bookstore chains, is virtual bookselling, via the Internet. With 6.2 million customers in 220 countries, Amazon.com is the leading on-line bookseller. Founded in 1995 by Jeff Bezos, it is now the third-largest bookseller in the United States, with net sales for the fourth quarter 2001 a record $1.12 billion. In addition to books, Amazon.com sells everything from music and electronics to kitchenware and toys. Consumers praise the convenience, efficiency, and heavy discounting. Amazon.com's success has prompted all of the major booksellers to offer on-line sales; Borders.com, in fact, recently partnered with Amazon.com to improve its Web site.

Bookselling is also accomplished without a bookstore, physical or virtual. In 1996, Oprah Winfrey launched the book club segment of her popular U.S. talk show. Publishers would send copies of already published novels to Winfrey's production company for consideration. If a title was selected, the publisher was asked to donate 10,000 copies to libraries and advised to order 650,000 copies of a hardcover, 800,000 copies of a paperback. No wonder: the first "Oprah's Book Club Selection," *Deep End of the Ocean* by Jacquelyn Mitchard, generated additional sales of 750,000 copies. Sales of *White Oleander* by Janet Fitch jumped from 25,000 copies to 1 million. This was the impact of a woman who simply declared that she wanted to "get Americans reading again." Single-handedly, Winfrey brought a whole new dimension—and hope—to publishing and bookselling, as well as the reading public (prompting the creation of neighborhood reading circles and book clubs). Few were surprised that, after Winfrey closed her book club in 2002 (citing a paucity of good titles to review), a half-dozen competitors opened their doors to bolster this new reading public.

BIBLIOGRAPHY

Adams, Michael. *Censorship: The Irish Experience.* Birmingham, Ala., 1968.

Basbanes, Lionel. *Patience and Fortitude: A Roving Chronicle of Book People, Book Places, and Book Culture.* New York, 2001.

The Bowker Annual Library and Book Trade Almanac. 46th ed. New York, 2001.

De Jonge, Peter. "Riding the Wild, Perilous Waters of Amazon.com." *New York Times Sunday Magazine*, 14 March 1999.

Getz, Malcolm. *Public Libraries: An Economic View.* Baltimore, 1980.

Hafner, Katie. "Gates's Library Gifts Arrive, but with Windows Attached." *New York Times*, 21 February 1999.

Hill, Alan. *In Pursuit of Publishing.* London, 1988.

Keating, Peter. *The Haunted Study.* London, 1989.

Lerner, Fred. *The Story of Libraries.* New York, 1999.

Link, Henry C., and Harry Arthur Hopf. *People and Books: A Study of Reading and Book buying Habits.* New York, 1946.

Lucas, E. V. *Reading, Writing and Remembering: A Literary Record.* London, 1933.

Lusty, Robert. *Bound to Be Read.* London, 1975.

MacArthur, Brian. "Rowling Books Unique Place in History." *The Times* (London), 21 December 2001, p. 8.

Max, D. T. "The Oprah Effect." *The New York Times Magazine*, 26 December 1999.

McAleer, Joseph. *Popular Reading and Publishing in Britain, 1914–1950.* Oxford, 1992.

McAleer, Joseph. *Passion's Fortune: The Story of Mills & Boon.* Oxford, 1999.

McMurtrie, Douglas C. *The Book: The Story of Printing and Bookmaking.* New York, 1943.

Mumby, Frank Arthur, and Ian Norrie. *Publishing and Bookselling.* 5th ed. London, 1974.

Olmert, Michael. *The Smithsonian Book of Books.* Washington, D.C., 1992.

Stevens, George, and Stanley Unwin. *Best-Sellers: Are They Born or Made?* London, 1939.

Unwin, Stanley. *The Truth about Publishing.* 3d ed. London, 1929.

Zeller, Brad. "Borders's 30th Anniversary." *Publisher's Weekly*, 19 November 2001, p. 30.

JOSEPH J. McALEER

BOTSWANA. *See* Southern Africa.

BOULTON, MATTHEW (1728–1809), English manufacturer and engineer.

Boulton played an entrepreneurial role alongside a number of partners in industry, of whom the most famous was James Watt. The standard view is that, compared to Watt's role, Boulton's role in the development of the steam engine was supportive, but overshadowed. He supplied commercial sense to the uncommercial imagination of the inventor. However, a case can be made that the importance of these roles should be reversed.

For one thing, Boulton's part in product design has been largely overlooked. His flair for design was more apparent in Boulton's other commercial undertakings—designing ornate and artistic items (such as silver plate and jewelry), what were called "toy goods" (i.e., decorative small metal items such as buckles), and later, coinage. In the Boulton and Watt partnership, Boulton's innovativeness in products, coupled with an entrepreneurial flair for marketing, meshed perfectly with Watt's command of technical design.

Boulton deliberately intended the great metal "manufactory" he designed and built at Soho, near Birmingham, to integrate large-scale production with merchandising, well before his partnership with Watt. Boulton had a vision for the Watt engine from the moment it was patented in 1769. He immediately propositioned that Watt join him at Soho, telling him that Watt would benefit in terms of finance, scale economies in production, and administering sales "to make for all the world." But Boulton did not obtain a share in the patent until Watt's Scottish patron, John Roebuck, went bankrupt in 1773; the Boulton-Watt partnership began in 1775. In fact, the question of scale economies in production did not arise immediately, as the early engines were largely assembled on site from components manufactured elsewhere. The manufactory was required mainly for project design and marketing, the real source of its scale economies. Boulton remarked to James Boswell in 1776, "I sell here, Sir, what all the world desires to have, Power." It was Boulton who pressured Watt into designing engines to work in the new factories of the Industrial Revolution, rather than just in pumping and mining operations. Watt long remained highly skeptical. Faced by any new prospect, Boulton's typical response was "can do"; Watt's was the opposite.

Engineers like Boulton's biographer, H. W. Dickinson, have regarded the Soho engine manufactory as the harbinger of mass production. In fact, it was the opposite. It relied extensively on the labor of multiskilled "fitters" to assemble each engine on a one-off basis. By contrast, as Henry Ford stated many years later, "in mass production, there are no fitters." But the one-off project design remains the standard means of producing what are termed "complex product systems" in large-scale engineering and construction. The later Soho Foundry of 1795 undertook much more of the production in-house, as by this time textile and other manufacturers wanted standardized engines with minimal assembly on-site, but this was managed mainly by Boulton's and Watt's sons.

How should we then judge the role of Boulton in the Boulton-Watt partnership (and others)? The celebrated business historian Alfred Chandler describes the successful industrial enterprise of modern times as undertaking "three-pronged investments" in "manufacturing, marketing and management." Boulton contributed innovations to all three functions, especially marketing. Watt's contribution came from a fourth function, largely overlooked by Chandler—technology. Their roles were basically complementary, though Boulton rather than Watt supplied the necessary integration of all four functions. The neat fit of their respective capabilities showed how even a two-person partnership could, as a very simple form of organization, fare better in economic activities than a single proprietor, as long as their complementary skills were properly integrated for the partnership's commercial benefit.

From a much broader point of view, Watt has overshadowed Boulton partly because technology has been given a larger role than organization in interpreting industrial history. But qualified engineers have downgraded the contribution of Watt to the history of technology, while modern economic historians have seriously questioned just how great the contribution of Watt's engine was to the Industrial Revolution in manufacturing. On the other side, the importance of organizational innovation, particularly the rise of the factory system, is commanding greater attention. Though Boulton was by no means unique, he played a demonstrably major part in the evolution of the factory system, and especially its orientation to markets. The real significance of Boulton and Watt was in coupling technological to organizational innovation.

BIBLIOGRAPHY

Lord, John. *Capital and Steam Power, 1750–1800*. 2d ed. London, 1966.
Roll, Eric R. *An Early Experiment in Industrial Organisation: Being a History of the Firm of Boulton & Watt, 1775–1805*. London, 1930.
Rolt, L. T. C., and J. S. Allen. *The Steam Engine of Thomas Newcomen*. London, 1977.
Tann, Jennifer, ed. *The Selected Papers of Boulton & Watt: The Engine Partnership*. Cambridge, Mass., 1981.

G. N. VON TUNZELMANN

BRAUDEL, FERNAND (1902–1985), French social scientist who incarnated the so-called second generation of the *Annales* school.

Intellectually, Braudel is known for four main emphases: the world-economy (*économie-monde*) as the unit of analysis; the existence of multiple social temporalities (especially the importance of the *longue durée*); his insistence on interscience; and his upside-down view of the relationship of capitalism to the market. He was extremely active in organizations and succeeded Lucien Febvre as the president of the Sixth Section of the École Pratique des Hautes Études in Paris. He was the founding administrator of the Maison des Sciences de l'Homme. He was the cofounder of the International Association of Economic History and its president (1962–1965). He served for some fifteen years as the president of the scientific committee of the very influential Istituto Internazionale di Storia Economica "Francisco Datini" at Prato. He taught at the Collège de France and was a member of the Académie Française; in the 1960s, he sought, unsuccessfully, to establish a faculty of social science at the Sorbonne in Paris.

His first great work, *The Mediterranean and the Mediterranean World in the Age of Philip II*, published first in 1949 and then in revised version in 1996, was essentially a long argument for his first two emphases: that of (1) the world-economy as the unit of analysis and that of (2) the *longue durée*. He conceived of the Mediterranean-world-as-a-whole as his unit of analysis, what he called an *économie-monde*, and he sought to explain its realities in terms of three social temporalities: the underlying socioecological structures of the *longue durée*, which were long lasting and slow to evolve; the medium-run cyclical shifts in the operation of the structures that he called *conjonctures;* and the short-run "events," which were the usual concern of political historians. He felt that without taking into account the often neglected structural bases of social interaction, researchers were doomed to a superficial appreciation of historical reality. His famous quip to summarize that view was, "events are dust."

If *The Mediterranean and the Mediterranean World* established his reputation as a great historian, his publication of *Capitalism and Civilization, 15th–18th Century* (1981) proved in many ways to be an even more radical contribution. (*Civilisation matérielle, économie et capitalisme*, 3 vols., Paris, 1981, translated by Siân Reynolds. An earlier version of the first volume appeared in English translation in 1973 as *Capitalism and Material Life, 1400–1800*, translated by Miriam Kochan.) He portrayed the modern (Western) world as if it were a house of three stories: the ground floor being the patterns of everyday life, the middle floor being the eternally resurgent exchange economy of the market, and the top floor being the realm of capitalism. Unlike both Adam Smith and Karl Marx, Braudel saw capitalism not as the achievement of a market economy but as the "anti-market," the domain of the monopolistic search for exceptional profits. The story of the modern world was, for Braudel, the story of the struggle between the market and capitalism, with the state acting most often as the guarantor of capitalism.

Braudel believed strongly in what he called "inter-science," which was for him more than just the rhetoric of interdisciplinarity. Rather, it represented the ecumenical coming together of scholars pursuing a single enterprise, in which history and social science were part of an undifferentiated cloth of social analysis. All his organizational efforts were directed toward implementing this view.

BIBLIOGRAPHY

Braudel, Fernand. "The Impact of the Annales School on the Social Sciences." *Review* 1.3–4 (Winter/Spring 1978).

Braudel, Fernand. *Civilization and Capitalism, 15th–18th Century*, vol. 3, *The Perspective of the World*. London, 1984.

Gemelli, Giuliana. *Fernand Braudel e l'Europa universale*. Venice, 1990. Published in French as *Fernand Braudel*. Paris, 1995.

Wallerstein, Immanuel. *Unthinking Social Science*. 2d ed. Part 5, "Revisiting Braudel." Philadelphia, 2001.

IMMANUEL WALLERSTEIN

BRAZIL continues to be one of the great underrealized economic powers of the world. At the end of the twentieth century, it ranked as one of the ten largest economies in the world but also as the fifth-largest population, with the result that per capita income levels placed it well below averages put forth by the Organization for Economic Cooperation and Development (OECD). A vast territorial expanse, thousands of kilometers of coastline, modest average population densities, and varied climate place Brazil undoubtedly among the top tier of nations in terms of economic potential. Yet Brazil has performed well behind its potential, as it was plagued over centuries by enduring problems: low rates of human capital formation, high transaction costs, underdeveloped capital markets, and pervasive and inefficient government intervention in the economy. In many respects, Brazil, despite its recent transition to growth, continues to exhibit the legacy of these obstacles.

Growth Record. The record of Brazilian economic performance in the colonial period (1500–1822) remains uncharted territory. Traditional historical descriptions of colonial boom-bust commodity cycles, which were often regionally specific, suffice in the absence of a more detailed statistical record. The first half century of the colony's existence was marked by heavy Portuguese interest in the dyewood indigenous to coastal Brazil. By the late 1500s, sugar cane cultivation propelled the colony's economic center of gravity to the northeast and toward heavy reliance on African slaves. In the mid-1600s, the discovery of large gold deposits in Brazil's interior for the first time pulled an appreciable share of the population—both free and slave—away from the littoral. By the time Brazil attained independence, its per capita export earnings were well below those of the United States. The economy in nineteenth-century Brazil grew, but population growth rivaled the expansion of national income, with the result that intensive growth was slight, less than .5 percent per year on average. Only at the turn of the century was there a perceptible transition to modern economic growth. Rates of per capita growth in gross domestic product (GDP) averaged more than 2 percent per annum in the first eight decades of the twentieth century. Though high levels of

BRAZILIAN INDUSTRY. Women sorting cashews at a factory in the port city of Natal, 1990. (© Paula Lerner/Woodfin Camp and Associates, New York)

debt and burdensome macroeconomic policies slowed growth later in the century, Brazil was at least no longer falling behind. Indeed, during the twentieth century Brazil moved forward at an impressive rate in comparison with most of the economies in the world. Within this transition to growth were significant shifts in population, the economy's output mix, the structure of employment, and the regional basis of Brazilian economic growth.

Structure and Change. In 1872, Brazil's first national population census revealed that one-third of the population, and one-half of the labor force, was employed in agriculture. The distribution of the labor force by activity before this time is unknown but was undoubtedly highly concentrated in agriculture throughout the colonial era. During the first half of the twentieth century, the share of the labor force in agricultural and extractive activities remained high, though began a steady decline after World War II. Like the labor force, output in the colonial era and during the nineteenth century was overwhelmingly agricultural, with early manufacturing surveys finding only small crafts shops and an occasional textile mill in the 1850s and 1860s. High value-added activities before the late nineteenth century were limited mainly to export agriculture. Sugar and cotton had been prominent Brazilian exports in the colonial era, and joining them in the nineteenth century were hides, rubber, and especially coffee. By 1900, Brazil accounted for more than one-half of world coffee production. Because of its preeminence as a coffee producer, Brazil's export economy and its putative social and political ramifications have garnered disproportionate attention from researchers. The position of exports in the economy's aggregate output mix actually declined during the age of export-led growth in the second half of the 1800s, as domestic-use agriculture and light industry accelerated their respective paces of expansion.

Manufacturing of any note came relatively late to Brazil. Capital goods, even for light industry, came mostly from abroad, and industry required high expected profits to be viable in a market with low purchasing power. Changing regulatory conditions enabled a rapid burst of industrial growth in the 1890s. Yet the country's first national economic census in 1920 showed that manufacturing accounted for only 20 percent of total private sector output. By the end of World War II, manufacturing's share had nearly doubled, at 38 percent. Significant regional shifts accompanied the birth of modern manufacturing during the decades immediately before and after the turn of the century. In the 1870s, the northeast of Brazil, its traditional economic center, and the emerging areas to the south were roughly equivalent in terms of exports per capita and probably similar in output per worker. The increasing geographic concentration of agricultural exports, incipient manufacturing in the country's center-south, and rigidities inhibiting internal geographic reallocation of labor created a large regional disparity. By 1939, per capita output in Brazil's northeast was only one-half of that in the rest of Brazil. The gap persisted through the twentieth century.

Population. Brazil's early population estimates are quite crude and incomplete. One hundred years after its discovery by the Portuguese, informed observers claimed about 100,000 residents for the colony, though the indigenous population was admittedly unknown. This figure grew to somewhere between 2 and 3 million persons by 1800. Population increased at least five fold between 1800 and 1900. By 1872, the first full population census found nearly 10 million Brazilians, of which 1.5 million were enslaved, either Africans or Brazilians of African ancestry. At the turn of the century, population growth accelerated even further. In 1900, the population was 17 million, while forty years later it had grown to 41 million. By the end of the century, it had increased to around 175 million, making Brazil one of the five largest societies in the world.

The main components of Brazilian population growth can be roughly sketched. Indigenes comprised a relatively low density population that the colonizers never were able to subjugate fully. A key element of colonial population growth was thus the importation of slaves from sub-Saharan Africa. Between the sixteenth century and the effective elimination of the slave trade to Brazil in 1850, some 10 million Africans arrived, mostly forced to work in agriculture and precious metals extraction. Brazil received more African slaves than any of the other New World economies. Yet, the slave population in Brazil never reproduced itself naturally. Uneven gender ratios among imported slaves, high mortality, and manumission combined to require continued acquisition of new slaves. With the cessation of the slave trade and the gradual emancipation of slaves, free immigration became an increasingly important source of population growth and labor supply in the last third of the nineteenth century. With the expansion of the coffee economy in the country's center-south, most immigrants went to São Paulo. In the peak period of immigration, from 1890 to 1913, 1.4 million foreign migrants came to São Paulo, mostly from the Mediterranean and eastern Europe. Later still, significant numbers of Japanese migrated to the same area. Though a large share of these migrants came initially as agricultural contract labor, many found opportunities as well in cities and towns. By the 1920s, Brazil's economic census revealed a small but rising share of foreign-born landowners in the areas of the heaviest settlement.

The character of Brazilian population growth worked against economic growth in several ways. Immigration and natural growth combined to give Brazil a young population. Twentieth-century gross annual birthrates were greater than 40 per 1,000 people until 1970, when they first began to fall off. High dependency ratios (defined as the share of the population fifteen years of age and younger) implied lower savings rates than would otherwise be obtained. In 1872, Brazil's dependency ratio was 0.35. In the context of growing immigration by mainly younger workers, by 1890 the dependency ratio had risen to 0.42 and did not fall below 0.40 for nearly a century. The demographic burden on the economy meant that export earnings and sustained capital inflows were indispensable for capital formation.

Not only did the demographic burden remain high in the twentieth century, but the population became increasingly urban, even dramatically so. In 1890, only 11 percent of Brazil's population could be found in cities of 10,000 or more persons. A century later, 77 percent of all Brazilians lived in urban areas. More than half the urban population resided not just in cities but in megalopolises, with 39 percent of the total population residing in cities with more than 1 million inhabitants. By the end of the twentieth century, Brazil was relatively young and urban.

Modern Economic Growth. Perhaps the most remarkable feature of Brazilian economic history was the abrupt transition to rapid economic growth at the start of the twentieth century. An array of changes in the last decades of the nineteenth century paved the way to improved economic growth. The expansion of coffee exports provided Brazil with the foreign exchange earnings, and thus potential, to import productivity-enhancing capital goods from abroad. That potential was ignited by technology, institutions, and policies along several fronts. High transport costs had long burdened product markets in Brazil and were probably the single most important obstacle to economic growth. Investments in railroads beginning in the late 1850s gradually alleviated this bottleneck, increasingly so after the mid-1880s. Repressive and arbitrary restraints on banking organizations and joint-stock companies also were loosened in the 1880s. The gradual elimination of slavery during the 1870s and 1880s made Brazil a more attractive region for European migrants, who possibly brought with them higher levels of human capital than were typical among native-born Brazilians at the time. In response to lower transport and start-up costs, manufacturing investment grew, and new firms emerged throughout much of Brazil. Changes in commercial law accelerated with the overthrow of the centralized constitutional monarchy and its replacement by a federal republic, and the modernization of commercial practices and rules fostered an acceleration in capital formation in industry in the 1890s. The republican system had at its core a fiscal federalism that provided further incentives to improved policymaking and economic expansion. Brazil was the leading target of British investment in Latin America until the 1880s and thereafter was second only to Argentina. Shortfalls in domestic savings and capital market development were remedied with foreign funds that comprised an appreciable share of Brazilian capital formation. On the eve of World War I, Brazil's transition to modern economic growth was fully underway.

From the 1930s through the 1970s, under both democratic and dictatorial regimes, the Brazilian economy sustained an impressively high rate of growth. The underpinnings of this growth varied. Statism served to push investment in manufacturing through a variety of policies. Import substitution became a conscious political and economic strategy of Brazilian governments. Foreign exchange rationing emerged as a constant feature of the economy, as planners sought to channel resources into specific sectors and regions. The burden of foreign-debt servicing grew as Brazil undertook new loans and as the currency devalued. Several features of this growth pattern are associated with some of the enduring economic challenges in Brazil. Investments in human capital were quite limited in the nineteenth century and indeed for much of the twentieth century. Wages, especially for unskilled and moderately skilled workers, had always been low and did not rise quickly in the twentieth century with the onset of economic growth. Inflationary finance was a big problem during much of the post-1930 period. Taken together, these elements had negative implications for the prospects of substantial improvements in the standards of living.

Standards of Living. Consistent indicators of the standard of living in Brazil over time are scarce, especially for the nineteenth century and before. The wages of unskilled workers in Rio de Janeiro from the 1850s through the 1920s were constant, on average, when adjusted for the cost of living. Industrial workers in São Paulo did enjoy rising real earnings during the first half of the twentieth century, but it is not clear the extent to which that pattern applied for the rest of Brazil. Probably the best available indicator for the twentieth century is life expectancy at birth, which climbed steadily from 1930 onward as infant mortality rates fell. The distribution of wealth and income was highly unequal in Brazil under slavery and has remained highly skewed in the twentieth century. Indeed, the rapid expansion of the unskilled labor force, low levels of literacy and educational enrollment, and high inflation in the second half of the century contributed to sustain one of the most unequal distributions of income on record. The Gini coefficients measuring the distribution of income worsened through the 1960s and 1970s. By 1980, the Gini index for Brazil was more concentrated than the average for Latin America as a whole, Africa, Asia, and the OECD economies.

Increasing economic openness, a newly diminished role for the state in the economy, and effective anti-inflation policies were accompanied by modest reversals of the highly skewed distribution of income during the 1990s. Yet, 10 percent of the population still commanded more than 50 percent of national product. Growth remained elusive, better than in the preceding decade but still below the trend established between 1900 and 1980. Improving the prospects for both growth and distribution will rest with the nation's ability to maintain openness, adhere to sound fiscal policies, increase the level of human capital, and foster efficiency.

[*See also* Portugal, *subentry on* Portuguese Empire.]

BIBLIOGRAPHY

Estatísticas históricas do Brasil: Séries econômicas, Demográficas e sociais de 1550a 1988. Rio de Janeiro, 1990.
Fishlow, Albert. "Origins and Consequences of Import Substitution in Brazil." In *International Economics and Development Essays in Honor of Raúl Prebisch*, edited by Luis Eugenio Di Marco. New York, 1972.
Holloway, Thomas H. *Immigrants on the Land: Coffee and Society in São Paulo, 1886–1934*. Chapel Hill, N.C., 1980.
Leff, Nathaniel H. *Underdevelopment and Development in Brazil*. London and Boston, 1982.
Peláez, Carlos Manuel, and Wilson Suzigan. *História monetária do Brasil*. Brasília, Brazil, 1981.
Summerhill, William R. "Transport Improvements and Economic Growth in Brazil and Mexico." In *How Latin America Fell Behind: Essays on the Economic Histories of Brazil and Mexico, 1800–1914*, edited by Stephen H. Haber. Stanford, Calif., 1997.
Suzigan, Wilson. *Indústria brasileira origem e desenvolvimento*. São Paulo, 1986.

WILLIAM SUMMERHILL

BRETTON WOODS SYSTEM. The United Nations Monetary and Financial Conference, which met at the Mount Washington Hotel in Bretton Woods, New Hampshire, from 1 July to 22 July 1944, had the ambitious goal of avoiding a repetition of currency and financial catastrophes that had destroyed the world economy in the late 1920s and early 1930s. The Depression was widely believed to be the outcome of unstable capital flows ("hot money") and competitive devaluations, and the conference aimed at tackling both these ills. The major features of the system as envisaged in 1944 were: a move to current account (but not capital account) convertibility; more or less fixed exchange rates (they might move by 1 percent from a central parity or "par value," fixed in respect to gold or to the U.S. dollar); changes in exchange rates would be made only in case of a "fundamental disequilibrium" (which never was defined unambiguously)—and if it involved a move of more than 10 percent, the newly created International Monetary Fund (IMF) might object; discrimination against transactions with surplus countries was permitted once their currency was determined to be a "scarce currency"; and the IMF could provide resources to cover temporary deficits while monetary and fiscal policy adjustment occurred.

It took much longer than expected for the major industrial countries to restore current account convertibility: the major European countries made this move only in 1959, and Japan only in 1964. By the time that the system really began to function, the major fear of the immediate postwar period, of dollar scarcity, had disappeared. The system as it actually operated differed in an important regard from the design of Bretton Woods. The dollar became the major reserve currency of the system (with a secondary role taken by the British pound), and the IMF played a much reduced role in reserve management from that envisaged by the founders of Bretton Woods, in particular by John Maynard Keynes.

The role of the dollar became the central problem of the Bretton Woods system in practice. One way of understanding this problem is in terms of the "dilemma" formulated by the Belgian economist Robert Triffin: if the United States did not run balance of payment deficits, there would be a shortage of reserves and a deflationary drag; if, on the other hand, the United States ran deficits, there would be a buildup of claims on the dollar, which eventually would generate a crisis of confidence similar to that of 1931, when Britain lost its credibility as a reserve center. In the mid-1960s, the United States took the Triffin analysis seriously, and supported an attempt to develop an alternative synthetic and multilateral reserve unit, which eventually became (in 1969) the Special Drawing Right (SDR) managed by the IMF.

By the late 1960s, however, capital flows had resumed (even though there were susbstantial controls on capital movements), and the focus of concern had changed. Some countries, notably France and Germany, accused the United States of exporting inflation through what General Charles de Gaulle referred to as the "exorbitant privilege" of making other countries hold claims on the United States and thus in practice making them finance the acquisitions of U.S. multilateral corporations or the Vietnam War.

The United States, on the other hand, looked at the current account surpluses of Germany and Japan, and saw in the reluctance of those countries to adjust the value of the deutsche mark and the yen an illegitimate effort to boost export performance and generate surpluses. Mercantilist expectations about trade policy increased, and the liberalized postwar trading order, probably the greatest reason for the economic successes of the 1960s, appeared at risk. The United States was trapped because it, unlike every other country, could not alter the value of its currency in the Bretton Woods system. In theory, it might have unilaterally changed the gold value of the dollar; but with almost every other currency fixed in dollars, not gold, the U.S. trade position would have been unaffected. The discussions of the final years of the Bretton Woods system thus concentrated less on the reserve issue than on the choice of an appropriate exchange-rate system, and in 1970 both the IMF and the Federal Reserve Board began using mathematical models to calculate a better system of exchange rates.

On 15 August 1971, President Richard Nixon "closed the gold window," ending the convertibility of the U.S. dollar into gold at $35 per ounce, and at the same time imposed a 10-percent surcharge on imports "to ensure that American products will not be at a disadvantage because of unfair exchange rates." The break with gold was a violation of the most basic of the principles on which the Bretton Woods system in practice had rested. The Group of Ten (the ten members of the IMF who had agreed on a scheme for additional lending, the General Arrangements to Borrow—in practice the ten largest Western industrial countries), during a meeting at the Smithsonian Institution (16–17 December 1971), succeeded in devising a new system of exchange rates, with slightly wider bands, and a new gold price for the dollar ($38 per ounce). However, the new arrangements broke down in March 1973 with very large capital movements in the expectation of exchange-rate changes. The new Second Amendment of the IMF's Articles of Agreement provided much more flexibility in the choice of exchange rates. Instead of referring to a "system of stable exchange rates," the IMF now would supervise a "stable system of exchange rates"—usually known to its critics as a "nonsystem."

The Bretton Woods system lived on in memory, seeming especially attractive because of high rates of growth that made the 1960s, the period in which the system had been operational, appear to have been "golden years." So it also became an inspiration for those who wanted to create regional currency schemes; in particular, the European Monetary System (1978) was intended by its founders to replicate the Bretton Woods system. Like its model, the European system suffered (by the second half of the 1980s) from an inability to change exchange rates, which generated speculative capital flows in anticipation of changes; and in 1992–1993 it broke down in a series of spectacular currency crises. Particularly after 1993, literature on Bretton Woods shifted from a discussion of its attractions and advantages to a focus on the lessons of the incompatibility of fixed exchange rates, monetary autonomy, and free movement of capital flows—a "trilemma" already recognized in the 1960s.

[*See also* Exchange Rates.]

BIBLIOGRAPHY

Bordo, Michael, and Barry Eichengreen, eds. *A Retrospective on the Bretton Woods System: Lessons for International Monetary Reform.* Chicago, 1993.

James, Harold. *International Monetary Cooperation since Bretton Woods.* New York, 1996.

McKinnon Ronald I. "The Rules of the Game: International Money in Historical Perspective." *Journal of Economic Literature* 31 (1993), 1–44.

Solomon, Robert. *The International Monetary System, 1945–76.* New York, 1977.

HAROLD JAMES

BROWN FAMILY. During the nineteenth century, Brown Brothers & Co. was the leading U.S. firm providing financial services for importers and exporters. With a network of branch offices in major ports, it specialized, first, in buying and selling foreign bills of exchange, mostly denominated in British pounds, and, second, in the issuance of letters of credit to Northern importers. For several decades, the firm also made advances to Southern exporters who shipped raw cotton on consignment to its office in Liverpool. The Browns' most important long-term competitor in the Anglo-American financial-services market was Baring Brothers & Co. After 1840 the Barings shifted their emphasis to the expanding U.S. capital market, leaving preeminence in the more mundane foreign-trade sector to the Browns.

The family partnership was founded by Alexander Brown, who migrated from northern Ireland to Baltimore in 1800. Starting as a linen importer, he soon was offering a variety of financial services to other international traders in Baltimore and its hinterlands. Over the first quarter century, the founder sent three of his sons to open branch offices of the partnership in Liverpool, Philadelphia, and New York. In Liverpool, and later in London, the firm was best known as Brown, Shipley & Co. After the New York office opened in 1825, it emerged as the focal point of the enterprise.

During the 1820s the Browns competed vigorously with the Second Bank of the United States in the expanding foreign-exchange market. Both enterprises had a network of branches and complementary agencies in the main Northern and Southern ports. The Second Bank was the premier seller of foreign exchange during this period, while the Browns held the second position in terms of sales volume. The partners' sterling bills typically sold at only slightly lower prices, within a range of 0.25 to 0.5 percent of the bank's rates. When the Second Bank lost its federal charter in 1836, the Browns assumed leadership in the U.S. foreign-exchange market, and the firm retained that position for most of the remainder of the century.

The Browns were also a dominant force in the letter-of-credit market. They collected fees ranging from 1 to 3 percent of customers' authorized credit lines for guaranteeing final payment by American importers of their foreign debts. The business was exceptionally lucrative because the firm's commitments were primarily contingent liabilities. The partnership needed to advance little of its own capital in handling these transactions; problems arose only periodically when American customers had difficulty in covering their overseas debts. The letter-of-credit market was highly oligopolistic because only a few firms with international reputations for financial rectitude were able to enter the field successfully.

Faced with increased competition from commercial banks in the early twentieth century, the Browns steadily lost market share. In 1930, the American partners agreed to a merger creating Brown Brothers, Harriman & Co., a private bank on Wall Street that continues to provide financial services for a wealthy clientele. Meanwhile, the firm's British partners operated Brown, Shipley & Co. as an independent enterprise in London until 1972, when it was acquired by the American securities firm Merrill Lynch & Co. The original Alexander Brown & Sons, based in Baltimore, functioned as an independent investment banking and brokerage firm until the 1990s, when it was absorbed by Deutsche Bank.

[*See also* Barings.]

BIBLIOGRAPHY

Chapman, Stanley. *The Rise of Merchant Banking.* London, 1984.
Perkins, Edwin J. *Financing Anglo-American Trade: The House of Brown, 1800–1880.* Cambridge, Mass., 1975.

EDWIN J. PERKINS

BRUGES. Now a tourist mecca and provincial capital in the federal state of Belgium, Bruges was once the leading commercial metropolis of northern Europe and first in a succession of trade-dominated cities that includes Antwerp, Amsterdam, and ultimately, London. The making of Bruges' commercial primacy in the fourteenth century was due to a complex admixture of elements ranging from broad changes in the geography of trade and transport to the unique political and social makeup of the city. In this, Bruges can serve as a model against which later commercial cities can be measured.

On the macro level, Bruges benefited from the widespread outbreak of warfare in Europe from the 1290s, which convulsed and disrupted trade routes and established economic relationships from Constantinople to Scotland. Though vast and varied in extent and duration, these conflicts caused a steep rise in transport and general transaction costs lasting well into the fifteenth century. The impact on trade and manufacture was profound, transforming the manufacture of cloth, trade in wool and other basic commodities, and the geographical organization of European long-distance trade with the decline of the Champagne fairs. As Italian and other merchants abandoned the overland trade routes to Champagne, opting instead for the direct sea route in an attempt to lower costs, a profound change in the geography of trade occurred.

Bruges stood ready to profit from the change. Long a governmental center and seaport of Flanders, the city had by 1300 amassed a considerable infrastructure of commercial buildings, distributed port facilities through a network of outports, and had even acted to curb the urban nemesis of fire in the commercial districts of the city. Comital and urban legal privileges had also provided

BRUGGHE

BRUGES. View of the city and its outskirts. Anonymous engraving, seventeenth century. (Bibliothèque Nationale, Paris/Giraudon/Art Resource, NY)

foreign merchant communities with far-reaching rights of self-government within Bruges as well as efficient means of legal redress in commercial matters. Densely urbanized Flanders also offered a rich commercial hinterland supplying both consumers and producers of rare commodities. All in all, Bruges emerged in the first decades of the fourteenth century as an unusually protective and responsive business setting.

Patterns of immigration and social organization reflected and reinforced a growing specialization in trade. Like all medieval cities, Bruges depended on immigration to sustain population, yet her immigrants came in larger numbers and from greater distances than to any other Flemish city. Skilled artisans were also disproportionately represented: of the thousand or so new immigrants between 1331 and 1375 who indicated an occupation, nearly 40 percent practiced the lucrative after-market trades such as tailoring, stocking manufacture, and gold and silver smithing. Striking as well was the high proportion of immigrants in the city's population. Between 1281 and 1408, some 20,000 people paid to be registered as citizens—this in a city whose population numbered between 40,000 and 45,000 throughout the era. Joining these new settlers were a large number of merchant colonies, with those from Italy, Iberia, England, and the German Hanse especially prominent. Numbering in the hundreds, sometimes in the thousands, these merchants did not reside in fortified enclaves but were dispersed throughout the commercial heart of the city in a variety of hostels and rented accommodations. Unique patterns of immigration, combined with the hosting of merchants, gave Bruges a kind of rollicking energy. Political power resided with the fluid, money-dominated social and political elite of the city, in which brokers/hostellers and other merchants exercised considerable power. All these elements gave Bruges a social profile uniquely its own.

Shifting trade and the jostling crowds packed into the commercial inns and public squares offered new business opportunities to natives and foreigners alike. Bruges merchants reoriented their efforts from direct trade to building various combinations of business in brokerage, hostelling, import/export, and industry. Often they invested in joint ventures with foreign merchants, exploiting Bruges' growing role as a clearing house of economic information. In turn, foreign merchants brought a variety of economic enterprises to the city, from Florentine and Lucchese merchant banks to English wool traders and Hanseatic wine importers. Some of these merchants developed into permanent residents, eventually joining the Bruges merchant elite. Others, like a number of Hanse merchants, operated taverns where predominantly German wine was sold, allowing importers a vertically integrated market often in partnership with Bruges hostellers. Such business permutations were nearly limitless.

Arising from and abetting such business was a payment and credit system of unique power and complexity. Composed of several segments, it sought to overcome the shortcomings of medieval currencies and the challenge of distance. First were the Italian merchant-banking companies who set up shop in Bruges throughout the fourteenth century. They brought with them a business based on bill-of-exchange transactions, providing a flexible and cheap means of remitting funds and extending credit between cities. They employed these innovations to dominate the trade in English wool, as well as in alum and other spices, with Bruges serving as the financial clearing house. Of equal importance was the financial segment forged by the cooperation of Bruges hostellers and money changers. Together they created a system of deposit holding and book transfers that not only mobilized investment capital through a fractional reserve system but also allowed a payment mechanism that obviated the need for the direct transfer of coin or bullion. A secondary result was credit creation for some local manufacturers, especially weaver/drapers. So common did leaving money on deposit with Bruges hostellers and money changers become that foreign merchants across northern Europe routinely used such deposits as payment even while far distant from the city. Thus Bruges became a center of both trade and finance by 1350.

Although inheriting the role of meeting place of the European south and north from the Champagne fairs, Bruges remained a great merchant city by reducing transaction costs through innovations in finance and business organization. These enabled the city to retain its dominance through the fifteenth century before changes in European trade and politics inexorably shifted commercial primacy to Antwerp. Thereafter Bruges sank to the second level of trading cities—chiefly as the site of the Spanish wool staple—there to remain until its renaissance as a tourist city from the nineteenth century until today.

BIBLIOGRAPHY

Houtte, J. A. van. *An Economic History of the Low Countries, 800–1800.* London, 1977.

Houtte, J. A. van. *De Geschiedenis van Brugge.* Tielt, Belgium, 1982.

Munro, John H. A. *Wool, Cloth, and Gold: The Struggle for Bullion in Anglo-Burgundian Trade, 1340–1478.* Toronto, 1972.

Nicholas, David. *Medieval Flanders.* London and New York, 1992.

Prevenier, Walter, and Wim Blockmans. *The Burgundian Netherlands.* Cambridge, 1986.

Prevenier, Walter, and Wim Blockmans. *The Promised Lands: The Low Countries under Burgundian Rule, 1369–1530.* Philadelphia, 1999.

Strohm, Reinhard. *Music in Late Medieval Bruges.* Oxford, 1985.

Verhulst, Adriaan E. *The Rise of Cities in North-West Europe.* Cambridge, 1999.

Wilson, Jean C. *Painting in Bruges at the Close of the Middle Ages: Studies in Society and Visual Culture.* University Park, Pa. 1998.

JAMES M. MURRAY

BRUNEL FAMILY. Sir Marc Isambard Brunel (1769–1849), French-born inventor and engineer, and his son Isambard Kingdom Brunel (1806–1854), English civil engineer and naval architect.

Born in France, the elder Brunel emigrated to New York in 1793 and designed numerous buildings as the city's engineer. In 1799 Brunel moved to England, where he invented machinery to manufacture wooden pulley blocks for sailing ships at Portsmouth dockyard. Brunel used sequential machine operations to produce 160,000 standardized pulley blocks per year with a tenfold increase in labor productivity. He invented other labor-saving machines, but they had little impact on British manufacturing.

Brunel also designed suspension bridges, floating piers, and a protective shield for tunneling under rivers. The shield supported the excavation and protected the miners from cave-ins while workers behind them built a permanent brick tube. In 1825 Brunel began work on a tunnel under the Thames River at London, completed in 1842 after overcoming floodings and capital shortages. Brunel was knighted for this feat, history's first true subaqueous tunnel.

Marc Brunel groomed his only son for greatness. Sent to France for mathematical education, then honing his skills in his father's office, the young Isambard Kingdom Brunel learned to manage major construction projects while directing work on the Thames tunnel. Seriously injured in 1828 by a sudden inundation, in 1830 Isambard designed a beautiful suspension bridge of record-breaking length for the Avon Gorge at Clifton. Brunel designed many graceful and innovative bridges, and in no area was his genius more evident.

In 1833 Isambard Brunel was named chief engineer for the Great Western Railway, and he designed and directed this railroad from London to Bristol—the longest yet proposed in the world. His most controversial decision—to lay rails 7 feet apart as opposed to 4 feet 8½ inches as on existing northern lines—was intended to promote high-speed traffic and smooth riding. His decision also reflected his striving for wealth, fame, and public honor —to "be first Engineer and example for all future ones," as he had written in his diary. Completed in stages by 1841, Brunel's Great Western was probably the world's most advanced railroad.

Brunel's contributions to shipbuilding were fundamental and reflected his lifelong commitment to speed and scale. In 1835 Brunel audaciously proposed an "extension" of the railroad to New York, and his *Great Western* (1837) was the first steamship to provide regular transatlantic service. Brunel's masterpiece, the iron-hulled *Great Britain* (1843), was the first large vessel driven by a screw propeller and the forerunner of all big modern ships. The

Great Eastern (1858), a commercial failure, was the largest ship built before 1900.

Unlike his father Marc, Isambard grew wealthy and purchased a country estate. Like his father, the younger Brunel found many outlets for his genius at a time when economic development needed many-sided engineers and professional specialization was just emerging. For an educated public, father and son were potent symbols of accelerating technical progress.

BIBLIOGRAPHY

Beamish, Richard. *Memoir of the Life of Sir Marc Isambard Brunel.* London, 1862.

Pugsley, Alfred, ed. *The Works of Isambard Kingdom Brunel: An Engineering Appreciation.* Cambridge, 1976.

Rolt, L. T. C. I*sambard Kingdom Brunel.* London, 1957; reprint, Harmondsworth, 1970.

Vaughan, Adrian. *Isambard Kingdom Brunel: Engineering Knight-Errant.* London, 1991.

JOHN P. MCKAY

BRUNNER FAMILY. The Brunner brothers, Henry Brunner (1838–1916), John Brunner (1842–1919) and Joseph Brunner (184?–1892), all pursued careers in the British chemical industry, but John Brunner achieved greatest prominence. He cofounded Brunner Mond, one of the major forerunners to Imperial Chemical Industries (ICI), before becoming a Liberal parliamentarian, party benefactor, and philanthropist. His political biographer found the uses to which Brunner put his worldly success more notable than the success itself. For an economic historian, the way Brunner attained success provides important insights into the changing nature of British business in the late nineteenth century.

The Brunner brothers were born in Liverpool, England, where they were raised in an educated, nonconformist environment by their Swiss-born father and Manx-born mother. John Brunner subsequently attributed his success in business to his Unitarianism, which he believed gave him courage and independence of thought as well as a sense of social responsibility. Yet opportunity and the ability to exploit that opportunity also were important, as the contrasting experiences of the Brunner brothers illustrate.

The oldest, Henry Brunner studied at the Zurich Polytechnic, then took a position as technical manager at the Widnes Leblanc alkali firm of John Hutchinson in 1861. After finishing his schooling and working at a Liverpool shipping firm, John Brunner joined the Hutchinson firm in a clerical position. John's responsibilities increased, and after going as far as was possible for a commercial employee by the late 1860s, he began to think about founding his own business. For the necessary technical contribution, he turned to the inventor Ludwig Mond, with whom he and Henry had become friends in their early days at Hutchinson.

Brunner and Mond investigated a number of potential ventures, including using the new Solvay ammonia soda process to establish an alkali plant. The ammonia soda process itself was not new. Solvay's breakthrough was in making it commercially viable, although in 1872 its viability was not clearly established. But Mond was enthusiastic, and Brunner accepted his friend's judgment. Their early decision allowed the two to secure a favorable license agreement with Solvay.

The new ammonia soda venture had a difficult startup period, but the two partners provided complementary expertise to overcome the hurdles they faced. Mond worked out how to implement the technology and made important improvements to it, while Brunner played an essential role in raising the necessary capital for the new, high-risk venture, building its markets, and running day-to-day operations. By 1881 output and profits had grown sufficiently for them to convert their partnership into a public company. This provided access to new sources of capital, allowing them to undertake a major plant expansion in the mid-1880s.

Henry Brunner became plant manager at Hutchinson in 1866 and part owner in 1881. The youngest brother, Joseph Brunner, became a Liverpool chemical broker. As part of a network of specialized intermediaries, he provided services to both Brunner Mond and the Leblanc firms by the mid-1880s. Henry's Leblanc firm and Joseph's chemical-brokering firm were among many similar firms in their industry; no single firm gained a substantial advantage that allowed it to dominate others. These small- to medium-sized firms were the mainstay of nineteenth-century business. By contrast Brunner Mond was among a number of large firms emerging in the 1880s. Brunner Mond's growth occurred partly because of an increase in demand for soda, but the main reason was because it had an advantage that allowed it to capture a major share of the soda market. The Solvay technology and a favorable license agreement had provided the opportunity to gain that advantage, but Brunner Mond's technical and commercial expertise also was necessary to exploit the opportunity.

As Brunner Mond grew, it came to rely on a pool of technical and commercial managers. Brunner retained close oversight over the company, attending most board meetings and corresponding with managers, and Mond did likewise on technical matters. But the founders also began to pursue other interests in the mid-1880s. Mond moved to London and devoted more time to other research projects, while Brunner entered Parliament, serving almost continuously as the Liberal member for Northwich from 1885 to before serving as president of the National Liberal Federation from 1911 to 1918. In Parliament, Brunner, one of a diminishing group of Radical Liberals, strongly supported Irish home rule, free trade, and reforms to education and working conditions. His political stance was mirrored by his private actions. He improved working conditions in his own company and made substantial donations to schools, libraries, and universities.

BIBLIOGRAPHY

Cohen, J. M. *The Life of Ludwig Mond*. London, 1956. The most informative account of Mond's life, but the role attributed to Brunner is considerably less than that conveyed by other authors, by original correspondence, and by other company papers in the Cheshire Record Office.

Hardie, D. W. F. *A History of the Chemical Industry in Widnes*. Liverpool, 1950.

Koss, Stephen E. *Sir John Brunner, Radical Plutocrat, 1842–1919*. Cambridge, 1970. The Focuses on Brunner's political life, but it does provide insights into his business and private lives. In contrast to other references, Koss states that Henry Brunner studied physics (not chemistry) in Zurich, which may explain why John did not form a partnership with his brother.

Reader, W. J. *Imperial Chemical Industries: A History*, vol. 1, *The Forerunners, 1870–1926*. London, 1970. Examines the formation and growth of Brunner Mond and the decline of the Leblanc firms. It also complements Koss's analysis of Brunner's political rivalry with the fellow northern, nonconformist industrialist William Lever by examining the acrimonious relationship that developed between their two businesses.

Warren, Kenneth. *Chemical Foundations: The Alkali Industry in Britain to 1926*. Oxford, 1980. Provides a more detailed analysis of the relative performance of Brunner Mond and the Leblanc firms.

DIANE HUTCHINSON

BUBBLE ACT OF 1720. The Bubble Act was passed by the English Parliament in June 1720, at the height of the South Sea Bubble, two months before the bubble burst. The act itself remained in force for 105 years and is often said to have constrained the organization of business and limited economic growth.

The act prohibited the formation of associations that presumed to act as corporate bodies and to raise transferable shares (resulting in limited liability of shareholders and the issue of equities on a stock market) without being duly incorporated by either Royal Charter or Special Act of Parliament. It provided for both severe criminal sanctions (including seizing the offenders' entire estate) and civil remedies to parties harmed. In addition, by declaring the illegality of an association, the act enabled the annulment of all contracts entered into by that association.

Three explanations are offered in the literature for the enactment of the Bubble Act. The first, from a public-benefit perception of regulation, suggests that it was promoted by those hostile to the development of the share market. It was a reaction to the South Sea Bubble, and intended to protect unwary investors and the public in general. The second explanation, from a public-choice approach to regulation, views incorporation as a commodity to be sold to groups of income-seeking entrepreneurs. The act was enacted by Parliament as an interested institution, in order to restore lost incomes after the bubbles of 1720 had bypassed parliamentary incorporation and evaded the payments involved in the process of negotiating incorporation by special act of Parliament. The third explanation views the act as a measure introduced by the South Sea Company itself to ensure the success of its scheme for converting the national debt into company shares. This scheme was designed both to relieve the government of irredeemable high-interest debt and to benefit the company, and it relied on a rise in the price of South Sea shares. The act was intended to block public investment in other bubble companies and to divert more money to buying South Sea shares. This third explanation suits both the interest-group and the public-benefit views of regulation, and may best fit the historical record of the legislative process and the priorities of those in power.

The market crash, and the taint of scandal that long continued to attach to incorporation, caused people to avoid the corporate form. For these reasons, the Bubble Act lay dormant, with the exception of a single prosecution in 1721, for its first eighty-seven years. In 1808, the act was revived; and, from then until its repeal in 1825, it served as the basis for criminal proceedings against over ten businesses that sought to raise share capital. These proceedings forced the courts to interpret the somewhat ambiguous act. In some cases, judges attempted to limit its scope and apply it only to fraudulent companies; in other cases, more conservative judges interpreted the act as applying to every unincorporated company. Decisions of the latter type raised questions about the legality of a large number of enterprises in key sectors of the economy and alarmed the business community. The act was finally repealed for reasons rooted in the boom of 1825 and the changing balance of power in that year among Members of Parliament with business interests, the government, and the judiciary.

The long-term effects of the Bubble Act are debated. It was not as well-defined a turning point as some historians claimed. It was not a major cause of Bubble or of the collapse, and it was relatively inconsequential in the period 1722 to 1807, when memories of it were dim among business attorneys and members of the general public. However, it was influential between 1808 and 1825 when it was high on political, legal, and business agendas. Even after the act was finally repealed, in 1825, its basic prohibition was established by conservative judges as a common-law prohibition. Only two decades later, with the introduction in 1844 of general and free incorporation, did the effects of the act finally end.

[*See also* Financial Panics and Crashes.]

BIBLIOGRAPHY

Banner, Stuart. *Anglo-American Securities Regulation: Cultural and Political Roots, 1690–1860*. Cambridge, 1998.

Carswell, John. *The South Sea Bubble*. Rev. ed. Dover, 1993.

Dickson, P. G. M. *The Financial Revolution in England: A Study in the Development of Public Credit, 1688–1756.* London, 1967.

DuBois, Armand B. *The English Business Company after the Bubble Act, 1720–1800.* New York, 1938.

Harris, Ron. "Political Economy, Interest Groups, Legal Institutions, and the Repeal of the Bubble Act in 1825." *Economic History Review* 50.4 (1997), 675–696.

Harris, Ron. *Industrializing English Law: Entrepreneurship and Business Organization, 1720–1844.* Cambridge, 2000.

Neal, Larry. *The Rise of Financial Capitalism: International Capital Markets in the Age of Reason.* Cambridge, 1990.

Patterson, Margaret, and David Reiffen. "The Effect of the Bubble Act on the Market for Joint Stock Shares." *Journal of Economic History* 50.1 (1990), 163–171.

Sperling, John G. *The South Sea Company: An Historical Essay and Bibliographical Finding List.* Boston, 1962.

RON HARRIS

BULLION refers to gold and silver used for monetary purposes. More specifically, bullion means uncoined precious metals, such as gold and silver bars or demonetized coins (i.e., coins that are not legal tender). The appreciation of gold and silver and their employment as money since ancient times is due to the specific characteristics of these metals. Their brilliant appearance and their resistance to corrosion are the reasons for their high value in most cultures. Furthermore, their remarkable malleability and softness permitted the manufacture of thin gold leaves and fine silver objects. It is easy to cut these metals into small pieces of the same size and mark them. Transportation costs for precious metals, like precious stones, were rather low because of their high value in relation to their weight and volume. Furthermore, these metals were available in many parts of the world in quantities that were large enough to supply the monetary demand of preindustrial societies. Therefore, gold bars were being used by the Egyptians as a monetary unit even as early as the reign of Menes (3100 BCE), and silver served as means of payment in Mesopotamia at the time of Hammurabi (1728–1686 BCE).

Gold production was restricted for a long time to surface activities, such as gold washing. Silver extraction required at least some basic underground mining techniques, and the ore gathered had to be refined and smelted. Whereas gold was usually refined with mercury (amalgamation), lead came to be added to the silver ores from the mid-fifteenth century (Seiger process).

In the ancient world, gold and silver were produced in many world regions. There are references to China and India as well as to the Middle East, Africa, and ancient America. In Europe, early sources on gold and silver mining mention the Carpathian Mountains and Bohemia. Phoenicians and Greeks also relied on production in the eastern Mediterranean area. The Romans conquered the Iberian Peninsula in order to gain access to its gold and silver riches. Besides larger mining districts, numerous small ventures existed that had local importance. By the end of the Roman Empire, the production of precious metals had become a capital-intensive enterprise worked by skilled and free laborers as well as by slaves. The political upheavals of the following period destroyed a larger part of the European mines. European gold production became almost insignificant; and from the thirteenth century, Christian territories were importing large quantities of African gold. The European bullion supply worsened when, during the first half of the fifteenth century, the mining centers of the Balkans were occupied by the Turks of the Ottoman Empire. At the same time, the Ottomans expelled Venetians and Genoese from their colonies in the eastern Mediterranean. Therefore, Europeans no longer had direct access to the North African gold trade with the Sudan, and precious metals could no longer be acquired from the Balkans. Such an insufficiency in European supplies of precious metals ultimately led to what many historians have called a "bullion famine" from the later fourteenth to the later fifteenth centuries. Even with the depopulations of this late-medieval period, the monetary situation was aggravated by the fact that the use of money spread, increasing the demand for precious metals not only in the Mediterranean but also in northwestern and central Europe.

Throughout the worsening bullion shortage, the search for new deposits was intensified, and mining and refining techniques were improved. As the famous work of Georgius Agricola, *De re metallica*, published in 1556, shows, methods for the drainage and transportation of ore from underground deposits to the surface were improved, employing a large number of water-powered wheels. In the case of silver mining, new refining techniques (Seiger), using lead to separate silver from argentiferous-cupric ores, were developed in order to be able to process vast deposits of low-grade ores in central Europe. The combination of these measures, as well as the search for new deposits, especially in the Alps (Tirol), Saxony, Bohemia, and Hungary, helped to overcome the "bullion famine" from the later fifteenth and early sixteenth centuries.

In addition, the Portuguese, in reaching West Africa and the "Gold Coast" by sea in the 1470s, had restored European access to the West African gold trade. During the first decades of the sixteenth century, the Portuguese were importing about 700 kilograms (1,540 pounds) of gold per year; between 1470 and 1550, the Portuguese had shipped 36 metric tons (39 short tons) of gold to Europe. Finally, the discovery and exploitation of the Caribbean gold mines at the beginning of the sixteenth century put an end to the European "bullion famine." Gold and especially silver from the mines of the American mainland became a major source of bullion supply from the mid-sixteenth century

GOLD BULLION. $1,250,000 in gold bullion at the Miners and Merchants Bank in Nome, Alaska, 1906. (Lomen Brothers, Nome/Prints and Photographs Division, Library of Congress)

onward. This was at first due to the discovery of new silver deposits in the Peruvian Andes (Potosí) and in northern Mexico (Zacatecas), which were exploited adopting the most sophisticated European techniques of the time. Subsequently, the refining techniques were improved, and the most significant achievement was the adoption of the mercury amalgamation process, previously used in refining gold, for silver production. Within a few years, ores with relatively small silver contents could be profitably exploited. The flow of American silver to Europe reached such an extent that European silver mines, whose production had peaked in the 1540s, could no longer sustain competition from the influx of the much cheaper Spanish American supplies. The American silver production itself had peaked between 1591 and 1595 (with mean annual outputs of 219,457 kilograms, or 482,800 pounds, from Potosí and Zacatecas), when about 274 tons of Peruvian and Mexican silver were reaching Seville each year.

From the later 1620s (when the mean annual outputs were now 178,490 kilograms, or 392,600 pounds), both the Peruvian and Mexican mines, suffering from the inexorable law of diminishing returns, entered a prolonged period of decline, though they briefly enjoyed some recovery in the early 1680s. At the same time, the Asian market was increasingly provided with Japanese silver. The European supply of precious metals was secured by an increasing Colombian gold production. At the end of the seventeenth century, Brazilian gold mining started and quickly became the world's largest supplier of gold, with annual mean outputs that rose from 4,760 kilograms (10,400 pounds) between 1701 and 1710 to a peak of 14,543 kilograms (32,000 pounds) between 1741 and 1750. During the eighteenth century, Brazil and Colombia together produced more than 1,150 metric tons of gold, and Africa supplied almost the same amount. Mexican silver mining recovered by the mid-eighteenth century and increased its output enormously. By the late 1790s, Mexico had become by far the world's biggest source of silver, with annual mean outputs of 619,495 kilograms (1.3 million pounds). After 1810, the wars of independence seriously afflicted the Latin American economies. Many mines were flooded and other mining fields were abandoned. Nevertheless, Mexican silver production recovered swiftly to reach a new peak of 240,828 kilograms (529,000 pounds) a year from 1816 to 1820.

From 1823 onward, Russian gold and silver became important. World bullion supply improved when, in the mid-nineteenth century, gold fields were discovered in California. In twenty-five years (1848–1873), the gold rush produced more gold than had been gathered on the American continent up until that time. In the 1850s, gold diggers moved from California to Australia. These ventures, just as those in Siberia, the Ural Mountains, Canada, the Philippines, New Guinea, and Alaska, were overshadowed by the discoveries in South Africa in 1885 on the reefs of the Witwatersrand. Shortly afterward in 1887 and 1888, the application of cyanide processing increased bullion production enormously; it marked the beginning of the industrialization of mining. In the twentieth century, gold production was concentrated in South Africa (about 700 tons per year), and silver production was centered in the American countries (about 4,500 tons per year).

The use of precious metals as a means of payment and a monetary base was restricted in time and space. In the ancient world, gold and silver coins had been struck in the Middle East, North Africa, and what became Europe. But in Africa south of the Sahara, pre-Columbian America, and many parts of Asia, including, for some time, even China, gold and silver served as jewelry, not as money. Other objects such as cowrie shells, coconuts, or copper pieces were used as means of payment. In Europe and the Western world, as well as in the European colonies, bullion lost gradually its monetary functions during the nineteenth and the twentieth centuries. Gold and silver were replaced by other metals, bank notes, and book money, a process whose origins can be traced back to the late Middle Ages. Silver was first demonetized in Great Britain, when, in 1821, a pure gold standard was introduced. In 1873, Germany and the Scandinavian countries followed suit. Mexico and the United States gave up silver in favor of gold as a monetary basis at the turn of the century. During World War I, the Great Depression, and World War II, the exchange of bank notes into gold had to be revoked temporarily, but the final blow against the gold standard occurred in 1971, when the United States had to suspend the free convertibility of the dollar into gold.

The relationship between gold and silver changed greatly over time. In ancient Mesopotamia, silver was appreciated more than gold, because silver mining required more technical skills than gold washing. This situation did not prevail, because gold is scarcer than silver and less affected by corrosion. By Roman times, gold had surpassed silver in value. This situation prevailed in the future. By the mid-thirteenth century, when western Europe resumed gold coinages (Genoa and Florence in 1252, Venice in 1284), the ratio of gold to silver values was 12:1, though by the mid-fourteenth century that ratio had fallen to 10:1, rising to 11:1 by the mid-fifteenth century. At the same time in India and China, silver had a considerably higher value. The discoveries and exploitation of the Latin American silver mines altered the gold-silver ratio considerably. Within less than a century, the value of silver in relationship to gold had dropped about 50 percent. By 1700, the gold-silver ratio in England had reached 15.5:1 and was about that as well in the Americas. In Asia, the bimetallic ratio had traditionally been much lower, because both economic and cultural factors had given silver a relatively higher value there than in Europe. In the early sixteenth century, the ratio was about 8:1 in India. In Europe for the next two centuries, the bimetallic ratio remained stable; but in India, with considerable influxes of silver during the seventeenth century, the bimetallic ratio rose to as much as 15:1 in 1660, though falling to 14:1 by 1680; and in subsequent centuries it fluctuated between 15:1 and 12:1. The divergence between gold and silver broadened once again with the introduction, in the late 1880s, of the cyanide process in silver and gold refining. The reduction in monetary functions and the introduction of a pure gold standard as a monetary base for most European countries during the nineteenth century led to a further fall in the relative value of silver. On the London market, just before World War I, gold was valued at almost 36 units of silver (and early in the twenty-first century, the bimetallic ratio fluctuates around 65:1).

The differing evaluations of gold and silver across various regions of the world, reflecting changing production patterns and monetary demands for the metals, have led to increased international bullion flows, even though most governments have traditionally imposed heavy restrictions on the bullion trade (such as in Europe from the late thirteenth century). From ancient times, African gold has poured into the Mediterranean in exchange for manufactured goods. During the later Middle Ages, the Venetians and Genoese exported European manufactures to North African ports in exchange for gold, which the Italians then used, in part, to purchase spices and silks from the Middle East and the Asian world. The revival in central European silver mining, from the 1460s, greatly enhanced the profits of the Italian trade with the Levant, especially because of the relatively higher value that silver commanded in the Asian world. Therefore, precious metals, and especially silver, poured increasingly into the East. West African gold and the first American gold boom offered Europeans additional riches with which to pay for Asian goods. American silver mining led to an increase of world bullion flows. The larger part of American silver and, later on, of American gold was brought to Europe. Here, the metals were used for intra-European trade and monetary circulation. But more important were the silver and gold exports, chiefly to Asia and Russia, via the Levant and the eastern Baltic. More than two-thirds of the American bullion that reached Europe was subsequently reexported in order to pay for foreign and exotic riches. Indeed, in the seventeenth century, about 70 percent of the values of Russian-Baltic and Asian merchandise acquired by Western trade were purchased with bullion, chiefly silver. By the early seventeenth century, European trade with Asia especially became increasingly dependent on a third route, especially for the Dutch, British, and French East India Companies: the transoceanic route via the Cape of Good Hope and the Indian Ocean. From Spanish America itself, part of the silver outflows went directly across the Pacific, chiefly in the trade between Acapulco in Mexico (New Spain) and the Spanish colonies in the Philippines (Manila). Therefore, the Mexican and Peruvian silver pesos (*reales de a ocho*) were used as stable global monetary unit for almost three centuries. These bullion flows came to an end after the Napoleonic Wars, which left Great Britain as the major economic power with direct access to African and South American gold production. Because of the expansion in the use and volume of paper money, the growing importance of bank accounts, and the lead position of London as a capital market, the nineteenth-century international bullion flows were chiefly directed by and through London. This did not prevent some regional silver coins from circulating far from their origins. This was the case with the Maria Theresia Taler, which was used as money in the Levant and in northeastern Africa well into the twentieth century.

Bullion in the form of bars, gold coins such as the sovereign and the guinea, and silver minted in the form of pesos or taler, circulated all over the world. They gradually lost their function as a means of payment only when industrialization required larger sums of money. Nonetheless, silver and gold retain part of their image as secure and unalterable riches, so that most central banks still use them as a monetary reserve.

BIBLIOGRAPHY

Ally, Russell. *Gold and Empire: The Bank of England and South Africa's Gold Producers, 1886–1926.* Johannesburg, South Africa, 1994.

Attman, Artur. *Dutch Enterprise in the World Bullion Trade, 1550–1800.* Göteborg, 1983.

Bakewell, Peter, ed. *Mines of Silver and Gold in the Americas.* Aldershot, U.K., 1997.

De Cecco, Marcello. *Money and Empire: The International Gold Standard, 1890–1914.* Oxford, 1974.

Flynn, Dennis O., and Arturo Giráldez, eds. *Metals and Monies in an Emerging Global Economy.* Aldershot, U.K., 1997.

Johnson, Marion. "The Cowrie Currencies of West Africa." *Journal of African History* 11.1 and 11.3 (1970), 17–48, 331–353.

Morineau, Michel. *Incroyables gazettes et fabuleux métaux: Les retours des trésors américaines d'après les gazettes hollandaises (XVIe–XVIIIe siècles).* Paris and Cambridge, 1985.

Munro, John H. *Bullion Flows and Monetary Policies in England and the Low Countries, 1350–1500.* Aldershot, U.K., 1992.

Richards, John F., ed. *Precious Metals in the Later Medieval and Early Modern Worlds.* Durham, N.C., 1983.

TePaske, John Jay. "New World Gold Production in Hemispheric and Global Perspective, 1492–1810." In *Monetary History in Global Perspective: 1500–1808*, edited by Clara Nuñez, pp. 21–32. Seville, Spain, 1998. Papers presented to session B-6 of the Twelfth International Economic History Congress.

RENATE PIEPER

BURIAL AND FUNERAL SERVICES. 11 September 2001 was perhaps the longest day in American history. It seemed to go on for months as smoke continued to rise from Ground Zero at the World Trade Center—and as determined workers sifted through the ruins with no hope of finding a survivor. That so many people would labor so long to recover human remains was a striking reminder of the emotional need of the living to honor the obligations felt toward the dead. This need has been demonstrated by most societies at most points in history. All societies encounter death, and all must find ways to dispose of the dead that are consistent with their values and beliefs.

Society's response to a death is not limited to the emotional bonds between the survivor and the deceased person as individuals. The death systems of preindustrial societies were permeated by fear of the dead, especially the newly dead (Kastenbaum, 2001). Danger was greatest during the period while the soul was still attached to the body and had not yet made a successful transition to the spirit realm. The corpse itself often was considered a potential source of harm because it was contaminated by the evil of death. The Old Testament book of Numbers in the Bible, for example, warns against contact with a corpse and stipulates the purification actions that must be taken. Furthermore, the soul of the deceased remained a threat to the community unless its journey had been eased by the appropriate rites of final passage (van Gennep, 1960).

Many band-and-village societies throughout the world believed that the soul was liberated and the danger lessened when only the bones remained. Tibetan "sky burial," in which the corpses were exposed for "purification" by vultures, is one such example. The corruptible flesh could also be removed through cremation. An alternative to shedding the corruptible flesh was whole-body burial after swaddling the corpse in the most effective wrapping materials available. (The word *mummy* itself derives from *mum*, a substance once used in the Middle East to seal the wrappings.) Both the physical disposition of the body and the accompanying rituals were intended to mollify the potentially dangerous dead and, if possible, earn their goodwill when crises arise in the future.

There are other significant functions of the funeral process that seem to have endured from ancient times to the present. These include closing the ranks against death by affirming the communal bonds among the living; establishing a time frame within which mourning and the disruption of ordinary activities can be contained; clearing the way for redistribution of the deceased's assets and powers; providing a sense of emotional closure (though seldom complete) that enables people to return to their own responsibilities, and thereby keep society going; and providing an acceptable rehearsal for one's own final exit from society. These functions are crucial to the viability of

FUNERALS. A service in progress in a small Portuguese village, 1989. (© Geoffrey Clifford/Woodfin Camp and Associates, New York)

society as well as to the those individuals whose lives have been most closely linked with the deceased.

"Paying Our Respects": Funeral Expenses in the Grand Tradition. There is no one-to-one relationship between the intensity of the love and grief associated with a death and the expenditure on funeral-related expenses. Pioneer settlers crossing the vast distances of North America had to bury their dearest companions by the side of a dusty trail with a simple marker and an improvised service. By contrast, elaborate tombs have been erected to house the remains of people nobody particularly liked because the next of kin could use this as an opportunity to flaunt their wealth and power. Unfortunately, though, there is often the perception that the funeral process must be elaborate and expensive enough to demonstrate the piety of the survivors, if not to aggrandize the deceased. Some of the most expensive (and, at times, artistic) creations of all human history have taken the form of tributes to the dead. It is instructive to remind ourselves of these extravagant ventures in order to gain perspective on attitudes and practices today.

The oldest and only surviving of the Seven Wonders of the Ancient World is the Great Pyramid of Giza (Cairo, Egypt) that Pharoah Khufu (c. 2560 BCE) ordered built for his tomb. The tomb of an otherwise undistinguished king of Caria (now in Turkey) is also on this elite list. Ready for occupancy around 350 BCE, this edifice was so impressive that King Mausolos's name became generic for *mausoleum* (though the structure itself was taken apart to fortify a

Crusader's fort in the early sixteenth century). Only half of the story of the Taj Mahal ("abode of the chosen one") is well known. Shah Jahan prepared this beautiful monument as a final love offering to his wife, Mumtaz Mahal. It seems to have been designed as a representation of heaven on earth. The other half of the story is that the Taj Mahal was part of an even more extensive building campaign that asserted Mogul rule over Northern India.

Three robust themes emerge from the study of death archaeology (e.g., Pearson, 2000). First, the strength and grandeur is intended to preserve some essence of the deceased through time. Second, the power asserted by the monument is intended to deter enemies and pass on to the rightful heirs. The history of grave robbing and vandalism, along with recyclings and natural disasters has not been kind to most of these intentions. Qin Shih Huang-Ti (c. 259–210 BCE) the first unifier of China, sought immortality with all the means at his disposal. His tomb represented a last-ditch attempt, replete with the now-famous terra cotta soldiers, chariots, and horses. His earthly power was soon overturned after his death, however, and apparently many of the tomb furnishings were stolen, although enough remained to make a striking impression. A veritable industry has been in existence since ancient times of looting the contents of tombs and even carrying off the building stones themselves. The practice of absconding with and selling the remains of martyrs and saints was so common that the Roman emperor Theodosius II (408–450 CE) found it necessary to increase the severity of the penalties (included in the influential Theodosian Code).

The third and most harrowing theme concerns the human expense of funeral-related endeavors. A great many tombs of the illustrious dead included the mass sacrifice of slaves, captives, commonfolk, concubines, and even ministers of state. The ultimate funeral expense is the death of others who fall within the power of the deceased. Less direct but more widespread was the further impoverishment of the population to construct such edifices as the Taj Mahal.

Methods and Expenses Today. The great age of tomb building is long past. Perhaps the great age of virtual memorials has started (Wertheim, 2000). The two most common modes of body disposal in the past—burial and cremation—are still dominant today, their relative popularity influenced by changing social and environmental circumstances. In general, there is a shift from whole-body burial to cremation (the "cremains" are sometimes buried, but often not).

Cremation has become the most common method in much of the world. Japan is the leader in this respect with more than 90 percent. Great Britain, another small and densely populated island nation, now cremates about three of every four corpses. About three of every five deaths throughout Europe and Australia/New Zealand are cremated. In the United States cremation is at an all-time high at about 25 percent and increasing (already the most common method in California, Florida, Arizona, and several other states). People who have moved to sunbelt states in their retirement years often select the cremation option as more convenient for shipping their remains back home, as well as for its lesser expense. The influence of religious tradition on choice of funeral-related events has diminished for many, though certainly not all, people. The still-developing story of cremation in America provides many insights into the ways that this nation has both preserved and altered its patterns of behavior and belief (Prothero, 2001).

Funeral and memorial activities are clearly caught up in a pattern of change. Some changes arise primarily from the funeral industry itself. The funeral industry took form as a consequence of the Civil War, with its brutally disfigured corpses that would have to be transported home over long distances. Embalming techniques, though primitive at first, helped to reduce the shock and horror. Eventually, the public assumed that all deaths should be in the hands of professionals and embalming conducted as a matter of course. Funeral "homes" were family businesses and the "undertakers" often respected as pillars of the community. Lawn-garden cemeteries, such as Mount Auburn in Cambridge, Massachusetts, started to emerge as an alternative to the increasingly crowded and often neglected church graveyards as public demand grew for a more comforting scene (Linden-Ward, 1989).

This fairly stable pattern could not go on forever in an ever-changing and sometimes convulsive society. Among the most destabilizing influences and responses:

1. A geographically mobile society attenuates its relationship with "home base" at the same time that much of small-town America shrivels in the raging stream of "progress."
2. The family funeral home becomes overmatched or absorbed by large corporations that have little or no connection to the local community.
3. The funeral industry comes in for a pounding by the media on charges of exorbitant pricing, blatant commercialism, and insensitivity (Jessica Mitford's *The American Way of Death*, 1963, was the opening salvo).
4. Memorial societies emerge, dedicated to simple and inexpensive funerals.
5. A growing number of people are attracted, while others explore a variety of alternative funerals with more decision making and participation by families and less control by the industry establishment.
6. Federal regulations increase almost exponentially—especially as a consequence of the AIDS epidemic, which intensified concerns about contagion.

The funeral industry has shown a measure of resourcefulness and adaptility to these changes. For example, a growing number of funeral directors welcome the opportunity for open dialog with family members in making arrangements that are most likely to meet their needs. Other members of the trade have become more evasive and defensive. Such organizations as the American Association of Retired People (AARP) have responded by offering potential consumers information and advice. The "traditional" funeral still takes place, but variations have become common.

Expense also varies. The AARP has determined that the average cost of a traditional funeral is $4,600. This figure does not include flowers, obituary notices and other amenities, nor the cost of the gravesite itself. There are significant regional differences, and often among competing funeral homes in the same area. Federal regulations now require funeral homes to disclose costs to potential consumers, so it is now somewhat easier to make comparisons.

Conclusion. Death-related customs cannot be separated from society's general beliefs, values, and tensions. Power motives have often dominated the send-off and memorialization of a society's "important" people. The affluent have made funerals a venue for conspicuous consumption, even when they present themselves as humble Puritans (Stannard, 1975). Meanwhile, the powerless have been confirmed in their helpless state by callous and degrading postmortem treatment. The African American experience offers many such examples (Holloway, 2002). The future of burial services in technologically advanced countries may be affected in ways we cannot now predict by changing family cultures, computer-assisted memorialization, and a continued decline in belief in the afterlife.

BIBLIOGRAPHY

Holloway, Karla F. C. *Passed On: African American Mourning Stories*. Durham, 2002.

Kastenbaum, Robert. *Death, Society, and Human Experience*. 7th ed. Boston, 2001. Grief, mourning, and funerals are considered here within the larger context of society's overall concern with death (includes definitions of death, suicide, homicide, dying, and end-of-life issues). Useful for a compact and up-to-date exploration of the way that we and other cultures live and die.

Kastenbaum, Robert. *And Away We Go: The Final Passage Through Life and Death*. Berkeley, in press.

Linden-Ward, Blanche. *Silent City on a Hill: Landscapes of Memory and Boston's Mount Auburn Cemetery*. Columbus, Ohio, 1989. Provides an overview of the development of lawn-garden cemeteries around the world as well as the history of Mount Auburn. Well illustrated.

Mitford, Jessica. *The American Way of Death*. New York, 1963. A surprise bestseller when it appeared, this book by a visiting English author criticized and mocked the American funeral industry to the delight of the general public.

Pearson, Mike Parker. *The Archeology of Death and Burial*. College Station, Tex., 2000. Snappy and engaging, this book is also a broad and reliable survey of its topic. An ideal introduction for the general reader with some detail that will be informative to most specialists as well.

Prothero, Stephen. *Purified by Fire: A History of Cremation in America*. Berkeley, 2001. Fortunately, the one and only book length treatment of this subject is also first-rate. Good scholarship, good writing.

Stannard, David E., ed. *Death in America*. Philadelphia, 1975. The most accessible source on dying, death, and funeral practices in early America.

Zbarsky, Ilya, and Samuel Hutchinson. *Lenin's Embalmers*. London, 1997.

ROBERT KASTENBAUM

BURMA. *See* Myanmar.

BUSINESS CYCLES. History illustrates the evolutionary nature of business cycle behavior. In economic systems that entail behavioral, institutional, structural, and policy changes, the nature of business cycles will evolve and change over time. For example, the process of economic growth of modern economies has undergone massive structural change in the past two hundred years. With industrialization, we would expect a lessening in the importance of agricultural cycles in influencing macroeconomic fluctuations. Similarly, policy regime changes have an observable effect on cyclical fluctuations. Business cycles during the rules-driven policy framework of the pre-1913 gold-standard epoch were very different from those of the interwar period; the fluctuations of the Bretton Woods–era after World War II were very different from those observed in other periods.

The perspective to business cycles found in the historical literature is one that emphasizes the existence of a multiplicity of cycles (of differing amplitude and period) coexisting in time, and with each cycle varying in importance over time. Economic historians have focused attention on three major cycles: the trade cycle, also known as the Juglar cycle, with an average period of 7 to 9 years; the Kuznets swing, or long swing, with an average period of 16 to 22 years; and the Kondratieff wave, which is assumed to have an average period of 50 to 60 years.

The Juglar (Trade) Cycle. The Juglar cycle has an average period of 7 to 9 years. A number of studies have argued that this is the dominant cycle influencing industrial economies over the period from 1870 to 1938 (Aldcroft and Fearon, 1972; Rostow, 1948). The path of British industrial production has often been seen as a good example of the prevalence and regularity of the Juglar cycle (Crafts et al., 1989). Aggregate industrial production fluctuated with peaks in 1873, 1882, 1889, 1899, 1907, 1913, 1920, 1929, and 1937.

The regularity and dominance of the Juglar cycle is partly a statistical artefact. In the case of Great Britain, a Juglar cycle was imposed on much of the historical data. For example, in reconstructing the industrial production index, Lewis (1978) imposed a cycle of nine years on *a priori* grounds. A Juglar cycle was imposed on iron and steel products, commercial building, clothing, printing, and chemicals, which account for over 28 percent of Lewis's total industrial production index and 35 percent of the manufacturing and construction index. This type of assumption reflects the belief that the Juglar cycle was dominant in the nineteenth century. In fact, the existence of independent evidence suggests a more complex cyclical pattern. The experience of other countries reinforces the idea of irregularity. In the case of Germany and the United States, the economy displays an irregular cycle with an average period of 10.8 years; but the economy also shows up a long swing of 20 years. The coexistence of these cycles suggests a more irregular cyclical path than is implied by the assumptions of earlier economic historians.

Over time we observe significant changes in the Juglar (trade) cycle. For example, volatility was significantly higher in the interwar period than in the pre-1913 era (Sheffrin, 1988; Backus and Kehoe, 1992). Over the postwar era the average period of the cycle fell to 4 to 5 years and amplitude fell significantly, relative to the interwar and the pre-1913 periods.

Kuznets Swings. The Kuznets swing refers to a variation in economic growth that is longer than the Juglar trade cycle but shorter than the Kondratieff wave. The actual length of the swings found varies with different studies, but something between 14 and 22 years is representative. The differing periods are partly the result of different statistical methods used to identify the swings. Kuznets swings are particularly important for our understanding of the period before 1913. During this period, long swings have been observed in a wide variety of variables, including GDP, balance of payments, productivity, money supply, investment, sectoral terms of trade, agricultural output, and migration (Solomou, 1987). The evidence also suggests that long swings are observed in a wide variety of countries, including Germany (Solomou, 1987; Metz and Spree, 1981), France (Lévy-Leboyer, 1978; Solomou, 1987), Canada (Harkness, 1968), Brazil (Catao, 1991), Argentina (Ford, 1974), Australia (Pope, 1984) and Japan (Ohkawa and Rosovsky, 1973; Minami, 1986).

For most countries during the interwar period, the long swings that were so pervasive before 1913 came to an end. The major factor behind this change is that the interwar epoch did not have an equivalent set of international adjustment mechanisms to the pre-1913 era. The pre-1913 gold standard survived for so long partly because there existed viable international adjustment mechanisms to national-specific shocks, including international migration, trade protection, and overseas investment (which stimulated the tradable sector). These adjustments manifested themselves in long swing fluctuations in a number of international economic variables, such as exports, overseas investment, and international migration. The interwar era saw an abrupt end of many of these adjustment mechanisms. Legislation in the New World restricted international labor mobility. The disintegration of world trade, partly due to protection policies and a collapse of overseas investment between 1928 and 1938, prevented export growth from stabilizing the effect of domestic demand shocks. Instead, adverse shocks left economies with high unemployment and low output levels. The "passing of the Kuznets cycle" in the interwar era is of central importance to business cycle experiences, just as the presence of Kuznets swings before 1914 represented the workings of various stabilizing cyclical adjustment mechanisms in the international economy (Abramovitz, 1968).

The case of the United States illustrates the importance of international economic-demographic linkages in generating long-swing adjustments. For most countries, once these international flows collapsed during the interwar period, the Kuznets swings that were so prevalent in medium-term growth fluctuations before 1913 come to an end. However, in a large economy such as that of the United States, intranational economic-demographic interactions continued to be important to the economy throughout the twentieth century (Hickman, 1974; Easterlin, 1968). Intranational labor and capital flows in a large integrated market, such as that of the United States, have had a large effect on medium-term growth swings for much of the twentieth century.

The Kondratieff Wave. The Kondratieff wave is a cycle of prices and output with an approximate period of 50 to 60 years. In some of the earlier literature, the Kondratieff wave has been used as a framework for understanding such epochs as the great depression of 1873 to 1896 and the Edwardian inflation of 1899 to 1913 (Kondratieff, 1925; Schumpeter, 1939). However, recent economic historians have found it difficult to describe business cycles in terms of Kondratieff waves. For example, the economic history of the period from 1873 to 1896 is written in terms of the "Myth of the Great Depression" (Saul, 1969). The empirical evidence suggests that we need to tread with care in the evaluation of Kondratieff waves. Most macroeconomic variables (such as GDP, investment, and industrial production) fail to display a Kondratieff wave growth pattern (Solomou, 1987).

In contrast, long cycles in prices have been noted, particularly over the period of the classical gold standard period before 1913 (Lewis, 1978; Rostow and Kennedy, 1979). In much of the macroeconomic history literature, long cycles in prices have been linked to the mean reversion of the price level under the gold standard (Bordo and Kydland, 1996). The argument is that a credible commitment to gold resulted in a predictable mean-reverting price level. Given that it took time for a shortage of gold to lead to gold discoveries, via increased search activity for gold, a long cycle in prices was generated. With the introduction of discretion-driven policy regimes in the twentieth century, this type of price adjustment ended. However, the hypothesis of mean reversion in the price level with a 50 to 60 year cycle should be evaluated more critically. Consider Figures 1 and 2, which provide plots of British and U.S. wholesale prices over the gold standard epoch. Formal statistical tests for mean reversion suggest that in a strict sense we fail to reject the idea of nonstationarity for a wide variety of long time periods. The evidence for Kondratieff long cycles in prices is also weak. The secular movements in U.S. prices provide some evidence of war-induced cyclicality in the Kondratieff frequency, but similar results are not observed for other gold-standard countries. For example, in the case of Great Britain, if there is a long cycle in prices, it is far longer than the Kondratieff cycle.

Given the historical discussion of multiple cycles, it is useful to describe the relevance of this perspective using modern time-series methods of decomposing trends and cycles. Solomou (1998) considers the empirical relevance of multiple-cycle models by employing the Kalman filter to describe cycles in GDP for Great Britain, France, Germany, and the United States during the period between 1870 and 1913. The cyclical path of all these economies is depicted as the sum of short and long cycles. For all the major industrial countries, the amplitude of the long swings is as large as the amplitude of the shorter cycles.

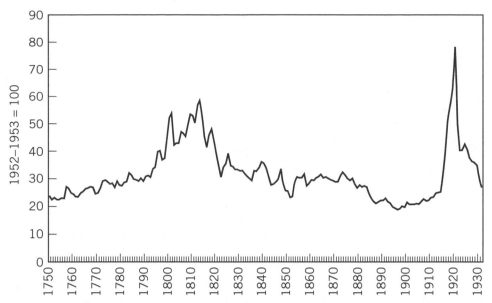

Figure 1. British wholesale prices, 1750–1931. SOURCE: Mitchell, Brain R. International Historical Statistics: Europe, 1750–1988. 3d ed. New York, 1992.

This perspective provides an alternative to Hicks's (1982) description of irregular fluctuations. One aspect of irregularity is that the epoch was influenced by cycles of different average periods. Accepting the idea of multiple cycles as reality suggests one way of capturing some of the observed irregularity.

Economic Depressions, 1873–1921. This section describes the major depressions observed between 1873 and 1921. The interested reader should consult the works of Matthews (1954), Gayer et al. (1975), and Hughes (1960) for detailed outlines of earlier depressions.

1873. The world economic boom of the 1860s and early 1870s culminated in the depression of 1872–1873. The boom was a time of extensive housing construction and railway building in all the major industrial countries. Prosperity ended first in the United States and France with peaks in 1872. In contrast, depression in Great Britain and Germany was more of a slowing down in the rate of growth rather than a sharp depression.

Depression in the United States was sharp. The move into a state of depression was signaled by financial crisis. Asset prices on the stock exchange fell, and many banks collapsed. The collapse of commodity prices reduced the ability of farmers and railway companies to repay loans. Without a central bank, the economic system had to bear the full impact of the shock with the resultant outcome of banking collapse and a credit squeeze. The high amplitude of the depression was related to financial crisis. The depression was also unusually long, lasting from 1873 to 1876. With depression, the economic-demographic feedback effects that sustained the boom moved into reverse. As

unemployment increased, immigration collapsed, resulting in a fall of housing and infrastructure construction. The length of depression was also related to the policy stance of the 1870s. In 1875 the decision to return to the gold standard at the prewar par value imposed considerable monetary deflation on the price level. Although money wages fell during the depression, real wages rose significantly, imposing constraints on profitability and investment.

While depression in the United States was sharp, depression in Great Britain, France, and Germany is best described as a growth pause. In France, the fall of industrial production and GDP was limited to 1873. Significant revival was observed from 1874. In fact, despite further adverse shocks to the agricultural sector in 1879, the French economy maintained growth momentum for most of the 1870s.

In Great Britain, a diversity of sectoral growth experiences kept the economy growing during the early 1870s, avoiding a deep depression. A strong construction boom kept building activity high until 1876. In fact, the economy faced a more severe downturn in 1878 and 1879 than it did in 1873. Two national-specific features help to explain the double-phased depression in Great Britain during the 1870s. First, as the major capital exporter in the world, the collapse of overseas investment between 1875 and 1879 had adverse effects on British exports. Second, the British economy faced adverse supply-side shocks in the late 1870s. The coupling of weather to the economic conditions of the key sectors of the period (including agriculture, construction, and energy demand) resulted in a major adverse supply-side shock arising from the extreme

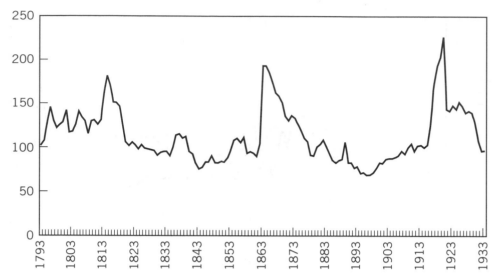

Figure 2. U.S. wholesale prices, 1793–1933. Source: Mitchell, Brian R. International Historical Statistics: The Americas, 1750–1988. 2d ed. New York, 1993.

weather conditions of the late 1870s. For example, in 1879 extreme weather conditions adversely affected agriculture, reducing British GDP by 1.5 percent (Solomou and Wu, 1999). The Bank of England's policy response to the conditions of the 1870s made the economic situation worse. The bank used the interest rate as an instrument of controlling gold reserves. Since the bank operated with a very low gold reserve, interest rates were sensitive to adverse balance-of-payment shocks. The collapse of exports in the early 1870s and the balance of payment effect of the supply-side shocks of the late 1870s forced a high nominal and real interest rate on the economy from 1876 to 1879. The situation was made worse by the fact that the 1870s saw the adoption of the gold standard by a number of major economies (including Germany and the United States), raising the international demand for gold and placing pressures on British gold reserves.

1883. The U.S. depression of the 1880s was not as deep or as long as that of the early 1870s. A marked boom followed a mild recession between 1884 and 1845 until 1892. From late 1882, profitability in the U.S. economy became strained, making it difficult to raise new capital for investment. The bad harvest of 1883 hit railway profits, leading to an even more significant fall in railway construction.

In Great Britain, the depression of 1883 was severe, lasting until 1886. Industrial production fell by 10 percent from 1883 to 1886 and unemployment peaked at 10.2 percent in 1886. The depression was perceived to be so severe that a Royal Commission on the Depression of Trade and Industry was established in 1886 to account for the phenomenon. A number of factors explain the length and severity of depression. Exports peaked in 1882 and col-

lapsed between 1883 and 1886. Since the British effective exchange rate was little changed during these years, the contraction of exports was mainly the result of a contraction of world incomes, as the core industrial economies moved into recession (Solomou and Catao, 2000). The Bank of England's monetary policy was also central to generating a depressed cyclical effect on the economy. With each upswing in economic growth, the bank had to raise interest rates to maintain gold reserves. Short-term rates were raised significantly between 1879 and 1882, pushing up the real interest rate. The era shows the early makings of a "stop-go" cycle under fixed exchange rate regimes.

The depression of the early 1880s had little effect on Germany. Although there was a pause in the growth rate in the early 1880s, growth picked up significantly from the mid-1880s. A number of favorable cyclical influences affected the German economy. During the early 1880s, the German real effective exchange rate was relatively low compared with other industrial countries, giving Germany an advantage to maintain export growth, despite adverse world income trends (Solomou and Catao, 2000). Thus, the only year that exports had an adverse effect on the economy was in 1885 when exports fell by 2 percent. The other major effect on the German business cycle of the early 1880s is the favorable effect arising from the agricultural sector. Agricultural protection and favorable weather conditions meant that the agricultural sector was booming.

France was enjoying rapid economic expansion until 1882, helped by a series of public works, known as the Freycinet Plan. Charles de Freycinet became Minister of Public Works in December 1877. The plan he introduced consisted of a 10-year plan to improve the transportation system as an economic development initiative. The plan fuelled a strong construction boom. However, by 1881 the plan was running out of steam, with the market showing an unwillingness to absorb so much government stock. The result was that by 1883, government expenditure contracted rapidly, adding deflationary pressures on the economy. Depression in France has also been blamed on the phylloxera epidemic that attacked the vineyards. This is only partially correct. In fact, conditions in agriculture were adverse due to a number of factors. Adverse weather conditions and increased international competition created significant problems for French agriculture throughout 1883–1889.

1893. The United States experienced a deep depression in 1893, similar in amplitude to that of 1873. The similarities are such that Simon Kuznets argued for a long swing of approximately 20 years' duration. Stock market values fell drastically, six hundred banks collapsed, and unemployment rose significantly. Domestic monetary factors impacted enormously on the American depression. The spread of the gold standard in the 1870s had resulted in a fall in the price of silver at the expense of American silver producers. The problems of silver producers and a general deflation since 1873 resulted in a movement in favor of bimetalism. The Sherman Silver Purchase Act raised questions about America's commitment to the gold standard. The Act required the Treasury to buy 4.5 million ounces of silver every month. Uncertainty surrounding the U.S. commitment to the gold standard resulted in the Treasury's loss of half its gold stock in 1890. Default by Argentina in 1890 brought home the risks of lending overseas, resulting in a fall in British lending to America. The election of 1892 raised the probability of an American exit from gold, resulting in a run on the dollar in 1893. The discount rate reached 18.1 percent by August 1893. Recession reduced the rate of capital inflow, forcing the export of gold to finance the U.S. trade deficit. Thus, at the heart of the U.S. depression of 1893 were domestic monetary factors resulting from a fear of devaluation.

The crisis of the 1890s broke out in Great Britain in November 1890 with the Barings crisis. Financial difficulties in Argentina meant that the British public became wary of Argentinean stock. When John & Francis & Co. Barings issued a £10 million loan in 1890 for public works in Buenos Aires, it proved a failure with 90 percent of the stock left with the bank. By November the bank was forced to suspend payments. The Bank of England raised the bank rate and committed itself to winding up the affairs of Barings & Co. with the help of the Bank of France. Although such actions meant that financial panic was brief, depression was not averted and lasted until 1893. Between 1890 and 1894, the monetary problems of some of the key primary producers and the significant capital reflow to the United Kingdom

resulted in a 10 percent appreciation of the British real effective exchange rate (Solomou and Catao, 2000). Combined with adverse income movements in many primary producing economies, British exports fell significantly, transmitting international shocks to the domestic economy.

1907. In the United States, signs that the boom of the early twentieth century was coming to an end were present from the end of 1906 into early 1907. Railway companies' profits were down, and after mid-1907, metal prices began to slump. Industrial production slowed before the monetary crisis that hit in the autumn of 1907. A financial panic developed when the National Bank of Commerce refused to honor the bills of the Knickerbocker Trust Company and set off a run on deposits. A stock market crisis followed at the end of October. Severe depression was observed in 1908. Industrial production fell by 17.1 percent in 1907–1908, unemployment rose sharply, and immigration fell by 40 percent during 1907–1908.

Germany was facing economic problems from the summer of 1906. Iron and steel orders were in decline in the second half of 1906, and construction activity was down early in 1907. A monetary crisis broke out in October 1907. Reichsbank reserves fell sharply, and the discount rate was raised to 7.5 percent. Industrial production growth stagnated to zero, exports fell, and unemployment rose.

In Great Britain, the Bank of England responded to the U.S. crisis by raising interest rates to 7 percent in November 1907. Monetary crisis was avoided, and by May 1908 the interest rate was brought down to 2.5 percent. However, depression was not avoided. Industrial production fell, exports fell, and unemployment rates doubled from 3.7 percent in 1907 to 7.8 percent in 1908.

The nature of depression in 1907–1908 illustrates a number of changed features relative to the past. First, the weight of the United States in core industrial production was rising over time, strengthening the transmission effects on the other major countries. As a result, core industrial production fell by nearly 10 percent during 1907–1908. Second, the degree of international synchronization was high. Only France had enough growth momentum to avoid the international effect of the depression of 1907–1908. Depression was becoming manifestly more of an international affair. The internationalization of the business cycle, a feature that has been noted for the interwar period (Backus and Kehoe, 1992; Eichengreen, 1994) has some of its roots in the pre-1913 period.

1920–1921. This was a depression year in all of the major industrial countries that attempted to bring to an end the post–World War I inflation, including Great Britain, France, and the United States. For Great Britain, this was the most severe slump experienced since the nineteenth century, being more severe in its effects than the depression of 1929 to 1932. In order to understand the depression of 1920–1921, we have to consider the inflationary path of the immediate post–World War I period. Postwar reconstruction generated both demand-pull and cost-push inflationary pressures. Between 1918 and 1920, the economy operated at full employment, with a rapid growth of demand for consumer and investment goods at home and abroad: this generated demand-pull inflationary pressures. Cost-push pressures were also present. Dowie (1975) emphasizes the importance of the introduction of the 8-hour day in 1919 as a major inflationary force: weekly working hours fell from 50 to 43.5, amounting to a 13 percent fall. The fall occurred without a reduction in weekly wages, which meant that real wages for a normal week rose by the full amount of the reduction in hours. The combined effects of demand and cost pressures on the British inflation rate caused it to rise faster than the U.S. rate.

At the same time, in November 1919 the British government announced the official policy intention of returning to the gold standard at the pre-1913 gold parity. Since a differential had arisen between U.K. and U.S. inflation rates between 1914 and 1919, the government was clearly announcing a forthcoming contractionary monetary policy stance. Given the system of flexible exchange rates that was introduced in 1919, the effect of the restrictive monetary policy announcement was to result in an "overshooting" of the real effective exchange rate (Broadberry, 1986). Such effects were compounded by expansionary monetary policy in the high inflation countries of Germany, France, Belgium, Italy, and central Europe. The restrictive monetary policy also led consumers to hold to inelastic inflationary expectations, reducing consumption and increasing money demand. This analysis implies that the rise in interest rates in April 1920 was not the impulse that pushed the economy into depression but a symbol that recessionary forces were well under way from late 1919, resulting from the deflationary monetary policy announcements and the wage-gap in the labor market.

One of the outstanding features of the depression of 1921 is the exceptionally large fall in British exports of 30 percent. However, the export collapse cannot be seen as an *exogenous* shock: under flexible exchange rates, the contractionary monetary policy and the supply-side changes in the labor market resulted in an appreciation of the real exchange rate, leading to a large fall in exports.

The severity of the British depression was unmatched by that of any other country. Both the United States and France saw relatively milder depressions (Patat and Luttala, 1990; Romer, 1988); while British GDP fell by 10 percent (Solomou and Weale, 1996), U.S. GDP fell by 2.4 percent (Romer, 1988) and French GDP by only 1.6 percent. The major difference in these relative experiences is to be found in different exchange-rate policies and supply-side conditions. Great Britain's commitment to an early return to the gold standard at the pre-1913 parity resulted in a rapid appreciation of the real exchange rate during 1919–1922 that had serious adverse output effects. In the case of France, there was a more gradualist approach to returning to the pre-1913 gold parity, which meant that monetary policy was eased in the middle of 1921. These different exchange-rate policies meant that monetary deflation was far more severe in Great Britain than the other major industrial countries. When combined with the adverse supply-side shift induced by the fall in hours of work in 1919, the British economy was faced with a very severe contraction. In contrast, Romer (1988) has noted the importance of favorable supply-side shifts in the American economy, induced by the collapse of production costs in 1920–1921.

The case of Germany further illustrates the importance of monetary policy during 1920–1921. In the same year, German GDP grew by more than 10 percent and exports by 21 percent, despite stagnation in world income growth. This is explained by a significantly depreciated exchange rate. The rapid depreciation of the nominal exchange rate resulted in a real depreciation that gave a large stimulus to exports; at the same time, high inflation reduced real wages with favorable supply-side effects on profitability and investment (Sommariva and Tullio, 1987). Depression in the leading capital suppliers also meant that there was an excess supply of liquidity in the world economy, some of which found its way as capital imports in the German economy as investors were speculating on a Reichmark appreciation (Holtfrerich, 1986).

[*See also* Stabilization Policies.]

BIBLIOGRAPHY

Abramovitz, Moses. "The Passing of the Kuznets Cycle." *Economica* 35 (1968), 349–367.

Aldcroft, Derek H., and Peter Fearon. eds. *British Economic Fluctuations, 1790–1939*. London, 1972.

Backus, David K., and Patrick J. Kehoe. "International Evidence on the Historical Properties of Business Cycles." *American Economic Review* 82.4 (1992), 864–888.

Bordo, Michael D., and Hugh Rockoff. "The Gold Standard as a Good Housekeeping Seal of Approval." *Journal of Economic History* 56.2 (1996), 389–426.

Broadberry, Stephen N. *The British Economy between the Wars: A Macroeconomic Survey*. Oxford, 1986.

Catao, Luis. "The Transmission of Long Cycles between Core and Periphery Economies: A Case Study of Brazil and Mexico." Ph.D. diss., University of Cambridge, 1991.

Crafts, N. F. R., S. J. Leybourne, and T. C. Mills. "The Climacteric in Late Victorian Britain and France: A Reappraisal of Evidence." *Journal of Applied Econometrics* 4.2 (1989), 103–118.

Dowie, J. "1919–1920 Is in Need of Attention." *Economic History Review* 28 (1975), 429–450.

Easterlin, Richard. *Population, Labor Force, and Long Swings in Economic Growth: The American Experience*. New York, 1968.

Ford, A. G. "British Investment in Argentina and Long Swings, 1880–1914." In *Essays in Quantitative Economic History*, edited by Roderick Floud. Oxford, 1974.

Gayer, Arthur D., Walt W. Rostow, and Anna J. Schwartz. *The Growth and Fluctuation of the British Economy, 1790–1850: An Historical, Statistical, and Theoretical Study of Britain's Economic Development.* New York, 1975.

Harkness, J. P. "A Spectral-Analytic Test of the Long Swing Hypothesis in Canada." *Review of Economics and Statistics* 50 (1968), 429–436.

Harvey, Andrew C. *Forecasting, Structural Time Series Models, and the Kalman Filter.* Cambridge, 1989.

Hickman, Bert G. "What Became of the Building Cycle?" In *Nations and Households in Economic Growth: Essays in Honor of Moses Abramovitz,* edited by Paul David and Melvin Reder. New York and London, 1974.

Hicks, John R. "Are There Economic Cycles?" In *Money, Interest, and Wages: Collected Essays on Economic Theory,* vol. 2, edited by J. R. Hicks. Oxford, 1982.

Holtferich, Carl-Ludwig. "U.S. Capital Exports to Germany, 1919–23 Compared to 1924–29." *Explorations in Economic History* (1986), 1–32.

Hughes, Jonathan R. T. *Fluctuations in Trade, Industry, and Finance: A Study of British Economic Development 1850–1860.* Oxford, 1960.

Kondratieff, Nikolai D. "The Major Economic Cycles." *Voprosy kon'iunktury* 1 (1925), 28–79. An abridged English translation appears as "The Long Waves in Economic Life." *Review of Economic Statistics* 17.6 (1935), 105–115.

Lévy-Leboyer, Maurice. "Capital Investment and Economic Growth in France." In *The Cambridge Economic History of Europe,* vol. 7, edited by P. Mathias and M. M. Postan. Cambridge, 1978.

Lewis, William A. *Growth and Fluctuations, 1870–1913.* London, 1978.

Matthews, Robin C. O. *A Study in Trade Cycle History: Economic Fluctuations in Great Britain, 1833–1842.* Cambridge, 1954.

Metz, R., and R. Sprec. "Kuznets-Zyklen im Wachstum der deutschen Wirtshaftwahrend des 19. und fruhen 20. Jahrhunderts." In *Konjunktur, Krise, Gesellschaft,* edited by D. Petzina and G. van Roon. Stuttgart, 1981.

Minami, Roshin *The Economic Development of Japan: A Quantitative Study.* London, 1986.

Ohkawa, Kozushi, and Henry Rosovsky. *Japanese Economic Growth: Trend Acceleration in the Twentieth Century.* Stanford, Calif., 1973.

Patat, Jean Pierre and Michel Luttala, *A Monetary History of France in the Twentieth Century.* Houndmills, U.K., 1990.

Pope, David. "Rostow's Kondratieff Cycle in Australia." *Journal of Economic History* 44.3 (1984), 729–753.

Romer, Christina. "World War I and Postwar Depression: A Reinterpretation Based on Alternative Estimates of GNP." *Journal of Monetary Economics* 22 (1988), 91–115.

Saul, S. B. *The Myth of the Great Depression, 1873–1896.* London and Basingstoke, U.K., 1969.

Sheffrin, Steven M. "Have Economic Fluctuations Been Dampened? A Look at Evidence Outside the United States." *Journal of Monetary Economics* 21 (1988), 73–83.

Schumpeter, Joseph A. *Business Cycles: A Theoretical, Historical, and Statistical Analysis of the Capitalist Process.* New York, 1939.

Solomou, Solomus N. *Phases of Economic Growth, 1850–1973: Kondratieff Waves and Kuznets Swings.* Cambridge, 1987.

Solomou, Solomus N. *Themes in Macroeconomic History: The U.K. Economy, 1919–1939.* Cambridge, 1996.

Solomou, Solomus N. *Economic Cycles.* Manchester, U.K., 1998.

Solomou, Solomus N., and L. A. V. Catao. "Real Exchange Rates 1870–1913: The Core Industrial Countries." *European Review of Economic History* (December 2002), 361–382.

Solomou, Solomus N., and M. R. Weale. "U.K. National Income 1920–1938: The Implications of Balanced Estimates." *Economic History Review* 49.1 (1996), 101–115.

Solomou, Solomus N., and W. Wu. "Weather Effects on European Agricultural Output 1850–1913" *European Review of Economic History* 3 (December 1999), 351–373.

Sommariva, Andrea, and Guiseppe Tullio. *German Macroeconomic History, 1880–1979: A Study in the Effects of Economic Policy on Inflation, Currency Depreciation, and Growth.* Basingstoke, U.K., 1987.

SOLOMOS SOLOMOU

BYZANTINE EMPIRE. The territory of the early Byzantine Empire encompassed Asia Minor, Syria, Palestine, Egypt, and the Balkans south of the Danube. Following Justinian's military campaigns in the sixth century CE, North Africa and southern Italy were brought under Byzantine control. Domination of the eastern Mediterranean ensured favorable conditions for the transfer of goods. Constantinople was the prime beneficiary. Demand from the capital, including the requirements of the imperial court and bureaucracy, the ecclesiastical hierarchy, the senatorial aristocracy, and an incalculable number of traders, craftsmen and laborers, made Constantinople the most important market in the eastern Mediterranean. Its population may have reached, at a rough estimate, some 400,000. It could not be sustained without special measures to provision the city, so the state organized regular shipments of grain from Egypt to Constantinople. Many other cities around the eastern Mediterranean experienced considerable prosperity during the fifth and sixth centuries, and the villages of Greece, Asia Minor, Syria, and Palestine became densely settled. In places with convenient access to large markets, there was scope for agricultural specialization, for example, the concentration on the cultivation of olives in some villages of northern Syria.

The strong imprint of the state on economic life must be emphasized. Coins produced at imperial mints were put into circulation through imperial expenditure, mainly by payments to the army and imperial officials. Revenues flowed regularly from the provinces back to Constantinople through the system of land taxation. Monetary and fiscal structures were based on a gold coin with a consistently high level of fineness. Taxation was generally demanded in gold and change given in low-value coinage. The state's exactions also included a range of obligations in kind, and in regions where there was serious military activity, these exactions had a severe impact on the resources of the local population.

Byzantine territory contracted sharply in the seventh century, when the Arabs conquered Egypt, Palestine, Syria, and North Africa, and the Slavs settled in large parts of the Balkan provinces. Byzantine territories in Asia Minor and Greece were affected by military campaigns. Most towns contracted sharply both in size and in the range of occupational specialization. The main area of expenditure in seventh- and eighth-century towns was the construction of fortifications. Rural society was also affected adversely by the difficult economic conditions, and the number of rural settlements declined sharply. The resources available to the state were reduced, and as provincial mints closed, leaving monetary production concentrated in Constantinople, the quantity of money in circulation declined. There was a greater emphasis on taxation in kind when compared with the fifth and sixth centuries.

Recovery from the economic contraction of the seventh and eighth centuries was a protracted process. Early signs of revival can be detected in the ninth and tenth centuries, and from the eleventh century there was a substantial increase in activity in all sectors of the economy. Similar economic progress and demographic growth can also be found in Catholic western Europe; and, indeed, this Byzantine revival was sustained more consistently in the European provinces. The expansion of rural settlements in Macedonia from the tenth century can be traced in archival documents. Independent peasants, who owned their own land and paid the land tax directly to the state, became a smaller part of the rural population. The majority of peasants rented land from either the state or large landowners. Income from imperial estates had become a more important source of revenue than the land tax by the twelfth century. Privileged landowners received concessions from the state entitling them to establish peasant households on their estates with exemptions from a range of fiscal obligations, on condition that the peasants were not already paying taxes or rents to the state. Regular fiscal reassessments were carried out to enforce the state's claims. The main importance of the grants of privileges was to protect landowners from an intensification of fiscal obligations as the peasant population on their estates increased. There was a substantial growth in the rural population of Macedonia between the tenth and early fourteenth centuries, and both landowners and the state benefited from the resulting increase in revenues.

The documentary evidence from Macedonia is complemented by the results of intensive archaeological surveys in other parts of Greece, which show a consistent pattern of expansion of rural settlements from the eleventh century. Agricultural production increased mainly through the greater availability of labor, but there is evidence of considerable expenditure on agricultural improvements by wealthy landowners. Some were involved in the creation of new settlements, but more usually money was spent on irrigation and the planting of vines and olives by landowners whose boats could ship the produce to large markets, especially Constantinople.

Expansion in the rural economy was accompanied by an urban revival and an increase in the quantity of money in circulation between the tenth and twelfth centuries.

Outside Constantinople, information from written sources is scanty, and historians are dependent on archaeological evidence to provide a framework of economic development. Urban settlements became more densely populated with a greater variety of crafts production and commercial activity. This was again most pronounced in the European provinces. In cities like Thessaloníki, Adrianople (present-day Edirne), and Thebes, the imperial and ecclesiastical bureaucracies stimulated demand. Thebes became the most important industrial center after Constantinople. It was famous for the high quality of its silk manufactures, a craft in which the city's substantial Jewish population was actively involved. Production in other cities like Corinth and Athens was, in contrast, geared to meeting local demands, although Corinth had considerable importance as an outlet for the produce of its region and as an administrative center. More intensive production in the rural economy stimulated economic activity in the towns of the European provinces of the empire in the twelfth century.

In Asia Minor, the economic pattern was more uneven. Economic revival in the tenth and eleventh centuries was interrupted by military instability after the Seljuk Turks occupied a large part of Asia Minor in the late eleventh century. Conditions became more unfavorable for economic activity in both town and country. The strengthening of Byzantine authority in western Asia Minor during the twelfth century and, especially, the establishment of the empire of Nicaea after the sack of Constantinople by the Fourth Crusade provided a platform for economic expansion. A growing population contributed to a more effective exploitation of agricultural resources, and the towns, especially Smyrna, prospered for much of the thirteenth century, until the region came increasingly under Ottoman Turkish domination toward the end of the century.

The coinage was debased substantially in the eleventh century. By the early 1080s, the gold nomisma was worth less than one-third of its original value. Its fineness was largely, but not entirely, restored in 1092 by Alexios I Komnenos, whose monetary reform created a more flexible system, better suited to commercial exchange. The new arrangement proved stable during the twelfth century. But the coinage was debased steadily from the thirteenth century, and the gold nomisma disappeared, except as a term of account, during the fourteenth century.

Different interpretations have been advanced to explain the debasement of the eleventh century. Although it is generally agreed that the acceleration of the process in the 1070s and 1080s was the result of a current budgetary deficit, the first phase of debasement has been explained in the same fiscal terms. But whether or not the state actually sought to promote economic expansion by increasing the money supply through such coin debasements cannot be ascertained; such theories seem to be anachronistic.

From the late eleventh century, the commercial activities of the Italian maritime republics in Byzantium increased significantly. The legal framework for this expansion was provided by the privileges granted to Venice, Pisa, and Genoa by successive emperors. In 1082, Alexios I granted the Venetians the right to trade in the empire without any obligation to pay the tax on commercial transactions. The Pisans and Genoese subsequently received less comprehensive privileges. Apart from Constantinople, the towns most regularly frequented by Venetian merchants were Corinth, Sparta, Thebes, and Almyrós. Primary produce, especially oil, was purchased and resold in Constantinople and Alexandria. Attempts by emperors to restrict the scope of the privileges proved unsuccessful because of the greater naval power of the Venetians.

Differing views have been expressed about the impact of the Italian traders on the Byzantine economy. The old view is that their trade grew at the expense of Byzantine rivals, damaging the economy. More recently, it has been suggested that their presence led to an increase in demand that benefited Byzantine landowners and peasants. Hendy has argued that the extent of Italian commerce in Byzantium has been exaggerated and that the total value of Venetian property in the empire in the later twelfth century was less than the wealth of a single Byzantine aristocrat.

After the soldiers of the Fourth Crusade sacked Constantinople in 1204 and installed a Latin emperor, Italian economic power increased substantially. Venice obtained control of a number of ports and islands, notably Crete, which were of great strategic value for the protection and development of its commerce. Venetians and the Genoese extended their commercial activities into the Black Sea, which they had not entered before the Fourth Crusade. Even after the restoration of Byzantine rule in Constantinople in 1261, the Venetians and Genoese played a dominant role in the commercial life of the capital. Although Byzantine merchants can be found in business partnerships with the Italians, the most lucrative areas of trade remained firmly under Italian control.

By 1300, the empire had lost control over Asia Minor, apart from a few isolated outposts. It still retained a substantial territorial base in Europe, where settlements were densely populated in the early fourteenth century, but imperial revenues were restricted by the extensive privileges that large landowners received. The flow of revenues to the state and to landowners was also reduced by a number of factors during the fourteenth century. Landownership was disrupted by the Serbian occupation of much of Macedonia in the middle of the century. Some landowners who had contacts with the Serbian monarch were able to retain their properties, but others lost theirs and had great difficulty in recovering them after the region was restored to Byzantine control. The Ottoman advance into Europe in the second half of the fourteenth century made conditions in the rural economy much more precarious. Demographic decline following the Black Death had a devastating impact on landowners' revenues, although the Byzantine evidence is less comprehensive than that for the medieval West. Numerous abandoned peasant holdings on monastic properties on the island of Lemnos were recorded in the 1350s and 1360s. Evidence for Macedonian lands belonging to the monasteries of Mount Athos suggests that between 1321 and 1409 the peasant population had fallen by about 80 percent. This reduction might have been aggravated by political and military factors, as peasants sought greater security in territory controlled by the Ottomans. As the Ottomans' pressure on Constantinople and Thessaloníki increased, conditions on the land still controlled by the Byzantines became more difficult, and productive agriculture was almost impossible. By the early fifteenth century, those who owned land inside the walls of these cities gained considerable opportunities from high levels of demand, and complaints of profiteering proliferated. Economic conditions remained unfavorable until the fall of the empire in 1453, when the stability provided by the Ottomans facilitated a revival of economic activity.

BIBLIOGRAPHY

Angold, Michael. *A Byzantine Government in Exile: Government and Society under the Laskarids of Nicaea, 1204–1261*. Oxford, 1975.

Cameron, Averil. *The Mediterranean World in Late Antiquity, AD 395–600*. London, 1993.

Haldon, John F. *Byzantium in the Seventh Century: The Transformation of a Culture*. rev. ed. Cambridge, 1997.

Harvey, Alan. *Economic Expansion in the Byzantine Empire, 900–1200*. Cambridge, 1990.

Hendy, Michael F. *Studies in the Byzantine Monetary Economy, c. 300–1450*. Cambridge, 1985.

Laiou-Thomadakis, A. E. *Peasant Society in the Late Byzantine Empire: A Social and Demographic Study*. Princeton, 1977.

Laiou-Thomadakis, A. E. "The Byzantine Economy in the Mediterranean Trade System: Thirteenth–Fifteenth Centuries." *Dumbarton Oaks Papers* 34/35 (1980–1981), 177–222.

ALAN HARVEY

C

CADBURY FAMILY. A family of Quaker manufacturers and philanthropists based in Bournville, Birmingham, England, the Cadburys have been active in the confectionery trades since the early nineteenth century, trading for much of their history as Cadbury Brothers. A series of twentieth-century mergers and acqusitions, notably with Fry's in 1919 and Schweppes in 1969, produced Cadbury-Schweppes, one of the largest blue-chip companies in the United Kingdom and the market leader in chocolate production, with a number of well-established brands. The Cadbury family has achieved household-name status in cocoa and chocolate products, but also is associated with ethical business practices, a highly developed welfare policy toward its factory workforce, and the creation of a model factory suburb in Bournville with a workers' housing association (the Bournville Village Trust). The firm has been a leading innovator in shop-floor participation through Works Councils, quality control, imaginative branding and marketing, early adoption and adaptation of continuous-process production techniques, and introduction of computer-based production, warehousing, and distribution.

Cadbury's confectionery business was originated by John Cadbury (1801–1899) in 1824 from a shop selling teas and cocoa products in Bull Street, Birmingham. By the 1850s, the firm had become a manufacturer in its own right and acquired a Royal Appointment to Queen Victoria; but in 1861, when the business was turned over to John's sons Richard (1835–1899) and George (1839–1922), it was close to bankruptcy. The brothers diversified the product range and embarked on a more aggressive marketing strategy, at the same time engaging in more direct control of the manufacturing process and producing a highly regarded unadulterated type of cocoa known as cocoa essence. The success of these innovations enabled Cadbury Brothers to move their operations to the famous "factory in a garden" at Bournville, then a rural district outside Birmingham, in 1879.

The striking success of Cadbury's after 1879 was closely linked with improving urban living standards, which saw cocoa consumption rise from 523,000 pounds in the 1820s to 22.5 million pounds by 1894. Cocoa consumption also had been associated with the temperance movement, which the Cadburys, as Quakers, firmly embraced, and no public houses (taverns) were allowed on the Bournville estate. Cadbury's selling proposition was based on high-quality, accurate measure and the use of unadulterated dairy products in manufacture. The firm introduced a corps of factory record clerks, known as "check-weighers," who exercised close control of the production process, and Cadbury chocolates acquired an unrivaled reputation for quality. In the interwar period following the merger with Fry's, the firm established production in Australia, Canada, South Africa, and Ireland. It also had diversified interests in the West African cocoa trades. Its product range came to be associated with the British Empire and was somewhat less successful in continental Europe and the United States.

After World War II, the Cadbury business gradually ceased to function as a family firm and mutated into a large corporation, particularly following the merger with Schweppes in 1969. By then the firm was clearly undercapitalized, and a takeover or a merger was inevitable. The new arrangements saw for the first time a non-Cadbury chairman of the business, Lord Watkinson. However, the family, although now only a minority shareholder, has produced two subsequent chairmen of the business, Adrian Cadbury (b. 1929, managing director, 1969–1974, chairman, 1975–1989) and Dominic (b. 1940, chairman, 1993–2000). In the 1980s, and 1990s, Cadbury-Schweppes made a number of acquisitions in the food, drink, and retail sectors, although many of them were later divested. The firm sold its U.S.-based confectionery manufacture to Hershey in 1988, but was at the same time able to acquire holding interests in French and Spanish chocolate firms. Although the firm is part of a large, variegated business in the food trades, including teas, soft drinks, and instant mashed potatoes, the "Cadbury" brand name is now reserved exclusively for chocolate products.

In social history, family members are as well known for their philanthropic work as their industrial activities. The Bournville factory estate became a model of social housing and was made an independent trust in 1900. Through the Bournville Day Continuation Schools, established in the 1920s, a comprehensive system of day-release classes for younger employees was established. The wife of George Cadbury, Elizabeth (1858–1951), was a driving force behind these educational initiatives. Richard Cadbury's daughter, Beatrice Cadbury Boeke (1884–1976), through her collaboration with the Dutch socialist-educationalist Cornelius Boeke, played a leading role in the development of working class education in England and the Netherlands. The Bournville buildings and facilities, including swimming pools for employees, schools, and a medieval-style village green, are much admired by conservationists. The family took some interest in politics and acquired the London *News Chronicle* in 1901, but sold its newspaper interests after World War II.

BIBLIOGRAPHY

Chinn, Carl. *The Cadbury Story: A Short History.* Studley, U.K., 1998.

Crosfield, John F. *The Cadbury Family.* 2 vols. Cambridge, 1985. A genealogical survey only.

Evans, D. Wyn. "Catalogue of the Cadbury Papers." University Library, Birmingham, 1973. Although there is no satisfactory history of the Cadbury business interests, substantial archives exist, such as this one.

Gardiner, Alfred G. *The Life of George Cadbury.* London, 1923.

Williams, Iolo A. *The Firm of Cadbury, 1831–1931.* London, 1931.

MARK STEELE

CALCUTTA, city in eastern India, the capital of the state of West Bengal, located on the east bank of the River Hooghly, about 80 miles (128 kilometers) upstream from the head of the Bay of Bengal, with a population of some 4.4 million as of the census of 1991. A city of commerce and manufacture, it is the second largest (after Bombay) in India and the dominant urban center of eastern India. In 1690, Job Charnock, an agent of the British East India Company, moved the company's headquarters in Bengal from the town of Hooghly to the village of Sutanati, which together with the neighboring villages of Govindpur and Dihi-Kalkatta eventually became part of Calcutta. The city's fortunes changed in the mid-eighteenth century when, in 1756, Siraj-ud-Daula's Mogul forces captured it. The following year the British retook Calcutta and, when the *nawab* (governor) had been overthrown after the battle of Plassey in June 1757, the city's political importance was changed considerably. The company was granted *diwani* (revenue collection and administrative) rights in the province in 1765, and the administrative machinery for the government of Bengal was moved to Calcutta in 1772. In 1773, Calcutta was recognized by Act of Parliament in London as the seat of colonial government for supreme authority over British India.

As British power was extended over the subcontinent, the whole of northern India became a supplier for the port of Calcutta. The construction of railways begun in the 1850s further quickened the tempo of business life in the city. Eastern India in general and Calcutta in particular became a British business enclave, with colonial managing agencies exercising total control over the three major industries of the region—jute mills, tea plantations, and collieries (coal mines and associated buildings). Starting in the 1920s and intensifying in the 1930s and the 1940s, there was also substantial Indian entrepreneurship in Calcutta, which developed new industries as well as some in which Europeans had predominated, notably jute mills

CALCUTTA. City scene, 1984. (© Dilip Mehta/Woodfin Camp and Associates, New York)

and collieries. Much of this was due to the Marwari community, originally from Rajasthan, who set up new firms and steadily bought shares of many European companies until they were poised to take over such firms. Perhaps the most important index of the emergence of Indian entrepreneurship, not merely in jute and coal but also other industries, was the founding of the Indian Chamber of Commerce, which under G. D. Birla's initiative was set up in 1926. It was to "speak for Indian business and political interests" and became the rival of the Bengal Chamber of Commerce, then controlled by the European managing agencies.

The commercial importance of Calcutta has continued since India's independence in 1947. The Calcutta port remains one of the most important in the country. The city is an important center for banking and finance; in 1991, there were some 715 banks. The Calcutta stock exchange plays an important part in India's financial market. Among the principal commodities manufactured in the city are engineering goods, electrical goods, and chemicals. Problems of labor unrest, however, pose a threat to the city's industrial future.

BIBLIOGRAPHY

Census of India, New Delhi, 1991. Series 26, West Bengal, *District Census Handbook*, part XIIA and XIIB, *Calcutta Metropolitan District*, Calcutta, 1997.

Goswami, Omkar. "Sahibs, Babus, and Banias: Changes in Industrial Control in Eastern India, 1918–50." *Journal of Asian Studies* 48 (1989), 289–309.

Prakash, Om. "European Commerical Enterprise in Precolonial India." In the *New Cambridge History of India*, vol. 2.5. Cambridge, 1998.

OM PRAKASH

CAMPBELL, JOSEPH (died 1900), canning entrepreneur, who founded a company that would, under the guidance of Arthur and John Dorrance, become a dominant U.S. prepared-foods firm.

In 1869, New Jerseyian Joseph Campbell, who had been a purchasing agent for a fruit-and-vegetable wholesaler, became a partner in Abraham Anderson's canning business in Camden. They canned vegetables, jams, mincemeat, various condiments, and, for a time in the 1870s, even chicken soup. Wanting to expand the business, Campbell bought out his more cautious partner in 1876 and brought in two new partners, one of whom was Arthur Dorrance, a wealthy timber and flour merchant. In 1894, Dorrance succeeded Campbell as president, though Campbell continued to take an interest in the firm. With Campbell's death in 1900, the association of the Campbell family with the business that bore its name ended.

In 1897, Dorrance hired his nephew, Dr. John T. Dorrance. At this time the firm was not really different from any of the other thousands of canneries in the area; but

Dr. Dorrance, who had trained as a chemist at the Massachusetts Institute of Technology and held a doctorate from the University of Göttingen, gave it a new focus. During his European training, Dorrance had acquired a fondness for having soup at meals; and he convinced his uncle to give him space for a laboratory to perfect a method of canning soup. Already sold in limited quantities in America, canned soup was expensive to ship because of its high water content. Dorrance used his training in experimental chemistry to develop industrial methods of producing condensed soups. Condensing the soup reduced the weight of the finished product, and so lowered its final cost to the consumer from thirty-five cents to ten cents a can. An equally important innovation was Dorrance's marketing method. Previously, producers had relied upon wholesalers to distribute and "brand" their goods. The Campbell's sales offices took over this function and dealt directly with retailers—a necessary step, as condensed soup was a "new" product, and canned soup had never had mass appeal. Demand had to be created. Consumers were persuaded to try the product by roving demonstrators and advertising.

Campbell's advertising effort was innovative in volume and technique. By 1920, the advertising budget had grown to $1 million, or 5 percent of total sales, an astounding amount by contemporary standards. Further, the company was the first to develop nationally recognized brand icons. The sweet, round-faced "Campbell Kids," who were to appear on advertisements for the company through the 1930s, first appeared in 1904. They appealed to people looking for a nutritious and economical product, and were instrumental in giving the firm a recognizable brand identity. Alfred Chandler argues that a combination of brand loyalty and established distribution channels allowed Campbell's and other mass producers of consumer goods to continue to dominate their respective industries for decades, despite the relatively low cost of their capital equipment and the ease with which competitors could copy their products.

BIBLIOGRAPHY

Chandler, Alfred. *The Visible Hand*. Cambridge, Mass., 1977.

Collins, Douglas. *America's Favorite Food: The Story of Campbell Soup Company*. New York, 1994.

SUSAN WOLCOTT

CANADA, country in North America that is the second largest in the world, occupying all the territory east of Alaska and north of the United States, including adjacent islands of the Arctic Archipelago. Newfoundland and the eastern seaboard were claimed for England by John Cabot in 1497; the Gaspé Peninsula and Saint Lawrence estuary were claimed for France by Jacques Cartier in 1524. The

French settled in 1605 and fur traders, explorers, and missionaries to the Native Americans became part of the French colonial expansion of the seventeenth and eighteenth centuries. The French established trading posts on the Bay of Fundy in 1605 and at Quebec on the Saint Lawrence River in 1608. Around the former trading post grew a small isolated settlement of subsistence farmers—the Acadians. Quebec was the more important settlement, but it functioned for its first fifty years merely as the trading post of a commercial venture into the New World. In this respect, Quebec closely paralleled English trading ventures in America; however, while to the south in the British colonies of New England and Virginia, substantial settlement was taking place, the Quebec colony attracted a mere handful of settlers. The longstanding population ratio of about one-tenth as many people in Canada as in what became the United States was established from the earliest years. Quebec was essentially concerned with the trade in furs, especially with beaver pelts to be used in Europe for making felt, a pressed and matted fabric that incorporates fine hairs. The aboriginal population produced the furs; the French merely traded, and that did not support a large, growing colony as agriculture might have.

The trading post at Quebec attracted a few supporting settlers, but as a commercial venture it faltered and, in 1663, was taken over as the Crown Colony of New France. Under the intendency of Jean Talon, the settlement was transformed into a more substantial colony; new settlers were brought in, and steps were taken to diversify the economy. That marked the beginning of a real settler economy in Canada. Land was granted, along feudal lines, to *seigneurs*, who had the responsibility of settling their tracts with *censitaires*. Settlers came from France on a contract basis. Soldiers brought in to defend the colony against the Iroquois were disbanded as settlers. To provide wives, young women were sent from the royal orphanages of France. The population increased rapidly, since these early colonists reproduced at the highest possible rates. By the beginning of the eighteenth century, France's Quebec colony had become an agricultural community that produced a range of crafts to support demand for a variety of nonagricultural goods. The urban, commercial, and craft component of Quebec's economy was, most probably, somewhat larger than in the British colonies to the south.

The fur trade remained the heart of Quebec's colonial economy. To provide an ever-expanding supply of beaver pelts, especially the *castor gras* (pelts worn long enough to have the coarse guard hairs rubbed off), the French were impelled to push farther into the interior. Thus, this small colony took the lead in exploring the lands to the west and south, and it laid claim for France to a huge area of North America. Competition for furs came from the British in two directions. The British settlers to the south, centered on Albany, also pushed their trade westward. After 1670, the British Hudson's Bay Company established trading posts to the north and west, thereby providing strong competition on that front. In addition to their competition with the British for furs, the French had to defend themselves continuously against the Iroquois—that raised the cost of operating the colony and constrained settlement to the near confines of the Saint Lawrence Valley.

In the meantime, the small French settlement on the Bay of Fundy had grown in numbers and was a relatively prosperous subsistence agricultural community, ingeniously using dikes to exploit the rich tidal marshes of the bay. Acadia, as this settlement was called, came under British rule in 1713. In 1755, because of worries over disloyalty to the British Crown as war loomed with France, the Acadians were rounded up and dispersed to colonies to the south. British New Englanders moved in to take over the established farms. Shortly before that, for strategic reasons, the British had established a new settlement at Halifax, to take advantage of the great harbor on the southeast coast of Nova Scotia. With additional Swiss and German settlers, as well as British, a new colonial economy was established in Nova Scotia.

In the first half of the eighteenth century, New France had developed primarily as a self-sufficient agricultural economy, yet no agricultural staple export was established. Tobacco could be grown, but it was not promoted as a colonial product. For a few years, the economy gained from provisioning the French fortress at Louisbourg on Cape Breton Island. Land in Canada was more abundant and the peasants became more prosperous than those in France. Still, that was not enough to attract many more settlers from the mother country. During French rule, no more than ten thousand people ever moved from France to Canada. They nevertheless reproduced with great rapidity. When the war erupted (called the French and Indian War by the British colonists and the Seven Years' War in Europe), Quebec fell to Britain. From 1763 onward, Canada became a part of the British Empire. Britain had acquired a largely agricultural economy of about seventy thousand inhabitants, thinly strung out along the valley of the Saint Lawrence River, with two prominent urban centers of about equal size—Quebec City, the Atlantic port and administrative center, and Montreal to its southwest, which would become the commercial center of the colony.

Under British Rule. Shortly after Canada came under British rule, the American Revolution brought a major shock and new settlers to Canada and the Maritime colonies. English-speaking Empire Loyalists, displaced from the newly established United States, suddenly increased Canada's population by about 30 percent. Most went to Nova Scotia, and the greatest portion settled on the west bank of the Bay of Fundy, in the Saint John River

Valley. There they gained recognition as a separate colony, New Brunswick. Others, including a number of blacks, remained in Nova Scotia. Together, they gave a substantial boost to the population of those colonies. A smaller fraction of Loyalists settled in Quebec, mainly along the upper Saint Lawrence, to the west of the existing French settlement; they immediately demanded British laws and institutions—met in 1791 by the partition of Canada into two separate colonies, Upper Canada and Lower Canada.

In addition to the four colonies (New Brunswick, Nova Scotia, Upper Canada, and Lower Canada), Prince Edward Island had been granted to a handful of British absentee landlords as a separate colony. A steady stream of migrants from Britain then arrived to augment the Maritime colonies while the Canadas continued to welcome land-seeking settlers from the United States. The British North American (BNA) colonies offered cheap land and integration into the British mercantile system. In the late 1700s, wheat, grown mostly in Lower Canada, was being exported to Britain, where prices were then at an all-time high. Nova Scotians were developing a trade in shipping to the West Indies. The fur trade, now in British hands, continued to be pursued vigorously from a headquarters in Montreal (although Americans competed from New York to the Pacific, especially John Jacob Astor, after the U.S. purchase of the Louisiana Territory from France in 1803). The most important trade, however, developed as a consequence of Britain's war with Napoleon in the early 1800s. By imposing high duties on European timber, Britain deliberately switched its source of supply to its North American colonies. With an abundance of Canadian standing pine (that high transport costs had made it unprofitable to exploit), the trade in squared pine timber soon expanded. By 1820, Canada had become the dominant supplier to the British market. New Brunswick, centered on its main port city of Saint John, became the foremost timber colony, but Canada also engaged in cutting and shipping timber. For most of the 1800s, wood exports continued to be the driving force of the Canadian economy. In the early 1830s, per capita timber exports were three times the value of U.S. per capita cotton exports.

In the early 1800s, Canada was still a largely subsistence agricultural economy, although one that offered several advantages. First, there was an abundance of good farm land; a second, there was an excellent internal transport system—a waterway. The entire settlement stretched in a thin band along the Saint Lawrence River and the Great Lakes of Ontario and Erie. This superb waterway provided Canada with the lowest transport costs to be found in the world. Overland hauls to the water were short and were aided by cold winters—with firm ground for wagons or, most often, snow cover for sleighs. A further advantage was the easy movement of people, publications, and ideas

between Canada and both Britain and the United States; for example, in the early 1800s Canadians quickly adopted American inventor Oliver Evans's improved flour mills, and they initiated steam navigation on the Saint Lawrence very shortly after Robert Fulton showed its commercial feasibility on the Hudson River in 1807. There were disadvantages faced by Canadians as well: Indian corn (maize), the most efficient feed crop, could not reliably be ripened. The settlement was excessively dispersed and low in density. But the chief limitation was the restricted ability to export wheat to Britain. After the high prices for wheat during the Napoleanic war period came to an end and Britain reimposed the Corn Laws, it was generally unprofitable to export wheat from Canada. A few good years offered glimmers of hope, and Upper Canada was able to specialize in the production of wheat to sell to Lower Canada, which had revenues from timber sales.

Canadians lobbied Britain, eventually with success, for exemption from the provisions of the Corn Laws, and they further reduced internal transport costs by investing heavily in canals: the Welland Canal, to skirt the Falls at Niagara, and the Lachine Canal, to bypass rapids above Montreal, both built in the 1820s. By 1848, Canada had completed a system of canals that allowed lake schooners and steamers freely to navigate the Great Lakes–Saint Lawrence system. Toward 1850, Canada's situation changed dramatically and modern economic growth clearly got underway. There were several elements to this change. First, there was a boom in wheat and flour exports, as commercial wheat farming began to pay. Exports of forest products also grew, as the British market for timber expanded and an export trade in pine boards was begun to the United States. From the 1842 reduction of the Timber Duty, Canadian sawmill operators found the U.S. market increasingly profitable, despite a relatively high tariff there on sawn boards. In 1854, a U.S.–Canada agreement provided for reciprocal free trade in raw products (defined to include milled flour and sawn boards). Canadian exports to the United States boomed at the same time as the market in Britain was especially strong. With open access to the U.S. market, Canadians found profitable opportunities in a wider range of agricultural products, including butter, hay, malting barley, feeder cattle, and horses.

This period was also Canada's first major era of railway building. In 1850, Canada possessed only one short rail line; by 1860, there was a substantial network of railways. The most ambitious was the Grand Trunk Railway of Canada, the longest single railway in the world when completed in 1859, and incorporating one of the great early railway bridges over the Saint Lawrence at Montreal; however, the Grand Trunk had been built parallel to the world's best inland waterway. The railway failed to generate enough traffic to be even close to profitable and was

QUEBEC. Advertising poster for the Canadian Pacific Railway, early 1900s. (Prints and Photographs Division, Library of Congress)

major center of the sawmill industry, built around a massive hydraulic power site.

The Canadian Federation. In 1867, the colony of Canada formed a political and economic union with the two maritime colonies of New Brunswick and Nova Scotia and became the Dominion of Canada. A third maritime colony, Prince Edward Island joined the federation in 1873. The people of BNA were attempting to forge an economic future. Land suitable for agriculture had just about run out, population was growing rapidly, and Canadians had begun to emigrate to the United States in large numbers—the dynamic seemed to have run out of the economy. The economic objectives of the Canadian Confederation were to create a larger and more closely integrated economy out of the several disparate colonies, to expand the nation by acquiring a huge territory of land where a new agricultural frontier might be created, and to promote industrialization using protectionist measures. The model of the United States, with a continuously moving agricultural frontier and a vigorously expanding industrial sector, was clearly in mind. The great land mass to the north and west was acquired from the Hudson's Bay Company; a new province of Manitoba was established in 1870 and two British colonies on the Pacific coast were induced to join the federation as the province of British Columbia in 1871. That completed the formation of Canada "from sea to sea." Provision was then made for freely granted homesteads in Manitoba and the Northwest Territories, and plans were made for a transcontinental railway to British Columbia. First, however, as part of the Confederation arrangement, a long and costly railway had to be built to link the central provinces of Canada with Nova Scotia on the Atlantic. That was done as a government enterprise.

Initially, economic development did not work out as hoped for. The depression of the 1870s was severe. The short-run boom, associated with investment in the construction of the Intercolonial Railway to the maritime provinces, ended just as the world economy was falling into depression; the western frontier failed to attract many settlers; arrangements ended for the railway to the Pacific. Industrialization for export had been blocked by high tariffs in the United States after the Civil War, and exports of agricultural products were restricted. Canadians continued to emigrate to the United States in large numbers. The economic prospects of the new Canadian federation looked bleak until 1879, when a policy was begun of fostering industrialization for the home market behind a high tariff, but had meager effect. Also in 1879, railway access to Manitoba, via the United States, brought a surge of settlement to that western province; it was short-lived because world wheat prices declined and several years of adverse climate conditions drew attention to the shortcomings of the Canadian west as a region of settlement.

rescued from bankruptcy only by the government of Canada, which took on a huge debt to meet the bond interest guarantees. Other, more sensible, railways were built from lake- and riverfront into the hinterland. Railway construction imparted a short-run boost to Canada's economy that reinforced the impression of the 1850s as a decade of prosperity.

During the 1850s, Canada's manufacturing sector was notably broadened, with the first steps taken in becoming an industrialized economy. Shipbuilding at Quebec and in the Maritime colonies was a major industry. Foundries, machine shops, and railway engine and rolling stock factories were established, and agricultural implements were manufactured in many locations. Sawmilling, traditionally the foremost industry of the economy, was shifted to large-scale plants, still mostly water powered, producing standard-dimension boards (deals) for export. Bytown (later, as Ottawa, to become the capital) emerged as a

In 1883, the Canadian Pacific Railway was completed, from the lakehead at Thunder Bay on Lake Superior to Winnipeg and the western plains; the entire road from Montreal to British Columbia was finished in 1885. A private enterprise, undertaken with an enormous subsidy, it provided the rail link essential to opening the Canadian west. Still, the settlers did not come, and Canadians continued to emigrate. Western settlement required the development of a technology for producing wheat in a region that was otherwise too arid—although accomplished by about 1890, the years immediately following were marked by especially unfavorable wheat prices. A cattle-ranching industry was established in the 1880s, and cattle raised in the foothills of the Canadian cordillera were exported to Britain. Manitoba eventually became known on world markets as a producer of high-quality hard wheat.

The late 1890s marked a pronounced turnaround of the Canadian economy. From 1896 until the outbreak of World War I in 1914, Canada experienced its most rapid and dramatic economic development. The growth of real per capita income averaged 3.6 percent annually. Much of the historical literature has attributed this to the settlement of the Canadian plains, the establishment there of an export wheat economy, and its secondary effects throughout the rest of the national economy. It seemed, finally, to be a vindication of the original Confederation plan. The settlement of western Canada did get underway, although at first in a relatively modest way, but the pace accelerated after 1905. From 1909 to 1913, Canada was receiving huge numbers of immigrants, many of them seeking free homestead land in the west. The emigration of Canadians to the United States slowed, with people going to western Canada instead. Americans also moved into the Canadian west, contributing almost one-third of all the settlers to the area. Branch railway lines were built throughout the plains area, and a network of towns and villages was rapidly put in place. New provinces of Alberta and Saskatchewan were established in 1905. Wheat acreage was expanded rapidly and, by the eve of World War I, Canada had emerged as one of the world's leading wheat exporters. During the same period, Canadian manufacturing expanded and urban centers grew rapidly—so the country became more urbanized at the same time that it extended its agricultural sector.

The extent to which this great burst of economic growth can be attributed to western settlement and the establishment of the "wheat economy" has been controversial among economic historians. Canada had experienced a full decade of unusually rapid growth from 1896 to 1907, before western settlement had much impact—and an alternative source of economic development needs to be emphasized. By the late 1890s, rapid industrialization was underway, independent of the influences of western settlement. There were two

elements: first was the technology of the Second Industrial Revolution; second was the maturing of several agricultural processing industries in central Canada (making butter, cheese, and cured pork for the British market). The most important constituents of Second Industrial Revolution technology were steel, chemical processes, and electricity; the largest and most direct impact on Canada came from steel. In the nineteenth century, Canadians had been unable to establish a coke-fueled iron industry, for want of either coal or iron ore, but in the last years of the century a modern steel industry was built with plants at three locations. Contrary to the view expressed by many Canadian economic historians, this was not a development induced by railway building in the west but was a more independent development, and it formed the single largest element in the vigorous Canadian industrialization of the time. Canada also made effective use of the chemical processes that were a prominent feature of late-nineteenth-century technology. The chemical production of paper from wood pulp was the most outstanding development, and it required large-scale production of such chemical agents as acids and alkalis. Electrolytic processes were also prominent, and such products as aluminum and carborundum played a central role. Then there was electricity—which soon pervaded all aspects of the economy. Canada electrified early and made effective use of its abundant hydraulic power sites to produce cheap electricity.

Canada's exploitation of the new technology of the Second Industrial Revolution, which imparted an accelerated economic growth, does not entirely explain why Canada grew more rapidly than some other countries with the same technological boost. Along with this major development, Canada got further benefits; in the late 1800s, Canada promoted exports from the agricultural production of central Canada. First and foremost was factory cheese. Canadians had been neither consumers nor producers of cheese, but a large market existed in Britain. In the 1860s, the technology of producing cheese in small local factories, built around a skilled cheesemaker, had been imported from upstate New York. By the 1870s, a successful export industry in a nonindigenous product had been developed. By the mid-1890s, it was important enough to have a perceptible aggregate effect. In the mid-1890s, cheese was the leading single commodity exported. Factory butter making was begun in the 1890s, and that industry also produced for the export trade, as did large-scale pork packing, which was established from the outset as an export industry to provide the British market with bacon.

From 1905 to 1914, settlers moved onto Canada's western plains and basically completed the settlement process. A great inflow of foreign capital occurred at the same time, which financed the railways and western urban infrastructure. Urbanization was especially rapid, with new cities in

the west; in central Canada, the leading cities of Montreal and Toronto grew substantially. By 1914, the many immigrants had made Canada's population increase by 46 percent, from 5.4 million in 1901 to 7.9 million. World War I had a severe impact on the Canadian economy. Canada's direct war effort was huge for its size. The military absorbed 600,000 men, more than 30 percent of those eighteen to forty-five in the census of 1911. About 60,000 died and many others returned injured and incapacitated from poisonous gases used at the front. During the war, capital accumulation dropped precipitously, as resources were redirected to unproductive war purposes. Real per capita income declined and until 1925 did not reattain its 1913 level—75 percent of that of the United States—an increase from the 60 percent level in the early 1870s. As a result of the war and postwar readjustment, Canadian living standards by the early 1920s had returned to 60 percent of the U.S. level. The one bright spot in the wartime economy was a large increase in wheat exports; however, following the ebullient settlement years just before the war, that increase led to an overexpansion of wheat production in regions too arid to sustain it. The consequence was large-scale farm abandonment in the early 1920s—greater than that of the 1930s dust-bowl conditions.

By the later 1920s, the Canadian economy had regained satisfactory growth that was chiefly led by the exploitation of the forest and the mineral resources of the Precambrian Shield. Manufacturing of paper newsprint for export, especially to the United States, and the mining and smelting of nonferrous metals led the expansion. Canada had become a leading industrial nation, and its entire range of manufacturing was growing. From 1923 to 1929, the output of Canadian manufactures rose almost three times as fast as manufacturing in the United States and Great Britain. Canada emerged in the 1920s as the second leading builder and exporter of automobiles (after the United States). The automobile industry also set the trend in another characteristic of the Canadian economy; it became dominated by branch plants of U.S. firms. Direct investment from the United States would continue to be a prominent and controversial feature of the Canadian economy for the next half century. By the 1920s, however, the economies of the Maritime provinces were lagging—the culmination of a trend that had started around the time of Confederation in 1867. Relatively isolated from the rest of the nation and stuck with small-scale enterprises, the Maritimes had not fully participated in the rapid growth of the "wheat boom" era. By the 1920s emigration from the Maritimes was so great that the region had almost no population growth for the decade. The economic problems of the Maritime provinces would continue to trouble the Canadian economy until at least the 1970s.

The Great Depression of the 1930s was severe in Canada. National income fell 30 percent from 1929 to the nadir in 1933, when unemployment averaged 24 percent; in a still largely agricultural economy—where farmers were never counted as unemployed—that was 38 percent of the nonagricultural workforce. Only the United States, of the leading industrial nations, suffered more severely. Recovery in Canada was delayed even longer than in the United States, partly because of the severity of conditions in the western agricultural region. World prices of wheat and other farm products had fallen drastically and, at the same time, the region was beset with a severe drought. Yet Canada had avoided the bank failures that were so prominent in the United States. In 1935, a central bank was established (Canada officially abandoned the gold standard in 1931, although as early as 1928 it had been violating gold-standard conditions).

In 1939, when World War II began, the Canadian economy was stimulated and brought out of the Depression. In general, the war helped the Canadian economy more than had been the case during World War I. Although Canada was in the war from the beginning, its direct involvement was proportionally smaller than it had been in World War I and there was greater long-term persistence to the many special production facilities that were established. Canada emerged from the war as one of the world's leading industrial nations; it had built up great capacity in the automotive and aircraft industries, although woodpulp paper and nonferrous metals continued to be leading sectors. Natural resources played an important role in the postwar growth of the Canadian economy—iron mines, a petroleum industry, and many hydroelectric generating projects were prominent. Large sums of capital were attracted from the United States, and a large inflow of labor—first from Europe then later from several areas of the third world—made immigration once again a major contributor to the growth of labor supply. Urbanization from the mid-1940s to the 1960s was especially rapid. At the beginning of the twenty-first century, the greater Toronto conurbation had surpassed Montreal as the leading city of the nation.

[See also American Indian Economies, *subentry on* Indigenous North American Economy.]

BIBLIOGRAPHY

Bliss, Michael. *Northern Enterprise: Five Centuries of Canadian Business*. Toronto, 1987. A very readable account of the evolution of business in Canada.

Easterbrook, William T., and Hugh G. J. Aitken. *Canadian Economic History*. 2d ed. Toronto, 1961. For many years the preeminent textbook and the quintessential presentation of the Canadian "staples interpretation," this is still useful for its detail.

Harris, R. Cole, and John Warkentin. *Canada before Confederation: A Study in Historical Geography*. New York, 1974; reprinted 1991 as Carleton Library Series 166.

McCalla, Douglas. *Planting the Province: The Economic History of Upper Canada, 1784–1870*. Toronto, 1993. An excellent account of the

early development of the most dynamic component of the Canadian economy.

McCalla, Douglas, and Michael Huberman. *Perspectives on Canadian Economic History*. 2d ed. Toronto, 1994. A good selection of useful articles from the periodical literature.

Marr, William L., and Donald G. Paterson. *Canada: An Economic History*. Toronto, 1980. The first attempt at a new and analytical economic history of the country—uneven but good on some topics.

Norrie, Kenneth, and Douglas Owram. *A History of the Canadian Economy*. 2d ed. Toronto, 1996. The most up-to-date general history of the Canadian economy.

Pomfret, Richard. *The Economic Development of Canada*. 2d ed. Scarborough, Ontario, 1993. Slender, but good on the more recent period and has a good bibliography.

Taylor, Graham D., and Peter A. Baskerville. *A Concise History of Business in Canada*. Toronto, New York, and Oxford, 1994. Not so concise at 500 pages, it is as much an economic history as just a history of business; offers a contrasting perspective and extensive references.

Urquhart, Malcolm C. *Gross National Product, Canada, 1870–1926: The Derivation of the Estimates*. Kingston and Montreal, 1993. The essential source of Canadian historical national income aggregates and their components.

Urquhart, Malcolm C., and Kenneth A. H. Buckley. *Historical Statistics of Canada*. Toronto, 1965. An indispensable compilation of statistical data. Although a more recent edition updates the data series, it leaves out some commentary and some of the earlier statistical series.

R. Marvin McInnis

CANALS. *See* Water Transportation, *subentry on* Canal Transportation.

CANTON. *See* Guangzhou (Canton).

CAPITALISM. The term *capitalism* was first used in English in 1854. The word *capital*, meaning "wealth," first appeared in 1611; Arthur Young first used the word *capitalist* in 1792.

Definition. It was the perceived importance of capital in production and growth that led to the invention of the term. The timing was no accident: when it came to giving a name to the economy and society that produced growth based primarily on laissez-faire principles, the term *capitalism* reflected the remarkable buildup of physical capital that industrialization and growth had produced. There is little doubt that contemporaries saw the highly visible evidence of factories, roads, bridges, canals, brickworks, and machinery as the most obvious and probably the most important feature of the new industrial growth economy.

In fact no term is so frequently used but so rarely defined as *capitalism*. Werner Sombart wrote in 1930, "It cannot be said that a clear-cut definition has ever been attempted" (p. 195). The term has been used differently by economists and historians. Economists take a narrow view, using it to answer questions about the determination of production, consumption, and distribution with the emphasis on the use of the market for resource allocation and of capital as a factor of production. Economists also have a precise theoretical model of an ideal form of capitalism, an economy in which all resources are privately owned and in which the market determines the allocation of all resources.

Such economies do not exist, and historians and economic historians, with broader interests than economists, use *capitalism* to describe a particular socioeconomic system in which a variety of factors, but particularly the distribution of the ownership of wealth (including human capital), determine the structures of social organization and government. They are also interested in the motivation and values in society that condition action; the opportunities that determine action and the customs and laws that restrain it; the evolution of interest groups (like trade unions), classes (loosely defined by income), voluntary associations, and political parties (which cooperate or conflict in pursuance of particular goals); and the interdependence of political, economic, and social institutions in the growth of wealth and the power of governments. Their concept of capitalism goes well beyond the market to examine more general social conditions and attempts to cope with the complexity of history.

The consequence of such differences between disciplines is disagreement and confusion, with the recognition of many types of capitalism (classified according to chronology or function), with debate about the origins of capitalism (in land or commerce), with speculation about the future of capitalism, and with the fiercest of arguments about the ills of capitalism, which are sometimes exaggerated because of the underlying anticapitalist mentality of many historians. Nevertheless, although there is no universally acceptable definition of capitalism, there is in political economy, in history, in the media, and in general discussion a broadly understood concept of capitalism based on what is perceived as the salient characteristic of all capitalist economies—the use of the market for allocation and distribution of goods and factors of production.

The Causes of Capitalism. *Capitalism* as a term leaves many questions unanswered, the most important of which is what caused capitalism? Historians have three explanations of the emergence of capitalism: first, the expansion and increasing efficiency of the market; second, the increasing accumulation of capital; and third, the change in values and motivation leading to the emergence of capitalist entrepreneurs. Put differently they are laissez-faire, industrialization and capital accumulation, and the "spirit of capitalism." Increasing trade provided the main stimulus. Geographical discoveries and the formation of European empires increasingly involved Europe and the rest of the world in mutually advantageous trade. The growth of the merchant class and the use of new financial instruments, such as double-entry bookkeeping, facilitated trade, the increasing use of the market, and capital accumulation. The most important explanation of capitalism, however, was given by the German sociologist Max Weber, who linked description with cause. To Weber the defining feature of capitalism as a unique system was its rationality in the forms of rational institutions, rational behavior, and most important "the presence of men with a rational ethic for the conduct of life" (Weber, 1961, p. 233). Rationality included a "rational organization of labour" (Weber, 1961, p. 232).

Capitalism, based on free wage labor, contrasted with other systems based on other forms of labor organization, such as slavery or serfdom. These developments led to a unitary state with "a professional administration . . . and law based on the concept of citizenship" (Weber, 1961, p. 232). The commercial instincts, with the propensity to barter and trade, were, as Adam Smith pointed out, almost universal, and the growth of commerce produced a strong economic incentive, which was translated into action by the development of institutions.

The question of definition is not resolved by considering the variety of causes that have been used to explain the development of capitalism. The literature on causes identifies the role of different variables in the explanations of economic growth. If capitalism is identified by the rise of free market economies, the rise of free market economies resulting in economic growth is explained by changes in institutions, technologies, ideologies, and population. And these are seen as interdependent. If capitalism in a particular economy is analyzed, in the case of England for example, the growth of freedoms, including economic freedom, and the limiting of the powers of government certainly promoted trade and growth. A nineteenth-century innovation was to identify a sequence of consequential stages, such as Karl Bücher's: household, town, national, and international in historical order. Other related characteristics emphasized included the rational evolution of a labor market. Maine noted the change of relationship from status to contract; Henri Sumner Pirenne stressed the importance of international, long-distance trade; George Unwin believed that increasing freedom resulted in the formation of voluntary organizations that were important in the market economy, being essential for voluntary collective action.

The Origins of Capitalism. The debate about the origins of capitalism centers on capital accumulation in two periods, the medieval period and the period leading up to the Industrial Revolution. Karl Marx, seeking the source of what he called "primitive accumulation" in the Middle Ages, found it in the dispossession of the small landowner and the consequent concentration of ownership of land, the accumulation of rent, and the powerlessness of the proletariat. This was also the view of Sombart, who after Marx and Weber was the most influential of the historians of capitalism. Sombart argued that the use of capital saved from ground rents and the entry of the holders of rents into the growing cities gave the impulse to the medieval development of capitalism. Other historians, including Pirenne and Henri Sée, argued that the capital for medieval development came from finance, commerce, and trade, especially foreign trade, particularly in Italy. From the twelfth century the essential features of capitalism—industrial enterprise, profits from trade, the provision of credit, rational commercial law—were found in the city-states of Italy. Sombart gave momentum to the search for the origins of accumulation in three related books that identified other stimuli to accumulation, including war (where costs gave scope for expanding banking and credit facilities), the demand for luxury production from the new wealthy class (which stimulated artisan production and had a demonstration effect), and the importance of the Jews, whose exclusion from many avenues of employment led to a concentration on finance.

The dramatic growth of fixed capital during the Industrial Revolution led to questions about the sources of capital and the adequacy of the supply. The answer lay in recognition of the wealth of the mercantilist economy, which made possible an important switch of resources from homes to factories, from conspicuous consumption to tools and machinery, from primitive transport to canals and surfaced roads; in the increasing sophistication of financial institutions and financial instruments; and in the development of the stock exchange. Earl J. Hamilton argued that the entry into Europe of silver from the Latin American colonies of Spain caused inflation, with wages lagging behind prices, leading to increased profits and capital accumulation. By the eighteenth century there existed both adequate wealth to finance the Industrial Revolution in England and a sophistication of financial institutions that channeled capital into more productive employment. The law merchant, using precedent and mercantile practice, gave legal security to property and person and encouraged the use of new legal instruments, including the joint stock company and the bill of exchange. Advances in science and technology were protected by patent laws that encouraged invention. The development of economics and political economy gave theoretical acceptance to laissez-faire and the removal of mercantilist restrictions on trade and industry. By the mid-nineteenth century England had a trinity of economic policies that favored capitalist growth: free trade, convertibility (the gold standard), and free factor mobility.

Capitalism and Freedom. Capitalism, however, created as well as solved problems, producing "progress" on the one hand and the need for "reform" on the other. The rapid growth of population, urbanization and its needs (for example, pure water), the increasing use of machinery (which often threatened health), the trade cycle (which caused periodic unemployment), and technological unemployment (which impoverished some historical activities, like hand-loom weaving, as new industries replaced old), and persistent poverty (which became more obvious in cities than in the countryside) led to remedial measures like the New Poor Law and the Factory Acts. Social ills, long endured, were publicized and investigated and became social problems to be solved by legislation and the establishment of a bureaucracy of control and regulation and by voluntary action. England led Europe in both economic growth and liberal reform, though the other countries of western Europe followed, obviously encouraged by England's success.

Capitalism as a term came into vogue in the second half of the nineteenth century to describe the industrializing growth economies of western Europe and later those of the rest of the world. These economies were productive and provided high and increasing levels of real income for their citizens. By 1900 western Europe, North America, parts of South America (for example, Argentina), some of the European colonies elsewhere in the world (for example, Australia, South Africa, New Zealand, and Japan), dominated world production and trade. Of these only Japan had a non-European background.

The capitalist economies were not only the most successful and wealthiest in the world, they were also the most liberal, with a high degree of individual freedom, strong intellectual respect for the individual and for the voluntary association of individuals, and strong legal protection for the individual and his or her property. Freedom was at the core of the development of both democracy and capitalism. The rise of European liberalism culminated in England in the eighteenth century with the Industrial Revolution and in the nineteenth century with a widening of the franchise and the growth of representative government. The remarkable success of England in the nineteenth century was proof of the efficacy of freedom in providing both progress and reform—progress in the form of a more productive economy, reform in the form of remedial action to alleviate the perceived ills of capitalism.

The relationship between capitalism and freedom—the market and democracy—was questioned in the twentieth century because of the existence of fascism (Spain, Italy, Germany) and of paternalistic democratic regimes (Singapore), all of which had modified capitalist economies. But the collapse of fascism and communism in Europe and the increasing use of the market in China reaffirmed the importance of freedom in the formation of capitalist economies and the conclusion that communism, in allowing the use of the market, encourages political freedom.

Economic History and the Stages of Capitalism. Economic history as a separate discipline dates from the mid-nineteenth century and developed under the influence of two major developments: the attempt of the English classical economists from Adam Smith to John Stuart Mill to explain wealth, progress, and the evolution of society; and the stages of history debate formulated by the German historical school. The German historians divided the history of mankind into stages, each with a distinct social and economic organization, and gave prime place to a historical methodology that derived economic theory from historical evidence. The longer-term history of Europe was divided into three periods—feudalism, mercantilism, and industrialization—each associated with a type of capitalism. In the period before industrialization the main source of development was merchant capitalism in international trade with the formation of colonial empires, the role of the merchant as capitalist, and the colonies serving as markets and sources of raw materials. This form of capitalism or mercantilism prospered with the help of strong central governments that kept close control of trade. As national states evolved under mercantilism, there came national policies for the conservation and increase of wealth by the control of trade while leaving considerable room for private property and private enterprise. A major step to the modern world was the transition from feudalism to capitalism, leading to freer labor, freer markets, and more rapid economic growth. By adopting laissez-faire policies, England came, in the second half of the nineteenth century, to resemble the ideal capitalism of the economists.

Marxism and Capitalism. As Joseph A. Schumpeter pointed out, "The term capitalism was, throughout the nineteenth century, hardly used except by Marxists and writers directly influenced by Marxism" (Schumpeter, 1954, p. 552). Marx's theory of capitalism came directly from David Ricardo, whose model of capitalism was beautifully simple. As population increased and began to press on food supplies, profits were continuously decreased by the rising cost of living owing to the increasing cost of food as agriculture moved to marginal land and, as more marginal land went into production, rising rents. There was therefore a tendency for profits to fall, real wages to remain constant, and rents to rise until the profits fell to zero and the economy became stationary. Marx's refinement of Ricardo used the idea of a conflict of interest between landlords and workers to argue that capitalism was subject to chronic underconsumption as wages were adjusted downward in an attempt to maintain the profit rate, resulting in the immiseration of workers, leading to revolution. A temporary respite came from imperialism. In the colonies profits were high because capital was scarce, and the low price of plentiful land made raw material cheap. Capital and consumer goods were exported to the colonies, and raw materials were imported by the metropolitan capitalist economy. Because of the greater power of the capitalist economy, it dominated the colony and exploited it.

Marx was also interested in the "social relations of production," the relation between the owners of the means of production (the bourgeoisie or the capitalists) and those who owned no capital and had only their labor to sell (the proletariat). The power of the capitalist increased with the increase in capital accumulation. Compulsory labor, characteristic of feudalism, gave way to free labor in capitalist economies in which labor was separated from the means of production (as cottage industry gave way to factory industry), leading to alienation. "Free" labor gave way to "contract" labor, and the worker lost security and status.

The main theses of Marxism were the theory of immiseration and the complementary theory of alienation, the theory of the declining profit rate, and the theory of imperialism based on the high profitability of exploitative colonial enterprise. There is no empirical evidence for any of these propositions as specified by Marx. Real wages have risen continuously in all capitalist economies, though with cyclical variations; the rate of return on capital in capitalist economies, though fluctuating, has shown no significant downward trends; and there is no significant margin between the profitability of investment at home and in the colonies. The immiseration thesis led to the longest, largest, and most heated debate about the Industrial Revolution—whether or not the workers' standard of living declined during industrialization to the point of misery. At no time, however, was there a sustained decline in real wages, although significant gains came only after almost a century of industrialization.

Capitalism in the Twentieth Century: The Keynesian Revolution and Managed Capitalism. Capitalism in the 1950s differed significantly from that in the 1850s. Although the term was and still is used and although it implies a significant (though reduced) use of the market in the allocation of resources, it is impossible to describe modern economies as "pure capitalism." An outstanding feature of twentieth-century capitalist economies was the growth of the public sector as measured by the percentage of the national income it absorbed. Generally it increased from about 10 percent in 1900 to over 40 percent by the end of the century. The question then reasonably asked was whether or not the economic system with such a high level of public expenditure was still to be regarded as capitalistic.

The increase in fact began in the nineteenth century with the rise of problems connected with industrialization, urbanization, and population increase and with the growing power of the working classes as they became enfranchised. It was seen also as a response to socialist criticism of capitalism, often inspired by Marx, which took two forms: first, the Fabian or Social Democrat arguments for reform of capitalism and the development of the welfare state; second, the Marxist argument that class conflict was leading inevitably to revolution and socialism. But no revolution in any of the advanced capitalist economies culminated in socialism. Rather, there were Europewide social reforms, the beginning of the welfare state and the widening of the franchise, and the increasing participation of government in social and economic affairs. Revolutions, when they came, were generally in economies that were still largely rural and that bore little resemblance to the conditions posited by Marx.

The first half of the twentieth century was critical for the history of capitalism, with declines both in market economies and in liberalism, political as well as economic. In spite of two world wars and the Great Depression, progress did continue, and living standards improved during a troubled half century. However, doubts grew about the stability and long-term prospects of capitalism, and the 1930s generated a literature of skepticism about its future: population was about to decline, technology no longer produced new inventions, frontiers throughout the world had been reached—all leading to a thesis of the stagnation of capitalism. These fears were not realized, but war and depression certainly led to a revision of economic theory and policy, resulting in a large expansion of government and, in the long run, a new type of capitalism. John Keynes provided the economic blueprint for this so-called managed capitalism, for the regulation and direction of economies to achieve desired ends. In his pamphlets *The End of Laissez-Faire* and *How to Pay for the War*, he pronounced the demise of the market economy and advocated demand management by government to provide economic stability and growth. World War II was fought by government-managed economies, and toward the end of the war planning for the postwar period anticipated an increase in government control, particularly to produce full employment, since unemployment was seen as the greatest social problem of the interwar years.

Keynes, like Adam Smith, was reacting to the economic problems of his times when he published *The General Theory of Employment, Interest, and Money* (1936). The experience of a world war, a troubled postwar period, and the Great Depression led him to consider economic stability and full employment the most desirable aims of economic policy. His theory, at one level, was simple. By manipulating a few macroeconomic variables, the government could manage the economy to achieve desirable objectives. Government intervention in the economy meant a strengthening and widening of its economic power, marking a decline in liberalism. The view that wise government management, in a partnership joining labor, business, and government, could cure most economic ills dominated economic theory and policy for nearly half a century.

The development of managed capitalism took place against the background of a debate in which capitalism was contrasted with socialism, a nonmarket system in which goods are produced and distributed by a bureaucracy based on a system of political allocation. The acceptance of two different systems of resource allocation dominated policy discussion about the desirability of capitalism as against socialism or socialism as against capitalism or the most desirable mix of the two systems. The debate about the merits of capitalism and socialism and the policy implications of preferring one system over the other can be encapsulated in one question: What is the proper role of government in economy and society? In capitalism the role of government is clearly smaller than in socialism. What then are the proper functions and limits of government agencies? In what areas of economic and social life should there be government intervention and how much? These questions are perhaps the most important in political theory and in economic policy. And in regard to terminology, at what stage, as the public sector increases, does capitalism cease to be capitalism?

The Study of Capitalism in the Twentieth Century. The interest of economic historians in capitalism was at its height in the first half of the twentieth century. In that period there was hardly an important economic historian who did not write about capitalism. Those who did include William Cunningham, W. J. Ashley, George Unwin, G. D. H. Cole, E. Lipson, R. H. Tawney, and Maurice Dobb in England; Max Weber, Werner Sombart, Henri Pirenne, Lujo Brentano, Amintore Fanfani, and Gino Luzatto in Europe; and N. S. B. Gras, John U. Nef, Earl J. Hamilton, and Joseph A. Schumpeter in the United States. However, the publication in 1942 of *Capitalism, Socialism, and Democracy* by Schumpeter and in 1944 of *The Great Transformation* by Karl Polanyi and *The Road to Serfdom* by F. A. Hayek, all three widely read and widely acclaimed, marked in one sense the end of an important stage in the long intellectual debate about the future of capitalism.

Many historians believed, as Schumpeter put it succinctly, that the achievements of modern capitalism included rapid economic growth, enhanced personal freedom "for all," and more "active sympathy for real and faked sufferings," and that even feminism uses "an essentially capitalist phenomenon" (Schumpeter, 1942, pp. 126–127). Schumpeter admired the capitalist entrepreneur but nevertheless thought capitalism was doomed. He believed, with Marxian fatalism, that "capitalist evolution will destroy the foundations of capitalist society" and prophesied, without any enthusiasm, the coming of socialism (Schumpeter, 1942, p. 42). He wrote that capitalism would be destroyed not from any inherent economic weakness but from its success and

the hostility raised and sustained against it by the intellectuals of Western society.

Polanyi believed capitalism was already dead. Tracing the history of capitalism from its beginnings in eighteenth-century England to its death in Europe and America even before the Great Depression of the 1930s and World War II of the 1940s, he believed capitalism had been so socially divisive that spontaneous social controls had emerged to regulate markets and finally to destroy laissez-faire and create the welfare state. Polanyi argued that "the human degradation of the labouring classes under early capitalism was the result of a social catastrophe not measurable in economic terms" and believed that capitalism was a system that broke both with history and human character and hence could have only a short existence (Polanyi, 1944, p. 293).

Friedrich Hayek saw capitalism as threatened with destruction and argued that the erosion of the self-regulating and impersonal market and its replacement by collective direction of all social forces to deliberately chosen goals was "the road to serfdom," along which political and personal freedoms would be destroyed as the final outcome of increasing government regulation of the economy. He, like Schumpeter, emphasized the importance of the intellectuals in influencing political and economic thought. If Schumpeter (1942, p. 153) recognized that the intellectual's "hostility increases instead of decreases, with every achievement of capitalist evolution," Hayek was prepared to attribute blame. "In every country that has moved towards socialism," Hayek wrote, "the phase in development in which socialism becomes a determining influence on politics has been preceded for many years by a period during which socialist ideals governed the thinking of the more active intellectuals" (Hayek, 1949, p. 417). The reasons Western intellectuals accepted for so long almost uncritically the claims of socialism to be economically more efficient and morally superior to capitalism are a mystery. "La trahison des clercs" (Benda, 1927) and "L'opium des intellectuals" (Aron, 1955) are difficult to explain or to justify decades of self-delusion.

The decline and fall of capitalism has long been predicted, especially by those who have wanted it to fail. The failure of capitalism is part of the historicist package, which includes also expectations of increasing class conflict and revolution. The classic exposition of inevitable conflict was made in the 1840s by Friedrich Engels, who prophesied that the next trade cycle would precipitate bloody revolution. Every change in fortunes since then has been hailed as the beginning of the end: the depression after 1870, World War I, the Great Depression of the 1930s, World War II, the dissolution of empires after 1945, the emergence of Russia as a great power, the depression of the 1970s, and the increased globalization of the 1990s. The inevitable revolution dissolving capitalism has not come, and much Marxist ingenuity has been exercised in explaining why it has been so slow in arriving. Prophesies have become more cautious, explicit in criticisms of capitalism rather than explicit in scenarios of decline. And some see the advent of socialism as inevitable but see that it will come gradually and peacefully rather than quickly and violently. New models of the transition from capitalism to socialism have appeared, based more on what is actually happening than on what Marx said should have happened over one century ago.

In spite of the predictions and expectations of decline, however, there has been nothing inevitable about the destruction of capitalism. Indeed this expectation has been argued to be the leading fantasy of the twentieth century. The combination of inflation and unemployment, the failure of governments to plan successfully to achieve specified aims, and a weakened belief in the possibility of managed capitalism led, in the 1980s, to a more realistic view of what governments could achieve and to the revival of liberal economic ideas and policies. "The fatal conceit," as Hayek (1989) described it, that societies could be transformed by design, had been shown unexpectedly difficult. The complexity of successful planning and the unintended consequences of well-intentioned plans had been fatal for the successful achievement of a socialist utopia and instead were leading to Leviathan.

The combination of liberal democracy and capitalism has been so successful that it has become the model by which states are judged and which the majority of states strive to create, albeit with one important modification that can be described as the "welfare coefficient," that is, the attempt to correct some of the presumed consequences of market "failures," like inequality of opportunities, presumed inequality of outcomes, externalities, and the trend toward monopoly and the restriction of competition. Although belief in socialism as a system has been somewhat discredited, there has been a growth of other anticapitalist criticisms centering on the environment (pollution, global warming, reduction of biodiversity), globalization (the effect of expanding capitalism on the underdeveloped world), and the alleged trivialization of culture (particularly as a result of advertising and cheap mass production), that have led to a modified form of liberalism with an enhanced government role (the third way, social market economy, the restoration of a civil society, and so forth). The criticisms of capitalism changed over its history, but always they have been shown to be biased, exaggerated, or wrong. Criticism emerged during the Industrial Revolution, when social problems were identified and investigated and attempts were made to remedy them by legislative action. These inquiries created a massive source from which Marx derived his theory of immiseration and the English Parliament its impulse for reform. Unfortunately these inquiries

were concerned with the ills of society and seldom its goods. Problems certainly existed, but those investigated by Parliament were not necessarily typical of England's economy and society. Nevertheless the social legislation that resulted marked the origins of the welfare state.

Social legislation in the nineteenth century concentrated on poverty and factory legislation; in the early twentieth century on industrial concentration that threatened the market system; by the mid-twentieth century on instability (the trade cycle) and unemployment. Little of this legislation was repealed, so the accumulation accounted for the increasing intervention of government in economic affairs. Gradually inequality and relative poverty commanded the attention of the legislators. The theoretical recognition of imperfect competition and the regulation of business to prevent monopoly in the United States and England, for example, became an essential part of managerial regulation. And toward the end of the twentieth century, after the failure of socialism, new problems enumerated above were recognized or invented to condemn capitalism. It is difficult to believe, however, that capitalism is seriously threatened by such criticisms. The productivity of capitalism, the high standard of living it has produced, and the nature of individual freedoms to choose employments and consumption patterns are its greatest attractions and should ensure, with adjustments, its survival.

[*See also* Markets.]

BIBLIOGRAPHY

CLASSICS AND INFLUENTIAL HISTORIES

Brentano, Lujo. *Die Anfänge des modernen Kapitalismus*. Munich, 1916.

Cunningham, William. *The Progress of Capitalism in England*. Cambridge, 1916.

Fanfani, Amintore. *Catholicism, Protestantism, and Capitalism*. London, 1935. (First published in 1934.)

Hayek, Friedrich. "The Intellectuals and Socialism." *University of Chicago Law Review* 16 (Spring 1949), 417–433.

Hayek, Friedrich, ed. *Capitalism and the Historians*. Chicago, 1954.

Hobson, John A. *The Evolution of Modern Capitalism*. New York, 1894.

Keynes, John Maynard. *The End of Laissez-Faire*. London, 1927.

Keynes, John Maynard. *How to Pay for the War*. London, 1940.

Lenin, V. I. *Imperialism: The Highest State of Capitalism*. New York, 1939. (First published in 1917.)

Maine, Henry Sumner. *Ancient Law*. London, 1861.

Marx, Karl. *Capital*. 3 vols. Chicago, 1906–1909. (First published in 1867, 1885, and 1894.)

Polanyi, Karl. *The Great Transformation*. New York, 1944.

Ricardo, David. *On the Principles of Political Economy and Taxation*. London, 1817.

Schumpeter, Joseph A. *Capitalism, Socialism, and Democracy*. New York, 1942.

Schumpeter, Joseph. *History of Economic Analysis*. New York, 1954.

Sée, Henri. *Modern Capitalism: Its Origin and Evolution*. London, 1928. (First published in 1926.)

Sombart, Werner. *Der Moderne Kapitalismus*. 3 vols. Leipzig, 1902–1927.

Tawney, R. H. *Religion and the Rise of Capitalism*. London, 1926.

Unwin, George. *Studies in Economic History*. London, 1927.

Weber, Max. *The Protestant Ethic and the Spirit of Capitalism*. New York, 1930. (First published in 1904–1905.)

Weber, Max. *General Economic History*. New York, 1961. (First published in 1927.)

ARTICLES AND BIBLIOGRAPHIES

Hamilton, Earl J. "American Treasure and the Rise of Capitalism." *Economica* 9 (November 1929), 338–357.

Knight, Frank H. "Historical and Theoretical Issues in the Problem of Modern Capitalism." *Journal of Economic and Business History* 1 (November 1928), 119–136.

Pejovich, Svetozar, ed. *Philosophical and Economic Foundations of Capitalism*. Lexington, 1983.

Pirenne, Henri. "The Stages in the Social History of Capitalism." *American Historical Review* 19 (April 1914), 494–515.

Postan, M. "Studies in Bibliography," part 1, "Medieval Capitalism." *Economic History Review* 4 (April 1933), 212–227.

Sombart, Werner. "Capitalism." In *Encyclopedia of the Social Sciences*, vol. 3, pp. 195–208. New York, 1930.

Tawney, R. H. "Studies in Bibliography," part 2, "Modern Capitalism." *Economic History Review* 4 (October 1933), 336–356.

CAPITALISM VERSUS SOCIALISM

Aron, Raymond. *L'opium des intellectuels*. Paris, 1955.

Benda, Julien. *La trahison des clercs*. Paris, 1927.

Dobb, Maurice H. *Studies in the Development of Capitalism*. New York, 1947.

Friedman, Milton. *Capitalism and Freedom*. Chicago, 1962.

Hayek, Friedrich. *The Fatal Conceit*. Chicago, 1989.

Pigou, A. C. *Socialism versus Capitalism*. London, 1937.

Sweezy, Paul M. *The Theory of Capitalist Development*. New York, 1942.

Tawney, R. H. *The Acquisitive Society*. New York, 1920.

Webb, Sidney, and Beatrice Webb. *The Decay of Capitalist Civilization*. New York, 1923.

R. M. HARTWELL AND STANLEY L. ENGERMAN

CAPITAL MARKETS *[This entry contains two subentries on capital markets before and after 1750.]*

Capital Markets before 1750

Capital markets as alternatives to bank finance as a means of financial intermediation between savers and investors and between lenders and borrowers must have existed informally at least as long as banking activity. The two forms of financial intermediation are often substitutes in the short run but must become complementary in the long run. Banks keep confidential the information given them by their borrowers when describing their investment plans; capital markets require borrowers to display their investment plans publicly so that the widest number of possible lenders can be tapped. In ancient Greece, banking functions were performed by the *trapezai*, who kept confidential the affairs of wealthy Athenians who borrowed from them. Public subscriptions for the finance of festivals or wars, however, were announced and solicited in the *agora*, the public market place. These were episodic, so they could not be the basis for sustained development of capital markets.

The first evidence of long-term debt that could be the basis for a capital market comes from the Italian city-state of Florence, which in 1356 founded the Monte Comune, which allowed holders of the city's debt to sell their claims to others in a secondary market. This must have been fairly active, as fifteenth-century direct taxes were based on the market value of the debt held by citizens, not the nominal value. But its importance for financial activity in Florence seems to have been small.

Modern capital markets can be dated from the creation of the permanent joint stock of the Dutch East India Company in 1609. Shareholders at that time could not withdraw from the enterprise or even vote on its operation; all they could do was draw dividends, which were determined by a ruling committee of seventeen directors appointed by the largest shareholders of the six participating cities, and sell their shares to anyone who might buy them. The capital of nearly 6.5 million florins was divided into transferable shares of 3,000 florins each and remained thus until the company was disbanded by the Batavian Republic under French domination in 1795. These shares, and artificial divisions of them into *ducatons*, formed the basis for the development of an active capital market in Amsterdam, the city that controlled four-ninths of the capital stock of the Dutch East India Company.

As the needs of war finance increased in the following century, bonds of individual cities and provinces and occasionally of the Generaliteit of the United Provinces of the Netherlands were traded as well. Trading activity was largely conducted by Sephardic Jews who were excluded by guild restrictions from many trades and professions. The techniques developed at the Amsterdam Beurs were transferred to London when the Bank of England, created in 1694 under William III, who was also the stadholder of the United Provinces, adopted the same format for registration and transfer of shares as that of the Dutch East India Company. Earlier joint-stock companies in England, such as the British East India Company, the Hudson's Bay Company, and the Royal African Company, also had periods of active stock trading, especially after the Stop of the Exchequer in 1672, which bankrupted the leading goldsmith bankers in London and redirected the investment activities of the remaining bankers away from government debt and into shares of joint-stock companies. Active traders included Jewish migrants from the Netherlands as well as other Dutch merchants and Huguenots from France, in addition to London merchants and goldsmith bankers.

The demands of war finance led in England and Scotland to the creation of successive large joint-stock companies that held long-term debt of the government as well as the sale of an increasing number and variety of patents that fostered the creation of joint-stock companies to exploit them. In the years 1719 and 1720, France attempted to imitate the British success with capital markets by creating joint-stock companies of their own with shares traded on their stock exchanges. Several Dutch provincial cities also experienced joint-stock company speculation intended to challenge the dominance of Amsterdam. The speculative boom and then collapse of the Mississippi Bubble in France, the South Sea Bubble in England, and the Dutch bubbles in several provinces forced each stock market in turn to change its character. In each case, the promoters of the new joint-stock company tried to inflate the price of its shares to encourage investors to purchase quickly, thinking they could sell out later at even higher prices. The Paris Bourse collapsed, with only desultory trading in shares of a much reduced French East India Company, which was forced out of its most profitable posts in India during the Seven Years' War. The Amsterdam Beurs, itself little affected by the bubbles, benefited along with London from the flight of capital from France.

However, the absence of banking institutions capable of providing liquidity in times of crisis caused Amsterdam's capital markets to suffer from later financial crises in 1763 and 1772. By then, a small number of merchant bankers dominated the capital market, which specialized in retailing shares in the loans they extended to various European states. The London market reemerged from the financial crashes of 1720 by reorganizing the South Sea Company, converting half its share capital into perpetual annuities bearing 5 percent interest, and enlarging the capital stock of the Bank of England and the British East India Company. Trade in these securities sustained a substantial corps of specialized traders who, supplemented by a migration of Amsterdam bankers in the decades after 1763, laid the basis for London's nineteenth-century dominance of the international capital markets.

BIBLIOGRAPHY

Carruthers, Bruce. *City of Capital: Politics and Markets in the English Financial Revolution*. Princeton, 1996.

Dickson, Peter G. M. *The Financial Revolution in England: A Study in the Development of Public Credit, 1688–1756*. London, 1967.

Murphy, Antoin E. *John Law: Economist Theorist and Policy-Maker*. Oxford, and New York. 1997.

Neal, Larry. *The Rise of Financial Capitalism: International Capital Markets in the Age of Reason*. Cambridge, 1990.

Riley, James C. *International Government Finance and the Amsterdam Capital Market, 1740–1815*. Cambridge, 1980.

Wilson, Charles. *Anglo-Dutch Commerce in the Eighteenth Century*. Cambridge, 1941.

LARRY NEAL

Capital Markets after 1750

It is now well established that capital markets predate the Industrial Revolution. Taking 1750 as the Industrial Revolution's approximate chronological point of departure

does not allow for a complete discussion of the origins of capital markets. (For these, see Neal, 1990.) Nevertheless, these markets underwent substantial changes after 1750. Two limits on this survey have been self-imposed. First, the geopolitical focus here is on a handful of those industrial countries that developed earliest, principally on Great Britain, western Europe, and the United States. Second, capital markets are understood as sets of institutions concerned with the purchase and sale of long-term financial investments. In other words, money market institutions, though doubtless important, receive little attention here.

At the beginning, capital markets in western Europe served almost exclusively the needs of financial investment in government securities. Eighteenth-century wars understandably fueled governments' financial demands, but the proven willingness of private savers to satisfy them are less easily explained. Rising upper- and middle-class incomes, though poorly documented, are part of the story, no doubt; and the relative rates of expected returns on alternative forms of investments, though even less well documented, are probably another. Such relative rates of return, however, need to be corrected for risk: the greater the risk, the higher the expected rate of return needed to hold investors' interest. Looking at the observable results, we see a soaring volume of government debt instruments in circulation coupled to trend-stationary or even declining real rates of returns. One explanation is increased public trust in governments' ability and willingness to honor their debt commitments. England's development over the eighteenth century is a case in point, as seen in Table 1. The rising ratio of debt to annual revenues may be seen as an additional index of increasing trust in the government. But what was the source of such trust? Scholars of English history have stressed two factors: (1) the establishment of a strong central state with an unquestioned power to tax (Brewer, 1989); and (2) the tailoring of government debt instruments to suit the preferences of middle-class investors (through standardization, easier and more transparent payment rules, etc.) (Neal, 1990 and 2000). The former was important, to be sure. The latter, however, really reflected a shift in government policy priorities favoring those middle-class investors, constituting England's "financial revolution" (Dickson, 1967) and giving that country its head start in the international development of capital markets. By the end of the eighteenth century, British government bonds—above all, the famous 3 percent "consols"—had become the center of the British capital market, highly liquid assets, everywhere tradable at the same price and yielding a return that was practically synonymous with the "opportunity cost" of financial capital (Neal, 1994).

Continental Europe had a similar long-term pattern, though with a considerable time lag and some other

TABLE 1. *Government Finances and Yield on Public Debt in England, 1695–1790*

YEAR	DEBT[a]	NET INCOME[a]	PRICES (1701=100)	YIELD, %
1695	8.4	4.1	116	8.0
1710	21.4	5.2	122	8.3
1730	51.4	6.3	95	3.3
1750	78.0	7.5	95	3.0
1770	131	11.4	100	3.9
1790	244	17.0	124	3.9

[a] In millions of pounds sterling.
SOURCES: Mitchell, 1962; and Homer, 1963.

important differences. Here, the Napoleonic Wars served as a catalyst. The heavy debt incurred in the war years had been financed in a great variety of ways, but after 1815 most countries followed the British model and consolidated and transformed their debt into marketable (fixed-interest) instruments, instruments that collectively called forth and then dominated the national capital markets. Examples are the *rentes* in France and the *Staatsschuldscheine* in Prussia. In the following decades, the yields of most of these instruments tended to fall, as they had done in Great Britain earlier. The main reason was, as for the English consols, their increasing attractiveness to capitalist investors as highly liquid assets. Nevertheless, in terms of neither sheer volume nor stability of yields did these debt instruments approach their British counterparts. At the close of the Napoleonic Wars, for example, Britain's outstanding debt has been estimated at around 840 million pounds sterling—something like two and a half times the country's national income—whereas the national debt of France and Prussia at about this time amounted to no more than 75 and 40 million pounds sterling—between one-fifth and one-fourth of the estimated national incomes of these countries (Feinstein, 1992; Sée, 1936; Goldsmith, 1985). The comparisons of yields described by Homer (1963) clearly show the greater stability (and lower levels) of the British securities. These differences were at once cause and effect of the greater importance of the British capital market for international transactions in government securities. Only at the end of the nineteenth century did a marked convergence of yields take place.

Capital markets in the United States also grew, at least initially, on the coattails of rising government debt. Shortly after the nation's founding, Alexander Hamilton's Federalist financial revolution, which involved the assumption and funding of debts of the individual states, generated some $65 million in new federal government bonds. These debt instruments soon found favor with investors, registered falling yields, and in general gave the country's

capital market a solid anchor (Sylla, 1998). In the following decades, however, development in the United States differed from that in Great Britain and continental Europe in that corporate stocks and bonds soon overtook government bonds in importance, at least collectively. According to Goldsmith (1985), by 1850 the latter represented no more than a quarter of outstanding securities, while in Great Britain and continental Europe their share still amounted to at least 60 percent. The U.S. Civil War weakened this contrast, but only temporarily. It reflects a basic structural difference, to which we shall return.

One of the striking characteristics of this phase of government security predominance was its internationalization or, to put it differently, the related rise of foreign portfolio investment. Not surprisingly, the British capital market led the way. By 1850, Great Britain may have become a net creditor to the amount of two hundred million pounds—a sum equal to about one-third of its estimated national income. Even the capital markets of continental Europe became active centers in facilitating the international flow of government securities. Thus, Spanish and Austrian loans were traded in Paris and Berlin, even though Prussian and French government bonds were being issued and traded in London and the economies of those countries were being described as "capital scarce" (Brockhage, 1910; *The Economist*, 1845; Levy-Leboyer, 1964). This pattern suggests capital market imperfections, in particular in the fact that investors may have found it easier to extend their preference for domestic government securities to foreign securities having the same characteristics (i.e., fixed-interest bonds based on governments' power to tax) than to consider a wider array of domestic financial opportunities.

The dominance of government securities in capital market development seems to have peaked in the second quarter of the nineteenth century. This followed from the rise of joint-stock companies with limited liability and especially from the spread of that most capital-intensive innovation, the railway. It was important historically, because, as Feinstein (1992) pointed out, "it is only with the provision of funds for this great innovation that the capital market becomes of real significance for the productive, as opposed to the financial, aspect of capitalism." Nevertheless, there was a direct connection between the two. The securities of railway companies proved to be apt heirs to the government securities they (in part) replaced. When railways came upon the scene in the 1830s they could be seen as civic improvements having public or governmental attributes. Close ties to government existed from the start. For example, there was the delegation of eminent domain rights and stipulations for carrying government troops and mail; and their securities resembled government debt. Like the latter, they mainly took the form of fixed-interest securities and even frequently adopted the practice, associated with government bonds, of providing for semiannual coupon payments.

Railway equity was much less widely traded. In Great Britain, the United States, and Germany, local investors expecting indirect gains from railways took up most of the common stock. When railway organizers felt it essential to sell common stock to a wider public, they frequently offered a fixed-interest payment to shareholders for the duration of the construction period. This came close to being a temporary form of preferred stock—another favored instrument of railway finance in the countries considered here (Baskin, 1988). Another, similar, practice was the issuance of convertible bonds offering an equity option exercisable after a specified time.

The idea behind all these devices was to gain investors' trust or, in modern terminology, to overcome the "informational asymmetry" of investor-enterprise financial relations. The enormous growth of railway securities issued over the nineteenth century underscores the success of such devices. By 1850 railways in Great Britain had a total financial capital of nearly 235 million pounds, a sum that made them collectively far and away Britain's most important financial investment (apart from government bonds). At the beginning of the twentieth century, their capital accounted for more than two-thirds of the nongovernment securities listed on the London stock exchange. In New York, at this same time, railway companies represented well more than half of all listed securities.

Most of this growth, however, took the form of fixed-interest securities. At the end of the nineteenth century, for instance, trading in railway bonds in the New York capital market represented something like ten times the value of equity transactions (*New York Commercial and Financial Chronicle*, 1900). Bondholding posed much weaker information needs than shareholding, suggesting that information problems persisted, although the desire of railway executives or insider groups to maintain enterprise control might also have been a motive behind limited equity issues.

In most of the countries surveyed here, joint-stock companies with limited liability had made their appearance in various branches of activity before the railway age. In Great Britain, for example, a speculative wave of investment in such companies peaked in the mid-1820s; and in the United States from the 1790s on, many banks, textile enterprises, and transportation and mining companies were founded as joint-stock companies. Some of their shares and bonds became objects of capital market activity. In terms of overall capitalization, however, the growth of private corporate securities as elements of capital market development really followed on the back of railway growth. For one thing, as Feinstein's survey suggested, the experience of investors with railway securities encouraged them to consider investment in the securities of other types of companies. Moreover, the successful establishment of railways as going concerns probably hastened the spread of general limited liability—a necessary legal condition of the introduction of industrial and commercial securities into the capital market, achieved in Britain in 1856 (Feinstein, 1992). In Germany, an incorporation boom in heavy industry marked the upswing of the 1850s; and with the advent of free incorporation laws in 1870, a great wave of incorporation took place (Tilly, 1990). In France, the legal breakthrough came in 1867, though access to the *Société en commandite par actions* long before that date weakened the restrictiveness somewhat (Freedeman, 1993). In the United States, the great corporate age came in the 1890s, on the heels of completion of the national transportation and communications network (Chandler, 1990).

For various reasons, then, in the last third of the nineteenth century the securities issued by industrial, commercial, and financial companies came to be an important element of the capital markets of the countries discussed. For some of these securities, indeed, an international market—operating via links between the national capital markets—could be fashioned. In spite of important common features, however, this development was marked by persistent international differences. One way of discussing them is to compare some of the financial ratios compiled by Raymond Goldsmith. Table 2 summarizes a selection of the relevant data.

Table 2 documents a number of differences. First, the growth of securities was relatively modest in Germany. Since Germany differed little from other countries with respect to growth of financial assets as a whole, this means that more finance in that country flowed via institutions, in particular through the banks, than in other countries, as discussed below. Second, the high degree of "securitization" of finance recorded here for Great Britain, though not surprising, would be even higher if the British holdings of foreign securities were added to the figures given here (which reflect domestic issuers). Third, securitization in the United States had just about caught up with that of Great Britain by 1913; and the proportion held in shares, rather than bonds, was even higher than in the latter country, reflecting the wide use made of the corporate business form in the United States. Fourth, French securitization was also striking; and, as in Great Britian, consideration of French holdings of foreign securities would raise that figure still more.

The figures just discussed are related to, but not identical with, the extent to which capital markets allocated finance in these countries. The mere issuance of securities did not and does not imply use of the capital markets. At one extreme, a company might sell new shares on the

TABLE 2. *Securities and Asset Structure, Five Countries, 1850–1913*

SECURITIES AS % OF TOTAL ASSETS	1850		1875		1913	
COUNTRY	GOVERNMENT	OTHER	GOVERNMENT	OTHER	GOVERNMENT	OTHER
Great Britain	13	6	7	8	5	18
Belgium	5	7	4	9	7	10
France	4	2	8	8	8	11
Germany	2	1	2	3	4	4
United States	3	8	5	13	2	15

SECURITIES AS % OF ASSETS OF FINANCIAL INSTITUTIONS IN:	1850	1875	1913
Great Britain	322	161	207
Belgium	527	232	167
France	525	268	139
Germany	109	80	62
United States	162	258	258

SOURCE: Goldsmith, 1985, Appendix A.

securities exchange to individual investors; but at the other extreme, a company in debt might convert itself into a corporation and its principal creditor into a major shareholder; then listing on the exchange would have no more than juridical significance—an important distinction that deserves more research.

And how open is the capital market? In recent years financial historians have stressed the difference between market-based and bank-based financial development. In the former, finance is largely a public affair and finance flows across open markets. Numerous sellers of securities confront numerous buyers and a basically competitive system of pricing predominates. In the latter, financial flows are largely private or at least semiprivate, a matter concerning, say, bankers and their customers, and one based mainly on bilateral negotiations. Where larger capital demands are involved, we see networks of bankers and financiers seeking a cooperative solution. The financial history of Great Britain and the United States has frequently been seen as prototypical market-based development, while Germany illustrates the bank-based case (Conti, 1992). This characterization, we note, fits the data in Table 2 almost perfectly.

Differences in financial patterns are naturally related to differing institutional development; and their discussion can usefully include a brief look at comparative banking history. In Great Britain, private banks, which predominated until the 1830s, were relatively small in scale and specialized. They operated in a highly competitive market, in particular in association with the use of bills of ex-

change as interregional means of payment and a highly liquid form of short-term credit (Pressnell, 1956; Neal, 1994 and 2000). The joint-stock banks that subsequently replaced them operated in essentially the same manner. They were strictly commercial banks, and they were only linked to the capital market through short-term call loans made to brokers. As noted earlier, the great weight of highly liquid government securities in that market made intermediaries there less important, analogous to the way highly liquid bills of exchange made bankers less important to customers in the money market who did not use banks. Highly competitive markets led to high volumes of business, specialization, and efficient flows of finance. These took place in open markets, based on widely distributed, virtually public, information.

In the United States, dual banking regulation, involving fiscal interests of both federal and state governments, encouraged the growth of many relatively small banks and kept those banks small. Like their British counterparts, they were strictly commercial banks, initially note issuers, and later deposit banks. Regulation and prudence, perhaps, precluded them from playing an important role in the securities market. In New York, to be sure, as an unintended result of government regulation, banks engaged in short-term financing of security exchange transactions, as in London, and New York had a significant concentration of powerful investment bankers, as exemplified by the legendary J. P. Morgan (Carosso, 1969). In both countries, securities exchanges became important vehicles of finance relative to banks and, above all, the true centers of capital

market activity. It is surely no accident that in both countries, also, these exchanges were private, essentially self-regulating organizations, born of the interest of financial intermediaries like stockbrokers and security dealers in establishing professional standards and, in effect, protection—from competitors, from charlatans, or both (Michie, 1986).

How different was development in Germany—and in the continental countries that followed the "German model." Here, private banks engaged in both commercial and investment banking activity; and with the advent of joint-stock banking in the 1850s, this combination—subsequently labeled "universal banking"—became typical of their operating procedures as well. Large-scale capital market transactions, such as issues of securities related to government and later railway finance, were undertaken by bankers and banks cooperating via syndicates built on personal networks. Only secondarily were the security exchanges used. Thus, they played a much less central role than in Great Britian and the United States. Security exchanges did become important centers for securities trading—for example, in Berlin—and new issues were usually undertaken in the hope that they could be marketed on those exchanges. But banks and their own networks became even more important. Interestingly, securities exchanges in Germany were semipublic organizations, subject to much more government control before 1914 than their Anglo-American counterparts. Indeed, initially the principal intermediaries at work there were the official brokers, whose monopoly of floor trading and price formation (or "call trading") probably kept transaction costs relatively high. Moreover, the autonomy they enjoyed was in a sense undermined by the fact that bankers were not only active members of these exchanges but usually a dominating force in setting procedural rules and conflict resolution (Wetzel, 1996). Government regulation restricting the operations of securities exchanges grew in nineteenth-century Germany, above all in the Security Exchange Law of 1896, while concentration in banking—embodied in the emergence of the "great banks" (Riesser, 1911)—continued apace. "Strong banks, weak markets" might be an appropriate title for this phase of German financial history.

The significance of these institutional differences can be seen in terms of the "economics of information." Under "normal" circumstances, a capital-using enterprise should enjoy better information concerning its own willingness and ability to honor its financial obligations than the investors providing the capital, especially shareholders,

since bondholders as a rule enjoy a legal claim on physical assets. "Informational asymmetry" must have been great in the nineteenth and early twentieth centuries, because legal requirements governing the supply of relevant financial information to investors were lax in the countries examined here. In countries in which universal banking predominated, however, banks obtained a rich supply of relevant information on the financial status of the enterprises whose securities they underwrote and marketed from their day-to-day commercial banking connection with the same enterprises. In order to maintain their credibility and reputation with their own depositors and shareholders, universal banks should take their monitoring duties seriously. On that assumption, the mobilization of capital for nonfinancial enterprise should be, *ceteris paribus*, easier, more continuous, and cheaper than under a more fragmented financial system. On the other hand, the distribution of gains of improved intermediation and diversification under such a system probably tended to favor the universal banks greatly, since no institution existed to monitor them. If an open securities market would impose more competition among intermediaries than the more concentrated system of large universal banks, this dimension of the comparison would favor the Anglo-American market-oriented system.

One point should be stressed in terms of rates of growth of new issues of nonfinancial securities, in terms of the realized ex post return on such equity, absolute and relative to estimated riskiness, and in terms of the cost of raising equity capital to nonfinancial corporate enterprise. Performance in Germany, a universal banking country, was better than that estimated for either Great Britain or the United States in the late nineteenth century (Calomiris, 1992; Tilly, 1986 and 1995). Even in the United States some banks did engage in universal banking, and they seem to have been more successful than strictly commercial banks (De Long, 1992; Ramirez, 1995; Smith and Sylla, 1996). Therefore, here is a presumption that universal banking, represents an efficiency-enhancing aspect of capital market development.

In spite of the differences just emphasized, some important common trends of pre-1914 capital market development do stand out. First, in all the countries considered here, financing by means of security issues and trading in the "secondary market" became more important (see, for example, Table 2). Second, an international market for many of the securities issued and traded in the national markets developed. The result was an increasing integration of financial capital, that is, "globalization," before 1914 (Neal, 1989). One indicator of this development was the observable pattern of secularly falling yields, in particular the marked decline in the national differences. Third, although in absolute terms the financing of industry via

◄ CAPITAL MARKET. Trading floor of the Tokyo Stock Exchange, 1988. (© Ken Jarecke/Woodfin Camp and Associates, New York)

security markets grew in most of these countries, the sums involved covered only a small share of industry needs; and even corporate industrial enterprise relied mainly on self-financing. Much of the evidence suggests the validity of a "pecking order" view of enterprise finance, in which growth built first, on inside finance, second, on external debt (bond issues), and only as a last resort, on outside equity. The limited and halting use of equity finance is interesting; it contradicts the neoclassical (Miller-Modigliani) view that financial structure does not matter (Baskin, 1988). Despite this limitation of pre-1914 capital market development, however, progress up to then was considerable. By some standards, indeed, the achievements of financial capitalism before 1914—international capital mobility, for instance—were not surpassed until the 1970s (Taylor, 1999).

Changes in pre-1914 capital market development were of lasting significance. Nevertheless, some important changes of the twentieth century deserve discussion. They all follow a rough U or inverted U pattern. One was the changing relative weight of government demand. World War I, for example, transformed the capital markets of our countries into vehicles for financing government deficits. The depression of the 1930s and in World War II further strengthened this tendency. Only in the 1970s did this weight begin to fall, driven, at least in the economically advanced countries, by growing issues of private securities. The rise and fall of government securities in the capital market corresponded roughly to a second tendency of the twentieth century: the fall and rise in the international mobility of financial capital. The crisis and world depression of the 1930s was marked by widespread debt default and losses to investors in foreign securities, an experience that virtually shut down international transactions in private securities (Eichengreen, 1996). In the postwar reconstruction of the world economy, national controls on international flows of financial capital were maintained at first. They were seen as an integral part of the Keynesian policies and fixed exchange rates of the Bretton Woods system; the breakdown of this system marked the return of international financial capital movements as a major factor in capital market development in the countries covered here.

Both of the changes just mentioned were related to a third significant shift in capital market conditions: the rise and fall of government regulation (of which controls on international capital flows were one part). In Germany it was a response to the crisis of the 1930s and then to the war aims and needs of the Third Reich (Wandel, 1993). Enduring results came in the United States with the Glass-Steagall Act of 1933, which required the separation of commercial and investment banking, and the Securities Exchange Act of 1934. The former weakened banker-financier control of corporate enterprise; the latter improved the flow of financial information to final investors, in effect further weakening the role of banks as capital market intermediaries.

Further New Deal measures along the same lines followed, reflecting an old American fear of concentrated financial capital and its power for evil. According to Smith and Sylla (1996), however, the principal long-term result was to strengthen corporate executives as against the ultimate investors—to enhance a dichotomy of "strong managers and weak owners" (Roe, 1994). Deregulation and financial innovation in the 1980s—in part a reaction to defects of the "strong managers" syndrome—began to weaken manager autonomy and strengthen the leverage of financial intermediaries and the ultimate investors behind them. This change was felt both in Europe, and in the United States. Indeed, it reflected an almost worldwide tendency, a pressure on national financial institutions and policies frequently summarized in that catchall word "globalization."

To understand this shift, it is useful to consider yet a fourth twentieth-century tendency: a significant social widening of the investor base, a change Sylla and Smith (1993) describe as "democratization of financial investment." In Europe, World War I brought middle-class investors into the capital markets, hitherto dominated by professionals and upper-class investors, on a much greater scale than earlier. This change was only partly reversed in the period of public debt retirement that followed in the twenties, although in Germany, where investors experienced repudiation and more or less permanent losses, capital market development may have been significantly braked (Holtfrerich, 1986). In the United States, the stock market collapse in 1929 followed on the heels of a stock market boom. The boom had been supported by the new middle-class investors and by new forms of financial organization that attracted their savings (e.g., the investment affiliates of commercial banks, investment trusts, and public utility holding companies). After the stock market collapse, the democratization of financial investment kept going in the United States. During World War II it was associated with government securities, and subsequently with the stocks and bonds of private corporations.

In both Europe and the United States, the social widening of financial investment also took the indirect form of relative growth in the importance of pension funds. Since the 1980s, their weight in the capital markets has increased dramatically. For example, in the United States by the mid-1990s it equaled more than 50 percent of ownership of outstanding corporate equity (Smith and Sylla, 1996). In Europe and the United States, by the end of the twentieth century, through pension funds, together with other investment funds, banks and insurance companies

TABLE 3. *Relative Capitalization of National Security Markets, 1988*

INDICATOR	U.S.A.	U.K.	GERMANY	FRANCE	ITALY
Exchange capitalization*	2457	705	238	223	134
World capitalization, %	28.51	8.18	2.76	2.59	1.55
World GNP, %	37.06	6.36	9.13	7.17	6.34

*U.S. billion dollars.
SOURCE: Curioni, 1994.

had come to constitute blocks of institutional investors that could have consequences for the capital market. By executing buy and sell orders for individual securities those investors could significantly affect their price and call forth potentially destabilizing "bandwagon" effects. Furthermore, corporate reorganization plans, mergers, and takeovers could be influenced decisively by the shareholder votes controlled by large institutional investors.

Such a development thus asks the question again, first raised at the beginning of the twentieth century in connection with the "money trust" and the "great banks," of whether we need public control of great concentrations of financial power. Restricting the institutions can weaken incentives to control the capital-using enterprises and enhance the danger of "free-riding" shareholders. Freeing them from restrictions could permit those institutions to keep the gains from control for themselves, at the expense of their own ultimate source of capital, the individual investors. This dilemma is likely to stay with us for some time—along with the tendency to "democratize" financial investment.

Finally, the national differences in openness of capital markets noted in Table 2 persisted up to the end of the twentieth century. As late as 1988, "securitization," as measured by the relative weight of capitalization of national security markets, differed considerably (note especially the Anglo-American lead in Table 3). All the evidence points to convergence since then. Incipient financial deregulation, and, probably more important, the long U.S. stock market boom of the 1990s pulling European capital markets into its bullish orbit, paved the way. Since then, much public commentary has stressed the new "culture of equity." Financial investment is spreading across Europe, and is especially prevalent in Germany. The United States has relaxed legal restrictions on universal banking, and in the major financial centers of the country, universal banks have become leading capital market institutions (Calomiris, 1998). For the world of finance surveyed in this article, at least, convergence looks like part of a long-term trend.

[*See also* Interest Rates.]

BIBLIOGRAPHY

Baskin, Jonathan. "The Development of Corporate Financial Markets in Britain and the United States, 1600–1900." *Business History Review* 62 (1988), 199–237.

Brewer, John. *The Sinews of Power: War, Money, and the English State, 1688–1783.* New York, 1989.

Brockhage, Bernhard. *Zur Entwicklung des preussisch-deutschen Kapitalexports.* Leipzig, 1910.

Calomiris, Charles. "Universal Banking 'American Style.'" *Journal of Institutional Economics* 154 (1998), 44–57.

Carosso, Vincent. *Investment Banking in America.* Cambridge, Mass., 1969.

Chandler, Alfred D. *Scale and Scope: The Dynamics of Industrial Capitalism.* Cambridge, Mass., 1990.

Curioni, Stefano. "Institutional Framework of the Italian Securities Market: a Long-Term Interpretation." Unpublished ms. Milan, 1994.

DeLong, Brad. "Money Trust." In *The New Palgrave Dictionary of Money and Finance*, edited by P. Newman, M. Milgate, and J. Eatwell. London, 1992.

Dickson, P. G. M. *The Financial Revolution in England: A Study in the Development of Public Credit, 1688–1756.* London, 1967.

Eichengreen, Barry. *Globalizing Capital.* Princeton, 1996.

Feinstein, Charles. "Capital Markets and Capitalism in Britain and Continental Europe before 1914." In *The New Palgrave Dictionary of Money and Finance*, edited by P. Newman, M. Milgate, and J. Eatwell. London, 1992.

Freedeman, Charles. *The Triumph of Corporate Capitalism in France, 1867–1914.* New York, 1993.

Goldsmith, Raymond. *Comparative National Balance Sheets: A Study of Twenty Countries, 1688–1978.* Chicago, 1985.

Holtfrerich, Carl-L. *The German Inflation, 1914–1923: Causes and Effects in International Perspective.* Berlin and New York, 1986.

Homer, Sidney. *A History of Interest Rates.* New Brunswick, N.J., 1963.

Lévy-Leboyer, Maurice. *Les banques europeennes et l'industrialisation internationale dans la première moitié du XIX siècle.* Paris, 1964.

Michie, Ranald. "The London and New York Stock Exchanges, 1850–1914." *Journal of Economic History* 46 (1986), 171–187.

Mitchell, B. R. *Abstract of British Historical Statistics.* Cambridge, 1962.

Neal, Larry. *The Rise of Financial Capitalism.* Cambridge and New York, 1990.

Neal, Larry. "How It All Began: The Monetary and Financial Architecture of Europe during the First Global Capital Markets, 1648–1815." *Financial History Review* 7 (2000), 117–140.

Neal, Larry. "The Finance of British Business." In *The Economic History of Britain since 1700*, edited by R. Houd and D. N. McCloskey. Cambridge, 1994.

North, Douglass, and Barry Weingast. "Constitutions and Commitment: The Evolution of Institutions Governing Public Choice in Seventeenth-Century England." *Journal of Economic History* 49 (1989), 803–832.

Platt, D. C. M. "British Portfolio Investment Overseas before 1870: Some Doubts." *Economic History Review* 33 (1980), 1–16.

Pollard, Sidney. "Capital Exports, 1870–1914: Harmful or Beneficial?" *Economic History Review* 38 (1985), 489–514.

Pressnell, Leslie. *Country Banking in the Industrial Revolution.* Oxford, 1956.

Ramirez, Carlos. "Did Morgan's Men Add Liquidity? Corporate Investment, Cash Flow, and Financial Structure at the Turn of the Century." *Journal of Finance* 50 (1995), 661–678.

Riesser, Jacob. *The German Great Banks and Their Concentration.* Washington, D.C., 1911.

Roe, Mark. *Strong Managers, Weak Owners: The Political Roots of American Corporate Finance.* Princeton, 1994.

Sée, Henri. *Französische Wirtschaftsgeschichte.* 2 vols. Jena, 1936.

Smith, George, and Richard Sylla. *Wall Street and the Capital Markets in the Twentieth Century.* New York, 1996.

Taylor, Alan. "International Capital Mobility in History. The Savings-Investment Relationship." NBER Working Paper No. 5743, 1996.

Tilly, Richard. "German Banking, 1850–1914." *Journal of European Economic History* 15 (1986), 113–152.

Tilly, Richard. "Banks and Industry: Lessons from History?" In *European Economic Integration as a Challenge to Industry and Government,* edited by Richard Tilly and Paul Welfens. Berlin, Heidelberg, and New York, 1995.

Tilly, Richard. *Vom Zollverein zum Industriestaat.* Munich, 1990.

Wandel, Eckhard. "Die Rolle der Banken bei der Finanzierung der Aufrüstung und des Krieges 1933 bis 1945." In *Geld und Währung vom 16. Jahrhundert bis zur Gegenwart,* edited by E. Schremmer. Stuttgart, 1993.

RICHARD TILLY

CARIBBEAN REGION *[This entry contains two subentries on the economic history of the Carribean region before and after the Emancipation period.]*

Pre-Emancipation Period

The settled islands of the Caribbean Sea include the four large islands of the Greater Antilles—Cuba, Hispaniola (the Dominican Republic and Haiti), Jamaica, and Puerto Rico—as well as a large number of smaller islands that make up the Lesser Antilles. Most of these islands are tropical in climate, with excellent soil for the production of a variety of crops, most importantly, sugar. Prior to the arrival of Columbus in the Caribbean, fewer than one million Native Americans lived there, most on the island of Hispaniola. As elsewhere in the Americas, contact with Europeans led to a significant decline in numbers, so that even today the Native-American population of the Caribbean is rather small.

Columbus's four voyages to the Caribbean entailed landings at many islands and led to Spanish domination of the islands of the Greater Antilles. Over the next centuries, the knowledge of the productive potential of the Caribbean led many European natives to seek to establish ownership and control over various of the islands, and the Caribbean became a major battleground for rival European powers. Spain's interests were focused on the mines of Mexico and Peru, so that the economic potential of its Caribbean possessions was not developed for more than two centuries. Nevertheless, it did take about one century after the Spanish arrival before western European nations began to explore and settle in the Caribbean, and, with periodic changes in ownership of individual islands, the economic basis of the Caribbean shifted to the British, the French, and the Dutch, with some smaller roles played by the Danes and, on a lesser scale, the Swedes.

The key economic events leading to British domination of the Caribbean economy was the settlement of previously unoccupied Barbados in 1624 and the capture of Jamaica from the Spanish in 1655. Barbados did not begin as a sugar colony. For the first half-century of its settlement, it was populated predominately by whites; and the major crop produced was tobacco. After the 1640s, with the transfer and development of sugar technology and organization, primarily from Brazil, Barbados rapidly increased its slave population via imports from Africa and produced mainly sugar for sale in Europe. Jamaica also had limited numbers of slaves in the mid-eighteenth century, producing less sugar than did Barbados and the Leeward Islands. French settlement of the Caribbean began at the end of the seventeenth century, based in the initial half-century upon tobacco production by whites before the shift to slaves, sugar, and coffee in the eighteenth century. The western part of Hispaniola, now Haiti, was recognized as belonging to France in 1697. In the second half of the eighteenth century, it became the region's major sugar and coffee producer; and it was possibly not only the most successful colony in the region, but also the area with the highest per capita output in the world. The Dutch colonies fell into two categories: Surinam, on the north coast of South America, was a producer of sugar and coffee, based on slave labor; and a series of small, mainly entrepôt islands, including Aruba and Curaçao, off the coast of Venezuela. The even-smaller Danish colony included three islands, combining sugar production and entrepôt functions.

These islands of the western Europeans had several features in common, which differentiated them from the Spanish Caribbean. After the initial period of settlement, these colonies were generally comprised of about 90 percent black slaves with only about 10 percent of the population being white. The major crop produced was sugar on plantations of one to three hundred slaves, who also produced foodstuffs and other crops in addition to the primary export crop. Sugar was primarily for export sale in European markets, under the mercantilist rules introduced by the European nations. Demographically, these areas were rather a disaster, with both whites and blacks experiencing rates of natural population decrease, via high mortality, particularly during the first years after arrival, and low fertility. To maintain the total slave population, continued imports of new slaves from Africa were necessary, and (including the Spanish Caribbean) nearly one-half of all transatlantic slave shipments went to the Caribbean. The cumulated number of slave arrivals was in excess of those alive in the black population in the nineteenth century. Incomes to the planters in the British, French, and Dutch colonies were quite high by contemporary standards, and the increased number of slave imports and the rising slave prices suggest that expansion was expected to continue.

FRENCH CARIBBEAN. *View of the Exportation of Sugar from the Colonies.* Painting by S. de Beauvernet, eighteenth century. (Musée de la Cooperation Franco-Américaine, Château Blerancourt, France/Gérard Blot/Réunion des Musées Nationaux/Art Resource, NY)

The circumstances of the Spanish Caribbean were quite different from those of the islands belonging to northwestern European nations for most of the period. Spain had early settled Cuba, Santo Domingo (the Dominican Republic), and Puerto Rico, but these were not initially considered to be important for sugar production and were not slave-based colonies. The number of whites exceeded that of blacks, and, given the relative economic unimportance of slaves at this time, there were more free coloreds than slaves. A dramatic shift occurred after the British capture of Havana for ten months in 1763, which led, after the British withdrawal, to a shift in Spanish policy. The opening up of Cuba to increased sugar production, trade in slaves, and sale of sugar in Europe, meant a movement of Cuban slaves from tobacco and coffee to sugar production on plantations, and an increase in the import of slaves. By the mid-nineteenth century, Cuba accounted for about one-half of the world's cane sugar output and maintained importation of slaves until the 1860s.

Throughout the eighteenth and early nineteenth centuries, there was a steady expansion of the slave-based plantation system, with increases in wealth, the output and value of sugar exports, and the prices paid for slaves in

Africa and in the Caribbean. This was the result both of European economic expansion that created a high demand for sugar, and of a series of technological and organizational changes, including improvements to mills and boiling equipment, that led to expanded productivity. The plantation system developed as a commercially based system of production and marketing, with substantial concern for controlling the labor force, but it also led to a set of labor incentives to provide for higher output of sugar and foodstuffs. The role of European merchants and refiners was also important to the productivity of the system.

This apparent growing wealth in the Caribbean underlines one of the major arguments about Caribbean economic history, flowing from the work of the Oxford-trained historian Eric Williams, who became the first prime minister of the newly independent nation of Trinidad and Tobago. Among his major arguments was the relationship between the slave and plantation system in the Caribbean and the Industrial Revolution in Great Britain at the end of the eighteenth century. To Williams, the profits from slavery and the slave trade, the increased Caribbean imports of British manufacturers made possible by the economic expansion in the Caribbean, and the ability of the Caribbean to attract capital flows from Great Britain, together served to spur British economic growth by generating favorable structural changes, permitting the British to become the world's first industrial nation. This has long been an interesting hypothesis linking two major historical events and because of some basic similarities in timing. But the relatively small magnitudes of Caribbean slavery, compared to the overall British economy, and the dependence of the argument upon the presumed importance of dynamic externalities and scale effects raise questions about the posited relationship and make attempts to describe the precise linkages somewhat unclear. The nation that carried the largest number of slaves, Portugal, did not experience the Industrial Revolution at this time, and none of the other European industrializations, including those with major slave colonies, such as France, relied on slave-generated earnings. The "Williams Thesis," however, remains one of the major historic debates; and, even if questions do remain, it is important in describing the economic relationships among four continents over several centuries.

Clearly, whatever the economic future looked like in 1790, within the next half-century the Caribbean was in severe decline. While the Marxist forecast was for a decline in the economies of slave societies because of their own internal limitations and the inability of slave economies to compete with the emerging free labor of the time, the decline of the Caribbean economies was due not to its own economic dynamics, but rather to political, religious, and military change in both the Caribbean and in the European metropolis. The conquest of Havana by the British in 1763, with a sharp increase in slave imports and in maritime trafficking, led the Spanish to change their laws concerning trade and production in Cuba. This led to the emergence of a new major source of sugar and of a large-scale demand for slave imports from Africa, thus influencing the returns to other Caribbean areas. The American Revolutionary War, and its outcome, caused a reduction in the supply of foodstuffs made available from the mainland to the British West Indies, influencing slave consumption and the costs of sugar production. Most dramatic was the 1791 to 1804 slave uprising in Saint-Domingue, previously the richest and most rapidly growing of all slave colonies. The success of the revolution meant the end of the sugar plantation system in Haiti and dramatic falloffs in sugar and coffee export production. While the decline of Haiti provided some boost to sugar production elsewhere, including the British West Indies, Haiti's economic recovery did not occur; and today Haiti is the poorest of all Caribbean nations. While the decline of the plantation system reflected in part the working preferences of the freed slaves, by the twentieth century, Haitian migrant workers formed an important part of the sugar plantation labor force in Cuba and the Dominican Republic.

Important in ending slavery and in the decline of the plantation was the success of the abolition movement, starting with the late eighteenth century. First, European nations passed laws to end the transatlantic slave trade. The Danes and the British (and the Americans) ended their slave trade in the first decade of the nineteenth century, and all the other Caribbean colonial powers (except Spain) ended their slave trade before 1820. The closing of the slave trade threatened to ultimately end slavery, given the fact that most areas had been experiencing negative rates of natural increase. At least two decades after the slave trade ended in the Caribbean, most European nations ended slavery in their other colonies. Emancipation of slaves could be immediate, after a period of required labor called apprenticeship, or else by a law freeing those born after a certain date, also after a required period of apprenticeship. Generally, emancipation came with compensation, based on slave prices, paid to the slaveowners.

Great Britain ended slavery in 1834 (and the period of apprenticeship in 1838) and Sweden in 1847. France's date of emancipation (except for the earlier one in Saint Dominique) was 1848, as was that of the Danish. The Dutch emancipation was in 1863, Puerto Rico in 1873, Cuba in 1886 (after the 1870 law of the free womb, freeing legally the children born to slave mothers after passage, while maintaining the slave status for the mother and with the child bound to the mother's master until age eighteen), and, last in the New World, Brazil in 1888 (preceded by a law of the free womb in 1871). In most cases, the impact of emancipation was to have the ex-slaves leave the plantations and seek work on small plots of land, whether for themselves or as wage labor for others. This meant a measured fall in the society's level of exports and output. There were a few exceptions, such as Barbados, where the high population density meant that ex-slaves had nowhere else to work (until willing to emigrate) than on plantations, an outcome that kept output high and was considered to be a sign of success by numerous contemporary observers. Alternatively, in those areas of the Caribbean with ample land and that had been growing rapidly before emancipation, importations of indentured labor from India and China and elsewhere, as well as in the Dutch areas, from Java, served to provide an expanding labor force with continued growth in sugar output. In these areas, sugar plantations — with a different form of labor supply—permitted an expanding economy. Most other islands, which could not prevent movement of laborers out of the plantation sector, suffered export declines.

[*See also* Cuba; Haiti; Jamaica; Slave Trade; *and* Sugar.]

BIBLIOGRAPHY

Bergad, Laird W., Fe Iglesias García, Marjá del Carman Barcia. *The Cuban Slave Market, 1790–1880*, Cambridge, 1995.

Emmer, Pieter C., ed. *General History of the Caribbean*, vol. 2, *New Societies: The Caribbean in the Long Sixteenth Century*. London, 1999.

Fick, Carolyn E. *The Making of Haiti: The Saint Dominigue Revolution from Below*. Knoxville, Tenn., 1990.

Higman, B.W., ed. *General History of the Caribbean*, vol. 6, *Methodology and Historiography of the Caribbean*. London, 1999.

Klein, Herbert S. *African Slavery in Latin America and the Caribbean*. Oxford, 1986.

Knight, Franklin W., ed. *General History of the Caribbean*, vol. 3, *The Slave Societies of the Caribbean*. London, 1997.

Oostindie, Gert, ed. *Fifty Years Later: Antislavery Capitalism and Modernity in the Dutch Orbit*. Pittsburgh, 1990.

Richardson, Bonham C. *The Caribbean in the Wider World, 1492–1992*. Cambridge, 1992.

Sheridan, Richard. *Sugar and Slavery: An Economic History of the British West Indies, 1623–1775*. Baltimore, 1973.

Solow, Barbara L., and Stanley L. Engerman, eds. *British Capitalism and Caribbean Slavery: The Legacy of Eric Williams*. Cambridge, 1987.

Williams, Eric. *Capitalism and Slavery*. Chapel Hill, N.C., 1944.

Williams, Eric. *From Columbus to Castro: The History of the Caribbean, 1492–1969*. London, 1970.

Watts, David. *The West Indies: Patterns of Development, Culture, and Environmental Change since 1492*. Cambridge, 1987.

STANLEY L. ENGERMAN

Post-Emancipation Period

The dates of slave emancipation differ from colony to colony, as do the ensuing sociopolitical and economic histories. The earliest Caribbean slave emancipation initiated an infectious socioeconomic transformation that eventually spread throughout the region. Haitian troops, following their own successful revolution against France that ended in 1803, influenced the 1821 granting of freedom for the slaves across Haiti's border in the Spanish half of Hispaniola (the Dominican Republic). Emancipation came later in the other Spanish Caribbean territories, and not until 1886 in Cuba. In the British islands, the official termination of slavery in 1834 was followed by a four-year "apprenticeship" everywhere except Antigua, so genuine freedom did not come about in most British Caribbean colonies until 1838. Slaves in the French and Danish Caribbean colonies were freed in 1848. The Dutch freed their slaves in 1863.

Despite emancipation throughout the region, all of the territories except Haiti remained firmly under colonial control, so the new, post-slavery systems of labor and livelihood unfolded everywhere on familiar lands, amid a social atmosphere clouded with animosities between plantation owners and workers. Local planter assemblies attempted to limit land ownership and the mobility of former slaves by passing restrictive laws; those were subsequently modified and sometimes rescinded by legal authorities in Europe. Where islands were sufficiently large, free men and women established village settlements as small-scale landholders, usually on sloping or on swampy lands that were unwanted by the ongoing plantations. In some places—notably Nevis, Saint Lucia, and Tobago—sharecropping systems were developed, in which former slaves delivered sugar-cane crops to planter-owned grinding mills for a negotiated percentage of the value. On the smallest islands, some of the men began to migrate away on wooden sailing vessels for wage labor—usually as seasonal cane-cutters—to the larger islands. Then they returned home, thereby establishing a tradition of seasonal migration, for which the Caribbean region is still known.

Various elements of physical geography were important to socioeconomic changes that occurred during the late 1800s. Island life was a limiting factor; in closing some opportunities, it encouraged migration, especially of "deckers" aboard the new steam vessels. Periodic drought on such low-lying islands as Antigua, Guadeloupe, and Barbados resulted in hardship for the planters and their laborers. Several seasonal hurricanes arrive annually— then without warning—until weather observation stations could try to relay information, using the undersea electric telegraph lines that were introduced in the 1870s. In 1898, a huge hurricane ravaged Barbados and Saint Vincent, then delivered a glancing blow to Saint Lucia on its way north. In August 1899, the "San Ciriaco" hurricane devastated Puerto Rico and the adjacent islands in the northeastern part of the region. Earth tremors also were common, mainly in the volcanic arc of the eastern Caribbean; in May 1902, the eruption of Mount Pelée in Martinique killed an estimated 40,000 people, and a simultaneous eruption in neighboring Saint Vincent killed another 1,500. The events captured newspaper headlines worldwide and inspired relief efforts from nearby island colonies, as well as from Europe and the United States.

After emancipation, the cultivation and initial processing of sugar cane remained the region's principal economic activity. Afro-Caribbean wage laborers worked the estate fields and in the grinding factories, under planter supervision, to produce the raw sugar then exported to Europe for its final refining (usually in London or Rouen, France). When some Caribbean freedmen united to demand higher wages, planters complained about labor "shortages" and worker "unreliability"—and so convinced colonial officials to enlarge local labor pools. Starting in 1838, the British Colonial Office approved bringing indentured workers to the Caribbean from India under five-year labor contracts. From then until 1917, more than 400,000 men and women came from the recruiting terminals of Calcutta and Madras to work on British Caribbean sugar-cane plantations, mainly in British Guiana (240,000), Trinidad (135,000), and Jamaica (33,000); smaller numbers were used throughout the other British islands. The French and the Dutch also brought people to the region from India; from 1852 to 1885, France imported nearly 100,000 to

Guadeloupe, Martinique, and French Guiana. Small numbers of indentured workers from Portuguese Madeira and China; then, somewhat later, from Dutch Indonesia.

Other problems contributed to the gradual reorientation and decline in sugar production, especially on the smaller islands. In 1846, the British Parliament, in an effort to increase trade with non-British cane-sugar producers elsewhere in the tropics, removed the preferential sugar prices for British West Indian sugar that had been in force since the Navigation Acts of the seventeenth century. Hardest hit were the "old islands" of Antigua, Saint Kitts, and Barbados, where, although sugar was still produced, depleted soils and antiquated infrastructures were unsuited for the new production methods. In the 1840s, the French constructed large steam-powered sugar-grinding mills in Guadeloupe and Martinique. The British in the 1870s installed steam mills and vacuum pans in Saint Lucia and Trinidad, which allowed the boiling of sugar juices at lower temperatures that produced unscorched, high-quality sugar crystals.

Yet local adaptations and improvements were no match for the changes in the world sugar industry that affected small-scale Caribbean sugar economies. By the end of the nineteenth century, British entrepreneurs in Fiji, South Africa, and Mauritius, Dutch planters in Indonesia, and U.S. companies in Cuba and the Dominican Republic had established enormous steam factories; often these were on previously untilled lands, thereby establishing economies of scale in cane-sugar production that could not be matched on the small Caribbean islands. Even more threatening was the increasing competition from beet sugar, grown in Europe, Russia, and, increasingly, the United States. Beet sugar had begun to gain importance in Europe in the 1820s and, at a global level, gained steadily on cane sugar, surpassing it early in the 1880s. That was partly in response to growing demands from European workers for diets that included more sugar, especially in pastries, sweets, and preserved or canned fruit.

Late in the 1800s, continental European governments introduced a complex system of payment incentives for their local sugar-beet producers that had direct and disastrous consequences for Caribbean sugar-cane economies. Refunds of internal excise taxes ("bounties") were based on improvements in local refining techniques, which led to massive European beet-sugar surpluses, which, in turn, drove down Caribbean sugar prices. From 1880 to 1883, the price of a 100 kilogram "quintal" of sugar exported from Guadeloupe fell from 70 francs to 25 francs. In 1884, the price of 100 pounds of sugar shipped from the British Caribbean islands fell from 19 shillings to 13 on the London market. The ensuing "bounty depression" in the Caribbean led to reduced cane acreage, depressed wages, failed businesses, lowered food imports and associated high levels of malnutrition, and general misery throughout the region—except in those few places no longer relying on sugar, such as Grenada with cacao and Dominica with coffee and limes. In 1897, a British Royal Commission traveled through the British West Indies to assess the economic impacts of the "bounty depression." It suggested the breaking up of large estates on several of the islands and the consolidation of cane production under central milling on others, recommendations with momentous long-term impacts for the region.

The opening of the twentieth century saw an increasingly restive Caribbean labor force chafing under what they considered unfair and inept colonial governments, as well as the emergence of the United States as a geopolitical power in the region. The U.S. construction of the Panama Canal from 1904 to 1914 attracted tens of thousands of Afro-Caribbean construction workers, mainly from Jamaica and Barbados but also from every other Caribbean colony, including those controlled by Denmark, France, and the Netherlands. U.S.–owned banana enclaves (mainly The United Fruit Company) along the Caribbean rim of Central America and some large sugar-cane cane estates (for Domino and others) in the Greater Antilles similarly attracted workers from the small islands, often on a seasonal basis. The money earned in those jobs helped lift the people of the region from the economic depression conditions of the 1880s and 1890s, and men returning home from these work experiences soon demanded more political power. During the Great Depression of the 1930s, a chain reaction of depression-induced labor riots occurred in the small island colonies of the British Caribbean. These disturbances are considered by West Indian historians as seminal events that helped lead to the relaxation of voting restrictions, to more home rule, and to eventual political independence. The French Caribbean colonies, taking a different direction, were assimilated politically as metropolitan departments of continental France in 1946. Although government payments (subsidies) have led to a reasonably high standard of living in the French Caribbean, concerns about local cultural autonomy there underlie ongoing discussions and commentary about still-possible political independence. The West Indies Federation, composed of the former British Caribbean colonies, was established in 1958; it disintegrated in 1961 when the large and prosperous members—Jamaica, Trinidad and Tobago, and Barbados—left the federation. Since then, nearly all the former British colonies have gained political independence. The former Dutch colonies—Aruba, Bonaire, and Curaçao in the south, and Saint Martin, Saba, and Saint Eustatius in the north—have internal political autonomy combined with continuing political and economic links with the Netherlands.

After World War II (1939–1945), when eventual political independence appeared inevitable for Caribbean colonies, local debate and discussion about the prospects for future economic development spawned important economic exchanges. The Saint Lucia–born Nobel laureate W. Arthur Lewis then authored a pamphlet entitled "The Industrialization of the British West Indies" that appeared in the *Caribbean Economic Review* (vol. 2, 1950, pp. 1–39), in which he advocated local industrialization financed by outside capital, to transform the region's small agrarian societies into prosperous, manufacturing ministates. Lewis's idea, often referred to as "industrialization by invitation," was subsequently countered by other West Indian economists—notably George Beckford of Jamaica. They took a more historical view of local economic problems and suggested that external capitalists would essentially reimpose the plantation economies that first created the region's underdevelopment; they also favored more government intervention in local economies.

Today, an inherited dependency on economic decisions made elsewhere continues to plague the region. As one example, the banana industries of the tiny states that were once the British Windwards—Grenada, Saint Vincent, Saint Lucia, and Dominica—prospered during the late twentieth century, owing to special price arrangements that gave them access to the British market. Negotiations among Britain, the United States, and the European Union may, however, result in the Windward bananas being undercut by cheaper U.S. growers' "dollar bananas" from Central America. The prosperous tourist-based economy of Barbados, which supports national living standards at the level of Hong Kong and Singapore, is ultimately based on the disposable income spent mainly by vacationing Americans—therefore it is subject to such factors as U.S. stock-market fluctuations. Sugar cane, although in relative decline, remains regionally important, yet its cultivation depends on guaranteed markets, such as the market assurance the French islands have as part of the European Union. The problems of the small Caribbean states going it alone have for decades inspired various multi-island trade groupings and associations, which have resulted in few tangible benefits for Caribbean peoples. Many individuals and families have emigrated to the colonizing country and to the nearby United States and Canada.

The Caribbean's most serious current problem cannot be appreciated without referring to the region's economic history. At the beginning of the twenty-first century, drug growing, processing, and trafficking have become the most remunerative business of the entire region. Cocaine from northwestern South America crosses the Caribbean to North America in every conceivable way—as does the new South American product, heroin. If demand for conventional crops (such as bananas in the Windwards) declines, marijuana (a fast-growing hemp crop) often takes their place. Increases in local crime in all the islands are attributed, more often than not, to drug smuggling and the protection of product and territories. Heretofore unheard of sums of cash generated from the drug trade are offered to tempt elected officials and civil servants, which threatens to undermine the integrity of local governments. Money laundering and the offshore banking industry are monitored closely by U.S. officials, who have attempted to extend U.S. authority into local territories and local waters with mixed success. Whether or not they collaborate with the United States, almost all Caribbean officials identify the problem as one of U.S. market demand. They maintain that the small islands of the Caribbean are just supplying the mid-latitude markets with tropical staples, thereby playing the same economic role that they have for centuries.

BIBLIOGRAPHY

Beckford, George L. *Persistent Poverty: Underdevelopment in Plantation Economies of the Third World.* New York, 1972.

Deerr, Noel. *The History of Sugar.* 2 vols. London, 1949–1950. Clear, illustrated discussions of historical sugar technologies, with detailed annual production data from the individual colonies.

Galloway, J. H. *The Sugar Cane Industry: An Historical Geography from Its Origins to 1914.* Cambridge, 1989.

Griffith, Ivelaw L. *Drugs and Security in the Caribbean: Sovereignty under Siege.* University Park, Pa., 1997.

Grossman, Lawrence S. *The Political Ecology of Bananas.* Chapel Hill, N.C., 1998. Bananas grown in Saint Vincent are traced from planting to the London market; excellent discussions of intervening transportation and marketing problems.

Knight, Franklin W., and Colin A. Palmer, eds. *The Modern Caribbean.* Chapel Hill, N.C., 1985. Slightly dated, but perhaps the best of the anthologies on the region, with original essays by leading scholars about economic histories.

Mintz, Sidney W. *Sweetness and Power: The Place of Sugar in Modern History.* New York, 1985. A classic analysis of the historical interrelationships between the Caribbean's slave-produced sugar and the emergence of the British working class.

Moreno Fraginals, Manuel, Frank Moya Pons, and Stanley F. Engerman, eds. *Between Slavery and Free Labor: The Spanish-Speaking Caribbean in the Nineteenth Century.* Baltimore, 1985. An indispensable set of articles, particularly useful in understanding the impact of the United States in the region.

Richardson, Bonham C. *Economy and Environment in the Caribbean: Barbados and the Windwards in the Late 1800s.* Gainesville, Fla., 1997. The effects of the sugar bounty depression.

Sutton, Paul, ed. *Europe and the Caribbean.* London, 1991. Emphasis is on recent political relationships.

Thomas, Clive Y. *The Poor and the Powerless: Economic Policy and Change in the Caribbean.* New York, 1988. A Guyanese economist provides poignant examples of the ways external economic control creates local hardships.

Tinker, Hugh. *A New System of Slavery: The Export of Indian Labour Overseas, 1830–1920.* London, 1974.

Williams, Eric. *From Columbus to Castro: The History of the Caribbean, 1492–1969.* London, 1970. The best of a number of regional historical surveys. This by the famous Trinidadian historian/statesman, with an excellent bibliography organized on the basis of the predominant languages of the region.

BONHAM C. RICHARDSON

CARNEGIE, ANDREW (1835–1919), industrialist and philanthropist.

Andrew Carnegie was a pivotal figure in the transformation of the United States from a rural agricultural giant into the dominant industrial power of the world. Carnegie exemplified the possibilities available to ambitious young men in the United States during the nineteenth century. His career spanned most of the major industrial fields—telegraphs, railroads, cotton textiles, oil, bridge building, iron, and steel. He achieved all of his success despite an inauspicious youth.

Young Carnegie was born in Scotland. His father was a hand-loom weaver who had been displaced by the power loom, so the family migrated to Pennsylvania in 1848. Andrew began working as a "bobbin boy" at a local cotton mill. He became an office boy and then a telegraph operator in Pittsburgh. He gained a mentor in Thomas A. Scott, a superintendent in the Pennsylvania Railroad. Scott employed Carnegie as his personal secretary and telegrapher. Carnegie absorbed Scott's business techniques and soon demonstrated his competence in railroad matters, eventually being promoted to director of the western division. He became acquainted with the Pennsylvania Railroad's pioneering use of cost-accounting principles, an acquaintance that he would apply to later business ventures.

Carnegie began investing in sleeper cars, oil, bridge building, and iron manufacturing. He extended his investment activities by becoming a bond salesman and speculator; he prospered in these activities and could have comfortably retired (at which point, he might have remained a footnote in the history of the Pennsylvania Railroad).

However, Carnegie's previous experiences positioned him to take advantage of the new technologies in the iron and, later, the steel industries. By 1865, he began managing the Keystone Bridge Company. He brought not only a fixation for cutting costs to the company, but he also began the process of vertical integration in the iron and steel industries by acquiring the Union Iron Company. He recognized that iron rails lacked durability and that there existed a nascent market for steel rails, so he entered the steel industry in 1872. Eventually, he merged his holdings into the Edgar Thomson Steel Works and, later, the Carnegie Brothers Company.

In these endeavors, Carnegie applied cost-accounting methods, continued to vertically integrate, and implemented innovations in production (championing the new Bessemer and the Thomas open-hearth processes for making steel). Indeed, he quickly scrapped his Bessemer furnaces when the Thomas process proved itself superior. He also gathered a coterie of highly competent associates, including Henry C. Frick (owner of coke fields) and Captain William R. Jones (a top steel maker). By using cost-accounting information, Carnegie could assess and im-

ANDREW CARNEGIE. Portrait (c. 1900) by Charles H. Davis and E. Starr Stanford (c. 1862–1917). (National Portrait Gallery, Smithsonian Institution, Washington, D.C./Art Resource, NY)

prove the performances of his managers. His tactics enabled Carnegie Steel to produce steel at lower costs than its rivals and to dominate the market for steel. Not only did Carnegie manufacture steel more cheaply than did his rivals, he succeeded in decreasing his costs for decades.

Although rivals often invited Carnegie to join in their various price-fixing schemes, his ability to produce more cheaply and his natural skepticism regarding pools usually led him to disdain such invitations. When the market for railroad steel dwindled in the late 1890s, rival steel producers were desperate to bolster prices; Carnegie's ability to decline their pool and quite plausibly drive them out of business led to their efforts to buy him out. By 1901, when Carnegie sold his share of Carnegie Steel to J. P. Morgan for more than $230 million, he could boast of having revolutionized the steel industry in America. At this juncture, America was the world's largest producer of steel.

While Carnegie sometimes espoused amicable relationships between management and labor unions, the Homestead Strike of 1892 was the major blemish on his public record. Carnegie and Frick decided to reduce the minimum wage and break the union at the Homestead Works. Frick enlisted Pinkerton guards to break the strike. A number of people were killed in the ensuing violence. Although Carnegie had not authorized the Pinkertons and had been out of the country at the time of the violence, he reaped unfavorable publicity because many people believed he tacitly approved of Frick's decision.

In perhaps his most-lasting achievement, Carnegie endowed numerous libraries across the country, Carnegie Mellon University, and other philanthropic endeavors. He distributed $350 million to these efforts. Indeed, in 1889 he wrote a two-part article in the *North American Review* on "Wealth," where he argued that capitalists should administer their wealth for the benefit of humanity. He concluded the first part of the article saying, "The man who dies thus rich dies disgraced." By this reckoning, Carnegie did not die disgraced.

BIBLIOGRAPHY

Hughes, Jonathan R. T. *The Vital Few.* New York, 1986. Contains a chapter on Carnegie.

DAVID G. SURDAM

CARTELS AND COLLUSION [*This entry contains four subentries, a historical overview and discussions of concentration and entry, price-fixing and vertical restrictions, and price discrimination.*]

Historical Overview

A cartel is a formal organization among firms designed to create market power. Although the actual structure of cartels varies greatly, each, essentially, is a collusive agreement among independent firms to coordinate production and distribution jointly, most often in order to restrict output and raise prices. The extent of the cartels' organization ranges from firms creating formal organizations with executive committees overseeing the cartels' operations to firms colluding simply through informal meetings among CEOs. However they organize, if a group of firms can coordinate the supply of a good and preclude entry, and if it faces relatively inelastic demand, it can control the price of its output in the quest for greater profits. Effective collusion is anticompetitive and results in a welfare loss to society since less of the product is supplied at a higher price.

Firms cooperate in a variety of ways. They can buy out other firms, thus merging individual small firms into larger ones. They can remain independent and have agreements on prices or outputs or both; these agreements can be formal with quota arrangements and monitoring structures, as in the case of cartels, or they can be relatively informal, as in the various forms of trade associations. In between these two poles, there are a variety of combinations that have relatively more or less independence among firms. These include pool arrangements, trusts, and forms of Konzerne (affiliated firms under a centralized organization, sometimes with government representation). They can organize to control only prices, to establish binding quotas, and/or to impose uniform trade conditions on their customers.

Whether firms can reach and maintain an agreement depends upon many factors. If there are relatively few firms with few potential entrants, the firms have an incentive to collude, and collusion is easier. If, in addition, the firms have good information about prices and demand conditions and have clear, effective ways to punish any defector or entrant, then cartel arrangements are likely to be stable. On the other hand, firms have an incentive to cheat once an agreement to curtail sales has been made. This "chiseling" makes such arrangements inherently unstable. The classic problem with collusive arrangements is that firms have an incentive to cheat on restrictive policies in the expectation that they can secure greater individual profits. Clearly, if all firms behave in this manner, the arrangement is not stable and collapses.

In both static and dynamic noncooperative collusive models, firms weigh the benefits and the costs of defection. Simply, collusion in the static case will be stable if profits are higher for fringe firms outside the market than for the colluding firms, and if member firms receive higher profits from membership than from defection. The fewer the firms, the more likely it is that these conditions will obtain. In the dynamic case, the important question involves the temporal tradeoff from compliance or defection. If the present discounted value of defection is large enough to offset the loss of cartel profit levels, then the cartel will break down. In part, this situation is a function of the discount rate. The higher the concentration of the industry is, the larger the range of discount rates that stabilizes the collusive arrangement.

If, however, antitrust policy is more active when there are fewer firms, then collusive behavior might be more likely in a sector with enough firms to preclude government intervention (see Werden and Baumann, 1986). Even if the number of firms is small, if member firms in a cartel have capital of different vintages and hence different costs, agreeing on a unified price might require low-cost firms with large quotas to make side payments to weaker firms to induce them to maintain the cartel price. Other factors such as the homogeneity of the product also can simplify arrangements; the more similar the product across firms, the easier it is to reach agreement. In addition, the ability to respond quickly and harshly to cheaters also makes arrangements easier. Stable cartels often are dominated by large producers; a large producer can both detect and respond to any infractions (e.g., diamonds with DeBeers and oil with Saudi Arabia).

The more information available on pricing, the more stable the cartel is. The more public the pricing information, the cheaper the detection of cheating is. Cartels without this advantage often have to hire accounting firms to police agreements, often at great cost and never with certainty of results. Clearly, the collusive group, no matter how internally stable, must preclude entry because the economic profits will attract new firms. Traditionally, it has been thought that the higher the excess capacity of cartel members is, the lower the stability of the collusion. However, recent models show that high capacity can yield harsh punishments that facilitate collusion; a firm could strategically choose some excess capacity to use in retaliation to any entry. The main issue here is whether the excess capacity is chosen or is the result of a negative demand shock.

Another factor that may help firms to collude is the number of markets in which the firms interact, or the multimarket contact of the firms. If firms meet in many markets, then cheating in any one can cause retaliation in the many other markets in which the firms compete. Firms understand these stabilizing features and often attempt to address them through "facilitating practices," or actions that attempt to stabilize collusion. These actions come in many forms, as in base-point pricing arrangements, vertical price controls, or formula pricing.

Examples of these business organizations, or at least attempts at them, can be found throughout almost any period in market economies. In the Middle Ages, the economy was highly regulated with laws governing entry into industry and labor mobility, with very restrictive apprenticeships and guilds that controlled labor and production. As trade and production expanded, regulation moved to secure higher profits through coordination. Cartel arrangements were attempted throughout Europe; for example, in 1283 the government of Venice ordered all Venetian merchants to form a cartel over goods imported from Alexandria. In 1331, wine merchants throughout southern France united to control prices. Often the masters of the guilds controlled production by allowing work by the members only when officially sanctioned. A fine example of this was in the building trades in London in the fourteenth century. In 1356, the Articles of London forbade any worker's accepting a job unless the masters could pledge that the worker had the necessary ability to complete the work. This effectively gave the masters local monopoly control over who worked and where they were able to work. As quickly as firms cooperated, governments attempted to limit the impact of their collusion. For example, the city of Coventry in 1517 prohibited daubers and rough masons from forming agreements among themselves and set wages for their labors.

In the fifteenth and sixteenth centuries, European producers attempted to secure their positions by gaining royal monopolies through exclusive sales arrangements and import restrictions, such as was the case with tin, felt, and pins in England. Throughout this period, masters and guilds continued to limit production through control of apprenticeships and production practices. A good example is the Hatmakers' Congress of 1777, which passed bylaws, inflicted fines on producers not in alignment, and prevented an increase in the number of apprentices. As industry grew, industrialists and merchants colluded to control prices, especially in periods of volatile or low prices. In the seventeenth and eighteenth centuries, producers joined in trying to control prices in iron and glass making and in textiles.

Late in the nineteenth century, European countries promoted national industry, often at the expense of trade. Closed markets, often through bilateral quota arrangements or protective tariffs, barred entry from foreign competition and were fertile ground for the domestic coordination of production. These organizations were called many different things to avoid the "cartel" label. In France, the term *entente* was frequently used, as well as the seemingly benign term *comptoir*. In Germany, the place of cartelization on the greatest scale, there were numerous terms: *Verband*, *Komptoir*, *Vereinigung*, *Gemeinschaft*, *Syndikat*, and *Konvention* were all used in association with various forms of intrafirm cooperation. The German word *Kartel* became anglicized as *cartel*, the word used today. (In the seventeenth century, *cartel* referred to an arrangement of prisoners of war. Liefmann claims that the word's current use is attributable to Eugen Richter and found its way into English usage at the turn of the twentieth century.) French firms also had agreements among themselves in the nineteenth century in most major heavy industries such as coal and steel.

As early as 1840 in Germany, local arrangements existed among steel firms, but more important regional cartels came at the end of the century. One of the first major combines was the Rheinisch-Westfälische Kohlensyndikat. The combination of several local groups into the Roheisen-Syndikat zu Düsseldorf, turned, after a few difficulties, into the Roheisen-Verband in 1910. After World War I, more concentration and cooperation occurred. In 1926, a giant steel trust was organized under the name Vereinigte Stahlwerke, with members the Rheinelbe-Union, the Thyssen group, the Phönix combine, and Rheinstahl. These groups controlled over thirty coal mines and steel mills. This joint-management structure allowed the groups to coordinate production and further to strengthen the agreements between them and other major producers such as Krupp, Klöckner, Hoesch, and the Guttehoffnugshütte, overseen by the German national cartel the Stahlwerks-Verband, which allocated quotas and set prices for most products.

Other collusive organizations grew up in industries such as the electrical industry (with arrangements between AEG and Siemens), dyestuffs (in which a major overarching trust was formed in 1925 out of the major collusive members), and potash (where a cartel was decreed by the Minister of Economic Affairs under a sales cartel known as the Kalissyndicat). Other nations, such as Belgium, Luxembourg, and Italy, also had various combines. This domestic cartelization led, rather naturally, to national groups combining with others to form international cartels, which attempted to control prices and distribution in major export markets. Dozens of these functioned during the interwar period; cartels were organized around most traded products: primary agricultural goods, chemicals and dyes, industrial minerals and inputs (coal, coke, copper, lead, and so on), and pharmaceuticals, (cocaine, for example, was controlled by the International Cocaine Convention, headquartered in Darmstadt).

In foodstuffs, many arrangements were made among producers and exporters of goods such as tea, sugar, and vegetable and animal fats. The tea industry, for example, was cartelized through arrangements among producer groups in India, Ceylon, and the Netherlands Indies. The International Tea Agreement of 1933 was signed by the India Tea Association, the Ceylon Association, and the Vereeniging voor de Thee Cultuur in Nederlandsh Indie. Later groups from China and Japan also coordinated production in conjunction with an overarching organization of growers, exporters, and governmental representatives in the International Tea Committee.

In heavy industries, arrangements were made among domestic cartels in industries such as steel, chemicals and pharmaceuticals, glass, and shipping. The steel industry was organized out of several agreements meant to control most exported steel products; arrangements were made in merchant bars, wire, plates, tubes, and so on. National cartels in Germany (Stahlwerksverband), France (Comptoir Siderurgique), and Belgium and Luxembourg (Cosibel) joined to form the International Steel Cartel with quotas and dictated prices for each product and within each major importing area. In order to perfect the possibilities for price discrimination across export markets, each major market had exclusive buyer organizations that were the sole importers of products from the International Steel Cartel. Later both Britain and the United States joined the international cartel. (Under the Sherman Antitrust Act, U.S. firms were not allowed to conspire to raise prices; but the U.S. firms were allowed to participate in the International Steel Cartel under provisions of the Webb-Pomerene Act.)

Agreements also were made for primary products such as diamonds, tin, aluminum, uranium, and oil. Perhaps one of the longest-lived cartels has been the DeBeers diamond cartel. In 1873, Cecil Rhodes formed a Diamond Syndicate between his mines and buyers' groups in Kimberly, South Africa. By 1880, Rhodes controlled all of the major South African mines. After Rhodes death in 1902,

Ernest Oppenheimer took over control of both DeBeers and the Diamond Syndicate, forging a highly vertically controlled industry with price and distribution controls throughout the world. DeBeers no longer controlled production merely in South Africa; it quickly organized buying and distribution arrangements with diamond-producing countries for rough stones. These joint ventures allowed DeBeers to control prices and allocate diamonds throughout the world. Only very recently has this system been challenged, owing to continued growth in production outside of South Africa and turmoil within the country.

Prior to World War I, cartels functioned throughout what would become the Soviet empire. Throughout the Urals, Siberia, and Central Asia sheet iron was controlled by the Krovlya syndicate, with the Prodamet syndicate controlling the iron market in Russia. In oil and oil products the Nobel group and the Mazut group combined in 1910, forming the Nobmaz cartel, which controlled 80 percent of the petroleum products going through the port of Astrakhan. Cartels functioned with the aid of large banks, and continued to develop up until 1914. After that, the Soviet economy was concentrated and controlled by the state, with various state collectives controlling production and allocation.

In Japan, much of the early industrialization was state-supported, and then was controlled after 1900 by the zaibatsu. These family-based organizations grew out of rapid economic transformations after the Meiji Restoration of 1868. At the turn of the twentieth century, large vertically and horizontally integrated enterprises controlled much of Japan's production: the Mitsui group controlled paper manufacturing, cotton spinning, and electrical machinery, the Mitsubishi group moved into shipbuilding; Sumitomo controlled steel and electric wire manufacturing, along with the Furukawa group; and Asano controlled cement making and oil refining. In reality, these groups are similar to the Konzerne of the interwar German economy, yet with a more direct family orientation than the German groups had. However, the Japanese groups did coordinate production and were the groups to work with the government and any other groups in any of the international arrangements mentioned above.

Depressed industries can, with government approval, create "depression cartels" that can last up to one year. Also, firms can apply to organize and streamline production with "rationalization cartels." This practice was attempted during the Great Depression in the United States through the National Industrial Recovery Act; however, the organizations thus created were deemed unconstitutional in 1935. In post-1950 Europe, steel firms were allowed to coordinate to "rationalize" production (i.e., plan production across firms and countries in order to lower costs). These government-sponsored cartels all have been failures; if anything, they have served only to restrain trade.

In the post-1945 era, the cartel that has most affected world markets has been the Organization of the Petroleum Exporting Countries, known as OPEC. Founding members were Iran, Iraq, Kuwait, Saudi Arabia, and Venezuela. These five were joined by eight others: Qatar (1961), Indonesia (1962), Libya (1962), United Arab Emirates (1967), Algeria (1969), Nigeria (1971), Ecuador (1973), and Gabon (1975). Ecuador and Gabon left the organization in the early 1990s. In the 1970s, these countries orchestrated a contraction in the world's supply of crude oil and sent oil prices up 300 percent. The supply shock from this move greatly affected industrialized nations; and a period of "stagflation," inflation with high unemployment, ensued. One of the features that kept the cartel functioning was the Saudis' very large reserves; in 1992 Saudi crude reserves were at about 36 billion tons, and the cumulative reserves of all other members were at about 65 billion tons, with the next largest holder, Iraq, at about 13 billion tons. Saudi Arabia could threaten to dump reserves and drive prices very low if it discovered cheating among OPEC members. The cartel functioned well until the start of the 1980s when the debt crisis and other factors (e.g., the availability of North Sea oil) caused defections and a collapse of prices. Recently, OPEC once again was able to reduce production and drive world prices upward.

Throughout time and space firms have attempted to combine into trusts and cartels in order to obtain market power. Production, distribution, and shipping all have been controlled in order to secure higher profits. From the medieval guilds and the first industrial groups in textiles to current arrangements in goods such as diamonds, steel, and crude oil, independent firms have attempted to organize, to control production, and to secure higher prices. Inherent instabilities have precluded most of these firms from colluding formally, but some collusive arrangements have existed for relatively long periods, affecting both national and international markets.

BIBLIOGRAPHY

Barbezat, Daniel. "A Price for Every Product, Every Place: The International Steel Export Cartel, 1933–1939." In *Coalitions and Collaboration in International Business*, edited by Geoffrey Jones, pp. 157–175. Elgar Reference Collection, International Library of Critical Writings in Business History, No. 7. Aldershot, U.K., 1993.

Barbezat, Daniel. "The *AVI* and the German Steel Cartels, 1929–1939." *Explorations in Economic History* 31 (April 1994), 479–500. Article showing that the German steel cartels were less able to secure high prices because of forced rebates. A cautionary tale showing that published prices are not always received prices.

Edwards, Corwin. *Control or Cartels and Monopolies: An International Comparison.* New York, 1967. Excellent description of post-1945 structures and antitrust policies throughout Europe and some parts of the rest of the world.

Ekelund, Robert B, Jr., Donald R. Street, and Robert D. Tollison. "Rent Seeking and Property Rights' Assignments as a Process: The Mesta Cartel of Medieval-Mercantile Spain." *Journal of European Economic History* 26.1 (Spring 1997), 9–35.

Griffin, James M., and Weiwen Xiong. "The Incentive to Cheat: An Empirical Analysis of OPEC." *Journal of Law and Economics* 40.2 (October 1997), 289–316.

Grossman, Peter Z. "The Dynamics of a Stable Cartel: The Railroad Express 1851–1913." *Economic Inquiry* 34.2 (April 1996), 220–236.

Hexner, Ervin. *International Cartels.* Chapel Hill, N.C., 1944.

Hillman, John. "The Impact of the International Tin Restriction Schemes on the Return to Equity of Tin Mining Companies, 1927–39." *Business History* 39.3 (July 1997), 65–80.

Liefmann, Robert. *Cartels, Concerns, and Trusts.* London, 1932. Classic account of the development of European cartels with special sections on international cartels and an interesting account of turn-of-the-century thought on the economic effects of cartelization.

Michels, Rudolf. *Cartels, Combines, and Trusts in Post War Germany.* New York, 1928. Classic description of post–World War I industrial development. Very good details about the German cartel laws and the cartels in the coal, iron and steel, electro-technical, dyestuff, and potash industries.

Morikawa, Hidemasa. *Zaibatsu: The Rise and Fall of Family Enterprise Groups in Japan.* Tokyo, 1992. Detailed study of development and implications of the zaibatsu through World War II.

Podolny, Joel M., and Fiona M. Scott Morton. "Social Status, Entry, and Predation: The Case of British Shipping Cartels 1879–1929." *Journal of Industrial Economics* 47.1 (March 1999), 41–67. Interesting paper examining whether the social status of an entrant owner impacted the predation behavior of the incumbent cartels, which finds that high-social-status entrants are significantly less likely (40 percent) to be preyed upon than the low-social-status entrants. Social status is taken as an indicator of an entrant's propensity to be a cooperative cartel participant.

Porter, Robert. "A Study of Cartel Stability: The Joint Executive Committee, 1880–1886." *Bell Journal of Economics* 14.2 (1983), 301–314. Study of the railroad cartel's ability to discern demand shocks from chiseling. See also Green, Edward, J., and Robert H. Porter, "Noncooperative Collusion under Imperfect Price Information." *Econometrica* 52.1 (1984), 87–100.

Sekiguchi, Sueo. "Industrial Adjustment and Cartel Actions in Japan." *Troubled Industries in the United States and Japan*, edited by Hong W. Tan and Shimada Haruo, pp. 189–207. RAND study series. New York, 1994.

Spar, Debora. *The Cooperative Edge: The Internal Politics of International Cartels.* Ithaca, N.Y., 1994. Excellent study of twentieth-century cartel developments in tin, uranium, diamonds, and aluminum.

Stigler, George. "A Theory of Oligopoly." *Journal of Political Economy* 72.1 (1964), 39–63. Classic study on the stability conditions for collusion.

Stocking, G. W., and M. W. Watkins. *Cartels in Action.* New York, 1946. Classic overview of the many early-twentieth-century cartels. Excellent source on the organization and operation of the various pre–World War II cartels.

Unwin, George. *Industrial Organization in the Sixteenth and Seventeenth Centuries.* Oxford, 1904. Solid history of early industrialization with good descriptions of early collusive attempts throughout Europe.

Werden, G. J., and M. G. Baumann. "A Simple Model of Imperfect Competition in Which Four Are Few but Three Are Not." *Journal of Industrial Economics* 34.3 (1986), 331–335.

DANIEL BARBEZAT

Concentration and Entry

If independent firms can combine into larger firms or collude and prevent other firms' entry, they can restrict output, raise prices, and receive economic profits. In competitive industries, firms are generally small and numerous and thus have no market power. Market conditions determine prices that competitive firms must charge; they have no power to affect prices. This situation is due to entry and exit; with industry profits, firms enter and drive prices down, and with industry losses, firms exit, forcing prices up. In competitive equilibrium, economic profits should be at or near zero. However, in some industries, such as steel or oil, enterprises naturally attain large market shares. In these cases, firms often combine to gain advantages in raw-material attainment and production efficiency. If, however, firms can block entry, or if market conditions make entry difficult, then the firms may exploit their size and maintain positive economic profits. In addition, if the number of firms is relatively low and can remain so because of barriers to entry, then the firms can strategically collude and sustain noncompetitive prices and profits. This is not to say that the mere existence of a small number of firms means that firms are exploiting market power and causing lost welfare.

Empirical studies of concentration have used two basic measures: the concentration ratio and the Herfindahl-Hirschman Index. The first is a simple sum of market shares, usually measured in terms of sales (also in terms of value added or employment) of the top firms, traditionally the top four firms. This number is easy to calculate and has been widely used, both in economic studies and in antitrust cases; however, it gives no indication of the concentration outside the top firms or the distribution among them. A market could have a high four-firm concentration ratio but a relatively low eight-firm ratio. Also, two markets might have identical four firm concentration ratios, but one firm might dominate most of the production in one market, whereas in the other the top four firms could be equally large. To address these issues of inequality among the largest firms, and between the largest firms and the rest of the firms, the Herfindahl-Hirschman Index is calculated as the sum of the squares of all the firms' market shares, so that it should be close to zero for a competitive industry and ten thousand for a monopoly.

However measured, concentration is due to a variety of factors. Clearly, in markets with large economies of scale, high fixed costs, and other natural barriers to entry, there are likely to be a few large firms. There need not be any collusion among firms nor any anticompetitive practices to bring about concentration. Historically, as the scale of both industry and agriculture expanded, firm and farm sizes increased as mechanization and large capitalization were introduced. Through the seventeenth century, labor productivity was generally low, and production required highly labor-intensive techniques. During this period, there were artificial barriers to entry, through either laws

supporting only certain producers or trade associations and guilds that limited the number of producers. As new techniques developed and more capital was employed, markets expanded, costs fell, the size of enterprises grew naturally, and markets became more concentrated.

The industrial development of Europe and America in the nineteenth and early-twentieth centuries exhibited large increases in concentration. Firm size(s) grew in many industries, developing from protoindustrialization, putting out systems to artisanal shops, on to actual factory work in textiles and other light manufacturing. The first very large businesses grew after 1850 with railroads and the new industrial production of steel with Sir Henry Bessemer's invention of the converter in 1856, bringing mass production to the steel industry. This natural process of large-scale production in high–fixed-cost enterprises is still evolving today in the economic development of the newly industrializing nations of the world. Attempts to change this process have been very costly, as evidenced by the disastrous forced microproduction units of the Great Leap Forward of Maoist China in the late 1950s and early 1960s.

Over the twentieth century, the U.S. market showed a good deal of turnover among the largest firms. The "great merger movement" over the ten years 1895 through 1904 was preceded by the formation of the Standard Oil Trust in 1882 and a variety of trusts and consolidations in other industries, such as sugar and lead. In fact, a study of factory size over the period 1879 to 1929 has shown that it doubled from 1869 through 1889 but only increased about a quarter between 1899 and 1929, suggesting that economies of scale were not an important motive for the merger wave. Perhaps as important were the aims of controlling prices, exploiting economies of scope, and introducing managerial efficiencies. The process of consolidation and merger continued through the next phase of industrial development. Studies have shown that of the 100 largest U.S. firms in 1909, only 36 remained among the top 100 in 1958, and only 21 by 1976. More detailed studies, though, have shown that much of this change was due to merger rather than liquidation, as the largest firms have had the highest survival rate.

The relationship between large firms and the government is often ambiguous. In Japan, after the Meiji Restoration the government along with large, powerful family conglomerates known as zaibatsu dominated industrial production. After about 1905, these family-controlled vertically and horizontally integrated combines no longer needed direct government support. Groups such as Mitsubishi (starting in shipbuilding), Mitsui (paper), and Sumitomo (steel) became industrial powers that controlled virtually all Japanese industry. Clearly, throughout the early development of European markets, monarchs established exclusive sales arrangements and supported firms in becoming large and powerful so that the monarchy could easily extract taxes from them. In more recent times, the relationship between larger firms and the political process has ranged between two extremes, with the firms having more influence through effective lobbying and encountering more difficulty with the close, incisive scrutiny of antitrust authorities. A number of studies of U.S. and British markets have shown that there is an important negative relationship between firm size and corporate income tax payments. Studies also have revealed that larger firms have to deal with more regulations than smaller ones and more often fight against antitrust cases brought against them. Whatever the case, the manufacturing sector became more competitive over the last quarter of the twentieth century, largely because of increased import competition, domestic antitrust activity, and reductions in minimum efficient scales. Transportation and communication network improvements have reduced the benefits of agglomeration. Since the service sector is generally less concentrated than manufacturing, collusion has been less in evidence in the service area.

The mere concentration of firms with large market shares is no longer seen as necessarily welfare-reducing. Some have argued that innovation and research may be stimulated by large firms because they have larger resources to devote to research and development. However, studies of U.S. firms have shown both large and small firms to be equally research intensive. Innovation does not seem at all to be the province of large firms only. Patents have come from many sources although often their widespread distribution has come about from large-firm activity, especially when there are imperfect capital markets. The overall welfare effects of concentrated markets are unclear; so the effects of entry or potential entry are multifaceted.

The ease of firm entry does help determine the level of concentration in a market. In addition to the structural factors listed above, many strategic factors account for ease or difficulty of entry. Large excess capacity and sunk costs can deter entry, as can very specialized skill requirements. Firms can punish entry through price lowering, and thus can deter entry with the threat of lowered prices. One of the ways firms hinder entry is by strategically increasing capacity, either creating a large excess capacity to use when a market is threatened or increasing size so as to lower marginal costs, thereby committing themselves to produce at the limit capacity if new firms enter. In special cases (e.g., contestable markets, or investments with sunk costs), such entry is less likely, even in the case of existing profits. In addition to changing capacity, firms can price so that potential entrants have no incentive to enter; here the models are of defensive limit-pricing and aggressive predatory pricing. In addition, if production itself is accompanied by steep learning curves, then incumbents can deter entry by moving quickly down the learning curve and keeping ahead of other potential producers. Finally, incumbents can exploit demand conditions by filling all the market niches through product differentiation (increasing the scope of their production), thus giving new entrants no foothold in markets.

When capacity is used strategically to deter entry, the incumbent firm moves first to set its capacity, which affects the amount that it can credibly threaten to produce if new firms attempt to enter, as in the standard Dixit-Spence framework. The classic case of this is that of Alcoa's aluminum production and the case brought against the firm in 1945 (*U.S.* v. *Aluminum Co. of America*, 1945). Patents gave Alcoa a superior cost advantage and precluded entry before 1909. In 1912, a consent decree forced Alcoa to refrain from making agreements with foreign producers and with utilities to bar electricity supply to other producers. Yet, by 1938, through aggressive business practice, Alcoa held over 90 percent of the market. In the judgment against Alcoa, it was found that the "doubling and redoubling" of capacity in anticipation of demand gave Alcoa a monopoly position though the exclusion of possible entry. This illustrates the use of capacity and the credible deterrence of possible entrants. Alcoa could easily respond to any entrant by increasing production and forcing prices down.

In addition to holding defensive capacity, if Alcoa, or another firm with market power, can control prices, then it can limit-price, that is, set a price in order to stop another firm from entering. This could mean that a firm could keep prices very high and drop them only with entry or the threat of entry, or that the firm could have some scale advantage that would force other firms to charge more in order to break even. Essentially, a firm without any special cost-advantage would have to keep prices low and receive near-competitive profits. An example often cited is DuPont's virtual monopoly on cellophane from 1924 through 1947. In spite of the monopoly, DuPont's prices fell over 80 percent through 1947, indicating that the social cost of this sort of limitation is low. Another classic example involves the consequences of the antitrust case brought against United Shoe Machinery (*U.S.* v. *United Shoe Machinery*, 1954). Because United Shoe Machinery held over 90 percent of the market, it was found to have monopolized the market even though the rates of its return on capital were at competitive levels. In its decision, the Supreme Court decided that it would review market shares after ten years. In response, United Shoe raised prices, and its rate of return nearly doubled. Increased profits, of course, attracted entry, and over fifty firms entered the market.

Another type of pricing to impede entry or even drive out incumbents is predatory pricing, which occurs when a firm lowers a price, often below unit costs, in order to drive out competitors or to preclude entry. Economists have long been leery of this sort of behavior, thinking that merger would be preferable to such costly attacks. However, not all firms are willing to sell; family-owned firms often do not want to lose managerial control. In addition, it is not always legal to merge, as in the U.S. case under Sherman antitrust scrutiny. The classic regulatory case is *Federal Trade Commission* v. *Standard Oil of New Jersey* (1911). However, Standard probably used forms of limit-pricing; whatever the case, Standard Oil was found guilty of noncompetitive behavior.

Clearer in its predation was the American Tobacco Company, which effectively used discriminatory pricing to attack firms in segmented markets in order to make them lose money and lower their market value. At the turn of the twentieth century, American Tobacco created bogus firms in various regional markets to apply below-cost pricing, forcing the existing firms to lose money and thus lowering the costs of acquiring these rivals. American Tobacco saved up to 60 percent of what it would have paid had it not used this low-price strategy. As a form of cartel control, selling below cost has stabilized cartels, for example, through dominant members such as Germany in the interwar steel cartels, South Africa in the diamond cartel, and Saudi Arabia in OPEC during the 1970s.

Finally, if an industry exhibits learning-by-doing advantages or high switching costs, entry is discouraged. In the learning-by-doing models, firms might have an incentive to produce even more (thus, to price less) than short-term costs would suggest. This means that what might appear to be predatory pricing might be a strategy for long-run attainment of even lower costs through learning-by-doing. A classic case of this is the early-nineteenth-century U.S. textile market and the early-twentieth-century rayon market, with firm production and strategy seemingly guided by these concerns.

BIBLIOGRAPHY

Bagwell, Kyle. "Informational Product Differentiation as a Barrier to Entry." *International Journal of Industrial Organization* 8.2 (1990), 207–223.

Baumol, William, John Panzar, and Robert Willig. *Contestable Markets and the Theory of Industrial Structure*. New York, 1982.

Church, Jeffrey, and Roger Ware. *Industrial Organization: A Strategic Approach*. New York, 2000. Excellent text explaining the theory and providing many examples; see especially Chapter 14, "Entry Deterrence," and Chapter 16, "Strategic Behavior: Applications."

Collins, Norman, and Lee Preston. "The Size Structure of the Largest Industrial Firms, 1909–1958." *American Economic Review* 51 (1961), 986–1011.

Dixit, A. "The Role of Investment in Entry Deterrence." *Economic Journal* 90 (1980), 95–106. The standard reference, with Spence below, showing how capacity can be used strategically to limit entry. Dixit's model differs from Spence's only in that the postentry game is Cournot, whereas Spence's is Bertrand.

Dunne, Timothy, Mark Robert, and Larry Samuelson. "Patterns of Firm Entry and Exit in U.S. Manufacturing Industries." *Rand Journal of Economics* 19.4 (1988), 495–515. Comprehensive examination of entry and exit of firms using manufacturing censuses of 1963, 1967, 1972, 1977, and 1982. Finds that entry is likely to be unsuccessful, and that most entrants are small.

Jarmin, R. S. "Learning by Doing and Competition in the Early Rayon Industry." *Rand Journal of Economics* 25 (1994), 441–454. Econometric work showing how investments were used to move down learning curves in order to reduce rivals' production.

Lamoreaux, Naomi. *The Great Merger Movement in American Business, 1895–1904*. New York, 1985.

Martin, Stephen. *Advanced Industrial Economics*. Cambridge, Mass., 1993. Excellent account of the literature as of its publication, with clear explanations of advanced articles; see especially Chapter 7, "Market Structure, Entry, and Exit."

McCraw, Thomas, and Reinhardt Forest. "Losing to Win: U.S. Steel's Pricing, Investment Decisions, and Market Share, 1901–1938." *Journal of Economic History* 49.3 (1989), 593–619. Examination of the constraints faced by U.S. Steel in pursuing entry-barring, collusive practices.

Mowery, David. "Industrial Research and Firm Size, Survival, and Growth in American Manufacturing, 1921–1946: An Assessment." *Journal of Economic History* 43.4 (1983), 953–980. Article showing that large firms were no more research-intensive than smaller firms, and that research seemed to improve growth for both small and large firms.

Nix, Joan, and David Gabel. "AT&T's Strategic Response to Competition: Why Not Preempt Entry?" *Journal of Economic History* 53.2 (1993), 377–387. Very interesting article exploring the reasons for AT&T's seemingly not using entry-barring pricing strategies after its patents expired.

O'Brien, Anthony Patrick. "Factory Size, Economies of Scale, and the Great Merger Wave of 1898–1902." *Journal of Economic History* 48.3 (1988), 639–649. Article showing that gaining economies of scale was not an important factor in the great merger wave.

Salamon, L. M., and J. J. Siegfried. "Economic Power and Political Influence: The Impact of Industry Structure on Public Policy." *American Political Science Review* 67 (1977), 1026–1043.

Spence, A. M. "Entry, Capacity, Investment, and Oligopoly Pricing," *Bell Journal of Economics* 8 (1977), 534–544.

DANIEL BARBEZAT

Price-Fixing and Vertical Constraints

In both highly competitive markets and more restrictive oligopolistic markets, firms use a variety of vertical controls over the pricing and the distribution of their products. The main means are tying, exclusive territory restraints, resale price maintenance, and exclusive dealing. In tying, firms link the purchase of one good with the forced purchase of another, as has been documented with computer purchases and the Windows operating system. With exclusive territory restraints, distributors are given guaranteed areas that cannot be contested by other distributors. Resale price maintenance is the practice of a supplier's setting the price that distributors must charge. Exclusive dealing is simply limiting retailers to carrying only one firm's products or limiting one firm's output to only one retailer, as has been the case throughout the auto industry. The actual practices and the welfare implications of these vertical policies depend upon a variety of conditions but especially on the relative competitive position of the industry.

Tying occurs for a variety of reasons. No one would question linking the sale of a car with tires, for instance, or the control of distributors' or franchises' supply purchases in order to ensure uniformity and quality. There could be clear efficiency gains for these types of tyings. However these practices can be exclusionary; they can limit competition by constraining entry. In Europe, tying has been paid little attention; but in both Germany and Spain, tying is deemed abusive when imposed by dominant firms. In Ireland, tying, for most purposes, is prohibited. In the United States, in Section 3 of the Clayton Act, tying is specifically precluded when it "substantially lessen(s) competition or tend(s) to create a monopoly." One of the first cases brought against IBM by the U.S. government concerned the tying of IBM's unpatented punch cards to the lease of its machines. IBM claimed that it wanted to control the quality of the cards since jams would reflect poorly on the firm and would increase the cost of service contracts. In *IBM* v. *U.S.* (1936), IBM was found guilty of limiting competition and ordered to allow the use of competitors' cards in leased machines. IBM did as it was told but still retained over 90 percent of the market after 1936. On the other hand, Kodak's 1954 consent decree resulted in a large change in market share. Kodak tied photo development to the purchase of Kodak film in the 1950s. Before the antitrust case in 1954, Kodak held about 90 percent share of photo processing; after the decree, Kodak divested much of its processing capability, and its share fell to about half the market. Many firms entered the industry, and prices fell. The general effects of tying depend upon market concentration and likelihood of entry.

Clearly, territorial constraints could be used to foster cartel arrangements. Firms can enhance market power through exclusive territories, using franchise fees to recoup distribution costs. However, the restraint is within a product and not across products. In the United States, the classic instance of this involved a truck manufacturer, the White Motor Company (*White Motor Company* v. *U.S.*, 1963), that had territorial restrictions on its franchises. The Supreme Court ruled that the existence of these arrangements were not illegal *per se* since they might actually increase White's ability to compete with larger producers. Even though a manufacturer can limit the number of outlets through which it chooses to sell its product, it cannot also divide up territories collusively among its outlets. In the *U.S.* v. *General Motors Corp.* (1966), General Motors was found to be in a conspiracy to restrain trade by coordinating territories among its dealers. In a market with a large degree of product differentiation, competition among distributors is especially important. Customer

loyalty to a product might be exploited by exclusive dealers with unique territories; in the case of soft drink producers, such as Coca-Cola and Pepsi-Cola, it has been estimated by the Federal Trade Commission that removal of these sorts of restrictions would save consumers over $200 million per year. The major issue with territorial restraints is that of whether the reduction in competition among distributors of the same product is outweighted by an increase in competition across products.

Resale price agreements are really vertical price controls. A manufacturer sets the price that its dealers have to charge. These arrangements have been prevalent in British markets and in the United States in pharmaceuticals, cosmetics, and small electric appliances. The early defining cases in the United States were *Dr. Miles Medical Co.* v. *John D. Park and Sons Co.* (1911) and *United States* v. *Colgate and Co.* (1919). In the first case, Miles, the producer, sued Park and Sons, a wholesaler, for receiving goods in the market and then undercutting prices. The Supreme Court ruled against Miles. With Colgate, the Court found that announced, enforced resale price agreements were not illegal *per se*. In the 1930s, retailers actually lobbied for and won passage of the Miller-Tydings Act, which enabled the use of strict resale price maintenance. In 1952, the act was strengthened by controlling "non-signers" under the McGuire Act. Finally, these practices were curtailed by the Consumer Goods Pricing Act of 1975. Since 1975, resale price arrangements have been legal only if retailers are wholly owned by producers or, as in the Colgate case above, the producer simply announces the resale prices and cuts off distribution for good if those prices are not charged.

Exclusive dealing has been practiced for a wide variety of reasons. In its 1985 "Vertical Restraints Guidelines" the U.S. Justice Department made it clear that exclusive dealing conducted by firms with market shares is unlikely to facilitate collusion or deter competition. The practices themselves are not illegal, but if they are shown to deter entry or support collusion, they can be challenged in court. As in tying, Section 3 of the Clayton Act is cited for infringements. An early example was the 1922 case of *Standard Fashion* v. *Magrane-Houston Co.*; since the designer held 40 percent of all dress-pattern outlets, the exclusive arrangement was judged illegal. Perhaps the automotive industry best illustrates the issues raised by exclusive sales arrangements in its dealerships and exclusive factory-authorized parts for service. Major cases have been launched against General Motors, most notably *F.T.C.* v. *General Motors Corp.* (1941). The cases have been judged on whether the claim could be made that quality was being preserved by allowing only certain products to be sold. When territories are given to dealers (territorial restraints) along with the prices to be charged (resale price maintenance), exclusive dealers can effectively be the agents stabilizing cartel arrangements and deterring entry. This was the structure within the many international cartel arrangements of the early-twentieth century.

BIBLIOGRAPHY

Aghion, Phillipe, and Patrick Bolton. "Contracts as a Barrier to Entry." *American Economic Review* 62.5 (1987), 388–401. Theoretical paper on the entry effects of exclusive dealing.

Barbezat, Daniel. "A Price for Every Product, Every Place: The International Steel Export Cartel, 1933–1939." In *Coalitions and Collaboration in International Business*, edited by Geoffrey Jones, pp. 157–175. Elgar Reference Collection, International Library of Critical Writings in Business History, No. 7, Aldershot, U.K., 1993. Examination of exclusive import merchants and third-degree price discrimination in the International Steel Export Cartel.

Gilligan, Thomas, "The Competitive Effects of Resale Price Maintenance." *Rand Journal of Economics* 17.4 (1986), 544–556.

Greer, Douglas. *Industrial Organization and Public Policy*. New York, 1992. Excellent background of the legal cases of each of the vertical restraints. See especially Chapter 19, "Vertical Market Restriction: Practice and Policy."

Heim, Carol. "Industrial Organization and Regional Development in Interwar Britain." *Journal of Economic History* 43.4 (1983), 931–952.

Martin, Stephen. *Advanced Industrial Economics*. Cambridge, Mass., 1993. Advanced theoretical treatment of issues with excellent bibliography. See especially Chapter 12, "Vertical Restraints."

Posner, R. A. *Antitrust Law: An Economic Perspective*. Chicago, 1976. Elaboration of the "Chicago School's" views on the competitive effects of vertical restraints and how they often add, rather than diminish, economic efficiency.

Rey, Patrick, and Joseph Stiglitz. "Vertical Restraints and Producers' Competition." *European Economic Review* 32.3-2 (1986), 561–568. Theoretical paper on the market-power enhancing effects of territorial restraints.

Shepard, Andrea, "Pricing Behavior and Vertical Contracts in Retail Markets." *American Economic Review* 80.2 (1990), 427–431. Examination of the effects of vertical contracts in the retail gasoline industry.

Whinston, Michael. "Tying, Foreclosure, and Exclusion." *American Economic Review* 80.4 (1990), 837–859. Theoretical paper on the market-power-enhancing effects of tying.

DANIEL BARBEZAT

Price Discrimination

Price discrimination occurs when a seller sells similar goods at different price-cost ratios, in the case of either similar (or identical) production costs but different selling prices or different production costs with similar (or identical) selling prices. In order to pursue this sort of pricing, a firm must have some market power; a competitive firm cannot choose its selling price. In addition, sellers must face and identify different demand groups with differing price elasticities. Finally, the different groups must be unable to sell to each other; otherwise the group receiving a good for a lower price could sell it for a guaranteed profit to the group charged a higher price. This arbitrage can be precluded by the groups' being widely separated in space or by the good's being a nontransferable good, such as a service. A classic example of precluding resale is quoted in Douglas Greer's industrial organization text; in the 1940s, the firm Rohm & Haas sold methyl methacrylate plastic for industrial use at \$.85 per pound and for dental use at \$45.00 per pound, clearly, there was a great incentive for industrial purchasers to sell to dentists. Rohm & Haas threatened to stop this resale by placing small amounts of arsenic or lead into the industrial plastic, thus stopping the resale through intervention of the Food and Drug Administration.

Broadly, there are three types of price discrimination. Under first-degree price discrimination a seller can sell each unit at the value of the marginal benefit for each consumer, thus extracting the full consumer surplus from consumers. This clearly provides more output than does the monopoly case, in which the firm cannot price-discriminate. Examples of this sort of discrimination are hard to find in practice. It is somewhat found in bazaar-type markets where consumers haggle individually at different times and thus pay different prices for the same products.

In second-degree discrimination a seller sells blocks of output at various prices, the price usually falling as the blocks move to greater quantities. This is similar to the first-degree case except that sellers extract less of the consumer surplus from consumers, given that they have to price in chunks of output. Scale discounts are very common in markets with large firms having market power or in associations of firms, such as those that characterized industry in western Europe in the nineteenth and early-twentieth centuries. For example, in prewar Britain this was practiced in many industries, such as cement, glass, and textiles. This was also the case in German, French, and Belgian steel and coal markets, as in many other markets dominated by producer organizations. Scale discounts also were common during the growth of U.S. industry; but the Clayton Act directly sought to control price discrimination, and the Robinson-Patman Act of 1936 specifically controlled discrimination against small purchasers. Robinson-Patman was enacted in direct response to small independent grocers and drugstore owners complaining about the price advantages that A&P could force out of wholesalers. The classic application for "primary level injuries," acts affecting sellers' markets, is the *Utah Pie* v. *Continental Baking Co.* (1967) case. Utah Pie, a local producer in Salt Lake City, had to fight three nationwide brands that were selling pies below cost in the Salt Lake area. Although Utah Pie was able to keep producing, it sued and eventually won its case in the Supreme Court. The benchmark case in U.S. regulation affecting buyers' markets, for "secondary level injuries," is *Federal Trade Commission* v. *Morton Salt* (1948). Morton Salt was selling table salt from \$1.60 per case down to \$1.35 per case, depending upon overall purchases. The Supreme

Court ruled against Morton, finding that this practice gave large buyers an undue competitive advantage over small buyers. As in the case with first-degree discrimination, more output is produced than under the single-monopoly case; but the concerns here are in the distributive effects, with small merchants being placed at a disadvantage.

Under third-degree price discrimination, a seller faces two separated demand curves with differing price elasticities. If the seller produces the good for both markets, its marginal costs of production are the same, but the marginal revenue curves in the two markets are different, thus yielding different prices. This is a common type of price discrimination and is typically found in export cartels with exclusive dealerships in importing countries. This is not merely "dumping," selling exports at a lower price than in protected domestic markets; rather, large firms set up exclusive foreign agents who sell under quasi-monopoly status. A fine example of this was the International Steel Export Cartel of the 1930s. Members Germany, France, Belgium, and Luxembourg established exclusive import merchants throughout Scandinavia and charged different prices to different countries, based on their relative steel demands. United States firms attempted these sorts of cartel arrangements in the 1930s under the Webb-Pomerene Act of 1918, which enables U.S. firms to collude over sales to foreign markets as long as their doing so does not harm U.S. markets.

Lastly, a special case of price discrimination is so-called predatory pricing, wherein a firm lowers price, often below unit costs, in order to drive competitors out, preclude their entry, or discipline collusive arrangements. Economists have long been leery of this approach, thinking that merger would be preferable to such costly attacks. However, the historical record demonstrates this sort of behavior.

BIBLIOGRAPHY

Barbezat, Daniel. "A Price for Every Product, Every Place: The International Steel Export Cartel, 1933–1939." In *Coalitions and Collaboration in International Business*, edited by Geoffrey Jones, pp. 157–175. Elgar Reference Collection, International Library of Critical Writings in Business History, No. 7. Aldershot, U.K., 1993.

Burns, Malcolm. "Predatory Pricing and the Acquisition Cost of Competitors." *Journal of Political Economy* 94.2 (1986), 266–296. Calculations of the savings of the tobacco trust's use of predatory pricing.

Greer, Douglas. *Industrial Organization and Public Policy*. New York, 1992. Excellent account of theory and application of the various sorts of price discrimination; see Chapter 14, "Price and Production Strategy in the Long Run: Theory and Evidence," and Chapter 15 for the application to public policy.

McGee, John. "Predatory Price Cutting: The Standard Oil (N.J.) Case." *Journal of Law and Economics* 1 (1958), 137–169. Classic dismissal of the use of predatory pricing.

Philips, Louis, *The Economics of Price Discrimination*. Cambridge, 1983. Highly technical account of all aspects of discrimination with analyses of welfare implications.

Scherer, F. M. *Industrial Market Structure and Economic Performance*. Chicago, 1980. Excellent source of examples of price discrimination

in the United States; see especially Chapter 21, "Antitrust Policy: Other Restrictions on Conduct."

DANIEL BARBEZAT

CARTHAGE. Carthage, founded as early as 814 BCE as a colony of the Phoenicians, traders from the Levant (in this case, Tyre), was located on a natural harbor in modern Tunisia on the North African coast. Though virtually all the historical references to Carthage come from writings of its enemies, the city surpassed the fame of any other Phoenician colony and had an agrarian base that supplemented its role as trading post and enabled a rapid period of urbanization. Though the legendary founding is set at 814 BCE, the archaeological record suggests no permanent residency until over half a century later. The archaeological record, however, is almost as scant as the written record. Much of Carthage's lingering fame comes from Rome's powerful testament to Carthage's influence in its choice to render the city uninhabitable for generations to come at the conclusion of the Third Punic War in 146 BCE.

Through the time of its power, from its ascendancy in the sixth century to its notorious destruction in the middle of the second century BCE, Carthage both traded and competed directly with the Greek city-states and Rome for control of the Mediterranean, in this process passing on valuable goods and military, navigation, and agricultural techniques from the entire known world of the day. Carthaginian territorial claims led to warfare with the Greeks in Sicily, Marseille, and Corsica, and later Rome and Carthage fought the Punic Wars throughout Europe and North Africa.

Opportunities for trade pushed the Carthaginians to explore not only the Mediterranean but also as far north as Britain, in search of tin, and down both sides of the African coast, likely reaching as far south as modern-day Senegal, mainly trading salt, cloth, and light arms for gold, ivory, and slaves. Carthage, begun as a colony itself, began to assert independence and found its own colonies as early as 654 BCE (at Ibiza). By 550 BCE, Carthage had established naval dominion over Sardinia and Sicily, and by the end of the sixth century treated with the newly formed Roman Republic for hegemonic control of these islands and other colonial outposts throughout the Mediterranean. With the fall of Tyre in 573 BCE, the Phoenician era shifted to the Punic era.

Coinage at Carthage began in the fifth century BCE and conformed both to the Attic and Phoenician standards. Local coinage did not appear until the third century, but prior to this time there is written record (from Aeschines) of a fiat currency, called "leather money," in circulation. Carthage earned the majority of its revenues through colonial tribute, tax revenues, and mines it controlled.

Estimates for Carthage's population (citizens and resident aliens) run as high as 700,000 people (from Strabo),

CARTHAGE. Destroyed by the Romans in 146 BCE the city was rebuilt on a new site by Augustus between 27 BCE and 14 CE. (Werner Forman Archive/Art Resource, NY)

but a more accurate figure, given the archaeological record, is perhaps 400,000 during the city's heyday in the third century BCE.

From Aristotle we know that Carthage garnered much respect from the Greeks for having a constitution. In essence an aristocracy with strong religious institutions, the main distinction between the Carthaginians and their contemporaries was Carthage's separation of political and military control. In addition, the citizens of Carthage used mercenaries for most of their warfare.

Written and archaeological evidence indicates that the ruling class had strong agrarian ties, and in particular the Barca family (which produced Hamilcar and Hannibal, among others) controlled significant agricultural land in addition to mines in Spain and Corsica. There are several accounts of an agricultural handbook, focused on sophisticated techniques for growing cereals, vines, and olives, thought valuable enough to translate into Greek and Latin. Also, Livy tells us that in 203 BCE Scipio Africanus proposes a significant contribution of 500,000 bushels of corn and 300,000 bushels of barley as a contribution toward a peace treaty, more fitting tribute from an agrarian society than from one whose power base came from traded gold and similar products.

Carthage, successfully built up through a combination of trading and navigation skills and sufficient agricultural resources and urban institutions, checked the growth rates of both Greek city-states and Rome and dominated the naval scene on the Mediterranean for almost four hundred years before a final and thorough defeat at the hands of the Roman Scipio Aemilianus. Carthage's remaining inhabitants scattered or were enslaved, the city's landholdings became a Roman province, and the Romans eventually began to rebuild the site over a century later, under Augustus.

BIBLIOGRAPHY

Aubet, Maria Eugenia. *The Phoenicians and the West: Politics, Colonies, and Trade.* Translated by Mary Turton. Cambridge, 1993.

Church, Alfred J., and Arthur Gilman. *The Story of the Nations,* vol. 4, *Carthage, or the Empire of Africa.* London, 1888.

Harden, Donald. *Ancient People and Places,* vol. 26, *The Phoenicians.* New York, 1962.

Heeren, A. H. L. *Historical Researches into the Politics, Intercourse, and Trade of the Carthaginians, Ethiopians, and Egyptians.* 2d ed. Translated from German by D. A. Talboys. London, 1857.

Moore, Karl, and David Lewis. *Birth of the Multinational: 2000 Years of Ancient Business History—From Ashur to Augustus.* Copenhagen, 1999.

Warmington, B. H. *Carthage.* London, 1960.

BROOKS KAISER

CASSAVA. *Cassava, yuca,* and *manioc* are all names for the same plant. The Taíno Indians bartered *cassabe* (bread made from cassava) to Christopher Columbus on the island he had named San Salvador on 12 October 1492. Since wheat fares poorly in the Caribbean, the Spaniards

CASSAVA. Harvest at the Mandioca Flour Plantation, Brazil, 1934. (*New York World-Telegram* and the *Sun* Newspaper Photograph Collection/Prints and Photographs Division, Library of Congress)

soon thereafter established a flourishing trade with the Tainos, of European-made beads, cloth, and metallic items for cassabe. The European sailors, especially, appreciated the new *cassabe* bread. Cassabe can be stored over a year without worm or mold infestation, unlike the wheat-based "ship's biscuit" that was the mainstay of their diet. Hispaniola's conquistadors subjected the Tainos to an annual tribute of gold, but in regions where there was no gold, they accepted payment in cassabe.

Cassava (*Manihot esculenta*) is a tuberous plant of the family *Euphorbiaceae* that is believed to have originated in Brazil. There are two varieties: bitter and sweet. The Tainos' ancestors brought cassava cultivation with them from the Orinoco and Amazon River valleys and perfected the tedious process of making cassabe from bitter yucca, which is extremely poisonous, releasing cyanic or prussic acid. The poison can be removed by fermentation or multiple washes, but the most common method is that used by the Taínos: wash the tubers, remove the brown outer coating, and grate the remaining white portion into a fine pulp.

Press the pulp, traditionally in a *cibucán* (tube of woven palm), then dry it in the sun. Finally, cook the resulting flour on a *burén* ("griddle"), causing it to mass into a simple cake, without other ingredients.

The roots of the cassava plant have only a one percent protein content, but they have twice the fiber than potatoes and more potassium. Most important, cassava per unit of cultivation, is higher in caloric content than any other agricultural crop, with the exception of sugar cane. Cassava grows in poor soils, tolerating the full sun of the tropics, but also grows in partial shade, does not rot in wet areas, lasts through droughts, and can be left in the ground for many months after maturation, to be harvested as needed.

Portuguese sailors introduced cassava to Africa in the early sixteenth century, where it quickly became a staple food in poor, sparsely populated regions. (Historians speculate that the resultant population expansion catalyzed the slave trade.) Today cassava is grown throughout tropical South America, the Caribbean, Africa, Asia, and

Indonesia. It is eaten boiled, fried, or baked, in the form of bread or pudding, or as toasted flour sprinkled on other foods. Cassava foods include *bammy* bread (Jamaica), *farofa* (Brazil), *balinghoy, kamoteng, kahoy, kalibre,* and *bangala* (Phillipines), and *gari, fufu,* and *farinah* (Africa). Outside the tropics, cassava is generally known only for the tapioca, a gelatinized starch pellet, derived from it.

Agriculturalists are seeking new ways to use cassava. It shows promise as an animal food, and its starch, which is viscous and resistant to freezing and shear stress, can be used in a wide range of nutritional and industrial processes. Cassava cultivation has helped several third and fourth world nations reduce their dependence on imported grains. Annual production is expected to reach 210 million tons by 2005.

BIBLIOGRAPHY

"Defensa de la causa de la yuca." *Food and Agricultural Organization of the United Nations* (FAO), <http://www.fao.org/Noticias/2000/000405-s.htm>. Explains the nutritional value of yuca (cassava) and some of the innovative ways scientists and agriculturalists attempt to expand its use and cultivation.

Food and Agricultural Organization of the United Nations. *Economía mundial de la yuca: Hechos, tendencias y perspectivas* (Economic World of Yuca: Facts, Tendencies and Perspectives). Rome, 2000.

Oviedo y Valdés, Gonzalo Fernández de. *Historia general y natural de las Indias.* In *Biblioteca de Autores Españoles,* vols. 117–121. Madrid, 1959. Initially published in 1535, Oviedo, an accomplished naturalist, wrote excellent descriptions of the early cultivation and processing of yucca (cassava) that he saw in the Americas. See in particular book 7, chapters 1 and 2. Sterling Stoudemire translated the natural history portion of Oviedo's work into English in 1959, and it was published by the University of North Carolina Press, though it is not considered to be a very good translation.

Tabío, Ernesto E. *Arqueología: Agricultura aborigen antillana.* Havana, 1989. A fascinating treatise on the South American Indians' development of yucca (cassava) from a poisonous wild plant to a cultigen and the transplantation to the Greater Antilles of the technology required to cultivate and process it.

Viola, Herman L., and Carolyn Margolis, eds. *Seeds of Change: Five Hundred Years since Columbus.* Washington and London, 1991. A collection of fifteen articles describing the agricultural exchanges between the Old and New Worlds since 1492, and their social and economic consequences.

Lynne A. Guitar

CATALONIA. The core of the Roman Tarraconensis province—the current Catalonia—began to acquire some distinctive features by the eighth century when Charlemagne created the "Marca Hispanica," which subsequently became part of the medieval kingdom of Aragon. The "reconquest" against the Muslims lasted for three centuries. By the eleventh century, Barcelona, its principal city and capital, became a central location for the slave and gold trades. During the following three centuries, Catalonia, as part of the kingdom of Aragon, built a Mediterranean-wide commercial network (and empire) that explains its leadership in maritime commercial law (the Consulat de Mar) as well as its specialization in cloth production and its advanced banking and monetary institutions.

Catalonia entered the early modern period weakened by the late medieval demographic crisis and civil wars. But the Sentencia Arbitral de Guadalupe, which King Ferdinand of Aragon issued in 1486 to end the peasant wars, meant the end of most of the feudal duties imposed on the Catalan peasantry. A class of peasant freeholders developed in the following centuries, during which Catalonia attracted a large number of French immigrants, who accounted for 25 percent of the population by 1600. But subsequently, when Philip IV demanded more and more taxes to finance the crown of Habsburg Spain, Catalonia sought but failed to gain independence in a long series of wars between 1640 and 1659. When Charles II had abandoned Spain's imperial ambitions, this region embarked on an economic recovery, based especially on wine trade with northwestern Europe. By 1700, a now prosperous Catalonia became keen defenders of the Habsburgs against the Bourbons. But in 1714, the victorious Bourbon king Philip IV removed its privileges and imposed a new regime (Nueva Planta) that unified the political and administrative systems of Aragon with those of Castile. It was the beginning of modern Spain.

The defeated Catalonia became an economic success. Catalan manufacturers gained free access to Castilian markets. Catalonia developed as a wine and spirits exporter to northern Europe, as a textile exporter to Spain, and as a manufacturing and services exporter to the Spanish American Empire. The direct access to the American colonial market completed the long "bonanza" of the eighteenth century. Meanwhile, aided by a protectionist commercial policy, Catalan manufacturers developed cotton textile production.

The outbreak of the French wars was a first signal of the fragility of the Catalan markets. When Napoleon's army invaded Spain, Catalan cotton manufacturers lost their American market to the British and the North Americans, and the European and Spanish markets to the British and the French. The previous state of affairs was never recovered. Only by 1840, and only after the end of the foreign invasions and the first Carlist civil war, did Catalan cotton manufacturing undergo an industrial revolution. Subsequently, Catalonia became the Spanish manufacturing region—the "Spanish mill"—and the most industrialized in the northern Mediterranean, but failed to develop as an exporting economy.

The loss of Cuba in 1898 weakened the Catalan economy. On the contrary, thanks to Spanish neutrality, the World War I years were prosperous. At the outbreak of the Civil War (1936), Catalonia was a completely industrial region with a large and highly unionized working class and a well-developed and long-established bourgeoisie, afraid of the anarchist mood and ready to accept Franco's coup d'état. Catalonia remained on the Republican side and underwent a social revolution that lasted more than two years.

After Franco's military victory, industrial development was halted in the 1940s because of a mixture of autarkic and regional policies. Starting in 1950, and for a quarter of a century, as Spain became increasingly open to foreign trade, Catalonia was well equipped in human capital and all kinds of externalities to take full advantage of the new opportunities. It doubled its population thanks to mass immigration from the rest of Spain. Catalonia is now a developed region, on the European Union GDP per capita average, with political autonomous status within democratic Spain. It has a dynamic capital, Barcelona, and a dense network of export-oriented small-and medium-sized firms, but no headquarters of any major multinational company.

BIBLIOGRAPHY

Nadal, Jordi, et al., eds. *Història econòmica de la Catalunya contemporània*. 6 vols. Barcelona, 1988–1994. The major collective work on nineteenth- and twentieth-century Catalan economic history with an introductory chapter on its early modern origins. Two volumes are devoted to the general evolution by centuries, while the other four are organized by sectors.

Thomson, James. *A Distinctive Industrialization: Cotton in Barcelona, 1728–1832*. Cambridge, 1992. The most relevant work on Catalan economic history published recently in English. Thomson tracks the century-long preparation of the Catalan Industrial Revolution of 1832–1861, departing from the most common views among Catalan researchers on its causal factors and its chronology.

Vilar, Pierre. *La Catalogne dans l'Espagne moderne: Recherches sur les fondements économiques des structures nationales*. 3 vols. Paris, 1962. The most important single academic work on Catalan economic history, an attempt at *histoire totale* that for decades has been highly influential on Catalan and Spanish historiography—not only economic. Half of the work is on the eighteenth century—concentrating on population, agriculture, and trade. The other half is on the geographical and the historical foundations. Vilar provides an unsurpassed summary of Catalan economic history up to 1700.

ALBERT CARRERAS

CATTLE are the largest, most numerous (excluding poultry), and most useful of farm animals. Their prime function has been, until recently, as beast of burden, pulling carts, providing power for mills and irrigation devices, drawing plows, and threshing grain with their hooves. Their dung is used as fertilizer, as a fuel (chips), and as a plaster in rural buildings. Their skins are used to make leather, their hooves glue; their horns were once drinking vessels. Since the late 1800s, their importance as providers of milk and beef has overtaken these functions, although they still remain the principal source of power on farms in many parts of the developing world. Like sheep and goats, cattle can digest cellulose and so convert grass into protein foods for humans. Although some plants can be consumed directly by humans, cattle eat plants and then are consumed by humans; this extra trophic level means that cattle produce fewer calories per hectare than do most plants. Nevertheless, cattle can eat natural vegetation on lands that could not be used for growing crops.

Early History. Modern cattle are descended from *Bos primigenius*, the extinct large long-horned aurochs or wild ox, whose natural range was Europe, North Africa, the north of the Indian subcontinent, and Burma. Its earliest evidence of domestication is found after that of sheep and goats, in Anatolia and the Greek region at about 8000 BP (before present). Modern European cattle, *Bos taurus*, are descended from these animals. The humped zebu and the sanga cattle that predominate in the tropics, *Bos indicus*, are of similar descent, but they may be an independent domestication, the first evidence of which is from the Baluchistan region at about 6000 BP. *Bos indicus* spread throughout eastern, southern, and southeastern Asia, where it later shared the plowing with the water buffalo (*Bubalus bubalus*). The water buffalo is an important source of draft power and milk in Asia; although a different species, it is a member of the same family as the wild ox and was domesticated in India in the third millennium BCE. *Bos taurus* spread north and west throughout Europe and Russia, and west into North Africa; the cattle of sub-Saharan Africa, however, are a cross between the humped zebu and long-horned Hamitic cattle. There is evidence for the milking of cattle in Southwest Asia (Near East) in the fourth millennium BCE, and of butter and cheese making there in the third millennium BCE. These dairying practices spread throughout most of Eurasia and into Africa. There is no early evidence for the milking of cattle in China or in eastern Southeast Asia, where milking remains unimportant among the contemporary Han Chinese, although it is practiced by ethnic minorities in western and northern China. Milking is also rare in much of central and western Africa, and this may be caused by a relatively high incidence of lactose intolerance or malabsorption among the population. The ox-drawn plow was first used in the Near East in the fourth millennium BCE; it was thereafter adopted in Europe, India, China, and North Africa, but it never reached sub-Saharan Africa, where the hand hoe was the principal agricultural implement. Until introduced by Europeans, neither the plow nor cattle were known in the Americas and Australasia.

Since the Middle Ages. In ancient Greece and Rome, cattle were used for plowing, little milk was consumed, and most meat was provided by sheep and goats. Cattle were then much more important in northern than in southern Europe, and in the north most of the major developments took place in livestock husbandry. In the Middle Ages, oxen (castrated bulls) were still kept mainly for draft, and they provided some manure. Other cattle were kept and fed on common land; they were not then specially bred for milk or meat, and neither food was important in the northern European diet. Livestock and crop production were not yet integrated. In the Low Countries during the fourteenth century, however, fodder crops, including roots, began to be grown in fallow years, and crop rotations included alfalfa and clover. These practices increased crop yields; legumes increased the nitrogen content in the soil (a fertilizer) and root crops were hoed, thus reducing weed growth. Livestock, especially cattle, were better fed there and the yield of meat, milk, and wool increased as a result of the integration of livestock and crop husbandry. Cattle were soon kept in stalls, bedded on the straw from cereal crops; dung and straw—farmyard manure—fertilized soils and increased crop yields. These, with other changes, culminated in an agricultural revolution in western Europe. Cattle were replaced by horses as draft animals in parts of France during the thirteenth century, but this was a slow process; ox-drawn plows remained in use in various parts of eastern and southern Europe until the 1950s. They were then replaced by tractors, in most cases, rather than by horses.

As long as cattle were poorly fed, kept on unenclosed land, and used mainly as draft animals—which was their main function until the nineteenth century—beef and milk were minor products. In the eighteenth century, however, better fed animals and a growing demand for beef led to attempts to breed improved stock. Cattle that gave higher yields of meat were soon bred in Britain, including the Aberdeen Angus, the Shorthorn, and the Hereford. Dairy cattle were improved later, notably the Friesian variety in the Netherlands. From the 1700s on- ward, these varieties were taken to areas of British colonial settlement in North America, South Africa, Australia, and New Zealand; the Shorthorn is now the most widely distributed breed worldwide. In the twentieth century, Charollais and Limousin cattle from France were adopted in many parts of Europe. European cattle have not thrived in the tropics, since they are ill adapted to heat and become susceptible to diseases; however, zebu have been successfully crossed with European breeds in the United States to tolerate heat, and they have been a success in the heat of Brazil.

The integration of livestock and crops did not occur in sub-Saharan Africa, where the plow and the ox were not in use. In India, cattle and water buffalo were used as draft animals, and the latter were milked; but Hindu tradition disallows the slaughter of cattle, and the shortage of crop land there inhibited full integration. In China and Southeast Asia, both cattle and water buffalo were used as draught animals but not for milk or meat; pigs and poultry, which are scavengers rather than grazers, were historically the principal livestock. In Japan, special hand-raised, pampered Kobe cattle have been bred to supply highest-quality marbled beef.

Nomadic Herding. In the Old World, although few cattle were kept on farms except in Europe, cattle were numerous in Africa and Asia but kept by nomadic herders rather than by sedentary farmers. Such peoples had no concept of land as private property, but they were rarely pure nomads, for some grain was essential. Their livestock were kept for blood (bloodletting was practiced) and for milk—rarely for meat—and in Africa were and are prized as symbols of prestige as much as for their economic value. Livestock were rarely sold but given as bride price or as fines. Nomads moved in search of grass growth, determined by seasonal rainfall, and kept not only cattle but sheep and goats—and, in the Middle East and Central Asia, camels. Nomadic movements were initially in the grasslands that fringe the arid zone of the Sahara, East Africa, and the Arabian Desert, as well as the steppes of southern Russia, Mongolia, and Siberia. In Eurasia, nomads tamed the horse in the third millennium BCE; on horseback, they threatened the Han Chinese civilization from the third century CE. They remained a potent political power in Russia until the eighteenth century, when the Russians began to occupy the steppes. In Africa, nomadism was a much later lifestyle, where, in contrast to Asia, cattle were the chief herded animals, and there were no horses.

With the growth and expansion of sedentary populations and civilizations, backed by military power, nomads were slowly excluded from the better watered land onto the edges of the deserts. In the twentieth century, the modern state tried to control nomadism and encouraged (in the Soviet Union and in Mongolia, forced) nomads to become sedentary livestock raisers, with mixed success. By the 1960s, there were less than 15 million nomads in the world (all in the Old World; there were never nomads in the Americas).

Ranching. Modern ranching is characterized by large, privately owned land holdings and herds of cattle (except in New Zealand) that graze on poor grasslands; like the nomads, ranchers have been driven from wetter areas by crop producers, who need to irrigate. Cattle are supervised by mounted herdsmen—once on horse, now often in motor vehicles—and are periodically rounded up and branded, to provide identification on open ranges. This distinctive system emerged in southern Spain during the *reconquista* of the 1400s, when Spain won its last battles against the Moors (Arabs who had occupied the Iberian Peninsula from 711 to 1492). The horse, the longhorn cattle, round-ups, the bolero jacket, branding, cattle drives, spurs, wide brimmed hats, the Moorish saddle, and other features were in the 1500s taken by the Spanish to Mexico, where the lasso was added, and by the Portuguese to

CATTLE. Fulbe herder's Zebu cattle, near Sokoto, Nigeria, 1959. (Eliot Elisofon/Eliot Elisofon Photographic Archives/National Museum of African Art, Smithsonian Institution, Washington, D.C.)

Brazil. Later, cattle ranching was established in Argentina, Uruguay, and New Mexico, and in the western United States in the 1800s. Until the mid-nineteenth century, cattle were raised on open communal lands, and the principal products were hides and tallow, which became important exports from Argentina in the early nineteenth century. In the late nineteenth century, these systems came under pressure from farming settlers who moved into the grasslands of the llanos (plains), pampas, and prairies to produce crops. The ranchers were then forced to buy land and, in the United States, enclosed their ranches with barbed wire—a new invention in the 1880s. Rising demand for beef from the cities of the eastern United States and western Europe created a growing market, but American longhorns provided poor meat and were replaced in the United States by Herefords and Shorthorns, and in Argentina by Aberdeen Angus. Railroads were then extended into the prairie and pampas, and soon canned meat was carried from meatpackers to urban markets; with the introduction of refrigerated railroad cars and ships from the 1870s onward, frozen and chilled meat was exported to Europe. In the United States, cattle were reared on the range but driven to and fattened in the Corn Belt, a practice that declined as grain was carried to feedlots nearer the range.

Modern ranching has become intensive, especially with efforts to improve feed quality and breeds. Cattle are raised in a similar manner in northern Australia and in parts of Africa, but the Americas—the principal region of raising cattle in this manner—accounts for 40 percent of world beef output.

Dairying. Both nomadic grazing and ranching are specialized ways of raising livestock, but most of the world's cattle are kept on mixed farms, where both crops and livestock are raised. Dairying became a specialism, however, by the mid-1800s. There were, by that time, regions in Europe that produced milk for butter and cheese making, generally in regions where either altitude or abundant rainfall made crop growing difficult but gave grass growth an advantage, such as in Brittany, the Alps, parts of western Britain, the Low Countries, and much of Scandinavia. Still, the consumption of fresh milk was negligible, and butter and cheese (fermented milk products) were eaten in only small quantities, until the rising incomes of the late nineteenth century allowed for increased demand. Milk output was spurred by the development of railroads, which allowed fresh milk to be marketed in distant urban centers (with the assistance of the milk churn, boiled glass bottles, and other methods of keeping milk fresh in transit). Also important were the adoption of laws that regulated human and animal hygiene in dairies, and those that limited the adulteration of milk. With pasteurization and the reduction of tuberculosis in herds during the 1920s and 1930s, health risks were reduced. Although cheese and butter had long been produced on farms in the United States, in the 1850s and 1860s, both began to be processed in factories. These methods were also slowly adopted in western Europe—and soon condensed, evaporated, and dried (powdered) milk were also produced in factories.

Milk production on the farm has been increased and improved by supplementing the main feed, grass, with oil-cake and grain, as well as by the mechanization of hay-making and milking, storing grass by silage, improved grass varieties, and the use of fertilizers. The animals have also been greatly improved, with dual-purpose breeds replaced by specialized milk producers, such as the Friesian in the late nineteenth century; since the 1930s, selected bulls, frozen sperm, and artificial insemination have been used to produce good milkers, and antibiotics have been given (and controversially added to feed) to cure cattle of diseases. Yet the great revolution has occurred largely in Europe and in European-settled areas, which account for more than 66 percent of all bovine milk production, 80 percent of the cheese, and 50 percent of the butter.

Market Problems. Additives to British and some European cattle feed have included pulverized animal parts (mainly sheep), which in their nervous systems harbor the pathogen that causes "mad cow disease," bovine spongiform encephalopathies (BSE). Its passing to humans has been recognized as Creutzfeldt-Jacob Disease (CJD)—an illness that paralyzes and kills. Britain has banned such feed and destroyed thousands of head of infected cattle. The European Union (EU) banned British beef in the late 1990s, but some tainted feed is still in existence in Europe and is being sold on the open and black markets, so all beef and dairy products have become suspect. In 2001, the first tainted feed was found in Texas and the cattle quarantined. The enormous beef-eating American public has had about a decade of grace before the adulterated feed was actually reported in the United States, although beef and dairy products from the rest of the world are used in U.S. prepared foods and in restaurants.

Cattle feed in the United States has had various problem additives publicized since the 1960s—including antibiotics, pesticides, steroids, and hormones (the most infamous is DES, diethylstilbestrol, a human carcinogen and teratogen). Additional concerns include genetically altered stock and transgenic foods, called genetically modified (GM) foods. The organic-foods and free-range industries are expanding as the public becomes aware of the problems. From a minor role in the rural economy of the western world, cattle have assumed a leading role. For example, the number of cattle in western and central Europe has doubled since 1800. In many of those countries, cattle and their products account for over one-third of total agricultural income.

BIBLIOGRAPHY

Clutton-Brock, Juliet. *A Natural History of Domesticated Mammals*. 2d ed. Cambridge, 1999. Good section on the domestication and early history of cattle.

Cockrill, W. Ross, ed. *The Husbandry and Health of the Domestic Buffalo*. Rome, 1974. Mainly modern regional studies, but some useful historical material.

Dale, Edward E. *The Range Cattle Industry: Ranching on the Great Plains from 1865 to 1925*. 2d ed. Norman, Okla., 1960

Fussell, George E. *The English Dairy Farmer, 1500–1900*. London, 1966.

Galaly, John G., and Douglas L. Johnson, eds. *The World of Pastoralism: Herding Systems in Comparative Perspective*. London, 1991. Mainly regional studies by anthropologists, but excellent introduction on livestock systems.

Grigg, David B. *The Agricultural Systems of the World: An Evolutionary Approach*. Cambridge, 1974. A historical world geography of major farming systems, including nomadism, dairying, and ranching.

Hall, Stephen J. G., and Juliet Clutton-Brock. *Two Hundred Years of British Farm Livestock*. London, 1995.

Leeds, Anthony, and Andrew P. Vayda, eds. *Man, Culture, and Animals: The Role of Animals in Human Ecological Adjustment*. Washington, D.C., 1965. Anthropolgical essays, including essays on the sacred cow, cattle in Africa, and ranching in the Americas.

Needham, Joseph. *Science and Civilisation in China*, vol. 6, *Biology and Biological Technology: Agriculture* by Francesca Bray. Cambridge, 1984.

Oldstone, Michael B. A. *Viruses, Plagues, and History*. Oxford and New York, 1998. Covers the history of Mad Cow Disease in chapter 13, pp. 158–172.

Postan, Michael M. *The Cambridge Economic History of Europe*, vol. 1, *The Agrarian Life of the Middle Ages*. 2d ed. Cambridge, 1966.

Slicher van Bath, B. H. *The Agrarian History of Western Europe, AD 500–1850*. London, 1963. Still the standard text.

David Grigg

CENTRAL AFRICA [*This entry contains three subentries on the economic history of central Africa during the ancient period, from 1500 to 1850, and from 1850 to the present.*]

Ancient Period

Central Africa is the least archaeologically explored region of Africa. Until scholars uncover direct evidence for plant and animal domestication, indirect evidence from historical linguistics and material culture must suffice for sketching out where and when the advent of food production took place. The story of this transition begins over five thousand years ago, and it involves the gradual mixing of Bantu-language-speaking immigrants with dispersed groups of people—hunter-gatherers and fishing communities—who already inhabited parts of Central Africa. Linguistic analyses of the over six hundred Bantu languages spoken today indicate that the earliest Bantu language–speakers were farmers, and that they originated in an area of what is now western Cameroon. At least nine different dispersals of Bantu-speakers created the first food-producing settlements in central and southern Africa, followed by others, each with its own dynamic.

Material evidence confirms this general trend. Early farming communities are identified by the presence of both polished stone tools and ceramics; by dating and mapping of such sites, a pattern emerges showing small-scale neolithic groups slowly spreading south and southeast from Cameroon between 3500 and 200 BCE. By the seventh century CE, most of the region was settled. These neolithic farming communities coexisted with some remaining hunter-gatherer and fisher groups, suggesting early exchange of food surplus and other products.

Central African farmers created several major food-production systems by adapting to the region's diverse environmental conditions. Again, much of the evidence comes from linguistic analyses. Vegeculture in the rainforests relied on yams, beans, and palm oil although gathered foods continued to be an important part of the diet. Protein came from goats, fish, and wild game, either trapped or hunted. Later, domesticated fowl were introduced. In the Great Lakes area, farmers engaged in forest vegeculture along with cereal growing and cattle herding, a combination that allowed for a relatively intensive food-production system to develop there. For the savannas south of the rainforest, early farmers practicing forest vegeculture were restricted to river valleys, leaving land open to cereal growers and herders who began moving in from the east about 500 CE, transforming food production in this area. Cattle-keeping had to be limited to the eastern portion of the savannas and only some parts of the west, areas that were inhospitable to tsetse flies (carriers of sleeping sickness). Also during the first half of the first millennium CE, the introduction and spread of banana cultivation, with its high yield per labor inputs, made greater food surpluses possible throughout the entire region.

Generally low population densities are suggested by the lack of proto-Bantu vocabulary items for market, caravan, and currency; hence trade probably was conducted on a relay basis. Evidence of social stratification comes from terminology distinguishing bush-dweller from farmer, and the practice of pawning people for debts owed. Differentiation of labor existed early on, with potters, raphia weavers, and salt-makers (sea and vegetal salt) evident in the proto-

Bantu linguistic record. During the middle period of Bantu dispersals, people of Central Africa began using and producing metals. Recent archaeological evidence indicates that the new metalworking technologies, while significant, were not revolutionary, since stone tool users coexisted alongside neighboring metal users. The earliest iron smelting was carried out in the east (Great Lakes area) from at least the sixth century BCE onward and in the western rainforests (present-day Cameroon and Gabon) from at least the fifth century BCE. By 500 CE, iron-smelting sites were widespread in the Congo basin, and metalworkers to the southeast in the Copperbelt were smelting copper and turning it into cast, smithed, and drawn-wire products.

It is not known for certain how labor was divided by gender during ancient times, but recent evidence strongly suggests a general, perhaps long-standing pattern: food gathering, plant domestication, and farming were the work of women, as were food preparation and pottery-making; men were most likely the hunters, fishers, clearers of land, raphia weavers, and metalworkers.

Linguistic analyses show three types of interlocking social groups making up the fabric of society. The smallest unit, the house, consisted of kinfolk, friends, clients, and other dependents; next came either the village, a clustered settlement including a number of different houses, or, in herding country, the neighborhood, a spatial network of dispersed houses with fenced-in land for cattle-keeping. Specific houses could be linked through marriage and age-grade institutions as well as the exchange of goods and services. Finally, the district was the largest unit of collective identity during this period. Leadership positions were achieved and held by men who exercised authority over both people and land, principles that were also reflected in religious belief, which centered on veneration of heroes and nature spirits. Healers and diviners performed a variety of therapeutic tasks for individuals and social groups.

Three main centers of economic and population growth developed from 800 CE onward: one based primarily on surplus food production, another tied to long-distance trade, and the last based on regional trade. These centers also were areas where early political centralization took place, but this early history is incompletely understood. In the western Great Lakes, by about 800, environmental pressures were building as a result of highly productive herding and banana cultivation. Competition among patrilineages over rights to increasingly scarce land created a new and larger-scale unit of social organization, the territorial chiefdom. Another center developed in the southeastern savannas where population growth, locally produced metal currencies, and greater economic inequality show up in the archaeological record from about 1000. Glass bead and cowrie currencies, used in the Indian

Ocean trade, attest to indirect links with foreign markets for the area's copper and ivory exports. Intensification of this trade spurred economic expansion, and, by 1500, the founding of the Luba and Rund kingdoms. Lastly, a thriving regional trade in iron goods, salt, fish, cloth, ceramics, and furs developed in the western rainforests around the lower Congo, served by cloth, metal, and nzimbu-shell currencies. The kingdoms of Loango, Tio, and Kongo emerged there before 1500, presumably from competitions among territorial leaders.

BIBLIOGRAPHY

Clist, Bernard, and Raymond Lanfranchi, eds. *Aux origines de l'Afrique centrale.* Libreville, Gabon, 1991. Excellent summaries and syntheses of the archaeological record for the region, minus the Great Lakes and Zambia.

Eggert, M. K. H. "Central Africa and the Archaeology of the Equatorial Rainforest: Reflections on Some Major Topics." In *The Archaeology of Africa: Food, Metals, and Towns*, edited by T. Shaw, P. Sinclair, B. Andah, and A. Okpoko, pp. 289–329. London, 1993. Archaeological evidence for the Congo basin, and trenchant critique of historical linguistics and its application in Central Africa.

Kriger, Colleen E. *Pride of Men: Ironworking in 19th Century West Central Africa.* Portsmouth, N.H., 1999. Includes a critical review of the scholarly literature of metalworkers in Central African history.

Phillipson, D. W. "Central Africa to the North of the Zambezi." In *UNESCO General History of Africa*, vol. 3, *Africa from the Seventh to the Eleventh Century*, edited by M. Elfasi, pp. 643–663. Berkeley, 1988. Archaeological evidence for the savannas south of the rainforests although the interpretation is flawed by an outmoded "Bantu expansion" theory and the questionable presumption that ceramic styles correlate neatly with social groups.

Schoenbrun, David Lee. *A Green Place, A Good Place: Agrarian Change, Gender, and Social Identity in the Great Lakes Region to the 15th century.* Portsmouth, N.H., 1998. Impressive and convincing interpretation of historical linguistics and archaeological evidence, providing a social and economic history of the Great Lakes.

Vansina, Ian. *Paths in the Rainforests: Toward a History of Political Tradition in Equatorial Africa.* Madison, Wis., 1990. History of the rainforested area of Central Africa, drawing on a host of different types of primary sources, especially historical linguistics (western Bantu languages).

Vansina, Jan. "Equatorial Africa before the Nineteenth Century." In *African History, from Earliest Times to Independence*, edited by P. Curtin, S. Feierman, L. Thompson, and J. Vansina, pp. 213–240. 2nd ed. London, 1995. Important synthesis of the evidence for early history of the savannas south of the rainforests.

Vansina, Jan. "New Linguistic Evidence and 'The Bantu Expansion.'" *Journal of African History* 30 (1995), 173–195. Critique of "Bantu expansion" theories, and discussion of recent Bantu language analyses and their implications. Vansina makes the point that language and linguistics are not neatly linked with archaeological "ceramic styles."

COLLEEN KRIGER

Central Africa from 1500 to 1850

The Atlantic Era in the economic history of Central Africa can be subdivided into two periods: the first, 1500 to 1660, was a time of continuity, when overseas trade with Europeans on the Atlantic coast developed without causing fundamental or widespread reorganization of Central African economies and societies; in contrast, the later period, 1660 to 1850, was a time of significant change, as overseas trade intensified, and slaves became the primary export. A hiatus in Indian Ocean trading and the rise of Atlantic commerce turned west Central Africa into the region's major economic center. As inland suppliers gradually oriented commercial networks toward entrepôts on the west coast, they transformed themselves into wealthy, independent elites posing challenges to the established social and political order. Most important, efforts to meet the increasing demand for slave exports created supply systems based on violence, generating unprecedented levels of insecurity and social inequality.

Production and Trade, 1500–1660. Central African workers organized their occupations according to variable combinations of local resources, seasonal patterns, and social divisions of knowledge and skill. Agricultural production continued to require more labor than any other economic activity, particularly during the rainy season, which could last from seven to ten months, depending on the area. Dry-season activities were fishing, trading, and certain kinds of craftwork such as iron- or copper-smelting and pottery-making. Complex work patterns developed, especially out of gendered differences in access to resources and technologies. The most important of these was in the agricultural sector, where men held rights to land use, and women, who had the technical expertise for planting, cultivating, and processing crops, were the farmers. People were the key to productivity, and it mattered greatly whether they were male or female.

Consumer demand was complex and strong enough by this time to encourage local and long-distance trading networks throughout the region. Trade goods ranged from perishables, such as agricultural surplus and domestic animals, to raw and processed materials and specialty manufactures. The most prominent commodities were salt, iron, copper, preserved fish, pottery, raphia cloth, prepared furs and skins, mats, baskets, and camwood (processed for cosmetic and medicinal use). Both men and women contributed to the trading sector: men as hunters, metalworkers, fishers, weavers, tree cultivators, and long-distance traders, and women as farmers, saltmakers, potters, and camwood processors. Demand for metals was such that copper-smelting intensified in the copperbelt from 1300 to 1600, and in the west smelters on the plateaus of the Tio kingdom produced significant amounts of iron from 1500 to 1700. Metals, cloth, salt, and shells were the main forms of currency.

External commerce with Europeans initially fitted into these already existing production and trading patterns; and from the time of the arrival of the first Portuguese ships in the late fifteenth century until the first decades of the nineteenth century, fierce competition was the norm. One sees evidence of this competitive climate in the rise and fall of different export entrepôts on the Atlantic coast and in the shifting locations of supply routes in the Central African interior, trends shaped by merchants and suppliers as they sought advantageous trading positions for themselves.

Portugal's first trading partner on the west Central African coast was the Kongo kingdom, whose port at Mpinda became its main overseas entrepôt until the breakaway of Soyo province in 1641. Early exports included copper, ivory, raphia cloth, skins, and honey, (produced by specialist workers in different geographic areas), and slaves (mostly war captives purchased inland at Malebo Pool with *nzimbu* shells); imports were mainly cloth, guns, beads, and alcohol. Commodity currencies that facilitated this trade flowed into Kongo's capital as tribute from the provinces: salt and nzimbu shells from the coast, raphia cloth from the east, and copper from the southern mountains.

Luanda became the next major Atlantic entrepôt in the region, having been established as an overseas trading station in the 1530s by Luso-African traders (men of mixed Portuguese and Central African descent) who operated between the mainland and São Tomé. Their primary trade route stretched northeastward to the Kongo capital and farther on to the Pool and Okango country, with raphia cloth as the main currency. At least some of that currency supply came from Loango, a kingdom north of the Congo River, carried by Vili traders along with valuable export products such as ivory, skins, camwood, and copper, all to be exchanged in Luanda for European imports. With Luanda's success came efforts by the Portuguese crown to tap into merchants' profits. The port became a colonial base in 1576, and soon thereafter Portuguese attempts at expansion touched off almost a century of sporadic armed conflict with the neighboring kingdom of Ndongo. After 1600, yet another set of trade routes connected Luanda with inland Mbundu kingdoms directly to the east and new sources of products and captives for export.

Atlantic commerce brought several American food crops to Central Africa, which transformed the food base and contributed to future development of long-distance trading operations. Groundnuts and new varieties of beans supplemented those that Central African women already grew, and maize gradually replaced the comparatively less hardy sorghum and millet. The crop making the greatest impact was cassava (manioc), grown in Loango as early as 1608 and in the Tio kingdom by the late 1600s. Replacing yams in many places, during the eighteenth and nineteenth centuries it was grown on a large scale along trade routes to feed caravan traffic, especially slave porters. One reason for cassava's success was its higher yield relative to yams, and the fact that it could be stored underground for up to two years as protection against famine. However, it had several drawbacks: it was of limited nutritional value; the land clearance it required encouraged growth of mosquitoes and the spread of disease; and it demanded laborious processing, whose burden fell entirely on women.

This formative period drew to a close with portents of future disruptions. Portugal never managed to effectively control the activities of its own merchants, nor did it win the allegiance of Luso-African entrepreneurs who were vital suppliers of export trade on the west Central African coast. To make matters worse, Portugal was dealt serious blows by the Dutch, who seized and occupied Luanda in the 1640s. Meanwhile, heavy investments in slaves by Kongo titleholders in the late sixteenth century eventually led to transformations in the kingdom's social and political structures. Female slaves, used mainly as concubines and domestic workers, enlarged the scale of elite houses, and male slaves served either as soldiers for the king and nobility or as agricultural producers for the capital and provincial towns (the latter effecting a breach in the gender division of labor). Hence the growing numbers of slaves supported powerful rival factions, sparking conflict and weakening the king's authority. As overseas commerce began to bypass Kongo's capital, the kingdom entered a period of economic decline and political fragmentation, which culminated in civil wars during the second half of the seventeenth century.

The Slaving Frontier, 1660–1850. Growth in scale and profitability of New World sugar production had repercussions on the African side of the Atlantic. During this period, the Portuguese lost their lead to other merchant groups, and west Central Africa became the most important continuous source of slaves in the Atlantic trade. Established ports continued to attract foreign ships while new ones arose, the most prominent examples being Benguela and Loango, which came to rival Luanda as the region's major entrepôt. Settled and developed after 1615 by Luso-African merchants avoiding trade regulations imposed in Luanda by the Portuguese crown, Benguela was the preferred destination of Brazilian trading firms during the eighteenth and nineteenth centuries. Dutch traders developed Loango into a major supply port by 1670, but they were soon overtaken by English and French competitors, who dominated commerce on the northern coast over the next century.

An important consequence of this expansion in overseas trading was the influx of capital into the region's economies although the issue has hardly been studied, and thus is poorly understood. Transactions were handled through the mechanism of "assortment bargaining," whereby the current value of a standardized assortment of overseas goods would be negotiated, and then the parties would agree upon the equivalent value in African goods. The latter, mostly slaves but also ivory, copper, wax, camwood, and other commodities, were valued by coastal brokers in terms of currencies used in their inland supply networks, such as raphia cloth. Overseas imports (cloth from Goa and Europe, metal cutlery, copper basins, guns and gunpowder, beads, cowrie shells, and alcohol) were assessed by Atlantic merchants in terms of their cost in European currency values. Some of these imports circulated in inland commodity currency networks, but not necessarily as counterfeit; imported cotton, for example, was so visibly different from raphia that it became a new kind of cloth currency, whereas copper basins could indeed be hammered or cast into counterfeit metal currency units. In other words, Atlantic trading transactions increased the money supply—commodities used in regional African currency systems—and variously transformed economic values beyond the coastal ports.

As slaves became the dominant export, the threat of enslavement spread eastward with the commercial frontier. Brokers selling human beings to foreign shippers received them from sources near and far: local people who had been judged guilty of a crime; local people who were debt pawns; victims of kidnapping; prisoners of war from neighboring countries; and, increasingly over time, slaves from the interior who were purchased by merchants and forced to the coast along river and caravan routes. During the eighteenth century, the peak period in the Atlantic trade, slaves exported from Loango were described as Teke, Mayombe, and Bobangi although these names refer primarily to inland merchant suppliers. The slaves themselves, by at least mid-century, were being torn from communities as far away as the Ubangi and Lulonga rivers in the inner Congo basin. Also by this time, Imbangala and Luso-African merchants were organizing caravans that directly linked Lunda and other savanna kingdoms to Luanda and Benguela.

Risks assumed by slave suppliers increased. Local trading systems dovetailed into external commerce all along the river and caravan routes, and merchants had to provision themselves accordingly. For purchase of slaves and other exportable goods inland, they received overseas imports on credit at the coast. In addition, they needed commodity currencies such as salt, iron, and copper that could buy the cassava, services, and other supplies necessary for a large, traveling entourage. Expansion of the commercial frontier meant longer caravan routes and much higher transport costs, but dependency on foreign creditors prevented slave suppliers from recovering these costs. Many Luso-African suppliers especially were driven out of the export business.

Detailed local histories portraying the impacts of enslaving so many human beings and exporting them from Central Africa remain to be written. General economic impacts are not difficult to discern, such as the development of complex, interconnected trading networks and the rise of powerful merchant groups in much of the region. Political histories for this period reveal how wealthy elites and warlords such as the Imbangala created new kingdoms and tribute-collecting systems based on their external commercial relations. Most significantly, this external trade became one in which people were violently uprooted and forcibly redistributed, changing the densities of population groups and sometimes skewing their age and sex ratios. Slaves exported from west Central Africa tended to be youths, adult men, and older women, a pattern often cited in ongoing questions about whether women were deliberately retained in Africa, and, if so, why they were. The debate hinges on the value of women's productive work versus their value as social and biological reproducers. Scholars who wish to pursue these issues would do well to emulate Harms's study of Bobangi society and focus on how work was divided by gender, how increased slave use could either reinforce or redefine men's and women's work, and the degree to which women were able to control birth rates in their communities.

[*See also* Slave Trade.]

BIBLIOGRAPHY

Austen, Ralph A, and Jonathan Derrick. *Middlemen of the Cameroons Rivers: The Duala and Their Hinterland, c. 1600–c. 1960.* Cambridge, 1999 Social and economic history that bridges the precolonial and colonial periods, tracing the transformation of a fisher society into one engaged in riverine and international commerce. Invaluable for its critical analysis of both written and oral sources.

Dupré, Marie-Claude, and Bruno Pinçon. *Métallurgie et politique en Afrique centrale* Paris, 1997 Analysis and interpretation of archaeological evidence for intensive iron smelting in the Tio kingdom during the sixteenth and seventeenth centuries.

Harms, Robert. *River of Wealth, River of Sorrow: The Central Zaire Basin in the Era of the Slave and Ivory Trade, 1500–1891.* New Haven, 1981. History of the rise and decline of the Bobangi, a major merchant group in the Congo basin, based on oral traditions, testimonies, and archival sources.

Harms, Robert. "Sustaining the System: Trading Towns along the Middle Zaire." In *Women and Slavery in Africa,* edited by Claire Robertson and Martin Klein, pp. 95–110. Madison, Wis., 1983. Case study of gender, class, labor, and birth control in Bobangi towns during the nineteenth century.

Henriques, Isabel de Castro. *Commerce et changement en Angola au XIXe siècle: Imbangala et Tshokwe face à la modernité.* 2 vols. Paris, 1995. Major investigation into several prominent Central African societies that were heavily involved as suppliers for the Atlantic trade. Includes excellent critiques of the sources and scholarly literature in Portuguese and French.

Hilton, Anne. *The Kingdom of Kongo.* Oxford, 1985. The first comprehensive history of Kongo to appear in English. Useful especially for its exhaustive exploitation of documentary sources in several European languages, its major weakness being an overreliance on anthropological theory with regard to social structure.

Kriger, Colleen E. *Pride of Men: Ironworking in 19th Century West Central Africa.* Portsmouth, N.H., 1999. Focuses on the prominent role of ironworkers in Central African economies and societies, including new evidence for production and trade of metalwares and iron currencies.

Martin, Phyllis. *The External Trade of the Loango Coast, 1576–1870.* Oxford, 1972. History of commerce on the coast north of the Congo River, though based primarily on European documentary sources.

M'Bokolo, E. "From the Cameroon Grasslands to the Upper Nile." In *UNESCO General History of Africa*, vol. 5, *Africa from the Sixteenth to the Eighteenth Century*, edited by B. A. Ogot, pp. 515–545. Paris, 1992. Excellent synthesis of current historical perspectives on societies along the northern Central African coast and in the Congo basin during the heyday of the Atlantic trade.

Miller, Joseph. *Way of Death: Merchant Capitalism and the Angolan Slave Trade, 1730–1830.* Madison, Wis., 1988. Major work on the South Atlantic commercial system, offering a pathbreaking intercontinental perspective that incorporates Portugal, Angola, and Brazil.

Thornton, John. *The Kingdom of Kongo: Civil War and Transition, 1641–1718.* Madison, Wis., 1983. Informed by exhaustive analyses of documentary sources and oral traditions, presents a convincing interpretation of the Kongo civil wars as the transformation of society over the long term rather than the decline of a kingdom.

Vansina, Jan. *The Children of Woot: A History of the Kuba Peoples.* Madison, Wis., 1978. History of a Central African kingdom that arose and prospered during the Atlantic Era by harnessing New World crops and adopting protectionist trading policies. The analysis is based on a variety of evidence including historical linguistics, oral traditions, ethnological studies, and archival sources.

Vansina, Jan. *Paths in the Rainforests: Toward a History of Political Tradition in Equatorial Africa.* Madison, Wis., 1990. Provides the foundation for understanding Central African societies before the Atlantic trade and during its formative period.

Vansina, Jan. "The Kongo Kingdom and Its Neighbors." In *UNESCO General History of Africa*, vol. 5, *Africa from the Sixteenth to the Eighteenth Century*, edited by B. A. Ogot, pp. 546–588. Paris, 1992. Synthesis of the major issues and themes in west Central African history during the Atlantic Era, focusing on Loango, Kongo, and Angola.

Volavka, Zdenka. *Crown and Ritual: The Royal Insignia of Ngoyo.* Toronto, 1998. History of a religious shrine in the lower Congo area with valuable new evidence for copperworking technology and trade before the twentieth century. Primary sources include scientific analyses of material culture, oral evidence, and archival sources in several European languages.

COLLEEN KRIGER

Central Africa from 1850 to the Present

The period since about 1850 covers the accelerating and deepening penetration of Central Africa by Europeans and European powers, the division of central African territories into dependencies and colonies, the independence of these colonies in the 1960s and 1970s, and the development of independent African states. Central Africa is still a region of low population density, and the total population of the central African states in 2000 was less than the population of Nigeria, in an area a little more than half the size of mainland China.

Around 1850, Central Africa had hardly been penetrated by Europeans or Arabs. The exceptions were the coastal areas of west-central Africa, which were drawn into the Portuguese slave trade after about 1500. The coastal areas of Cameroon, Gabon, and the Congo were supplying most of British, French, and Portuguese slaves by the early nineteenth century, or around 1 million slaves between 1815

and 1850. By 1850, though, the slave trade in west-central Africa was declining, and the region saw the arrival of "legitimate" commerce that involved increasing penetration of the inland by European traders and their agents. Trading caravans extended from the coast of Congo and Angola deep into the Congo basin and the highlands of Angola, reaching into modern-day Zambia. The thinly populated and largely subsistence-oriented pre-colonial economies were slowly drawn into the growing international economy of the nineteenth century.

Colonial history proper begins in the last three decades of the nineteenth century, a period during which the international economy was depressed. Expansion of trade led to a fall in the prices of primary commodities and protectionist pressures, factors that also influenced the growing interest of Europeans in Central Africa. Especially attractive were such goods as ivory and wild rubber, which bucked the trend of falling world commodity prices. Expanding commercial activity on the Atlantic coast attracted the interest of German, French, and Belgian colonial entrepreneurs; and at the Berlin Conference of 1884–1885, the various European claims on Central Africa were settled and colonial boundaries were drawn.

Unable and unwilling to invest heavily in west-central Africa, the European powers initially devised a system of economic development based on concessionary companies, a solution unique to Central Africa. The concessionary companies were given large swathes of Central Africa to exploit at will; this led to the rapid depletion of natural resources, such as wild rubber, ivory, and timber. This brutal exploitation triggered a more direct involvement of European governments in an area that was vast, underpopulated, and offered few established trade networks or cooptable native states. Central African economic history was shaped by a number of common themes: in particular, low population density and geography presented challenges to the formation of large-scale political units. One of the main challenges was the mobilization of labor, which often involved the use of taxation and regulations forcing Africans to work in mines and on plantations or forcing them to cultivate certain crops. Overreliance on the exploitation of a small number of primary products (such as minerals, timber, rubber, and ivory) made the region vulnerable to world economic cycles and hindered the development of its agricultural potential during the colonial period and after independence; this limited indigenous economic development and led to unusually high urbanization rates. Colonial governments in the region were highly interventionist, regulating land use and migration with little interest in promoting indigenous African economic activity. After independence, central African states retained strong control of economies that remained heavily dependent on a few primary products, which now included petroleum. Widespread corruption and mismanagement since independence contributed to the continued economic underdevelopment of the region.

Cameroon. In Cameroon, the period before the 1880s was characterized by the influence of the slave trade, which had begun to decline and was slowly replaced by the export of "legitimate" goods, in particular, ivory and palm kernels. Goods were collected, hunted, or farmed inland and channeled to the coast through African traders who then exchanged them for cloth, liquor, firearms, and metals. The initial priority of the colonial economy was large-scale plantation production rather than the small-scale African agricultural production that dominated in West Africa; Cameroon became the only example of a successful plantation economy in a formal African colonial context. Large-scale plantations required labor; and an important aspect of colonial administration was the mobilization of African labor, using coercive methods including forced recruitment and taxation although policies gradually became more supportive of African production of food crops for local consumption and export. Cameroon's economy was transformed as railways were constructed and a large number of indigenous people migrated in response to German labor requirements in road and railway construction as well as porterage. Also, large areas of Cameroon were handed over to concessionary companies, who continued the collection and hunting of wild rubber and ivory using African labor. A policy of increased African agricultural production for the world market continued after World War I, encouraging an indigenous market response, especially in cocoa and coffee production. At independence, Cameroon was an economy dominated by a small number of agricultural exports and subsistence production, a negligible industrial sector, and strong dependence on imported manufactured and industrial goods. The economy was relatively market oriented and was relatively economically and politically stable in the first two decades of independence. After 1980, the abandonment of fiscal prudence coincided with increased oil production, and the economy was forced into painful economic adjustment.

Congo-Brazzaville (Republic of the Congo). The area north of the Congo estuary came under French control in the late nineteenth century. Major European involvement in the area began with the granting of large tracts of land to concessionary companies, who were given a free hand in the exploitation of rubber in particular. The extractive activities of the concessionary companies involved brutal use of forced labor. Congo-Brazzaville eventually became part of French Equatorial Africa (AEF), France's poorest colonial outpost. An example of the often heavy-handed colonial regime was the construction of the Congo-Ocean railway line in the 1920s and 1930s, which required enormous amounts of forced labor and resulted in the deaths of thousands of workers. The concessionary companies' legacy of plunder was gradually replaced by a trade economy after World War I, involving mostly gathered and hunted goods. This orientation dominated the economy of the Congo until independence. African domestic producers were heavily taxed in an attempt to make AEF financially self-sufficient, and there was no development of major employment opportunities. So the Congo became heavily urbanized, with up to one-half of the population seeking employment in petty trading or services. Investment in the Congo was minimal, and the territory was heavily subsidized by France. After independence, Europeans remained dominant in commerce and production. Independent Congo carried out radical socialist economic experiments, the failure of which led to the introduction of structural adjustment policies in the late 1980s. The Congo has become increasingly dependent on oil production, neglecting domestic agricultural production, which limits employment creation and reinforces the pattern of urbanization and high urban unemployment. Economic development is stifled by the prevalence of civil war.

Gabon. French colonial involvement in Gabon began in the 1880s. Gabon's natural resources, in particular wild rubber and ivory, were initially exploited by concessionary companies in order to minimize metropolitan financial involvement. The interwar years witnessed the emergence of what was to become, until recently, Gabon's dominant economic activity: the production and export of timber, in particular, the versatile *okume* softwood. Timber was logged in the interior rain forests using African labor that was often coerced. The logs were floated downriver, minimizing investment in infrastructure, and Gabon developed an enclave economy centered on timber and run by French companies. Because of an underdeveloped agricultural sector, there were few employment opportunities for Africans, a fact that helps account for the very high degree of urbanization. Independent Gabon began developing its mineral resources, especially petroleum, manganese, and uranium, from the 1960s onward, and the Gabonese economy is now dominated by petroleum production. Oil has allowed Gabon to enjoy one of the highest levels of income per capita in Africa, and French strategic interests in petroleum and uranium have contributed to high levels of political stability. Overspending in response to Gabon's oil bonanza forced the country into painful structural adjustment programs, and the country's mineral wealth has been highly unevenly spread.

Democratic Republic of the Congo (Zaire). Democratic Republic of the Congo, formerly Zaire, is the largest of the countries covered in this article, and attempts at controlling the vast economic resources of the Congo basin stand at the beginning of the "scramble for Africa" in the 1880s. Its early colonial economic history as a personal

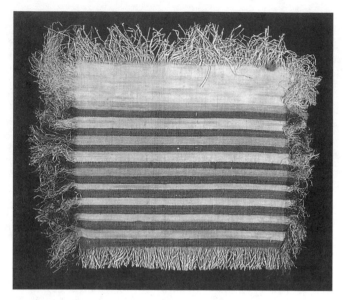

CLOTH CURRENCY. Raffia cloth, Democratic Republic of the Congo, early twentieth century. The value was negotatied based on variations in width and the quality of the weave. (Gift of S. M. Harris/Franko Khoury/National Museum of African Art, Smithsonian Institution, Washington, D.C.)

domain of the Belgian king was based on the violent and unrestrained exploitation of natural and human resources, in particular wild rubber, which was in great demand overseas and which was largely exhausted within twenty years. Exploitation was carried out by concessionary companies who were given exclusive rights over vast areas of the Congo basin, a system that is now thought to have cost up to 10 million Africans their lives. In the interwar years, increasing investment in the production and processing of agricultural exports meant an increasing involvement of African producers in the cash-and-wage economy, especially after the failure of plans for extensive European settlement. But the colonial government also engaged in forced cultivation, especially of cotton; and the increasing role of mineral extraction meant that the main focus of colonial economic policy in Congo became labor recruitment for railway construction and mining. Economic policy was subsequently modified in the postwar years to provide greater freedoms for African producers, but the agricultural potential remains largely undeveloped. Congo attracted vast foreign investment in mining during the colonial years, and mining required large numbers of unskilled workers. Labor mobilization initially involved forced physical relocation and required a large number of migrant workers; later, a policy of "labor stabilization" encouraged the movement of entire families to permanent compounds in the mining zones and the spread of health and social policies in urban areas. But rural Congo was viewed mostly as an enormous labor reservoir as well as the source of agricultural production for urbanized mineworkers. These facts remained salient after independence in 1960, when the Congolese (and Zaïrean) economy and polity were dominated by a small and increasingly corrupt elite. Economic policy since independence has been disastrous. An infamously predatory and fiscally irresponsible government owed its persistence to the support of the United States during the cold war and to the strategic value of its resources. Congo became a "failed state" with wasted physical and human resources and its vast mineral wealth once more the object of preying outsiders.

Angola. As the southernmost supplier of slaves in western Africa, Angola was able to evade controls on slaving longest; and although Portugal abolished the trade in 1875, slaves were exported until before World War I. By the mid-nineteenth century, ivory, wax, and wild rubber had become Angola's main export products, collected from far inland and transported to the coast by African long-distance traders. As the economically weakest of the African colonial powers, Portugal was vitally interested in Angola's resources and in guaranteed markets, even small ones; Angola became the most important market for Portuguese cotton textiles by 1900. European cotton, sugar, and coffee plantations were established, benefiting from the continued use of local slave labor. Competition for slaves from outside Angola led Portugal to institute a policy of compulsory labor that initially had a small impact because populations was so dispersed. Many Portuguese settlers were small-scale, uneducated farmers, and competition with Africans for land and labor intensified. But most immigrants were petty traders, and there was little investment in the economy: In 1910, Angola was still dominated by small trading rather than plantations or mines. The colonial grasp then grew stronger; head taxes were enforced more widely, forced labor became widespread—enforced through local chiefs and headmen. Forced cultivation, especially of cotton, had the effect of shifting production risk toward African peasant producers. Land in potential coffee plantation areas was taken from Africans as European immigration was encouraged after 1926 although most immigrants worked in relatively unskilled urban jobs competing with Africans who had migrated to urban centers. One of the major projects using African labor was the construction of a railroad linking the Congolese copper mines to Angolan ports. After World War II, coffee production expanded, carried out mostly by Portuguese small farmers who prevailed in competition with African planters because of their preferential access to credit and markets as well as to compulsory labor. Only small numbers of Africans were able to establish themselves as export farmers, and the only example of progressive social policies was found in the expanding diamond mines. As a consequence, violence erupted in 1960, sparking a guerilla war that lasted forty years and resulted in the almost complete emigration of European settlers when Angola achieved independence in 1974 as a Marxist-Leninist state. Oil and diamond production began to dominate the economy, with revenues fueling the highly destructive civil war. The economy came completely under state control, leading to extreme corruption, hyperinflation, and the increasing need for economic stabilization and adjustment.

Zambia. The territory of present-day Zambia is landlocked and was therefore not part of an early precolonial coastal trading economy. Its connection to the world economy was established in the second half of the nineteenth century. Competition for slaves and ivory meant that many Africans were taken and transported to the Atlantic and Indian Ocean slaving ports. Zambia was transformed by the commercial attention it received from the British South Africa Company (BSAC), which was granted a royal charter in 1889, giving it the sole rights to exploit Zambia's natural and human resources. The BSAC saw Zambia as a labor reservoir for the coal and gold mines of Southern Rhodesia (now Zimbabwe) as well as the copper mines of the Belgian Congo, and the most extensive investment until the 1930s was the railway connecting the Katanga mines to the Indian Ocean. A hut tax encouraged labor migration to the copper mines and to the European farming estates in Southern Rhodesia. Although European immigration to Zambia was encouraged, it never became a major area of settlement; most Europeans were attached to mining and administration. The large-scale exploitation of copper began in the early 1930s, and Zambia soon became a major copper exporter. More than half of the African male population migrated to the mining areas, accounting for the high levels of urbanization. Labor turnover was high, working conditions were bad, and a formal color bar prevented the professional advancement of Africans in the mines, although conditions improved from the late 1940s. The first decade after independence in 1964 was a period of prosperity as copper markets boomed, but Zambia's fortunes soon turned as prices slumped. A heavily government-led economy tied to a socialist development model provided little investment or opportunities for employment or diversification.

BIBLIOGRAPHY

Amin, Samir, and Catherine Coquery-Vidrovitch. *Histoire économique du Congo 1880–1968*. Dakar, Senegal, 1969.
Austen, Ralph. *African Economic History*. London, 1987.
Barnes, James F. *Gabon: Beyond the Colonial Legacy*. Boulder, 1992.
Birmingham, David, and Phyllis M. Martin, eds. *History of Central Africa*. 2 vols. Harlow, Essex, U.K., 1983.
Birmingham, David, and Phyllis M. Martin, eds. *History of Central Africa: The Contemporary Years since 1960*. London and New York, 1998.
DeLancey, Mark W. *Cameroon: Dependence and Independence*. Boulder, 1989.
Hochschild, Adam. *King Leopold's Ghost*. Boston, 1998.
Hodges, Tony. *Angola: From Afro-Stalinism to Petro-Diamond Capitalism*. Oxford, 2001.
Manning, Patrick. *Francophone Sub-Saharan Africa, 1880–1995*. Cambridge, 1998.
Munro, J. Forbes. *Africa and the International Economy, 1800–1960*. London, 1976.
Roberts, Andrew. *A History of Zambia*. New York, 1976.
Wickins, Peter. *An Economic History of Africa, 1880–1980*. Oxford, 1986.

WOLFRAM LATSCH

CENTRAL AMERICAN COUNTRIES. Spanish rule in Central America ended in 1821 without the bloodshed and upheaval that characterized the end of empire in many other parts of Latin America. This peaceful transition to independence should have provided an ideal background for the new states. First, with the end of the Spanish monopoly, they were free to trade directly with other countries. Second, they were able to exploit their unique geography for the transport of goods and people from the Atlantic to the Pacific by the shortest routes.

These opportunities, however, were wasted. After a brief and voluntary annexation by Mexico, the five former provinces of the Spanish Captaincy General of Guatemala formed the Central American Federation in 1823. Regional rivalries led to civil war and the breakup of the federation in 1838. The independence of Costa Rica, El Salvador, Guatemala, Honduras, and Nicaragua dates from that time, whereas Panama only came into existence as a separate state in 1903, having been until then a province of Colombia.

The new states lacked a strong export sector, and tax collection was too low to support effective public administration. The fledgling nations were further weakened by the rivalry between the United Kingdom and the United States of America for control over any trans-isthmian transport link that might be built. In the case of Nicaragua, the state was so weak that it was unable to resist the political ambitions of a former slaveowner from the United States, William Walker, who declared himself president of the republic in the 1850s and was only finally defeated by the joint efforts of all Central American countries in 1860.

The struggle for political stability and the search for profitable exports were closely linked. Exports made imports possible, and the tax on imports was the most important source of government revenue. Thus, until exports started to expand, there was little chance of political stability; and without political stability the promotion of new exports proved elusive.

This vicious circle began to be broken after the 1850s. Export growth, in particular, accelerated during and after the adoption of economic reforms by liberal governments in the 1870s. These reforms emphasized private ownership of property and led to the alienation of communal lands occupied mainly by the Indian populations. Migration was promoted through the grant of state lands taken from the Indians, and the displaced Indian population was forced to seek work outside the subsistence sector.

HONDURAS. Harvesting bananas for the United Fruit Company (now the Tela Railroad Company), 1989. (© Mireille Vautier/Woodfin Camp and Associates, New York)

The liberal reforms mainly encouraged the growth of the coffee sector, although Honduras remained dependent on mining throughout the nineteenth century. Even so, everywhere except in Costa Rica, exports did not exceed $10 per head by the end of the century. Government income grew in line with imports, and the Central American states began to emerge as nations. Power was concentrated in a small group associated with the export sector, although an enlightened group in Costa Rica—where landholdings were small and depended on family labor in the absence of a significant Indian population—had begun to promote universal primary education by the 1890s.

Land and labor had ceased to be constraints on the growth of the economies as a result of the liberal reforms, but capital remained desperately scarce. State efforts to promote infrastructure through bond finance were largely unsuccessful, and the railway age came late to Central America (the exception being Panama, not yet a separate state, where a trans-isthmian rail link was opened in 1855). When railroads did finally arrive in the last quarter of the nineteenth century, they paved the way for the promotion of banana exports, which rapidly came to rival coffee in all countries except El Salvador.

The banana industry at first consisted of a large number of domestic producers and a handful of foreign companies engaged in foreign trade. With the formation of the United Fruit Company (UFCO) in 1900, the character of the industry changed abruptly, as independent producers virtually disappeared. Three foreign companies handled all exports until the end of the 1920s, when further mergers reduced the number of companies to two.

The banana companies were quick to exploit their monopsony position and drove a hard bargain with the region's governments (including Panama after its independence in 1903). Taxes were low, the companies functioned as enclaves, and the states' degrees of freedom were further restricted by their dependence on the companies for credit in times of crisis.

By the end of the 1920s, the countries of Central America had become extremely dependent on coffee and banana exports, although Panama also depended on the ship canal that had been opened under U.S. control in 1914 (and was finally handed over to Panama on 31 December 1999). The export sector represented up to 40 percent of a country's gross domestic product (GDP), and much of the nonexport sector depended on the fortunes of exports. Governance, however, remained fragile. Guatemala suffered from serious inflationary problems up to 1923; and Nicaragua was occupied by U.S. marines for most of the period from 1909 to 1933, with U.S. officials in charge of customs duties until 1947. Panama continued to reflect its origins as a U.S. geopolitical project (the U.S. dollar has always been the official currency). Costa Rica, despite a brief military dictatorship between 1917 and 1919, had enjoyed greater stability than the other countries, deeper reforms, and by all accounts a higher standard of living, attributable to high levels of literacy and modest amounts of income and wealth inequality.

The 1930s depression hit Central America hard. The price of coffee collapsed, banana exports shrank, and government income imploded. The Honduran government was even reduced to paying its civil servants in postage stamps. Countries were forced to default on their external debt, most of which was owed to European governments. Civil unrest led to dictatorial rule in several countries and abandonment of the modest reform progams adopted in some. Recovery had to await an improvement in the net barter terms of trade after 1932, but agriculture for domestic consumption thrived in some areas because of import substitution (the high levels of trade dependence in the 1920s meant that many foodstuffs were imported at that time).

Manufacturing, in contrast to the experience of larger Latin American countries, showed almost no progress. The shortage of capital, the absence of infrastructure, and the small size of the market were insurmountable obstacles in the 1930s. Panama, however, benefited from the recovery of world trade after 1932, with economic activity in the Canal Zone sustained by the large U.S. presence and the employment of local Panamanians in the work force.

Without exception, the six nations of Central America followed the U.S. lead during World War II. In return, they were absorbed into a U.S. project for Latin America that helped to sustain output, employment, and incomes. German property was confiscated, and this action brought valuable assets into state hands in several countries. Coffee was marketed under special wartime arrangements, and the U.S. government encouraged the production and export from Central America of new commodities to replace those lost to the U.S. economy as a result of the Japanese occupation of Asia. External trade was almost entirely routed through the United States, and the European presence—secondary to that of the United States even before World War I—became negligible. The region's infrastructure improved significantly as a result of wartime priorities; the Pan-American Highway, for example, was pushed south as far as Panama. This opened up the possibility of intraregional trade, and several countries were able to export fruits and vegetables to the population in the Canal Zone.

The final months of World War II pushed political reform onto the agenda, and the position of the region's dictators was much weakened. The Somoza family survived in Nicaragua, but only after a deal had been struck with the labor movement. Costa Rica, particularly after a brief civil war in 1948, laid the foundations for a welfare state and nationalized the banks. However, the Cold War had a negative impact on the reform process in the rest of the region, and the triumph of the counterrevolutionary movement in Guatemala in 1954 ushered in thirty years of military rule there.

While the rest of Latin America chose this moment to turn its back on export-led growth, Central American countries aggressively promoted new exports. The stranglehold of coffee and bananas was finally broken, with cotton, beef, and sugar entering the export list. Panama began to experiment with service exports in the areas of shipping, banking, and insurance. All the Central American countries benefited from the redistribution of the U.S. sugar quota for Cuba after 1960.

The diversification of primary exports provided foreign exchange, currency stability, and low inflation. However, it did not lead to the growth of modern manufacturing, because of the small size of the national markets. Population growth had risen to nearly 3 percent by the 1960s; but even Guatemala—the largest country—had only five million people by the end of the decade, with a Central American total population of less than twenty million. Widespread poverty and a large subsistence economy reduced the size of the markets even further.

The solution to this problem was found in regional integration. In 1960 the five northern countries (Panama remained outside) formed the Central American Common Market (CACM) with a specific emphasis on industrialization. Intraregional exports jumped from less than 5 percent of total exports in 1960 to 25 percent in 1970, and almost all this trade was in manufactured goods. Multinational companies, previously uninterested in the manufacturing sector, were quick to take advantage of the CACM.

Much of the growth of the CACM was due to trade diversion, that is, the replacement of cheaper imports from outside the region with more expensive imports from a partner. This worked to the disadvantage of Honduras, which had been the least successful country at attracting direct foreign investment into its manufacturing sector. After a brief war with El Salvador in 1969 (due in the main to migration from densely populated El Salvador), Honduras left the CACM. In the 1970s, the CACM functioned with greatly reduced effectiveness although the total value of trade continued to grow.

The commodity price boom in the world economy after the first oil crisis in 1973 brought a substantial improvement in the net barter and income terms of trade. It also brought inflation and external indebtedness, as in the rest of Latin America. By 1980, Costa Rica had already defaulted on its external obligations. The debt problem obliged all countries to reduce their imports, but these restrictions also affected intraregional trade. By the mid–1980s the value of intraregional trade had fallen to one-third of its previous peak, and the CACM was virtually dead.

The collapse of the CACM was linked to the regional political crisis. The triumph of the Sandinista revolution in Nicaragua in 1979 soon brought confrontation with the United States. The guerrilla movements in El Salvador and Guatemala gained in strength and led to civil war. The U.S. government turned against General Manuel Noriega—its former ally—in Panama, briefly occupying the country in

1989. Only Costa Rica escaped the political turmoil and social upheaval. The GDP per head fell throughout the region in the 1980s, and emigration—mainly to the United States but also to Costa Rica—accelerated.

Electoral defeat of the Sandinistas in 1990 brought a change in the region's fortunes. The civil wars in El Salvador and Guatemala came to an end, and Panama began the task of reconstruction after the U.S. invasion. Efforts were made to revive regional integration, this time with the participation of Panama. All governments once again emphasized export promotion with the value of both extra- and intraregional exports rising rapidly in the 1990s. Costa Rica, as so often in the past, was particularly successful in applying the new growth model.

Despite the improved performance of the 1990s, many parts of Central America remain extremely underdeveloped. Honduras and Nicaragua are among the poorest countries in Latin America. El Salvador and Guatemala, while enjoying a higher GDP per head than their poorer neighbors, suffer from widespread poverty and a low tax burden that makes it difficult for the state to carry out its functions properly. Costa Rica and Panama have a higher standard of living than the other Central American countries—closer to the Latin American average—with much lower levels of poverty. All these countries, however, remain vulnerable to natural disasters, whose impacts have been exacerbated by damage to the environment from the development process of the last half century.

[*See also* American Indian Economies, *subentries on* Aztec Economy *and* Maya Economy; *and* Spain, *subentry on* Spanish Empire.]

BIBLIOGRAPHY

Bulmer-Thomas, Victor. *The Political Economy of Central America since 1920*. Cambridge, 1987. Does not include Panama, but the period since 1920 is examined in detail.

Euraque, Dario. *Reinterpreting the Banana Republic: Region and State in Honduras, 1870–1972*, Chapel Hill, N.C., 1996.

Karnes, Thomas. *Tropical Enterprises: Standard Fruit and Steamship Company in Latin America*. Baton Rouge, La., 1978. The United Fruit Company's great rival, Standard Fruit, is examined here.

Kepner, Charles, and Jay Soothill. *The Banana Empire: A Case Study in Economic Imperialism*. New York, 1935. A classic study of the operations of the United Fruit Company in the region.

Lindo-Fuentes, Hector. *Weak Foundations: The Economy of El Salvador in the 19th Century, 1821–1898*. Berkeley, 1990.

Schoonover, Thomas. *Germany in Central America: Competitive Imperialism, 1821–1929*. Tuscaloosa, Ala., 1998. A competent survey of the economic links between Germany and Central America.

Torres Rivas, Edelberto. *History and Society in Central America*. Austin, 1993. Although there is no single book that covers the economic history of the whole period, this is an excellent overview by a leading Central American sociologist.

Williams, Robert. *Export Agriculture and the Crisis in Central America*. Chapel Hill, N.C., 1986. Studies the emergence of nontraditional exports after 1950.

VICTOR BULMER-THOMAS

CENTRAL ASIA. The Central Asian region, including the current states of Kazakhstan, Uzbekistan, Turkmenistan, Kyrgyzstan, Tajikistan, and Mongolia, has been shaped by its central location, connecting China to the West. Trade routes from Persia or China to Europe, especially during Han China, the entity known as the "Turk Empire" of the sixth century, and the Mongol Empire of the thirteenth century, stimulated economic and cultural development. Since the fifth century BCE, Central Asia has been continuously conquered and reconquered by different polities seeking the riches that could be gained through taxes levied on the trade though the area.

Humans evolved in warm regions. To settle in colder regions, such as Central Asia, social and technological adaptations, such as the use of fire and concentration on hunting rather than gathering to find food, clothing, and shelter, were needed. The aridity of the region made it too dry to support farming without irrigation in most areas, so in prehistoric times the hunter-gatherer lifestyle remained dominant. Early pastoral diets were based on meat and the fermented milk of sheep, goats, cattle, horses, and camels. Most of the region is desert with grassland, in which a thin growth of vegetation provides fodder for herders and nomads but is quickly extinguished, requiring frequent mobility. Oases provide pockets of denser settlement sustained by trade and the use of irrigation agriculture to grow cereal crops, like barley and wheat. These oases were the foundation for small trading states, such as Samarkand and Bukhara (in modern Uzbekistan), which eventually developed into prosperous cities.

Secondary Products Revolution. During the so-called "secondary products revolution" in 4000 BCE, new techniques were developed enabling more intensive use of livestock, such as for riding and pulling chariots and the production of blood, milk, and hair. The people of Central Asia became nomadic pastoralists and developed simple forms of agriculture, a way of life that lasted until the early twentieth century. This largely self-sufficient system limited material accumulation, which decreased the possibility of division of labor and inequalities in wealth and rank. There was some division of labor, as women took care of dwellings and made garments, while men controlled animals and fought, but women undertook male tasks during emergencies. The constant movement and amount of space necessary for a group, compounded with instability between years because of varied herd sizes, led to constant fighting for pastureland and raiding of neighboring tribes, and Central Asian people developed strong military skills. With new weaponry developed early in the first millennium BCE, such as more accurate bows and arrows, powerful pastoral leaders were able to form relatively stable alliances with smaller tribal groups, enabling them to mobilize large armies.

Widespread warlike migrations spread over large areas of inner Eurasia.

Empires. The first empire to rule over a large portion of Central Asia was the Achaemenid Empire, which controlled much of the area during the fifth century BCE while maintaining the authority of local rulers, who paid tributes to the empire. The peace established during this time, along with official road building, stimulated trade throughout the empire, as inner Eurasian trade networks became linked with Iran, Mesopotamia, and the Mediterranean. Agriculture was improved by the introduction of Persian irrigation techniques and new plants, such as peaches, apricots, and possibly sugarcane and oranges. Writing was introduced during this time by Persian officials as well as a post-horse service for official mail. By 400 BCE parts of Central Asia had freed themselves from Achaemenid control, and not until the Arab conquests of the seventh century CE was so large an area of Central Asia again incorporated into one empire. In 329 BCE much of the area was annexed by Alexander the Great into the Macedonian Empire. Macedonian control only lasted half a century, but it had a huge effect through the foundation of new cities, the acceleration of commerce, and the introduction of Greek commerce and culture. The conquest also caused much damage, including the near destruction of the trade city of Samarkand, but new towns were built with walls to protect them. The introduction of a new calendar and commercial laws stimulated trade and travel, and the link with Mediterranean civilization encouraged the exchange of ideas.

From 200 to 133 BCE, Mongolia, Manchuria, Siankiang, and eastern Central Asia were dominated by the Hsiung-nu, a pastoral nation on the Mongolian frontier of China. In 133 BCE the Chinese emperor Wu-ti, having heard about the wealthy lands of Central Asia in his travels, attacked the Hsiung-nu to establish the Han Empire. This began China's first successful attempt to establish diplomatic and commercial links with Central Asia. During this period trade increased between China and the West along the Silk Road, which turned into a major international trade route, linking all of Eurasia into a single system of regular commercial exchanges. Silk dominated the route because of its lightness, low bulk, and high value, but other commodities were traded as well. The power of the Han Empire eventually began to decline around 220 CE owing to internal divisions, at which point the Hsiung-nu briefly regained power but quickly lost it. Some Hsiung-nu refugees moved west, mixed with local populations, and became the group known as the Huns. The western migration of the Huns led to the Turkicization of inner Eurasia, as Iranian-speaking pastoralists were replaced by groups speaking Turkic languages, dominating the central and western steppes by 500 CE and much of southern Central Asia by 1000 CE.

During the Kushan Empire, which ruled over the first and second centuries CE, international trade increased dramatically along the Silk Road as resources in animal transport improved. Eastbound caravans brought gold, precious metals and stones, ivory, coral, spices, tea, paper, textiles, horses, and chinaware, while westbound caravans transported furs, ceramics, incense, cinnamon bark, rhubarb, and bronze weapons. Oasis cities, such as Samarkand and Bukhara, became thriving centers for trade. Ideas and information also traveled along the Silk Road, and Buddhism reached Central Asia during this time. Widespread political stability, royal support for irrigation, and booming trade networks enabled great economic prosperity. Vineyards thrived as irrigation systems became more advanced, enabling the appearance of commercial wine makers in Samarkand and Bukhara. Horses were bred commercially, especially in the Ferghana region in modern Kazakhstan. Agricultural methods improved with the use of iron implements, wooden plows, and metal plowshares for farming cereals, fruits, and fodder crops. The downfall of the Kushan Empire was caused by the conquest of the Northwest territories by Sassanian Persians in the fourth century CE, after which the oasis cities declined until the first Turkish Empire of 552 BCE. A group of Mongolian tribes, led by T'u-men, gained power after the split of the Wei dynasty in northern China. They extracted resources from the Chinese as well as from commercial towns and cities of Central Asia. However, most of their income came from trade, not tribute. After conquering the steppes of Kazakhstan, they grew rich trading silk, linens, gold, jade, vases, clothing, and wine for steppe produce, such as horses. They opened north silk roads to Byzantium, which stimulated the revival of trade and cultural contacts across Eurasia, causing a boom period for the city of Samarkand until the fall of the empire around 630 CE.

Islamic conquerors entered Central Asia in the mid-seventh century, making their base in the city of Merv in modern Turkmenistan and settling fifty thousand Arabs there. Most became farmers, putting down strong roots in the area. They next conquered Bukhara, Balkh, Samarkand, and Khorezm in modern Uzbekistan, up to the Syr Darya River in Kazakhstan. The first mosque in Central Asia was built in Bukhara, establishing the city's future as a major center of Islamic learning. Under Islamic rule, irrigation systems were extended and modernized, and a water wheel moved by animals and watermills were developed. Wheat, grain, fruits, and vegetables were grown along with sugar beets brought in from India. Cotton, flax, and wool were also produced, making textiles the leading industry of the region. Commercial wealth expanded, supporting a luxurious lifestyle for aristocrats in the cities. Great works of architecture, art, and literature were created, and literacy spread widely in the towns. Economic prosperity enabled population growth during this time, as improved agriculture meant

RUINS OF JIAOHE CITY, CHINA. During the Tang Dynasty (618–907), a permanent garrison of 6,000 men was stationed at Jiaohe to guard caravans and police the Silk Road. (Jiaohe City, Xinjiang Province, China/Werner Forman Archive/Art Resource, NY)

the cities could support a larger population. In the eighth century international rivalries arose over Mawara'n-nahr (present-day Turkmenistan, Uzbekistan, and parts of Kazakhstan), with the armies of Islam, Tibet, and Tang China battling for control of the area. Chinese victories over the Tibetan armies destroyed their chances, and China's defeat by Muslim armies in the battle of Talas in 751 ended Chinese ambitions over Central Asia for nearly a millennium. The Muslim caliphate could then consolidate control over Khorasan, the region of modern Turkmenistan and Afghanistan, and Mawara'n-nahr, in modern Uzbekistan, and begin the slow process of conversion from a multitude of religions to Islam. This process began in major towns and by the tenth century was nearly complete even in the countryside.

The Samanid dynasty of the tenth century revived the Islamic Empire, turning the region into the most prosperous and intellectually creative area in the Islamic world. The Samanids were regional governors centered in Bukhara. They were the first Central Asian rulers to use armies of slaves from the steppes, which had far-reaching consequences throughout the Islamic and Central Asian world. The separation of military and civilian population linked fiscal and military power, as agrarian and commercial revenues translated into military power. The strong government in Bukhara created the preconditions for commercial and economic expansion, and Bukhara became one of

the most important cities in the Islamic world. Other cities, such as Samarkand, also thrived, and economic and commercial growth throughout the region increased the size and number of provincial towns. Samarkand was known for its paper manufacture, learned from the Chinese after the battle of Talas in 751, and the production of glass, which was traded along the Silk Road to China. Bukhara became famous for its textiles, as well as the Islamic scholars who came to the city from the entire Muslim world. The engineering demands for building and maintaining the irrigation canals necessary for these cities encouraged original work in mathematics. Rice, wheat and other cereal products, cotton, and fruit were the main products grown. Trade expanded, especially with eastern Europe, where silk and cotton goods, silver and copper bowls and plates, weapons, and jewelry were sent in exchange for furs, amber, honey, sheepskins, and other raw materials. Trade along the Silk Road also flourished. However, during the second half of the tenth century the power of the Samanids began to decline, and an economic crisis developed. Poor maintenance of irrigation canals allowed the desert to encroach on the land used for agriculture, and land values fell. The government increased taxes on arable land to compensate for revenue losses, and many peasants moved to cities, working as household slaves or in weaving and spinning establishments. Throughout the eleventh century, without a strong government to maintain law and order and care for irrigation systems, water shortages occurred, the standard of living fell, and tribes of bandits roamed freely, destroying cultivated fields.

In the twelfth century Mongolia was a region of loose tribal confederations, such as the Tatars, Karait, and Naiman. Genghis Khan rose to power in 1206, conquering the other tribes and absorbing them into the Mongol Empire. Under his rule the Mongols swept through northern China in 1211 and conquered the Qara-Khitan realm in 1218, which gave the Mongols control over the trade routes between China and the Middle East. In 1220 Genghis conquered Bukhara and Samarkand. The Mongols caused a great deal of destruction in the conquered areas but rebuilt the cities to be better and stronger. Genghis established a Pax Mongolia, which allowed for safe travel from Crimea to Korea, permitting merchandise and ideas to move long distances. Mongol rulers further encouraged trade by standardizing weights and measures, suppressing banditry, holding villages responsible for maintaining roads, and building bazaars to encourage foreign merchants. The stability of this period, in addition to the economic prosperity caused by trade, allowed for the growth of literature, arts, and architecture. Genghis Khan's conquests transformed the nomadic tribal society into a feudal society, in which military leaders were able to reap the benefits of their conquests through tribute without giving up their traditional mode of life. However, constant military campaigns took conquered tribespeople away from their work in cattle breeding and led to high death rates. Agricultural development came to a halt owing to damage to many irrigation systems during the conquest period, and many other irrigation systems were destroyed afterward by neglect. The Mongols were forced to rely increasingly on slave labor at home and foreign troops in their campaigns abroad, deporting civilians from Persia and northern China to Siberia and Mongolia to weave, mine, and make tools and weapons. Genghis died in 1227, and his kingdom was divided among his four sons, in accordance with Mongol tradition. Jöchi, the eldest, was given the land from the Yenisey River and the Aral Sea westward (modern Kazakhstan and western Siberia.) This area became known as the Golden Horde, which became an Islamic state in 1313. The cities of the Golden Horde, such as Urganj in modern Uzbekistan, were close to the transcontinental caravan route and became thriving centers of craftsmanship and commerce. Chinese and Central Asian luxuries, grain, cattle, horses, slaves, fur, wood, and fish were shipped to Egypt, Syria, Italy, and Byzantium in exchange for textiles, cloth, jewelry, precious metals, perfume, and fruit. The prosperity of the Mongol Empire collapsed in 1348, when the Black Death struck the region and spread along the trade routes. Domestic stability ended as the area became further fragmented, and the empire began to disintegrate during the fifteenth century owing to internal strife. It was divided into independent khanates that feuded bitterly. This instability allowed Russia to begin its slow invasion of the area, conquering Siberia during the late sixteenth century and moving gradually toward Central Asia.

Artistic and intellectual life in the area was revived by the Timurid Empire in modern Uzbekistan that lasted from 1370 to the early 1500s. This Turkic dynasty achieved greatness in literature, art, and architecture and turned Samarkand into a new center for Islamic culture and scientific learning, but it eventually fell victim to incessant war with Uzbek tribes. In the early sixteenth century Uzbeks began to conquer the remnants of the Timurid Empire, but Vasco da Gama's discovery of the sea route between Europe and the Far East (1498) decreased the importance of Central Asia as a trade route. The transcontinental caravan trade, which had been the main source of prosperity to the area through tolls, began its steady decline. Central Asian rulers no longer had the resources to purchase firearms, and their power decreased. The area was now governed by many small khanates, surviving on the slave trade and exorbitant taxation of the population, who were no match for the Russian armies.

Russian Expansion. There were several causes of Russian expansion in Central Asia. The first Russian expedition into Turkmenistan in 1716 sent Peter the Great seeking a route for Russian trade with southern Asia and the Middle East. Central Asia was also seen as a market for Russian exports, such as grain, sugar, tobacco, cloth, and metal items, in addition to the possibility of importing cattle, leather, wool, rugs, and spices. In the 1730s Kazaks and Kyrgyzes asked for Russian protection from plundering raids in exchange for a tribute of furs along with enhanced Russian trade interests. Whenever possible Russian governors and generals pushed the fortified frontier south into lands in present-day Kazakhstan, where political authority was divided among weak states. It was easy for Russians to extend their control over these lands, and by the end of the eighteenth century they were under Russian rule. Irregularities in the U.S. cotton supply during the U.S. Civil War created additional motivation for Russian expansion, as Central Asia was viewed as a potential cotton producer. In the 1870s Russians began the pattern of transferring land from grain cultivation to cotton cultivation, expanding Central Asia's cotton production to Kyrgyzstan and Tajikstan. Russian colonization eroded the traditional nomadic way of life for many tribes in the region through a series of land codes between 1867 and 1891 in order to force agricultural settlement and make taxes easier to collect. The codes reduced pastureland and isolated many groups from their traditional grazing land and water resources, and many thousands of nomads and their herds died of hunger. In 1876 the remnants of the khanate of Kokand were annexed into Russia and made a part of Turkestan. In the succeeding years military expeditions brought the lands west of the Amu Darya to the Caspian Sea under Russian control. By 1884 the Russian conquest of Central Asia was complete, and the Russian frontier met the frontiers of Persia, China, and Afghanistan.

[*See also* Silk Road.]

BIBLIOGRAPHY
Christian, David. *A History of Russia, Central Asia, and Mongolia.* Oxford, 1998.
D'Encausse, Helene Carrere. *Islam and the Russian Empire: Reform and Revolution in Central Asia.* London, 1988.
Frye, Richard N. *Bukhara: The Medieval Achievement.* Norman, Okla., 1965.
Hambly, Gavin. *Central Asia.* London, 1969.

CENTRAL BANKING. Central banks are important institutions charged with the conduct of monetary policy. Their functions have sometimes been exaggerated and greater claims have been made for their powers than is wise. This essay describes their responsibilities and how these are fulfilled. It also outlines their origins and development, giving particular attention to the key function of lender of last resort.

Functions of a Central Bank. The principal function of a central bank is control of monetary policy. In a country with a floating exchange rate, the central bank has control of the money supply. If it operates within a fixed exchange-rate system, it lacks this control and must accept the monetary policy of the dominant country in the fixed exchange-rate system. In the former case, in which it has control of the money stock, it issues the money base, sometimes called high-powered money. (Some of the institutions that later became central banks were often referred to as banks of issue.) Control of the money base means responsibility for controlling the money supply and therefore the power to determine short-term nominal interest rates. Ordinarily, the principal objective of the bank is price stability, and the operating procedure has usually been through short-term interest rates, although these rates may not indicate clearly the intention of policy. By acting through interest rates, the central bank controls the growth of the monetary base, and that has an impact on the economy through many channels. The influence over interest rates means that the bank has some part to play in the determination of the nominal exchange rate since there is a relationship, albeit a complex one, between interest rates and exchange rates. Where there are exchange controls in place (as there were for most of the twentieth century), the central bank is often responsible for administering such controls. Because central banks have an influence over interest rates, they are effectively debarred from carrying out commercial business; if a significant part of their business were commercial banking, a conflict could arise between their macroeconomic obligations and their microeconomic obligations. For example, macro policy may require an increase in interest rates, while competition with other banks could result in pressures to reduce rates. There is also a risk of central banks helping their own customers. For these reasons there should be no commercial rivalry. (It is because some continental European banks were engaged in commercial rivalry in the late nineteenth century that they could not be considered true as central banks until they had shed their commercial functions in some cases not until the twentieth century.)

Central banks perform other possible functions. They are commonly, though not necessarily, the government's bank. That originated in part from the establishment of banks by government charter and the obligation imposed to look after the government's accounts. But this clearly makes sense from the point of view of the operation of monetary policy, since the biggest borrower in the financial markets has so often been the government. And it usually follows, though again it need not do so, that the bank manages at least some of the government's debt. (This can be used in the operation of monetary policy.) Some banks have had responsibility for all the debt. However, for small countries it is likely that there are fund managers (perhaps even in another country) better placed to do that, though for political reasons they are not used as often as they might be if purely financial concerns dominate.

Stability in the financial system is a major goal, and various means of achieving this have been tried. Encouraging prudence or allowing commercial banks to find their own way to prudence is a good start. But shocks can still hit the banking system, and prudence may not be enough on its own to protect it. Supporting such a prudent system in its role as lender of last resort is the other main task of the central bank. But central banks have been led into supervision of the banking sector, and to the regulation of it, in an attempt at further promoting stability. There is no widespread agreement on how, or even if, regulation and supervision should be carried out. Deposit insurance has also been widely introduced to bolster stability, and it often falls to the central bank to administer such schemes. Central banks have sometimes been charged with other functions, such as providing full employment and contributing to economic growth. These are now recognized as lying outside the influence of the banks. Central bank may also be encouraged to promote commercial banking in their economies.

History. Central banks today generally have similar origins. They were not set up as central banks. The first institutions were usually established as government banks carrying out the business of government. That commonly involved lending to governments, possibly on favorable terms. Initially, they did not necessarily have sole right to issue notes, but that was something they invariably acquired before too long. However, if the principal defining characteristic of a central bank is, as some would argue, as lender of last resort, then their proper founding dates come even later. Thus, although it is often remarked that the Swedish Riksbank (founded in 1668) was the first central bank, this is highly misleading. There was no concept of central banking in the seventeenth century, and the Riksbank assumed all the core functions of a central bank only in the late nineteenth century.

Ignoring these difficulties for the moment, some indications can be given of the growth of these institutions before specifying more precisely when they took on their more properly defined role. Only a handful of institutions existed in the nineteenth century, and even by 1900 there were only 18 of them. For reasons explained later, there was another burst of activity in the interwar years, and by 1940 there were 40. That number had risen to 75 by 1960, to 149 in 1990, and further still to 173 in 1998. The upper limit must be the number of countries in the world. This in itself may grow or shrink. However, in the current century there is the prospect of the number of central banks falling. For example, following the formation of the European Central Bank (ECB), all the individual-country central banks will disappear. The numbers employed in these institutions are quite impressive, though it is likely that the peak has been reached. The biggest central bank is probably the Peoples Bank of China, which has employed around 100,000 in recent years. The Russian Federation Bank is also large with 40,000. Not surprisingly, given its origins and structure, the U.S. Federal Reserve is the third, largest employer with 23,000, while the German Bundesbank and the Bank of France are not far behind with roughly 16,000 each. The Bank of England, by contrast, has fewer than 3,000. Of course, when the European Central Bank takes over completely, then the numbers in Europe will be greater than those of the U.S. Fed.

In the late nineteenth century, attention was directed to the usefulness of an institution to manage the gold standard. Around that time, the real origins of central banking began. The Bank of England is said to have been the first, its beginnings as a mature central bank dating from the 1870s. During World War I, central banks generally lost what independence they had, and it is not surprising that considerable inflation followed, as governments printed money to finance wartime expenditure. The mood following the war was to return to the world of pre-1914. Independence was restored, and central banks were established to ensure responsible behavior in monetary matters.

But no sooner had this happened than the Great Depression turned the world's attention to banks and central banks as the progenitors of the economic collapse. This, in addition to World War II and the influence of Keynesian ideas on the management of the economy, saw the loss of independence and the misuse of central banks by governments. The mood after World War II was also one which favored freeing colonial territories and establishing new sovereign countries. A concomitant surge in new banks took place. Where there had been currency boards or simply commercial banks of the imperial country, there now appeared central banks.

The next burst of growth came toward the end of the twentieth century, again with the establishment of new countries or, more often, the restoration of once-independent countries to their former status, following the breakup of the Soviet empire and of Yugoslavia. Clearly, no one can predict the changing number of banks in the future. It will depend on whether the drive to form bigger political or monetary unions, such as the European Union, is offset by the demands for smaller units of peoples who wish to direct their own destinies.

The Lender of Last Resort. If a precondition for economic growth is macroeconomic stability, a prerequisite for macrostability is monetary and financial stability. This suggests the important of the central bank, for it stands at the center of the financial system and wields considerable power. It should be able by a variety of means to promote, if not to ensure, monetary and financial stability. The main issue is how to achieve that stability. It is the prime purpose of the lender of last resort to deliver financial stability. As noted in the introduction, it is the role of lender of last resort that best captures the essence of central banking. But what exactly does the term mean? There has been, and continues to be, disagreement on the subject. The main area of disagreement lies in whether the central bank should come to the rescue of an individual financial institution that has fallen into difficulty or whether it should concern itself only with the operation of the system as a whole.

On the question of whether it should bail out a failing bank, the argument in favor is that a large bank in difficulty (for whatever reason) will induce worry among depositors of other banks about their own institutions. If sufficiently worried, they would move into either cash or other instruments and so endanger the system. It is therefore said to be sensible for the central bank to make sure that the first bank does not fail. The principal objection to this is that it introduces a moral hazard and so weakens the whole system. If a bank can count on the central bank coming to its rescue, the bank is encouraged to engage in imprudent behavior. If the price of risk falls, then the quantity of risk consumed rises. For that reason alone, bail outs should be avoided.

BANK OF ENGLAND. London, circa 1901. (George Grantham Bain Collection/Prints and Photographs Division, Library of Congress)

Some argue that if the largest banks failed, it would have disastrous consequences for the system and they must therefore be saved—the "too-big-to-fail" doctrine. Apart from other predictable consequences, such as banks forming themselves into units that qualify for rescue, there are more serious objections to this. The main one is that if an institution fails, then it needs an injection of capital. If it is so large that it matters to the whole system, then no central bank would be in a position to provide the necessary capital. It would in effect have to raise the new capital from government—that is to say, from the taxpayer. In other words, it would have to make a fiscal decision. There is already sufficient concern over the power of central banks (run by unelected officials) without allowing them to take fiscal action as well as monetary.

What then should the bank do, and how can it do it? The proper behavior is for the bank to provide for the liquidity needs of the market as a whole. As the sole issuer of money (cash), a central bank can always produce the necessary liquidity no matter how much is required. Thus, if one bank falls into difficulty for reasons of bad management—usually overlending on poor security—it should fail. But if

there is a consequent threat of a bank run, a financial crisis, then that clearly threatens financial stability, and the central bank should provide sufficient liquidity to meet the demands of the otherwise well-run banks. Because it prints money, it can do that endlessly. But the central bank will choose to provide it to those who bring good securities, and at an increasing price. Banks with good liquid assets need never fear the inability to get cash in times of need. Banks taking greater risks and carrying less acceptable commercial paper in their balance sheets will have more difficulty. During the Great Depression, was the failure of the U.S. Federal Reserve to provide the required liquidity even on good security that intensified the severity of that depression. The learning of that lesson allowed the central bank to avert anything similar in 1987, when the stock market collapsed in similar fashion.

The ideal way for the central bank to provide liquidity to the market is to do so anonymously. This needs the appropriate institutional structure, but when in place it allows the central bank simply to keep the market supplied with funds without becoming involved with any one bank and thereby raising the moral hazard issue.

Because the central bank is key to the working of the financial system and indeed the whole economy, other occasions may arise when it sees the need to address a particular problem. This could mean organizing the rescue of a major institution. It could be that unfortunate and unpredictable circumstances arise that endanger a particular bank. The central bank may then use its influence to organize a rescue by encouraging other institutions to raise capital and to reconstitute the failing firm. This is entirely acceptable and useful. However, it is more properly called crisis management. It probably involves no lending at all and should not be confused with the role of lender of last resort.

The lender-of-last-resort role is, then, at the heart of central banking. But it is important to stress that it should mean lending to the market as a whole, not to an individual institution. Of course, there are still difficulties. A central bank needs to acquire the appropriate reputation for good and careful behavior before it can act in this way successfully. The risk is that if the central bank does not know how or when to act, it could provide too much liquidity and cause inflation. This is a problem in young countries—often developing economies—and there is no easy way out of the problem. Reputation does take time to build.

Main Central Banks of the World. The origins, development, and approaches of the central banks in the principal industrial countries have been different. The five biggest economies in the world that operate the main central banks are the United States, the United Kingdom, Germany, France, and Japan. (The European Central Bank has only recently been established, and its future is not yet clear.) Different experience is found in developing countries and in other parts of the developed world, too. But it is worth giving brief outlines of the main banks.

The Bank of England can claim to be the oldest central bank in the world. The bank was formed in 1694 as a monopoly joint-stock bank and the government's bank. Its charter was renewed every twenty years, and by the end of the eighteenth century, it had grown to a point where it dominated the monetary system. It was granted sole note-issuing rights in 1844, and after a long learning process (and the development of institutions around it), it emerged in the 1870s as a true central bank. It was in that decade that it became a lender of last resort in the modern sense. Where there had been financial crises throughout its existence up to 1866, there was none after that date. It continued to be a private bank until it was nationalized in 1946, but it had begun to lose its autonomy long before that. Poor inflationary experience in the post–World War II decades was among the principal reasons for restoring it to an independent position in 1997.

The U.S. Federal Reserve was founded primarily to combat financial instability. The U.S. economy had been much more volatile than the British and some other European economies, and it had experienced frequent and damaging banking panics in the second half of the nineteenth century. The National Monetary Commission was set up to investigate causes and find solutions. It took evidence from around Europe, and the outcome was the founding of the Fed in 1913. It is made up of twelve regional banks with the chairmanship residing in Washington, D.C. The most important regional bank for most of the Fed's history was in New York because of the significance of the financial sector located around Wall Street. The Fed has had a checkered history. It is held responsible for the Great Depression in the interwar years but enjoyed great prestige in the last twenty or so years of the twentieth century under the chairmanship first of Paul Volcker and then of Alan Greenspan. Although its articles set out many goals for the bank and chairmen continue to talk in terms of these goals, in fact it concentrates heavily on the one thing it can properly do: provide sound money and hence stable prices. The extent of its independence has long been discussed, but it is widely agreed that it is one of the more independent central banks.

Although the Bundesbank is one of the youngest of the big central banks, it does have some important predecessors. The Prussian State Bank, founded in 1846, is the obvious beginning. That was converted to the Reichsbank in 1876 following the unification of Germany in 1871. Within continental Europe, the tradition was one in which large universal banks developed. In Germany, these were quite large, and it is open to question whether the Reichsbank could have operated as a lender of last resort before the twentieth century. Further, it continued to transact commercial business and was therefore in competition with the other big banks. It presided over the worst inflation in German history in 1923. All of this mattered for the constitution of the new bank founded after World War II. The model for that was essentially the U.S. Fed. From 1948 to 1957, a system of regional banks operated—the Banks deutsche Lander. Following that in 1958, the Bundesbank was founded. For a number of reasons it developed a good reputation, and with considerable independence, it provided Germany with less inflation than most other countries. Its life, however, has been a short one as it is now subsumed in the ECB.

The Bank of France was founded in 1800. That followed the disastrous experience with a paper currency, the assignat, and the wild inflation of the 1790s. However, it, too, for reasons similar to the Reichsbank, had to wait until the twentieth century before it was considered a central bank. It probably never had much independence and lost whatever it had when it was nationalized in 1945. It regained independence in the 1990s in preparation for its demise as a branch of the European Central Bank.

The Bank of Japan (Nippon Ginko) was founded in 1882. It quickly became the government's bank and began issuing its notes in 1885. In 1942, a major amendment was passed in the Bank of Japan Act. Its objectives included "the regulation of the currency, the facilitation of credit and finance, and the maintenance and fostering of the credit system, pursuant to the national (economic) policy." At that stage, the bank became totally subordinate to the ministry of finance. It appears to have been highly successful through most of its life, though this may simply reflect the path of the Japanese economy for much of the twentieth century. It was less successful in the deflationary decade at the end of the twentieth century.

Theory. The theory governing central bank behavior lies at the heart of modern monetary economics. It is well known, and has been since the time of David Hume in the eighteenth century, that stable money is associated with stable prices. That is, if the quantity of money is allowed to grow or can be managed to grow in line with the growth of the real economy, then stable prices will follow. The long-run relationship is remarkably strong. However, in the short run circumstances arise that appear to call for action on the part of the bank. A recession may be looming, and the need for some easing in monetary policy may be advisable. But any such expansion carries with it the danger of inflation if it is not reversed when the appropriate time arrives. In other words, there is a conflict between the short run and the long run.

At one time, it was believed that there was a clear trade-off between inflation and output growth (a Phillips curve) and that careful management could bring whatever results were required. But that view was attacked almost as soon as it appeared. It was then greatly modified to the point that it became accepted that there was no more than a short-run relationship of that kind (Phillips curve). But before the practice had been corrected, the world experienced considerable inflation (in the 1970s) while output remained stagnant. The short-run relationship can be abused by administrations in their pursuit of reelection. Abuse indeed occurred, and it was for this reason (as well as the return of floating exchange rates) that independent central banks reemerged.

The central task is to provide price stability, and the question is how best to operate to achieve this. Several ways are possible, and debate on the issues persists. Three alternative approaches are available: money-supply control, interest-rate targeting, and exchange-rate targeting. In effect, the latter two reduce to one when covered interest parity holds. Does it then matter whether a central bank controls the money supply or operates on interest rates? One is a quantity and the other a price, and on the surface, it would not seem to matter which the bank chooses. However, the bank faces a constantly changing world, and it matters how the central bank and the rest of the market perceive the changes. The changes, however, are not always easy to read. They can be both real and monetary; some changes might be anticipated, while others are not. More important, some changes are permanent, while others are transitory. Frequently, it is difficult to distinguish between the latter when they occur. The central bank's strategy should be to try to reduce uncertainty to a minimum. Academic debate is divided on this but perhaps inclines to controlling money supply and allowing interest rates to adjust.

Supervision/Regulation. The general case for the supervision of the banking system is based on the need for financial stability. Some would argue that proper use of the lender-of-last-resort function in conjunction with a prudent banking system should be sufficient to ensure stability. The question is, how is a well-behaved banking system encouraged? Can it learn caution on its own, or must it be given a set of guidelines by which to abide? If the answer is the former, then there is no case for statutory regulation. If the answer is the latter, then there is a case. It is nevertheless important to remember that supervision/regulation should do something other than what is covered by the laws of the land. The banking system need not be concerned with fraud, for instance, since that would be a duplication of powers.

There is a difference between supervision and regulation. The first implies oversight and possibly some suggestions on appropriate behavior. The second bears the clear implication of policing and disciplining and would have to carry the threat of penalty to be effective. If there is a case for supervision, as against regulation, it must be that there is some use in collecting information. Thus, the supervisory body could ask for different types of information according to changing circumstances. It could then monitor particular developments in the markets. But based on this scenario, the supervisor would be toothless. In the end, would this add to anything that banks would do on their own?

Regulation suggests backup: something can be done about any errant member of the regulated group. This usually means enforcement, by some appointed body, of the rules set out in statutes. But even where there is self-regulation, the suggestion is that the group as a whole will take responsibility for its membership and will keep members in line with best practice. Under regulation, the rules as well as the penalties for noncompliance must be mad clear, and an institution must be appointed to enforce the rules. That institution has almost invariably been the central bank, though it need not have been. The case for leaving regulation to the central bank is a strong one, for the main point is that the bank pursues financial stability by means of the lender of last resort. This function must be supported by a well-behaved banking system. If there is a case at all for supervision and regulation, it would seem that the central bank should carry out these tasks.

The main measures taken by regulators have aimed at limiting risk. The separation of commercial banking and investment banking is one such measure. Capital requirements are another important (and commonly used) measure. Sometimes, deposit insurance is introduced. And occasionally, limits are placed on the proportion of a balance sheet that can be lent to any one customer. Serious objections have been raised against all of these measures. The first measure has broken down in recent years. The second raises the question of the quality of the capital and/or the assets against which the capital has been set. Deposit insurance might produce the opposite effect of what is intended because it tends to encourage risk taking. The final measure raises the question of who would best know what a bank's lending policies should be.

The history of regulation has not been an entirely happy one. In some countries, such as the United States, it has been argued that regulation was as much responsible for problems in the system as solving them. In a country such as the United Kingdom, relatively light self-regulation contributed to a system in which there were no financial crises. Even if it were shown that regulation made a positive contribution to stability, the cost of enforcement would have to be assessed. The cost may be too high in relation to the benefits.

Independence. To what extent should a central bank be free of political interference? This emerged as an issue in the 1980s and 1990s after the world experienced a long period of sustained inflation. It was clear that some countries had performed substantially better than others, and the question was, What was responsible for the difference? The preceding and accompanying academic debate showed that inflation was a consequence of lax monetary policy—of monetary growth exceeding the growth of the economy. If governments could manipulate monetary policy and surprise the electors, they could generate the appearance of good economic conditions just prior to an election. A large number of studies indicated that there was a close and positive relationship between the degree of central bank dependence and the rate of inflation. However, these studies were restricted to the period following the mid-1970s, for it was only then that floating exchange rates allowed governments their own monetary policy. But perhaps causality ran the other way: low inflation was desired and insistence on central bank independence followed. Either way, they certainly seemed to go together.

Attention also focused on the precise definition and extent of independence. Some kinds of independence had more serious consequences for democracy. After all,

central bankers were unelected, and it was important to decide on the extent of their freedom. Two broad views of independence emerged. One was "instrument" or "operational" independence. The other was goal independence. In the first, governments would decide the rate of inflation and leave the central bank to produce it. Such a contract would be better if it were for a reasonable period. In the second case, the central bank would be left to decide on the rate of inflation. For instance, it might be required to produce stable prices and left to decide what that meant. In the second instance, there is a greater loss of democracy. To some extent, that could be offset by complete openness and accountability.

The question is sometimes raised, If there is a body with independence in monetary policy, why is there none for fiscal policy? The answer is surely that there are a large number of objectives for fiscal policy as well as a problem of priorities. This is the essence of politics. For monetary policy, following acceptance of a vertical Phillips curve, there was a single objective. And so long as the institution could be monitored and made accountable, the democratic deficit was kept to a minimum.

The nineteenth century saw relative freedom. That was curtailed in World War I. Some restoration of freedom came at the end of the war but was set back by both the Great Depression and the World War II. Then came a period of greatest dependence (followed by the greatest inflation). In the last two decades of the twentieth century, the vogue for independence took hold and reached its apotheosis in the creation of the European Central Bank.

This essay has outlined the origins and development of central banking. Most of this refers of necessity to the twentieth century. The central function is that of the lender of last resort. The main lesson to be learned from the experience is that central banks can do one thing: provide price stability, the underpinnings of financial and macroeconomic stability. These, in turn, are necessary conditions for economic growth. Beyond that particular ability, however, the powers of central banks are limited.

BIBLIOGRAPHY

Capie, Forrest, et al. *The Future of Central Banking.* Cambridge and New York, 1994.

Conant, Charles A. *A History of Modern Banks of Issue.* London, 1909.

Hawtrey, Ralph G. *The Art of Central Banking.* London, 1932.

Kisch, C. H., and W. A. Elkin. *Central Banks* New York, 1928.

Smith, Vera. *The Rationale of Central Banking and the Free Banking Alternative.* Westminster, U.K., 1936.

Sprague, Oliver M. W. *History of Crises under the National Banking System* Washington, D.C., 1910.

Timberlake, Richard H. *Central Banking in the United States.* Chicago, 1993.

Toniolo, Gianni, ed. *Central Bank's Independence in Historical Prespective.* New York, 1988.

FORREST CAPIE

CENTRAL SOUTH AMERICAN STATES. The Gran Chaco region includes southeastern Bolivia, northeastern Argentina, and the northern half of Paraguay; it has for most of its history remained marginal to the economies of South America. The region is a large and densely wooded flood plain in the center of the continent, in which there are virtually no rocks or economically desireable mineral deposits. During the winter, the region is very dry, and many of the water sources (including some rivers) disappear. In the summer, abundant rainfall brings about vigorous plant growth but also heat, mosquitoes, and flooding. Such ecological conditions have never sustained large human populations or much agriculture, except on the Chaco's fringes. By the nineteenth century, the Chaco's major ethnic groups included the agricultural Chiriguanos (Ava-Guaraní) along the northwestern border, the hunting-and-gathering Matacos (now also known as Weenhayek or Wichí) and Chulupí in the southcentral region, and the Tobas and Pilagá in the central and eastern regions.

From the 1500s to the early 1800s, Spain and Portugal colonized most of South America. With national independence in the 1810s, the colonial era's Roman Catholic missions were closed in the Chaco, and the Indians regained control over the region. Some members of the Salta elites in Argentina tried to turn the former missions into sheep farms and cloth factories, using the indigenous labor, but those efforts failed because of Indian resistance. Efforts to develop European-style agriculture along the Pilcomayo and Bermejo rivers, as well as riverboat service from the interior to the River Plate region, also failed. The Bolivian government was especially interested in river navigation during the 1830s, as a way to find access to Atlantic ports; however, its attempts to colonize the Chaco and explore the waterways did not succeed. In fact, until the mid-to-late 1800s, landlords and local officials paid fees to the Indians to keep them as "allies" or to pasture their cattle on land that, on paper, belonged to the ranchers. Thus, the Indians used their military superiority to gain access to scarce goods from creole society (criollos were Europeans born in the New World), in a type of tribute system. In most cases, that involved the providing of imported textiles to war chiefs, who redistributed the goods to their followers; the system assured that the warrior faction and warfare remained paramount within indigenous societies. Indian women, who had previously produced most of the clothing, lost status within indigenous societies during the early 1800s.

In the 1860s, the Chaco's indigenous populations began to engage in the surrounding national economies, which came about for three reasons.

1. The criollos of Bolivia and Argentina began to use the Chaco for extensive cattle ranching. The trend was especially notable in Argentina, where by the 1870s the government gave out vast land grants for ranching in a tract called Colonia Rivadavia; its settlement became possible because whites got access to repeating rifles, which provided them a great military advantage. The Huacaya War (1874–1878) in southeastern Bolivia brought the end to an alliance of Chiriguano and Toba peoples. The 1880 military invasion into the Chaco by Argentine Colonel Benjamin Victorica defeated many of the Mataco and Toba peoples in the southcentral Chaco.

2. After 1860, Franciscan missions flourished both on the Bolivian and Argentine sides of the Chaco. Although the friars attempted to shield their charges from landlord abuses, most mission Indians went to work on nearby ranches or haciendas. Then, too, the sugar cane plantations of Salta and Jujuy provinces, on the western fringes of the Chaco in Argentina, contracted with tens of thousands of seasonal workers for the harvest every year. The plantations sent labor contractors into the Chaco to recruit Indians. Contractors paid chiefs to bring their subjects to the plantations, where they lived in precarious housing. By the 1880s, this migration led to a serious labor drain on the Bolivian side, where Indians escaped slavelike conditions on local farms and ranches. Among the Chiriguano, Argentina became known as *Mbaporenda* ("the land where there is work"), where Indians could earn clothing, mules, and guns, could drink alcohol, and could consume goods not available at home. Colonization schemes (such as the creation of the town of Villamontes by turning over the old Franciscan missions along the Pilcomayo to the German merchant firm Staudt and Company) had also failed. In that case, the Germans had planned to dam the Pilcomayo and create a development of vast irrigated acreage. Instead, the land became concentrated in the hands of a few ranchers when the company found it impossible to build the dam. U.S. oil exploration and production by the Standard Oil Company also did not help the local people, as the American firm preferred to hire Argentine crews.

3. On the Argentine side of the Chaco, and especially after the last "pacifying" expedition of 1911 (where Indians were hunted, killed, relocated, and so on), the Argentine army became involved in labor recruitment for the plantations. With the encouragement of the plantation owners and as a means of "civilizing" the natives, army patrols moved from Indian village to Indian village, forcing the adults to go to the plantations during harvest time. This system broke down only in the 1930s, when plantation owners purchased large estates in the Andean highlands in the provinces of Salta and Jujuy, then obligated their resident peasants to work in the lowlands. Likewise, in Bolivia, more and more peasants from the southern highlands began to work in the lowland sugar cane fields, so the proportion of Chaco Indians in the plantation labor force decreased.

The 1930s were a period of great turmoil in the Chaco region. Foremost, in the Chaco War of 1932 to 1935, Bolivia fought Paraguay—and more than one hundred thousand soldiers were killed, with many more captured. That caused the depopulation of the region, with the Indians either escaping into the Argentine Chaco's refugee camps or taken into the interior by the Paraguayans as war captives. After the war, many Indians remained in Argentina; most had become dependent on the government's support and did not return to their original territories. In the aftermath of the war, ranchers took over much of the indigenous land that had been vacated; thus, the Indian population became concentrated on the fringes of the Chaco, to serve as a marginal and poorly paid labor reserve. From the 1930s onward, the economic situation in the Chaco changed substantially. Oil and natural gas were found and they provided large resources both for Argentina and Bolivia, but this capital-intensive industry did not create many jobs. The cotton boom of the 1930s and 1940s fizzled when the lands quickly became exhausted. Mennonite farmers settled in the Chaco by the Paraguayan government in 1928—engaged in some agriculture and much ranching, and that providing some jobs for indigenous peoples. Lumber companies continued to harvest timber throughout the Chaco, but their clear-cutting techniques brought about tremendous ecological problems (erosion of topsoil by wind and weather, loss of oxygen producers, increased heat, etc.).

The Indians today live in their own settlements close to Tartagal, Argentina. In addition to occasional employment on ranches and in urban centers, they subsist on the making of handicrafts for sale in Argentine cities. With the privatization of the state-run Argentine and Bolivian oil companies (YPF and YPFB, respectively) their employment has decreased and even creoles are leaving for jobs outside the region. The current economic situation for the Chaco region is bleak; the shrinking of governments and government programs has diminished state subsidies throughout the region. The 1990s integration of the countries into MERCOSUR, a trading bloc, has marginalized the Gran Chaco region even more, given its poverty-stricken, poorly educated population and its lack of natural resources.

[See also American Indian Economies, *subentry on* Inca Economy; Andean Region; *and* Spain, *subentry on* Spanish Empire.]

BIBLIOGRAPHY

Langer, Erick D. *Economic Change and Rural Resistance in Southern Bolivia, 1880–1930*. Stanford, Calif., 1989. General overview of colonization, ranching, missions, and effects of oil companies in southeastern Bolivia.

Langer, Erick D. "Foreign Cloth in the Lowland Frontier: Commerce and Consumption of Textiles in Bolivia, 1830–1930." In *The Allure of the Foreign: The Role of Imports in Post-Colonial Latin America*, edited by Benjamin S. Orlove, pp. 93–112. Ann Arbor, 1997. Discusses use of textiles as tribute goods for Chiriguano Indians in the early nineteenth century.

Maybury-Lewis, David. "Lowland Peoples of the Twentieth Century." In *The Cambridge History of Native Peoples of the Americas*, vol. 3, part 2, edited by Frank Salomon and Stuart B. Schwartz, pp. 872–948. Cambridge, 1999.

Miller, Elmer S., ed. *Peoples of the Gran Chaco*. Westport, Conn., 1999. Compendium of contemporary economic activities of Chaco peoples by distinguished anthropologists.

Teruel, Ana, and Omar Jerez, eds. *Pasado y presente de un mundo postergado*. San Salvador de Jujuy, 1998. Collection of works on the Argentine and Bolivian Chaco, which includes missions, plantations, living conditions, and the political integration of Indians into the state.

Whiteford, Scott. *Workers from the North: Plantations, Bolivian Labor and the City in Northwest Argentina*. Austin, 1981.

ERICK D. LANGER

CERAMICS. Well preserved in the archaeological record, ceramics (fire-hardened clay vessels, plates, tiles, and plaques) can be traced from the Neolithic era, with production sites known worldwide from about 12,000 to 6,000 years ago. The history of ceramics is then one of an ancient technology, in which clay is fired into stone. Yet the field of developmental economic history has taken a disparaging view of much of the industry. For example, earthenware, whether made by hand or thrown on a potter's wheel, is considered "primitive," so little comment is made concerning the fact that some household and industrial pottery never needed change in basic form or function—earthenware still serves us well. The developmental approach that seeks to describe "improvement," therefore, misses much that is interesting and may obscure the general role of labor-intensive production and innovation within traditional or small-scale enterprises.

Like earthenware, stoneware is a useful example of the importance of taking a long view. Stoneware is a form of high-fired ceramics, and its history shows innovations in different ways at different times; also, that production could expand without any innovation. Stonewares became important in England during the late seventeenth century, and they contributed to the expansion of the industry in the first half of the eighteenth century, as England became industrialized. If England alone is considered, it would seem that stoneware was an "invention" there, based on experimentation in the Midlands and London. Yet stoneware had been produced in many places well before the seventeenth century—the earliest is known from the Bronze Age of Mesopotamia (c. 2700–2200 BCE). It is known from China about 1500 BCE; it was important in Japan and Korea from the fifth century CE; it was first made in medieval Europe only in the thirteenth century. Commercially advanced pottery production was possible without stoneware, for it was hardly made at all by the successful

Roman industry (c. 200 BCE to 500 CE). No matter how advanced some parts of the industry were, others were rooted in the past; for example, cooking pots were made by hand locally throughout the Roman Empire at the same time that large quantities of fine earthenwares were produced for household use. In the twentieth century, hand-built cooking and storage vessels, little different from those made thousands of years before, continued to be made for daily use in Africa, India, and South America. The long view, therefore, emphasises continuity and does not limit the focus to European industrialization.

Techniques. Ceramics are made from clays that are shaped in various ways and hardened by heat. A series of processes is needed to make ceramics of any kind, and archaeological evidence about its production has provided the long view about many techniques. Ceramic wares have been excavated at ancient sites of all kinds, including production sites. These have been compared to observations of "traditional" production methods in Africa, Asia, and the Americas, experimental kiln firings, and conventional historical documents. Clays are found abundantly in many areas of the world, and they were not at first transported more than about a kilometer (0.6 mile or so), although they were traded over many hundreds of miles in the Americas and in post-medieval Europe. Decorative clays, various pigments, and glazing materials were used in smaller quantities and were transported from greater distances than clays or the heavy fuels needed to fire them. The more sophisticated the wares, the more varied the raw materials; stoneware and the even higher-fired porcelains needed careful preparation and mixing of clay with other materials, because the high heat (1400°C) made them liable to distort in the firing. In the nineteenth and twentieth centuries, "industrial" ceramics (for dinnerware and household use) were mixed from white "ball" clays, local clays, and other additions; china clay and calcined animal bone were used to make bone china. Baking and storage vessels, by contrast, could still be made industrially from most types of local clay.

Hand-built pottery, typically formed by building pots from coils of clay, resists heat better than wheel-thrown vessels, so these methods survived alongside the potter's wheel for cooking vessels and were still used in the twentieth century. The potter's wheel was an ancient invention that dates from the fourth millennium BCE in the early civilizations of Mesopotamia; such wheels were turned by hand or by an apprentice. Gradually, they were improved to be easier to use and faster, with double wheels—the lower wheel turned by the foot, the upper having the wheelhead for the pot. The modern kick-wheel, with a vertical iron shaft, dates from the sixteenth century CE in Europe. The wheel speeded production and gave regular shapes, although the clay needed to be very plastic. In the Americas,

the potter's wheel was unknown and most ordinary wares were hand built. Until the nineteenth century in Europe, molds were not normally important to large scale production, except for the fine *terra sigillata* industry of the Roman Empire, in which large amounts of fine, decorated earthenware was made on an "industrial" scale in both standard and complex patterns. In the Americas, very fine wares were mold made. In China, Japan, and Korea, molds were used for figures and decoration. Nineteenth- and twentieth-century European industrial wares relied on various semimechanized molding processes, both for plates and hollow wares. Pot surfaces were usually decorated in some way, including the burnishing and polishing of the surface, carving the surface, the addition of clays and molded decorations to the surface, glazes, painting, and stamping. Industrial pottery usually has printed transfers applied but some is still painted by hand.

Firing the pottery was a key stage at all times, for reliable results were (and still are) essential. Pottery may be fired in hearths or pits with such fuels as brush, wood, or grass; evidence from prehistoric pottery suggests that it was fired at a relatively low temperature (750–800°C), with a short firing time. Evidence for well-constructed kilns begins at about 4000 BCE in Asia and about 2700 BCE in the ancient Near East; then they became widespread in the Old World. Most kilns were made of durable materials with one or more fireplaces, often round in shape with various ways of stacking the vessels and enclosing the roof. They allowed higher temperatures (900–1200°C for firing earthenware and up to 1350°C for firing stoneware and porcelain) and greater control over the firing. Greek vases, for example, required precise control over firing to bring out the color of the painting (achieved by a three-phase firing, using oxidation and reduction techniques to get the red and the black colors characteristic of this ware). Square kilns were typical of the European Delftware industry of the 1600s. Some Asian kilns differ from anything found elsewhere—built as a series of hearths up a hillside and shared between workshops; firing took place at the bottom of the slope, with fuel supplements at points along its extent, giving precise control and high temperatures (over 1300°C). They date from about 1100 CE and were not adopted elsewhere, even when control and high temperatures were needed. Industrial development in Europe relied on large "bottle" ovens fired with coal; in the late 1930s, there were some two thousand such ovens in Stoke-on-Trent. By 1965, not one was still in use, replaced by continuously fired, tunnel ovens.

Most important to the ceramics industry was the development or acquisition of reliable technology, which enabled various types of pottery to be made. The nature of the processes also influenced the commercial and organizational sides of the industry. The need for local, bulky raw materials and skilled workers concentrated production in favorable places. The use of potter's wheels, kilns, and other tools resulted in concentrations of workshops. Where production increased—as in the Roman Empire, or Jingdezhen (China) in the seventeenth century, or North Staffordshire (England) in the eighteenth century—the workshops grew. In North Staffordshire, there was some use of power and large numbers of ovens; the largest, at Stoke-on-Trent, had more than twenty bottle ovens by the late nineteenth century.

Capital and Costs. In most prehistoric societies, the making of pottery was (as far as is known) subsidiary to farming and was based around a homestead, with handmade, open-fired pots produced. There is evidence of exchange or trade in many kinds of early wares, both in the Old World and the New World, which suggests that early pottery had a "value." Where production resulted in workshops, after kilns and the potter's wheel were in use, such specialization allows for estimates of capital and costs. Excavations reveal that even early potteries had separate areas for the stages of production; potteries of two to ten people are known from Mesopotamia as early as 2100 or 2000 BCE. Professional early workshops are also known from Dynastic Egypt and the adjacent Near East; Iron Age Britain; the Greek city-states and the Roman Empire; Korea, China, Japan, Southeast Asia, and India; medieval Europe; and in the Mesoamerican and Andean regions of the New World.

Small commercial workshops in Europe and Colonial America had little working capital, so the buildings and kilns predominated in the value of the enterprise; tools were of lesser value although not of lesser importance. Potteries making high-quality wares (such as painted Delft ware) or technically advanced wares (such as stoneware) invested relatively less in buildings and relatively more in working capital for the stock of wares and the money due for wares already provided. Resources were needed to be invested in sales, and this was financed by the producers; some mid-eighteenth century enterprises in England allowed three to six months credit to wholesalers in an extensive sales network, thus requiring working capital. The early industrial manufacturers also required working capital for stock and for credit, so the proportion invested in the buildings was smaller than in the other aspects of the business.

Labor was the greatest explicit cost, as is usual in a manual-skill trade; even in the mid-twentieth century, skilled labor continued as the most important cost. (Labor was also important when work was done by family members, since the workers might have been doing something else.) The other significant cost was fuel, which was very important to the early potteries. (Where cash costs are not the concern, in families, collecting wood or brushwood can be considered as the opportunity cost of growing and or gathering the fuel.) The industrial use of kilns from the mid-eighteenth century onward in Europe and North America reduced the relative cost of fuel, and it was further reduced, relatively, in the nineteenth century.

Demand. Pottery was and is used in households and industry, and it is thus found in most places where people have lived from the Neolithic era onward—Egyptian tombs, Sumerian markets, Roman villas and military camps, medieval villages and port towns, and pre-Columbian communities in North and South America. Few societies made no use of pottery, but they include the early settlements in Anglo-Saxon England and the Viking areas of settlement in Northern Europe, in which wood, leather, and fabric were used to store, serve, and transport goods; some Native Americans used baskets, leather, and wooden containers. Three levels of demand exist for pottery (as for much else): ordinary, luxury, and middle. Pottery fulfilled ordinary purposes in food storage, preparation, cooking, and serving. A general overview of the place of ceramics in High Renaissance European household life is depicted in many Dutch and Flemish genre paintings of the sixteenth and seventeenth centuries, where kitchen and peasant scenes show jugs, plates, bowls, and cooking utensils used alongside wooden platters, baskets, metal serving dishes and cooking pots. Even then, simple earthenware may not have been owned by the poorest in that era; for example, in England in the early eighteenth century, only about a third of the lowest classes owned earthenware (as derived from household inventories at their deaths).

At the high end of society, some pottery was intended to be special, from Bronze Age decorated funerary beakers, to Egyptian tomb ware, to painted Greek vases, to the porcelains made in Korea, China, and Japan. Asian porcelains and celadon wares are good examples of luxury production, with the most valuable produced for and under the patronage of the imperial courts and the elites. Korean celadonwares (made from the tenth to the fourteenth century CE) were intended for elite use and in Buddhist rituals; they were made in strictly controlled, specialist settlements in the southwest of the peninsula, where more than a hundred kiln sites have been identified. Porcelain, a very high-fired translucent ceramic, first made in China in the sixth century CE, was intended as an item of conspicuous consumption. After 1330, some Chinese blue on white porcelain (cobalt blue painted onto a white body and glazed) was produced in Jingdezhen under the patronage of the imperial court; it was soon admired by Europeans.

The largest demand always came from people in the middle ranks of society. An early example was Roman *terra sigillata*, a red earthenware with a fine surface finish and molded decorations. A comprehensive range of such

PORCELAIN. Artisans stack vases in the kiln for firing. Ming dynasty (1368–1644), China. (Gulistan Palace, Tehran, Iran/SEF/Art Resource, NY)

vessels were made for table and kitchen—essential tableware for millions in the Roman Empire for almost six hundred years, from the first century BCE to the Byzantine era. Made in Gaul (France), Italy, and Germany, it benefited from the trade networks and economic infrastructure of the Roman Empire. A second example of attractive, mass-produced wares aimed at the middle social ranks was "China-ware," imported to Europe in quantity from the middle of the seventeenth century. This ware was made up of a range of cups, bowls, tea service, and other small pieces that sold for the relatively modest sum of about sixpence each in eighteenth-century England. In the early eighteenth century, one to two million pieces a year were imported to England—with a hundred thousand pieces a year of that reexported to the British colonies. As early as the 1720s, a third of the middle ranks in London owned some China-ware (according to their inventories at death). The demand strength from the middle market can also be seen from the sustained growth of the English ceramic industry (concentrated in North Staffordshire), which was based on fine types of wares for household use. By the 1780s, the fine earthenware sector that served this market,

had grown to account for an estimated four-fifths of the British industry. In the twenty-first century, a worldwide middle-class market—for an increased range of decorated tea sets, tablewares, and other everyday items—continues, with earthenwares, stonewares, bone china, and porcelain supplied both locally and through imports.

Trade and Distribution. Archaeological evidence shows that prehistoric pottery was distributed beyond the limits of the area in which it had been made; there is also good evidence for significant long-distance trade in historical times. Again, these include the Roman Empire, the trade in China-ware, and internal trade in eighteenth-century England, just before major industrial change. Pottery was relatively heavy and, in all three cases, water transport was crucial; in the Roman Empire and in eighteenth-century Europe, it cost about five times as much to take goods overland as by river and twenty-five times as much to carry them overland as by sea.

The Roman Empire had established a comprehensive trade network; their fine wares were distributed around the Mediterranean and throughout Europe. Pottery was transported among bulk items and thus was associated with high-value goods, such as oil and wine. Central Gaulish (French) ware was distributed to virtually every Roman-British site of the second century CE, as demonstrated by the supply of cooking pots to the Roman army from Dorset to the length of Hadrian's Wall. In China by the twelfth century CE, the ceramic trade was well established to Vietnam, Malaysia, Indonesia, India, Africa, Japan, and Korea. China's porcelain was taken by the Silk Road to Europe in very small amounts by the fourteenth century, then very large amounts were shipped from the late seventeenth century by Dutch, Portuguese, and English traders. Trade with China both increased production in China and stimulated the development of new forms of decorated ware in Europe—Delftware, fine earthenware, and white-bodied bone china. The growth of the pottery industry in eighteenth-century England relied on a complex network of wholesale and retail dealers centered largely on London, where dealers redistributed large amounts of that China-ware through the British East India Company auctions. They also distributed the output of most of the North Staffordshire stoneware and fine earthenware potteries. The network was focused on London and the seaports that traded to North America and the West Indies, but it also supplied retailers in urban centers and market towns throughout England and Scotland. This effective network sustained production growth in England during the eighteenth and nineteenth centuries, when other European and American wares became both desirable and available.

In the twentieth century, the U.S. ceramics industry produced space-age materials that can sustain the high heat of leaving Earth's gravity plus the cold temperatures of space plus reentry and the plunge into the chill waters of the ocean before recovery—all without cracking. Consumers have used a version of this fine-bodied Pyro-ceram™ for freezer-to-oven-to-table ware since about 1960.

BIBLIOGRAPHY

Crossley, David. *Post-Medieval Archaeology in Britain*. Leicester, U.K., 1990.

Freestone, Ian, and David Gaimster. *Pottery in the Making: World Ceramic Traditions*. London, 1997. The best overview, with excellent illustrations from some thirty places and times as early as 12,000 BCE. It offers technological insight, some economic detail, and a very comprehensive bibliography.

Greene, Kevin. *Roman Pottery*. London, 1992.

Lloyd, Seton. *The Archaeology of Mesopotamia*. London, 1978.

McCarthy, Michael R., and Catherine M. Brookes. *Medieval Pottery in Britain, AD 900–1600*. Leicester, 1988.

Medley, Margaret. *The Chinese Potter*. 3d ed. London, 1989.

Rice, Prudence M. *Pottery Anaysis: A Sourcebook*. Chicago, 1987.

Sinopoli, Carla M. *Approaches to Archaeological Ceramics*. New York, 1991.

Vainker, S. J. *Chinese Pottery and Porcelain*. London, 1991.

Weatherill, Lorna M. "The Growth of the Pottery Industry in England, 1660–1815." Ph.D. diss., London School of Economics, 1981. Also a facsimile by Garland Publications, New York, in the series Outstanding Theses from the LSE, 1986.

Weatherill, Lorna M. *Consumer Behaviour and Material Culture in Britain, 1660–1760*. 2d ed. London, 1996.

Williams, Dyfri. *Greek Vases*. 2d ed. London, 1999.

Young, Hilary. *English Porcelain, 1745–1995*. London, 1999.

LORNA SCAMMELL

CEREALS. Most encyclopedias define cereals broadly as any grass yielding starchy seeds, known commonly as grains, suitable for food. These include wheat, rice, rye, oats, barley, corn or maize, and sorghum. It is possible to simplify this list, because it has been estimated that world grain production rests largely on three of those grains— rice, wheat, and maize. At the end of the twentieth century, wheat occupied more farmland than any other food crop. It is also the cereal crop that can be traced back the furthest in antiquity, with consistent archaeological evidence of the use of wild varieties dating from about the tenth millennium BCE. Rice, the second largest cereal in terms of human consumption, is the staple in much of Asia, from which some 90 percent of rice derives. Maize, though originating in the Western Hemisphere, is the most widely distributed food crop, exceeded in acreage only by wheat. Therefore, in their own ways, the three principal cereals occupy important positions in world agriculture. Together they account for 90 percent of total grain consumption. Rice is almost all consumed by humans (including alcohol), much of the maize is consumed by animals or is used for industrial purposes, and wheat is mainly produced for human consumption, though animals consume a small but still significant proportion.

The economic history of these three main cereals is deserving of much wider attention than it can receive here, therefore it is more useful to identify the main issues that interest economic historians. There are three such issues. The first is the triumph of wheat and the wheaten loaf. There has been a marked convergence in Europe and North America toward grain production that is almost entirely wheat dominated and therefore a human consumption that is based on wheaten bread. The economic history of cereals in the Western world is the triumph of wheat production over the other bread grains. The second question is the international integration of the rice trade, especially during and following the second half of the nineteenth century. The third question, which relates to the second, is the international diffusion of these cereal grains. The focus of most interest is on maize, or Indian corn, as it was originally known. Indigenous to the New World, it is now a staple in much of Africa and elsewhere.

Wheat. There are few measurements of the distribution and growth of the various cereal crops before the modern period. Using Britain as a touchstone runs the risk of exaggerating the length of time wheat has been triumphant; nevertheless, there was a crop census as long ago as 1801 covering (albeit incompletely) England and Wales. It is an important benchmark for measuring the production of cereals in the midst of the first Industrial Revolution. The 1801 Crop Returns were a "let's find out" survey conducted at the height of the French wars, when a series of bad harvests had rendered Britain vulnerable to famine conditions. It was a survey of the principal cereal crops, the pulses, and the principal root crops. The cereals were wheat, barley, oats, and rye. At this time, there was also the modest growth of cereals in combination, usually wheat with rye, known as maslin, which was found fairly extensively in northern England in Durham, Northumberland, and the three ridings of Yorkshire (and also in Warwickshire). Barley and oats were also grown in combination, a blend called muncorn, which in 1801 was recorded spasmodically in Shropshire. Cereal blends were also known as blendings and blendcorn.

It is not unusual to read in texts that by 1800 almost the entire population of England and Wales subsisted on wheat. The 1801 survey dispels that belief, though it does show some fairly clear lines of cereal use. Wheat was the chief crop and therefore the bread grain of preference in almost every county of south, southwest, east, and midland England. In northern England, north of and including Staffordshire and Derbyshire, oats was the main crop. The writing was on the wall. In those counties where oats was the lead crop, wheat was almost always the second crop, but the reverse was not invariable. Barley was much more commonly the second crop to wheat in southern Britain. For the cereals alone in terms of cultivated acreage, perhaps 42 percent of England was under wheat, followed by 33 percent under oats and 24 percent under barley. The county pattern in Wales was less clear, but the English and Welsh distribution was unequivocal. Oats was the leading cereal (42 percent), with barley second (32 percent) and wheat third (25 percent). In both countries, there was a residual 1 percent under rye or rye blends. The pattern of cereal production and consumption is confused during this period because as many as nine of the twenty-two harvests that occurred in the French revolutionary and Napoleonic War years were deficient. The governments of the day faced supply problems of many sorts, including food, and the exhortation was to reduce wheat consumption and to explore ways of substituting rice, oats, and barley. Nevertheless, the geographical distribution obtained from the 1801 returns is almost certainly more or less correct, though the supremacy of wheat by this time was by no means final.

In about 1800, probably less than 70 percent of the population in England and Wales ate wheat, and less than 60 percent in Britain as a whole. Estimates from Scotland and Ireland are scarce, though the view is that they subsisted largely on oatmeal and potatoes until well into the nineteenth century. Charles Smith, a miller and amateur economist of the mid-eighteenth century, suggested that 62.5 percent of the population of Britain was wheat eating, though on the basis of other contemporaries, this was probably an exaggerated estimate. Thus the precise distribution of grain eating in Britain is a little unclear for the early decades of the Industrial Revolution, but it seems fairly certain that the subsequent history emphasized wheat. No doubt there was an important relationship with urbanization early on. It is estimated that 81 percent of the population of Britain was eating wheaten bread by 1850. Later in the nineteenth century, there is a clear link with the great surge of bulk importation once the new wheat lands of North America had been opened up and iron-clad, steam-powered bulk carriers superseded timber ships powered by sails. The Russian wheat trade to Britain preceded this development. In the face of North American competition, Russia turned its attention from Britain to central Europe, and the development of new wheat lands in the annexed territories to the south and east of the Russian heartland supplied the pasta-based diet of southern Europe. Throughout the period from 1860 to 1914, the Russians supplied from a quarter to a third of the world trade in wheat.

The wheat revolution of the Northern Hemisphere was more or less complete by the end of the twentieth century, but it had already occurred in Britain by 1900, with 96 percent of the British population consuming wheaten bread. Only in Scotland did use of oats in bread and other products persist to any degree. In other regions of Europe, wheat was in the ascendant by the nineteenth century,

replacing rye, traditionally a cereal of preference, in France and Germany. Rye is more frost resistant than wheat. In the period 1885 to 1889, the per capita consumption of wheat in the British Isles was 5.47 bushels; in France, it was 7.11 bushels; and in Belgium, Italy, and Switzerland, it was over 5 bushels per head. By the 1930s, per capita wheat consumption in Britain had actually declined, as it had in the other major wheat-eating countries. This reflected a growing variety in diets rather than substitution of other grains. It is too simplistic to explain the wheaten bread revolution in terms simply of living standards in which the superior bread grains were triumphant. Even in poor areas, wheat has displaced other traditional grains. The persistent laggards in conversion have been the Scandinavian countries. These patterns are partly related to environmental influences, duration of growing season, and habit and custom, but all influences are in turn affected by increasingly global markets and fashions. By the 1980s, the northern European countries remained outposts of rye bread consumption. There was a large minority grain consumption based on rye in Denmark (26 percent as compared with 63 percent based on wheat), in the former Federal Republic of Germany (17 percent as compared with 70 percent), and in Sweden (21 percent as compared with 76 percent). It is important to note here that bread was not the only way by which these grains were consumed. Malting and distilling and the production of beer and spirits has always been an important use of bread grains, especially barley, in Europe.

Rice. If wheat has been triumphant in the Western world, then rice is easily its equivalent in the East. On the eve of World War I, rice was the staple food crop for about half the world's population. It was centered in monsoon Asia, India, Burma, the Malayan Peninsula, Java, Siam, Indochina, China, and Japan. Throughout the second half of the nineteenth century, rice was not only the most common cereal in use in the world, it was also traded extensively, though it still only accounted for about 10 percent of the total world trade in cereals in the early twentieth century. Yet, by any measure, the importance of rice has attracted the attention of economic historians as a traded commodity. By the late nineteenth century, rice had become part of an integrated international market directly linked to the wheat trade, for which it was a substitute. Unlike wheat, however, which was almost entirely used for human consumption, rice was also used for other purposes, such as the production of starch, paper, animal feed, and spirits. That gave added impetus to its position as a traded good.

Rice can be grown almost anywhere under certain conditions. Water supply rather than monsoon per se is favorable to rice production, coupled with a particular mode of cultivation. Thus rice cultivation developed outside the monsoon regions of Asia, with which it is mostly associated.

Rice was a trade good in Greek and Roman times, and wider European cultivation can be traced to the Moors in Spain and the Turks in southern Europe. But it was not until rice was produced in Northern Italy (Piedmont and Lombardy) in the fifteenth century that it became an established if limited European commodity. It became a more familiar European crop through its production in the British colony of South Carolina and subsequently in neighboring Georgia and also through the British political control of Bengal. Fairly early in the eighteenth century, it became a regular traded item with northern European countries, especially the German states. Much of the trade passed through Britain before reexport to Europe or directly through the main northern European ports, like Hamburg.

The import of rice into England and Wales grew from 3,000 tons in the first decade of the eighteenth century to 80,000 tons in the 1730s and more than 150,000 tons by the 1760s, which was the decade when Britain ceased to be self-sufficient in wheat and wheat flour. Therefore, for much of the time before the 1760s, it was as much an industrial import, or destined for reexport, as it was an essential food import. Upwards of 99 percent of this rice came from North America, and at the end of the century, almost 90 percent still came from North America. During the dearth conditions (for traditional cereals) of the 1790s, the British government sought supplies from Italy and South Carolina to substitute for native British bread supplies. But during the nineteenth century, the Asian trade to Britain took off, based on British and Dutch colonial development in British India (especially Bengal), Burma, and Java. South Carolina and Georgia were casualties of this trade. By the 1840s, 84 percent of British rice imports came from Asia, and British Burma and Bengal became the greatest rice exporters in the world.

The rule in the late nineteenth century was that the rice trade for rice eaters west of the Malay Peninsula was dependent for supplies on Bengal, and for rice eaters east of the peninsula the supply came from Cochin China (Vietnam) and Siam. Burma provided nonfood rice for Europe. Singapore became a major distribution center. By World War I, Burmese rice more generally became a source of staple food in Asia, but in Siam, Indochina, and Burma, rice accounted for more than half the total exports.

Questions in economic history have revolved around whether or not the international rice trade had become integrated by the late nineteenth century and the extent to which it became a substitute for wheat. The consensus of opinion based on the analysis of price movements of both commodities suggests a positive answer on both counts.

Maize. In the late twentieth century, about 40 percent of the crops grown in Africa had their origins in the New World. No other part of the world has so influenced the agriculture of another part of the world, except for the spread of plants from the cradle of civilization in Southwest Asia to Europe several millennia ago. The spread of corn or maize from the Americas to Europe, then to Africa, took place in the last five hundred years, especially in the first two centuries of that period. With the opening up and development of the Americas, both maize and potatoes were seen as higher yielding crops than European grains. The Spanish and Portuguese quickly introduced maize in the wake of Christopher Columbus, and the crop subsequently spread rapidly to Mediterranean and other southern European lands. Further diffusion by the Ottoman Empire left its legacy in Southeast Europe, where it has remained a major crop. The opening up of Africa south of the Sahara by Europeans from the fifteenth century saw the further spread of New World maize. The Turks introduced it from the north through Egypt, from where it spread further south and west.

But perhaps the biggest influence was by those whose direct colonization and trade with the New World and with West Africa meant the direct introduction of maize from America to Africa. This took place early in the sixteenth century. The diffusion of the crop was both rapid and widespread and the result of European expansion and colonialism on both sides of the Atlantic. To that extent, it cannot be divorced from the Atlantic trade system and in particular the slave trade. Indeed, almost certainly it was an important ingredient in maintaining the profitability of the slave trade because it was employed as a slave staple food, both indigenously in West Africa and also as a staple for those slaves shipped across to the Americas. It allowed European slave ships to arrive at the African coast laden with cargoes of trade goods, since they could acquire maize for slave consumption in the middle passage in Africa. Besides, maize was innately cheaper than traditional European cereals.

The advantage of maize in tropical Africa, which helped to make it the most rapidly diffused crop of all, was that where the rainfall was suitable it was possible to get two crops a year. The crop became common in the sub-Guinean zone and in the Congo basin by the seventeenth century and diffused rapidly to become common on the Gold Coast in the eighteenth century. By the late sixteenth century, it had reached East Africa, and by the nineteenth century it was found more or less throughout the continent.

The legacy of introduction, especially through the Portuguese, lives on to a degree in Europe. In the early 1980s, maize in Portugal represented 23 percent of total grain-based consumption, second to wheat with 57 percent (and rice with 14 percent). And the legacy of diffusion through the Ottoman Empire survived well into the late twentieth century, this time in southern Europe. Over 40 percent of Albanian grain consumption was based on maize in about 1965, nearly a quarter of Romanian grain consumption about 1980, and 13 percent of Yugoslavian grain consumption in the early 1980s. The cultivation of maize also experienced a resurgence in France after World War II.

Maize, or corn as it is more popularly known in North America, has been a staple of the North American farming system, especially in the twentieth century. It gives rise to the appellation the "Corn Belt," a district of huge-scale farming that spreads from South Dakota and Nebraska eastward to Ohio. It is a system of agriculture based on livestock—principally pigs but also cattle—in which corn provides the main livestock feed. At the end of the twentieth century, the United States produced about half of the world's corn. After China, the other major producers are Brazil, Mexico, and the Argentine. For the economic historian, the intriguing questions concerning maize include its international diffusion, its class-specific place in human consumption, and the regional differences in its use as a fodder crop or a direct source of human nutrition.

[*See also* Animal Husbandry *and* Rice Farming.]

BIBLIOGRAPHY

Coclanis, Peter A. "Distant Thunder: The Creation of a World Market in Rice and the Transformation It Wrought." *American Historical Review* 98.4 (1993), 1050–1078.

Collins, Edward J. T. "Dietary Change and Cereal Consumption in Britain in the Nineteenth Century." *Agricultural History Review* 23.1 (1975), 97–115.

Collins, Edward J. T. "Why Wheat? Choice of Food Grains in Europe in the Nineteenth and Twentieth Centuries." *Journal of European Economic History* 22.1 (1993), 7–38.

Grigg, David B. *The Agricultural Systems of the World: An Evolutionary Approach.* Cambridge, 1974.

Hohenberg, Paul. "Maize in French Agriculture." *Journal of European Economic History* 6.1 (1977), 63–101.

Latham, Anthony J. H., and Larry Neal. "The International Market in Rice and Wheat, 1868–1914." *Economic History Review* 36.2 (1983), 260–280.

Miracle, Marion P. "The Introduction and Spread of Maize in Africa." *Journal of African History* 6 (1965), 39–55.

Petersen, Christian. *Bread and the British Economy, circa 1770–1870.* Aldershot, U.K., 1995.

Turner, Michael E. "Arable in England and Wales: Estimates from the 1801 Crop Return." *Journal of Historical Geography* 7.3 (1981), 291–302.

MICHAEL TURNER

CEYLON. *See* Sri Lanka.

CHAD. *See* Sudan, *subentry on* Central Sudan.

CHAEBOL. The Chinese character combination for the Korean word *chaebol* is identical to that used for the Japanese term zaibatsu. For this reason, and because many of the postwar South Korean *chaebol* share similarities with prewar Japanese zaibatsu—to some extent, *chaebol* imitating their Japanese counterparts—it is possible to employ as a definition of *chaebol* the one describing zaibatsu: a collection of diversified enterprises under the ownership of a single family or an extended family. However, because the Korean family system differs from the Japanese family system in important respects—blood ties are preeminent in Korea but are sometimes superseded by fictive ties in Japan, and prewar Japanese inheritance was not partible, whereas Korean inheritance emphasizes division of property among sons—it must be kept in mind that being owned by a family has different implications in the two societies.

The *chaebol* have concentrated substantial economic power in their hands. For instance, during the 1970s the top five *chaebol* (Samsung, Hyundai, Lucky-Goldstar, and Daewoo are the big four) accounted for over 18 percent of value added in manufacturing, over 15 percent in construction, and nearly 23 percent in finance and insurance. Forty-six *chaebol*, including lesser *chaebol* such as Sunkyong, Ssangyong, Hyosung, Hanjin, and Kia as well as the big four, accounted for almost 43 percent of manufacturing value added, 37 percent of value added in construction, and 32 percent of value added in finance and insurance. Samsung has been especially active in electronics, textiles, and insurance; Hyundai in automobiles, industrial machinery, and shipbuilding; Daewoo in computer products, automobiles, finance, and shipbuilding; and Lucky-Goldstar in electronic and chemical products.

Has the instability of South Korea's growth since the onset of the Asian financial crisis in 1997 weakened the *chaebol*? Recent studies and journalistic accounts of bankruptcies of major *chaebol* companies suggest that many *chaebol*-affiliated companies are indeed in trouble; but the *chaebol* are deeply rooted in the Korean economic structure and are unlikely to disappear.

The structure of the *chaebol* varies. Some are set up as family proprietorships; some are controlled by a holding company as were most of the zaibatsu after 1920; and some are tied together through cross-shareholding of stock, a form of alliance characteristic of postwar *keiretsu*. In general the founder of the *chaebol* exercises very decisive leadership over the determination of strategy and structure for the enterprises that he controls (there are no female heads of *chaebol*).

There are important similarities between postwar South Korean *chaebol* and prewar Japanese zaibatsu. In both countries, the closed model of family ownership and the diversified financial/industrial empire played a crucial role during early industrialization; and in both countries technically trained salaried managers—engineers—have played a crucial role in the day-to-day decision making of the vast industrial/financial empires. Three reasons help to account for the similarity: entrepreneurial talent and capital was scarce in both nations during early industrialization; the state pursued a strategy of favoring large financial and industrial empires and fostering close government-business relations in order to implement nascent industrial policy; and the prewar Japanese zaibatsu (especially the *shinzaibatsu*) were very active in Korea during the period when Korea was a colony of Japan (1910–1945), thereby serving as a model for Korean entrepreneurs.

However, there are also important differences between zaibatsu, *keiretsu*, and *chaebol*. Korean *chaebol* tend to be very closed, the family monopolizing most of the stock issued by the enterprises (certain zaibatsu prior to 1930 were similar). Moreover, key strategic decision making tends to be in the hands of the founding entrepreneur and his sons, a pattern not particularly evident in prewar Japan with the exception of zaibatsu such as Mitsubishi and Yasuda during the heyday of their founders. Also, unlike many zaibatsu, most Korean *chaebol* do not have a general trading company. Perhaps the most important difference lies in the nature of the family systems in the two countries. As noted, Korean society practices partible inheritance, so that there is a strong probability that many of the individual *chaebol* will break apart upon the death of the founder, various sons inheriting chunks of the industrial/financial empire. Understanding that Asian family patterns vary substantially and that this variance has important implications for economic development is one of the most important lessons to draw from a comparison of Korean *chaebol* with Japanese zaibatsu.

[*See also* Keiretsu *and* Zaibatsu.]

BIBLIOGRAPHY

Amsden, Alice. *Asia's Next Giant: South Korea and Late Industrialization*. New York, 1989. This general study of postwar South Korean economic development emphasizes the role of the *chaebol* in pioneering structural change by diversifying into heavy industries such as shipbuilding. It argues that government subsidies were essential. It also argues that diversifying from a base in light industry—cotton textiles, for instance—was difficult. The technological sophistication of the industry was too low to support this diversification. Rather, diversifying from a more technologically demanding industry such as cement manufacturing seems to have been key to South Korea's successful transition from an economy whose engine of growth was light manufacturing to an economy whose engine of growth was heavy manufacturing.

Hattori, Tamio. "The Relationship between Zaibatsu and Family Structure: The Korean Case." In *Family Business in the Era of Industrial Growth: Its Ownership and Management*, edited by Akio Okochi and Shigeaki Yasuoka, pp. 121–142. Tokyo, 1984. This study examines the performance and organization of forty-six *chaebol* (the same Chinese characters are used for *chaebol* as for zaibatsu; so the author, writing for a Japanese audience, employs the term *zaibatsu*) in postwar Korea. It breaks the *chaebol* down into three groups: those monopolized by a proprietor or a family, those controlled by a holding company, and those held together by reciprocal stockholding. The author also compares Korean *chaebol* to prewar Japanese zaibatsu and to postwar Japanese *keiretsu*. Hattori notes that because family-run partnerships or holding companies in Japanese zaibatsu held the assets of the extended family as a collective unit, Japanese zaibatsu did not tend to fissure. By contrast, *chaebol* may break apart because under rules of the Korean family system, partible inheritance usually is practiced.

McNamara, Dennis L. *The Colonial Origins of Korean Enterprise, 1910–1945*. Cambridge, 1990. This study, written as a contribution to the study of the political economy of prewar Korea and postwar South Korea, emphasizes the relationship between monopoly positions in industries and close relations between the state and large business concerns. It discusses how Japanese zaibatsu played the dominant role in financing industrial investment in prewar Korea, and it describes how Korean-owned *chaebol* emerged during the colonial period by imitating the practices of the Japanese-owned zaibatsu.

Steers, Richard M., Yoo Keun Shin, and Gerardo R. Ungson. *The Chaebol: Korea's New Industrial Might*. New York, 1989. This study emphasizes five characteristics of the postwar *chaebol* in South Korea: family control, paternalistic authoritarian leadership, centralized planning, entrepreneurial orientation, and the fostering of close relations between government and the *chaebol* leadership. It examines in detail the four major *chaebol*—Samsung, Hyundai, Lucky-Goldstar, and Daewoo—and compares the *chaebol* of postwar Korea to the *keiretsu* of postwar Japan.

CARL MOSK

CHANDLER, ALFRED D. (born 1918), business historian

Alfred du Pont Chandler, Jr. was the most influential figure among American and world business historians in the second half of the twentieth century. Born in 1918, he came from a moderately wealthy business family; his father was a representative of Baldwin Locomotive in Buenos Aires. Despite his traditional family middle name, he was not a blood relative of the Wilmington du Ponts, though he grew up as a member of their social set.

An early interest in Southern history at Harvard College and the University of North Carolina gave way to business history in his Harvard doctoral dissertation (published in 1956) on Henry Varnum Poor, the railroad stock analyst and his own great-grandfather. Another important formative influence was wartime service in the U.S. Navy, which culminated in his analyzing aerial reconnaissance photographs to evaluate the effectiveness of Allied bombing of Japan and Germany, an experience that taught him the importance both of supply lines for materials and power and of key sectors in the economy. Intellectually, his exposure to Talcott Parsons and historical sociology was a stronger influence than that of any historian, but he benefited from participation with a remarkable group of scholars who formed the Harvard Research Center in Entrepreneurial History.

His professional career developed at MIT (1950–1963), Johns Hopkins (1963–1971, where he edited the papers of Theodore Roosevelt and Dwight D. Eisenhower), and

Harvard (from 1971, when he was appointed to the endowed Straus Chair of Business History and where he has remained an active Emeritus Professor, having published in 2001 Inventing the Electronic Century: The Epic Story of the Consumer Electronics and Computer Industries).

Chandler published many articles, notably in Harvard's *Business History Review*, but his work is best exemplified in three key (and much translated and reissued) books on big business: *Strategy and Structure* (1962), *The Visible Hand* (1977), and *Scale and Scope* (1990). What differentiates these works is Chandler's capacity to generalize on the basis of careful empirical work. Though not a theorist, by combining detailed work in the archives with a broad examination of a wide range of secondary works, he was able to gain insights that had eluded many others studying the messy facts of history. That creative capacity is the key to Chandler's influence both abroad and at home, as well as in other disciplines. A striking aspect of his work is that it has been more frequently cited by economists, sociologists, and management scientists than by economic historians, and even more widely cited than the work of his contemporary and Nobel Prize winner Douglass North. Chandler was awarded the Pulitzer Prize for *The Visible Hand*.

Chandler's *Strategy and Structure*, based on case studies of DuPont, General Motors, Standard Oil, and Sears Roebuck, demonstrated that these companies were the first to adopt a multidivisional organization (the "M-form") for managing diversified enterprises whose growth had been driven by new technologies and changing markets. The revolutionary thesis was validated by comparisons with other large American corporations and was profoundly influential in business schools because it showed that a change in strategy is likely to be successful only when accompanied by a change in the organizational structure used to manage it. *The Visible Hand* is an economic historian's book: essentially a collective biography of the large firms that created the modern American industrial economy, with particular emphasis on the processes of horizontal and vertical integration, and the replacement of market integration (Adam Smith's "the invisible hand") by managerial hierarchies.

The germ of his later emphasis on organizational learning, which played its part in reinforcing the dominance of the resource-based theory of the firm in industrial economics, is also perceptible in this book and his next, *Scale and Scope*. The latter was driven by a quest to explain why the German and American economies grew twice as fast as the British in the twentieth century, finding an explanation in the more successful economies' more effective "three-pronged investment" in manufacturing, marketing, and management in the top two hundred companies that shaped their development, particularly in the capital-intensive industries of the second industrial revolution.

Key to the explanation was Britain's overreliance on the family company and management hierarchies that were too small.

Critics of Chandler's work on the U.S. economy have concentrated on his omissions: particularly his lack of attention to labor and human resources, and the absence of an understanding of the state's role in shaping the modern economy through antitrust legislation and in many other ways. The charge is correct but misplaced; focus is essential in a scholarly career, and Chandler can hardly be called narrow by the standards of most economic historians, as he was deep in his chosen field. The criticism of the international perspectives in *Scale and Scope* has been more substantive. Although the narrative power of Chandler's European examples has been much admired, his comparative analytical framework has puzzled specialists in European economic history.

Most of the dimensions on which German and British business can be compared (some of the data being generated by Chandler's students), from the adoption of the M-form organization or integrated steel plants, family control of enterprise, the proportion of company employment devoted to management, or of enterprises quoted on the stock exchange, to the growth and stability of large companies, typically show Germany and Britain to be much nearer to each other than to the United States; and when a country has been closer or sooner in Americanization, that country usually has been Britain.

Moreover, new economic historians using national income accounting techniques have recently demonstrated that differences among the three countries' primary and service sectors are far more important in explaining variations in their national performance than the industrial enterprises on which Chandler concentrated. The quantitative facts have, then, been shown to be sharply at odds with Chandler's narratively developed international hypothesis.

To the question of why has Chandler been the most influential business historian in business history and an inspiration to so many younger scholars, the answer, as in the case of Gerschenkron, is that scholars who attack big subjects—who are few—are both more creatively innovative and also more frequently wrong. In short, they are risk takers. Totally dedicated to scholarly inquiry, Chandler insisted on asking the big questions, and his success in bringing new facts and perspectives to bear on big issues remains a good role model for the profession, from one of its creative giants.

BIBLIOGRAPHY

Chandler, Alfred D. *Strategy and Structure: Chapters in the History of Industrial Enterprise*. Cambridge, Mass., 1962.

Chandler, Alfred D. *The Visible Hand: The Managerial Revolution in American Business*. Cambridge, Mass., 1977.

Chandler, Alfred D. *Scale and Scope: The Dynamics of Industrial Capitalism*. Cambridge, Mass., 1990.

McCraw, Thomas K., ed. *The Essential Alfred Chandler: Essays toward a Historical Theory of Big Business*. Boston, 1988.

LESLIE HANNAH

CHARITIES, organizations designed to provide assistance to those considered to be in some form of need. Although they have since the twentieth century given help to cultural activities, research, and education, they are normally thought of and will be treated here as Western institutions that focus their attention on the poor. As such, they have been major providers of assistance. Two key themes dominate the historiography of charities in the Western world: first, the continuities and changes in their choices among the sections of the poor to be helped and the form of that aid; second, the relationship between charities and state organizations in the raising of funds and in the distribution of resources.

In ancient times, wealthy Greeks and Romans frequently made charitable gifts; they were careful to ensure that a record of the gift was carved into their tombs as monuments to their own goodness. The novelty of the early Christian approach to charity, itself derived from Judaic and other Near Eastern religious traditions, was that charity was for the glory of God as well as for the benefit of the recipient. In the late Middle Ages, there was a belief among Roman Catholics that charitable gifts would so please God that the donor's time in purgatory would be reduced. The recipients of charity in that period were not only the very poor but also those who were particularly religious and "the shame-faced poor" (people who had suffered a decline in circumstances but were too proud to beg). The most important charitable institutions were confraternities and hospitals. In confraternities (lay and religious voluntary organizations), activities of piety and charity were inextricably intertwined to meet the needs of the members, primarily and often exclusively; but sometimes they ranged beyond that. They were very numerous, and in 1521, Venice, for example, had at least one hundred twenty small confraternities and five large ones. Hospitals, many run by religious foundations, met the needs of travelers and pilgrims, the sick, and the aged. In the fourteenth century, foundling hospitals (some that became orphanages) began to be established for abandoned babies.

Church dominance over charitable foundations began to be rivaled in the fifteenth century by wish on the part of donors to perpetuate their own memories and to glorify their cities. They built various structures as important statements of their wealth, power, and taste—the foundling hospital in Florence, for example, was funded by a wealthy merchant and designed by the great Renaissance architect Filippo Brunelleschi. This process through which lay people began to supersede the religious in the organization and management of charities did not necessarily imply a lessening of a religious motivation; in the sixteenth century and the seventeenth, under the impact of the Reformation and Counter-Reformation, it was perhaps heightened. In the early sixteenth century, in the face of serious economic and social problems, a new phase of charitable activity was begun. The focus was then on those poor who were perceived to be nonproductive—beggars or idle. Distinguishing between the deserving and the undeserving poor, a concern evident from the fifteenth century, now became and remained part of the mindset of the organizers of both charities and welfare arrangements. Charity became concerned not so much with the glorification of God in the act of giving but more with the outcome of giving, in the creation of a moral, disciplined, and godly society. In part, this was achieved by creating institutions within whose walls those who offended the moral and productive majority might, it was hoped, be housed, helped, or reformed. The cities and towns of Europe erected grandiose buildings for the reform of the ungodly.

By the late eighteenth century, the impact of charity and the management of charities were much criticized. The trustees of some seemed to spend more on dinners for themselves than on resources for the poor; funds were used to establish and consolidate power relationships. A sense among reformers that the church (especially the Roman Catholic), which still ran most charities, was itself corrupt, led to a widespread belief that new charitable initiatives were necessary. Many of the new reformers, both in Europe and in North America, were Protestant (and some were Jewish). They called themselves "philanthropists," a word that in some quarters became associated with a secular approach to charity, one which embodied an antipathy to church-related charity. Underlying it, however, was an approach similar to that which had inspired reform in the sixteenth century—a belief that those who offended against the mores of society could be reformed, a belief with which Christians (and Jews) were happy to be associated. In the late eighteenth century and the nineteenth, prostitutes, "juvenile delinquents," the insane, and criminals could, it was hoped, be reclaimed if preventive measures were taken or if placed in a suitable environment; the charities worked with state organizations toward these ends. Those not in need of incarceration might be removed from the environments that were thought to be harmful to them: for example, slum children and orphans from the Atlantic seaboard sent to the Midwest of the United States, under the auspices of the Children's Aid Society from 1854 onward; some eighty thousand children sent from British cities to Canada between 1870 and 1914. During the late eighteenth century, in an attempt to strengthen the distinction between deserving and undeserving and to prevent the misuse of charities, there was

CHARITIES. Food aid at the Domochedonski Boarding School and Orphanage, Moscow, Russia, 1992. (© Chuck Nacke/Woodfin Camp and Associates, New York)

much emphasis on visiting the poor in their homes. Upper middle-class women were thought to be particularly suited to this, and many found volunteer work (part-time unpaid employment) helping charitable agencies. In some cases, it went beyond this (in Ireland, for example, the number of nuns rose sharply, many of them working for charitable organizations). Eventually, this concept of charitable concern and good works was to lead to the twentieth-century occupation of social worker, with schools of social work at the university graduate level.

How important were charities to the poor? In the makeshift economies in which many of the poor scraped an existence, charities were one among a range of resources. Normally, only people within an institution found their total subsistence needs met by charitable aid, and they were always a societal minority of those in receipt of charity. Most charity was delivered to people in their homes; in the 1770s, in Grenoble, France, for example, there were up to four hundred inmates in the hospital, but an additional thirty-five hundred received home relief. Large proportions of populations could come within the ambit of charities. In the late 1700s, just over one-third of the population of Florence was estimated to be in need of alms, which rose to more than two-thirds in crisis years. In the early 1800s in Amsterdam, about one-quarter of the population was helped by charities on a regular basis. These seem to be typical levels. Widows with children, workers with large families, children, the sick, the infirm, and the elderly were those who, over the centuries and

across cultures, were most likely to receive charitable aid. It was available in many forms; in addition to large institutions giving aid within their own walls or in beneficiaries' homes, there were innumerable bequests and endowments in wills that might provide dowries for girls, apprenticeships for boys, or almshouses for the elderly.

Some argue that in northern Europe, the nuclear family structure made it likely that, in the course of the life cycle, working-class children or the elderly would need support from charity or state institutions. Equally plausible is the argument that the poor made use of charitable institutions wherever they existed. In Milan in the 1840s, the foundling hospital ran an open-door policy, and working-class Milanese regularly consigned to its care any children born to them after two; in Bologna, where provision was scarce, such children remained with their families. Charities also created economic networks that became difficult to dismantle, indicating that with the power relationships entrenched in any form of charity, the poor had some leverage. Foundling hospitals, for example, had considerable effects on the surrounding societies; if babies in them were to have any chance of living, wet nurses had to be provided. Thus, in the rural hinterlands of large urban foundling hospitals, as in France and Russia, economies developed around the income from wet nursing.

Voluntary and state charitable activity are not always easy to distinguish. England was unique in having, from the late sixteenth century onward, a system of relief for the poor, based on taxation. Elsewhere, such systems were developed in the eighteenth and nineteenth centuries; funds for the support of the poor until then, and after, came from donations given voluntarily, although at times the administration of them might be entrusted to municipal or state officials. The role of charities arguably diminished from about the 1880s, with the first movements toward what would emerge as welfare states in the mid-twentieth century. The truth in this cannot be denied, since the scale of state spending on social security escalated; however, historians now reject an analysis wherein charities were replaced by state welfare organizations. Rather, they depict a "mixed economy" of welfare institutions from about 1500. They find charities working in a range of relationships with municipal and national state organizations—and they put emphasis more on the increase in total supply of welfare than on the replacement of one agency, charities, by another, the state.

[*See also* Poor Relief.]

BIBLIOGRAPHY

Barry, Jonathan, and Colin Jones, eds. *Medicine and Charity before the Welfare State*. London, 1991.

Cavallo, Sandra. *Charity and Power in Early Modern Italy: Benefactors and Their Motives in Turin, 1541–1789*. Cambridge, 1995.

Cunningham, Hugh, and Joanna Innes, eds. *Charity, Philanthropy and Reform: From the 1690s to 1850*. Basingstoke, U.K., 1998.

Daunton, Martin, ed. *Charity, Self-Interest and Welfare in the English Past*. London, 1996.

Hands, Arthur R. *Charities and Social Aid in Greece and Rome*. London, 1968.

Henderson, John, ed. "Charity and the Poor in Medieval and Renaissance Europe." *Continuity and Change*, Special Issue, 3.2 (1988), 137–311.

Henderson, John, and Richard Wall, eds. *Poor Women and Children in the European Past*. London, 1994.

Jones, Colin, *The Charitable Imperative: Hospitals and Nursing in Ancien Regime and Revolutionary France*. London, 1989.

Prochaska, F. K. *Women and Philanthropy in Nineteenth-Century England*. Oxford, 1980.

Pullan, B. *Rich and Poor in Renaissance Venice: The Social Institutions of a Catholic State, to 1620*. Oxford, 1971.

Woolf, Stuart. *The Poor in Western Europe in the Eighteenth and Nineteenth Centuries*. London, 1986.

HUGH CUNNINGHAM

CHAVEZ, CESAR (1927–1993), American agricultural labor leader, born in Arizona, where his paternal grandfather owned a 160-acre farm near Yuma.

After losing the land to foreclosure in the Great Depression of the 1930s, Chavez and his family moved to California and joined the ranks of migrant agricultural laborers. California's "industrialized agriculture" has always depended on labor. Originally part of Mexico, California's land grants during the early 1800s had created tracts too large for a single family to farm without additional labor or machinery. At the close of the Mexican War, California was ceded to the United States in 1848 and became a state in 1850. Soon, transportation improvements—first the Transcontinental Railroad in 1869, then the refrigerated railroad car—opened a nationwide market for the region's perishable fruits and vegetables. That type of produce was often unsuited to mechanization; it was too fragile for machine harvesting, or it did not ripen at a uniform pace. Consequently, an enormous supply of migratory, seasonal labor was essential to expand California agriculture.

The transient harvest laborers in California included Native Americans in the eighteenth century; Chinese, Japanese, and Filipinos in the nineteenth century; and Mexicans in the twentieth century. The U.S. government had accorded special status to Mexicans through the bracero program (1942–1965). Thousands of Mexican residents were regularly given temporary permits to work in U.S. agriculture. Initially intended to alleviate the labor shortage of World War II, the bracero program was used by growers to secure an economically and politically vulnerable labor force. By hiring braceros, landowners could undercut the demands of U.S. residents for higher wages or greater control.

The early attempts to unionize U.S. agricultural workers were largely unsuccessful. During the first half of the twentieth century, the International Workers of the World (IWW), the Trade Union Unity League of the Communist Party, the Congress of Industrial Organizations (CIO), and the American Federation of Labor (AFL) had each, in turn, attempted to organize California's farm labor. Chavez's father had been a member of the National Farm Laborers Union, an offshoot of the Southern Tenant Farmers Union, whose efforts had been hampered by the power of the growers, by the huge pool of available labor in Mexico, and by U.S. federal law—the National Labor Relations Act of 1935 had affirmed labor's right to organize and bargain collectively through its own representatives, but agricultural employees were explicitly excluded from the legislation.

While working with the Community Service Organization (CSO) to register U.S. voters in the 1950s, Cesar Chavez became increasingly concerned about the economic plight of California's Mexican Americans—U.S. citizens whose livelihood was often tied to low-wage, hazardous farm work. In 1962, after the organization rejected his proposal for greater involvement in agriculture, Chavez resigned as director, and he formed the National Farm Workers Association (NFWA). By 1964, this new union had some one thousand dues-paying members and had coordinated a number of small strikes. In September 1965, Chavez agreed to honor a strike against table-grape growers by the Agricultural Workers Organizing Committee (AWOC), a Filipino-led union that was sponsored by the joint AFL–CIO. The growers attempted to circumvent this activist union by offering the United Brotherhood of Teamsters (originally a union for truckers) a "sweetheart contract," in which the Teamsters would be allowed to unionize the workers and negotiate wages. In return, the Teamsters promised not to challenge the growers on any issues involving farm management or workplace conditions. The result was the first union representation election ever held in agriculture. The Teamsters, however, lost to the new United Farm Workers (UFW) union, a merger of the NFWA and AWOC, headed by Chavez. By 1970, the UFW represented 85 percent of California's table-grape industry. The UFW then became the most influential agricultural labor union in American history—owing, in part, to Chavez's own background as a migrant worker in a state where 70 percent of harvest pickers were of Mexican descent.

Chavez was innovative in his methods (using strikes, fasts, marches, and picketing). Because the vast stretches of agricultural land in California rendered picket lines ineffective for strikes, Chavez introduced a new weapon against the growers: the nationwide consumer boycott. This approach, backed by Chavez's commitment to nonviolence, was particularly powerful during the civil-rights era of the 1960s. In 1972, the UFW became affiliated with the AFL-CIO, although Chavez worried that such formal recognition would require the UFW to comply with the 1947 Taft-Hartley Act's prohibition of secondary boycotts, thereby denying the UFW its most important tool—union demonstrations at stores that sold boycotted grapes and lettuce. As UFW contracts expired in the early 1970s, growers invited the Teamsters (a seemingly more employer-friendly union) to organize their workers. By 1973, the UFW had lost 75 percent of its membership, and some organizers were jailed. Chavez appealed to California's liberal Democratic governor, Jerry Brown, and in 1975 Brown signed California's Agricultural Labor Relations Act; this was the first state law to govern farmlabor organizing in the continental United States, and it guaranteed representation by secret ballot. In the aftermath, the Teamsters ceded the organization of field workers to the UFW, and membership rose to more than fifty thousand by 1978.

The UFW's influence declined during the conservative Republican presidency of the 1980s, and a debate began within the union as to whether to focus narrowly on labor issues or, as Chavez advocated, more broadly on Chicano (Mexican-American) civil rights. Although he died in 1993, Cesar Chavez remains a potent symbol for farm workers throughout the United States.

BIBLIOGRAPHY

Daniel, Cletus E. "Cesar Chavez and the Unionization of California Farm Workers." In *Labor Leaders in America*, edited by Melvyn Dubofsky and Warren Van Tine, pp. 350–382. Urbana, 1987.

Day, Mark. *Forty Acres: Cesar Chavez and the Farm Workers*. New York, 1971.

Galarza, Ernesto. *Farm Workers and Agri-business in California, 1947–1960*. Notre Dame, Ind., 1977.

Gómez-Quinones, Juan. *Mexican-American Labor, 1790–1990*. Albuquerque, 1994.

Griswold del Castillo, Richard, and Richard A. Garcia. *Cesar Chavez: A Triumph of Spirit*. Norman, Okla., 1995.

Levy, Jacques. *Cesar Chavez: Autobiography of La Causa*. New York, 1975.

London, Joan, and Henry Anderson. *So Shall Ye Reap*. New York, 1970.

Taylor, Ronald. *Chávez and the Farm Workers*. Boston, 1975.

KERRY A. ODELL

CHEMICAL INDUSTRIES *[This entry contains three subentries, an introduction and discussions of chemical industries before and after 1850.]*

An Introduction

The chemical industry is clearly important, one of the largest industries in the United States, Great Britain, and Germany, and yet it is hard to define. The boundaries of the industry are defined by custom and practice, and thus by historical accidents, rather than by logic. Furthermore, the concept of a chemical industry has been projected back to a period when no chemical industry in the modern sense existed. One can define it as the industry that changes the chemical composition of its raw materials or one that produces (more or less) pure chemicals. The first definition would include the manufacture of steel, pottery, and even cakes, but not the extraction of natural soda. The latter would encompass the water industry (on the grounds that even water is a chemical), but exclude plastics. For many years, the chemical industry was largely whatever the large corporations (DuPont, ICI, BASF) chose to make—explosives, paint, or magnetic tapes—but the industry has always contained many small firms, many of which have left no traces. Pharmaceutical products are sometimes considered to be part of the chemical industry, and at other times, they are rigorously excluded. The industry's products are often divided into inorganic and organic. The term *inorganic* covers any product that does not contain carbon. However, sodium carbonate (soda), a major product that contains carbon, is considered to be inorganic. Millions of tons of the leading inorganic chemicals, notably sulfuric acid and soda, have been made for many years and hence are often called "heavy" chemicals. By contrast, some inorganic chemicals, for laboratory or pharmaceutical use, were made in small quantities, usually in a state of high purity, and were called "fine chemicals," a term also used for similar organic chemicals. Organic chemicals became a distinct branch of the industry following the beginning of synthetic dye manufacture in the late 1850s and became significant only around the beginning of the twentieth century. As the production volume of certain organic chemicals mounted during the 1920s and 1930s, the term *heavy organic chemicals* was adopted.

The history of the chemical industry can be traced back to the small-scale manufacture of various inorganic chemicals in antiquity. It became economically important, however, only after the introduction of the lead chamber process for sulfuric acid in the 1740s. Over the following century, the chemical industry developed into a complex of interlocking processes. Sulfuric acid, made cheaply using the well-established lead chamber process, was used to make soda (the Leblanc process) and fertilizers. The products of the chemical industry were used by metal producers and the textile industry, as well as soap and glass manufacturers.

Between 1856 and 1866, two young men, Ernest Solvay and William Henry Perkin (both born in 1838) established the basis for a completely new chemical industry. Solvay, a Belgian entrepreneur, developed a new way of making soda by reacting brine with carbon dioxide and ammonia, which avoids the energy costs and excessive pollution of the Leblanc process. His process was introduced to Great Britain, the undisputed leader of the soda industry, by the German chemist Ludwig Mond. While he was still an undergraduate at the Royal College of Chemistry in London, Perkin created a new synthetic dye, mauve, from the coal-tar product aniline. Lacking light-fastness, mauve soon passed out of use, but the synthesis of the important natural dye alizarin by Perkin and independently by Heinrich Caro of the German firm BASF in 1869 set the stage for the development of a new industry based on coal tar, hitherto a noxious waste product. By the 1880s, the dye companies were exploring the possible manufacture of pharmaceuticals from coal tar.

When World War I broke out in 1914, Germany dominated the organic chemical industry. The export of German dyes was blocked by the Royal Navy, and to fill the gap, new organic chemical industries had to be created in Great Britain and the United States. America had a modest pharmaceutical industry and was a major producer of explosives but had previously imported most of its chemicals. Indeed, potash was still made from wood ashes well into the nineteenth century. The consolidation of the chemical industry after the war led to the establishment of several large firms, notably IG Farben in Germany, ICI in Great Britain, and Allied Chemicals in the United States. DuPont diversified from explosives into chemicals and polymers. During the interwar period, the key technology was hydrogenation: the reaction of hydrogen at high pressures with nitrogen (from the air) to form ammonia—crucial for fertilizer and explosives manufacture—and with pulverized coal to make synthetic gasoline. The production of synthetic gasoline declined as cheap petroleum from the Middle East became available in the 1950s, but the Haber-Bosch ammonia process has remained important.

After World War II, the chemical industry entered a period of unprecedented growth, at first in the United States and then in Europe and East Asia. This growth was based on two different sectors: plastics (including synthetic fibers) and pesticides. As the earlier products became mature, as with nylon, or unacceptable in the case of DDT, profits were generated by a new generation of polymers (aramid fibers) and pesticides (glyphosphate). The situation in West Germany was changed dramatically by the breakup of IG Farben and the loss of its leading factories in what became East Germany. The successor companies to IG Farben (BASF, Bayer, Hoechst) became more innovative and internationally minded, resulting in their rapid expansion during the late 1950s and 1960s.

At the beginning of the 1970s, most of the industry's larger companies had been in existence for several decades, profits from its products, notably plastics, were still good if slowly declining, and its public image was still respectable despite the publication of Rachel Carson's *Silent Spring* in 1962. Three decades later, the scene was completely transformed. As a consequence of disasters such as Love Canal in the United States, Seveso in Italy, and Bhopal in India, the public image of the industry took a battering. Many of the major players renamed themselves and rearranged their component parts. They dropped traditional lines of manufacture and research, mostly aiming to convert themselves into producers of niche products or pharmaceuticals, or even as genetic engineers. ICI switched from being a British industrial giant into a medium-sized specialty firm with no strong national identification. Similarly, the genetically modified crop firm Monsanto had been a conventional producer of plastics and pesticides in the 1960s. It is characteristic of changes in the industry that the privately owned and hitherto largely unknown Huntsman Corporation is now one of the largest firms in the chemical sector.

BIBLIOGRAPHY

Aftalion, Fred. *A History of the International Chemical Industry.* Translated by Otto Theodor Benfey. 2d ed. Philadelphia, 2001. Originally published as a history of chemistry, Aftalion's book is of variable quality and lacks references. Unlike any other book in this field, it has the virtue of covering the evolution of the industry in France, Germany, and the United States up to the 1980s.

Arora, Ashish, Ralph Landau, and Nathan Rosenberg. *Chemicals and Long-Term Growth: Insights from the Chemical Industry.* New York, 1998. A series of essays that cover the history of the chemical industry since 1850, with particular reference to Great Britain, Germany, United States, and Japan. In contrast to earlier histories, there is a strong economic focus with chapters on monetary, fiscal, and trade policies, and on the financing of the chemical industry.

Haber, L. F. *The Chemical Industry during the Nineteenth Century: A Study of the Economic Aspects of Applied Chemistry in Europe and North America.* Oxford, 1958.

Haber, L. F. *The Chemical Industry, 1900–1930: International Growth and Technological Change.* Oxford, 1971. Taken together, these two volumes are by far the best history of the industry and the only economic history. Excellent coverage of developments in the leading countries (Great Britain, Germany, the United States) but less strong on smaller countries such as the Netherlands.

Hardie, D. W. F., and J. Davidson Pratt. *A History of the Modern British Chemical Industry.* Oxford, 1966. A technically oriented overview of the development of the British chemical industry that concentrates on the period between 1870 and 1955. Useful (but now outdated) brief histories of numerous British companies and trade associations.

Haynes, Williams. *American Chemical Industry: Background and Beginnings.* 6 vols. New York, 1945–1954. Five decades later, this magisterial set is still the only history of the American chemical industry. Volume 6 provides short histories of the individual companies, which are inevitably dated.

Homburg, Ernst, Anthony S. Travis, and Harm G. Schröter, eds. *The Chemical Industry in Europe: Industrial Growth, Pollution, and Professionalization.* Dordrecht, Netherlands, 1998.

Morris, Peter J. T., Hugh L. Roberts, and W. Alec. Campbell, eds. *Milestones in 150 Years of the Chemical Industry.* Cambridge, 1991. Collection of overviews of different sectors of the chemical industry arranged according to their end uses. The focus of the essays ranges from the technical to semipopular but provides considerable information in a single volume.

Multhauf, Robert P. *The History of Chemical Technology: An Annotated Bibliography.* New York and London, 1984. A comprehensive guide to the history of the chemical industry, with brief annotations by a leading scholar, but oriented toward the history of technology rather than economic history.

Russell, Colin A., ed. *Chemistry, Society, and Environment: A New History of the British Chemical Industry.* Cambridge, 2000. A pioneering attempt to combine the history of the chemical industry with environmental history. In many respects, however, it is a fairly traditional account of the industry's development, and it only covers developments in Great Britain.

Taylor, F. Sherwood. *A History of Industrial Chemistry.* London, 1957. In many respects, this is still the best history of chemical technology from the early Egyptians to the petrochemical industry in the 1950s, with clear explanations of the processes involved. Unfortunately, it also largely ignores the economic and corporate history of the industry, and obviously is now rather dated.

Travis, Anthony S., et al., eds. *Determinants in the Evolution of the European Chemical Industry, 1900–1939.* 2 vols. Dordrecht, Netherlands, 1998. These two volumes of essays by leading scholars in the field complement, but do not replace, the work of L. F. Haber. They represent a mixture of case studies and national surveys, economic history, and history of chemical technology.

PETER J. T. MORRIS

Chemical Industries before 1850

The problem of defining the chemical industry in the period before 1850 is particularly acute. Indeed, it would be possible to argue that there was no single "chemical industry" at that time. Rather, there was a number of different industries that can be considered a part of the chemical industry as it is understood today. In this entry, I will take a narrower position in defining the industry, for it seems excessive to cover industries that no one would now regard as being part of the chemical industry, such as the porcelain industry.

In the period between 1700 and 1850, the chemical industry was predominantly an industry based on the manufacture of inorganic chemicals. This is not surprising. Inorganic chemistry is the chemistry of a large number of elements, while organic chemistry is the chemistry of one element, carbon. Organic chemistry is complex and became a mature science only during the nineteenth century. Furthermore, natural products provided many of the needs currently supplied by the synthetic organic chemical industry.

Copperas Industry. The chemical industry in the seventeenth and early eighteenth century was largely a copperas industry. This is rather confusing, as the copperas industry has long disappeared and has nothing to do with copper. Copperas is an old name for the pale green crystals of hydrated iron (II) sulfate, which were prepared by the action of air on cheap iron pyrites (fool's gold) over a period of several weeks. The liquors from this process were "matured" in wooden vats before being boiled (for three weeks) with iron dust. Copperas was later used as a mordant in dyeing, but most of it was strongly heated to produce sulfuric acid. The by-product of this reaction, iron (III) oxide, was valued as an abrasive (jeweler's rouge) and a pigment.

The bleaching of cloth, linen in particular, was a major technological bottleneck in the early eighteenth century. The cloth went through several stages from plant to fabric, but there was little point in speeding up any of these processes while the finished cloth was soaked in potash and staked out in fields to be bleached slowly by the sun. Around the beginning of the eighteenth century, the Dutch used sour buttermilk (a by-product of butter making) as a bleach, but this was only a modest improvement, and buttermilk was not always available. Both quicklime and sulfuric acid were then tried, but there was understandable concern that these caustic chemicals would attack the cloth. Even so, diluted sulfuric acid still took four months to bleach linen fabrics. The breakthrough came in 1789 when the French chemist Claude Berthollet discovered that chlorine gas destroyed colors. A weak solution of chlorine and potash in water was then developed as a bleaching agent. In 1799, Charles Tennant and Charles Macintosh of Glasgow invented a cheap bleaching powder, made by reacting chlorine with quicklime. This was easily transported to the textile factories, where cloth could be bleached in a matter of hours.

Macintosh had already established the Scottish alum industry in Hurlet near Paisley in 1796. Alum (potassium aluminum sulfate) was known to the ancient Greeks and had been used for thousands of years as a mordant to affix red madder dye to cloth. A product of volcanic activity, it was relatively rare in nature, and for many years it was a papal monopoly. In the seventeenth century, an alternative source of alum was discovered in Yorkshire. The local shale was burned with wood and the liquor, produced by running water through the burnt shale, was treated with alkalies to produce alum. The yield was low but the market was good, and copperas was produced as a by-product. Macintosh found coal-mine waste that had been weathered for two centuries, thus permitting the easy extraction of the alum it contained. The business prospered, and alum works were also erected at Campsie, north of Glasgow. Another Scottish chemical manufacturer, Peter Spence, took out a patent for alum manufacture in 1845, and within a decade, he had set up alum works in Manchester and at Goole in Yorkshire.

The copperas process produced strong acid, even the fuming sulfuric acid associated with the German city of Nordhausen, but it was neither cheap nor abundant. It appears that the manufacture of sulfuric acid by burning sulfur in glass vessels began during the seventeenth century in Germany, from whence it diffused to France and the Netherlands. Joshua Ward used this process at his works at Twickenham near London from 1736 onward, and in 1749, he added niter (potassium nitrate) to the sulfur, which drastically increased the yield. By this time, John Roebuck and Samuel Garbett had already replaced the expensive and delicate glass vessels with chambers constructed from cheap and easily worked lead sheets. They constructed their first lead chamber works in Birmingham in 1746, followed by a second factory in Prestonpans near Edinburgh three years later. Over the next century, lead chamber works sprang up in many places, even in remote Welsh valleys, to supply the local tinplate industries. The potassium nitrate used in the process was expensive and was also needed for gunpowder manufacture. Although it was known by 1827 that the nitrogen oxides liberated during the reaction could be absorbed in sulfuric acid, the method of recovering these nitrogen oxides from the acid had to wait until John Glover's idea of passing hot gas from the sulfur burners through the nitrated acid was implemented in 1858. The sulfur itself was a Sicilian monopoly, and this was broken only in 1838, when Thomas Farmer introduced a new method of producing the intermediate sulfur dioxide by burning iron pyrites at Kennington in London.

The lead chamber process was developed for the metalworking trade, but the major consumers of cheap sulfuric acid were eventually located elsewhere, in the Leblanc soda industry and the fertilizer industry. The alkalies, sodium carbonate (soda) and potassium carbonate (potash), had been made for centuries by burning plants and then running water through the resulting ash. Soda was made in France and Spain by burning marine plants, notably *Salsoda soda*. Potash (extracted from the ashes of fern, bracken, and gorse) was more common in Great Britain. Another major source was wood ashes from the Baltic ports and the American colonies. Caustic potash (lye) was made by packing the ashes into a barrel with quicklime and then trickling water through the barrel.

Alkalies made this way were obviously dilute and supplies could be uncertain. One alternative was kelp, made by burning seaweed in Scottish islands. Nevertheless, a cheaper method had to be found as the demand from the textile industries, glassmakers, and soap manufacturers continued to grow. James Keir, a Scottish glass manufacturer in Stourbridge, England, near Birmingham, attempted with some success to make soda at his chemical works in nearby Tipton by treating sodium sulfate with quicklime in the late 1770s. The French were particularly active in this field; Nicolas Leblanc, like Roebuck a physician, was working on the same process as Keir. His breakthrough came in 1789, when Jean-Claude de la Métherie published a method of making soda by heating sodium sulfate with coal. Although this process did not work, his paper gave Leblanc the idea of adding coal to a mixture of sodium sulfate and quicklime. With the help of his patron, the duke of Orleans, Leblanc set up a small factory in 1791 to manufacture soda at Saint-Denis near Paris. The factory and the duke soon became victims of the French Revolution. Although Napoleon returned the factory to Leblanc in 1802, he lacked the capital to revive it and committed suicide in 1806.

However, the Leblanc process soon prospered on the other side of the English Channel. It was brought to Tyneside, probably in 1816, by William Losh, who had collaborated with the great innovator Archibald Cochrane, ninth earl of Dundonald, to make soda in the 1790s. Losh also studied chemistry in Paris in 1791. The industry took off after the abolition of salt duty in 1823. The process required sulfuric acid to convert salt (sodium chloride) into sodium sulfate, which was then heated with coal and limestone in a revolving furnace to produce "black ash," containing soda and calcium sulfide. The soda was extracted with water, leaving a foul-smelling waste product called *galligu*. The original process was wasteful. It also damaged the environment by releasing acidic hydrogen chloride gas into the atmosphere and creating huge heaps of nauseating *galligu* outside the works. William Gossage, an alkali manufacturer in Stoke Prior near Leominster in Worcestershire, in 1836 developed a tower that dissolved the noxious hydrogen chloride gas in water. Although this was a step in the right direction, it produced hydrochloric acid, for which there was only a limited market and which was allowed to pollute local water courses. His tower was not generally adopted until the 1860s.

CHEMICAL INDUSTRY. Factory of Powers and Weightman, manufacturing chemists, Philadelphia. Lithograph by Longacre and Co., circa 1800. (Prints and Photographs Division, Library of Congress)

Nonetheless, the Leblanc process had the virtue of manufacturing cheap and reliable soda on a huge scale. It replaced the copperas industry and the lead chamber process as the defining activity of the chemical industry, a position it held for many years. Large centers of alkali manufacture sprang up in Great Britain and Europe, and for the first time, the chemical industry dominated entire towns.

Although lime and bones had been added to the soil since the Middle Ages and various chemists had written about the application of chemistry to agriculture (notably the earl of Dundonald and Humphry Davy), the modern fertilizer industry can be dated to the manufacture of "superphosphate of lime" in Deptford on the Thames by John Bennet Lawes in 1841. Superphosphate was made by treating used animal charcoal, from the neighboring sugar refineries, and bones with sulfuric acid. John Ball of Burwell near Cambridge began the manufacture of superphosphate from coprolite (fossilized dung) in 1851. By this time, ammonium sulfate from gasworks was slowly replacing animal (and human) waste in its various forms as the main source of nitrogenous fertilizer.

Bones (and other animal waste such as hides and hoof) were a valuable raw material for the chemical industry between 1780 and 1850. Animal bones were used to make the important pigment Prussian blue. And even before they were used to make superphosphate, bones treated with sulfuric acid were heated with charcoal to produce white phosphorus. Glue, bone black, and sal ammoniac were also derived from animal waste. In the late eighteenth and early nineteenth centuries, ammonia was also produced from urine and soot.

Pigments were an important branch of the chemical industry in this period. White lead (basic lead carbonate) was made by corroding lead sheets with acetic acid. The expensive green pigment verdigris (basic copper acetate) was similarly made by corroding copper sheets with vinegar. Scheele's green (copper arsenite) was cheaper (and even more poisonous) but came into general use only in the early nineteenth century. Prussian blue was first made in Berlin in 1704, and the process was soon taken up in Tyneside. It was made by boiling potash and iron filings with blood and hide trimmings, then treating the resulting "prussiate of potash" (potassium ferrocyanide) with copperas. Red lead was made by strongly heating litharge (lead monoxide). Naples yellow was produced by heating glass of antimony (antimony oxide) with litharge. The chrome colors—lemon yellow (barium chromate) and chrome yellow (lead chromate)—were commercialized in the 1830s.

Origins of the Organic Chemical Industry. In contrast to the enormous development of the inorganic chemical industry, with its lead chambers and black-ash revolvers, the organic chemical industry was still both fragmentary and small in 1850. The early organic chemical industry was largely rural and was based on the distillation of wood. The origins of wood distillation are surprisingly obscure. But they stemmed from the heating of wood to produce fine charcoal for gunpowder and good quality wood tar for rope making and the caulking of ships' hulls during the second half of the eighteenth century. Although it had been known since the time of Johann Glauber (1604–1670) that heating wood yielded wood spirit and pyroligneous acid, their exploitation was limited until 1800, when pyroligneous acid was identified as acetic acid. It is possible that the first wood distilleries were founded around Glasgow, drawing on cheap Scottish timber. Turnbull and Company set up a distillery in the Vale of Leven around the end of the eighteenth century and its main works at Camlachie in 1813. The Camlachie works finally closed in 1965. By 1820, the industry was established in England (mainly using scrap wood), Germany, and Austria; the U.S. industry began on a small scale in 1830. Acetic acid produced by the distillation of wood was used to make mordants for dyeing and pigments, notably copperas, white lead, and verdigris. Although methanol and acetone were isolated from wood spirit as early as 1812, their commercial exploitation did not begin until the 1850s.

Derived from plants and insects, the manufacture of natural dyes and their use in textile dyeing remained a largely empirical technology until the nineteenth century. Nonetheless, there were important links between dyeing and the chemical industry. The discovery in 1758 that Scottish lichens could be used as dyes (cudbear) drew the MacIntosh family into the chemical industry. The introduction of the "cold vat" process for indigo in the early eighteenth century created a new demand for copperas and potash. Around 1740, Saxe blue, the first synthetic dye, was made by treating indigo with fuming sulfuric acid. During the eighteenth century, the growing use of certain metallic salts (mordants) to fix dye to fabrics, particularly in calico printing, generated a large market for alum, copperas, lead acetate, and, subsequently, aluminium acetate. In 1827, Pierre Robiquet used sulfuric acid to extract "garacine" from madder, which produced more brilliant colors. The yellow explosive picric acid, discovered by the eccentric chemist Peter Woulfe in 1771, was produced as a wool dye in 1845, and other manufacturers soon sprang up. The last of the pre-mauve synthetic dyes, Murexide, was made by treating uric acid (from guano) with ammonia and nitric acid, but its commercial exploitation by Depoully Frères of Paris did not begin until 1855.

Worldwide Development. Before 1800, it is difficult to make national comparisons. In Great Britain, Queenborough and Deptford on the Thames were important locations for the copperas industry in the seventeenth century, and the industry was also developed on Tyneside in the second half of the eighteenth century. London was a stronghold of small factories, often producing high-value fine chemicals. The Birmingham area, with its metalworking industries, was another early center of chemical

production. The Leblanc soda industry was initially concentrated in Tyneside and in Glasgow. The alum industry was also located in North Yorkshire, around Whitby, and in the Glasgow area. In 1823, James Muspratt started Leblanc soda manufacture in Liverpool, and he later opened works at Newton, near Saint Helens. With its glass industry and nearby soap manufacturers, Saint Helens became a center of the alkali industry in the 1830s and 1840s. Widnes, a small village on the Mersey River near Saint Helens, became an attractive site for the industry when the railway and the canal linked up there in 1833. John Hutchinson established the first alkali works in 1848, and by the 1860s, Widnes had become the undisputed leader of the English chemical industry.

The Dutch chemical industry was important but entered a period of relative decline in the late eighteenth century. It was concentrated in the Zaan area to the northwest of Amsterdam and, to a lesser extent, in Rotterdam and Utrecht. In contrast to the British chemical industry, it was broadly based, manufacturing a wide range of products including white lead, borax, smalt (cobalt blue), mercury compounds, nitric acid, and madder. There was a strong internal market (pottery, linen, and calico printing), but the export trade was also important. The Liège area (outside the Dutch republic) was an early center of the sulfuric acid, copperas, and alum industries. The first lead chamber plant in the Netherlands was built around 1774 in Amsterdam by J. Farquharson & Company. Although two other plants appear to have existed between 1790 and 1810, the first two long-lived sulfuric acid factories in the Netherlands, Ketjen in Amsterdam and Smits in Utrecht, were established in 1835. By contrast, the first Leblanc soda works in the Netherlands (Ketjen) was not erected until 1860.

Despite the advanced state of chemistry in eighteenth-century France, the chemical industry developed relatively slowly. The first lead chamber works, near Rouen in Normandy, was not constructed until 1774, and although it was short-lived, it did stimulate the construction of other lead chamber plants around Rouen. After the Restoration in 1814, the Marseille area became the center of the Leblanc soda industry, partly because the French soap industry was already concentrated there. The glass company Saint Gobain set up its acid and soda factory at Chauny in Picardy in 1810. The chemical industry was also carried on around Paris and Lyon and in the north around Amiens and Lille.

Germany had been one of the leaders of the chemical industry in the seventeenth century but, thereafter, lagged behind Great Britain. In the early nineteenth century, its chemical works were small and scattered. Like London, Berlin was a center of small factories that supplied the local industries. The first lead chamber plant in Berlin was built in 1837. The Giulini brothers erected a chemical factory in Wohlgelegen near Mannheim in 1810 and commenced the manufacture of soda there in 1837. The first Leblanc soda factory in Germany was started in 1827 in Käferthal, also near Mannheim, but its equipment was moved to the Neuschloss works near Worms in the following year. Eventually, in 1854, these two factories combined with the Leblanc works in Heilbronn (founded by Gustav Clemm and Christian Böhringer in 1851) to form the Verein Chemische Fabriken, Mannheim.

The first lead chamber plant in the United States was erected by John Harrison in 1793 in Philadelphia, and the city remained an important center of the chemical industry until the twentieth century. Harrison's own firm was taken over by DuPont in 1917. The Leblanc process was not taken up in the United States before 1850 as wood was cheap and plentiful. The potash industry was based in western New York, Pennsylvania, and Ohio, leading to the growth of the glass and soap industries in Pittsburgh and Cincinnati. The white lead industry was also important. It was founded in Philadelphia by Samuel Wetherill in 1804, and by 1850, the industry also existed in Pittsburgh, Cincinnati, and Saint Louis.

Before 1800, chemical works were generally small, by modern standards, and although the factories often existed for a century or more, the tenure of the owners (either individuals or partners) were often short-lived (i.e., Roebuck and Prestonpans). With the rise of the Leblanc soda industry, long-lived companies began to emerge. The partnership of Tennant, Knox, and Company was founded in 1797 and changed its name to Charles Tennant and Company in 1814. Although the alkali works became part of the United Alkali Company in 1890, the company still exists. The Bealey family ran lead chamber works in Radcliffe in Lancashire from 1791 until well into the twentieth century, latterly under the style of Richard Bealey and Sons. In the United States, Farr and Kunzi of Philadelphia (founded in 1818), specializing in medicinal and fine chemicals, became Powers and Weightman in 1847 and merged with its Philadelphia rivals Rosengarten & Sons (originally founded in 1822) in 1905. Finally, in 1927, Powers-Weightman-Rosengarten merged with Merck; the last Rosengarten on the board of Merck died in 1990.

[*See also* Oil Industry.]

BIBLIOGRAPHY

Campbell, W. A. *The Chemical Industry*. London, 1971. Good introduction to the chemical industry before 1860, with clear descriptions of the technology but biased in favor of British developments.

Clow, Archibald, and Nan L. Clow. *The Chemical Revolution: A Contribution to Social Technology*. London, 1952. A pioneering work that describes in rich detail the impact of the chemical industry on the Industrial Revolution. It overstates the importance of the Scottish industry and is dated by its use of Lewis Mumford's evolutionary classification of technologies.

Fox, Robert, and Augustí Nieto-Galan. *Natural Dyestuffs and Industrial Culture in Europe, 1750–1880*. Canton, Massachusetts, 1999. A collection of papers that illustrates the impact of science on the dye industry before mauve.

Haber, Ludwig F. *The Chemical Industry during the Nineteenth Century: A Study of the Economic Aspects of Applied Chemistry in Europe and North America*. Oxford, 1958. The best economic history of the industry in this period and particularly good for the development of the industry outside Great Britain, but it is weak on smaller countries such as the Netherlands.

Haynes, Williams. *American Chemical Industry*, vol. 1, *Background and Beginnings*. New York, 1954. The only history of the early American chemical industry. Haynes is particularly good on the personal element and the social context.

Morris, Peter J. T., and Colin A. Russell. *Archives of the British Chemical Industry, 1750–1914: A Handlist*. Faringdon, U.K., 1988. Offers a feel for the early chemical industry through its brief histories of numerous companies, most of them small and hitherto unknown, and a guide to the sadly depleted primary sources.

Musson, Albert E., ed. *Science, Technology, and Economic Growth in the Eighteenth Century*. London, 1972. Contains useful (if somewhat dated) papers on "Vitriol in the Industrial Revolution" by Archibald and Nan Clow and on "The Macintoshes and the Origins of the Chemical Industry" by D. W. F. Hardie.

Russell, Colin A., ed. *Chemistry, Society, and Environment: A New History of the British Chemical Industry*. Cambridge, 2000. A comprehensive and readable history of the industry from its origins up to the 1970s but restricted to Great Britain.

Smith, John Graham. *The Origins and Early Development of the Heavy Chemical Industry in France*. New York and Oxford, 1979. An excellent scholarly history, based on archival sources, of the development of inorganic chemicals in eighteenth- and early-nineteenth-century France. Rich in details and sensitive to the political, social, and economic contexts, Smith's work is limited by its focus on France.

Warren, Kenneth. *Chemical Foundations: The Alkali Industry in Britain to 1926*. Oxford, 1980. A wonderfully clear description of the growth of the British alkali industry, which also acknowledges developments elsewhere.

PETER J. T. MORRIS

Chemical Industries after 1850

As the twenty-first century begins, the chemical industry is one of the largest manufacturing industries in the world, selling products worth more than $1.67 trillion and employing over 10 million people. The United States produces approximately 28 percent of the global chemical output; Japan, 13 percent; Germany, 6 percent; France, 4 percent; and the United Kingdom (Great Britain) 3 percent. About 30 percent of this output is traded internationally. The chemical industry is the largest manufacturing industry in the United States, the second-largest in Europe after food and kindred products, and the second-largest in Japan after electrical machinery. On a value-added basis, it is responsible for about 11.3 percent of total U.S., 10 percent of total European, and 13.8 percent of total Japanese manufacturing.

In all leading national economies, chemical production represents a strikingly similar share of gross domestic product (GDP): 4.1 percent in the U.S. (2 percent in terms of value-added), 4.4 percent in Japan, 5.4 percent in Germany, 3.6 percent in the United Kingdom, and 5.5 percent in France, suggesting that chemicals are an indispensable part of large economies. Mikolaj Piskorski's data on exchange relationships between industries in the United States confirm the central role of chemicals in a modern economy. When the entire U.S. economy is classified into seventy-seven distinct industries, the chemical industry ranks ninth in terms of how important it is to the functioning of all other industries in the economy. Not surprisingly, the wholesale sector leads this centrality ranking, followed by government enterprises and new construction—all of which exchange significant output with virtually all other sectors in the economy. If one counts only relationships in which a focal industry exchanges goods with another industry that amounts to 5 percent of the focal industry's output, the chemical industry sells to or buys from fifty different industries. By contrast, the average U.S. industry sells to or buys from forty-one industries.

The major supply industries for chemical production at the beginning of the twenty-first century are wholesale (accounting for 10 percent of inputs), electricity (8 percent), petroleum (7 percent), and natural gas (6 percent). The major buyers of chemicals are the health care (accounting for 21 percent of outputs), plastics (16 percent), textile (8

percent), paper (5 percent), and rubber industries (5 percent). A look back to the middle of the nineteenth century reveals that the most important inputs and outputs of the chemical industry have changed dramatically over the past 150 years. In 1850, the main inputs were coal, salt, pyrites, and sulfur. The main outputs, in turn, were alkalies and acids. Demand for these heavy chemicals increased dramatically during the nineteenth century because alkalies and acids played an important supporting role in the first Industrial Revolution as inputs to the rapidly expanding textile, soap, glass, and steel industries. Aside from these high-volume inorganic chemicals, the industry produced only a few pigments and a small number of low-volume organic chemicals in the middle of the nineteenth century. One of the central characteristics of the chemical industry is that it experienced a continuous stream of process and major product innovations over the next 150 years and thereby acquired a diverse product portfolio of well over seventy thousand different chemical substances. The main product categories at the beginning of the twenty-first century range from the traditional acids to food additives and preservatives (see Figure 1).

The constant expansion of the industry's product portfolio has led to a dramatic growth in chemical output since the middle of the nineteenth century (see Table 1). At the turn of the twenty-first century, chemical production in

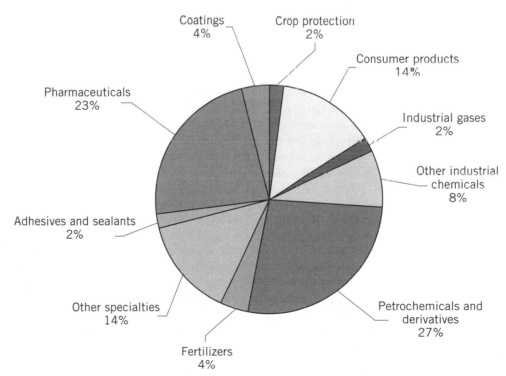

FIGURE 1. Global chemical production by segment, 2000. SOURCE: American Chemical Council. Guide to the Business of Chemistry. Arlington, Va., 2001.

TABLE 1. *Production of Chemicals in Billion US $ and Country Shares*

YEAR	UNITED STATES		GREAT BRITAIN		JAPAN		GERMANY		FRANCE		WORLD TOTAL
1850	0.005										
1860	0.0047										
1870	0.0194										
1877							0.6	20%			3
1880	0.0386										
1890	0.0594										
1895							1				
1900	0.0626										
1905	0.0921										
1913	3.4	34%	1.1	11%	0.15	2%	2.4	24%	0.85	9%	10
1927	9.45	42%	2.3	10%	0.55	2%	3.6	16%	1.5	7%	22.5
1935	6.8	32%	1.95	9%	1.3	6%	3.7	18%	1.6	8%	21
1938	8.0	30%	2.3	9%	1.5	6%	5.9	22%	1.5	6%	26.9
1951	71.8	43%	14.7	9%	6.5	4%	9.7	6%	5.9	4%	166
1970	49.20	29%	7.60	4%	15.30	9%	13.60	8%	7.20	4%	171
1980	168.34	23%	31.77	4%	79.23	11%	59.29	8%	38.60	5%	719
1990	309.10	24%	44.70	4%	162.80	13%	100.50	8%	66.30	5%	1248
2000	460.00	28%	50.70	3%	218.40	13%	100.00	6%	73.00	4%	1669

Notes: The second column for each country indicates the world production share for the particular country.

Figures are in billion U.S. $ except: 1870, 1913, 1927, 1935, 1939 in billion reichsmark; 1951 in billion deutsche mark.

Because the statistical definition of the chemical industry was not always the same in each country, the numbers in this table need to be interpreted as estimates rather than exact figures. The U.S. share in 1913 is exaggerated because it includes petroleum refining, which is not included in the European figures. Haber (1971) puts American production in 1913 at around 1.53 billion reichsmark (my calculation), placing it about halfway between Germany and Great Britain. Figures for Germany between 1951 and 1990 refer to West Germany.

SOURCES: Haeber. *Chemische Industrie.* vol. 4 (1952), 890–891; VCI. *The German Chemical Industry in Figures*, 1977; CEFIC. *Historical Sequence*; American Chemical Council. *Guide to the Business of Chemistry*, 2001.

the United States, for example, is approximately 3,730 times larger (in constant dollar terms) than in 1850. At that point, Great Britain had the biggest economy in the world and was by far the largest producer of chemicals. The country's output of 304,000 tons of soda in 1867 and 590,000 tons of sulfuric acid in 1870 was much larger compared with Germany's 33,000 tons of soda and 43,000 tons of sulfuric acid. British production of these two heavy chemicals—they represent a rough proxy for overall economic activity during the nineteenth century just as semiconductor production serves as such a proxy for the leading industrial countries at the turn of the twenty-first century—was respectively eleven and seventeen times higher on a per capita basis than that of Germany.

In 1870, the United States produced only 93,700 tons of sulfuric acid, ten times less than Great Britain on a per capita basis, and imported most alkalies from Great Britain. But the German and U.S. chemical industries subsequently grew much faster than Great Britain's. German growth was fueled to a considerable extent by the development of new chemical technologies, whereas the United States until around 1930 developed its own chemical industry largely by importing European chemical technologies and adapting them to the American context.

By 1910, Germany produced around 500,000 tons of soda, thereby reducing Great Britain's lead on a per capita basis to about 2.3 to 1. With an output of 1.6 million tons of sulfuric acid in 1913, Germany surpassed British production by 350,000 tons and even pulled ahead when measured on a per capita basis (1.05 to 1). Parallel to the growth of its overall economy, the United States by World War I had become the largest sulfuric acid producer in the world with 2.2 million tons of output. On a per capita basis, this was nearly as much as Great Britain (0.9 to 1). Great Britain, however, still produced approximately twenty times as much sulfuric acid as Japan, reflecting the relative underdevelopment of the Japanese economy at the time. Although the synthetic dye industry had been pioneered in Great Britain, Germany's production of 137,000 tons of highly valued dyes in 1913 gave it about a 19 to 1 lead on a per capita basis when compared with a British output of 5,000 tons. With a world market share of about 85 percent in synthetic dyes and the largest share in new pharmaceuticals, the German chemical industry had captured a dominant position in organic chemicals similar to the one Great Britain had enjoyed in soda half a century earlier.

Because of its undisputed leadership in organic chemicals, Germany by 1913 possessed the largest chemical

TABLE 2. *Share of Chemical Exports (in %) by Country of Origin: 1899–2000*

EXPORTS FROM	1899	1913	1929	1937	1950	1959	1990	2000
United Kingdom	19.6	20.0	17.5	16.0	17.9	15.0	8.4	6.6
France	13.1	13.1	13.5	9.9	10.1	8.6	9.1	7.8
Germany[1]	35.0	40.2	30.9	31.6	10.4	20.2	17.7	12.1
Other Western Europe[2]	13.1	13.1	15.3	19.4	20.5	21.1	31.7	32.0
United States	14.2	11.2	18.1	16.9	34.6	27.4	13.2	14.1
Canada	0.4	0.9	2.5	2.9	5.2	4.4	1.8	1.6
Japan	0.4	1.0	1.8	3.0	0.8	3.1	5.4	6.1
Other	4.2	0.3	0.4	0.3	0.5	0.2	12.8	19.8
Total	100.0	100.0	100.0	100.0	100.0	100.0	100.0	100.0
Total in billion $ U.S.	0.26	0.59	1.04	0.98	2.17	5.48	309.2	566.0

[1] West Germany between 1950 and 1990.

[2] Belgium, Luxembourg, Italy, the Netherlands (except in 1899 and 1913), Spain (only 1990 and 2000), Sweden, and Switzerland.

SOURCES: Maizels, A. *Industrial Growth and World Trade*; American Chemical Council. *Guide to the Business of Chemistry*.

industry in the world and was also the largest exporter with a 40.2 percent global share (see Table 2). But since chemicals proved to be such an important strategic asset in twentieth-century warfare, the United States, Great Britain, and France, in the wake of World War I, would never again allow themselves to become as dependent on German organic chemicals as they had been on the eve of the war. With the rapid development of the American chemical industry in the first half of the twentieth century, of the Japanese chemical industry in the second half of the twentieth century, and the growth of East Asian economies more recently, the British and German share of world production and exports has decreased substantially since World War I, but Germany at the turn of the twenty-first century continues to be the second-largest chemical exporter in the world after the United States. Furthermore, Germany still has the largest positive trade balance in chemicals ($22.8 billion), followed by Ireland ($17.3 billion), the Netherlands ($11.2 billion), Switzerland ($8.3 billion), and the United States ($6.3 billion). Building on two centuries of cumulative technological innovation, western Europe continues to have a strong positive trade balance ($68.2 billion), North America has a small negative one ($ – 8.5 billion), and Asia Pacific has a larger negative one ($ – 27.8 billion). Over 35 percent of contemporary world trade in chemicals is intrafirm in nature because the large companies increasingly invest in all major markets in the world and sell output to their international subsidiaries. More and more, prices for commodity chemicals are determined by global supply and demand because the diffusion of petrochemical technology through specialized engineering firms (SEFs), which build turnkey plants, has created a slew of new producers close to the sources of the oil and gas.

Technological Developments and Their Importance to the Industry. Three types of innovations have recurred throughout the history of the chemical industry. The first type involves the creation of processes for making chemical substances that are also found in nature but occur naturally in limited quantity or are cheaper to produce in an industrial plant. The Haber-Bosch nitrogen fixation process (1912) and synthetic indigo process (1897) are cases in point. The second type of innovation involves the substitution of an existing industrial process for a more efficient one, such as the Solvay ammonia soda process (1864), which replaced the Leblanc soda process. Such new processes often work with raw materials that are cheaper or produce by-products that are more valuable in the market. The depletion of high quality raw materials has also frequently forced chemical firms to develop skills for obtaining higher yields from difficult-to-extract sources or to develop processes that could operate with lower-quality raw materials. The third type of innovation involves the creation of chemical substances that do not naturally occur on earth. The vast majority of synthetic dyes, including the first one—mauve—invented in 1856 by William Henry Perkin (1838–1907), as well as the majority of modern pharmaceuticals, falls into this category. The 118 chemical elements found in the universe to date can form many more stable combinations (the so-called molecules) than were present on earth before human beings acquired sufficient chemical knowledge to deliberately create synthetic compounds. It is this sheer limitless number of possible molecules that has provided the opportunity for continuous product innovations in the chemical industry.

The steady growth of the chemical industry since the middle of the nineteenth century came about because all three types of innovations appeared in regular frequency. Some innovations have provided a particularly large boost to the growth of the industry; and it is therefore customary to identify the stages in the development of the chemical industry with the most important new products or process technologies—organic chemistry, electrochemicals, high-pressure technologies, polymer chemistry, petrochemicals, plant protection chemicals, rational drug design, and the like. The development of the Solvay ammonia soda process, the Haber-Bosch high-pressure ammonia process, synthetic indigo, and the polyester fiber processes collectively provide a window on the challenges that need to be overcome in developing a commercially viable chemical technology.

Since the early nineteenth century, a number of people had tried to develop an ammonia soda process, but nobody had been able to solve the problem of recovering a sufficient amount of ammonia in the process to make it economically viable. After much additional trial and error, Ernest Solvay (1838–1922) succeeded in removing the final technical obstacles to the creation of an ammonia soda process that could compete with the Leblanc process. Solvay patented every stage of his process. Later, he sold licenses to his process around the world and forced his licensees to share their technical improvements with him. The efficiency of the process was increased substantially in the decades after the original plant was built. At the turn of the twentieth century when chlorine could be manufactured electrochemically, the Leblanc process, which as a side product also made bleaching powder and caustic, had lost its final advantage. From that point, all new soda plants worked the 25 percent cheaper Solvay process.

Much of the innovative work in chemical technology is concerned with taking a product that can be made on a laboratory scale and developing a process that works on an industrial scale. Because the problems of scaling up a laboratory reaction to an industrial process are substantial, an entire academic discipline of chemical engineering designed to master these technological challenges has developed since the late nineteenth century. Professor Adolf von Baeyer (1835–1917) synthesized indigo in 1880, winning in 1905 the Nobel Prize in chemistry for this work. Nevertheless, it took seventeen years of research and development that involved intensive collaboration among many academic and firm chemists before BASF had a commercially viable process. Without innovations in inorganic chemicals, such as the new contact sulfuric acid process that could deliver a hitherto unavailable strength of the acid, synthetic indigo would not have been able to wipe out all indigo plantations within a short period. Germany dominated the chemical industry in 1913 because it had the strongest scientific base in chemistry from which firms could draw in their innovation efforts. In terms of its eco-

nomic impact, the single most significant academic-industrial collaboration was the one between the physical chemist Fritz Haber (1868–1934) and the BASF chemist-engineer Carl Bosch (1874–1940). Their high-pressure catalytic process to synthesize ammonia directly from nitrogen and hydrogen gave the world a cheap source of fertilizers and won both men independently the Nobel Prize in chemistry, Haber in 1918 and Bosch in 1931. The fixation of atmospheric nitrogen had been on the agenda of chemists for decades, and many different approaches had been tried unsuccessfully since 1780 before the Haber-Bosch process emerged. Unlike many other chemical processes that do not survive for long because a better one is developed, the Haber-Bosch process continues to be the chief source of ammonia in the world. The high-pressure technology developed by Bosch was later employed in the synthesis of methanol and hydrogenation of coal to petroleum.

Early in the twentieth century, chemists in Europe and the United States began to study the science of long-chained molecules (polymer chemistry) that would later provide the founding for plastics, synthetics fibers, and rubber. Signaling the beginning of American technological leadership in the chemical industry, Wallace H. Carothers (1896–1937) and his team at DuPont developed the first artificial fiber, nylon, in the 1930s. Of the hundreds of synthetic fibers studied during the twentieth century, only about a dozen have the properties to compete successfully in quality and price with the natural fibers such as cotton, wool, silk, and flax. The most economically significant synthetic fiber to date is polyester, which was originally developed in 1941 by John Rex Winfield (1901–1966) and J. T. Dickson in England. For polyester to become the second-most important textile fiber after cotton, much additional research money and manpower had to be invested on the part of the makers of the petrochemical raw materials, the chemical companies producing the fiber, the dye firms, and the textile and apparel makers. The successful introduction of a chemical invention more often than not is a large collective process.

Market Structures. Market structures have changed dramatically in the chemical industry since 1850. Given that thousands of different products compose the industry, it is impossible to identify a general trend in development of market structures. Except for the period between World War I and War II, when most major chemical markets with the exception of the United States were cartelized—often with one large company, such as IG Farben in Germany and ICI in Great Britain, taking a dominant position—the industry was at least moderately competitive. (The formation of IG Farben was orchestrated by Carl Bosch and Carl Duisberg [1861–1935], while the merger of all large British chemical firms into ICI was led by Sir Harry McGowan

[1874–1961, later Lord McGowan] and Sir Alfred Mond [1868–1930, in 1928 Lord Melchett] to counter the competitive threat posed by IG Farben.) Monopolies typically existed only for limited periods of time when a firm acquired a patent that guaranteed a legal monopoly for not more than twenty years.

A large number of other chemical markets have been characterized by an oligopoly because entry barriers either in the form of large amounts of capital or technical and organizational know-how required to operate at a competitive scale were substantial enough to keep new entrants away. The German dominance in the synthetic dye industry was built in large part on the ability of such firms as Bayer, BASF, and Hoechst to exploit economies of scope in dye production and marketing. For many chemicals, large-scale production increases the efficiency of a chemical process. Since Ralph Landau's (1916–) Scientific Design developed the petrochemical ethylene oxide in 1953, the scale at which new plants for this chemical are built has increased at least twenty fold. Chemical engineers long worked with the rule of thumb that capital costs increase only by 60 percent of the increase in a chemical process plant's capacity.

Many of the early firms that became successful in the chemical industry, such as BASF and DuPont, have remained leading players by investing substantial capital every year into research and development (R&D) and diversifying into new product lines. The R&D laboratory as a routine function of the corporation was invented in the German dye industry and gave those firms that pioneered this new organizational form a large advantage over their rivals. To adapt chemical technology to American conditions and later to develop genuinely new technologies such as polymer chemistry, U.S. chemical firms before 1950 created R&D laboratories in larger numbers than any other sector in the U.S. economy. Five hundred sixteen, or 26 percent of the total of 2,303 R&D labs created in the United States before 1950, were formed in the chemical industry. This provided the basis for the countless U.S. chemical innovations after World War II.

One significant determinant of the market structure in the petrochemical segment of the industry after World War II was that many of the key petrochemical processes were acquired (and sometimes even developed) by specialized engineering firms such as Kellogg, the Lumus Company, Foster-Wheeler, and Stone & Webster. These firms licensed their technologies all over the world, allowing many countries such as Japan to build significant domestic chemical industries. By facilitating entry into the petrochemical industry, the SEFs have made the industry more efficient. But overcapacities in the commodities sector have also eroded profit margins and led to significant restructuring of the industry since the 1980s. The Japanese

chemical industry has found it more difficult to restructure because the large business groups such as Mitsubishi, Mitsui, and Sumitomo, which dominated Japan during the twentieth century, were reluctant to sell or merge their chemical business with that of rival groups. Hence, Japanese chemical firms have generally achieved lower profits in recent decades compared with the large American chemical firms.

Environmental and Work Safety Regulation. Many chemical manufacturing processes create waste products that can be harmful to the environment and human health when not properly handled. Without careful planning and monitoring, chemical plants also harbor significant risks to the life of workers and the population in the vicinity. This has been true from the beginning of the industry, not just in recent decades that were marked by a number of disastrous chemical accidents. With the dramatic growth of the British alkali industry after 1850, more and more complaints were filed by people who had property in the vicinity of alkali plants and who suffered from the noxious fumes the factories released. This led to the so-called Alkali Act in 1864 that regulated how much hydrochloric acid fumes plants could release into the atmosphere.

When companies complied with the act by channeling much of their waste products into rivers, the British legislature passed another act that regulated the discharge of polluting wastes into rivers. Early synthetic dye production also caused significant environmental hazards. Fuchsin, which was invented in 1858, was originally manufactured with the help of substantial quantities of arsenic acid. Two years later, Jakob Müller-Pack (1825–1899) became the second fuchsin manufacturer in the city of Basel, but his business was bankrupted in 1864 by the compensation it had to pay to victims of the arsenic water poisoning caused by his plant.

Following scientific recommendations of three chemistry professors, the government then outlawed the use of arsenic acid in dye production and required that all dye factories build pipes to carry their waste away in the Rhine River. In the early days of the synthetic dye industry, it was also common for firms in Switzerland and Germany to settle disputes by making cash reparation payments to neighbors who complained that the fumes from the dye factories ruined white laundry drying in open air on adjacent properties. As these examples illustrate, the chemical industry from the beginning had to cope with environmental hazards, but in the nineteenth century only government officials and those who lived in the vicinity of plants generally perceived these hazards.

Although the chemical industry in the first half of the twentieth century enjoyed the general reputation of being a high-tech sector that improved life considerably, a number of accidents in recent decades shocked the general

CHEMICAL INDUSTRIES. Plastic container manufacturing plant, Nancalpan, Mexico, 1985. (© Stephanie Maze/Woodfin Camp and Associates, New York)

public, and extensive media coverage cemented the negative image that the chemical industry had acquired starting in the 1960s. The most prominent accidents took place in 1976, 1984, and 1986. First, dioxin, one of the most toxic chemicals known to date, escaped from a chemical plant just north of Milan, Italy. Wind carried the toxic cloud to the municipality of Seveso, where about 37,000 people were exposed to chemicals, some of whom came down with health problems only a few hours later. Four percent of local farm animals died, and the remaining 80,000 were killed to prevent contamination from filtering up the food chain. In 1984, the leakage of toxic chemicals at a Union Carbide plant in Bhopal, India, resulted in the death of 3,800 people and led to $470 million in compensation payments. Only two years later, a fire at a Sandoz plant in Switzerland caused significant pollution of the Rhine River and, together with the Seveso accident, came to symbolize in the public mind the dangers of chemical production

in densely populated Europe. The leakage of toxic chemicals that had been buried for decades in the Love Canal forced the evacuation of local residents in 1980 and galvanized the U.S. public to address the nation's toxic waste problems.

More than a century of unprecedented economic growth in all sectors of industry had created pollution levels by the 1960s that turned many rivers in industrialized countries into poisonous streams and the air over large metropolitan areas into a significant health hazard. Many a scientific committee warned about a possible environmental collapse. At this point, the public at large became concerned about the living conditions on the planet. The rise of the environmental consciousness of the general population produced unprecedented levels of new regulations in all industrialized countries during the second half of the twentieth century to protect air, water, and soil. Governments also created environmental protection agencies to coordinate state policies in cleaning up and protecting the environment. As a result of a slew of tougher regulations, average environmental spending in the chemical industry rose from about 3 percent of total operational investment in the 1940s to more than 6 percent in the 1960s and reached about 20 percent by the early 1990s. Initially, the chemical industry in the industrialized countries tried to resist many regulations because they would increase the cost of production. In recent years, however, the industry has learned that it is to its advantage to take a proactive approach toward regulations and to engage in self-regulation through such initiatives as Responsible Care that commits members of all the world's major chemical industry trade associations to continually improve health, safety, and environmental performance.

Since 1970, the American chemical industry, for example, has spent $36 billion for pollution abatement and control. Thanks to stringent government regulation and recent industry self-regulation, chemical industry emissions in the United States are down by 65 percent since 1988, although industry output is up by 30 percent. From an environmental point of view, the globalization in the chemical business is likely to aid the environment because companies from industrialized countries tend to build plants that meet the same environmental and safety standards as the plants back home.

In the major industrialized countries, governments and trade unions have been active for more than a hundred years in improving the working conditions in chemical plants. An investigation of death rates at the end of the nineteenth century brought to light the fact that the chemical industry had the highest rate of all industries with 98 per 1,000 compared with 57 per 1,000 for all employed males. A century later, working conditions in chemical plants of the industrialized world improved dramatically.

In the United States, which can be taken as representative of all major chemical-producer countries, the occupational injury and illness rates (per 100 full-time employees) are less than half of the manufacturing sector as a whole (4.4 versus 9.2).

Aside from eliminating many hazardous jobs and implementing effective safety programs, the chemical industry has significantly fewer labor accidents at the turn of the twenty-first century because plant employees are less prone to fatigue. Twelve-hour shifts common in the mid-nineteenth century have been reduced to about eight hours in the chemical industries of the major industrial countries. Workers in some departments of British alkali plants put in as much as 84 hours per week until 1889, when the introduction of additional shifts reduced the work hours significantly. Across the channel, the workweek of an average plant employee in the German chemical industry decreased continually from 72 hours per week in 1872, to 62 hours per week in 1900, to 57 hours per week 1913, and to an average of 37.5 hours at the turn of the twenty-first century.

Sources of Industrial Leadership. Between 1850 and 2000, leadership positions in the chemical industry have changed from Great Britain to Germany and later to the United States as radical product innovations created entirely new branches of the industry, as large markets opened up in North America and Japan, and as petroleum replaced coal as the key feedstock for organic chemicals. But there is also much continuity in industrial leadership. Many of the companies that dominated the industry in the beginning of the twentieth century—BASF, Bayer, Dow and DuPont—continue to be the largest chemical enterprises in the world because, as first movers, they have continually invested in new technologies and built large capabilities in management, production, and distribution. Significant competitive advantages were created and lost by national industries—but not overnight. Industrial strength in the chemical industry is, in essence, the product of long-term investments.

The economic history of the chemical industry is also consistent with Dennis Mueller's general findings (*Profits in the Long Run*, Cambridge and New York, 1986) that only companies which are able to introduce new innovations time and again, such as Merck, or companies which establish a particularly strong brand in the mind and hearts of consumers, such as Coca-Cola, can achieve above normal returns in the long run. Chemical innovations that were at one point reaping large profits—synthetic dyes, fertilizers, petrochemicals—are no longer sources of abnormal profits because market forces have brought them down to normal levels. However, companies that develop a stream of new therapeutic substances, for example, continue to reap above normal returns.

Pharmaceuticals, plastics, artificial fibers, and synthetic dyes are only the most visible products of the chemical industry that have made modern life more enjoyable on a physical level. Even when we take into consideration the environmental damage that chemical production has caused at various times, chemicals are in large measure the reason that citizens of the industrialized world need no longer claim that life is poor, nasty, short, and brutish.

[*See also* Oil Industry *and* Synthetic Fibers Industry.]

BIBLIOGRAPHY

Aftalion, Fred. *A History of the International Chemical Industry: From the 'Early Days' to 2000.* 2d ed. Philadelphia, 2001.

Ashish Arora, Ralph Landau, and Nathan Rosenberg, eds. *Chemicals and Long-Term Economic Growth: Insights from the Chemical Industry.* New York, 1998. The following chapters are most relevant for further reading: "Evolution of Industry Structure in the Chemical Industry" by Ashish Arora and Alfonso Gambardella, pp. 379–414; "Chemicals: A U.S. Success Story" by Ashish Arora and Nathan Rosenberg, pp. 71–102; "The Evolution of Corporate Capability and Corporate Strategy within the World's Largest Chemical Firms: The Twentieth Century in Perspective" by Alfred D. Chandler, Jr., Takashi Hikino and David Mowery, pp. 415–458; "Monetary, Fiscal, and Trade Policies in the Development of the Chemical Industry" by Barry Eichengreen, pp. 265–306; "Structure and Performance of the Chemical Industry under Regulation" by Kian Esteghamat, pp. 341–378; "The Japanese Puzzle" by Takashi Hikino, Tsutomo Harada, Yoshio Tokuhisa and James Yoshida, pp. 103–106; "The Process of Innovation" by Ralph Landau, pp. 139–180; "On the Making of Competitive Advantage: The Development of the Chemical Industries in Britain and Germany since 1850" by Johann Peter Murmann and Ralph Landau, pp. 27–70; and "Technological Change in Chemicals: The Role of the University-Industry Interface" by Nathan Rosenberg, pp. 193–230.

Garfield, Simon. *Mauve: How One Man Invented a Color That Changed the World.* New York, 2001.

Haber, L. F. *The Chemical Industry during the Nineteenth Century.* Oxford, 1958.

Haber, L. F. *The Chemical Industry, 1900–1930.* Oxford, 1971.

Homburg, Ernst, Anthony S. Travis, and Harm G. Schröter, eds. *The Chemical Industry in Europe, 1850–1914: Industrial Growth, Pollution, and Professionalization.* Dordrecht and Boston, 1998.

Landau, Ralph. *Uncaging Animal Spirits: Essays on Engineering, Entrepreneurship, and Economics.* Cambridge, Mass., 1994.

Landes, David S. *The Unbound Prometheus: Technological Change and Industrial Development in Western Europe from 1750 to the Present.* New York, 1969.

Mokyr, Joel. *The Lever of Riches: Technological Creativity and Economic Progress.* New York, 1990.

Murmann, Johann Peter. *Knowledge and Competitive Advantage: The Coevolution of Firms, Technology, and National Institutions.* New York, 2003.

Smil, Vaclav. *Enriching the Earth: Fritz Haber, Carl Bosch, and the Transformation of World Food Production.* Cambridge, Mass., 2001.

Spitz, Peter H. *Petrochemicals: The Rise of an Industry.* New York, 1988.

Travis, Anthony S., Harm G. Schröter, Ernst Homburg, and Peter J. T. Morris, eds. *Determinants in the Evolution of the European Chemical Industry, 1900–1939: New Technologies, Political Frameworks, Markets, and Companies.* Dordrecht and Boston, 1998.

ONLINE RESOURCES

American Chemical Council. <http://www.americanchemistry.com/>.

Chemical Industries Association (Great Britain). <http://www.cia.org.uk/>.

European Chemical Industry Council. <http://www.cefic.be/>.

International Council of Chemical Associations. <http://www.icca-chem.org/>.

Search Engine for Chemical Industry Information. <http://chemindustry.com/>.

Synthetic Dye Industry Project. <http://johann-peter.murmann.name/dye-project.htm>.

JOHANN PETER MURMANN

CHICAGO. The importance of the Chicago area was clear to the first Europeans to pass through it, Father Jacques Marquette and Louis Joliet (1673), who were seeking a route from the Great Lakes to the Mississippi River. Its few residents at the turn of the nineteenth century were white fur traders; Native Americans had used the spot as a place to meet and trade, but there is no evidence of their regular habitation. The strategic importance of the site where the Chicago River joins Lake Michigan led to the cession by Native Americans to the United States of six square miles of this land by treaty in 1795, and to the construction of Fort Dearborn in 1803. By the mid-1820s, Chicago had fourteen taxpayers and thirty-five voters. Most of the taxable property belonged to John Jacob Astor's American Fur Company, the only major business.

Lake Michigan did not offer Chicago a natural harbor. In 1830, ships bringing provisions to Fort Dearborn had to anchor half a mile offshore. Even before incorporation of Chicago was contemplated, the federal government appropriated funds to dredge the sand at the Chicago River's mouth. By the 1840s, lake vessels regularly entered the river, the logical western terminus for Great Lakes traffic.

When Chicago incorporated in 1833, the population was 350. The 1835 census counted 3,265 people. By 1850, the population was nearly 30,000. At the time of the great fire in 1871, roughly 325,000 lived there.

The year 1848 was important for three reasons. The first regional telegram arrived in January, and in April the first through telegram arrived from the East Coast. That same April, the Illinois and Michigan Canal opened. Canal construction engendered real estate development and land speculation, and attracted immigrants to the area. Completion of the canal provided a dominant market for the Illinois River valley, which previously had shipped its agricultural surpluses downstream to Saint Louis. Finally, in October, Chicago's first railroad, the Galena and Chicago Union, made its inaugural run, connecting the lead-mining area around Galena with lake-shipping facilities and serving the needs of farms along the route.

Gradually railroad systems were assembled from such roads. Chicago became the western terminus for the most important eastern roads and the eastern terminus for the most important western railroads. Of major importance to Chicago's growth was the fact that competition among rails, the canal, and the lake kept freight rates relatively low. Chicago later became a hub for airlines, as the initial routes were allocated in the manner in which the railroads carried U.S. mail. Today, it is a center for data movement as fiberoptic lines have been laid along the railroad rights-of-way.

Chicago interests quickly dominated four industries: grain, lumber, mail-order, and meatpacking. Among the companies taking advantage of Chicago's railroad network were: retailers such as Marshall Field, Montgomery Ward, and Sears & Roebuck; producers such as Armour, Cudahy, Morris, Swift, and Wilson (who made up Chicago's "Big Five" meatpackers); printer R. R. Donnelley; the McCormick Reaper Works; and ultimately U.S. Steel.

From 1857 on, Chicago's iron and steel industry grew quickly. By 1898, the largest producer in the west was Illinois Steel Corporation, south of the city on Lake Michigan. That year, with assistance from J. P. Morgan, Judge Elbert Gary transformed Illinois Steel into Federal Steel, and, three years later, into U.S. Steel. Gary became its president in 1903. Two years later, U.S. Steel decided to build both a larger plant and a city named for Gary.

In the 1850s, the Chicago Board of Trade (incorporated in 1850) and other civic groups addressed the city's greatest woe: mud. In 1852, Chicago became the first North American city to construct a comprehensive sewer system, resolving its problem of flatness by the simple but costly expedient of elevating buildings and streets. George Pullman came to Chicago to help raise buildings, then returned to build his palace cars that became emblematic of the town. To alleviate the inevitable pollution in the Chicago River and Lake Michigan, a new water system with an intake point farther offshore was constructed during the Civil War. The city's growth continued to threaten the water supply; so the canal was deepened, and new pumps were added. The opening of these works in 1871 formally reversed the flow of the Chicago River.

There were four dominant influences on Chicago's development between 1870 and 1900. First, the great fire of 1871 burned four square miles, including the entire downtown; but because of its crucial position on the railroad network, Chicago was quickly rebuilt. The fire proved to be little more than a short-run disruption. A second event was labor conflict, which began shortly after the Civil War. Contributing to this strife was continued deflation, the growth of large corporations, and renewed European immigration. Chicago witnessed the Haymarket Square riot in 1886 and the Pullman strike of 1894. Conflict accelerated with the Great Migration of African Americans, who began arriving in the city around World War I. Third, in 1889,

CHICAGO. View of the Wrigley Building and Tribune Tower on Michigan Avenue at the Chicago River, 1930. (© Stock Montage, Inc.)

Chicago annexed 125 square miles of former suburbs. Some 225,000 people became Chicagoans, making the city's population more than 1,000,000. Finally, the Columbian Exposition of 1893 was a celebration of the city's future. Daniel Burnham's design contributed to the ascendancy of Chicago architecture, which included the invention of the modern skyscraper. His monumental plan for Chicago contributed to the professionalization of both architects and city planners. The exposition also demonstrated the many uses of electrical power. In time, Samuel Insull built an electrical network centered on Chicago.

Before the turn of the twentieth century, Chicago was *the* Midwestern metropolis. Its manufacturing industries continued to exploit the area's natural resources, but service industries using transportation networks also grew rapidly. In the twentieth century, the latter would outpace the former. By 2000, Carl Sandburg's "city of the big shoulders" had only 40 percent of the manufacturing jobs it had in 1960.

Much of the city's infrastructure was built or expanded during the 1930s with money from the WPA or the PWA. Federal dollars also contributed to a second round of infrastructure development, particularly expressway construction, that took place in the 1950s and 1960s under Mayor Richard J. Daley.

Suburbanization of business began as early as the 1920s, but the trend accelerated after World War II as the population shifted. Automobiles, trucks, and airplanes pulled production away from the city center; the port and the railroad lost their locational importance. Chicago's African-American population, which doubled in the 1910s as a result of the Great Migration, doubled again in the 1940s. Hispanics began arriving in large numbers in the 1960s, and Asian immigration accelerated in the 1970s. In 1999, the total population of the Chicago metropolitan area was 7.8 million people, 4.1 million of whom were employed. The city of Chicago had 54.5 percent of the population of Cook County but only about half of the employed. It had 38.3 percent of the population of the metropolitan area but only about a third of the workers. Even so, total employment in the city had continued to increase.

At the dawn of the twenty-first century, downtown Chicago continues to thrive, but it increasingly depends on activities that benefit from face-to-face contact and those that require a central location. It remains a locus of finance, law, and government. The health services industry is now the city's largest employer; manufacturing is no longer in the top ten. Chicago has a strong attraction for accounting, advertising, and journalism. Its distinguished cultural institutions and athletic teams contribute to the amenities of living in the metropolitan area.

BIBLIOGRAPHY

Andreas, A. T. *History of Chicago from the Earliest Time to the Present.* 3 vols. Chicago, 1884.

Belcher, Wyatt Winston. *The Economic Rivalry between St. Louis and Chicago, 1850–1880.* New York, 1947.

Cain, Louis P. *Sanitation Strategy for a Lakefront Metropolis: The Case of Chicago.* De Kalb, Ill., 1978.

Cronon, William. *Nature's Metropolis: Chicago and the Great West.* New York, 1991.

Einhorn, Robin L. *Property Rules: Political Economy in Chicago, 1833–1872.* Chicago, 1991.

Miller, Donald L. *City of the Century: The Epic of Chicago and the Making of America.* New York, 1996.

Pierce, Bessie Louise. *A History of Chicago.* 3 vols. New York, 1937, 1940, 1957.

Spinney, Robert G. *City of Big Shoulders: A History of Chicago.* De Kalb, Ill., 2000.

LOUIS P. CAIN

CHILD CARE. Historical and anthropological studies help us understand that the ways babies are born, nursed, cradled, dressed, and helped to learn to walk are not universal; instead, they correspond to religious, social, and economic constraints characteristic of specific societies. The infinite variety of caretaking practices and the

CHILD CARE. Children at a day care center in Havana, Cuba, 1998. (© Betty Press/Woodfin Camp and Associates, New York)

corresponding modes of social organization and ways of representing children are astonishing. Certain societies organized by family lineage place great emphasis on the idea that the child is the incarnation of an ancestor: This view has considerable influence on the way members of that society organize childbirth, name the baby, interpret its cries, and so on. The bonds between the baby and the spirits are very strong, hence the need to take certain precautions regarding newborn infants.

In the West, it is important to distance children from their animal nature and from sin as early as possible, according to notions transmitted by Christianity. This effort has led to specific practices concerning baptism, swaddling, and protecting the baby's head, which is understood to be the seat of the soul. These very divergent conceptions have a rational basis that nineteenth-century observers and ethnographers could not fathom, imbued as they were with scientific rationalism, for the conceptions in question can be grasped only by observers who can detach themselves from their own representations of reality. We are better situated today to grasp the rational basis for such practices, owing to a proliferation of studies and the questioning of a universal model dominated by the West.

Infant care, and before that pregnancy and childbirth, were unquestionably women's business in all ancient societies. Women—mothers, neighbors, or midwives—advised the pregnant woman, helped her at home during childbirth, and provided initial care for the baby. Men were not viewed as useful; at best, the father prepared the fire for heating water or ran to get the midwife. In Europe, obstetricians began to intervene in the seventeenth century, but only if there was a problem. Even then they worked discreetly, without seeing the woman's body.

The increasing medicalization of birth in the nineteenth and twentieth centuries brought about radical changes: from then on, childbirth took place outside of the family home; the costs of childbirth were covered by society (through a social security system); and men, as professionals authorized to use instruments, gained control of the field. But the movement took hold slowly; it gained dominance only in the second half of the twentieth century, and it is not at all uniform throughout the world.

Breast-Feeding and Wet Nurses. As a general rule, mothers nursed their own children, on demand, for quite a long period (up to two years). The prevailing conception was that nursing was an extension of gestation: milk was viewed as a whitened form of the mother's blood, hence the incompatibility between nursing and sexual relations. Abstinence between spouses was imposed during the entire period of nursing, which explains the recourse to polygamy among certain peoples.

Another solution was the replacement of the mother with a wet nurse. The division of labor on this point is quite ancient: it is attested by the Code of Hammurabi (eighteenth century BCE), which punishes the wet nurse for taking another child to replace a child who has died. The same practice is found in Babylon, in ancient Egypt, in Greece, and in Rome. Rich families delegated nursing chores to live-in wet nurses, who were often slaves. Such delegation presupposed reasoning along economic lines that attributed a higher value to the goods produced by the mother in activities other than nursing than to those produced by nursing itself: a hierarchy of values assigned nursing lower status than goods, such as the woman's social role or her fertility. For wet nurses, mother's milk had a market value that was attested by the wages they received.

Recourse either to live-in nurses (among wealthy families) or to nurses who took children into their own homes (in more modest milieus) became quite extensive throughout Europe starting in the Renaissance, when mercantile activity was developing: in the well-known case of Florence, large numbers of city children were sent to the neighboring countryside. Account books make it possible to reconstitute in great detail the rhythm of placements, the ages of the children placed, the wages paid, and even the clothes given to wet nurses.

Similar practices prevailed in China in the seventeenth century: recourse to wet nurses among families at the highest social levels was the norm, although the practice was criticized by neo-Confucianists. The urbanized Europe of craftsmen and merchants attributed increasing importance to women's work in stalls and workshops; this accounts for the extension of recourse to wet nurses to these milieus. In London, Lyon, and Paris, thousands of children moved between city and country, spending their early years away from their families.

While these practices decreased in frequency in Anglo-Saxon countries after the eighteenth century, in the Latin world they continued throughout the nineteenth century, under the name "nursing industry" or "mercenary nursing." They persisted into the industrial era, with market mechanisms, such as the intervention of intermediaries (called *meneurs*, "leaders," in France), the establishment of fee scales based on social demand, the organization of recruitment centers for wet nurses and of placement zones based on the social origin of the child, and so on.

Influences of Technology. Around 1840, two technological developments, the vulcanization of rubber and industrial production of molded glass baby bottles, made it possible for babies to be bottle fed, including by nurses. Toward the end of the nineteenth century in France, the monthly wage scale—eighteen to twenty-five francs for bottle feeding by a nurse in the country, thirty-five to forty francs for breast-feeding by a nurse in the country, and eighty to one hundred francs for breast-feeding in the child's home—situates the first category among the lowest wages but the last among the best-paid domestic servants.

Still quite common around 1900 in Europe, placing children in the care of nurses gradually disappeared starting with World War I: the model of the mother taking direct care of her own child became dominant and remained so until the 1960s, when salaried work by mothers imposed a multiplication of modes of child care, collective and private. The traditional modes (family, nurses) were complemented by collective child-care systems, such as day nurseries, drop-in centers, and preschools.

Treatment of Children. In certain countries, quite different issues were at stake in the circulation of children. In Oceania, it was traditionally possible for a parent to claim a child that had just been born. The biological parents were required to give the child away. The biological mother could continue to nurse her child, but the adoptive mother provided food for the nursing mother and thus, vicariously, for the child. A child was never given to a sterile woman, who was thought to be incapable of growing *taros*, the tuberous plants that were a staple of the everyday diet.

The circulation of children was quite different in sub-Saharan Africa, and remains so today, since the gift of children can compensate for differences in fertility. But children are also entrusted to others in order to reinforce ties among members of the same lineage, to ensure the family's social advancement via the child, or to allow some family member to profit from the child's capacity to work. Children are often placed in cities and some are able to go to school. In contrast to the European practice of farming out nursing infants, it is rare in Africa for children to be handed over to another family while they are nursing.

Certain categories of children have not been well treated—especially, in Christian countries, children born out of wedlock. Traditionally left exposed on public roads and dependent on the goodwill of strangers, these children were finally taken in by large hospices: these were the first institutions in both Europe and China that organized the responsibility for very young children, brought in wet nurses from the outside, and covered the costs. Between 1780 and 1868, when the tower (*la ruota*) was closed, more than 220,000 children passed through the convent of Santa Catarina alla Ruota in Milan. These children had only a slim chance of survival, since the mortality rate reached 50 percent; however, a significant number (40 percent) finally returned to their parents, proving that abandonment was also a temporary recourse for families in economic difficulty. In the twentieth century, the practice of abandonment decreased considerably, but certain forms can reappear, as attested, for example, by the African children whose parents die of AIDS.

For most children, early childhood was a period of significant risks: infant mortality could be as high as two to three hundred per thousand. Even today, in certain countries the infant mortality rate is more than one hundred per thousand. To protect the health of children, families turned for centuries to magic and/or religious means: they carried out such rites as prophylactic baths or massages, which also had real relational benefits. Starting at birth, the child was cleaned with water or oil and was purified by having someone blow in its ears to dislodge the evil spirits.

In Europe, when a child did not seem to be growing normally, it was taken to a spring consecrated to a saint or to the Virgin; either the child or a piece of its clothing was plunged into the holy water. Certain places specialized in curing given illnesses. Everywhere, babies were supplied with amulets or protective medallions: in Islamic countries, little leather bags containing a verse from the Qur'ān were worn around babies' necks. In Europe, babies wore strings of coral beads intended to help with teething. To treat sicknesses like measles, people turned to analogic medicine: everything that recalled the color red had healing properties (for example, red cloth, red curtains). Vaccination in the nineteenth century, and the systematic surveillance of the health of young children later on, along with other economic and social factors, account for the significant reduction in infant mortality at the end of the nineteenth century in Europe. However, considerable inequality remained, both between geographical regions and between social classes.

Children Become Consumers. In traditional societies, babies did not pollute, and they consumed very little. Except on special occasions, they wore clothes made at home from scraps of old clothing. Diapers—"flags" that covered babies' bottoms—were made from worn-out sheets. Shirts, caps, jackets, swaddling clothes, and other items were made at home. Older children's clothes were handed down to the younger ones. In warm countries, where infants were carried constantly on their mothers' backs, their clothing was reduced to the minimum: the prophylactic necklace.

The child's entrance into the cycle of consumption is a recent phenomenon: it began in the nineteenth century, when mass production supplied layette items in cotton and wool along with toys, cradles, bottles, and even sterilized milk, at lower and lower prices. The notion of the child as capital developed during this period in relation to national efforts to increase infant survival, raise the level of education, and supply society the labor force it needed.

The externalization of expenditures, limited until then, became a widespread phenomenon after World War II in industrialized countries: babies became major consumers of diapers, industrial milk, and special furniture, before beginning to prescribe family spending more generally later on. The cost of a child may have become one of the reasons for a drop in birth rates—to the point of the one-child family in such countries as Italy, Spain, and Japan.

Limiting the number of births is a phenomenon that can be traced from the eighteenth century in western Europe and from later dates in many other countries. Traditionally, birth control entailed post partum abstinence and on-demand breastfeeding, which ensured a space of at least two years between births. The other ways of controlling the number of children included mortality, and, in Europe, delaying the age of marriage.

As the Anglican pastor Thomas Malthus (1766–1834) indicated, mortality is one of the obstacles ("negative checks") to population growth. But recourse to wet nurses exposed women to a new and premature conception: this may be one of the causes of contraception in Europe. To slow down population growth, Malthus himself advocated abstention and late marriage. But couples tended to choose contraception or even abortion instead (Malthus considered these means illicit). Family size decreased in Europe and North America in the nineteenth century; everywhere in the world it declined markedly after World War II, under the influence of the economic and social changes and national policies.

Adult aspirations to happiness have become concentrated on fewer and fewer children, and the physical and psychological investment in the child—often an only child—is much more intense than ever before.

BIBLIOGRAPHY

Boswell, John. *The Kindness of Strangers: The Abandonment of Children in Western Europe from Late Antiquity to the Renaissance.* New York, 1998.

Fildes, Valerie. *Breasts, Bottles, and Babies: A History of Infant Feeding.* Edinburgh, 1986.

Fildes, Valerie. *Wet Nursing: A History from Antiquity to the Present.* New York, 1988.

Fildes, Valerie, Lara Marks, and Hilary Marland, eds. *Women and Children First: International Maternal and Infant Welfare, 1870–1945.* London, 1992.

Furth, Charlotte. "Concepts of Pregnancy, Childbirth, and Infancy in Ch'ing Dynasty China." *Journal of Asian Studies* 46.1 (1987), 7–32.

Gelis, Jacques. *L'arbre et le fruit: La naissance dans l'Occident moderne.* Paris, 1984.

Hunecke, Volker. *I trovaletti di Milano.* Bologna, 1999.

Kertzer, David I. *Sacrificed for Honor: Italian Infant Abandonment and the Politics of Reproductive Control.* Boston, 1993.

Klaus, Alisa. *Every Child a Lion: The Origins of Maternal and Infant Health Policy in the United States and France, 1890–1920.* New York, 1993.

Lallemand, Suzanne. *La circulation des enfants en société traditionnelle: Prêts, dons, échange.* Paris, 1993.

Mause, Lloyd de. *The History of Childhood.* London, 1991.

Mead, Margaret. *Sex and Temperament in Three Primitive Societies.* New York, 1935.

Meckel, Richard A. *Save the Babies: American Public Health Reform and the Prevention of Infant Mortality, 1850–1929.* Baltimore, 1990.

Rollet, Catherine. *La politique à l'égard de la petite enfance sous la IIIe République.* Paris, 1990.

Rollet, Catherine, and Marie-France Morel. *Des bébés et des hommes: Traditions et modernité des soins aux tout-petits.* Paris, 2000.

Sussman, George D. *Selling Mothers' Milk: The Wet-Nursing Business in France, 1715–1914.* Urbana, Chicago, and London, 1982.

CATHERINE ROLLET
Translated from French by Catherine Porter

CHILD LABOR. The words *child labor* evoke the image of British novelist Charles Dickens's "dark satanic mill," where in the 1800s little children worked long hours as factory hands and as sooted chimney sweeps. The words invoke the turn-of-the-century photographs of Lewis Hines, who in the United States captured the images of young girls and boys with dirty faces and tattered clothing working in fields, factories, and the mines of industrializing America. Their small stature, slender frame, and young faces easily distinguished them from adult workers. Children who work, whether paid or unpaid, to produce a good or a service that can be sold in the marketplace for money are considered child laborers. A "child" is a young person (usually dependent on adults for his or her livelihood, whether they are parents, relatives, other adults, or government officials), but the exact ages of childhood depend on the country, culture, and period under consideration. Apart from slavery and family farms, the practice of putting children to work in the West was first recorded in the Middle Ages, when children spun thread to be woven in their father's loom. The practice of having children help or work was part of their training and education. Whether it was working in the fields or assisting in the family's trade, children from the age of three and four contributed to the family enterprise in working-class families before the Industrial Revolution. The idea of children working to increase family income was not viewed by parents or society as cruel or abusive but was recognized as necessary for survival. Parents had worked when they were young, and the same was expected of their offspring.

Preindustrial Child Labor. Most of the children who worked in the fields worked with their families and were not hired laborers who received a wage but, instead, augmented the parents' productivity. Some children were, however, hired labor, who received room and board with a farmer instead of a wage. These children, called "servants" or "servants in husbandry," were often sons and daughters of paupers who served out apprenticeships that were negotiated by their parents (usually for seven years). They usually worked longer hours, more days, and had fewer holidays than the children working with their families. Some children were employed as helpers in domestic production (or what is called "cottage industry") or as domestic servants. Girls and boys worked in a vast array of industries as dressmakers, hat makers, and earthenware painters to name just a few. These "sweated trades," as they are often referred to in the literature, were practiced in workshops located in the family home or in sheds attached to the backs of cottages, where there were as few as three and as many as two hundred workers. The workshop hours and conditions varied considerably and depended on the trade and the owner. In Great Britain, from sunup to sundown, workshops expected as many hours as those needed on farms; in some trades, like dressmaking, the hours were even longer (averaging fifteen), while in others, like pottery, the hours were shorter (ten to twelve). Another group of child laborers who worked in the home for extremely long hours consisted of domestic servants. Unlike the child workers in the "sweated trades" who lived at home, domestic servants lived with the family for whom they worked. Typically, girls became domestic servants and, although their work was considered productive (cooking, cleaning, caring for babies, etc.), it was unpaid work because the girls received room, board, and training in the domestic skills important for marriage. This job also required children to work long hours, because domestic servants were expected to respond at all hours, as needed.

Industrial Child Labor. As Great Britain industrialized, from 1760 to 1830, young children also began to work outside the home in factories and mines. Although the majority of children continued to work in traditional occupations throughout the Industrial Revolution, the employment and exploitation of children as young as three and four in the textile mills and the coal mines especially captured the attention of novelists, historians, and economic historians. The extent of the employment of children and the role that child labor played in the British Industrial Revolution has been a hotly debated topic (see Hermann Freudenberger, Francis Mather, and Clark Nardinelli [1984], Marjorie Cruickshank [1981], and Carolyn Tuttle [1999] on the large proportion of the textile [50 percent] and mining [30 percent] work force that were children). Based on the large numbers of children working in these industries, the essential tasks they performed, and the importance of these industries to industrialization, some researchers have concluded that child labor played a crucial role in the British Industrial Revolution. In contrast, Hugh Cunningham (1990) found sufficient evidence from the *Report on the Poor Laws in 1834* to argue the opposite; he claims that the idleness of children (without mandatory schooling) was more of a problem during the Industrial Revolution than was employment. This conflicting evidence indicates that a national labor market for children did not exist but that the labor market for children was segmented by region and industry, with employment high in industrial towns and low in rural villages.

Sara Horrell and Jane Humphries (1995) and Carolyn Tuttle (1999) argue that children's role in production and the family changed dramatically during industrialization. In preindustrial, traditional economies, children had worked in the fields and in homes as auxiliary workers. Once small enterprises formed, children helped their parents or a neighbor in production. As the country began to industrialize, some children left the farm and home to work for a stranger in a factory or mine. The child workers were then no longer mere auxiliary workers but primary workers who could perform as well, and sometimes better, than adults in the production process. For children, the nature and conditions of work changed dramatically; they no longer worked with their family under the supervision of a parent but in a large establishment alongside other children. They were bound by a contract that set their work hours and the number of days they worked, predetermined the length of their breaks and holidays, and established rules about daily conduct, all of which had to be followed to avoid fines or punishment.

The factory debate. Whether this initial group of industrial child laborers were exploited is a subject of debate. The pessimists argue that the abuses were considerable and that child labor during the British Industrial Revolution was dramatically different from child labor during other periods of British history. In the mid- to late-1800s, Karl Marx and Frederick Engels (and in 1920, J. L. and Barbara Hammond) painted a picture of greedy industrialists who employed children as young as five for twelve to sixteen hours a day, six days a week; the children worked in hot, stuffy, overcrowded factories to earn as little as four shillings per week. The optimists, however, argue that the pessimist position exaggerates the extent of the deplorable conditions and abuses because they relied on biased evidence from the *Factory Inspector Reports* (1831–1832 [706] XV). Instead, S. J. Clapham (1904), Clark Nardinelli (1990), and Andrew Ure (1835) claimed that factory work did not seem to be any worse for children than work on the farm or at home and that the wages were clearly better.

This factory debate did attract the attention of the British populace, and it eventually swayed the sentiments of Parliament to interfere on behalf of children. Reformers passed the First Factory Act of 1802 that set maximum hours for children at twelve and improved the conditions of cotton mills. During the nineteenth century, as many as fifteen child-labor laws were eventually passed in Great Britian to reduce the employment of children in textile factories and mines. Several historians view these laws as instrumental in reducing the employment of children in Great Britain, whereas others argue the opposite, because the fines were negligible and the laws were not adequately enforced.

Child labor in Europe and in the United States. Child labor also played a role in the industrialization of other European countries and in North America. According to Rene De Herdt (1996), child labor during the nineteenth century was associated with industrialization and poverty in Belgium; children there worked in almost every sector of the economy (agriculture, craft industries, and brickyards) and tended to be concentrated in the spinning mills of Ghent and the coal mines of Wallonia. Enriqueta Cura (1996) argues that in Catalonia (Spain), from 1850 to 1920,

child labor was associated with industrialization and the family life cycle; as mechanization and automation moved work out of the home and into the factory, the relatively high wages of children replaced the mother's contribution to family income. In the United States, children were an important source of labor during industrialization, and Juliet Mofford (1997) reports that in 1880, some 1 million U.S. children (under age sixteen) worked in the economy. By 1900, 1.7 million children worked in U.S. industry.

The Labor Market for Children. In Great Britain, the labor market for children was competitive except for instances of subcontracting. T. S. Ashton (1964), David Landes (1969), and Clark Nardinelli (1990) have documented the large number of producers that coexisted and competed for consumers' money—ranging from small-scale producers in the cottage industry to large-scale factories in urban centers. The existence of a monopsony was also unlikely, despite the concentration of the British textile industry in the North and the mining industry in the South. Evidence from the *Factory Returns of 1836 and 1850* shows that there were numerous textile factories in the manufacturing districts and no counties with only one factory. Similarly, the *1842 Report on the Mines* show forty-eight collieries (coal mines and processing sheds) in Derbyshire, eighty collieries in Yorkshire, and 164 collieries in Lancashire. The labor market was not competitive, however, when parents "hired" their own children to assist them; this system of subcontracting was used in textile spinning, where spinners hired their own "piecers," and in coal mining, where the hewers hired their own "putters." In these cases, children were hired, trained, supervised, and paid by their parents.

Supply. The supply of child labor varied with the attitudes of parents, the fertility rate, and the existence and effectiveness of government legislation that became directed at the curbing of child labor. The attitudes of parents varied considerably among cultures and changed with time, as many countries developed or adopted a different view of childhood. In Europe, because work was part of poor childhoods and was not frowned upon by society, poverty increased the supply of child labor. Poor families had difficulty surviving, so putting their children to work outside the home often meant that the family might continue. Although the contribution that child labor made to family income may have been relatively small in preindustrial societies, it still helped to improve the family's position. Then, when countries began to industrialize, the opportunities created for children in the marketplace put the dream within reach, of crawling out of poverty and bettering the family's economic position. In New England in 1800, children, on average, could earn one-sixth to one-fourth of an adult man's wages. In the Northern textile factories of 1830s Great Britain, children could earn, on average, one-third of an adult man's wages. In Belgium in 1846, a survey of Ghent workers revealed that a factory child could earn one-fifth to one-third of an adult man's wages.

Some cultures thought of childhood as a time when the young acquired the skills and the training to become independent, self-supporting adults. The age at which this learning begins and the form it takes (apprenticeships or schooling) depends on the cultural traditions of the people within a local, regional, or national sphere. J. A. Gathia (1983) and Ramesh Kanbargi (1988) have shown that in India, many feel that the learning process should start soon after birth, when the human body is soft, flexible, and pliable, because a child can learn to twist, bend, stretch, or assume the different positions required by specific jobs. Other cultures have viewed childhood as a time to treasure children, which discouraged the employment of children. Osamu Saito (1996) reported this type of attitude to be prevalent in Japan during the mid-nineteenth century. Consequently, few young children but more juveniles worked in factories as Japan industrialized.

An increased birth rate or decreased infant mortality rate might increase the supply of child labor. This factor may have been important during the 1800s demographic revolution in Great Britain, yet a positive relationship between the dependency rate and the supply of child labor does not always occur. For example, in the United States, the steady decline in the birth rates between 1820 and 1840 did not reduce the nineteenth-century child labor force by much. Government policies have been established to discourage the employment of children and thereby decrease the labor supply, and mandatory schooling laws require children to attend. Schooling laws originally depended on the date of passage, the size of the fine, and the strictness of enforcement. In Great Britain, education laws were not originally a deterrent to child labor, because elementary education was not compulsory until 1881. Belgium had passed its schooling law relatively early, in 1842; although the law required each community to establish one free primary school for the poor, most of those children still worked because the law was not compulsory. Some historians would argue that it takes more than laws to change the supply of child labor—it also takes a change in societal attitudes about the value of education. These attitudes are best illustrated with the case of Japan just before industrialization. In 1872, the new Meiji government passed the Educational Ordinance, which declared the education of children a national priority. Osamu Saito (1996) reported that primary school enrollment had increased by 1905 and that the employment of young children was then relatively low in Japan as compared with Great Britain, Belgium, and France.

Demand. The demand for child labor has varied, depending on the relative costs of inputs, the labor require-

CHILD LABOR. Fourteen-year-old boy working in the mule room at the Berkshire Cotton Mills in Adams, Massachusetts, 1916. (Lewis W. Hine/Prints and Photographs Division, Library of Congress)

ments of the technology, and the existence and enforcement of deterrent legislation. Producers keep costs down by hiring children, whose wages were and are the lowest of all workers; so demand for child labor exists because children can substitute for adults when the production process requires unskilled workers. With industrialization, the demand for child labor increases for another reason. The centralization of production in modern industry meant a loss of worker autonomy and a new work discipline. The new emphasis on regular hours, punctuality, constant attendance, conformity, and obedience made it especially difficult for the early factory owners to recruit workers. Children who were by nature submissive and obedient were, therefore, the most desirable recruits for the new factory regime.

There is considerable debate regarding the impact of technological change on the demand for child labor. William Lazonick (1979) and Clark Nardinelli (1990) have argued that most of the mechanization that occurred with the Industrial Revolution was labor-saving and required only a few children to assist adults. In Great Britain's textile industry, they point to the invention of the common mule (1779), the self-actor (1829) and the power loom (1785) as examples of inventions that created the need for assistants but did not lead to the replacement of adults with children. As these machines were refined and enlarged, moreover, the demand for child labor fell. In contrast, Carolyn Tuttle (1999) has argued that the technological innovation that accompanied the Industrial Revolution (mechanization, automation, and the centralization of production) increased the demand for child labor, because it was labor-intensive, labor-substituting, or labor-specific technological change. The centralization of production increased the possibilities of specialization, and the division of labor reduced many procedures to simple one-step tasks, and these increased the demand for children (labor-intensive). Instead of increasing the number of auxiliary workers, inventions like the water-frame (1769), the self-actor, and the power loom, which mechanized and automated the process of spinning and weaving, allowed children to substitute for adult workers (labor-substituting). In some work situations, the demand for child labor increased because children had a comparative advantage through small size or agility (labor-specific).

Child Labor in Developing Countries. Today, child labor continues to play a role in the industrialization of developing countries. The International Labor Organization (ILO) and the United Nations Center on Human Rights have stated that child labor is prevalent in nearly all developing countries. In 1996, the ILO estimated that at least 250 million children between the ages of five and fourteen are workers. Asia employs the greatest number of children, with India employing roughly 44 million child laborers. Family poverty, the cultural views of childhood, and the cost of labor are offered as explanations in developing countries, despite child labor legislation. The ILO views poverty as the primary factor, with child labor as a part of a family survival strategy or to help when a major household crisis occurs. In many cultures, regardless of the family's economic status, custom dictates that children work as part of the maturation process, to become independent of one's family. Critics of child labor believe that children are used mainly as cheap labor, which allows a country to produce competitive products. Others argue that children are employed because they have a comparative advantage, as, for example, in tying small knots to make carpets (in Nepal), in stooping over to weave carpets with nimble fingers and supple bodies (in India), and in carrying coal from narrow mine tunnels, owing to their small stature (in northeast India).

Today, such children no longer work in the formal sector, in large factories or mills, but have moved to the informal sector where child labor laws do not apply or are not strictly enforced. They work in small sheds, cottages, garages, and shops, performing many of the same tasks as their predecessors during the British Industrial Revolution. Children still spin and weave cotton, silk, and wool in the textile industries of Brazil, India, and Mexico. Children carry dirt and sift out precious metals in tin, chromium, and gold mines of Colombia and Brazil. Children sew cloth in the garment industries of Bangladesh, Brazil, Guatemala, Indonesia, Morocco, the Philippines, and Thailand. Children harvest agricultural products by cutting sisal leaves in Brazil, picking coffee in Africa, and picking fruits and vegetables in Mexico and parts of the United States. Other children work under verandas, in fields, and in greenhouses. Children crouch at looms to make hand-knotted carpets in Egypt, India, Morocco, and Pakistan.

International organizations, government officials, and labor leaders have joined forces to try to break the persistence of child labor in developing countries with only moderate success. Unlike the child labor that arose during the industrialization of Europe and North America in the eighteenth and nineteenth century, child labor today exists despite both child labor laws and mandatory schooling laws. Clearly, there are lessons to be learned from the past that shed light on the persistence of child labor today.

BIBLIOGRAPHY

Ashton, T. S. *The Industrial Revolution, 1760–1830.* Oxford, 1964. A seminal book that summarizes the economic changes of the British Industrial Revolution.

Clapham, S. J. *The Lancashire Cotton Industry.* Manchester, 1904.

Cruickshank, Marjorie. *Children and Industry.* Manchester, 1981.

Cura, Enriqueta Camps i. "Family Strategies and Children's Work Patterns: Some Insights from Industrializing Catalonia, 1850–1920." In *Child Labour in Historical Perspective, 1800–1985: Case Studies from Europe, Japan and Colombia*, edited by Hugh Cunningham and Pier Paolo Viazzo, pp. 57–71. Florence, 1996. The economic, social, and cultural factors contributing to the use of child labor in Britain, Belgium, Spain, Japan, and Colombia.

Cunningham, Hugh. "The Employment and Unemployment of Children in England, c. 1680–1851." *Past and Present* 126 (1990), 115–150.

De Herdt, Rene. "Child Labour in Belgium: 1800–1914." In *Child Labour in Historical Perspective, 1800–1985: Case Studies From Europe, Japan and Colombia*, edited by Hugh Cunningham and Pier Paolo Viazzo, pp. 23–39. Florence, 1996.

Engels, Frederick. *The Conditions of the Working Class in England.* Translated from German by the Institute of Marxism-Leninism, Moscow. London, 1845.

Freudenberger, Hermann, Francis J. Mather, and Clark Nardinelli. "A New Look at the Early Factory Labour Force." *Journal of Economic History* 44 (1984), 1085–1090.

Gathia, J. A. "Child Workers in the Informal Sector: Role of NGOs—Some Reflections." In *Women and Child Workers in Unorganized Sector*, edited by K. D. Gangrade and J. A. Gathia, chapter 7. New Delhi, India, 1983.

Hammond, J. L., and Barbara Hammond. *The Skilled Labourer, 1760–1832.* London, 1920.

Horrell, Sara, and Jane Humphries. "The Exploitation of Little Children: Child Labor and the Family Economy in the Industrial Revolution." *Explorations in Economic History* 32.4 (1995), 485–516.

International Labour Office. *Child Labour: Targeting the Intolerable.* Geneva, 1996.

Kanbargi, Ramesh. "Child Labour in India: The Carpet Industry of Varanasi." In *Combatting Child Labour*, edited by Assefa Bequele and Jo Boyden, pp. 93–108. Geneva, 1988.

Landes, David. *The Unbound Prometheus*. Cambridge, 1969. A seminal book on the British Industrial Revolution.

Lazonick, William. "Industrial Relations and Technical Change: The Case of the Self-Acting Mule." *Cambridge Journal of Economics* 3 (1979), 231–262.

Marx, Karl. *Capital*, vol. 1. Chicago, 1906. Several good translations from the German *Das Kapital* (3 vols., 1867–1894) are available.

Mofford, Juliet H., ed. *Child Labor in America*. Carlisle, Mass., 1997.

Nardinelli, Clark. *Child Labor and the Industrial Revolution*. Bloomington, Ind., 1990.

Saito, Osamu. "Children's Work, Industrialism, and the Family Economy in Japan, 1872–1926." In *Child Labour in Historical Perspective 1800–1985: Case Studies from Europe, Japan, and Colombia*, edited by Hugh Cunningham and Pier Paolo Viazzo, pp. 73–90. Florence, 1996.

Tuttle, Carolyn. *Hard at Work in Factories and Mines: The Economics of Child Labor during the British Industrial Revolution*. Boulder, Colo., 1999.

Ure, Andrew. *The Philosophy of Manufactures*. London, 1835.

U.S. Department of Labor. *By the Sweat and Toil of Children: The Use of Child Labor in American Imports*, vol. 1. Washington, D.C., 1994. The first of seven volumes of confirmed information on today's employment of children in developing countries. An excellent starting point for anyone researching child labor in Latin America, China, Africa, and India.

Ware, Caroline. *The Early New England Cotton Manufacture*. New York, 1966.

CAROLYN TUTTLE

CHILDREN. The contemporary view held by Western industrialized nations that children are innocent, fragile, and vulnerable individuals who are both physically and emotionally dependent on adults for their survival has its roots in 1700s Europe. Before that, children in Europe and colonial America were viewed as "imperfect adults" who were to be seen and not heard. Once children could survive without their mothers, wet nurses, or nannies, they joined the community and mingled with adults in all aspects of life—in the streets, fields, workshops, and social establishments. The child's world and the adult's world were not different or separate. As Lawrence Stone noted in *The Family, Sex, and Marriage in England, 1500–1800* (London, 1977), England viewed children as rational, responsible individuals who had to work as hard as adults to sustain themselves. This view of childrens' socioeconomic role changed in time and varied by class.

Role of Children in Family and Society. Among the European upper classes, parents began to view their children as nonadults, distinct from themselves, in the thirteenth century. Children of the noble and middle classes were no longer dressed like adults; they began to wear robes and false sleeves, which indicated that they were to be handled carefully. Between the fifteenth century and the seventeenth, formal schooling was substituted for apprenticeship in the education of noble and middle-class children. By the eighteenth century, such children were no longer viewed as "imperfect" adults but as a source of amusement and gratification for adults. Mothers adopted a new coddling attitude and the health and education of children became a chief preoccupation for all wealthy parents. In contrast, from the early Middle Ages to the fifteenth century, apprenticeship was a way of life for European children of the working class. They learned their manners and a trade by serving adults and by participating in adult life. For majority, from the peasant and laboring classes, this type of training was usual into the nineteenth century and the early twentieth. In the United States, the federal child labor laws were passed only in 1938 (mainly through the Fair Labor Standards Act). In France, during the nineteenth century, Colin Heywood (*Childhood in Nineteenth-Century France*, Cambridge, 1988) reported that rural childhoods were short because of the longstanding tradition of putting children to work on the farm, beginning at age seven. Similarly, Ivy Pinchbeck and Margaret Hewitt's research on *Children in English Society* (London, 1973) found that children were viewed as "little adults" in Great Britain and, by law, were held accountable for their actions at age seven. This mature image of children of the lower classes were reinforced in cities and towns, where children were dressed like adults and some even frequented ale houses and brothels. Today, the preindustrial view of children of the working class as "miniature adults" who must share their parents' toil persists in many developing countries. International organizations and government officials have attempted to protect these children by asking countries to adopt the United Nations Convention on the Rights of the Child (passed in 1989), which establishes basic rights to food, shelter, medical care, and education for children under the age of eighteen.

Most social and economic historians (J. L. and Barbara Hammond, Ivy Pinchbeck, Margaret Hewitt, John Rule, Edward Shorter and Lawrence Stone) concur that children of poor and working-class parents in preindustrial economies had very different roles in the family than those of the upper classes. In John Rule's *The Experience of Labour in Eighteenth Century English Industry* (New York, 1981), he observed that the presence of children in a poor family created a family life cycle. Typically, the birth of a child drained a young family's income and plunged them into poverty. Once the child was physically able to work, he or she began to add more to the family's income than he or she consumed. As the child or children grew older and contributed more to the family's enterprise, family income reached its peak. Once a child left home to marry and form a new household, income decreased and the family began the descent into poverty again. Given this cycle, the more children a family had, the greater the potential income they might generate at its peak. In economic terms, children were viewed as positive assets that became productive after very little investment. This stands in sharp contrast to today's children of industrialized nations, who require a considerable investment of time and money before becoming productive members of the economy.

The role of children in the family and in society affects the motivation to have children. Identifying the factors that alter that motivation and how they may vary by class and change through time have been instrumental in examining fertility rates. Specifically, demographers have observed a significant decline in fertility (from an average of six or more births per women to two) and in mortality rates as countries industrialized, birth control and improved hygiene and health care contributed to these changes. This is contrary to Robert Malthus's prediction from his *An Essay on the Principal of Population* (1798; rev. ed. 1803) that economic growth would cause world population to increase faster than the food supply and lead to malnutrition and a subsistence standard of living. Consequently, several economists and demographers have developed models to analyze family behavior in an attempt to understand the causes of the demographic transition that accompanied economic modernization. Theodore Schultz (1973, 1974) and Richard Easterlin (1985) have created a model where the number of children born to a mother, and survive, is thought to be determined by the interactions between the supply and the demand for children. Therefore, fertility is affected by the parents' motivation for wanting (or demanding) children and is responsive to changes in economic conditions. In these fertility models, Gary Becker (1960, 1991) views children as consumption or production goods, while Schultz views them as forms of human capital. The main sources of the demand for children in this framework are the following: (1) to enjoy as a consumption good; (2) to acquire as a production or investment good; and (3) to secure as insurance against crises, tragedies, and poverty in old age.

The "Demand" for Children. Becker (1973) models the demand for children by using the theory of demand for consumer durables—where children are considered a consumption good because they are a source of personal satisfaction for parents; the number of children a couple has then depends on the value placed on a child (as a good) in relation to other goods. In that context, the demand for children is affected by three factors: parents' tastes, the "price" of having and raising children, and the level of family income. People who want to have children have certain "tastes," or "preferences," whereby children provide them

"utility," or satisfaction—the stronger their "tastes," the higher their demand for children. Easterlin (1985) argues that modernization tends, on balance, to lower the demand for children; urbanization and the introduction of new consumer goods decrease household "tastes" for children relative to other goods, while increasing the desire to purchase the new goods and enjoy the new lifestyle—which becomes incompatible with having children. Becker claims that the cost of having and raising children rises with modernization.

According to the law of demand, if children are costly to bear and raise, then the number of children demanded decreases as the cost of having and raising them increases. In Becker's model, the net cost, the "price," of having children is equal to the present value of expected outlays, plus the imputed value of the parents' services, minus the sum of the present value of the expected money return, minus the imputed value of the child's services. Thus, the value of the parents' nonmarket work, the discomfort and risks of pregnancy and delivery, the costs of avoiding pregnancies and deliveries, as well as the expenditures on food, clothing, and education—all are part of the costs of having a child. Becker argues that the market value of the mother's time in producing and rearing children is a significant portion of the total costs of having a child. This implies that the industrialization of the household, as articulated by Barbara Bergmann in *The Economic Emergence of Women* (New York, 1986), would lead to an increase in the demand for children, because cooking and cleaning becomes less time intensive with inventions like frozen food, dishwashers, and laundry washers and dryers. That effect must have been small, however, because there was a large decline in fertility in developed countries since 1900, which may be understood in light of women's increased labor force participation and earning power during the twentieth century. The demand for children decreased because the opportunity cost of the mother's time (what she could earn in the market) increased, which also increased the net cost of having and rearing children.

The demand for children may increase from a decrease in the net cost of having children in economies where young children work and contribute to family income (on the farm, in the family enterprise, or in the market). In preindustrial economies, children of poor and working-class families have been and continue to be important contributors to family output and income, both in the agricultural sector and the informal sector (or cottage industry). The custom of putting young children to work (at home or in the work place) was present in preindustrial Great Britain, France, Belgium, Spain, and the United States; it persists today especially in Brazil, Colombia, Guatemala, Mexico, Pakistan, Thailand, and Zimbabwe. An increase in the earning potential of children may increase the working-class family's demand for children. Thus, this model would predict an increase in the demand for children with industrialization. Child labor in industrializing Great Britain, Belgium, France, Spain (in Catalonia), Japan, Colombia, and the United States was used primarily in the textile mills but also as a notable part of the workforces in glass factories, tobacco factories, match factories, paper mills, and mines.

Work or School? Becker's third factor in influencing the family's demand for children is the level of family income. The income factor is not straightforward, however, because nineteenth-century trends for urban families have contradicted the prediction of economic theory. Industrialization, if accompanied by an increase in the standard of living, should cause the family's demand for children to increase. This can be explained theoretically if children are considered a normal good, then a rise in family income would increase the number of children a family would desire. According to economists and demographers Halvor Gille (1960), Gwendolyn Johnson (1960), and Clyde Kiser (1960), the relationship between fertility and wealth during modernization among urban families became partially or completely negative in Europe and the United States. Jacob Mincer (1963) explained this contradiction by arguing that the effective "price" of children increases with rising income, because the wives of men with higher incomes also have greater earning potential. R. J. Willis (1973) argued that the increase in income creates an increase in the net cost of having children; he claimed that the effective "price" of children increases with income, because the wives of men with higher incomes also have higher values of time. Richard Easterlin's (1985) relative income hypothesis predicts two opposing responses to an increase in income (relative to the previous generation). On the one hand, an increase in the father's income relative to his father would cause his demand for children to increase; on the other hand, if the relative income of the wife also increases, the demand for children would fall.

Gary Becker and Gregg Lewis (1973), however, offered a very different explanation. They claimed that the effective "price" of children rises with income, because of the interaction between the quantity and quality of children (they define *quantity* as the number of children and *quality* as the level of expenditure spent on a child). Their theory predicts a strong negative relationship between the quantity and quality of children because of the interaction of these two variables in the family's utility function (the shadow price of quality depends on quantity and the shadow price of quantity depends on quality). For example, the "price" of having high-quality children is greater with the more children (quantity) had by the family. Thus, the more money spent on a child, the higher the quality—and this implies that when family income increases, parents choose to have better "quality" children, rather than more children.

Hugh Cunningham (1996) argues that toward the end of the nineteenth century there was a new valuation of childhood in Britain, which led to the end of child labor and a decline in working-class in family size. The psychic value of each child began to increase and to exceed the economic value of each child. The balance of power within the working-class family economy changed, and the flow of economic resources began to go from parents to children, rather than from children to parents. Children stopped working and contributing to family income as parents began investing in their childrens' education. Economists would say that children went from being a production good (source of money income) to a consumption good (source of satisfaction) within the family. The great exception to this trend among industrializing nations was Japan, where the psychic value of children was always high, with children viewed as "little treasures." Children under ten were not expected to work or contribute to the family's income. As Osamu Saito's research (1996) on child labor revealed, Japanese parents placed a greater value on young children's education than on their wages. Since the economic returns for young children were negligible, Japanese families were smaller than those of other industrialized countries, because the "demand" for children was lower.

According to Schultz (1973, 1974), children are viewed as heterogeneous forms of human capital (or investments). Parents may make the investment because they derive satisfaction, productive services and, possibly, income from their children. The specific form of human capital depends on the age of the child as well as the general wealth of the family and the country. In rich countries, parents may acquire current and future personal satisfaction from their children whether they are young toddlers or teenagers. In poor countries, parents may also receive income or contributions to their future real income, depending on the age of the child; until they are old enough to work, the return or rewards in having young children is psychic. Once a child can work in poor countries, the rewards increase, because of useful work they perform in unpaid work (helping the family enterprise) or in paid work (outside the home). The level of investment that each parent makes in a child depends on the relative cost in terms of time and money that child bearing and rearing requires—compared to the relative return, in terms of personal satisfaction and the work or income a child provides. For example, an increase in the number of opportunities for a child to work will increase the potential contribution a child can make to family income, which would increase the demand for children. Michael Anderson (*Family Structure in Nineteenth Century Lancashire*, Cambridge, 1971) and David Levine (*Reproducing Families: The Political Economy of English Population History*, Cambridge, 1987) use this model to explain the larger family size of the working class in the English industrial cities of Lancashire and Manchester, where a child's contribution to family income was important during the Industrial Revolution.

For several reasons, an increase in the economic value of education decreases the demand for children. Becker (1991) and Easterlin (1985) argued that compulsory education may increase the relative cost (or "price") of children, by reducing their potential contribution to family income in the form of child labor. In addition, education improves the income-earning potential of women, which raises their opportunity cost of time and thereby decreases the demand for children. Easterlin also pointed out that the rise of education decreases the "taste" for children because it offers alternative lifestyles that are incompatible with children. He also argued that education can lead to smaller families, because it leads to higher standards with regard to child care and rearing that put a greater emphasis on the "quality" of children over the quantity. Many economic historians would argue that the impact of schooling on the employment of children, their net cost, and their parents' demand were not substantial until after countries experienced industrialization. David Mitch (*The Rise of Popular Literacy in Victorian England: The Influence of Private Choice and Public Policy*, Philadelphia, 1992) and E. G. West (*Education and the Industrial Revolution*, London, 1975) concur that the increase in school enrollment in Great Britain occurred late in the nineteenth century, with laws passed only in 1891. Levine even showed that the fertility decline in Great Britain was completed before comprehensive schools admitted their first students. The same was true for Belgium, as Rene De Herdt (1985) found, that despite passing its first labor law during the early stages of industrialization in 1842, parents continued to send their children to work because the law did not make schooling compulsory.

The existence of legislation that prohibits children from working or requires them to attend school reduces the family's economic returns from children by imposing fines, which would reduce the net wage received by working children. In the case of child labor laws, the existence of fines and the cost of reporting imposes an implicit tax on the employer's demand for child labor—and, properly enforced, child labor laws carrying significant fines should decrease the demand for children. The impact of child labor laws on the employment of children remains a hotly debated topic. Economic historian Clark Nardinelli (1980) has argued their insignificance in reducing child labor in Great Britain, while international organizations, like the International Labor Organization and the International Confederation of Free Trade Unions, lament their ineffectiveness today in developing countries.

Children as Insurance. Parents often view their children as a form of insurance against illness, unemployment, and old age. In preindustrial and early industrial societies, there was typically one person within the household who earned the greatest portion of family income. Although other household members contributed to this person's productive effort, or worked independently in the market, their combined contributions might be smaller. Therefore, the family's survival depended on the ability of one individual to earn a large enough income that, when supplemented by other family members' contributions, was sufficient to provide the necessities. If this primary provider were to become ill, disabled, or unemployed, the children were a way to insure the family against the resulting sudden and dramatic decline in income. Economic historians Enriqueta Cural (1996), Osamu Saito (1996), and development economists Mead Cain and A. B. M. Mozumder (1981) show how child labor was part of a family strategy for poor and working-class families in Catalonia, Japan, and rural South Asia, respectively. Several young children (each with a low earning potential) or an older child (with a higher earning potential) could secure employment that might almost replace the breadwinner's contribution and allow the family to maintain roughly the same standard of living. Poor and working-class parents also looked on their children as "old-age insurance," to guarantee themselves a more comfortable standard of living in old age (before pensions and various versions of welfare and social security were enacted in the twentieth century). The need for children as a provision for old age and its impact on fertility were noted by demographers E. A. Wrigley and R. S. Schofield in *The Population History of England, 1541–1871: A Reconstruction* (Cambridge, 1981). They asserted that when deciding on how many children to try to have (in a time of no birth control but high infant death), young parents considered the time when they could no longer work. Poor parents with no source of income might stay with one of their surviving sons or daughters who had a new household. The grown children might provide them with food, shelter, and health care. As a family's savings increased or other forms of insurance and pensions became available (life insurance, social security, private pension funds), this motive would disappear, thereby decreasing the demand for children.

[*See also* Child Care; Child Labor; Family Structures and Kinship; *and* Household.]

BIBLIOGRAPHY

Becker, Gary. "An Economic Analysis of Fertility." In *Demographic and Economic Change in Developed Countries.* New York, 1960. Papers presented at a conference of the Universities-National Bureau Committee for Economic Research, examining population change and its economic effects.

Becker, Gary. *A Treatise on the Family.* Cambridge, 1991.

Becker, Gary, and Gregg Lewis. "On the Interaction between the Quantity and Quality of Children." *Journal of Political Economy* 81.2, part 2 (1973), S279–S288. This entire issue is devoted to an analysis of fertility.

Cain, Mead, and A. B. M. Mozumder. "Labor Market Structure and Reproductive Behaviour in Rural South Asia." In *Child Work, Poverty, and Underdevelopment,* edited by Gerry Rodgers and Guy Standing, pp. 245–281, Geneva, 1981.

Cunningham, Hugh. "Combatting Child Labour: The British Experience." In *Child Labour in Historical Perspective, 1800–1985: Case Studies from Europe, Japan, and Colombia,* edited by Hugh Cunningham and Pier Paolo Viazzo, pp. 41–53, Florence, 1996. Available from the Italian office of UNICEF and contains an insightful interdisciplinary examination of child labor in several countries as they industrialized.

Cura, Enriqueta. "Family Strategies and Children's Work Patterns: Some Insights from Industralzing Catalonia, 1850–1920." In *Child Labour in Historical Perspective, 1800–1985; Case Studies from Europe, Japan, and Colombia,* edited by Hugh Cunningham and Pier Paolo Viazzo, pp. 57–71, Florence, 1996.

De Herdt, Rene. "Child Labour in Belgium: 1800–1914." In *Child Labour in Historical Perspective, 1800–1985: Case Studies from Europe, Japan, and Colombia,* edited by Hugh Cunningham and Pier Paolo Viazzo, pp. 23–39, Florence, 1996.

Easterlin, Richard, and Eileen Crimmins. *Fertility Revolution: A Supply-Demand Analysis.* Chicago, 1985.

Gille, Halvor. "An International Survey of Recent Fertility Trends." In *Demographic and Economic Change in Developed Countries,* pp. 17–35, Princeton, 1960.

Hammond, J. L., and Barbara Hammond. *Town Laborer.* New York, 1937.

Johnson, Gwendolyn. "Differential Fertility in European Countries." In *Demographic and Economic Change in Developed Countries,* pp. 36–76, Princeton, 1960.

Kiser, Clyde. "Differential Fertility in the United States". In *Demographic and Economic Change in Developed Countries,* pp. 77–116. Princeton, 1960.

Mincer, Jacob. "Labor Force Participation of Married Women." In *Aspects of Labor Economics.* New York, 1963.

Nardinelli, Clark. "Child Labor and the Factory Acts." *Journal of Economic History* 40.4. (1980), 739–755.

Saito, Osamu. "Children's Work, Industrialism and the Family Economy in Japan, 1872–1926." In *Child Labour in Historical Perspective, 1800–1985: Case Studies from Europe, Japan, and Colombia,* edited by Hugh Cunningham and Pier Paolo Viazzo. pp. 41–53, Florence, 1996.

Schultz, Theodore W. "The Value of Children: An Economic Perspective." *Journal of Political Economy* 81.2, part 2 (1973), S2–S13.

Schultz, Theodore W. *Economics of the Family: Marriage, Children, and Human Capital.* Chicago, 1974.

Shorter, Edward. *The Making of the Modern Family.* New York, 1975.

Trattner, Walter I. *Crusade for the Children: A History of the National Child Labor Committee and Child Labor Reform in America.* Chicago, 1970.

Willis, R. J. "A New Approach to the Economic Theory of Fertility." *Journal of Political Economy* 81.2, part 2 (1973), S14–S64.

CAROLYN TUTTLE

CHILE. Chile began its existence on the periphery of the Spanish Empire. After the conflict of independence, the new nation had to struggle in the 1820s with its large distance from its trading partners (primarily Peru and Great Britain), its small population, and its poorly developed transportation network. The population has increased from more than a million in 1835 to more than 15 million in the first years of the twenty-first century. Most Chileans are mestizos, a mixture of white and Indian. While most people worked in the countryside into the early twentieth century, international trade, particularly the export of minerals, drove economic improvement. Today, the country is highly urbanized with more than 5 million living in the capital city of Santiago. The nation has a grass domestic product (GDP) of more than U.S. $75 billion, which means a per capita income of more than U.S. $4,900. It is relatively prosperous in comparison with most other Latin American nations. It has a middle class, severe smog in the capital, and a highly unequal distribution of income and wealth.

A major element in Chile's development can be traced to size alone and the difficulties of overcoming a small internal market. Other elements are the legacy of the Spanish Empire, the evolution of forced-labor and debt-peonage systems, and the monopoly of key resources, especially land, in the hands of the few. A final aspect is the result of international markets, since Chile has rarely had strong leverage in its terms of trade. The outcome has been a nation with high levels of vulnerability to foreign markets and, sometimes, to the goals of foreign governments and corporations.

The Nineteenth Century. Independent Chile's first governments were liberal, and by the mid-1820s, the new state was deeply in debt. In 1829, landlords and merchants under the leadership of Diego Portales (1793–1837) rebelled against the liberals. They won the conflict and imposed the Constitution of 1833 and a government dominated by the president. Elite rule provided fairly stable government, and by the late 1830s, the economy was growing.

Santiago was the administrative center while Valparaíso became the nation's chief port. Customs duties, primarily imports, provided a major part of the government's income. Tariffs also protected the interests of agriculture but not of manufacturing. A pattern appeared by the 1840s that would characterize the rest of the century. Key exports that were developed in the nation's north or south were marketed through London exchanges. The new wealth was spent in Santiago, either by the government or by a landed class seeking a cosmopolitan life. Major export booms occurred in the late 1830s with silver mining in northern Chañarcillo, in the late 1840s with southern wheat farming around Concepción, and in the 1850s and 1860s with northern copper mining around Copiapó.

The population increased slowly but steadily and remained centered near Santiago. Large estates dominated the countryside; most Chileans were landless and worked as illiterate tenant farmers, day laborers drifting from one estate to another, or worked in the mines. They endured high mortality and a short life span.

Chile's economy changed dramatically in the War of the Pacific (1879–1883), when it seized the nitrate provinces of Bolivia (Antofagasta) and Peru (Tarapacá). Sodium nitrate (*salitre*) became the world's major source of commercial fertilizer and also was used to produce iodine and explosives. Chilean policies during the war handed ownership to a group of British speculators, led by John T. North, the "Nitrate King." A conflict between the British interests and President José Manuel Balmaceda (1840–1891) was an underlying element in the Civil War of 1891, won by Balmaceda's congressional opponents. The presidency was weakened, and British interests dominated the sector until it unraveled in the 1920s.

The Twentieth Century. When nitrates waned in the 1920s, copper became the key export, providing up to 50 percent of the GDP in the 1950s and 1960s. United States corporations Anaconda and Kennecott dominated copper production and export. In 1971, Chile nationalized the copper mines, and they have remained in state hands.

The government's financial stability turned on export cycles. Domestic taxes increased, but the government relied heavily on an export duty on nitrates and then on direct imposts on the copper companies. The nitrate duties, for example, paid between 25 and 50 percent of annual expenditures in the early part of the century. In cyclical downturns, the government borrowed from abroad to cover expenditures, leading to a financial crisis in 1931. The state covered other obligations by printing money, and inflation became endemic after the 1890s, reaching 300 percent or higher in the early 1970s.

Economic growth was unevenly distributed, geographically and by sectors. Santiago boomed, the southern provinces languished, and the nitrate and copper zones received little state investment. Industry and finance centered in Santiago, as did real estate speculation. Agriculture gained markets in the mining labor force and the growing urban population but was hurt by state controls on food prices. Hacendados (landholders) counted on a cheap labor force, and the state did not extend labor protections to the countryside until the political crisis of the late 1960s and early 1970s. Even after sustained growth in the 1980s and 1990s, 10 percent of the population took more than 40 percent of the income; the bottom quarter of the population was destitute.

Chile moved from a rural nation to an urban one in the first quarter of the twentieth century. The government spent more heavily on the cities where the votes were, providing infrastructure and schools. In a pattern common in Latin America, rural workers moved to the cities. Housing was scarce, and, by the 1940s, Santiago authorities complained about unsanitary conditions in burgeoning shantytowns.

The shift from rural to urban and the expansion of suffrage triggered changes in public economic policies. Anarchists and socialists pressured for decent wages and working conditions in the first decade of the century. In 1938, a center-left Popular Front won the presidency and began to create a social welfare state. In 1970, Salvador Allende (1908–1973) won the presidency by plurality and promised a "Chilean Road to Socialism." Political polarization occurred and was accompanied by a deepening economic crisis of inflation and the international cutoff of credit (led by the United States). The military overthrew Allende in a bloody coup on 11 September 1973 and established the dictatorship of General Augusto Pinochet Ugarte. The regime relied on murder, torture, and forced exile to cement its control.

Pinochet abolished democratic procedures and the social welfare state. During his sixteen years in power, he reduced tariffs, ended labor rights, opened the country to foreign investment, and promoted nontraditional exports, such as wine, fruit and vegetables, paper and pulp, and fish. Crises occurred from 1974 to 1975 and from 1982 to 1984, but the economy grew sharply after 1985, setting off international praise for the "Chilean model." When Pinochet lost a plebiscite under his own constitution (1980), the civilian Concertación won, in part, by promising not to change the dictator's policies. The economy grew even faster in the 1990s (sometimes as high as several percent per year), although this growth has been subject to sharp downsizing and persisting inequality.

[*See also* American Indian Economies, *subentry on* Inca Economy *and* Spain, *subentry on* Spanish Empire.]

BIBLIOGRAPHY

Banco Central de Chile. <http://www.bcentral.cl/>

Bauer, Arnold J. *Chilean Rural Society from the Spanish Conquest to 1930.* Cambridge, 1975.

Blakemore, Harold. *British Nitrates and Chilean Politics, 1886–1896: Balmaceda and North.* London, 1974.

Collins, Joseph, and John Lear. *Chile's Free-Market Miracle: A Second Look.* Oakland, Calif., 1995.

Loveman, Brian. *Chile: The Legacy of Hispanic Capitalism.* 3d ed. New York, 2001.

Mamalakis, Markos J. *The Growth and Structure of the Chilean Economy: From Independence to Allende.* New Haven, 1976.

Martínez, Javier, and Alvaro Díaz. *Chile: The Great Transformation.* Washington, D.C., and Geneva, 1996.

Monteón, Michael. *Chile in the Nitrate Era: The Evolution of Economic Dependence, 1880–1930.* Madison, Wis., 1982.

Monteón, Michael. *Chile and the Great Depression: The Politics of Underdevelopment.* Tempe, Ariz., 1998.

Moulian, Tomás. *Chile actual: Anatomía de un mito.* Santiago de Chile, 1997.

Salazar Vergara, Gabriel. *Labradores, peones y proletarios: Formación y crisis de la sociedad popular chilena del siglo XIX.* Santiago de Chile, 1985.

MICHAEL MONTEÓN

CHINA

CHINA [*This entry contains five subentries on the economic history of China during ancient and feudal times; during the Tang, Song, and Yuan dynasties; during the Ming and Qing dynasties; during the republican period; and under communism.*]

Ancient and Feudal China

Recent archaeological excavations have shown that the Chinese tradition was formed out of many different Neolithic cultures starting from about 7000 BCE and was not a single stream expanding from a single source in the Yellow River valley. Historically, Chinese culture incorporated ideas, beliefs, social practices, and even languages of a diverse group of tribes living in the huge area of subcontinental East Asia, comprising many different ecosystems. The economic basis of the society was intensive agriculture: in the north the main crop was millet, later wheat, and, in the south, rice; and many other local and regional natural resources were exploited. On the periphery and in the interstices of Chinese polities, numerous groups continued to practice hunting and gathering. True nomadism evolved in the steppes to the north from about 1000 BCE onward, and nomads interacted continuously with sedentary Chinese peoples throughout the historical period. Silk and hemp were of exceptional value for the production of cloth, and ceramics, jade working, lacquer production, and bone carving came to be typical Chinese handicrafts. In the middle and late Neolithic period (5000–2000 BCE), social differentiation and stratification became highly elaborated, craft specialization developed, warfare became endemic, and large walled settlements protected communities ruled by chieftains, who were able to command the labor of their subjects.

The Early Bronze Age. Although the historical existence of the first Chinese dynasty in traditional Chinese records, the Xia, is still a matter of dispute among specialists, the second, the Shang, is known from both archaeological and epigraphic sources as having ruled large parts of the north China plain from the mid-second millennium BCE to 1046 or 1045 BCE. The king stood at the apex of a religious, political, and economic hierarchy. In the religious sphere, he mediated between Heaven, the ancestors and spirits of nature, and humans through pyromancy; and his ability to influence the ancestors through divination and sacrifice legitimated his political power. Records of divinations were inscribed on oracle bones that provide the first written Chinese historical documents. In sacrifice, drinking and eating were the essential part of the ceremonies; and enormous numbers of bronze ritual vessels, manufactured using the piece-mold method, have been discovered. The king himself was probably considered to be a sacred or magical person, possibly even a shaman, capable of conferring victory in battle and good harvests, and communicating with the dead ancestors and the gods.

In political terms, the king was the head of a conical patrilineal clan and was allied to other lineages by marriage. Like the royal lineage, these allies were based in separate walled towns that bore the same name as the lineage. Towns and cities were both ritual and administrative centers. Craftsmen seem to have held relatively high social status, but were bound to aristocratic lineages and were not independent entrepreneurs. Goods used in rituals flowed to the center and were then redistributed by the king to his allies. He needed to redistribute resources in order to maintain his prestige: his paramountcy may have been recognized only as long as he could keep the system of redistributing wealth operational. Thus there existed only barter and exchange of goods; there was no money, nor was there a market economy in Shang times. Economic activity was particularly obvious in the areas of hunting and grain production. Hunting was used to acquire meat for sacrifice to the ancestors and as food for the royal entourage and for the training of soldiers. Grain was also used in sacrifice, for making wine, and for food. The two activities of hunting and agriculture were closely related. Shang soldiers organized by lineages into groups of one hundred to three hundred went out to burn an area and capture and kill its animals. The burned vegetation fertilized the soil, and the fields were incorporated into the Shang state network. As the Shang expanded, they encountered other tribes living on the periphery and killed large numbers of enemy as human sacrifices. These other groups began to adopt some of the Shang's technology and possibly political organization in order to resist their aggressors. In the late Shang, therefore, local bronze-making cultures with distinct regional styles developed, such as the Guanghan culture in Sichuan province, and the northern bronze cultures in the steppes.

Western and Eastern Zhou. The second phase of the Bronze Age was ushered in when the Shang dynasty was conquered by a coalition of peoples to their west, led by the Zhou king Wu, in 1046 or 1045 BCE. Later, in their turn, the Zhou were defeated by a coalition of rebels and nomadic tribesmen in 770 BCE and were forced to abandon their capital and move east to Luoyang. Thus the period from 1046 to 771 BCE is known as the Western Zhou, and the period after 770 to 256 BCE is called the Eastern Zhou. Only in the last few years have archaeological discoveries been made confirming that the Zhou had reached a high level of technical competence prior to the conquest. They possessed advanced ceramic and bronze technology, large palace complexes of sophisticated design, and a tradition of oracle bone divination—evidence that they, like the Shang, had developed religious specialization and had gained the diplomatic skills to organize numerous tribes under their banner to fight for control of the Shang dominions. They used the principle of primogeniture for transmission of the throne and claimed that the Shang had become morally corrupt and that the Zhou supreme deity in Heaven (Tian) had transferred the right to rule, the mandate of Heaven, to them. The Zhou king was responsible for ensuring that the human realm was in harmony with the cosmic order. Only he had the right to perform the rituals to Heaven and Earth, to the dead Zhou kings, and, for example, the ritual first tilling of the soil in the sacred field that heralded the beginning of the agricultural cycle.

The Question of Feudalism. The Zhou sought to control the territory they had conquered by conferring on members of the Zhou royal lineage and their chief supporters walled towns and garrisons. The Zhou simply did not have the human resources or the administrative skills to exploit and govern the conquered peoples and land by themselves. Thus the various states they established (one estimate is that there were close to two thousand such states at the beginning of the Western Zhou) were scattered throughout the vast eastern plains and were connected to the royal court by ties of blood and marriage. This system of governance, known to historians as the *fengjian* system, has been equated by modern scholars to feudalism, with the conclusion that the Western Zhou system of governance was similar to that of medieval Europe. Among the most important evidence is that found in later texts recording what appear to be feudal investiture ceremonies, as well as the records on recently discovered genuine Zhou bronzes, similarly recording donations of items of prestige value, often military equipment, and sometimes of lands and persons, with charges by the Zhou king for the recipients to perform some kind of task for him.

Some scholars claim that the Zhou was a "feudal empire," others that the Western and Eastern Zhou period was dominated by city-states and regional city-state systems. Archaeologically speaking, each state was based on walled towns that were ritual centers of aristocratic lineages. The governing body of each state was composed of the ruler's own male lineage and related and nonrelated lineages whose heads held ministerial rank. Below them were the mass of the peasants, whose activities are not recorded. The lineages fought among themselves for political dominance, and gradually power centered on only one or two lineages, and a centralized administrative structure developed. Most aristocratic lineages were wiped out in the warfare, and the administration came to be run by poor *shi* or knights who had been distantly related to the more powerful lineages but who had no land on which to support themselves or any other means of support. They owed their loyalty solely to the lord of the centralized state, who employed them for either administrative or military skills, both of which depended on education. Thus the administration began to be staffed by educated individuals: Confucius (died 479 BCE) was the first private teacher of such knights.

Springs and Autumns and Warring States of China. From 770 BCE on, the Zhou remained kings merely in name and they maintained only ritual authority over their vassals. The latter waged continual wars against each other until gradually the smaller states were absorbed by the larger, so that by the fourth century BCE only seven major regional city-states were left. Finally, in 221 BCE, the first emperor of Qin conquered his last rivals, unified the whole of China, and founded the empire. By approximately 600 BCE, currency in the form of metal and bolts of cloth had made its appearance, and the economy gradually developed from one of barter-exchange to one based on money and markets. The cash was primarily of bronze cast in the shape of knives (in the east), two-pronged spades (in the center), or rounds with square holes (in the west); but gold was also circulated in the southern state of Chu, as were silver and lead. Cast-iron technology was developed first for agricultural implements, including heavy turn-plows, and vessels, and then for weapons, such as long swords and sabers. Social organization began to be more elaborate, and urbanization spread. Many cities were located on trade routes, were highly internally differentiated, and were home to a large and diverse population of peasants, artisans, entrepreneurs, aristocrats, and slaves: Linzi, the capital of Qi, had seventy thousand families. Private and state-sponsored merchants traded across state boundaries and with neighboring regions, such as the far south and the steppes to the north, and increased communication between different parts of China helped to develop regional economic specialization. The peasantry also came to be involved in state affairs. They were taxed in kind, primarily grain produced by men and cloth woven by women, and provided corvée labor for the state and manpower for the armies. The more astute and skilled of the merchants and lower orders were promoted by the rulers of the independent city-states, initiating social mobility. They rose up the social hierarchy to replace the aristocrats who were being eliminated in the wars, and they sought to influence rulers by advocating a bewildering variety of philosophical, political, and economic policy alternatives. Confucians eschewed the profit motive, whereas Mohists encouraged it; Daoists and agriculturalists urged a return to self-sufficient peasant production; legalists promoted agriculture and denigrated trade.

The State of Qin. In the mid-fourth century BCE, Wei Yang, Lord Shang, initiated a series of political, social, legal, and economic reforms in the state of Qin that laid the foundations for the unification of China in 221 BCE. Lord Shang promoted agriculture and warfare, reorganized the land tenure system, expanding the size of the acre to 240 paces, and divided fields by pathways running north to south and east to west. He organized the population into a hierarchy that stretched from five family units, through villages, districts, and counties, to the central authorities, and controlled individual behavior by the institution of a system of mutual responsibility. Individuals were obliged to denounce crimes of members of their unit or face prosecution themselves.

A large body of Qin legal statutes and documents discovered in a tomb in 1975 has revealed how deeply involved the Qin state was in the economy. Although private businesses were permitted to exist, it managed a complex system of workshops and foundries operated by highly organized specialists. Much work was performed by slaves and criminals serving hard-labor sentences. The quality of products was carefully monitored, each item was given a manufacturer's mark, and continued poor performance was punished with fines. The higher up the managerial hierarchy, the heavier was the fine. Qin officials supervised the markets, mandating that every item for sale of more than one cash in value had to have a price tag. Sales taxes were collected in the markets as well as at passes, where traffic was controlled by a system of passports and tallies. Merchants were registered separately from other members of the population, some becoming exceptionally wealthy, and all had to declare their wealth for tax purposes: poll and labor taxes were imposed that depended on age and on social status for males, determined by a merit-ranking system of seventeen grades awarded primarily on the basis of success in battle. Although it is clear that private land ownership and the buying and selling of land were tolerated, much of the land was either cultivated directly by the state or leased to tenant farmers, who were allotted slaves to help them work the fields if they had gained success in battle by cutting off enemy heads. The Qin developed an extremely sophisticated system of reporting and storing grain revenue, and recording weather conditions and damage to crops and farm animals, and maintained a state- and empirewide system of officially run granaries and a complex system for checking income and disbursements. The precise quantities of grain to be handed out to officials as salaries and to feed convicts and slaves were fixed by statutory law, as was the exchange rate between cash and bolts of cloth used as money. Although it is unlikely that the Qin economy was based on slave labor, the state relied heavily on a wide variety of convict labor supervised by a complex bureaucratic hierarchy to construct massive public-works projects, such as the Great Wall, canals such as the one that linked north and south China, drainage and irrigation networks, and numerous palaces and parks.

BIBLIOGRAPHY

Barnes, Gina. *The Rise of Civilization in East Asia: The Archaeology of China, Korea, and Japan.* London, 1996.

Chang, Kwang-chih. *Shang Civilization.* New Haven and London, 1980.

Chang, Kwang-chih. *The Archaeology of Ancient China.* 4th ed. New Haven and London, 1986.

Hsu, Cho-yun. *Ancient China in Transition: An Analysis of Social Mobility, 722–222 BC.* Stanford, Calif. 1965.

Hsu, Cho-yun, and Katheryn M. Linduff. *Western Chou Civilization.* New Haven and London, 1988.

Hulsewé, A. F. P. *Remnants of Ch'in Law: An Annotated Translation of the Ch'in Legal and Administrative Rules of the 3rd Century BC. Discovered in Yünmeng Prefecture, Hu-pei Province, in 1975.* Leiden, 1985.

Li, Xueqin. *Eastern Zhou and Qin Civilizations.* New Haven and London, 1985.

Swann, Nancy Lee, trans. *Food and Money in Ancient China: The Earliest Economic History of China to AD 25.* Princeton, 1950.

Wu, Baosan. *Xian Qin jingji sixiang shi* (History of Pre-Qin Economic Thought). Beijing, 1996.

ROBIN D. S. YATES

Tang, Song, and Yuan Dynasties

The Tang and Song dynasties (618–1279 CE) lasted for six centuries and marked the High Middle Ages of imperial China (221 BCE–1911 CE). There were advancements in technological inventions, the development of new institutions, a rise in total factor productivity, an expansion of markets, a spread of specialization, growth in population and urbanization, and a geographic shift of the economic center. As commonly recognized, it was the era during which China led the world in science, technology, and administration. It was also the era of the most intensive growth ever recorded in world history. The Yuan dynasty (1279–1368 CE), imposed by Mongol conquest, ended that growth.

Tang (618–907 CE). The Tang dynasty was built on the achievements of the Sui (581–618 CE), an unpopular and short-lived regime, known for its mismanagement of the economy. The Sui, however, bequeathed two important socioeconomic factors: the Grand Canal and the lesson of its fiscal blunders. The canal facilitated a southward shift of the economic center, and the fiscal problems led to a package of reforms. Generally, the Tang dynasty provided both political strength and economic prosperity. China's population was then relatively stable, at forty to fifty million taxpayers. The Tang had expanded its territory, established flourishing foreign trade, and developed an extraordinary output in literature and the arts. The most important event was the shift of the economic center to the south, where land yield levels and population density reached unprecedented heights. The early Tang rulers succeeded in political reform by establishing a meritocracy, based on selective recruitment, known as the "imperial examinations," and assessment procedures called "surveillance and promotion." The selection of officials was based on a Confucian curriculum, while their promotion was based on socioeconomic indexes. County magistrates, for example, who managed to have agricultural output increase by at least 20 percent were promoted by one rank, with a 30 percent increase in salary. The impact of the reform went far beyond the state apparatus, since a bureaucratic homogeneity lowered transaction costs throughout the economy. Meritocracy led to social mobility, which in turn generated socioeconomic dynamics, and the prestige of educational qualifications stimulated the literacy rate.

During the Tang dynasty, growth was based on success in agriculture in combination with new technology and favorable institutions. As control over China's southern territories was consolidated, the "southern plow," a new plow type for paddies, began to spread. Light in weight and using a single draft animal, its maneuverability and low investment cost made it superior to the heavy "northern plow," which took two or three cattle to pull. Members of the Confucian literati made considerable efforts to introduce this new equipment. Institutionally, the "land-equalization system" had guaranteed farming households access to lifetime leaseholding of a piece of state land, called the "ever-holding estate." By the late Tang era, the land was privatized, with legal protections for private ownership. With state promotion, equal inheritance of private land then became the norm, and parents bequeathed their property (farming land and permanent houses) equally among their sons (and sometimes among daughters). The economic rationale was to replicate as many farming households as possible, to increase the imperial tax base. Late Tang policy affected even its army: two-thirds of the military were employed at some one thousand state-run farming colonies.

Tang agricultural taxes were light and predictable. Under the land-equalization system, a tax package called the "rent-corvée-poll" was introduced. Taxes were paid in kind at a fixed amount: rent in grain and poll in corvée (a labor draft system) and silk. With land privatization, taxation was reformed to be "two-seasonal taxes," at a rate of 7 percent of the total grain output (11 *sheng* of grain per *mu* in 769 CE). The earlier poll in corvée and silk, equivalent to about two months per man of work, was abolished. Taxes were allowed to be paid in cash (official coinage), an institutional endorsement for commercial farming. As the tax system left leeway for farming households to produce more crops, Tang revenues increased. Huge quantities of taxed grain were shipped through the Grand Canal to China's north—more than one million metric tons each year during the middle Tang era. Much of it was used to pay the military's salaries, so the grain facilitated an exchange economy, especially along the frontiers. Cash crops became common. In the early Tang era, apart from the planting of mulberry trees (to feed silkworms), which was made a legal obligation under the state lease, tea was grown in most of the southern provinces. Commercial tea growers, called "tea farmers," became highly specialized. Their quality products formed the backbone of the "tea-for-horse" trade between China and its nomadic neighbors to the west and north. The trade continued until the end of the seventeenth century, when tea found its new market—Europe and, eventually, the Americas.

China's handicraft industry experienced strong growth during the Tang. Bronzes, silks, lacquers, ceramics, and papermaking formed the base of China's manufacturing sector. The annual output of the Tang mint from 713 to 741 CE was one billion mass-produced bronze coins. Large quantities of China's products were, at that time, exported to Japan, Southeast Asia, West and Central Asia, and East Africa. Shipping and overseas trade stimulated the development of Tang-era maritime technology. By the late Tang dynasty, boats and ships with large loading capacities for the canal and sea were standardized, and the use of sail at sea became the norm. The invention of the "Tang handy ruler" and the "star-measuring ruler" to fix the latitude of ships' positions revolutionized seagoing. Sea routes then rapidly expanded, which marked a turning point in history, as China's maritime trade eclipsed its traditional overland trade. As shipping costs fell, some sea routes were frequently used for the silk trade; thus, "silk routes" soon linked China to regions of the western Pacific and northern Indian oceans. As a consequence of maritime trade expansion, the Tang pharmacy became unprecedentedly dependent on overseas medicaments: rhinoceros horns, frankincense, myrrh, turtle shell, clove, and ambergris, to name just a few.

Tang-era merchants were protected by law and were entitled to live in walled cities. They were taxed, in most cases, at a low 3.3 percent of goods traded. In 714 CE, the Tang imperial court instituted the Bureau for Maritime Trade, and it appointed a commissioner for maritime trade to promote and regulate the foreign trade. Rights and autonomy of foreign traders were protected. According to Tang law, foreign offenders were subject to their own laws if their own people were involved; they were only subject to Tang law if different peoples were affected. With the boom of trade, such urban centers as the capital, Changan, and large coastal towns became cosmopolitan, with foreign merchants, imported goods and animals, exotic dancers, and black immigrants highly visible. In 879 CE, rebels under Huang Chao allegedly massacred, in Guangzhou (Canton) alone, some one hundred thousand foreigners—Muslims, Jews, Christians, and Zoroastrians—which reflected the sizeable foreign communities in China (from the Middle East, Europe, Persia, India, and Southeast Asia).

Song (960–1279 CE). The Song dynasty emerged after a short but chaotic period known as the Five Dynasties (907–960 CE) The economy soon recovered and then surpassed all previous records for growth. It was a period of intensive growth—characterized by promarket state policies, advancing technology, prosperous urbanization, and widespread trade networks.

The Song developed two subperiods: the Northern Song (960–1127 CE), which thrived in technology and manufacturing; and the Southern Song (1127–1279 CE), which thrived in landholding and commerce. First recorded during the Northern Song were applications of the portable compass, gunpowder, firearms, movable-type printing, paper currency, the peddle boat, and deep drilling for minerals. Many elements of modern capitalism were then present in society. Quality porcelains and brocade textiles began to be produced commercially. The capital city Kaifeng, the largest city in Asia, was estimated to produce annually 150,000 tons of iron. In addition, a green revolution started to change China's landscape, with newly experimental multicrop farming. The result was output growth. The number of taxpayers increased as well to some seventy million in 1190 (unparalleled until 1753).

The Northern Song bureaucracy's main achievement was nationwide registration for taxation and maintained law and order. There were four main registration categories: farming acreage (called a "fishscale survey"); land productivity (under "five grades"); land ownership (in the form of "owners' certificates" and "tenants' registration"); and tax-payable households/population (called "taxpayers' rolls"). As the proportion of state-owned land was reduced, the registration represented a major step toward recognizing, monitoring, and regulating a predominantly private farming sector. The surveillance costs for the state proved to be increasingly high, however, as more and more people dodged taxes, despite relatively low tax rates. Despite tax and land reforms under Wang Anshi (1021–1086), the state's finances were further weakened. Soon there was a trend toward absentee landlordism. Northern Song officials found a solution, by splitting land ownership and cultivation rights. In the south, a type of lifetime landholding rights—with fixed sharecropping (50 50 division of lands and produce being the norm there) called "permanent leaseholding rights"—was developed, since the price of agricultural land was high. As southern agriculture became productive enough to support a class of absentee landlords, the permanent leaseholding rights also became subject to market speculation.

Administratively, the Northern Song regime turned out to be not very successful. An overcentralized superstructure, designed to avoid a recurrence of any internal factionalism, resulted in a poorly organized national defence system and inefficient government finances. Eventually, in 1127, under the joint pressure of internal rebellion and external invasion, half of the Song territory was lost to the Tartars, and the capital was moved south. This territo-rial loss had profound effects on the Song economy; there was a decline in manufacture and rise in intensive farming. The sack of Kaifeng by the Tartars destroyed for good the Song iron industry and the Kaifeng-based northern market network. Kaifeng's population and economic power never fully recovered until the Ming dynasty (1368–1644 CE). The mass migration of the fleeing northern population to the south caused a sudden population explosion there. New agricultural technology was soon needed as a response to the demographic shift and the consequent land-price surge. Land-saving innovations were developed to intensify the use of good land, while marginal land was brought under cultivation. Intensive irrigation and the frequent top-dressing of fertilizers were commonplace. Dry-farming was reintroduced to high elevations. Not only were terraced fields built on hillsides but water-surface space was also used, with plots built out onto wooden rafts. New sets of tools were then developed, including the water-lifting devices of an "ox-pulled water pump" and a labor-saving "seedling boat."

The categories of landholding were changed, as well, with the northern refugees (registered as "guests") forming the single largest tenant group for farming; the early invention of the permanent leaseholding rights were spread more widely and the concept of subleasing land was developed. Rent was divided further between the primary rent ("plot rent") and the secondary rent ("topsoil rent"). The subleaser became a broker of the tillage rights. The unprecedented level of total productivity enabled the agricultural surplus to support not only the increased rent-seeking groups but also economic specialization and diversification. This is especially evident in the densely populated Lake Tai region, in the lower reaches of the Yangzi River valley, an area which was redeveloped for rice exporting. The region also produced top-quality silk in large quantities. To process the silk, a semimechanical foot-powered spinner was designed for the rural handicrafts industry. As the Southern Song developed rapid concentration of land ownership, North China under the Tartar Jin administration (1127–1234) launched a campaign to lure farmers to resettle in the North, to enlarge the Jin tax base. Stable and egalitarian landholdings were offered by the Tartar state. These soon resulted in the reverse migration of a large number of Chinese who had little to lose from leaving the south.

During the Song dynasty, with a tax rate of 2 to 5 percent of the goods' value, market expansion accelerated. In the northern cities, permanent street markets were established and regular fairs were held in large temples (called "temple fairs"). Kaifeng had two large daily fairs, the "morning market" and "night market." Wholesale agents for staple goods were well entrenched in the cities. An increasing number of foreigners migrated to China. One such group

SONG DYNASTY. *Going Up the River at the Spring Festival,* silk scroll painting showing port and market scenes, possibly in the old capital of Kaifeng. (Beijing Palace Museum, Imperial Palace, Beijing/Werner Forman Archive/Art Resource, NY)

that lived in the hinterland was the "Kaifeng Jews," whose Arab counterparts had concentrated in the ports. After the loss of the northern territory to the Tartars, Song merchants soon reconnected China withthe outside world by sea routes. The reduced sailing costs, from developments during the Tang dynasty, made feasible the Song sea-trade expansion to South Asia, Southeast Asia, and East Africa. Flourishing foreign trade then led to a boom in ship building. By 1276, there were some twenty thousand Song ships, with seven thousand large seagoing vessels. Tertiary industry increased strongly also—restaurants, hotels, clinics, and money dealers—all of which supported business and the urban lifestyle.

An increasing budget deficit from huge defense expenditures forced the Song state to practice proto-mercantilistic policies. During the Northern Song, there were at least ten different government schemes to interfere with trading in grain, tea, wine, salt, and horses. Later, maritime trade was targeted by the Southern Song authorities, since much of the revenue from land and poll taxes was lost to the Tartars. Customs law was established to reassure the merchants of their rights, and duty rates were also fixed. Official titles were also granted to those who attracted maritime business. Even imperial envoys were sent overseas to lure foreign traders. The Song government then became directly involved in profiteering through monopolizing imports. The gamble paid off as the maritime duty revenue increased fourfold from 1099 to 1159. At the end of the Song era, government revenue from commercial taxes was 70 percent of its total—a record that remained unbroken until the Qing dynasty (1644–1911). As the Song economic growth seemed unstoppable, an external shock came from invading Mongols in 1279, which once again changed China.

Yuan (1279–1368 CE). The Song dynasty became the victim of its own economic success, in that its wealth attracted the Mongols to China's north to plunder China's wealth. Song military weakness, in comparison with its economic might, paid the ultimate price: for the first time, China—as a whole—was conquered by an alien society, with no native Chinese political enclave or administration left in the territory. By reunifying North and South China, the Mongol invasion and conquest dramatically altered socioeconomic conditions.

Superficially, during the Mongol Yuan period, a *pax Mongolia* replaced the early *pax Sinica*: China's nominal territory expanded about 30 percent beyond the Great Wall, north into Mongolia, Manchuria, and Siberia; the long-distance transport system was improved; and overland foreign trade along the "silk roads" was resumed. The extravagant façade of the Yuan Empire deeply impressed visitors like Marco Polo. Yet inside China, the Mongol invasion and conquest was considered a nationwide disaster and was a major discontinuity in China's technological and economic growth. Under early Mongol rule, Chinese labor and capital were destroyed on a large scale. In the north, the population loss was as high as 86 percent, from the state genocidal policy of the invaders. Chinese who survived the killing were made slaves or serfs (called "forced laborers"), and they totaled some 14.1 million (derived from 2.8 million registered households). Vast areas of farming were first devastated and then enclosed for the Mongol army and their temples, as well as for individual aristocrats and officials (some 38 million *mu* in total = 2.5 million hectares). Livestock belonging to the Chinese were confiscated, and autumn tillage for the second crop was forbidden because of the need for grazing land for Mongol horses. This upset the normal production cycle of the Chinese farmers.

Such destruction reduced Mongol revenues, a point made by Yelü Chucai, a Yuan-era courtier from Persia who argued that the Chinese could better be exploited than killed. The Mongols soon decided to revive agriculture and, in 1261, the Agriculture Promotion Bureau was established. Official posts were then created in larger numbers than during the Song dynasty, to take charge of rural production and water control. Books on agronomy were compiled and distributed in the hope that Chinese farmers would relearn what had been lost after the Mongol invasion and conquest. Still, much of the possible positive effect of the Mongol institutions was offset by the economic disincentives for the Chinese through rent-seeking by the predatory Mongol state (as reflected by Mongol taxation). The Yuan land tax was about 3 percent of the average yield of the period—3 *sheng* (2.2 kilograms = 5 pounds per *mu*)—considerably lower than that under the Tang. But the Yuan poll tax was much higher—at 30 *sheng* per head (22 kilograms = 50 pounds)—equivalent to the total output of 3 *mu* of the average farming land, or 44 percent of an adult's subsistence income. This pattern was designed to benefit the landowners, a large number of whom were Mongols and their associates from central Asia, and to exploit the tillers, who were exclusively Chinese.

The Mongols imposed as many as thirty-two indirect taxes on consumer goods, such as calendars, porcelain, firewood, medicine, coal, meat, and vegetables. In addition, there were two surcharges exclusively on the Chinese population, called "cash contribution" and "annual silver," at one *liang* and four *liang* of silver per household, respectively. (Five *liang* was at least a year's subsistence wage for an adult, more than 20 percent of a family's subsistence

income.) Each farming household was also taxed at 22.3 *jin* (830 grams = 1.8 pounds) of silk floss, which in 1260 tripled Tang rates. During the Yuan, silk became an international currency for foreign trade, and the Mongols could not get enough of it. Along with taxing their Chinese subjects in silk, the Mongols not only imposed a strict ban on their use of silk but also forced them to grow the newly introduced cotton plant (from the Near East and East Africa) as a substitute for Chinese clothing to extract the maximum quantity of silk from the Chinese population.

Toward that same end, the Mongols tried to revive China's commerce after they devastated it during the first phase of conquest. Therefore, the Song trade policies were carefully copied, and some former Song trade officials of non-Chinese background were reappointed. Special funds were earmarked for state–private maritime trade joint ventures, and the Yuan government charged an annual return of 30 percent from such investments. Apart from silk, large quantities of porcelain were also gathered by the Yuan state for trade. As a result, trade routes were expanded both overland and by sea. Based on a Song joint-venture method, a scheme called "government-invested ships" was established, which combined government ships with merchant expertise in maritime trade. Discriminative tax regimes and rates were raised in favor of the ruling Mongols. When the Yuan-era tax rate on commerce was 10 percent. These rates on commerce were, however, always lower than those imposed on agriculture and on Chinese households. Although the Mongols actively promoted trade, their real revenue base undoubtedly remained Chinese agriculture, especially the farming sector in the South, from which they gained 70 percent of their annual revenue—including some 12 million *shi* of grain (900,000 metric tons), over 1 million *jin* of silk floss (600 tons), and a half million rolls of silk cloth. As the Chinese were then excluded from the profitable silk and ceramics trades, the main beneficiaries of the Yuan overseas trade were the Mongols and their non-Chinese associates.

Mongol discrimination also affected the Chinese literati. First, the Tang-Song imperial examinations were abolished for eighty of the ninety-six-year Mongol rule. People from the Middle East and Europe, called "the colored-eye races," were instead employed in large numbers in the Yuan bureaucracy. Second, Buddhism (a different sect from what the Chinese were used to) replaced Confucianism as the state religious philosophy. Such changes not only destroyed the tradition of the Confucian state but also ended China's balanced sociopolitical and socioeconomic equilibrium. By the end of the Yuan dynasty, the population in China proper had slowly recovered to the Tang level of 50 million registered taxpayers. Yet as the tax burden was increased many times, there was no significant improvement in the average living standards. Transaction costs in the Yuan economy increased dramatically, while economic opportunities were systematically denied the Chinese. Not surprisingly, no significant technological progress ensued, as literature, theater, and the arts became the main arenas for Chinese creativity. A socioeconomic renaissance in China occurred only after the Mongol rule was toppled.

BIBLIOGRAPHY

Deng, Kent G. *Development versus Stagnation: Technological Continuity and Agricultural Progress in Premodern China.* New York, London, and Westport, Conn., 1993.

Deng, Kent G. *Chinese Maritime Activities and Socioeconomic Development c. 2100 BC–1900 AD.* New York, London, and Westport, Conn., 1997.

Deng, Kent G. "The Foreign Staple Trade of China in the Premodern Era." *The International History Review* 19.2 (1997), 253–283.

Deng, Kent G. *The Premodern Chinese Economy—Structural Equilibrium and Capitalist Sterility.* London and New York, 1999.

Deng, Kent G. *Maritime Sector, Institutions, and Sea Power of Premodern China.* New York, London, and Westport, Conn., 1999.

Elvin, Mark. *The Pattern of the Chinese Past.* Stanford, Calif., 1973.

Hartwell, Ronald M. *Iron and Early Industrialism in Eleventh-Century China.* Chicago, 1963.

Jones, Eric L. *The European Miracle.* Cambridge, 1981.

Jones, Eric L. *Growth Recurring: Economic Change in World History.* Oxford, 1988.

Jones, Eric L. "The Real Question about China: Why Was the Song Economic Achievement Not Repeated?" *Australian Economic History Review* 30.2 (1990), 5–22.

Langlois, John D., ed. *China under Mongol Rule.* Princeton, 1981.

Maddison, Augus. *Chinese Economic Performance in the Long Run.* Paris, 1998.

Mokyr, Joel. *The Lever of Riches.* New York and Oxford, 1990.

Needham, Joseph, ed. *Science and Civilisation in China.* Cambridge, 1954–1994.

Rossabi, Morris. "The Tea and Horse Trade with Inner Asia during the Ming." *Journal of Asian History* 4 (1970), 136–168.

Shiba, Yoshinobu. *Commerce and Society in Sung China.* Translated by Mark Elvin. Ann Arbor, 1970.

Temple, Robert. *The Genius of China: 3,000 Years of Science, Discovery, and Invention.* New York, 1986.

Twitchett, Denis. "Merchant, Trade and Government in Late T'ang." *Asia Major* 14.1 (1968), 63–95.

KENT G. DENG

Ming and Qing Dynasties

Sixteenth-century Europeans returned from the coasts of Asia with tales of vast, wealthy societies. For centuries the dream of Oriental riches had been their primary incentive for trade, exploration, and warfare. Jesuit missionaries at the Chinese court, hoping for mass conversions, praised the rulers' wisdom and the country's prosperity. In the eighteenth century, anticlerical French writers saw China as a secular, rational government based on light taxation and respect for agriculture. Montesquieu retaliated by insisting on the despotism of the East. But nineteenth-century Britons portrayed China as corrupt, backward, and decaying, a target for reform and invasion. Myths about

China's society and economy have constantly driven Western perceptions and actions; only rarely did uncomfortable facts seep through the cultural screens. Western social theory, from Adam Smith and Malthus to Marx and Weber, was erected on the foundations of these uninformed views.

Chinese likewise embraced unrealistic visions of their neighbors, seeing many of them as uncivilized, even subhuman, but regarding others, such as Indian Buddhists, as admirable. These competing stereotypes have inevitably influenced study of the economic history of China. Since the 1980s, the opening of China's imperial archives to Western scholars has markedly improved empirical studies of the economy, but only recently have scholars begun to grapple with its complexities in a truly comparative way.

Periodization. The term "Ming-Qing China" refers to the dynasties of the Ming (1368–1643 CE) and the Qing (1644–1911 CE). Carving up time this way does not fit well with economic cycles. Five periods fit better: (1) the reversion to agrarianism after the collapse of the Mongol (Yuan dynasty), circa 1400 to 1500; (2) the revival of commerce, and global contact, 1500 to 1640; (3) seventeenth-century crisis and recovery, 1640 to 1680; (4) the long eighteenth-century expansion, 1680 to 1850; (5) internal and external crises, reconstruction, and revolution, 1850 to 1949. In this periodization, population growth, commercialization, and rising agricultural productivity have alternated with shorter periods of instability and disintegration. Aggregate economic trends have coincided only imperfectly with political transitions, and the timing of cycles has varied greatly by region.

Demography. China's population was close to 75 million in 1400 and 450 million in 1900. At an average annual growth rate of 0.36 percent, it had increased from 22 percent to 28 percent of the world's population. Steady, slow growth was interrupted by two short declines. Aggregate population probably reached 150 to 175 million by 1600, dropped to about 100 to 150 million by 1650, then rose to over 300 million in 1800 and to 410 million in 1850, declined by 50 to 60 million during the midcentury rebellions, and recovered to 430 million by the end of the nineteenth century. If foreigners and Chinese agree on one thing, it is that China has a large population. However, China's population is not so huge as it seems, and the underlying causes of China's growth are often misinterpreted. Europe, after all, rose in this period from 60 million to 400 million. Europeans thought that early and universal marriage for women kept Chinese breeding up to the limits of subsistence. Confucian norms supporting large extended families seemed to bear out this stereotype, but modern demographic studies have destroyed these claims (Lee and Feng, 1999). In fact, Chinese families carefully regulated reproduction in response to the price of grains;

caloric intakes were well above the minimum; households on average were not large (about five persons); and life expectancies at birth of thirty to thirty-five years were comparable, if not better than, most of those of early-modern Europe. The Chinese female average total marital fertility of 6.3 was much lower than Europe's. The image of a large, rapidly growing, poor population on the brink of starvation must be replaced with one of a large, fairly well-fed, slowly growing society, constantly pushing agricultural techniques and commercial exchange to exhaust the resources of the land.

Gender. Historians are only beginning to understand the close links between China's family structure and economic development. Instead of myths of an unchanging patriarchal hierarchy, they now engage in a much more nuanced exploration of how commerce and state institutions shaped family roles. Women were not visible in the public sphere, but within the household they had considerable autonomy. Elite women, a surprisingly high number of whom were literate, managed complex household economies, which involved not only textile production and servants but considerable interaction with the outside world. Popular literature features many variations on the classic traveling salesman story, in which a woman left alone by her husband on a business trip conducts an affair with a local decadent youth. Religious pilgrimages and temple fairs allowed women to leave their kinship network to conduct business or illicit liaisons. Puritanical literati who denounced women for focusing on personal adornment were preaching against the tide.

The general impression is that in the sixteenth century commercialization and mobility undermined patriarchal restrictions, whereas in the seventeenth and eighteenth centuries the moralistic Qing state pushed women back into their traditional roles of reproduction and domestic economy. Spinning and weaving validated women's crucial contributions to the household, but these production functions began to become professionalized industries dominated by males producing for the market. Bound feet and female infanticide revealed the terrible price of female subordination. On the other hand, some enlightened male scholars denounced footbinding and infanticide, an extensive network of orphanages collected abandoned children, and widespread adoption preserved family lines with no male heir while relieving poor families of the economic burden of childrearing. Within the harsh constraints set by nature and custom, Chinese families still adjusted their gender and economic roles to improve their circumstances.

Agriculture. The miraculous productivity of Chinese agriculture supported the demands of the population. The cultivated land area usually increased along with population, but was the increase cause or consequence of increasing population, or both? Larger populations meant more labor and increased demand for trade, especially in regions with efficient water transport. Yields on paddy rice fields increased as density grew. As textile industries boomed in the lower Yangzi delta (Jiangnan), farmers turned to cash cropping, converting grain fields to production of cotton and silk. The grain-rich middle Yangzi provinces sent their surplus downstream in exchange for manufactured textiles. Rising demand stimulated improved production technologies. New World crops—tobacco, sweet potatoes, peanuts, and chili peppers—enhanced the diet, spread cultivation up eroded hillsides, and generated further trade opportunities. Mountainous Fujian, in the southeast, for example, exported tobacco and tea to the more prosperous deltas of Guangdong and Jiangnan, and imported grain from Taiwan. Regional specialization tied the empire together. During the mostly peaceful eighteenth century, guilds, customs duties, and warfare presented few obstacles to the flow of people and goods. Correlations of grain price movements around the country indicate increasing market integration.

Expanding frontiers encouraged pioneer settlements. The Ming armies that conquered the southwest were followed by civilian settlers and merchants. The Qing rulers enlarged China's territorial size dramatically in the eighteenth century, adding 7.2 million square kilometers to the empire and nearly tripling its size. Much of the land in Central Asia was desert, but Taiwan and Manchuria offered fertile fields. Peasant farmers also pushed out along internal frontiers, moving into mountains, clearing sandbars, and filling in entire lakes with paddy fields.

Where peasant farmers gained, trees, tigers, and non-Han natives lost. Faced with the Han juggernaut, forests disappeared, animals were driven to extinction, and native peoples either accommodated themselves to Han methods as "cooked" intensive farmers, or fled to even more remote areas, where, as "raw" barbarians, Qing military forces hunted them down. Calling China's agrarian experience, paradoxically, "three thousand years of unsustainable growth," Mark Elvin (Elvin and Liu, 1995) highlights the continual race between the escalating demands of a growing population for a better life and the new technologies of resource extraction, which increasingly impacted the environment.

Cities and Macroregions. China is not only a huge agrarian but also a huge urban society. Networks of exchange supported an elaborate hierarchy reaching from central metropolises down to thirty-eight thousand market towns (with small urban populations). Beijing, with 850,000 people, remained the largest city in the world into the nineteenth century. Below Beijing, major provincial capitals dominated their regions because of their concentration of administrative and transportation resources. Cities such as Xi'an in the northwest, Chengdu in Sichuan, or Guangzhou (Canton) in the south stood at the top of both administrative and commercial hierarchies. Other major commercial centers, such as Hankow, had no administrative rank. In the lower Yangzi, especially, numerous large cities competed for prominence in cultural, economic, and bureaucratic status. Yangzhou had culture, as well as a prime location at the base of the Grand Canal; Hangzhou prospered from coastal trade; Suzhou reigned supreme over the textile industry and landscape gardens of cultured gentlemen. Upstart Shanghai, created as a treaty port in the nineteenth century, would come to surpass all of China's cities in its reputation for splendor, squalor, dynamism, and intrigue. The "shock city" of China's modern age, it rooted its enormous industrial vitality in the trade and transport network of the lower Yangzi region where it was embedded.

State and Economy. Subtle relationships between the imperial state and the economy have generated much exciting research. Old images of a static, agrarian bureaucracy need substantial revision. Even though Confucius ranked the merchant below the farmer, officials and elites did not neglect commerce. They knew how to form joint ventures or to lend official funds at interest. The Yongzheng emperor (r. 1723–1735) told his officials not to block trade routes and made them invest in roads and waterways. The empire's prime concern was domestic and international order. Profit-seeking merchants could help stave off unrest by shipping grain to famine-struck regions. When grain rioters, as in Europe, blocked boats taking grain out of a deficit area, local officials put down the unrest and ensured that subsistence needs were met. Magistrates protected property rights by enforcing contracts and adjudicating complex rent and inheritance disputes. Thousands of ever normal granaries across the empire bought and sold grain to maintain stable prices. A vast information-collecting apparatus informed top officials of monthly prices, harvest, and rainfall everywhere. In all these ways, Qing officials tried to keep the peace while also protecting a stable environment for business.

Foreign trade presented special problems. Under the label "tribute," the Ming emperors allowed exchanges of large amounts of tea and silk for poor horses, to prevent nomadic raids on the northwestern frontier. The Qing had a different solution: as Manchus, they knew Central Asia well. With their aggressive military campaigns, they decimated the rival Mongolian state and fostered active trade with Russia and Central Asia under imperial supervision. When Europeans arrived on the south coast with their unusual cargoes of woolens and opium, they at first accepted the same managed trade structure that was applied on the continental frontier. But the peculiar insistence of British and Americans on "free trade" for opium (banned in England), combined with uncontrollable Chinese smuggling,

undermined this officially chartered trade and led to war. China's "tribute system," a flexible set of arrangements for handling multitudes of dignitaries and traders, continued to define East Asian regional trading structures through the nineteenth century. It finally was destroyed by the rival pretensions of other imperial powers, the British and later the Japanese, who could not tolerate alternate visions of a global trading order.

Technology. Far too many historians still have the mistaken impression that significant technological change in China stopped after 1433, with the return home of the last of the great imperially chartered ships, used for voyages into the southern seas. These vessels represented impressive feats of shipbuilding and navigation and the culmination of a maritime age, from 900 to 1433 CE, during which millions of Chinese set their sights on Southeast Asia and beyond. In view of Columbus's serendipitous stumble onto New World shores a few decades later, it is hard to resist evoking missed opportunities.

China's technological evolution did not stop after 1433. The disastrous arrival of the Portuguese, whose method of trade was to plunder every vessel they met, generated an antimaritime orientation among Chinese officials in the sixteenth century, but private Chinese shipping still dominated the Southeast Asian and Indian seas. Through the seventeenth century, Chinese civilian merchant ships still far outweighed in size and cargo those of the Dutch, Portuguese, and English in South Asian waters. The Ming emperors made a rational decision to redirect their efforts toward the northwest frontier, the source of nomad raids. Their response produced China's second greatest civil engineering achievement: the Great Wall. Completed as a nearly continuous bulwark only in the 1570s, it represented a massive mobilization of construction, organizational, and logistical technologies. Linking the garrisons on the wall to the interior also required extensive cooperation with the merchants of the lower Yangzi, who shipped supplies to the northwest in return for salt monopoly licenses.

An even greater infrastructure project completed at this time was the Grand Canal. Originally built in the seventh century to bring grain supplies from the south to the north, it came into its own in the sixteenth century as a major artery of military and commercial communication. Soon, merchant barge-owners elbowed out military quartermasters, defying official complaints. Canny traders had discovered how to convert this national security investment, equivalent to America's interstate highway system, into their own gain. Less conspicuous technological changes were dispersed through the paddy fields in the form of better seeds, new crops, water pumps, and sugar cane crushing mills.

China chose not to invest in naval gunnery, but, on land, the generals quickly adopted new gunpowder weaponry, which the Jesuits had brought back home. The Jesuits' dubious claim that they knew how to cast cannon gave them credibility in spreading the Christian message: they distributed guns and Bibles promiscuously to the Ming, peasant rebels, and the Qing alike. Under Jesuit tutors, the Kangxi emperor (r. 1662–1722) studied Euclid and trigonometry, very useful for planning military campaigns, and commissioned a cartographic survey of the empire for strategic ends. His main rivals, the Zunghar Mongols, also commissioned foreigners to cast cannon and make maps. This arms race stimulated imperial interest in technological advance. Military technological slowdown dates only from the late eighteenth century, after all serious rivals had been crushed.

Implications. China, from the sixteenth to the eighteenth centuries, had nearly all of the necessary ingredients for successful economic growth. The population grew, but not too fast; commercialized agriculture generated demands for trade; labor and capital mobility integrated markets; domestic peace and frontier expansion offered space for growth. Agrarian and military technologies advanced gradually. As for values, although China had no Protestants, the country had thrifty families who saved for the long run; rationalization of exchange; extensive information collection; and a literate elite, some of whom discussed practical political economy.

This leads one to the conclusion that Europe's Industrial Revolution was neither deeply rooted in uniquely Western values nor due to the gradual outgrowth of a special early-modern economy. Historians now must presume a rough similarity in the per capita standard of living in the advanced regions of China and that of Europe in the eighteenth century; and if this is so, scholars must reexamine the sources of Europe's industrial achievements in the nineteenth century and question their theories of social change.

By 1850, however, Europeans spurted ahead while the Chinese declined into turmoil. China lost successive wars with European powers, and a spectacular series of rebellions wracked nearly every part of the empire, depopulating the countryside and disrupting commerce. Up to fifty million people died. After 1870, both China and Japan launched movements to strengthen their industrial and military capabilities, but only Japan succeeded, becoming in 1895 the next on the list of China's oppressors. The most vivid images of China as a land of famine and despair derive from its hapless state in the late nineteenth century.

Rather than list all the possible causes of what Kenneth Pomeranz has called the great divergence, I shall emphasize a few major points. "Feudal" Confucian values or foreign aggression alone does not account for China's plight. The focus must be on frontier conquest, environmental constraints, and institutional sclerosis. Conquest was the

hallmark of the early Qing state. From 1620 to 1760, imperial expansion drove improvements in military technology, the rationalization of government, and the famine-relief system. Securing the people's livelihood produced good soldiers and ensured that the military did not burden the peasantry. New territories facilitated migration, technological diffusion, equalization of regions, and the spread of markets. When expansion stopped after 1760, gradually the steam went out the system. Just as Europe was being catapulted into the Napoleonic Wars, the Qing state was divesting itself of its military, retaining only those forces needed for local control.

China was also unlucky in its periphery. Because Qing armies moved into the interior of Eurasia instead of across the seas, they conquered deserts, steppes, and oases, instead of forests, fertile lands, and silver mines. Europeans improved their man/land ratios by exploiting the vast "ghost acreage" of the New World, leaving room and incentives for labor-saving innovation at home. China's population also pushed outward, but Central Eurasia had no vast amber waves of grain. Unlucky for China, its coal, too, was in the periphery, not close to river transport like England's.

To ecology one must add institutional factors. The Chinese universal empire worked on different principles from those of the European state system. The imperial ideal recognized that all people had defensible economic and social claims. Hungry people must be fed; interregional trade must be encouraged; peace must be preserved. Europe was able to "exploit" (or capitalize on opportunities presented by) radical inequalities, including coerced labor in its peripheries, that were seldom seen in China, but were found in serfdom in Russia and eastern Europe, in American slavery, and in South American haciendas.

The competitive European state system fostered continual warfare as an instrument of national economic development. Colonialism extended this pattern of domination worldwide. China's rulers aimed to create a balance between regions, not a hierarchical core–periphery structure. As inland regions caught up with advanced areas, aided by sponsored migration, the gaps that produced complementary trade were reduced. Unlike those of Europe, handicrafts spread from core to periphery without obstruction; so the lower Yangzi lost its markets, and slowed down. These were the costs of balanced growth.

Persistent local disorder, a result of ecological pressure, undermined these imperial goals. After the big rebellions died down, bandits, local feuding families, and officials exacting protection rents blocked regional trading networks. As the balanced imperial structure unraveled, treaty-port coastal areas progressed, but neglected peripheries became more isolated. By the twentieth century, rural areas off the beaten track had gone backward in measurable ways: in market integration, in decline of public works, in environmental sustainability, in state control and social order.

China's crisis was an interrelated mix of military weakness, domestic disorder, institutional decay, ecological crisis, and cultural ferment, so complex that its best and brightest could not save the empire. Now, after another agonizing century, the Chinese economy is booming, but the political institutions and ecology are still problematic. The lost balance of the flourishing age has not been retrieved, but the imperial model still conditions the policies of the modern nation-state.

BIBLIOGRAPHY

Bernhardt, Kathryn, and Philip Huang, eds. *Civil Law in Qing and Republican China*. Stanford, Calif., 1994. Argues for the important role of civil law in regulating economic and social conflicts.

Brook, Timothy. *The Confusions of Pleasure: Commerce and Culture in Ming China*. Berkeley, 1998. Superb synthesis of the transformation of China by commercialization.

Dunstan, Helen. *Conflicting Counsels to Confuse the Age: A Documentary Study of Political Economy in Qing China, 1644–1840*. Ann Arbor, 1996. Detailed translation and annotation of official discussions of economic policy.

Elvin, Mark, and Ts'ui-jung Liu, eds. *Sediments of Time: Environment and Society in Chinese History*. Cambridge, 1995. Pioneering essays in environmental history.

Lee, James Z., and Wang Feng. *One Quarter of Humanity: Malthusian Mythology and Chinese Realities*. Cambridge, 1999. Provides convincing empirical proof of a revisionist view of China's demographic dynamics.

Li, Bozhong. *Agricultural Development in Jiangnan, 1620–1850*. New York, 1998. Demonstrates the intensification, rising productivity, and modernization of agriculture as a major component of China's economic boom.

Li, Lillian M. *China's Silk Trade: Traditional Industry in the Modern World*. Cambridge, 1981. Discusses both premodern technology and the failures of modern industrialization efforts.

Marks, Robert B. *Tigers, Rice, Silk, and Silt: Environment and Economy in Later Imperial South China*. Cambridge, 1998. Shows how commerce, land clearance, and local ecologies interacted in this prospering region over a thousand years.

Mazumdar, Sucheta. *Sugar and Society in China: Peasants, Technology, and the World Market*. Cambridge, 1998. In contrast to other studies, stresses the limitations of markets and constraints on mobility found in some parts of South China. Provides excellent details on technology of sugar cane production and links to South and Southeast Asian markets.

Millward, James A. *Beyond the Pass: Economy, Ethnicity, and Empire in Qing Central Asia, 1759–1864*. Stanford, Calif., 1998. Examines the impact of imperial policies on the commercial economy of Xinjiang.

Naquin, Susan, and Evelyn Rawski. *Chinese Society in the Eighteenth Century*. New Haven, 1987. Somewhat outdated, but the best survey of this period.

Perdue, Peter C. *Exhausting the Earth: State and Peasant in Hunan, 1500–1850*. Cambridge, 1987. Describes land settlement, water conservancy, immigration, and property relations over the long term.

Perkins, Dwight H. *Agricultural Development in China, 1368–1968*. Chicago, 1969. Filled with valuable data on agrarian output and trade.

Pomeranz, Kenneth. *The Great Divergence: China, Europe, and the Making of the Modern World Economy*. Princeton, 2000. Makes a powerful argument that China was a strong contender until 1850 for global economic leadership.

Rawski, Thomas G., and Lillian M. Li, eds. *Chinese History in Economic Perspective*. Berkeley, 1992. Contains articles on grain, population, labor, women and capital markets from the eighteenth to the twentieth centuries.

Skinner, G. William, ed. *The City in Late Imperial China*. Stanford, Calif., 1977. Includes Skinner's highly influential macroregional analysis, and detailed studies of regions and urban centers.

Skinner, G. William. "Presidential Address: The Structure of Chinese History." *Journal of Asian Studies* 44.2 (1985), 271–292. Outlines the major regional economic cycles of the last thousand years.

Will, Pierre-Etienne, and R. Bin Wong, eds. *Nourish the People: The State Civilian Granary System in China, 1650–1850*. Ann Arbor, 1991. Massive empirical analysis of this key institution.

Wong, R. Bin. *China Transformed: Historical Change and the Limits of European Experience*. Ithaca, N.Y., 1997. Broad-ranging comparative analysis of European and Chinese economies, social structures, and institutions, looking at Europe from China and vice versa.

PETER C. PERDUE

Republican Period

The Chinese Revolution of 1911 marked the end of 267 years of imperial rule under the Qing government (1644–1911) and ushered in the short Republican period in Chinese history. Running between 1912 and 1949, it ended with the military defeat of Jiang Jieshi (Chiang Kaishek) and the Guomindang (Kuomintang or KMT) by Mao Zedong and the Communists and the establishment of the People's Republic of China (PRC) in 1949. The Guomindang subsequently fled to and governed Taiwan under the banner of the Republic of China, ceding power in elections in 1998.

Unlike Meiji Japan (1868–1911), the end of the old order in China failed to herald any sharp break in institutions, policies, or external relations. The problem of a weak central government, endemic to the late Qing, was recurrent throughout the Republican period. In fact at no time between 1912 and 1949 did a single government exercise unified control over all of China. Manchuria (Northeast China), for example, was de facto ruled by the Japanese between 1931 and 1945. Although new policies and relationships between the state and the economy began to emerge during the course of the Nationalist or Nanjing Decade (1928–1937), any effect was obviously short-lived. The Chinese economy was severely disrupted first by the Sino-Japanese War (1937–1945) and then by civil war (1945–1949).

The performance of the economy over the short period in Chinese economic history that includes the last few decades of the Qing dynasty and runs up through 1937, however, has become a source of renewed debate and interest. Conventional wisdom and an earlier historiography tied in part to the outcome of China's protracted civil war holds that over this period the land-scarce and primarily agrarian Chinese economy experienced enormous difficulty in accommodating a modest population; that development of a modern sector was severely limited, and its effect, like that of the international economy on China, was largely confined to the treaty ports; that inequality in the countryside widened, accompanied by a growing urban-rural split; and that a host of institutional and political constraints inhibiting economic growth were not removed until after 1949.

More recently each of these views has come under careful review and assessment. This has been aided by revisionist work on Qing economic and political history, the post-1978 market-liberalizing and open economic reforms in the PRC, and the economic success of Taiwan after 1949 under the KMT (and the Asia miracle more generally), each of which has provided a new lens through which to examine the Republican period. Although severe data limitations for the early twentieth century and for the late Qing dynasty seriously handicap empirical analysis and determination of long-run trends, emerging is a slightly more positive, albeit nuanced and geographically differentiated, view of the extent of economic growth during the late nineteenth century and the twentieth century.

This alternative perspective, while acknowledging continued and significant domestic constraints on economic development and internal weaknesses, highlights: (1) the role of access to new technology and knowledge acquired through China's ongoing economic opening and integration with the international economy; (2) the combined influence of new internal and external factors on demand, resource allocation, and accumulation in major segments of the Chinese economy; (3) the largely positive interactions between China's emerging modern sector and its traditional economy; and (4) the slow emergence of new facilitating institutions. This reinterpretation raises interesting parallels (and contrasts) between China's post-1978 reopening to the international economy and that occurring a century earlier and recalls the important positive legacy of the period on post-1949 developments, especially that in industry. It remains to reconcile this assessment with the much more favorable interpretation now offered for the comparative level development achieved during the mid-Qing dynasty.

Though assessment of longer-run economic trends is difficult and open to debate, it is much easier to provide a snapshot of China's basic economic structure and endowment circa the early 1930s (1931–1936), owing largely to the work of Ta-chung Liu and Kung-chia Yeh (1965). At that time China was still a predominantly agrarian economy with a population of between 500 and 550 million people. Nearly two-thirds of its GNP originated in agriculture, and probably three-quarters of its labor force derived all or most of its income from agriculture. The rest came from earnings in traditional nonagricultural sidelines, such as handicraft textiles. Despite a huge continental landmass, less than 15 percent of China's land was cultivatable, and land per capita in the countryside was less than an acre per capita. The distribution of landownership in farming was also highly skewed, with a quarter of rural Chinese households landless and a third of all land rented. Using largely traditional methods, however, land productivity in China was among the highest in the world, and roughly 40 percent of farm output was marketed.

China had a small nascent modern sector comprising parts of industry, construction, transportation, and finance that totaled 10 percent of GDP. This sector was largely confined to China's urban population, which at its pre-1949 level made up slightly less than 10 percent of the country's population. Although much of the early investment in the modern sector was by foreigners under the protective cover of the treaty ports, by the 1930s three-quarters or more of ownership was Chinese. By the standards of the time China was also a fairly open economy, with imports and exports combined representing nearly an eighth of GNP. It was also a major beneficiary of foreign direct investment, largely from the United Kingdom, Germany, and Japan, and in the 1930s it was the host of 6 percent of the total world stock of FDI. On the other hand, the government sector only commanded between 5 and 10 percent of GDP, much of which went for military expenditure and debt payment. China remained, however, a poor country compared to the West. Maddison's estimates suggest per capita GDP for the early 1930s of approximately U.S. $600 (1990 international $), which ranks China among the world's poorest at that time. Life expectancy was probably only in the vicinity of thirty years or perhaps slightly less.

Much more difficult to assess is the full extent of the growth and structural change that occurred in the Chinese economy over the course of the late nineteenth century and the early twentieth century and the influence of these processes on per capita incomes and China's long-run economic trajectory. Not open to much debate is the growth that occurred in China's industry and modern sector or in its foreign trade. Although smuggling became a more serious issue in the early 1930s under KMT tariff reform (which significantly increased tariffs in a move to protect domestic industry), a combination of low tariffs and the British administration of China's maritime customs contributed to a fairly accurate recording of Chinese trade. On the other hand, China's modern sector does not predate the 1890s, and its growth can be tracked reasonably well. Estimates by John Chang, Thomas Rawksi (1989), and others suggest that China's modern industry, much of it in labor-intensive light industry such as textiles, grew roughly 7 to 8 percent per annum between 1912 and 1918 and between 1931 and 1936 (and by a similar rate between the 1890s and the 1930s). These rates of growth are comparable to that enjoyed by Japan during a similar period in its economic development. Growth in the entire modern sector was slightly less. Foreign trade, on the other hand, grew in real terms at a rate of approximately 4 percent per annum before being affected by the downturn in external demand in the 1930s and experienced a marked shift in its composition over the period.

The weakest link in current assessments of long-run growth is estimates for the rate of agricultural growth over the period, followed by estimates for the traditional nonagricultural sector, including handicraft manufacturing, transportation, and finance. The latter are important because of the sector's potential disruption by modern counterparts and thus the interaction between the modern and traditional sectors. Unresolved issues over the rate of population growth following the Taiping Rebellion in the mid-nineteenth century only compound the problems of converting aggregate growth rates into per capita figures. With roughly two-thirds of total GDP coming from agriculture in the 1930s, estimates of the rate of growth in the economy and empirical assessments of the period hinge pivotally on growth in the farm sector.

Existing estimates for the rate of agricultural output growth in the early twentieth century suggest growth only marginally in excess of population. Unfortunately estimates for the value of agricultural output made for 1914 to 1918 (and thus growth between 1914 and 1918 and between 1931 and 1936) are seriously problematic. These calculations draw on estimates that either not much is known about, for example, changes in cultivated acreage made by the National Agricultural Research Bureau, or that were the product of a weak national reporting system, for example, cropping pattern data from the Ministry of Agriculture and Commerce for the years 1914 to 1918. They also assume that yields remained the same over the entire period. Farm output estimates reconstructed for the 1880s, on the other hand, are simply not usable.

Limitations in "conventional" data for agriculture for the period have spawned the use of alternative measures of the pace of economic activity widely used in historical economics. These include data on farm wages, productivity estimates in nonfarm sectors that competed with agriculture for labor, marketing and trade data, and consumption and nutrition data. These data suggest growth in excess of population, although there are important regional differences. The use of these data has been criticized, largely for the assumptions that reportedly underlie their use, for example, competitive markets in China. The much more serious issue is simple measurement errors in these data that imply confidence intervals that encompass both the growth and no-growth cases. At a minimum there does not

seem to be much disagreement that Chinese agriculture was able to accommodate population growth at earlier per capita output levels and that agriculture in major parts of China experienced an accelerated commercialization over the period. However, more empirical work will be required to resolve ongoing debates over the extent of growth in agriculture and the Chinese economy prior to its disruption in 1937.

Even if the empirical record ultimately shows more growth than previously believed, the pre– and post–World War II experiences of China's land-scarce Asian counterparts, for example, Korea, Japan, and Taiwan, as well as those of China under the post-1978 economic reform, identify a number of important factors that were still largely missing from China during the first half of the twentieth century. Growth in agriculture in each of these contexts has been heavily dependent on the introduction of new high-yielding varieties that entail the substitution of the complementary inputs of chemical fertilizer and water for land (the scarce resource). Essential to the development and spread of these varieties has been significant public investment in seed research and development; coordinated public and private investment in farm infrastructure, notably irrigation and drainage; and the development of farm extension services. These experiences highlight the fundamental role of technological supply (as opposed to demand) constraints in agriculture in these land-scarce economies and the complex political economy influencing public investment decisions and technological innovation in agriculture.

Although the Nationalist government embarked on a similar path for agriculture in the mid-1930s, its program and effort were rather limited. Any significant benefits probably were not realized until after 1949, when the introduction of new hybrids (based on earlier breeding work) was combined with increases in investment in rural infrastructure under the rural communes. Ironically the full benefits of this new technology in China were not to be realized by farmers until the problem of poor incentives under the communes was removed with the reintroduction of family farming in the PRC in 1978 and the implementation of market-liberalizing reforms.

Finally, in each of these successful cases, the state has played an important role in the development process, albeit not always exactly the same. This extended from undertaking infrastructure investment, such as that in human capital and transportation, to fostering an economic and institutional environment conducive to the development of new administrative, organizational, and technical skills so vital to the successful absorption, adaptation, and assimilation of new technologies from outside. Throughout much of the Republican period the state was largely devoid of any capacity in this regard and usually more concerned about internal and external threats and political survival. This makes the growth observed during the period all the more significant. Without being too deterministic, it also portends the positive consequences of the economic and institutional reforms observed in China after 1978 as well as those in Taiwan several decades earlier.

BIBLIOGRAPHY

Brandt, Loren. *Commercialization and Agricultural Development: Central and Eastern China, 1870s–1930s.* New York, 1989.

Huang, Philip. *The Peasant Economy and Social Change in North China.* Stanford, Calif., 1985.

Huang, Philip. *The Peasant Economy and Rural Development in the Yangzi Delta.* Stanford, Calif., 1990.

Liu, Ta-chung, and Kung-chia Yeh. *The Economy of the Chinese Mainland: National Income and Economic Development.* Princeton, 1965.

Myers, Ramon. *The Chinese Peasant Economy: Agricultural Development in Hopei and Shandong, 1890–1940.* Cambridge, Mass., 1970.

Perkins, Dwight, ed. *China's Modern Economy in Historical Perspective.* Stanford, Calif., 1975.

Rawski, Thomas. *Economic Growth in Prewar China.* Berkeley, 1989.

Richardson, Phillip. *Economic Change in China, c.1800–1950.* Cambridge, 1999.

Schran, Peter. "China's Demographic Evolution, 1850–1953, Reconsidered." *China Quarterly* (1978).

LOREN BRANDT

Communist China

Before 1949 China had experienced the beginnings of industrialization, but development had been hampered by foreign invasion, war, and civil war. The resumption of development became possible with the military victory of the Chinese Communist Party and the establishment of the People's Republic of China in October 1949. The new government scored a number of early successes, as it controlled inflation, rehabilitated industry, and distributed land to farmers. By the early 1950s the government had embarked on a program of "forced draft" industrialization. For the following half century the experience of rapid industrial growth fueled by high rates of investment was a constant. In virtually all other respects, however, the economic history of post-1949 China divides into two distinct periods—before and after 1978—that could hardly have been more different.

The period before 1978 was dominated by a socialist industrialization strategy, government control of the economy, and a virtual exclusion of markets. Institutions from the Soviet Union were adapted to create a planned economy that evolved through instability and policy inconsistencies into a distinctive Maoist variant of the socialist model. After 1978 China tentatively began a program to reform—and ultimately to abandon—the planned economy and make the transition to a market economy. Since 1978 the reinstatement of market forces has been a main priority,

and the economy has become increasingly integrated into the global economy. In addition, after 1978, growth accelerated, and living standards increased rapidly.

Maoist China, 1949–1978. During the mid-1950s the Chinese government gradually adopted the essential elements of a Soviet-style economic system. Government control was gradually extended over the economy, and resources were allocated according to planners' commands, rather than price and profitability signals. During 1955 and 1956 farmers were organized into agricultural collectives, reversing what had been a program of voluntary cooperation among farm households newly endowed with their own land. In the cities, factories and other large-scale economic organizations were systematically nationalized.

As the government established its control over the price system, it used that control to channel resources into the government budget. Farmers were required to deliver agricultural produce to the government monopoly at low fixed prices. Relative prices of industrial products were high, especially those of manufactured consumer goods. With low farm prices and low wages, government-run factories were in a position to harvest large surpluses for government use. These surpluses were channeled through the budget into industrial investment. Total investment, as a share of gross domestic product (GDP), surpassed 25 percent in 1954, and most of this was government investment in heavy industry. The first Five Year Plan was drawn up to cover the years 1953 to 1957, with the investment plan focused on 156 large industrial projects imported from the Soviet Union.

Reflecting its high priority in the socialist plan, industry grew rapidly, sustaining an average annual growth rate of 11.4 percent from 1952 to 1978, according to official figures. Progress was also made in spreading basic health care and literacy, and life expectancy grew from approximately fifty in the 1950s (estimates vary) to sixty-eight in 1981 (based on the 1982 census). The Maoist period thus saw a sustained process of modernization, industrialization, and structural change in Chinese society. Gross domestic product, again according to official figures, grew 6 percent annually through 1978, and with population growth at 2 percent, per capita GDP grew 4 percent per year. Overall performance was somewhat less impressive than these figures indicate, however. In the first place, agriculture was a chronic weak spot in the economy, with output growing much more slowly at 2.8 percent and with agriculture seemingly unable to produce adequate food and also release sufficient workers to the modern sector. Moreover official data overstate the real growth performance, because the distorted price system tended to overweight rapidly growing industrial sectors and because other official data procedures produce upward bias. Unfortunately no definitive recalculation of growth rates has yet been done. Finally, because an increasing share of national output was devoted to investment—and an increasing share was wasted—per capita consumption in urban and rural areas grew by 3 percent and 1.8 percent respectively, considerably below the growth of per capita GDP.

At first during the mid-1950s it appeared that the Chinese regime would successfully avoid the worst excesses of past Soviet experience in establishing agricultural collectives and nationalizing the urban economy with relatively little economic disruption or loss of life. However, almost immediately after the achievements of the mid-1950s Mao Zedong, the supreme leader, began to intervene in economic policy in an erratic and ultimately disastrous fashion. Mao pushed for a "Great Leap Forward" between 1958 and 1960. The leap was a utopian mass mobilization that aimed to dramatically accelerate the pace of economic growth, ushering in a communism of abundance within a few years. National leaders mistakenly believed that bumper harvests had released constraints on the economy, and false reports from local officials encouraged the delusions of top leaders. Farmers were organized into huge communes with thirty thousand or more households that set up free social services and dining halls and organized huge labor armies for agricultural and industrial pursuits. Under the slogan "walking on two legs," commune members were sent to work in "backyard steel mills," developing small-scale, low-technology factories, while at the same time large urban factories with modern technology recruited millions of new workers from the countryside.

The Great Leap Forward led to disaster. Some fifty million prime agricultural workers left the farms, and agricultural output began to drop markedly. Planners failed to heed warning signs and increased agricultural procurements from already high levels, so almost 40 percent of the 1959 grain harvest was taken by the state and 35 percent of the 1960 harvest. Famine began in poorer agricultural provinces that could least afford to turn over nonexistent surpluses to the government. In Sichuan Province cumulative excess deaths from hunger and disease between 1959 and 1961 amounted to 14 percent of the population; in Anhui and Henan Provinces excess deaths were 7 percent of the population. According to the best estimates, twenty-five to thirty million excess deaths were recorded between 1959 and 1961. The Great Leap Forward famine was one of the worst twentieth-century famines anywhere in the world. Although the Chinese government has confirmed the basic facts about the famine, the event and its causes are rarely discussed inside China.

In 1961 planners belatedly began to rectify the worst policies of the Great Leap Forward policies. Farmers were sent back to the farm, compulsory procurements were reduced, food imports began, and a realistic set of economic

COMMUNIST CHINA. "Long live the general line!" proclaims a Chinese poster, 1961. (International Institute for Social History, Amsterdam)

priorities was adopted by planners. Yet even after its worst effects were liquidated, the leap had an enduring negative legacy. To prevent a recurrence of workers exiting agriculture, rural-to-urban migration was effectively halted by a system of household registration rigidly stratified into rural and urban. As all urban jobs were assigned by the state, job mobility disappeared within the urban sector as well.

Moreover, just as the economy was beginning to recover, Mao intervened again to radicalize Chinese policy and plunged China into a renewed period of economic and political turmoil. During 1964 industrial investment suddenly increased and was refocused on a costly program of dispersed, defense-related plants in remote inland areas known as the "Third Front." Beginning in 1966 the so-called "Cultural Revolution" led to a profound disruption of China's politics and institutions that lasted until Mao's death in 1976. The Cultural Revolution (CR) was primarily a political movement, and the leadership had learned enough from the Great Leap Forward disaster to prevent the CR from leading directly to economic catastrophe. But the CR was nonetheless extremely damaging to China's institutional health and long-run economic performance. Universities were closed through most of the CR, and supplies of skilled manpower declined. Seventeen million urban secondary school graduates were sent to the countryside, where many felt trapped and underutilized. Output growth slowed as the stock of incomplete investment projects steadily grew.

By the early 1970s China's economic system had been significantly altered from its original Soviet model. While remaining a command economy, a kind of Maoist economic system had emerged. This system was relatively decentralized, less dependent upon huge factories, and less effectively planned than the Soviet model. A particularly striking development was the development of small-scale rural industries, later called "township and village industries" or TVEs. Harking back to the Great Leap Forward, rural industries were promoted—carefully this time—to serve agriculture with cement, machinery, and fertilizer.

China during this phase was largely isolated internationally and came close to autarchy. A side effect of the Great Leap Forward had been the rupturing of previously close relations with the Soviet Union. Soviet advisers were abruptly removed from China in mid-1960, and China thereafter lacked an adequate source of modern technology for its growing industry. There was no foreign investment, and total foreign trade (exports plus imports) amounted to only 5 percent of GDP in 1971. Even provinces and regions within China were encouraged to become self-sufficient.

In this environment a kind of austerity socialism prevailed. Bonuses and other material incentives were largely eliminated. Socialist idealism was compulsory, and the military presence was pervasive. Overall, industry continued to grow, and a particularly striking achievement was the creation of a large domestic petroleum industry. But behind the facade of growth, economic and social institutions were increasingly rigid and fragile.

Reformist China, Post-1978. The death of Mao in 1976 broke the political paralysis of the Cultural Revolution. At a key Communist Party meeting in December 1978, veteran party leaders Deng Xiaoping and Chen Yun reemerged to assume control of economic policy. By mid-1979 a broad program of economic reforms had been adopted that included openness to some foreign investment, relaxation of rural policies, and experimentation with industrial reforms. The commitment to reform was vague and without a clear objective, but veteran leaders brought in younger leaders to push reforms forward.

China's approach to market transition over the next two decades was very different from the rapid dismantling of the state systems in Russia and Eastern Europe. China generally maintained the institutions inherited from the Maoist era, only gradually reshaping them to meet the needs of a market economy. Privatization played virtually no role in the urban enterprise sector until the late 1990s, almost twenty years after the initiation of reform. Instead, the key policy initiative was the reduction of entry barriers protecting state monopolies. New entrants—initially from rural areas and especially township and village enterprises—reshaped the competitive landscape and eroded the protected position of state firms. State firms in turn were given increased autonomy and more powerful incentives in an attempt to revitalize them to meet the competitive challenges. Market forces were introduced on the margin, drawing resources into relatively high-value uses, but the system as a whole remained highly distorted. As market forces grew, they put increasing pressure on policy makers to address deep-seated institutional distortions. Remarkably policy makers were generally able to address critical economic problems and provide the bare essentials necessary to sustain growth.

With reform China's GDP growth accelerated to 9.7 percent per annum from 1978 to 1998. Since population growth declined to 1.3 percent, per capita GDP growth doubled from the pre-reform 4 percent to 8 percent between 1978 and 1998. As in the earlier period, growth rates are overstated in official data, but plausible revisions do not challenge the remarkable acceleration in growth that took place after 1978. Industrial output growth increased from 11 percent to 15 percent, but agricultural growth accelerated from 2.8 percent to 6.6 percent. Consumption growth in both rural and urban areas accelerated to over 6 percent per year. Sustained growth of this scale contributed to substantial changes in Chinese society, including the slackening of controls on population and job mobility, accelerated migration and urbanization, and the emergence of a consumer society.

Rural areas were the first to see substantial change. Increased autonomy to rural collectives led gradually—but seemingly inexorably—to a system of contracting land to individual farm households. Farmers agreed to turn over a stipulated quantity of grain—the price of which was raised from the punitive levels prevailing at the end of the CR—and received control over their land and net incomes. When farm output increased dramatically in 1983–1984, it convinced wavering government leaders to embrace reforms and push for a more fundamental market transition. The relaxation of controls over the rural economy also fueled a rapid growth in the township and village enterprises (TVEs) that had grown up during the CR. TVEs were increasingly given the freedom to produce whatever the market demanded. Given pervasive shortages of manufactured goods and the distorted price system that privileged industrial production, TVEs were extremely profitable, and lowered entry barriers led to an explosion in activity. Rapid improvements in farm efficiency allowed households to shift labor to off-farm activities, and agricultural workers dropped from 70 percent to 50 percent of the national labor force by 1996.

Policy makers sought to replicate the rural success in urban areas. They began to allow markets to develop alongside the administered economy, creating a two-tiered system of plan and market. State-owned firms were allowed to sell at market prices as long as they fulfilled their planned deliveries at planned prices. At the same time state-owned firms faced new competitive pressures, especially from TVEs. Factory managers were given generous incentives to maintain or increase profitability, and management authority was decentralized. Industrial growth accelerated as well, but inflation surged, too.

Reforms of the external sector began quickly in the early reform period. Policy makers needed foreign exchange to renew technology imports after years of isolation; but they were hesitant to open domestic markets to foreign trade, worried that inefficient indigenous firms and distorted prices would lead to trade imbalances. Instead, special economic zones or SEZs—similar to the export processing zones pioneering in Taiwan and elsewhere in East Asia— were set up in southern China beginning in 1979. Export processing arrangements and externally oriented foreign investment were permitted in order to facilitate China's reentry into world markets. Trade growth was fueled by the restructuring of existing export production networks in Hong Kong and Taiwan, as labor intensive activities were moved to the Chinese mainland. Trade and foreign direct investment both grew rapidly. After 1992 China also began to offer access to domestic markets to foreign investors (even though import barriers remained high). Foreign companies responded with a flood of incoming foreign investment that exceeded U.S. $40 billion each year from 1996, making China by far the largest developing country destination for foreign direct investment. China's total trade soared from 10 percent of GDP in 1978 to 44 percent of GDP in 2000, and half of China's exports were produced by foreign-invested firms.

After the mid-1990s China's approach to market transition began to display significant changes. The previous strategy of introducing market forces to aid in the dissolution of the planned economy had been made irrelevant by its own success. Chinese policy makers faced difficult problems adapting inadequate institutions to the increasing demands of a dynamic and increasingly market-oriented economy. State-owned enterprises shed 40 percent of their workforce between 1992 and 2000. Privatization became an important component in policy, although it continued to be downplayed. Large firms undertook partial privatization by listing on the stock market and selling off minority stakes; smaller firms were privatized by local governments through a variety of forms. Tax systems were restructured, and the banking system faced significant challenges. The will to continue the process of system transformation was symbolized by China's entry into the World Trade Organization (WTO) at the beginning of 2002. By joining the WTO, China committed to a substantial opening of its domestic economy to foreign goods, lowering import barriers that had remained stubbornly high until then. Moreover WTO membership implied a commitment to rules of government regulation and to locking in the transition process. Particularly important were the commitments to accept foreign participation in service sectors, such as finance and telecommunications, which had remained, until that time, the last redoubt of state monopoly ownership and control. In the early part of the twenty-first century the dynamism of economic growth and structural transformation appeared to be leading toward a full transition to a market economy.

BIBLIOGRAPHY

Byrd, William, and Qingsong Lin, eds. *China's Rural Industry: Structure, Development and Reform*. New York, 1990. In-depth institutional analysis by an international team of scholars.

Comprehensive Statistical Data and Materials on 50 Years of New China. National Bureau of Statistics, Department of Comprehensive Statistics. Beijing, 1999. Easily accessible source of official data, with headings in Chinese and English.

Joseph, William, Christine Wong, and David Zweig, eds. *New Perspectives on the Cultural Revolution*. Cambridge, Mass., 1991. Includes reassessments of rural industry, the Third Front, and central-local relations during the Cultural Revolution.

Knight, John, and Lina Song. *The Rural-Urban Divide: Economic Disparities and Interactions in China*. Oxford, 1999. Combines microeconomic analysis based on survey data with broad structural view.

Lin, Justin Yifu, Fang Cai, and Zhou Li. *The China Miracle: Development Strategy and Economic Reform*. Hong Kong, 1996. The section on the socialist development strategy is especially good.

Lin, Justin Yifu, and Dennis Tao Yang. "Food Availability, Entitlements, and the Chinese Famine of 1959–1961." *The Economic Journal* 110 (January 2000), 136–158.

Maddison, Angus. *Chinese Economic Performance in the Long Run*. Paris, 1998. An alternative calculation that sets a floor to plausible growth rates.

Naughton, Barry. *Growing Out of the Plan: Chinese Economic Reform, 1978–1993*. New York, 1995. Comprehensive coverage of industry, macroeconomics, and transition strategy.

Riskin, Carl. *China's Political Economy: The Quest for Development since 1949*. New York, 1991. A thoughtful reconsideration of the goals and shortcomings of economic system and development strategy under Mao.

BARRY NAUGHTON

CHRYSLER, WALTER (1875–1940), American industrialist.

The first automobile bearing Walter Chrysler's name was assembled in 1924. Within five years, his company rivaled Ford and General Motors for leadership in the industry, rising to number two in the U.S. automobile market by 1933, ahead of Ford. In recognition of this extraordinary accomplishment, *Time* magazine would name him its second man of the year, after Charles Lindbergh.

Born in Kansas, Chrysler rejected a university education, opting instead to complete an apprenticeship at the shops of Union Pacific in 1897, and spending the next fifteen years gaining practical experience in numerous railway maintenance shops. In 1910, he moved to Pittsburgh, where he was responsible for the design and manufacture of locomotives for the American Locomotive Works.

His talent for organizing manufacturing works caught the attention of James Storrow, head of General Motors' finance committee. Looking for someone to bring order to GM, he made Chrysler works manager at Buick in 1912. Chrysler quickly turned Buick into a profitable division of GM, abandoning much of the technology borrowed from the older carriage trade. Borrowing from the railway manufacturing sector, where profit margins were low, he tightened accounting practices and formalized the piecework payment system. Pursuing the same strategy as Ford at Highland Park, he designed special-purpose machines, and around 1913 or 1914 he set up a crude moving assembly line.

In 1916, Durant regained control of General Motors and enticed Chrysler to become president of Buick and GM vice-president in charge of operations, at an annual salary of $500,000. The arrangement was short-lived. Chrysler grew disenchanted with Durant and in 1920 announced his retirement. However, Chrysler's talent for organizing production systems was well known and in a few months he was approached by Willys Overland, with an offer to rescue the troubled firm at an annual salary of $1,000,000. The attempt failed, and Willys Overland was liquidated in 1921. Before this collapse, he was courted by the owners of Maxwell Motors. Chrysler saw potential in the floundering Maxwell and by 1923 had become president of that company. In 1924, he introduced the Chrysler Six, a car that sold for $1,500 and featured advanced engineering and stylish design. In 1925, the company was renamed the Chrysler Corporation. Still a relatively small producer of midpriced vehicles, Chrysler entered the volume market dominated by Ford and GM through his purchase of Dodge in 1928, introducing the Plymouth that same year.

Chrysler's contribution to the automobile industry and the evolution of mass production have long been underappreciated. The changes at Buick during 1912 and 1913 clearly anticipated the production system that would come to dominate the industry after 1919. Of equal interest is the management structure Chrysler pioneered. He abandoned the personal-owner-managed model found at most early vehicle companies, including Ford, moving to an impersonal professional management structure that allowed

WALTER CHRYSLER. (Daimler-Chrysler Historical Collection)

Chrysler to maintain firm control over operations in Detroit from its corporate headquarters in New York. This organization facilitated Chrysler's expansion to become a multimarket vehicle supplier in the 1920s, and underscored the sound engineering and marketing methods that secured Chrysler's position among the U.S. "big three." His goal was to create an organization that eliminated the human factor and was based on scientific principles.

BIBLIOGRAPHY

Chrysler, Walter P. *Life of an American Workman.* New York, 1937.

Curicio, Vincent. *Chrysler: The Life and Times of an Automotive Genius.* New York, 2000.

Edsforth, Ronald. "Walter Percy Chrysler." In *American National Biography*, edited by John Garraty, vol. 4, pp. 859–861. New York, 1999.

Fox, Steven. "I Like to Build Things." *American Heritage of Inventions and Technology* 15.1 (1999), 20–30.

WAYNE LEWCHUK

CLAN LAND. In early agrarian societies, it was commonplace to find the ownership of land exercised by kin-based descent groups known as lineages. In some parts of the world (western Europe), these landowning kin-groups did not survive the spread of feudalism. In other parts (Africa and South Asia), they have survived to the present day. Why they originated in the first place can be explained in a number of ways; but once farming had developed and communities began to invest significant amounts of labor in preparing the ground or had cause to protect grazing resources against other claimants, control over specific blocks of land became a powerful contributory factor to their formation. In such societies, right of claim to land and its product was based on whether one's ancestors had occupied the land.

Though cognatic or bilateral groups also existed, most lineages were unilineal, tracing descent either patrilineally or matrilineally. The former type was the more common form, accounting for about 70 percent of all lineage-based societies and found widely in parts of Africa (the Nuer of Ghana), South Asia (the Kachin of Burma), and the Americas (the Yanomama in Amazonia), as well as Europe (the medieval Irish *fine* and Welsh *gwely*). The latter type also was found in the Pacific (the Trobriand islanders) and South Asia (the Nayar of south India), parts of Africa (the Bemba of central Africa), and America (the Crow Indians), but everywhere was localized in occurrence. As landholding groups, patrilineal and matrilineal groups differed in one important respect: right of claim among patrilineal groups was traced back through a man's father, with the land of each lineage becoming divided between sons, fathers, grandfathers, and so on; in matrilineal societies, it was traced from daughters back to mothers, and so on. In the latter case, boys went to live in their mother's home settlement, to be brought up by their mother's brother, that is, their uncle; so the typical matrilineal farming community comprised daughters and mothers together with their sons and their brothers.

Structurally, kin groups ranged from minimal lineages embracing kin linked across no more than three or four generations to maximal lineages that could embrace all males linked across as many as ten or more generations. As the size of the kin group grew, the kin ties often became more generalized; and, as they did so, maximal lineages tended to merge into clans. Though the term is sometimes used in other senses, clans typically comprised maximal lineages or groupings of lineages in which common descent from an apical ancestor was claimed but could not be specified, and could even be putative or assumed.

As landholding groups, lineages and clans embraced a multitude of arrangements. On the one hand, land could be owned by the lineage, with individual kinsmen being given use rights in particular plots or holdings. On the other, lineages might form part of a larger network of clanship under the leadership of a chief, with the latter initially assuming a jurisdiction over all clan lands on behalf of the entire clan and its constituent lineages; and, in time, some chiefs came to exercise such overall control absolutely (as among Scottish highland clans), in a form that could differ little from feudalism. In between these two extremes lay a welter of intermediate forms. Patrilineal lineages, for example, were prone to regular fission in response to growth, new lineages being formed once established ones had become too big. These fissionable tendencies meant that the older core areas of landholding became progressively fragmented between lineages that could be quite shallow in terms of their generational depth. Patrilineal lineages also tended to be expansionist in their approach to land, not only pushing freely into unoccupied space but also competing aggressively to displace rival lineages or clans from occupied land.

BIBLIOGRAPHY

Fortes, Meyer. *Kinship and the Social Order: The Legacy of Lewis Henry Morgan.* London, 1969.

Fox, Robin. *Kinship and Marriage: An Anthropological Perspective.* Harmondsworth, 1967.

Parkin, Robert. *Kinship: An Introduction to Basic Concepts.* Oxford, 1997.

Radcliffe-Brown, Alfred R., and Cyril D. Forde, eds. *African Systems of Kinship and Marriage.* Oxford, 1950.

Schneider, David M. *American Kinship: A Cultural Account.* 2d ed. Chicago, 1980.

ROBERT. A. DODGSHON

CLAPHAM, JOHN (1873–1946), economic historian.

The eminent economic historian T. S. Ashton once said that all the best economic historians were born within a ten-mile radius of the center of Manchester. He may well have had Sir John Clapham in mind, and certainly he qualifies as one of them by that criterion. Born in Manchester in 1873 into a sober nonconformist family, Clapham became a conforming Christian steeped in the Victorian middle-class values of his family. He was to become a pioneer in economic history. Clapham was by training and temperament an empiricist. He knew a great deal of economic theory, having been taught by Alfred Marshall, and history (his first subject), for which his mentors were Lord Acton and William Cunningham. He taught history at Cambridge and was elected a fellow of King's College in 1898. But Marshall encouraged Clapham to go to Leeds as professor of economics in 1902. Clapham returned to Cambridge in 1908 as a lecturer and in 1928 became the first professor of economic history at Cambridge. The following year he gave an inaugural lecture entitled, "The Study of Economic History." He is sometimes said to have been the first to delineate the study of economic history.

In 1935 Clapham was elected a member of King's College, Cambridge, where John M. Keynes was bursar. Apparently Clapham disliked Keynes and disagreed with his approach to economics. When the London School of Economics left London for Cambridge in wartime in 1940, Keynes found accommodation for Frederick August Hayek at King's, and Clapham became a great friend of Hayek's.

Clapham was vice provost of King's from 1933 to 1943. He was elected president of the British Academy in 1940 and remained as such until his death in 1946 at the age of seventy-two. He was knighted in 1943. He was also president of the Economic History Society.

Clapham believed the economic historian should be above all a measurer. The questions he pursued were how large, what part of the whole economy was involved, how long did it last, and how often did it happen? His emphasis was on the achievement of a correct record of events, and he resisted the temptation to generalize. He was concerned with precision and used statistics to achieve that, but he was more concerned with writing attractive narrative and avoiding the dangers of making the subject arid. He succeeded greatly in that aim.

Clapham's first book on the woollen and worsted industries, which he called an exercise in descriptive economics, was published in 1907. In 1921 his pioneering comparative study of the economic development of France and Germany, a conventional economic history, was published. There followed his three-volume economic history of modern Britain in 1928, 1932, and 1938, hailed at the time as the best economic history written. And in the 1940s he produced the two-volume study of the history of the Bank of England. Originally intended to celebrate the bank's 250th birthday, the book was published in 1944. It had its critics (though Ashton and Richard Sayers were admirers). But it is a remarkable testament to Clapham's empiricism that sixty years on it remained the first work to turn to for anyone interested in the development of the bank, a reliable account of its history.

BIBLIOGRAPHY

Mathias, Peter. "Sir John Clapham." In *International Encyclopaedia of Social Sciences*. New York, 1968.

Postan, Michael. "Sir John Clapham." *Economic History Review* 161 (1946), 56–59. Clapham's obituary.

Usher, Abbot P. "Sir J. H. Clapham and the Empirical Reaction in Economic History." *Journal of Economic History* 11.2 (1951), 148–153.

FORREST CAPIE

CLIMATE AND CLIMATE HISTORY.

The global climate of the last millennium is reconstructed using evidence from both "natural" and documentary evidence. Natural data are essential for those periods of history and those regions of the world for which documentary evidence is sparse or nonexistent. For example, annual growth rings in long-lived trees (dendrochronological data) provide the backbone for the climate history of precolonial North America and northern Eurasia. Conditions in high altitudes and latitudes are documented from annual strata of snowfall accumulation in ice cores drilled into high mountain and polar ice caps or from the historical position of glacier tongues.

Marine biologists study the density of living coral reefs two hundred to eight hundred years of age found in shallow tropical oceans. Annually laminated sediments from coastal basins or lake beds generate data about temperature, solar radiation, and precipitation. However, for investigations into the human dimension of climatic change, the time resolution of most data from natural archives is inadequate.

Documentary Evidence. Historical climatology, which serves as an interface between climatology and history, critically reviews and interprets human archives. It is directed toward three objectives:

1. reconstructing weather and climate as well as natural disasters prior to the creation of scientific meteorological stations,
2. investigating the vulnerability of past societies to climatic extremes and natural disasters, and
3. exploring past discourses on and social representations of climate.

Studies in historical climatology were promoted by the French historian Emmanuel Le Roy Ladurie and by the English climatologist Hubert H. Lamb. In the framework of European Union (EU) research programs during the 1990s, climate historians improved their methodologies and developed common standards.

Whereas documentary evidence is well researched in Europe and in East Asia, investigations have hardly begun in Latin America, and the evidence for Africa is spotty. In the Islamic world and in precolonial India the possibly abundant evidence is unexplored.

Documentary evidence is classified into descriptive and proxy data. Descriptive data include chroniclers' narratives of weather patterns and natural disasters memorable to a particular region or town. Chinese historians have drawn upon annual climate observations in local gazetteers maintained by local gentry in nearly every local district. To more objectively portray the character of extreme events, European and Chinese chroniclers referred to the duration of snow cover or the freezing of water bodies, stages in the development of crops, and high and low water levels. African climate history draws on long-term chronologies of lake levels and rivers (for example, the Nile) supplemented by African famine-drought chronologies and the observations of early European explorers.

Weather diaries were kept in Japan from about 1000 BCE. In Europe systematic daily weather observations were promoted by the rise of planetary astronomy from the late fifteenth century. In the late seventeenth century regular instrumental measurements (air pressure, temperature, precipitation) were initiated. Subsequently many elites took such measurements. In 1780 Karl Theodor, elector of the Palatinate (southwestern Germany), created a first short-lived international network equipped with standardized instruments. In 1860 national meteorological networks came into being, but in many parts of the globe regular measurements were not taken before the early twentieth century.

Indirect (proxy) measures of climate are drawn mostly from administrative records. These may yield long, continuous, and quasi-homogeneous series of data that can be calibrated with instrumental measurements. Proxy data may reflect the beginning of agricultural activities, such as the grain or vine harvest; agricultural production, for example, the yield of vineyards; the time of freezing and thawing of seaports or inland waterways; or the time of religious ceremonies. For example, the blossoming of the sweet cherry trees around Kyoto, Japan, was recorded from the Middle Ages. Records of rogations (that is, standardized religious ceremonies to put an end to a meteorological stress situation) are a promising source for the Spanish-speaking world. In Spain rogations were recorded in the account books of both the municipalities and the church.

Usually the evidence available for a given month or season is converted to ordinal indices for temperature and precipitation. Computing transfer functions with instrumental series allows assessments of temperature and precipitation for the preinstrumental period. Series of indices are included in statistical models to reconstruct monthly mean air pressure at sea level for the eastern North Atlantic–European region (25° west to 30° east longitude and 35° north to 70° north latitude) back to 1659.

Climatic Trends and Anomalies. Paleoclimatologists and climate historians have assembled robust evidence that the world's climate changed significantly during the last millennium. They describe four phases: a "medieval warm period" to 1300; a transitory interval from 1300 to 1550; a subsequent cool phase to the late nineteenth century called the "Little Ice Age" because glaciers in most regions of the globe expanded during that time; and the warmest period, partly a consequence of the increased greenhouse effect, after 1950. However, such generalizations on the global level mask a broad array of contrasting regional and local trends. Moreover to investigate human vulnerability to climatic stress, the perspective of "ages" needs to be broken down to regional monthly or seasonal temperature and precipitation patterns. So far this level of detail is only available for Europe and China.

Iceland. Evidence shows a cooling in Iceland between the late thirteenth century and the mid-fourteenth century, whereas the period from 1390 to 1430 was relatively mild. From 1580 the data suggest a multidecadal cooling, during which milder decades (the 1610s, 1641–1660, 1700–1730) alternated with severe ones (1620–1640, the 1690s, 1730–1800). In the nineteenth century the seasonal variability

was greater, with more extremely cold months than in the twentieth century.

Central Europe. Winters in Central Europe, after a cold phase in the twelfth century, were prevailingly warm from 1180 to 1300. Up to 1900 the winter half year was colder than subsequent winters, owing to more frequent and sustained advection of cold-dry continental air masses from the (north)east. Severe winters were frequent in the periods 1306 to 1328, 1430 to 1490, 1565 to 1615, 1655 to 1710, 1755 to 1860, and 1880 to 1895. From 1365 to 1400, from 1520 to 1560, and from 1610 to 1650 moderate winters prevailed. Springs were extremely cold in the 1690s and in the 1740s.

Summers do not show distinct long-term characteristics. Those in the thirteenth century were prevailingly warm and dry. In the fourteenth century clusters of cold and wet summers occurred repeatedly (for example, in the 1310s and the 1340s). From 1380 to 1430 and again from 1530 to 1565 the summer half year was as warm as today. Over the last third of the sixteenth century cold spells and long rains in midsummer expanded at the expense of warm anticyclonic weather. This tendency culminated in the 1590s. Summers at the beginning and the end of the seventeenth century were prevailingly cool, and those from 1630 to 1687 were moderate. In the 1700s several warm decades (the 1720s, the 1730s, and the 1780s) were noted in England and central Europe, whereas the first half of the nineteenth century, particularly the 1810s, were markedly cooler.

Russia. Winters in Russia became more severe at the end of the sixteenth century, in particular from 1620 to 1680 and in the first half of the nineteenth century. In the summer half year droughts were frequent in the periods 1201 to 1230, 1351 to 1380, and 1411 to 1440. A period of comparatively warm conditions in all seasons stands out during the first half of the sixteenth century. Subsequently, cold spells occurred more often from 1590 to 1620 and from 1690 to 1740 with a peak in the 1730s. Droughts occurred frequently from 1640 to 1659 and from 1680 to 1699. The six decades from 1770 to 1830 were warm, and droughts were frequent from 1801 to 1860. Summers from 1890 to 1920 were by far the coldest in the last five hundred years and included an unusually large number of extreme dry and wet seasons.

China. In South China the thirteenth century was the warmest of the last millennium. Three cold periods, 1470 to 1520, 1620 to 1740, and 1840 to 1890, have been identified, the 1650s by far the coldest decade. Rainfall during the seventeenth century was extremely variable. Temperatures during the eighteenth century, unlike in Europe, rarely climbed to twentieth-century levels, but precipitation conditions were more favorable. Climate variability increased markedly throughout the nineteenth century to a maximum in the early twentieth century. In North China

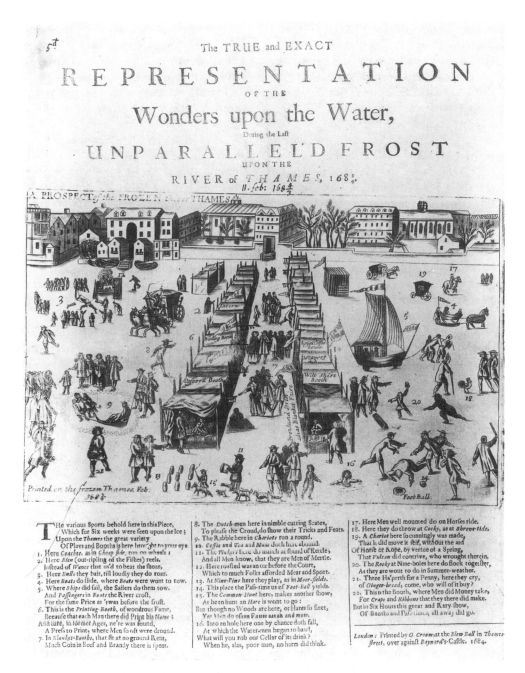

FROST. Fair on the frozen Thames River, London, 1683–1684. Broadsheet, February 1684. (The Fotomas Index, U.K.)

two cold periods, 1500 to 1690 and 1800 to 1860, stand out over the last six centuries. Considering all seasons, the period from 1650 to 1670 was the coldest, but the summer half year was almost equally cold from 1580 to 1600.

The Mediterranean. After a cold twelfth century, the period 1200 to 1400 was warm in the Southwest. Annual precipitation in Morocco was generally lower from the sixteenth century to the nineteenth century. In Catalonia (northeastern Spain) dry spells in the winter half year were

frequent in the mid-sixteenth century but were almost absent from 1580 to 1620. Numerous autumnal floods were reported from 1580 to 1630. The island of Crete (eastern Mediterranean) experienced twenty-one winters marked by cold or excessive rains between 1547 and 1645, whereas in twenty-five years the rains failed. From 1680 to 1710 Arctic air repeatedly penetrated into the eastern or western Mediterranean with devastating effects on crops and fruit trees (for example, in 1709). In Catalonia autumnal floods were remarkably frequent from 1770 to 1800 and again from 1840 to 1870.

Africa. In most regions of Africa the critical issue is the annual precipitation during the monsoon. Annual rainfall levels (that is, isohyetes) mark the boundaries of vegetation zones, for example, in West Africa between the Sahelian cattle zone and the savanna, where rain-fed crops are grown. During wetter periods isohyets advanced northward; during dryer periods they moved to the south. In West Africa a wet period stands out from 700 BCE to 1300 CE. It was followed by a drier period from 1300 to 1500. Between 1500 and 1700 rainfall was more plentiful than in the preceding period or in the twentieth century, and at that time the savanna zone extended to the town of Timbuktu (16° north latitude). From the eighteenth century the zones receded again. By 1850 they had moved two hundred to three hundred kilometers to the south. Black cattle raisers retreated, and Arab camel nomads advanced in the wake of this shift. In the 1820s and 1830s most of the continent experienced a pattern of drought and below-average rainfall. Probably such conditions prevailed until 1850. In the late nineteenth century the situation changed. From 1870 to 1900 increased rainfall characterized much of the continent. Lake levels and the discharge of major streams exceeded the twentieth-century average.

Greenland, Canada, the United States. At Camp Century, Greenland, the coldest conditions seem to have been in the seventeenth century. In northern Canada summer temperatures were generally low from 1570 to 1860. In the northern United States no prolonged periods of cool temperatures were evident between 1640 and 1820. In the western United States average conditions from 1602 to 1900 were warmer and drier compared to the period after 1900. Regional droughts were more frequent during the eighteenth century and after 1920, whereas few droughts were recorded in the second half of the nineteenth century.

Mexico. In Mexico wet conditions characterized much of the Aztec period (1445–1521). Since the mid-1550s the climate of central Mexico has been characterized by a prolonged drought that was particularly acute during the 1590s, 1620s, 1690s, 1770 to 1790, and the late 1800s.

South America. Both Spanish and Portuguese America experienced a trend toward greater aridity in the 1700s compared to the 1600s. Dendroclimatic evidence for the Santiago de Chile area indicates higher than average rainfall from 1450 to 1600, whereas droughts became frequent over the subsequent centuries (for example, 1637–1640, 1770–1773, the 1790s, and the 1810s). In the Buenos Aires region of Argentina the 1700s were drier than the previous century. Prolonged droughts were recorded in the 1690s, the 1710s, the 1750s, and from 1771 to 1774.

Pacific and Indian Oceans. The El Niño Southern Oscillation (ENSO) is the result of a cyclic warming and cooling of the surface ocean of the central and eastern Pacific that strongly affects rainfall in the areas around the Pacific Ocean and the Indian Ocean. Archival data suggest that ENSO episodes from 1600 to 1900 had more intense global effects than those of the twentieth century. For example, the worst droughts in the colonial period in India (mid-1590s, 1629–1633, 1685–1688, 1788–1793, and 1877–1878) were ENSO–connected failures of the monsoon. For the last two events the global dimension can be demonstrated. Besides ENSO, large volcanic eruptions (for example, the 1815 explosion of Tambora in Indonesia) also induced global weather anomalies.

Historical Significance of Climatic Change. The issue of the impact of climatic change on history is controversial. It should not be overlooked that both "climate" and "history" are blanket terms of such a levels of abstraction that relationships between them cannot be investigated according to the rules of scientific methodology. To become more meaningful, the issue needs to be broken down to lower scales of analysis, for example, by putting a focus on specific human activities or needs in relation to a given set of climatic variables. Regarding preindustrial societies, this concerns primarily the availability of biomass (for example, food, fodder) and energy (for example, wind, waterpower, draft animals) in the secondary processes of population dynamics (for example, patterns of disease and epizootics and fertility of people and livestock), and in the third place, transport and communications, and in military and naval operations. Undoubtedly beneficial climatic effects tend to enlarge the scope of human action, whereas climatic shocks restrict it or even lead to emergency situations. Which climatic constellations mattered for energy availability and population dynamics depends on the environmental, cultural, and historical context.

Models of climatic effects on society are often framed as a chain of causation. Climatic patterns have a first-order or biophysical impact on agricultural production and on the outbreak of diseases or epizootics. These may have second-order effects on prices of food or raw materials, which may then ramify into the wider economy and society (third-order impacts). The farther away from first-order impacts, the greater the complexity of the factors masking the climatic effect. It is also clear that it is easier to investigate the effects of short-term (annual and perennial) impacts. Dealing with the effects of multidecadal climate variations requires accounting for modifications in the economic, institutional, and environmental setting so great as to vitiate any attempt at strict comparison or measurement. Most climatic impacts were related to food scarcity or famines.

A multifactor model of subsistence crises is described in Figure 1. Crises were triggered by a slump in overall agricultural production. This could be a consequence of

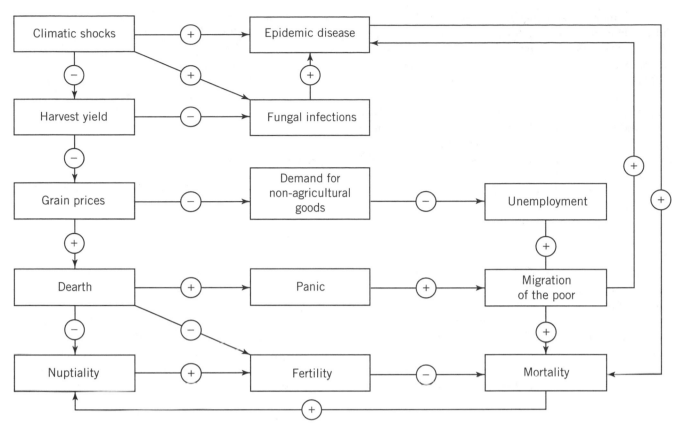

FIGURE 1. A Model of demographic and subsistence crises. SOURCE: Dupâquier, 1989. Reprinted with the permission of Cambridge University Press.

warfare, climatic effects, or both. In Central Europe severe crises (for example, 1569–1574, 1586–1589, 1593–1597, 1627–1629, 1692–1694, 1769–1772, 1816–1817, 1853–1855) were connected to a cumulation of unfavorable weather patterns, including long rains in autumn, cold springs, and rainy midsummers, which made the traditional risk-minimizing strategies, such as diversification of crop mix, ineffective. Rainfall is the limiting factor in the subtropical and tropical zone; in higher latitudes it is summer warmth.

Connections between climatic anomalies and diseases are complex. Some diseases, such as cholera, are promoted by drought; others, such as measles, are promoted by insufficient nutrition; and still others, such as bubonic plague, are not climate related. However, it was established that moldy grain, resulting from wet harvest periods, was likely to contain microfungi that had an immuno-suppressive effect. Thus poor people who ate this grain were more susceptible to all kinds of infections. Ernest Labrousse's theory of preindustrial trade cycles considers the harvest the critical determinant influencing urban income and rural employment levels. A sharp rise in food prices promoted the widespread unemployment, begging, and vagrancy that propagated infectious diseases, which,

rather than famine, were the primary cause of increased crisis mortality.

Crises represented a major challenge for political and social systems. Rather than investigating changes in average values, (historical) climatology should focus on changes in the frequency and severity of extremes. For example, in Russia and China drought and heavy rainfall both were detrimental to the agrarian economy. Growing evidence indicates that exogenous shocks (including natural disasters) tended to cluster rather than distribute randomly through time axis as is often believed. This makes it possible to distinguish between periods of high and low climatic stress.

An example is sixteenth-century Europe. It has been shown that the number of cold anomalies increased substantially from 1565 to 1600. A model investigating the effects of temperature and precipitation on rye prices in Germany showed that in this period climate became more significant for food prices than population levels and increases in the money supply. This is even more obvious for wine production, which, as a consequence of an almost uninterrupted series of cold summers from 1585 to 1600, nearly collapsed across a large region from Switzerland to Hungary.

This climate variation probably had a global dimension, judging from the evidence for Iceland, Russia, India, and Mexico. The near collapse of vine production had far-reaching consequences for the revenues of institutions, such as the Habsburg crown, and for major social groups that depended on vine growing. The social historian Wolfgang Behringer investigated the way such changes were perceived in a society highly vulnerable to meteorological shocks. Many peasant communities suffered such large collective damage from the effects of continuous crop failures that they pressed authorities to sanction witch-hunts. Thousands of witches were burned as scapegoats of climatic change.

The loss of the Norse settlement in Greenland in a period of lowered temperatures and severe weather around the mid-fourteenth century is a prime example of the impact of changing climate on human population. However, studies suggest that, while periods of unfavorable climatic fluctuations may have played a role in bringing Western settlement to an end, their cultural vulnerabilities to environmental change left the Norse far more subject to disaster than their Inuit neighbors.

BIBLIOGRAPHY

Barlow, Lisa K., Jon P. Sadler, and Thomas H. McGovern. "Interdisciplinary Investigations of the End of the Norse Western Settlement in Greenland." *Holocene* 7.4 (1997), 489–499.

Bradley, Raymond S. *Palaeoclimatology: Reconstructing Climates of the Quaternary*. 2d ed. Orlando, 1999.

Bradley, Raymond S., and Philip D. Jones, eds. *Climate since AD 1500*. 2d ed. London, 1996.

Claxton, Robert H. "The Record of Drought and Its Impact in Colonial Spanish America." In *Themes in Rural History of the Western World*, edited by Richard Herr, pp. 194–226. Ames, Iowa, 1993.

Dupâquier, Jacques. "Demographic Crises and Subsistence Crises in France, 1650–1725." In *Famine, Disease, and the Social Order in Early Modern Society*, edited by John Walter and Roger Schofield, pp. 189–200. Cambridge, 1989.

Fleming, James Rodger. *Historical Perspectives on Climate Change*. New York, 1998.

Grove, Richard H., and John Chappell, eds. *El Niño, History, and Crisis*. Isle of Harris, Scotland, 2000.

Frenzel, Burkart, Christian Pfister, and Birgit Gläser, eds. *Climatic Trends and Anomalies in Europe, 1675–1715*. Stuttgart, 1994.

Harington, Charles R., ed. *The Year without a Summer? World Climate in 1816*. Ottawa, 1992.

Hughes, Malcolm K., and Henry F. Diaz. *The Medieval Warm Period*. Dordrecht, Netherlands, 1994.

Kates, Robert, Jesse H. Ausubel, and Mimi Berberian, eds. *Climate Impact Assessment: Studies of the Interaction of Climate and Society*. Chichester, U.K., 1985.

Luterbacher, Jürg, et al. "Reconstruction of Monthly Mean Sea Level Pressure over Europe for the Late Maunder Minimum (1675–1715): "A Key Period for Studying Decadal Scale." *Climatic Change* 49 (2001), 441–462.

Martin Vide, Javier, and Mariano Barriendos Vallvé. "The Use of Rogation Ceremony Records in Climatic Reconstruction: A Case Study from Catalonia (Spain)." *Climatic Change* 30 (1995), 201–221.

McCann, James. "Climate and Causation in African History." *International Journal of African Historical Studies* 32.2–3 (1999), 261–279.

O'Hara, Sarah, and Sarah E. Metcalfe. "Reconstructing the Climate of Mexico from Historical Records." *Holocene* 5.4 (1995), 485–490.

Pfister, Christian, Brázdil Rudolf, and Rüdiger Glaser, eds. *Climatic Variability in Sixteenth Century Europe and Its Social Dimension*. Dordrecht, Netherlands, 1999.

Richards, John F. *The Unending Frontier: Environmental History in the Early Modern World*. Berkeley and Los Angeles, 2001.

Rotberg, Robert I., and Theodore K. Rabb, eds. *Hunger and History: The Impact of Changing Food Production and Consumption Patterns on Society*. Cambridge, 1983.

Wang, Shao Wu. "Reconstruction of Temperature Series of North China from 1380s to 1980s." *Science in China*, series B, 34.6 (1991), 751–759.

Wigley, Tom M. L., Martin J. Ingram, and Graham Farmer, eds. *Climate and History: Studies in Past Climates and Their Impact on Man*. Cambridge, 1981.

CHRISTIAN PFISTER

CLIOMETRICS is the application of economic theory and quantitative techniques to study history. The name comes from joining *Clio* (the muse of history), with *metrics* ("to measure") and was coined by economist Stanley Reiter, who, while collaborating with economic historians Lance Davis and Jonathan Hughes, was "musing" about for a word that described the work they were discussing.

This subfield of economic history emerged in the United States in the late 1950s. Economic history in the United States had a significant quantitative component, but newer scholars complained that many important economic issues were misinterpreted because of a failure to unite economic theory and quantitative historical data, and pushed their colleagues to employ economic theory along with measurement so that they could assess the historical performance of the economy.

The value of the new approach was convincingly displayed in one of the first cliometric papers, by Conrad and Meyer (1958). Rather than examine the motives of slaveholders or review the accounts of particular plantations, the authors approached the subject as an investment problem. Was slavery profitable? Would it have toppled under its own weight without the necessity of a civil war? Conrad and Meyer modeled slave owners as investors with a capital asset subject to depreciation and maintenance costs. They examined historical data on cotton yields, the slaves' average life spans, and the prices of inputs and output, and calculated that owning slaves was more profitable than other potential investments.

Instead of imprecise qualitative statements such as "it is difficult to exaggerate the importance of this," cliometrics provides precise estimates of economic magnitudes and economic relationships. The cliometric approach quickly ended a number of ongoing debates in American economic history. Using a simple trade model, estimates of demand and supply elasticities, and colonial price measures, for example, cliometric research estimated the per-capita burden of the Navigation Acts as a percentage of national income and found it to be much smaller than earlier supposed. Cliometricians were the first historians to harness computers, which allowed them to find totals and averages quickly, but also to estimate economic relationships and marginal effects—heretofore hidden in voluminous but previously mute and unusable bodies of archival data. The numbers-based approach often requires inferring missing numbers and some of the most important cliometric conclusions have been reached by setting up explicit "counterfactuals"—comparing the historical economy to what would have been if a certain policy, event, or invention had not happened.

Key dates in the cliometric "revolution" include the 1957 meeting of the National Bureau of Economic Research's Conference on Income and Wealth at which Conrad and Meyer presented their slavery paper; and, the first meeting of the Purdue Conference on the Application of Economic Theory and Quantitative Techniques to Problems of History, in 1960, at which Robert Fogel presented his early research on American railroads. This conference became an annual event known as the Cliometrics Conference, which continues today with funding from the National Science Foundation. By the mid-1960s the "new economic history" had become the subject of considerable interest among economists, and economics departments eagerly hired the hordes of new cliometricians.

One way to gauge the progress of cliometrics is to examine the pages of the leading economic history journal. In the early 1950s less than 2 percent of the pages in the *Journal of Economic History* were in cliometric articles—those that used measurement (tables) and explicit economic theory. This figure subsequently climbed to 10 percent in the late 1950s, 16 percent in the early 1960s, 43 percent in the late 1960s, and 72 percent in the early 1970s. In the late 1950s, some saw cliometrics as a new fad, but by the 1970s it was the standard operating procedure for American economic historians.

Amid the flood of early cliometric research, several works stand out, including Douglass North's *The Economic Growth of the United States, 1790–1860* (1961), Robert Fogel's *Railroads and American Economic Growth* (1964), and Fogel and Stanley Engerman's *Time on the Cross: The Economics of American Negro Slavery* (1974). Indeed, Fogel and North's research was so influential that, in 1993, the Royal Swedish Academy cited them "for having renewed research in economic history by applying economic theory and quantitative methods in order to explain economic and institutional change" and awarded them the Nobel Prize in Economics, as "pioneers in . . . cliometrics."

Cliometrics has its critics. Traditional economic historians complain that it is not history because its findings are driven by theoretical assumptions. Many historians find its methods, models, and multivariate regressions incomprehensible and no longer keep up with research in economic history. Some simply complain that the cliometric approach is boring and takes the romance out of history. Cliometricians themselves, especially Douglass North, have argued that mainstream cliometrics is too wedded to static neoclassical theory and have challenged it to expand its horizons to examine the impact and evolution of economic institutions. In the past couple of decades, cliometrics has spread beyond the United States, sinking deep roots in Europe. However, despite cliometric's auspicious beginnings, most economists are not convinced that they need to study economic history and many see economic history as just another field of applied economics.

The Cliometric Society, founded under the leadership of Donald McCloskey and Samuel Williamson in 1983, has more than 400 members. It holds conferences, publishes a newsletter, and can be found on the Internet at www.eh.net/Clio.

BIBLIOGRAPHY

Conrad, Alfred H., and John R. Meyer. "The Economics of Slavery in the Ante Bellum South." *Journal of Political Economy* 66 (1958), 95–130.

Whaples, Robert. "A Quantitative History of the Journal of Economic History and the Cliometric Revolution." *Journal of Economic History* 51.2 (June 1991), 289–301.

SAMUEL H. WILLIAMSON AND ROBERT WHAPLES

CLOCK MAKING AND TIME MEASUREMENT.

With the possible exception of the Maya, ours is the most time-obsessed culture the world has ever known. The Hopi language has no word for time and no verb tenses; the traditional Nuer of East Africa have no means of measuring time apart from the succession of their daily or seasonal activities. Studies of these and many other cultures clearly reveal that there is no universal human intuition of time. How, then, did the culture of the modern industrialized world become so uniquely time-conscious? The answer is complex, but surely no one would deny the major role played by the mechanical clock. David S. Landes (1983) has called it "one of the great inventions in the history of mankind—not in a class with fire and the wheel, but comparable to movable type in its revolutionary implications."

Before the invention of the mechanical clock in the late thirteenth century, sundials and waterclocks were the primary means of timekeeping. These instruments were used to measure time in ancient Egypt, and continued to be used in the Greek, Roman, and medieval worlds. The key distinction between the ancient sundial and the present way of telling time is that the sundial divided the daylight period into twelve equal parts, so that the hours varied in length throughout the year, each summer hour being longer than a winter hour. Although water clocks easily could have been made to measure hours of equal duration, most of them were ingeniously engineered to show the same "temporary" hours recorded by the sundial.

The medieval cities of Europe were filled with a cacophony of bell signals tied to the natural rhythm of day and night as measured by the temporary hours. The public mechanical clock, which was technically incompatible with the making of hours of variable length, gradually began to replace unique signals geared to special audiences with an abstract sign that eventually would change the way people conceived of time. Ultimately, the clock would lift time out of its relationship to the visible rhythm of day and night and make it something abstract and autonomous, an entity unto itself that could be used rather than merely lived through.

Not only did the clock count hours of equal length, but it produced them in a radically new manner. Earlier timekeeping devices had used something that flowed to track the passage of time: water, sand, the slow flow of sunlight across a dial. The reasoning was that time, which seems to move continuously and evenly in the same direction, ought to be tracked by something else that does the same. However, it turns out that nothing flows at nearly a steady-enough pace to measure time precisely. Surprisingly, time is best tracked not by something that flows, but by something that oscillates at a regular interval and whose beats can be counted.

This was the brilliant innovation embodied in the escapement, the regulator of mechanical clocks. The most widely used early escapement was known as the verge-and-foliot (Figure 1). In this device, a horizontal bar, the foliot, is attached to a vertical rod, the verge, from which project two pallets at right angles to each other. The pallets engage a saw-toothed escape wheel driven by the force of gravity on a falling weight. As the escape wheel turns, it is abruptly stopped when caught by the top pallet of the verge. This causes the foliot to oscillate, reversing the rotation of the verge so that the wheel escapes from the top pallet, only to be caught by the lower one. Again the foliot oscillates, causing the verge to turn and release the wheel from the bottom pallet. The wheel thus advances (or "escapes") by one tooth for each double oscillation. On and on the foliot oscillates, causing the escape wheel to move slowly and steadily, tooth-by-tooth, as it is caught and released, caught and again released, by the two pallets. A series of geared wheels transmits the count of the oscillations to the hand(s) on the clock face.

All later clocks, whether their oscillators are mechanical, quartz crystal, or atomic, still embody the principle of this first instrument. All are devices for maintaining and counting oscillations. The stupendous improvements in timekeeping accuracy during the past seven hundred years have resulted primarily from (1) increasing the frequency

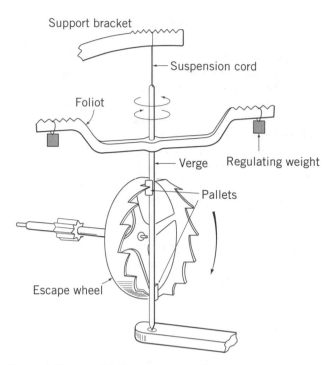

FIGURE 1. Verge-and-foliot escapement. SOURCE: Howse, 1980.

and the precision of the oscillator and (2) giving the oscillator greater control over the clock by isolating it from outside interference, either from the clock's mechanism or from temperature and pressure changes in the atmosphere.

The Early Clocks. The origins of the mechanical clock still elude historians. It almost certainly was invented somewhere in western Europe late in the thirteenth century, and probably by monks, because of their extreme concern with the temporal regimentation of daily life and because they were one of the few segments of medieval society with enough mathematical education to work out the clock's gearing. The accuracy of the first clocks was very low; the best could keep time only to within about fifteen minutes a day. The period of oscillation of the foliot was mechanically derived, all of the gears were cut by hand, and the various functions of the clock were so tightly bound together that any tiny change in one of them would trickle through the whole mechanism and cause the clock to become inaccurate.

These inaccuracies seemed not to matter; mechanical clocks were the technological sensation of their age. Every town wanted one. Huge iron clocks mounted in the towers of town halls or churches began to appear in northern Italy, and then spread rapidly to the German empire, the Netherlands, France, and England. The very earliest clocks had no face or hands and did not strike the hours; they just sounded an alarm that alerted the bell ringer to pull the rope. The first clock that struck the hours automatically was erected in Milan in 1336; by the end of the fourteenth century, some clocks had begun to strike on the quarter hour; and during the fifteenth century, clock faces began to appear, so that the acoustic indication of the time was finally joined by a visual sign.

A few terms still in use derive from this period—"a quarter to four" and "half past eight"—hark back to an age when these were the smallest divisions into which the clock could divide time. And "3 o'clock" is a shortened version of "3 *of* the clock," from an age when it was still necessary to indicate the particular mode of timekeeping.

By the early fourteenth century, the hour was beginning to replace the day as the basic unit of labor time in the textile industry. Because wages played a large role in the textile industry's production costs, clock time led not only to greater efficiency but to savings. Time thrift is also expressed as an individual moral virtue in writings of the period, and the greatest support for that came from chamber clocks used in the home. Like the public clocks, the earliest chamber clocks were weight-driven, but they were made of brass rather than iron. People were so enamored of the new clock time that they wanted to keep it with them on journeys or, better yet, wear it on their persons; but for that a power source of falling weights would not do. By the early fifteenth century, a coiled steel spring (mainspring) began to be used as the motive force in portable clocks; and by the end of the century, it had been sufficiently miniaturized to work in watches. Most of these watches were heavy, thick objects with beautifully ornamented cases and could be afforded only by royalty or the very wealthy.

The Pendulum. There was greater and greater demand for clocks, and yet the instruments still could not keep good time. Not until nearly four centuries after the invention of the mechanical clock did the first great breakthrough in accuracy occur. In 1583, Galileo (1564–1642) discovered that the swing of a pendulum takes the same amount of time whether it makes a wide arc or a small one, and the duration of a pendulum's swing depends on how long the pendulum is, not on the width of its swing. Unlike a foliot, a pendulum has a natural period of oscillation because its motion is controlled by gravity. If a pendulum could be made to control a clock, it would run quite effortlessly and with a degree of precision far beyond that previously achieved with much greater effort. Although in his old age Galileo devised a design for a pendulum clock, the first one was built by Salomon Coster under the direction of Christiaan Huygens (1629–1695) in The Hague in 1657.

With the natural oscillation of the pendulum now serving as the clock's time divider, there was spectacular improvement in accuracy. Clocks for the first time could accurately measure minutes. Further improvement came from the discovery that at forty-five degrees north latitude, a 39.1-inch pendulum would complete its swing in precisely one second. By the 1670s, clocks with seconds-beating pendulums were keeping time to within ten seconds per day.

Although pendulums transformed the accuracy of stationary clocks, they clearly could not be used in watches. Around 1675, both Robert Hooke (1635–1702) and Christiaan Huygens claimed to have invented the balance spring, which coiled and uncoiled at a fixed rate and thus provided a natural periodicity to control a watch's mechanical oscillator. Like the pendulum in stationary clocks, the balance spring brought watches into a new realm of accuracy.

Time and Space. Despite the radical improvement in accuracy of clocks and watches, the time they told was strictly local. Each city was an isolated island of time, and travelers found out what time it was when they arrived. This would have been a nightmare had there been any sort of communication system, but there was none. Until the mid-eighteenth century, travel on land was no faster than it had been during the Roman Empire.

The only vehicles doing any traveling worthy of the name were ships at sea, and it was here that the first efforts were made to relate the time of day to the turning planet. The purpose actually had nothing to do with time; instead it was to save lives and valuable cargo. Sailors could determine their latitude by measuring the angle between the horizon and either the sun at noon or the North Star, but could not determine their longitude with any precision and thus had no idea how far east or west they had gone. Ships crashed on rocky coasts at night, fortunes in cargo were lost, and crews died of scurvy and thirst because trips took weeks longer than anticipated.

Even the Greeks of the third century BCE knew that longitude, unlike latitude, could be understood as a function of time. If it takes twenty-four hours for the earth to turn through 360 degrees, then every hour it rotates through fifteen degrees of longitude (and each degree of longitude amounts to four minutes of time). If a ship had a clock that continuously showed the correct time at zero degrees longitude, that time could be compared with the local time at sea (found on another clock reset daily to correlate the midpoint of the sun's path through the sky with noon); and the difference between the two times could be translated into degrees of longitude. But the clock that could keep precise time after weeks or even months on a rolling ocean did not exist, and there seemed to be no hope that it ever would—until a self-taught Yorkshire clockmaker named John Harrison (1693–1776) devoted his entire life to whittling away every source of friction and finding ways to compensate for the expansion and contraction of the metals in clocks caused by the huge temperature changes during a long sea voyage. Harrison built four chronometers, before the last, the historic H.4 (a watch only five inches in diameter), finally—in 1762—proved that its precision timekeeping could be used to calculate the longitude at sea correctly. No one then could have imagined that by the early twentieth century the time at zero degrees longitude would be arriving by radio signals, or that a global positioning system (GPS) armed with atomic clocks would be pinpointing ships' locations before the end of that century.

A town is not a moving ship, however, and on land pinpoint accuracy can present a problem when travel begins to require greater communication between distant places. The first modern communication system was the railroad, and the use of zone time resulted directly from the clash between the jumble of local times of the cities and the time used by the railroads. Trains could not keep changing their clocks so that they would match the local times of their destinations; but if they failed to do so, their passengers missed the trains. In England, the trains all kept Greenwich mean time, and the towns had precise local times; yet even in that small country, there was great confusion. By 1855, less than a quarter-century after a railway system had got under way, nearly all public clocks had been set to Greenwich mean time. This effectively put all of Britain into one time zone. The electric telegraph had been invented in 1836, and by 1852 telegraph lines laid alongside the major railroad tracks were telegraphing the time from the Royal Observatory in Greenwich to cities throughout Britain at least once a day.

The conflict between local and railway time was vastly compounded in such a huge country as the United States, and matters were made even worse because the many railway companies each kept their own times as well. To quote the father of the American time-zone system, Charles Dowd (1825–1904): "The traveler's watch was to him but a delusion; clocks at stations stared each other in the face defiant of harmony either with one another or with surrounding local time and all wildly at variance with the traveler's watch, baffling all intelligent interpretation." The temporal chaos also was responsible for many train wrecks because trains on the same track used different times. Dowd's idea was to use four time zones across the United States, each covering fifteen degrees of longitude and varying by one hour. In the final plan, these zones were based on Greenwich as the prime meridian (zero degrees longitude). On Sunday, 18 November 1883, at noon, the plan was enacted for the railways and most public clocks. For the first time, all clocks struck at the same moment, marking the four different hours of their zones, and all minute hands were in the same position.

By 1883, only England, Sweden, the United States, and Canada had zone times based on the Greenwich meridian; other countries still tended to use their own capitals as prime meridian. When a few far-sighted people such as Canadian railway engineer Sandford Fleming (1827–1915) broached the idea of wrapping one unified system of time around the world, it was clear that the first step would have to be the adoption of a single prime meridian used by all countries. At the International Meridian Conference held in 1884, it was resolved to make Greenwich the universal prime meridian. This vote set in motion changes that would create the temporal world now taken for granted. Once Greenwich was accepted as the prime meridian, country after country gradually adopted zone time. It was a slow process; France did not join until 1911, Mexico waited until 1922, and Liberia held out until 1972. Today, the turning earth has become a clock face with the time zones its numerals.

The Quartz and Atomic Revolutions. Despite the progress in relating time to the revolving planet, at the end of the nineteenth century most pendulum clocks could keep time only to about a tenth of a second per day. Another breakthrough would have to be made to give the degree of precision required for today's communication, power, and navigation systems; and no further perfection of the pendulum clock would be able to accomplish it.

The great period of invention and development of the mechanical clock, which lasted nearly seven hundred years, is over. In a digital clock, there are no moving parts; it has just a battery, a capsule containing a quartz crystal, and a bit of electronic circuitry. Yet the principle of the very first mechanical clock is retained in this device: a battery generating electricity has replaced the falling weight as the source of power; a quartz crystal has taken the place of the foliot or the pendulum as the oscillating time divider; and instead of an escapement and gear train, an integrated circuit now counts the crystal's vibrations, reduces their thousands of beats per second into the language of time, and transmits this language to the clock face.

When pressure or an electrical current is applied to certain crystals, they can be made to vibrate at a very constant frequency. By the 1920s, quartz crystals were keeping radio broadcast waves on a set frequency; so inventors wondered, if the vibrations of a quartz crystal were stable enough to keep radio waves on a fixed frequency, could they also be used to regulate a clock? This question was asked and answered by the Americans Joseph Horton and Warren Marrison in 1928, when they built the first clock regulated by the vibrations of a quartz crystal. Its accuracy, within one or two thousandths of a second per day, was far greater than anything a pendulum clock ever could achieve. The first quartz crystal clock was installed at the Greenwich Observatory in 1939, but another thirty years would pass before the technology could be sufficiently miniaturized for commercial use. Once it was, there was no turning back; quartz watches now make up about 99 percent of the market.

Although their accuracy is more than adequate for wrist watches, it does not approach the timekeeping requirements of today's navigation, power, and communication systems. In navigation, a time error of a millionth of a second can result in a position error of half a mile; planes can miss runways, missiles can hit the wrong targets, and spacecraft can sail past the planets they were sent to study. These catastrophes do not often occur because modern society is literally held together by electronic technology that routinely communicates by signals synchronized to billionths of a second. This exquisite accuracy is due to the cesium atomic clock, which was developed during the 1950s, and whose steady improvements since that time have recently produced an atomic clock that will not gain or lose a second in twenty million years! The oscillator in the clock vibrates at a frequency of 9,192,631,770 cycles per second, which is the frequency of the radiation emitted or absorbed when the outermost electron of the cesium atom flips its magnetic direction relative to that of the nucleus. Now the second may be governed by the laws of quantum physics, but atomic clocks—just like the earliest iron tower clocks—are still simply devices for maintaining and counting regular oscillations.

Manufacture and International Competition. The work on the huge tower clocks of the fourteenth century was done by craftsmen in the immediate region (blacksmiths, bell founders, carpenters, bricklayers, ropers), who returned to their primary jobs once the clock was finished. "Clockmaker" was a recognized profession by the fourteenth century, and the making of the clock itself was overseen by a clockmaker(s), who often traveled to the site for the job. Unfortunately, these early clocks did not have very long life spans; rarely could twenty years go by before they began to break down. Clockmakers were as much repairmen as original constructors, and they spent a lot of time traveling back to the sites of their earlier clocks to get them going again.

As the demand for clocks grew, and the profession became more structured, the ad hoc division of labor among workmen from other fields became a division among workers devoted full-time to making clocks. Shops devoted to smaller, domestic timepieces separated from those making tower clocks, and later a similar division occurred between those making clocks and watches. The instrument's case and dial were subcontracted out to specialists early on, as were the springs, because the coiling of spring steel was a task too arcane for even the most competent clockmaker. Guilds came late: a clockmaker's guild formed in Paris in 1544, one for watchmakers in Geneva in 1601, and another in London in 1631.

Centers for clock- and watchmaking were concentrated north of the Alps: Geneva became such a center in the sixteenth century, and others arose in Paris, London, Augsburg, and Nuremberg. Not only were most timepieces made by Protestants in northern Europe, but so were most users. When Louis XIV revoked the Edict of Nantes in 1685, he nearly destroyed the French watchmaking industry, as hundred of Protestant clockmakers fled, primarily to England and Switzerland, to escape persecution.

England hardly needed that help; from 1675 to 1775 it dominated the industry, both in the quality of its timepieces and commercially. Not only did this period witness the work of such legendary horologists as Thomas Tompion, George Graham, and Thomas Mudge; it also saw Britain take the lead in inventing machines for making clock parts. There were machines for cutting the teeth of gear wheels and for drawing pinion wire. Brass now could be pressed rather than hammered, and there were lathes and drills and a variety of other tools for turning out uniform parts that only had to be filed down by the clock's assembler. The parts were made in workers' cottages, and then all were gathered together and the watch assembled.

Geneva was second to England in industry dominance in the eighteenth century. An active watchmaking industry had flourished there since the mid-sixteenth century, and descendants of Huguenot refugees from France still worked in the trade. Because Switzerland had a tiny home market, Geneva was forced to export, and had established trade links throughout Europe as well as with Turkey and China. Genevans would sell what was wanted to anyone who wanted it, and their enterprising spirit kept them scrambling to meet demand until the very end of the eighteenth century. Then the industry went into temporary decline because of a challenge from its own backyard—tiny Swiss villages high in the Jura Mountains north of Geneva.

The hardy Jura villagers raised cattle and made lace, and their life was not easy. When watchmaking was introduced early in the eighteenth century, they eagerly undertook it, and by the end of the century they were undercutting Geneva in price, if not in quality. They had low-cost skilled workers and a division of labor so refined that the making of a single watch involved contributions from more than one hundred people. By the 1780s, factories were appearing in the mountain towns, with machines producing standardized parts.

Geneva was never able to compete with Jura prices, but after a generation it recovered, focusing on high-end products, as it still does. Geneva and the Jura undersold Britain, France, Germany, and everyone else during the nineteenth century. By around 1870, two-thirds of the world's watch output by value came from Switzerland. This development is astonishing, considering that the Industrial Revolution had been born in Britain, which led the world in almost every other field of manufacture. Britain's early network of railroads had heightened time consciousness and the demand for watches, but in the nineteenth century many of its people bought Swiss watches. The British watchmaking industry was too set in its ways to innovate, in either manufacturing techniques or products, so its watches were no better than the Swiss but were much higher-priced.

The only threat to the Swiss came from Americans. In the first decade of the nineteenth century, Eli Terry (1772–1852) introduced the mass production of clocks, and by midcentury Aaron Dennison's Waltham Watch Company was accomplishing the far more difficult feat of mass-producing watches. Although Europeans had built machines for producing uniform parts, it was Americans who first made the interchangeability of parts the governing principle of manufacture, and they were able to produce huge numbers of timepieces without sacrificing accuracy. America had no pool of cheap labor and so found a way to substitute machines for people.

The Swiss rose to the challenge by gradually adopting American production techniques, and by the turn of the twentieth century over half of the world's watches still came from Switzerland. The Swiss were quicker than the Americans to respond to the new taste for wristwatches over pocket watches after World War I; and with a few ups and downs, they still had over half the world market until quartz watches began to be manufactured commercially in the 1970s.

The Swiss understood the quartz technology but they failed to realize that it was the foundation of a revolution. The Japanese and the Americans, perhaps because they were already manufacturing other electronic devices, led the way. Unlike mechanical timepieces, quartz technology does not require skilled labor, and by 1980 a large, unskilled, low-wage workforce had already made Hong Kong the world's leading exporter of watches. In 2000, some 80 percent of the 700 million watches manufactured came from Hong Kong and China.

The modern world is an edifice built upon the precise measurement of time; but its cornerstone, put in place seven hundred years ago, was a revolutionary machine that measured time not by something that flows, but by something that oscilllates at a regular interval and whose beats can be counted.

BIBLIOGRAPHY

Barnett, Jo Ellen. *Time's Pendulum: The Quest to Capture Time—From Sundials to Atomic Clocks*. New York, 1998.

Blaise, Clark. *Time Lord: Sir Sanford Fleming and the Creation of Standard Time*. New York, 2000.

Boorstin, Daniel. J. *The Discoverers*. New York, 1985. Perhaps the only work of overarching synthesis to highlight the importance of time measurement (first section).

Borst, Arno. *The Ordering of Time*. Chicago, 1993.

Dohrn-van Rossum, Gerhard. *History of the Hour: Clocks and Modern Temporal Orders*. Chicago, 1996. A detailed history of clock development and its social impact, focusing on the pre-pendulum era.

Gimpel, Jean. *The Medieval Machine: The Industrial Revolution of the Middle Ages*. New York, 1976.

Howse, Derek. *Greenwich Time*. Oxford, 1980. Chronicles the role played by the Royal Observatory in Greenwich and its clocks in astronomy, navigation, and the standardization of time.

Hunter, John. *An Illustrated History of Timepieces*. New York, 1991.

Jesperson, James, and Jane Fitz-Randolph. *From Sundials to Atomic Clocks: Understanding Time and Frequency*. New York, 1977. Classic study that puts difficult material about time and frequency into language comprehensible to the layperson.

Klein, H. Arthur. *The World of Measurements*. New York, 1974.

Landes, David S. *Revolution in Time: Clocks and the Making of the Modern World*. Cambridge, Mass., 1983. Comprehensive yet wonderfully readable story of all aspects of development of the mechanical clock.

Le Goff, Jacques. *Time, Work and Culture in the Middle Ages*. Chicago, 1980.

O'Malley, Michael. *Keeping Watch: A History of American Time*. New York, 1990.

White, Lynn T., Jr. *Medieval Technology and Social Change*. Oxford, 1962.

Whitrow, G. J. *Time in History: Views of Time from Prehistory to the Present Day*. Oxford, 1988. Encyclopedic examination of the concepts and instruments of time measurement in all cultures.

JO ELLEN BARNETT

CLOTHING TRADES. Through much of the medieval and early modern periods, the production of clothing in Europe was dominated by highly structured guilds. These city-based organizations oversaw the stitching of men and women's garments, the cobbling of shoes and boots, and the creation of hats, gloves, and other accessories. Guilds trained and monitored workers, enforcing quality and prices. They also attempted to enforce their monopoly over production, to assure an orderly and profitable market in commodities essential for comfort and display. Masters and journeymen produced exquisite garments for elite buyers, as well as basic commodities for local and outlying consumers. Some regions produced such superior products that they dominated sales throughout Europe; for example, Milan was the unrivaled source for silk stockings in the sixteenth and seventeenth centuries. However, supplementary production and repair of clothing also took place in the households of laborers, particularly in rural and suburban communities outside guild control. The skills of these men and women were not as well developed as those of guild members, but their labor was cheaper. As the economy grew and the demand for clothing rose from the sixteenth century onward, these semiskilled workers were key to the growing production of apparel.

Guilds were not static, however. New guilds were established as items of clothing assumed greater importance. For example, a guild for knitted beret makers was formally established in Mantua in 1513. Hand-knitting employed the poor in many parts of Europe. In England, the stocking knitting frame was invented about 1590 and spread throughout various parts of England over the seventeenth century. This invention led to the development of an extensive machine-made stocking industry that used the putting-out system of production, where rural laborers knit stockings on frames for national and overseas markets. The stocking frame was one of the earliest technological innovations in clothing production. Although spinning equipment and looms of various sorts had been used since ancient times in the production of cloth, the stocking frame was one of the earliest technological innovators in clothing production. Stocking frames spread throughout continental Europe from the second half of the seventeenth century. The timing of this technological breakthrough coincided more with other innovations in spinning and weaving than it did with the broader changes occurring at the same time in the clothing trades. The most important technological innovation would be the sewing machine in the mid- nineteenth century. Prior to that, transformations in production were brought about through the reorganization of labor, rather than the introduction of new technology.

Growth and Innovation. A combination of factors stimulated changes within the clothing trades from 1500 to 1800. The popularization of fashion played an important role. As cities in western Europe grew, enriched by colonial and overseas trade, the fascination with novelties also spread. The widening middle classes defined themselves through the purchase and display of material goods, especially dress. Some imitated the tastes of the aristocracy; but many other groups created distinctive styles appropriate to their political, economic, religious, and social orientations. Simultaneously, the retail sale and distribution of apparel became more advanced, speeding the movement of clothes and accessories from workshop to consumer. Recognizing the economic power of fashion, in the 1660s, France claimed to be the arbiter of taste for Europe, a position the country maintained in elite fashions for nearly three centuries. The French silk industry, as well as couturiers and fashion publishing, benefited from this hegemony; however, the rising demand for small luxuries affected the underlying structures of the clothing industries in more dramatic ways. These changes were felt throughout all western nations. The growth of popular consumerism stimulated the production and sale of a plethora of inexpensive accessories—handkerchiefs, hats, hosiery, caps, gloves, aprons, sleeves, and head-clothes—affordable items that were purchased more frequently than their more costly counterparts. Men and women bought ephemeral fashion items at a faster rate, gradually setting aside older consumer habits, such as the purchase of only long-lasting garments. New patterns of consumerism were emerging.

Collective demand was one part of a two-pronged process that transformed the clothing trade. Equally important was the role of institutional demand, particularly as represented by the military. The rise of the nation-state, with large military forces, created new fiscal structures necessary to build fleets and provision armies. One element of this structure was the contracted production of apparel. The financing of wars enabled investors to profit from government contracts for clothing. The urgent need for basic apparel, which came following declarations of war, linked financiers to contractors, subcontractors to needlewomen. In cities and ports, masses of cheap female labor were organized to produce bales of shirts, trousers, jackets, and waistcoats for sailors, soldiers, and marines. By 1700, tens of thousands of garments were produced by English contractors. By the end of the eighteenth century, contractors could assemble many times that quantity of garments. Indeed, one English naval contractor produced over six hundred thousand garments between 1780 and 1782. This system of production was organized around the centralized cutting of fabric, a putting-out system of stitching, and centralized warehousing and distribution. Low-wage female labor was the basis and mainstay of this production system.

The Modern Age in Fashion. By 1800, the tailoring of men and women's garments was sharply differentiated between custom tailoring, made-to-measure for specific clients, and ready-made apparel. Journeymen tailors were primarily wage laborers; guild power had eroded. Similarly, most needlewomen worked either for contractors or for the mid- and large-scale retailers who emerged in the nineteenth century. The pattern of large-scale production put in place to dress the military was adapted for civilian markets. Companies like E. Moses & Son, of London, and Brooks Brothers, of New York, flourished over the nineteenth century, fitting the common man in ready-to-wear garments. Later they strived for a more fashionable aura. Both companies built elaborate retail premises. They recognized that, to attract customers, shopping had to be a pleasurable experience. By the mid-nineteenth century, E. Moses & Son promised customers elegant showrooms and fitting rooms, with a selection of garments second to none. With the spread of chain stores, clothes manufacturing and retailing became closely interconnected.

Mass production did not begin with the factory, nor did the putting-out system end with the spread of clothing factories. Factory production was well established by the 1860s, initially with the knitting trades, with English firms like I. & R. Morley, one of the giants of knitting. Both systems of production depended on a gendered division of labor, with lower wages paid to women and girls. Clothing factories multiplied in all industrialized nations following the invention and diffusion of effective sewing machine technology in the mid-nineteenth century—sewing machines suited both home sewing and factory production. Output increased and competition intensified between companies and countries. Manufacturers found that the

CLOTHING TRADE. Men pulling racks of clothing on busy sidewalk in New York's garment district, 1955. (*New York World-Telegram* and the *Sun* Newspaper Photograph Collection/Prints and Photographs Division, Library of Congress)

two systems of production were in fact complementary. Factory production and sweatshop putting-out work continued in tandem. Low wages and poor working conditions were common, especially among sweatshop outworkers laboring in their tenement apartments for pennies a garment; their working conditions became the focus of reformers. Western nations gradually worked to end sweatshop labor and improve factory conditions. However, these production patterns persisted. Low-wage female labor continued to be the mainstay of this industry, even as, over the twentieth century, clothing production shifted to other regions of the world. After 1950, the industry began to falter in the industrialized western nations and to flourish in the newly industrializing regions. Manufacturers based in Asia and Central and South America, for example, enjoyed far lower labor costs than manufacturers in other areas of the West. A global market for clothing challenged the earlier industrial dominance of western textile and clothing manufacturers.

The character and production of clothing experienced substantial changes in most parts of the world, not only the West. The Japanese kimono is a case in point. These straight-cut robes became standard wear from about the Heian period (794–1191). Initially based on Chinese styles, kimonos exemplified the economic, political, and technological character of the era in which they were produced, as well as the social rank of the wearer. The basic structure of this garment made them easy to stitch, requiring no concession to the shape of the body. The textiles in these garments were the key differentiating features, from basic hemp kimonos tied with cord and worn by rural laborers, to the twelve layers of colored silk kimonos worn by court women of the Edo period (1603–1868). Asian textile designs, introduced by Dutch and Portuguese traders of the economically expansive Edo period, encouraged local production of printed fabrics. The diversification of craft production accelerated, and factory-based textile production became a leading sector. By 1900, Japanese manufacturers were competitive internationally.

Over the twentieth century, the clothing trades became international in terms of not only production, but also fashion. Western styles spread to all corners of the globe, providing Asian manufacturers further scope to develop regional textile and clothing industries. By the end of the century, a standardized and simplified pattern of everyday dress, which included running shoes, jeans, T-shirt or shirt, was adopted by some, if not most, of the population in most parts of the world. The standardization of appearance promises to proliferate, dependent on the combined inter-action of fashion, production, and trade. Differentiations in dress, arising from taste, social, or religious differences, sustain some regional clothing trades. But clothing is made and worn within an increasingly unitary system of production and style.

[*See also* Cotton Industry; Fashion Industry; Linen Industry; Silk Industry; Textiles; *and* Wool Industry.]

BIBLIOGRAPHY

Abé, Takeshi, and Osau Saito. "From Putting-out to the Factory: A Cotton-weaving District in Late-Meiji Japan." *Textile History* 19.2 (1988), 143–158.

Breward, Christopher. *The Hidden Consumer: Masculinities, Fashion, ,and City Life, 1860–1914.* Manchester, 1999.

Burke, Peter. "Res et Verbe: Conspicuous Consumption in the Early Modern World." In *Consumption and the World of Goods*, edited by John Brewer and Roy Porter, pp. 148–161. London, 1993.

Bythell, Duncan. *The Sweated Trades: Outwork in Nineteenth-Century Britain.* London, 1978.

Chapman, Stanley. "I. & R. Morley: Colossus of the Hosiery Trade and Industry, 1799–1965." *Textile History: Special Issue on the History of the Ready-Made Clothing Industry* 28.1 (1997), 11–28.

Coffin, Judith. *The Politics of Women's Work: The Paris Garment Trades, 1750–1915.* Princeton, 1996.

Gamber, Wendy. *The Female Economy: The Millinery and Dressmaking Trades, 1860–1930.* Urbana, Ill., 1997. Examines the American experience of these trades.

Godley, Andrew, guest ed. *Textile History: Special Issue on the History of the Ready-Made Clothing Industry* 28.1 (1997). A collection with articles from a range of chronological and geographic perspectives.

Green, Nancy L. *Ready-to-Wear and Ready-to-Work: A Century of Industry in Paris and New York.* Durham, N.C., 1997.

Harte, Negley, ed. "Fabrics and Fashions: Studies in the Economic and Social History of Dress." *Textile History: Special Issue* 22.2 (1991). Focuses on articles from the late medieval period to the early twentieth century, from a primarily British perspective.

Lemire, Beverly. *Dress, Culture, and Commerce: The English Clothing Trade before the Factory, 1660–1800.* London, 1997.

Lemire, Beverly. *Fashion's Favourite: The Cotton Trade and the Consumer in Britain, 1660–1800.* Oxford, 1991.

Miller, Michael B. *The Bon Marché: Bourgeois Culture and the Department Store, 1869–1920.* Princeton, 1981.

Nakaoka, Tetsuro, Kayoko Aidawa, Hisao Miyajima, Takao Yoshii, and Tamotsu Nishizawa. "The Textile History of Nishijin (Kyoto): East Meets West." *Textile History* 19.2 (1988), 117–142.

Roche, Daniel. *The Culture of Clothing: Dress and Fashion in the Ancien Régime.* Cambridge, 1994.

Schmiechen, James A. *Sweated Industries and Sweated Labor: The London Clothing Trades, 1860–1914.* Urbana, Ill., 1984.

Sigsworth, Eric W. *Montague Burton: The Tailor of Taste.* Manchester, 1990. A case study of one of the most important British manufacturer/retailers.

Thirsk, Joan. "The Fantastical Folly of Fashion: The English Stocking Knitting Industry, 1500–1700." In *Textile History and Economic History*, edited by N. B. Harte, and K. G. Ponting. Manchester, 1973. A classic study of the early impact of popular fashion.

Uchida, Hoshimi. "Narrow Cotton Stripes and Their Substitutes: Fashion, Technical Progress, and Manufacturing Organization in Japanese Popular Clothing, 1850–1920." *Textile History* 19.2 (1988), 159–170.

BEVERLY LEMIRE

COAL BASINS. The coal basin is a territory created at the time of intensive use of mineral fuel for manufacturing (from the early nineteenth century to the mid-twentieth century, according to different countries). The territory is organized around the collieries that dictate the laying out of roads, railways, and canals and the building of houses and other infrastructure. Moreover, industries using a huge amount of fuel—iron and steel plants, glassmaking factories, and brick and tile furnaces—gathered close to coal pits to avoid prohibitive transport costs. One of the oldest and most typical coal basins, the Borinage (Belgium) "is not a region bound by fixed limits," wrote an observer of Valenciennes, France, in 1850. "It is a whole of coal shafts that could extend or retract according to the discovery of new seams or to the closure of redundant pits."

In the nineteenth century, coal mining was one of the most labor-intensive activities. Therefore, collieries needed to amass a large work force close to coal pits. Usually, coal mining firms built up entire new communities of houses (called *corons* in France and Belgium) and provided the working population with basic urban infrastructures, like hospitals, churches, shops, and so on, creating entire towns. During the phase of development, coal basins were populated by immigrants and their families, who were attracted by the prospect of higher wages and other material advantages. After some decades, however, the mining population continued to develop, mainly through natural growth. Urban expansion was usually too fast to allow for urban planning. Therefore, most of the big coal basins, like the Ruhr and the Upper Silesia, became an unmanageable urban chaos by the end of the nineteenth century. Planning programs only appeared in the early twentieth century, when local authorities and coal mining companies decided to reorganize the urban landscape. The main characteristic of that landscape is the intertwining of industrial plants, houses, networks of transport, and so on.

Coal was the main location factor for heavy industry. Iron and steel industries in particular moved from woodlands to coal basins in the early nineteenth century, when the new technology of coke smelting was adopted. Moreover, the development of coal and iron production was determined by transport costs. Therefore, railway technology was closely linked to coal basins. Indeed, the first railways were set up by coal mining companies to carry coal (from Darlington to Stockton on Tees in 1825 and from Saint-Étienne to Lyon in 1826). With the railway, the full development of the coal basin as a site of heavy industry could proceed. In the mid-nineteenth century, most of the main industrial basins developed, including the north of France, Borinage-Charleroi and Seraing (Belgium), Lyon and Saint-Étienne, Ruhrgebiet, Upper Silesia, and finally Donbas in the late nineteenth century.

Destructions during World War I provided the opportunity for urban planning and modernization in the coalfields of Nord–Pas-de-Calais (France) and to a lesser extent in Belgium. During the interwar period and after World War II, European coal basins relied on a new labor force from Poland, Italy, Turkey, and North Africa to fill the places left by local workers increasingly attracted to healthier jobs in the steel industry and other industrial sectors. The working-class society in most European coal basins became multiethnic communities that persist today. From the 1960s onward, the decline of coal mining—owing to the use of other fuels, like natural gas and oil, for domestic heating and industrial energy supply—and the restructuring of the iron and steel industries have dramatically altered all the coal basins. They have suffered from mass unemployment, obsolete infrastructures, and a lack of investments in housing and economic activities. In the 1970s, most of the old coal basins were depressed areas urgently requesting programs for regeneration. National and regional authorities (like the Land of North-Rhine-Westphalia) and the European Coal and Steel Community had to take initiatives for industrial redeployment and labor conversion, which have been successful in some cases, like the Ruhr Valley, but not successful in many other coal basins (Borinage, Donbas). The fact that old industrial plants and redundant collieries do not lend themselves to rehabilitation remains the main problem of coal basins today.

Ruhr Valley. The Ruhrgebiet, the major industrial area of Germany since 1850, took its name from the Ruhr River, a tributary of the Rhine. The coalfield extends from the left bank of the Rhine east to Hamm and from the Ruhr River north to the Lippe River. In the late eighteenth century, the Ruhr Valley was still a poor rural area with only small market towns (Essen, Bochum, Dortmund, Unna) along the Hellweg, a medieval road. Industry started slowly in the 1740s and 1750s, when some merchants of Mülheim-am-Ruhr launched a coal trade from the local coal mines and when charcoal furnaces (Sankt-Antonihütte in 1743 and a furnace at Sterkrade in 1782, where Friedrich Krupp's family started (later known as the Gutehoffnungshütte), operated on the iron ore seams around Essen.

After 1815, the Ruhr, now part of the Prussian kingdom, took advantage of the establishment of the Zollverein (1834) to develop coal mining and iron smelting. The discovery of a high-quality coal seam (*Fettkohle* suitable for coking) in the Ruhr area dictated the location of ironworks around Essen and Mülheim. In 1849, coke was first used in the Friedrich-Wilhemshütte at Mülheim, and the railroad reached the region, opening new possibilities for trade. Liegeois entrepreneurs introduced mining and metallurgical technology and capital, stimulating a first wave of rapid industrialization in a liberal economic context. In

TABLE 1. *Coal Output in Oberbergamtsbezirk Dortmund, 1815–1989*

PERIODS	MILLIONS OF TONS	PERIODS	MILLIONS OF TONS
1815–1819	0.4	1905–1909	79.5
1820–1824	0.4	1910–1914	99.6
1825–1829	0.5	1915–1919	89.3
1830–1834	0.7	1920–1924	82.9
1835–1839	0.9	1925–1929	114.5
1840–1844	1.1	1930–1934	86.9
1845–1849	1.3	1935–1939	118.1
1850–1854	2.4	1940–1944	125.2
1855–1859	3.6	1945–1949	65.5
1860–1864	5.8	1950–1954	112.5
1865–1869	9.7	1955–1959	121.3
1870–1874	13.9	1960–1964	116.4
1875–1879	18.2	1965–1969	97.3
1880–1884	25.2	1970–1974	84.6
1885–1889	30.9	1975–1979	70.5
1890–1894	37.9	1980–1984	67.0
1895–1899	48.2	1985–1989	59.4
1900–1904	62.3		

SOURCES: Fischer, W., 1989, p. 33; Holtfrerich, C.–L., *Quantitative Wirtschaftsgeschichte des Ruhrkohlenbergbaus im 19. Jahrhundert*, Dortmund, 1973, pp. 16–19; Koellmann, W., "Beginn der Industrialisierung," Dusseldorf, 1990, p. 36; Hempel, G., *Die deutsche Montanindustrie. Ihre Entwicklung und Gestaltung*, Essen, 1969, p. 200; *Statistik des Kohlenwirtschaft. Zahlen zur Kohlenwirtschaft*, Essen, 1991; Tenfelde, K., *Sozialgeschichte der Bergarbeiterschaft an der Ruhr im 19. Jahrhundert*, Bonn, 1981, pp. 602–603.

the 1850s, ironworks flourished: Gutehoffnungshütte at Oberhaussen, Friedrich-Wilhemshütte at Mülheim, Herrmannshütte (Hoesch) at Hörde, Phönix near Ruhrort, and Alfred Krupp at Essen. In 1860, the Ruhr already offered the highest concentration of blast furnaces and coal mines in the world, while Bochumer Verein and Alfred Krupp monopolized steel output.

An early integration of coal mines and ironworks, called *Hüttenzechen*, characterizes the Ruhr industry. The first such integration occurred in 1854, when the Gutehoffnungshütte bought a mine to supply its coke ovens. Soon after others flourished, including Bochumer Verein, Krupp (1868), Dortmunder Union (1872), Hoerder Verein, and Phönix. These *Hüttenzechen* paved the way to the mixed concerns (*Konzern*) of the twentieth century. The ironworks also stimulated heavy engineering, such as Friedrich-Harkort-works at Wetter or Märkische-Maschinenbauansthal A.G. (which later merged into DEMAG) and the rise of coal output (from 1.3 million tons in 1845–1849 to 13.9 million tons in 1870–1874 and nearly 100 million tons in 1913).

In 1865, Alfred Krupp (1812–1887) adopted the Bessemer process using Spanish ore. With the German annexation of a major part of the Lorraine in 1871, the Ruhr also had access to Lorraine *minette*, an abundant but low-quality iron ore. The *minette* stimulated the adoption of the Thomas-Gilchrist process by both the Hoerde works and the Rheinische-Stahlwerke (Ruhrort) in September 1879. Ruhr steelmakers, such as Krupp at Essen and August Thyssen (1842–1926) at Hamborn, dominated the European market, while Hugo Stinnes (1870–1924) became the leader in coal mining and trade. Powerful cartels organized production and trade, including Rheinisch-Westfälisches-Kohlensyndikat (1893) and Roheisensyndikat (1896), which paved the way to the creation of the Deutsche Stahlwerksverband in 1904.

Industrialization and urbanization proceeded in three steps. Between 1830 and 1860, it was mainly in the Ruhr Valley, where coal mines created numerous coal villages around Witten. When industrialization reached the northern part along the Hellweg, cities like Rurhort, Mülheim, Essen, Bochum, and Dortmund faced an exponential population growth from 1860 onward. It was only at the end of the nineteenth century that industrialization reached the northern periphery and industrial cities such as Oberhausen, Gelsenkirchen, and Recklinghausen. The Ruhrgebiet was also the focus of an impressive labor migration not only from other parts of Germany but also from Poland.

After World War I, the Ruhr lost access to Lorraine iron ore. The "reparations" that required shipments of coal and coke to France and the occupation by French and Belgian troops in January 1923 precipitated the economic crisis (1921–1925). After a short recovery, the economic crisis of 1930–1931, followed by the arrival of Adolf Hitler (1933) placed the Ruhr industrialists in a situation of being forced to supply the Nazi economy and rearmament. In 1944–1945, the Ruhr was a major target for the Allied attacks: 30 percent of the coal mines and the main ironworks were damaged. After the war, dismantling the Ruhr industry was contemplated, but after 1947 a more realistic project of controlled rebuilding was launched under the direction of the International Authority for the Ruhr (1949), replaced in 1952 by the European Coal and Steel Community.

In the 1950s and 1960s, a new process of integration marked the rebirth of the Ruhr economy, dominated now by three groups of *Konzern*, energy producers (Ruhrkohle A.G., created in 1969, in the gas and electricity sector), steelmakers (August-Thyssen-Hütte, Hoesch, Klöckner, Krupp, Demag, Gutehoffnungshütte), and the chemical industry. In the 1970s and 1980s, a huge process of industrial rationalization and modernization deeply transformed the Ruhrgebiet.

Donetz Coal Basin. The Donetz Coal Basin—also known as "Old Donbass," mainly in what today is Ukraine—covers twenty-five thousand square kilometers

TABLE 2. *Industrial Output of the Ruhr (millions of tons).*

YEARS	COAL	COKE	PIG IRON	CRUDE STEEL
1850	1.96	0.07	0.01	—
1860	4.27	0.19	0.13	*0.2
1870	11.57	0.34	0.36	*0.5
1880	22.36	1.30	0.76	*0.8
1890	35.51	3.76	1.33	*2.0
1900	60.12	8.91	3.01	*4.3
1913	114.22	25.05	8.20	10.11
1923	41.80	9.75	2.92	3.91
1925	104.34	22.57	8.00	9.89
1929	123.58	26.52	10.98	13.17
1932	73.72	14.83	3.42	4.63
1939	130.18	34.17	12.86	**15.08
1950	103.33	24.28	***9.39	9.70
1957	123.20	39.77	14.80	19.51
1965	110.90	34.72	18.33	24.68
1974	78.17	27.15	23.65	30.28

* From Weber, W., "Entfaltung der Industriewirtschaft," p. 263.
** 1938
*** 1953
SOURCE: Holz, J. M., 1977, p. 127.

inside the loop of the Donetz River before it reaches the Don. The largest town of the Donbass, Stalino, formerly Yuzovka, is the administrative center of the largest mining district of the European part of the former Soviet Union.

Coal was discovered there in 1721 and began to be exploited intensively after 1869, when the first railway reached the Donetz. In 1872, a Welshman, John Hugues, set up an ironworks at Yuzovka. In 1884, a railroad linked Krivoï Rog, a huge iron ore deposit 150 miles farther west, and stimulated coal mining and ironworks in the Donbass. With British, French, and Belgian capital, technological transfers, and skilled engineers, more than forty blast furnaces were in operation in the 1890s. The Belgian Cockerill Company played a leading role in the Donetz industry. In 1886, Eugène Sadoine (administrator of the Cockerill Company) founded the Société Métallurgique Dniéprovienne du Midi de la Russie to supply the new Donetz blast furnaces with Krivoï Rog's iron ore. In 1894, Cockerill and the Dniéprovienne created the Société des Charbonnages du Centre du Donbass (also known as Almaznaïa) to supply Cockerill's ironworks with cheap coke. This initiative stimulated other Belgian and French enterprises to invest in the Donetz, where more than 50 percent of the capital was foreign. The output of pig iron increased from 2 million tons in 1900 to 4.7 million in 1914, and coal output jumped from 1 million tons in 1880 to 16.7 in 1910. On the eve of the revolution, the Donetz was producing 75 percent of the Russian pig iron and nearly 90 percent of the coal. However, the tsarist regime made no effort to develop engineering industries.

After the revolution, the Donetz became a strategic issue during the fuel crisis of 1921. During the New Economic Policy (NEP) of 1921 to 1926, most of the mines of the Donetz were gathered in the Donugol trust, while the Council of Labor and Defence (STO) imposed a special commission to mobilize the coal resources. From 920 small mines in 1920, the number fell to 179 in October 1923, while the output of coal increased to supply the national demand for fuel for railways and industry. The pre-war level of coal output was regained in 1924 (12.2 million tons), and production continued to rise rapidly to nearly 70 million tons in 1936 and 94 million tons in 1940. Indeed, the First Five-Year Plan (1927–1932) strongly supported the development of ironworks and large coal mines, such as the United State Political Department Mine in the Nesvetai District (OGPU), the Artyem Mine of the Sevkavugol Trust in the Shakhty District, and the Young Communar Mine of the Artyemugol Trust. At that time, the Irmino Mine (near Uspenskoye) came to symbolize Soviet industry, and one of its miners, Aleksey Stakhanov, came to represent the heroic Soviet industrial worker. Under the Second Five-Year Plan, giant ironworks appeared (Kramatorskoye heavy engine-building works, Voroshilovgrad locomotive-building works, Makeevka metallurgical works) along with several chemical plants and an agricultural machine-building works in Rostov-on-the-Don.

Between 1941 and 1942, the Donetz was devasted. In 1945, coal output fell to thirty million tons. During the Fourth Five-Year Plan (launched in 1946), coal mines and steelworks were rebuilt as they had been in the 1930s. However, since 1928 a shift in the industrial location in favor of Ural, Kuznetsk, and Siberia reduced the share of the Donetz basin in total coal production (from 87 percent in 1913 to 60 percent in 1937).

In the 1960s and 1970s, coal mines and the steel industry continued to supply the heavy engineering of the Don region: electrical engineering, machine-tool manufacture, a tractor plant, and other agricultural machinery in Rostov-on-Don and Odessa. Even though a relative industrial decline and a deterioration of the working conditions in the mines are observed from the late 1980s, the Donetz remains the main industrial center of the Ukrainian Republic.

U.S. Coal Basins. In the early twentieth century, three main coal seams were exploited; the Appalachian Mountains, the Great Lakes region (Indiana, Illinois), and the west central region (Iowa, Missouri, Kansas). Coal was also exploited in Colorado. In 1908, the northern Appalachian Mountains (Pennsylvania and Ohio) and Illinois produced 330 million short tons of coal per year or 79 percent of the U.S. output.

The Appalachian coal seam, one of the richest deposits in the world, offers a wide spectrum of coal, from bituminous coal to high-quality anthracite. The anthracite de-

TABLE 3. *Donbass Coal Field Output of Coal (millions of tons)*

YEARS	OUTPUT	YEARS	OUTPUT
1855	0.1	1926	19.6
1860	0.1	1927	27.3
1865	0.2	1928	31.0
1870	0.3	1929	31.0
1875	0.9	1930	30.5
1880	1.3	1931	45.0
1885	1.9	1933	52.5
1890	2.8	1934	60.0
1895	4.9	1935	69.3
1900	10.8	1936	77.5
1905	12.9	1937	76.9
1910	16.7	1940	94.3
1915	26.6	1945	30.3
1917	24.8	1950	78.0
1918	8.9	1955	126.0
1919	5.5	1960	172.1
1920	4.5	1965	194.3
1921	5.4	1970	207.1
1922	7.2	1975	223.0
1923	8.1	1980	197.1
1924	12.2	1985	189.0
1925	12.5	1990	165.0

SOURCES: Gruner, E., and Bousquet, G., *Atlas général des houillères. Deuxième partie: Texte*, Paris, 1911, p. 320; Scwartz, H., *Russia's Soviet economy*, London, 1951, p. 214; Kubijovyc, V., *Encyclopedia of Ukraine*, vol.1, Toronto, 1985, pp. 530–531; *Coal Information 1992*, International Energy Agency, Paris, 1992, p. 65.

posits in northeastern Pennsylvania were already known in the early nineteenth century, when the anthracite of Schuylkill County was used locally as domestic fuel. In the mid-nineteenth century, the improvement of water transportation and the railways opened the expanding market of the bourgeoning cities of the eastern coast. Sulfur-free anthracite of Pennsylvania was mainly used by railway companies and in homes. Around 1850, three-quarters of all the coal used was transformed into steam power and mechanical work. In the 1840s, anthracite also was used by the ironworks of Pennsylvania and the eastern Great Lakes states, and the use of coke in conjunction with anthracite started before the Civil War.

The bituminous coalfield of the northern Appalachians, located close to the ocean, sent coal by railways to the Atlantic harbors. The bituminous coal of the southern Appalachian Mountains (from Alabama to Pennsylvania), suitable for producing coke, began to be used by ironworks after the Civil War. From 1850 onward, the bituminous coal of Pennsylvania, West Virginia, Ohio, and Illinois had two main outlets, the railways and the iron industry. After 1860, the valleys of the Ohio River and its tributaries (Monongahela, Youghiogheny, Allegheny,

TABLE 4. *Relative Weight of Regions (in percentages) in the Output of Coal, 1870–1950*

	1870	1890	1910	1930	1950
Middle Atlantic[a]	76.53	58.39	47.89	36.52	26.90
Great Lakes[b]	17.01	19.12	19.95	17.40	20.35
Southeast[c]	3.02	11.27	21.56	38.34	46.60
Plains[d]	2.78	5.73	3.23	2.22	1.84
Mountain[e]	0.18	3.67	4.97	4.01	3.53
Other regions	0.48	1.82	2.4	1.51	0.78
Total in millions of short tons (=100%)	33.0	157.8	501.6	536.9	560.0

[a]New York, New Jersey, Pennsylvania, Delaware, Maryland, District of Columbia

[b]Ohio, Indiana, Illinois, Michigan, Wisconsin

[c]Virginia, West Virginia, Kentucky, Tennessee, North Carolina, South Carolina, Georgia, Florida, Alabama, Mississippi, Arkansas, Louisiana

[d]Minnesota, Iowa, Missouri, North Dakota, South Dakota, Nebraska, Kansas

[e]Montana, Idaho, Wyoming, Utah, Colorado

SOURCE: Perloff, H. S., et al., *Regions, Resources, and Economic Growth*, Lincoln, *Nebr.*, 1960, p. 213.

Conemaugh, and Beaver) became the cradle of the American iron and steel industry. Coal was carried to the coke ovens of Connellsville and to the ironworks of western Pennsylvania, especially Pittsburgh. Around Pittsburgh, coal began to be exploited when ironworks were set up during the War of 1812. Linked to the iron industry, coal mining expanded around the city during the Civil War, when the ironworks and mines supplied the Union army with fuel and armament. In the 1870s, numerous glass factories further increased the demand for coal.

In 1873, Andrew Carnegie introduced the Bessemer converter to produce cheap steel in the Edgar Thomson Works near Pittsburgh. The adoption of the Bessemer process (and after 1878, the Thomas-Gilchrist process) strengthened coal mining and heavy industry in western Pennsylvania. A new steel industry using the Bessemer process flourished around Chicago, while the steel industry of Birmingham marked the beginning of intensive coal mining in Alabama. Between 1870 and 1890, larger and more efficient blast furnaces raised the average furnace output sixfold. In the 1890s, the steel industry drifted in the direction of the Great Lakes region when the Mesabi ores (Minnesota) supplied the steel industry. The heavy industry of Chicago was reinforced by the expansion of the engineering and automobile industries.

On the other hand, the coal mines of the Tug, Kanawha, and New Rivers, tributaries of the Ohio River, sent their output to the Mississippi River and the Atlantic harbors (Portsmouth, Norfolk, Newport News, Lambert Point, Sewall Point) for export to Europe. After 1920, a decline in coal production and consumption began that lasted until 1932. The gradual recovery that started in 1933 culminated in 1943 in exactly the same record consumption previously reached in 1918—651 million tons. Stimulated by the serious coal shortage overseas following the end of World War II, production reached its all-time high in 1947 (688 million tons) but began to decline afterward.

BIBLIOGRAPHY

Abelshauser, W. *Der Ruhrkohlenbergbau seit 1945: Wiederaufbau, Krise, Anpassung.* Munich, 1984.

Berg, W. *Wirtschaft und Gesellschaft in Deutschland und Großbritannien im Überzang zum "organisierten Kapitalismus." Unternehmer, Angestellte, Arbeiter und Staat im Steinkohlenbergbau des Ruhrgebietes und von Südwales, 1850–1914.* Berlin, 1984.

Dobb, Maurice. *Soviet Economic Development since 1917.* London, 1972.

Feige, Ullrich. *Bergarbeiterschaft zwischen Tradition und Emanzipation: Das Verhältnis von Bergleuten und Gewerkschaften zu Unternehmern und Staat im westlichen Ruhrgebiet um 1900.* Düsseldorf, 1986.

Fischer, W. *Statistik der Bergbauproduktion Deutschlands, 1850–1914.* Saint Katharinen, Germany, 1989.

Holz, J. M. *La Ruhr du "Kohlenpott" à la région urbaine.* Paris, 1977.

Kortus, B. "Donbas and Upper Silesia—A Comparative Analysis of the Industrial Regions." *Geographia Polonica* 2 (1964), 183–192.

Mckay, J. P. *Pioneers for Profit: Foreign Entrepreneurship and Russian Industrialization, 1885–1913.* Chicago and London, 1970.

Leboutte, René. *Vie et mort des bassins industriels en Europe, 1750–2000.* Paris, 1997.

Pierenkemper, T. *Die westfälischen Schwerindustriellen, 1852–1913: Soziale Struktur und unternehmerischer Erfolg.* Göttingen, 1979.

Pounds, N. J. G. *The Ruhr: A Study in Historical and Economic Geography.* London, 1952.

Pounds, N. J. G. *An Historical Geography of Europe, 1800–1914.* Cambridge, 1993.

Ruhrgebiet im Industriezeitalte: Geschichte und Entwicklung. 2 vols. Düsseldorf, 1990.

Schlieper, Andreas. *150 Jahre Ruhrgebiet: Ein Kapitel deutscher Wirtschaftsgechichte.* Düsseldorf, 1986.

Schurr, Sam H., and Bruce C. Netshert. *Energy in the American Economy, 1850–1975: An Economic Study of Its History and Prospects.* Baltimore, 1960.

Steinberg, Heinz Günter. "Das Ruhrgebiet im 19. und 20. Jahrhundert. Ein Verdichtungsraum im Wandel." In *Selbstverlag der Geographischen Kommission für Westfalen.* Münster, 1985.

Stepanov, P., ed. *Donetz Coal Basin (Donbass).* International Geological Congress, 12th session, USSR, 1937. Leningrad and Moscow, 1937.

Tenfelde, Klaus. *Sozialgeschichte der Bergarbeiterschaft an der Ruhr im 19. Jahrhundert* (1977). Reprint, Bonn, Germany, 1981.

Wiel, Paul. *Wirtschaftsgeschichte des Ruhrgebietes: Tatsachen und Zahlen, Siedlungsverband Ruhrkohlenbezirk.* Essen, Germany, 1970.

RENÉ LEBOUTTE

COATS FAMILY. The Coats family of Paisley, Scotland, leading cotton-thread manufacturers, whose firm, J. & P. Coats, formed in 1830 by brothers James (1803–1845) and Peter (1808–1890), became an outstanding multinational enterprise in the early twentieth century. Although many firms, including Clark & Co., were engaged in the manufacture of the new textile material in the town famous for its shawl, J. & P. Coats opted for export to the United States. Two other brothers supported the infant business: Thomas (1809–1883) became a partner in 1833 and later took charge of the Paisley mill; more important, between 1840 and 1860, Andrew (1814–1900), an emigrant merchant, organized a profitable network of agencies for the American market, which continued to expand, particularly after the introduction of Singer's sewing machine in 1851. American production, under the supervision of James (1834–1913), Peter's son, began at the Conant Thread Company in Pawtucket, Rhode Island, in 1869. By the early 1880s, seven other members of the second generation joined their family firm; Archibald (1840–1912) was the chairman from 1884 to 1912, and Thomas G. (1846–1922) from 1912 to 1922.

Events of the 1890s enabled J. & P. Coats eventually to dominate both the British and the American markets. After the company went public in 1890, a large amount of money became available, and several professional managers, particularly Otto E. Philippi (1846–1917), a German sales expert, were admitted to the board. In 1896, it took over archrival Clark & Co. and two other major British competitors, and within the next two years it acquired their four American subsidiaries. Also, the company secured a formidable position in many other foreign markets by aggressively pursuing a policy of export and local production. In addition to those in the United States and four other countries, factories were acquired or built in nine more countries between 1896 and 1914. J. & P. Coats was perhaps the most active of the early British multinationals, making some fifty-three direct investments, for both manufacture and sale, in fifteen countries on four continents before 1914.

Eight members of the third generation, including William H. Coats (1866–1928), the chairman from 1922 to 1928, took part in company management after the 1896 merger. The family-dominated board gradually created an advanced managerial hierarchy, resembling a decentralized multidivisional (M-form) structure, to cope with the extensive business interests. Ultimately, J. & P. Coats was a highly profitable conglomerate unlike other British amalgamations of the day, becoming the world's largest textile company and Britain's largest manufacturing company in terms of capital by the 1910s.

The Coats thread's fame as a world product persisted throughout the twentieth century, as did the management tradition although it gradually weakened. In 1981, one of the two directors from the fourth generation, William D. Coats (born 1924), became the chairman of Coats Patons. Five years later he stepped down when the company was taken over by Vantona Viyella to become Coats Viyella.

Until then, the Coats family (in total, twenty-two members from four generations) had had leading roles in the cotton thread–making industry for more than 150 years.

BIBLIOGRAPHY

Cairncross, Alexander K., and J. B. K. Hunter. "The Early Growth of Messrs J. & P. Coats, 1830–83." *Business History* 29.2 (1987), 157–177.

Hunter, J. B. K. "Archibald Coats," "Otto Ernst Philippi," and "Thomas Coats." In *Dictionary of Scottish Business Biography 1860–1960*, vol. 1, edited by A. Slaven and S. Checkland, pp. 329–335, 389–392. Aberdeen, 1986.

Kim, Dong-Woon. "From a Family Partnership to a Corporate Company: J. & P. Coats, Thread Manufacturers." *Textile History* 25.2 (1994), 185–225.

Kim, Dong-Woon. "J. & P. Coats as a Multinational before 1914." *Business and Economic History* 26.2 (1997), 526–539.

Kim, Dong-Woon. "The British Multinational Enterprise in the United States before 1914: The Case of J. & P. Coats." *Business History Review* 72.4 (1998), 523–551.

DONG-WOON KIM

COCKERILL, JOHN (1789–1840), was the youngest son of William Cockerill, an engineer forced to leave England in 1797.

Cockerill was born in Haslingden, Lancashire, and his family settled in Verviers (Belgium), a textile city where William was commissioned in 1799 by two merchant-entrepreneurs to build spinning jennies. In 1814, John and his brother James became managers of the workshop created by their father in Liege to build textile machinery and steam engines. After the Battle of Waterloo, John Cockerill took advantage of the formation of the United Kingdom of the Netherlands to champion the policies of King Willem I on industrialization. In 1816 he received official support to establish ironworks using British technology. On 17 January 1817, Willem I sold his estate at Seraing (near Liège) to Cockerill. The king, who intended to modernize the industry of the southern part of the Netherlands (Wallonia) and to support the free trade of the northern merchants, was closely associated with Cockerill's factory, whose trademark seal included the phrase *Koninglijk Établissement te Seraing*. In addition to a policy of moderate import–export duties and protective measures in favor of nascent industrialization, Willem I established the Fund for National Industry (1821), which became the main source of capital for Cockerill's enterprises, and the Société Générale pour favoriser l'industrie nationale (1822), based in Brussels.

However, Seraing's ironworks faced difficulties not only in launching a coke blast furnace but also in going beyond the economic stagnation of 1819 to 1822. Naval Lieutenant G. M. Roentgen, comparing the situation of the Belgian iron industry to the British one, emphasized in a January 1823 report the promising plans for Seraing. In May 1823 the government approved an association (loan contracts) with John Cockerill, with his brother James giving up his participation. With the help of the Scottish engineer David Mushet, Cockerill managed to set up an integrated iron-works (1823–1826), consisting of a coal mine, an internal railroad, coke ovens, a blast furnace (used only in 1826), puddling furnaces, rolling mills, and an "icon factory." Seraing's ironworks became the main supplier of the state itself and the Netherlands Steamboat Company. In spite of many financial problems, Cockerill managed not only to develop Seraing's ironworks but also to create several factories elsewhere in Germany, France, and Catalonia.

Belgian independence (1830–1831) put Cockerill, considered an Orangist, on shaky ground; and the new Belgian government at first refused him any financial support. In 1833 the association between the Dutch government and Cockerill was finally liquidated. The Belgian State decided to lend Cockerill capital, and above all to create a railway network (1835), an initiative that stimulated Seraing's ironworks. In 1835 Cockerill delivered the first locomotive and tons of rails to the Belgian State. He also produced steamships and steam engines. The economic crisis of 1837–1838 forced Cockerill to liquidate his assets in February 1839. While the enterprise was put under the control of a special commission, Cockerill took advantage of a moratorium to travel to St. Petersburg with the idea of launching new industrial plants; but on his way back to Belgium he died, on 19 June 1840 in Warsaw, a victim of typhus. Seraing was immediately reorganized by his nephew Conrad-Gustave Pastor. The enterprise was transformed into a limited company (Société Anonyme John Cockerill, 1842), which performed extremely well thereafter.

BIBLIOGRAPHY

Fremdling, Rainer. "John Cockerill: Pionierunternehmer der Belgisch–Niederländischen Industrialisierung." *Zeitschrift für Unternehmensgeschichte* 26.3 (1981), 179–193.

Mahaim, Ernest. "Les débuts de l'Etablissement John Cockerill à Seraing: Contribution à l'histoire des origines de la grande industrie au Pays de Liège." *Vierteljahrschrift für Sozial- und Wirtschafsgeschichte* 4 (1905), 627–648.

Westebbe, Richard M. "State Entrepreneurship: King Willem I, John Cockerill, and the Seraing Engineering Works, 1815–1840." *Explorations in Entrepreneurial History* (Research Center in Entrepreneurial History, Harvard University) 8.1 (1956), 205–232.

RENÉ LEBOUTTE

COCOA. The botanical origins of cocoa (*Theobroma cacao*) lie in the Upper Amazon, and wild cocoa still grows scattered throughout the American tropics, a small, lower story forest tree with large pods that contain seeds, called beans. Theobromine, an alkaloid in the beans, is a mildly addictive stimulant. Cocoa was first cultivated in orchards in Mesoamerica in pre-Columbian times. As an integral part of the Maya and Aztec civilizations, cocoa had its own god, and its consumption was at first restricted to elites. The beans were roasted and ground to make a fine powder, then brewed into an unsweetened drink, mixed with spices, and usually drunk cold. Dried beans were also widely used as currency throughout Mesoamerica by the time of the Spanish Conquest in the 1520s. The Spaniards were entranced by tales of cocoa at Aztec banquets, and some believed that it was an aphrodisiac. In establishing New Spain, they swept away social restrictions to the drink and created a new form, drunk hot, sweetened with cane sugar, and flavored with vanilla or cinnamon. In this mode, the drink enjoyed great success around the Caribbean Basin, across the Pacific in the Spanish-owned Philippines Islands, and in Catholic southern Europe by the seventeenth century; by the eighteenth century, it had spread into northern Europe and into the North American colonies, where it was sometimes prepared with milk, through trade with the Dutch after they broke away from rule by Spain. In New Spain, cocoa was also mixed into a dark sauce for meats, with hot pepper and spices, called *mole poblano*.

Until the 1880s, cocoa came almost exclusively from the Americas, although the tree was introduced into Asia in about 1650 and into Africa in about 1820. Production in the Americas came to be associated with estates that used African slaves—typical of the Caribbean Basin, notably Venezuela, the largest producer of the eighteenth century. Cocoa estates were smaller than those growing sugar cane, however, and were sometimes owned by "free persons of color." The estates of coastal Ecuador employed free labor from an early date, and they dominated the world market from the 1820s to the 1880s. Smallholder production persisted in much of Mesoamerica, and in South America the Roman Catholic missionaries encouraged Native Americans to forage in the Amazon Basin for wild cocoa.

Technical innovations from the 1870s to the 1900s led to the development in Europe and North America of chocolate confectionery, milk chocolate, and low fat cocoa beverages. As incomes rose, such products became items of mass consumption in the industrialized world, with some help from the anti-alcohol temperance campaigners. Most of chocolate's name brands, still sold today, originated at that time. The shift to a mass market led to a switch away from the Criollo varieties of cocoa—fine tasting, but slow to mature, low yielding, short lived, and vulnerable to a wide array of pests and diseases. The more robust Forastero varieties became the norm, their bitter taste partly overcome by a lengthier fermentation of the cocoa beans during processing.

In response to the new demand, export volumes grew at a fast and fairly regular pace (only seriously interrupted in the 1940s by World War II). Prices were much more volatile, as it did not prove economically viable to replant cocoa in the same land. That led to unpredictable production bottlenecks, since sharp price increases triggered massive waves of planting by pioneers chopping down virgin forests. As the trees came into production only some five years later, gluts then brought prices crashing down. Such volatility was worsened by market manipulation—first by cartels of planters starting in the 1890s, then by associations of governments starting in the 1960s.

As exports grew, the New World became a minor player, in part because its best-located virgin forests had been exhausted, then pests and diseases ravaged the aging trees. Estate agriculture had also become a burden, as there were no economies of scale in growing cocoa. With the abolition of slavery and debt peonage, the estates could rarely meet labor costs in times of low cocoa prices. Although the estates survived as large producers in the south of Bahia state in Brazil, in the 1990s, they too ran out of virgin forest. The focus of production in the twentieth century thus shifted to Old World smallholders, in partnership with vigorous mercantile diasporas. In West Africa, the island of São Tomé's Portuguese estates lost their early lead, however, to indigenous farmers in Ghana and southwestern Nigeria. As state-marketing boards pushed farm-gate prices below production costs in the 1970s, Ivory Coast smallholders became the main producers, although throughout West Africa forests were dwindling fast. Asia entered the cocoa market in the 1970s; there, Malaysian estates proved to be uneconomical, unable to make profits when cocoa prices headed downward. Today, the Bugis smallholders and traders of southern Sulawesi, Indonesia, are the most dynamic growers and traders of cocoa, but they too face vanishing forests and a local pest, the pod-borer moth.

BIBLIOGRAPHY

Clarence-Smith, William G. *Cocoa and Chocolate, 1765–1914*. London, 2000.

Clarence-Smith, William G., ed. *Cocoa Pioneer Fronts since 1800: The Role of Smallholders, Planters and Merchants*. London, 1996.

Coe, Sophie, and Michael Coe. *The True History of Chocolate*. London, 1996.

Dand, Robin. *The International Cocoa Trade*. Cambridge, 1993.

Harwich, Nikita. *Histoire du chocolat*. Paris, 1992.

Ruf, François. *Booms et crises du cacao, les vertiges de l'or brun*. Paris, 1995.

Young, Allen M. *The Chocolate Tree: A Natural History of Cocoa*, Washington, D.C., 1994.

WILLIAM G. CLARENCE-SMITH

COFFEE. Coffee, the second most valuable exported legal commodity (after oil), is the primary delivery system for caffeine, the world's most widely taken psychoactive drug, and it provides a livelihood (of sorts) for over 20 million people. The daily wage of the average coffee laborer would purchase one cup of coffee in a trendy coffee bar in the developed world.

From its original natural home on the mountainsides of Ethiopia, coffee's cultivation has spread in a girdle around the globe in some fifty countries between the Tropics of Cancer and Capricorn. It is a small understory tree that grows to approximately 20 feet if unpruned, with a brief, mildly aromatic white blossom, followed by the production of a coffee berry, or *cherry*, which is red in most varieties. Like peanuts, coffee beans usually grow in facing pairs, surrounded by layers of silver skin, parchment, mucilage, and outer skin. Plants that lack sufficient boron can produce a single bean called a peaberry, which is prized by some consumers.

Although there are many species of *Coffea*, only two are grown widely as commercial crops: *Coffea arabica*, the original bean found in Ethiopia, which accounts for 75 percent of the world's crop, and *Coffea canephora*, commonly known as *robusta*, which accounts for the rest. *Arabica* trees grow best on mountainsides in semitropical regions where the weather neither freezes nor gets too hot. *Robusta*, which withstands higher heat and is more disease-resistant, is generally considered inferior to *arabica* in taste, and it contains twice the caffeine.

Coffee's tumultuous history has had a powerful impact on the world's economy, environment, and lifestyle. Probably in the fifteenth century, an Ethiopian first roasted the beans and ground them for an infusion in hot water, and the coffee beverage as we know it was born. Its cultivation jumped across the Red Sea to Yemen, and the Turks traded coffee beans throughout their empire during the sixteenth century.

The Arabs attempted to maintain a monopoly, but the Dutch smuggled out fertile seeds, beginning cultivation in the East Indies in the seventeenth century. They enslaved natives of Ceylon, Java, and other islands, forcing them to grow coffee.

European travelers brought back tales of this strange black Arab brew. In 1650 the first European coffeehouse opened in Oxford, England, and over the next fifty years, coffee took Europe by storm. In London alone there were two thousand coffeehouses by 1700. Coffee consumption changed lifestyles. Until then, alcoholic intake had predominated. Coffee and coffeehouses provided intellectual meeting places that helped spawn art, business, and revolution.

The French spread coffee cultivation to the New World, beginning in Martinique in 1723, then Santo Domingo (Dominican Republic and Haiti), and elsewhere, using imported African slaves as coffee laborers. By 1790 half of the world's coffee was grown on Haiti. The following year a successful slave revolt destroyed the plantations.

Near the end of the nineteenth century, a fungus, *Hemileia vastatrix*, called coffee leaf rust, wiped out the coffee plantations in the East Indies. *Robusta*, which was

COFFEE. Mangebetu man spreading coffee to dry, Mongomasi, Zaire (present-day Democratic Republic of the Congo), 1972. (Eliot Elisofon/Eliot Elisofon Photographic Archives/National Museum of African Art, Smithsonian Institution, Washington, D.C.)

discovered in the Belgian Congo, was resistant to the fungus, and therefore began to replace *arabica* in some places.

By that time coffee cultivation had spread throughout much of Central and South America, with Brazil the largest producer. In the meantime the British had switched primarily to tea, but after the Boston Tea Party of 1773, it was a patriotic duty to drink coffee in the American colonies. Although Europeans traditionally imported the highest quality beans, Americans drank the most coffee per capita. Industrial coffee roasting began in the 1860s, and branded U.S. coffee companies made coffee a valuable international commodity by 1900, when a glut in Brazil began the boom-bust cycle that continues to this day. Although various quota control systems have been implemented over the years, none have been satisfactory. The International Coffee Agreement, begun in 1962, collapsed in 1989.

The "specialty" coffee trend, from which Starbucks sprang, began as a grassroots movement in the United States in the 1960s and 1970s, rediscovering the joys of high-quality, fresh-roasted *arabica* beans in reaction to instant coffee and mass-produced, poor-quality blends that included more and more *robusta* in the years after World War II. Some of the world's best *arabica* beans are grown in countries such as Costa Rica, Guatemala, Kenya, Colombia, Sumatra, Jamaica, Hawaii, and Papua New Guinea.

In the latter part of the twentieth century, concern over the poor nutrition, housing, and education of coffee laborers resulted in the sale of fair-trade coffee in Europe and the United States. Fair-trade beans are certified to come from cooperatives of small farms, and the growers are guaranteed a reasonable price. Yet fair trade impacts only a minority of coffee laborers. Because shade-grown coffee provides an important habitat for migratory birds, "bird-friendly" coffee has also found a niche market, along with organic coffee.

Technology has had small impact on coffee cultivation. Machine harvesting is sometimes used in Brazil and Hawaii, but steep slopes require hand-picking in most other countries. Both the "dry" method of processing (removing naturally dried husks) and the "wet" method (removing the skin, fermenting and washing off the mucilage, then drying and stripping the parchment) are labor intensive. The wet method requires more labor and costs more. It is generally used for superior, high-grown beans.

Because roasted coffee grows stale quickly, roasting and packaging have traditionally been done in consuming countries. One result has been that most of the profits from coffee have gone to developed, industrial countries. The three major coffee roaster/retailers are the multinationals Nestlé, Philip Morris, and Procter & Gamble, though there are many smaller roasters, and Starbucks has become the world's dominant specialty retail coffee beverage purveyor. The success of Starbucks stems as much from its social function (providing a pleasant place to meet and talk) as from its coffee.

Beginning in the 1990s, Vietnam became a huge factor in coffee cultivation, flooding the market with cheap *robusta* beans and causing prices to decline to disastrously low levels by the early twenty-first century. Some coffee growers simply abandoned their farms.

Health concerns about coffee go back to the first Arab coffeehouses of the sixteenth century. Caffeine is an addictive drug, and people can suffer from severe withdrawal headaches. Yet scientific reports of the early 1980s, which implicated caffeine in everything from cancer to birth defects, turned out to be false alarms and have not been replicated. Taken in moderation, coffee appears to have no ill effects on most people, and it may even have some benefits. Pregnant and nursing mothers should consider cutting out caffeine, however, since it flows through to the fetus and turns breast milk into a kind of natural latte.

BIBLIOGRAPHY

Bates, Robert H. *Open-Economy Politics: The Political Economy of the World Coffee Trade*. Princeton, 1997.

Bersten, Ian. *Coffee Floats, Tea Sinks: Through History and Technology to a Complete Understanding*. Sydney, Australia, 1993.

Davids, Kenneth. *Coffee: A Guide to Buying, Brewing & Enjoying*. 4th ed. Santa Rosa, Calif., 1991.

Illy, Francesco, and Riccardo Illy. *The Book of Coffee: A Gourmet's Guide*. New York, 1992.

Pendergrast, Mark. *Uncommon Grounds: The History of Coffee and How It Transformed Our World*. New York, 1999. Comprehensive social and economic history.

Ukers, William H. *All About Coffee*. 2d ed. New York, 1935. Classic text, available as reprint from Specialty Coffee Association of America.

Weinberg, Bennett Alan, and Bonnie K. Bealer. *The World of Caffeine: The Science and Culture of the World's Most Popular Drug*. New York, 2001.

MARK PENDERGRAST

COINAGE. *See* Money and Coinage.

COKE SMELTING. Coke is a fuel made from coal; it has been processed to remove most of the gases. Coke then burns with intense heat and little smoke and was used industrially from the 1660s onward. Ironmaking in Europe during modern times was accomplished by the indirect process—iron ore was first smelted in a blast furnace to pig iron before being refined to malleable wrought iron in the forge. In both processes, the fuel used was charcoal. By 1700, most of the important industries in Britain replaced charcoal with coal, but not the iron industry, despite some significant experimentation during the seventeenth century. In 1709, however, Abraham Darby (1678–1717), manage to make pig iron at his blast furnace in Coalbrookdale, Shropshire, using local coal as fuel. The explanation for Darby's success is still not clear, but his earlier involvement in the brass industry, which made him familiar with the smelting of copper using coal, has been considered, along with the qualities of Shropshire coal. Darby's achievement has been hailed as a major advancement in the history of technology, but more than four decades passed before coke smelting spread beyond Shropshire; also, coke-smelted pig iron was suitable only for casting. Darby mainly used his coke iron for thin-walled castings, with only a fraction refined to wrought iron.

Not until the 1750s did forgemasters in Britain begin to use coke iron in their forges. The reason for this long delay has been debated. T. S. Ashton noted (1924) the inferior quality of the pig iron made and that Darby managed to keep his novelty a secret. Since then, Charles Hyde (1977) reported that price differences acted in favor of charcoal-made pig iron, and that it was the rise in charcoal prices after the mid-eighteenth century that promoted the shift to coke smelting. Hyde's explanation has also been challenged, since it seems that something must have happened to enhance the quality of coke-smelted pig iron. One aspect of furnace practices that did change during the late 1700s was the supply of air. Improvements in blowing technology—the use of cast-iron blowing cylinders, sometimes combined with steam engines—made it possible both to increase the temperature in the furnace and erect larger furnaces. The result might also have had a positive effect on quality.

After the mid-eighteenth century, the number of coke-fired blast furnaces increased from only three to some two hundred and thirty in 1810. At the same time, the number of charcoal blast furnaces declined, from about seventy to only a handful. Production volumes rose from some 30,000 tons to more than 350,000 tons for the same period. Connected with these trends were the spatial restructuring of the industry, which resulted in its concentration. The development of coke smelting meant that fewer but larger production units—often containing several blast furnaces as well as forges and mills—were located to the coalfields to replace the many small and scattered furnaces that had used charcoal as fuel.

BIBLIOGRAPHY

Ashton, Thomas S. *Iron and Steel in the Industrial Revolution*. Manchester, 1924.

Harris, John R. *The British Iron Industry 1700–1850*. Houndmills, England, 1988.

Hyde, Charles K. *Technological Change and the British Iron Industry, 1700–1870*. Princeton, 1977.

GÖRAN RYDÉN

COLLECTIVE ACTION is the pursuit by groups of the common interests of their members. Until the mid-1950s, political scientists assumed that such common interests and collective action were easily identified and pursued. However, the Harvard-trained economist and social scientist Mancur Olson (1932–1998) demonstrated that the problem of collective action is to explain why individuals acting in their private interests can fail to secure the provision of goods and services that are collectively in the interests of all. Although much of individual action is refracted through collective organizations designed to further the common interests of their members, self-interest—or calculative rationality—tends to drive a self-seeking individual not to join. The difference between private goods (where the benefits of consumption are confined exclusively to the paying customer) and public goods (where even those who have not paid toward the cost cannot be excluded from enjoying the benefits) is the primary cause. Thus the rational individual will calculate that it is better for others to pay the costs of collective action while personally opting to travel free. The greater the number of such rational calculators with a common interest, the less likely it is that an organization will be capable of collective action; it will tend to remain either latent or weak.

Olson's approach has been criticized for its very narrow view of self-interest, but it has yielded powerful results, notably in explaining limited collective action by social classes (defined by their relationship to the means of production) in the modern period. Even when individuals are aware of their own class interests and reject the class interests of others, the rational bourgeois may concentrate on running the business, and the rational proletarian may expect to enjoy the benefits of social revolution without paying the costs, figuring that one revolutionary more or less will make little difference. Thus the terminology of "collective action" has tended to replace that of "class conflict," and research has focused on mobilization strategies and the creation of collective social and moral interests that outweigh individual economic calculation, enabling "latent" interest groups to become actual and pursue collective action.

The examples of successful collective action are manifold. Ancient civilizations erected major edifices and enormous statues in a collective effort to appease gods or to venerate ancestors. It is not known exactly how the enormous stone heads of Rapa Nui (Easter Island) were quarried on one side of the island and then moved, carved, and erected on the other, but collective action is the only logical assumption. On a more modest scale, the irrigation systems of medieval and early-modern Iran, the *qanats*, were built and maintained over many generations by collective action of villagers. Groups of producers or consumers frequently engage in collective action to influence prices, market arrangements, or the legislative framework. In medieval European cities, artisans sought to control price, quality, and supply through a guilds system. The origin of the Indian caste system, one based on occupation, can be fruitfully examined in terms of producers using endogamy to control labor supply over many generations and so bring collective benefits of higher and more secure incomes. Indeed, the classic examples of collective action in the modern period are business lobbies for protection, subsidy, and restricted entry and the efforts of labor unions to raise wages for their members.

The ability of groups to overcome the problems posed by free riding for public goods depends, according to Olson, in part on the structural characteristics of the group, especially on its size, and in part on the strategy it pursues. In a group of n similar people, each derives only one divided by n ($1/n$) of the total benefit that might accrue from collective action. The incentive to contribute to collective action is only $1/n$ of what is optimal for the group. The disincentive increases as n increases. Large groups can easily remain latent. Thus, the thousands of ordinary stockholders in a modern corporation are almost invariably controlled with some ease by the board of directors. Individual shareholders have no incentive to work in the collective interest; they will gain only a trifling amount from any change in dividend policy, and managers typically enjoy unchallenged authority. Large groups have two main solutions, the more obvious one being coercion. Governments, even of the most laissez-faire hue, have recognized the potential benefits from collective action to provide defense, stable markets, and security of private property. They have also acknowledged that voluntary contributions to the cost of such services are unreliable and have universally relied upon compulsory taxation revenues. Alternatively, large groups may provide "selective incentives" in the form of private benefits to induce individuals to join and contribute to the pursuit of collective action. For example, professional organizations have provided solely to their own members insurance against malpractice suits and technical journals (private goods) so that they can finance lobbying on behalf of the profession as a whole (collective action).

Smaller organizations face their own problems; clearly the constraints of size do not apply. In a market environment, collective action requires 100 percent participation from all potential members; so a holdout has enormous bargaining power and may demand concessions unacceptable to the majority. The failure of British staple export industries to conclude voluntary price-fixing and market-sharing agreements in the early 1930s illustrates the difficulties. In nonmarket situations, small groups typically have to confront asymmetry among members. If one member makes disproportionate gains from the collective action, it has a much larger incentive to bear the costs, and its complaints about "unfair" burdens are unlikely to be credible. The best-known applications are military alliances, notably NATO, where the United States has carried a huge share of the costs, but also has drawn

LABOR PROTEST. *The Human Tide.* Painting by Giuseppe Pellizza da Volpedo (1868–1907). (Galleria d'Arte Moderna, Villa Reale, Milan/Alinari/Art Resource, NY)

substantial economic and political benefits from peace and stability in western Europe, so that its efforts to redistribute alliance costs have been largely unsuccessful.

Collective Action, Public Choice Theory, and New Institutional Economics. This approach to the study of collective action is but one aspect of the application of economic analysis to political behavior, or public choice theory. The leading exponents are two economists from the Virginia School (founded at the Thomas Jefferson Center in the University of Virginia at Charlotte), Gordon Tullock (born 1922) and James M. Buchanan (born 1919, Nobel laureate in 1986). Mancur Olson served as president of the Public Choice Society (1972–1974). The first major public choice landmark was a study by the political (later urban) economist Anthony Downs (born 1930), *An Economic Theory of Democracy* (New York, 1957). Downs suggested that government would supply vote-maximizing policies financed by spending policies that would lose it the minimum number of votes. Downs concluded that democratic governments would favor producers rather than consumers, would be explicitly redistributive, and would experience budgetary strains. Tullock and Buchanan have sounded a more pessimistic note, portraying modern democracies as ripe for exploitation by organized collective interests. Rational voters, whether individual electors or members of the legislature, are poorly informed about the issues on which they vote except where they have a sectional interest. Public choice theorists argue that much of the initiative in public policy making devolves to self-aggrandizing bureaucrats and organized interests, which support political campaigns in return for transfers of resources through favourable policies. Buchanan also distinguished between decision costs (the transaction costs involved in reaching a decision) and external costs (which decision makers pass to others). If a decision is made by a small group, decision costs are minimal, and external costs, which are deflected, are maximal. If a decision is made by a large majority, the converse holds.

Transaction cost analysis is associated particularly with leaders of the new institutional economics (notably Douglass North, born 1920; Oliver Williamson, born 1932) but also has profoundly shaped the analysis of collective action. The new institutionalists also have focused on incentive structures, collective groups, and government, but with a less inherently critical tone than in public choice theory. New institutionalists are concerned with the devising of rules to limit opportunistic behavior, reduce uncertainty, and limit the cost of transacting as exchange relations have become more complex and impersonal in the processes of economic development. In this approach, the restrictive impact of narrow interest groups can be (more than) offset if they establish enforceable codes of conduct that commit parties to coordinated exchange. Thus, North and others have argued that the merchant guilds of the Italian city-states and the German Hansa played positive roles in the late-medieval commercial revolution in Europe between the eleventh and fourteenth centuries, despite their narrowness and restrictive functions. Equally, institutionalists view the modern state and bureaucracy in a more neutral light than do public choice theorists. For institutionalists, central protection of property rights and enforcement of legal rules to regulate contracts, corporate behavior, and the financial sector can reduce transaction costs and promote economic development. Both new institutionalists and public choice theorists agree that the capture of the state by narrow interest groups is socially wasteful.

Collective Action and National Economic Performance. From these and diverse other influences has sprung an institutional approach to explaining economic performance. Among the competing varieties of institutional analysis, the most influential, but controversial, has been Olson's interpretation of why growth rates differ over time and between nations. Its central element is the distributional coalition, which is the fully formed, mature interest group in public choice (rent-seeking) clothing. There are two important extensions to the theory developed in his earlier work. The first gives even greater emphasis to time. In stable conditions, distributional coalitions can, in time, evolve methods for overcoming their collective action problems, and, once established, they tend to collapse or disappear only under violent repression. Thus, stable societies have a rich texture of organizations for collective action and accordingly suffer losses of efficiency and dynamism, the felicitously termed conditions of institutional "arthritis" and "sclerosis." It follows that societies that can re-create internal stability and order after a convulsion has destroyed organizations for collective action should, for a time, grow extremely rapidly. This approach clearly predicts that societies with long periods of stability and immunity from invasion (such as the United Kingdom and the United States) will grow slowly, but also that spurts of growth will occur in countries that have experienced institutional destruction in war (most of Western Europe and Japan after 1945) or jurisdictional integration (the widening of the national market and simultaneous establishment of a government that could be influenced by larger lobbies than previously existed, such as the United States in the nineteenth century and Holland during its Golden Age in the seventeenth century).

Olson also introduced the notion of an encompassing interest, a distributional coalition whose activities could be growth-enhancing. A group representing a large proportion of the society will not have an incentive to engage in rent seeking because it must internalize onto its members much of the costs of such antisocial behavior. Encompassing groups will pursue strategies that increase the national product rather than fight over its distribution. Olson thus could explain the successes of the neocorporatist economies of northwestern Europe, especially in the 1970s when they appeared to make more rapid and appropriate adjustments to external shocks by collective action than their more decentralized neighbors. Thus, the economies that best withstood the pressures of stagflation in the 1970s were those with encompassing labor-market institutions. That basic argument also has been extended to account for differences in post-1950 rates of labor productivity growth among Organization for Economic Cooperation and Development (OECD) countries. The idea that collective action through neocorporatist arrangements could be economically beneficial became widely accepted in the 1980s. Since the 1990s, however, growth rates generally have slowed, and in the 1990s some neocorporatist countries suffered substantial relative deterioration in economic performance. Thus the impact of encompassing organizations on performance has been highly controversial, not least because Olson's early work provided a long list of reasons why such groups would remain latent or weak, and his analysis of growth assumed that countries with encompassing interests would remain economically strong. Olson later reflected that encompassing organizations were usually created by quasi-constitutional settlements, often under pressure from powerful governments or occupying powers, and subsequently were subject to an inevitable process of devolution into narrower, special-interest organizations under pressure from external shocks. This version fits the pattern of centripetal tendencies that brought Sweden's encompassing labor unions and employers' organizations much pain in the later 1990s. However, it does not fit other neocorporatist economies of the late 1990s so snugly, and fails to explain why the equally violent external disturbances of the 1930s persuaded Swedish distributive coalitions to become more rather than less encompassing and to cement rather than fracture the pattern of collective decision taking.

Similar difficulties have arisen with the use of time and sociopolitical stability. Olson emphasizes the need for long periods of stability to allow distributional coalitions to establish and multiply, but signs of distributional arthritis can take centuries (as with medieval guilds and the Indian caste system) or a couple of decades (as with the developed economies since 1945) to emerge. The theory cannot predict how much time is needed for the various processes. Similarly, political and social upheaval are uncertainly treated. There is no real distinction between those wars and revolutions that threatened growth-inhibiting groups and those that reinforced them. Much has been made of the power of Olson's theory to explain post-1945 economic performance, but it fails completely to account for differences in growth rates after 1918. German economic historians, moreover, have noted that their nation's defeat in World War I saw institutional destruction in the replacement of an autocratic regime by a democratic system and the creation of corporatist frameworks in industry, but did not produce faster growth until the reintroduction of many of the Weimar institutions in the late 1940s.

Olson sought to construct a parsimonious theory with substantial explanatory power; that is, one able to explain many diverse phenomena using a narrow set of assumptions. Justly critical of monocausal explanations, as might be expected from one analyzing change over the very long run in economies open to all manner of external influences, he did not pretend, as have some followers and critics, that collective action could wholly explain any aspect of economic performance. The cataloging of exceptions to and problems with theories of collective action does not, of course, refute the analysis. Whether this approach can be quantified and empirically tested, as Olson clearly hoped, is another matter. The ambiguities about both the treatment of time and definitions of "encompassing" and "narrow," as well as "institutional destruction" and "jurisdictional integration," make quantification uncertain. Nevertheless, there is a very general agreement among social scientists that institutions, whether Olsonian collective groups or the new institutionalists' codes of behavior, do profoundly matter in the shaping of national and international economic performance. In the very long run (a span to which collective action and institutional approaches necessarily apply), differences in national economic performance have been subtle; and scholars are still searching for authoritative methods of isolating the contribution of distributional coalitions.

BIBLIOGRAPHY

WORKS BY MANCUR OLSON

The Logic of Collective Action: Public Goods and the Theory of Groups (hereafter *Logic*). Cambridge, Mass., 1965. A brilliant and compelling exploration of the problems of externalities and public goods.
With Richard Zeckhauser. "An Economic Theory of Alliances." *Review of Economics and Statistics* 47.3 (1965), 266–279. Application of the theory of *Logic* to military alliances; develops perceptive insights into the funding of NATO. *The Rise and Decline of Nations: Economic Growth, Stagflation and Social Rigidities*. New Haven, 1982. A massively influential application of the analysis of his *Logic* to understanding variations in economic growth; the foundation of many "institutional" accounts of economic performance.
"Devolution of the Nordic and Teutonic Economies." *American Economic Review* 85.2 (1995), 22–27. An attempt to explain why encompassing interests cannot remain encompassing.
Edited with Satu Kähkönen. *A Not-so-Dismal Science: A Broader View of Economies and Societies*. Oxford, 2000. Posthumously published; contains important overviews by Olson, Oliver Williamson, Russell Hardin, Joel Mokyr, and Pranab Bardhan.

WORKS ON INSTITUTIONS AND COLLECTIVE ACTION

Booth, Alan, Joseph Melling, and Christoph Dartmann. "Institutions and Economic Growth: The Politics of Productivity in West Germany, Sweden and the United Kingdom, 1945–55." *Journal of Economic History* 57.2 (1997), 416–444. Sympathetic but critical assessment of Olson's approach; with a reply by Olson.
Bruno, Michael, and Jeffrey D. Sachs. *The Economics of Worldwide Stagflation*. Cambridge Mass., 1985.
Crafts, N. F. R., and Gianni Toniolo. *Economic Growth in Europe since 1945*. Cambridge, 1996. Contains important institutional analyses by Barry Eichengreen, Olson, and Karl-Heinz Pacqué.
Hardin, Russell. *Collective Action*. Baltimore, 1982. Reviews much of the literature stimulated by Olson's *Logic*.
Mueller, Dennis C., ed. *The Political Economy of Growth*. New Haven, 1983. Papers from a conference called to discuss early drafts of *RADON*. Many useful contributions.
North, Douglass C. *Institutions, Institutional Change, and Economic Performance*. New York, 1990. The classic account of the institutional requirements for economic development.
Reisman, David. *Theories of Collective Action: Downs, Olson, and Hirsch*. London, 1990. Perceptive and entertaining survey that has much to say on public choice theory.
Sandler, Todd. *Collective Action: Theory and Applications*. Ann Arbor, 1992. Thorough, balanced assessment.
Williamson, Oliver E. *The Economic Institutions of Capitalism*. New York, 1985. This and North's volume are the classic historically aware texts of new institutional economics.

ALAN BOOTH

COLLECTIVE AGRICULTURE AND COLLECTIVIZATION. Agriculture, or the production of food and fiber for domestic consumption, processing, and export is a mode of economic activity fundamental to economic development. Historical, regional, and country experiences with agricultural activity differ significantly from one another. In addition to the obvious natural differences, there are significant differences in the role of the state, the nature of organizational arrangements used (often termed the economic system), the policies implemented, and the resource mix available. Collective, as opposed to private agriculture, has historically involved special organizational arrangements and policies, specifically production, and sometimes consumption, on a group or collective basis combined with significant socialized, as opposed to individual, incentives. This essay explores the framework and nature of collective arrangements, the historical experiences with varying organizational and policy arrangements, and the degree of success achieved in different national settings.

Understanding Collective Agriculture. In a less-developed nation, the role played by agriculture, from the earliest stages of backwardness through the process of economic growth and development, can vary depending upon a number of factors. However, agriculture is frequently an important sector (judged by its importance in total output and its utilization of inputs), becoming a focal point for initiating and sustaining the process of economic growth and development as a country moves beyond the very early stages of rural backwardness.

Agriculture and agrarian reform: The emergence of institutions. As economic development proceeds, agrarian reform focuses on both organizational and policy changes designed to move toward what is often termed the creation of modern agriculture (Nafziger, 1998; Ray, 1998). As development proceeds, it is anticipated that agricultural productivity will increase, facilitating the growth of agricultural output while at the same time allowing the transfer of resources (for example, labor) to the emerging urban/industrial sector, a process guided by market and/or state policies and institutions.

Agrarian reform focuses on institutional and policy changes, and especially the development of a legal infrastructure to underpin the changing nature of resource use, for example, different ways to organize the use of land, labor, and capital. In broad terms, institutional arrangements may be private (based upon some variant of private property rights and the emergence of family farms), collective (based upon public property and some concept of cooperative production arrangements) or state, generally with state ownership and some elements of collective organizational arrangements. Thus, the role of the state is important as an agent of change during the process of agricultural modernization, and, from a policy perspective, there exists a major dichotomy in both theory and practice between private as opposed to socialized organizational arrangements. The focus is on the nature of property rights, the nature of the organizational hierarchy used in agriculture, the nature of decision making and incentive arrangements.

Concept of collective agriculture. Collective agricultural arrangements have varied widely throughout history. It is, however, useful to identify first the major reasons why collective agriculture has been appealing, and second, the differing ways in which collective agriculture has been implemented, specifically the role of the state. There are two broad characteristics that are useful in identifying the nature of differing collective arrangements. These characteristics are ideological and economic.

First, collective agriculture is often based upon ideological considerations that may or may not in turn be based on Marxian concepts (Dorner, 1975). As such, motives for the creation of collective agricultural arrangements have been largely egalitarian in nature. For example, the motivation behind two major world examples of collective agriculture (the kolkhoz in the Soviet Union, the commune in China) and variants in a number of less-developed nations were partially (officially) ideological in nature, based, at least in theory, upon Marxian concepts. However, the creation of the kibbutz in Israel was based not on Marxian ideas, but rather upon the pursuit of egalitarian objectives.

Second, collective agriculture has been pursued on largely economic grounds, specifically, the basis of the co-op as an appealing organizational form, in addition to varying other perceptions, such as alleged advantages of sharing (for example inputs) and scale. The cooperative form of organization, whether used in industry or agriculture, differs fundamentally from its market twin (the family farm), in the sense that decision-making arrangements differ, and labor participation and effort are usually rewarded by the payment of a dividend (in money, in kind, or some combination of both), rather than by a contractual wage. This aspect of collective, as opposed to private agriculture, is of fundamental importance and has spawned a large body of theoretical and empirical literature (Bonin, Jones, and Putterman, 1993).

A second major characteristic that helps to identify important differences among variants of collective agriculture is the manner in which the collective form was implemented, and especially the role of the state in this process. First, there are examples of collective agriculture, generally in poor settings, in which landless families join together in some form of cooperative production, a primary objective being the acquisition of land.

Second, collective agriculture has often been implemented by the state, clearly an important explanation (in addition to ideological considerations) in both China and the Soviet Union. Notice that in these cases, the nature and process of implementation is critical to understanding the performance of collective agriculture.

Although these characteristics of varying types of collective agriculture are basic, as we examine real-world examples, it will become obvious that these basic characteristics capture many of the important features of the collective experience, even over long periods of time and in many widely varying political and natural settings.

Organization of collective agriculture. The forms of collective agriculture observed in real-world settings differ significantly, not only in terms of their organizational architecture, but also in terms of the manner in which they were implemented. For example, the manner in which the Israeli kibbutz (and variants of this form in Israel) were implemented differ fundamentally from the controversial process of collectivization in the Soviet Union during the 1930s.

We will observe that the results of collective agriculture, measured by traditional indicators, such as the growth of output and productivity, are controversial, deserving our attention. For example, while the role of the kibbutz in Israel and the role of the kolkhoz in the Soviet Union differ fundamentally in many dimensions, their results also differ markedly. These differing results are in part a result of different forms of implementation, variants of the organizational architecture of collective arrangements, internal decision-making arrangements, and varying incentive arrangements.

In light of the controversial nature of collective agriculture, the various arrangements used, and important differences in their implementation, why has collective agriculture sustained an appeal in many parts of the world over a long span of years? There are a variety of explanations.

First, and possibly most important to many, there is the appeal of achieving an egalitarian outcome through the socialization of production, and, most important, the equalization and socialization of incentives related to production. The nature of this appeal has varied (or fluctuated) considerably over time and also by region, a factor helping to explain the varying degrees of interest through time in the collective experience. Fundamental to the collective experience, however, is the assumption that rewards should be based upon conceptions of need, not specifically upon labor participation and effort. Moreover, rewards should be social rather than private in character. The kibbutz is a dominant example historically.

Second, in many less-developed nations, there is an appeal that the socialization of production can reap the benefits of scale, benefits that are viewed as unavailable through small-scale, individual farms. The advantages of scale were viewed as important in the Soviet Union during the command era and in China.

Third, many underdeveloped countries view the socialization of agriculture as a means to put the state in charge of a sector critical to the process of economic growth and economic development. In such cases as China and the USSR, the role of the state in the development of collective agriculture has been dominant. A major role for the state is in some cases an element of the command economy, justified by the broader appeal of state management of resources. It is also, however, a role justified on the basis of altering the distribution of the product of the agricultural sector, specifically providing the state with direct access to output.

Fourth, there is a strong and persevering economic underpinning of collective agriculture, namely the theory of the co-op. Although theorizing about the nature of a co-op as a production organization extends well beyond agriculture, the pathbreaking work of Benjamin Ward (1958) opened a lengthy and continuing discussion regarding the co-op and its differences from the more usual capitalist (market) enterprise as a decision-making unit. This body of literature is especially important because it presents a theory of the cooperative form of organization in an era when the nature of organizational arrangements is central to the microeconomic theory of the decision-making unit. Moreover, the appeal of the cooperative organizational form has been extended well beyond narrowly economic considerations to include what might be termed the human dimension in the contemporary discussion of the participatory economy.

Finally, a great deal of attention has focused on collective agriculture as a result of the major contemporary (and recent historical) examples of collective agriculture and the major controversies surrounding these examples. These major examples merit our attention in terms of their organizational arrangements, their implementation and operation, and finally their successes and failures.

Collective Agriculture: The Major Cases. To further understand collective agriculture, it is necessary to examine three prime examples: the Soviet kolkhoz, the Chinese commune, and the Israeli kibbutz.

Collective agriculture in the USSR. The collective farm (kolkhoz) emerged on a major scale during the process of collectivization (after 1928) in the USSR (Davies, 1980). As implemented, the collective farm was based in part upon experimentation during the 1920s, the main issues being the manner in which production and consumption would be organized. During the controversial process of collectivization, it had been widely argued in the USSR that the key to rapid Soviet industrialization would be the extraction of an agricultural surplus, and this would be done by the state through organizational arrangements other than markets.

Thus, while the process of collectivization was cloaked within an ideological framework, the motives were fundamentally economic with a major state role and both policies and mechanisms designed to change the framework and terms of trade between the city and the countryside. The market as a mechanism to connect the peasant and the state was to be eliminated, giving the state direct access to the agricultural product at relatively low prices. The process of collectivization was sudden, rapid, costly, and, many would argue, had a long-lasting impact on the controversial performance of Soviet agriculture in general and the collective farm in particular.

In theory, the kolkhoz was a co-op, though many aspects of participation that might be voluntary were not in fact voluntary, and the managerial arrangements differed from those that would be expected in a co-op (Stuart, 1972). Specifically, the management of the kolkhoz was designed to use strong state and Party control set in a typical hierarchial agency setting. Although consumption was generally not communal, there was an attempt to socialize incentives, and the system of payment of labor (the labor day or *trudoden*) widely used until the mid 1960s, attracted widespread attention. It did base rewards on a residual, a system bearing close formal resemblence to the theory of the co-operative.

The labor-day system was quite simple. As peasants fulfilled tasks (rated in labor units) assigned, for example, by brigade leaders, the labor units assigned to each task would be earned and recorded as the work was completed. At the end of the year (more frequently in later years), the state extracted product (compulsory deliveries at low state set prices) from the collective farm, after which the remaining or residual product would be available to determine the value of each labor unit. Specifically, the state would extract grain (for example), leaving each farm with a residual amount of grain and hence an amount of grain for each labor day. This value of the labor day (in terms of grain) could then be used to determine the earnings of any peasant working on the farm. Unlike the state farms in the Soviet Union in which workers were paid a contractual wage, the collective farms were not budget financed but rather self-financed, thus conceptually bearing a major burden of accumulation not borne by state farms.

COLLECTIVE FARM. Peasants marching to work in the fields, Soviet Union, circa 1930. (David King Collection)

Assessing the effectiveness of the collective farm in the Soviet experience is a difficult task. In part this difficulty stems from the fact that the sorts of data that would be needed (for example, input and output data by farm type, region, and so on), were generally not available. There are also, however, important conceptual issues. If the collective farm was a mechanism to "extract the surplus" did this in fact happen? There are several important themes relating to the issue of performance.

First, there is significant literature assessing the issue of measuring and assessing the contribution of the collective farm sector to early Soviet industrialization. This literature challenges the traditional view that the collective farm was a major net contributor to accumulation, or that the process of collectivization enhanced the share of product extracted by the state from the countryside.

Second, there is substantial literature that assesses the productivity of Soviet agriculture in general and Soviet collective agriculture in particular. It is reasonable to conclude that the lack of growth of agricultural productivity, indeed the decline in total factor productivity after the 1950s, was a major factor leading to growing state subsidies and food (especially grain) imports in the Soviet Union and the continuing shift away from collective farms toward state farms in a process termed agro-industrial integration (Wong and Ruttan, 1990). Thus, Soviet agriculture was often characterized as the "Achilles' heel" of the Soviet economy, not able to fulfill many of the functions expected from a modern agricultural sector.

Third, the process of collectivization has always been and remains controversial. The manner in which the process unfolded was costly in terms of destruction of capital stock, reduction of peasant morale, and the loss of human life, all arguably affecting the long-term productivity of this sector.

Finally, the collective farm has been viewed as an organizationally ineffective mechanism for organizing production. It lacked the resources and access to capital necessary for modernization, and, most important, it utilized an incentive system widely argued to be ineffective.

China: The commune. The collective agriculture of China has understandably been compared to arrangements in the Soviet Union, and yet there are important differences that should be emphasized. The origin and implementation of collective agriculture in China after the Communist Party assumed power in 1949 were different from the Soviet experience. Moreover, the organizational arrangements and policies implemented were quite different from those implemented in the Soviet Union (Lardy, 1983). In part, these differences reflect a learning process from earlier Soviet mistakes.

China did not have a period of experimentation but rather chose to reject private peasant farming, with Marxist ideological concepts and economic aspects as basic motivating forces. The implementation of the commune system was evolutionary, rather than the immediate and turbulent experience of collectivization as in the Soviet Union, although the extreme secrecy of the Mao era makes careful analysis difficult.

Land reform took place in China between 1948 and 1952, and it was accompanied by the creation of mutual aid teams (MATs). By 1954, some 60 percent of peasant households were MAT members. The same year marked the introduction of producer co-operatives, largely based upon economic motives (especially the advantages of scale). By the end of 1955, roughly 60 percent of peasant households were in producer co-ops with land owned by the co-op. Decision making was centralized, implementing state targets, and payment was a residual after obligations to the state had been met. A private sector was sustained for the production of vegetables.

From 1956 to 1957, collectives were introduced, a major difference being a greater degree of socialization as opposed to the co-ops and larger scale. In 1958, the collectives were amalgamated to form communes, the final state of agricultural change during the 1950s. The communes differed fundamentally from their predecessors. They became the unit of local government, and production included output beyond agriculture. The communes shifted away from the concept of a residual payment for work done, and the importance of the private sector was significantly reduced.

This system remained in existence until 1978, when China introduced dramatic changes effectively bringing collective agriculture to an end. These changes fundamentally altered the organization of Chinese agriculture, introducing leasing arrangements and local agricultural markets in the context of family farming. After 1978, the performance of Chinese agriculture improved significantly from earlier modest increases in output, though comparisons with the secretive pre-1978 era are difficult.

Israel: The kibbutz. Because it is a collective, the kibbutz has received a great deal of attention, although the dominant organizational form in Israel is a cooperative, the *moshav*. The kibbutz is of great interest in that it differs fundamentally from the Soviet kolkhoz. Although the first kibbutz was formed in 1909, most kibbutzim were in fact formed after Israeli independence in 1948. Unlike the Soviet kolkhoz, entry to and exit from a kibbutz is voluntary, and rewards for kibbutz members are not traditionally based upon work input.

The kibbutz is managed by the General Assembly, although in practice the Secretariat (elected by the general assembly) is the operational manager supervising the various (production) divisions of the kibbutz. The distribution of products from the kibbutz into the Israeli economy takes place through Federations, important to the overall structure of the kibbutz.

The most fundamental contemporary issue facing the kibbutzim is their future under changed and changing circumstances. First, the kibbutz as an organizational form was originally founded on the basis of altruism, although sustaining this altruism is difficult in fundamentally changing circumstances. Second, a major change in Israel, as elsewhere, is the shift away from a substantially rural, labor-based economy toward an urban industrial-based economy. Third, the most immediate outcome of a changing environment is changing organizational and allocation arrangements within the kibbutz, leading many to question their future as the egalitarian basis of work and payment for work disappears (Rosner, 2000). In ownership, work, and consumption, there has been a continuing shift away from communal and toward private economic activity.

Collective agriculture in less-developed countries. Although precise codification is virtually impossible, there are nevertheless many countries (mostly less developed) in which some variant of collective agriculture has been practiced with varying organizational arrangements, motivated by both ideological and economic incentives, but under very different natural and historical settings. In many of these cases, collectivization was pursued in contemporary times, but also reversed to varying degrees, for example, in Guyana, Madagascar, Mozambique, Cambodia, and South Yemen. Given the significant variations among these types of cases, generalizations about performance and related outcomes are inappropriate (Pryor, 1992).

Collective Agriculture: An Assessment. A comprehensive and general assessment of the performance of collective versus private agriculture would be a daunting task for two major reasons. First, the objectives of collective agriculture have differed significantly in different settings. Second, and possibly more important, the absence of microeconomic data for collective and private agriculture in comparable settings makes comparative analysis very difficult. However, some general conclusions beyond those noted for specific cases can be made from the available empirical evidence.

First, the Soviet collective farm was widely viewed as a mechanism through which the state could acquire an agricultural surplus for the purpose of financing economic development. This issue has been the subject of controversy, the result of which has been empirical evidence to suggest that collectivization did not lead to an important change in the net flow of resources between the rural and urban sectors of the Soviet Union during the 1930s.

Second, many empirical studies, for example, climatic analog studies, estimates of production functions, and the like, have generally concluded that collective agriculture is less efficient than private agriculture, although these studies are not conclusive in the absence of necessary microeconomic data (Boyd, 1991).

Third, where there have been broader social objectives, for example, in the case of the kibbutz, one cannot argue that the particular organizational variant failed in a setting where both the conditions of existence and the objectives changed. The latter might be better served by a different set of organizational arrangements.

Finally, quite apart from a degree of skepticism about the efficiency of cooperative arrangements, these arrangements remain of theoretical and practical interest precisely because of both economic and often admired noneconomic characteristics.

[*See also* Property Rights in Land, *subentry on* Communal Control.]

BIBLIOGRAPHY

Bonin, John P., Derek C. Jones, and Louis Putterman. "Theoretical and Empirical Studies of Producer Cooperatives: Will the Twain Ever Meet?" *Journal of Economic Literature* 31.3 (September 1993), 1290–1320.

Boyd, M. L., *Performance and System Choice: East European Agricultural Development*. Boulder, 1991.

Davies, R. W., *The Collective Farm, 1919–1930*. Cambridge, Mass., 1980.

Dorner, Peter, ed. *Cooperative and Commune: Group Farming in the Economic Development of Agriculture*. Madison, Wis., 1975.

Kanovsky, Eliyahu. *The Economy of the Israeli Kibbutz*. Cambridge, Mass., 1966.

Lardy, Nicholas R., *Agriculture in China's Modern Economic Development*. Cambridge, 1983.

Nafziger, E. Wayne. *The Economics of Developing Countries*. 3d. ed. Upper Saddle River, N.J., 1998.

Pryor, Frederic L. *The Red and the Green: The Rise and the Fall of Collectivized Agriculture in Marxist Regimes*. Princeton, 1992.

Ray, Debraj. *Development Economics*. Princeton, 1998.

Rosner, Menahem. "Future Trends of the Kibbutz: An Assessment of Recent Changes." Institute for the Study and Research of the Kibbutz, Haifa, 2000.

Stuart, Robert C. *The Collective Farm in Soviet Agriculture*. Lexington, Mass., 1972.

Ward, Benjamin. "The Firm in Illyria: Market Syndicalism." *The American Economic Review* 48.4 (September 1958), 566–589.

Wong, Lung-Fai, and Vernon Ruttan. "A Comparative Analysis of Agricultural Productivity Trends in Centrally Planned Economies." In *Soviet Agriculture: Comparative Perspectives*, edited by Kenneth R. Gray, pp. 23–47. Ames, Iowa, 1990.

ROBERT C. STUART

COLOMBIA. In 1830–1831, Colombia, at the time called New Granada, emerged as an independent state. Of its population of 1.6 million, roughly 99 percent lived in the northwestern 46 percent of its territory, dominated by three branches of the Andes. Nearly four-fifths of the people inhabited the mountainous interior of this populated area, and the other fifth lived on or near the Caribbean Coast. Approximately 53 percent of the territory, the lowland tropical plains in the east and south, were only lightly peopled and attracted significant colonization only after 1950.

The Andes fragmented the populace of the interior into many small pockets, with large spaces between them virtually uninhabited. In the nineteenth century, overland freight was carried by mules at high cost (35 to 50 cents per ton mile on mountain slopes in dry weather; 60 to 90 cents in time of rain, if mule owners would risk their animals at all). Most food was consumed locally or regionally. Only items of relatively high value (for example, handwoven textiles, cacao) were traded over long distances. Short stretches of railway (565 kilometers constructed between 1870 and 1904) and more significant additions after 1905 aimed to facilitate exports. Colombia did not approach having an integrated national market until highway construction (1930–1960) permitted the introduction of more efficient truck haulage.

Until the 1930s, the interior was linked to the Atlantic economy chiefly by the Magdalena River, which until about 1848 was navigated almost entirely by poled boats. These often took two months to reach the river port serving the relatively populous eastern cordillera. With the bulk of its people isolated in the interior, Colombia was, in per capita terms, among the least-successful exporters in Latin America. Until 1845, its only significant export was gold, which was sufficiently valuable to bear high freight costs. Antioquia supplied the greater part of Colombia's gold and had the most active regional economy.

Rising prices and the liberalization of British trade policy in the 1840s encouraged export of tobacco from the upper Magdalena Valley. Tobacco exports (1845–1865) fueled increased imports, making possible continuous steamboat service on the Magdalena River. The tobacco trade, though limited in scale, encouraged experiments, with variable results, with exports of other tropical commodities, including cinchona bark and other forest products, indigo, cotton, and palm-fiber hats. Colombia remained a marginal exporter of tropical products until it began to focus on coffee. Coffee cultivation had begun around Cúcuta in the 1830s as an extension of the coffee culture in neighboring Venezuela. With the failure of tobacco and other commodities, the interior provinces turned to coffee after 1865. By 1890, coffee had become the chief export, but its most vigorous growth occurred after 1910. By 1929, Colombia produced 10 percent of the world crop. At first, large haciendas led coffee production; subsequently, small- and medium-scale growers came increasingly to the fore. Coffee transformed Colombia economically. It made intensive use of previously underutilized mountain slopes. As a relatively reliable large-scale export, it provided an economic base for transportation development and generated capital for the establishment of manufacturing, while numerous small cultivators helped provide industry with a consumer base.

Early manufacturing (1880–1905) primarily processed food for an emerging urban population. After 1905, electrically powered textile plants, encouraged by protectionist policies, supplied growing domestic markets. As these industries depended upon imported machinery and raw materials, the two world wars brought pauses in otherwise substantial growth. In the 1940s, the state supported enterprises in iron, steel, rubber, and chemicals. After 1945, foreign manufacturers of tires, automobiles, and pharmaceuticals established factories in Colombia's protected market. To facilitate imports of machinery by national manufacturers, coffee exports were taxed, and efforts were made to develop other export commodities. Consumer goods continued to dominate. In 1970, capital goods represented 7.7 percent of industry, intermediate goods 38.2 percent.

Commercial agriculture (cotton, vegetable oils, sugar cane) grew rapidly after 1950, aided by policies facilitating the importation of machinery, fertilizer, and insecticides. Production of basic foods lagged, however, leading to increasing food imports.

With negligible immigration and high mortality rates, the population grew slowly in the nineteenth century, (1.3 to 2.0 percent per annum). In the twentieth century population growth accelerated as mortality rates fell while birthrates remained high (3.8 percent per annum in the 1930s; 4.4 percent in 1951–1964). Rural violence after 1946 and insufficient land in conditions of unequal distribution induced many rural people to migrate from traditionally settled areas. Some went to previously unexploited tropical lowlands in the southeast, where coca became the most profitable crop, high freight costs discouraging alternative ones. (Since 1980, exports of illegal drugs have eclipsed the value of coffee.) Many more rural folk migrated to the cities. Whereas Colombia's population was 69 percent rural and 31 percent urban in 1938, by 1985 the situation was reversed, with 30.4 percent rural and 69.5 percent urban. Swelling migration to the cities around 1965 provided the context for a vigorous birth control program, which contributed to a rapid drop in the birthrate (2.4 percent per annum by 1993).

Concerned by slowing economic growth, Colombian policy makers in 1990 adopted a program of economic liberalization, hoping thereby to develop internationally competitive industry. This policy seems largely to have failed. With continuing violence inducing still more rural-urban migration, urban unemployment remains a problem.

[*See also* Spain, *subentry on* Spanish Empire.]

BIBLIOGRAPHY

Berry, R. Albert, ed. *Essays on Industrialization in Colombia*. Temple, Ariz., 1983.
Berry, R. Albert, and Ronald Soligo, eds. *Economic Policy and Income Distribution in Colombia*. Boulder, 1980.
Cohen, Alvin, and Frank R. Gunter, eds. *The Colombian Economy: Issues of Trade and Development*. Boulder, 1992.
Díaz-Alejandro, Carlos F. *Foreign Trade Regimes and Economic Development: Colombia*. New York, 1976.
McGreevey, William Paul. *An Economic History of Colombia, 1845–1930*. Cambridge, 1971.
Ocampo, José Antonio. *Colombia y la economía mundial, 1830–1910*. Bogotá, 1987.
Ospina Vásquez, Luis. *Industria y protección en Colombia, 1810–1930*. Medellín, Colombia, 1955.
Safford, Frank, and Marco Palacois. *Colombia: Fragmented Land, Divided Society*. New York, 2002.
Tirado Mejía, Alvaro, ed. *Nueva historia de Colombia*, vol. 5, *Economía, café, industria*. Bogotá, 1989.

FRANK R. STAFFORD

COMMAND ECONOMIES. The command economy (CE) refers to the economic system that directed resources in the Soviet Union, eastern Europe, China, and Vietnam prior to reform. North Korea and Cuba still maintain a CE. The CE is alternatively called a "planned socialist," a "centrally planned," or an "administrative-command" economy. It has also been called an economy of inherent shortage (Kornai, 1980). The CE was created in the Soviet Union in the early 1930s. Although the CE was based ideologically on Karl Marx's theory of lower and higher stages of socialism, it was created by the Bolshevik leadership largely without a blueprint and on the basis of trial and error. The CE was installed as an instrument for raising investment, raising military power, and creating an economy that was largely independent of the encircling hostile capitalist powers.

The leaders of the Soviet Union did not create the CE until more than a decade after they achieved power with the Bolshevik Revolution of 1917. When an abortive effort was made by Vladimir Lenin to move directly to a CE during the Russian civil war (1918 and 1921), the "war communism" system resulted in economic ruin. Particularly damaging was state requisitioning of all agricultural "surpluses" from peasant households. By 1920, the economy produced less than half of its prewar level. In March 1921, Lenin announced the New Economic Policy, or NEP. NEP was a mixed economic system based on small peasant land holdings, a proportional agricultural tax, private retail trade, and the amalgamation of industrial enterprises into trusts and syndicates under the direction of a Supreme Economic Council. NEP spawned an impressive economic recovery; prewar production levels were achieved in 1926 according to official statistics.

Origins of the Command Economy. The decision to abandon NEP for a CE was made in the late 1920s after an extensive debate between the right (Nikolai Bukharin and Alexei Tomsky) and left (Leon Trotsky) wings of the Communist Party, called the Great Industrialization Debate (Erlich, 1960). The left wing advocated forced industrialization based on forced saving from the peasantry. The

nineteenth century. When in 1475 the city of Kaffa in Crimea, administered by Italian merchants, was conquered by the Ottomans, Armenian traders and merchants were as many as two-thirds of the population there. After the big deportation of the Armenians of Julfa (now Dzhul'-fa) in 1590, ordered by the Persian Shah Abbas I (1571–1629), the survivors set the center of their transit trade in New Julfa (near the Persian capital) where they established the famous Company of the Armenian Traders of Julfa, which built its wealth on the long-distance trade of silk, luxury goods, and spices from China and India to northern Europe. Even modern members of the Armenian diaspora in Europe, Iran, and North America are mostly engaged in commercial pursuits.

The Huguenots who left France after the revocation of the Edict of Nantes in 1685 and emigrated to Ireland, England, Prussia, and America brought their commercial and industrial skills, which contributed to the development of industries and trades. For example, a large group went to Geneva (which was Calvinist) and established the Swiss watch industry there. In Ulster during the seventeenth and eighteenth centuries, the Huguenots helped establish linen cloth manufacturing. Various branches of manufacturing were introduced by the French Huguenots who settled in Prussia at the end of the seventeenth century. The Parsis (from Iran) who settled in India, the China Seas (Macau, Hong Kong), and East Africa specialized in business, long-distance trade, and banking. With the European geographical expansions and the establishment of colonial rule in Southeast Asia and West and East Africa during the nineteenth and twentieth centuries, Lebanese Christians, Chinese, and Indians have contributed to the establishment of commercial economies in the European colonial empires. Chinese from the southern provinces of China established trading establishments in Indonesia and Malaya as early as the ninth century. After the establishment of colonial rule by European countries in the Indonesian archipelago, the ethnic Chinese controlled the retail trade; when the Dutch left Indonesia, this control extended to the wholesale trade. They also acted as bankers to local producers and as middlemen to peasants by supplying goods in return for agricultural produce. At the same time, they controlled most branches of industry, trucking, and river transportation. The same is true of the ethnic Chinese in Thailand.

Given their occupational selection into crafts and trade, members of commercial and trade diasporas have also displayed a common preference for urban locations.

Occupational Specialization. Various explanations have been proposed to account for the occupational specialization of some diasporas into urban, skilled occupations, such as crafts and trade. Some scholars have maintained that members of diasporas ended up in urban,

skilled occupations in the destination countries because the pool of migrants mostly consisted of highly skilled individuals who already held these occupations in their own countries. Alternatively, in his theory on the economics of small minorities, Simon Kuznets (1901–1985), starting from the assumption that for noneconomic reasons (i.e., religious identity) a minority group has distinctive cultural characteristics within a larger population, has argued that the noneconomic goal of maintaining cohesion and group identity can lead minority members to prefer to be concentrated in selected industries and selected occupations.

Avner Greif has linked the successful economic performance of trade and commercial diasporas to the mutual pooling of resources, common linguistic skills, and the network of personal and family relations combined with the use of community sanctions, which reduced transactions costs. His study focuses on the Maghribi traders, the Jewish merchants engaged in long-distance trade in the Mediterranean in the high Middle Ages. Yet, his argument can be applied to other trade and commercial diasporas. According to Greif's argument, diasporas succeeded because small but distinctive minorities could reduce opportunistic behavior by fellow members by effectively excluding or ostracizing members who deviated from mutually agreed norms of economic behavior or abused the trust of other members of the diaspora. Once trust existed among members of a small group, and once cooperative norms were established, members of minorities were well equipped to take over long-distance trade because they could find kinsmen at long distances who they knew would not behave opportunistically.

In contrast to theories that rely on internal factors within the diasporas to explain their occupational specialization, other arguments have focused on the sociopolitical environment. Thus, Cecil Roth asserted that the medieval prohibitions set by European rulers against land ownership by the Jews explain why the Jews did not engage in farming and became almost exclusively associated with trade and crafts. The exclusion of Jews from guild membership in medieval and early modern Europe would account for the further segregation of Jews into moneylending and the medical profession. Similarly, the Agricultural Law of 1870 in Indonesia against land ownership by ethnic Chinese has been set forth to explain the exclusion of the Chinese diaspora from farming and agricultural activities.

Discriminatory taxation of diaspora members is another factor that has been considered to explain their occupational choice. Members of many diasporas have usually been required to pay a poll tax. This has been the case of the ethnic Chinese in Southeast Asia, or non-Muslims in the Muslim empire. In some instances, the type of taxation might have discouraged members of the diasporas from engaging in certain occupations. For example, Salo Baron contended that the deteriorating profitability of agriculture and discriminatory taxation of Jewish farmers in the late Roman Empire might explain the shift of Jews from agriculture to crafts and trade, a transition that started in that period and reached its apogee after the Arab and Muslim expansions.

The relationship between diaspora members on one hand and the local population and rulers on the other hand has been double-edged. Rulers have usually tolerated and often protected the diasporas as they appreciated the comparative advantage of these minorities in terms of labor skills, communication abilities, and availability of capital and credit they could supply. For example, members of most diasporas were employed as tax farmers: this is true for the Jews in the Muslim empire and in Spain, the ethnic Chinese in Southeast Asia, the Germans in Russia, and the Armenians in the late Ottoman Empire. At the same time, rulers often regulated to their own advantage the businesses in which diaspora members were engaged. Thus, town and state governments taxed the Jewish moneylenders and asked them to advance loans to the governments themselves. In exchange, they offered protection to the Jewish minority against possible violence from the local populations. Similarly, the European colonial powers in Southeast Asia and Africa protected the ethnic Chinese and the Indian middleman minorities; in the Middle Ages, Muslim rulers extended the same protection to Christian and Jewish merchants. In some instances, though, rulers substituted one diaspora for another if they perceived the change to be advantageous for them. Thus, in nineteenth-century Hungary, the Jews took the jobs that once were held by the urban German diaspora. In the Ottoman Empire, Catholic Levantines, who held the leadership in crafts and trade in the fifteenth century, were replaced by the Jews in the sixteenth and partly the seventeenth centuries, followed by the Greeks until the beginning of the nineteenth century and the Armenians during the nineteenth century.

The concentration of most diasporas into urban, skilled occupations brought a noticeable divergence in the living standards of their members compared with those of the indigenous populations. The members of the commercial and trade diasporas were, on average, more affluent than the majority of the population in the countries in which they lived.

BIBLIOGRAPHY

Armstrong, John A. "Mobilized and Proletarian Diasporas." *American Political Science Review* 70.2 (1976), 393–408. An excellent article that provides a taxonomy of diasporas, the main features of various diasporas, and many historical examples.

Bruneau, Michel, ed. *Diasporas*. Paris, 1995. A very fine collection of essays covering many trade and commercial diasporas.

Cator, Writser Jans. *The Economic Position of the Chinese in the Netherlands Indies*. Chicago, 1936.

Cohen, Robin. *Global Diasporas: An Introduction*. London, 1997.

Cohen, Shaye J. D., and Ernest S. Frerichs, eds. *Diasporas in Antiquity*. Atlanta, 1993.

Greif, Avner. "Contract Enforceability and Economic Institutions in Early Trade: The Maghribi Traders' Coalition." *American Economic Review* 83.3 (June 1993), 525–548.

Kuznets, Simon. "Economic Structure and Life of the Jews." In *The Jews: Their History, Culture, and Religion*, edited by Louis Finkelstein, vol. 2, pp. 1597–1666. New York, 1960.

Sandjian, Avedis. *The Armenian Communities in Syria under Ottoman Dominion*. Cambridge, Mass., 1965.

MARISTELLA BOTTICINI

COMMERCIAL PARTNERSHIPS. It has been argued that the economic preeminence of the West rests on its ability to combine many people's resources by developing new methods of business organization and capital formation. Since antiquity commercial partnerships—any associations of persons who share ownership of some goods or enterprise—have enabled businesspeople to organize and finance their trades using someone else's resources. Yet the practice of doing business with other people's resources became a basic feature of only Western commercial life. It took root in the Middle Ages with the emergence of both multiple *commenda* partnerships and the family firm and culminated in the mid-nineteenth century with the introduction of the modern corporation as a limited-liability joint-stock company. Today commercial enterprises typically adopt the form of proprietorships, limited partnerships, or corporations.

The proprietorship or ordinary partnership (*société en nom collectif*) agglomerates the capital of various individuals, all of whom are jointly and severally liable for the partnership's obligations. The limited partnership (*société en commanditeé*) distinguishes between the managing partners, who are jointly liable for the whole of the firms' debts, and the passive partners or equity investors, whose liability is limited to the amounts they have invested in the partnership. Both the proprietorship and the limited partnership are legally dissolved each time a partner dies or decides to leave the firm. The closing of the partnerships is followed by the distribution of the profit or loss among the partners in proportion to their capital investments. In sharp contrast, the corporation (*société anonyme*) offers unlimited liability for all equity investors, ensures the continuity of the corporation independently of the partners' status, and enables capital to be raised by the sale of readily marketable shares or stocks. The investor's stockholding determines his or her share of the profit or loss through both the disbursement of dividends and the capital gains and losses realized in secondary markets.

The oldest form of business partnership is the proprietorship, which dates back to the Greco-Roman *societas* contract. This survived into medieval times under the name *compagnia* and was utilized throughout Europe, from the Baltic in the north and England in the west to the Mediterranean in the south. Although occasionally found in maritime trade, it was mainly used for land-based commercial and industrial enterprises. In the Muslim world, however, it was extensively used also in maritime trade.

Commenda. By the thirteenth century the new *commenda* partnership became the dominant means of bringing together resources of labor and capital in commercial ventures throughout the western Mediterranean, thereby contributing greatly to the commercial prosperity of cities like Genoa, Venice, Pisa, Ragusa, Marseille, Barcelona, Valencia, and so forth. There were two types of *commenda* contracts. In the standard unilateral *commenda* or *accomendatio* the merchant did not supply any capital, assumed no liability if a loss occurred, and received one-fourth of the net profit in return for his or her labor. In the standard bilateral *commenda* or *societas maris* the merchant provided one-third of the capital, bore one-third of the capital loss, and was entitled to one-half of the net profit in return for both his or her work and risky investment (one-fourth plus three-fourths on the one-third merchant's capital equals one-half). The merchant's remuneration from his or her labor was therefore the same under both contractual forms, if the venture was funded entirely through a single partnership. However, when amalgamating funds, the bilateral *commenda* typically established that the one-fourth profit that accrued to the merchant for his or her work in a unilateral *commenda* should be converted into the profit of the bilateral *commenda* before dividing it in half.

In contrast with the medieval *compagnia* and the Islamic partnership (*shirka*), the investing partner in a *commenda* was not liable for the enterprise's obligations to third parties and might or might not participate in the venture's management. In Genoa, for example, the *commenda* operated mostly as a service contract to handle the investor's business abroad. In Venice, however, the *commenda*, known as *collegantia*, worked primarily as a financial contract through which investors of all means and conditions, including women, priests, public officials, artisans, and other persons without business experience as well as merchants themselves, mobilized their savings and diversified their portfolios in long-distance trade. Indeed it was common practice for merchants to raise capital through the sale of ownership in sea ventures by means of multiple *commenda* partnerships. For example, in 1234 Rodolfo Suligo combined funds through *commenda* partnerships from at least sixteen Venetian investors. Similarly the Marseille merchant Nicolas Marinier, sailing for Messina on the *Saint Gilles* in 1248, entered into at least fourteen *commenda* partnerships with different investors.

A *commenda*-type partnership (the *wederlegginge*, the *fürlegung*) was also known among the Hanseatic and the southern Germany merchants but not among the English. Yet the Germans made little use of this type of partnership, and like the English they conducted their business abroad in person or through their agents, that is, consigning their merchandise to salaried factors, commission agents, or fellow merchants for a share of the profit. The Muslim equivalent of the *commenda* partnership (the *quirad* or *mudharabah*) dates from the seventh century and persisted into modern days, probably because Islamic law did not develop more sophisticated means of business associations.

The evolution of the Western *commenda* suggests that these contracts were designed to secure the best possible allocation of risk, given the merchant's ability to engage in fraud by understanding the true profit and thus by embezzling the difference. Before the adoption of the *commenda*, the sea loan had been the dominant contract in Mediterranean trade. The sea loan was a fixed-payment loan with the particular feature that the investor took the risk of loss by shipwreck, piracy, or confiscation in foreign lands and was therefore allowed a higher rate of return. The papacy declared this contract to be usurious in 1236 as a supplement to Gregory IX's more general condemnation of usury in the *Decretales* of 1234, but by this time the transition from the sea loan to the *commenda* had been fully accomplished. In contrast with the *commenda*, in the sea loan merchant took all the commercial profit and risk, thereby forgoing mutually beneficial risk sharing. The *commenda* thus replaced the sea loan when and where various institutional arrangements provided the information required to enforce better commercially contingent contracts, despite the merchant's claims.

Both the sea loan and the *commenda* contracts stipulated that the investor bore liability for loss at sea or from the action of the enemy in proportion to his or her capital investment. The merchant was therefore partially insured against the "risk of sea and people," but he or she did not enjoy as much insurance as with premium insurance contracts, which established a coverage payment to compensate the merchant who suffered a marine loss. It has been shown that the sea loan and the *commenda* optimally shared the risk associated with costly sea ventures, whereas pure marine insurance contracts were better suited to less risky and costly ventures. Thus in fact the sea loan and the *commenda* actually gave way to insurance as an independent form of business when commerce lost many of its adventurous features and wealth accumulation from commerce reduced the former scarcity of capital. During the fourteenth and fifteenth centuries, sea ventures were commonly funded through risk-free bills of exchange, insured through premium contracts, and organized by means of commission agents who resided permanently abroad.

Family Firm. Furthermore during the thirteenth century, a distinctive type of *compagnia*, the family firm, also emerged in various inland cities of north central Italy, such as Lucca, Siena, Piacenza, and above all Florence. By mid-century a handful of exceptionally large family firms, the Bardi, Peruzzi, and Acciaiuoli companies, were engaged in both trading and finance over a wide geographical area. Just to give an idea of these firms' sizes, consider that in 1335 the assets of the Bardi company were valued at about 4.5 times the English king's net income as late as 1433, and the firm's staff, in the range between 120 and 150 employees, matched even the mighty bureaucracy of the age, the Avignon papacy, with its 250 administrators. It has been conjectured that these super-companies were created extraordinarily large so they could advance the huge loans required to obtain trading privileges from the English and southern Italian rulers, who were in desperate need of these large sums to finance their military campaigns. Thus the super-companies got involved in trading and finance, both of which proved profitable. But subsequently, shortly before the Black Death, these super-companies perished when the specific circumstances that had led to their emergence disappeared. In particular improvements in English administration reduced the king's need for continuous financing by private companies, and the increased regulations and taxation of the grain trade considerably diminished the scope for profitable trading with southern Italy.

Despite the merits of this argument, it accounts neither for the family firm's nonappearance among the Muslim Karimi merchants, who nevertheless obtained the commercial protection of the Egyptian sultan in return for massive loans during the late twelve century, nor for the family firm's persistence in the West, albeit if in a smaller version, such as the late-fourteenth-century Alberti and Datini companies, the fifteenth-century Medici bank, or the myriad of small family firms that even today constitute the basic business unit of the industrialized countries.

The family firm has also been viewed as an essentially quasi-permanent ordinary partnership that emerged, independently of its size, in response to the agency problems associated with the separation between ownership and control. Operating through branches was potentially efficient, but it did require the branch managers to maintain control over the partners' commercial business abroad, enabling them to act opportunistically. The family firm, however, did not mitigate this problem by using partner's relatives to work abroad, nor was it a fundamentally family concern. For example, none of the branches of the Medici bank was headed by a Medici, and only eighteen of the Peruzzi company's eighty-eight employees in 1336 were related to any partner. Also only five of the twenty-three partners of the Bonsignori company from Siena were blood related in 1298. Nonetheless a few family firms, such as the South German Fugger company and the typical sixteenth-century Venetian family partnership, were strictly family-based.

The family firm, unlike the ordinary partnership, provided credible signals that it would operate for a long period. By systematically renewing their articles of association, the Peruzzi company lasted from 1275 to 1343 and the Medici bank from 1397 to 1494. This might have enabled the operation of a (bilateral) reputation mechanism through which the carrot of high salaries and long-term employment, on the one hand, and the stick of firing and legal suits, on the other hand, motivated agents, family members or not, to refrain from acting opportunistically. Indeed the family firms paid high salaries, employed the same branch managers and officials for long periods of time, sometimes for life, and hired exclusively fellows from their home cities to facilitate, if necessary, the agents' punishment by means of the legal system. Moreover the evolution of the family firms' internal organization seems to have reflected a process of learning whereby better incentive and control schemes were adopted following the collapse of the three big super-companies, indicating that agency costs were perceived as having contributed to the super-companies' decline. In particular, whereas the Bardi, Peruzzi, and Acciaiuoli companies remunerated their branch managers with high but fixed salaries, the later Medici bank invariably used junior and subordinated partners, who as such received a share of profits and were held unlimited liable for all the branch debts. In addition the Medici bank applied more accurate and regular financial controls and benefited from improved bookkeeping techniques.

Despite several changes in their internal organization, the Italian family firms retained their basic structure as unlimited- and joint-responsibility partnerships throughout the centuries, most likely because this enhanced their ability to solicit deposits from the general public. Indeed the Italian family firms accepted time deposits in amounts about ten times the firms' own capital.

The multiple *commenda* partnerships and the family firm were among the first associations in western Europe that provided the means to organize complex trade and channel the capital resources of the public at large into that trade. More collectivist societies, such as the eleventh-century Maghribi traders who operated in the Muslim Mediterranean or the Chinese diaspora, established neither multiple *commenda* contracts nor family firms. Instead, they conducted business through coalitions or family networks that limited the accumulation of capital and labor to the exogenous size of the merchants' group, thereby constraining their potential for growth.

Joint-Stock Company. During the Middle Ages the nature of long-distance trade did not preclude the successful operation of small-scale business, but the oceanic commerce and colonization required vastly larger-scale organizations, much longer-term ventures of a year or more, and thus vastly larger capitals. The West met that need by developing joint-stock companies, which first appeared in Portugal during the fifteenth century, became a regular feature of the English and Dutch colonial trade during the sixteenth and seventeenth centuries, and then diffused to the mining, banking, and transportation industries.

The joint-stock company originated in the multiple *commenda* partnerships, whereby capital was raised by the sale of shares of ownership, later called *stock*. Like the family firm, the joint-stock company was an ordinary partnership through which the owners both held jointly the stock—hence the term *joint-stock*—and were liable for the companies' debts to the extent of all their property. This of course discouraged most potential investors from buying stock. A few joint-stock companies enjoyed, however, the status of corporations: the English, Dutch, and French East India Companies, the Hudson's Bay Company, and the Bank of England among others. Corporate status allowed the business venture a separate legal entity and granted its shareholders limited liability, but incorporation was an expensive and cumbersome procedure until the mid-nineteenth century (1856–1857 in England, 1863 in France).

Within ten years after this limited-liability legislation some five thousand British companies organized or reorganized themselves as limited-liability corporations. Nevertheless two-thirds of the existing firms chose to remain unincorporated, mainly for fear of lessening their ability to solicit loans, since this legislation obviously transferred risk from equity holders to bondholders. On the Continent the slow pace by which firms adopted corporate status was enhanced by the ease of forming limited partnerships, which provide full protection for nonactive investors. The limited partnership or *société en commandite*, which also derives from the medieval *commenda* and was first contemplated in 1408 by the Statues of Florence, was incorporated into law by the Napoleonic Commercial Code in 1807 and then spread throughout continental Europe. In the United States of America, however, the corporation proliferated from the mid-nineteenth century.

BIBLIOGRAPHY

Brealey, R. A., and S. C. Myers. *Principles of Corporate Finance*. New York, 1991.

Carlos, Ann, and Stephen Nicholas. "Theory and History: Seventeenth Century Joint-Stock Chartered Trading Companies." *Journal of Economic History* 56.4 (December 1996), 916–924.

De Roover, R. *The Organization of Trade*, vol. 3. of *The Cambridge Economic History of Europe*, edited by M. Postan, E. Rick and M. Miltey. Cambridge, 1965.

Hunt, Edwin S., and James M. Murray. *A History of Business in Medieval Europe, 1200–1550*. Cambridge Medieval Textbooks. Cambridge and New York, 1999.

Greif, Avner. *Historical Institutional Analysis*. Cambridge, forthcoming.

Tracy, James D., ed. *The Rise of Merchant Empires: Long Distance Trade in the Early Modern World, 1350–1750*. Cambridge, 1994.

YADIRA GONZÁLEZ DE LARA

COMMERCIAL POLICY [*This entry contains three subentries, on tariffs, non-tariff barriers, and customs unions.*]

Tariffs

Abraham Lincoln is reported to have said, "I don't know much about the tariff. But I know this much. When we buy manufactured goods abroad, we get the goods and the foreigner gets the money. When we buy manufactured goods at home, we get both the goods and the money." Sadly, that complete misapprehension of international exchange has continued to be common among politicians and a wider public down to the present day, in spite of a long history of tariff use.

The tariff is but one of a large number of measures used in commercial policy. For different reasons at different times other instruments have been used, and on occasion complete bans have been placed on some items (for example, Edward III's statute of 1337 in England that prohibited the import of wool into England). More commonly there have been quotas—stipulated quantities of goods allowed entry. In recent times the latter have sometimes been dressed up as "voluntary export restraints"; that is, agreements have been struck between two countries with one supposedly offering voluntarily to restrict its exports to the other. Usually more difficult to identify, but nevertheless frequently of importance, are invisible barriers to trade: measures that may be called safety regulations or health regulations but are in fact intended to place a foreign supplier at some disadvantage compared to the domestic supplier. These devices have been widely used and are clearly one way of evading some free-trade international agreements.

Tariffs at least have the merit of being transparent and to some extent can be captured in different measures. Tariffs have been of two principal kinds: specific and ad valorem. Specific tariffs level a specified monetary amount on a fixed quantity of goods, for example, £10 per ton of steel. Irrespective of the price of steel, the tariff would remain at £10 per ton. This would obviously represent a variable burden to the importer, according to how the price of steel moved over time. The ad valorem tariff, which has been much more common than specific tariffs, is a percentage of the imported price, say 10 percent.

It has never been easy to measure the scale of tariffs, to make a comparison between countries or even between products within a country. One way of measuring the protectionist stance of a country is to take an arithmetic average of all the tariffs in use. However, there is no allowance in this for weighting the relative importance of each item, and it is difficult to agree on the appropriate method of weighting. One widely accepted measure is the ratio of duties collected to total imports. This suffers from the disadvantage that if an exceptionally high tariff completely shut out the import of a product, then no duties would be collected at all. Further, if a finished product were taxed at the same rate as some input required in the production of the finished product, then one good would have an advantage (or less of a disadvantage) over the other. So a net tariff might be calculated as the difference between the tariff on the final product and that on the inputs used. A refinement can be made to this by expressing the net tariff as a proportion of the value added, the so-called effective tariff.

Tariffs can be used either for revenue raising or for protectionist purposes. Some of the earliest tariffs were for revenue, but in recent times they have been almost without exception for protectionist purposes, even if claimed to be for revenue. In the early modern period (roughly the two hundred years or so before 1700) the financial needs of the Crown or the state were met in the main from customs duties and excise duties. So, for example, in England there were import duties on wine and tobacco, products that were not produced domestically. In the absence of views on these substances' possible deleterious effects on users, these tariffs can be seen as designed essentially for revenue. There were duties on exports too that were clearly a revenue measure. However, as tax systems became more extensive, there were other, more effective means of collecting revenue; and tariffs used in trade were clearly for protectionist purposes.

Main Trends. The use of tariffs has varied over the centuries, with alternating phases of increasing levels and declining levels. As just implied, part of the explanation for their long-term relative decline is found in the increasing sophistication of tax systems so that at least they tended to be used less for revenue purposes; but they did not disappear, because of their protectionist role.

Across the centuries there have been several waves of protection in the world economy. In the eighteenth century, when mercantilist philosophy and policy prevailed, there was widespread protection with relatively high tariffs (some for revenue purposes). This trend lasted well into the nineteenth century, but the coming of laissez-faire policies began to reverse it (in some countries faster than others), and the period from about 1850 to the 1880s was characterized by increased openness in international trade. Nationalism, however, was asserting itself at the end of the century, accompanied by a new resort to protection, which began to spread again. Since World War I (itself an outcome of these nationalist tensions) failed to resolve the problems that had produced it, protection worsened in the interwar years, reaching a peak in the depression years of 1929–1933 as countries sought solution in autarky. Not surprisingly, this protectionism contributed to the dramatic collapse in international trade in the 1930s and to some of the poor economic performance of the decade. Some would go so far as to argue that it brought the rise of Hitler and World War II. It was a goal of the victors in World War II to ensure liberalization of trade in the postwar world; and there did follow a long period of increasing freedom, overseen by new institutions designed for the purpose (such as the General Agreement on Tariffs and Trade—GATT), with only relatively minor hiccups along the way.

Within these long-term trends, it has been suggested that the economic cycle has played a role, for example, that economic depression was responsible for increased protection. Generally this theory does not stand up, or at least whatever general relationship there may be is too complex to disentangle. Nevertheless, it is true that in the severe contraction called the Great Depression (1929–1932/1933) increased tariffs were imposed around the world. In the United States there was the famous Smoot-Hawley tariff, and in the United Kingdom a policy of free trade that had been followed for almost a century was reversed when a general tariff was introduced. The British at that point also introduced imperial preference, a system that gave preferential treatment to members of the British Empire and particularly irked the United States.

Advantages and Disadvantages. It is much easier to discuss the disadvantages of tariffs than their advantages. Figure 1 illustrates what tariffs do. This diagram represents the market for a particular product, with price measured on the vertical axis and quantity on the horizontal axis. In an economy without international trade there is a demand for the product, shown as *DD*, and there is a supply, shown as *SS*. These lines intersect at *Z* and produce a price of £15, and at that price 350 units are bought and sold. Then suppose that international trade takes place, and all the sales of this product in the world occur at a price of £10. Then domestic suppliers are replaced, in large part, by foreign suppliers. Domestic suppliers are reduced to an output of 200 units, as total sales go up to 800 units at the lower price.

Now imagine that a tariff of 20 percent is introduced. That raises the price to £12, and allows domestic suppliers to raise their output to 300 but cuts total demand to 700 units. Imports have been reduced from 600 units (800–200) to just 400 units. Furthermore, the state collects revenue of £800—the area *LMNO*—the amount of the tariff (£2) multiplied by the number of units paying the tariff (400). Moreover, there are what are called deadweight losses (losses that are not captured by anyone else anywhere),

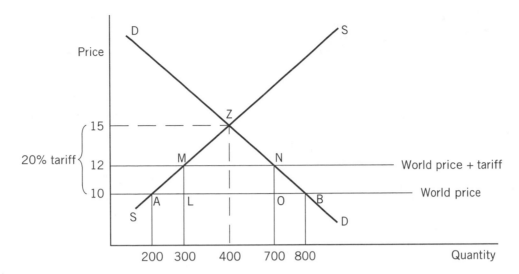

FIGURE 1. The effect of a tarrif.

which are equal to the sum of the two triangles *ALM* and *OBN*, also, coincidentally, equal in value to £200.

In summary, when there was a move from a closed economy to one with international trade, prices came down and more was consumed—the objective of economic life. When the tariff was imposed, it moved sales back toward the original position and so reduced economic welfare. (The two triangles referred to are called welfare triangles.) The losses incurred are due to the production of domestic goods that are inferior to foreign goods (that is, they cost more to produce the same quality), plus the restriction of total consumption, and the wasted resources used in the administrative costs incurred in policing and enforcing the tariff. Clearly some people have been made better off— the producers who are allowed to produce more. However, their gains have been more than offset by the losses that the consumers have had to bear

An argument long made in favor of tariffs is the "infant industry" argument. It is argued that some countries might have a potentially profitable industry that simply cannot get started because its competitors are too well established elsewhere, and thus it is currently impossible to compete. The argument at base is that there are economies of scale to be reaped, but it takes time to grow to the size necessary to benefit from them. A tariff that kept out the foreign product (or greatly diminished it) would allow the domestic industry to grow to the appropriate size; then the tariff could be removed. There are two main problems with this: in practice it becomes very difficult to remove a tariff once it is in place; and, more important, if there is such a fledgling industry, there are means superior to tariffs by which it can become established. For example, it could borrow in the capital markets, confident that in the longer term it could repay the loans from the benefits that

would flow. This approach would avoid the distortions that come with the tariff.

In addition to these microeconomic aspects of the tariff, there are other considerations at the macroeconomic level. It is sometimes argued that tariffs can be used as employment-promoting policies or for purposes of income distribution. They can be so used, but these objectives can be better achieved by other means. There are also possibilities for the trade account. Under a fixed exchange rate, the tariff certainly can have an impact. Under floating exchange rates, the tariff is not effective and simply leaves a burden of administrative costs. Under fixed rates, however, there is a complicated story, with implications for the money supply. Tariffs are effective insofar as they reduce imports and work to correct a trade deficit—but that is only the first step. Raising tariffs raises the domestic money supply and lowers the foreign money supply; so prices rise in the domestic economy, and competitiveness is reduced (that is, the country's goods are more expensive than those of other countries). This situation has implications for the trade account, but tariffs generally are regarded as useful for improving the balance of trade.

Mercantilism. Mercantilism is an economic and political philosophy that prevailed during the period from around 1600 to the early nineteenth century, a definition that needs some modification. Mercantilism actually means many things and according to the meaning attached can be regarded with anything between approval and distaste. The term was understood in the seventeenth century; and insofar as it was a system, it reached its apogee (at least in England but also elsewhere) in the eighteenth century.

The term seems to have its origin in the phrase that Adam Smith used to characterize the economy of his time

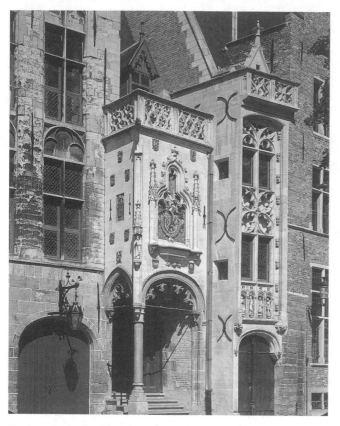

TARIFFS. Loge des Portefaix (porter's lodge), porch of Pierre de Luxembourg, and the Grand Tonlieu, house in Bruges where foreign merchants were taxed, 1470–1478. (Erich Lessing/Art Resource, NY)

and earlier: "the mercantile system," a phrase that Smith probably picked up from the Physiocrats in France. At worst mercantilism was guilty of confusing wealth with money; in its more sophisticated forms it was widely accepted as serious economic thinking. However, because of that association of wealth and money, a strong desire often was expressed for the accumulation of gold and silver. Indeed, in its most extreme version that became the principal objective of macroeconomic policy.

When around 1630 Thomas Mun published *England's Treasure from Forraign Trade*, he argued that the flow of money came from the balance of trade. It was then but a short step to argue for a surplus in the trade accounts; thus it became policy to promote exports and discourage imports. Exports were promoted with subsidies and imports discouraged by duties. The emphasis tended to be on manufactures, for it was principally merchants who advocated the policy, doing what is today called lobbying or rent seeking. As still happens, they dressed the policy up in other ways, arguing, for example, that it was the good of, and the strength of, the state in which they were interested. The policy also extended to other means by which the balance

of trade could be improved, such as the control of shipping. The latter was responsible for the Navigation Acts, dating from the 1660s and repeatedly revised, which legislated for the carriage of English-traded goods in English ships.

Mercantilism was thus a protectionist philosophy. It varied somewhat from country to country, with its main tenets as outlined above. Although it became a complex of ideas and policies, the balance of trade was central and often was built into legislation. Wherever it held, the doctrine's motivation centered on state power, the objective being national gain. The interests of the individual were seen as secondary to those of the state.

Mercantilism was displaced in part by the laissez-faire school developing at the beginning of the nineteenth century, or rather it was displaced for a while. Not every country adopted laissez-faire; and even for those who did, it had effectively come to an end by World War I. Jacob Viner, an eminent international economist, commented on World War I as marking "the end of the intermission in mercantilism."

Laissez-faire was a reaction against the lobbying of merchants, against what Adam Smith called the conspiracy of merchants. Mercantilism began to be condemned for being corrupt (as was clearly likely, given the nature of the policy-making process) and disastrous in its economic consequences. The main thrust of these new views was that economic affairs were best left free from the interference of the state. Smith had argued in *The Wealth of Nations* that optimum wealth would be achieved from the actions of individuals alone. It did not matter that they were unenlightened, or acting out of self-interest; that outcome would be superior to any arrangement that involved the state directing affairs. There were very few exceptions to this conclusion although Smith himself allowed at least one, that of defense. Other commentators have been prepared to see a bigger role for the state in, for example, the provision of a framework for well-defined and enforceable property rights. Others would still add more.

State intervention interfered with the freedom of consumers to demand as they chose and so distorted what was produced. The influence of laissez-faire was extensive in the course of the nineteenth century, not least because Britain was at that point the leading economy in the world and the principal exponent of these freedoms. In the twentieth century there was, for a variety of reasons, some retreat from laissez-faire, and the emphasis in developed countries shifted to the distribution of income; but as the century closed, it was clear that liberalization of markets was triumphing again. The disappointing performance of controlled economies compared to those that were freer prompted a move toward more market activity.

Political Economy of the Tariff. If there are more disadvantages than advantages to protection, the question might legitimately be asked, why has there been, and is there still, so much protection in the world economy? A major part of the answer to that undoubtedly lies in the politics, or the political economy, of the tariff. Indeed most analysis of protection in recent decades has been carried out within a public-choice framework; this is, there is the application of explicit economic models to politics. Most economists assume that market participants—firms, consumers, and others—pursue their own self-interest as utility or profit maximizers. Public-choice analysis asks why *all* economic agents should not be treated in the same way, be they public or private-sector. Politicians and voters explicitly behaving in such a way should be brought into the analysis. This formal treatment of interest-group behavior began in the 1960s, examining the costs and the benefits of policies to different groups, and the profitability or otherwise of these groups' lobbying for a policy.

The gainers generate a demand for protection, and the government is the source of the supply. The views of nongainers can be influential, but consumers are generally too scattered to organize resistance in an efficient and profitable way. Producers, however, have a clear incentive to lobby, but not without costs. The likelihood is that there will be a process of exchange between government and organized interests. (As noted, this is what gave considerable impetus to mercantilism.) So the government provides tariff legislation in exchange for some form of support, financial or electoral. As a monopoly producer of legislation, it faces a demand curve that is the expression of the payments it will be offered. It will have cost curves that are the sum of the forgone costs of depriving another group in some ways, by either lessening protection or providing free trade, plus the actual cost of legislation. The government will maximize gains by delivering a certain amount of protectionist legislation at a price that is the outcome of the intersection of these marginal cost and marginal revenue curves.

This kind of analysis is likely to be more applicable in some countries than in others. Some have argued that Britain had institutions that produced an incorruptible civil service and law-abiding citizens, in contrast to the United States, which had no such tradition. The American system invited lobbying, and the British made it difficult for it to be successful.

Lobbying alone cannot explain all the protection that exists. The principal alternative explanation lies in the power of ideas, be they bad or good ones. Again returning to mercantilism, there was lobbying involved, but there was also a powerful belief in the balance of trade and the confusion of wealth with money. This idea tended to produce the notion that any job saved by restricting imports added to the total of employment—a bad idea that could find expression in someone as distinguished as Abraham Lincoln.

Many other ideas have played a part in shaping commercial policy; for example, there is "fairness"—the need to avoid social disruption from foreign competition. There is also the powerful force of economic nationalism.

Long-Term Effects. In this description of tariffs, essentially the immediate, or short-term, effects were considered. There are long-term effects as well, which are perhaps more serious than the immediate ones. The most serious criticism of the protective tariff is that in the long run the kind of lobbying that is encouraged will lead to corruption and destroy the normal competitive economic climate. Clearly, whether that occurs depends in part on other factors, but it continues to be a risk.

Although it is difficult to provide a precise measure of the degree of protection in force at any time, there are the reasonable approximations, as indicated above; and they can be used as a start in examining the relationship between protection and economic growth. When the multiplicity of factors responsible for economic growth are considered, it is not surprising to find that the damaging effects of protection may not look very large—ignoring the further difficult question of deciding what would be large and what not. Still, some of the calculations made for developing countries at a time, in the 1950s and 1960s and later, when they were using protection (misguidedly) as a means to development, did turn out to be significant in terms of their size against gross domestic product (GDP).

There is another issue, namely, that there are as many ways of defeating tariffs as there are tariffs. All kinds of devices are employed, some perfectly legitimate and others not, to avoid tariffs. This often results in ludicrously detailed tariff schedules as bureaucrats try to specify as tightly as possible the product they wish to tax. In turn those in whose interest it lies to defeat the tariff are encouraged to be imaginative in circumventing the new specification. All of this contributes to distortions in the allocation of resources; that is, the welfare triangles (described above) grow in size. Incidentally, although these triangles can be measured precisely and give good indications of deadweight losses, it has been argued that the losses they represent are in fact considerably greater than those shown in the calculation.

Serious long-term effects of protection result from shielding domestic industry from the changing competitive forces in the rest of the world. Many of the cost-cutting techniques going on more generally are ignored, and the industry is likely to become ever less productive compared to overseas competitors—a circumstance that, in turn, will support its demands for continuing protection. It becomes less and less clear where comparative advantage might lie. Sclerosis inevitably sets in as new technology fails to be adopted. Industries become senile, and the case is then argued for protection for them, just as there was a case for protecting infant industries. The argument is that something must be done to ease their decline. The damage that tariffs do is cumulative.

BIBLIOGRAPHY

Ashley, Percy. *Modern Tariff History*. London, 1910.

Bhagwati, Jagdish. *Protectionism*. Cambridge, Mass., 1998.

Capie, Forrest, ed. *Protectionism in the World Economy*. Aldershot, U.K., 1992.

Capie, Forrest. *Tariffs and Growth*. Manchester, 1994.

Corden, Warner M. *The Theory of Protection*. London, 1971.

Gordon, Margaret. *Barriers to World Trade: A Study of Recent Commercial Policy*. New York, 1941.

Leipman, Heinrich. *Tariff Levels and the Economic Unity of Europe*. London, 1938.

Schattschneider, Elmer E. *Politics, Pressure, and the Tariff*. New York, 1935.

Taylor, Arthur, J. *Lassez-faire and State Intervention in Nineteenth-Century Britain*. London, 1992.

FORREST CAPIE

Nontariff Barriers

The variety and complexity of nontariff trade barriers (NTBs) appear to be limited only by the imaginations of their designers. In the trade policy literature, the term has come to apply broadly to any nontariff trade-distorting interference—even if not, strictly speaking, a "barrier." The most readily identified instruments are quantitative restrictions, such as import quotas, licenses, and foreign exchange controls. However, the number and complexity of other nontariff trade-distorting instruments has increased in recent decades with the size and bureaucratic capabilities of the state. Besides more obvious border-policy substitutes to tariffs (i.e., various quantitative restrictions and nontariff border charges), governments also use a wide range of "behind-the-border" policies that qualify as NTBs, including internal administrative procedures, regulatory policies, and legal restraints, which may be discriminatory to foreign producers. (See Table 1.) NTBs tend to be either blunter or less transparent instruments than tariffs, and are often more subject to rent seeking by domestic interest groups.

Some trade analysts have declared the incidence of NTBs to be on the rise, particularly since the mid-1960s, at least relatively, because of the decline in tariff protection under the General Agreement on Tariffs and Trade (GATT) since 1947. But because of the continued difficulties of measuring both past and current levels of NTB incidence, it is unknown whether nontariff protection has increased in an absolute sense. It seems untenable to imagine that trade-distorting governmental interventions are currently at a historical peak, although behind-the-border constraints on trade may not have been binding in former periods of high border-policy protection.

As far as we know, acts of trade exclusion were present at the dawn of European civilization. Blunt, though not strictly enforceable, NTB devices, such as complete prohibitions of imports or exports, appear to have predated tariffs. Early modern mercantilist policy relied more heavily on prohibitions than tariffs, carried from earlier medieval municipal policies. At those times, trade prohibitions more often were associated with guild regulations, which protected guild members, whether inhabitant or foreigner. However, import prohibitions as a tool of protectionism (in the modern sense) were not unknown in the late Middle Ages. Eli Heckscher (1955) encountered import prohibitions in thirteenth-century northern Italian city-states erected to protect local industry, often combined with exclusive bilateral trading treaties, a practice that continued

TABLE 1. *Classes of Nontariff Barriers*

QUANTITATIVE RESTRICTIONS	Prohibitions, voluntary export restraints, import and export quotas or licenses, domestic content or mixing requirements, exchange controls, reciprocal trade requirements
NONTARIFF CHARGES	Variable levies (equal to the difference between official fixed and foreign prices), countervailing duties to offset subsidies, advance deposit requirements for imports, or discriminatory border tax adjustments
GOVERNMENT ENTERPRISE, REGULATION, OR LEGAL INTERVENTIONS	Government subsidies or procurement policies, state trading, legal monopolies, exclusive franchises, controls over foreign investment, antidumping or "fair trade" laws
ADMINISTRATIVE BARRIERS	Customs valuation policies (which value imports at official rather than market prices), and cumbersome customs classification or clearance procedures
TECHNICAL BARRIERS	Health and sanitary regulations, quality standards, safety and industrial regulations, packaging and labeling regulations, including trademarks, advertising, and media regulations

into the twentieth century. Well-known eighteenth-century trade liberalization agreements (e.g., the Anglo-French Eden treaty of 1786) often took the form of replacing prohibitions with tariffs. Yet import prohibitions continued to be at the center of nineteenth-century trade negotiations. The comprehensive system of prohibitions set up by Napoleon under the Continental Blockade remained largely in effect until the Anglo-French treaty of 1860.

The resurgence of late nineteenth-century protectionism in Europe involved both tariff and nontariff barriers. Post-1879 Germany took the lead in protectionist innovation, using grain import certificates, juridical enforcement of quota-based cartels, and so forth. Germany's grain trade restrictions included mixing requirements, not unlike domestic content requirements today. Prohibitions on imports of live cattle, hogs, and certain meats, imposed ostensibly for sanitary reasons, resemble modern-day "technical barriers." Drawbacks, bounties, and other subventions were also important instruments of national trade policies during that time. Legally backed multilateral quota-based international cartels and commodity agreements, such as the International Steel Cartel of 1926 and the international sugar agreement in 1931, became important features of the interwar industrial landscape.

It is widely believed that 1931 was a watershed year as the first time import quotas and licensing arrangements (the NTBs most associated with the first half of the twentieth century) replaced tariffs as the principal instruments of national protectionist policies. The conditions of uncertainty surrounding the 1930s abandonment of the gold standard provided impetus for their sudden, widespread adoption at that time. Countries remaining on the gold standard, such as France and Switzerland, experienced staggering surges in imports. To halt deteriorating trade balances, they abruptly imposed import quotas and exchange controls.

The quota was preferred over the tariff for two reasons. First, in many cases tariffs could not be increased without abrogating existing treaties. Second, relative price changes were so violent that tariffs, customarily specific rather than ad valorem, were deemed too difficult to administer fairly. How quota policies were first imposed, then revised, is instructive of their intent. France first imposed global quotas, which fixed the quantity of imports of a given item but not its origins. The de facto first-come first-served policy provoked objections from disadvantaged, more distant trading partners and caused them to ship goods in anticipation of quota announcements. In the interest of justice to former trading partners, French officials altered their former policy either by assigning quotas by country of origin or by issuing import licenses.

Applied first and most comprehensively in France, the suddenness and extent of diffusion of import quota or exchange controls in Europe, the United States, Japan, and elsewhere is remarkable. Import and exchange controls and behind-the-border restrictions were often implemented in combination, imposing several layers of bureaucracy, to restrict exchange outflows and goods inflows. Their aim was to alleviate balance of payments pressures. Reimplemented after World War II, the pervasive systems of quantitative restrictions were eliminated significantly only after 1955, within the framework of GATT.

Less transparent NTBs have become more prominent as successful multilateral negotiations in tariff reduction progressed under GATT. Some argued that achievements (especially in the Kennedy Round, 1963 to 1967) in tariff reductions came only because officials knew less visible NTBs could be used as substitutes. Efforts to reduce less visible discriminatory trade policies face greater, if not insurmountable, challenges. The immediate problem is an inadequate ability to identify and measure them. A more fundamental problem is that policies now under scrutiny for distorting trade are widely recognized as legitimate instruments of domestic policy. Concerns have mounted over so-called "technical barriers," which include regulations to establish national standards of quality, health, or safety, packaging, trademark and media regulations, antitrust laws, industrial policies, and legal remedies, such as "fair trade" laws. Internationally uniform standards can eliminate the trade-distorting effects. However, efforts at multilateral agreements to establish uniformity of standards face strong political opposition because they would restrict the sovereign rights of nations to use these regulatory devices for domestic policy.

BIBLIOGRAPHY

Bairoch, Paul. "European Trade Policy, 1815–1914." In *The Cambridge Economic History of Europe*, vol. 8, edited by Peter Mathias and Sidney Pollards. Cambridge, 1989.

Baldwin, Robert E. *Nontariff Distortions of International Trade*. Washington, D.C., 1970.

Cline, William, et al. *Trade Negotiations in the Tokyo Round: A Quantitative Assessment*. Washington, D.C., 1978.

Deardorff, Alan V., and Robert M. Stern. *Measurement of Nontariff Barriers*. Ann Arbor, 1998.

Gerschenkron, Alexander. *Bread and Democracy in Germany*. Berkeley, 1943.

Grieco, Joseph M. *Cooperation among Nations: Europe, America, and Non-Tariff Barriers to Trade*. Ithaca, N.Y., 1990.

Haight, Frank Arnold. *A History of French Commercial Policies*. New York, 1941.

Heckscher, Eli. *Mercantilism*. 2d ed. 2 vols. London, 1955.

Heuser, Heinrich. *Control of International Trade*. London, 1939.

Hexner, Ervin. *International Cartels*. Westport, Conn., 1946.

Hillman, Jimmye S. *Nontariff Agricultural Trade Barriers*. Lincoln, Nebr., 1978.

Sykes, Alan O. *Product Standards for Internationally Integrated Goods Markets*. Washington, D.C., 1995.

Wilcox, Clair. *A Charter for World Trade*. New York, 1949.

Yates, P. Lamartine. *Food Production in Western Europe*. London, 1940.

ALAN D. DYE

Customs Unions

For the purposes of this article *customs unions* are defined as free trade unions of two or more countries having a common external tariff vis-à-vis all other countries. This distinguishes them from *free trade areas*, whose members trade freely among themselves but retain their own individual tariffs on trade with the rest of the world. From a taxonomical perspective, these two institutions belong to the "lowest form" of international economic integration; the highest is a complete economic union (Balassa, 1976). Indeed, interest in customs unions has by and large derived from the possibility that they might serve as springboards to fuller integration, up to and including that of the nation-building kind. They are still a topic of considerable relevance, as recent discussions of the North American Free Trade Agreement (NAFTA) and the Latin American Mercosur suggest.

Commonsense judgments have often seen customs unions as a kind of halfway house between our protectionist reality and the economist's ideal of a world of free trade. Economic theory, however, does not support such a view. Though a rough consensus still prevails with respect to the optimality of (multilateral) free trade, "it does not follow that any movement toward free trade improves existing protected positions" (Kindleberger, 1963, p. 323). Even if attention is restricted to the customs union member countries, the net economic gains (or "welfare effects") of customs unions are hard to assess. They depend on whether "trade-creation" effects are greater than "trade-diversion" effects, and these depend, in turn, "on the elasticities of supply and demand within the union, the height of the tariff, and the differences in costs among home, partner, and world producers" (Kindleberger, 1963, p. 326). It is no easy task to determine whether the circumstances under which customs unions can be presumed to enhance the welfare of the affected populations are present. Nevertheless, empirical studies of this question abound. These studies do tend to agree that the net gains to customs union members from joining are, at best, modest—almost negligible. For this reason, scholarly treatment of customs unions has frequently turned to a second presumed effect: their importance as foundations of, or stepping stones to, political unification.

Assessments of customs unions have drawn heavily on economic history. That is the approach here. We begin with what was undoubtedly the most celebrated historical case of customs unions, the German *Zollverein*, born in 1834, though conceived a decade or so earlier. Germany's rapid industrialization and political unification in the decades that followed 1834 suggest that the *Zollverein* embodied both of the customs union effects mentioned above. More than sixty years ago, however, the economic historian, Sir John Clapham, warned that the *Zollverein's* alleged contribution to industrialization was subject to the fallacy *post hoc ergo propter hoc*. More recent research has confirmed Clapham's scepticism: the foundations of German industrialization were being laid well before the *Zollverein* was born; and the factors driving that industrialization—the application of new, imported technologies, the accumulation of capital, or the labor supply—did not derive their strength primarily from the *Zollverein*, if at all (Clapham, 1936, pp. 96–97; Tilly, 1990, pp. 41–42). It also follows that the estimated net economic gains ("social savings") attributable to the *Zollverein* have turned out to be small, certainly not more than 1 percent of the estimated national income of the times (Dumke, 1981). Given the hefty annual fluctuations in harvest returns, prices, and foreign trade—in the 1830s a good deal higher than the cited 1 percent of national income—it is not surprising that contemporaries took no notice of the *Zollverein's* presumed effects on industrial growth (Tilly, 1990).

The smallness of the *Zollverein's* measured economic effects has led some historians to view it primarily as a vehicle for German unification. That interpretation, however, proves unsatisfactory. First, it projects political goals of the 1860s into the 1820s and 1830s, where they make an ill fit. Second, the identification of political-diplomatic goals alone fails to provide a mechanism of causation (other than war). It therefore makes sense to look elsewhere. Following Henderson (1959) and Dumke (1984) we see fiscal needs of the German states as the crucial causal element and principal initial achievement of the *Zollverein*.

The first step came with the Prussian Customs Union of 1818, a result of the need to consolidate the new territories acquired in the peace treaty of 1815. Prussia's rulers soon discovered that modest duties imposed on trade on the borders of a larger territory generated higher revenues and at lower collection costs than anticipated. The foreign territory between Prussia's eastern and western provinces, however, motivated those same rulers to negotiate trade agreements with the other, much smaller, German states. By 1830, moreover, Prussia was also concerned with the political stability of those states, and thus offered them a generous share in expected customs revenues as a means of shoring up their financially weak and aristocratic regimes. These revenues, one should note, did not depend on the willingness of the estates assemblies in those states to grant new taxes. The result: Prussia obtained its unobstructed internal trade corridor and the smaller German states a welcome source of revenue. In the years that followed, the substantial growth in customs revenues—on a per capita basis they grew between 1834 and 1842 by more than 5 percent per year—held the *Zollverein* together. That is, its strength lay not in politics, but political economy.

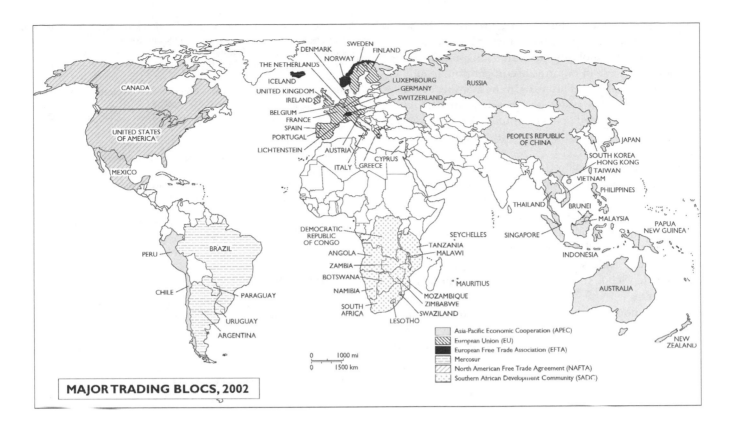

MAJOR TRADING BLOCS, 2002

Asia-Pacific Economic Cooperation (APEC)
European Union (EU)
European Free Trade Association (EFTA)
Mercosur
North American Free Trade Agreement (NAFTA)
Southern African Development Community (SADC)

The foregoing should not suggest that the German *Zollverein* had no long-run economic consequences. I mention just two. One concerns German monetary integration. The need to apportion revenues among the several states necessitated agreement on exchange rates between the various existing moneys of account, in particular between the taler of northern Germany and the gulden of the southern states. This came about at a time (1837 and 1838) when metallic money was not only the standard but also the principal means of payment. When, in the 1850s, an agreement was reached that made the silver taler *de facto* the basic money in the *Zollverein* states, full monetary integration (which came in the 1870s) was in sight (Holtfrerich, 1988). The second economic effect involved railways. They were launched in Germany in the 1830s, and were probably promoted more consistently and on less particularist lines than they would have been without the *Zollverein*'s integrating presence.

In the historiography of customs unions the *Zollverein* stands virtually alone as a nineteenth-century success story. In contrast, the Austro-Hungarian customs union, begun in 1850, has not received much attention. Only indirectly, as a sorely missed institution in the interwar European economy, have scholars acknowledged its importance (Svennilson, 1957). That is interesting, for according to Komlos's work, the estimated net gains to the Austro-Hungarian economies were on the same modest order of magnitude as those estimated for the German *Zollverein*, 1.0 to 1.5 percent of national income (Komlos, 1983). The collapse of that union in 1918, however, has been interpreted as a major disaster. That makes sense, since (by 1918) the costs of readjusting to new trade barriers, after years of cumulative adaptation to their absence, will naturally have been higher than the initial measured benefits. The same argument would apply to the German *Zollverein*.

The German *Zollverein* has frequently been seen as a model for subsequent experiments in economic integration. That is particularly true of the European Economic Community (EEC), which started out as a customs union of the three Benelux countries (Viner, 1950; Fischer, 1961; Henderson, 1981). Perhaps it was seen as a model out of the hope (or fear) that political unification must follow economic integration, as it did in the German case. But the differences between the two cases of integration are so great that the comparison hardly seems worth making. For one thing, the EEC has had no parallel to the dominant position of Prussia (which accounted for well over half of the German population at the *Zollverein*'s founding and whose size and organization provided the "social capital" that facilitated the latter's start). Instead, the EEC's driving force was the French aim for economic and political security tradable against West Germany's goal of regaining its political sovereignty and acceptance in the community of nations.

A second difference is that the EEC was, from the beginning, more than a customs union: it was to be an economic union, with factor mobility but with a large number of exceptions to the rule of unionwide competition, mainly because of powerful vested interests in the member countries (Milward, 1992). The result was "horse trading" in which each country obtained special protection for its internationally inefficient, but domestically powerful, interest groups.

A third difference lay in the conscious character of the EEC's construction. From the start it was seen as a potentially powerful instrument for promoting economic growth; one idea was the realization of economies of scale in the larger, common market, rather than on the U.S. model (Scitovsky, 1958). No such notions motivated German political leaders in the 1830s, though a few outsiders—Friedrich List, for example—did see the *Zollverein* in that light.

One common strand does deserve mention. EEC member countries enjoyed relatively rapid economic growth in the years following the union's founding, as did most of the German states after 1834, but in both cases, a number of factors other than economic union were probably more important causes of that growth. And as in the *Zollverein* case, the estimated net gains for member states from joining the EEC turned out to be relatively small, on the same order of magnitude of around 1 percent of the estimated national incomes (Johnson, 1958; Krauss, 1972; Balassa, 1975). The social costs to the member countries of leaving the Economic Union (EU) now, however, would no doubt be much higher, just as it would have been to the individual German states, say, in the 1860s, which reminds us that economic unions, like customs unions, are historical, path-dependent phenomena.

BIBLIOGRAPHY

Balassa, Bela. "Types of Economic Integration." In *Economic Integration: Worldwide, Regional, Sectoral*, edited by F. Machlup. London, 1976.

Balassa, Bela. "Trade Creation and Diversion in the European Common Market." In *European Economic Integration*, edited by Bela Balassa. Amsterdam, 1975.

Berding, Helmut, ed. *Wirtschaftliche und politische Integration in Europa im 19. und 20. Jahrhundert*. Göttingen, 1984.

Clapham, John. *The Economic Development of France and Germany, 1815–1914*. 4th ed. Cambridge, 1936.

Dumke, Rolf H. "Der Deutsche Zollverein als Modell ökonomischer Integration." In *Wirtschaftliche und politische Integration in Europa im 19. und 20. Jahrhundert*, edited by Helmut Berding. Göttingen, 1984.

Dumke, Rolf H. "Die wirtschaftlichen Folgen des Zollvereins." In *Deutsche Wirtschaftsgeschichte im Industriezeitalter*, edited by W. Abelshauser and D. Petzina. Düsseldorf, 1981.

Fischer, Wolfram. "Der Deutscher Zollverein, die Europäische Wirtschaftsgemeinschaft, und die Freihandelszone." *Europa-Archiv* 16 (1961), 1–16.

Henderson, William O. *The German Zollverein*. London, 1959.

Holtfrerich, Carl-L. "The Monetary Unification Process in Nineteenth-Century Germany. Relevance and Lessons for Europe Today." In *Monetary Regimes and Monetary Institutions—Issues and Perspectives in Europe*, edited by M. De Cecco and A. Giovannini. Cambridge, 1988.

Johnson, Harry. "The Gains from Freer Trade with Europe: An Estimate." *Manchester School* 26 (1958), 247–255.

Kindleberger, Charles. *International Economics*. 3d ed. Homewood, Ill., 1963.

Komlos, John. *The Habsburg Monarchy as a Customs Union: Economic Development in Austria-Hungary in the Nineteenth Century*. Princeton, 1983.

Krauss, Melvyn B. "Recent Developments in Customs Union Theory: An Interpretative Survey." *Journal of Economic Literature* 10 (1972), 413–436.

Milward, Alan. *The European Rescue of the Nation-State*. London, 1992.

Scitovsky, Tibor. *Economic Theory and Western European Integration*. Stanford, Calif., 1958.

Svennilson, Ingvar. *Growth and Stagnation in the European Economy*. Geneva, 1954.

Tilly, Richard. *Vom Zollverein zum Industriestaat*. Munich, 1990.

Viner, Jacob. *The Customs Union Issue*. New York, 1950.

RICHARD TILLY

COMMON-FIELDS SYSTEM. *See* Property Rights in Land, *subentry on* Communal Control.

COMMON GOODS. Common goods are those perceived to be available to a society without the effort of that society's members. Examples are natural resources, such as land, forests, air, water, and minerals, which are often owned by clans, tribes, communities, or nations instead of by individuals, families, or firms, as with private goods. The focus here is on land.

The classic problem with common goods is that each individual member of the community will have an incentive to overuse the resource since not using it would imply that another user would appropriate the benefit of its use. Even worse, present overuse may reduce future productivity, giving rise to the "tragedy of the commons" (Hardin, 1968).

If common goods, but not private goods, are vulnerable to tragedies of the commons, why should society designate such resources as common goods? Answers to this question vary considerably. An extreme view is that resources remain as common goods only out of ignorance, but the credibility of this view is weakened by its confusing common property rights with open access (the absence of property rights). When property rights exist but are vested in the community, the community may avoid overuse by prohibiting use by outsiders and regulating use by community members. At another extreme is the view that private-property rights result from illegal actions of the ruling class for their own private benefit and do not imply efficiency.

More interesting and realistic, however, are positions in between, many of which hinge on the existence of transaction costs of creating and maintaining any given property-rights regime. Two types of transaction costs can be distinguished: the costs of regulating use of resource owners and those of excluding use by nonowners. Whereas the former rise with the number of individuals who are allowed access to the (common) resource, the latter rise with the number of individual (private) parcels into which the resource is divided. Hence, there is a trade-off between the net benefits of private relative to common property, suggesting that both the magnitude and the direction of these net benefits could vary with environmental conditions.

Since enforcement costs feature heavily among the exclusion costs of private-goods regimes, the proponents of such regimes may rely heavily on the state to invest in institutions for property-rights enforcement. Among the benefits of privatizing land rights are: the ability to make land-use decisions more quickly, allocate land more efficiently, invest more substantially, and provide collateral for obtaining credit and access to capital. On the other hand, common-property regimes can be advantageous if they result in greater equity and thereby greater cooperation, greater pooling of information and resources, greater flexibility in the face of locally varying environmental risks, and internalization of potential externalities (i.e., keeping the benefits or costs from spilling over to other owners; Platteau, 2000).

Geographically, despite methodological difficulties, existing studies tend to substantiate many of the alleged benefits of private goods in situations where markets are well developed, but also those of common goods in much of Africa and Asia characterized by conditions favorable to common goods.

For historical applications, a common hypothesis is that as a resource becomes more valuable, the benefits of privatizing and more sharply defining property rights increase, thereby inducing such an institutional change (Demsetz, 1967). Some studies of recent history (e.g., Libecap, 1989), provide strong support for this hypothesis. However, the further back in history one goes, the more difficult it becomes to explain when or why certain apparent changes in property regimes occurred.

No evidence of common property can be found in either the classical river-valley civilizations or the Greek or Roman civilizations. Indeed, Roman law did not even recognize common property as a legitimate form of property. There is, however, evidence of common property at the northern and eastern fringes of these societies, for example, among the Dorian tribes that moved into Greece from the north, Germany, Scandinavia, parts of Great Britain, Central Asia, and central and eastern Europe in Roman times. In most of these cases, land and sometimes other resources belonged to the clan, only much later getting divided into subclans and then households (Orwin and Orwin, 1954; Davisson and Harper, 1972).

In much of western Europe, however, when feudal lords had trouble holding onto their serfs during the late Middle Ages, some feudal estates were converted into rental properties. Perhaps somewhat later, others were at least partially transformed into varying forms of common property. One such form was the open-field system of England and France, which facilitated cooperation in plowing and certain other activities as well as complementarities between agriculture and husbandry. Another was a more completely communal system, as in the monastic orders and pioneered by the Cistercians, who introduced a number of important innovations in both agriculture and husbandry.

Still later, as various conditions—such as the price of grains relative to animal products, population, technology, and institutions—changed, the open-field strips and other forms of commons were consolidated and privatized in a series of enclosure movements. These changes took place from the fifteenth to the nineteenth centuries—earlier in England, later in central and eastern Europe, and latest in Australia and the American West. In some of the earlier cases, enclosures were associated with conversion from mixed farming to husbandry. Opposition to enclosure by commoners varied in intensity from one locality to another. Debate remains keen among economic historians on the reasons for such trends and variations.

[*See also* Environment; Fisheries and Fish Processing; Forests and Deforestation; Mining; Soil and Soil Conservation; Water Resources; *and* Whaling.]

BIBLIOGRAPHY

Davisson, William I., and James E. Harper. *European Economic History*, vol. 1, *The Ancient World*. New York, 1972.
Demsetz, Harold. "Toward a Theory of Property Rights." *American Economic Review* 57 (May 1967), 347–359.
Hardin, Garett. "The Tragedy of the Commons." *Science* 162 (December 1968), 1243–1248.
Libecap, Gary D. *Contracting for Property Rights*. Cambridge, 1989.
Orwin, Charles S., and Christabel S. Orwin. *The Open Fields*. Oxford, 1954.
Platteau, Jean-Philippe. *Institutions, Social Norms and Economic Development*. Reading, U.K., 2000.

JEFFREY B. NUGENT

COMPANY TOWNS. Company towns have developed throughout the world in such industries as mining, quarrying, and lumbering, which were located in isolated, largely unsettled areas. The locations vary from coal company towns in the United States, Great Britain, and Germany, to towns near diamond mines in South Africa, to defense manufacturing towns in Russia, to lumber camps in various places throughout the world, to oil derricks offshore and in the Alaskan tundra. Company towns at times arose in less-isolated settings. Southern textile mills in the United States, for example, built company towns in agricultural areas and on the outskirts of cities in the late nineteenth and early twentieth centuries. Other industries provided subsidized housing for their more-skilled workers in the suburbs of expensive cities, a practice that continues into the twenty-first century.

The nature of company towns often depended on the expected life of the town. In lumbering, where timber was exhausted within a year or two, the towns often consisted of temporary bunkhouses. In the coal industry, where seams lasted ten to thirty years, the companies built towns with housing ranging from cheap shanties for young bachelors to more spacious houses for skilled workers. Towns with larger populations offered more amenities because economies of scale lowered the cost of providing housing. Newer towns offered better and more modern facilities. Towns blessed with more spacious and less-mountainous locations typically could offer better housing at lower cost. Some of the larger employers also experimented with welfare capitalism, providing better housing and services to attract and keep more productive workers.

Opportunities for women in company towns varied across industries. Until the latter part of the twentieth century, virtually no women were allowed in the mines. Their income opportunities in isolated towns were often limited to taking in boarders or doing laundry, although in England in the nineteenth century a number of wives in colliery towns opened shops in their homes. In contrast, in New England textile towns in the early 1800s, the primary workforce was young, unmarried women, while in Southern textile towns, women and children often contributed a substantial portion of the family's earnings from the mill.

Company towns have often been cited as monopolies, but this emphasis has been overstated. The company's ability to exploit a local monopoly on housing and stores was limited by the extent of competition from nearby stores; by regional, national, or international competition for workers from employers located in company towns or in other independent towns; and by collective action of the workers. Modern studies of British mining communities in the nineteenth century show that the mines with company housing were often in direct competition with collieries located in more-densely populated areas where miners owned their own homes. In the United States in the early 1900s, where coal company towns were more widespread, the miners displayed a high degree of mobility across towns. As a result, company house rents were often lower than the rents in independent cities and towns. Coal company store prices were higher in some areas, partly because of higher costs of transporting goods to the area,

while prices at coal company stores and nearby independent stores were often similar. Typically, companies had to match higher monthly rents and store prices with similar increases in wages.

Company towns have often been viewed with suspicion because the employer hired the police and owned the property, housing, and stores. Dissatisfactions that were spread across store owner, landlord, mayor, police, and employer in the typical town all were focused on the employer in the company town. The towns in the United States developed a union-busting image based on the nature of housing leases and the hiring of private police. The leases made the housing contingent on employment, allowed shorter notice for eviction, and allowed the company control over visitors. Many companies claimed that they rarely enforced the leases, and they often deferred rental payments when work was slow or the tenant was sick or injured. On the other hand, some companies used the clauses to keep union men out and to evict workers when they struck. In some towns, evictions and violations of civil liberties by company guards contributed to some of the most violent episodes in labor history.

Union busting, however, was probably not the primary reason for the existence of company towns. The desire to avoid unionization was common to all employers, but company towns existed largely in areas isolated from other industrial and agricultural activity. The isolation gave both workers and employers reasons for seeking company housing. By renting, workers could move easily and avoid being tied to a single company. Employers had incentives to own the housing and store to prevent an independent from obtaining a local monopoly position. An independent could freely exploit the monopoly at the expense of the employer, who was forced to pay higher wages to compete for workers in the regional labor market. The importance of isolation is best illustrated by the demise of company towns in many regions. As population densities increased and more employers set up shop in the area, many company towns made the transition to independent towns. In areas that remained isolated when the resource played out, the workers and the companies moved out, leaving ghost towns behind.

BIBLIOGRAPHY

Allen, James B. *The Company Town in the American West*. Norman, Okla., 1966.

Benson, John. *British Coalminers in the Nineteenth Century: A Social History*. Dublin, 1980.

Brandes, Stuart D. *American Welfare Capitalism, 1880–1940*. Chicago, 1976.

Carstens, Peter. *In the Company of Diamonds: De Beers, Kleinzee, and the Control of a Town*. Athens, Ohio, 2001.

Fishback, Price. *Soft Coal, Hard Choices: The Economic Welfare of Bituminous Coal Miners, 1890–1930*. New York, 1992.

Gaddy, Clifford G. *The Price of the Past: Russia's Struggle with the Legacy of a Militarized Economy*. Washington, D.C., 1996.

Hall, Jacquelyn Dowd et al. *Like a Family: The Making of a Southern Cotton Mill World.* Chapel Hill, N.C., 1987.

Shifflett, Crandall. *Coal Towns: Life, Work, and Culture in Company Towns of Southern Appalachia, 1880–1960.* Knoxville, Tenn., 1991.

PRICE VANMETER FISHBACK

COMPARATIVE ADVANTAGE AND ECONOMIC SPECIALIZATION.

Comparative advantage is among the most profound and important concepts in economics. It provides the theoretical basis for specialization, a core element in models of market development and the transition to the modern economy since Adam Smith. Although primarily associated with theories of international trade, the concept can also be applied to individuals, firms, and regions—indeed to any institution or economic activity in which specialization plays a role.

Eighteenth-century authorities adopted absolute rather than comparative advantage to explain specialization. Individuals choose the occupation to which their talents are best suited, establishing a division of labor that generates the highest rewards for all. So too, national economies exhibit absolute advantages in the production of some goods rather than others and maximize their incomes by concentrating on those activities. In the Enlightenment world of a systematic and superior natural order, each individual's and each nation's advantage complements all others. As David Hume observed, "Nature, by giving a diversity of geniuses, climates, and soils, to different nations, has secured their mutual intercourse and commerce, as long as they all remain industrious and civilized."

Theories of Comparative Advantage. David Ricardo developed the theory of comparative advantage to address the simple yet fundamental question of what happens to trade if one country has an absolute advantage in all products relative to another. His answer was that it would specialize in the activity in which it had the greatest relative advantage, leaving its second-best activity to the other nation. (This result assumes that the two countries are of similar size; if one is much larger than the other, incomplete specialization will result). Both countries gain from trade, able to consume more goods by participating in exchange than would otherwise be possible.

Ironically, Ricardo's example, which argued from the assumption that Portugal had absolute advantage (in terms of comparative labor costs) in the production of textiles and wine over England, seems implausible for the early nineteenth century. Rather, it is probable that England had an absolute advantage in textiles and Portugal in wine (given the allocation of skills, capital, and, in the case of wine, sunshine, and warmth). Indeed, much trade in historical (and contemporary) settings seems likely to have been governed by absolute rather than comparative advantage.

While comparative (and absolute) advantage has become a ruling paradigm in the analysis of trade flows, it is fundamentally a proposition about how production decisions are shaped at the regional and national levels. In its modern formulation, the theory of comparative advantage starts from a consideration of production decisions in autarky (a state without trade). In a hermetically closed economy, production possibilities are shaped by the array of internal factor endowments (labor, capital, land, materials) and local technological capacity for transforming these into goods and services.

The structure of output will be determined by the confluence of supply and domestic demand. Some goods will be cheap and others relatively expensive. As long as autarky is maintained, prices will diverge across borders, except in the peculiar case of identical factor endowments, tastes, and technology. With the introduction of trade to this system of closed economies, arbitrage tends to break down the divergences. Economies export goods that command higher autarky prices abroad than at home. In a world unfettered by restrictions on trade, exchange continues until goods prices are equalized everywhere.

International trade in commodities thus reflects the shape of production advantages—economies export those goods in which they have a relative advantage (via more abundant factor endowments or superior technology) in exchange for goods in which they have a relative disadvantage. Supply conditions dictate specialization. Although differences in tastes could certainly contribute to trade, demand explanations have been derogated in modern treatments, which usually begin from the assumption that tastes are identical and homothetic.

The notion of the transition from autarky to trade, while clearly artificial and stylized, nonetheless provides a useful way of thinking about the origins of specialization in newly settled regions. Thus North America before 1600 and Australia before 1800 had only limited, localized internal markets with restricted potential for division of labor. Integration into the world economy dramatically increased opportunities for specialization, permitting potential comparative advantage to be fully (if gradually) realized. Once the tyranny of distance was conquered and settlers adapted to their new environment, staple agriculture took root (sugar in Barbados, tobacco in the Chesapeake, wool in New South Wales), shaped by the intersection of European demand and colonial production possibilities.

If specialization is limited by the extent of the market, the extent of the market is in turn dependent on the technology of transportation. Falling freight rates throughout the nineteenth and twentieth centuries stimulated the growth of trade and increased market integration. New technologies in transoceanic shipping, from clipper to steamship and oil tanker, were a vital part of the process, but sequential improvements in internal transportation, from canal to railroad to highway trucking, were also important. Transportation thus acts as a permissive factor, enabling economies to realize their comparative advantage. But what determines specialization?

The dominant modern theory is the Heckscher-Ohlin model, named for two Swedes: Eli Heckscher, the economic historian who first developed the idea, and his pupil, Bertil Ohlin, who systematized it. Heckscher (1950, p. 278) identified the "prerequisites for initiating international trade . . . as *different relative scarcity* [of factors] . . . as well as *different proportions between factors of production in different commodities*." Thus whereas the classical (Ricardian) model emphasizes comparative costs (via technological differences) as the basis of trade, the neoclassical (Heckscher-Ohlin) model focuses on comparative (and divergent) factor endowments, predicting that, under conditions of free trade, countries export commodities that use its abundant factors intensively and import goods intensive in its scarce factors. Factors include not only land, labor and capital, but also local attributes (climate, mineral deposits, skills, soil types, and so forth).

An important corollary of the Heckscher-Ohlin model is the factor price equalization theorem, which (in its strong form) states that the flow of goods not only equalizes their prices but also the prices of the factors of production. Commodity trade is thus a substitute for factor mobility across borders. Heckscher espoused a weaker form of the theorem, in which trade promotes partial convergence. He also argued that factor prices should be corrected for productivity differences across countries, a suggestion that finds support in empirical analysis (for example, Estevadeordal and Taylor, 2002) and which suggests some reconciliation with classical arguments attributing trade to technological differences between countries, which have been otherwise displaced.

One implication of factor price convergence, whether partial or complete, is that there are winners and losers from trade and specialization. Abundant factors command higher prices; the premium to scarcity falls. Political consequences follow. Thus falling freight rates after 1870 (due to cheaper transatlantic shipping and transcontinental railroads) unleashed the American invasion of Europe (Part I—agriculture). European governments responded by instituting tariffs to protect their key agricultural sectors (and the significant voting bloc they represented) against falling incomes. Much the same reaction took place in response to the American invasion (Part II—manufacturing) that began to take off in the 1890s.

A pure story of an economy governed by the dictates of comparative advantage is therefore likely to be incomplete. Tariffs and quotas are designed to protect the factor incomes of politically significant constituents, be they farmers or landlords, workers or capitalists, from the consequences of import shocks. Subsidies to senescent industries that maintain political power even while their economic strength is in decline, such as U.S. and U.K. steel in the twentieth century, are classic examples of the use of the government purse to subvert the dictates of comparative advantage.

Policies are not always defensive; they may be motivated to assist catch-up to more advanced economies by protecting infant industries or by stimulating the growth of crucial factor endowments (for example, educational reforms to promote human capital investment or state banking to promote capital accumulation). Such policy devices were recommended by nationalist economists of the nineteenth century, from Alexander Hamilton to Friedrich List, were apparent in some nineteenth century "latecomers" to industrialization, and have been identified as a component of the success of the Asian tigers since 1945 (see Heller, 1976, on Japan; Lee, 1995, on Korea).

Evolving Trade and Specialization. An understanding of how trade flows and patterns of specialization evolve over time—the dynamics of comparative advantage—requires the historian to go beyond the limitations of the textbook version of the Heckscher-Ohlin model with its assumptions of static factor endowments and complete factor price equalization in a world of free trade. The crucial issues involve changes in endowments (domestic and foreign) relative to global demand and in the mechanism by which factors are mapped into production (technology). Technological change may promote (or reduce) intensive use of certain factors, thereby altering relative factor prices and shaping production outcomes. Changes in domestic endowments relative to global supply and demand can alter the basis of comparative advantage (the Rybcyzinski effect). So too can changes in global supply and demand relative to domestic supplies (the latter communicated to the domestic economy via changes in relative factor prices).

Market forces help determine the evolving structure of factor endowments over time and thus the basis for specialization. In one direction, the higher returns to abundant resources generated by trade stimulates factor deepening—pushing back the frontiers of settlement in land-abundant regions, intensive mineral exploration in economies rich in natural resources, rising birth rates in labor-abundant societies—all developments that tend to *widen* differences between countries over time. But this process tends to generate a reaction, since factors are free to move across borders in response to (and thereby reducing) differential rates of return. Commodity trade promoted factor price convergence in the late nineteenth century (O'Rourke and Williamson, 1994), but the real wage differences that motivated labor migration in such large numbers between 1870 and 1913 (as many as fifty million migrants across national boundaries) and the divergences in rates of return on investment that prompted the significant transfer of capital from the Old to the New World in the same period emphasize that the process was far from complete. Factor migration tends to *narrow* differences between countries as endowments become increasingly similar.

The influence of evolving endowments is clearly evident in the case of the United States. Land abundance in the early nineteenth century had established a comparative advantage in agriculture. The newly emergent manufacturing sector of mid-century was dominated by agricultural processing industries, from cotton textiles and flour milling to shoemaking and woodworking. By the end of the century American comparative advantage had shifted to another corollary of land abundance—natural resource–intensive production (Wright, 1990). The technological complementarity between extractive and (capital-intensive) heavy industries (coal, iron ore, and steel, for example) encouraged capital accumulation (Findlay, 1995), helping to catapult the United States toward industrial dominance in the global economy.

The natural resource intensity of U.S. trade declined after 1940 owing to two interlocking developments: the discovery and marketing of new sources of raw materials overseas, which reduced America's relative abundance, and the falling cost of transporting materials, which undermined the local benefits of resource richness by creating a global market for materials available to all. Hence countries like Japan were able from the 1950s onward to export steel and other capital-intensive industrial products, such as automobiles, using only imported resources.

A somewhat different interpretation has been attached to the evolving pattern of comparative advantage in Britain after 1870. Britain's industrial leadership in the nineteenth century was also based on natural resource abundance, notably coal. But the failure to restructure British industry during the "Second Industrial Revolution," when coal and the steam engine fell from grace in favor of electricity and the internal combustion engine, has been attributed to underinvestment in human capital formation relative to the United States and Germany. The trade data appear to support this interpretation. Britain's comparative advantage in manufactures was in unskilled, labor-intensive, capital-neutral, human capital–scarce activities throughout 1870 to 1939 (Crafts and Thomas, 1986), a period identified with the rise of "high wage, technologically sophisticated, human capital intensive activities" among more progressive economies (Crafts, 1983).

The factor proportions model tells a good story but has drawbacks. Most significant is the limited empirical support for its primary proposition, namely that there is a systematic relationship among factor endowments, factor intensities in production, and the pattern of international trade at any point in time. This is the conclusion of Antoni Estevadeordal and Alan Taylor (2002) for international trade about 1913, a finding that accords with analyses of late-twentieth-century data. Not only do factor endowments not explain much of the trade that did take place, but there was much less trade than the diversity of endowments across countries would predict. Notably capital and labor seem to play almost no role in determining commodity flows across borders. Resources (land and minerals) do matter, but not as much as might be expected. An inability to explain trade in any given year does not necessarily indicate that the model is irrelevant to change over time, however; it adds a powerful cautionary note to the standard narratives.

Historians are interested not only in the sources of comparative advantage but also in its outcomes, most notably in its impact on specialization. If an economy specializes in products that embody its comparative advantage, what products are they? The process of economic development involves the rise and fall of certain industries, but these are not the same industries in every case. Understanding which industries rise to significance and which are in secular decline provides clues about the sources of comparative advantage, especially in relation to the possible limitations of the factor proportions model.

Revealed Comparative Advantage. One measure of the degree of specialization by product is an economy's revealed comparative advantage (RCA). RCA is calculated as the ratio of a country's share of global exports by commodity or industry to its share in all global exports. The higher the ratio, the greater the revealed comparative advantage; ratios below 1 indicate a comparative disadvantage. Each country (or region) exhibits a mix of comparative advantage and disadvantage across commodities. This approach does not test the hypothesis of comparative advantage, nor does it investigate its sources; it simply determines which countries specialize in which goods and to what degree.

Comparing RCA indices over time measures how quickly specialization changes. It is usually a slow process, as might be expected. Moreover certain industries seem to remain at the top or bottom of the ranking of a country's export intensities for long periods of time. The United States, for example, has maintained a world leadership in agricultural machinery throughout the past 150 years while never developing a competitive edge in textiles. India, by contrast, has exhibited a consistent high profile in textiles and leather goods for the past century. But in certain economies, rapid changes in RCA take place. Between 1953 and 1971, for example, Japan's export ranking in synthetic fabrics rose from sixty-seventh (out of seventy-three product categories) to first place, while its RCA in cotton yarn fell from fifth to sixty-seventh (Balassa, 1977).

The empirical evidence for the twentieth century suggests that persistence in specialization is the norm for mature economies and also for countries locked into underdevelopment. Volatile RCA indices are characteristic of periods of industrialization, deindustrialization, or other episodes of significant structural change (such as the transition from command to market economy or vice versa). In the half-century since 1950, persistence dominates RCA for manufactured goods in the United States, the United Kingdom, Canada, and continental Europe; the rankings of export intensity for Japan, Korea, and Singapore indicate radical changes in specialization.

Stability was more widespread in the first half of the twentieth century. Only two out of a sample of eleven industrial and semi-industrial economies showed (statistically) significant changes in their comparative advantage in manufactures over this period (Crafts, 1989). In Britain's case this was due to the declining importance of the mid-Victorian staples (textiles, iron and steel, rail and ship, agricultural and industrial equipment) and growing expertise in alcohol and tobacco, and "fancy goods." Canada's change was due primarily to an increasing comparative advantage in metal manufactures.

Persistence can occur in a factor proportions model if factor intensities evolve in a balanced way across industries over time while relative endowments remain stable. The evidence on factor proportions among U.S. industries over time supports this idea. Between 1880 and 1987 capital-labor and materials-labor ratios increased sharply, but the ranking of industries by factor intensity was highly stable. Unstable RCA results from economies experiencing differential relative growth in factors (for example, high capital accumulation or exhaustion of local resources). Thus Japanese comparative advantage after World War II shifted from labor-intensive to capital- and skill-intensive production, responding to capital imports and high domestic savings rates and the accretion of skills emanating from postwar educational reforms (Heller, 1976).

An alternative interpretation for persistence, outside the factor proportions tradition, posits that industrial leadership is governed by hysteresis or path dependency, so that an economy's comparative advantage today is determined by its comparative advantage yesterday. One possibility is that export performance reflects the "first-mover advantages" of the technological leader. The first mover can sustain its competitive advantage through learning by doing and innovation, thus making it hard for laggards to catch up. To this explanation may be added the potential effects of increasing returns as well as the opportunity for agglomeration effects owing to external economies, especially at the local or regional levels.

Clearly any explanation of specialization over time has to account for the high degree of locational stability of some industries and the footloose nature of others. It seems sensible therefore to consider an eclectic interpretation of the dynamics of comparative advantage, in which some sectors are governed by factor endowments, some by technology, and some by path dependency. Such an approach might also help us understand and overcome the limitations of the factor proportions model, most notably its inability to provide a comprehensive explanation for patterns of trade and specialization in all cases and all times.

[*See also* Commercial Policy, *subentry on* Tariffs.]

BIBLIOGRAPHY

Balassa, Bela. "'Revealed' Comparative Advantage Revisited: An Analysis of Relative Export Shares of the Industrial Countries, 1953–1971." *Manchester School* 45 (December 1977), 327–344.

Balassa, Bela. "The Changing Pattern of Comparative Advantage in Manufactured Goods." *Review of Economics and Statistics* 61 (May 1979), 259–266.

Crafts, N. F. R. "Revealed Comparative Advantage in Manufacturing, 1899–1950." *Journal of European Economic History* 18 (Spring 1989), 127–137.

Crafts, N. F. R., and Mark Thomas. "Comparative Advantage in UK Manufacturing Trade, 1910–1935." *Economic Journal* 96 (September 1986), 629–645.

Estevadeordal, Antoni, and Alan Taylor. "A Century of Missing Trade?" *American Economic Review* 92 (March 2002), 383–393.

Findlay, Ronald. *Factor Proportions, Trade, and Growth*. Cambridge, Mass., 1995.

Heckscher, Eli. "The Effect of Foreign Trade on the Distribution of Income." In *Readings in the Theory of International Trade*, edited by Howard S. Ellis and Lloyd A. Metzler, pp. 272–300. Homewood. Ill., 1950.

Heller, Peter S. "Factor Endowment Change and Comparative Advantage: The Case of Japan, 1956–1969." *Review of Economics and Statistics* 58 (August 1976), 283–292.

Hume, David. "Of the Jealousy of Trade." In *Essays, Moral, Political, and Literary*, pp. 347–352. Dublin, 1779.

Lee, Jaimin. "Comparative Advantage in Manufacturing as a Determinant of Industrialization: The Korean Case." *World Development* 23 (July 1995), 1195–1214.

O'Rourke, Kevin, and Jeffrey Williamson. "Late-Nineteenth-Century Factor-Price Convergence: Were Heckscher and Ohlin Right?" *Journal of Economic History* 54 (December 1994), 892–916.

Ricardo, David. *On the Principles of Political Economy and Taxation*. London, 1817.

Wright, Gavin. "The Origins of American Industrial Success, 1879–1940." *American Economic Review* 80 (September 1990), 651–668.

MARK THOMAS

COMPUTER INDUSTRY. One broad measure of the power of a computer is the number of so-called floating-point operations (such as adding together two numbers) a machine can perform in a second. The first truly digital computer, the ENIAC of 1946, cost some $750,000 to produce—something like $6,265,000 in 1998 dollars—and

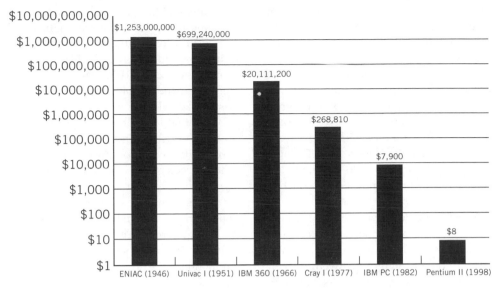

FIGURE 1. The decreasing cost of computing power. 1998 dollars per MFLOPS. SOURCE: Kurzweil, 1999, pp. 320–321.

could perform 5,000 calculations per second. A circa 1998 Pentium II computer cost about $1,500 and can perform 200 million calculations per second. That is about $1.25 billion per MFLOPS (million floating-point operations per second) for the ENIAC—and about $8 per MFLOPS for the Pentium II. (See Figure 1.)

This phenomenal decline in the cost of computing power has been mirrored in an equally phenomenal growth in the computer industry. What underlies this growth? Both the computer and the semiconductor technology that came to support it benefited from what economists now call general-purpose technologies (GPTs). Such technologies (and their attendant systems of skill and knowledge) typically develop in response to specific technological puzzles or bottlenecks, but they ultimately generate principles and techniques that are applicable to a wide variety of otherwise distinct output sectors of the economy. Nathan Rosenberg (*Inside the Black Box*, Cambridge, 1976), described this process as technological convergence. Because it permits the same technological knowledge to be reused many times at low cost, technological convergence generates the something-for-nothing effect economists call increasing returns, a phenomenon at the heart of economic growth.

The rapid performance improvements and price declines experienced by the semiconductor and computer industries trace to the status of these technologies as GPTs. Perhaps the most important GPT is the planar process, the basic technique for fabricating increasingly large numbers of transistors on a single chip. But there are other related GPTs as well, including the integrated circuit, standardized memory, the microprocessor, the von Neumann stored-program architecture of computers, and modular computer platforms.

Emergence of Electronic Computing. The ancestry of the computer goes back at least to the Jacquard loom, which was clearly a programmable numerical-control device. But the electronic computer, using vacuum-tube and later solid-state circuitry, emerged from government-sponsored work during World War II. The U.S. Army contracted with J. Presper Eckert and John W. Mauchly of the Moore School at the University of Pennsylvania for a device to solve ballistics problems and to help in the printing of range tables for artillery. By November 1945, they had produced the Electronic Numerical Integrator and Computer (ENIAC), the first fully operational all-electronic digital computer—a behemoth occupying 1,800 square feet, boasting 18,000 tubes, and consuming 174 kilowatts of electricity. The end of the war reduced the urgency of the goal of calculating range tables, and the first major task given the ENIAC was actually to perform calculations for the development of the hydrogen bomb.

The computer opened up wide possibilities for technological convergence. In part, this convergence arose because of the falling cost of computation—attendant eventually on the falling cost of semiconductors—which allowed the device to be used in a wide range of applications requiring numerical computation and, later, information processing more generally. But a specific innovation in the design of digital computers was also central to the device's wide potential. In the summer of 1944, the mathematician John von Neumann learned by accident of the Army's ENIAC project. Von Neumann began advising the Eckert-Mauchly team, which was working on the development of a new machine, the EDVAC. Out of this collaboration came the concept of the stored-program computer: Instead of being hard-wired, the EDVAC's instructions were to be stored in memory to facilitate modification. A single hardware design could thus be quickly adapted to a variety of different uses through what came to be called software. Von Neumann's abstract discussion of the stored-program concept circulated widely and served as the logical basis for virtually all subsequent computers. The stored-program idea was also contained in the work of Alan Turing in England, and the first functioning storable-program computer was run for the first time on 21 June 1948, at the University of Manchester.

Universities continued to play an important role throughout the early life of the technology. Indeed, the computer has been called "the most remarkable contribution of American universities to the last half of the twentieth century." Beyond the invention of the computer itself, universities played an ongoing role in spurring the industry by helping to create the wholly new discipline of computer science. The dominance of American universities in computer science (and their success in research and graduate education more generally) helped lure to the United States the best and the brightest from around the world, most of whom never returned to their home countries.

Government, especially military, support for the computer remained significant throughout the 1950s, and government funding helped spark important technical developments like ferrite-core memory, which emerged from the military-funded Whirlwind project at the Massachusetts Institute of Technology (MIT). But government research support had little to do with the success of the commercial computer industry.

Computers for Business. By 1951, Eckert and Mauchly had joined Remington Rand, where they produced the UNIVAC, whose first model went to the Census Bureau. But Remington Rand was not the company that rose to dominance in the industry. Nor was it General Electric, RCA, or some other existing giant of electronics. Rather, the company that quickly became synonymous with the digital computer was the International Business Machines Corporation. IBM started life in 1911 as Computer-Tabulating Recording Company, a maker of punch-card tabulating machines that sprang from the pioneering work of Herman Hollerith in the nineteenth century. In 1914, Thomas J. Watson Sr. gained control of the company, eventually changed its name to International Business Machines Corporation, and developed its capabilities in mechanical information devices.

It was the Korean War, along with the sponsorship of Thomas Watson Jr., son of reigning Thomas Watson Sr., that spurred IBM's development of electronic computers. A "defense calculator" project led to the IBM 700 series of computers. IBM's greatest commercial successes, however, came from the low-priced 650, of which 1,800 units were sold, and later the 1400 series, of which some 12,000 units were sold. Whereas the high-end 700-series machines were perceived as "IBM UNIVACs," it was the 650, often called the Model T of computing, that thrust IBM into industry leadership.

By the mid 1960s, however, IBM found itself riding herd on a multiplicity of physically incompatible systems—the various 700-series computers and the 1400 series, among others—each aimed at a different use. Relatedly, and more significantly, software was becoming a serious bottleneck. By one estimate, the contribution of software to the value of a computer system had grown from 8 percent in the early days to something like 40 percent by the 1960s. And writing software for so many incompatible systems greatly compounded the problem. In what *Fortune* magazine called "the most crucial and portentous—as well as perhaps the riskiest—business judgment of recent times," IBM decided to "bet the company" on a new line of computers called the 360 series. The name meant to refer to all the points of the compass, for the strategy behind the IBM 360 was to replace the diverse and incompatible systems with a single modular family of computers. Instead of having one computer aimed at scientific applications, a second aimed at accounting applications, and so forth, the company would have one machine for all uses. This was not to be a homogeneous or undifferentiated product; but it was to provide a framework in which product differentiation could take place while retaining compatibility.

The IBM 360 was the first major computer platform: a shared, stable set of hardware, software, and networking technologies on which users could build and run computer applications. To put it another way, the IBM 360 was a modular system, albeit one that remained mostly closed and proprietary despite the efforts of the "plug compatible" industry to pick away at its parts. The essence of such a system is compatibility among the components, which, in the case of a computer platform, is maintained by (often de facto) interface standards. A large literature has arisen describing the positive-feedback character of technical standards: The more users adopt a platform, the more desirable that platform becomes to others, leading to a "virtuous circle" and pressure for the dominance of a single platform. The IBM 360 did indeed become a dominant platform, a prototype form of general-purpose technology in the computer industry.

The IBM 360 reinforced IBM's dominant position in the computer industry. Until technological change eventually unseated the mainframe computer itself, IBM's dominance was never challenged, despite the best attempts of both foreign governments and the U.S. government itself. Foreign governments set up programs to create "national champions" in IBM's image—with moderate success in Japan and dismal failure in Europe. And American antitrust policies and federal procurement practices tried hard to prop up IBM's weak domestic competitors—also with little success.

The growth of the computer industry was also spurred by the creation of a set of general-purpose technologies in the basic building blocks of computers—semiconductors. In 1959, engineers at a small firm called Fairchild developed a new technique for making semiconductors, the planar process, in which various layers of semiconductor material and interconnections were built up on a flat surface by what are essentially techniques of chemical processing. The planar process has become the basis of all semiconductor fabrication since, including, of course, the integrated circuit (IC), for which the process is of critical importance. Integrated circuits are semiconductor devices containing an entire circuit of transistors and other devices on a single "wafer," or chip. The IC held out the promise of overcoming a developing bottleneck in the mass fabrication of transistor-based systems, often called the "tyranny of numbers." As systems became more complex, requiring interconnections among hundreds of transistors, assembly costs mounted; more important, complex systems became vulnerable to the failure of any single connection or component. By fabricating an entire circuit using the techniques of semiconductor manufacture, the "monolithic" approach could yield greater reliability.

As significant as the innovation of the IC was, the planar process is arguably the more important technological breakthrough, not merely because it underlay the IC but because it provided the paradigm or technological trajectory the industry was to follow. The most dramatic economic feature of IC production is the increase in the number of transistors that can be fabricated in a single IC. Transistor counts per IC increased from 10 to 4,000 in the first decade of the industry's history, from 4,000 to more than 500,000 in the second decade, and from 500,000 to 100 million in the third decade. The 10 million-fold increase in the number of transistors per IC has been accompanied by only modest increases in the cost of processing of a wafer and almost no change in the average costs of processing the individual IC. This factor alone has been responsible for the enormous cost reduction in electronic circuitry since the birth of the IC. Electronic systems comparable in complexity to vacuum-tube or transistor systems costing millions of dollars can be constructed for a few hundred dollars, a magnitude of cost reduction that it is virtually unprecedented in the history of manufacturing. The cheapness of electronic functions has reduced the costs of electronic systems relative to mechanical ones and lowered the relative price of electronic goods in general—developments that have had a major effect on the industrial structure of the electronics and IC industries.

As the market for computers picked up speed, the symbiosis between computers and semiconductors became stronger. In contrast to IBM, which did not begin using ICs until 1970, IBM's competitors, such as RCA and Burroughs, adopted ICs more quickly in an effort to gain an advantage. This led to a dynamic interaction in which competition among computer makers drove the demand for ICs, which lowered IC prices by moving suppliers faster along their learning curves, which in turn fed back on the price of computers. The result was a self-reinforcing process of growth for both industries. Indeed, the falling prices of semiconductor logic fueled a second computer revolution, that of the minicomputer.

In November 1960, a small start up firm called Digital Equipment Corporation sold its first PDP-1 computer. Much slower than a mainframe, it was also much cheaper and incorporated many of the principles of interactive computing that DEC's founders, Kenneth Olsen and Harlan Anderson, had learned on the government-funded Whirlwind project at the Massachusetts Institute of Technology. In the 1960s, DEC incorporated into its machines the idea of timesharing, also invented at MIT, and in the 1970s introduced the VAX line of minicomputers that would thrust the company into the number two position worldwide behind IBM. Among the other firms to enter the minicomputer market were Scientific Data Systems, Data General (founded in 1968 by defectors from DEC), Prime Computer, Hewlett-Packard, Wang, and Tandem.

Growth of Smaller Machines. Mainframes and minicomputers inhabited separate, if slightly overlapping, market niches, and both segments grew. By the 1980s, however, both niches were invaded rapidly by smaller machines, driven by the accelerating imperatives of miniaturization and increasing power in microelectronics. Two new general-purpose technologies were of signal importance: the standardized dynamic random-access memory (DRAM) chip and the microprocessor.

By the late 1960s, it became economical to replace with solid-state circuitry the clumsy ferrite-core memory on which mainframes like the 360 had originally relied. While many semiconductor firms saw customization as key to competitive advantage, Intel, a start-up firm spun off from Fairchild in 1968, bet on standardized solid-state memory, creating the first DRAM. The mass-production economies that standardization permitted quickly wiped out any benefit to customized chips. Since DRAMs could remember any kind of information, they served as cheap general-purpose information-storage devices.

The other innovation, the microprocessor, was an integrated circuit designed not to store information but rather to provide on a single chip the information-processing capability of a digital computer. In 1969, a Japanese manufacturer asked Intel to design the logic chips for a new electronic calculator. Marcian E. ("Ted") Hoff Jr., the engineer in charge of the project, thought the Japanese design was too complicated to produce. The then-current approach to the design of calculators involved the use of many specialized hardwired circuits to perform the various calculator functions. Influenced by the von Neumann architecture of minicomputers, Hoff reasoned that he could simplify the design enormously by creating a single programmable IC rather than the set of dedicated logic chips the Japanese had sought. By using relatively simple general-purpose logic circuitry that relied on programming information stored elsewhere, Hoff effectively substituted cheap DRAM memory (then Intel's major product) for relatively expensive special-purpose logic circuitry. The result was the Intel 4004, the first microprocessor. One-sixth of an inch long and one-eighth of an inch wide, the 4004 was roughly equivalent in computational power to early vacuum-tube computers that filled an entire room. It also matched the power of a 1960s IBM computer whose central processing unit was about the size of a desk.

The microprocessor found uses in a wide variety of applications involving computation and computer control. But it did not make inroads into the established mainframe or minicomputer industries, largely because it did not initially offer the level of computing power these larger machines could generate using multiple logic chips. Instead, the microprocessor opened up the possibility of a wholly new kind of computer—the microcomputer.

The first microcomputer is generally acknowledged to have been something called the MITS/Altair, which graced the cover of *Popular Electronics* magazine in January 1975. Essentially a microprocessor in a box, the machine's only input/output devices were lights and toggle switches on the front panel, and it came with a mere 256 bytes (not megabytes or even kilobytes) of memory. But the Altair was, at least potentially, a genuine computer. Its potential came largely from a crucial design decision: The machine incorporated a number of open "slots" that allowed for additional memory and other devices to be added later. These slots were hooked into the microprocessor by a network of wires called a bus. This modular approach emerged partly in emulation of the design of minicomputers and partly because hobbyists and the small firm supplying them would have been incapable of producing a desirable (that is, more capable) nonmodular machine within any reasonable time. In effect, the hobbyist community captured the machine and made it a truly open modular system. The first clone of the Altair—the IMSAI 8080—appeared within a matter of months, and soon the Altair's architecture—eventually known as the S-100 bus because of its 100-line structure—became an industry standard.

This standard dominated the hobbyist world. But the machine that took the microcomputer into the business world adopted a distinctive architecture, built around a Motorola rather than an Intel microprocessor. Stephen Wozniak and Steven Jobs had started Apple Computer in 1976, quite literally in the garage of Jobs's parents' house. The hobbyist Wozniak, also influenced by the architecture of minicomputers, insisted that the Apple be an expandable system—with slots—and that technical details be freely available to users and third-party suppliers. With the development of word processors like WordStar, database managers like dBase II, and spreadsheets like VisiCalc, the machine became a tool of writers, professionals, and small businesses. Existing computer companies were slow to develop competing microcomputers, largely because they saw the machines as a small fringe market. But as business uses increased and microcomputer sales rose, some computer makers saw the opportunity to get a foothold in a market that was complementary to, albeit much smaller than, their existing product lines. By far the most significant entry was that of IBM. On 12 August 1981, IBM introduced the computer that would become the paradigm for most of the 1980s.

In a radical departure, IBM produced the machine outside the control of company procurement policies and practices. Philip Donald Estridge, a director of the project, knew that to meet the deadline he had been given, IBM would have to make heavy use of outside vendors for parts and software. The owner of an Apple II, Estridge was also impressed by the importance of expandability and an open architecture. He insisted that his designers use a modular bus system that would allow expandability, and he resisted all suggestions that the IBM team design any of its own add-ons. Because the machine used the Intel 8088 instead of the 8080, IBM needed a new operating system. A tiny Seattle company called Microsoft agreed to produce such an operating system, which it in fact bought from another small Seattle company and rechristened the system MS-DOS, for Microsoft Disk Operating System.

Few people inside or outside IBM foresaw the sweeping changes the personal computer (PC) would make in computer markets. In April 1981, four months before the official announcement of the IBM PC, IBM gave presentations estimating it would sell 241,683 PCs over five years. In fact, IBM shipped 250,000 PCs in one month. By 1983, the PC had captured 26 percent of the market, and an estimated 750,000 machines were installed by the end of that year. The IBM standard largely drove out competing alternatives during the decade of the 1980s. This happened in part because of the strength of the IBM name in generating network effects, principally because it created the expectation among users that the key vendor would continue to provide services long into the future and that a wide array of complementary devices and software would rapidly become available. But in large measure the "tipping" of the market

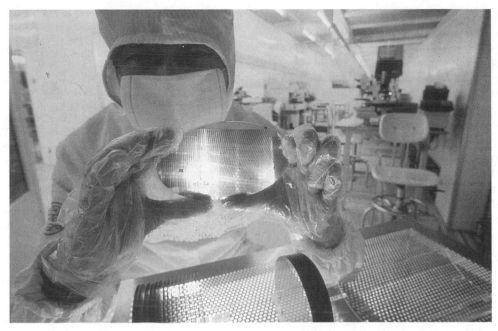

COMPUTERS. Worker examines a microchip wafer in the cleanroom of a computer factory in South Korea, 1999. (© Nathan Benn/Woodfin Camp and Associates, New York)

to the IBM PC standard was a result of the openness of the IBM system, which could be easily copied by others, and the eagerness of Microsoft to license MS-DOS to all comers.

As it had with the 360/370 series, IBM had created a dominant computer platform. But, in the case of the PC, the dominance of the platform would not translate into a dominant market share for IBM. Because of the strategy of outsourcing and the standards it necessitated, others could easily imitate the IBM hardware, in the sense that any would-be maker of computers could obtain industry-standard modular components and compete with IBM. A legion of clones emerged that offered IBM compatibility at usually a price lower than what IBM charged. By 1986, more than half of the IBM-compatible computers sold did not have IBM logos on them. By 1988, IBM's worldwide market share of IBM-compatible computers was only 24.5 percent. IBM's choice of an open modular system was a two-edged sword that gave the company a majority stake in a standard that had grown well beyond its control. For reasons that are debated in the literature but that likely have to do both with strategic mistakes by IBM and with the inherently strong positions of key suppliers in controlling their proprietary "bottleneck" technologies—the microprocessor and the operating system—Intel and Microsoft gained control of the standard that IBM had originally sponsored. The PC architecture is now often referred to as the "Wintel" (Windows/Intel) platform.

The rapid quality-adjusted price decline in microcomputers resulted not only from the declining price of computing power attendant on successive generations of Intel (and other) processors but also from the vibrant competition and innovation at the level of hardware components and applications software that resulted from the open modular design of the PC. A decentralized and fragmented system can have advantages in innovation to the extent that it involves the trying out of many alternate approaches simultaneously, leading to rapid trial-and-error learning. Moreover, the microcomputer benefited from technological convergence: It turned out to be a technology capable of taking over tasks that had previously required numerous distinct—and more expensive—pieces of physical and human capital. By the early 1980s, a microcomputer costing $3,500 could do the work of a $10,000 standalone word processor, while keeping track of the books like a $100,000 minicomputer and amusing the kids with space aliens like a 25-cents-a-game arcade machine.

Take over of Personal Computers. The personal computer grew rapidly in a niche that existing mainframes and minicomputers had never filled. Quickly, however, the microcomputer's niche began to encroach on the territory of its larger rivals, driven by the rapidly increasing densities and decreasing prices of memory chips and microprocessors. In the early 1980s, a class of desktop machines called workstations arose to challenge the dominance of the minicomputer in scientific and technical applications. As in the case of personal computers, the workstation market was driven by open technical standards and competitio within the framework of what was largely a modular system.

Initially, these workstations used microprocessor and operating systems—reduced-instruction-set-computing (RISC) microprocessors and variants of the UNIX operating system—that were different from those of personal computers. By the early 1990s, however, the same process of increasing power and decreasing cost began pushing the Windows-Intel platform into what is today a dominance of the workstation space. At the same time, workstations hooked together (or hooked to personal computers) began to take over many of the functions of larger minicomputers and mainframes.

By the 1990s, networks of fast, cheap smaller machines were widespread, a development accelerated by the spectacular growth of the Internet. This growth had a significant negative effect on the makers of larger computers, notably the Boston-area minicomputer makers. Many went bankrupt; and, in a telling development, the flagship maker of microcomputers—DEC—was acquired by Compaq, a maker of microcomputers. IBM was forced into major restructuring and a refocusing of its capabilities on software, smaller computers, and networks. New firms like 3Com and Cisco Systems sprang up in the late 1980s and the 1990s and prospered on the growth of network computing, although some of the luster fell from the Internet economy in 2000 when stock prices collapsed from all-time highs.

The development of network computing further reinforced American dominance in the industry. The most successful foreign competitors, such as Hitachi and Fujitsu, had succeeded in emulating the IBM model just in time to be undone along with IBM. And, although Japanese electronics firms found roles as competent suppliers of parts to the personal computer industry, a proprietary domestic PC strategy prevented them from taking any important role in systems design in the open-standards industry that swept the world market.

The trend of technological convergence seems likely to continue. The convergence of computer technology with consumer electronics and telecommunications is well underway. Many are skeptical that the costs of computing power can continue to decline at the same rates as they have so far, and perhaps microcomputers as currently conceived are reaching saturation levels. But technology always has the potential to surprise. Some are touting system-level integration, as the next breakthrough in which entire systems, not just microprocessors or memory, are created by planar techniques on wafers of silicon.

[*See also* Information and Communication Techonology.]

BIBLIOGRAPHY

Baldwin, Carliss Y., and Kim B. Clark. "Sun Wars: Competition within a Modular Cluster." *In Competing in the Age of Digital Convergence*, edited by David B. Yoffie, pp. 123–157. Boston, 1997.

Bresnahan, Timothy F., and Franco Malerba. "Industrial Dynamics and the Evolution of Firms' and Nations' Competitive Capabilities in the World Computer Industry." In *The Sources of Industrial Leadership*, edited by David C. Mowery and Richard R. Nelson, pp. 79–132. New York and Cambridge, 1999.

Campbell-Kelley, Martin, and William Aspray. *Computer: A History of the Information Machine*. New York, 1996.

Carroll, Paul B. *Big Blues: The Unmaking of IBM*. New York, 1993.

Chposky, James, and Ted Leonsis. *Blue Magic: The People, Power, and Politics behind the IBM Personal Computer*. New York, 1988.

Ferguson, Charles H., and Charles R. Morris. *Computer Wars: How the West Can Win in a Post-IBM World*. New York, 1993.

Fisher, Franklin M., James W. McKie, and Richard B. Mancke. *IBM and the U.S. Data Processing Industry*. New York, 1983.

Flamm, Kenneth. *Creating the Computer*. Washington, D.C., 1988.

Freiberger, Paul, and Michael Swaine. *Fire in the Valley*. Berkeley, 1984.

Garud, Raghu, and Arun Kumaraswamy. "Changing Competitive Dynamics in Network Industries: An Exploration of Sun Microsystems' Open Systems Strategy." *Strategic Management Journal* 14 (1993), 351–369.

Kurzweil, Raymond. *The Age of Spiritual Machines*. New York, 1999.

Langlois, Richard N. "External Economies and Economic Progress: The Case of the Microcomputer Industry." *Business History Review* 66.1 (1992), 1–52.

Langlois, Richard N., and Paul L. Robertson. *Firms, Markets, and Economic Change: A Dynamic Theory of Business Institutions*. London, 1995.

Moritz, Michael. *The Little Kingdom: The Private Story of Apple Computer*. New York, 1984.

Mowery, David C., ed. *The International Computer Software Industry*. New York and Oxford, 1996.

Pugh, Emerson W. *Building IBM: Shaping an Industry and Its Technology*. Cambridge, 1991.

Rifkin, Glenn, and George Harrar. *The Ultimate Entrepreneur: The Story of Ken Olsen and Digital Equipment Corporation*. Chicago, 1988.

Usselman, Steven W. "IBM and Its Imitators: Organizational Capabilities and the Emergence of the International Computer Industry." *Business and Economic History* 22 (1993), 1–35.

RICHARD N. LANGLOIS

CONGO. *See* Central Africa.

CONSTRUCTION INDUSTRY [*This entry contains three subentries, discussions of technological change, industrial organization and markets, and regulation.*]

Historical Overview and Technological Change

The construction industry comprises all those organizations and persons concerned with the process by which building and civil engineering works (following the activities listed in the International Standard Industrial Classification [ISIC]) are procured, produced, altered, repaired, maintained, and demolished. This includes companies, firms and individuals working as consultants, main and subcontractors, material and component producers, equipment suppliers, and builders' merchants. The industry has a close relationship with clients and financiers. This definition was the result of discussions at a conference organized by the International Council for Research and Innovation in Building and Construction in 1999.

The industry encompasses various parts:

1. Housing: The fundamental need for shelter is one of the basic driving forces that leads to the development of a building industry, but housing usually remains a specific sector, financed and organized differently from the rest of the building industry.
2. Building: The development of settlements, villages, and towns involves the construction of shops, schools, offices, factories, warehouses, and so on. Buildings generally require diverse components and materials and a large number of specialized crafts.
3. Civil engineering: In the Middle Ages, the engineer was a military man. In the United Kingdom, it was with the development of the canals that the profession of civil engineering was developed. Civil engineering projects tend to involve vast amounts of earthmoving by men or machines and a small number of large-scale activities. They include canals, roads, airports, dams, and irrigations systems.
4. Repair and maintenance: The output of the construction industry requires repair and maintenance; otherwise, it will degrade. Indeed, repair and maintenance usually represents approximately half of construction activity for most developed countries.

What the Industry Produces. The products of the industry from earliest times are closely related to the availability of local materials.

Preindustrialization. Originally, settlements were formed for common protection against wild animals and for mutual help. In the early stages of development, most projects were for the provision of simple buildings, housing, small workshops, and farm buildings. Settlements developed into villages and later into towns and cities, and buildings became more sophisticated and generally of higher quality and were more durable.

Building was done by the members of the community; and this informal approach to construction survives to the present day, in the shadow of the formal industry. The building industry developed as towns were established. Susan Reynolds describes the characteristics of a town as a settlement where a significant proportion of the population lives from trade, industry, and administration, forming distinct social units, separate from the surrounding countryside. The development of towns also led to the need for transportation and communications, requiring roads, bridges, harbors, and ports.

The earliest great buildings, where longevity and prestige were important, were made of large blocks of stone, sometimes transported over enormous distances, for example, Stonehenge, the pyramids, and, more recently, cas-

tles and cathedrals. Interestingly, Louis Francis Salzman describes how "the building of a church might be spread over generations, but a castle would be of little use if not completed with the utmost rapidity . . . ."

The building industry tends to use locally produced materials and products, even in Europe, partly because of the cost of transportation; but in developing countries, locally produced materials are the norm. In tropical developing countries, one of the materials used for housing is woven coconut palms. In the Nile delta, the traditional building material until well into the twentieth century was Nile mud. In temperate climates, timber is a much-used material and, where it has been available, stone, followed at a later stage of development by clay products, such as bricks and roof tiles. One key feature of many of these materials is that they can easily be replaced or are so robust that they can be re-used. It is not unusual to find ruins being used as a source of building materials.

Wherever trees grow, they have been used for timber. Timber was very widely used for cheaper construction and for small-scale construction. Compared to other materials, it is only moderately strong, but it is easier to work than the stronger materials. But timber's greatest disadvantage is its flammability, leading to many famous great conflagrations. During the twentieth century, developments in fire retardants and glues led to a more widespread use of timber in many circumstances.

Postindustrialization. As industrialization develops, there is an increasing need for large robust buildings for industry. Factories, warehouses, offices, and shops are all a consequence of industry and commerce. Thus, the emphasis in a country at the early stage of development is on factories and works and later on commercial rather than residential buildings. As populations move to meet the needs of industry and commerce, a mass market for housing develops; and, as wealth is created, there is a need for more prestigious and substantial buildings. At the same time, and partly as a result of these demands, new materials and such composite materials as reinforced and prestressed concrete enable designers and builders to meet these needs with innovative solutions.

Despite the early and diverse use of iron, particularly for nails, as far back as the Middle Ages, and steel for specialized items, such as the hard edges of tools, iron was rarely used as a major building material until the building of such structures as Ironbridge in Shropshire, United Kingdom (1777–1778), the Crystal Palace for the Great Exhibition in London (1851), and the Eiffel Tower for the Paris Exhibition (1889). However, the impact of iron and steel on the construction industry was most significant after the development of processes that enabled vast quantities of steel to be produced cheaply and of consistently high quality. Thus, in the United Kingdom as well as in the United States, it

CAST-IRON CONSTRUCTION. The Reading Room of the Bibliothèque Nationale, Paris. One of the first modern cast-iron constructions, the nine cupolas are supported by slim cast-iron columns. The library is an example of the new architecture of France's Second Empire (1852–1870). (Bibliothèque Nationale, Paris/Erich Lessing/Art Resource, NY)

was not until the late nineteenth century that major use was made of steel as a structural material. In places like Chicago, this enabled the development of much higher buildings than had previously been built. For example, the sixteen-story Monadnock building of 1891 was an office building with load-bearing walls of brick that were six feet thick at the base. If they had been much thicker than this, there would not have been space between the walls. The limit had been reached for load-bearing masonry construction. But at the same time, many buildings in American cities were already being built using a skeleton steel frame construction, leading eventually to much taller buildings with usable floor area at all levels. As a result of the Great Chicago Fire (1871), in which most of the buildings in the central business district were destroyed, and with easy access to steel, Chicago became the birthplace of modern architecture. Hugh Dalziel Duncan points out the significance of the fact that the new buildings of Chicago were not built by the city, by religious organizations, by educational institutions, or by private groups as palatial edifices: they were built by businessmen and they were built for profit.

Reinforced concrete frames also emerged, the earliest example of which is the Ingalls building in Cincinnati, completed in 1903. By combining the compressive strength of concrete with the tensile strength of steel, and casting shapes on site, large, strong, and complex structures are possible. To increase the load-bearing capacity of reinforced concrete, the technique of prestressing involves stretching the reinforcement before pouring the concrete, so that once the concrete is cured, the steel puts the element under compression, thus enabling much greater load-bearing capacity.

It is important not to underestimate the impact of major items of equipment, such as cranes, concrete batching plants, and various handling and lifting machinery on building sites, as well as earthmoving machinery, which enabled the construction of airports, roads, and harbors.

The widespread use of steel and concrete in structures depends upon the availability of a transportation system that enables the delivery of bulky materials to their point of use. Thus the development of railways, canals, roads, and shipping is a prerequisite for the development of a modern construction industry. The developments in the use and availability of steel and reinforced concrete were probably the most important developments in building materials. But modern buildings are possible because of

Law of Primitive Socialist Accumulation, formulated by the theorist of the left wing, E. A. Preobrazhensky, called for a state grain purchasing monopoly that would acquire grain from the peasantry at low prices and resell at market prices in order to generate a "surplus" for industrialization. The right wing favored more moderate industrialization and continued private ownership in agriculture and trade; while the left favored superindustrialization and complete state ownership. After allying himself with the moderate right wing to purge his main rival, Trotsky, Josef Stalin and his cohorts opted for the left-wing program in 1928 and 1929 with their choice of the ambitious variant of the First Five-Year Plan and of forced collectivization of agriculture.

Stalin's Great Leap Forward of the 1930s required a new "command" economic system managed by general directives of the Communist Party, translated into concrete tasks by an economic bureaucracy, to be fulfilled by economic agents in enterprises and industrial ministries. In December 1930, Stalin replaced rival Alexei Rykov with his closest associate, Vyacheslav Molotov, as prime minister. It was the task of Stalin's team of Molotov, Sergo Ordzhonokidze (heavy industry), Anastas Mikoyan (light industry), Vladimir Kuibyshev (State Planning Commission), and Lazar Kaganovich (transportation), to create an economic system for superindustrialization and collectivization.

The loose planning and administration of the 1920s, which had been directed by the Supreme Economic Council and the Ministry of Finance, was replaced by a system of industrial ministries, dominated by the Ministry of Heavy Industry. National plans were compiled by the State Planning Commission (Gosplan), based on decrees issued by the supreme state and party bodies, the Council of Ministers, and the Politburo. The system's directors comprised an interlocking directorate of less than ten party leaders, occupying both state and party positions. Although Stalin had, by the early 1930s, emasculated his most potent rivals, he ruled the country in this early period through the Politburo (Davies, 1996). By the late 1930s, formal meetings of the Politburo virtually ceased, and Stalin ran the country through his own decrees or informal committees (Khlevnyuk, 1996).

Although the fiction was maintained that the collectivization of agriculture was voluntary, peasants were forced by the army, militia, and party loyalists into collective farms. Resistance in the countryside to collectivization was fierce, and the Soviet countryside broke out in armed rebellion. Hundreds of thousands of "wealthy" peasants, called kulaks, were either killed or deported or fled to the city. Peasants slaughtered their livestock rather than turning them over to the collective farm, resulting in the decimation of draft animals. Stalin was forced to begin a program of massive tractor production to replace the lost draft power of animals (Hunter and Szrymer, 1991). Although agricultural production stagnated during the early years of collectivization, state collections of grain soared, due to the state's firm control over agricultural production. The collective farm shifted the burden of crop failures to peasant households because collective farmers were paid the residual production that remained after compulsory deliveries at prices set by the state.

Operations. The guiding principles of the command economy created in the 1930s were: domination of economic decision making by the Communist Party—the so-called leading role of the party; high rates of capital formation; administrative planning of material and labor balances; collectivized agriculture; rationing of consumer goods during periods of imbalances between consumer income and the availability of consumer goods; supervision and management of enterprises by industrial ministries, and one-man management and responsibility within production units (such as enterprises and industrial ministries). Other guiding principles were autarky in trade, with exports regarded as a necessary evil required to buy crucial inputs, and a strong national defense. These guiding principles remained in place until the eventual collapse of the CE system in the late 1980s.

Although planning was supposedly based on five-year plans, the actual operational plans of the CE were monthly, quarterly, and annual plans. Despite the massive public attention devoted to five-year plans, they were not used in preparing operational plans. The frequent adjustment of operational plans of all types calls into question whether the CE was a planned economy, or a resource-managed economy (Zaleski, 1980); that is, one in which ad hoc administrative decisions made after plans were completed actually guided resource allocation.

Although enterprises were given detailed output-input-financial plans, enterprise managers exercised considerable autonomy over enterprise inputs, outputs, and technology. Managerial autonomy is explained by the multiple and conflicting targets, imperfect monitoring by the center, and severe penalties for plan failure (Berliner, 1957; Granick, 1954). Managers could earn substantial bonuses and privileges for plan fulfillment, but they faced a "ratchet effect" if they produced more than the plan: overfulfillment meant more difficult plans in the next planning period. Managers developed an informal supply network to protect themselves from the uncertainties of the formal supply system, and they used misleading accounting practices to show plan fulfillment. Because they were rewarded primarily for fulfilling physical output targets, they showed little interest in quality, assortment, or reducing costs. New technologies were regarded as threats to plan fulfillment, and new products were not priced to encourage

COMMAND ECONOMY. Auto factory, Nizhni Novgorod, Soviet Union, 1931. The city was named Gorki between 1932 and 1990. (David King Collection)

innovation. Investment choices were particularly difficult in the absence of capital charges and a time-preference discount rate.

The CE substituted administrative for market resource allocation. Although the Soviet literature emphasized the scientific nature of Soviet planning, in reality, resources were allocated by simple administrative balances in which planners tallied resource availabilities against the demands on these resources. Most balancing was done within the industrial ministries, but Gosplan prepared several hundred national balances. The key material balances were the "funded" industrial commodity balances planned at the center (Gregory and Stuart, 2000). The supply of each funded commodity equaled current production plus imports (minus exports). Interindustry demand was compiled from input requests from the various industrial ministries, requests that were based on input norms established by the center. Although the center was supposed to prepare "scientific norms" reflecting the latest technology, most norms were simply based on historical experience.

Other key balances of the CE were the labor balance and the consumer goods balance. The labor balance operated by placing graduates from institutions of higher and specialized technical education into first jobs. The higher education system was operated largely by the industrial ministries. The consumer goods balance attempted to equilibrate household disposable income with the supply of consumer goods at established prices. According to this consumer balance philosophy, household saving was the consequence of excess demand—a phenomenon Soviet authorities called the "savings overhang." Unlike market economies in which household saving is usually welcomed, Soviet authorities feared the inflationary consequences of savings.

Attempts were made over the years to improve the quality of material balance planning. In the 1960s and 1970s, there was considerable interest in mathematical economics, particularly in input-output economics and linear programming, as ways to improve Soviet planning. Despite attempts to computerize planning and to create computerized scientific input norms and quality measures, the planning system in effect in the mid-1980s was virtually the same as that of the mid-1930s.

The primary objective of Soviet industrial planning was to find a workable balance—not to seek an optimal resource allocation (Bergson, 1964). The effort required to achieve a workable balance was so time-consuming that planners tended to make only small alterations from the existing allocation in each planning period. Planning was done, in the Soviet parlance, "from the achieved level." New technologies required new supply relationships and disrupted established balances; they were therefore shunned at both the enterprise and the ministerial levels.

Even after the advent of computers, the center could plan relatively few commodities. Most actual planning was done within industrial ministries and by large enterprises themselves. The contract system operated below the level of planning and remains poorly understood. Moreover, a large array of products was allocated by market or quasi-market forces. Retail prices were typically set to clear the market to avoid the need for rationing. Enterprise managers adjusted relative wages of employees by reclassification, by bonuses, or by using fictitious positions to supplement wages. Collectivized agricultural households were allotted small private plots on which they could grow fruit and vegetables, which they were free to market. A thriving second economy (Grossman, 1977) supplied households with services. Such private activities were tolerated because they provided safety valves to compensate for planning errors and mistakes.

Performance. The command economic system oversaw the forced industrialization of the Soviet Union between 1928 and 1937. Structural changes in favor of investment, heavy industry, industrial labor and urbanization, and public ownership that required fifty or more years in market economies took place in less than a decade. According to the most widely cited estimates (Bergson, 1961), Soviet real GNP growth was rapid between 1928 and 1940, although much more rapid in the prices of early than of later years. Soviet growth was interrupted by the outbreak of World War II (Harrison, 1996). Soviet growth from the end of World War II through the early 1960s was again rapid, although not as rapid as in Germany or Japan during this period. Starting in the mid-1960s, Soviet economic growth began to decline in terms of both output and factor productivity. This declining pattern of growth, under the long tenure of Leonid Brezhnev, came to be called the "period of stagnation."

Reform. Under the Stalin dictatorship, criticism of the CE was not permitted. Propaganda held that "scientific planning" was superior to any other economic system and that failures were due to human error and deliberate sabotage. The latter type of thinking culminated in the Great Purge of 1937 and 1938 during which a significant portion of the Soviet leadership was either executed or imprisoned. After Stalin's death in 1953, the new collective leadership under Nikita Khrushchev and then Leonid Brezhnev permitted more open discussion of reform. Khrushchev himself permitted the printing of Liberman's reform proposals in Pravda in 1962, and a major reform was introduced in September 1965. Although a number of reforms were announced proposing the introduction of hard budget constraints, more managerial autonomy, decentralized investment, and the like, the system remained unchanged, and the declining pattern of economic growth continued.

The Soviet leadership attempted to break the declining pattern of growth with the appointment of Mikhail Gorbachev in 1985 to the post of general secretary of the Communist Party. The reform-minded Gorbachev began the perestroika reforms of openness, democratization, and economic decentralization. In 1987, a new enterprise law was enacted that gave enterprises considerable autonomy and weakened the power and control of the ministries and Gosplan. In effect, perestroika destroyed the CE without putting a new economic system in place. Although Gorbachev had promised an acceleration of economic growth, perestroika resulted in further declines, so that, by the late 1980s, economic growth had become negative. The weakening of central state and party power encouraged independence movements in the fifteen Soviet republics; Lithuania was the first Soviet republic to gain independence. With the failure of the August 1991 coup against Gorbachev, the Soviet Union collapsed; it was formally disbanded in December 1991. Boris Yeltsin, who had earlier been elected president of the Russian Federation, assumed the reins of power from Gorbachev.

The Soviet Union broke up into fifteen newly independent states. The Russian Republic was the largest, accounting for more than 60 percent of the population of the former Soviet Union. Each newly independent state began the process of transition from a CE to some form of a market economy.

The Command Economy: Eastern Europe and Asia. After World War II, the CE was exported to eastern Europe, where it was installed virtually as a carbon copy of the Soviet model in countries like Poland, Czechoslovakia, Hungary, Romania, Bulgaria, and Albania. Yugoslavia, under Marshall Tito, broke with the Soviet leadership in the early 1950s and installed a form of worker-managed socialism. The CE was also installed in China, Vietnam, Mongolia, and later in Cuba with the ascendancy to power of Fidel Castro.

China's version of the CE differed from that of the Soviet Union in that China remained largely a poor agricultural economy. China collectivized more slowly than the Soviet Union had. During "normal" periods, China's economic growth was relatively rapid, but it was interrupted by traumatic political upheavals ordered by Chairman Mao—the Great Leap Forward of 1958 to 1960 and the Cultural Revolution of 1966 to 1969 (Eckstein, 1977; Naughton, 1998).

Deng Xiaoping, Mao's successor, initiated a series of liberalizing reforms in 1978 (Lardy, 1984). These reforms basically decollectivized agriculture, liberalized foreign trade, and created new ownership forms for trade and industry. The Deng reforms were carried through consistently, making China one of the world's fastest growing economies over the past two decades.

Transition from Command to Market Economy. Of the twenty-five or more former command economies, relatively few have made a successful transition from the command to a market system. With the exception of China, all suffered a transitional recession during the early years of transition. The relatively few success stories—Poland, Hungary, the Czech Republic, Slovenia, and the three Baltic states—lost about 25 percent of their output during the first few years of transition before returning to positive growth. Other former CEs, in particular in Russia and the Ukraine, lost 50 percent of their output. In all cases, transition was accompanied by significant inflation, bordering on hyperinflation, during the first few years of transition. Even after returning to positive growth, the transition "failures" have grown slowly, if at all, suggesting that decades will be required before they recover pretransition output levels.

The CE was the most important social experiment of the twentieth century. The task of transforming former CEs into market economies has proven difficult, and, of the more than twenty-five former CEs, only a handful have made the successful transition to a market-type economy to date.

[*See also* China, *subentry on* Communist China; Marxism and Marxist Historiography; *and* Russia, *subentry on* Communist Russia.]

BIBLIOGRAPHY

Bergson, Abram. *The Economy of Soviet Planning.* New Haven, 1964.
Bergson, Abram. *The Real National Income of Soviet Russia Since 1928.* Cambridge, Mass., 1961.
Berliner, Joseph. *Factory and Manager in the USSR.* Cambridge, Mass., 1957.
Davies, R.W. *Crisis and Progress in the Soviet Economy, 1931–33.* Basingstoke, U.K., 1996.
Eckstein, Alexander. *China's Economic Revolution.* New York, 1977.
Erlich, Alexander. *The Soviet Industrialization Debate, 1924–28.* Cambridge, Mass., 1960.
Granick, David. *Management of Industrial Firms in the USSR.* New York, 1954.
Gregory, Paul, and Robert Stuart. *Russian and Soviet Economic Structure and Performance.* 7th ed. Reading, Mass., 2000.
Grossman, Gregory. "The Second Economy of the USSR." *Problems of Communism* 26 (1977), 25–40.
Harrison, Mark. *Accounting for War: Soviet Production, Employment, and Defense Burden, 1940–45.* New York, 1996.
Hunter, Holland and Janusz Szyrmer. *Faulty Foundations: Soviet Economic Policies, 1928–1940.* Princeton, 1992.
Khlevnyuk, Oleg. *Politburo: Mekhanizmy politicheskoi vlasti v 1930-e gody.* Moscow, 1996.
Lardy, Nikolaus. *China in the World Economy.* Washington, D.C., 1984.
Naughton, Barry. *Growing Out of the Plan.* Cambridge, 1998.
Kornai, Janos. *Economics of Shortage.* Amsterdam, 1980.

PAUL R. GREGORY

COMMERCIAL AND TRADE DIASPORAS.

A diaspora is any ethnic group without a territorial base within a given polity, and whose social, economic, and political networks cross the borders of nation-states. In particular, trade and commercial diasporas refer to those diasporas whose members specialized in trade and commercial activities, or more generally, in urban, skilled occupations. Historical examples include the Jews in the last two millennia, the Parsi (Zoroastrian) diaspora from Iran, the Huguenots in early modern and modern western Europe,

the Armenians, the Greeks in the Ottoman Empire, the Germans throughout eastern Europe in modern times, the Chinese in many areas of Southeast Asia from the fifteenth to the twentieth century, the Indian middleman minorities of East Africa and Malaya, the Pakistanis in Great Britain, and the Lebanese Christians in eighteenth-century Egypt and contemporary West Africa.

Characteristics and Traits. Each trade and commercial diaspora has its unique features. Yet, most of them share common traits. Some diasporas, such as the Jews and the Parsis, had a permanent character because they lacked a homeland or territorial base to which they could eventually return. In contrast, other diasporas, such as the Germans in eastern Europe in modern times and the Chinese in Southeast Asia, were temporary because the people belonging to these diasporas were a segment of a larger population with a stable territorial base. Either way, Commercial diasporas are commonly formed by religious minorities, often the object of religious persecution.

Commercial and trade diasporas (and diasporas in general) have been characterized by strong linguistic skills, often consisting of the ability to speak and write in both their own language and alien languages. This enabled members of a diaspora to maintain communication networks within the group and to use alien languages for practical reasons. Thus, the Jews have continued to write in the Hebrew alphabet while employing Arabic, Persian, Romance, and Germanic dialects. In Southeast Asia, the ethnic Chinese learned the colonial powers' languages.

Maintaining the common original language is one of the means to enhance the organization of a diaspora. Other mechanisms include the establishment of communal institutions, such as the commercial coalitions among the Jews in the Mediterranean in the high Middle Ages, or the Chinese societies known as *Houei*; the development of commercial laws, norms, or codes of behavior whose enforcement is delegated to courts within the communities; and strong endogamic marriage strategies.

Trade and commercial diasporas have been credited for the emergence and growth of commercial economies, industrial development, and the transmission of innovative economic and business techniques. Diaspora members have displayed a striking occupational role specialization as most of them held urban, skilled jobs as middlemen, shopkeepers, craftsmen, traders, bankers, and medical doctors. Long-distance trade was one of the main occupations of Radanite Jews in the ninth century: these merchants traveled from France to India and China and back, bringing to Europe many products previously unknown. Long-distance trade was also the main occupation of Spanish and Portuguese Jews in medieval and early modern times, whereas the Armenians controlled the overland trade between Europe and the Middle East until the equally innovative developments in the production of glass walling, windows, elevators, heating, and ventilation.

Prefabrication. Prefabrication refers to the practice of manufacturing products off-site, in a controlled environment, and then delivering them to site for installation. It is used widely in the construction industry in order to locate the production process away from the unpredictability of conditions on the building site and bring it into an indoor environment. In temperate climates, this can reduce the impact of bad weather. But, regardless of climate, prefabrication usually allows for better supervision and, therefore, quality.

Buildings. Prefabricated buildings are rarely whole buildings transported to site, simply because of the size of buildings. In trying to meet as quickly as possible the huge demand for dwellings in the United Kingdom during and after World War II, "prefab" houses were factory made, delivered in flat-pack form, then fastened together on site and placed on a concrete slab. In order to create heavier buildings, prefabrication has tended toward the manufacture of modular items that can be bolted together on site, and this is more often called industrialized or system building. The aim of this kind of prefabrication is to reduce but not eliminate the need for above-ground site work and, by reducing the need for skilled site labor, to increase the capacity of the industry to construct dwellings quickly. The development of large apartment buildings in various European cities, such as those in Paris and Moscow, was based on the use of various types of prefabricated modules. These practices were clearly very widespread. They have also produced buildings that are rarely liked. However, the techniques continue to be used with some success. Indeed, in Japan, Toyota has produced dwellings using techniques similar to those used for the manufacture of cars. If all the apartments occupy the same space, then a consumer need only make a choice from a limited range in a catalog. While system building is aimed at producing whole buildings, the principle has also been applied to components of buildings, for more general use.

Components. The prefabrication of components has become one of the most important means for making the construction industry more productive. Factory-made window frames and door sets reduce the demand for joiners on building sites, as they can be installed by semiskilled operatives. Similarly, heating and ventilation equipment can be designed to be centralized into one or more large boxes that can be factory made, delivered, and installed as a unit. In office buildings, the restrooms can now be produced as "pods" that are completely finished inside, requiring nothing more than locating and connecting to the electricity, waste, and water services.

One essential aspect of the increasing use of components is the development of modular sizes. Modularization has made it much simpler to select components for use in all sorts of buildings because there is some conformity of size between various manufacturers. In the United States, where factory-made components seem to be more widely used than anywhere else, designers can choose from a very wide range, and catalogs are produced with part numbers and supplier details. The practice here is very close to designing by assembling "kits-of-parts."

Sophisticated civil-engineering projects. Major civil engineering projects are not just a feature of the modern world, as the Seven Wonders of the Ancient World attest. In addition, the Great Wall of China, an enormous feat by any reckoning at 6,400 kilometers long, was commenced in the seventh century BCE and was built over a period of some two thousand years. Hill forts were built in the United Kingdom well into the Iron Age. The need for water has often been the motivating factor behind great feats of civil engineering. The Romans were accomplished engineers and builders. One famous surviving example is France's Pont du Gard, built in the first century BCE, to bring water to the town of Nîmes. On a much larger scale, in Sri Lanka, irrigation reservoirs called "tanks" were created. From 274 CE, the great tanks were built and are still in use, the largest of which is a reservoir of 4,670 acres.

The difference between historical and modern civil engineering projects, then, is not a difference of scale or of vision. In the United Kingdom, Thomas Telford (1757–1834) designed and supervised the construction of the Menai Strait suspension bridge, opened in 1826, supporting a span of 579 feet between the towers. The designs in modern civil engineering projects involve mathematical calculation, intensive use of plant and machinery, as well as modern materials. An example is the 31-mile (50-kilometer) Channel Tunnel, joining England to France by rail, up to 131 feet below the seabed. This involved enormous purpose-built tunnel-boring machines that started at opposite ends and were navigated with great precision toward each other.

Quality, durability, and longevity. There is wide variability in expectations of the life of buildings. In the United Kingdom, sixty years is not an unusual life expectancy for a building, although about 15 percent of the current housing stock is more than one hundred years old. By contrast, the Japanese use twenty years as a typical life expectancy for a dwelling, but usually they last for forty to sixty years. The difference in longevity may simply be due to the fact that in the United Kingdom, the stock of dwellings is predominantly of brick and masonry, whereas in Japan, timber is more usual for dwellings.

The quality of work in the construction industry is variable. The work is largely custom-made, site-based, and geographically dispersed. No trade can be continuously employed on one site, so there is disruption as labor moves

CIVIL ENGINEERING. Construction of the Semmering Railroad line, the first mountain railroad built across high mountains in lower Austria, by Carl Ritter von Ghega (1802–1860). (Technisches Museum, Vienna/Erich Lessing/Art Resource, NY)

from one site to another. The industry has characteristics that make consistency of output difficult to achieve. Moreover, much of what is built is produced in response to particular markets. Some customers of the industry are either unwilling or unable to pay for high quality. Further, the way that a building is designed and supervised has a significant impact on the quality of the product.

Old buildings that have survived are not typical. There is no reason to suppose that buildings used to be of a higher quality, or longer lasting, generally. We see only those that have survived, and the vast majority did not.

The industry is very skill-intensive; and although the move of some of the processes into factories has reduced the need for some skills, there is still a pressing need for skilled and experienced operatives, the shortage of which is a perennial problem everywhere.

Repair and maintenance in relation to size of stock. The need for repair and maintenance increases as the stock increases, but it is common for this need to be overlooked. Most developing countries neglect repair and maintenance to the detriment of the stock. The planned economies of the Soviet Bloc had no adequate provision for repair and maintenance. As a consequence, some of the buildings are beyond repair. In developed countries, approximately half of the activity of the construction industry is repair and maintenance, but there are problems even with assessing how much work is done in this sector because much of it takes place informally. Indeed, in many countries there are no statistics collected for construction repair and maintenance.

Relation to the Economy. The construction industry is vital to the national economy. It produces on average across the world around a tenth of all the goods and services produced. Just as important is that it produces about half the investment, which is essential to the present and future well-being of the economy.

Economic characteristics of construction. Governments are major influences on the construction industry because they control the economic parameters in which the industry works, such as the rate of interest and the system of taxation. In addition, governments and other public-sector agencies are clients for much large building and civil-engineering work. These characteristics provide the key to the interrelationship between the industry and the economy. The sheer size of the construction industry and the investment goods it provides mean that changes in output affect the size of the national product both directly and indirectly, but it also means that what is happening to the construction industry must be a matter of national concern. It is too big and too important to ignore.

Fluctuations and their effects. Three types of fluctuations affect the construction industry: demand, seasonal, and work flow.

Fluctuations in demand. The characteristics and behavior of the construction industry have been similar throughout history. Even in the Middle Ages, there were substantial fluctuations in output, and these continue to the present time. The key to this lies partly in the nature of investment goods:

· The value of the product is high in relation to the income of the purchaser.
· In many cases, the product is required not for its own sake, but for the flow of services that it generates, for example, factory building, living accommodation, or transportation and communications.
· The products of the construction industry have a long life, and the stock is therefore high in relation to annual production so that small fluctuations in the demand for the stock of buildings have large repercussions on the demand for new building.

Another reason for fluctuations in demand is that most of the products of the industry will be required only if certain other factors are favorable, for example, the level of demand in the economy as a whole, the availability of mortgages for house purchases, and the economic climate in which government makes decisions about the level of social services. The dependence on government as a client means that it is able to increase or reduce the demands on the industry by actions on its own proposed projects, in addition to the indirect control it is able to exert on overall investment through control of credit and interest rates.

Construction contractors rely on work other than competitive contracting to balance fluctuations in demand. Historically, their efforts were directed to controlling their supplies by building up large skilled and unskilled labor forces, and owning their own plant.

Overall demand for certain types of work changes due to the state of the economy. This has effects upon the diversification policy of companies that are particularly susceptible because of low profit margins and the importance of cash flow. Such fluctuations lead to insolvencies in construction companies.

Seasonal fluctuations. Seasonal fluctuations are caused by weather patterns and by the demands of other activities, like agriculture, especially in less-developed countries. Regardless of economic cycles, the construction industry has always been subject to seasonal cycles. Fewer customers want to build in the winter than in the summer. Moreover, certain construction operations are susceptible to inclement weather, making construction longer and more expensive in the winter. Various ways of overcoming these problems have been in operation throughout history.

For example, in ancient Egypt, construction work on pyramids was dovetailed into the agricultural seasons. Similarly, in England for many generations, the builder was often the undertaker and sometimes also the coal merchant. The demand for building work was lower in the winter, but the death rate was higher and the demand for coal greater so that fluctuations in overall workload could be ironed out. This applied throughout the trades because masons could be used for gravestones as well as building; joiners could be used for making coffins; and the builders had a yard for storing coal and carts for funerals and fuel deliveries.

Fluctuations in work flow. The volume and type of work change during the execution of any project. The demand for labor fluctuates during the process because, for example, excavation and foundation building require very different skills and materials from roofing and finishing. This kind of fluctuation can be smoothed out if a contractor has a very large flow of work, so that operatives can be moved from one to site to another. However, if there is little work, or if the projects are widely dispersed geographically, other solutions are employed. Typically, work is subcontracted to local specialists. For these reasons, general contractors are either very large (such as the big six in Japan), or they subcontract the majority of their work, as is now general practice in the United Kingdom.

Government intervention. Although the construction industry has a substantial impact on the health of the economy, governments have not attempted to influence its effect until relatively recently. In general, when they have commissioned work, they have acted solely for the successful completion of that particular project. In 1253, as Salzman reports, Henry III (1207–1272) wrote to his treasurer and his clerk of works "we command you as you wish our love towards you to be continued, that you in no wise fail that the chambers which we ordered to be made at Westminster for the use of the knights be finished on this side of Easter, even though it should be necessary to hire a thousand workman a day for it." The English kings even resorted to pressed labor, on pain of imprisonment. This is a clear example of the way that clients and governments have historically focused on the industry's products without understanding any effects of the industry on the economy. This changed during the twentieth century.

Because the construction industry plays such an important part in the economy, its activity is affected by government plans for national development. Although various governments have attempted to develop their construction industries, few have done it seriously or with much success. For example, Nigeria's national plan included the construction industry, and Singapore established a Construction Industry Development Board. Most countries in their development plans consider the building of infrastructure without considering the impact on the construction industry or how the construction industry might be able to respond.

The twentieth century has seen the emergence of international bodies with an interest in development. Such agencies as the World Bank, the European Bank for Reconstruction and Development, the Asian Development Bank, and European Union programs frequently commission capital projects as a catalyst for development. Some of the practices of these agencies are out of step with modern thinking. For example, World Bank projects often have too many tendering contractors by today's standards. Moreover, the size of a project is so great that it excludes the participation of local contractors and does not consider the impact of the method of organization of the contract on the local construction industry. Also, governments have played a major role in the planning and in the regulation of the quality of buildings, particularly in response to disasters. For example, the Great Fire of London in 1666 led to legislation about party walls between dwellings; a similarly destructive fire in Chicago in 1871, earthquakes, and other disasters frequently led to revisions to building codes and regulations.

Activity related to development. In terms of economic development, the demand for durable and high-quality buildings arises only once the basic needs for life are met. Thus, less-developed countries have a low demand for the products of the construction industry as a proportion of their income. As a country industrializes, the demand for construction accelerates rapidly. But in advanced industrialized countries, it declines. Once the stock of building is sufficiently high, the need for new construction decreases, but the need for repair and maintenance and for rehabilitation increases, according to Ranko Bon and David Crosthwaite.

Organization of the Industry: From Crafts to Trades and Professions. Specialization in the labor used in building began very early as those undertaking building work were found to be particularly good at certain tasks. Monks building their early churches in wattle and daub and thatch did the work themselves. But when the more difficult task of masonry arose, the monks did the simpler work but lay craftsmen performed most of the work. In Europe, the earliest craftsmen were the masons, who were divided into various specialist skills, and the carpenters. More specific parts of buildings were provided by tilers, slaters, thatchers, plumbers, glaziers, smiths, painters, plasterers, and later bricklayers, and so on. In England, specialist craftsmen organized themselves from the beginning of the thirteenth century in a system of craft guilds. They were strictly local and, in general, membership of one town's guild did not confer membership of another. This was not suitable for masons who were constantly on the move, and they formed "lodges" or temporary associations where they worked. This division of crafts remains similar today and applies over large parts of the world. Louis Francis Salzman documents the development in the United Kingdom of architects from master masons and carpenters of the fourteenth century to independent designers of buildings who eventually became more closely associated with architects from a more artistic background, such as Sir Christopher Wren (1632–1723), the designer of Saint Paul's Cathedral in London. In the United Kingdom, the role of the modern architect was crystallized with the formation of the Royal Institute of British Architects in 1850. In this role, architects took charge of the whole process of ascertaining what the client wanted, designing the building, and supervising its construction. Christopher Powell explains that the new profession of quantity surveyor (measurer) began to emerge in the 1820s, whose role was concerned with cost prediction, dealing with bidding, and measuring work in progress for the purposes of interim payments. Over the last few decades, many more specialized roles have emerged, such as project manager and construction manager, and a comprehensive description of the full range of roles has been provided by Will Hughes and John Murdoch. Although many of these practitioners have their own associations, they have not achieved the status of separate professional institutions as the role is often filled by members of the existing professions.

In many countries, particularly those not influenced by British practice, the development of the role of the architect has not been as significant as that of the engineer in forming the modern construction industry.

While the crafts were developing, self-building was continuing, particularly in rural areas. The habit of repairing and maintaining one's own property has led to a substantial do-it-yourself (DIY) industry, particularly in the United Kingdom but increasingly elsewhere. While it was originally the practice for the client to employ each of the necessary crafts directly, some master masons and carpenters took the step of taking responsibility for the whole project and employed their own tradesmen so that they could operate as building contractors. In this situation, the early contractors were able to provide the design and the construction as required, but they were often employed to build only a part of a project, alongside other contractors and tradesmen employed by the client. In some contracts, the builder was called upon to supply materials, but in others the employer provided them. During the centuries prior to industrialization, practices were clearly very diverse. In the United Kingdom, during the Industrial Revolution, general contactors emerged. In one of the few detailed historical studies of building contracts, Richard Moore describes how Thomas Cubitt in London began to trade as a general contractor in the early part of the nineteenth century, and this is usually acknowledged as the origin of general contracting. Prior to this, it was the usual practice for tradesmen, such as carpenters, to subcontract their work to others. Cubitt employed all the craftsmen he needed and paid them regular wages. In order to sustain this labor force and pay for yards and business premises, the peaks and troughs of contracted work were smoothed by speculative house building. In the twentieth century, contractors continued the practice of speculative house building for two reasons: first, to invest surplus cash in land, and second, to use the positive cash flow from contracts to finance the building of houses. In modern times, there is a growing tendency for contractors to use their positive cash flows to invest in projects, rather than house building. This investment comes about when governments encourage the use of private sector capital to procure public services, known variously as private finance initiative (PFI), public/private partnerships (PPP), or build, own, operate, and transfer (BOOT). The financial structure of contractors is, therefore, very complex and has led to the development, particularly since World War II, of large building and civil engineering contracting organizations. Most countries have major contractors, many of whom operate internationally, but recently, through mergers and acquisitions, some of these now have an annual turnover larger than the GDP of many small countries, for example, Skanska, Dragados, and Turner, three major multinational construction conglomerates. However, major contractors may have an unexpectedly small work force because large portions of their work are subcontracted to others. The largest construction giants are actually conglomerates, with a number of different business types contributing to the group's profits. This may include not only construction activities, but also design consultancy and service provision, as well as investment and property development. The most recent developments in the way that contractors have diversified and formed into groups are merely the latest step in a long history during which successful contractors have sought to engage in business activities whose cycles counteract those of building.

Subcontractors have always been a feature of the construction industry. Since medieval times, it was quite normal to encounter both labor-only subcontracting and supply-and-fix subcontracting. In the former, materials are supplied and the subcontractor provides only the labor. In the latter, the subcontractor provides the materials and components. Even when general contractors have a large work force, they still subcontract specialist items of work and use subcontractors alongside their own work force to deal with peaks in demand. It should be noted that labor-only subcontracting is frowned upon in some countries; for example, in some circumstances, it is illegal in France and Germany.

General contracting of the kind where the contractor employs most of the work force is a relatively recent phenomenon, and it is no surprise to see a trend over the last few decades of the twentieth century away from direct employment toward subcontracting. In construction, therefore, it is extremely unlikely that there would be a direct relationship between volume of business and size of work force. But most firms in the construction industry are small. This is because of the size and geographical distribution of projects, including repair and maintenance. Numerically, most of the jobs are small. Even large projects lead to many small contracts because of subcontracting. Apart from planned economies, this size distribution of contractors is virtually universal: in just about any country, there is a handful of large companies and a huge number of small ones.

One of the features of many construction industries is that contractors need very little capital because payment is usually made for work in progress, often on a monthly basis. At the same time, they are often able to delay payments to their suppliers and subcontractors until after they have received payment for work done each month. In this way, construction contracts are cash positive throughout the building period, and successful contractors can invest surplus cash for the duration of a project. Competition for work is frequently based on lowest price, and contractors are dependent for their profits on relatively small margins combined with the manipulation of cash flow. For these reasons, contractors are susceptible to insolvency. Insolvency risks and the mechanisms that have emerged for protecting both clients and suppliers are dealt with at length by Will Hughes, Patricia Hillebrandt, and John Murdoch (1998). While the risk of insolvency is higher in the construction industry than in any other, the difference is only very marginal during boom periods but higher during a recession.

Organization of Projects. Complex tasks require diverse skills. Construction projects, generally, are complex. Even in a fairly simple medieval building, there were a number of different materials and trades; but in a modern building, the number of different skills that are required is vast. Moreover, most buildings are not replicas of others, except for certain types of housing, and they are built over a wide geographical area, each process taking place in a definite sequence. So although it is possible to generalize about the way that construction projects are organized, every project is, in fact, different.

Historically, the owner, the financier, and the user were the same person. This remains true for purpose-built dwellings for the financially well-off, but such projects are rare. From the ownership and rental of land, it is a small step to the ownership and rental of buildings. As Ranko Bon points out, compared to other goods, buildings became objects of exchange rather late in human development. According to Christopher Powell, independent developers acting as intermediaries between landowners and people with interests in completed buildings were well established by 1800 in the United Kingdom. Thus the financiers of building projects may or may not be the ultimate users. Indeed, the procurement of finance for a construction project has always been a major step in the process. Financial arrangements aside, a variety of options has evolved for organizing the processes in construction procurement. The separation of responsibility for design from responsibility for building has been a key feature in the evolution of the role of the architect.

In its most simple form, building work has always included design. Historically, a client would have approached someone to build something, and the builder would have decided how to do it. This simple approach became known as design-and-build and typically dominated the craft-based, preindustrial construction sector. As the industry evolved along the lines described earlier, the emergence of separate specialist trades led to the need for clients to engage each specialist directly. "Separate trades contracting" was widespread until general contractors appeared in nineteenth-century England, for example. Design and construction became separated as the architectural and civil engineering professions institutionalized during the nineteenth century. This led to their focusing on design and restricting their role in the construction process to ensuring that their designs were properly constructed.

A lot of experimentation has taken place among large, continuing clients of the industry. Much of this has revolved around developing long-term business relationships with a limited number of designers, contractors, and specialists, and a move away from price as the only means of selection. It remains to be seen how successful this will be as countries everywhere grapple with the difficulty of understanding and organizing construction projects.

BIBLIOGRAPHY

Bon, Ranko. *Building as an Economic Process*. 2d ed. London, 2001.
Bon, Ranko, and David Crosthwaite. *The Future of International Construction*. London, 2000.
Bowley, Marion. *Innovations in Building Materials*. London, 1960.
Bowley, Marion. *The British Building Industry: Four Studies in Response and Resistance to Change*. Cambridge, 1966.
Campagnac, Elisabeth, and Vincent Nouzille. *Citizen Bouygues, ou, L'histoire secrèt d'un grand patron*. Paris, 1988.
CIB (1999) TG29 on Construction in Developing Countries: Definitions. In "Managing Construction Industry Development in Developing Countries: Report on the First Meeting of the CIB Task Group 29 (TG29)." Arusha, Tanzania, 21–23 September 1998. CIB Report No. 229. International Council for Research and Innovation in Building and Construction, Rotterdam, pp. xii–xiii.
Duncan, Hugh Dalziel. "The Chicago School: Original Principles." In *Chicago's Famous Buildings*, edited by Ira J. Bach, pp. xi–xvii. 3d ed. Chicago, 1980.
Hillebrandt, Patricia M. *Analysis of the British Construction Industry*. London, 1984.
Hillebrandt, Patricia M. *Economic Theory and the Construction Industry*. 3d ed. London, 2000.
Hoskins, William George. *The Making of the English Landscape*. 2d ed. London, 1988.
Hughes, Will, Patricia Hillebrandt, and John Murdoch. *Financial Protection in the UK Building Industry: Bonds, Retentions, and Guarantees*. London, 1998.
Hughes, Will, and John Murdoch. *Roles in Construction Projects: Analysis and Terminology*. London, 2001.
Ive, Graham, and Stephen Gruneberg. *The Economics of the Modern Construction Sector*. London, 2000.
Lewis, John Parry. *Building Cycles and Britain's Growth*. London, 1965.
Low, Sui Pheng. *The Role of Construction and Marketing in Economic Development: A Framework for Planning*. London, 1994.
Moore, Richard. *Response to Change: The Development of Non-Traditional Forms of Contracting*. Ascot, England, 1984.
Murdoch, John, and Will Hughes. *Construction Contracts: Law and Management*. 3d ed. London, 2000.
Ofori, George. *The Construction Industry: Aspects of Its Economics and Management*. Singapore, 1991.
Powell, Christopher. *The British Building Industry since 1800: An Economic History*. 2d ed. London, 1996.
Raftery, John. *Principles of Building Economics: An Introduction*. Oxford, 1991.
Reynolds, Susan. *An Introduction to the History of English Medieval Towns*. Oxford, 1977.
Ruddock, Leslie. *Economics for Construction and Property*. London, 1992.
Ruegg, Rosalie, and Harold Marshall. *Building Economics: Theory and Practice*. New York, 1990.
Salzman, Louis Francis. *Building in England down to 1540: A Documentary History*. London, 1952.
Sebestyén, Gyula. *Construction: Craft to Industry*. London, 1998.
Stone, Peter Albert. *Building Economy: Design, Production, and Organisation : A Synoptic View*. 3d ed. Oxford, 1983.
Turin, Duccio A., ed. *Aspects of the Economics of Construction*. London, 1975.
Wells, Jill. *The Construction Industry in Developing Countries: Alternative Strategies for Development*. London, 1986.

WILL HUGHES AND PATRICIA HILLEBRANDT

Industrial Organization and Markets

The history of construction can be divided into three basic regimes: nonmarket, traditional, and modern. Each regime is defined by the role of the owner. In nonmarket regimes, the owner is responsible for design, organization, and construction. In traditional regimes, the owner is responsible for design and organization but hires labor for the actual construction. In modern regimes, the owner plays almost no role in physical construction. Design, organization, supervision, and construction are all carried out by others. Broadly speaking, traditional organization follows nonmarket and precedes modern, but there is considerable overlap.

Nonmarket Construction. For most of history, in most places, people have built their own houses and barns with the help of family and neighbors but with little or no wage labor. Nonmarket construction has not disappeared today. It is common in countries where property rights are insecure and squatters find it hard to raise capital for construction on land they do not own. In developed economies, "do it yourself" is common for the simplest construction, especially renovation and repair.

Larger projects can be built outside the market, with volunteer or coerced labor. Many societies have used slave labor. Government construction has often employed coerced labor. The roads in ancient Rome, for example, were built, in large part, by Roman soldiers. In early modern Europe, many governments reserved the right to impress building craftsmen for military projects. And in many places, including much of nineteenth-century United States, taxpayers could choose to work off their taxes by working on local road construction.

Traditional Construction. The defining feature of the traditional construction regime was the direct participation of the owner. The owner hired a master builder, generally a carpenter or mason, with whom he shared responsibility for design and organization and to whom he delegated day-to-day responsibility for supervision, but the owner remained involved in major decisions and controlled costs. Most of the workers were paid directly by the owner. The owner was able to participate because both he and the craftsman worked within an understood vernacular architecture, and the general process and final product were understood by all parties.

Payment was structured to reward honesty. Craftsmen who worked largely without supervision were generally paid for output, not time. If the construction was simple, the craftsmen might negotiate a fixed price for a whole building. A fixed price effectively addresses the principal-agent problem by making the builder the residual claimant, but a fixed price, agreed on in advance, does not allow for changes during construction and could only be employed for very simple buildings. For more complex construction, we find, in places as diverse as medieval Europe, early-nineteenth-century North America, and ancient Babylon, that much work was paid "by the measure," a form of piecework. Owner and craftsman would agree in advance on a price per unit (area or volume) of brickwork or wall. After the craftsman had completed the work, a third party, the quantity surveyor, would be responsible for measuring the finished construction and determining how much brickwork or plaster had been completed. This measure determined what the owner owed the craftsman. The system encouraged price fixing, but it limited the planning and supervision required from the owner, allowed the craftsman to adapt construction to the particular site, and provided a third party to evaluate the work.

Skilled workers were organized by craft. Carpenters, masons, bricklayers, plasterers, and painters among others, trained as apprentices, working for a master craftsman. (In almost all cases, the traditional industry was dominated by men.) Once training was completed, the apprentice was a journeyman, working by day or by piece. Once he began to accept jobs directly from building owners, he became a master. In some places, the crafts were organized into guilds, which might have the power to set wages and control working conditions, training, entry, and quality of work. In other places, guilds were weak or nonexistent and the worker's progress was determined by market conditions. In general, the skilled construction craftsmen were among the best paid workers in traditional economies, although few became wealthy. Large numbers of unskilled workers were also employed in construction. These laborers were rarely literate or organized; we know less about them.

Modern Construction. Around the time that the Industrial Revolution emerged in Europe and North America, the modern construction industry began to replace the traditional across newly industrialized economies. The owners of structures slowly relinquished their control over the design, organization, and supervision of construction. The shift was not driven by a sudden change in the technology of building, although there were and continue to be incremental improvements. Rather the rising complexity of structures pushed the owner out of the process. The owners' control was not replaced by any single organizing institution like the factory that emerged to dominate manufacturing. Instead, an array of institutions and practices developed to organize the growing number of professionals responsible for building—the architects, engineers, builders, craftsmen, and laborers—and to encourage them to be both efficient and honest. The resulting industry is a welter of independent professionals, small and large firms, suppliers, subcontractors, and spot-labor markets, rather than an industry of large, integrated, hierarchical firms. But it would be a mistake to see the organizational variety as backward or insensitive to the demands of the market. On the contrary, the variety is the result of exquisite sensitivity to demands, technology, principal-agent issues, competition, market power, credit, and government.

For many structures, especially houses, the market replaced the owner as the source of discipline. Developers (often, but not always, builders) borrow money, buy or lease land, and build on speculation, selling complete structures to owners who play no part in their construction. The future owners are able to choose among buildings constructed by different builders, and the competitive market aligns the builders' incentives with the desires of the owners.

Some structures are unique and must be built to order. Without a competitive market in complete structures, another mechanism must be found to replace the owner's supervision. In modern construction, the owner's oversight is (largely) replaced by the plan and the fixed bid. The owner buys a plan from an architect or engineer, then hires a separate builder to build the plan for a fixed fee. This creates a competitive market in construction, with the owner hiring the builder who tenders the lowest credible bid. Separating design and construction fixes the incentive problem, but it is clumsy. In speculative building, where the market provides incentives, builders work directly with designers. For some structures, design and construction cannot be separated despite the dangers of collusion. In the construction of infrastructure such as roads and bridges, the engineer must work closely with the builder because the site conditions, revealed as construction goes forward, often determine the cost. Fixed price bids are hard to enforce in the construction of infrastructure and such construction is famous for cost overruns and for corruption.

The organization of the actual construction—the mix of employees and subcontractors on the building site—also balances incentives against efficient organization. The market, or the fixed bid, aligns the builders' interests with those of the owner, but the builder must find a way to pass the incentive down to the workers actually constructing the building. Organizing within a single firm makes close coordination of different tasks easier, but it blunts the incentive to work quickly and efficiently. Organizing through contracts and subcontracts rewards each craftsman for working efficiently, saving on supervision, but makes close coordination more difficult. Keeping employees in a firm from project to project also maintains firm specific human capital, but decreases the flexibility of the firm. Organizing through contracts and subcontracts allows the builder to tailor the workforce to the project. Economies of scale across multiple construction sites appear to be limited, and building firms tend to be no larger than necessary to handle the technical demands of their particular kind of construction. Big projects are built by large firms; small projects are built by small firms. The supply of credit and of building supplies also affects firm size. Firms that operate in areas with well-developed credit and land markets are actually smaller because when credit is available modest entrepreneurs can borrow to buy land and to build. Therefore the industry tends to be local, entry is relatively easy, and building is generally quite competitive.

These relationships can best be illustrated by the different histories of the organization of heavy construction and of residential construction. Engineering and construction (E&C) firms, which build big engineering projects such as steel mills and power plants, are among the largest and the most integrated in the construction industry. Building a big piece of complicated infrastructure requires a skilled and experienced workforce and a high degree of coordination and quality control, all demands that favor the large, integrated firms. The E&C firms generally own specialized capital equipment. Clients and financiers also want the security that comes with reputation and capital. Because large E&C firms are vertically integrated and thus able to provide all of the skilled workers needed, they are not limited to working in their local market. The first E&C firms built the railroads in England, and the same firms found they could export their building teams, first to other nations in Europe and later to Africa, Asia and the Americas. Today the largest E&C firms are multinational, constructing dams, tunnels, and oil drilling platforms all over the world.

Firms that build housing, on the other hand, are almost always local. They exhibit a range of sizes and a much greater dependence on subcontracting. The variation in size is driven by differences in the markets for land, credit, labor, and building supplies, as can be seen in the history of the housing industry in the United States. In the United States, almost all single-family homes built since 1840 have used the same technology, the balloon frame, built with nails and dimension lumber. In the nineteenth century, small builders dominated where credit and land markets were well developed. The houses of early-nineteenth-century Philadelphia and late-nineteenth-century Boston were built by thousands of independent craftsmen, often house carpenters. These small entrepreneurs could borrow money and buy or lease land in the well-developed credit and land markets of those cities. Where craftsmen found it harder to borrow or to buy land, such as in nineteenth-century New York, large-scale developers would organize and fund construction, hiring the builders as subcontractors. After World War II in the United States, credit was widely available to builders of all sizes, and the size and level of integration of a builder were determined by the size of the development that was constructed. The small builders built a few houses on scattered lots. The large firms that emerged built larger housing developments. The largest companies, like the Irvine Company in California, used fewer subcontractors and more employees than their smaller competitors. They also hired their own full-time architects, provided financing to buyers, and took on some community planning responsibilities of local government.

Small or large, builders absorb significant risk. Because new buildings are investments, the demand for building fluctuates widely over the business cycle. Most builders and subcontractors work on credit, increasing the risk they face as the interest rates rise and fall. If they are developers, they also absorb market risk, the risk that the value of the building will not be what they expect. Panics and

CONSTRUCTING SKYSCRAPERS. *Riveting the Last Beam*, photograph of construction on the Empire State Building, New York, 1931. (Lewis W. Hine/Courtesy George Eastman House, Rochester, N.Y.)

recessions can hit small builders very hard. The continued success of the small entrepreneurs, despite the high level of risks, suggests the importance of market incentives in ensuring efficient construction.

Labor. The organization of construction labor mirrors the organization of building firms. First, the division between worker and builder is not always clear. A skilled worker may work for wages on one job and contract as an independent entrepreneur on another. Second, firms and markets are not the only organizing institutions. Unions

play a much larger role in the organization of construction than they do in other industries.

The division between skilled craftsman and builder is somewhat blurred in construction, but over the past several centuries the distance between the skilled worker and the builder has grown. The people who organize and supervise construction are less and less likely to ever pick up a hammer. Over the past two centuries, the growing complexity of construction has also increased the number of crafts, and the number of subcontractors, individuals who are independent businessmen but who do not organize entire building projects. The increasing mechanization in the building supply industry, on the other hand, has increased the proportion of premanufactured components and has, in many crafts, actually decreased the level of skill required. A house carpenter in 1820 had to know how to build his own windows. A house carpenter in 1890, in most of northern Europe and the United States, could buy premanufactured windows, ready to install.

Labor unions, not employers, often wield the most control over wages, entry, and the conditions of work. Labor unions often physically run the local labor market; employers go to the union hall to find skilled employees. Because building is local and work is organized through the union, members can expect to work together repeatedly, which strengthens the community and lowers the cost of organizing and maintaining an effective union. Labor unions are sometimes able to manipulate local building markets and extract monopoly rents by raising wages and prices. Because building is local and a local monopoly can reap significant rents if it can control wages and entry, the firms are small, numerous, highly competitive, and cannot form an effective monopoly. The labor unions are larger and control the supply of a key input—skilled labor. They can sometimes raise wages and earn monopoly rents.

Construction unions are often large enough to be politically powerful in a democracy. Labor unions are likely to be most effective where they are able to influence government to enforce union agreements on wages, training, and working conditions. Government support strengthens labor unions in many European countries, increasing the control they wield. In the United States, where federal law does not impose national wage agreements on local construction, labor unions are more successful in central cities and less successful in suburbs (although the central city unions have declined in power as the central cities have declined in importance). At the turn of the twentieth century, the most powerful construction unions in the United States were in Seattle and San Francisco, where labor was scarce.

The effect of unions on efficiency and innovation has been widely studied, but with no firm conclusions. Unions will, in theory, try to limit entry, raise wages, and thereby raise costs and lower productivity. On the other hand, the union is more likely to internalize the benefits of innovations than are the fragmented construction firms, and so may help disseminate information and training. In countries that show significant variation in levels of unionization, such as the United States, the effects of unions are hard to detect. On the other hand, in the United States, union and nonunion localities compete, so wide variations in productivity and price are unlikely.

Unskilled workers are much harder to organize. Construction has traditionally offered jobs to unskilled and often undocumented workers in many developed economies. Work can be extremely uncertain. In many places, true "spot markets" emerge—street corners where the unskilled gather and foremen know to come to hire a worker or six for the day, generally for cash and without paying taxes. These informal markets are very old, but they leave few records, and little is known of their history.

BIBLIOGRAPHY

Bishir, Catherine, Charlotte V. Brown, Carl R. Lounsbury, and Ernest H. Wood. *Architects and Builders in North Carolina: A History of the Practice of Building.* Chapel Hill, N.C., 1990.

Frampton, Kenneth, and Kunio Kudo. *Japanese Building Practice from Ancient Times to the Meiji Period.* New York, 1997.

Goldthwaite, Richard A. *The Building of Renaissance Florence: An Economic and Social History.* Baltimore, 1980.

Linder, Marc. *Projecting Capitalism: A History of the Internationalization of the Construction Industry.* Westport, Conn., 1994.

Louw, Hentie. "The Mechanization of Architectural Woodwork in Britain from the Late Eighteenth to the Early Twentieth Century and Its Practical, Social and Aesthetic implications." *Construction History,* part 1, *The Period c.1790 to c.1860,* 8 (1992), 21–54; part 2, *Technological Progress c.1860 to c.1915,* 9 (1993), 27–50; part 3, *The Retreat of the Handicrafts,* 11 (1995), 51–71; part 4, *The End of an Era,* 12 (1996), 19–40.

Morrell, David. *Indictment.* London, 1987.

Powell, Christopher. *The British Building Industry since 1800: An Economic History.* 2d ed. London, 1996.

Rilling, Donna J. *Making Houses, Crafting Capitalism: Builders in Philadelphia 1790–1850.* Philadelphia, 2001.

Satoh, Akirah. *Building in Britain.* Translated by Ralph Morton. Cambridge, 1995.

Warner, Sam Bass, Jr. *Streetcar Suburbs.* 2d ed. Cambridge, Mass., 1978.

Woods, Mary N. *From Craft to Profession: The Practice of Architecture in Nineteenth-Century America.* Berkeley, 1999.

Woodward, Donald. *Men at Work: Labourers and Building Craftsmen in the Towns of Northern England, 1450–1750* (Cambridge Studies in Population, Economy and Society in Past Times, vol. 26). Cambridge, 1995.

REBECCA MENES

Regulation

The regulation of construction is as old as written law. The law code of King Hammurabi of Babylon, the oldest surviving written law code, regulated real estate markets, fixed wages in construction, and established penalties for poor construction. Since 1780 BCE the governments of the world have continued to regulate construction employment, the quality and nature of structures, land use, and real estate and credit markets.

Regulation of employment and of structures has traditionally been enforced with the help of craft guilds or unions. In Japan guilds and regulation developed during periods of political stability and disappeared during political upheavals. Guilds do not guarantee regulation will develop. In Renaissance Florence construction guilds existed, but construction was largely unregulated. But because craft guilds generally help enforce traditional regulations, the rules tend to favor skilled craftspeople by raising wages and limiting entry. On the other hand, regulation may benefit buyers as well. In the traditional construction industry, the buyer and the master craftspeople work together on design, organization, and supervision of construction. A trained craftsperson can cheat a less-knowledgeable buyer by overcharging or delivering shoddy construction. Regulations that fix prices and mandate minimum standards may limit these problems, although at a price.

Governments have always been willing to regulate aspects of construction beyond employment and safety, but their ability was constrained by the limits of traditional government. In Japan in 1751 the centralized, bureaucratic government of the Tokugawa Shogunate (1573–1868) successfully regulated the style, size, and plan of houses for the different official classes of society. But in England the relatively weak government of Queen Elizabeth I was not able to limit the growth of London. In 1580 a royal edict forbade new construction within five miles of the city, but with no institutions to enforce the edict, building continued.

As the early modern nation-states evolved into modern democracies, the machinery of the state grew, and with it grew the ability to regulate construction. In some countries, such as Germany, governments continued to regulate employment in construction. In other nations, like the United States, employment regulation declined. But control over other aspects of construction grew everywhere. Regulation of structures increased from a few rules to complex "uniform building codes" that mandate standards for nearly every system in a building. Land use controls increased from a few poorly enforced restrictions on noxious activities to complete systems of urban and regional planning and land use control. Regulation grew in response to the economic growth and urbanization of the Industrial Revolution, to changes in transportation that reshaped cities, and to rising distrust in private real estate markets. In many nations, including France, Germany, and Belgium, the government has regulated urban rents since World War I and has built large amounts of public housing to alleviate the inevitable shortages of housing. But even in nations like the United States, where nearly all construction is carried out in the private sector, the industry is highly regulated.

Contagious disease and fire are classic examples of urban externalities, and they created demand for building regulations to control them. As scientific knowledge about public health grew during the nineteenth century, middle-class reformers pressed governments to insist on minimum standards for ventilation and plumbing, both to help the poor and to protect all city residents from cholera and other diseases. As cities grew more dense, the danger of fire also grew. Largely wooden cities of nineteenth-century America were especially vulnerable to citywide conflagrations. Individual owners bought fire insurance and ignored the threat their flammable buildings posed to neighbors. But when a whole city burned, insurance companies failed. It was the insurance companies who pushed most vigorously for rules requiring fire-resistant construction.

The role of building codes is more complex. They do mandate construction designed to withstand fire, earthquake, and hurricane where appropriate, but they also regulate construction details, such as door and window dimensions, meant largely to simplify and coordinate design. Building codes, used all over the world, were developed with the cooperation of the construction industry because they help coordinate the work of the independent contractors who work together on every job site and because they provide a mechanism for establishing best practice in a fragmented industry. However, building codes can attract corruption and rent seeking. On the one hand, any single builder may want to cheat on any particular project. Where governments are weak or corrupt, the local inspectors can be bought off. The corruption is only revealed when an earthquake or fire destroys buildings. On the other hand, some craftspeople may try to manipulate building codes to increase demand for their services. Prefabricated housing, for example, is banned in many urban areas, which raises the price of the cheapest housing.

The introduction of trucks and private cars revolutionized the geographic organization of cities. Suddenly economic activity could be located just about anywhere. Most governments responded by expanding their land use controls. The kind of controls each country adopted reflected the different political institutions it inherited. For example, in both Britain and the United States most land use decisions are made by the local governments. But in the United States local governments are fragmented and independent, with dozens or even hundreds of individual municipal governments in a metropolitan area. In Britain there are fewer local governments per metropolitan area, and they are more dependent on the central government for their authority. In the United States each suburb makes its own land use (zoning) policy with no oversight. The result is American cities with sprawling, low-density suburbs, filled with large, relatively inexpensive, owner-occupied middle-class housing, but also with poor central cities and communities segregated by income and by race. In Britain the local town or county council makes decisions for a much larger chunk of a metropolitan area (often the whole city), and the decisions can be appealed to the national level. The result is English cities with smaller, more expensive housing in higher-density urban and inner-suburban communities and more countryside kept open near the cities.

The regulation of construction continues to change because the power to alter the built environment is the power to affect any activity that takes place in buildings. In the United States in the 1960s the federal government introduced building regulations meant to protect the environment, such as requiring low-flow toilets and showerheads. In 1990 the Americans with Disabilities Act mandated that new construction be designed to accommodate the disabled. And there is a growing movement in the United States for municipal governments to work together to coordinate metropolitanwide land use control to suppress suburban growth or "sprawl." In some parts of the world the basic institutions are still developing. In Latin America and in the former Socialist world, improved property rights and real estate markets are encouraging construction.

BIBLIOGRAPHY

Booth, Philip. *Controlling Development*. London, 1996.
Cullingworth, J. B. *The Political Culture of Planning: American Land Use Planning in Comparative Perspective*. London, 1993.
Fischel, William A. *An Economic History of Zoning and a Cure for Its Exclusionary Effects*. Forthcoming.
Frampton, Kenneth, Keith Vincent, and Kunio Kundo. *Japanese Building Practice from Ancient Times to the Meiji Period*. New York, 1997.
Glaeser, Edward, and Joseph Gyourko. "The Impact of Zoning on Housing Affordability." National Bureau of Economic Research, Working Paper no. 8835. March 2002.
Haar, Charles M., and Jerold S. Kayden. *Zoning and the American Dream: Promises to Keep*. Chicago, 1989.
Knowles, C. C., and P. H. Pitt. *The History of Building Regulation in London, 1189–1972*. London, 1972.
Popper, Frank. "Understanding American Land Use Regulation since 1970." *Journal of the American Planning Association* 54 (1988), 291–301.
Wermiel, Sara. E. *The Fireproof Building: Technology and Public Safety in the Nineteenth Century American City*. Baltimore, 2000.

REBECCA MENES

CONSUMER CREDIT. Consumer credit allows household expenditures to exceed income, either in the very immediate term, when the relative timing of spending and of income streams differ, or over a longer term, when household deficit spending is the norm. The oldest form of consumer credit is informal extension of credit by merchants or service providers. Variously called merchant credit, store credit, or service credit, this form is typically characterized by the absence of a signed contract between the two parties. The volume of such credit is difficult to track; little more than merchant account books gauge its extent.

For centuries, pawnbrokers have aided working-class families. Household goods or other personal property is typically offered as collateral in exchange for a money loan, often at extremely high interest rates and on a relatively short term. If the loan is not repaid, the collateral is forfeited. Paul Johnson claims in *Saving and Spending* that pawning was common among the English working class throughout the nineteenth and twentieth centuries.

Exorbitant interest rates charged by pawnbrokers led to regulation. Pawnbroking in England was legislated by the Pawnbrokers Act of 1872. In the United States, a Uniform Small Loan Law that served as a guide for state-level regulation was proposed in 1916.

Installment credit began in the mid-1800s but burgeoned in industrialized countries worldwide with encouragement from durable goods' manufacturers as a strategy for marketing their goods. In the United States and England, growth was especially pronounced in the 1920s. In other countries, installment credit use expanded greatly only after World War II. With an installment contract, consumers obtained durable goods for a small down payment and regular, typically monthly, installment payments. Legal ownership but not possession of the goods remained with the seller, who could repossess the goods if the contract was breached. No money was lent. The legal distinction between installment selling and money lending allowed sales finance companies to skirt usury laws.

Charge plates offered by department stores to regular customers were the late 1920s precursor to modern-day bank credit cards. BankAmericard and Master Charge were established in the United States in the late 1950s. Their 1960s marketing practice of mailing millions of unsolicited cards led to increased regulation protecting consumers from liability for unauthorized charges. In the 1970s, the cards were marketed aggressively in Europe and Asia.

Home equity loans are the most recent innovation in consumer credit. Homeowners can borrow for any purpose against the accumulated equity in their homes. Failure to repay can result in foreclosure.

Usage. Consumers' use of credit in the United States increased markedly in the twentieth century, as seen in Table 1. Debt service burdens have increased more slowly than debt-to-income ratios because of increases in average contract length. Moreover, the increase in the aggregate debt-to-income ratio overstates the typical indebted household's debt burden: as more households acquire consumer debt, aggregate debt-to-income ratios increase.

By the end of the twentieth century, consumer credit was common throughout the Organization for Economic

TABLE 1. *Consumer Credit Outstanding in the United States*

	TOTAL CONSUMER CREDIT OUTSTANDING (BILLION U.S.$)	OUTSTANDING CREDIT/ DISPOSABLE INCOME (PERCENT)
1920	3.0	4.1
1940	8.3	11.0
1960	60.0	16.4
1980	349.4	17.3
2000	1525.0	21.8

SOURCES: 1920, 1940: U.S. Bureau of the Census, *Historical Statistics of the United States*, Series X551 (credit) and F9 (income); 1960, 1980: *Economic Report of the President 2000*, Table B75 (credit) and B28 (income); 2000: Federal Reserve Statistical Release <http://www.federalreserve.gov/Releases/G19/20010207/>; 2000: Bureau of Economic Analysis <http://www.bea.doc.gov/bea/newsrel/pi1200.pdf>

Cooperation and Development (OECD) countries. Outstanding debt-to-income ratios in OECD countries in the 1990s range from well over one in Japan to close to zero in Greece and Switzerland (Table 2). With a handful of exceptions, most European nations had ratios significantly lower than that of the United States, while Canada's was comparable.

Historical Importance. Expansion of consumer credit is viewed by many as a vital component of the rise of consumerism. Consumerism, generally understood to be the development of a cultural ethos that places value on increased consumer choices, dates in the United States from the early twentieth century. Active marketing of consumer credit, coupled with efforts by industry specialists to improve the public's image of household indebtedness, placed credit at the center of the cultural maelstrom and secured its acceptance.

Economic functions of the various types of consumer credit differed. So too did the factors associated with changes in use. Unexpected income declines or expense increases—in the language of the permanent income hypothesis, large transitory income or expenses—lead to increased demand for merchant credit or small-loan lending in order to maintain the usual consumption pattern. The household members must ultimately adjust their income, spending, or saving plans to retire the debt.

On the other hand, buying durable goods on the installment plan simply shifts timing of saving from before to after the goods' acquisition. Because the successful completion of an installment contract requires a steady income stream, demand for installment credit is unrelated to transitory changes in income and instead depends on long-run expected income.

Economic Impact of Consumer Credit. Installment credit and consumer durable goods are complements. Increased availability of installment credit apparently facili-

tated the initial increased demand for durable goods, though the empirical evidence is readily available only for the United States and the United Kingdom. Once the resulting revolution in consumer durables transpired, further increases in the use of installment credit were primarily triggered by increased demand for durable goods. Most empirical evidence indicates little if any price sensitivity of demand for consumer credit, at least within the usual range of interest rates, contract length, and down payments.

Before installment credit use could increase, two conditions had to be met. First, at least in the United States, society's attitudes needed to change from viewing acquisition of debt as a source of shame to viewing it as evidence of responsible financial behavior. Advertising, popular fiction, and articles in a wide variety of popular magazines all contributed to a relatively rapid change in attitudes. Second, in any economy, families whose income stream was erratic could not expect to complete an installment contract. Commitment to an installment contract therefore required increased labor force attachment. Some scholars have argued that increased use of installment credit explains increased married women's labor force participation rates before World War II, but a more reasonable interpretation reverses the causality.

Some modern economists have considered the impact of increased consumer indebtedness on household spending and the macroeconomy. Frederic Mishkin developed the "balance sheet approach," which allows for separate effects of assets and of liabilities. Financial asset holdings increase future spending for durable goods and housing while nonmortgage debt holdings decrease such spending. The effect of debt is substantially greater in absolute value than that of financial assets. Mishkin applied the model to the Great Depression: real liability increases from increased debt acquisition and price deflation, coupled with decreased liquid assets due to the 1929 stock market crash, led, in his view, to decreased demand for consumer durable goods in the 1930s.

The extent to which consumer spending declined in the United States in 1930 was unique in American history, leading to the argument that the extent of the negative effect of indebtedness on future household spending depends upon the magnitude of the penalty incurred when households default on consumer debt (Olney, 1999, 319–335). Penalties became less stringent over time and especially between 1933 and 1937. As a result, the collapse of consumer spending in the United States during the Great Depression was a unique historical response to high consumer indebtedness coupled with very expensive default penalties.

Saving and Investment. Effects of consumer debt in national income accounting are often misunderstood.

TABLE 2. *Consumer Credit Outstanding in OECD Countries, 1990s*

	CONSUMER CREDIT OUTSTANDING, GRANTED BY (MILLION U.S.$)			
	FINANCIAL INSTITUTIONS	NON-FINANCIAL ENTERPRISES	TOTAL	OUTSTANDING CONSUMER CREDIT/GDP RATIO[1] (PERCENT)
Japan[2]	3,242,798		3,242,798	122
Sweden	105,814	0	105,814	40
Austria	48,620		48,620	33
Australia	67,112	279	67,391	25
Norway	16,073	0	16,073	22
Canada	89,945	1,258	91,203	15
United States	754,996	70,263	825,259	13
Germany	222,194		222,194	11
United Kingdom	73,287	3,678	76,965	8
Finland	8,505		8,505	7
Belgium	11,355	196	11,551	6
France	66,842		66,842	6
Spain	34,325	0	34,325	6
Netherlands	12,478		12,478	3
Italy	20,682	0	20,682	2
Portugal	2,189		2,189	2
Greece	415		415	1
Switzerland	3,510		3,510	1

SOURCES: Consumer credit data from Organisation for Economic Cooperation and Development, *Financial Statistics Monthly,* Section 2, *Domestic Markets—Interest Rates*, 1 January 1998, Table D.6. GDP data from *Statistical Abstract of the United States*, Tables 1365 (2000 edition), 1374 (1995 edition), and 1355 (1998 edition).

[1]Credit data are for various times from June 1989 (Australia) through November 1997 (Netherlands). For each country, the GDP estimate is within one year of the credit data. For example, Austria's credit data is credit outstanding as of 30 June 1992 and the GDP data used to compute the credit-to-GDP ratio is for the year 1992.

[2]Japanese data include operating funds lent to retailers who offer consumer credit, so is an overstatement of consumer credit outstanding.

When an item is purchased with credit, the full purchase price of the product is recorded as expenditure when the item is acquired. As the debt is retired, the payments are counted as saving. While this pattern strikes many people as odd—they, after all, feel they are "spending money" when they make loan payments—it is consistent with a guiding principle of national income accounting: record as expenditure those amounts most tightly correlated with the employment required to produce the item. The result is that personal saving rates fall when debt is acquired and, *ceteris paribus*, rise in subsequent years as the debt is retired.

In the last quarter-century, Americans increased their credit card usage, in part substituting credit cards for installment buying of appliances and furniture. Saving rates plummeted as overall debt acquisition grew, as seen in Table 3.

Consumer debt, which is largely immune to changes in interest rates, uses funds that might otherwise be available for business investment. To the extent debt-financed consumer spending does not enhance productivity, the long-run impact of increased consumer debt is potentially a

TABLE 3. *Debt and Saving Relative to Disposable Income*

YEAR	INSTALLMENT (NONREVOLVING) DEBT-TO-INCOME	CREDIT CARD (REVOLVING) DEBT-TO-INCOME	SAVING RATE
1970	17.2	0.7	9.4
1980	14.6	2.7	10.2
1990	12.8	5.6	7.8
2000	12.3	9.5	−0.1

SOURCES: 1970, 1980, 1990: *Economic Report of the President 2001*, Tables B-75 (debt), B-28 (saving rate, disposable income); 2000: Bureau of Economic Analysis <http://www.bea.doc.gov/bea/newsrel/pi1200.pdf> Federal Reserve Statistical Release <http://www.federalreserve.gov/Releases/G19/ 20010207/>.

decline in economic growth. The size effect is potentially large: In the United States in 2000, total consumer debt was $1,525 billion and investment spending was only slightly higher at $1,834 billion.

Overall, increased availability and use of consumer credit has expanded consumer choices and enjoyment of goods and services.

BIBLIOGRAPHY

Board of Governors of the Federal Reserve System. *Consumer Instalment Credit*. Washington, D.C., 1957. Four-volume report of extensive study of consumer credit in the United States. Contains extensive bibliographic footnotes.

Calder, Lendol. *Financing the American Dream: A Cultural History of Consumer Credit*. Princeton, 1999. Argues that the rise of consumer credit in America created worker discipline.

Goldsmith, Raymond W. *A Study of Saving in the United States*, vol. 1. Princeton, 1955. The classic study of saving, replete with a multitude of data and thorough source notes.

Johnson, Paul. *Saving and Spending: The Working-Class Economy in Britain, 1870–1939*. Oxford, 1985. Chapter 6 provides thorough history of credit use in Britain, including extensive discussion of pawnbroking.

Mandell, Lewis. *The Credit Card Industry: A History*. Boston, 1990. A thorough history of the credit-card industry in the United States, but the absence of any footnotes or bibliography limits its usefulness.

Mishkin, Frederic S. "The Household Balance Sheet and the Great Depression." *Journal of Economic History* 38 (December 1978), 918–937. Argues for separate consideration of household assets and liabilities in the determination of household spending.

Olney, Martha L. *Buy Now, Pay Later: Advertising, Credit, and Consumer Durables in the 1920s*. Chapel Hill, N.C., 1991. Links the rise of installment credit and consumer durables revolution. Chapter 4 focuses on credit.

Olney, Martha L. "Avoiding Default: The Role of Credit in the Consumption Collapse of 1930." *Quarterly Journal of Economics* 114 (February 1999), 319–335. Argues the consumption collapse in the United States during the Great Depression was a unique response to rapid 1920s growth in installments financing coupled with severe penalties for default.

Phelps, Clyde William. *The Role of the Sales Finance Companies in the American Economy*. Baltimore, 1952. Published by a sales finance company, contains a thorough history of the sales finance industry in the United States.

Robinson, Louis N., and Rolf Nugent. *Regulation of the Small Loan Business*. New York, 1935. A perspective on small lending from the architects of United States small-lending regulation.

Seligman, Edwin R. A. *The Economics of Installment Selling: A Study in Consumers' Credit with Special Reference to the Automobile*. New York, 1927. An epic study of installment credit, solicited by General Motors but widely regarded as objective and thorough.

MARTHA L. OLNEY

CONSUMPTION *[This entry contains four subentries, on consumer durables, leisure, non-durables, and services.]*

Consumer Durables

Consumer durables are defined as goods purchased by consumers for use over a relatively long period of time. The distinction between a nondurable and a durable good is thus a matter of degree. Undoubtedly, there have always been durable and nondurable goods—from the early caveman and cavewoman to contemporaries in the high-tech global economy; but for the purposes of this article, the emphasis is on that class of durable goods associated with the rise of the mass market for durables, such as automobiles and household appliances, which date from the turn of the twentieth century.

The phenomenon is associated at least initially with developed economies, where disposable incomes were such that the large majority of the population were able to extend their purchases beyond the necessities of food, clothing, fuel, and shelter to a range of other goods that promised new experiences in leisure activities (radio, television, videocassette recorder, car) and/or to alleviate some of the hard manual work involved in housework (washing machines, vacuum cleaners, freezers). Consumer durables treated in these terms relate to those goods that ultimately came to be enjoyed by the majority of the population and thereby excludes those that were acquired only by the more affluent in previous centuries (Brewer and Porter, 1993).

For economic and social historians, the phenomenon is of interest for three distinct, not necessarily mutually exclusive, areas of inquiry: what explains the diffusion of consumer durables through society, what are the implications of this diffusion for the economy as a whole, and what are the implications for the household and for the individual? The study of consumer durables is of intrinsic interest in its own right, but also for the wider implications for the economy and society. It is a subject that has attracted macroeconomists wishing to incorporate specific expenditure patterns into predictions of economic growth, social historians assessing the impact of changing patterns of leisure, feminist historians working on the use of time in the home and women's labor force participation, as well as microhistorians working on technological change in industry. The aim here is to highlight key areas of interest and debate for different branches of the economic history profession.

What explains how and why consumer durables diffuse through society? Three main theories have been used: macroanalyses of consumer demand, diffusion models, and new home economics. Macroanalysis concentrates on explaining expenditure on durable goods over time and has identified price, income, depreciation, existing stocks, and household formation as the important influences. In these terms, demand for consumer durables is explained in terms of price and income effects, but also in terms of the need for new and replacement goods. Diffusion models were initially based on the work of epidemiologists in their study of the spread of disease through society. The spread of consumer durables was likened to the spread of an infectious illness, was plotted as an S-shaped (sigmoid) curve, and drew attention to specific stages in the development of markets for such goods. A three-stage process was identified: initially the goods are expensive, are perceived as luxuries, and are bought by only the most affluent. The second stage is associated with diffusion through the "middling" ranks of society, while the third describes mass production for a mass market. Both macro- and diffusion analysis stress the importance of income and price effects. Diffusion models, however, add technological change as the instrumental variable that causes inflection points in the curve leading to different stages in the process. It is technology that leads to the price reductions, which makes the goods ultimately affordable to the majority of the population. The additional insight was that of "contagion," which underlined the importance of understanding how and why consumers learned of new goods and acquired the desire to own them (Deaton and Muellbauer, 1980; Houthakker and Taylor, 1970; Pyatt, 1964). The third approach is grounded in household supply decision, where consumer durables are treated as an input into household production (Becker, 1991). Instead of aggregate income and price effects, this stresses household formation, the allocation of work in the home, and the labor supply decision of household members.

The implications of such patterns for the household and for the economy are less easily understood, but have in the literature revealed important linkages between consumer durable acquisition and a range of key areas of interest. We have already stressed the importance of technological change as the key supply-side factor explaining how and why such goods came within the province of the majority of consumers. This in turn has been linked to changes in the production processes (for example, the mass production of motor vehicles) and to institutional change. Investigations into the price effects, for example, have revealed that purchase costs alone do not explain diffusion patterns: the supply of credit has been equally instrumental. This, in turn, has led to investigations into the role of financial institutions in identifying and then supplying hire purchase and rental credit. Innovation in the financial markets has thus been an important factor in the growth of demand for consumer goods (Olney, 1991). Contagion theories may stress inflection points and income and price effects as explanatory variables in the growth process, but they also see the diffusion of durable goods as depending on "infection," that is, they see the desire to own such goods as largely a matter of learning, imitation, and information. Not surprisingly, advertising, the role of the media, and cultural norms thus become key components of our understanding of how and why consumers acquire the information and the taste for consumer durable acquisition (Olney, 1991).

What are the implications for the economy? Consumer durable acquisition, unlike food, may be postponed, particularly where consumers are seeking to replace existing goods. Consumers can choose to delay purchases. Such decisions, in the aggregate, may cause large fluctuations in expenditure and thus instability in the economy. In some periods, fluctuations have been deliberately used as policy to control expenditure, as in the 1950s and 1960s in the United Kingdom. Control of consumer expenditure became an instrinsic part of macroeconomic policy as expansion of aggregate demand was seen as a necessary component of growth strategy. But such a policy was also inconsistent with balance-of-payments equilibrium under a fixed exchange-rate regime. Hence the 1950s and 1960s were characterized by abrupt switches in policy between periods of expanding demand to stimulate growth and restrictive practices to counter the resulting balance-of-payments deficits. In both periods, changes in marginal tax rates, short-run interest rate shifts, and hire-purchase controls directed to containing overall levels of aggregate demand fell particularly on consumer durables, whose purchase could be delayed. Consumer durable acquisition thus became an integral part of the public policy regime in this period—and hence of critics who see the attempt to manage the economy through controls of household expenditure at this time as undermining the United Kingdom's comparative economic growth.

Consumer durables are also, and increasingly, seen as crucial in our understanding of the household labor supply decision and in particular in the role of women in the home and in the paid labor market. The gender implications of the diffusion of consumer durables has been one of the most fruitful avenues of research in recent years, reflecting in part the profusion of work by feminist historians seeking to understand continuity and change in women's lives over time. In theory, one might expect the introduction of goods that promised to reduce the hard physical labor involved in housework as making a significant difference in the lives of women.

In practice, scholars have questioned whether such promises were realized (Cowan, 1983; de Grazia and Furlogh, 1991; Hardyment, 1998). Household technology did not reallocate work in the home away from women, nor did it necessarily release their time: consumer durables never questioned cultural norms that housework was "women's work," nor could they overcome patriarchal norms in the workplace that assigned low-paid, low-status jobs to women. In the wider scheme of economic and social analyses, fertility control, access to education, and a reduction of discrimination in the workplace have been more important in women's lives than have consumer durables. Consumer goods designed to alleviate housework have certainly reduced the physical toil of housework and thereby improved the lives of many women, but most historians would now question their impact on labor-force participation patterns or indeed the allocation of work within the home. Now, as in the past, most housework is performed by women—whether or not they are in paid work outside the home. Analyses of patterns of consumption moreover have suggested that households have assigned greater priority to leisure goods rather than housework goods, a preference, as some historians have termed it, for time-using rather than time-saving goods (Bowden and Offer, 1994). The consumer durable that takes care of children has yet to be invented.

[*See also* Luxury Trades.]

BIBLIOGRAPHY

Becker, G. S. *A Treatise on the Family.* Cambridge, Mass., 1991.

Bowden, Susan, and Avner Offer. "Household Appliances and the Use of Time: The United States and Britain since the 1920s." *Economic History Review* 47.4 (November 1994), 725–748.

Brewer, John, and Roy Porter, eds. *Consumption and the World of Goods.* London, 1993.

Cowan, Ruth S. *More Work for Mother: The Ironies of Household Technology from the Open Hearth to the Microwave.* New York, 1983.

Deaton, Angus, and John Muellbauer. *Economics and Consumer Behaviour.* Cambridge, 1980.

De Grazia, Victoria, and Ellen Furlough, eds. *The Sex of Things: Gender and Consumption in Historical Perspective.* Berkeley, 1991.

Dunnett, Peter J. S. *The Decline of the British Motor Industry: Effects of Government Policy, 1945–1979.* London, 1980.

Hardyment, Christina. *From Mangle to Microwave: the Mechanisation of Household Work.* Cambridge, 1988.

Houthakker, H. S., and L. D. Taylor. *Consumer Demand in the United States: Analyses and Projections.* 2d ed. Cambridge, Mass., 1970.

Olney, Martha L. *Buy Now, Pay Later: Advertising, Credit, and Consumer Durables in the 1920s.* Chapel Hill, N.C., 1991.

Pyatt, F. G. *Priority Patterns and the Demand for Household Durable Goods.* Cambridge, 1964.

SUE BOWDEN

Leisure

Peasant Society. Within the confines of peasant society, the individual's labor and leisure activities formed an integral part of a far wider behavioral pattern. Via a linked system of landholding, social status, work intensity, and consumption, this behavioral pattern extended to every aspect of village life. Viewed in a secular perspective, it was only from the eleventh century that the archetypal two-or-three-field system and associated village complex of peasant holdings firmly established itself on the European scene. Then for almost a millennium all over Europe, where this agrarian regime prevailed, the peasant, in order to achieve his hierarchically determined levels of con-

sumption, established a common but complex pattern of labor deployment. This included up to 264 workdays per year for each family member. This comprised about 144 days of farm work, necessary to satisfy familial self-consumption, and 120 days of "dead time" when, free from the agricultural round, labor could be deployed in commerce and/or manufacturing to provide for familial cash requirements. Thus, in periods of high population pressure and weak labor markets, as in the late thirteenth and sixteenth centuries, peasants in England and Poland fully utilized the "dead time" available to them, working the full complement of 264 days. With the reduction in seigniorial obligations in fifteenth-century England or post-Emancipation Russia, however, the peasant was able to substitute leisure for cash, in the latter instance creating popular, so-called *bytovye* holidays.

The corollary of this hierarchically ordered and technologically determined system of work was an equally structured program of nonwork or leisure. It encompassed both a fixed element of about 100 days and a variable one of up to 120 days a year, available to the peasant after he had satisfied the family's cash requirements. This time was not, however, homogeneous and varied in nature, utility, and form. Within the fixed hundred or so holy days, ordained by the church for man's rest, the peasant enjoyed a series of holidays, sanctified by the church, which marked the high points of the agricultural year. In part they afforded the relaxation necessary after periods of sustained labor. Their significance within the peasant community was, however, far wider than that. They were also the occasion to propitiate those unseen forces that controlled the villagers' agricultural destiny with ceremonies to secure fertility and good weather, and times when they sought to sanctify that social order ordained by God to control and direct the vagaries inherent in their own nature. God's time was therefore common time, when the whole village relaxed and took the opportunity to assuage common fears, anxieties, and to assert common values. Yet its importance should not be exaggerated.

Those days chosen by the villagers themselves for their relaxation were of much greater significance. Amid that considerable amount of unsanctified time, certain periods enjoyed a fixity and importance that was paralleled only in the observance of the major holy days. Even when forced by economic circumstances to abandon their free time, they clung with such an extraordinary tenacity to certain days in January and February (Saturnalia or the Feast of Fools) and May (Floralia) that it is impossible to doubt the significance of these holidays. As in the case of the holy days, these civil festivities were sanctioned for much more than bodily rests. While both men and women utilized the holy day to reveal the lighter side of their character in corporate displays of thanksgiving, so they employed these civil days of profanity to reveal the darker side of their natures. These were times of rebellion against the proper order of things. Acts were committed that were explicable only in terms of the periodic release necessary in a rigidly ordered, hierarchical society.

In the realms of labor and leisure, such time, when the calendar day coincided with the work- or leisure day to create a round of uninterrupted activity, was, however, exceptional. Labor and leisure were normally inextricably intertwined on an intradiurnal basis. The peasant's normative experiences were encompassed within the realms of flexible time. This could be structured to emphasize differences in status or permitted those adjustments, which the peasant had to make, in changing economic circumstances in order to maintain their state of material prosperity. How such adjustments were made can best be illustrated in terms of an important element in the diurnal round—mealtimes. William Harrison, topographer, in 1570, considering the period of some forty years since his youth, during which the peasantry had increasingly to work to maintain their earnings, declared that,

> "Heretofore there has been much time spent in eating and drinking than commonly is in these days, for whereas of old we had breakfasts in the forenoon, beverages or nuncheons after dinner, and thereto reresuppers (ie. second or late suppers)generally when it was time to go to rest. . . . Now these odd repasts . . . are very well left and each one in manner . . . contented himself with dinner and supper only. . . ."

In this instance, during the years from about 1530 to 1570, the English peasants, being forced to work harder in order to maintain their material prosperity, secured the time for this extra work by abandoning breakfast and afternoon drinking.

Throughout that period, from the eleventh to the nineteenth century and beyond, where a two-or-three-field system and a nucleated village complex prevailed and provided the spatial environment for a peasant society, leisure time continued to provide the peasantry with opportunities for many activities. It afforded them playtime to take their bodily ease and recreation. It provided liturgical time to praise their God, and common time to assuage their mutual fears, dissipate tensions, and affirm their allegiance to a common value system.

Urban Society. The experience of those who enjoyed the status of industrial worker or townsman at this time did not differ greatly from that of their brethren in the countryside. Life continued to move to the tempo of the agricultural round, craft activity displaying marked temporal discontinuities as men set aside their tools to work in the town fields. A common work pattern, moreover, engendered a common pattern of leisure activity. Urban ceremonials paralleled in both their form and function those of the countryside. Subsequently, as improved agricultural supply systems allowed the townsman to divorce himself from the round of rustic pursuits, and an unfavorable demographic regime necessitated a continuous inmigration from the countryside, time here assumed a more specific and measured character, but within an allocatory structure, which continued to extol traditional values. At this time, the prevailing ordering of leisure time changed only through extension. In Scotland, the monarch's birthday was publicly celebrated from the time of the Restoration of King Charles II. On such occasions in the burghs, the authorities directed festivities along theatrical lines. In a variety of ways, during the daytime at least, the urban elites were able to exemplify, in the form of the festivities, the traditional virtues of corporate identity and the hierarchical ordering within their community as well as providing a show of their own loyalty to the monarchy. As night fell, however, they were forced to surrender their control over leisure time to the lower orders. In such a way, men were able once again by traditional means to provide themselves with a release from the constraints of a highly ordered civil society and to indulge the baser instincts, which had been suppressed throughout the rest of the year.

Effects of Economic Growth. Economic growth, first experienced in the northwestern European nations (England and the Low Countries), totally transformed the environment in which the populace both worked and played. Improved agricultural supply systems allowed those engaged in industrial-commercial activity, to divorce themselves from the round of rustic pursuits and assume a functionally separate identity from the farmer and agricultural laborer. This trend, moreover, was reinforced contemporaneously by changes in labor markets. Relentless population pressure, which was felt throughout Europe, when combined with technological change in Anglo-Netherlands agriculture, fundamentally undermined the position of the peasant producer. By the mid-seventeenth century, the peasants' position had become untenable as the dependent elements of their value system became mutually incompatible. Over the next half century, some of them joined the ranks of "cottagers-paupers." Others abandoned peasant society. They assumed the work ethic of the "professional" laborer. Yet it would be anachronistic to perceive members of this new labor force in modern terms. A minor ideology, which had characterized a diminutive group within peasant society, in England during the late seventeenth century had come to command almost universal acceptance.

At the beginning of the eighteenth century, therefore, industrial and commercial activity enjoyed a no more prominent position (in terms of share in employment or national income) in the English economy than it had in

CONSUMPTION. *Peasant Wedding,* painting by Peter Bruegel the Elder, c. 1565. (Kunsthistorisches Museum, Vienna)

1500. Yet the old symbiotic relationship, which had existed between the two activities in peasant society, had been split asunder. Industrial-commercial and agricultural workers came to inhabit separate and discrete worlds. They labored to new rhythms, conditioned not only by changing economic circumstances but also by the work disciplines of the newly emergent forms of industrial organization. This was particularly noticeable in the work patterns of those enterprises that operated on a small-scale, often workshop basis. Here the hinge on which the week swung was the payment for work done on Saturday night. With no set hours, the week would have a desultory start and gradually pick up the tempo toward a final burst of intense activity, up to eighteen hours at a stretch, on Friday and Saturday. Work would often be ignored completely on Monday, and even again on the next day—Saint Monday and Holy Tuesday had become the workers' sardonic response to the loss of the old saints' days from the holiday calendar. In terms of its incidence, this work regime peaked in the first two decades of the nineteenth century but declined extremely quickly thereafter. In the mining industries, and particularly coal mining, it persisted much longer. In England and the United States, seasonal demand patterns and a differential access to markets, coupled with a supply heterogeneity across mines, all served to limit operational time to only 220 to 240 days per year, perpetuating a pattern of labor and leisure similar to that in urban workshops.

The Nineteenth Century to Modern Times. From the 1830s, however, as the impact of the Industrial Revolution made itself felt in England and factory production became the norm, a new pattern was superimposed on the workers' patterns of labor and leisure: a working year of 286 to 308 working days divided into 5½- to 6-day working weeks. This pattern of labor and leisure time, moreover, was not long in universalizing itself. Nor was this process confined to the English-speaking world, which rapidly assimilated the mores of the English Industrial Revolution, sometimes with even greater fervor than in England, as was found in the United States with a late-nineteenth-century norm of a 308-day working year. Even in a nation like Russia, where traditional patterns of labor and leisure persisted among the peasantry, factory workers labored in accordance with internationally recognized norms—on average toiling some 308 days (of ten hours each) a year. Local traditions could be maintained, but only if they could be accommodated in terms of those norms. The pattern for the future was clear. Whenever and wherever the factory was established, so too was its discipline.

To maintain the new system, it was necessary for factory owners to impose an increasing intensity of labor on their workforces. The task was a formidable one, but as late-seventeenth-century Englishmen of the "industrious sort" were only too aware when they chided the laborer for his idleness and underconsumption, what was required was structural change—a permanent upward shift in levels of the workers' income expectations. In part such a process was inherent in the process of innovation, widening the range of consumer goods available. More important perhaps was the commercialization of leisure itself. Entrepreneurs, by tapping into the leisure time of a heterogeneous labor force and evolving imaginative methods of realizing cash from the promotion of sporting activities, were able to establish a widely based, high-profile consumer service industry. Already by 1800 in England the commercialization of leisure had been achieved. During subsequent years, in the English-speaking world (the United Kingdom, United States, and Australia) at least such entrepreneurs ensured that their products would figure significantly in the widening consumption packages of the working population. The workers steadily increased their labor intensity in order, at least in part, to enjoy the leisure they had left to them.

Elsewhere the situation was very different. In pre-Revolutionary Russia, the impetus to the introduction of Western-style sports came from members of the foreign managerial group, who saw in the organization of soccer teams, the opportunity to alleviate social tensions and encourage corporate loyalties among the workforce. Nor was this situation exceptional in continental Europe. The absence of a popular sports tradition dating from preindustrial times and the relative backwardness of commercialization combined here, as in pre-Revolutionary Russia, to limit the development of commercialized leisure for a working-class market. "English sports" were largely introduced into the new industrial towns via the initiatives of members of the new urban elites (Agnelli and Fiat in Milan, Peugeot in Sochaux, the textile industry in northern France, and Bata' in Prague). It was only in the 1950s that here, sporting activities emancipated themselves from such narrow industrial objectives. Rapidly rising incomes provided an increasingly large proportion of the population with the means to acquire the products of sporting promoters. Symptomatic of the age was the creation in 1955 of the European Cup, which every year is having more success and is attracting a wider public. Support of a team was no longer confined to a narrow industrial milieu. It provided a point of identification for the individual in relation to his local community and his nation—an affirmation of his position in the prevailing civil order. It also provided the environment for rebellion against that civil order. Alienation found expression in soccer hooliganism. Illicit market forces provided the occasions for uncontrolled indulgence in violence, sex, and drugs providing that release from the constraints of a highly ordered civil society and allowing the indulgence of those baser instincts, which had been suppressed throughout the rest of the year.

BIBLIOGRAPHY

Archbald, Hugh. *The Four Hour Day in Coal.* New York, 1922.

Blanchard, Ian. "Consumption and Hierarchy in English Peasant Society, 1400–1600." *Chicago Economic History Workshop Papers* 20 (1980), 1–12.

Blanchard, Ian. "Konsumpcja ne wsi angielskiej, 1580–1680 (English Peasant Consumption: The End of an Epoch, 1580–1680)." *Kwartalnik Historii Kultury Materialnij* 30.1 (1982), 27–42.

Blanchard, Ian, ed. *Labour and Leisure in Historical Perspective, Thirteenth to Twentieth Centuries.* Stuttgart, 1994.

Bogucka, Maria. "Space and Time as Factors Shaping Polish Mentality from the 16th to the 17th Century." *Acta Poloniae Historica* 66 (1992), 40–62.

James, Mervyn. "Ritual, Drama, and Social Body in the Late Medieval English Town." *Past and Present* 98 (1983), 3–29.

Malcolmson, Robert W. *Popular Recreations in English Society, 1700–1850.* Cambridge, 1973.

Reid, Douglas. A. "The Decline of Saint Monday, 1766–1876." *Past and Present* 71 (1976), 76–101.

IAN BLANCHARD

Non-Durables

Non-durable goods sustain life. Of the three essentials of Homo sapiens' material existence—food, clothing, and shelter—the first two are non-durables. Indeed, throughout most of human existence, the quest for non-durables dominated all other economic activity. In the most primitive societies, non-durable consumption meant, literally, the ingestion of plants and animals, and it was the difference between life and death. A larger and more diverse set of consumer goods and services accompanied the economic development of the past six millennia or so. Indeed, the diminution of the relative importance of the essential nondurables has been a key indicator of that progress. In more recent centuries, the monetization of market transactions determined the way consumers obtained goods and services and the way economists came to define and measure consumption. Today, among economists, the term generally means an expenditure for some good or service, and it is a key indicator of economic well-being over time and across countries.

The importance of consumption as an economic indicator has a long history. In *Inquiry into the Nature and Causes of the Wealth of Nations* (1789, vol. 1, p. 179), Adam Smith claimed. "Consumption is the sole end and purpose of all production," Despite this admonition, historically, when analyzing economic well-being, economists relied more heavily on production and income data than on consumption data. Indeed, to this day, much of the consumption data in the national income and product accounts are generated from production figures. Partly, this situation results from the relative difficulty of obtaining consumption data, at least at the household level. From the time economic activity was first organized outside the household, there were many more consuming units than there were producing units, and a large proportion of consumption was of home-produced goods consumed behind closed doors. Also, for various reasons (often associated with tax and customs collecting, census taking, and so forth), governments collected more output and income data than consumption data. As a result, economic historians have reconstructed a much less extensive set of cross-country time series on consumption than they have on production. These difficulties notwithstanding, the importance of consumption in interpreting long-run economic growth and cyclical activity, among other things, has led to the collection of a large body of consumption data.

Although the classifications and major categories vary somewhat from country to country and across agencies that collect consumption data, non-durable goods typically include expenditures for food and beverages, clothing and shoes, fuel for private transportation, fuel for heating, tobacco, toiletries, stationery, and newspapers. Generally speaking, these data are available from two primary sources. The national income and product accounts include aggregate consumption of non-durables by category, and household-level surveys typically include consumption by households of various incomes or demographic groups.

The aggregate figures, which represent an important part of the expenditure side of national income, are generally derived from one of two techniques. The so-called direct method involves the actual collection of sales data, typically at the retail level. Because such data are not always available, the so-called commodity flow method is also used. Interestingly, commodity flow figures are actually output data adjusted for transportation costs, markup, net exports, and inventory changes. Today, these data are typically collected and processed by national governments, such as the U.S. Commerce Department's Bureau of Economic Analysis, or other agencies, such as the United Nations (UN) or the Organization for Economic Cooperation and Development (OECD). The OECD, for example, reports non-durable consumption data for many countries in its *Quarterly National Accounts*, and the UN has published figures on at least some non-durable consumption categories for many countries since 1950. For a handful of countries, economic historians have reconstructed consumption figures, including non-durable categories, back to the nineteenth century. Most notable for their length, range, and consistency among these efforts are the U.S. estimates derived by Stanley Lebergott (1993, 1996) and the British figures produced by Charles Feinstein (1972).

Since time immemorial, the primary components of consumption have been the two main non-durable categories: food (including beverages) and clothing. The nineteenth-century German statistician Ernst Engel posited, among other things, that the proportion of income spent on food would decline as incomes rose, while that spent on clothing would remain relatively constant (Engel's Laws). In recent centuries, at least at the aggregate level, the shares of income spent on both food and clothing have fallen. Today, overall consumption represents roughly 60 to 70 percent of gross domestic product (GDP) in the leading industrial countries of Japan, the United Kingdom, and the United States, and non-durable consumption composes between 20 and 30 percent of consumption in those countries. These ratios tend to be higher in earlier stages of economic development, and in general, non-durables' share of consumption has been falling since as far back as aggregate data are available, a phenomenon that has generally accompanied modern economic growth. In the United States, for example, food and clothing alone composed nearly 75 percent of consumption expenditures in 1900, and in the United Kingdom, as late as 1950, more than half of consumption expenditures still went toward purchases of food and clothing.

The aggregate results often mask interesting behavior at the household level, so the other primary source of non-durable consumption data comes directly from records of household consumption or expenditures. Prior to the late nineteenth century, these data were generated from surveys typically of poor or working-class households and typically during periods of economic distress. The data from many of these original studies, surveys, and so forth have subsequently been processed and their data made available by government agencies or scholars. As a result, the citations, summaries, and in some cases actual data from these original sources are in secondary sources. For example, George Grantham (1993) summarizes some early (pre-1850) French surveys; Sally Horrell and Jane Humphries (1992) do the same for the United Kingdom before 1880; Lee A. Craig (2002) reviews the U.S. efforts after 1880; and C. Zimmerman and F. Williams (1935) describe household expenditure studies from a number of other countries between 1850 and the early 1930s. In more recent decades, national governments have occasionally maintained such surveys. In the United States, for example, the Department of Labor has conducted consumer expenditure surveys since the 1950s.

Because the non-durable consumption data contain, among other things, information on food consumption, they generally play a key role in any number of historical debates concerning the standard of living, economic growth, business cycles, and the distribution of income. For example, agriculture's role in industrialization in the eighteenth and nineteenth centuries is linked with the amount of food that ultimately left the farm to be

Food. Store in Vienna, Austria, 1984. (© Adam Woolfitt/Woodfin Camp and Associates, New York)

consumed by nonagricultural households. If one subtracts the food consumed by farm households from farm production, then the remainder represents an estimate of the marketable surpluses that could be consumed by nonagricultural households and therefore the potential amount of agricultural labor that could be released for industrialization. More on-farm consumption suggests smaller marketable surpluses, and thus less labor could be "released" from the agricultural sector (Grantham, 1993, 1995).

Although Engel observed that food consumption did not rise proportionally with income, the very nature of food consumption changed with the rising incomes that accompanied modern economic growth. Specifically, the ratio of the value of food and beverage products ultimately consumed to the initial value of food and beverages as agricultural products rose fairly dramatically (roughly 50 percent) during industrialization (Clark et al., 1995), which demonstrates that the processing, transporting, and marketing of food increased in relative importance over time. In addition, in Britain at least, the composition of consumption changed as well, with alcohol, tea, and sugar among the most prominent gainers, suggesting that higher incomes were used disproportionally to purchase goods other than those containing basic nutrients. Even after 1850, there were further increases in the consumption of tobacco, tea, and sugar (Mokyr, 1988), reinforcing the point.

In one way or another, many of the debates concerning the major components of non-durable consumption ultimately compose part of a larger debate among economic historians on the interpretation of industrialization and the onset of modern economic growth (Mokyr, 1988). The evidence from standard economic indicators, such as incomes, wages, and aggregate consumption, suggests an "optimistic" interpretation of early economic growth; however, other measures, such as mortality, stature, and the distributions of income and consumption, suggest, though not without controversy, a more "pessimistic" interpretation. The future of these debates will continue to depend partly though crucially on the history of the patterns of non-durable consumption.

The changing composition of non-durable consumption has also played an important role in interpreting changes in and among socioeconomic classes over time. Economic growth tends to have two impacts on the distribution of incomes. While growth typically shifts the entire distribution upward, not all classes move up at the same rate, thus the "economic distance" between classes changes with growth. Furthermore, changes in consumption do not necessarily match those of income. Employing U.S. household-level surveys, Clair Brown (1994) found that although income inequality increased over the course of the twentieth century—that is, the distance between classes increased—measures of distance in consumption actually narrowed—that is, the variety and "status" of goods consumed by the poorer classes grew more rapidly than their incomes. There are two reasons for this apparently paradoxical finding. First, as noted, the consumption of the basic non-durables, food and clothing, does not expand proportionally with income. Thus, beyond some elemental level, increases in income are disproportionly spent on variety and status goods—a class interpretation of Engel's Law. Second, by the end of the twentieth century, households in the lowest socioeconomic classes consumed roughly 14 percent more than their incomes (Craig, 2002), a result largely attributable to government transfers.

BIBLIOGRAPHY

Brown, Clair. *American Standards of Living, 1918–1988.* Oxford, 1994.

Clark, Gregory, Michael Huberman, and Peter H. Lindert. "A British Food Puzzle, 1770–1850." *Economic History Review* 48.2 (1995), 215–237.

Craig, Lee A. "Consumer Expenditures." In *Historical Statistics of the United States,* millennial ed. New York, 2002.

Grantham, George W. "Divisions of Labour: Agricultural Productivity and Occupational Specialization in Pre-Industrial France." *Economic History Review* 46.3 (1993), 478–502.

Grantham, George W. "Food Rations in France in the Eighteenth and Nineteenth Centuries: A Reply." *Economic History Review* 48.4 (1995), 774–777.

Feinstein, Charles H. *National Income, Expenditure, and Output of the United Kingdom, 1855–1965.* Cambridge, 1972.

Horrell, Sally, and Jane Humphries. "Old Questions, New Data, and Alternative Perspectives: Families' Living Standards in the Industrial Revolution." *Journal of Economic History* 52.4 (1992), 849–880.

Lebergott, Stanley. *Pursuing Happiness: American Consumers in the Twentieth Century.* Princeton, 1993.

Lebergott, Stanley. *Consumer Expenditures: New Measures and Old Motives.* Princeton, 1996.

Mokyr, Joel. "Is There Still Life in the Pessimists' Case? Consumption during the Industrial Revolution." *Journal of Economic History* 48.1 (1988), 69–92.

Toutain, J.-C. "Food Rations in France in the Eighteenth and Nineteenth Centuries: A Comment." *Economic History Review* 48.4 (1995), 769–773.

Zimmerman, Carle C., and Faith Williams. *Studies in Family Living in the United States and Other Countries.* Washington, D.C., 1935.

LEE A. CRAIG

Services

The meaning of services and their place in consumption and production have been discussed for many years. Some early observers maintained that all production consists of services. In *The Nature of Capital and Income,* Irving Fisher suggested the following definition: "An instrument renders a service when, by its means, a desirable event is promoted or an undesirable event prevented" (p. 336). An instrument here is an "individual article of wealth" (p. 333), but services could also be provided by human beings. "For instance, the services of a loom consist in changing yarn into cloth, or what is called weaving. Similarly, a plow performs the service of changing the soil in a particular manner; a bricklayer, of changing the positions of bricks . . ." (p. 19).

Definitions. A common definition today focuses on differences between commodities and services. A commodity can be weighed, measured, touched (in principle), and stored; but these characteristics do not pertain to services, which are immaterial and thus not storable or transportable. Services are said to be produced and consumed in one and the same moment in an interaction between a producer and a consumer. A related definition is that a service means a change in the condition of a person or a good belonging to some economic unit brought about as a result of the activity of some other economic unit, with prior agreement between the persons or the economic units. However, all definitions are problematic because services are very heterogeneous, perhaps more so than goods. It is often maintained that the productivity of service production has grown at a slower pace than that of goods production, or even has been unchanged. An example is that the time required for an orchestra to play a certain symphony by Beethoven has not changed since his lifetime. However, this is not necessarily a good illustration because productivity also is concerned with the quality of the service. Moreover, there are questions of, for instance, how to play the symphony, the quality of the musical instruments, concert venues, amplifiers, and so on, as well as the number of people who can listen to the orchestra. The music could be played in a concert hall for three hundred listeners or on television for an audience of one million. It also could be recorded, and then a great number of people could listen to it for many years. The latter situation is sometimes regarded as a shift of demand from services to goods, that is, from the services produced in a concert hall to the use of recording at home. Similar examples include changing from cinema to video cassette recorders and from commercial laundries to washing machines. These examples suggest how tricky definitions of production and consumption of goods and services are. Should, for instance, part of the listening to a compact disc (CD) be regarded as service consumption and part as goods consumption, and if so, how should one discriminate between these categories? Consequently, it is advisable to use practical definitions of services, which is particularly important in a historical context.

The symphony case is an example of Baumol's cost disease, namely, that the relative prices in a technologically nonprogressive sector—in this case the one providing cultural services—increase over time, and the same is true for employment shares. Thus the nominal but not the deflated output share of the nonprogressive sector increases over time. Relatively more and more resources must be devoted to this sector if it is to remain viable, and these resources are taken from the "productive" parts of the economy. This phenomenon is said to be characteristic of a large portion of the service sector, which therefore grew in the second half of the twentieth century.

Services generally include anything from totally unqualified work such as selling newspapers on the street to work performed by "superskilled" people with specialized education. Production and productivity changes over time also can vary greatly between different sectors of the economy. This great variation is illustrated by the following classification (or some variation of it), which is used in historical national accounts.

Transport and communication	*Private services*	*Public services*
Bus traffic	Attorneys	Military services
Coach services	Pharmacies	Ecclesiastical services
Domestic aviation	Banking	Education
Foreign aviation	Private health care	Health care
Horse-drawn transports	Hair dressers	Administration
International shipping	Insurance	Police
Lorry traffic	Retail and wholesale trade	Fire brigades
Postal services	Hotels and restaurants	Sanitation
Railways	Cultural and amusement services	
Stevedoring		
Taxi traffic	Religious services (other than public church)	
Telecommunications		
Timber-floating	Dentists and doctors	
Tramways	Veterinarians	
	Paid domestic services	
	Unpaid domestic services	
	Services of wellings	

Such a categorization could also be made in other ways. In an economic-historical context the following division could be used:

- *New services*: education, medical services, social care.

- *Goods-related services*: transport services, trade, banking and insurance, legal services, hotels and restaurants.
- *Society-related services*: administration, maintenance of law and order (the night-watcher's state services).
- *Old services*: paid domestic services, religious services.

These categories are not pure and simple; instead, they overlap. Part of banking and insurance could, for instance, be allocated to society-related services, or to new services. Generally, however, this distribution provides an appropriate basis for analyzing changes over time.

Quantitative Issues. In the late 1990s, according to the Organization for Economic Cooperation and Development (OECD), services constituted more than 70 percent of total production in a number of wealthy countries, for instance, the United States, Denmark, and France, and the arithmetic average for all OECD countries was 67 percent. Agriculture with its ancillaries made up only a small fraction, on average slightly over 3 percent, and industry about 30 percent. In looking at historical performance, a typical and familiar pattern can be discerned. In the course of economic growth, agriculture's share has gone down conspicuously, and industry's share has increased, but that increase has become smaller, and in the decades following World War II it was even reversed to a decrease. Meanwhile services, whose proportion for many years had changed erratically or grown more slowly than that of industry, began to expand.

The composition of expenditures has changed in a similar way, linked to changes in demand patterns. Over time, total private consumption as a fraction of gross domestic product (GDP) has diminished while the shares of investment and government consumption have grown. Within private consumption, tendencies differ between different countries as to service-share changes. Private service consumption often has decreased or remained rather stable as a proportion of GDP but increased in relation to private goods consumption. Taken together, the total service share, that is, the sum of private and public service consumption in relation to total expenditures, has tended to grow. These tendencies can be illustrated with Swedish figures, which showed a clear picture of a long-term relative decrease in total consumption, from about 90 percent to 75 percent of GDP between 1875 and 1975. Conversely, there has been an expansion of investment's share of GDP. Within the relatively shrinking consumption, the private goods share decreased from 67 percent to 45 percent and private services from 18 percent to 12 percent of GDP. Public services meanwhile grew fourfold, from 5 percent to 21 percent, and thereby services as a whole increased. Thus, the long-term expanding parts of total expenditures were public services and investment. In recent decades these items have stayed at a high level.

New services, as defined above, are to a great extent performed under the auspices of the welfare society. Their share of total service production in Sweden increased from a few percentage points in the early nineteenth century to about one-third by the end of the twentieth century. During the same time span, old services decreased from around 25 percent to next to nothing. Taken together, the share of these two categories was about the same during the whole period or increased only slightly. Consequently, the other two categories (goods-related and society-related services), taken together, also showed small long-term changes, and this is also true for each of them individually. Thus, services for consumption did increase, but not very much, as a portion of total service production, and the increase was concentrated in the period after World War II.

Seen from another angle, service consumption has long grown at roughly the same pace as total production, as also mentioned above. In the postwar period, however, there was a distinct increase in service consumption relative to GDP, and in the 1990s this tendency was even more clear.

These changes are often alleged to characterize the present society as a "service society," a "postindustrial society," an "information society," a "knowledge society," or something similar. The reason for this is that services have become more and more important in production, employment, and other economic fields in comparison to goods. Whether these changes—which are also connected to the rapidly developing information and communication technology (ICT)—mean a radical change from an industrial society to something new is not at all clear. Therefore, the present society is sometimes also considered a neo-industrial society.

BIBLIOGRAPHY

Baumol, William J. "The Case for Subsidizing the Arts." *Challenge* 38 (September/October 1995), 52–56.

Baumol, William J., and William G. Bowen *Performing Arts: The Economic Dilemma*, New York, 1966.

Bryson, J. R., and P. W. Daniels *Service Industries in the Global Economy*, vols. 1 and 2. Cheltenham, U.K., 1998.

Elfring, Tom. *Service Employment in Advanced Economies. A Comparative Analysis of Its Implications for Economic Growth*. Groningen, 1988.

Fisher, Irving. *The Nature of Capital and Income*. London, 1906.

Gershuny, J. *After Industrial Society: The Emerging Self-Service Economy*. London, 1978.

Gershuny, J., and I. Miles. *The New Service Economy: The Transformation of Employment in Industrial Societies*. London, 1983.

Hill, T. P. "On Goods and Services." *Review of Income and Wealth* 23 (1977), 315–338.

Illeris, Sven, *The Service Economy: A Geographical Approach*. West Sussex, U.K., 1996.

Krantz, Olle. "New Estimates of Swedish Historical GDP since the Beginning of the Nineteenth Century." *Review of Income and Wealth*. 34 (1988), 165–181.

Krantz, Olle. "Service Production in Historical National Accounts." *Review of Income and Wealth* 40 (1994), 19–41.

Maddison, Angus. *Monitoring the World Economy*. Paris, 1995.

Tiongson, Erwin, R. "Baumol's Cost Disease Reconsidered." *Challenge* 40.6 (November/December 1997), 117–122.

OLLE KRANTZ

CONTRACT ENFORCEMENT AND LEGAL SYSTEMS.

Contracts are written or spoken agreements between or among individuals. The use of contracts through history has largely been as a commitment device in support of trade, which has long been an important source of growth and a conduit for new technology and new ideas. How does trade occur, though, between strangers? Philip Curtin defines the problem clearly: "People with a different way of life are strangers by definition; their ways seem unpredictable, and the unpredictable is probably dangerous as well. Communication itself is difficult . . . . These problems in cross-cultural understanding in general have meant that cross-trade has almost always been carried out through special institutional arrangements to help guarantee the mutual security of the two sides" (Curtin, 1984, p. 1).

Contracting is one of those important institutional arrangements. Typically, contracts imply some form of legal enforcement; the forms of legal enforcement have been varied and have changed over time. The changes in enforcement over time form the foundation of this summary, which focuses on trade with strangers, the use of trading agents, and the problem of ruler expropriation of merchant profits in return for contract enforcement. In all three of these cases, the sequential nature of the exchange creates a commitment problem and the associated need for enforcement. They all rely on the repeated interactions among merchants and customers, merchants and agents, and merchants and rulers to create value and often on the reputations formed in those repeated interactions as an enforcement tool. This survey concentrates on pre-eighteenth-century trade and contract enforcement, illustrating the evolution that led up to the legal, third-party institutional context of modern contracts.

Contract enforcement, whether formal or informal, is an important component of the institutional foundations of exchange. There are three general ways to solve the problem of whom to trust. The first is to rely on ethics, normative rules about behavior, to get people to be honest. The second is to use courts as third parties to enforce contracts. The final one is to structure relations so that contracts are self-enforcing. Contracts and the promise of enforcement reduce uncertainty, increase the probability of commitment on the parts of agents and trading partners, and increase the likelihood of and volume of trade. As with modern exchange and contracts, the focus is on the deterrence of bad behavior through creating expectations of what would happen as a consequence of breaching the contract.

Early Medieval Contracts. Changes in contract enforcement through history mirror the evolution of trading patterns. Specifically, contract enforcement institutions reflected and were shaped by technological change and patterns of trade (Greif, 2000, pp. 252–254). Trading patterns evolved from the tenth century onward in three general ways: from local trade among families and close-knit ethnic groups to long-distance trade among strangers; from personal exchange to impersonal exchange; and from self-enforcing contracts to third-party enforcement of contracts, reinforced by the development of nation-states by the fifteenth century. These changes and the institutional innovations supporting them captured the benefits of technological change in shipping, navigation, printing, and writing, among other things. These general patterns illustrate the extent to which contract enforcement is a matter of information, the ability to observe behavior and outcomes, the incentives that lead to mutually beneficial exchange, and trust.

The single most important change in trade and contract enforcement between the tenth century and the eighteenth century was the substantial increase in long-distance trade. Trustworthiness is crucial to the success of long-distance trading ventures. Depending on somebody else, an agent, to take goods far away and sell them on your behalf requires trusting that person. The circumstances around long-distance ventures pose special threats to the creation of trust arising from the very nature of the trade. Exchanges over long distances made it hard for partners to observe either trader effort or actual outcomes. Furthermore, in the early medieval period there was uncertainty about the duration of the trip, market conditions, pirates, and other variables that could affect the profitability of a voyage. Trading ventures were small-scale and personal, often self-financed, with the partners splitting up after each trip.

Early medieval trade, such as the trade around the Mediterranean rim in the tenth and eleventh centuries, relied on close family and cultural or religious connections to create incentives for traders to maximize profits from the principal's perspective. The share of trade that was impersonal or among strangers was relatively small. Other patterns of trade at the time reflect these characteristics, including internal trade in China (Elvin, 1973; Curtin, 1984, ch. 6) and internal European trade (McNeill, 1982). Curtin points out that cross-cultural trade that occurred in this period tended to take certain forms, in which the early

institution used to create commitment was the trade settlement. In trade settlements, merchants built relationships with local artisans and subsequently built networks of trade settlements. Over time, these networks became established trade routes (Curtin, 1984, p. 3; DeRoover, 1963; Williamson, 2001).

Avner Greif (1989) analyzed the self-enforcing long-distance trade contracts of the Maghribi Trade Coalition of Alexandria, Egypt. The details of his analysis illustrate the importance of reputation in enforcing contracts. Traders in the coalition operated under conditions of substantial uncertainty. They often had several trading ventures going at once, which allowed them to lower risks. Their relations were characterized by what seems to be an amazing amount of flexibility for the period. Traders delegated a great deal of authority to their agents, trusting them to make important business decisions on the spot. This trust was not based on the use of courts. There are few mentions of courts in the records, and when courts are mentioned, it is frequently to complain about how long they are taking to settle disputes.

The coalition combined several methods to ensure that its members had an incentive to remain honest. The first was to pay the other members they dealt with a premium. The source of this premium was the gain from cooperation. By raising the gains to the agent from cooperating, paying a premium raised the cost of cheating—anyone who cheated would be giving up even more future income. They also based payment on a commission derived from revenue, not a piece rate or a fixed fee. The revenue-based commission aligned the agent's incentives to maximize profits with the principal's. In addition to paying a premium, the members of the coalition agreed never to deal with someone who had been caught cheating. In game-theoretic terms, this punishment in perpetuity of cheating greatly increased the expected costs of cheating.

Another source of evidence is the structure of trading relations. Members of the coalition worked together on different terms from long-distance traders elsewhere in Europe. In much of Europe, principals paid agents some form of wage, and joint investments were rare. However, in the coalition it was not unusual for the agent to invest with the principal. This arrangement made sense, since the agent was already investing his or her most valuable asset, reputation, in the venture. When the agent was also part owner, he or she could be counted on to make decisions that reflected the interests of other investors.

Thus contracts were self-enforcing through a reputation mechanism among principals and agents. The use of reputation allowed them to link past performance to future rewards in a way that gave them an incentive not to cheat. Because the coalition members refused ever to deal again with cheaters, a cheater was sacrificing so much future income that cheating never paid.

If the coalition was so successful, why did it not grow larger? A larger group would not have worked as well, because personal reputation mechanisms weaken as the number of individuals in the reputation network increases. The success of the coalition depended on the existence of abundant low-cost, high-quality information. After a certain point, increasing the size of the group would raise the cost of gathering information while lowering the quality of the information. In addition, technological change in shipping and navigation increased the range of travel and therefore increased trade with strangers. This change reinforced decreases in the efficacy of personal information networks and reputation mechanisms.

Medieval and Early Renaissance Contracts. The next large trend in institutional change in contract enforcement came with medieval and early Renaissance trade up to approximately 1600. Increased long-distance and impersonal trade characterized this period, as did the evolution of contract enforcement away from personal, decentralized information mechanisms. Interlocking trade networks grew among Asia, northern Africa, the Ottoman Empire, and northern and southern Europe.

Another example of information networks and reputation in contract enforcement was the trade fair and the use of the Law Merchant (*Lex Mercatoria*). The Law Merchant was a private code of laws in which judges, who might be local officials or local merchants, heard and resolved disputes (Milgrom et al., 1990, p. 10). Information on judges' actions traveled from fair to fair, so judges and merchants could see the decisions at other fairs.

As in the case of the Maghribi Trade Coalition, information was the primary factor that shaped this enforcement institution. The Law Merchant did not replace reputation mechanisms; its role was to make the reputation mechanism work more effectively to promote honest trade, even among strangers. It did so by reducing the merchants' transaction costs of enquiring after their trading partners. The most important characteristic of the Law Merchant was that this institution arose to enforce contracts and create honest trade after trading communities had grown large and long-distance trade was profitable but before the rise of third-party enforcement through the state. Private judges adjudicated cases, but in order for the judgments to have any effects, enforcement had to be credible. Thus, as with the Maghribi Trade Coalition, ostracism and not trading with those who cheated had to be upheld. The Law Merchant provided a way to bring together and use decentralized information about who had cheated. The repetition of interactions, even among strangers, made the reputation mechanism work. Repetition also gave merchants incentives to obey the Law Merchant, to not trade with cheaters, to provide evidence against cheaters, and to follow the decisions of the judges.

This period also saw the growth of the great trading city-states of Italy, which increasingly served as intermediaries for silk, cotton, tea, sugar, and spices between Asia and Europe (Braudel, 1981; Lopez, 1971). In northern Europe, institutions like the Hanseatic League created a healthy environment for long-distance trade by limiting the predation and expropriation opportunities of rulers.

In general, contract enforcement in this period relied on networks of interlocking relationships to centralize dispersed information about contract compliance with others and to distribute that information from particular transactions to potentially interested parties, such as future trading partners. Technological change continued to play an important role, particularly in the dissemination of and improvement of the printing press in reducing the transaction costs of sharing information among strangers.

This period also saw the increasing importance of rulers' *ex ante* commitments not to expropriate the profits of alien merchants (Greif, 2000, p. 261). One illustration of an institutional change to address this possibility was the growth of merchant guilds (Greif et al., 1994). Merchant guilds served as coordination mechanisms to counterbalance the ruler's ability to expropriate profits and to change his or her valuation of the expected future value of the merchants' profits. They did so by conditioning future trade (and all of the associated benefits that came with it, including tax revenue for the ruler) on past protection from the ruler.

Early Modern Contracts. The early modern period after 1600 saw the ascendancy of the Dutch and then English merchant and banking industries. For example, both the British East India Company and the Dutch East India Company were founded at this time, after a century of prosperous trade network extension, to capture the rents from long-distance maritime trade (Tracy, 1900). Such activities led to increasing globally integrated trade. Trade network extension and the exploration of countries in Asia and the Western Hemisphere led to the discovery of gold and silver deposits, which flowed through the European economies as a consequence. This period also saw a dramatic increase in international capital flows, facilitated by the entrepreneurial fervor of Italian, Dutch, and English banking industries between 1600 and 1800. Increased precious metal flows, capital flows, and goods movement kept the pressure on contract enforcement institutions to continue supporting trade and deterring cheating.

The backbone of this rise of global merchant capitalism was the ability to enforce impersonal contracts among strangers, and this enforcement evolved during the early modern period to incorporate more written contracts and third-party enforcement. This third-party enforcement largely took the form of courts administered by the burgeoning nation-states, progressing beyond and incorporating the centralized, yet decentralized, information mechanism embedded in the earlier Law Merchant.

The seventeenth century also saw an increase in the use of banking and financial systems as information networks supporting and enforcing contracts (Neal and Quinn, 2001). London's growth as a credit hub, even without a central bank, depended on using bankers' networks to monitor overseas agents. Bankers' networks also spread default information and enforced the collection of international claims. The web of enforcement tools they used included both formal, legal means and these informal networks.

One of the most important changes in contract enforcement occurred in the late seventeenth century, after the Glorious Revolution of 1688 in England. Douglass North and Barry R. Weingast (1989) argue that the political changes in the wake of the Glorious Revolution shifted political power toward Parliament and away from the monarch, and the institutional changes that accompanied that shift helped create secure property rights and reduced the ability of the monarch to expropriate wealth. Thus political change that enabled the government to commit to less confiscatory behavior increased the security of contract enforcement among merchants, bankers, and others, thereby reducing transaction costs of exchange.

As in the medieval period, further incremental technological change in shipping and navigation reinforced the incentives to engage in long-distance trade by changing the risk, return, and time tradeoffs in shipping relative to overland transport. As shipping became relatively less risky and time-consuming because of increased navigational precision, the returns to long-distance trade increased, which further fed the need to have effective third-party contract enforcement for trades among merchants in a network. Many of these merchants came from different nation-states, so increased trade among them prodded the question of one nation recognizing another nation's contract law. Such negotiations formed the beginnings of commercial treaties among nations.

Over the course of the subsequent centuries, contract enforcement evolved to the formal, document-based, court-enforced legal institution associated with modern commercial capitalism. Indeed, the modern credit system and the use of credit cards over the Internet is the current culmination of centuries of evolution of information and reputation mechanisms from supporting per-

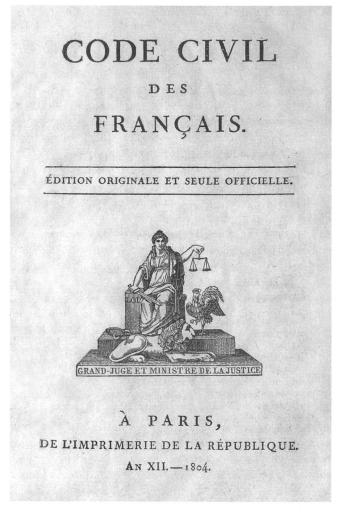

LEGAL CODE. Title page of the French civil code, 1804. The first section contains the Napoleonic code. (Châteaux de Malmaison et Bois-Preau, Rueil-Malmaison, France/Réunion des Musées Nationaux/Art Resource, NY)

sonal, local trade with self-enforcement to supporting impersonal, long-distance trade with third-party enforcement. Technological change has played a crucial role in enabling this multilayered evolution from personal to impersonal and local to long-distance. As a result of the confluence of technology and contract enforcement, individuals over several centuries have benefited tremendously from the reduction of uncertainty, risk, transaction costs, transport costs, and time involved in exchange.

The end result (thus far) of this progression has been the replacement of personalized with impersonalized exchange and the replacement of self-enforcement with third-party enforcement as more institutions specialized in the development of trustworthiness. The modern world has increasingly been more productive with much less personal knowledge than people used to have. Only the reputations of a few intermediary, transaction-cost-reducing firms are needed. Such levels of ignorance about the reputations of trading partners would have been unthinkable in the past. The modern world is more productive with less information because the institutions used have far more information content than did the systems used in the past. Contract enforcement has evolved to the use of firms that specialize in getting good information about specific things. Each of these specialists knows more about less; taken together they know more (and better) than their predecessors.

BIBLIOGRAPHY

Braudel, Fernand. *Civilization and Capitalism: Fifteenth-Eighteenth Century*. New York, 1981.

Curtin, Philip. *Cross-Cultural Trade in World History*. Cambridge, 1984.

DeRoover, Raymond. "The Organization of Trade." In *Cambridge Economic History of Europe*, vol. 3, *Economic Organization and Policies in the Middle Ages*. Cambridge, 1963.

Elvin, Mark. *The Pattern of the Chinese Past*. Stanford, Calif., 1973.

Greif, Avner. "Reputation and Coalitions in Medieval Trade: Evidence on the Maghribi Traders." *Journal of Economic History* 49 (1989), 857–882.

Greif, Avner. "The Fundamental Problem of Exchange: A Research Agenda in Historical Institutional Analysis." *European Review of Economic History* 4 (2000), 251–284.

Greif, Avner, Paul Milgrom, and Barry Weingast. "Coordination, Commitment and Enforcement: The Case of the Merchant Guild." *Journal of Political Economy* 102 (1994), 745–776.

Lopez, Robert. *The Commercial Revolution of the Middle Ages*. Englewood Cliffs, N.J., 1971.

McNeill, William. *The Pursuit of Power: Technology, Armed Force, and Society since AD 1000*. Chicago, 1982.

Milgrom, Paul, Douglass North, and Barry Weingast. "The Role of Institutions in the Revival of Medieval Trade: The Law Merchant, Private Judges, and the Champagne Fairs." *Economics and Politics* 2 (1990), 1–23.

Neal, Larry, and Stephen Quinn. "Networks of Information, Markets, and Institutions in the Rise of London as a Financial Centre, 1660–1720." *Financial History Review* 8.1 (2001), 7–26.

North, Douglass, and Barry Weingast. "Constitutions and Commitment: The Evolution of Institutions Governing Public Choice in Seventeenth-Century England." *Journal of Economic History* 49 (1989), 803–832.

Postan, M. M. *Medieval Trade and Finance*. Cambridge, 1973.

Rosenberg, Nathan, and Robert Birdzell. *How the West Grew Rich*. New York, 1986.

Tracy, James, ed. *The Rise of Merchant Empires*. Cambridge, 1990.

Williamson, Dean. "Transparency, Contract Selection, and the Maritime Trade of Venetian Crete, 1303–1351." Mimeo, U.S. Department of Justice, 2001.

LYNNE KIESLING

CONTRACT LABOR AND THE INDENTURE SYSTEM.

The indenture system, an integral part of European overseas expansion, was the use of explicit, legal, multiyear, forward-labor contracts to facilitate transoceanic migration of workers from labor-plentiful to labor-scarce areas. The vast majority of workers entered the system voluntarily, trading contracts on their future labor in exchange for transportation to a new land, usually because passage costs were greater than their savings and because borrowing money without collateral in the country of origin was prohibitively expensive owing to the lender's inability to enforce repayment. Most servants were unmarried young adult male laborers moving from places such as Europe, India, China, Japan, and Melanesia to places of newly expanded commercial agriculture in the Americas, Australia, and South Africa, and on numerous tropical islands. The typical adult contract was between three and five years.

The large-scale use of the indenture system was evident by the early seventeenth century, first appearing in the European transatlantic trade among English, Scots, and Irish workers moving to the British Caribbean and North American colonies. By the eighteenth century, sizable numbers of French and German servants joined this trade, going primarily to Canada and the Pennsylvania region, respectively. The transatlantic indenture system disappeared among British, Irish, and French migrants by the Napoleonic Era, and among German migrants by 1820. Throughout this period, approximately half of all transatlantic migrants from these countries were indentured, representing approximately one-half million people. Immigrant servants were the dominant labor force in their colonies in the early seventeenth century, but by 1700 slaves south of Pennsylvania and colonial-born workers north of Virginia had eclipsed indentured servants in numerical importance.

In the nineteenth century, the abolition of slavery led to a return of the indenture system as a vehicle for providing bound-labor replacements for freed slave labor, especially on tropical sugar plantations. Between 1834 and 1918 slightly more than 1,500,000 indentured servants from India, 250,000 from China, 80,000 from Japan, 50,000 from Portuguese Atlantic islands, and 100,000 from Melanesia were sent to British, French, Dutch, Spanish, German, and American colonies in the Caribbean, the Indian Ocean, South and West Africa, Malaya, Australia, Peru, Hawaii, Fiji, and Samoa. These migratory streams had a much higher indentured-to-free passenger ratio than the European transatlantic migratory streams of the seventeenth and eighteenth centuries.

The Servant Contract and Its Enforcement. The typical indentured servant contract was a preprinted, standardized, single-page form with blanks spaces positioned where individually negotiated hand-written terms could be added. The negotiating parties signed the contract, and occasionally officials at either the embarkation or the debarkation port recorded the terms to prevent fraud. Contracts completely specified the destination, payment of passage, contract commencement data, length of servitude, and whether the master had the right to sell the servant to a third party. Contracts also stated that servants would be given a customary sum, called freedom dues, upon contract completion. These payments were fixed by statutory law in most colonies. In the pre-1820 European trade, freedom dues were typically two complete suits of clothing; in the post-1830 Asian trade, freedom dues were typically return-passage tickets. The servant's work effort and the master's provisioning effort were incompletely specified, both contractually and legally. For example, contracts typically stated only that the servant was to perform customary labor, and the master was to provide meat, drink, apparel, and lodging.

Because the servant's transoceanic passage was paid before the labor commenced, the servant had an incentive to shirk and/or run away to work for a master who would not deduct the passage cost from the servant's compensation. To counter such incentives, breech of contract by running away was criminalized in law, and harsher penalties were imposed on runaways in servant-receiving areas, such as more whippings and forced contract extensions, compared with those imposed on servant labor in Europe. The incentive to shirk was remedied through the contract's incompleteness. The tasks performed by servants were too varied and unpredictable from day to day, if not from hour to hour, for them to be contractually specified completely; and although the servant's work effort was observable to the master, it was not easily verifiable to an outside agent, such as a court. Given the rarity of repeat contracting and the legal limits placed on physical coercion, the master may have been able to counter servant shirking only through adjusting provisions. The day-to-day execution of the servant contract became a series of simultaneous exchanges between master and servant. Masters reduced or increased the quantity and the quality of provisions in response to servant shirking or diligence; consequently servants would adjust their shirking or diligence to the optimal amount. Purposefully leaving the master's provisioning effort contractually incomplete was necessary to insure the optimal execution of servant contracts.

The Recruitment and Shipping of Servants. The markets for recruiting and shipping servants evolved over time. Before 1820 in the European transatlantic trade, markets were relatively unregulated and competitive. At embarkation ports prospective servants bargained with shippers over the length of servitude required to secure transportation to chosen destinations. The terms of the servant contract were fixed before sailing. At debarkation the shipper sold the contract at auction to the highest bidder, thereby recouping the shipping expense. Competition led to servants signing the shortest labor contract necessary to secure passage and to shippers earning no economic profit on servant cargo. With contracts fixed prior to embarkation, servants were insured against, while shippers bore the risk of, errors in forecasting the amount for which the labor needed to sell to cover the cost of passage, as well as unforeseen changes in the servant's labor productivity during the voyage.

Although the opportunity cost of passage (freight space and provisions) was relatively constant across servants, servant labor productivity per unit time was not. Less productive servants had to sign longer contracts than more productive servants in order to sell their contracts for the same passage cost. Servant registration and auction evidence confirms this behavior. Contract lengths were systematically and negatively related to measures of servant productivity known at embarkation, whereas auction prices in America were systematically unrelated to measures of servant productivity known at embarkation. In America auction prices were very narrowly distributed and exhibited few forecast errors. Finally, shipping evidence indicates that the approximately 15 percent higher passage fares charged for servants relative to free passengers (who paid cash in advance) compensated shippers for the additional default risk (mortality, morbidity, and escape) and opportunity cost of capital associated with servant cargo compared with free passenger cargo.

By the mid-eighteenth century a new variant, called redemption servitude, was increasingly used in the transatlantic trade. It most likely evolved out of the recruitment methods used by the Dutch East India Company. Although German migrants used it first and exclusively after the 1720s, some British and Irish servants also used this variant. Instead of signing a forward-labor contract at embarkation, prospective migrants signed fixed-debt passage contracts that required them to sell themselves into servitude at debarkation, if necessary, to clear the debt with the shipper.

Redemption shifted the voyage and forecast risk from shipper to migrant. With passage debts, but not contract lengths, fixed before embarkation, shippers were insured against, and migrants bore the risk of, errors in forecasting the amount labor needed to sell for the passage debt contracted and for unforeseen changes in the servant's labor productivity during the voyage. Migrants accepted the increased risk of this variant for two reasons. First, redemption gave migrants increased flexibility in designing servant contracts, in particular allowing them to negotiate restrictive contingency clauses into their servant contracts and to select their own master upon debarkation. Family groups, more prominent among German compared with British immigrant servants, found this flexibility valuable. Second, redemption solved the "lemons" problem in the German servant trade.

Unlike British immigrant servants, many Germans incurred varying debts before the voyage while migrating to and while searching for work or migration opportunities in Holland. Shippers in Dutch ports assumed these debts when agreeing to transport these Germans to America. Thus, German servants had to sell in America for enough to cover both the cost of passage and the cost of any prevoyage debts assumed by the shipper. Under the older system of fixing contract lengths before the voyage, when servant contracts were all expected to sell for the same passage cost, buyers in America could infer the expected relative productivity of arriving servants from contract lengths: a longer contract implied that the shipper thought the servant was less productive. If contract lengths varied because of both differences in servant productivity and differences in servant prevoyage debts, then buyers in America could not infer the expected relative productivity of arriving servants from contract lengths. Risk-averse buyers would interpret longer contracts as a signal of lower productivity—that these servants were lemons—rather than as due to the possessing higher prevoyage debts. As a result, they would offer too low a price per contract length for German servants who had high prevoyage debts. The redemption variant, by fixing debts at embarkation and letting contract lengths vary at auction in America to clear the market, solved this information problem.

In the post 1830 Asian transoceanic trade, markets were more regulated than the transatlantic ones, in part to make the trade appear less like slavery. For example, in the Melanesian trade to Queensland, Australia, the British government fixed the length of all labor contracts at three years, fixed servant wages at a minimum of six pounds per annum, did not allow unrestricted recruiting, and did not allow servants to be openly auctioned at debarkation. Only when planters officially requested a given number of servants, and secured this request by posting bonds, were shippers licensed to proceed and recruit that number in exchange for a fee-per-recruit determined before the voyage. The servants who landed were assigned by officials to each planter according to the number each had initially requested.

The profit-maximizing response by shippers to the fixing of the fee-per-recruit before the voyage and to the nonauction of servants at debarkation was to minimize the cost per recruit, which led to recruiting of the cheapest workers, who were typically the least productive, and occasionally to kidnapping. The British government's correction for this regulatory-induced behavior was yet more regulation. Recruits were required to be inspected, at the planters' expense for age and illness, with those who were deemed to be too young or sick rejected. The inspection measures, however, less than exacting. The government also required officials to travel on recruiting voyages to ensure that recruits were volunteers.

The End of Transoceanic Servitude. The European transatlantic trade in servants ended because servant supplies disappeared, not because American demand dried up. Prospective European migrants found better employment alternatives to servitude, such as military service during the Napoleonic Era in either Europe or India, or found better alternatives to servitude for financing passage to America, such as securing remittances from family and friends already in America or funding migration out of savings, which became increasingly easy as income rose and passage fares fell during the nineteenth century. The post-1830 Asian transoceanic indenture systems often were ended by government regulation or prohibition, in conjunction with the shifting fortunes of the global sugar industry. For example, the Melanesian trade to Queensland was ended in 1903 by legislative fiat as part of the "White Australian Policy" influencing the process of Australian confederation. The government's provision of a protected home market for Queensland sugar and subsidies for sugar produced by "white" labor were necessary to gain the industry's acquiesce for ending the Melanesian trade.

The legacy of these indenture systems can be seen in sizable populations of descendants of these transplanted peoples in diverse locations around the globe, such as Western Europeans in North America; Asian Indians in Fiji, South Africa, and the Caribbean; Japanese in Hawaii and Peru; Chinese in North America, South Africa, and the Caribbean; and Melanesians in Australia.

BIBLIOGRAPHY

Beckles, Hilary McD. *White Servitude and Black Slavery in Barbados, 1627–1715.* Knoxville, Tenn., 1989.

Emmer, P. C., ed. *Colonialism and Migration: Indentured Labour before and after Slavery.* Dordrecht, 1986.

Galenson, David W. *White Servitude in Colonial America.* Cambridge, 1981.

Galenson, David W. "The Rise and Fall of Indentured Servitude in the Americas: An Economic Analysis." *Journal of Economic History* 44.1 (1984), 1–26.

Grubb, Farley. "The Market for Indentured Immigrants: Evidence on the Efficiency of Forward-Labor Contracting in Philadelphia, 1745–1773." *Journal of Economic History* 45.4 (1985), 855–868.

Grubb, Farley. "Redemptioner Immigration to Pennsylvania: Evidence on Contract Choice and Profitability." *Journal of Economic History* 46.2 (1986), 407–418.

Grubb, Farley. "The Long-Run Trend in the Value of European Immigrant Servants, 1654–1831: New Measurements and Interpretations." *Research in Economic History* 14 (1992), 167–240.

Grubb, Farley. "The Statutory Regulation of Colonial Servitude: An Incomplete-Contract Approach." *Explorations in Economic History* 37.1 (2000), 42–75.

Grubb, Farley, and Tony Stitt. "The Liverpool Emigrant Servant Trade and the Transition to Slave Labor in the Chesapeake, 1697–1707: Market Adjustments to War." *Explorations in Economic History* 31.3 (1994), 376–405.

Moogk, Peter N. "Reluctant Exiles: Emigrants from France in Canada before 1760." *William and Mary Quarterly* 46.3 (1989), 463–505.

Morris, Richard B. *Government and Labor in Early America.* New York, 1946.

Northrup, David. *Indentured Labor in the Age of Imperialism, 1834–1922.* Cambridge, 1995.

Richardson, Peter, and Shula Marks, eds. *International Labour Migration.* Hounslow, U.K., 1984.

Shlomowitz, Ralph. "Markets for Indentured and Time-Expired Melanesian Labour in Queensland, 1863–1906: An Economic Analysis." *Journal of Pacific History* 16.2 (1981), 70–91.

FARLEY GRUBB